2004 | WORLD DEVELOPMENT INDICATORS

The World Bank

"When we read statistics, we must see real people. When we confront problems, we must cast them as opportunities. When we doubt our energy or question our faith in development, we must take fresh resolve from the reality that on our work depends the fate of millions."

Barber Conable, 1922–2003
President, World Bank, 1986–91

2004 | WORLD DEVELOPMENT INDICATORS

If you have questions or comments about this product, please contact:

Development Data Center
The World Bank
1818 H Street NW, Room MC2-812, Washington, DC 20433, USA
Hotline: 800 590 1906 or 202 473 7824; fax 202 522 1498
Email: data@worldbank.org
Web site: www.worldbank.org or www.worldbank.org/data

ISBN 0-8213-5729-8

FOREWORD

Development is about people. But to measure development and see its effect on people, we need good statistics. Statistics that tell us that life expectancy in the last 40 years has gone up 20 years in developing countries, more than in all the time before that. That literacy has improved. That infant mortality and maternal mortality have decreased. And that fewer people are living in extreme poverty.

However, the statistics also tell us that malnutrition and disease still claim the lives of millions of young children. That millions more never receive a primary education. And that in countries at the center of the HIV/AIDS epidemic, life expectancy has been falling. Of the 6 billion people on the planet today, 5 billion live in developing countries. But in the next 30 years the world's population will grow by 2 billion—from 6 billion to 8 billion—and all but 50 million of them will live in today's developing countries. What will their lives be like? We hope, much better than today.

The Millennium Development Goals set specific targets for improving people's lives. They were proposed and adopted by the General Assembly of the United Nations—not as vague and lofty statements of our good intentions, but as a practical guide to what can and should be accomplished by the international community in the opening quarter of the 21st century. That is why they were presented so clearly, with precise, quantified targets, based on widely accepted statistical indicators. Setting goals and measuring progress toward them in a transparent process is a proven management technique for holding our focus, avoiding wasteful diversions of effort, and encouraging robust public discussion of both means and ends.

Since the adoption of the Millennium Development Goals another important step in deepening the international consensus on development was the Monterrey Conference on Financing for Development. At Monterrey developing countries recognized the need to put reducing poverty and achieving the human and environmental goals of the Millennium Declaration at the center of their development programs. Developed countries accepted an obligation to uphold their share of a partnership for development by providing resources, opening trade, and relieving the burden of debt on the poorest countries. That consensus requires monitoring not only the outcomes in developing countries—but also the policies and actions of rich countries and development agencies to meet their commitments.

A comprehensive development strategy calls for a comprehensive set of statistics. Any user of *World Development Indicators* recognizes the many gaps in sound, available information. At the World Bank we are committed to working with our partners to improve the quality and availability of development statistics. This effort starts with strengthening national statistical systems in developing countries. But it must be matched by a commitment of the international community to provide the necessary technical and financial support.

The World Bank's mission statement asks us to "fight poverty with passion and professionalism for lasting results." Ultimately, it is the results that count. If we act now with realism and foresight based on good information, if we think globally and allocate our resources accordingly, we can make a lasting difference in people's lives.

James D. Wolfensohn
President
The World Bank Group

ACKNOWLEDGMENTS

This book and its companion volumes, *The World Bank Atlas* and *The Little Data Book,* are prepared by a team coordinated by David Cieslikowski. Team members are Mehdi Akhlaghi, Mahyar Eshragh-Tabary, Richard Fix, Amy Heyman, Masako Hiraga, M. H. Saeed Ordoubadi, Sulekha Patel, Eric Swanson, K. M. Vijayalakshmi, Vivienne Wang, and Estela Zamora, working closely with other teams in the Development Economics Vice Presidency's Development Data Group. The CD-ROM development team included Azita Amjadi, Ramgopal Erobelly, Reza Farivari, and William Prince. The work was carried out under the management of Shaida Badiee.

The choice of indicators and text content was shaped through close consultation with and substantial contributions from staff in the World Bank's four thematic networks—Environmentally and Socially Sustainable Development, Human Development, Poverty Reduction and Economic Management, and Private Sector Development and Infrastructure—and staff of the International Finance Corporation and the Multilateral Investment Guarantee Agency. Most important, the team received substantial help, guidance, and data from external partners. For individual acknowledgments of contributions to the book's content, please see the *Credits* section. For a listing of our key partners, see the *Partners* section.

Communications Development Incorporated provided overall design direction, editing, and layout, led by Meta de Coquereaumont and Bruce Ross-Larson. The editing and production team consisted of Joseph Costello, Elizabeth McCrocklin, Christopher Trott, and Elaine Wilson. Communications Development's London partner, Grundy & Northedge, provided art direction and design. Staff from External Affairs oversaw publication and dissemination of the book.

PREFACE

Four years have passed since the Millennium Development Goals sharpened the focus on measuring the results of development—not the number of projects undertaken or the dollars spent, but the improvements in people's lives. The emphasis on quantitative targets and the requirement for monitoring progress on country poverty reduction strategies have increased the demand for statistics. And that showed us how deficient the statistical systems are in many parts of the developing world. Good statistics are not just a technical issue— they are a development issue, requiring concerted action by the entire global community. As Trevor Manuel, South Africa's minister of finance, has put it, "If you can't measure it, you can't manage it."

That is why data, statistics, and indicators are at the heart of the results agenda. Governments need them. Politicians need them. Managers of development programs need them. And citizens need them—to hold governments accountable for their actions and their results.

The global effort to improve the quality of development statistics has three pillars:

- Strengthening the capacity of developing countries to produce, analyze, and use reliable statistics.
- Providing financial support to countries expanding their statistical capacity.
- Improving the quality and availability of international statistics for monitoring global progress.

Much is already happening. Around the world, 37 developing countries have prepared strategic plans to guide their statistical development. The African Development Bank is systematically carrying out statistical assessments in 47 countries in that region, a key step in identifying shortcomings and constraints and in better targeting support. The Trust Fund for Statistical Capacity Building, managed by the World Bank, has provided grants to support statistical projects in more than 60 countries.

Interagency cooperation is much stronger than it was even two years ago. Joint efforts have improved the measurement of such indicators as child mortality and immunizations. And the International Comparison Program is proceeding with an ambitious plan to measure purchasing power parities in more than 100 countries.

Much has been achieved, but much remains to be done. The Second Roundtable on Development Results—held at Marrakech, Morocco, and sponsored by the multilateral development banks and the Development Assistance Committee of the Organisation for Economic Co-operation and Development—identified six broad sets of actions to improve national and international statistics:

- Mainstream the strategic planning of statistical systems and help all low-income countries prepare national statistical development strategies by 2006.
- Strengthen preparations for the 2010 censuses. A core source of development statistics, censuses underpin the ability to monitor progress toward the Millennium Development Goals.
- Increase financial support for statistical capacity building. Countries that adopt good policies for their statistical systems should receive the financial support they need for their statistics.
- Set up an international household survey network to coordinate and improve the effectiveness of international survey programs.
- Undertake urgent improvements needed to monitor the Millennium Development Goals for 2005.
- Increase the accountability of the international statistical system.

Good quality information is not produced overnight. We plan today for better information tomorrow. In doing so, we must be careful not to overburden fragile national systems. We must also recognize that the cost of making mistakes and allocating resources inefficiently can dwarf the cost of producing good statistics.

World Development Indicators reflects the strengths and weaknesses of the international statistical system. As development statistics improve, the results will appear here—as we continue striving to meet the needs of policymakers, researchers, commentators, and interested citizens. You can find out more about our products at http://www.worldbank.org/data. And you can send queries and comments to data@worldbank.org.

Shaida Badiee, Director
Development Data Group

TABLE OF CONTENTS

FRONT

 # 1. WORLD VIEW

2. PEOPLE

3. ENVIRONMENT

TABLE OF CONTENTS

4. ECONOMY

5. STATES AND MARKETS

6. GLOBAL LINKS

BACK

PARTNERS

Defining, gathering, and disseminating international statistics is a collective effort of many people and organizations. The indicators presented in *World Development Indicators* are the fruit of decades of work at many levels, from the field workers who administer censuses and household surveys to the committees and working parties of the national and international statistical agencies that develop the nomenclature, classifications, and standards fundamental to an international statistical system. Nongovernmental organizations and the private sector have also made important contributions, both in gathering primary data and in organizing and publishing their results. And academic researchers have played a crucial role in developing statistical methods and carrying on a continuing dialogue about the quality and interpretation of statistical indicators. All these contributors have a strong belief that available, accurate data will improve the quality of public and private decisionmaking.

The organizations listed here have made *World Development Indicators* possible by sharing their data and their expertise with us. More important, their collaboration contributes to the World Bank's efforts, and to those of many others, to improve the quality of life of the world's people. We acknowledge our debt and gratitude to all who have helped to build a base of comprehensive, quantitative information about the world and its people.

For easy reference, this section includes Web addresses for organizations that maintain Web sites. The addresses shown were active on 1 March 2004. Information about the World Bank is also provided.

International and government agencies

Bureau of Verification and Compliance, U.S. Department of State

The Bureau of Verification and Compliance, U.S. Department of State, is responsible for international agreements on conventional, chemical, and biological weapons and on strategic forces; treaty verification and compliance; and support to ongoing negotiations, policymaking, and interagency implementation efforts.

For information, contact the Public Affairs Officer, Bureau of Verification and Compliance, U.S. Department of State, 2201 C Street NW, Washington, DC 20520, USA; telephone: 202 647 6946; Web site: www.state.gov/t/vc.

Carbon Dioxide Information Analysis Center

The Carbon Dioxide Information Analysis Center (CDIAC) is the primary global climate change data and information analysis center of the U.S. Department of Energy. The CDIAC's scope includes anything that would potentially be of value to those concerned with the greenhouse effect and global climate change, including concentrations of carbon dioxide and other radiatively active gases in the atmosphere; the role of the terrestrial biosphere and the oceans in the biogeochemical cycles of greenhouse gases; emissions of carbon dioxide to the atmosphere; long-term climate trends; the effects of elevated carbon dioxide on vegetation; and the vulnerability of coastal areas to rising sea levels.

For information, contact the CDIAC, Oak Ridge National Laboratory, PO Box 2008, Oak Ridge, TN 37831-6335, USA; telephone: 865 574 0390; fax: 865 574 2232; email: cdiac@ornl.gov; Web site: http://cdiac.esd.ornl.gov.

Deutsche Gesellschaft für Technische Zusammenarbeit

The Deutsche Gesellschaft für Technische Zusammenarbeit (GTZ) GmbH is a German government–owned corporation for international cooperation with worldwide operations. GTZ's aim is to positively shape political, economic, ecological, and social development in partner countries, thereby improving people's living conditions and prospects.

The organization has more than 10,000 employees in some 130 countries of Africa, Asia, Latin America, and Eastern Europe.

For publications, contact Deutsche Gesellschaft für Technische Zusammenarbeit (GTZ) GmbH Corporate Communications, Dag-Hammarskjöld-Weg 1-5, 65760 Eschborn, Germany; telephone: 49 0 6196 79 1174; fax: 49 0 6196 79 6196; email: presse@gtz.de; Web site: www.gtz.de.

Food and Agriculture Organization

The Food and Agriculture Organization (FAO), a specialized agency of the United Nations, was founded in October 1945 with a mandate to raise nutrition levels and living standards, to increase agricultural productivity, and to better the condition of rural populations. The organization provides direct development assistance; collects, analyzes, and disseminates information; offers policy and planning advice to governments; and serves as an international forum for debate on food and agricultural issues.

Statistical publications of the FAO include the *Production Yearbook, Trade Yearbook,* and *Fertilizer Yearbook.* The FAO makes much of its data available online through its FAOSTAT and AQUASTAT systems.

FAO publications can be ordered from national sales agents or directly from the FAO Sales and Marketing Group, Viale delle Terme di Caracalla, 00100 Rome, Italy; telephone: 39 06 5705 5727; fax: 39 06 5705 3360; email: Publications-sales@fao.org; Web site: www.fao.org.

International Civil Aviation Organization

The International Civil Aviation Organization (ICAO), a specialized agency of the United Nations, was founded on December 7, 1944. It is responsible for establishing international standards and recommended practices and procedures for the technical, economic, and legal aspects of international civil aviation operations. The ICAO works to achieve the highest practicable degree of uniformity worldwide in civil aviation issues whenever this will facilitate and improve air safety, efficiency, and regularity.

To obtain ICAO publications, contact the ICAO, Document Sales Unit, 999 University Street, Montreal, Quebec H3C 5H7, Canada; telephone: 514 954 8022; fax: 514 954 6769; email: sales_unit@icao.int; Web site: www.icao.int.

International Labour Organization

The International Labour Organization (ILO), a specialized agency of the United Nations, seeks the promotion of social justice and internationally recognized human and labor rights. Founded in 1919, it is the only surviving major creation of the Treaty of Versailles, which brought the League of Nations into being. It became the first specialized agency of the United Nations in 1946. Unique within the United Nations system, the ILO's tripartite structure has workers and employers participating as equal partners with governments in the work of its governing organs.

As part of its mandate, the ILO maintains an extensive statistical publication program. The *Yearbook of Labour Statistics* is its most comprehensive collection of labor force data.

Publications can be ordered from sales agents and major booksellers throughout the world and ILO offices in many countries or from ILO Publications, 4 route des Morillons, CH-1211 Geneva 22, Switzerland; telephone: 41 22 799 6111; fax: 41 22 798 8685; email: publns@ilo.org; Web site: www.ilo.org.

International Monetary Fund

The International Monetary Fund (IMF) was established at a conference in Bretton Woods, New Hampshire, United States, on July 1–22, 1944. (The conference also established the World Bank.) The IMF came into official existence on December 27, 1945, and commenced financial operations on March 1, 1947. It currently has 184 member countries.

The statutory purposes of the IMF are to promote international monetary cooperation, facilitate the expansion and balanced growth of international trade, promote exchange rate stability, help to establish a multilateral payments system, make the general resources of the IMF temporarily available to its members under adequate safeguards, and shorten the duration and lessen the degree of disequilibrium in the international balance of payments of members.

The IMF maintains an extensive program for developing and compiling international statistics and is responsible for collecting and reporting statistics on international financial transactions and the balance of payments. In April 1996 it undertook an important initiative to improve the quality of international statistics, establishing the Special Data Dissemination Standard (SDDS) to guide members that have, or seek, access to international capital markets in providing economic and financial data to the public. In 1997 the IMF established the General Data Dissemination System (GDDS) to guide countries in providing the public with comprehensive, timely, accessible, and reliable economic, financial, and sociodemographic data. Building on this work, the IMF established the Data Quality Assessment Framework (DQAF) to assess data quality in subject areas such as debt and poverty. The DQAF comprises dimensions of data quality such as methodological soundness, accuracy, serviceability, and accessibility. In 1999 work began on Reports on the Observance of Standards and Codes (ROSC), which summarize the extent to which countries observe certain internationally recognized standards and codes in areas including data, monetary and financial policy transparency, fiscal transparency, banking supervision, securities, insurance, payments systems, corporate governance, accounting, auditing, and insolvency and creditor rights.

The IMF's major statistical publications include *International Financial Statistics, Balance of Payments Statistics Yearbook, Government Finance Statistics Yearbook,* and *Direction of Trade Statistics Yearbook.*

For more information on IMF statistical publications, contact the International Monetary Fund, Publications Services, Catalog Orders, 700 19th Street NW, Washington, DC 20431, USA; telephone: 202 623 7430; fax: 202 623 7201; telex: RCA 248331 IMF UR; email: pub-web@imf.org; Web site: www.imf.org; SDDS and GDDS bulletin board: http://dsbb.imf.org.

International Telecommunication Union

Founded in Paris in 1865 as the International Telegraph Union, the International Telecommunication Union (ITU) took its current name in 1934 and became a specialized agency of the United Nations in 1947. The ITU is unique among international organizations in that it was founded on the principle of cooperation between governments and the private sector. With a membership encompassing telecommunication policymakers and regulators, network operators, equipment manufacturers, hardware and software developers, regional standards-making organizations, and financing institutions, ITU's activities, policies, and strategic direction are determined and shaped by the industry it serves.

The ITU's standardization activities, which have already helped foster the growth of new technologies such as mobile telephony and the Internet, are now being put to use in defining the building blocks of the emerging global information infrastructure and in designing advanced multimedia systems that deftly handle a mix of voice, data, audio, and video signals. ITU's continuing role in managing the radio-frequency spectrum ensures that radio-based systems such as cellular phones and pagers, aircraft and maritime navigation systems, scientific research stations, satellite communication systems, and radio and television broadcasting continue to function smoothly and provide reliable wireless services to the world's inhabitants. And ITU's increasingly important role as a catalyst for forging development partnerships between government and private industry is helping bring about rapid improvements in telecommunication infrastructure in the world's developing economies.

The ITU's main statistical publications are the *ITU Yearbook of Statistics* and the *World Telecommunication Development Report.*

Publications can be ordered from ITU Sales and Marketing Service, Web site: www.itu.int/ITU-D/ict/publications/index.htm; telephone: 41 22 730 6141 (English), 41 22 730 6142 (French), and 41 22 730 6143 (Spanish); fax: 41 22 730 5194; email: sales@itu.int; telex: 421 000 uit ch; telegram: ITU GENEVE; Web site: www.itu.int.

National Science Foundation

The National Science Foundation (NSF) is an independent U.S. government agency whose mission is to promote the progress of science; to advance the national health, prosperity, and welfare; and to secure the national defense. It is responsible for promoting science and engineering through almost 20,000 research and education projects. In addition, the NSF fosters the exchange of scientific information among scientists and engineers in the United States and other countries, supports programs to strengthen scientific and engineering research potential, and evaluates the impact of research on industrial development and general welfare.

As part of its mandate, the NSF biennially publishes *Science and Engineering Indicators,* which tracks national and international trends in science and engineering research and education.

Electronic copies of NSF documents can be obtained from the NSF's online document system (www.nsf.gov/ pubsys/ods/index.html) or requested by email from its automated mailserver (getpub@nsf.gov). Documents can also be requested from the NSF Publications Clearinghouse by mail, at PO Box 218, Jessup, MD 20794-0218, USA, or by telephone, at 301 947 2722. For more information, contact the National Science Foundation, 4201 Wilson Boulevard, Arlington, VA 22230, USA; telephone: 703 292 5111; Web site: www.nsf.gov.

Organisation for Economic Co-operation and Development

The Organisation for Economic Co-operation and Development (OECD) was set up in 1948 as the Organisation for European Economic Co-operation (OEEC) to administer Marshall Plan funding in Europe. In 1960, when the Marshall Plan had completed its task, the OEEC's member countries agreed to bring in Canada and the United States to form an organization to coordinate policy among industrial countries. The OECD is the international organization of the industrialized, market economy countries. Representatives of member countries meet at the OECD to exchange information and harmonize policy with a view to maximizing economic growth in member countries and helping nonmember countries develop more rapidly.

The OECD has set up a number of specialized committees to further its aims. One of these is the Development Assistance Committee (DAC), whose members have agreed to coordinate their policies on assistance to developing and transition economies. Also associated with the OECD are several agencies or bodies that have their own governing statutes, including the International Energy Agency and the Centre for Co-operation with Economies in Transition.

The OECD's main statistical publications include *Geographical Distribution of Financial Flows to Aid Recipients, National Accounts of OECD Countries, Labour Force Statistics, Revenue Statistics of OECD Member Countries, International Direct Investment Statistics Yearbook, Basic Science and Technology Statistics, Industrial Structure Statistics, Trends in International Migration,* and *Services: Statistics on International Transactions.*

For information on OECD publications, contact the OECD, 2, rue André Pascal, F-75775 Paris Cedex 16, France; telephone: 33 1 45 24 81 67; fax: 33 1 45 24 19 50; email: sales@oecd.org; Web sites: www.oecd.org and www.oecd.org/bookshop.

Stockholm International Peace Research Institute

The Stockholm International Peace Research Institute (SIPRI) was established by the Swedish Parliament as an independent foundation in July 1966. SIPRI conducts research on questions of conflict and cooperation of importance for international peace and security, with the aim of contributing to an understanding of the conditions for peaceful solutions to international conflicts and for a stable peace.

SIPRI's research work is disseminated through books and reports as well as through symposia and seminars. SIPRI's main publication, *SIPRI Yearbook,* serves as a single authoritative and independent source on armaments and arms control, armed conflicts and conflict resolution, security arrangements, and disarmament. *SIPRI Yearbook* provides an overview of developments in international security, weapons and technology, military expenditure, the arms trade and arms production, and armed conflicts, along with efforts to control conventional, nuclear, chemical, and biological armaments.

For more information on SIPRI publications contact SIPRI at Signalistgatan 9, SE-169 70 Solna, Sweden; telephone: 46 8 655 97 00; fax:46 8 655 97 33; email: sipri@sipri.org; for book orders: http://home.sipri.se/publications.html; Web site: www.sipri.org.

United Nations

The United Nations and its specialized agencies maintain a number of programs for the collection of international statistics, some of which are described elsewhere in this book. At United Nations headquarters the Statistics Division provides a wide range of statistical outputs and services for producers and users of statistics worldwide.

The Statistics Division publishes statistics on international trade, national accounts, demography and population, gender, industry, energy, environment, human settlements, and disability. Its major statistical publications include the *International Trade Statistics Yearbook, Yearbook of National Accounts,* and *Monthly Bulletin of Statistics,* along with general statistics compendiums such as the *Statistical Yearbook* and *World Statistics Pocketbook.*

For publications, contact United Nations Publications, Room DC2-853, Department I004, 2 UN Plaza, New York, NY 10017, USA; telephone: 212 963 8302 or 800 253 9646 (toll free); fax: 212 963 3489; email: publications@un.org; Web site: www.un.org.

United Nations Centre for Human Settlements (Habitat), Global Urban Observatory

The Urban Indicators Programme of the United Nations Centre for Human Settlements (Habitat) was established to address the urgent global need to improve the urban knowledge base by helping countries and cities design, collect, and apply policy-oriented indicators related to development at the city level.

In 1997 the Urban Indicators Programme was integrated into the Global Urban Observatory, the principal United Nations program for monitoring urban conditions and trends and for tracking progress in implementing the goals of the Habitat Agenda. With the Urban Indicators and Best Practices programs, the Global Urban Observatory is establishing a worldwide information, assessment, and capacity building network to help governments, local authorities, the private sector, and nongovernmental and other civil society organizations.

Contact the Co-ordinator, Global Urban Observatory and Statistics, Urban Secretariat, UN-HABITAT, PO Box 30030, Nairobi, Kenya; telephone: 254 2 623119; fax: 254 2 623080; email: habitat.publications@ unhabitat.org or guo@unhabitat.org; Web site: www.unhabitat.org.

United Nations Children's Fund

The United Nations Children's Fund (UNICEF), the only organization of the United Nations dedicated exclusively to children, works with other United Nations bodies and with governments and nongovernmental organizations to improve children's lives in more than 140 developing countries through community-based services in primary health care, basic education, and safe water and sanitation.

UNICEF's major publications include *The State of the World's Children* and *The Progress of Nations*.

For information on UNICEF publications contact the Chief, EPS, Division of Communication, UNICEF, 3 United Nations Plaza, New York, NY 10017, USA; telephone: 212 326 7000; fax: 212 303 7985; email: pubdoc@unicef.org; Web site: www.unicef.org and www.un.org/Publications.

United Nations Conference on Trade and Development

The United Nations Conference on Trade and Development (UNCTAD) is the principal organ of the United Nations General Assembly in the field of trade and development. It was established as a permanent intergovernmental body in 1964 in Geneva with a view to accelerating economic growth and development, particularly in developing countries. UNCTAD discharges its mandate through policy analysis; intergovernmental deliberations, consensus building, and negotiation; monitoring, implementation, and follow-up; and technical cooperation.

UNCTAD produces a number of publications containing trade and economic statistics, including the *Handbook of International Trade and Development Statistics*.

For information, contact UNCTAD, Palais des Nations, 8-14, Avenue de la Paix, 1211 Geneva 10, Switzerland; telephone: 41 22 907 1234; fax: 41 22 907 0043; email: info@unctad.org; Web site: www.unctad.org.

United Nations Educational, Scientific, and Cultural Organization, Institute for Statistics

The United Nations Educational, Scientific, and Cultural Organization (UNESCO) is a specialized agency of the United Nations established in 1945 to promote "collaboration among nations through education, science, and culture in order to further universal respect for justice, for the rule of law, and for the human rights and fundamental freedoms . . . for the peoples of the world, without distinction of race, sex, language, or religion."

The UNESCO Institute for Statistics' principal statistical publications are the *Global Education Digest* (GED) and regional statistical reports, as well as the on-line database.

For publications, contact the UNESCO Institute for Statistics, C.P. 6128, Succursale Centre-ville, Montreal, Quebec, H3C 3J7, Canada; telephone: 514 343 6880; fax: 514 343 6882; email: uis@unesco.org; Web site: www.unesco.org; and for the Institute for Statistics: www.uis.unesco.org.

United Nations Environment Programme

The mandate of the United Nations Environment Programme (UNEP) is to provide leadership and encourage partnership in caring for the environment by inspiring, informing, and enabling nations and people to improve their quality of life without compromising that of future generations.

UNEP publications include *Global Environment Outlook* and *Our Planet* (a bimonthly magazine).

For information, contact the UNEP, PO Box 30552, Nairobi, Kenya; telephone: 254 2 621234; fax: 254 2 624489/90; email: eisinfo@unep.org; Web site: www.unep.org.

United Nations Industrial Development Organization

The United Nations Industrial Development Organization (UNIDO) was established in 1966 to act as the central coordinating body for industrial activities and to promote industrial development and cooperation at the global, regional, national, and sectoral levels. In 1985 UNIDO became the 16th specialized agency of the United Nations, with a mandate to help develop scientific and technological plans and programs for industrialization in the public, cooperative, and private sectors.

UNIDO's databases and information services include the Industrial Statistics Database (INDSTAT), Commodity Balance Statistics Database (COMBAL), Industrial Development Abstracts (IDA), and the International Referral System on Sources of Information. Among its publications is the *International Yearbook of Industrial Statistics.*

For information, contact UNIDO Public Information Section, Vienna International Centre, PO Box 300, A-1400 Vienna, Austria; telephone: 43 1 26026 5031; fax: 43 1 21346 5031 or 26026 6843; email: publications@unido.org; Web site: www.unido.org.

World Bank Group

The World Bank Group is made up of five organizations: the International Bank for Reconstruction and Development (IBRD), the International Development Association (IDA), the International Finance Corporation (IFC), the Multilateral Investment Guarantee Agency (MIGA), and the International Centre for Settlement of Investment Disputes (ICSID). Established in 1944 at a conference of world leaders in Bretton Woods, New Hampshire, United States, the World Bank is the world's largest source of development assistance. In 2003 the World Bank provided $18.5 billion in development assistance and worked in more than 100 developing countries, bringing finance and technical expertise to help them reduce poverty.

The World Bank Group's mission is to fight poverty and improve the living standards of people in the developing world. It is a development bank, providing loans, policy advice, technical assistance, and knowledge sharing services to low- and middle-income countries to reduce poverty. The Bank promotes growth to create jobs and to empower poor people to take advantage of these opportunities. It uses its financial resources, trained staff, and extensive knowledge base to help each developing country onto a path of stable, sustainable, and equitable growth in the fight against poverty. The World Bank Group has 184 member countries.

For information about the World Bank, visit its Web site at www.worldbank.org. For more information about development data, contact the Development Data Group, World Bank, 1818 H Street NW, Washington, DC 20433, USA; telephone: 800 590 1906 or 202 473 7824; fax: 202 522 1498; email: data@worldbank.org; Web site: www.worldbank.org/data.

World Health Organization

The constitution of the World Health Organization (WHO) was adopted on July 22, 1946, by the International Health Conference, convened in New York by the Economic and Social Council of the United Nations. The objective of the WHO, a specialized agency of the United Nations, is the attainment by all people of the highest possible level of health.

The WHO carries out a wide range of functions, including coordinating international health work; helping governments strengthen health services; providing technical assistance and emergency aid; working for the prevention and control of disease; promoting improved nutrition, housing, sanitation, recreation, and economic and working conditions; promoting and coordinating biomedical and health services research; promoting improved standards of teaching and training in health and medical professions; establishing international standards for biological, pharmaceutical, and similar products; and standardizing diagnostic procedures.

The WHO publishes the *World Health Statistics Annual* and many other technical and statistical publications.

For publications, contact the World Health Organization, Marketing and Dissemination, CH-1211 Geneva 27, Switzerland; telephone: 41 22 791 2476; fax: 41 22 791 4857; email: publications@who.int; Web site: www.who.int.

World Intellectual Property Organization

The World Intellectual Property Organization (WIPO) is an international organization dedicated to helping to ensure that the rights of creators and owners of intellectual property are protected worldwide and that inventors and authors are thus recognized and rewarded for their ingenuity. This international protection acts as a spur to human creativity, pushing forward the boundaries of science and technology and enriching the world of literature and the arts. By providing a stable environment for the marketing of intellectual property products, WIPO also oils the wheels of international trade.

WIPO's main tasks include harmonizing national intellectual property legislation and procedures, providing services for international applications for industrial property rights, exchanging intellectual property information, providing legal and technical assistance to developing and other countries facilitating the resolution of private intellectual property disputes, and marshalling information technology as a tool for storing, accessing, and using valuable intellectual property information.

A substantial part of its activities and resources is devoted to development cooperation with developing countries.

For information, contact the World Intellectual Property Organization, 34, chemin des Colombettes, CH-1211 Geneva 20, Switzerland; telephone: 41 22 338 9734; fax: 41 22 740 1812; email: ebookshop@wipo.int; Web site: www.wipo.int.

World Tourism Organization

The World Tourism Organization is an intergovernmental body entrusted by the United Nations with promoting and developing tourism. It serves as a global forum for tourism policy issues and a source of tourism know-how. The organization began as the International Union of Official Tourist Publicity Organizations, set up in 1925 in The Hague. Renamed the World Tourism Organization, it held its first general assembly in Madrid in May 1975. Its membership includes 141 countries, seven territories, and some 350 Affiliate Members representing the private sector, educational institutions, tourism associations, and local tourism authorities.

The World Tourism Organization publishes the *Yearbook of Tourism Statistics, Compendium of Tourism Statistics,* and *Travel and Tourism Barometer* (triannual).

For information, contact the World Tourism Organization, Calle Capitán Haya, 42, 28020 Madrid, Spain; telephone: 34 91 567 8100; fax: 34 91 571 3733; email: infoshop@world-tourism.org; Web site: www.world-tourism.org.

World Trade Organization

The World Trade Organization (WTO), established on January 1, 1995, is the successor to the General Agreement on Tariffs and Trade (GATT). The WTO has 144 member countries and is the only international organization dealing with the global rules of trade between nations. Its main function is to ensure that trade flows as smoothly, predictably, and freely as possible. It does this by administering trade agreements, acting as a forum for trade negotiations, settling trade disputes, reviewing national trade policies, assisting developing countries in trade policy issues—through technical assistance and training programs—and cooperating with other international organizations. At the heart of the system—known as the multilateral trading system—are WTO's agreements, negotiated and signed by a large majority of the world's trading nations and ratified by their parliaments.

The WTO's *International Trade Statistics* is its main statistical publication, providing comprehensive, comparable, and up-to-date statistics on trade.

For publications, contact the World Trade Organization, Publications Services, Centre William Rappard, rue de Lausanne 154, CH-1211, Geneva 21, Switzerland; telephone: 41 22 739 5208 or 5308; fax: 41 22 739 5792; email: publications@wto.org; Web site: www.wto.org.

Private and nongovernmental organizations

Containerisation International

Containerisation International Yearbook is one of the most authoritative reference books on the container industry. It has more than 850 pages of data, including detailed information on more than 560 container ports in more than 150 countries and a review section that features two-year rankings for 350 ports. The information can be accessed on the Web at www.ci-online.co.uk, which also provides a comprehensive online daily business news and information service for the container industry.

For more information, contact Informa UK at 69-77 Paul Street, London, EC2A 4LQ, UK; telephone: 44 1206 772061; fax: 44 1206 772563; email: webtechhelp@informa.com.

Euromoney Publications PLC

Euromoney Publications PLC provides a wide range of financial, legal, and general business information. The monthly magazine *Euromoney* is an authoritative source of detailed yet concise information on the trends and developments in international banking and capital markets and carries a semiannual rating of country creditworthiness.

For information, contact Euromoney Publications PLC, Nestor House, Playhouse Yard, London EC4V 5EX, UK; telephone: 44 870 90 62 600; email: customerservice@euromoney.com; Web site: www.euromoney.com.

Institutional Investor, Inc.

Institutional Investor, Inc., develops country credit ratings every six months based on information provided by leading international banks. It publishes the monthly magazine *Institutional Investor,* and InstitutionalInvestor.com strives to be the gateway to all Institutional Investor publications online, offering selected articles from its 40 publications.

For information, contact Institutional Investor, Inc., 225 Park Avenue South, New York, NY 10003, USA; telephone: 212 224 3800; email: info@iiplatinum.com; Web site: www.institutionalinvestor.com.

International Data Corporation

International Data Corporation (IDC) is a premier global market intelligence and advisory firm in the information technology and telecommunications industries. IDC analyzes and predicts technology trends to enable clients to make strategic, fact-based decisions on information technology purchases and business strategy. More than 700 IDC analysts in 50 countries have provided local expertise and insights on technology markets for 40 years.

For further information on IDC's products and services, contact IDC, Corporate Headquarters, 5 Speen Street, Framingham, MA 01701 USA; telephone: 508 872 8200; Web site: www.idc.com.

International Road Federation

The International Road Federation (IRF) is a nongovernmental, not-for-profit organization with public and private sector members in some 70 countries. The IRF's mission is to encourage and promote development and maintenance of better and safer roads and road networks. It helps put in place technological solutions and management practices that provide maximum economic and social returns from national road investments.

The IRF believes that rationally planned, efficiently managed and well-maintained road networks offer high levels of user safety and have a significant impact on sustainable economic growth, prosperity, social well-being, and human development.

The IRF has a major role to play in all aspects of road policy and development worldwide. For governments and financial institutions, the IRF provides a wide base of expertise for planning road development strategy and policy. For its members, the IRF is a business network, a link to external institutions and agencies and a business card of introduction to government officials and decisionmakers. For the community of road professionals, the IRF is a source of support and information for national road associations, advocacy groups, companies, and institutions dedicated to the development of road infrastructure.

The IRF publishes *World Road Statistics*.

Contact the Geneva office at chemin de Blandonnet 2, CH-1214 Vernier, Geneva, Switzerland; telephone: 41 22 306 0260; fax: 41 22 306 0270; or the Washington, DC, office at 1010 Massachusetts Avenue NW, Suite 410, Washington, DC 20001, USA; telephone: 202 371 5544; fax: 202 371 5565; email: info@irfnet.com; Web site: www.irfnet.org.

Moody's Investors Service

Moody's Investors Service is a global credit analysis and financial opinion firm. It provides the international investment community with globally consistent credit ratings on debt and other securities issued by North American state and regional government entities, by corporations worldwide, and by some sovereign issuers. It also publishes extensive financial data in both print and electronic form. Its clients include investment banks, brokerage firms, insurance companies, public utilities, research libraries, manufacturers, and government agencies and departments.

Moody's publishes *Sovereign, Subnational and Sovereign-Guaranteed Issuers*.

For information, contact Moody's Investors Service, 99 Church Street, New York, NY 10007, USA; telephone: 212 553 0377; fax: 212 553 0882; Web site: www.moodys.com.

Netcraft

Netcraft is an Internet services company based in Bath, United Kingdom. Netcraft's work includes the provision of network security services and research data and analysis of the Internet. It is an authority on the market share of Web servers, operating systems, hosting providers, Internet service providers, encrypted transactions, electronic commerce, scripting languages, and content technologies on the Internet.

For information, visit www.netcraft.com.

PricewaterhouseCoopers

Drawing on the talents of 120,000 people in 139 countries, PricewaterhouseCoopers provides industry-focused assurance, tax, and advisory services for public and private clients in corporate accountability, risk management, structuring and mergers and acquisitions, and performance and process improvement.

PricewaterhouseCoopers publishes *Corporate Taxes: Worldwide Summaries* and *Individual Taxes: Worldwide Summaries*.

For information, contact PricewaterhouseCoopers, 1177 Avenue of the Americas, New York, NY 10036, USA; telephone: 646 471 4000; fax: 646 471 3188; Web site: www.pwcglobal.com.

The PRS Group, Inc.

The PRS Group, Inc., is a global leader in political and economic risk forecasting and market analysis and has served international companies large and small for more than 20 years. The data it contributed to this year's *World Development Indicators* come from the *International Country Risk Guide,* a monthly publication that monitors and rates political, financial, and economic risk in 140 countries. The guide's data series and commitment to independent and unbiased analysis make it the standard for any organization practicing effective risk management.

For information, contact The PRS Group, Inc., 6320 Fly Road, Suite 102, East Syracuse, NY 13057-9358, USA; telephone: 315 431 0511; fax: 315 431 0200; email: custserv@PRSgroup.com; Web site: www.prsgroup.com or www.ICRGOnline.com.

Standard & Poor's Equity Indexes and Rating Services

For more than 140 years Standard & Poor's, a division of the McGraw-Hill Corporation, has been a preeminent global provider of independent highly valued investment data, valuation, analysis, and opinions and is still delivering on that original mission.

The S&P 500 index, one of its most popular products, is calculated and maintained by Standard & Poor's Index Services, a leading provider of equity indexes. Standard & Poor's indexes are used by investors around the world for measuring investment performance and as the basis for a wide range of financial instruments.

Standard & Poor's *Sovereign Ratings* provides issuer and local and foreign currency debt ratings for sovereign governments and for sovereign-supported and supranational issuers worldwide. Standard & Poor's Rating Services monitors the credit quality of $1.5 trillion worth of bonds and other financial instruments and offers investors global coverage of debt issuers. Standard & Poor's also has ratings on commercial paper, mutual funds, and the financial condition of insurance companies worldwide.

For information on equity indexes, contact Standard & Poor's Index Services, 55 Water Street, New York, NY 10041, USA; telephone: 212 438 1000; email: index_services@sandp.com; Web site: www.spglobal.com.

For information on ratings contact the McGraw-Hill Companies, Inc., Executive Offices, 1221 Avenue of the Americas, New York, NY 10020, USA; telephone: 212 512 4105 or 800 352 3566 (toll free); fax: 212 512 4105; email: ratingsdirect@standardandpoors.com; Web site: www.ratingsdirect.com.

Standard & Poor's Emerging Markets Data Base

Standard & Poor's Emerging Markets Data Base (EMDB) is the world's leading source for information and indices on stock markets in developing countries. The EMDB was the first database to track emerging stock markets. It currently covers 53 markets and more than 2,200 stocks. Drawing a sample of stocks in each EMDB market, Standard & Poor's calculates indices to serve as benchmarks that are consistent across national boundaries. Standard & Poor's calculates one index, the S&P/IFCG (Global) index, that reflects the perspective of local investors and those interested in broad trends in emerging markets and another, the S&P/IFCI (Investable) index, that provides a broad, neutral, and historically consistent benchmark for the growing emerging market investment community.

For information on subscription rates, contact S&P Emerging Markets Data Base, 55 Water Street, 42nd Floor, New York, NY, 10041-0003; Telephone: 212 438 2046; Fax: 212 438 3429; Email: indexservices@sandp.com; Web site: www.standardandpoors.com.

World Conservation Monitoring Centre

The World Conservation Monitoring Centre (WCMC) provides information on the conservation and sustainable use of the world's living resources and helps others to develop information systems of their own. It works in close collaboration with a wide range of people and organizations to increase access to the information needed for wise management of the world's living resources.

Committed to the principle of data exchange with other centers and noncommercial users, the WCMC, whenever possible, places the data it manages in the public domain.

For information, contact the World Conservation Monitoring Centre, 219 Huntington Road, Cambridge CB3 0DL, UK; telephone: 44 12 2327 7314; fax: 44 12 2327 7136; email: info@unep-wcmc.org; Web site: www.unep-wcmc.org.

WORLD CONSERVATION
MONITORING CENTRE

World Information Technology and Services Alliance

The World Information Technology and Services Alliance (WITSA) is a consortium of 53 information technology industry associations from around the world. WITSA members represent more than 90 percent of the world information technology market. As the global voice of the information technology industry, WITSA is dedicated to advocating policies that advance the industry's growth and development; facilitating international trade and investment in information technology products and services; strengthening WITSA's national industry associations by sharing knowledge, experience, and information; providing members with a network of contacts in nearly every region; and hosting the World Congress on Information Technology.

WITSA's publication, *Digital Planet 2002: The Global Information Economy,* uses data provided by the International Data Corporation.

For information, contact WITSA, 1401 Wilson Boulevard, Suite 1100, Arlington, VA 22209, USA; telephone: 703 284 5333; fax: 617 687 6590; email: ahalvorsen@itaa.org; Web site: www.witsa.org.

World Resources Institute

The World Resources Institute is an independent center for policy research and technical assistance on global environmental and development issues. The institute provides—and helps other institutions provide—objective information and practical proposals for policy and institutional change that will foster environmentally sound, socially equitable development. The institute's current areas of work include trade, forests, energy, economics, technology, biodiversity, human health, climate change, sustainable agriculture, resource and environmental information, and national strategies for environmental and resource management.

For information, contact the World Resources Institute, Suite 800, 10 G Street NE, Washington, DC 20002, USA; telephone: 202 729 7600; fax: 202 729 7610; email: front@wri.org; Web site: www.wri.org.

USERS GUIDE

Tables

The tables are numbered by section and display the identifying icon of the section. Countries and economies are listed alphabetically (except for Hong Kong, China, which appears after China). Data are shown for 152 economies with populations of more than 1 million, as well as for Taiwan, China, in selected tables. Table 1.6 presents selected indicators for 56 other economies—small economies with populations between 30,000 and 1 million and smaller economies if they are members of the International Bank for Reconstruction and Development (IBRD) or, as it is commonly known, the World Bank. The term *country,* used interchangeably with *economy,* does not imply political independence, but refers to any territory for which authorities report separate social or economic statistics. When available, aggregate measures for income and regional groups appear at the end of each table.

Indicators are shown for the most recent year or period for which data are available and, in most tables, for an earlier year or period (usually 1990 in this edition). Time-series data are available on the *World Development Indicators* CD-ROM and in *WDI Online.*

Known deviations from standard definitions or breaks in comparability over time or across countries are either footnoted in the tables or noted in *About the data.* When available data are deemed to be too weak to provide reliable measures of levels and trends or do not adequately adhere to international standards, the data are not shown.

Aggregate measures for income groups

The aggregate measures for income groups include 208 economies (the economies listed in the main tables plus those in table 1.6) wherever data are available. To maintain consistency in the aggregate measures over time and between tables, missing data are imputed where possible. The aggregates are totals (designated by a *t* if the aggregates include gap-filled estimates for missing data and by an *s,* for simple totals, where they do not), median values (*m*), weighted averages (*w*), or simple averages (*u*). Gap filling of amounts not allocated to countries may result in discrepancies between subgroup aggregates and overall totals. For further discussion of aggregation methods, see *Statistical methods.*

Aggregate measures for regions

The aggregate measures for regions include only low- and middle-income economies (note that these measures include developing economies with populations of less than 1 million, including those listed in table 1.6).

The country composition of regions is based on the World Bank's analytical regions and may differ from common geographic usage. For regional classifications, see the map on the inside back cover and the list on the back cover flap. For further discussion of aggregation methods, see *Statistical methods.*

Statistics

Data are shown for economies as they were constituted in 2002, and historical data are revised to reflect current political arrangements. Exceptions are noted throughout the tables.

Additional information about the data is provided in *Primary data documentation.* That section summarizes national and international efforts to improve basic data collection and gives information on primary sources, census years, fiscal years, and other background. *Statistical methods* provides technical information on some of the general calculations and formulas used throughout the book.

Data consistency and reliability

Considerable effort has been made to standardize the data, but full comparability cannot be assured, and care must be taken in interpreting the indicators. Many factors affect data availability, comparability, and reliability: statistical systems in many developing economies are still weak; statistical methods, coverage, practices, and definitions differ widely; and cross-country and intertemporal comparisons involve complex technical and conceptual problems that cannot be unequivocally resolved. Data coverage may not be complete because of special circumstances or for economies experiencing problems (such as those stemming from conflicts) affecting the collection and reporting of data. For these reasons, although data are drawn from the sources thought to be most authoritative, they should be construed only as indicating trends and characterizing major differences among economies rather than offering precise quantitative measures of those differences. Discrepancies in data presented in different editions of the *World Development Indicators* reflect updates by countries as well as revisions to historical series and changes in methodology. Thus readers are advised not to compare data series between editions of the *World Development Indicators* or between different World Bank publications. Consistent time-series data for 1960–2002 are available on the *World Development Indicators* CD-ROM and in *WDI Online.*

Except where otherwise noted, growth rates are in real terms. (See *Statistical methods* for information on the methods used to calculate growth rates.) Data for some economic indicators for some economies are presented in fiscal years rather than calendar years; see *Primary data documentation.* All dollar figures are current U.S. dollars unless otherwise stated. The methods used for converting national currencies are described in *Statistical methods.*

Country notes

China. On July 1, 1997, China resumed its exercise of sovereignty over Hong Kong, and on December 20, 1999, it resumed its exercise of sovereignty over Macao. Unless otherwise noted, data for China do not include data for Hong Kong, China; Taiwan, China; or Macao, China.

Democratic Republic of Congo. Data for the Democratic Republic of Congo (Congo, Dem. Rep., in the table listings) refer to the former Zaire. (The Republic of Congo is referred to as Congo, Rep., in the table listings.)

Czech Republic and Slovak Republic. Data are shown whenever possible for the individual countries formed from the former Czechoslovakia—the Czech Republic and the Slovak Republic.

Eritrea. Data are shown for Eritrea whenever possible, but in most cases before 1992 Eritrea is included in the data for Ethiopia.

Germany. Data for Germany refer to the unified Germany unless otherwise noted.

Jordan. Data for Jordan refer to the East Bank only unless otherwise noted.

Serbia and Montenegro. On February 4, 2003, the Federal Republic of Yugoslavia changed its name to Serbia and Montenegro.

Timor-Leste. On May 20, 2002, Timor-Leste became an independent country. Data for Indonesia include Timor-Leste through 1999 unless otherwise noted.

Union of Soviet Socialist Republics. In 1991 the Union of Soviet Socialist Republics came to an end. Available data are shown for the individual countries now existing on its former territory (Armenia, Azerbaijan, Belarus, Estonia, Georgia, Kazakhstan, Kyrgyz Republic, Latvia, Lithuania, Moldova, Russian Federation, Tajikistan, Turkmenistan, Ukraine, and Uzbekistan). External debt data presented for the Russian Federation prior to 1992 are for the former Soviet Union. The debt of the former Soviet Union is included in the Russian Federation data after 1992 on the assumption that 100 percent of all outstanding external debt as of December 1991 has become a liability of the Russian Federation. Beginning in 1993 the data for the Russian Federation have been revised to include obligations to members of the former Council for Mutual Economic Assistance and other countries in the form of trade-related credits amounting to $15.4 billion as of the end of 1996.

República Bolivariana de Venezuela. In December 1999 the official name of Venezuela was changed to República Bolivariana de Venezuela (Venezuela, RB, in the table listings).

Republic of Yemen. Data for the Republic of Yemen refer to that country from 1990 onward; data for previous years refer to aggregated data for the former People's Democratic Republic of Yemen and the former Yemen Arab Republic unless otherwise noted.

Changes in the System of National Accounts

World Development Indicators uses terminology in line with the 1993 United Nations System of National Accounts (SNA). For example, in the 1993 SNA *gross national income* (GNI) replaces *gross national product* (GNP). See *About the data* for tables 1.1 and 4.9.

Most economies continue to compile their national accounts according to the 1968 SNA, but more and more are adopting the 1993 SNA. Economies that use the 1993 SNA are identified in *Primary data documentation*. A few low-income economies still use concepts from older SNA guidelines, including valuations such as factor cost, in describing major economic aggregates.

Classification of economies

For operational and analytical purposes the World Bank's main criterion for classifying economies is GNI per capita. Every economy is classified as low income, middle income (subdivided into lower middle and upper middle), or high income. For income classifications see the map on the inside front cover and the list on the front cover flap. Low- and middle-income economies are sometimes referred to as developing economies. The use of the term is convenient; it is not intended to imply that all economies in the group are experiencing similar development or that other economies have reached a preferred or final stage of development. Note that classification by income does not necessarily reflect development status. Because GNI per capita changes over time, the country composition of income groups may change from one edition of *World Development Indicators* to the next. Once the classification is fixed for an edition, based on GNI per capita in the most recent year for which data are available (2002 in this edition), all historical data presented are based on the same country grouping.

Low-income economies are those with a GNI per capita of $735 or less in 2002. Middle-income economies are those with a GNI per capita of more than $735 but less than $9,076. Lower-middle-income and upper-middle-income economies are separated at a GNI per capita of $2,935. High-income economies are those with a GNI per capita of $9,076 or more. The 12 participating member countries of the European Monetary Union (EMU) are presented as a subgroup under high-income economies.

Symbols

..

means that data are not available or that aggregates cannot be calculated because of missing data in the years shown.

0 or 0.0

means zero or less than half the unit shown.

/

in dates, as in 1990/91, means that the period of time, usually 12 months, straddles two calendar years and refers to a crop year, a survey year, an academic year, or a fiscal year.

$

means current U.S. dollars unless otherwise noted.

>

means more than.

<

means less than.

Data presentation conventions

- A blank means not applicable or, for an aggregate, not analytically meaningful.
- A billion is 1,000 million.
- A trillion is 1,000 billion.
- Figures in italics refer to years or periods other than those specified.
- Data for years that are more than three years from the range shown are footnoted.

The cutoff date for data is February 1, 2004.

1 WORLD VIEW

The Millennium Development Goals put the world community on a time table. When 189 member states of the United Nations adopted the Millennium Declaration in September 2000, they looked backwards to 1990 and ahead to 2015 and gave themselves 25 years to produce substantial improvements in the lives of people. At the time, it was clear that in many places development progress had slowed and would have to be accelerated if the ambitious targets of the Millennium Development Goals were to be achieved.

As in the past four editions, this section of *World Development Indicators* reviews progress toward the major development goals. Until recently we have been gauging progress toward the Millennium Development Goals based on the record of the 1990s. Now, we are closer to 2015 than to 1990, and we are getting our first look at the record of the 21st century. There are hopeful signs. Global poverty rates continue to fall. Fewer people are living in extreme poverty, after an increase in the late 1990s. In countries that have laid a good foundation for growth, indicators of social development are also improving. But progress is uneven. Slow growth, low educational achievement, poor health, and civil disturbances remain obstacles for many.

It is still too early to conclude that the world as a whole is on track to achieve the Millennium Development Goals—or that it is not. What is clear is that the goals remain a great challenge and that hard work lies ahead.

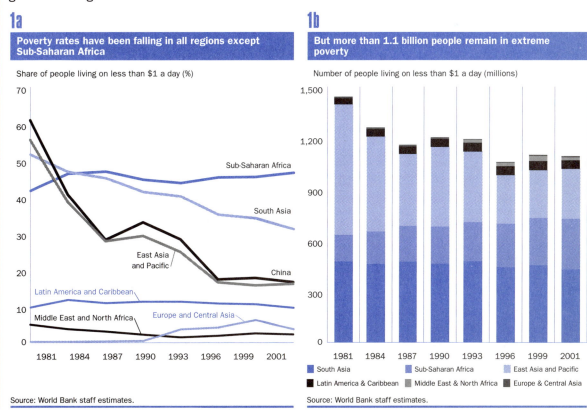

1a

Poverty rates have been falling in all regions except Sub-Saharan Africa

Share of people living on less than $1 a day (%)

Source: World Bank staff estimates.

1b

But more than 1.1 billion people remain in extreme poverty

Number of people living on less than $1 a day (millions)

South Asia | Sub-Saharan Africa | East Asia and Pacific
Latin America & Caribbean | Middle East & North Africa | Europe & Central Asia

Source: World Bank staff estimates.

1 Eradicate extreme poverty . . .

The first Millennium Development Goal calls for cutting in half the proportion of people living in extreme poverty—and those suffering from hunger—between 1990 and 2015. A poverty line of $1 a day ($1.08 in 1993 purchasing power parity terms) has been accepted as the working definition of extreme poverty in low-income countries. In middle-income countries a poverty line of $2 a day ($2.15 in 1993 purchasing power parity terms) is closer to a practical minimum, and national poverty lines may be set even higher.

In 1990, 1,219 million people, 28 percent of the population of low- and middle-income countries, lived on less than $1 a day. Over the next 11 years gross domestic product (GDP) in low- and middle-income countries grew 31 percent, and by 2001 the poverty rate had fallen to 21 percent. During the same period population in those countries grew by 15 percent to 5 billion, leaving about 1,100 million people in extreme poverty.

New estimates of poverty rates, based on reexamination of household survey data back to 1981, show that global trends in poverty reduction have been dominated by rapid growth in China and the East Asia and Pacific region. GDP per capita more than tripled while the proportion of people in extreme poverty fell from 56 percent to 16 percent. Poverty also fell in South Asia over the past 20 years, and while the decline was not as rapid, almost 50 million fewer people were living in extreme poverty by 2001. But in Sub-Saharan Africa, where GDP per capita shrank 14 percent, poverty rose from 41 percent in 1981 to 46 percent in 2001, and an additional 140 million people were living in extreme poverty. Other regions have seen little or no change. In the early 1990s the transition economies of Europe and Central Asia experienced a sharp drop in income. Poverty rates rose to 6 percent at the end of the decade before beginning to recede.

Continued progress in poverty reduction depends on economic growth and the distribution of income. Growth without poverty reduction is at least a theoretical possibility, and in regions such as Latin America, where the distribution of income is less equitable, the poverty reducing effects of growth are weaker. In looking ahead, income distribution is assumed to remain unchanged on average. If projected growth remains on track through 2015, global poverty rates measured at $1 a day will fall to 12.7 percent—less than half the 1990 level of 28 percent—and 363 million fewer people will live in extreme poverty than at the beginning of the 21st century.

Poverty rates will fall fastest in East Asia and Pacific outside of China, but the huge reduction in the number of people below the $1 a day poverty line in China will dominate global totals. In Europe and Central Asia and in the Middle East and North Africa, where poverty rates measured at $1 a day are low, a continuation of current trends will cut poverty rates to half their current levels. South Asia, led by continuing growth in India, is likely to reach or exceed the target. But growth and poverty reduction are proceeding more slowly in Latin America and the Caribbean, which will not reach the target unless growth picks up. The most difficult case is Sub-Saharan Africa, where poverty has increased since 1990 and will, on present trends, fall very slowly in the next 11 years, unless there is a major change in prospects.

1c

Most regions are on a path to cut extreme poverty by half by 2015

Share of people living on less than $1 (or $2) a day (%)

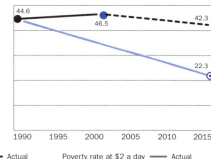

Source: World Bank staff estimates.

New poverty estimates trace the decline of global poverty levels over the last two decades

1d

With continuing growth the number of people living in extreme poverty will fall

People living on less than $1 a day (millions)

Region	1981	1984	1987	1990	1993	1996	1999	2001
East Asia & Pacific	767	558	424	472	416	287	282	284
China	606	421	308	377	336	212	224	212
Europe & Central Asia	1	1	2	2	17	20	30	18
Latin America & Caribbean	36	46	45	49	52	52	54	50
Middle East & North Africa	9	8	7	6	4	5	8	7
South Asia	475	460	473	462	476	441	453	428
Sub-Saharan Africa	164	198	219	227	241	269	292	314
Total	**1,451**	**1,272**	**1,169**	**1,219**	**1,206**	**1,075**	**1,117**	**1,101**
Excluding China	845	850	861	841	870	863	894	888

1e

And the proportion of people in extreme poverty will reach an all-time low in 2015

Share of people living on less than $1 a day (%)

Region	1981	1984	1987	1990	1993	1996	1999	2001
East Asia & Pacific	55.6	38.6	27.9	29.6	25.0	16.6	15.7	15.6
China	61.0	40.6	28.3	33.0	28.4	17.4	17.8	16.6
Europe & Central Asia	0.3	0.3	0.4	0.5	3.7	4.2	6.2	3.7
Latin America & Caribbean	9.7	11.8	10.9	11.3	11.3	10.7	10.5	9.5
Middle East & North Africa	5.1	3.8	3.2	2.3	1.6	2.0	2.6	2.4
South Asia	51.5	46.8	45.0	41.3	40.1	35.1	34.0	31.1
Sub-Saharan Africa	41.6	46.3	46.8	44.6	43.7	45.3	45.4	46.5
Total	**39.5**	**32.7**	**28.4**	**27.9**	**26.2**	**22.3**	**22.2**	**21.3**
Excluding China	31.5	29.8	28.4	26.1	25.5	24.0	23.7	22.8

1f

But more than 2 billion people will live on less than $2 a day

People living on less than $2 a day (millions)

Region	1981	1984	1987	1990	1993	1996	1999	2001
East Asia & Pacific	1,151	1,104	1,024	1,117	1,080	922	900	868
China	858	809	732	830	807	650	630	596
Europe & Central Asia	8	9	8	58	78	97	111	93
Latin America & Caribbean	99	119	115	125	136	117	127	128
Middle East & North Africa	52	50	53	51	52	61	70	70
South Asia	821	859	911	958	1,005	1,022	1,034	1,059
Sub-Saharan Africa	288	326	355	382	409	445	487	514
Total	**2,419**	**2,466**	**2,466**	**2,689**	**2,759**	**2,665**	**2,730**	**2,733**
Excluding China	1,561	1,657	1,734	1,858	1,952	2,015	2,101	2,137

1g

And more than half the population of South Asia and Sub-Saharan Africa will be very poor

Share of people living on less than $2 a day (%)

Region	1981	1984	1987	1990	1993	1996	1999	2001
East Asia & Pacific	83.4	76.3	67.4	69.9	64.8	53.3	50.3	47.6
China	86.3	78.0	67.0	72.6	68.1	53.4	50.1	46.7
Europe & Central Asia	1.9	2.0	1.7	12.3	16.6	20.6	23.5	19.7
Latin America & Caribbean	26.9	30.4	27.8	28.4	29.5	24.1	25.1	24.5
Middle East & North Africa	28.9	25.2	24.2	21.4	20.2	22.3	24.3	23.2
South Asia	89.1	87.2	86.7	85.5	84.5	81.2	77.7	76.9
Sub-Saharan Africa	73.3	76.1	76.1	75.0	74.3	74.8	75.7	76.3
Total	**65.9**	**63.4**	**59.8**	**61.6**	**60.1**	**55.3**	**54.2**	**52.8**
Excluding China	58.3	58.0	57.2	57.6	57.2	56.0	55.6	54.8

Source: World Bank staff estimates.

1 ... and reduce hunger and malnutrition

The world produces enough food to feed everyone, but hunger remains a persistent problem. Although famines and droughts cause terrible short-term crises and grab most of the headlines, the root cause of hunger is poverty. The Food and Agriculture Organization (FAO) estimates that worldwide there are more than 840 million people who are chronically undernourished, most of them living in low-income countries. But there are hungry people everywhere, including 10 million undernourished people living in industrial countries.

Undernourishment means consuming too little food to maintain normal levels of activity. The FAO sets the average requirement at 1,900 calories a day. Among the less severely affected the average daily shortfall is less than 200 calories a person. In the FAO's estimation extreme hunger occurs with a shortfall of more than 300 calories, but the needs of individuals vary with age, sex, and height. Adding to the problems of undernourishment are diets that lack essential nutrients and illnesses that deplete nutrients.

The Millennium Development Goals call for cutting the prevalence of hunger to half of its 1990 levels by 2015. Prevalence rates have been falling in most regions, but too slowly to achieve the 2015 target, and in many regions the number of hungry people continues to grow. By 2001 only the East Asia and Pacific and Latin America and the Caribbean regions had fewer undernourished people than 10 years earlier. Countries that have succeeded in reducing hunger had higher economic growth, especially in their agricultural sector and rural regions. They have also had lower population growth and lower rates of HIV infection.

Malnutrition in children often begins at birth, when poorly nourished mothers give birth to underweight babies. Improper feeding and child care practices contribute to the harm done by an inadequate diet, putting poor children at a permanent disadvantage. Malnourished children develop more slowly, enter school later, and perform less well. And malnutrition is an underlying factor in more than half the deaths of children under age five.

Progress in reducing child malnutrition has been fastest in East Asia and Pacific. where child malnutrition rates declined by 33 percent, and South Asia, where rates declined 25 percent. But many countries, especially in Sub-Saharan Africa, lag far behind. In many others data are inadequate for tracking progress. In the 74 countries with two or more observations since 1988, only 29 are currently on track to achieve the target by 2015. But faster progress is possible. Programs to encourage breastfeeding and to improve the diets of pregnant and lactating mothers along with micronutrient supplementation help to prevent malnutrition. Appropriate care and feeding of sick children, oral rehydration therapy, control and treatment of parasitic diseases, and programs to treat vitamin A deficiency have all been shown to reduce malnutrition rates.

1h

The undernourished are everywhere

Prevalence of undernourishment (%)

Source: FAO 2003, *The State of Food Insecurity in the World*.

1i

Malnourished children are among the most vulnerable

Prevalence of underweight children (%)

Source: WHO and World Bank staff estimates.

2 Achieve universal primary education

Education is the foundation of democratic societies and globally competitive economies. It is the basis for reducing poverty and inequality, increasing productivity, enabling the use of new technologies, and creating and spreading knowledge. In an increasingly complex, knowledge-dependent world, primary education, as the gateway to higher levels of education, must be the first priority. The Millennium Development Goals call on the world to ensure that by 2015 all children are able to complete a course of primary education. This target can be achieved—and it must be, if all developing countries are to compete in the global economy.

Progress toward this target is commonly measured by the net enrollment ratio—the ratio of enrolled children of official school age to the number of children of that age in the population. Ratios at or near 100 percent imply that all children will receive a full primary education. But lower ratios are ambiguous. Schools may fail to enroll all students in the first grade, or many students may drop out in later grades. Chad, for example, reports a net enrollment rate of almost 60 percent, but barely 20 percent complete the final year of primary education. Primary completion rates—the proportion of each age group finishing primary school—directly measure progress toward the Millennium Development Goal. To achieve 100 percent completion rates, school systems must enroll all children in first grade and keep them in school throughout the primary cycle. To reach the target of universal primary education by 2015, school systems with low completion rates will need to start now to train teachers, build classrooms, and improve the quality of education.

Three regions—East Asia and Pacific, Europe and Central Asia, and Latin America and the Caribbean—are on track to achieve the goal. Many countries in these regions have already reached the target. China, Mexico, and Russia are at or near full enrollment. Others, such as Brazil, Bulgaria, and Laos made rapid progress in the 1990s and are likely to reach the target by 2015. But three regions, with 150 million primary school-age children, are in danger of falling short. Sub-Saharan Africa lags farthest behind, with little progress since 1990. South Asia has chronically low enrollment and completion rates. And completion rates in the Middle East and North Africa stagnated in the 1990s. But even in these regions some countries have made large gains. Removing impediments and reducing costs can boost enrollments. Malawi and Uganda lowered school fees but could not provide spaces for all the new students. Many countries face the challenge of improving school quality while attracting and keeping more children in school.

If current trends persist, children in more than half of developing countries will not complete a full course of primary education in 2015. But faster progress is possible, and successful countries have set an example by:
- Committing a higher share of their budgets to public education.
- Managing to efficiently control costs.
- Providing an adequate level of complementary inputs.
- Keeping pupil-teacher ratios around 40 and repetition rates below 10 percent.

Many poor countries cannot afford the cost of expanding their education systems to reach the goal. They will need help from donors that are prepared to make long-term commitments to supporting education. The World Bank estimates the financing gap in low-income countries at $2.4–3.7 billion a year (Bruns, Mingat, and Rakotomalala 2003, p. 13).

1j

To reach the goal, all children need to complete primary school

Average primary school completion rate, 2000–02 (%)

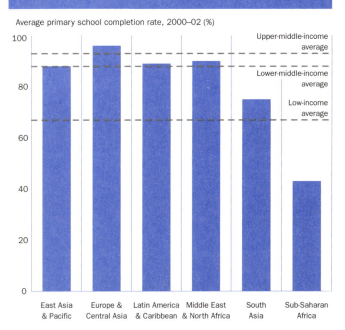

Source: World Bank staff estimates.

1k

Schools need to do more to lower costs and attract students

Reasons for leaving primary school

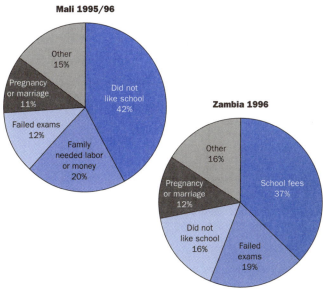

Source: Demographic and Health Survey EdData Education Profiles (www.dhseddata.com).

3 Promote gender equality and empower women

Gender disparities exist everywhere in the world. Women are underrepresented in local and national decisionmaking bodies. They earn less than men and are less likely to participate in wage employment. And in many low-income countries girls are less likely to attend school.

Evidence from around the world shows that eliminating gender disparities in education is one of the most effective development actions a country can take. When a country educates both its boys and its girls, economic productivity tends to rise, maternal and infant mortality rates usually fall, fertility rates decline, and the health and educational prospects of the next generation improve. With this in mind, the Millennium Development Goals call for eliminating gender disparities in primary and secondary school by 2005 and at all levels by 2015. But all regions except Latin America are still short of the first target.

The differences between boys' and girls' schooling are greatest in regions with the lowest primary school completion rates and the lowest average incomes. In South Asia girls' enrollment in primary schools is 12 points lower than boys', and only 61 percent of girls complete primary school compared with 86 percent of boys. One consequence is that illiteracy rates among young women ages 15–24 are almost 40 percent in South Asia and 26 percent in Sub-Saharan Africa, and in both regions they are more than half again as high as those of young men. The disparities are even greater in the Middle East and North Africa, a region of higher average incomes but a long history of neglecting female education.

The failure to educate women has consequences for development. A recent study (Klasen 1999) estimates that if countries in South Asia, Sub-Saharan Africa, and the Middle East and North Africa had closed the gender gap in schooling between 1960 and 1992 as quickly as East Asia did, their income would have grown by an additional 0.5 to 0.9 percentage point per year. In Africa this would have meant close to doubling per capita income growth.

What does improving girls' enrollments require? Mainly overcoming the social and economic obstacles that stop parents from sending their daughters to school. For many poor families the economic value of girls' work at home exceeds the perceived returns to schooling. Improving the quality and affordability of schools is a first step. The World Bank's Girls' Education Initiative outlines many gender-sensitive strategies and interventions, including construction of toilet blocks and water sources in schools, provision of nursery and preschool centers where girls can leave younger siblings, abolition of school fees and uniforms, and provision of free or subsidized textbooks. Overcoming women's disadvantages in the labor force and increasing their representation in public life will also help encourage girls to attend and stay in school. Progress is possible. Over the past decade gender differences at the primary level have been eliminated or greatly reduced in Algeria, Angola, Bangladesh, China, the Arab Republic of Egypt, and The Gambia.

Because the Millennium Development Goals are mutually reinforcing, progress toward one goal affects progress toward all the others. Success in many of the goals will have positive impacts on gender equality, just as progress toward gender equality will further other goals. Increasing opportunities for women will also contribute toward the goal of reducing poverty, educating children, improving health, and better managing environmental resources.

1l

Many girls still do not have equal access to education

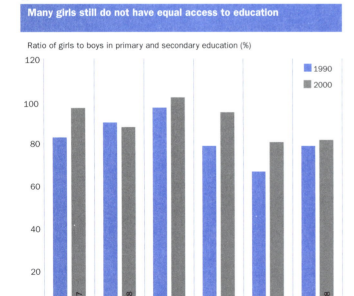

Ratio of girls to boys in primary and secondary education (%)

Source: United Nations Economic, Scientific and Cultural Organization and World Bank staff estimates.

1m

Literacy rates have been rising as more children remain in school, but girls lag behind boys

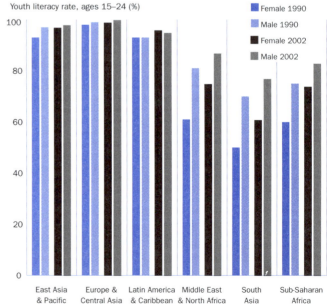

Youth literacy rate, ages 15–24 (%)

Source: United Nations Economic, Scientific and Cultural Organization and World Bank staff estimates.

4 Reduce child mortality

Every year more than 10 million children in developing countries die before the age of five. Rapid improvements before 1990 gave hope that mortality rates for infants and children under five could be cut by two-thirds in the following 25 years. But progress slowed almost everywhere in the 1990s. And no region, except possibly Latin America and the Caribbean, is on track to achieve the target. Progress has been particularly slow in Sub-Saharan Africa, where civil disturbances and the HIV/AIDS epidemic have driven up rates of infant and child mortality in several countries. For the region the under-five mortality rate stands at 171 deaths per 1,000 live births.

Child mortality is closely linked to poverty. In 2002 the average under-five mortality rate was 122 deaths per 1,000 live births in low-income countries, 42 in lower-middle-income countries, and 21 in upper-middle-income countries. In high-income countries the rate was less than 7. For 70 percent of the deaths the cause is a disease or a combination of diseases and malnutrition that would be preventable in a high-income country: acute respiratory infections, diarrhea, measles, and malaria.

Improvements in infant and child mortality have come slowly in low-income countries, where mortality rates have fallen by only 12 percent since 1990. Upper-middle-income countries have made the greatest improvement, reducing average mortality rates by 36 percent. But even this rate of improvement falls short of that needed to reach the target. There is evidence that improvements in child mortality have been greatest among the better-off. In 20 developing countries with disaggregated data, child mortality rates fell only half as fast for the poorest 20 percent of the population as for the whole population. In Bolivia, which is nearly on track to achieve the target, under-five mortality rates fell 34 percent among the wealthiest 20 percent but only 8 percent among the poorest. In Vietnam mortality rates also fell among the better-off but scarcely changed for the poor. But in Egypt in the late 1990s under-five mortality fell faster among the poor than among the general population. In the effort to reach the Millennium Development Goals, the poor do not need to be left behind.

Just as child deaths are the result of many causes, reducing child mortality will require multiple, complementary interventions. Raising incomes will help. So will increasing public spending on health services. But a greater effort is needed to ensure that health care and other public services reach the poor. Access to safe water, better sanitation facilities, and improvements in education, especially for girls and mothers, are closely linked to reduced mortality. Also needed are roads to improve access to health facilities and modern forms of energy to reduce dependence on traditional fuels, which cause damaging indoor air pollution. The Millennium Development Goals remind us of the need to look at health and health care from the broadest possible perspective.

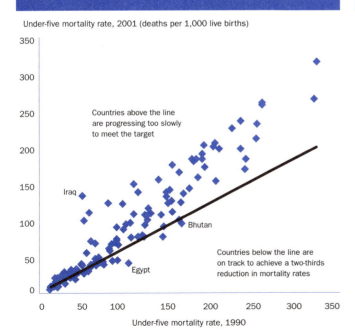

1n

Few countries are on track to meet the child mortality target

Under-five mortality rate, 2001 (deaths per 1,000 live births)

Countries above the line are progressing too slowly to meet the target

Countries below the line are on track to achieve a two-thirds reduction in mortality rates

Iraq

Bhutan

Egypt

Under-five mortality rate, 1990

Source: World Bank staff estimates.

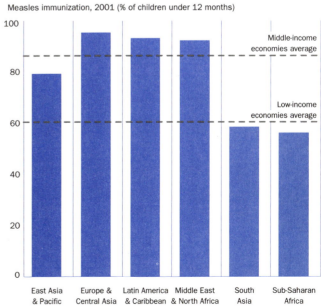

1o

To reduce early childhood deaths, immunization programs must be extended and sustained

Measles immunization, 2001 (% of children under 12 months)

Middle-income economies average

Low-income economies average

East Asia & Pacific / Europe & Central Asia / Latin America & Caribbean / Middle East & North Africa / South Asia / Sub-Saharan Africa

Source: WHO, UNICEF, and World Bank staff estimates.

5 Improve the health of mothers

In rich countries 13 women die in childbirth for every 100,000 live births. In some poor countries 100 times more women die. Overall, more than 500,000 women die each year in childbirth, most of them in developing countries. What makes maternal mortality such a compelling problem is that it strikes young women undergoing what should be a normal function. They die because they are poor. Malnourished. Weakened by disease. Exposed to multiple pregnancies. And they die because they lack access to trained health care workers and modern medical facilities.

The Millennium Development Goals call for reducing the maternal mortality ratio by three-quarters between 1990 and 2015, or an average of 5.4 percent a year. Maternal mortality is difficult to measure accurately. Deaths from pregnancy or childbirth are relatively rare and may not be captured in general-purpose surveys or surveys with small sample sizes. Maternal deaths may be underreported in countries that lack good administrative statistics or where many women give birth outside the formal health system. For these reasons, efforts to monitor maternal mortality often rely on proxy indicators or statistical models.

The share of births attended by skilled health staff is frequently used to identify where the need for intervention is greatest. Only 56 percent of women in developing countries are attended in childbirth by a trained midwife or doctor. In Latin America, where the share of births attended by skilled health personnel is high, maternal mortality is relatively low. But in Africa, where skilled attendants and health facilities are not readily available, it is very high.

The maternal mortality ratio measures the risk of a woman dying once she becomes pregnant. Women who have more pregnancies are exposed more often to the risk of maternal death and thus face a higher lifetime risk of death due to pregnancy or childbirth. The greatest number of maternal deaths each year occur in populous India, which has a maternal mortality ratio of 540 per 100,000 and a lifetime risk of maternal death of 1 in 48. But in little Togo, with a similar maternal mortality ratio but higher fertility rate, women are exposed to almost twice the risk of death (AbouZhar and Wardlaw 2003).

New estimates of trends in maternal mortality suggest that all regions, except possibly the Middle East and North Africa, will fall short of the 2015 target (World Bank 2003). Across the developing world 17 percent of countries, with almost a third of the population of developing countries, are on track to achieve the maternal mortality target. In Sub-Saharan Africa, where maternal mortality ratios are on average the highest, the rate of improvement is expected to be less than in any region except Europe and Central Asia.

Significant progress in reducing maternal mortality will require a comprehensive approach to providing health services: deaths in childbirth often involve complications, such as hemorrhaging, that require fully equipped medical facilities, accessible roads, and emergency transportation. Causes of complications during pregnancy and childbirth include inadequate nutrition, unsafe sex, and poor health care. Gender inequality in controlling household resources and making decisions also contributes to poor maternal health. Early childbearing and closely spaced pregnancies increase the risks for mothers and children. Access to family planning services helps women plan whether and when to have children. Fewer pregnancies means a lower lifetime exposure to the risk of maternal mortality.

1p

Extreme risks of dying from pregnancy or childbirth in some regions

Lifetime risk of maternal death, 2000

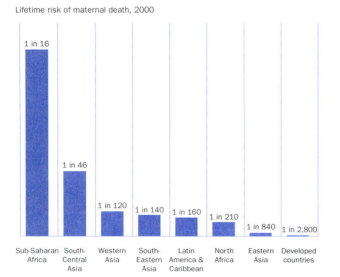

The lifetime risk of maternal death is the risk of an individual woman dying from pregnancy or childbirth during her lifetime. A 1 in 3,000 lifetime risk represents a low risk of dying from pregnancy or childbirth, while a 1 in 100 lifetime risk is a high risk of dying.

a. Excludes Australia, Japan, and New Zealand.
Source: AbouZhar and Wardlaw 2003.

1q

The presence of skilled health staff lowers the risk of maternal death

Births attended by skilled health staff, 1995–2000 (% of total)

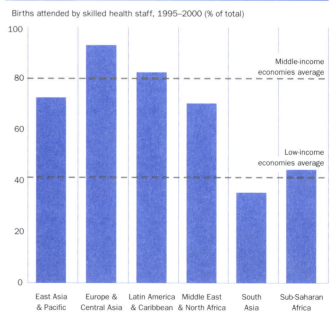

Source: World Bank staff estimates.

6 Combat HIV/AIDS, malaria, and other diseases

Epidemic diseases exact a huge toll in human suffering and lost opportunities for development. Poverty, civil disturbances, and natural disasters all contribute to, and are made worse by, the spread of disease. In Africa the spread of HIV/AIDS has reversed decades of improvements in life expectancy and left millions of children orphaned. It is draining the supply of teachers and eroding the quality of education.

HIV has infected more than 60 million people worldwide. Each day 14,000 people are newly infected, more than half of them below age 25. The Millennium Development Goals have set the target of reducing prevalence among 15–24 year olds by 25 percent by 2005 in the most severely affected countries and by 2010 globally. At the end of 2002, 42 million adults and 5 million children were living with HIV/AIDS—more than 95 percent of them in developing countries and 70 percent in Sub-Saharan Africa. There were almost a million new cases in South and East Asia, where more than 7 million people now live with HIV/AIDS. Projections suggest that by 2010, 45 million more people in low- and middle-income countries will become infected unless the world mounts an effective campaign to halt the disease's spread. But there are success stories: Brazil, Thailand, and Uganda are controlling the spread of HIV/AIDS. Thailand has reduced the number of new infections from 140,000 a decade ago to 30,000 in 2001.

The World Health Organization (WHO 2002) estimates that 300–500 million cases of malaria occur each year, leading to 1.1 million deaths. Almost 90 percent of cases occur in Sub-Saharan Africa, and most deaths are among children younger than five. Malaria is a disease of poverty: almost 60 percent of deaths occur among the poorest 20 percent of the population. The disease is estimated to have slowed economic growth in African countries by 1.3 percent a year (World Bank 2001). Because children bear the greatest burden of the disease, the Millennium Development Goals call for monitoring efforts focusing on children under five. An effective means of preventing new infections is the use of insecticide-treated bednets. Vietnam, where 16 percent of children sleep under treated bednets, has made significant strides in controlling malaria. But in Africa only 7 of 27 countries with survey data reported rates of bednet use of 5 percent or more. The emergence of drug-resistant strains of malaria has increased the urgency of finding new means of treatment and prevention.

Tuberculosis kills some 2 million people a year, most of them 15–45 years old. The emergence of drug-resistant strains of tuberculosis; the spread of HIV/AIDS, which reduces resistance to tuberculosis; and the growing number of refugees and displaced persons have allowed the disease to spread more rapidly. Each year there are 8 million new cases—2 million in Sub-Saharan Africa, 3 million in Southeast Asia, and more than a quarter million in Eastern Europe and the former Soviet Union. Poorly managed tuberculosis programs allow drug-resistant strains to spread. WHO has developed a treatment strategy—directly observed treatment, short course (DOTS)—that emphasizes positive diagnosis followed by a course of treatment and follow-up care. DOTS produces cure rates of up to 95 percent, even in poor countries. While some countries have made rapid progress in DOTS detection rates, those with high tuberculosis burdens are not increasing detection rates toward the 70 percent target.

1r

HIV strikes at youth—and women are particularly vulnerable

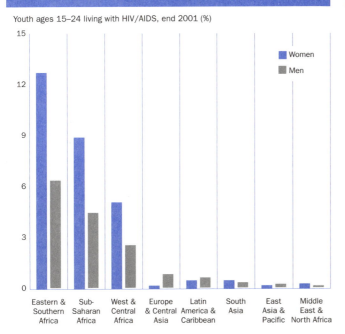

Youth ages 15–24 living with HIV/AIDS, end 2001 (%)

Source: Joint United Nations Programme on HIV/AIDS.

1s

Treated bednets are a proven way to combat malaria, but they are still not widely used

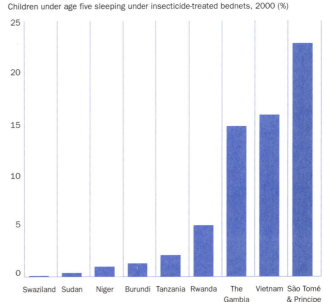

Children under age five sleeping under insecticide-treated bednets, 2000 (%)

Source: World Health Organization.

7 Ensure environmental sustainability

Sustainable development can be ensured only by protecting the environment and using its resources wisely. Because poor people are often dependent on environmental resources for their livelihood, they are most affected by environmental degradation and by natural disasters, such as fires, storms, and earthquakes, whose effects are worsened by environmental mismanagement.

The Millennium Development Goals draw attention to some of the environmental conditions that need to be closely monitored—changes in forest coverage and biological diversity, energy use and the emission of greenhouse gases, the availability of adequate water and sanitation services, and the plight of slum dwellers in rapidly growing cities.

As a result of economic and demographic growth most developing regions have increased their carbon dioxide emissions, primarily due to the burning of fossil fuels such as coal, oil, and natural gas, and land-use practices. In the last decade carbon dioxide emissions have increased by 25 percent in low-income countries, though from a significantly lower level than in other income groups. Globally, the increase in carbon dioxide emissions has slowed in the last decade, and annual emissions per capita have declined from 4.1 metric tons to 3.8 a year. Still, greenhouse gases accumulate and increase the risk of climate changes, which will affect all of us for generations to come.

Lack of clean water and basic sanitation is the main reason that diseases transmitted by feces are so common in developing countries. In 1990 diarrhea resulted in 3 million deaths, 85 percent of them among children. In 2000, 1.2 billion people still lacked access to a reliable source of water that was reasonably

protected from contamination, 40 percent of them in East Asia and Pacific and 25 percent in Sub-Saharan Africa. Improved sanitation services and good hygiene practices are also needed to reduce the risk of disease. A basic sanitation system provides disposal facilities that can effectively prevent human, animal, and insect contact with excreta. Such systems do not, however, ensure that effluents are treated to remove harmful substances before they are released into the environment. Meeting the Millennium Development Goals will require providing about 1.5 billion people with access to safe water and 2 billion with access to basic sanitation facilities between 2000 and 2015.

The world is rapidly urbanizing. While the movement of people to cities may reduce immediate pressure on the rural environment, it increases people's exposure to other environmental hazards. The United Nations Human Settlements Programme (UN Habitat 2003) estimates that in 2001, 924 million people lived in slums, where they lack basic services, live in overcrowded and substandard housing, and are exposed to unhealthy living conditions and hazardous locations. The Millennium Development Goals call for improving the lives of at least 100 million slum dwellers by 2020. Polluted air is one of many hazards faced by urban dwellers. Poor people, who live in crowded neighborhoods close to traffic corridors and industrial plants, are likely to suffer the most. Every year an estimated 0.5–1.0 million people die prematurely from respiratory and other illnesses associated with urban air pollution (World Bank 2002i). Much can be done to improve the lives of slum dwellers by improving basic infrastructure, mitigating environmental hazards, increasing access to education and health services, and empowering them to control and manage their own lives.

1t

Greenhouse gas emissions rise with income

Per capita emissions of carbon dioxide (metric tons)

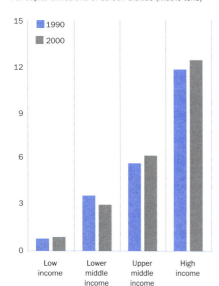

Source: Carbon Dioxide Information Analysis Centre and World Bank staff estimates.

1u

Access to water and sanitation services will require large investments

Share of population with access to an improved source, 2000 (%)

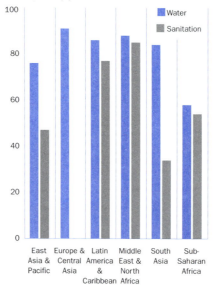

Source: World Health Organization, UNICEF, and World Bank staff estimates.

1v

Slums are growing in newly urbanized areas

Number of urban residents (millions)

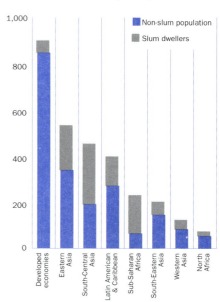

Note: United Nations–defined regions.
Source: UN Habitat 2003.

8 Develop a global partnership for development

The eighth and final goal complements the first seven. It commits wealthy countries to work with developing countries to create an environment in which rapid, sustainable development is possible. It calls for an open, rule-based trading and financial system, more generous aid to countries committed to poverty reduction, and relief for the debt problems of developing countries. It draws attention to the problems of the least developed countries and of landlocked countries and small island developing states, which have greater difficulty competing in the global economy. And it calls for cooperation with the private sector to address youth unemployment, ensure access to affordable, essential drugs, and make available the benefits of new technologies.

Important steps toward implementing the global partnership envisioned in the Millennium Declaration were taken at international meetings held in 2001 in Doha, which launched a new "development round" of trade negotiations, and in 2002 at the International Conference on Financing for Development held in Monterrey, Mexico, where developed and developing countries reached a new consensus stressing mutual responsibilities for reaching the Millennium Development Goals. The Monterrey Consensus calls for developing countries to improve their policies and governance aimed at increasing economic growth and reducing poverty and for developed countries to increase their support, especially by providing more and better aid and greater access to their markets.

What is at stake? Greater access to markets in rich countries for the exports of developing country goods and services could generate substantial gains in real incomes and reduce the

number of people living in poverty in 2015 by 140 million more than in current projections. But progress on trade issues has slowed since the Doha meetings, and the subsequent World Trade Organization meetings at Cancun failed to reach agreement on outstanding issues, particularly the agricultural policies of high-income economies. Subsidies to agriculture by Organisation for Economic Co-operation and Development members were greater than $300 billion in 2002. By distorting world prices and restricting access to markets, subsidies hurt growth in the agricultural sector, where many of the poorest people work. Trade in manufactured goods faces fewer barriers. But tariff peaks are used selectively to keep out exports of developing countries.

The force of the Monterrey Consensus is that more aid should go to countries with good track records and to support reform programs that produce results. After falling throughout most of the last decade, aid levels rose in 2002, and commitments made during or following the Monterrey Conference would increase the real level of aid by $18.6 billion dollars more in 2006. This is a substantial increase, but it will fall short of the $30–50 billion extra needed to meet the identified needs of the poorest countries to set them on the path to achieving the Millennium Development Goals. The quality of aid is important as well. Aid is most effective in reducing poverty when it goes to poor countries with good economic policies and sound governance and advances country-owned poverty reduction programs. But about a third of official development assistance goes to middle-income economies. And when aid flows are affected by geopolitical considerations, donors may overlook weaknesses in the recipient country's policies and institutions.

1w

Aid has increased, but not by as much as domestic subsidies to agriculture

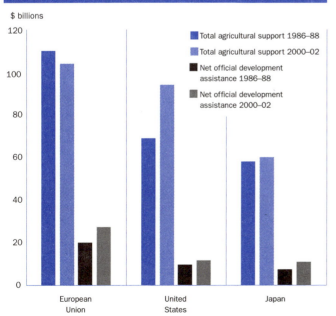

$ billions

Legend:
- Total agricultural support 1986–88
- Total agricultural support 2000–02
- Net official development assistance 1986–88
- Net official development assistance 2000–02

Source: Organisation for Economic Co-operation and Development, Development Assistance Committee, and World Bank staff estimates.

1x

New commitments by donors, the first major increase in more than a decade, will still meet only a fraction of the need

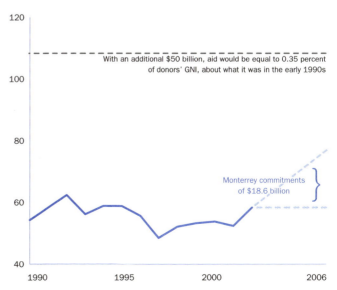

Net official development assistance ($ billions)

With an additional $50 billion, aid would be equal to 0.35 percent of donors' GNI, about what it was in the early 1990s

Monterrey commitments of $18.6 billion

Source: Organisation for Economic Co-operation and Development, Development Assistance Committee, and World Bank staff estimates.

Goals, targets, and indicators

Goals and targets from the Millennium Declaration | **Indicators for monitoring progress**

Goal 1   Eradicate extreme poverty and hunger

Target 1	Halve, between 1990 and 2015, the proportion of people whose income is less than $1 a day	1	Proportion of population below $1 (PPP) a day [a]
		1a	Poverty headcount ratio (percentage of population below the national poverty line)
		2	Poverty gap ratio [incidence x depth of poverty]
		3	Share of poorest quintile in national consumption
Target 2	Halve, between 1990 and 2015, the proportion of people who suffer from hunger	4	Prevalence of underweight children under five years of age
		5	Proportion of population below minimum level of dietary energy consumption

Goal 2   Achieve universal primary education

Target 3	Ensure that, by 2015, children everywhere, boys and girls alike, will be able to complete a full course of primary schooling	6	Net enrollment ratio in primary education
		7	Proportion of pupils starting grade 1 who reach grade 5 [b]
		8	Literacy rate of 15- to 24-year-olds

Goal 3   Promote gender equality and empower women

Target 4	Eliminate gender disparity in primary and secondary education, preferably by 2005, and in all levels of education no later than 2015	9	Ratios of girls to boys in primary, secondary, and tertiary education
		10	Ratio of literate women to men ages 15–24
		11	Share of women in wage employment in the nonagricultural sector
		12	Proportion of seats held by women in national parliaments

Goal 4   Reduce child mortality

Target 5	Reduce by two-thirds, between 1990 and 2015, the under-five mortality rate	13	Under-five mortality rate
		14	Infant mortality rate
		15	Proportion of one-year-old children immunized against measles

Goal 5   Improve maternal health

| Target 6 | Reduce by three-quarters, between 1990 and 2015, the maternal mortality ratio | 16 | Maternal mortality ratio |
| | | 17 | Proportion of births attended by skilled health personnel |

Goal 6   Combat HIV/AIDS, malaria, and other diseases

Target 7	Have halted by 2015 and begun to reverse the spread of HIV/AIDS	18	HIV prevalence among pregnant women ages 15–24
		19	Condom use rate of the contraceptive prevalence rate [c]
		19a	Condom use at last high-risk sex
		19b	Percentage of 15- to 24-year-olds with comprehensive correct knowledge of HIV/AIDS [d]
		19c	Contraceptive prevalence rate
		20	Ratio of school attendance of orphans to school attendance of nonorphans ages 10–14
Target 8	Have halted by 2015 and begun to reverse the incidence of malaria and other major diseases	21	Prevalence and death rates associated with malaria
		22	Proportion of population in malaria-risk areas using effective malaria prevention and treatment measures [e]
		23	Prevalence and death rates associated with tuberculosis
		24	Proportion of tuberculosis cases detected and cured under directly observed treatment, short course (DOTS)

Goal 7   Ensure environmental sustainability

Target 9	Integrate the principles of sustainable development into country policies and programs and reverse the loss of environmental resources	25	Proportion of land area covered by forest
		26	Ratio of area protected to maintain biological diversity to surface area
		27	Energy use (kilograms of oil equivalent) per $1 GDP (PPP)
		28	Carbon dioxide emissions per capita and consumption of ozone-depleting chlorofluorocarbons (ODP tons)
		29	Proportion of population using solid fuels
Target 10	Halve, by 2015, the proportion of people without sustainable access to safe drinking water and basic sanitation	30	Proportion of population with sustainable access to an improved water source, urban and rural
		31	Proportion of population with access to improved sanitation, urban and rural

Goals and targets from the Millennium Declaration	Indicators for monitoring progress
Target 11 By 2020, to have achieved a significant improvement in the lives of at least 100 million slum dwellers	**32** Proportion of households with access to secure tenure

Goal 8	**Develop a global partnership for development**	

Goals and targets	Indicators
Target 12 Develop further an open, rule-based, predictable, nondiscriminatory trading and financial system Includes a commitment to good governance, development and poverty reduction—both nationally and internationally	Some of the indicators listed below are monitored separately for the least developed countries (LDCs), Africa, landlocked countries and small island developing states. **Official development assistance (ODA)** **33** Net ODA, total and to the least developed countries, as a percentage of OECD/DAC donors' gross national income **34** Proportion of total bilateral, sector-allocable ODA of OECD/DAC donors to basic social services (basic education, primary health care, nutrition, safe water and sanitation) **35** Proportion of bilateral official development assistance of OECD/DAC donors that is untied
Target 13 Address the special needs of the least developed countries Includes tariff and quota free access for the least developed countries' exports; enhanced programme of debt relief for heavily indebted poor countries (HIPC) and cancellation of official bilateral debt; and more generous ODA for countries committed to poverty reduction	**36** ODA received in landlocked countries as a proportion of their gross national incomes **37** ODA received in small island developing states as proportion of their gross national incomes
Target 14 Address the special needs of landlocked countries and small island developing states (through the Programme of Action for the Sustainable Development of Small Island Developing States and the outcome of the 22nd special session of the General Assembly)	**Market access** **38** Proportion of total developed country imports (by value and excluding arms) from developing countries and from the least developed countries, admitted free of duty **39** Average tariffs imposed by developed countries on agricultural products and textiles and clothing from developing countries **40** Agricultural support estimate for OECD countries as a percentage of their gross domestic product **41** Proportion of ODA provided to help build trade capacity
Target 15 Deal comprehensively with the debt problems of developing countries through national and international measures in order to make debt sustainable in the long term	**Debt sustainability** **42** Total number of countries that have reached their HIPC decision points and number that have reached their HIPC completion points (cumulative) **43** Debt relief committed under HIPC Debt Initiative **44** Debt service as a percentage of exports of goods and services
Target 16 In cooperation with developing countries, develop and implement strategies for decent and productive work for youth	**45** Unemployment rate of 15- to 24-year-olds, male and female and total [f]
Target 17 In cooperation with pharmaceutical companies, provide access to affordable essential drugs in developing countries	**46** Proportion of population with access to affordable essential drugs on a sustainable basis
Target 18 In cooperation with the private sector, make available the benefits of new technologies, especially information and communications	**47** Telephone lines and cellular subscribers per 100 people **48a** Personal computers in use per 100 people **48b** Internet users per 100 people

Note: Goals, targets, and indicators effective September 8, 2003.

a. For monitoring country poverty trends, indicators based on national poverty lines should be used, where available. b. An alternative indicator under development is "primary completion rate." c. Among contraceptive methods, only condoms are effective in preventing HIV transmission. Since the condom use rate is only measured among women in union, it is supplemented by an indicator on condom use in high-risk situations (indicator 19a) and an indicator on HIV/AIDS knowledge (indicator 19b). Indicator 19c (contraceptive prevalence rate) is also useful in tracking progress in other health, gender, and poverty goals. d. This indicator is defined as the percentage of 15- to 24-year-olds who correctly identify the two major ways of preventing the sexual transmission of HIV (using condoms and limiting sex to one faithful, uninfected partner), who reject the two most common local misconceptions about HIV transmission, and who know that a healthy-looking person can transmit HIV. However, since there are currently not a sufficient number of surveys to be able to calculate the indicator as defined above, UNICEF, in collaboration with UNAIDS and WHO, produced two proxy indicators that represent two components of the actual indicator. They are the percentage of women and men ages 15–24 who know that a person can protect herself from HIV infection by "consistent use of condom," and the percentage of women and men ages 15–24 who know a healthy-looking person can transmit HIV. e. Prevention to be measured by the percentage of children under age five sleeping under insecticide-treated bednets; treatment to be measured by percentage of children under age five who are appropriately treated. f. An improved measure of the target for future years is under development by the International Labour Organization.

1.1 Size of the economy

	Population	Surface area	Population density	Gross national income		Gross national income per capita		PPP gross national income [a]			Gross domestic product	
	millions	thousand sq. km	people per sq. km	$ billions	rank	$	rank	$ billions	Per capita $	rank	% growth	Per capita % growth
	2002	2002	2002	2002[b]	2002	2002[b]	2002	2002	2002	2002	2001–02	2001–02
Afghanistan	28[c]	652	43	..	..	..[d]	..	..	..	..	..	..
Albania	3	29	115	4.6	120	1,450	120	16	4,960	112	4.7	4.1
Algeria	31	2,382	13	53.8	48	1,720	114	173[e]	5,530[e]	103	4.1	2.5
Angola	13	1,247	11	9.3	89	710	146	24[e]	1,840[e]	163	15.3	12.0
Argentina	36	2,780	13	154.0	27	4,220	74	387	10,190	72	−10.9	−12.0
Armenia	3	30	109	2.4	145	790	144	10	3,230	139	12.9	13.6
Australia	20	7,741	3	384.1	14	19,530	29	539	27,440	19	2.7	1.4
Austria	8	84	97	192.1	20	23,860	18	233	28,910	12	1.0	0.8
Azerbaijan	8	87	94	5.8	108	710	146	25	3,010	142	10.6	9.8
Bangladesh	136	144	1,042	51.1	51	380	171	241	1,770	165	4.4	2.6
Belarus	10	208	48	13.5	80	1,360	124	55	5,500	105	4.7	5.2
Belgium	10	31	315	237.1	18	22,940	21	291	28,130	16	0.7	0.2
Benin	7	113	59	2.5	144	380	171	7	1,060	185	6.0	3.3
Bolivia	9	1,099	8	7.9	96	900	140	21	2,390	149	2.8	0.5
Bosnia and Herzegovina	4	51	81	5.4	112	1,310	125	..	..	..	3.9	2.5
Botswana	2	582	3	5.1	114	3,010	88	13	7,740	84	3.1	2.1
Brazil	174	8,547	21	494.5	12	2,830	91	1,300	7,450	86	1.5	0.3
Bulgaria	8	111	72	14.1	78	1,770	111	56	7,030	87	4.8	5.5
Burkina Faso	12	274	43	2.9	139	250	187	13[e]	1,090[e]	184	4.6	2.1
Burundi	7	28	275	0.7	179	100	206	4[e]	630[e]	204	3.6	1.7
Cambodia	12	181	71	3.8	126	300	178	25[e]	1,970[e]	159	5.5	3.6
Cameroon	16	475	34	8.7	94	550	156	30	1,910	162	4.4	2.3
Canada	31	9,971	3	702.0	8	22,390	23	907	28,930	11	3.3	2.3
Central African Republic	4	623	6	1.0	171	250	187	4[e]	1,170[e]	183	−0.8	−2.2
Chad	8	1,284	7	1.8	151	210	194	8	1,010	187	9.9	6.7
Chile	16	757	21	66.3	43	4,250	73	147	9,420	76	2.1	0.9
China	1,280	9,598[f]	137	1,234.2	6	960	136	5,792[g]	4,520[g]	125	8.0	7.3
Hong Kong, China	7	..	..	167.6	25	24,690	16	187	27,490	18	2.3	1.3
Colombia	44	1,139	42	79.6	42	1,820	109	269[e]	6,150[e]	98	1.6	0.0
Congo, Dem. Rep.	52	2,345	23	5.0	115	100	206	32[e]	630[e]	204	3.0	0.0
Congo, Rep.	4	342	11	2.2	147	610	153	3	710	202	3.5	0.6
Costa Rica	4	51	77	16.1	75	4,070	77	34[e]	8,560[e]	81	3.0	1.2
Côte d'Ivoire	17	322	52	10.2	87	620	152	24	1,450	177	−1.8	−3.8
Croatia	4	57	80	20.3	66	4,540	71	45	10,000	74	5.2	5.2
Cuba	11	111	103	..	..	..[h]	..	..	..	..	..	..
Czech Republic	10	79	132	56.0	46	5,480	68	152	14,920	55	2.0	2.1
Denmark	5	43	127	162.6	26	30,260	9	164	30,600	8	2.1	1.8
Dominican Republic	9	49	178	..	..	..[h]	..	54[e]	6,270[e]	97	4.1	2.5
Ecuador	13	284	46	19.1	70	1,490	118	43	3,340	138	3.4	1.8
Egypt, Arab Rep.	66	1,001	67	97.6	37	1,470	119	253	3,810	132	3.0	1.1
El Salvador	6	21	310	13.6	79	2,110	101	31[e]	4,790[e]	120	2.1	0.4
Eritrea	4	118	43	0.8	173	190	196	4[e]	1,040[e]	186	1.8	−0.5
Estonia	1	45	32	5.7	109	4,190	75	16	11,630	63	6.0	6.5
Ethiopia	67	1,104	67	6.5	102	100	206	52[e]	780[e]	200	2.7	0.5
Finland	5	338	17	124.2	29	23,890	17	136	26,160	25	1.6	1.4
France	59	552	108	1,362.1[i]	5	22,240[i]	24	1,609	27,040	21	1.2	0.7
Gabon	1	268	5	4.0	123	3,060	87	7	5,530	103	3.0	0.8
Gambia, The	1	11	139	0.4	193	270	184	2[e]	1,660[e]	169	−3.1	−5.7
Georgia	5	70	74	3.4	135	650	151	12[e]	2,270[e]	152	5.6	6.6
Germany	82	357	236	1,876.3	3	22,740	22	2,226	26,980	22	0.2	0.0
Ghana	20	239	89	5.5	111	270	184	42[e]	2,080[e]	156	4.5	2.7
Greece	11	132	82	123.9	30	11,660	48	200	18,770	43	4.0	3.6
Guatemala	12	109	111	21.0	64	1,760	112	48[e]	4,030[e]	129	2.2	−0.4
Guinea	8	246	32	3.2	137	410	169	16	2,060	157	4.2	2.0
Guinea-Bissau	1	36	51	0.2	203	130	205	1[e]	680[e]	203	−7.2	−9.8
Haiti	8	28	301	3.6	129	440	165	13[e]	1,610[e]	172	−0.9	−2.7

Size of the economy

	Population	Surface area	Population density	Gross national income		Gross national income per capita		PPP gross national income [a]			Gross domestic product	
									Per capita			Per capita
	millions	thousand sq. km	people per sq. km	$ billions	rank	$	rank	$ billions	$	rank	% growth	% growth
	2002	2002	2002	2002 [b]	2002	2002 [b]	2002	2002	2002	2002	2001–02	2001–02
Honduras	7	112	61	6.3	105	930	138	17 [e]	2,540 [e]	147	2.5	0.0
Hungary	10	93	110	53.7	49	5,290	69	133	13,070	58	3.3	3.6
India	1,049	3,287	353	494.8	11	470	161	2,778 [e]	2,650 [e]	146	4.6	3.0
Indonesia	212	1,905	117	149.9	28	710	146	650	3,070	141	3.7	2.3
Iran, Islamic Rep.	66	1,648	40	112.9	33	1,720	114	438	6,690	91	6.7	5.1
Iraq	24	438	55	..	..	.. [h]	..	..	..	..	..	..
Ireland	4	70	57	90.3	38	23,030	20	116	29,570	9	6.9	5.4
Israel	7	21	318	105.2	35	16,020	37	125	19,000	41	–0.8	–2.7
Italy	58	301	196	1,100.7	7	19,080	30	1,510	26,170	24	0.4	0.4
Jamaica	3	11	242	7.0	100	2,690	93	10	3,680	134	1.1	0.3
Japan	127	378	349	4,323.9	2	34,010	7	3,481	27,380	20	0.3	0.2
Jordan	5	89	58	9.1	92	1,760	112	22	4,180	127	4.9	2.0
Kazakhstan	15	2,725	6	22.6	62	1,520	117	84	5,630	101	9.8	10.1
Kenya	31	580	55	11.2	85	360	174	32	1,010	187	1.0	–0.9
Korea, Dem. Rep.	22	121	187	..	..	.. [d]	..	..	..	..	..	..
Korea, Rep.	48	99	483	473.0	13	9,930	53	808	16,960	51	6.3	5.7
Kuwait	2	18	131	38.0	55	16,340	36	41 [e]	17,780 [e]	47	–1.0	–3.3
Kyrgyz Republic	5	200	26	1.4	158	290	181	8	1,560	175	–0.5	–1.5
Lao PDR	6	237	24	1.7	153	310	176	9	1,660	169	5.0	2.6
Latvia	2	65	38	8.1	95	3,480	86	21	9,190	77	6.1	7.0
Lebanon	4	10	434	17.7	72	3,990	79	20	4,600	123	1.0	–0.3
Lesotho	2	30	59	1.0	170	550	156	5 [e]	2,970 [e]	143	3.8	2.8
Liberia	3	111	34	0.5	190	140	201	..	..	..	3.3	0.8
Libya	5	1,760	3	..	..	.. [j]	..	..	..	..	..	..
Lithuania	3	65	54	12.7	81	3,670	83	35	10,190	72	6.7	7.1
Macedonia, FYR	2	26	80	3.5	132	1,710	116	13	6,420	95	0.7	0.6
Madagascar	16	587	28	3.8	124	230	191	12	730	201	–12.7	–15.2
Malawi	11	118	114	1.7	154	160	200	6	570	207	1.8	–0.2
Malaysia	24	330	74	86.1	40	3,540	84	207	8,500	82	4.1	1.9
Mali	11	1,240	9	2.7	142	240	189	10	860	192	4.4	1.9
Mauritania	3	1,026	3	0.8	175	280	183	5 [e]	1,790 [e]	164	3.3	0.8
Mauritius	1	2	597	4.7	118	3,860	81	13	10,820	67	4.4	3.4
Mexico	101	1,958	53	597.0	9	5,920	66	887	8,800	80	0.9	–0.5
Moldova	4	34	129	1.7	155	460	164	7	1,600	173	7.2	7.6
Mongolia	2	1,567	2	1.1	167	430	166	4	1,710	167	4.0	2.8
Morocco	30	447	66	34.7	58	1,170	128	111	3,730	133	3.2	1.6
Mozambique	18	802	24	3.6	128	200	195	18 [e]	990 [e]	189	7.7	5.6
Myanmar	49	677	74	..	..	.. [d]	..	..	..	..	..	..
Namibia	2	824	2	3.5	131	1,790	110	14 [e]	6,880 [e]	89	2.7	0.6
Nepal	24	147	169	5.5	110	230	191	33	1,370	179	–0.5	–2.7
Netherlands	16	42	477	377.6	15	23,390	19	458	28,350	15	0.2	–0.4
New Zealand	4	271	15	52.2	50	13,260	44	81	20,550	39	4.3	2.8
Nicaragua	5	130	44	3.8	125	710	146	13 [e]	2,350 [e]	150	1.0	–1.6
Niger	11	1,267	9	2.0	149	180	197	9 [e]	800 [e]	195	3.0	–0.1
Nigeria	133	924	146	39.5	54	300	178	106	800	195	–0.9	–3.1
Norway	5	324	15	175.8	23	38,730	3	166	36,690	3	1.0	0.4
Oman	3	310	8	19.9	67	7,830	59	33	13,000	59	0.0	–2.3
Pakistan	145	796	188	60.9	45	420	168	284	1,960	160	2.8	0.4
Panama	3	76	40	11.8	83	4,020	78	18 [e]	6,060 [e]	99	0.8	–0.7
Papua New Guinea	5	463	12	2.8	140	530	158	12 [e]	2,180 [e]	153	–0.5	–2.8
Paraguay	6	407	14	6.4	103	1,170	128	25 [e]	4,590 [e]	124	–2.3	–4.4
Peru	27	1,285	21	54.0	47	2,020	103	130	4,880	117	4.9	3.3
Philippines	80	300	268	82.4	41	1,030	134	356	4,450	126	4.4	2.3
Poland	39	313	127	176.6	22	4,570	70	404	10,450	70	1.4	1.4
Portugal	10	92	111	109.1	34	10,720	50	181	17,820	46	0.4	0.2
Puerto Rico	4	9	436	..	..	.. [k]	..	..	..	..	..	..

	Population	Surface area	Population density	Gross national income		Gross national income per capita		PPP gross national income[a]			Gross domestic product	
									Per capita			Per capita
	millions	thousand sq. km	people per sq. km	$ billions	rank	$	rank	$ billions	$	rank	% growth	% growth
	2002	2002	2002	2002[b]	2002	2002[b]	2002	2002	2002	2002	2001–02	2001–02
Romania	22	238	97	41.7	53	1,870	108	145	6,490	93	4.3	4.8
Russian Federation	144	17,075	9	306.6	16	2,130	99	1,165	8,080	83	4.3	4.8
Rwanda	8	26	331	1.8	150	230	191	10[e]	1,260[e]	182	9.4	6.3
Saudi Arabia	22	2,150	10	186.8	21	8,530	57	277[e]	12,660[e]	60	1.0	−1.8
Senegal	10	197	52	4.6	119	470	161	15[e]	1,540[e]	176	1.1	−1.2
Serbia and Montenegro	8[l]	102	..	11.6[l]	84	1,400[l]	123	..	..	..	4.0	35.7
Sierra Leone	5	72	73	0.7	177	140	201	3	500	208	6.3	4.2
Singapore	4	1	6,826	86.1	39	20,690	27	99	23,730	31	2.2	1.4
Slovak Republic	5	49	..	21.3	63	3,970	80	68	12,590	61	4.4	4.4
Slovenia	2	20	98	20.4	65	10,370	52	36	18,480	45	2.9	3.6
Somalia	9	638	15	..	..	..[d]	..	..	..	..	..	..
South Africa	45	1,221	37	113.4	32	2,500	94	445[e]	9,810[e]	75	3.0	1.8
Spain	41	506	82	596.5	10	14,580	40	868	21,210	36	2.0	1.6
Sri Lanka	19	66	293	16.1	74	850	142	67	3,510	135	4.0	2.7
Sudan	33	2,506	14	12.2	82	370	173	57[e]	1,740[e]	166	5.5	3.3
Swaziland	1	17	63	1.4	159	1,240	127	5	4,730	122	3.6	1.7
Sweden	9	450	22	231.8	19	25,970	12	230	25,820	26	1.9	1.5
Switzerland	7	41	184	263.7	17	36,170	4	232	31,840	7	0.1	−0.7
Syrian Arab Republic	17	185	92	19.1	69	1,130	130	59	3,470	136	2.7	0.3
Tajikistan	6	143	45	1.1	164	180	197	6	930	191	9.1	8.5
Tanzania	35	945	40	9.7[m]	88	290[m]	181	20	580	206	6.3	4.1
Thailand	62	513	121	123.3	31	2,000	104	425	6,890	88	5.4	4.7
Togo	5	57	88	1.3	161	270	184	7[e]	1,450[e]	177	4.6	2.4
Trinidad and Tobago	1	5	254	8.8	93	6,750	63	12	9,000	79	2.7	2.1
Tunisia	10	164	63	19.5	68	1,990	105	63	6,440	94	1.7	0.6
Turkey	70	775	90	173.3	24	2,490	95	438	6,300	96	7.8	6.1
Turkmenistan	5	488	10	..[h]	..	..	..	23	4,780	121	14.9	13.1
Uganda	25	241	125	5.9	107	240	189	33[e]	1,360[e]	180	6.7	3.8
Ukraine	49	604	84	37.9	56	780	145	234	4,800	119	4.8	5.6
United Arab Emirates	3	84	38	..[k]	..	..	..	77[e]	24,030[e]	30	1.8	−5.0
United Kingdom	59	243	246	1,510.8	4	25,510	13	1,574	26,580	23	1.8	1.5
United States	288	9,629	31	10,207.0	1	35,400	6	10,414	36,110	4	2.4	1.4
Uruguay	3	176	19	14.6	77	4,340	72	26	7,710	85	−10.8	−11.3
Uzbekistan	25	447	61	7.8	98	310	176	41	1,640	171	4.2	2.9
Venezuela, RB	25	912	28	102.3	36	4,080	76	131	5,220	110	−8.9	−10.5
Vietnam	80	332	247	34.8	57	430	166	185	2,300	151	7.0	5.8
West Bank and Gaza	3	..	..	3.6	130	1,110	131	..	..	..	−19.1	−22.5
Yemen, Rep.	19	528	35	9.1	91	490	160	15	800	195	3.6	0.5
Zambia	10	753	14	3.5	133	340	175	8	800	195	3.3	1.6
Zimbabwe	13	391	34	..	..	..[d]	..	28	2,180	153	−5.6	−6.7
World	**6,199 s**	**133,895 s**	**48 w**	**31,720 t**		**5,120 w**		**48,462 t**	**7,820 w**		**1.9 w**	**0.7 w**
Low income	2,495	33,612	77	1,070		430		5,269	2,110		4.0	2.1
Middle income	2,738	67,886	41	5,056		1,850		15,884	5,800		3.1	2.3
Lower middle income	2,408	54,969	45	3,372		1,400		12,749	5,290		4.9	4.1
Upper middle income	329	12,917	26	1,682		5,110		3,145	9,550		−1.2	−2.4
Low & middle income	5,232	101,498	53	6,123		1,170		21,105	4,030		3.3	2.0
East Asia & Pacific	1,838	16,301	116	1,768		960		7,874	4,280		6.7	5.8
Europe & Central Asia	473	24,206	20	1,023		2,160		3,263	6,900		4.6	5.1
Latin America & Carib.	525	20,450	26	1,721		3,280		3,650	6,950		−0.8	−2.2
Middle East & N. Africa	306	11,135	28	685		2,240		1,733	5,670		3.0	1.0
South Asia	1,401	5,140	293	638		460		3,453	2,460		4.3	2.6
Sub-Saharan Africa	689	24,267	29	311		450		1,174	1,700		2.8	0.5
High income	966	32,397	31	25,596		26,490		27,516	28,480		1.6	1.0
Europe EMU	305	2,474	125	6,207		20,320		7,850	25,700		0.8	0.5

a. PPP is purchasing power parity; see *Definitions*. b. Calculated using the World Bank *Atlas* method. c. Estimate does not account for recent refugee flows. d. Estimated to be low income ($735 or less). e. The estimate is based on regression; others are extrapolated from the latest International Comparison Programme benchmark estimates. f. Includes Taiwan, China; Macao, China; and Hong Kong, China. g. Estimate based on bilateral comparison between China and the United States (Ruoen and Kai, 1995). h. Estimated to be lower middle income ($736–$2,935). i. GNI and GNI per capita estimates include the French overseas departments of French Guiana, Guadeloupe, Martinique, and Réunion. j. Estimated to be upper middle income ($2,936–$9,075). k. Estimated to be high income ($9,076 or more). l. Excludes data for Kosovo. m. Data refer to mainland Tanzania only.

Size of the economy | 1.1

About the data

Population, land area, income, and output are basic measures of the size of an economy. They also provide a broad indication of actual and potential resources. Population, land area, income—as measured by gross national income (GNI)—and output—as measured by gross domestic product (GDP)—are therefore used throughout *World Development Indicators* to normalize other indicators.

Population estimates are generally based on extrapolations from the most recent national census. For further discussion of the measurement of population and population growth, see *About the data* for table 2.1 and *Statistical methods*.

The surface area of a country or economy includes inland bodies of water and some coastal waterways. Surface area thus differs from land area, which excludes bodies of water, and from gross area, which may include offshore territorial waters. Land area is particularly important for understanding the agricultural capacity of an economy and the effects of human activity on the environment. (For measures of land area and data on rural population density, land use, and agricultural productivity, see tables 3.1–3.3.) Recent innovations in satellite mapping techniques and computer databases have resulted in more precise measurements of land and water areas.

GNI (or gross national product in the terminology of the 1968 United Nations System of National Accounts) measures the total domestic and foreign value added claimed by residents. GNI comprises GDP plus net receipts of primary income (compensation of employees and property income) from non-resident sources.

The World Bank uses GNI per capita in U.S. dollars to classify countries for analytical purposes and to determine borrowing eligibility. See the *Users guide* for definitions of the income groups used in *World Development Indicators*. For further discussion of the usefulness of national income as a measure of productivity or welfare, see *About the data* for tables 4.1 and 4.2.

When calculating GNI in U.S. dollars from GNI reported in national currencies, the World Bank follows its *Atlas* conversion method. This involves using a three-year average of exchange rates to smooth the effects of transitory exchange rate fluctuations. (For further discussion of the *Atlas* method, see *Statistical methods*.) Note that growth rates are calculated from data in constant prices and national currency units, not from the *Atlas* estimates.

Because exchange rates do not always reflect international differences in relative prices, this table also

shows GNI and GNI per capita estimates converted into international dollars using purchasing power parity (PPP) rates. PPP rates provide a standard measure allowing comparison of real price levels between countries, just as conventional price indexes allow comparison of real values over time. The PPP conversion factors used here are derived from price surveys covering 118 countries conducted by the International Comparison Program. For Organisation for Economic Co-operation and Development (OECD) countries data come from the most recent round of surveys, completed in 1999; the rest are either from the 1996 survey, or data from the 1993 or earlier round and extrapolated to the 1996 benchmark. Estimates for countries not included in the surveys are derived from statistical models using available data.

All economies shown in *World Development Indicators* are ranked by size, including those that appear in table 1.6. The ranks are shown only in table 1.1. (*World Bank Atlas* includes a table comparing the GNI per capita rankings based on the *Atlas* method with those based on the PPP method for all economies with available data.) No rank is shown for economies for which numerical estimates of GNI per capita are not published. Economies with missing data are included in the ranking process at their approximate level, so that the relative order of other economies remains consistent. Where available, rankings for small economies are shown in *World Bank Atlas*.

Growth in GDP and growth in GDP per capita are based on GDP measured in constant prices. Growth in GDP is considered a broad measure of the growth of an economy, as GDP in constant prices can be estimated by measuring the total quantity of goods and services produced in a period, valuing them at an agreed set of base year prices, and subtracting the cost of intermediate inputs, also in constant prices. For further discussion of the measurement of economic growth, see *About the data* for table 4.1.

Definitions

- **Population** is based on the de facto definition of population, which counts all residents regardless of legal status or citizenship—except for refugees not permanently settled in the country of asylum, who are generally considered part of the population of their country of origin. The values shown are midyear estimates for 2002. See also table 2.1. • **Surface area** is a country's total area, including areas under inland bodies of water and some coastal waterways.
- **Population density** is midyear population divided by land area in square kilometers. • **Gross national income (GNI)** is the sum of value added by all resident producers plus any product taxes (less subsidies) not included in the valuation of output plus net receipts of primary income (compensation of employees and property income) from abroad. Data are in current U.S. dollars converted using the *World Bank Atlas* method (see *Statistical methods*). • **GNI per capita** is gross national income divided by midyear population. GNI per capita in U.S. dollars is converted using the *World Bank Atlas* method. • **PPP GNI** is gross national income converted to international dollars using purchasing power parity rates. An international dollar has the same purchasing power over GNI as a U.S. dollar has in the United States. • **Gross domestic product (GDP)** is the sum of value added by all resident producers plus any product taxes (less subsidies) not included in the valuation of output. Growth is calculated from constant price GDP data in local currency. • **GDP per capita** is gross domestic product divided by midyear population.

Data sources

Population estimates are prepared by World Bank staff from a variety of sources (see *Data sources* for table 2.1). The data on surface and land area are from the Food and Agriculture Organization (see *Data sources* for table 3.1). GNI, GNI per capita, GDP growth, and GDP per capita growth are estimated by World Bank staff based on national accounts data collected by Bank staff during economic missions or reported by national statistical offices to other international organizations such as the OECD. Purchasing power parity conversion factors are estimates by World Bank staff based on data collected by the International Comparison Program.

Millennium Development Goals: eradicating poverty and improving lives

	Eradicate extreme poverty and hunger			Achieve universal primary education	Promote gender equality		Reduce child mortality		Improve maternal health		
	Share of poorest quintile in national consumption or income %	Prevalence of child malnutrition Weight for age % of children under age 5		Primary completion rate %	Ratio of female to male enrollments in primary and secondary school[a] %		Under-five mortality rate per 1,000 live births		Maternal mortality ratio per 100,000 live births Modeled estimates	Births attended by skilled health staff % of total	
	1990–2002 [b,c]	1990	2002	2000/01–2002/03 [b,d]	1990/91	2001/02 [d]	1990	2002	2000	1990	1995–2000 [b]
Afghanistan	..	..	..	..	*50*	..	260	257	1,900	..	12
Albania	9.1	..	*14*	100	90	102	42	24	55	..	99
Algeria	7.0	*9*	*6*	96	80	99	69	49	140	*77*	92
Angola	..	*20*	*31*	..	..	..	260	260	1,700	..	45
Argentina	3.1 [e]	..	..	100	..	103	28	19	82	*96*	98
Armenia	6.7	..	*3*	74	..	104	60	35	55	..	97
Australia	5.9	..	..	..	96	99	10	6	8	*100*	100
Austria	8.1	..	..	..	90	97	9	5	4	..	100 [f]
Azerbaijan	7.4	..	*17*	100	94	98	106	96	94	..	84
Bangladesh	9.0	66	*48*	77	72	105	144	73	380	..	12
Belarus	8.4	..	..	131	..	102	21	20	35	..	100
Belgium	8.3	..	..	..	97	106	9	6	10	..	100 [f]
Benin	..	..	*23*	45	..	65	185	151	850	..	66
Bolivia	4.0	11	..	89	89	98	122	71	420	*38*	69
Bosnia and Herzegovina	9.5	..	*4*	77	..	..	22	18	31	*97*	100
Botswana	2.2	..	*13*	91	107	102	58	110	100	..	94
Brazil	2.0	7	..	82	..	103	60	37	260	*76*	88
Bulgaria	6.7	..	..	94	94	98	16	16	32	..	..
Burkina Faso	4.5	..	..	29	61	70	210	207	1,000	..	31
Burundi	5.1	..	*45*	27	82	78	184	208	1,000	..	25
Cambodia	6.9	..	*45*	71	..	84	115	138	450	..	32
Cameroon	5.6	15	..	57	82	85	139	166	730	*58*	60
Canada	7.0	..	..	..	94	100	9	7	6	..	98
Central African Republic	2.0	..	..	..	61	..	180	180	1,100	..	44
Chad	..	..	*28*	22	..	55	203	200	1,100	..	16
Chile	3.3	..	*1*	96	98	100	19	12	31	..	100
China	4.7	*17*	*10*	102	81	..	49	38	56	*50*	76
Hong Kong, China	5.3	..	..	..	..	..	..	..	..	..	..
Colombia	2.7	*10*	*7*	90	*104*	103	36	23	130	76	86
Congo, Dem. Rep.	..	..	*31*	..	*69*	..	205	205	990	..	61
Congo, Rep.	..	..	..	58	*88*	87	110	108	510	..	..
Costa Rica	4.2	3	..	90	96	101	17	11	43	*98*	98
Côte d'Ivoire	5.5	..	..	48	..	69	157	191	690	45	63
Croatia	8.3	..	..	90	97	101	13	8	8	..	100
Cuba	..	..	*4*	100	101	97	13	9	33	..	100
Czech Republic	10.3	*1*	..	..	94	101	11	5	9	..	99
Denmark	8.3	..	..	..	96	102	9	4	5	..	100 [f]
Dominican Republic	5.1	*10*	*5*	95	..	109	65	38	150	*92*	98
Ecuador	3.3	..	..	99	*97*	100	57	29	130	*66*	69
Egypt, Arab Rep.	8.6	10	*4*	91	78	93	104	39	84	*37*	61
El Salvador	2.9	15	..	86	*100*	97	60	39	150	*52*	90
Eritrea	..	..	*40*	33	*82*	75	147	80	630	..	21
Estonia	6.1	..	..	103	*99*	99	17	12	63	..	..
Ethiopia	9.1	*48*	*47*	18	68	69	204	171	850	..	6
Finland	9.6	..	..	..	105	106	7	5	6	..	100 [f]
France	7.2	..	..	..	98	100	9	6	17	..	99 [f]
Gabon	..	..	*12*	92	..	96	96	85	420	..	86
Gambia, The	4.0	..	*17*	69	64	86	154	126	540	44	55
Georgia	6.4	..	..	92	94	105	29	29	32	..	96
Germany	8.5	..	..	..	*94*	99	9	5	8	..	100 [f]
Ghana	5.6	30	..	59	..	89	125	97	540	*40*	44
Greece	7.1	..	..	..	93	101	11	5	9	..	..
Guatemala	2.6	..	..	59	..	93	82	49	240	..	41
Guinea	6.4	..	*33*	..	43	..	240	165	740	*31*	35
Guinea-Bissau	5.2	..	*25*	..	..	65	253	211	1,100	..	35
Haiti	..	27	*17*	..	..	..	150	123	680	*23*	24

	Eradicate extreme poverty and hunger			Achieve universal primary education	Promote gender equality		Reduce child mortality		Improve maternal health		
	Share of poorest quintile in national consumption or income %	Prevalence of child malnutrition Weight for age % of children under age 5		Primary completion rate %	Ratio of female to male enrollments in primary and secondary school [a] %		Under-five mortality rate per 1,000 live births		Maternal mortality ratio per 100,000 live births Modeled estimates	Births attended by skilled health staff % of total	
	1990–2002 [b,c]	1990	2002	2000/01–2002/03 [b,d]	1990/91	2001/02 [d]	1990	2002	2000	1990	1995–2000 [b]
Honduras	2.7	18	17	70	103	..	61	42	110	45	56
Hungary	7.7	2	..	..	96	100	16	9	16	..	..
India	8.9	64	..	77	68	79	123	90	540	..	43
Indonesia	8.4	..	25	107	91	98	91	43	230	32	64
Iran, Islamic Rep.	5.1	..	..	123	80	96	72	41	76	..	90
Iraq	..	12	16	..	75	76	50	125	250	54	72
Ireland	7.1	..	..	..	99	..	9	6	5	..	100
Israel	6.9	..	..	..	99	100	12	6	17	..	99 [f]
Italy	6.5	..	..	..	95	98	10	6	5	..	..
Jamaica	6.7	5	..	90	97	101	20	20	87	79	95
Japan	10.6	..	..	..	96	100	6	5	10	100	100
Jordan	7.6	6	..	98	93	101	43	33	41	87	97
Kazakhstan	8.2	..	..	99	..	98	52	99	210	..	99
Kenya	5.6	..	..	56	..	97	97	122	1,000	50	44
Korea, Dem. Rep.	..	..	28	..	..	..	55	55	67	..	97
Korea, Rep.	7.9	..	..	..	93	..	9	5	20	98	100
Kuwait	..	..	..	..	97	104	16	10	5	..	98
Kyrgyz Republic	9.1	..	6	94	100	99	83	61	110	..	98
Lao PDR	7.6	..	40	73	75	83	163	100	650	..	19
Latvia	7.6	..	..	90	96	101	20	21	42	..	100
Lebanon	..	..	..	68	..	102	37	32	150	..	89
Lesotho	1.5	16	18	65	124	105	148	132	550	..	60
Liberia	..	..	27	..	..	..	235	235	760	..	51
Libya	..	..	..	..	..	103	42	19	97	..	94
Lithuania	7.9	..	..	106	93	99	13	9	13	..	..
Macedonia, FYR	8.4	..	..	95	94	98	41	26	23	..	97
Madagascar	4.9	41	33	41	..	..	168	135	550	57	46
Malawi	4.9	28	25	55	79	..	241	182	1,800	55	56
Malaysia	4.4	25	..	..	98	104	21	8	41	..	97
Mali	4.6	..	33	39	57	..	250	222	1,200	..	41
Mauritania	6.2	48	32	46	67	92	183	183	1,000	40	57
Mauritius	..	..	..	108	98	98	25	19	24	..	99
Mexico	3.1	17	..	96	96	101	46	29	83	..	86
Moldova	7.1	..	..	80	103	..	37	32	36	..	99
Mongolia	5.6	12	..	107	107	112	107	71	110	..	97
Morocco	6.5	10	..	68	67	85	85	43	220	31	40
Mozambique	6.5	..	..	22	73	77	240	205	1,000	..	44
Myanmar	..	32	..	71	95	98	130	108	360	..	56
Namibia	1.4	26	..	95	111	104	84	67	300	68	78
Nepal	7.6	..	48	73	53	83	143	83	740	7	11
Netherlands	7.3	..	..	..	93	97	8	5	16	..	100
New Zealand	6.4	..	..	..	96	104	11	6	7	..	100
Nicaragua	3.6	..	10	75	..	105	66	41	230	..	67
Niger	2.6	43	40	21	54	67	320	264	1,600	15	16
Nigeria	4.4	35	..	..	76	..	235	201	800	31	42
Norway	9.6	..	..	..	97	101	9	4	16	100	100 [f]
Oman	..	24	..	72	86	98	30	13	87	..	95
Pakistan	8.8	40	..	..	47	..	138	101	500	19	20
Panama	2.4	6	..	86	96	101	34	25	160	..	90
Papua New Guinea	4.5	..	..	59	77	97	101	94	300	..	53
Paraguay	2.2	4	..	89	95	98	37	30	170	53	71
Peru	2.9	11	7	98	93	..	80	39	410	46	59
Philippines	5.4	34	..	90	..	102	63	37	200	..	58
Poland	7.3	..	..	95	96	98	19	9	13	..	99 [f]
Portugal	5.8	..	..	..	99	102	15	6	5	98	100
Puerto Rico	..	..	..	..	..	..	..	..	25	..	..

	Eradicate extreme poverty and hunger			Achieve universal primary education	Promote gender equality		Reduce child mortality		Improve maternal health		
	Share of poorest quintile in national consumption or income %	Prevalence of child malnutrition Weight for age % of children under age 5		Primary completion rate %	Ratio of female to male enrollments in primary and secondary school [a] %		Under-five mortality rate per 1,000 live births		Maternal mortality ratio per 100,000 live births Modeled estimates	Births attended by skilled health staff % of total	
	1990–2002 [b,c]	1990	2002	2000/01–2002/03 [b,d]	1990/91	2001/02 [d]	1990	2002	2000	1990	1995–2000 [b]
Romania	8.2	*6*	3	94	95	100	32	21	49	..	98
Russian Federation	4.9	..	6	99	..	100	21	21	67	..	99
Rwanda	..	*29*	24	25	98	94	173	203	1,400	*26*	31
Saudi Arabia	..	..	..	66	82	94	44	28	23	..	91
Senegal	6.4	*22*	23	49	*69*	85	148	138	690	..	58
Serbia and Montenegro	..	..	2	..	96	101	30	19	11	..	99
Sierra Leone	..	*29*	27	..	67	..	302	284	2,000	..	42
Singapore	5.0	..	..	..	89	..	8	4	30	..	100
Slovak Republic	8.8	..	..	..	*98*	101	15	9	3	..	..
Slovenia	9.1	..	..	96	*97*	101	9	5	17	*100*	100 [f]
Somalia	..	..	26	..	..	..	225	225	1,100	..	34
South Africa	2.0	..	..	90	103	101	60	65	230	..	84
Spain	7.5	..	..	..	99	102	9	6	4	..	..
Sri Lanka	8.0	..	33	108	99	..	26	19	92	..	97
Sudan	..	..	11	..	75	86	120	94	590	..	86 [f]
Swaziland	2.7	..	10	74	..	93	110	149	370	..	70
Sweden	9.1	..	..	..	97	115	6	3	2	..	100 [f]
Switzerland	6.9	..	..	..	92	96	8	6	7	..	..
Syrian Arab Republic	..	..	7	89	82	92	44	28	160	..	76 [f]
Tajikistan	8.0	..	..	101	..	88	127	116	100	..	71
Tanzania	6.8	*29*	..	58	97	100	163	165	1,500	*44*	36
Thailand	6.1	..	..	91	94	95	40	28	44	..	99
Togo	..	*25*	..	84	59	69	152	140	570	*31*	49
Trinidad and Tobago	5.5	..	6	108	98	101	24	20	160	..	96
Tunisia	6.0	*10*	4	98	82	100	52	26	120	*69*	90
Turkey	6.1	..	..	95	77	85	78	41	70	..	81
Turkmenistan	6.1	..	12	..	..	..	98	86	31	..	97
Uganda	5.9	*23*	23	67	..	..	160	141	880	*38*	39
Ukraine	8.8	..	3	98	..	100	22	20	35	..	100
United Arab Emirates	..	..	..	..	96	100	14	9	54	..	96
United Kingdom	6.1	..	..	..	97	110	10	7	13	..	99
United States	5.4	..	..	..	95	100	10	8	17	*99*	99
Uruguay	4.8 [e]	*6*	..	95	..	105	24	15	27	..	100
Uzbekistan	9.2	..	..	98	..	98	65	65	24	..	96
Venezuela, RB	3.0	8	4	58	101	104	27	22	96	..	94
Vietnam	8.0	*45*	34	104	..	93	53	26	130	..	70
West Bank and Gaza	..	..	..	66	..	..	..	..	..	..	..
Yemen, Rep.	7.4	*30*	..	68	..	56	142	114	570	*16*	22
Zambia	3.3	*25*	28	59	..	..	180	182	750	*51*	43
Zimbabwe	4.6	*12*	..	..	96	95	80	123	1,100	*70*	73
World	.. w	.. w	.. w	.. w	*84 w*	.. w	95 w	81 w	403 w	.. w	60 w
Low income	..	..	..	74	*74*	84	144	121	657	..	41
Middle income	..	..	..	98	84	..	51	37	106	..	80
Lower middle income	..	..	9	97	82	..	54	40	112	..	78
Upper middle income	..	..	..	89	96	101	34	22	67	..	92
Low & middle income	..	..	..	86	*80*	..	103	88	440	..	56
East Asia & Pacific	*19*	*15*	100	83	..	59	42	115	..	72	
Europe & Central Asia	..	..	..	97	..	97	44	37	58	..	93
Latin America & Carib.	..	..	..	87	..	102	53	34	193	..	82
Middle East & N. Africa	..	..	..	91	79	91	77	54	165	..	70
South Asia	64	..	..	78	*68*	81	130	95	566	..	35
Sub-Saharan Africa	..	..	..	48 [g]	*79*	..	187	174	917	..	44
High income	..	..	..	..	96	101	9	7	13	..	99
Europe EMU	..	..	..	..	97	100	9	6	10	..	..

a. Break in series between 1997 and 1998 due to change from International Standard Classification of Education 1976 (ISCED76) to ISCED97. For information on ISCED, see *About the data* for table 2.10. b. Data are for the most recent year available. c. See table 2.7 for survey year and whether share is based on income or consumption expenditure. d. Data are preliminary. e. Urban data. f. Data refer to period other than specified, differ from the standard definition, or refer to only part of a country. g. Represent only 60% of the population.

About the data

This table and the following two present indicators for 17 of the 18 targets specified by the Millennium Development Goals. Each of the eight goals comprises one or more targets, and each target has associated with it several indicators for monitoring progress toward the target. Most of the targets are set as a value of a specific indicator to be attained by a certain date. In some cases the target value is set relative to a level in 1990. In others it is set at an absolute level. Some of the targets for goals 7 and 8 have not yet been quantified.

The indicators in this table relate to goals 1–5. Goal 1 has two targets between 1990 and 2015: to reduce by half the proportion of people whose income is less than $1 a day and to reduce by half the proportion of people who suffer from hunger. Estimates of poverty rates can be found in table 2.5. The indicator shown here, the share of the poorest quintile in national consumption, is a distributional measure. Countries with less equal distributions of consumption (or income) will have a higher rate of poverty for a given average income. No single indicator captures the concept of suffering from hunger. Child malnutrition is a symptom of inadequate food supply, lack of essential nutrients, illnesses that deplete these nutrients, and undernourished mothers who give birth to underweight children.

Progress toward achieving universal primary education is measured by primary school completion rates. Before last year's *World Development Indicators*, progress was measured by net enrollment ratios. But official enrollments sometimes differ significantly from actual attendance, and even school systems with high average enrollment ratios may have poor completion rates. Estimates of primary school completion rates have been calculated by World Bank staff using data provided by the United Nations Educational, Scientific, and Cultural Organization (UNESCO) and national sources.

Eliminating gender disparities in education would help to increase the status and capabilities of women. The ratio of girls' to boys' enrollments in primary and secondary school provides an imperfect measure of the relative accessibility of schooling for girls. With a target date of 2005, this is the first of the goals to fall due. The targets for reducing under-five and maternal mortality are among the most challenging. Although estimates of under-five mortality rates are available at regular intervals for most countries, maternal mortality is difficult to measure, in part because it is relatively rare.

Most of the 48 indicators relating to the Millennium Development Goals can be found in the *World Development Indicators*. Table 1.2a shows where to find the indicators for the first five goals. For more information about data collection methods and limitations, see *About the data* for the tables listed there. For information about the indicators for goals 6, 7, and 8, see *About the data* for tables 1.3 and 1.4.

Definitions

• **Share of poorest quintile in national consumption or income** is the share of consumption or, in some cases, income that accrues to the poorest 20 percent of the population. • **Prevalence of child malnutrition** is the percentage of children under age five whose weight for age is more than two standard deviations below the median for the international reference population ages 0–59 months. The reference population, adopted by the World Health Organization in 1983, is based on children from the United States, who are assumed to be well nourished. • **Primary completion rate** is the number of students successfully completing (or graduating from) the last year of primary school in a given year, divided by the number of children of official graduation age in the population. • **Ratio of female to male enrollments in primary and secondary school** is the ratio of female students enrolled in primary and secondary school to male students. • **Under-five mortality rate** is the probability that a newborn baby will die before reaching age five, if subject to current age-specific mortality rates. The probability is expressed as a rate per 1,000. • **Maternal mortality ratio** is the number of women who die from pregnancy-related causes during pregnancy and childbirth, per 100,000 live births. The data shown here have been collected in various years and adjusted to a common 1995 base year. The values are modeled estimates (see *About the data* for table 2.17). • **Births attended by skilled health staff** are the percentage of deliveries attended by personnel trained to give the necessary supervision, care, and advice to women during pregnancy, labor, and the postpartum period; to conduct deliveries on their own; and to care for newborns.

1.2a

Location of indicators for Millennium Development Goals 1–5

Goal 1. Eradicate extreme poverty and hunger

1. Proportion of population below $1 a day (table 2.5)
2. Poverty gap ratio (table 2.5)
3. Share of poorest quintile in national consumption (tables 1.2 and 2.7)
4. Prevalence of underweight in children under five (tables 1.2 and 2.17)
5. Proportion of population below minimum level of dietary energy consumption (table 2.17)

Goal 2. Achieve universal primary education

6. Net enrollment ratio (table 2.11)
7. Proportion of pupils starting grade 1 who reach grade 5 (table 2.12)
8. Literacy rate of 15- to 24-year-olds (table 2.13)

Goal 3. Promote gender equality and empower women

9. Ratio of girls to boys in primary, secondary, and tertiary education (see ratio of girls to boys in primary and secondary education in table 1.2)
10. Ratio of literate females to males among 15- to 24-year-olds (tables 1.5 and 2.12)
11. Share of women in wage employment in the nonagricultural sector (table 1.5)
12. Proportion of seats held by women in national parliament (table 1.5)

Goal 4. Reduce child mortality

13. Under-five mortality rate (tables 1.2 and 2.19)
14. Infant mortality rate (table 2.19)
15. Proportion of one-year-old children immunized against measles (table 2.15)

Goal 5. Improve maternal health

16. Maternal mortality ratio (tables 1.2 and 2.16)
17. Proportion of births attended by skilled health personnel (tables 1.2 and 2.16)

Data sources

The indicators here and throughout this book have been compiled by World Bank staff from primary and secondary sources. Efforts have been made to harmonize these data series with those published by the United Nations Millennium Development Goals Web site (www.un.org/millenniumgoals), but some differences in timing, sources, and definitions remain.

Millennium Development Goals: protecting our common environment

	Combat HIV/AIDS and other diseases			Ensure environmental sustainability						Develop a global partnership for development	
	HIV prevalence % ages 15–24[a]		Incidence of tuberculosis per 100,000 people	Carbon dioxide emissions per capita metric tons		Access to an improved water source % of population		Access to improved sanitation facilities % of population		Unemployment % ages 15–24	Fixed line and mobile phone subscribers per 1,000 people[b]
	Male	Female									
	2001	2001	2002	1990	2000	1990	2000	1990	2000	2002	2002
Afghanistan	..	..	333	0.1	0.0	..	13	..	12	..	2
Albania	..	..	27	2.2	0.9	..	97	..	91	..	348
Algeria	..	..	52	3.2	2.9	..	89	..	92	..	74
Angola	2.2	5.7	335	0.5	0.5	..	38	..	44	..	15
Argentina	0.9	0.3	46	3.4	3.9	94	..	82	..	32	396
Armenia	0.2	0.1	77	*1.1*	1.1	..	..	..	..	..	162
Australia	0.1	0.0[c]	6	15.6	18.0	100	100	100	100	12	1,178
Austria	0.2	0.1	15	7.4	7.6	100	100	100	100	5	1,275
Azerbaijan	0.1	0.0[c]	82	*6.4*	3.6	..	78	..	81	..	220
Bangladesh	0.0[c]	0.0[c]	221	0.1	0.2	94	97	41	48	*11*	13
Belarus	0.6	0.2	83	*9.3*	5.9	..	100	..	..	..	346
Belgium	0.1	0.1	14	10.1	10.0	..	..	..	..	16	1,280
Benin	1.2	3.7	86	0.1	0.3	..	63	20	23	..	41
Bolivia	0.1	0.1	234	0.8	1.3	71	83	52	70	*9*	172
Bosnia and Herzegovina	..	..	60	*1.1*	4.8	..	..	..	..	..	433
Botswana	16.1	37.5	657	1.7	2.3	93	95	60	66	..	328
Brazil	0.6	0.5	62	1.4	1.8	83	87	71	76	*18*	424
Bulgaria	..	..	48	8.6	5.2	..	100	..	100	*38*	701
Burkina Faso	4.0	9.7	157	0.1	0.1	..	42	..	29	..	13
Burundi	5.0	11.0	359	0.0	0.0	69	78	87	88	..	11
Cambodia	1.0	2.5	549	0.0	0.0	..	30	..	17	..	30
Cameroon	5.4	12.7	188	0.1	0.4	51	58	77	79	..	50
Canada	0.3	0.2	6	15.4	14.2	100	100	100	100	14	1,013
Central African Republic	5.8	13.5	338	0.1	0.1	48	70	24	25	..	5
Chad	2.4	4.3	222	0.0	0.0	..	27	18	29	..	6
Chile	0.4	0.1	18	2.7	3.9	90	93	97	96	*19*	659
China	0.2	0.1	113	2.1	2.2	71	75	29	40	*3*	328
Hong Kong, China	0.0	0.0	93	4.6	5.0	..	..	..	..	*11*	1,507
Colombia	0.9	0.2	45	1.6	1.4	94	91	83	86	*36*	286
Congo, Dem. Rep.	2.9	5.9	383	0.1	0.1	..	45	..	21	..	11
Congo, Rep.	3.3	7.8	395	0.8	0.5	..	51	..	..	..	74
Costa Rica	0.6	0.3	15	1.0	1.4	..	95	..	93	13	362
Côte d'Ivoire	2.9	8.3	412	1.0	0.7	80	81	46	52	..	83
Croatia	0.0	0.0	47	*3.5*	4.4	..	..	..	..	37	952
Cuba	0.1	0.0[c]	12	3.0	2.8	..	91	..	98	..	*52*
Czech Republic	0.0	0.0	13	*13.4*	11.6	..	..	..	..	16	1,211
Denmark	0.1	0.1	13	9.9	8.4	..	100	..	..	7	1,522
Dominican Republic	2.1	2.8	95	1.3	3.0	83	86	66	67	*23*	317
Ecuador	0.3	0.2	137	1.6	2.0	71	85	70	86	*15*	231
Egypt, Arab Rep.	..	..	29	1.4	2.2	94	97	87	98	..	177
El Salvador	0.8	0.4	60	0.5	1.1	66	77	73	82	*11*	241
Eritrea	2.8	4.3	268	..	0.1	..	46	..	13	..	9
Estonia	2.5	0.6	55	*16.2*	11.7	..	..	..	..	*22*	1,001
Ethiopia	4.4	7.8	370	0.1	0.1	25	24	8	12	..	6
Finland	0.0[c]	0.0[c]	10	10.6	10.3	100	100	100	100	21	1,391
France	0.3	0.2	14	6.3	6.2	..	..	..	..	20	1,216
Gabon	*2.3*	*4.7*	248	7.0	2.8	..	86	..	53	..	240
Gambia, The	0.5	1.4	230	0.2	0.2	..	62	..	37	..	101
Georgia	0.1	0.0[c]	85	*2.8*	1.2	..	79	..	100	*20*	234
Germany	0.1	0.0[c]	10	*11.1*	9.6	..	..	..	..	10	1,378
Ghana	1.4	3.0	211	0.2	0.3	53	73	61	72	..	33
Greece	0.1	0.1	20	7.1	8.5	..	..	..	..	26	1,337
Guatemala	0.9	0.8	77	0.6	0.9	76	92	70	81	..	202
Guinea	*0.6*	*1.4*	215	0.2	0.2	45	48	55	58	..	15
Guinea-Bissau	1.1	3.0	196	0.8	0.2	..	56	44	56	..	9
Haiti	4.1	5.0	319	0.2	0.2	53	46	23	28	..	33

Millennium Development Goals: protecting our common environment 1.3

	Combat HIV/AIDS and other diseases			Ensure environmental sustainability						Develop a global partnership for development	
	HIV prevalence % ages 15–24[a]		Incidence of tuberculosis per 100,000 people	Carbon dioxide emissions per capita metric tons		Access to an improved water source % of population		Access to improved sanitation facilities % of population		Unemployment % ages 15–24	Fixed line and mobile phone subscribers per 1,000 people[b]
	Male	Female									
	2001	2001	2002	1990	2000	1990	2000	1990	2000	2002	2002
Honduras	1.2	1.5	86	0.5	0.7	83	88	61	75	6	97
Hungary	0.1	0.0c	32	5.6	5.4	99	99	99	99	13	1,037
India	0.3	0.7	168	0.8	1.1	68	84	16	28	..	..
Indonesia	0.1	0.1	256	0.9	1.3	71	78	47	55	..	92
Iran, Islamic Rep.	0.0c	0.0c	29	3.9	4.9	..	92	..	83	..	220
Iraq	..	..	167	2.7	3.3	..	85	..	79	..	29
Ireland	0.1	0.1	13	8.5	11.1	..	..	..	..	8	1,266
Israel	0.1	0.1	10	7.4	10.0	..	..	..	..	19	1,422
Italy	0.3	0.3	8	7.0	7.4	..	..	..	..	26	1,419
Jamaica	0.8	0.9	8	3.3	4.2	93	92	99	99	..	704
Japan	0.0c	0.0c	33	8.7	9.3	97	96	98	99	10	1,195
Jordan	..	..	5	3.2	3.2	97	96	98	99	..	355
Kazakhstan	0.1	0.0c	146	15.3	8.1	..	91	..	99	..	195
Kenya	6.0	15.6	540	0.2	0.3	45	57	80	87	..	52
Korea, Dem. Rep.	..	..	160	12.3	8.5	..	100	..	99	..	21
Korea, Rep.	0.0c	0.0c	91	5.6	9.1	..	92	..	63	8	1,168
Kuwait	..	..	26	19.9	21.9	..	..	..	..	..	723
Kyrgyz Republic	0.0	0.0	142	2.4	0.9	..	77	..	100	..	88
Lao PDR	0.0c	0.0c	170	0.1	0.1	..	37	..	30	..	21
Latvia	0.9	0.2	78	4.8	2.5	..	..	..	..	21	695
Lebanon	..	..	14	2.5	3.5	..	100	..	99	..	426
Lesotho	17.4	38.1	726	..	..	..	78	..	49	..	56
Liberia	..	..	247	0.2	0.1	..	..	..	..	..	3
Libya	..	..	21	8.8	10.9	71	72	97	97	..	127
Lithuania	0.2	0.0c	66	5.8	3.4	..	67	..	67	29	746
Macedonia, FYR	0.0	0.0	41	5.5	5.5	..	..	..	..	..	448
Madagascar	0.1	0.2	234	0.1	0.1	44	47	36	42	..	14
Malawi	6.3	14.9	431	0.1	0.1	49	57	73	76	..	15
Malaysia	0.7	0.1	95	3.0	6.2	..	..	..	..	..	567
Mali	1.4	2.1	334	0.0	0.1	55	65	70	69	..	10
Mauritania	0.4	0.6	188	1.3	1.2	37	37	30	33	..	104
Mauritius	0.0c	0.0c	64	1.1	2.4	100	100	100	99	..	559
Mexico	0.4	0.1	33	3.7	4.3	80	88	70	74	5	401
Moldova	0.5	0.1	154	4.8	1.5	..	92	..	99	..	238
Mongolia	..	..	209	4.7	3.1	..	60	..	30	..	142
Morocco	..	..	114	1.0	1.3	75	80	58	68	..	247
Mozambique	6.1	14.7	436	0.1	0.1	..	57	..	43	..	19
Myanmar	1.0	1.7	154	0.1	0.2	..	72	..	64	..	8
Namibia	11.1	24.3	751	0.0	1.0	72	77	33	41	11	145
Nepal	0.3	0.3	190	0.0	0.1	67	88	20	28	..	15
Netherlands	0.2	0.1	8	10.0	8.7	100	100	100	100	6	1,362
New Zealand	0.1	0.0c	11	6.8	8.3	..	..	..	..	11	1,070
Nicaragua	0.2	0.1	64	0.7	0.7	70	77	76	85	20	70
Niger	0.9	1.5	193	0.1	0.1	53	59	15	20	..	3
Nigeria	3.0	5.8	304	0.9	0.3	53	62	53	54	..	19
Norway	0.1	0.0c	6	7.5	11.1	100	100	..	..	11	1,578
Oman	..	..	11	7.1	8.2	37	39	84	92	..	255
Pakistan	0.1	0.1	181	0.6	0.8	83	90	36	62	13	34
Panama	1.9	1.3	47	1.3	2.2	..	90	..	92	29	311
Papua New Guinea	0.3	0.4	254	0.6	0.5	40	42	82	82	..	14
Paraguay	0.1	0.0c	70	0.5	0.7	63	78	93	94	14	336
Peru	0.4	0.2	202	1.0	1.1	74	80	60	71	15	152
Philippines	0.0c	0.0c	320	0.7	1.0	87	86	74	83	19	233
Poland	0.1	0.0c	32	9.1	7.8	..	..	..	..	44	554
Portugal	0.4	0.2	47	4.3	5.9	..	..	..	..	12	1,247
Puerto Rico	..	..	7	3.3	2.3	..	..	..	..	21	662

1.3 Millennium Development Goals: protecting our common environment

	Combat HIV/AIDS and other diseases			Ensure environmental sustainability						Develop a global partnership for development	
	HIV prevalence % ages 15–24 [a]		Incidence of tuberculosis per 100,000 people	Carbon dioxide emissions per capita metric tons		Access to an improved water source % of population		Access to improved sanitation facilities % of population		Unemployment % ages 15–24	Fixed line and mobile phone subscribers per 1,000 people [b]
	Male 2001	Female 2001	2002	1990	2000	1990	2000	1990	2000	2002	2002
Romania	0.0 [c]	0.0 [c]	148	6.7	3.8	..	58	..	53	18	430
Russian Federation	1.9	0.7	126	13.3	9.9	..	99	..	..	..	362
Rwanda	4.9	11.2	389	0.1	0.1	..	41	..	8	..	16
Saudi Arabia	..	..	42	11.3	18.1	..	95	..	100	..	361
Senegal	0.2	0.5	242	0.4	0.4	72	78	57	70	..	77
Serbia and Montenegro	..	..	38	12.4	3.7	..	98	..	100	..	489
Sierra Leone	2.5	7.5	405	0.1	0.1	..	57	..	66	..	18
Singapore	0.1	0.2	43	13.8	14.7	100	100	100	100	5	1,258
Slovak Republic	0.0	0.0	24	8.4	6.6	..	100	..	100	37	812
Slovenia	0.0	0.0	21	6.2	7.3	100	100	..	..	16	1,341
Somalia	..	..	405	0.0	..	..	..	..	..	..	13
South Africa	10.7	25.6	558	8.3	7.4	86	86	86	87	56	410
Spain	0.5	0.2	30	5.5	7.0	..	..	..	..	22	1,330
Sri Lanka	0.0 [c]	0.0 [c]	54	0.2	0.6	68	77	85	94	24	96
Sudan	1.1	3.1	217	0.1	0.2	67	75	58	62	..	27
Swaziland	15.2	39.5	1,067	0.6	0.4	..	..	..	..	..	95
Sweden	0.1	0.0 [c]	5	5.7	5.3	100	100	100	100	13	1,625
Switzerland	0.5	0.4	8	6.4	5.4	100	100	100	100	6	1,534
Syrian Arab Republic	..	..	44	3.0	3.3	..	80	..	90	..	147
Tajikistan	0.0	0.0	109	3.7	0.6	..	60	..	90	..	39
Tanzania	3.5	8.1	363	0.1	0.1	38	68	84	90	..	24
Thailand	1.1	1.7	128	1.7	3.3	80	84	79	96	6	365
Togo	2.0	5.9	361	0.2	0.4	51	54	37	34	..	45
Trinidad and Tobago	2.4	3.2	13	13.9	20.5	91	90	99	99	..	528
Tunisia	..	..	23	1.6	1.9	75	80	76	84	..	169
Turkey	..	..	32	2.6	3.3	79	82	87	90	20	629
Turkmenistan	0.0	0.0	94	7.2	7.5	..	..	..	..	..	79
Uganda	2.0	4.6	377	0.0	0.1	45	52	..	79	..	18
Ukraine	2.0	0.9	95	11.5	6.9	..	98	..	99	24	300
United Arab Emirates	..	..	18	33.0	21.0	..	..	..	..	..	1,010
United Kingdom	0.1	0.1	12	9.9	9.6	100	100	100	100	11	1,431
United States	0.5	0.2	5	19.3	19.8	100	100	100	100	12	1,134
Uruguay	0.5	0.2	29	1.3	1.6	..	98	..	94	34	472
Uzbekistan	0.0 [c]	0.0	101	5.3	4.8	..	85	..	89	..	74
Venezuela, RB	0.7	0.1	42	5.8	6.5	..	83	..	68	23	369
Vietnam	0.3	0.2	192	0.3	0.7	55	77	29	47	..	72
West Bank and Gaza	..	..	27	..	..	..	..	..	..	..	180
Yemen, Rep.	..	..	92	0.7	0.5	..	69	32	38	..	49
Zambia	8.1	21.0	668	0.3	0.2	52	64	63	78	..	21
Zimbabwe	12.4	33.0	683	1.6	1.2	78	83	56	62	..	55
World	**0.8 w**	**1.3 w**	**142 w**	**4.1 w**	**3.8 w**	**74 w**	**81 w**	**45 w**	**56 w**		**286 w**
Low income	1.1	2.4	226	0.8	0.9	66	76	30	43		40
Middle income	0.6	0.8	108	3.8	3.4	76	82	47	61		316
Lower middle income	0.6	0.8	116	3.6	3.0	75	81	45	59		263
Upper middle income	0.6	0.4	43	5.7	6.2	..	..	..	..		431
Low & middle income	0.9	1.6	164	2.5	2.2	71	79	39	52		162
East Asia & Pacific	0.2	0.2	147	1.9	2.1	71	76	35	47		155
Europe & Central Asia	1.1	0.4	88	10.3	6.7	..	91	..	..		424
Latin America & Carib.	0.7	0.5	67	2.2	2.7	82	86	72	77		294
Middle East & N. Africa	..	..	57	3.3	4.2	..	88	..	85		159
South Asia	0.3	0.6	176	0.7	0.9	72	84	22	34		42
Sub-Saharan Africa	4.1	9.3	358	0.9	0.7	53	58	54	54		31
High income	0.3	0.1	18	11.8	12.4	..	..	..	..		1,283
Europe EMU	0.2	0.1	15	8.4	8.0	..	..	..	..		1,360

a. Data are an average of high and low estimates. b. Data are from the International Telecommunication Union's (ITU) *World Telecommunication Development Report 2003*. Please cite the ITU for third-party use of these data. c. Less than 0.05.

About the data

The Millennium Development Goals address issues of common concern to people of all nations. Diseases and environmental degradation do not respect national boundaries. Epidemic diseases, wherever they persist, pose a threat to people everywhere. And damage done to the environment in one location may affect the well-being of plants, animals, and human beings in distant locations.

The indicators in the table relate to goals 6 and 7 and the targets of goal 8 that address youth employment and access to new technologies. For the other targets of goal 8, see table 1.4.

Measuring the prevalence or incidence of a disease can be difficult. Much of the developing world lacks reporting systems needed for monitoring the course of a disease. Estimates are often derived from surveys and reports from sentinel sites that must be extrapolated to the general population. Tracking diseases such as HIV/AIDS, which has a long latency between contraction of the virus and the appearance of outward symptoms, or malaria, which has periods of dormancy, can be particularly difficult. For some of the most serious illnesses international organizations have formed coalitions such as the Joint United Nations Programme on HIV/AIDS (UNAIDS) and the Roll Back Malaria campaign to gather information and coordinate global efforts to treat victims and prevent the spread of disease.

Antenatal care clinics are a key site for monitoring sexually transmitted diseases such as HIV and syphilis. The prevalence of HIV in young people provides an indicator of the spread of the epidemic. Prevalence rates in the older population can be affected by life-prolonging treatment. The table shows the estimated prevalence among men and women ages 15–24. The incidence of tuberculosis is based on data on case notifications and estimates of the proportion of cases detected in the population.

Carbon dioxide emissions are the primary source of greenhouse gases, which are believed to contribute to global warming.

Access to reliable supplies of safe drinking water and sanitary disposal of excreta are two of the most important means of improving human health and protecting the environment. There is no widespread program for testing the quality of water. The indicator shown here measures the proportion of households with access to an improved source, such as piped water or protected wells. Improved sanitation facilities prevent human, animal, and insect contact with excreta but do not include treatment to render sewage outflows innocuous.

The eighth goal—to develop a global partnership for development—takes note of the need for decent and productive work for youth. Labor market information, such as unemployment rates, is still generally unavailable for most low- and middle-income economies. Fixed telephone lines and mobile phones are among the telecommunications technologies that are changing the way the global economy works. For more information on goal 8, see table 1.4.

Definitions

• **Prevalence of HIV** is the percentage of people ages 15–24 who are infected with HIV. • **Incidence of tuberculosis** is the estimated number of new tuberculosis cases (pulmonary, smear positive, extrapulmonary). • **Carbon dioxide emissions** are those stemming from the burning of fossil fuels and the manufacture of cement. They include carbon dioxide produced during consumption of solid, liquid, and gas fuels and gas flaring. • **Access to an improved water source** refers to the percentage of the population with reasonable access to an adequate amount of water from an improved source, such as a household connection, public standpipe, borehole, protected well or spring, or rainwater collection. Unimproved sources include vendors, tanker trucks, and unprotected wells and springs. Reasonable access is defined as the availability of at least 20 liters a person a day from a source within 1 kilometer of the dwelling. • **Access to improved sanitation facilities** refers to the percentage of the population with access to at least adequate excreta disposal facilities (private or shared but not public) that can effectively prevent human, animal, and insect contact with excreta. Improved facilities range from simple but protected pit latrines to flush toilets with a sewerage connection. To be effective, facilities must be correctly constructed and properly maintained. • **Unemployment** refers to the share of the labor force without work but available for and seeking employment. Definitions of labor force and unemployment differ by country. • **Fixed line and mobile phone subscribers** are telephone mainlines connecting a customer's equipment to the public switched telephone network, and users of portable telephones subscribing to an automatic public mobile telephone service using cellular technology that provides access to the public switched telephone network.

1.3a

Location of indicators for Millennium Development Goals 6–7

Goal 6. Combat HIV/AIDS, malaria, and other diseases

18. HIV prevalence among 15- to 24-year-old pregnant women (tables 1.3 and 2.18)

19. Knowledge and use of methods to prevent HIV transmission*

20. School attendance of orphans and nonorphans*

21. Prevalence and death rates associated with malaria*

22. Proportion of population in malaria-risk areas using effective malaria prevention and treatment measures* (see children sleeping under treated bednets in table 2.15)

23. Tuberculosis prevalence and death rates (see incidence of tuberculosis in tables 1.3 and 2.18)

24. Proportion of tuberculosis cases detected and cured under directly observed treatment, short-course (table 2.15)

Goal 7. Ensure environmental sustainability

25. Proportion of land area covered by forest (table 3.4)

26. Ratio of area protected to maintain biological diversity to surface area (table 3.4)

27. Energy use (kilograms of oil equivalent) per $1 of GDP (PPP) (see GDP per unit of energy use in table 3.8)

28. Carbon dioxide emissions per capita (table 3.8) and consumption of ozone-depleting chlorofluorocarbons*

29. Proportion of population using solid fuels (see combustible renewables and waste as a percentage of total energy use in table 3.7)

30. Proportion of population with sustainable access to an improved water source (tables 2.15 and 3.5)

31. Proportion of urban population with access to improved sanitation (table 2.15)

32. Proportion of population with access to secure tenure (table 3.11)

* No data available in the *World Development Indicators* database.

Data sources

The indicators here throughout this book have been compiled by World Bank staff from primary and secondary sources. Efforts have been made to harmonize these data series with those published on the United Nations Millennium Development Goals Web site (http://www.un.org/millenniumgoals), but some differences in timing, sources, and definitions remain.

1.4 Millennium Development Goals: overcoming obstacles

	Official development assistance (ODA) by donor	ODA for basic social services[a] % of total sector-allocatable ODA	Market access to high-income countries								Support to agriculture
			Goods (excluding arms) admitted free of tariffs %		Average tariff on exports of least developed countries						
					Agricultural products %		Textiles %		Clothing %		
	Net ODA % of donor GNI										% of GDP
	2002	2000–02	1996	2002	1996	2002	1996	2002	1996	2002	2002
Australia	0.26	17.7	98.3	96.1	0.5	0.2	10.0	6.2	31.2	19.6	0.4
Canada	0.28	22.4	78.3	64.5	3.5	2.9	10.9	7.4	22.4	17.9	0.8
European Union			94.4	99.8	3.3	0.8	0.0	0.2	0.0	0.9	1.3
Austria	0.26	14.7	..	..	..	..			..	..	..
Belgium	0.43	20.4	..	..	..	..			..	..	..
Denmark	0.96	7.8	..	..	..	..			..	..	..
Finland	0.35	14.3	..	..	..	..			..	..	..
France	0.38	..	..	..	..	..			..	..	..
Germany	0.27	10.3	..	..	..	..			..	..	..
Greece	0.21	3.9	..	..	..	..			..	..	..
Ireland	0.40	30.8	..	..	..	..			..	..	..
Italy	0.20	10.7	..	..	..	..			..	..	..
Luxembourg	0.77	*19.8*	..	..	..	..			..	..	..
Netherlands	0.81	26.7	..	..	..	..			..	..	..
Portugal	0.27	3.1	..	..	..	..			..	..	..
Spain	0.26	11.5	..	..	..	..			..	..	..
Sweden	0.83	11.8	..	..	..	..			..	..	..
United Kingdom	0.31	29.9	..	..	..	..			..	..	..
Japan	0.23	4.8	57.0	85.7	10.1	12.0	1.7	0.7	0.0	0.0	1.4
New Zealand	0.22	8.3	..	..	..	..			..	..	0.3
Norway	0.89	15.1	..	..	..	..			..	..	1.5
Switzerland	0.32	19.8	50.8	93.3	8.5	5.8	0.0	0.0	0.0	0.0	2.0
United States	0.13	27.0	22.6	51.2	5.3	3.1	7.2	6.3	15.5	14.6	0.9

	HIPC decision point[b]	HIPC completion point[c]	Estimated total nominal debt service relief $ millions		HIPC decision point[b]	HIPC completion point[c]	Estimated total nominal debt service relief $ millions
Benin	Jul. 2000	Mar. 2003	460	Madagascar	Dec. 2000	Floating	1,500
Bolivia	Feb. 2000	Jun. 2001	2,060	Malawi	Dec. 2000	Floating	1,000
Burkina Faso	Jul. 2000	Apr. 2002	930	Mali	Sep. 2000	Mar. 2003	895
Cameroon	Oct. 2000	Floating	2,000	Mauritania	Feb. 2000	Jun. 2002	1,100
Chad	May 2001	Floating	260	Mozambique	Apr. 2000	Sep. 2001	4,300
Congo, Dem. Republic	Jul. 2003	Floating	10,389	Nicaragua	Dec. 2000	Jan. 2004	4,500
Côte d'Ivoire	Mar. 1998	..	800	Niger	Dec. 2000	Floating	900
Ethiopia	Nov. 2001	Floating	1,930	Rwanda	Dec. 2000	Floating	800
Gambia	Dec. 2000	Floating	90	São Tomé & Principe	Dec. 2000	Floating	200
Ghana	Feb. 2002	Floating	3,700	Senegal	Jun. 2000	Floating	850
Guinea	Dec. 2000	Floating	800	Sierra Leone	Mar. 2002	Floating	950
Guinea-Bissau	Dec. 2000	Floating	790	Tanzania	Apr. 2000	Nov. 2001	3,000
Guyana	Nov. 2000	Dec. 2003	877	Uganda	Feb. 2000	May. 2000	1,950
Honduras	Jul. 2000	Floating	900	Zambia	Dec. 2000	Floating	3,850
Madagascar	Dec. 2000	Floating	1,500				

a. Includes basic health, education, nutrition, and water and sanitation services. b. Except for Côte d'Ivoire the date refers to the HIPC enhanced framework. The following countries also reached decision points under the original framework: Bolivia in September 1997, Burkina Faso in September 1997, Côte d'Ivoire in March 1998, Guyana in December 1997, Mali in September 1998, Mozambique in April 1998, and Uganda in April 1997. c. Except for Côte d'Ivoire the date refers to the HIPC enhanced framework. The following countries also reached completion points under the original framework: Bolivia in September 1998, Burkina Faso in July 2000, Guyana in May 1999, Mali in September 2000, Mozambique in July 1999, and Uganda in April 1998.

Achieving the Millennium Development Goals will require an open, rule-based global economy in which all countries, rich and poor, participate. Many poor countries, lacking the resources to finance their development, burdened by unsustainable levels of debt, and unable to compete in the global marketplace, need assistance from rich countries. For goal 8—develop a global partnership for development—many of the indicators therefore monitor the actions of members of the Development Assistance Committee (DAC) of the Organisation for Economic Co-operation and Development (OECD).

Official development assistance (ODA) has declined in recent years as a share of donor countries' gross national income (GNI). The poorest countries will need additional assistance to achieve the Millennium Development Goals. Recent estimates suggest that $30–60 billion more a year would allow most of them to achieve the goals, if the aid goes to countries with good policies. At the United Nations International Conference on Financing for Development in 2002 many donor countries made new commitments that, if fulfilled, would add $18.6 billion to ODA.

One of the most important actions that high-income economies can take to help is to reduce barriers to the exports of low- and middle-income economies. The European Union has announced a program to eliminate tariffs on developing country exports of "everything but arms," and the United States has launched a special program of concessions to exports from Sub-Saharan Africa.

The average tariffs in the table were calculated by the World Trade Organization (WTO). They reflect the tariff schedules applied by high-income OECD members to exports of countries designated "least developed countries" (LDCs) by the United Nations. Agricultural commodities and textiles and clothing are three of the most important categories of goods exported by developing economies. Although average tariffs have been falling, averages may disguise high tariffs targeted at specific goods (see table 6.6 for estimates of the share of tariff lines with "international peaks" in each country's tariff schedule). The averages in the table include ad valorem duties and ad valorem equivalents of non-ad valorem duties.

Subsidies to agricultural producers and exporters in OECD countries are another form of barrier to developing economies' exports. The table shows the value of total support to agriculture as a share of the economy's gross domestic product (GDP). Agricultural subsidies in OECD economies are estimated at $318 billion in 2002.

The Debt Initiative for Heavily Indebted Poor Countries (HIPCs) is the first comprehensive approach to reducing the external debt of the world's poorest, most heavily indebted countries. It represents an important step forward in placing debt relief within an overall framework of poverty reduction. While the initiative yielded significant early progress, multilateral organizations, bilateral creditors, HIPC governments, and civil society have engaged in an intensive dialogue about its strengths and weaknesses. A major review in 1999 led to an enhancement of the original framework.

• **Net official development assistance (ODA)** comprises grants and loans (net of repayments of principal) that meet the DAC definition of ODA and are made to countries and territories in part I of the DAC list of recipient countries. • **ODA for basic social services** is aid reported by DAC donors for basic health, education, nutrition, and water and sanitation services. • **Goods admitted free of tariffs** are the value of exports of goods (excluding arms) from least developed countries admitted without tariff, as a share of total exports from LDCs. • **Average tariff** is the simple mean tariff, the unweighted average of the effectively applied rates for all products subject to tariffs. • **Agricultural products** comprise plant and animal products, including tree crops but excluding timber and fish products. • **Textiles and clothing** include natural and synthetic fibers and fabrics and articles of clothing made from them. • **Support to agriculture** is the value of subsidies to the agricultural sector. • **HIPC decision point** is the date at which a heavily indebted poor country with an established track record of good performance under adjustment programs supported by the International Monetary Fund and the World Bank commits to undertake additional reforms and to develop and implement a poverty reduction strategy. • **HIPC completion point** is the date at which the country successfully completes the key structural reforms agreed on at the decision point, including developing and implementing its poverty reduction strategy. The country then receives the bulk of debt relief under the HIPC Debt Initiative without further policy conditions. • **Estimated total nominal debt service relief** is the amount of debt service relief, calculated at the decision point, that will allow the country to achieve debt sustainability at the completion point.

1.4a

* No data available in the World Development Indicators database.

Data sources

The indicators here, and where they appear throughout the rest of the book, have been compiled by World Bank staff from primary and secondary sources. The WTO, in collaboration with the UN Conference on Trade and Development and the International Trade Centre, provided the estimates of goods admitted free of tariffs and average tariffs. Subsidies to agriculture are compiled by the OECD.

Women in development

	Female population	Life expectancy at birth		Pregnant women receiving prenatal care	Teenage mothers	Literacy gender parity index	Labor force gender parity index		Women in non-agricultural sector	Unpaid family workers		Women in parliaments
		years								Male	Female	
	% of total	Male	Female	%	% of women ages 15–19	ages 15–24			% of total	% of male employment	% of female employment	% of total seats
	2002	2002	2002	1995–2002[a]	1995–2002[a]	2002	1990	2002	2000–02[a]	2000–02[a]	2000–02[a]	2003
Afghanistan	49.0	43	44	37	..	..	0.5	0.6	..	..	..	..
Albania	48.9	72	76	95	..	1.0	0.7	0.7	41.1	..	..	6
Algeria	49.4	69	72	79	..	0.9	0.3	0.4	12.2	..	..	6
Angola	50.5	45	48	66	..	..	0.9	0.9	..	..	..	16
Argentina	50.9	71	78	95[b]	..	1.0	0.4	0.5	42.9	0.7	1.8	31
Armenia	51.4	71	79	92	6	1.0	0.9	0.9	..	1.1	0.8	5
Australia	50.1	76	82	100[b]	..	..	0.7	0.8	48.1	0.4	0.7	25
Austria	51.3	76	82	100[b]	..	..	0.7	0.7	43.5	1.4	3.7	34
Azerbaijan	50.9	62	69	66	..	..	0.8	0.8	45.4	..	..	11
Bangladesh	49.7	62	63	40	35	0.7	0.7	0.7	22.9	10.1	73.2	2
Belarus	53.1	63	74	100	..	1.0	1.0	1.0	56.0	..	..	10
Belgium	50.9	75	82	..	..	..	0.7	0.7	44.8	..	..	35
Benin	50.7	51	55	81	22	0.5	0.9	0.9		..	..	6
Bolivia	50.2	62	65	83	14	1.0	0.6	0.6	36.4	5.2	11.1	19
Bosnia and Herzegovina	50.5	71	77	99	..	1.0	0.6	0.6	..	..	..	17
Botswana	50.2	38	38	91	..	1.1	0.9	0.8	44.8	16.9	17.4	17
Brazil	50.7	65	73	86	18	1.0	0.5	0.6	45.7	..	..	9
Bulgaria	51.4	69	75	..	..	1.0	0.9	0.9	50.2	..	..	26
Burkina Faso	50.4	42	44	61	25	0.5	0.9	0.9	..	..	..	12
Burundi	51.0	42	42	78	..	1.0	1.0	0.9	..	..	..	18
Cambodia	51.2	53	56	38	8	0.9	1.2	1.1	51.7	31.6	53.3	7
Cameroon	50.0	48	49	75	31	..	0.6	0.6	..	..	..	9
Canada	50.5	76	82	..	..	..	0.8	0.9	48.8	0.1	0.3	21
Central African Republic	51.2	42	43	62	36	0.7	..	..	..	..	..	7
Chad	50.5	47	50	42	39	0.8	0.8	0.8	..	..	..	6
Chile	50.5	73	79	95[b]	..	1.0	0.4	0.5	36.6	..	..	13
China	48.4	69	72	90	..	1.0	0.8	0.8	39.2	..	..	22
Hong Kong, China	50.9	78	83	..	..	..	0.6	0.6	45.5	..	..	..
Colombia	50.5	69	75	91	19	1.0	0.6	0.6	49.1	5.1	7.1	12
Congo, Dem. Rep.	50.4	45	46	68	..	..	0.8	0.8	..	..	..	..
Congo, Rep.	51.0	50	54	..	..	1.0	0.8	0.8	..	..	..	9
Costa Rica	50.1	75	80	70	..	1.0	0.4	0.5	40.1	2.5	3.6	35
Côte d'Ivoire	49.2	45	46	88	31	0.7	0.5	0.5	..	..	..	9
Croatia	51.7	70	78	..	..	1.0	0.7	0.8	45.9	2.4	7.8	21
Cuba	50.0	75	79	100	..	1.0	0.6	0.7	37.8	..	..	36
Czech Republic	51.2	72	79	99[b]	..	..	0.9	0.9	46.6	0.2	1.1	17
Denmark	50.5	75	79	..	..	..	0.9	0.9	48.9	..	..	38
Dominican Republic	49.3	64	70	98	21	1.0	0.4	0.5	34.3	..	..	17
Ecuador	49.8	69	72	69	..	1.0	0.3	0.4	41.4	4.4	10.2	16
Egypt, Arab Rep.	49.1	67	71	53	9	0.8	0.4	0.4	19.6	8.2	26.0	2
El Salvador	50.9	67	73	76	..	1.0	0.5	0.6	31.2	..	..	11
Eritrea	50.4	50	52	49	23	..	0.9	0.9	..	..	..	22
Estonia	53.5	65	77	..	..	1.0	1.0	1.0	51.7	0.8	0.9	19
Ethiopia	49.8	41	43	27	16	0.8	0.7	0.7	..	..	..	8
Finland	51.2	75	82	100[b]	..	..	0.9	0.9	50.2	0.6	0.4	38
France	51.4	76	83	99[b]	..	..	0.8	0.8	46.3	..	..	12
Gabon	50.4	52	54	94	33	..	0.8	0.8	..	..	..	9
Gambia, The	50.5	52	55	91	..	..	0.8	0.8	..	..	..	13
Georgia	52.5	69	78	95	..	..	0.9	0.9	48.6	23.2	40.2	7
Germany	50.9	75	81	..	..	..	0.7	0.7	45.5	0.5	2.1	32
Ghana	50.2	54	56	88	14	1.0	1.0	1.0	..	..	..	9
Greece	50.8	75	81	..	..	1.0	0.5	0.6	40.5	4.2	14.7	9
Guatemala	49.6	63	69	60	22	0.9	0.3	0.4	39.2	..	..	9
Guinea	49.7	46	47	71	37	..	0.9	0.9	..	..	..	19
Guinea-Bissau	50.6	44	47	62	..	..	0.7	0.7	..	..	..	8
Haiti	50.9	50	54	79	18	1.0	0.8	0.7	..	..	..	4

Women in development

	Female population	Life expectancy at birth		Pregnant women receiving prenatal care	Teenage mothers	Literacy gender parity index	Labor force gender parity index		Women in non-agricultural sector	Unpaid family workers		Women in parliaments
		years			% of women	ages				Male % of male	Female % of female	% of total
	% of total	Male	Female	%	ages 15–19	15–24			% of total	employment	employment	seats
	2002	2002	2002	1995–2002[a]	1995–2002[a]	2002	1990	2002	2000–02[a]	2000–02[a]	2000–02[a]	2003
Honduras	49.7	63	69	83	..	1.0	0.4	0.5	51.7	..	..	6
Hungary	52.3	68	77	..	..	1.0	0.8	0.8	46.1	0.4	1.0	10
India	48.4	63	64	60	21	..	0.5	0.5	17.1	..	..	9
Indonesia	50.1	65	69	89	12	1.0	0.6	0.7	29.7	..	..	8
Iran, Islamic Rep.	49.8	68	70	77	..	..	0.3	0.4	..	..	..	4
Iraq	49.2	61	64	77	..	..	0.2	0.3	..	..	..	8
Ireland	50.5	74	80	..	..	..	0.5	0.5	46.5	0.8	1.5	13
Israel	50.3	77	81	..	..	1.0	0.6	0.7	48.5	0.2	0.7	15
Italy	51.5	75	82	..	..	1.0	0.6	0.6	40.6	3.0	6.0	12
Jamaica	50.8	74	78	99	..	1.1	0.9	0.9	45.8	..	..	12
Japan	51.1	78	85	..	..	..	0.7	0.7	40.4	1.6	10.1	7
Jordan	48.3	70	74	96	6	1.0	0.2	0.3	20.8	..	..	6
Kazakhstan	51.6	57	67	91	7	1.0	0.9	0.9	..	..	..	10
Kenya	49.8	45	46	76	21	1.0	0.8	0.9	37.8	..	..	7
Korea, Dem. Rep.	49.7	61	64	..	..	..	0.8	0.8	..	..	..	20
Korea, Rep.	49.7	71	78	..	..	..	0.6	0.7	41.5	1.8	19.5	6
Kuwait	46.7	75	79	95	..	1.0	0.3	0.5	..	..	..	0
Kyrgyz Republic	51.1	61	70	97	9	..	0.9	0.9	44.8	..	..	10
Lao PDR	50.0	53	56	27	..	0.8	..	..	..	..	..	23
Latvia	54.1	65	76	..	..	1.0	1.0	1.0	52.7	4.2	4.9	21
Lebanon	50.8	69	73	87	..	..	0.4	0.4	..	..	..	2
Lesotho	50.3	37	39	85	..	0.6	0.6	..	..	..	12	
Liberia	49.7	46	48	85	..	0.6	0.6	0.7	..	..	..	8
Libya	48.3	70	75	81	..	0.9	0.2	0.3	..	..	..	..
Lithuania	52.9	68	78	..	..	1.0	0.9	0.9	51.3	2.8	3.5	11
Macedonia, FYR	50.0	71	76	100	..	..	0.7	0.7	41.9	..	..	
Madagascar	50.1	54	57	71	36	..	0.8	0.8	..	..	..	4
Malawi	50.8	37	38	91	33	0.8	1.0	0.9	12.2	..	..	9
Malaysia	49.4	70	75	..	..	1.0	0.6	0.6	36.5	..	..	10
Mali	50.9	40	42	57	40	0.5	0.9	0.9	..	..	..	10
Mauritania	50.4	49	53	64	16	0.7	0.8	0.8	..	..	..	4
Mauritius	50.5	69	76	..	..	1.0	0.4	0.5	39.0	..	..	6
Mexico	51.4	71	77	86	..	1.0	0.4	0.5	37.2	6.8	12.5	23
Moldova	52.4	63	71	99	..	1.0	0.9	0.9	52.7	4.7	10.7	13
Mongolia	50.3	64	67	97	..	1.0	0.9	0.9	..	..	..	11
Morocco	50.0	66	70	42	..	0.8	0.5	0.5	26.6	..	..	11
Mozambique	51.4	40	42	76	40	0.6	0.9	0.9	..	..	..	30
Myanmar	50.3	55	60	76	..	1.0	0.8	0.8	..	..	..	..
Namibia	50.5	42	41	91	..	1.0	0.7	0.7	48.8	..	..	26
Nepal	48.7	60	60	28	21	0.6	0.7	0.7	..	..	..	6
Netherlands	50.5	76	81	..	..	..	0.6	0.7	44.3	0.2	1.1	37
New Zealand	51.1	76	81	95[b]	..	..	0.8	0.8	50.9	0.6	1.2	28
Nicaragua	50.2	67	71	86	27	1.1	0.5	0.6	..	..	..	21
Niger	50.6	46	47	41	43	0.4	0.8	0.8	..	..	..	1
Nigeria	50.6	45	46	64	22	1.0	0.5	0.6	..	..	..	5
Norway	50.4	76	82	..	..	..	0.8	0.9	48.3	0.2	0.5	36
Oman	47.4	73	76	100	..	1.0	0.1	0.2	25.3	..	..	..
Pakistan	48.3	63	65	43	..	0.6	0.3	0.4	7.9	16.7	50.1	22
Panama	49.6	73	77	72	..	1.0	0.5	0.6	41.7	..	..	10
Papua New Guinea	48.5	56	58	78	..	..	0.7	0.7	..	..	..	1
Paraguay	49.6	69	73	89	..	1.0	0.4	0.4	38.4	..	..	9
Peru	49.7	68	72	84	13	1.0	0.4	0.5	34.6	4.7	11.5	18
Philippines	49.6	68	72	86	7	1.0	0.6	0.6	42.2	..	..	18
Poland	51.4	70	78	..	..	..	0.8	0.9	46.9	4.0	6.8	20
Portugal	52.0	73	79	..	..	1.0	0.7	0.8	46.3	1.1	3.2	19
Puerto Rico	51.9	72	81	..	..	1.0	0.5	0.6	39.0	0.2	1.0	..

Women in development

	Female population	Life expectancy at birth		Pregnant women receiving prenatal care	Teenage mothers	Literacy gender parity index	Labor force gender parity index		Women in non-agricultural sector	Unpaid family workers		Women in parliaments
		years		%	% of women ages 15–19	ages 15–24			% of total	Male % of male employment	Female % of female employment	% of total seats
	% of total	Male	Female									
	2002	2002	2002	1995–2002[a]	1995–2002[a]	2002	1990	2002	2000–02[a]	2000–02[a]	2000–02[a]	2003
Romania	51.1	66	74	..	..	1.0	0.8	0.8	45.7	10.4	29.1	11
Russian Federation	53.3	60	72	..	..	1.0	0.9	1.0	49.7	..	..	8
Rwanda	50.4	39	40	92	7	1.0	1.0	1.0	..	..	..	49
Saudi Arabia	45.9	71	75	90	..	1.0	0.1	0.2	14.2	..	..	0
Senegal	50.2	51	54	79	22	0.7	0.7	0.7	..	..	..	19
Serbia and Montenegro	50.2	70	75	..	..	..	0.7	0.8	..	..	..	8
Sierra Leone	50.9	36	39	68	..	..	0.6	0.6	..	..	..	15
Singapore	48.7	76	80	..	..	1.0	0.6	0.6	46.9	0.3	1.7	16
Slovak Republic	51.4	69	77	98[b]	..	1.0	0.9	0.9	51.9	0.1	0.2	19
Slovenia	51.3	72	80	98[b]	..	1.0	0.9	0.9	47.7	3.8	7.0	12
Somalia	50.4	46	49	32	..	..	0.8	0.8	..	..	..	..
South Africa	51.7	46	48	94	16	1.0	0.6	0.6	..	0.7	1.4	30
Spain	51.1	75	82	..	..	1.0	0.5	0.6	39.3	1.0	3.3	28
Sri Lanka	50.6	72	76	98	..	1.0	0.5	0.6	46.6	..	..	4
Sudan	49.7	57	60	60	..	0.9	0.4	0.4	..	..	..	10
Swaziland	51.7	44	44	87	..	1.0	0.6	0.6	29.6	..	..	3
Sweden	50.3	78	82	..	..	..	0.9	0.9	50.7	0.3	0.4	45
Switzerland	50.4	77	83	..	..	..	0.6	0.7	47.2	..	..	27
Syrian Arab Republic	49.5	68	73	71	..	1.0	0.3	0.4	17.4	..	..	12
Tajikistan	50.1	64	70	71	..	1.0	0.7	0.8	51.6	..	..	13
Tanzania	50.4	43	44	49	25	1.0	1.0	1.0	..	..	..	22
Thailand	50.8	67	72	92	..	1.0	0.9	0.9	46.8	16.4	39.8	9
Togo	50.3	49	51	73	19	0.8	0.7	0.7	..	..	..	7
Trinidad and Tobago	50.1	70	75	92	..	1.0	0.5	0.5	39.9	1.0	0.6	19
Tunisia	49.5	71	75	92	..	0.9	0.4	0.5	..	..	..	12
Turkey	49.5	68	73	68	10	1.0	0.5	0.6	18.9	10.2	51.3	4
Turkmenistan	50.5	61	68	98	4	1.0	0.8	0.8	..	..	..	26
Uganda	50.0	43	44	92	31	0.9	0.9	0.9	..	..	..	25
Ukraine	53.5	63	74	..	..	1.0	1.0	1.0	53.0	0.8	1.7	5
United Arab Emirates	34.4	74	77	97	..	1.1	0.1	0.2	13.8	..	..	0
United Kingdom	50.8	75	80	..	..	..	0.7	0.8	49.7	0.2	0.5	18
United States	51.1	75	80	99[b]	..	..	0.8	0.9	48.4	0.1	0.1	14
Uruguay	51.5	71	79	94	..	1.0	0.6	0.7	46.5	..	..	12
Uzbekistan	50.3	64	70	97	10	1.0	0.8	0.9	37.9	..	..	7
Venezuela, RB	49.7	71	77	94	..	1.0	0.5	0.5	39.6	..	..	10
Vietnam	50.6	67	72	68	6	1.0	1.0	1.0	..	..	..	27
West Bank and Gaza	49.3	71	75	..	..	..	..	..	..	6.0	27.3	..
Yemen, Rep.	49.0	57	58	34	16	0.6	0.4	0.4	..	..	..	0
Zambia	50.2	37	37	93	32	0.9	0.8	0.8	..	..	..	12
Zimbabwe	49.9	39	39	93	21	1.0	0.8	0.8	20.2	..	..	10
World	**49.6 w**	**65 w**	**69 w**	..		**0.9 w**	..	..	..	..	..	
Low income	49.2	58	60			0.9	..	..	..	..	..	
Middle income	49.6	68	72			1.0	..	..	..	..	..	
Lower middle income	49.5	67	72			1.0	..	..	..	..	..	
Upper middle income	50.8	70	77			1.0	..	..	..	..	..	
Low & middle income	49.5	63	66			0.9	..	..	..	..	..	
East Asia & Pacific	48.9	68	71			1.0	..	..	..	..	..	
Europe & Central Asia	52.0	64	73			1.0	..	..	..	..	..	
Latin America & Carib.	50.7	68	74			1.0	..	..	..	..	..	
Middle East & N. Africa	49.2	67	70			0.9	..	..	..	..	..	
South Asia	48.5	62	64			0.8	..	..	..	..	..	
Sub-Saharan Africa	50.2	45	47			0.9	..	..	..	..	..	
High income	50.6	75	81			..	..	..	..	..	..	
Europe EMU	51.0	75	82			..	..	..	42.8	..	..	

a. Data are for the most recent year available. b. Data refer to a period other than specified, differ from the standard definition, or refer to only part of a country.

About the data

Despite much progress in recent decades, gender inequalities remain pervasive in many dimensions of life—worldwide. But while disparities exist throughout the world, they are most prevalent in poor developing countries. Gender inequalities in the allocation of such resources as education, health care, nutrition, and political voice matter because of the strong association with well-being, productivity, and economic growth. This pattern of inequality begins at an early age, with boys routinely receiving a larger share of education and health spending than do girls, for example.

Because of biological differences girls are expected to experience lower infant and child mortality rates and to have a longer life expectancy than boys. This biological advantage, however, may be overshadowed by gender inequalities in nutrition and medical interventions, and by inadequate care during pregnancy and delivery, so that female rates of illness and death sometimes exceed male rates, particularly during early childhood and the reproductive years. In high-income countries women tend to outlive men by four to eight years on average, while in low-income countries the difference is narrower—about two to three years. The difference in child mortality rates (table 2.19) is another good indicator of female social disadvantage because nutrition and medical interventions are particularly important for the 1–5 age group. Female child mortality rates that are as high as or higher than male child mortality rates might be indicative of discrimination against girls.

Having a child during the teenage years limits girls' opportunities for better education, jobs, and income and increases the likelihood of divorce and separation. Pregnancy is more likely to be unintended during the teenage years, and births are more likely to be premature and are associated with greater risks of complications during delivery and of death.

In many countries maternal mortality (tables 1.2 and 2.16) is a leading cause of death among women of reproductive age. Most maternal deaths result from preventable causes—hemorrhage, infection, and complications from unsafe abortions. Prenatal care is essential for recognizing, diagnosing, and promptly treating complications that arise during pregnancy. In high-income countries most women have access to health care during pregnancy, but in developing countries an estimated 35 percent of pregnant women—some 45 million each year—receive no care at all (United Nations 2000b). This is reflected in the differences in maternal mortality ratios between high- and low-income countries.

Women's wage work is important for economic growth and the well-being of families. But restricted access to education and vocational training, heavy workloads at home and in nonpaid domestic activities, and labor market discrimination often limit women's participation in paid economic activities, lower their productivity, and reduce their wages. A gender labor force parity index of less than 1.0 shows that women have lower activity rates than men. However, a gender labor force parity index of 1.0 or more does not necessarily imply equality in employment opportunities. Women's unemployment rates tend to be higher than men's (table 2.4), and in many countries a large proportion of women who are reported as employed are unpaid family workers. Women's wage employment also tends to be concentrated in the agricultural sector.

Nonsalaried men tend to be self-employed, while nonsalaried women tend to be unpaid family workers. There are several reasons for this. Most women have less access to credit markets, capital, land, training, and education, which may be required to start up a business. Cultural norms may prevent women from working on their own or from supervising other workers. Also, women may face time constraints due to their traditional family responsibilities. Because of biases and misclassification substantial numbers of employed women may be underestimated or reported as unpaid family workers even when they work in association or equally with their husbands in the family enterprise.

Women are vastly underrepresented in decisionmaking positions in government, although there is some evidence of recent improvement. Gender parity in parliamentary representation is still far from being realized. In 2003 women represented 15 percent of parliamentarians worldwide, compared with 9 percent in 1987. Without representation at this level, it is difficult for women to influence policy.

For information on other aspects of gender, see tables 1.2 (Millennium Development Goals: eradicating poverty and improving lives), 2.3 (employment by economic activity), 2.4 (unemployment), 2.12 (education efficiency), 2.13 (education outcomes), 2.16 (reproductive health), 2.18 (health risk factors and future challenges), and 2.19 (mortality).

Definitions

• **Female population** is the percentage of the population that is female. • **Life expectancy at birth** is the number of years a newborn infant would live if prevailing patterns of mortality at the time of its birth were to stay the same throughout its life. •**Teenage mothers** are the percentage of women ages 15–19 who already have children or are currently pregnant. • **Pregnant women receiving prenatal care** are the percentage of women attended at least once during pregnancy by skilled health personnel for reasons related to pregnancy. • **Literacy gender parity index** is the ratio of the female literacy rate to the male rate for ages 15–24. • **Labor force gender parity index** is the ratio of the percentage of women who are economically active to the percentage of men who are. According to the International Labour Organization's (ILO) definition, the economically active population is all those who supply labor for the production of goods and services during a specified period. It includes both the employed and the unemployed. While national practices vary in the treatment of such groups as the armed forces and seasonal or part-time workers, in general the labor force includes the armed forces, the unemployed, and first-time job seekers, but excludes homemakers and other unpaid caregivers and workers in the informal sector. • **Women in nonagricultural sector** refer to women wage employees in the nonagricultural sector as a percentage of total nonagricultural employment. • **Unpaid family workers** are those who work without pay in a market-oriented establishment or activity operated by a related person living in the same household. • **Women in parliaments** are the percentage of parliamentary seats in a single or lower chamber occupied by women.

1.5a

Income and gender affect children's access to basic health care

Medical treatment of fever, by income quintile and gender (%)

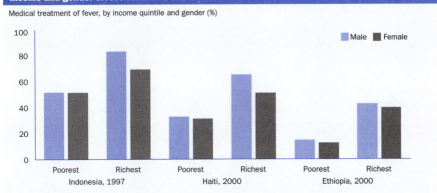

Boys are more likely to receive treatment for fever than girls. But poverty has a larger impact than gender on access to basic health care.

Source: Demographic and Health Survey data.

Data sources

The data on female population and life expectancy are from the World Bank's population database. The data on pregnant women receiving prenatal care are from United Nations Children's Fund's (UNICEF) *State of the World's Children 2004*. The data on teenage mothers are from Demographic and Health Surveys by Macro International. The data on the literacy gender parity index are from the UNESCO Institute for Statistics. The data on the labor force gender parity index are from the ILO database *Estimates and Projections of the Economically Active Population, 1950–2010*. The data on unpaid family workers are from the ILO database *Key Indicators of the Labour Market*, third edition. The data on women in parliaments are from the United Nations' *World's Women: Trends and Statistics 2000*.

	Population	Surface area	Population density	Gross national income				Gross domestic product		Life expectancy at birth	Adult literacy rate	Carbon dioxide emissions
						PPP [a]						
					Per capita		Per capita		Per capita		%	
	thousands	thousand sq. km	people per sq. km	$ millions	$	$ millions	$	% growth	% growth	years	ages 15 and older	thousand metric tons
	2002	2002	2002	2002 [b]	2002 [b]	2002	2002	2001–02	2001–02	2002	2002	2000
American Samoa	69	0.2	344	..	.. [c]	..	..	..	..	..	..	286
Andorra	68	0.5	136	..	.. [d]	..	..	..	..	..	..	..
Antigua and Barbuda	69	0.4	157	671	9,720	717	10,390	2.9	1.5	75	..	352
Aruba	97	0.2	511	..	.. [d]	..	..	..	..	..	..	1,924
Bahamas, The	314	13.9	31	..	.. [d]	..	..	..	..	70	..	1,795
Bahrain	698	0.7	983	7,326	10,500	11,298	16,190	3.5	1.4	73	89	19,500
Barbados	269	0.4	626	2,365	8,790 [e]	3,943	14,660	–2.1	–2.4	75	100	1,176
Belize	253	23.0	11	750	2,970	1,390	5,490	3.7	1.3	74	77 [f]	780
Bermuda	63	0.1	1,260	..	.. [d]	..	..	..	..	..	..	462
Bhutan	851	47.0	18	512	600	..	..	7.7	4.8	63	..	396
Brunei	351	5.8	67	..	.. [d]	..	..	..	..	77	94 [f]	4,668
Cape Verde	458	4.0	114	572	1,250	2,252 [g]	4,920 [g]	4.6	1.9	69	76	139
Cayman Islands	39	0.3	150	..	.. [d]	..	..	..	..	..	..	286
Channel Islands	149	0.2	745	..	.. [d]	..	..	..	..	79	..	..
Comoros	586	2.2	263	228	390	990	1,690 [g]	3.0	0.5	61	56	81
Cyprus	765	9.3	83	9,372	12,320	14,201 [g]	18,560 [g]	2.0	1.5	78	97 [f]	6,423
Djibouti	693	23.2	30	590	850	1,412	2,040 [g]	1.6	–0.3	44	..	385
Dominica	72	0.8	96	216	3,000	357	4,960	–5.2	–5.2	77	..	103
Equatorial Guinea	482	28.1	17	437	930 [h]	4,390	9,110 [g]	16.2	13.3	52	..	205
Faeroe Islands	46	1.4	33	..	.. [d]	..	..	..	..	..	..	649
Fiji	823	18.3	45	1,750	2,130	4,385	5,330 [g]	4.1	3.3	70	93 [f]	725
French Polynesia	240	4.0	66	..	.. [d]	..	..	..	..	74	..	542
Greenland	57	410.5	0	..	.. [d]	..	..	..	..	69	..	557
Grenada	102	0.3	300	361	3,530	673	6,600	1.2	–0.8	73	..	213
Guam	159	0.6	289	..	.. [d]	..	..	..	..	78	..	4,071
Guyana	766	215.0	4	656	860	3,020	3,940 [g]	–1.1	–1.6	62	..	1,598
Iceland	284	103.0	3	7,940	27,960	8,305	29,240	–0.5	–1.2	80	..	2,158
Isle of Man	75	0.6	125	..	.. [d]	..	..	..	..	..	..	..

About the data

The table shows data for 56 economies with populations from 30,000 to 1 million and smaller economies if they are members of the World Bank. Where data on gross national income (GNI) per capita are not available, an estimated range is given. For more information on the calculation of GNI (or gross national product in the 1968 System of National Accounts) and purchasing power parity (PPP) conversion factors, see *About the data* for table 1.1. Since 2000 this table has excluded France's overseas departments—French Guiana, Guadeloupe, Martinique, and Réunion—for which GNI and other economic measures are now included in the French national accounts.

Definitions

• **Population** is based on the de facto definition of population, which counts all residents regardless of legal status or citizenship—except for refugees not permanently settled in the country of asylum, who are generally considered part of the population of their country of origin. The values shown are midyear estimates for 2002. See also table 2.1. • **Surface area** is a country's total area, including areas under inland bodies of water and some coastal waterways. • **Population density** is midyear population divided by land area in square kilometers. • **Gross national income** (GNI) is the sum of value added by all resident producers plus any product taxes (less subsidies) not included in the valuation of output plus net receipts of primary income (compensation of employees and property income) from abroad. Data are in current U.S. dollars converted using the World Bank *Atlas* method (see *Statistical methods*). • **GNI per capita** is gross national income divided by midyear population. GNI per capita in U.S. dollars is converted using the *World Bank Atlas* method. • **PPP GNI** is gross national income converted to international dollars using purchasing power parity rates. An international dollar has the same purchasing power over GNI as a U.S. dollar has in the United States. • **Gross domestic product** (GDP) is the sum of value added by all resident producers plus any product taxes (less subsidies) not included in the valuation of output. Growth is calculated from constant price GDP data in local currency. • **Life expectancy at birth** is the number of years a newborn infant would live if

Key indicators for other economies

	Population	Surface area	Population density	Gross national income				Gross domestic product		Life expectancy at birth	Adult literacy rate	Carbon dioxide emissions
						PPP a						
		thousand sq. km	people per sq. km	$ millions	Per capita $	$ millions	Per capita $	% growth	Per capita % growth	years	% ages 15 and older	thousand metric tons
	thousands 2002	2002	2002	2002 b	2002 b	2002	2002	2001–02	2001–02	2002	2002	2000
Kiribati	95	0.7	130	91	960	..	..	2.8	0.6	63	..	26
Liechtenstein	33	0.2	205	..	..d	..	..	..	..	..	..	..
Luxembourg	444	2.6	171	17,523	39,470	23,659	53,290	1.1	0.2	78	..	8,482
Macao, China	439	..	..	6,335i	14,600i	9,618	21,910g	10.1	8.9	79	91f	1,634
Maldives	287	0.3	957	622	2,170	..	..	5.6	3.0	69	97	498
Malta	397	0.3	1,241	3,678	9,260	7,030	17,710	1.5	1.0	78	93	2,814
Marshall Islands	53	0.2	265	126	2,380	..	..	4.0	4.0	..	..	..
Mayotte	160	0.4	400	..	..c	..	..	..	..	60	..	..
Micronesia, Fed. Sts.	122	0.7	174	240	1,970	..	..	0.8	–0.8	69	..	..
Monaco	32	0.0	16,842	..	..d	..	..	..	..	..	..	..
Netherlands Antilles	219	0.8	274	..	..d	..	..	..	..	76	97	9,929
New Caledonia	220	18.6	12	..	..d	..	..	..	..	74	97f	1,667
Northern Mariana Islands	76	0.5	159	..	..c	..	..	..	..	..	..	..
Palau	20	0.5	43	136	6,820	..	..	3.0	3.0	..	..	242
Qatar	610	11.0	55	..	..d	..	..	..	..	75	84f	40,685
Samoa	176	2.8	62	251	1,430	981	5,570g	1.9	0.7	69	99	139
São Tomé and Principe	154	1.0	160	46	300	..	..	4.1	2.1	66	..	88
Seychelles	84	0.5	187	569	6,780	..	..	0.3	–2.1	73	92f	227
Solomon Islands	443	28.9	16	256	580	705g	1,590g	–2.7	–5.3	69	..	165
San Marino	28	0.1	277	..	..d	..	..	..	..	..	..	..
St. Kitts and Nevis	46	0.4	128	301	6,540	494	10,750	2.1	–0.1	71	..	103
St. Lucia	160	0.6	262	600	3,750	793	4,950	0.0	–1.2	74	..	322
St. Vincent and the Grenadines	117	0.4	300	330	2,820	607	5,190	1.1	0.2	73	..	161
Suriname	433	163.3	3	841	1,940	..	..	3.0	2.1	70	..	2,118
Timor-Leste	780	14.9	52	402	520	..	..	..	..	..	..	..
Tonga	101	0.8	140	146	1,440	689	6,820g	1.6	1.6	71	99f	121
Vanuatu	206	12.2	17	221	1,070	587	2,850g	–0.3	–2.7	69	..	81
Virgin Islands (U.S.)	110	0.3	324	..	..d	..	..	..	..	78	..	13,106

a. PPP is purchasing power parity; see *Definitions*. b. Calculated using the World Bank *Atlas* method. c. Estimated to be upper middle income ($2,936–$9,075). d. Estimated to be high income ($9,076 or more). e. Included in the aggregates for high-income economies on the basis of earlier data. f. Census data. g. The estimate is based on regression; others are extrapolated from the latest International Comparison Programme benchmark estimates. h. Included in the aggregates for low-income economies on the basis of earlier data. i. Refers to GDP and GDP per capita.

prevailing patterns of mortality at the time of its birth were to stay the same throughout its life. • **Adult literacy rate** is the percentage of adults ages 15 and older who can, with understanding, read and write a short, simple statement about their everyday life. • **Carbon dioxide emissions** are those stemming from the burning of fossil fuels and the manufacture of cement. They include carbon dioxide produced during consumption of solid, liquid, and gas fuels and gas flaring.

Data sources

The indicators here and throughout the book were compiled by World Bank Group staff from primary and secondary sources. More information about the indicators and their sources can be found in the *About the data*, *Definitions*, and *Data sources* entries that accompany each table in subsequent sections.

2| PEOPLE

The ultimate aim of development is to improve human welfare in a substantial way. But development has often bypassed the poor, and so attacking poverty directly through its many dimensions has become an urgent global priority.

To accelerate progress in human development, economic growth is, of course, necessary. But it is not enough. Because the most significant asset of people poor is their labor, the most effective way to improve their welfare is to increase their employment opportunities and the productivity of their labor through investments in human capital—the product of education and improvements in health and nutrition. Thus freedom from illiteracy (figure 2a) and freedom from illness are two of the most important ways that poor people can escape poverty. But although developing countries have made large investments in human capital, assisted by the private sector and official development agencies, good health and basic education remain elusive to many. To reinforce this paramount task of development, the Millennium Development Goals set specific targets for poverty reduction, education, status of women, and health, among others, in order to measure improvements in people's lives (see section 1 for a fuller discussion of the Millennium Development Goals).

The challenge for governments is formidable. They need to provide not only services that are linked to human development, but also effective mechanisms that reduce vulnerability to economic shocks, ill health, and disability. This section tracks the progress countries have made in developing their human capital and in reducing the vulnerability of their people.

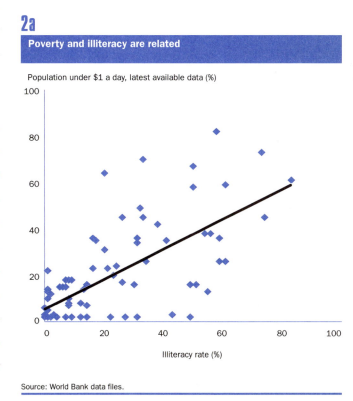

2a

Poverty and illiteracy are related

Population under $1 a day, latest available data (%)

Illiteracy rate (%)

Source: World Bank data files.

Population in sustainable development

In the second half of the 20th century the world population underwent unprecedented growth—from 2.5 billion in 1950 to 6 billion in 1999—even as the population growth rate was declining. The decline was triggered largely by a drop in fertility rates. Between 1950–55 and 2002 fertility rates halved, from 5.1 to 2.6 births per woman. Thus while the world population grew at 1.5 percent a year during 1980–2002, it is expected to grow more slowly, at 1 percent a year, during 2002–15, benefiting from continuing fertility declines (table 2.1). But most developing countries will not benefit from this decline. Between 2002 and 2015 roughly 1 billion people will be added to the world, and most (95 percent) will be born in low- and middle-income countries. Despite the increase in mortality rates brought on by AIDS, the fastest growing region will be Sub-Saharan Africa, and the largest number of people will be added in Asia. And the populations of some high-income and Eastern European countries will continue their decline.

Research shows that changes in population growth, age structure, and spatial distribution interact closely with development. Fertility decline in high-fertility countries, by slowing population growth, can have important economic benefits by reducing the number of children relative to the working age population. This can create a unique opportunity to increase investments in health, education, and infrastructure. Unfortunately, in many of the poorest countries that most need such a break, high levels of unwanted fertility and the pervasive HIV/AIDS pandemic are prematurely curtailing such opportunity. Together, the continuing dependency of youthful populations and the premature deaths of young adults prevent countries from benefiting from their demographic transition.

Enabling poverty reduction

In many developing countries agriculture is still the main economic activity for both men and women (table 2.3). But as economies grow, more people work for wages. The enlarged proportion of working-age populations in countries undergoing fertility decline provides for increased labor force participation (table 2.2). This contributes to economic growth, especially when it occurs in the formal sector. In developing countries gross domestic product (GDP) grew 4.3 percent a year in the 1990s, and the share of people living on less than $1 a day fell from 28.3 percent to 21.6 percent. By 2000, 137 million fewer people were living in extreme poverty (table 2.5). And if projected growth remains on track, global poverty rates will fall to 12.5 percent by 2015, meeting the global Millennium Development Goal target of halving the 1990 poverty rate.

Progress in reducing poverty has been uneven. But because many poor people continue to be excluded from all but the lowest level of economic activity, there are large gaps

2b

Defining income poverty

The most familiar definition of poverty uses a composite measure of total household consumption per member (with adjustments for household size and composition), derived from household surveys. Poor people are then defined as living in households below a particular threshold of this measure of consumption. But many surveys do not include consumption data, which are difficult to collect. Another approach, used by the World Bank, is to aggregate indicators of a household's asset ownership and housing characteristics into an index and then rank households into quintiles according to this index. These are typically referred to as asset or wealth quintiles.

Source: World Bank data files.

in social indicators between the rich and poor, confirming the persistence of deprivation (box 2b; table 2.6). Globally, much of the decline in income poverty took place in East Asia, where sustained growth in China has lifted more than 150 million people out of poverty since 1990. And faster growth in India has led to a modest decline in the number of poor people in South Asia. But in other regions the number of poor people has increased even as their share in the population has declined—and in Europe and Central Asia both the number and the share of poor people have risen. Unemployment is high in many of the formerly centrally planned economies, with long-term unemployment hovering around 40–50 percent of total unemployment in Croatia, the Czech Republic, and Hungary in 2002 (table 2.4).

Enhancing security for poor people

Poor people face many risks. They face labor market risks, often having to take precarious jobs in the informal sector and to put their children to work to increase household income. In Sub-Saharan Africa one in four children ages 10–14 was in the labor force in 2002 (table 2.8). Poor people also face health risks, with illness and injury having both direct and opportunity costs. In South Asia nearly 80 percent of all spending on health comes from private sources, much of it out of pocket, exposing many poor households to the impoverishing effects of needed health care (table 2.8).

Enhancing security for poor people means reducing their vulnerability to ill health and economic shocks. Market-based insurance and pension schemes can reduce risk significantly, but they play only a minor role in many developing countries. In 16 developing countries public spending on pensions amounted to less than 0.5 percent of GDP in the 1990s (table 2.9). To increase the security of poor people, national poverty reduction strategies must support their immediate consumption needs and protect their assets by ensuring access to basic services. Education, health, and

2c

Why public services fail poor people

Public services are failing the poor in four ways:

- Public spending on health and education is typically enjoyed by people who are not poor. In Nepal the richest 20 percent of the population benefits from 46 percent of education spending, while the poorest 20 percent gets just 11 percent.
- Even when public spending is reallocated to the poor, very little of it reaches frontline public service providers. In Uganda in the early 1990s primary schools received an average of just 13 percent of nonsalary spending allocations intended for them, and poorer schools received much less.
- There is a high degree of absenteeism among teachers, doctors, and nurses in public sector facilities. A survey of primary health care in Bangladesh found a 74 percent absentee rate among doctors.
- The poor quality of service, opportunity costs of travel time to schools or health facilities, and cultural factors create lack of demand or weak demand for services.

Source: World Bank, *World Development Report 2004.*

nutrition services are often the most needed and most valued by poor people. Yet many governments fail the poor in the provision of these services (box 2c).

Remaining and emerging challenges in building human capital

Investments in education widen horizons, making it easier for people to take advantage of new opportunities and helping them to participate in social and economic life. But despite increased spending on education, particularly primary education (table 2.10), enrollment rates remain low in many countries (table 2.11), and primary completion rates are even lower (table 2.12), hampering achievement of the Millennium Development Goal target of universal primary education by 2015. Most children who do not attend primary school, or who drop out early, live in poor households and in poor countries (table 2.12). But in many poor countries there is also a gender dimension to school attendance, reflecting traditional biases against girls' education and reliance on girls' contributions to the household. One consequence of this imbalance: higher rates of illiteracy among women. In 2002, 33 developing countries had female literacy rates of 60 percent or lower (table 2.13). And in predominantly illiterate societies there is likely to be less pressure for those who cannot read or write to achieve literacy.

The Millennium Development Goals for health cover health status, nutritional status, illness, mortality rates, and reproductive health. The public sector is the main provider of health care in developing countries—training medical personnel, investing in hospitals, and directly providing medical care (table 2.14). To reduce inequities, many countries have emphasized primary health care, including immunization, sanitation, access to safe drinking water, and safe motherhood initiatives (tables 2.15 and 2.16). But the Millennium Development Goals remain unattainable for many countries. Some 20 countries have rates of child malnutrition greater than 30 percent (table 2.17). An estimated 40 million people are living with HIV/AIDS, an unprecedented public health challenge (table 2.18), and more than half a million women in developing countries die each year during childbirth, often because births are not attended by trained personnel (figure 2d). And the reemergence of old diseases such as tuberculosis in Europe and Central Asia and parts of South and East Asia has put severe strains on health budgets. A high prevalence of disease puts a brake on poverty reduction. Beyond its direct impact on a household's living standards through out-of-pocket spending, ill-health has an indirect impact on labor productivity and the number of hours people can work.

*　　　*　　　*

There are many ways to measure poverty and its effects on people's lives. The indicators reported here suffer from many shortcomings, noted in *About the data* for each table. But taken together, the indicators provide a broad picture of how well different economies are doing in reducing poverty, enhancing human security, and building human capital—and how large a task still lies ahead.

2d

Poor women are much less likely to receive expert care in childbirth

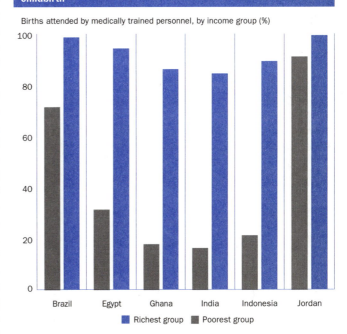

Births attended by medically trained personnel, by income group (%)

Source: World Bank data files.

	Total population			Average annual population growth rate		Population age composition			Dependency ratio dependents as proportion of working-age population		Crude death rate	Crude birth rate
	millions			%		Ages 0–14	% Ages 15–64	Ages 65+	Young	Old	per 1,000 people	per 1,000 people
	1980	**2002**	**2015**	**1980–2002**	**2002–15**	**2002**	**2002**	**2002**	**2002**	**2002**	**2002**	**2002**
Afghanistan	16.0	28.0[a]	38.8	2.6	2.5	43.8	53.4	2.8	0.8	0.1	21	49
Albania	2.7	3.2	3.5	0.7	0.8	28.0	64.9	7.1	0.4	0.1	6	17
Algeria	18.7	31.3	38.3	2.4	1.5	34.6	61.4	4.0	0.6	0.1	5	22
Angola	7.0	13.1	18.9	2.8	2.8	47.6	49.5	2.9	1.0	0.1	19	50
Argentina	28.1	36.5	42.9	1.2	1.2	27.3	63.0	9.8	0.4	0.2	8	19
Armenia	3.1	3.1	3.0	0.0	–0.1	21.6	68.7	9.7	0.3	0.1	8	9
Australia	14.7	19.7	21.7	1.3	0.8	20.2	67.4	12.4	0.3	0.2	7	13
Austria	7.6	8.0	8.0	0.3	–0.1	16.2	67.9	15.9	0.2	0.2	10	9
Azerbaijan	6.2	8.2	9.0	1.3	0.7	27.7	65.0	7.3	0.4	0.1	7	16
Bangladesh	85.4	135.7	166	2.1	1.5	36.2	60.5	3.3	0.6	0.1	8	28
Belarus	9.6	9.9	9.3	0.1	–0.5	17.4	68.8	13.8	0.3	0.2	14	9
Belgium	9.8	10.3	10.4	0.2	0.1	17.1	66.2	16.7	0.3	0.3	10	11
Benin	3.5	6.6	9.0	2.9	2.4	45.4	51.9	2.7	0.9	0.1	13	38
Bolivia	5.4	8.8	10.9	2.3	1.7	38.7	56.9	4.4	0.7	0.1	8	29
Bosnia and Herzegovina	4.1	4.1	4.2	0.0	0.2	17.8	71.7	10.6	0.2	0.1	8	12
Botswana	0.9	1.7	1.8	2.9	0.4	41.8	56.0	2.2	0.7	0.0	23	30
Brazil	121.6	174.5	201	1.6	1.1	27.9	66.8	5.3	0.4	0.1	7	19
Bulgaria	8.9	8.0	7.3	–0.5	–0.7	14.8	68.9	16.3	0.2	0.2	14	9
Burkina Faso	7.0	11.8	15.6	2.4	2.1	47.0	50.3	2.7	0.9	0.1	19	43
Burundi	4.1	7.1	8.8	2.4	1.7	45.7	51.8	2.6	0.9	0.0	20	39
Cambodia	6.8	12.5	15.1	2.8	1.5	42.0	55.1	2.8	0.8	0.1	12	27
Cameroon	8.8	15.8	19.7	2.7	1.7	41.3	55.0	3.7	0.8	0.1	16	36
Canada	24.6	31.4	33.5	1.1	0.5	18.4	68.8	12.8	0.3	0.2	7	11
Central African Republic	2.3	3.8	4.6	2.3	1.5	42.1	54.4	3.5	0.8	0.1	20	36
Chad	4.5	8.3	12.1	2.8	2.8	48.8	48.3	2.9	1.0	0.1	16	45
Chile	11.1	15.6	17.8	1.5	1.0	27.4	65.3	7.3	0.4	0.1	5	17
China	981.2	1,280.4	1,389.5	1.2	0.6	24.2	68.6	7.2	0.4	0.1	8	15
Hong Kong, China	5.0	6.8	7.0	1.4	0.2	16.2	72.3	11.4	0.2	0.2	5	7
Colombia	28.4	43.7	51.4	2.0	1.2	31.9	63.3	4.8	0.5	0.1	6	21
Congo, Dem. Rep.	27.9	51.6	75.2	2.8	2.9	47.8	49.6	2.6	1.0	0.1	18	45
Congo, Rep.	1.8	3.7	5.2	3.2	2.8	46.7	50.2	3.2	0.9	0.1	14	44
Costa Rica	2.3	3.9	4.7	2.5	1.4	30.5	63.8	5.8	0.5	0.1	4	20
Côte d'Ivoire	8.2	16.5	20.2	3.2	1.6	41.8	55.6	2.6	0.8	0.0	17	37
Croatia	4.6	4.5	4.3	–0.1	–0.3	16.4	68.1	15.5	0.2	0.2	12	10
Cuba	9.7	11.3	11.7	0.7	0.3	20.7	69.0	10.3	0.3	0.1	8	12
Czech Republic	10.2	10.2	9.9	0.0	–0.2	15.8	70.4	13.8	0.2	0.2	11	9
Denmark	5.1	5.4	5.4	0.2	0.1	18.5	66.6	14.9	0.3	0.2	11	12
Dominican Republic	5.7	8.6	10.1	1.9	1.2	32.5	63.0	4.5	0.5	0.1	7	23
Ecuador	8.0	12.8	15.4	2.2	1.4	33.2	62.0	4.8	0.5	0.1	6	23
Egypt, Arab Rep.	40.9	66.4	80.9	2.2	1.5	34.1	61.6	4.2	0.6	0.1	6	24
El Salvador	4.6	6.4	7.9	1.5	1.6	35.0	60.1	5.0	0.6	0.1	6	26
Eritrea	2.4	4.3	5.6	2.7	2.0	44.7	52.7	2.6	0.8	0.1	13	38
Estonia	1.5	1.4	1.3	–0.4	–0.6	16.5	68.4	15.1	0.2	0.2	14	9
Ethiopia	37.7	67.2	87.3	2.6	2.0	45.7	51.5	2.8	0.9	0.1	20	40
Finland	4.8	5.2	5.3	0.4	0.1	17.8	67.0	15.2	0.3	0.2	10	11
France	53.9	59.5	61.8	0.4	0.3	18.7	65.2	16.1	0.3	0.2	10	13
Gabon	0.7	1.3	1.7	2.9	2.2	40.4	54.1	5.6	0.7	0.1	15	35
Gambia, The	0.6	1.4	1.8	3.5	1.9	40.4	56.3	3.3	0.7	0.1	14	37
Georgia	5.1	5.2	4.7	0.1	–0.8	19.2	67.1	13.8	0.3	0.2	10	8
Germany	78.3	82.5	80.3	0.2	–0.2	15.1	68.1	16.9	0.2	0.2	10	9
Ghana	11.0	20.3	25.2	2.8	1.7	42.5	53.0	4.5	0.8	0.1	13	29
Greece	9.6	10.6	11	0.4	0.3	14.8	66.8	18.4	0.2	0.3	11	9
Guatemala	6.8	12	16.3	2.6	2.3	42.9	53.7	3.5	0.8	0.1	7	33
Guinea	4.5	7.7	9.8	2.5	1.8	44.0	53.4	2.6	0.8	0.0	17	38
Guinea-Bissau	0.8	1.4	2.0	2.7	2.6	44.2	52.3	3.5	0.8	0.1	20	49
Haiti	5.4	8.3	10.3	2.0	1.7	39.6	56.9	3.5	0.7	0.1	14	32

Population dynamics **2.1**

	Total population (millions)			Average annual population growth rate (%)		Population age composition (%)			Dependency ratio (dependents as proportion of working-age population)		Crude death rate (per 1,000 people)	Crude birth rate (per 1,000 people)
	1980	2002	2015	1980–2002	2002–15	Ages 0–14 2002	Ages 15–64 2002	Ages 65+ 2002	Young 2002	Old 2002	2002	2002
Honduras	3.6	6.8	8.9	2.9	2.1	41.1	55.5	3.4	0.7	0.1	6	30
Hungary	10.7	10.2	9.6	−0.2	−0.4	16.5	68.8	14.6	0.2	0.2	13	10
India	687.3	1,048.6	1,231.6	1.9	1.2	32.8	62.2	5.0	0.5	0.1	9	24
Indonesia	148.3	211.7	245.5	1.6	1.1	29.8	65.4	4.8	0.5	0.1	7	20
Iran, Islamic Rep.	39.1	65.5	77.5	2.3	1.3	30.8	64.4	4.7	0.5	0.1	6	18
Iraq	13.0	24.2	31.1	2.8	1.9	40.1	56.9	3.0	0.7	0.1	8	29
Ireland	3.4	3.9	4.3	0.6	0.8	21.4	67.4	11.2	0.3	0.2	8	15
Israel	3.9	6.6	7.9	2.4	1.4	27.5	62.8	9.7	0.4	0.2	6	20
Italy	56.4	57.7	55.1	0.1	−0.3	14.1	67.2	18.7	0.2	0.3	11	9
Jamaica	2.1	2.6	3.0	0.9	1.0	30.1	62.9	6.9	0.5	0.1	6	20
Japan	116.8	127.2	124.6	0.4	−0.2	14.3	67.6	18.1	0.2	0.3	8	9
Jordan	2.2	5.2	6.8	3.9	2.2	37.8	59.1	3.1	0.6	0.1	4	28
Kazakhstan	14.9	14.9	15.5	0.0	0.3	25.3	67.0	7.7	0.4	0.1	12	15
Kenya	16.6	31.3	37.5	2.9	1.4	42.6	54.8	2.7	0.8	0.0	16	35
Korea, Dem. Rep.	17.2	22.5	24.0	1.2	0.5	26.0	67.7	6.4	0.4	0.1	11	17
Korea, Rep.	38.1	47.6	50.0	1.0	0.4	21.0	71.8	7.2	0.3	0.1	7	12
Kuwait	1.4	2.3	3.0	2.4	1.9	25.1	73.1	1.7	0.3	0.0	3	20
Kyrgyz Republic	3.6	5.0	5.8	1.5	1.1	32.5	61.4	6.1	0.5	0.1	7	20
Lao PDR	3.2	5.5	7.3	2.5	2.1	42.1	54.4	3.5	0.8	0.1	12	36
Latvia	2.5	2.3	2.1	−0.4	−0.7	15.8	69.1	15.2	0.2	0.2	14	8
Lebanon	3.0	4.4	5.2	1.8	1.2	30.9	63.2	5.9	0.5	0.1	6	19
Lesotho	1.3	1.8	2.0	1.5	0.9	41.7	53.1	5.2	0.8	0.1	23	33
Liberia	1.9	3.3	4.4	2.6	2.2	44.3	53.0	2.7	0.8	0.1	20	43
Libya	3.0	5.4	6.9	2.6	1.8	33.0	63.4	3.6	0.5	0.1	4	27
Lithuania	3.4	3.5	3.3	0.1	−0.4	18.2	67.8	13.9	0.3	0.2	12	9
Macedonia, FYR	1.9	2.0	2.2	0.3	0.5	21.9	67.7	10.4	0.3	0.2	9	14
Madagascar	8.9	16.4	22.5	2.8	2.4	44.4	52.6	3.0	0.8	0.1	12	39
Malawi	6.2	10.7	13.6	2.5	1.8	44.7	51.9	3.5	0.9	0.1	25	45
Malaysia	13.8	24.3	29.6	2.6	1.5	33.3	62.4	4.3	0.5	0.1	5	22
Mali	6.6	11.4	15.6	2.5	2.4	47.2	50.0	2.9	0.9	0.1	22	48
Mauritania	1.6	2.8	3.6	2.5	2.0	43.1	53.7	3.1	0.8	0.1	15	35
Mauritius	1.0	1.2	1.4	1.0	0.9	25.2	68.5	6.3	0.4	0.1	7	17
Mexico	67.6	100.8	120.6	1.8	1.4	32.9	62.0	5.1	0.5	0.1	4	20
Moldova	4.0	4.3	4.1	0.3	−0.2	21.1	67.9	11.1	0.3	0.2	13	11
Mongolia	1.7	2.4	2.9	1.8	1.3	32.5	63.5	4.0	0.5	0.1	6	23
Morocco	19.4	29.6	35.4	1.9	1.4	33.5	62.2	4.3	0.5	0.1	6	21
Mozambique	12.1	18.4	22.7	1.9	1.6	42.5	53.8	3.7	0.8	0.1	21	40
Myanmar	33.7	48.8	55.7	1.7	1.0	32.3	63.1	4.5	0.5	0.1	12	23
Namibia	1.0	2.0	2.3	3.0	1.1	41.8	54.4	3.8	0.8	0.1	21	35
Nepal	14.6	24.1	31.1	2.3	2.0	40.4	55.8	3.8	0.7	0.1	10	32
Netherlands	14.2	16.1	16.7	0.6	0.3	18.4	67.8	13.8	0.3	0.2	9	12
New Zealand	3.1	3.9	4.4	1.1	0.8	22.1	66.2	11.7	0.3	0.2	7	14
Nicaragua	2.9	5.3	7.0	2.7	2.0	41.5	55.4	3.1	0.7	0.1	5	29
Niger	5.6	11.4	16.3	3.3	2.7	48.9	48.8	2.3	1.0	0.0	20	49
Nigeria	71.1	132.8	169.4	2.8	1.9	43.7	53.7	2.6	0.8	0.0	17	39
Norway	4.1	4.5	4.7	0.5	0.3	19.8	65.2	15	0.3	0.2	10	12
Oman	1.1	2.5	3.4	3.8	2.2	42.3	55.1	2.7	0.8	0.0	3	26
Pakistan	82.7	144.9	192.8	2.5	2.2	40.6	56.0	3.3	0.7	0.1	8	33
Panama	2.0	2.9	3.5	1.9	1.2	30.4	63.9	5.7	0.5	0.1	5	20
Papua New Guinea	3.1	5.4	6.9	2.5	1.9	41.1	56.5	2.4	0.7	0.0	10	33
Paraguay	3.1	5.5	7.2	2.6	2.0	38.8	57.7	3.5	0.7	0.1	5	30
Peru	17.3	26.7	31.5	2.0	1.3	32.4	62.7	4.9	0.5	0.1	6	22
Philippines	48.0	79.9	98.2	2.3	1.6	36.5	59.6	3.9	0.6	0.1	6	26
Poland	35.6	38.6	38.4	0.4	0.0	18.2	69.4	12.4	0.3	0.2	9	9
Portugal	9.8	10.2	10.2	0.2	0.0	17.2	67.6	15.2	0.3	0.2	11	12
Puerto Rico	3.2	3.9	4.2	0.9	0.7	23.6	66.2	10.2	0.4	0.2	8	15

	Total population (millions)			Average annual population growth rate (%)		Population age composition (%)			Dependency ratio (dependents as proportion of working-age population)		Crude death rate (per 1,000 people)	Crude birth rate (per 1,000 people)
						Ages 0–14	Ages 15–64	Ages 65+	Young	Old		
	1980	2002	2015	1980–2002	2002–15	2002	2002	2002	2002	2002	2002	2002
Romania	22.2	22.3	21.4	0.0	–0.3	17.2	69.1	13.7	0.2	0.2	13	10
Russian Federation	139.0	144.1	134.5	0.2	–0.5	16.9	70.2	12.9	0.2	0.2	15	10
Rwanda	5.2	8.2	10.0	2.1	1.6	46.6	50.3	3.1	0.9	0.1	22	44
Saudi Arabia	9.4	21.9	30.8	3.9	2.6	40.4	56.6	2.9	0.7	0.1	4	31
Senegal	5.5	10.0	12.8	2.7	1.9	44.0	53.3	2.7	0.8	0.1	13	35
Serbia and Montenegro	9.8 b	8.2	10.7	0.4 c	2.1	19.8	66.3	13.9	0.3	0.2	12	12
Sierra Leone	3.2	5.2	6.7	2.2	1.9	44.1	53.3	2.6	0.8	0.0	25	44
Singapore	2.4	4.2	4.8	2.5	1.1	21.1	71.4	7.5	0.3	0.1	5	11
Slovak Republic	5.0	5.4	5.4	0.3	0.0	18.8	69.8	11.4	0.3	0.2	10	11
Slovenia	1.9	2.0	1.9	0.1	–0.2	15.2	70.4	14.4	0.2	0.2	10	9
Somalia	6.5	9.3	14.0	1.6	3.1	47.9	49.7	2.4	1.0	0.0	18	50
South Africa	27.6	45.3	47.0	2.3	0.3	32.1	63.4	4.5	0.5	0.1	20	25
Spain	37.4	40.9	41.5	0.4	0.1	15.0	68.0	17.0	0.2	0.2	9	10
Sri Lanka	14.6	19.0	21.9	1.2	1.1	25.6	67.8	6.5	0.4	0.1	6	18
Sudan	19.4	32.8	42.6	2.4	2.0	39.7	56.8	3.5	0.7	0.1	10	33
Swaziland	0.6	1.1	1.3	3.0	1.2	42.2	55.0	2.9	0.8	0.1	18	35
Sweden	8.3	8.9	9.0	0.3	0.1	17.7	64.8	17.5	0.3	0.3	11	11
Switzerland	6.3	7.3	7.5	0.6	0.2	16.7	67.8	15.5	0.2	0.2	9	10
Syrian Arab Republic	8.7	17.0	22.0	3.0	2.0	39.0	57.8	3.1	0.7	0.1	4	29
Tajikistan	4.0	6.3	7.2	2.1	1.0	37.6	57.9	4.6	0.6	0.1	7	23
Tanzania	18.6	35.2	43.9	2.9	1.7	45.0	52.6	2.4	0.9	0.0	18	38
Thailand	46.7	61.6	66.3	1.3	0.6	23.2	70.3	6.4	0.3	0.1	8	15
Togo	2.5	4.8	6.2	2.9	2.0	43.6	53.3	3.2	0.8	0.1	15	36
Trinidad and Tobago	1.1	1.3	1.4	0.8	0.8	24.3	69.3	6.4	0.4	0.1	7	16
Tunisia	6.4	9.8	11.5	1.9	1.3	28.2	65.8	6.0	0.4	0.1	6	18
Turkey	44.5	69.6	81.3	2.0	1.2	28.4	65.8	5.9	0.4	0.1	7	22
Turkmenistan	2.9	4.8	5.7	2.3	1.3	34.7	60.9	4.4	0.6	0.1	8	22
Uganda	12.8	24.6	33.6	3.0	2.4	49.0	49.1	1.9	1.0	0.0	18	44
Ukraine	50.0	48.7	44.7	–0.1	–0.7	16.5	68.8	14.7	0.2	0.2	15	9
United Arab Emirates	1.0	3.2	3.7	5.1	1.1	25.5	71.6	2.9	0.4	0.0	4	17
United Kingdom	56.3	59.2	59.6	0.2	0.0	18.4	65.6	16.1	0.3	0.2	10	11
United States	227.2	288.4	319.9	1.1	0.8	21.1	66.4	12.5	0.3	0.2	9	14
Uruguay	2.9	3.4	3.6	0.6	0.6	24.5	62.9	12.6	0.4	0.2	10	16
Uzbekistan	16.0	25.3	30.0	2.1	1.3	35.4	60.0	4.6	0.6	0.1	6	20
Venezuela, RB	15.1	25.1	30.3	2.3	1.4	33.0	62.5	4.5	0.5	0.1	5	23
Vietnam	53.7	80.4	92.4	1.8	1.1	31.4	63.3	5.3	0.5	0.1	6	19
West Bank and Gaza	..	3.2	4.9	..	3.2	45.8	50.9	3.2	0.9	0.1	4	35
Yemen, Rep.	8.5	18.6	27.3	3.5	2.9	45.7	51.6	2.7	0.9	0.1	10	41
Zambia	5.7	10.2	11.9	2.6	1.2	44.9	52.9	2.2	0.8	0.0	23	39
Zimbabwe	7.1	13.0	14.1	2.7	0.6	44.0	52.8	3.1	0.8	0.1	21	29
World	**4,430.1 s**	**6,198.5 s**	**7,090.7 s**	**1.5 w**	**1.0 w**	**29.2 w**	**63.7 w**	**7.1 w**	**0.5 w**	**0.1 w**	**9 w**	**21 w**
Low income	1,561.8	2,494.6	3,044.0	2.1	1.5	36.5	59.3	4.2	0.6	0.1	11	29
Middle income	2,038.1	2,737.8	3,039.0	1.3	0.8	26.4	66.5	7.1	0.4	0.1	8	17
Lower middle income	1,801.0	2,408.5	2,658.4	1.3	0.8	26.1	66.9	7.0	0.4	0.1	8	17
Upper middle income	237.0	329.3	380.6	1.5	1.1	28.9	63.7	7.4	0.5	0.1	6	19
Low & middle income	3,599.8	5,232.4	6,083.0	1.7	1.2	31.2	63.1	5.7	0.5	0.1	9	22
East Asia & Pacific	1,359.4	1,838.3	2,036.9	1.4	0.8	26.3	67.2	6.5	0.4	0.1	8	16
Europe & Central Asia	425.8	472.9	478.2	0.5	0.1	20.9	67.9	11.2	0.3	0.2	12	13
Latin America & Carib.	356.4	524.9	619.4	1.8	1.3	30.9	63.6	5.5	0.5	0.1	6	21
Middle East & N. Africa	173.7	305.8	382.7	2.6	1.7	35.3	60.7	4.0	0.6	0.1	6	24
South Asia	901.3	1,401.5	1,683.7	2.0	1.4	34.2	61.2	4.6	0.6	0.1	9	26
Sub-Saharan Africa	383.2	688.9	882.1	2.7	1.9	43.8	53.3	3.0	0.8	0.1	18	39
High income	830.2	966.2	1,007.7	0.7	0.3	18.3	67.3	14.4	0.3	0.2	9	12
Europe EMU	285.5	305.5	305.2	0.3	0.0	16.0	67.2	16.8	0.2	0.2	10	10

a. Estimate does not account for recent refugee flows. b. Includes population for Kosovo until 2001. c. Data are for 1980–2001.

Population estimates are usually based on national population censuses, but the frequency and quality of these vary by country. Most countries conduct a complete enumeration no more than once a decade. Pre- and post-census estimates are interpolations or extrapolations based on demographic models. Errors and undercounting occur even in high-income countries; in developing countries such errors may be substantial because of limits in the transport, communications, and other resources required to conduct a full census.

The quality and reliability of official demographic data are also affected by the public trust in the government, the government's commitment to full and accurate enumeration, the confidentiality and protection against misuse accorded to census data, and the independence of census agencies from undue political influence. Moreover, the international comparability of population indicators is limited by differences in the concepts, definitions, data collection procedures, and estimation methods used by national statistical agencies and other organizations that collect population data.

Of the 152 economies listed in the table, 125 (about 82 percent) conducted a census between 1995 and 2003. The currentness of a census, along with the availability of complementary data from surveys or registration systems, is one of many objective ways to judge the quality of demographic data. In some European countries registration systems offer complete information on population in the absence of a census. See *Primary data documentation* for the most recent census or survey year and for the completeness of registration.

Current population estimates for developing countries that lack recent census-based data, and pre- and post-census estimates for countries with census data, are provided by national statistical offices, the United Nations Population Division, and other agencies. The standard estimation method requires fertility, mortality, and net migration data, which are often collected from sample surveys, some of which may be small or limited in coverage. The population estimates are the product of demographic modeling and so are susceptible to biases and errors because of shortcomings in the model as well as in the data. Population projections are made using the cohort component method.

The growth rate of the total population conceals the fact that different age groups may grow at very different rates. In many developing countries the population under 15 was earlier growing rapidly but is now starting to shrink. Previously high fertility rates and declining mortality rates are now reflected in the larger share of the working-age population.

Dependency ratios take into account the variations in the proportions of children, elderly people, and working-age people in the population. Separate calculations of young-age and old-age dependency suggest the burden of dependency that the working-age population must bear in relation to children and the elderly. But dependency ratios show the age composition of a population, not economic dependency. Some children and elderly people are part of the labor force, and many working-age people are not.

The vital rates shown in the table are based on data derived from birth and death registration systems, censuses, and sample surveys conducted by national statistical offices, United Nations agencies, and other organizations. The estimates for 2002 for many countries are based on extrapolations of levels and trends measured in earlier years.

Vital registers are the preferred source of these data, but in many developing countries systems for registering births and deaths do not exist or are incomplete because of deficiencies in the coverage of events or of geographic areas. Many developing countries carry out special household surveys that estimate vital rates by asking respondents about births and deaths in the recent past. Estimates derived in this way are subject to sampling errors as well as errors due to inaccurate recall by the respondents.

The United Nations Statistics Division monitors the completeness of vital registration systems. The share of countries with at least 90 percent complete vital registration increased from 45 percent in 1988 to 55 percent in 2002. Still, some of the most populous developing countries—China, India, Indonesia, Brazil, Pakistan, Bangladesh, Nigeria—do not have complete vital registration systems. Fewer than 30 percent of births and 40 percent of deaths worldwide are thought to be registered and reported.

International migration is the only other factor besides birth and death rates that directly determines a country's population growth. From 1990 to 2000 the number of migrants in high-income countries increased by 23 million. About 175 million people currently live outside their home country, accounting for about 3 percent of the world's population. Estimating international migration is difficult. At any time many people are located outside their home country as tourists, workers, or refugees or for other reasons. Standards relating to the duration and purpose of international moves that qualify as migration vary, and accurate estimates require information on flows into and out of countries that is difficult to collect.

• **Total population** of an economy includes all residents regardless of legal status or citizenship—except for refugees not permanently settled in the country of asylum, who are generally considered part of the population of their country of origin. The values shown are midyear estimates for 1980 and 2002 and projections for 2015. • **Average annual population growth rate** is the exponential change for the period indicated. See *Statistical methods* for more information. • **Population age composition** refers to the percentage of the total population that is in specific age groups. • **Dependency ratio** is the ratio of dependents—people younger than 15 or older than 64—to the working-age population—those ages 15–64. • **Crude death rate** and **crude birth rate** are the number of deaths and the number of live births occurring during the year, per 1,000 population estimated at midyear. Subtracting the crude death rate from the crude birth rate provides the rate of natural increase, which is equal to the population growth rate in the absence of migration.

The World Bank's population estimates are produced by its Human Development Network and Development Data Group in consultation with its operational staff and country offices. Important inputs to the World Bank's demographic work come from the following sources: census reports and other statistical publications from national statistical offices; Demographic and Health Surveys conducted by national agencies, Macro International, and the U.S. Centers for Disease Control and Prevention; United Nations Statistics Division, *Population and Vital Statistics Report* (quarterly); United Nations Population Division, *World Population Prospects: The 2002 Revision;* Eurostat, *Demographic Statistics* (various years); Centro Latinoamericano de Demografía, *Boletín Demográfico* (various years); and U.S. Bureau of the Census, International Database.

	Labor force participation rate				Labor force				
	% ages 15–64				Total millions		Average annual growth rate %	Female % of labor force	
	Male		Female						
	1980	2002	1980	2002	1980	2002	1980–2002	1980	2002
Afghanistan	89.3	87.6[a]	49.8	50.3[a]	6.8	11.7[a]	2.4	34.8	35.8[a]
Albania	86.1	85.5	60.6	65.8	1.2	1.6	1.3	38.8	41.5
Algeria	80.4	79.8	19.1	33.8	4.8	11.0	3.7	21.4	29.0
Angola	91.7	90.1	77.8	74.8	3.5	6.1	2.5	47.0	46.2
Argentina	86.4	84.3	32.6	44.1	10.7	15.7	1.8	27.6	34.4
Armenia	77.4	78.2	68.1	71.1	1.4	1.6	0.4	47.9	48.6
Australia	86.6	82.8	52.0	67.1	6.7	10.0	1.8	36.8	44.0
Austria	84.9	78.6	54.4	56.6	3.4	3.8	0.5	40.5	40.4
Azerbaijan	77.8	78.0	67.4	61.3	2.7	3.7	1.4	47.5	44.7
Bangladesh	90.9	87.8	70.2	67.9	40.3	72.4	2.7	42.3	42.5
Belarus	83.4	80.9	74.3	73.4	5.1	5.3	0.2	49.9	48.9
Belgium	79.8	72.3	41.3	51.8	3.9	4.3	0.4	33.9	41.1
Benin	86.9	82.5	77.8	75.4	1.7	3.0	2.7	47.0	48.3
Bolivia	85.9	83.5	39.6	49.4	2.0	3.6	2.7	33.3	38.0
Bosnia and Herzegovina	77.8	78.0	37.0	49.1	1.6	1.9	0.8	32.8	38.2
Botswana	84.9	83.9	72.2	66.5	0.4	0.8	3.0	50.1	45.1
Brazil	89.4	87.2	35.7	47.0	47.7	81.7	2.5	28.4	35.5
Bulgaria	82.7	77.3	70.4	70.8	4.6	4.1	–0.6	45.3	48.0
Burkina Faso	94.2	89.9	82.8	77.7	3.8	5.8	1.9	47.6	46.5
Burundi	93.9	93.9	86.9	85.4	2.3	3.9	2.4	50.2	48.6
Cambodia	85.9	86.2	85.2	84.8	3.7	6.6	2.7	55.4	51.5
Cameroon	89.8	86.0	49.6	51.7	3.7	6.5	2.6	36.8	38.2
Canada	86.0	82.8	57.3	72.0	12.2	16.8	1.5	39.5	46.0
Central African Republic	..	..	..	..	1.2	1.8	1.9	..	..
Chad	91.7	89.1	68.3	70.6	2.2	4.0	2.7	43.4	44.8
Chile	81.4	81.9	28.7	43.8	3.8	6.5	2.4	26.3	34.5
China	91.4	89.2	75.5	79.5	538.7	769.3	1.6	43.2	45.2
Hong Kong, China	86.1	85.0	50.5	56.3	2.5	3.6	1.7	34.3	37.2
Colombia	83.1	83.5	26.6	52.2	9.4	19.4	3.3	26.2	39.1
Congo, Dem. Rep.	87.6	84.7	65.8	62.5	12.4	21.4	2.5	44.5	43.3
Congo, Rep.	86.3	83.4	57.2	58.7	0.8	1.5	3.1	42.4	43.5
Costa Rica	88.8	84.3	24.3	40.9	0.8	1.6	3.2	20.8	31.6
Côte d'Ivoire	91.5	87.3	45.5	45.5	3.3	6.7	3.2	32.2	33.6
Croatia	80.5	75.2	53.2	59.7	2.2	2.1	–0.1	40.2	44.4
Cuba	83.4	85.1	39.7	57.4	3.7	5.6	1.9	31.4	39.9
Czech Republic	84.8	82.6	75.1	74.5	5.3	5.7	0.3	47.1	47.2
Denmark	88.3	84.4	71.3	76.7	2.7	2.9	0.3	44.0	46.5
Dominican Republic	86.3	86.7	30.5	44.0	2.1	3.9	2.8	24.7	31.4
Ecuador	86.9	85.6	22.5	35.7	2.5	5.1	3.2	20.1	28.7
Egypt, Arab Rep.	83.5	82.3	29.3	38.3	14.3	25.9	2.7	26.5	31.0
El Salvador	89.6	87.2	32.2	50.7	1.6	2.8	2.7	26.5	37.3
Eritrea	88.4	86.6	78.1	76.6	1.2	2.2	2.6	47.4	47.4
Estonia	85.4	81.7	79.3	74.1	0.8	0.8	–0.3	50.6	48.9
Ethiopia	86.9	85.6	60.2	58.6	16.9	28.9	2.4	42.3	41.0
Finland	79.3	75.6	68.3	71.7	2.4	2.6	0.3	46.5	48.2
France	81.6	75.2	55.2	62.3	23.8	27.0	0.6	40.1	45.3
Gabon	87.7	85.3	67.6	66.5	0.4	0.6	2.2	45.0	44.8
Gambia, The	93.0	90.0	71.2	70.7	0.3	0.7	3.4	44.8	45.2
Georgia	81.1	79.2	71.0	66.6	2.6	2.6	0.0	49.3	46.8
Germany	86.6	81.0	56.2	62.8	37.5	41.1	0.4	40.1	42.4
Ghana	83.0	82.4	82.8	81.0	5.2	9.7	2.8	51.0	50.4
Greece	83.5	78.3	31.8	48.7	3.8	4.6	0.9	27.9	38.2
Guatemala	91.7	88.3	27.6	39.9	2.3	4.5	3.0	22.4	30.1
Guinea	91.7	87.0	83.2	79.6	2.3	3.7	2.1	47.1	47.2
Guinea-Bissau	92.4	90.6	59.7	59.5	0.4	0.7	2.4	39.9	40.5
Haiti	85.5	82.4	64.2	58.1	2.5	3.6	1.6	44.6	42.8

	Labor force participation rate				Labor force				
	% ages 15–64				Total millions		Average annual growth rate %	Female % of labor force	
	Male		Female						
	1980	**2002**	**1980**	**2002**	**1980**	**2002**	**1980–2002**	**1980**	**2002**
Honduras	90.4	87.1	31.9	43.6	1.2	2.6	3.6	25.2	32.6
Hungary	84.8	78.2	62.0	61.1	5.1	4.9	–0.2	43.3	44.8
India	88.6	86.8	47.8	45.0	299.5	470.2	2.0	33.7	32.5
Indonesia	85.8	84.7	45.6	59.1	58.6	104.2	2.6	35.2	41.2
Iran, Islamic Rep.	83.9	79.8	20.6	32.8	11.7	21.1	2.7	20.4	28.4
Iraq	80.1	76.3	16.3	20.4	3.5	6.8	3.0	17.3	20.4
Ireland	85.0	79.4	34.7	44.7	1.3	1.7	1.3	28.1	35.0
Israel	81.9	79.2	42.0	57.5	1.5	2.9	3.1	33.7	41.7
Italy	81.8	78.7	39.2	50.3	22.6	25.7	0.6	32.9	38.7
Jamaica	85.7	83.8	72.6	74.8	1.0	1.4	1.7	46.3	46.2
Japan	86.1	84.9	52.1	62.4	57.2	68.0	0.8	37.9	41.7
Jordan	78.7	79.3	14.6	29.4	0.5	1.6	5.0	14.7	25.6
Kazakhstan	82.3	79.9	70.5	68.9	7.0	7.4	0.2	47.6	47.1
Kenya	91.7	89.2	77.7	76.8	7.8	16.3	3.3	46.0	46.1
Korea, Dem. Rep.	82.5	84.5	65.7	66.8	7.5	11.8	2.1	44.8	43.3
Korea, Rep.	77.6	79.8	50.2	59.1	15.5	24.6	2.1	38.7	41.8
Kuwait	86.3	79.8	21.0	43.9	0.5	1.0	3.1	13.1	32.1
Kyrgyz Republic	79.9	77.7	68.8	68.1	1.5	2.2	1.6	47.5	47.2
Lao PDR	..	..	..	..	1.7	2.6	2.1	..	..
Latvia	84.8	82.4	77.9	74.6	1.4	1.3	–0.5	50.8	50.5
Lebanon	77.7	81.1	21.4	33.3	0.8	1.6	2.9	22.6	30.1
Lesotho	87.8	85.0	50.0	49.9	0.5	0.7	1.4	37.9	37.0
Liberia	87.3	83.6	55.7	56.1	0.8	1.3	2.3	38.4	39.6
Libya	85.6	77.5	23.3	27.1	0.9	1.6	2.3	18.6	24.0
Lithuania	83.2	81.1	74.7	70.9	1.8	1.8	0.0	49.7	48.0
Macedonia, FYR	80.2	76.2	46.8	57.3	0.8	1.0	0.8	36.1	42.0
Madagascar	91.3	88.9	72.5	70.5	4.3	7.8	2.7	45.2	44.7
Malawi	89.6	86.4	81.4	78.4	3.1	5.2	2.3	50.6	48.4
Malaysia	84.6	81.2	42.8	51.3	5.3	10.3	3.0	33.7	38.3
Mali	92.3	89.7	75.9	73.6	3.4	5.6	2.2	46.7	46.1
Mauritania	91.4	87.5	71.5	65.0	0.8	1.3	2.3	45.0	43.5
Mauritius	85.2	83.7	28.5	42.0	0.3	0.5	1.9	25.7	33.0
Mexico	85.8	85.6	31.1	42.7	22.0	42.3	3.0	26.9	33.8
Moldova	82.8	79.5	74.6	69.9	2.1	2.2	0.1	50.3	48.4
Mongolia	90.4	86.2	75.7	77.3	0.8	1.2	2.2	45.7	47.1
Morocco	84.6	82.6	38.1	44.3	7.0	12.1	2.5	33.5	34.9
Mozambique	92.6	90.3	86.8	83.3	6.7	9.6	1.6	49.0	48.4
Myanmar	90.4	89.4	69.7	68.5	17.1	26.1	1.9	43.7	43.4
Namibia	87.7	82.9	55.2	56.9	0.4	0.8	2.8	40.1	41.0
Nepal	90.6	86.2	58.6	58.4	7.1	11.3	2.1	38.8	40.5
Netherlands	81.0	78.2	38.2	56.3	5.6	7.5	1.3	31.5	40.9
New Zealand	85.8	82.2	46.0	68.1	1.3	2.0	1.8	34.3	45.2
Nicaragua	88.6	86.2	34.8	51.2	1.0	2.2	3.6	27.6	36.6
Niger	95.2	92.6	73.6	71.1	2.8	5.4	3.0	44.6	44.3
Nigeria	89.1	86.2	50.0	49.7	29.5	52.9	2.7	36.2	36.7
Norway	83.5	81.0	59.8	73.9	1.9	2.4	0.9	40.5	46.5
Oman	88.3	77.9	7.4	22.1	0.3	0.7	3.3	6.2	18.9
Pakistan	88.2	86.4	27.7	38.7	29.3	55.3	2.9	22.7	29.5
Panama	82.4	82.8	37.3	47.5	0.7	1.3	2.8	29.9	35.7
Papua New Guinea	90.2	87.7	71.2	69.1	1.5	2.7	2.5	41.7	42.4
Paraguay	91.9	87.6	34.1	39.5	1.1	2.1	2.8	26.7	30.4
Peru	82.0	81.6	25.8	37.7	5.4	10.4	3.0	23.9	31.9
Philippines	84.5	83.1	46.0	51.8	18.7	34.2	2.7	35.0	38.0
Poland	84.2	77.8	67.7	66.2	18.5	19.9	0.3	45.3	46.5
Portugal	88.5	82.4	53.4	63.3	4.6	5.2	0.5	38.7	44.1
Puerto Rico	72.5	74.1	31.3	42.2	1.0	1.5	1.7	31.8	37.8

	Labor force participation rate				Labor force				
	% ages 15–64				Total millions		Average annual growth rate %	Female % of labor force	
	Male		Female						
	1980	2002	1980	2002	1980	2002	1980–2002	1980	2002
Romania	83.6	77.0	69.1	61.3	10.9	10.7	–0.1	45.8	44.5
Russian Federation	84.3	79.7	74.7	72.2	76.0	77.6	0.1	49.4	49.2
Rwanda	95.1	94.4	87.4	85.4	2.6	4.4	2.4	49.1	48.7
Saudi Arabia	86.3	81.1	9.6	24.5	2.8	7.2	4.4	7.6	17.7
Senegal	88.9	86.8	63.2	63.5	2.5	4.4	2.5	42.2	42.6
Serbia and Montenegro	81.4	76.4	50.5	58.6	4.5 [b]	3.9	0.6 [c]	38.7 [b]	43.1
Sierra Leone	86.8	84.6	44.6	46.9	1.2	2.0	2.1	35.5	37.1
Singapore	84.7	82.6	47.4	54.7	1.1	2.0	2.8	34.6	39.2
Slovak Republic	83.5	82.4	69.4	74.3	2.5	3.0	0.8	45.3	47.7
Slovenia	81.9	75.4	67.0	65.1	1.0	1.0	0.2	45.8	46.6
Somalia	89.6	87.2	66.2	64.6	3.0	4.0	1.3	43.4	43.4
South Africa	85.1	82.0	46.5	50.2	10.3	18.1	2.5	35.1	37.9
Spain	84.5	80.0	32.5	48.5	14.0	18.1	1.2	28.3	37.5
Sri Lanka	83.7	81.8	32.3	47.0	5.4	8.4	2.0	26.9	36.9
Sudan	88.6	85.9	30.8	36.5	7.1	13.2	2.8	26.9	30.0
Swaziland	86.4	83.1	41.5	44.5	0.2	0.4	3.2	33.5	37.8
Sweden	85.4	83.9	69.3	81.2	4.2	4.8	0.6	43.8	48.1
Switzerland	89.9	90.2	51.9	65.4	3.1	3.9	1.1	36.7	40.8
Syrian Arab Republic	82.1	80.5	23.6	31.1	2.5	5.6	3.7	23.5	27.6
Tajikistan	79.6	77.3	68.3	63.6	1.5	2.5	2.3	46.9	45.2
Tanzania	89.9	88.3	86.0	82.7	9.5	18.1	2.9	49.8	49.0
Thailand	89.3	89.9	79.7	77.9	24.4	37.5	2.0	47.4	46.2
Togo	89.9	87.2	54.7	55.0	1.1	2.0	2.7	39.3	40.0
Trinidad and Tobago	85.6	81.1	39.7	49.7	0.4	0.6	1.5	31.4	34.9
Tunisia	84.8	83.2	34.5	40.6	2.2	4.0	2.7	28.9	32.1
Turkey	87.5	84.9	47.8	53.6	18.7	33.7	2.7	35.5	38.1
Turkmenistan	81.4	80.4	69.9	67.4	1.2	2.1	2.7	47.0	45.9
Uganda	93.4	91.0	83.3	81.2	6.6	12.1	2.7	47.9	47.6
Ukraine	82.7	78.4	73.7	69.7	26.4	24.9	–0.3	50.2	48.8
United Arab Emirates	94.9	87.9	16.0	34.2	0.6	1.6	4.7	5.1	15.9
United Kingdom	89.2	83.3	57.0	67.1	26.9	29.6	0.4	38.9	44.3
United States	83.8	81.0	58.2	70.1	110.1	148.3	1.4	41.0	46.2
Uruguay	85.3	82.5	37.3	59.4	1.2	1.6	1.3	30.8	42.2
Uzbekistan	78.6	77.9	70.4	68.1	6.5	11.0	2.4	48.0	46.9
Venezuela, RB	83.9	83.0	32.3	47.3	5.2	10.5	3.2	26.7	35.4
Vietnam	89.9	83.8	74.9	77.5	25.6	41.8	2.2	48.1	48.7
West Bank and Gaza	..	..	..	..	..	..	..	..	..
Yemen, Rep.	83.0	84.1	28.5	31.9	2.5	5.9	3.9	32.5	28.3
Zambia	89.5	87.2	69.2	66.8	2.4	4.4	2.8	45.4	44.6
Zimbabwe	87.4	86.3	67.4	67.0	3.2	6.1	2.9	44.4	44.5
World	**87.5 w**	**85.3 w**	**57.3 w**	**60.8 w**	**2,036.6 s**	**3,028.6 s**	**1.8 w**	**39.1 w**	**40.7 w**
Low income	88.4	86.4	53.8	54.4	683.4	1,138.6	2.3	37.4	37.7
Middle income	88.2	85.9	61.9	65.1	978.8	1,419.4	1.7	40.5	42.2
Lower middle income	88.7	86.3	64.2	67.2	885.1	1,276.7	1.7	41.2	42.8
Upper middle income	84.8	82.5	44.3	49.0	93.7	142.7	1.9	34.2	37.0
Low & middle income	88.3	86.1	58.5	60.3	1,662.3	2,558.0	2.0	39.2	40.2
East Asia & Pacific	90.3	88.1	70.8	75.1	704.1	1,049.3	1.8	42.6	44.5
Europe & Central Asia	83.6	79.8	69.0	66.7	214.1	239.3	0.5	46.7	46.3
Latin America & Carib.	86.7	85.4	33.2	46.0	128.8	229.6	2.6	27.8	35.2
Middle East & N. Africa	83.2	80.8	24.8	33.8	53.9	105.0	3.0	23.8	28.6
South Asia	88.7	86.7	47.9	47.1	388.7	629.8	2.2	33.8	33.6
Sub-Saharan Africa	89.2	86.6	63.0	62.2	172.7	305.1	2.6	42.0	42.0
High income	84.4	81.1	52.6	63.5	374.3	470.6	1.0	38.4	43.4
Europe EMU	83.7	78.7	47.2	56.9	123.0	141.6	0.6	36.4	41.4

a. Estimate does not account for recent refugee flows. b. Includes labor force for Kosovo until 2001. c. Data are for 1980–2001.

The labor force is the supply of labor available for the production of goods and services in an economy. It includes people who are currently employed and people who are unemployed but seeking work as well as first-time job-seekers. Not everyone who works is included, however. Unpaid workers, family workers, and students are among those usually omitted, and in some countries members of the military are not counted. The size of the labor force tends to vary during the year as seasonal workers enter and leave it.

Data on the labor force are compiled by the International Labour Organization (ILO) from labor force surveys, censuses, establishment censuses and surveys, and various types of administrative records such as employment exchange registers and unemployment insurance schemes. For some countries a combination of sources is used. While the resulting statistics may provide rough estimates of the labor force, they are not comparable across countries because of the noncomparability of the original data and the different ways the original sources may be combined.

For international comparisons the most comprehensive source is labor force surveys. Despite the ILO's efforts to encourage the use of international standards, labor force data are not fully comparable because of differences among countries, and sometimes within countries, in their scope and coverage. In some countries data on the labor force refer to people above a specific age, while in others there is no specific age provision. The reference period of the census or survey is another important source of differences: in some countries data refer to people's status on the day of the census or survey or during a specific period before the inquiry date, while in others the data are recorded without reference to any period. In developing countries, where the household is often the basic unit of production and all members contribute to output, but some at low intensity or irregular intervals, the estimated labor force may be significantly smaller than the numbers actually working (ILO, *Yearbook of Labour Statistics* 1997).

The labor force estimates in the table were calculated by World Bank staff by applying labor force participation rates from the ILO database to World Bank population estimates to create a series consistent with these population estimates. This procedure sometimes results in estimates of labor force size that differ slightly from those in the ILO's *Yearbook of Labour Statistics*. The labor force participation rate of the population ages 15–64 provides an indication of the relative size of the supply of labor.

But in many developing countries children under 15 work full or part time. And in some high-income countries many workers postpone retirement past age 65. As a result, labor force participation rates calculated in this way may systematically over- or under-estimate actual rates. High participation rates are found in Sub-Saharan Africa, where men and women cannot afford to forgo work, because of a lack of social protection. The largest gap between men and women in labor force participation is observed in the Middle East and North Africa, where low participation of women in the work force also brings down the overall labor force participation rate.

In general, estimates of women in the labor force are lower than those of men and are not comparable internationally, reflecting the fact that for women, demographic, social, legal, and cultural trends and norms determine whether their activities are regarded as economic. In many countries large numbers of women work on farms or in other family enterprises without pay, while others work in or near their homes, mixing work and family activities during the day. Countries differ in the criteria used to determine the extent to which such workers are to be counted as part of the labor force. In most economies the gap between male and female labor force participation rates has been narrowing since 1980.

• **Labor force participation rate** is the proportion of the population ages 15–64 that is economically active: all people who supply labor for the production of goods and services during a specified period.
• **Total labor force** comprises people who meet the ILO definition of the economically active population. It includes both the employed and the unemployed. While national practices vary in the treatment of such groups as the armed forces and seasonal or part-time workers, the labor force generally includes the armed forces, the unemployed, and first-time job-seekers, but excludes homemakers and other unpaid caregivers and workers in the informal sector.
• **Average annual growth rate of the labor force** is calculated using the exponential endpoint method (see *Statistical methods* for more information).
• **Females as a percentage of the labor force** show the extent to which women are active in the labor force.

Data sources

The labor force participation rates are from the ILO database *Estimates and Projections of the Economically Active Population, 1950–2010*. The ILO publishes estimates of the economically active population in its *Yearbook of Labour Statistics*.

2.3 Employment by economic activity

	Agriculture[a]				Industry[a]				Services[a]			
	Male % of male employment		Female % of female employment		Male % of male employment		Female % of female employment		Male % of male employment		Female % of female employment	
	1980	2000–02[b]	1980	2000–02[b]	1980	2000–02[b]	1980	2000–02[b]	1980	2000–02[b]	1980	2000–02[b]
Afghanistan	66	..	86	..	9	..	12	..	26	..	2	..
Albania	..	..	..	..	..	..	..	..	..	..	..	..
Algeria	27	..	69	..	33	..	6	..	40	..	25	..
Angola	67	..	87	..	13	..	1	..	20	..	11	..
Argentina	..	1	..	0[c]	..	30	..	12	..	69	..	87
Armenia	..	..	..	..	..	..	..	..	..	..	..	..
Australia	8	6	4	3	39	30	16	10	53	64	80	87
Austria	..	5	..	6	..	43	..	14	..	52	..	80
Azerbaijan	..	37	..	43	..	14	..	7	..	49	..	50
Bangladesh	..	53	..	77	..	11	..	9	..	30	..	12
Belarus	..	..	..	..	..	..	..	..	..	..	..	..
Belgium	4	..	2	..	44	..	18	..	51	..	79	..
Benin	66	..	69	..	10	..	4	..	24	..	27	..
Bolivia	..	6	..	3	..	39	..	14	..	55	..	82
Bosnia and Herzegovina	26	..	38	..	45	..	24	..	30	..	39	..
Botswana	..	22	..	17	..	26	..	14	..	51	..	67
Brazil	*34*	24	*20*	16	*30*	27	*13*	10	*36*	49	*67*	74
Bulgaria	..	..	..	..	..	..	..	..	..	..	..	..
Burkina Faso	92	..	93	..	3	..	2	..	5	..	5	..
Burundi	..	..	..	..	..	..	..	..	..	..	..	..
Cambodia	..	71	..	70	..	9	..	12	..	20	..	18
Cameroon	65	..	87	..	11	..	2	..	24	..	11	..
Canada	7	4	3	2	37	33	16	11	56	64	81	87
Central African Republic	79	..	90	..	5	..	1	..	15	..	9	..
Chad	82	..	95	..	6	..	0[c]	..	12	..	4	..
Chile	22	18	3	5	27	29	16	13	51	53	81	83
China	..	..	..	..	..	..	..	..	..	..	..	..
Hong Kong, China	2	0[c]	1	0[c]	47	27	56	10	52	73	43	90
Colombia	2	33	1	7	39	19	26	17	59	48	74	76
Congo, Dem. Rep.	62	..	84	..	18	..	4	..	20	..	12	..
Congo, Rep.	42	..	81	..	20	..	2	..	38	..	17	..
Costa Rica	34	22	6	4	25	27	20	15	40	51	74	80
Côte d'Ivoire	60	..	75	..	10	..	5	..	30	..	20	..
Croatia	..	16	..	15	..	37	..	21	..	47	..	63
Cuba	30	..	10	..	32	..	22	..	39	..	68	..
Czech Republic	13	6	11	3	57	50	39	28	30	44	50	68
Denmark	..	5	..	2	..	36	..	14	..	59	..	85
Dominican Republic	..	21	..	2	..	26	..	17	..	53	..	81
Ecuador	..	10	..	4	..	30	..	16	..	60	..	79
Egypt, Arab Rep.	45	27	10	39	21	25	13	7	33	48	69	54
El Salvador	51	34	10	4	21	25	21	22	28	42	69	74
Eritrea	79	..	88	..	7	..	2	..	14	..	11	..
Estonia	..	10	..	4	..	42	..	23	..	48	..	73
Ethiopia	..	..	..	..	..	..	..	..	..	..	..	..
Finland	15	7	12	4	45	40	23	14	39	53	65	82
France	10	2	7	1	45	34	22	13	46	64	71	86
Gabon	59	..	74	..	18	..	6	..	24	..	21	..
Gambia, The	78	..	93	..	10	..	3	..	13	..	5	..
Georgia	..	53	..	53	..	12	..	6	..	35	..	41
Germany	..	3	..	2	..	44	..	18	..	52	..	80
Ghana	..	..	..	..	..	..	..	..	..	..	..	..
Greece	*26*	15	*42*	18	*34*	30	*18*	12	*40*	56	*40*	70
Guatemala	..	50	..	18	..	18	..	23	..	27	..	56
Guinea	86	..	97	..	2	..	1	..	12	..	3	..
Guinea-Bissau	81	..	98	..	3	..	0	..	17	..	3	..
Haiti	..	..	..	..	..	..	..	..	..	..	..	..

Employment by economic activity | 2.3

	Agriculture [a]				Industry [a]				Services [a]			
	Male % of male employment		Female % of female employment		Male % of male employment		Female % of female employment		Male % of male employment		Female % of female employment	
	1980	2000–02 [b]	1980	2000–02 [b]	1980	2000–02 [b]	1980	2000–02 [b]	1980	2000–02 [b]	1980	2000–02 [b]
Honduras	..	..	..	..	..	..	..	..	..	..	..	..
Hungary	..	9	..	4	..	42	..	26	..	49	..	71
India	..	..	..	..	..	..	..	..	..	..	..	..
Indonesia	57	..	54	..	13	..	13	..	29	..	33	..
Iran, Islamic Rep.	..	..	..	..	..	..	..	..	..	..	..	..
Iraq	21	..	62	..	24	..	11	..	55	..	28	..
Ireland	..	11	..	2	..	39	..	14	..	50	..	83
Israel	8	3	4	1	39	34	16	12	52	62	79	86
Italy	13	6	16	5	43	39	28	20	44	55	56	75
Jamaica	..	..	..	..	..	..	..	..	..	..	..	..
Japan	9	5	13	5	40	37	28	21	51	57	58	73
Jordan	..	..	..	..	..	..	..	..	..	..	..	..
Kazakhstan	..	..	..	..	..	..	..	..	..	..	..	..
Kenya	23	20	25	16	24	24	9	10	53	57	65	75
Korea, Dem. Rep.	39	..	52	..	37	..	20	..	24	..	28	..
Korea, Rep.	..	9	..	12	..	34	..	19	..	57	..	70
Kuwait	2	..	0	..	36	..	3	..	62	..	97	..
Kyrgyz Republic	..	..	..	..	..	..	..	..	..	..	..	..
Lao PDR	77	..	82	..	7	..	4	..	16	..	13	..
Latvia	..	18	..	12	..	35	..	16	..	47	..	72
Lebanon	13	..	20	..	29	..	21	..	58	..	59	..
Lesotho	26	..	64	..	52	..	5	..	22	..	31	..
Liberia	69	..	89	..	9	..	1	..	22	..	10	..
Libya	16	..	63	..	29	..	3	..	55	..	34	..
Lithuania	..	20	..	12	..	34	..	21	..	45	..	67
Macedonia, FYR	..	23	..	25	..	36	..	30	..	41	..	46
Madagascar	73	..	93	..	9	..	2	..	19	..	5	..
Malawi	..	..	..	..	..	..	..	..	..	..	..	..
Malaysia	34	21	44	14	26	34	20	29	40	45	36	57
Mali	86	..	92	..	2	..	1	..	12	..	7	..
Mauritania	65	..	79	..	11	..	2	..	25	..	19	..
Mauritius	29	..	30	..	19	..	40	..	47	..	31	..
Mexico	..	24	..	6	..	28	..	22	..	48	..	72
Moldova	..	52	..	50	..	18	..	10	..	31	..	40
Mongolia	..	..	..	..	..	..	..	..	..	..	..	..
Morocco	..	..	..	..	..	..	..	..	..	..	..	..
Mozambique	72	..	97	..	14	..	1	..	14	..	2	..
Myanmar	..	..	..	..	..	..	..	..	..	..	..	..
Namibia	52	33	42	29	22	17	10	7	27	49	47	63
Nepal	..	..	..	..	..	..	..	..	..	..	..	..
Netherlands	..	4	..	2	..	31	..	9	..	64	..	86
New Zealand	*13*	12	*7*	6	*38*	32	*19*	12	*48*	56	*73*	82
Nicaragua	..	..	..	..	..	..	..	..	..	..	..	..
Niger	..	..	..	..	..	..	..	..	..	..	..	..
Nigeria	..	..	..	..	..	..	..	..	..	..	..	..
Norway	10	6	6	2	41	33	13	9	49	58	81	88
Oman	52	..	24	..	21	..	33	..	27	..	43	..
Pakistan	..	44	..	73	..	20	..	9	..	36	..	18
Panama	..	29	..	6	..	20	..	10	..	51	..	85
Papua New Guinea	76	..	92	..	8	..	2	..	16	..	6	..
Paraguay	*2*	39	*0* c	20	*35*	21	*13*	10	*63*	40	*86*	69
Peru	..	11	..	6	..	24	..	10	..	65	..	84
Philippines	60	45	37	25	16	18	15	12	25	37	48	63
Poland	..	19	..	19	..	40	..	18	..	40	..	63
Portugal	..	12	..	14	..	44	..	23	..	44	..	63
Puerto Rico	8	3	0 c	0 c	27	27	24	14	65	69	75	86

2.3 Employment by economic activity

	Agriculture [a]				Industry [a]				Services [a]			
	Male % of male employment		Female % of female employment		Male % of male employment		Female % of female employment		Male % of male employment		Female % of female employment	
	1980	2000–02 [b]	1980	2000–02 [b]	1980	2000–02 [b]	1980	2000–02 [b]	1980	2000–02 [b]	1980	2000–02 [b]
Romania	22	40	39	45	52	30	34	22	26	30	27	33
Russian Federation	..	..	..	..	..	..	..	..	..	..	..	..
Rwanda	88	..	98	..	5	..	1	..	7	..	1	..
Saudi Arabia	45	..	25	..	17	..	5	..	39	..	70	..
Senegal	74	..	90	..	9	..	2	..	17	..	8	..
Serbia and Montenegro	..	..	..	..	..	..	..	..	..	..	..	..
Sierra Leone	63	..	82	..	20	..	4	..	17	..	14	..
Singapore	2	0 [c]	1	0 [c]	33	31	40	18	65	69	59	81
Slovak Republic	..	8	..	4	..	48	..	26	..	44	..	71
Slovenia	..	10	..	10	..	46	..	29	..	43	..	61
Somalia	69	..	90	..	12	..	2	..	19	..	8	..
South Africa	..	..	..	..	..	..	..	..	..	..	..	..
Spain	20	8	18	5	42	42	21	15	38	51	61	81
Sri Lanka	*44*	..	*51*	..	*19*	..	*18*	..	*30*	..	*28*	..
Sudan	66	..	88	..	9	..	4	..	24	..	8	..
Swaziland	..	..	..	..	..	..	..	..	..	..	..	..
Sweden	8	3	3	1	45	36	16	11	47	61	81	88
Switzerland	8	5	5	3	47	36	23	13	46	59	72	84
Syrian Arab Republic	..	..	..	..	..	..	..	..	..	..	..	..
Tajikistan	..	..	..	..	..	..	..	..	..	..	..	..
Tanzania	..	..	..	..	..	..	..	..	..	..	..	..
Thailand	68	50	74	48	13	20	8	17	20	30	18	35
Togo	70	..	67	..	12	..	7	..	19	..	26	..
Trinidad and Tobago	..	..	..	..	..	..	..	..	..	..	..	..
Tunisia	33	..	53	..	30	..	32	..	37	..	16	..
Turkey	*4*	24	*9*	56	*36*	28	*31*	15	*60*	48	*60*	29
Turkmenistan	..	..	..	..	..	..	..	..	..	..	..	..
Uganda	..	..	..	..	..	..	..	..	..	..	..	..
Ukraine	..	22	..	17	..	39	..	22	..	33	..	55
United Arab Emirates	5	9	0 [c]	0 [c]	40	36	7	14	55	55	93	86
United Kingdom	4	2	1	1	48	36	23	11	49	62	76	88
United States	5	3	2	1	39	32	19	12	56	65	80	87
Uruguay	..	6	..	2	..	32	..	14	..	62	..	85
Uzbekistan	..	..	..	..	..	..	..	..	..	..	..	..
Venezuela, RB	20	15	2	2	31	28	18	12	49	57	79	86
Vietnam	..	..	..	..	..	..	..	..	..	..	..	..
West Bank and Gaza	22	9	25	26	43	32	25	11	36	58	50	62
Yemen, Rep.	60	..	98	..	19	..	1	..	21	..	1	..
Zambia	69	..	85	..	13	..	3	..	19	..	13	..
Zimbabwe	..	..	..	..	..	..	..	..	..	..	..	..
World	.. w	.. w	.. w	.. w	.. w	.. w	.. w	.. w	.. w	.. w	.. w	.. w
Low income	..	..	..	..	..	..	..	..	..	..	..	..
Middle income	..	..	..	..	..	..	..	..	..	..	..	..
Lower middle income	..	..	..	..	..	..	..	..	..	..	..	..
Upper middle income	..	16	..	8	..	32	..	19	..	51	..	73
Low & middle income	..	..	..	..	..	..	..	..	..	..	..	..
East Asia & Pacific	..	..	..	..	..	..	..	..	..	..	..	..
Europe & Central Asia	..	..	..	..	..	..	..	..	..	..	..	..
Latin America & Carib.	..	21	..	9	..	27	..	14	..	52	..	76
Middle East & N. Africa	..	..	..	..	..	..	..	..	..	..	..	..
South Asia	..	..	..	..	..	..	..	..	..	..	..	..
Sub-Saharan Africa	..	..	..	..	..	..	..	..	..	..	..	..
High income	8	4	6	3	41	35	22	15	51	60	72	82
Europe EMU	..	5	..	4	..	40	..	16	..	55	..	80

a. Data may not add up to 100 because of workers not classified by sector. b. Data are for the most recent year available. c. Less than 0.5.

Employment by economic activity | **2.3**

The International Labour Organization (ILO) classifies economic activity on the basis of the International Standard Industrial Classification (ISIC) of All Economic Activities. Because this classification is based on where work is performed (industry) rather than on what type of work is performed (occupation), all of an enterprise's employees are classified under the same industry, regardless of their trade or occupation. The categories should add up to 100 percent. Where they do not, the differences arise because of workers who cannot be classified by economic activity.

Data on employment are drawn from labor force surveys, household surveys, establishment censuses and surveys, administrative records of social insurance schemes, and official national estimates. The concept of employment generally refers to people above a certain age who worked, or who held a job, during a reference period. Employment data include both full-time and part-time workers. There are, however, many differences in how countries define and measure employment status, particularly for students, part-time workers, members of the armed forces, and household or contributing family workers. Where the armed forces are included, they are allocated to the service sector, causing that sector to be somewhat overstated relative to the service sector in economies where they are excluded. Where data are obtained from establishment surveys, they cover only employees; thus self-employed and contributing family workers are excluded. In such cases the employment share of the agricultural sector is severely underreported.

Countries also take very different approaches to the treatment of unemployed people. In most countries unemployed people with previous job experience are classified according to their last job. But in some countries the unemployed and people seeking their first job are not classifiable by economic activity. Because of these differences, the size and distribution of employment by economic activity may not be fully comparable across countries (ILO, *Yearbook of Labour Statistics 1996*, p. 64).

The ILO's *Yearbook of Labour Statistics* and its database *Key Indicators of the Labour Market* report data by major divisions of the ISIC revision 2 or ISIC revision 3. In this table the reported divisions or categories are aggregated into three broad groups: agriculture, industry, and services. Classification into such broad groups may obscure fundamental shifts within countries' industrial patterns. Most economies report economic activity according to the ISIC revision 2, although a group of economies moved to ISIC revision 3. The use of one classification or another should not have a significant impact on the information for the three broad sectors presented in this table.

The distribution of economic activity by gender reveals some interesting patterns. Industry accounts for a larger share of male employment than female employment worldwide, whereas a higher proportion of women work in the services sector. Employment in agriculture is also male-dominated, although not as much as industry.

Segregating one sex in a narrow range of occupations significantly reduces economic efficiency by reducing labor market flexibility and thus the economy's ability to adapt to change. This segregation is particularly harmful for women, who have a much narrower range of labor market choices and lower levels of pay than men. But it is also detrimental to men when job losses are concentrated in industries dominated by men and job growth is centered in service occupations, where women often dominate, as has been the recent experience in many countries.

There are several explanations for the rising importance of service jobs for women. Many service jobs—such as nursing and social and clerical work—are considered "feminine" because of a perceived similarity to women's traditional roles. Women often do not receive the training needed to take advantage of changing employment opportunities. And the greater availability of part-time work in service industries may lure more women, although it is not clear whether this is a cause or an effect.

• **Agriculture** corresponds to division 1 (ISIC revision 2) or tabulation categories A and B (ISIC revision 3) and includes hunting, forestry, and fishing. • **Industry** corresponds to divisions 2–5 (ISIC revision 2) or tabulation categories C–F (ISIC revision 3) and includes mining and quarrying (including oil production), manufacturing, construction, and public utilities (electricity, gas, and water). • **Services** correspond to divisions 6–9 (ISIC revision 2) or tabulation categories G–P (ISIC revision 3) and include wholesale and retail trade and restaurants and hotels; transport, storage, and communications; financing, insurance, real estate, and business services; and community, social, and personal services.

2.3a

Women tend to suffer disproportionately from underemployment

Underemployment as share of total employment (%)

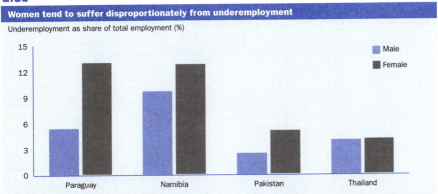

Time-related underemployment includes people who work less than the normal duration of work, as defined by national authorities, but who desire and seek to work additional hours. More women tend to be underemployed than men, as discrimination and women's household responsibilities may make it more difficult for them to have stable and high-paid work.

Source: International Labour Organization, *Key Indicators of the Labour Market,* third edition.

Data sources

The employment data are from the ILO database *Key Indicators of the Labour Market,* third edition.

	Unemployment						Long-term unemployment			Unemployment by level of educational attainment		
	Male % of male labor force		Female % of female labor force		Total % of total labor force		% of total unemployment			% of total unemployment		
							Male	Female	Total	Primary	Secondary	Tertiary
	1980	2000–02 [a]	1980	2000–02 [a]	1980	2000–02 [a]	2000–02 [a]	2000–02 [a]	2000–02 [a]	1999–2001 [a]	1999–2001 [a]	1999–2001 [a]
Afghanistan	..	..	..	..	..	..	..	..	..	..	..	..
Albania	..	18.8	..	28.4	5.6	22.7	..	..	..	..	..	..
Algeria	..	33.9	..	29.7	..	29.8	..	..	..	..	..	..
Angola	..	..	..	..	..	..	..	..	..	..	..	..
Argentina	..	14.1	..	16.4	2.3	17.8	..	..	..	..	..	..
Armenia	..	..	..	..	..	..	72.2	70.8	71.6	..	..	..
Australia	5.0	6.2	7.4	5.8	5.9	6.0	25.9	17.1	22.1	54.3	31.5	14.0
Austria	1.6	3.5	2.3	3.8	1.9	3.6	25.8	24.2	25.1	36.0	57.6	6.4
Azerbaijan	..	1.1	..	1.5	..	1.3	..	..	..	4.5	35.4	60.1
Bangladesh	..	3.2	..	3.3	..	3.3	..	..	..	54.3	22.7	8.4
Belarus	..	1.9	..	2.6	..	2.3	..	..	..	7.9	15.3	76.9
Belgium	5.5	6.2	15.0	7.8	9.1	6.9	45.8	53.3	49.4	50.0	34.9	15.1
Benin	..	..	..	..	..	..	..	..	..	..	..	..
Bolivia	..	4.5	..	6.2	..	5.2	..	..	..	60.2	32.5	4.4
Bosnia and Herzegovina	..	..	..	..	..	..	..	..	..	..	..	..
Botswana	..	14.7	..	17.2	..	15.8	..	..	..	..	..	..
Brazil	2.8	7.5	2.8	11.9	2.8	9.4	..	..	..	26.1	20.2	2.5
Bulgaria	..	20.2	..	18.4	..	19.4	..	..	..	36.7	53.0	10.3
Burkina Faso	..	..	..	..	..	..	..	..	..	46.8	19.3	5.6
Burundi	..	..	..	..	..	..	..	..	..	..	..	..
Cambodia	..	1.5	..	2.2	..	1.8	..	..	..	..	..	..
Cameroon	..	..	..	..	..	..	..	..	..	..	..	..
Canada	7.0	8.1	8.2	7.1	7.5	7.7	9.9	8.4	9.3	30.7	30.3	39.0
Central African Republic	..	..	..	..	..	..	..	..	..	..	..	..
Chad	..	..	..	..	..	..	..	..	..	..	..	..
Chile	10.6	7.5	10.0	8.5	10.4	7.8	..	..	..	22.7	54.9	21.6
China	..	..	..	..	4.9	3.1	..	..	..	..	..	..
Hong Kong, China	3.9	8.4	3.4	6.0	3.8	7.3	..	..	..	..	..	..
Colombia	7.5	11.6	11.5	19.1	9.1	17.9	..	..	..	22.8	57.2	17.2
Congo, Dem. Rep.	..	..	..	..	..	..	..	..	..	..	..	..
Congo, Rep.	..	..	..	..	..	..	..	..	..	..	..	..
Costa Rica	5.3	5.6	7.8	7.9	5.9	6.4	8.9	13.3	10.9	71.6	15.2	10.0
Côte d'Ivoire	..	..	..	..	..	..	..	..	..	..	..	..
Croatia	3.4	13.4	8.2	18.5	5.3	15.2	..	..	56.4	19.1	71.3	9.1
Cuba	..	..	..	..	..	3.3	..	..	..	..	..	..
Czech Republic	..	5.9	..	9.0	..	7.3	50.2	51.0	50.6	27.3	69.1	3.6
Denmark	6.5	4.2	7.6	4.3	7.0	4.3	17.1	22.1	19.5	35.1	44.9	20.0
Dominican Republic	..	9.4	..	26.0	..	15.6	2.2	1.3	1.6	..	..	..
Ecuador	..	7.1	..	16.2	..	11.0	..	..	..	26.8	50.8	20.2
Egypt, Arab Rep.	3.9	5.1	19.2	22.7	5.2	9.0	..	..	..	..	..	..
El Salvador	..	8.0	..	3.5	12.9	6.2	..	..	..	..	..	..
Eritrea	..	..	..	..	..	..	..	..	..	..	..	..
Estonia	..	12.9	..	12.2	..	12.6	..	..	..	19.3	62.7	18.1
Ethiopia	..	..	..	..	..	..	..	..	..	26.9	61.3	8.1
Finland	4.6	9.0	4.7	9.1	4.7	9.0	30.0	22.6	26.2	38.2	45.8	16.0
France	4.1	7.9	9.1	10.1	6.1	8.9	30.2	33.1	31.7	..	..	..
Gabon	..	..	..	..	..	..	..	..	..	..	..	..
Gambia, The	..	..	..	..	..	..	..	..	..	..	..	..
Georgia	..	11.6	..	10.7	..	11.0	..	..	..	5.5	33.1	61.4
Germany	..	8.7	..	8.3	..	8.6	44.9	48.7	46.6	26.8	60.4	12.8
Ghana	..	..	..	..	..	..	..	..	..	..	..	..
Greece	3.3	6.2	5.7	14.6	2.4	9.6	47.1	55.7	52.4	35.1	49.4	14.5
Guatemala	..	2.5	..	4.3	1.7	3.1	..	..	..	..	..	..
Guinea	..	..	..	..	..	..	..	..	..	..	..	..
Guinea-Bissau	..	..	..	..	..	..	..	..	..	..	..	..
Haiti	..	..	..	..	..	..	..	..	..	..	..	..

Unemployment 2.4

	Unemployment Male % of male labor force		Female % of female labor force		Total % of total labor force		Long-term unemployment % of total unemployment			Unemployment by level of educational attainment % of total unemployment		
							Male	Female	Total	Primary	Secondary	Tertiary
	1980	2000–02 [a]	1980	2000–02 [a]	1980	2000–02 [a]	2000–02 [a]	2000–02 [a]	2000–02 [a]	1999–2001 [a]	1999–2001 [a]	1999–2001 [a]
Honduras	8.6	3.4	6.0	4.7	7.3	3.8	..	..	..	..	..	..
Hungary	..	6.1	..	5.4	..	5.8	47.1	41.7	44.8	35.4	60.5	4.1
India	..	..	..	..	..	..	..	..	..	29.0	40.3	30.7
Indonesia	..	..	..	..	..	6.1	..	..	..	46.0	36.6	6.7
Iran, Islamic Rep.	..	..	..	..	..	..	..	..	..	..	..	..
Iraq	..	..	..	..	..	..	..	..	..	..	..	..
Ireland	11.4	4.6	8.2	3.7	10.5	4.2	35.9	18.2	29.4	60.8	20.8	16.1
Israel	4.1	10.1	6.0	10.6	4.8	10.3	..	..	..	20.7	44.2	34.1
Italy	4.8	6.9	13.2	12.2	7.6	9.0	58.0	61.6	59.9	49.1	41.9	7.2
Jamaica	16.3	..	39.6	..	27.3	..	24.4	36.2	31.7	..	..	..
Japan	2.0	5.6	2.0	5.1	2.0	5.4	34.8	21.6	29.7	21.5	53.4	24.8
Jordan	..	11.8	..	20.7	..	13.2	..	..	..	..	..	..
Kazakhstan	..	..	..	..	..	..	..	..	..	7.2	52.5	40.3
Kenya	..	..	..	..	..	..	..	..	..	..	..	..
Korea, Dem. Rep.	..	..	..	..	..	..	..	..	..	..	..	..
Korea, Rep.	6.2	3.5	3.5	2.5	5.2	3.1	3.1	1.2	2.5	26.1	51.0	22.9
Kuwait	..	0.8	..	0.6	..	0.8	..	..	..	..	11.9	2.7
Kyrgyz Republic	..	..	..	..	..	8.6	..	..	..	33.4	55.7	10.9
Lao PDR	..	..	..	..	..	..	..	..	..	..	..	..
Latvia	..	14.1	..	11.5	..	12.8	..	..	..	24.6	67.0	8.2
Lebanon	..	..	..	..	..	..	..	..	..	..	..	..
Lesotho	..	..	..	..	..	..	..	..	..	..	..	..
Liberia	..	..	..	..	..	..	..	..	..	..	..	..
Libya	..	..	..	..	..	..	..	..	..	..	..	..
Lithuania	..	19.7	..	14.2	..	13.8	..	..	57.8	15.4	55.8	28.8
Macedonia, FYR	15.6	31.7	32.8	32.3	22.0	31.9	..	..	..	34.0	52.1	7.8
Madagascar	..	..	..	..	..	..	..	..	..	..	..	..
Malawi	..	..	..	..	..	..	..	..	..	..	..	..
Malaysia	..	..	..	..	..	3.9	..	..	..	..	..	..
Mali	..	..	..	..	..	..	..	..	..	..	..	..
Mauritania	..	..	..	..	..	..	..	..	..	..	..	..
Mauritius	..	5.6	..	12.6	..	8.0	..	..	..	35.5	63.9	..
Mexico	..	2.4	..	2.4	..	2.4	1.0	0.3	0.7	51.5	23.9	22.2
Moldova	..	8.7	..	5.9	..	7.3	..	..	..	..	..	..
Mongolia	..	..	..	..	..	..	..	..	..	..	..	..
Morocco	..	..	..	..	..	..	..	..	..	..	..	..
Mozambique	..	..	..	..	..	..	..	..	..	..	..	..
Myanmar	..	..	..	..	..	..	..	..	..	..	..	..
Namibia	..	28.3	..	39.0	..	33.8	..	..	..	..	..	..
Nepal	..	..	..	..	..	..	..	..	..	..	..	..
Netherlands	4.3	2.8	5.2	3.6	4.6	3.1	21.5	20.7	21.1	49.5	35.9	13.2
New Zealand	..	5.0	..	5.3	..	5.2	14.9	10.0	12.6	0.5	44.5	19.2
Nicaragua	..	12.8	..	9.4	..	11.2	..	..	..	56.3	23.4	14.7
Niger	..	..	..	..	..	..	..	..	..	..	..	..
Nigeria	..	..	..	..	..	..	..	..	..	..	..	..
Norway	1.2	4.1	2.1	3.7	1.6	3.9	8.1	3.7	6.2	25.0	50.0	22.6
Oman	..	..	..	..	..	..	..	..	..	..	..	..
Pakistan	3.0	6.1	7.5	17.3	3.6	7.8	..	..	..	..	..	..
Panama	6.3	10.5	13.3	18.2	8.4	13.2	24.0	35.7	29.3	47.0	35.5	11.3
Papua New Guinea	..	..	..	..	..	..	..	..	..	..	..	..
Paraguay	3.8	..	4.8	..	4.1	..	..	..	..	..	..	..
Peru	..	7.5	..	10.0	..	8.7	..	..	..	15.8	54.9	28.3
Philippines	3.2	9.4	7.5	10.3	4.8	9.8	..	..	..	..	..	..
Poland	..	19.1	..	20.9	..	19.9	45.1	52.0	48.4	19.1	76.8	4.2
Portugal	3.3	4.2	12.1	6.1	6.7	5.1	31.9	31.4	31.6	73.3	13.6	8.1
Puerto Rico	19.5	13.0	12.3	9.1	17.1	11.4	..	..	..	..	..	..

	Unemployment						Long-term unemployment			Unemployment by level of educational attainment		
	Male % of male labor force		Female % of female labor force		Total % of total labor force		% of total unemployment			% of total unemployment		
							Male	Female	Total	Primary	Secondary	Tertiary
	1980	2000–02 [a]	1980	2000–02 [a]	1980	2000–02 [a]	2000–02 [a]	2000–02 [a]	2000–02 [a]	1999–2001 [a]	1999–2001 [a]	1999–2001 [a]
Romania	..	7.1	..	5.9	..	6.6	..	..	..	20.6	72.7	5.5
Russian Federation	..	9.3	..	8.5	..	8.9	..	..	..	16.8	41.6	41.6
Rwanda	..	..	..	..	..	..	..	..	..	60.7	24.1	5.9
Saudi Arabia	..	..	..	..	..	..	..	..	..	..	..	..
Senegal	..	..	..	..	..	..	..	..	..	..	..	..
Serbia and Montenegro	..	22.6	..	22.1	..	22.3	..	..	..	..	..	..
Sierra Leone	..	..	..	..	..	..	..	..	..	..	..	..
Singapore	2.9	3.5	3.4	3.4	3.0	3.4	..	..	..	25.5	26.9	32.0
Slovak Republic	..	18.6	..	18.7	..	18.6	..	..	..	19.8	77.1	3.0
Slovenia	..	5.6	..	6.3	..	5.9	58.6	61.4	59.9	33.3	63.2	5.3
Somalia	..	..	..	..	..	..	..	..	..	..	..	..
South Africa	..	26.1	..	33.3	..	29.5	..	..	..	..	..	..
Spain	10.4	8.0	13.1	16.4	11.1	11.4	31.6	41.8	37.5	57.1	19.7	22.2
Sri Lanka	..	6.8	..	11.2	..	8.2	..	..	..	41.0	..	56.1
Sudan	..	..	..	..	..	..	..	..	..	..	..	..
Swaziland	..	..	..	..	..	..	..	..	..	..	..	..
Sweden	1.9	5.6	2.6	4.7	2.2	5.2	23.0	18.1	20.9	28.6	56.6	13.1
Switzerland	0.2	2.8	0.3	3.1	0.2	2.9	19.0	23.9	21.3	43.0	43.0	14.0
Syrian Arab Republic	3.8	8.0	3.8	23.9	3.9	11.2	..	..	..	..	..	..
Tajikistan	..	..	..	..	..	..	..	..	..	..	..	..
Tanzania	..	..	..	..	..	..	..	..	..	..	..	..
Thailand	1.0	1.8	0.7	1.7	0.8	1.8	..	..	..	70.6	7.2	19.2
Togo	..	..	..	..	..	..	..	..	..	..	..	..
Trinidad and Tobago	8.0	..	14.0	..	10.0	..	20.3	34.7	27.6	38.2	60.7	0.8
Tunisia	..	..	..	..	..	..	..	..	..	..	..	..
Turkey	*9.0*	10.9	*23.0*	9.9	*10.9*	10.6	26.4	34.5	28.5	60.1	29.0	8.4
Turkmenistan	..	..	..	..	..	..	..	..	..	..	..	..
Uganda	..	..	..	..	..	..	..	..	..	..	..	..
Ukraine	..	11.2	..	11.0	..	11.1	..	..	..	8.6	27.3	64.1
United Arab Emirates	..	2.2	..	2.6	..	2.3	..	..	..	..	..	..
United Kingdom	8.3	5.6	4.8	4.4	6.8	5.1	26.4	17.0	22.8	33.7	44.4	12.7
United States	6.9	5.9	7.4	5.6	7.1	5.8	8.9	8.1	8.5	20.3	35.3	44.4
Uruguay	..	11.5	..	19.7	..	17.2	..	..	..	50.7	21.2	27.8
Uzbekistan	..	..	..	..	..	..	..	..	..	..	..	..
Venezuela, RB	..	11.6	..	14.6	5.9	12.8	..	..	..	57.9	24.0	14.4
Vietnam	..	..	..	..	..	..	..	..	..	..	..	..
West Bank and Gaza	..	27.3	..	14.1	..	25.5	..	..	..	..	..	..
Yemen, Rep.	..	..	..	..	..	..	..	..	..	..	..	..
Zambia	32.7	..	59.0	..	42.2	..	..	..	..	..	..	..
Zimbabwe	..	..	..	..	..	..	..	..	..	16.4	81.8	0.8
World	.. w	.. w	.. w	.. w	.. w	.. w	.. w	.. w	.. w	30.0 w	40.2 w	25.2 w
Low income	..	..	..	..	..	..	..	..	..	30.0	41.4	27.9
Middle income	..	..	..	..	4.8	4.9	..	..	..	..	..	..
Lower middle income	..	..	..	..	4.9	4.3	..	..	..	..	..	..
Upper middle income	..	..	..	..	..	9.0	..	..	..	34.8	52.5	11.3
Low & middle income	..	..	..	..	..	..	..	..	..	28.8	40.0	25.8
East Asia & Pacific	..	..	..	..	4.7	3.7	..	..	..	..	..	..
Europe & Central Asia	..	11.3	..	11.1	..	11.1	..	..	..	21.3	45.8	32.6
Latin America & Carib.	..	..	..	..	..	9.2	..	..	..	31.3	28.3	9.6
Middle East & N. Africa	..	..	..	..	..	..	..	..	..	..	..	..
South Asia	..	..	..	..	..	..	..	..	..	29.3	40.3	31.0
Sub-Saharan Africa	..	..	..	..	..	..	..	..	..	..	..	..
High income	5.5	5.4	7.0	6.7	6.0	6.2	24.7	22.8	24.1	31.1	41.8	25.9
Europe EMU	5.5	7.9	10.8	11.6	7.1	9.8	40.7	44.6	42.8	42.1	43.7	13.3

a. Data are for the most recent year available.

About the data

Unemployment and total employment in an economy are the broadest indicators of economic activity as reflected by the labor market. The International Labour Organization (ILO) defines the unemployed as members of the economically active population who are without work but available for and seeking work, including people who have lost their jobs and those who have voluntarily left work. Some unemployment is unavoidable in all economies. At any time some workers are temporarily unemployed—between jobs as employers look for the right workers and workers search for better jobs. Such unemployment, often called frictional unemployment, results from the normal operation of labor markets.

Changes in unemployment over time may reflect changes in the demand for and supply of labor, but they may also reflect changes in reporting practices. Ironically, low unemployment rates can often disguise substantial poverty in a country, while high unemployment rates can occur in countries with a high level of economic development and low incidence of poverty. In countries without unemployment or welfare benefits, people eke out a living in the informal sector. In countries with well-developed safety nets, workers can afford to wait for suitable or desirable jobs. But high and sustained unemployment indicates serious inefficiencies in the allocation of resources.

The ILO definition of unemployment notwithstanding, reference periods, the criteria for those considered to be seeking work, and the treatment of people temporarily laid off and those seeking work for the first time vary across countries. In many developing countries it is especially difficult to measure employment and unemployment in agriculture. The timing of a survey, for example, can maximize the effects of seasonal unemployment in agriculture. And informal sector employment is difficult to quantify where informal activities are not registered and tracked.

Data on unemployment are drawn from labor force sample surveys and general household sample surveys, censuses, and other administrative records such as social insurance statistics, employment office statistics, and official estimates, which are usually based on information drawn from one or more of the above sources. Labor force surveys generally yield the most comprehensive data because they include groups not covered in other unemployment statistics, particularly people seeking work for the first time. These surveys generally use a definition of unemployment that follows the international recommendations more closely than that used by other sources and therefore generate statistics that are more comparable internationally.

In contrast, the quality and completeness of data from employment offices and social insurance programs vary widely. Where employment offices work closely with social insurance schemes and registration with such offices is a prerequisite for receipt of unemployment benefits, the two sets of unemployment estimates tend to be comparable. Where registration is voluntary and where employment offices function only in more populous areas, employment office statistics do not give a reliable indication of unemployment. Most commonly excluded from both these sources are discouraged workers who have given up their job search because they believe that no employment opportunities exist or do not register as unemployed after their benefits have been exhausted. Thus measured unemployment may be higher in countries that offer more or longer unemployment benefits.

Women tend to be excluded from the unemployment count for various reasons. Women suffer more from discrimination and from structural, social, and cultural barriers that impede them from actively seeking work. Also, women are often responsible for the care of children and the elderly or for other household affairs. They may not be available for work during the short reference period, as they need to make arrangement before starting work. Furthermore, women are considered to be employed when they are working part-time or in temporary jobs in the informal sector, despite the instability of these jobs and that they may be actively looking for more secure employment.

Long-term unemployment is measured in terms of duration, that is, the length of time that an unemployed person has been without work and looking for a job. The underlying assumption is that shorter periods of joblessness are of less concern, especially when the unemployed are covered by unemployment benefits or similar forms of welfare support. The length of time a person has been unemployed is difficult to measure, because the ability to recall the length of that time diminishes as the period of joblessness extends. Women's long-term unemployment is likely to be lower in countries where women constitute a large share of the unpaid family workforce. Women in such countries have more access than men to nonmarket work and are more likely to drop out of the labor force and not be counted as unemployed.

Unemployment by level of educational attainment provide insights into the relationship between the educational attainment of workers and unemployment. Besides the limitations to comparability raised for measuring unemployment, the different ways of classifying the level of education across countries may also cause inconsistency. The level of education is supposed to be classified according to International Standard Classification of Education 1997 (ISCED97). For more information on ISCED97, see *About the data* for table 2.10.

Definitions

• **Unemployment** refers to the share of the labor force without work but available for and seeking employment. Definitions of labor force and unemployment differ by country (see *About the data*).
• **Long-term unemployment** refers to the number of people with continuous periods of unemployment extending for a year or longer, expressed as a percentage of the total unemployed. • **Unemployment by level of educational attainment** shows the unemployed by level of educational attainment, as a percentage of the total unemployed. The levels of educational attainment accord with the International Standard Classification of Education 1997 of the United Nations Educational, Cultural, and Scientific Organization (UNESCO).

Data source

The unemployment data are from the ILO database *Key Indicators of the Labour Market,* third edition.

	National poverty line								International poverty line				
	Population below the poverty line				Population below the poverty line					Population below $1 a day	Poverty gap at $1 a day	Population below $2 a day	Poverty gap at $2 a day
	Survey year	Rural %	Urban %	National %	Survey year	Rural %	Urban %	National %	Survey year	%	%	%	%
Afghanistan		..	..	..		..	..	..		..	..	..	..
Albania	2002	29.6		25.4		..	..	..	2002 [a]	<2	<0.5	11.8	2.0
Algeria	1995	30.3	14.7	22.6	1998	16.6	7.3	12.2	1995 [a]	<2	<0.5	15.1	3.8
Angola		..	..	..		..	..	..		..	..	..	..
Argentina	1995	..	28.4		1998		29.9		2001 [b]	3.3	0.5	14.3	4.7
Armenia	1996	48.0	58.8	54.7	1998–99	44.8	60.4	53.7	1998 [a]	12.8	3.3	49.0	17.3
Australia		..	..	..		..	..	..		..	..	..	..
Austria		..	..	..		..	..	..		..	..	..	..
Azerbaijan	1995	..	..	68.1	2001	..	..	49.6	2001 [a]	3.7	<1	9.1	3.5
Bangladesh	1995–96	55.2	29.4	51.0	2000	53.0	36.6	49.8	2000 [a]	36.0	8.1	82.8	36.3
Belarus	1998	..	..	33.0	2000	..	..	41.9	2000 [a]	<2	<0.5	<2	0.1
Belgium		..	..	..		..	..	..		..	..	..	..
Benin	1995	..	..	33.0		..	..	..		..	..	..	..
Bolivia	1997	77.3		63.2	1999	81.7	..	62.7	1999 [a]	14.4	5.4	34.3	14.9
Bosnia and Herzegovina	2001–02	19.9	13.8	19.5		..	..	..		..	..	..	..
Botswana		..	..	..		..	..	..	1993 [a]	23.5	7.7	50.1	22.8
Brazil	1990	32.6	13.1	17.4		..	..	..	2001 [b]	8.2	2.1	22.4	8.8
Bulgaria	1997	..	..	36.0	2001	..	..	12.8	2001 [a]	4.7	1.4	16.2	5.7
Burkina Faso	1994	51.0	10.4	44.5	1998	51.0	16.5	45.3	1998 [a]	44.9	14.4	81.0	40.6
Burundi	1990	36.0	43.0			..	..	..	1998 [a]	58.4	24.9	89.2	51.3
Cambodia	1993–94	43.1	24.8	39.0	1997	40.1	21.1	36.1	1997 [a]	34.1	9.7	77.7	34.5
Cameroon	1996	59.6	41.4	53.3	2001	49.9	22.1	40.2	2001 [a]	17.1	4.1	50.6	19.3
Canada		..	..	..		..	..	..		..	..	..	..
Central African Republic		..	..	..		..	..	..	1993 [a]	66.6	38.1	84.0	58.4
Chad	1995–96	67.0	63.0	64.0		..	..	..		..	..	..	..
Chile	1996	..	..	19.9	1998	..	..	17.0	2000 [b]	<2	<0.5	9.6	2.5
China	1996	7.9	<2	6.0	1998	4.6	<2	4.6	2001 [a]	16.6	3.9	46.7	18.4
Hong Kong, China		..	..	..		..	..	..		..	..	..	..
Colombia	1995	79.0	48.0	60.0	1999	79.0	55.0	64.0	1999 [b]	8.2	2.2	22.6	8.8
Congo, Dem. Rep.		..	..	..		..	..	..		..	..	..	..
Congo, Rep.		..	..	..		..	..	..		..	..	..	..
Costa Rica	1992	25.5	19.2	22.0		..	..	..	2000 [b]	2.0	0.7	9.5	3.0
Côte d'Ivoire		..	..	..		..	..	..	1998 [a]	15.5	3.8	50.4	18.9
Croatia		..	..	..		..	..	..	2000 [a]	<2	<0.5	<2	<0.5
Cuba		..	..	..		..	..	..		..	..	..	..
Czech Republic		..	..	..		..	..	..	1996 [b]	<2	<0.5	<2	<0.5
Denmark		..	..	..		..	..	..		..	..	..	..
Djibouti	1996	86.5	..	45.1		..	..	..		..	..	..	..
Dominican Republic	1992	49.0	19.3	33.9	1998	42.1	20.5	28.6	1998 [b]	<2	<0.5	<2	<0.5
Ecuador	1994	47.0	25.0	35.0		..	..	..	1998 [b]	17.7	7.1	40.8	17.7
Egypt, Arab Rep.	1995–96	23.3	22.5	22.9	1999–2000	..	..	16.7	2000 [a]	3.1	<0.5	43.9	11.3
El Salvador	1992	55.7	43.1	48.3		..	..	..	2000 [b]	31.1	14.1	58.0	29.7
Eritrea	1993–94	..	..	53.0		..	..	..		..	..	..	..
Estonia	1995	14.7	6.8	8.9		..	..	..	1998 [a]	<2	<0.5	5.2	0.8
Ethiopia	1995–96	47.0	33.3	45.5	1999–2000	45.0	37.0	44.2	1999–2000 [a]	26.3	5.7	80.7	31.8
Finland		..	..	..		..	..	..		..	..	..	..
France		..	..	..		..	..	..		..	..	..	..
Gabon		..	..	..		..	..	..		..	..	..	..
Gambia, The	1992	..	..	64.0	1998	61.0	48.0	..	1998 [a]	59.3	28.8	82.9	51.1
Georgia	1997	9.9	12.1	11.1		..	..	..	2001 [a]	2.7	0.9	15.7	4.6
Germany		..	..	..		..	..	..		..	..	..	..
Ghana	1992			50.0	1998	49.9	18.6	39.5	1999 [a]	44.8	17.3	78.5	40.8
Greece		..	..	..		..	..	..		..	..	..	..
Guatemala	1989	71.9	33.7	57.9	2000	74.5	27.1	56.2	2000 [b]	16.0	4.6	37.4	16.0
Guinea	1994	..	..	40.0		..	..	..		..	..	..	..
Guinea-Bissau	1991	..	..	48.7		..	..	..		..	..	..	..

	National poverty line							International poverty line				
		Population below the poverty line				Population below the poverty line				Population below $1 a day	Poverty gap at $1 a day	Population below $2 a day	Poverty gap at $2 a day
	Survey year	Rural %	Urban %	National %	Survey year	Rural %	Urban %	National %	Survey year	%	%	%	%
Guyana	1993	..	..	43.2	1998	..	..	35.0	1998[b]	<2	<0.5	6.1	1.7
Haiti	1987	..	..	65.0	1995	66.0	..	..	..	..	..	..	..
Honduras	1992	46.0	56.0	50.0	1993	51.0	57.0	53.0	1998[b]	23.8	11.6	44.4	23.1
Hungary	1993	..	..	14.5	1997	..	..	17.3	1998[b]	<2	<0.5	7.3	1.7
India	1993–94	37.3	32.4	36.0	1999–2000	30.2	24.7	28.6	1999–2000[a]	34.7	8.2	79.9	35.3
Indonesia	1996			15.7	1999			27.1	2002[a]	7.5	0.9	52.4	15.7
Iran, Islamic Rep.		..	..	..		..	..	..	1998[a]	<2	<0.5	7.3	1.5
Iraq		..	..	..		..	..	..	..	..	..	..	..
Ireland		..	..	..		..	..	..	..	..	..	..	..
Israel		..	..	..		..	..	..	..	..	..	..	..
Italy		..	..	..		..	..	..	..	..	..	..	..
Jamaica	1995	37.0	..	27.5	2000	25.1	..	18.7	2000[a]	<2	<0.5	13.3	2.7
Japan		..	..	..		..	..	..	..	..	..	..	..
Jordan	1991	..	..	15.0	1997	..	..	11.7	1997[a]	<2	<0.5	7.4	1.4
Kazakhstan	1996	39.0	30.0	34.6					2001[a]	<2	<0.5	8.5	1.4
Kenya	1994	47.0	29.0	40.0	1997	53.0	49.0	52.0	1997[a]	23.0	6.0	58.6	24.1
Korea, Dem. Rep.		..	..	..		..	..	..	..	..	..	..	..
Korea, Rep.		..	..	..		..	..	..	1998[b]	<2	<0.5	<2	<0.5
Kuwait		..	..	..		..	..	..	..	..	..	..	..
Kyrgyz Republic	1997	64.5	28.5	51.0	1999	69.7	49.0	64.1	2001[a]	<2	<0.5	27.2	5.9
Lao PDR	1993	48.7	33.1	45.0	1997–98	41.0	26.9	38.6	1997–98[a]	26.3	6.3	73.2	29.6
Latvia		..	..	..		..	..	..	1998[a]	<2	<0.5	8.3	2.0
Lebanon		..	..	..		..	..	..	..	..	..	..	..
Lesotho		..	..	..		..	..	..	1995[a]	36.4	19.0	56.1	33.1
Liberia		..	..	..		..	..	..	..	..	..	..	..
Libya		..	..	..		..	..	..	..	..	..	..	..
Lithuania		..	..	..		..	..	..	2000[a]	<2	<0.5	13.7	4.2
Macedonia, FYR		..	..	..		..	..	..	1998[a]	<2	<0.5	4.0	0.6
Madagascar	1997	76.0	63.2	73.3	1999	76.7	52.1	71.3	1999[a]	49.1	18.3	83.3	44.0
Malawi	1990–91	..	..	54.0	1997–98	66.5	54.9	65.3	1997–98[a]	41.7	14.8	76.1	38.3
Malaysia	1989	..	..	15.5					1997[b]	<2	<0.5	9.3	2.0
Mali	1998	75.9	30.1	63.8		..	..	..	1994[a]	72.8	37.4	90.6	60.5
Mauritania	1996	65.5	30.1	50.0	2000	61.2	25.4	46.3	2000[a]	25.9	7.6	63.1	26.8
Mauritius		..	..	..		..	..	..	..	..	..	..	..
Mexico	1988	..	..	10.1		..	..	..	2000[b]	9.9	3.7	26.3	10.9
Moldova	1997	26.7	..	23.3		..	..	..	2001[a]	22.0	5.8	63.7	25.1
Mongolia	1995	33.1	38.5	36.3		..	..	..	1995[a]	13.9	3.1	50.0	17.5
Morocco	1990–91	18.0	7.6	13.1	1998–99	27.2	12.0	19.0	1999[a]	<2	<0.5	14.3	3.1
Mozambique	1996–97	71.3	62.0	69.4		..	..	..	1996[a]	37.9	12.0	78.4	36.8
Myanmar		..	..	..		..	..	..	..	..	..	..	..
Namibia		..	..	..		..	..	..	1993[b]	34.9	14.0	55.8	30.4
Nepal	1995–96	44.0	23.0	42.0		..	..	..	1995[a]	37.7	9.7	82.5	37.5
Netherlands		..	..	..		..	..	..	..	..	..	..	..
New Zealand		..	..	..		..	..	..	..	..	..	..	..
Nicaragua	1993	76.1	31.9	50.3	1998	68.5	30.5	47.9	2001[a]	45.1	16.7	79.9	41.2
Niger	1989–93	66.0	52.0	63.0		..	..	..	1995[a]	61.4	33.9	85.3	54.8
Nigeria	1985	49.5	31.7	43.0	1992–93	36.4	30.4	34.1	1997[a]	70.2	34.9	90.8	59.0
Norway		..	..	..		..	..	..	..	..	..	..	..
Oman		..	..	..		..	..	..	..	..	..	..	..
Pakistan	1993	33.4	17.2	28.6	1998–99	35.9	24.2	32.6	1998[a]	13.4	2.4	65.6	22.0
Panama	1997	64.9	15.3	37.3		..	..	..	2000[b]	7.2	2.3	17.6	7.4
Papua New Guinea	1996	41.3	16.1	37.5		..	..	..	..	..	..	..	..
Paraguay	1991	28.5	19.7	21.8		..	..	..	1999[b]	14.9	6.8	30.3	14.7
Peru	1994	67.0	46.1	53.5	1997	64.7	40.4	49.0	2000[b]	18.1	9.1	37.7	18.5
Philippines	1994	53.1	28.0	40.6	1997	50.7	21.5	36.8	2000[a]	14.6	2.7	46.4	17.2
Poland	1993	..	..	23.8		..	..	..	1999[b]	<2	<0.5	<2	<0.5

	National poverty line								International poverty line				
		Population below the poverty line				Population below the poverty line				Population below $1 a day	Poverty gap at $1 a day	Population below $2 a day	Poverty gap at $2 a day
	Survey year	Rural %	Urban %	National %	Survey year	Rural %	Urban %	National %	Survey year	%	%	%	%
Portugal		..	..	..		..	..	..	1994 [b]	<2	<0.5	<0.5	<0.5
Puerto Rico		..	..	..		..	..	..		..	..	..	..
Romania	1994	27.9	20.4	21.5		..	..	..	2000 [a]	2.1	0.6	20.5	5.2
Russian Federation	1994	..	..	30.9		..	..	..	2000 [a]	6.1	1.2	23.8	8.0
Rwanda	1993	..	..	51.2		..	..	..	1983–85 [a]	35.7	7.7	84.6	36.7
Saudi Arabia		..	..	..		..	..	..		..	..	..	..
Senegal	1992	40.4	..	33.4		..	..	..	1995 [a]	26.3	7.0	67.8	28.2
Serbia and Montenegro		..	..	..		..	..	..		..	..	..	..
Sierra Leone	1989	76.0	53.0	68.0		..	..	..	1989 [a]	57.0	39.5	74.5	51.8
Singapore		..	..	..		..	..	..		..	..	..	..
Slovak Republic		..	..	..		..	..	..	1996 [b]	<2	<0.5	2.4	0.7
Slovenia		..	..	..		..	..	..	1998 [a]	<2	<0.5	<2	<0.5
Somalia		..	..	..		..	..	..		..	..	..	..
South Africa		..	..	..		..	..	..	1995 [a]	7.1	1.1	23.8	8.6
Spain		..	..	..		..	..	..		..	..	..	..
Sri Lanka	1990–91	22.0	15.0	20.0	1995–96	27.0	15.0	25.0	1995–96 [a]	6.6	1.0	45.4	13.5
Sudan		..	..	..		..	..	..		..	..	..	..
Swaziland	1995	..	..	40.0		..	..	..		..	..	..	..
Sweden		..	..	..		..	..	..		..	..	..	..
Switzerland		..	..	..		..	..	..		..	..	..	..
Syrian Arab Republic		..	..	..		..	..	..		..	..	..	..
Tajikistan		..	..	..		..	..	..	1998 [a]	10.3	2.6	50.8	16.3
Tanzania	1991	40.8		38.6	2000–01	38.7		35.7	1993 [a]	19.9	4.8	59.7	23.0
Thailand	1990	..	..	18.0	1992	15.5	10.2	13.1	2000 [a]	<2	<0.5	32.5	9.0
Togo	1987–89	..	..	32.3		..	..	..		..	..	..	..
Trinidad and Tobago	1992	20.0	24.0	21.0		..	..	..	1992 [b]	12.4	3.5	39.0	14.6
Tunisia	1990	13.1	3.5	7.4	1995	13.9	3.6	7.6	2000 [a]	<2	<0.5	6.6	1.3
Turkey		..	..	..		..	..	..	2000 [a]	<2	<0.5	10.3	2.5
Turkmenistan		..	..	..		..	..	..	1998 [a]	12.1	2.6	44.0	15.4
Uganda	1993	..	..	55.0	1997	..	..	44.0		..	..	..	..
Ukraine	1995	..	..	31.7		..	..	..	1999 [b]	2.9	0.6	45.7	16.3
United Arab Emirates		..	..	..		..	..	..		..	..	..	..
United Kingdom		..	..	..		..	..	..		..	..	..	..
United States		..	..	..		..	..	..		..	..	..	..
Uruguay		..	..	..		..	..	..	2000 [b]	<2	<0.5	3.9	0.8
Uzbekistan	2000	30.5	22.5	27.5		..	..	..	2000 [a]	21.8	5.4	77.5	28.9
Venezuela, RB	1989	..	..	31.3		..	..	..	1998 [b]	15.0	6.9	32.0	15.2
Vietnam	1993	57.2	25.9	50.9		..	..	..	1998 [a]	17.7	3.3	63.7	22.9
West Bank and Gaza		..	..	..		..	..	..		..	..	..	..
Yemen, Rep.	1998	45.0	30.8	41.8		..	..	..	1998 [a]	15.7	4.5	45.2	15.0
Zambia	1996	82.8	46.0	69.2	1998	83.1	56.0	72.9	1998 [a]	63.7	32.7	87.4	55.4
Zimbabwe	1990–91	35.8	3.4	25.8	1995–96	48.0	7.9	34.9	1990–91 [a]	36.0	9.6	64.2	29.4

a. Based on expenditure. b. Based on income.

Poverty

About the data

International comparisons of poverty data entail both conceptual and practical problems. Different countries have different definitions of poverty, and consistent comparisons between countries can be difficult. Local poverty lines tend to have higher purchasing power in rich countries, where more generous standards are used than in poor countries. Is it reasonable to treat two people with the same standard of living—in terms of their command over commodities—differently because one happens to live in a better-off country? Can we hold the real value of the poverty line constant across countries, just as we do when making comparisons over time?

Poverty measures based on an international poverty line attempt to do this. The commonly used $1 a day standard, measured in 1985 international prices and adjusted to local currency using purchasing power parities (PPPs), was chosen for the World Bank's *World Development Report 1990: Poverty* because it is typical of the poverty lines in low-income countries. PPP exchange rates, such as those from the Penn World Tables or the World Bank, are used because they take into account the local prices of goods and services not traded internationally. But PPP rates were designed not for making international poverty comparisons but for comparing aggregates from national accounts. Thus there is no certainty that an international poverty line measures the same degree of need or deprivation across countries.

This year's edition of the *World Development Indicators* (like those of the past four years) uses 1993 consumption PPP estimates produced by the World Bank. The international poverty line, set at $1 a day in 1985 PPP terms, has been recalculated in 1993 PPP terms at about $1.08 a day. Any revisions in the PPP of a country to incorporate better price indexes can produce dramatically different poverty lines in local currency.

Problems also exist in comparing poverty measures within countries. For example, the cost of living is typically higher in urban than in rural areas. So the urban monetary poverty line should be higher than the rural poverty line. But it is not always clear that the difference between urban and rural poverty lines found in practice properly reflects the difference in the cost of living. In some countries the urban poverty line in common use has a higher real value than does the rural poverty line. Sometimes the difference has been so large as to imply that the incidence of poverty is greater in urban than in rural areas, even though the reverse is found when adjustments are made only for differences in the cost of

living. As with international comparisons, when the real value of the poverty line varies, it is not clear how meaningful such urban-rural comparisons are.

The problems of making poverty comparisons do not end there. More issues arise in measuring household living standards. The choice between income and consumption as a welfare indicator is one issue. Income is generally more difficult to measure accurately, and consumption accords better with the idea of the standard of living than does income, which can vary over time even if the standard of living does not. But consumption data are not always available, and when they are not there is little choice but to use income. There are still other problems. Household survey questionnaires can differ widely, for example, in the number of distinct categories of consumer goods they identify. Survey quality varies, and even similar surveys may not be strictly comparable.

Comparisons across countries at different levels of development also pose a potential problem, because of differences in the relative importance of consumption of nonmarket goods. The local market value of all consumption in kind (including consumption from own production, particularly important in underdeveloped rural economies) should be included in the measure of total consumption expenditure. Similarly, the imputed profit from production of nonmarket goods should be included in income. This is not always done, though such omissions were a far bigger problem in surveys before the 1980s. Most survey data now include valuations for consumption or income from own production. Nonetheless, valuation methods vary. For example, some surveys use the price in the nearest market, while others use the average farm gate selling price.

Wherever possible, consumption has been used as the welfare indicator for deciding who is poor. Where consumption data are unavailable, income data are used. Beginning with last year's *World Development Indicators,* there has been a change in how income surveys are used. Before that, average income was adjusted to accord with consumption and income data from national accounts. This approach was tested using data for more than 20 countries for which the surveys provided both income and consumption expenditure data. Income gave a higher mean than consumption but also greater income inequality. These two effects roughly canceled each other out when poverty measures based on consumption were compared with those based on income from the same survey; statistically, there was no significant

difference. So income data are used to estimate poverty directly, with no adjustment of the income mean.

In all cases the measures of poverty have been calculated from primary data sources (tabulations or household data) rather than existing estimates. Estimation from tabulations requires an interpolation method; the method chosen was Lorenz curves with flexible functional forms, which have proved reliable in past work. Empirical Lorenz curves were weighted by household size, so they are based on percentiles of population, not households.

Definitions

• **Survey year** is the year in which the underlying data were collected. • **Rural poverty rate** is the percentage of the rural population living below the national rural poverty line. • **Urban poverty rate** is the percentage of the urban population living below the national urban poverty line. • **National poverty rate** is the percentage of the population living below the national poverty line. National estimates are based on population-weighted subgroup estimates from household surveys. • **Population below $1 a day** and **population below $2 a day** are the percentages of the population living on less than $1.08 a day and $2.15 a day at 1993 international prices. As a result of revisions in PPP exchange rates, poverty rates cannot be compared with poverty rates reported in previous editions for individual countries. • **Poverty gap** is the mean shortfall from the poverty line (counting the nonpoor as having zero shortfall), expressed as a percentage of the poverty line. This measure reflects the depth of poverty as well as its incidence.

Data sources

The poverty measures are prepared by the World Bank's Development Research Group. The national poverty lines are based on the World Bank's country poverty assessments. The international poverty lines are based on nationally representative primary household surveys conducted by national statistical offices or by private agencies under the supervision of government or international agencies and obtained from government statistical offices and World Bank country departments. The World Bank has prepared an annual review of its poverty work since 1993. *Partnerships in Development: Progress in the Fight against Poverty* is forthcoming.

Social indicators of poverty

| | Survey year | Prevalence of child malnutrition | | Under-five mortality rate | | Child immunization rate | | Contraceptive prevalence | | Births attended by skilled health staff[a] | |
| | | Weight for age % of children under age 5 | | per 1,000 | | Measles % of children ages 12–23 months[b] | | % of women ages 15–49 | | % of total | |
		Poorest quintile	Richest quintile	Poorest quintile	Richest quintile	Poorest quintile	Richest quintile	Poorest quintile	Richest quintile	Poorest quintile	Richest quintile
Armenia	2000	3	2	61	30	68	74[c]	16	29	93	100
Bangladesh	2000	60	29	140	72	59	86	37	50	4	42
Benin	1996	37	19	208	110	49	80	1	9	34	98
Bolivia	1998	14	3	147	32	58	85	7	46	20	98
Brazil	1996	12	3	99	33	78	90	56	77	72	99
Burkina Faso	1998–99	38	26	239	155	33	69	2	16	18	75
Cambodia	2000	52	34	155	64	44	82	13	25	15	81
Cameroon	1998	33	9	199	87	37	78	1	17	28	89
Central African Republic	1994–95	37	20	193	98	31	80	1	9	14	82
Chad	1996–97	50	29	171	172	12	39	0[d]	5	3	47
Colombia	2000	9	3	39	20	74	85	54	66	64	99
Comoros	1996	36	18	129	87[c]	51	86	7	19	26	85
Côte d'Ivoire	1994	31	13	190	97	31	79	1	13	17	84
Egypt, Arab Rep.	2000	7	2	98	34	95	99	43	61	31	94
Eritrea	1995	51	25	152	104	37	92	0[d]	19	5	74
Ethiopia	2000	49	37	159	147	18	52	3	23	1	25
Gabon	2000	19	8	93	55	34	71	6	18	67	97
Ghana	1998	33	12	139	52	61	87	8	18	18	86
Guatemala	1998	34	10	78	39	80	91	5	60	9	92
Guinea	1999	29	17	230	133	33	73	1	9	12	82
Haiti	2000	24	8	164	109	43	63	17	24	4	70
India	1999	61	26	141	46	28	81	29	55	16	84
Indonesia	1997	..	..	109	29	59	85	46	57	21	89
Jordan	1997	9	3	42	25	90	93	28	47	91	99
Kazakhstan	1999	5	6	82	45	74	76[c]	49	55	99	99
Kenya	1998	32	10	136	61	64	89	13	50	23	80
Kyrgyz Republic	1997	13	8	96	49	82	81	44	54	96	100
Madagascar	1997	45	32	195	101	32	79	2	24	30	89
Malawi	2000	33	13	231	149	80	90	20	40	43	83
Mali	2001	39	17	248	148	40	77	4	18	21	86
Mauritania	2000–01	37	18	98	78	42	86	0[d]	17	15	93
Morocco	1992	17	2	112	39	62	95	18	48	5	78
Mozambique	1997	37	14	278	145	33	94	1	17	18	82
Namibia	1992	36	13	110	76	69	79	5	57	51	91
Nepal	2001	57	31	130	68	61	83	24	55	4	45
Nicaragua	2001	16	3	64	19	76	94	50	71	78	99
Niger	1998	52	37	282	184	23	66	1	18	4	63
Nigeria	1990	40	22	240	120	35	70	1	12	12	70
Pakistan	1990	54	26	125	74	28	75	1	23	5	55
Paraguay	1990	6	1	57	20	48	69	21	46	41	98
Peru	2000	15	1	93	18	81	92	37	58	21	99
Philippines	1998	..	..	80	29	68	92	20	29	21	92
Rwanda	2000	27	14	246	154	84	89	2	15	17	60
Senegal	1997	..	..	181	70	..	..	1	24	20	86
South Africa	1998	..	..	87	22	74	85	34	70	68	98
Tanzania	1999	32	22	160	135	63	89	6	32	29	83
Togo	1998	32	12	168	97	35	63	3	13	25	91
Turkey	1998	17	3	85	33	64	89	24	48	53	98
Uganda	2000–01	27	12	192	106	49	65	11	41	20	77
Uzbekistan	1996	25	13	70	50	96	93	46	52	92	100
Vietnam	1997	..	..	63	23	64	88	47	56	49	99
Yemen, Rep.	1997	56	30	163	73	16	73	1	24	7	50
Zambia	2001	33	20	192	92	81	88	11	53	20	91
Zimbabwe	1999	18	6	100	62	80	86	41	67	57	94

a. Based on births in the five years before the survey. b. Refers to children who were immunized before 12 months or, in some cases, at any time before the survey (between 12–23 months).
c. The data contain large sampling errors because of the small number of cases. d. Less than 0.5.

About the data

The data in the table describe the health status and use of health services by individuals in different socioeconomic groups within countries. The data are from Demographic and Health Surveys conducted by Macro International with the support of the U.S. Agency for International Development. These large-scale household sample surveys, conducted periodically in developing countries, collect information on a large number of health, nutrition, and population measures as well as on respondents' social, demographic, and economic characteristics using a standard set of questionnaires. The data presented here draw on responses to individual and household questionnaires.

The table defines socioeconomic status in terms of a household's assets, including ownership of consumer items, features of the household's dwelling, and other characteristics related to wealth. Each household asset on which information was collected was assigned a weight generated through principal component analysis. The resulting scores were standardized in relation to a standard normal distribution with a mean of zero and a standard deviation of one. The standardized scores were then used to create break points defining wealth quintiles, expressed as quintiles of individuals in the population rather than quintiles of individuals at risk with respect to any one health indicator.

The choice of the asset index for defining socioeconomic status was based on pragmatic rather than conceptual considerations: Demographic and Health Surveys do not provide income or consumption data but do have detailed information on households' ownership of consumer goods and access to a variety of goods and services. Like income or consumption, the asset index defines disparities in primarily economic terms. It therefore excludes other possibilities of disparities among groups, such as those based on gender, education, ethnic background, or other facets of social exclusion. To that extent the index provides only a partial view of the multidimensional concepts of poverty, inequality, and inequity.

Creating one index that includes all asset indicators limits the types of analysis that can be performed. In particular, the use of a unified index does not permit a disaggregated analysis to examine which asset indicators have a more or less important association with health status or use of health services. In addition, some asset indicators may reflect household wealth better in some countries than in others—or reflect different degrees of wealth in different countries. Taking such information into account and creating country-specific asset indexes with country-specific choices of asset indicators might produce a more effective and accurate index for each country. The asset index used in the table does not have this flexibility.

The analysis has been carried out for 54 countries, with the results issued in country reports. The table shows the estimates for the poorest and richest quintiles only; the full set of estimates for more than 70 indicators is available in the country reports (see *Data sources*).

2.6a

Education lowers birth rates dramatically for rich women, but not for poor ones

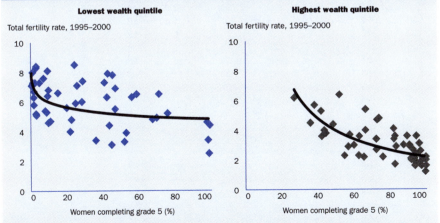

Lowest wealth quintile

Total fertility rate, 1995–2000

Women completing grade 5 (%)

Highest wealth quintile

Total fertility rate, 1995–2000

Women completing grade 5 (%)

It is well known that women's education strongly affects the number of children they bear. But the effect varies with the wealth of the household. Education greatly reduces fertility rates among wealthy women, but the effect is very weak among poor women.

Source: Demographic and Health Survey data.

Data sources

The data are from an analysis of Demographic and Health Surveys by the World Bank and Macro International. Country reports are available at http://www.worldbank.org/poverty/health/data/index.htm.

	Survey year	Gini Index	Percentage share of income or consumption						
			Lowest 10%	Lowest 20%	Second 20%	Third 20%	Fourth 20%	Highest 20%	Highest 10%
Afghanistan		..	..	..	..	..	..	..	..
Albania	2002 a,b	28.2	3.8	9.1	13.5	17.3	22.8	37.4	22.4
Algeria	1995 a,b	35.3	2.8	7.0	11.6	16.1	22.7	42.6	26.8
Angola		..	..	..	..	..	..	..	..
Argentina c	2001 d,e	52.2	1.0	3.1	7.2	12.3	21.0	56.4	38.9
Armenia	1998 a,b	37.9	2.6	6.7	11.3	15.4	21.6	45.1	29.7
Australia	1994 d,e	35.2	2.0	5.9	12.0	17.2	23.6	41.3	25.4
Austria	1997 d,e	30.0	3.1	8.1	13.2	17.3	22.9	38.5	23.5
Azerbaijan	2001 a,b	36.5	3.1	7.4	11.5	15.3	21.2	44.5	29.5
Bangladesh	2000 a,b	31.8	3.9	9.0	12.5	15.9	21.2	41.3	26.7
Belarus	2000 a,b	30.4	3.5	8.4	13.0	17.0	22.5	39.1	24.1
Belgium	1996 d,e	25.0	2.9	8.3	14.1	17.7	22.7	37.3	22.6
Benin		..	..	..	..	..	..	..	..
Bolivia	1999 a,b	44.7	1.3	4.0	9.2	14.8	22.9	49.1	32.0
Bosnia and Herzegovina	2001 a,b	26.2	3.9	9.5	14.2	17.9	22.6	35.8	21.4
Botswana	1993 a,b	63.0	0.7	2.2	4.9	8.2	14.4	70.3	56.6
Brazil	1998 d,e	59.1	0.5	2.0	5.7	10.0	18.0	64.4	46.7
Bulgaria	2001 d,e	31.9	2.4	6.7	13.1	17.9	23.4	38.9	23.7
Burkina Faso	1998 a,b	48.2	1.8	4.5	7.4	10.6	16.7	60.7	46.3
Burundi	1998 a,b	33.3	1.7	5.1	10.3	15.1	21.5	48.0	32.8
Cambodia	1997 a,b	40.4	2.9	6.9	10.7	14.7	20.1	47.6	33.8
Cameroon	2001 a,b	44.6	2.3	5.6	9.3	13.7	20.4	50.9	35.4
Canada	1998 d,e	33.1	2.5	7.0	12.7	17.0	22.9	40.4	25.0
Central African Republic	1993 a,b	61.3	0.7	2.0	4.9	9.6	18.5	65.0	47.7
Chad		..	..	..	..	..	..	..	..
Chile	2000 d,e	57.1	1.2	3.3	6.6	10.5	17.4	62.2	47.0
China	2001 a,b	44.7	1.8	4.7	9.0	14.2	22.1	50.0	33.1
Hong Kong, China	1996 d,e	43.4	2.0	5.3	9.4	13.9	20.7	50.7	34.9
Colombia	1999 d,e	57.6	0.8	2.7	6.6	10.8	18.0	61.9	46.5
Congo, Dem. Rep.		..	..	..	..	..	..	..	..
Congo, Rep.		..	..	..	..	..	..	..	..
Costa Rica	2000 d,e	46.5	1.4	4.2	8.9	13.7	21.7	51.5	34.8
Côte d'Ivoire	1998 a,b	45.2	2.2	5.5	9.6	13.6	20.1	51.1	35.9
Croatia	2001 a,b	29.0	3.4	8.3	12.8	16.8	22.6	39.6	24.5
Cuba		..	..	..	..	..	..	..	..
Czech Republic	1996 d,e	25.4	4.3	10.3	14.5	17.7	21.7	35.9	22.4
Denmark	1997 d,e	24.7	2.6	8.3	14.7	18.2	22.9	35.8	21.3
Dominican Republic	1998 d,e	47.4	2.1	5.1	8.6	13.0	20.0	53.3	37.9
Ecuador	1998 a,b	43.7	0.9	3.3	7.5	11.7	19.4	58.0	41.6
Egypt, Arab Rep.	1999 a,b	34.4	3.7	8.6	12.1	15.4	20.4	43.6	29.5
El Salvador	2000 d,e	53.2	0.9	2.9	7.4	12.4	20.2	57.1	40.6
Eritrea		..	..	..	..	..	..	..	..
Estonia	2000 d,e	37.2	1.9	6.1	12.1	15.9	22.0	44.0	28.5
Ethiopia	2000 a,b	30.0	3.9	9.1	13.2	16.8	21.5	39.4	25.5
Finland	2000 d,e	26.9	4.0	9.6	14.1	17.5	22.1	36.7	22.6
France	1995 d,e	32.7	2.8	7.2	12.6	17.2	22.8	40.2	25.1
Gabon		..	..	..	..	..	..	..	..
Gambia, The	1998 a,b	38.0	1.5	4.0	7.6	12.3	20.8	55.2	38.0
Georgia	2001 a,b	36.9	2.3	6.4	11.4	16.1	22.6	43.6	27.9
Germany	2000 d,e	28.3	3.2	8.5	13.7	17.8	23.1	36.9	22.1
Ghana	1999 a,b	30.0	2.1	5.6	10.1	14.9	22.8	46.6	30.0
Greece	1998 d,e	35.4	2.9	7.1	11.4	15.8	22.0	43.6	28.5
Guatemala	2000 d,e	48.3	0.9	2.6	5.9	9.8	17.6	64.1	48.3
Guinea	1994 a,b	40.3	2.6	6.4	10.4	14.8	21.2	47.2	32.0
Guinea-Bissau	1993 a,b	47.0	2.1	5.2	8.8	13.1	19.4	53.4	39.3
Guyana	1999 a,b	43.2	1.3	4.5	9.9	14.5	21.4	49.7	33.8
Haiti		..	..	..	..	..	..	..	..

Distribution of income or consumption | **2.7**

	Survey year	Gini Index	Percentage share of income or consumption						
			Lowest 10%	Lowest 20%	Second 20%	Third 20%	Fourth 20%	Highest 20%	Highest 10%
Honduras	1999 [d,e]	55.0	0.9	2.7	6.7	11.8	19.9	58.9	42.2
Hungary	1999 [a,b]	24.4	2.6	7.7	13.4	18.0	23.4	37.5	22.8
India	1999–2000 [a,b]	32.5	3.9	8.9	12.3	16.0	21.2	41.6	27.4
Indonesia	2002 [a,b]	34.3	3.6	8.4	11.9	15.4	21.0	43.3	28.5
Iran, Islamic Rep.	1998 [a,b]	43.0	2.0	5.1	9.4	14.1	21.5	49.9	33.7
Iraq		..	..	..	..	..	..	..	..
Ireland	1996 [d,e]	35.9	2.8	7.1	11.8	15.8	22.0	43.3	27.6
Israel	1997 [d,e]	35.5	2.4	6.9	11.4	16.3	22.9	44.3	28.2
Italy	2000 [d,e]	36.0	2.3	6.5	12.0	16.8	22.8	42.0	26.8
Jamaica	2000 [a,b]	37.9	2.7	6.7	10.7	15.0	21.7	46.0	30.3
Japan	1993 [d,e]	24.9	4.8	10.6	14.2	17.6	22.0	35.7	21.7
Jordan	1997 [a,b]	36.4	3.3	7.6	11.4	15.5	21.1	44.4	29.8
Kazakhstan	2001 [a,b]	31.3	3.4	8.2	12.5	16.8	22.9	39.6	24.2
Kenya	1997 [a,b]	44.5	2.3	5.6	9.3	13.6	20.2	51.2	36.1
Korea, Dem. Rep.		..	..	..	..	..	..	..	..
Korea, Rep.	1998 [d,e]	31.6	2.9	7.9	13.6	18.0	23.1	37.5	22.5
Kuwait		..	..	..	..	..	..	..	..
Kyrgyz Republic	2001 [a,b]	29.0	3.9	9.1	13.2	16.9	22.5	38.3	23.3
Lao PDR	1997 [a,b]	37.0	3.2	7.6	11.4	15.3	20.8	45.0	30.6
Latvia	1998 [d,e]	32.4	2.9	7.6	12.9	17.1	22.1	40.3	25.9
Lebanon		..	..	..	..	..	..	..	..
Lesotho	1995 [a,b]	63.2	0.5	1.5	4.3	8.9	18.8	66.5	48.3
Liberia		..	..	..	..	..	..	..	..
Libya		..	..	..	..	..	..	..	..
Lithuania	2000 [a,b]	31.9	3.2	7.9	12.7	16.9	22.6	40.0	24.9
Luxembourg	2000 [d,e]	30.8	3.5	8.4	12.9	17.1	22.7	38.9	23.8
Macedonia, FYR	1998 [a,b]	28.2	3.3	8.4	14.0	17.7	23.1	36.7	22.1
Madagascar	2001 [a,b]	47.5	1.9	4.9	8.5	12.7	20.4	53.5	36.6
Malawi	1997 [a,b]	50.3	1.9	4.9	8.5	12.3	18.3	56.1	42.2
Malaysia	1997 [d,e]	49.2	1.7	4.4	8.1	12.9	20.3	54.3	38.4
Mali	1994 [a,b]	50.5	1.8	4.6	8.0	11.9	19.3	56.2	40.4
Mauritania	2000 [a,b]	39.0	2.5	6.2	10.6	15.2	22.3	45.7	29.5
Mauritius		..	..	..	..	..	..	..	..
Mexico	2000 [d,e]	54.6	1.0	3.1	7.2	11.7	19.0	59.1	43.1
Moldova	2001 [a,b]	36.2	2.8	7.1	11.5	15.8	22.0	43.7	28.4
Mongolia	1998 [a,b]	44.0	2.1	5.6	10.0	13.8	19.4	51.2	37.0
Morocco	1998–99 [a,b]	39.5	2.6	6.5	10.6	14.8	21.3	46.6	30.9
Mozambique	1996–97 [a,b]	39.6	2.5	6.5	10.8	15.1	21.1	46.5	31.7
Myanmar		..	..	..	..	..	..	..	..
Namibia	1993 [d,e]	70.7	0.5	1.4	3.0	5.4	11.5	78.7	64.5
Nepal	1995–96 [a,b]	36.7	3.2	7.6	11.5	15.1	21.0	44.8	29.8
Netherlands	1994 [d,e]	32.6	2.8	7.3	12.7	17.2	22.8	40.1	25.1
New Zealand	1997 [d,e]	36.2	2.2	6.4	11.4	15.8	22.6	43.8	27.8
Nicaragua	2001 [d,e]	55.1	1.2	3.6	7.2	11.3	18.3	59.7	45.0
Niger	1995 [a,b]	50.5	0.8	2.6	7.1	13.9	23.1	53.3	35.4
Nigeria	1996–97 [a,b]	50.6	1.6	4.4	8.2	12.5	19.3	55.7	40.8
Norway	2000 [d,e]	25.8	3.9	9.6	14.0	17.2	22.0	37.2	23.4
Oman		..	..	..	..	..	..	..	..
Pakistan	1998–99 [a,b]	33.0	3.7	8.8	12.5	15.9	20.6	42.3	28.3
Panama	2000 [d,e]	56.4	0.7	2.4	6.5	11.2	19.6	60.3	43.3
Papua New Guinea	1996 [a,b]	50.9	1.7	4.5	7.9	11.9	19.2	56.5	40.5
Paraguay	1999 [d,e]	56.8	0.6	2.2	6.5	11.5	19.5	60.2	43.6
Peru	2000 [d,e]	49.8	0.7	2.9	8.3	14.1	21.5	53.2	37.2
Philippines	2000 [a,b]	46.1	2.2	5.4	8.8	13.1	20.5	52.3	36.3
Poland	1999 [a,b]	31.6	2.9	7.3	11.8	16.2	22.2	42.5	27.4
Portugal	1997 [d,e]	38.5	2.0	5.8	11.0	15.5	21.9	45.9	29.8
Puerto Rico		..	..	..	..	..	..	..	..

	Survey year	Gini Index	Percentage share of income or consumption						
			Lowest 10%	Lowest 20%	Second 20%	Third 20%	Fourth 20%	Highest 20%	Highest 10%
Romania	2000 a,b	30.3	3.3	8.2	13.1	17.4	22.9	38.4	23.6
Russian Federation	2000 a,b	45.6	1.8	4.9	9.5	14.1	20.3	51.3	36.0
Rwanda	1983–85 a,b	28.9	4.2	9.7	13.2	16.5	21.6	39.1	24.2
Saudi Arabia		..	..	..	..	..	..	..	..
Senegal	1995 a,b	41.3	2.6	6.4	10.3	14.5	20.6	48.2	33.5
Serbia and Montenegro		..	..	..	..	..	..	..	..
Sierra Leone	1989 a,b	62.9	0.5	1.1	2.0	9.8	23.7	63.4	43.6
Singapore	1998 d,e	42.5	1.9	5.0	9.4	14.6	22.0	49.0	32.8
Slovak Republic	1996 d,e	25.8	3.1	8.8	14.9	18.7	22.8	34.8	20.9
Slovenia	1998–99 d,e	28.4	3.6	9.1	14.2	18.1	22.9	35.7	21.4
Somalia		..	..	..	..	..	..	..	..
South Africa	1995 a,b	59.3	0.7	2.0	4.3	8.3	18.9	66.5	46.9
Spain	1990 d,e	32.5	2.8	7.5	12.6	17.0	22.6	40.3	25.2
Sri Lanka	1995 a,b	34.4	3.5	8.0	11.8	15.8	21.5	42.8	28.0
St. Lucia	1995 d,e	42.6	2.0	5.2	9.9	14.8	21.8	48.3	32.5
Sudan		..	..	..	..	..	..	..	..
Swaziland	1994 d,e	60.9	1.0	2.7	5.8	10.0	17.1	64.4	50.2
Sweden	2000 d,e	25.0	3.6	9.1	14.0	17.6	22.7	36.6	22.2
Switzerland	1992 d,e	33.1	2.6	6.9	12.7	17.3	22.9	40.3	25.2
Syrian Arab Republic		..	..	..	..	..	..	..	..
Tajikistan	1998 a,b	34.7	3.2	8.0	12.9	17.0	22.1	40.0	25.2
Tanzania	1993 a,b	38.2	2.8	6.8	11.0	15.1	21.6	45.5	30.1
Thailand	2000 a,b	43.2	2.5	6.1	9.5	13.5	20.9	50.0	33.8
Togo		..	..	..	..	..	..	..	..
Trinidad and Tobago	1992 d,e	40.3	2.1	5.5	10.3	15.5	22.7	45.9	29.9
Tunisia	2000 a,b	39.8	2.3	6.0	10.3	14.8	21.7	47.3	31.5
Turkey	2000 a,b	40.0	2.3	6.1	10.6	14.9	21.8	46.7	30.7
Turkmenistan	1998 a,b	40.8	2.6	6.1	10.2	14.7	21.5	47.5	31.7
Uganda	1999 a,b	43.0	2.3	5.9	10.0	14.0	20.3	49.7	34.9
Ukraine	1999 a,b	29.0	3.7	8.8	13.3	17.4	22.7	37.8	23.2
United Arab Emirates		..	..	..	..	..	..	..	..
United Kingdom	1999 d,e	36.0	2.1	6.1	11.4	16.0	22.5	44.0	28.5
United States	2000 d,e	40.8	1.9	5.4	10.7	15.7	22.4	45.8	29.9
Uruguay c	2000 d,e	44.6	1.8	4.8	9.3	14.2	21.6	50.1	33.5
Uzbekistan	2000 a,b	26.8	3.6	9.2	14.1	17.9	22.6	36.3	22.0
Venezuela, RB	1998 d,e	49.1	0.6	3.0	8.4	13.7	21.6	53.4	36.3
Vietnam	1998 a,b	36.1	3.6	8.0	11.4	15.2	20.9	44.5	29.9
West Bank and Gaza		..	..	..	..	..	..	..	..
Yemen, Rep.	1998 a,b	33.4	3.0	7.4	12.2	16.7	22.5	41.2	25.9
Zambia	1998 a,b	52.6	1.1	3.3	7.6	12.5	20.0	56.6	41.0
Zimbabwe	1995 a,b	56.8	1.8	4.6	8.1	12.2	19.3	55.7	40.3

a. Data refer to consumption shares by percentiles of population. b. Ranked by per capita consumption. c. Urban data. d. Data refer to income shares by percentiles of population.
e. Ranked by per capita income.

Inequality in the distribution of income is reflected in the percentage shares of income or consumption accruing to segments of the population ranked by income or consumption levels. The segments ranked lowest by personal income receive the smallest shares of total income. The Gini index provides a convenient summary measure of the degree of inequality.

Data on personal or household income or consumption come from nationally representative household surveys. The data in the table refer to different years between 1989 and 2002. Footnotes to the survey year indicate whether the rankings are based on per capita income or consumption. Each distribution is based on percentiles of population—rather than of households—with households ranked by income or expenditure per person.

Where the original data from the household survey were available, they have been used to directly calculate the income (or consumption) shares by quintile. Otherwise shares have been estimated from the best available grouped data.

The distribution data have been adjusted for household size, providing a more consistent measure of per capita income or consumption. No adjustment has been made for spatial differences in cost of living within countries, because the data needed for such calculations are generally unavailable. For further details on the estimation method for low- and middle-income economies, see Ravallion and Chen (1996).

Because the underlying household surveys differ in method and type of data collected, the distribution data are not strictly comparable across countries. These problems are diminishing as survey methods improve and become more standardized, but achieving strict comparability is still impossible (see *About the data* for table 2.5).

Two sources of noncomparability should be noted in particular. First, the surveys can differ in many respects, including whether they use income or consumption expenditure as the living standard indicator. The distribution of income is typically more unequal than the distribution of consumption. In addition, the definitions of income used usually differ among surveys. Consumption is usually a much better welfare indicator, particularly in developing countries. Second, households differ in size (number of members) and in the extent of income sharing among members. And individuals differ in age and consumption needs. Differences among countries in these respects may bias comparisons of distribution.

World Bank staff have made an effort to ensure that the data are as comparable as possible.

Wherever possible, consumption has been used rather than income. Income distribution and Gini indexes for high-income countries are calculated directly from the Luxembourg Income Study database, using an estimation method consistent with that applied for developing countries.

• **Survey year** is the year in which the underlying data were collected. • **Gini index** measures the extent to which the distribution of income (or, in some cases, consumption expenditure) among individuals or households within an economy deviates from a perfectly equal distribution. A Lorenz curve plots the cumulative percentages of total income received against the cumulative number of recipients, starting with the poorest individual or household. The Gini index measures the area between the Lorenz curve and a hypothetical line of absolute equality, expressed as a percentage of the maximum area under the line. Thus a Gini index of 0 represents perfect equality, while an index of 100 implies perfect inequality. • **Percentage share of income or consumption** is the share that accrues to subgroups of population indicated by deciles or quintiles. Percentage shares by quintile may not sum to 100 because of rounding.

Data sources

The data on distribution are compiled by the World Bank's Development Research Group using primary household survey data obtained from government statistical agencies and World Bank country departments. The data for high-income economies are from the Luxembourg Income Study database.

	Urban informal sector employment		Youth unemployment		Children in the labor force		Female-headed households		Pension contributors			Private health expenditure
	% of urban employment		Male % of male labor force ages 15–24	Female % of female labor force ages 15–24	% ages 10–14			% of		% of labor force	% of working-age population	% of total
	Male 1995–2001[a]	Female 1995–2001[a]	1995–2002[a]	1995–2002[a]	1980	2002	Year	total	Year			2001
Afghanistan	..	..	..	..	28	24		..		..	..	47.4
Albania	..	..	..	..	4	0		..	1995	32.0	31.0	35.4
Algeria	..	..	..	..	7	0		..	1997	31.0	23.0	25.0
Angola	..	..	..	..	30	26		..		..	..	36.9
Argentina	..	..	31	33	8	2		..	1995	53.0	39.0	46.6
Armenia	..	..	..	..	0	0	2000	28	2002	64.4	48.3	58.8
Australia	..	..	13	12	0	0		..		..	..	32.1
Austria	..	..	5	6	0	0		..	1993	95.8	76.6	30.7
Azerbaijan	..	..	..	..	0	0		..	1996	52.0	46.0	*24.9*
Bangladesh	..	..	11	10	35	27	1999–2000	8	1993	3.5	2.6	55.8
Belarus	..	..	..	..	0	0		..	1992	97.0	94.0	13.3
Belgium	..	..	16	15	0	0		..	1995	86.2	65.9	28.3
Benin	50	41	..	..	30	26	2001	20	1996	4.8	..	53.1
Bolivia	..	..	7	10	19	10	1998	19	1999	14.8	13.3	33.7
Bosnia and Herzegovina	..	..	..	..	1	0		..		..	..	63.2
Botswana	..	..	38	47	26	14		..		..	..	33.8
Brazil	27	27	15	22	19	14	1996	20	1996	36.0	31.0	58.4
Bulgaria	..	..	42	35	0	0		..	1994	64.0	63.0	17.9
Burkina Faso	..	..	..	..	71	40	1998–99	6	1993	3.1	3.0	..
Burundi	..	..	..	..	50	48		..	1993	3.3	3.0	41.0
Cambodia	..	..	..	..	27	23	2000	25		..	..	85.1
Cameroon	..	..	..	..	34	22	1998	22	1993	13.7	11.5	62.9
Canada	..	..	15	12	0	0		..	1992	91.9	80.2	29.2
Central African Republic	..	..	..	..	..	..	1994–95	21		..	..	48.8
Chad	..	..	..	..	42	36	1996–97	21	1990	1.1	1.0	24.0
Chile	..	..	17	22	0	0		..	2001	54.8	34.9	56.0
China	..	..	..	..	30	6		..	1994	17.6	17.4	62.8
Hong Kong, China	..	..	14	9	6	0		..		..	..	..
Colombia	..	..	32	41	12	6	2000	27	1999	35.0	29.3	34.3
Congo, Dem. Rep.	..	..	..	..	33	28		..		..	..	55.6
Congo, Rep.	..	..	..	..	27	25		..	1992	5.8	5.6	36.2
Costa Rica	..	..	12	16	10	4		..	1998	50.6	38.5	31.5
Côte d'Ivoire	..	..	..	..	28	18	1998–99	14	1997	9.3	9.1	84.0
Croatia	..	..	35	40	0	0		..	2001	67.0	57.0	18.2
Cuba	..	..	..	..	0	0		..		..	..	13.8
Czech Republic	..	..	15	17	0	0		..	1995	85.0	67.2	8.6
Denmark	..	..	9	5	0	0		..	1993	89.6	88.0	17.6
Dominican Republic	..	..	16	34	25	12	1999	32	2001	26.8	17.7	63.9
Ecuador	..	..	11	20	9	4		..	2002	23.2	14.9	49.7
Egypt, Arab Rep.	..	..	14	37	18	8	2000	11	1994	50.0	34.2	51.1
El Salvador	..	..	14	10	17	13		..	1996	26.2	25.0	53.3
Eritrea	..	..	..	..	44	38	1995	30		..	..	34.9
Estonia	..	..	19	26	0	0		..	1995	76.0	67.0	22.2
Ethiopia	39	65	..	..	46	41	2000	23		..	..	59.5
Finland	..	..	21	20	0	0		..	1993	90.3	83.6	24.4
France	..	..	18	23	0	0		..	1993	88.4	74.6	24.0
Gabon	..	..	..	..	29	12	2000	25	1995	15.0	14.0	52.1
Gambia, The	..	..	..	..	44	33		..		..	..	50.6
Georgia	21	7	20	20	0	0		..	2000	41.7	40.2	62.2
Germany	..	..	11	8	0	0		..	1995	94.2	82.3	25.1
Ghana	..	..	..	..	16	11		..	1993	7.2	9.0	40.4
Greece	..	..	19	34	5	0		..	1996	88.0	73.0	44.0
Guatemala	..	..	..	..	19	13	1998–99	19	1999	22.8	19.3	51.7
Guinea	..	..	..	..	41	30	1999	12	1993	1.5	1.8	45.9
Guinea-Bissau	..	..	..	..	43	36		..		..	..	46.2
Haiti	..	..	..	..	33	22	2000	42		..	..	46.6

Assessing vulnerability

	Urban informal sector employment		Youth unemployment		Children in the labor force		Female-headed households		Pension contributors			Private health expenditure
	% of urban employment		Male % of male labor force ages 15–24	Female % of female labor force ages 15–24	% ages 10–14			% of		% of labor force	% of working-age population	% of total
	Male 1995–2001[a]	Female 1995–2001[a]	1995–2002[a]	1995–2002[a]	1980	2002	Year	total	Year			2001
Honduras	..	..	7	8	14	7		..	1999	20.6	17.7	46.9
Hungary	..	..	13	12	0	0		..	1996	77.0	65.0	25.0
India	54	41	..	..	21	11	1998–99	10	1992	10.6	7.9	82.1
Indonesia	..	..	12	15	13	7	1997	12	1995	8.0	7.0	74.9
Iran, Islamic Rep.	..	..	..	..	14	2		..	2000	30.0	15.9	58.1
Iraq	..	..	..	..	11	2		..		..	..	68.2
Ireland	..	..	9	7	1	0		..	1992	79.3	64.7	24.0
Israel	..	..	19	18	0	0		..	1992	82.0	63.0	30.8
Italy	..	..	23	31	2	0		..	1997	87.0	68.0	24.7
Jamaica	..	..	24	46	0	0		..	1999	44.4	45.8	57.9
Japan	..	..	11	9	0	0		..	1994	97.5	92.3	22.1
Jordan	..	..	..	..	4	0	1997	9	1995	40.0	25.0	53.0
Kazakhstan	..	..	..	..	0	0	1999	33	2001	38.0	28.3	39.6
Kenya	..	..	..	..	45	38	1998	31	1995	18.0	24.0	78.6
Korea, Dem. Rep.	..	..	..	..	3	0		..		..	..	26.6
Korea, Rep.	..	..	10	7	0	0		..	1996	58.0	43.0	55.6
Kuwait	..	..	..	..	0	0		..		..	..	19.0
Kyrgyz Republic	33	25	..	..	0	0	1997	26	1997	44.0	42.0	51.3
Lao PDR	..	..	..	..	31	25		..		..	..	44.5
Latvia	..	..	20	21	0	0		..	1995	60.5	52.3	47.5
Lebanon	..	..	..	..	5	0		..		..	..	..
Lesotho	..	..	38	59	28	20		..		..	..	21.1
Liberia	..	..	..	..	26	14		..		..	..	24.1
Libya	..	..	..	..	9	0		..		..	..	44.0
Lithuania	50	27	31	26	0	0		..	2002	77.0	60.0	29.5
Macedonia, FYR	..	..	..	..	1	0		..	1995	49.0	47.0	15.1
Madagascar	..	..	..	..	40	33	1997	21	1993	5.4	4.8	34.1
Malawi	..	..	..	..	45	30	2000	26		..	..	65.0
Malaysia	..	..	..	..	8	2		..	1993	48.7	37.8	46.3
Mali	..	..	..	..	61	50	2001	11	1990	2.5	2.0	61.4
Mauritania	..	..	..	..	30	21	2000–01	29	1995	5.0	4.0	27.6
Mauritius	..	..	..	..	5	1		..	1995	60.0	57.0	40.5
Mexico	18	22	5	6	9	4		..	1997	30.0	31.0	55.7
Moldova	..	..	..	..	3	0		..		..	..	44.2
Mongolia	..	..	..	..	4	1		..	2002	61.4	49.1	27.7
Morocco	..	..	16	15	21	0	1992	16	2000	17.3	11.3	60.7
Mozambique	..	..	..	..	39	32	1997	26	1995	2.0	2.1	32.6
Myanmar	..	..	..	..	28	22		..		..	..	82.2
Namibia	..	..	33	41	34	16	1992	30		..	..	32.2
Nepal	60	76	..	..	56	41	2001	16		..	..	70.3
Netherlands	..	..	6	6	0	0		..	1993	91.7	75.4	36.7
New Zealand	..	..	12	11	0	0		..		..	..	23.2
Nicaragua	..	..	20	20	19	11	1997–98	30	1999	14.3	13.3	51.5
Niger	..	..	..	..	48	43	1998	13	1992	1.3	1.5	60.9
Nigeria	..	..	..	..	29	23	1999	16	1993	1.3	1.3	76.8
Norway	..	..	12	11	0	0		..	1993	94.0	85.8	14.5
Oman	..	..	..	..	6	0		..		..	..	19.3
Pakistan	64	61	11	29	23	14	1991	7	1993	3.5	2.1	75.6
Panama	..	..	25	37	6	2		..	1998	51.6	40.7	31.0
Papua New Guinea	..	..	..	..	28	16		..		..	..	11.0
Paraguay	..	..	12	17	15	5	1990	16	2001	18.0	12.0	61.7
Peru	..	..	13	14	4	2	2000	19	2001	31.0	19.0	45.0
Philippines	16	19	17	23	14	4	1998	14	1996	28.3	13.6	54.8
Poland	..	..	44	44	0	0		..	1996	68.0	64.0	28.1
Portugal	..	..	10	14	8	1		..	1996	84.3	80.0	31.0
Puerto Rico	..	..	23	16	0	0		..		..	..	..

	Urban informal sector employment		Youth unemployment		Children in the labor force		Female-headed households		Pension contributors			Private health expenditure
	% of urban employment		Male % of male labor force ages 15–24	Female % of female labor force ages 15–24	% ages 10–14			% of		% of labor force	% of working-age population	% of total
	Male 1995–2001[a]	Female 1995–2001[a]	1995–2002[a]	1995–2002[a]	1980	2002	Year	total	Year			2001
Romania	..	..	18	17	0	0		..	1994	55.0	48.0	20.8
Russian Federation	10	9	24	26	0	0		..		..	..	31.8
Rwanda	..	..	..	..	43	41	2000	36	1993	9.3	13.3	44.5
Saudi Arabia	..	..	..	..	5	0		..		..	..	25.4
Senegal	..	..	..	..	43	26	1997	18	1998	4.3	4.7	41.2
Serbia and Montenegro	..	..	..	..	0	0		..		..	..	20.8
Sierra Leone	..	..	..	..	19	13		..		..	..	39.0
Singapore	..	..	4	6	2	0		..	1995	73.0	56.0	66.5
Slovak Republic	..	..	39	36	0	0		..	1996	73.0	72.0	10.7
Slovenia	..	..	15	18	0	0		..	1995	86.0	68.7	25.1
Somalia	..	..	..	..	38	31		..		..	..	55.4
South Africa	16	28	58	53	1	0	1998	41		..	..	58.6
Spain	..	..	18	27	0	0		..	1994	85.3	61.4	28.6
Sri Lanka	..	..	20	31	4	1		..	1992	28.8	20.8	51.1
Sudan	..	..	..	..	33	27		..	1995	12.1	12.0	81.3
Swaziland	..	..	42	48	17	12		..		..	..	31.5
Sweden	..	..	14	12	0	0		..	1994	91.1	88.9	14.8
Switzerland	..	..	7	4	0	0		..	1994	98.1	96.8	42.9
Syrian Arab Republic	..	..	..	..	14	2		..		..	..	56.1
Tajikistan	..	..	..	..	0	0		..		..	..	71.1
Tanzania	60	85	..	..	43	36	1999	23	1996	2.0	2.0	53.3
Thailand	..	..	7	6	25	11		..	1999	18.0	17.0	42.9
Togo	..	..	..	..	36	26	1998	24	1997	15.9	15.0	51.4
Trinidad and Tobago	..	..	22	31	1	0		..		..	..	56.7
Tunisia	..	..	..	..	6	0		..	2000	40.0	23.0	24.3
Turkey	10	6	21	18	21	7	1998	10	1997	37.1	27.4	*36.8*
Turkmenistan	..	..	..	..	0	0	2000	26		..	..	26.7
Uganda	..	..	..	..	49	43	2000–01	27	1994	8.2	..	42.5
Ukraine	5	5	23	25	0	0		..	1995	69.8	66.1	32.2
United Arab Emirates	..	..	6	6	0	0		..		..	..	24.2
United Kingdom	..	..	13	9	0	0		..	1994	89.7	84.5	17.8
United States	..	..	13	11	0	0		..	1993	94.0	91.9	55.6
Uruguay	..	..	29	42	4	1		..	1995	82.0	78.0	53.7
Uzbekistan	..	..	..	..	0	0	1996	22		..	..	25.5
Venezuela, RB	..	..	20	28	4	0		..	1999	23.6	18.2	37.9
Vietnam	..	..	..	..	22	4	1997	24	1998	8.4	10.0	71.5
West Bank and Gaza	..	..	..	..	..	..		..		..	..	..
Yemen, Rep.	..	..	..	..	26	18	1997	9		..	..	65.9
Zambia	..	..	..	..	19	15	2001–02	22	1994	10.2	7.9	46.9
Zimbabwe	..	..	17	11	37	26	1999	33	1995	12.0	10.0	54.7
World			**.. w**	**.. w**	**20 w**	**11 w**						**40.8 w**
Low income			..	..	25	18						73.7
Middle income			..	..	21	5						48.9
Lower middle income			..	..	23	5						52.8
Upper middle income			21	27	6	2						42.3
Low & middle income			..	..	23	12						53.0
East Asia & Pacific			..	..	27	6						61.2
Europe & Central Asia			..	..	3	1						27.6
Latin America & Carib.			17	24	13	8						52.0
Middle East & N. Africa			..	..	14	4						40.7
South Asia			..	..	23	14						78.4
Sub-Saharan Africa			..	..	35	28						58.7
High income			12	13	0	0						37.9
Europe EMU			14	17	1	0						26.5

a. Data are for the most recent year available.

About the data

As traditionally defined and measured, poverty is a static concept, and vulnerability a dynamic one. Vulnerability reflects a household's resilience in the face of shocks and the likelihood that a shock will lead to a decline in well-being. Thus it depends primarily on the household's asset endowment and insurance mechanisms. Because poor people have fewer assets and less diversified sources of income than the better-off, fluctuations in income affect them more.

Poor households face many risks, and vulnerability is thus multidimensional. The indicators in the table focus on individual risks—informal sector employment, youth unemployment, child labor, female-headed household, income insecurity in old age, private health expenditure—and the extent to which publicly provided services may be capable of mitigating some of these risks. Poor people face labor market risks, often having to take up precarious, low-quality jobs in the informal sector and to increase their household's labor market participation through their children. Income security is a prime concern for the elderly. And affordable access to health care is a primary concern for all poor people, for whom illness and injury have both direct and opportunity costs.

For informal sector employment, the data are from labor force and special informal sector surveys, various household surveys, surveys of household industries or economic activities, surveys of small and micro enterprises, and official estimates. The international comparability of the data is affected by differences among countries in definitions and coverage and in the treatment of domestic workers and those who have a secondary job in the informal sector. The data in the table are based on national definitions of urban areas established by countries. For details on these definitions, see the notes in *Data sources*.

Youth unemployment is an important policy issue for many economies. Experiencing unemployment may permanently impair a young person's productive potential and future employment opportunities. In this table unemployment among youth ages 15–24 is presented, but the lower age limit for young people could be determined by the minimum age for leaving school, so age groups could differ across countries. Also since this age group is likely to include school leavers, the level of youth unemployment varies significantly over the year as a result of different school opening and closing dates. The youth unemployment rate shares similar limitations on comparability to the general unemployment rate. For further information, see *About the data* for table 2.4.

Reliable estimates of child labor are difficult to obtain. In many countries child labor is officially presumed not to exist and so is not included in surveys or in official data. Underreporting also occurs because data exclude children engaged in agricultural or household activities with their families. Available statistics suggest that more boys than girls work. But the number of girls working is often underestimated because surveys exclude girls working as unregistered domestic help or doing full-time household work to enable their parents to work outside the home.

The data on female-headed household are from recent Demographic and Health Surveys. The definition and concept of the female-headed household differ greatly across economies, making cross-country comparison difficult. In some cases it is assumed that a woman cannot be the head of any household in which an adult male is present, because of sex-biased stereotype. Users need to be cautious when interpreting the data.

The data on pension contributors come from national sources, the International Labour Organization, and International Monetary Fund country reports. Coverage by pension schemes may be broad or even universal where eligibility is determined by citizenship, residency, or income status. In contribution-related schemes, however, eligibility is usually restricted to individuals who have made contributions for a minimum number of years. Definitional issues—relating to the labor force, for example—may arise in comparing coverage by contribution-related schemes over time and across countries (for country-specific information, see Palacios and Pallares-Miralles 2000). Coverage of the share of the labor force covered by a pension scheme may be overstated in countries that do not attempt to count informal sector workers as part of the labor force.

The expenditure on health in a country can be divided into two main categories by source of funding: public and private. Public health expenditure consists of spending by central and local governments, including social health insurance funds. Private health expenditure includes private insurance, direct out-of-pocket payments by households, spending by nonprofit institutions serving households, and direct payments by private corporations. In countries where the share of out-of-pocket spending is large, poor households may be particularly vulnerable to the impoverishing effects of health care needs.

Definitions

• **Urban informal sector employment** is broadly characterized as employment in urban areas in units that produce goods or services on a small scale with the primary objective of generating employment and income for those concerned. These units typically operate at a low level of organization, with little or no division between labor and capital as factors of production. Labor relations are based on casual employment, kinship, or social relationships rather than contractual arrangements. • **Youth unemployment** refers to the share of the labor force ages 15–24 without work but available for and seeking employment. Definitions of labor force and unemployment may differ by country (see *About the data*). • **Children in the labor force** refer to the share of children ages 10–14 active in the labor force. • **Female-headed households** refer to the percentage of households with a female head. • **Pension contributors** refer to the share of the labor force or working-age population (here defined as ages 15–64) covered by a pension scheme. • **Private health expenditure** includes direct (out-of-pocket) spending by households, private insurance, spending by nonprofit institutions serving households (other than social insurance), and direct service payments by private corporations.

Data sources

The data on urban informal sector employment and youth unemployment are from the International Labour Organization (ILO) database *Key Indicators of the Labour Market,* third edition. The child labor force participation rates are from the ILO database *Estimates and Projections of the Economically Active Population, 1950–2010.* The data on female-headed household are from Demographic and Health Surveys by Macro International. The data on pension contributors are drawn from Robert Palacios and Montserrat Pallares-Miralles's "International Patterns of Pension Provision" (2000), and updates. For further updates, notes, and sources, go to "Knowledge and information" on the World Bank's Web site on pensions (http://www.worldbank.org/pensions). The data on private health expenditure for developing countries are largely from the World Health Organization's *World Health Report 2003* and updates, from household surveys, and from World Bank poverty assessments and sector studies. The data on private health expenditure for member countries of the Organisation for Economic Co-operation and Development (OECD) are from the OECD.

2.9 Enhancing security

		Public expenditure on pensions			Public expenditure on health	Public expenditure on education	
	Year	% of GDP	Year	Average pension % of per capita income	% of GDP **2001**	% of GDP **2001/02** [a]	Per student % of GDP per capita **2001/02** [a]
Afghanistan		..	..	..	2.7	..	..
Albania	1995	5.1	1995	36.4	2.4	..	..
Algeria	1997	2.1	1991	75.0	3.1	..	..
Angola		..	..	..	2.8	2.8	..
Argentina	1994	6.2	..	..	5.1	*4.6*	*14.5*
Armenia	2002	2.5	1996	18.7	3.2	3.2	14.3
Australia	1997	5.9	1989	37.3	6.2	4.6	16.5
Austria	1995	14.9	1993	69.3	5.5	*5.8*	..
Azerbaijan	1996	2.5	1996	51.4	*0.6*	3.5	12.4
Bangladesh	1992	0.0	..	..	1.5	2.3	11.2
Belarus	1997	7.7	1995	31.2	4.8	*6.0*	..
Belgium	1997	12.9	..	..	6.4	*5.9*	..
Benin	1993	0.4	1993	189.7	2.1	3.3	14.2
Bolivia	2000	4.5	..	..	3.5	*5.5*	15.0
Bosnia and Herzegovina		..	..	..	2.8	..	..
Botswana		..	..	..	4.4	*8.6*	*7.1*
Brazil	1997	9.8	..	..	3.2	4.0	12.7
Bulgaria	1996	7.3	1995	39.3	3.9	*3.2*	*15.6*
Burkina Faso	1992	0.3	1992	207.3	2.0	..	..
Burundi	1991	0.2	1991	57.4	2.1	3.6	25.6
Cambodia		..	..	..	1.7	2.0	7.6
Cameroon	1993	0.4	..	..	1.2	*3.2*	*12.2*
Canada	1997	5.4	1994	54.3	6.8	*5.2*	*9.1*
Central African Republic	1990	0.3	..	..	2.3	*1.9*	..
Chad	1997	0.1	..	..	2.0	*2.5* [d]	*14.2*
Chile	2001	2.9	1993	56.1	3.1	*3.9*	*15.1*
China	1996	2.7	..	..	2.0	*2.2*	*11.5*
Hong Kong, China		..	..	..	..	..	..
Colombia	1994	1.1	1989	72.2	3.6	4.4	19.5
Congo, Dem. Rep.		..	..	..	1.5	..	..
Congo, Rep.	1992	0.9	..	..	1.4	*0.1*	..
Costa Rica	1997	4.2	1993	76.1	4.9	4.7	19.1
Côte d'Ivoire	1997	0.3	..	..	1.3	*4.6*	*22.0*
Croatia	2001	13.2	..	..	7.3	*4.2*	*5.8*
Cuba	1992	12.6	..	..	6.2	*8.5*	*42.6*
Czech Republic	1999	9.8	1996	37.0	6.7	4.4	20.6
Denmark	1997	8.8	1994	46.7	7.0	*8.3*	*37.7*
Dominican Republic	2000	0.8	2000	42.0	2.2	2.4	..
Ecuador	2002	1.4	2002	55.3	2.3	..	..
Egypt, Arab Rep.	1994	2.5	1994	45.0	1.9	..	..
El Salvador	1997	1.3	..	..	3.7	2.5	*8.6*
Eritrea	2001	0.3	..	..	3.7	2.7	..
Estonia	2002	6.7	1995	56.7	4.3	*7.4*	*27.5*
Ethiopia	1993	0.9	..	..	1.4	*4.8*	..
Finland	1997	12.1	1994	57.4	5.3	*5.9*	..
France	1997	13.4	..	..	7.3	*5.8*	..
Gabon		..	..	..	1.7	*3.9*	*8.7*
Gambia, The		..	..	..	3.2	*2.7*	..
Georgia	2000	2.7	1996	12.6	1.4	2.5	..
Germany	1997	12.1	1995	62.8	8.1	*4.5*	..
Ghana	1996	1.1	..	..	2.8	*4.1*	..
Greece	1993	11.9	1990	85.6	5.2	*3.8*	..
Guatemala	1995	0.7	1995	27.6	2.3	*1.7*	..
Guinea		..	..	..	1.9	*1.9*	..
Guinea-Bissau		..	..	..	3.2	*2.1*	..
Haiti		..	..	..	2.7	..	..

Enhancing security

		Public expenditure on pensions			Public expenditure on health	Public expenditure on education	
	Year	% of GDP	Year	Average pension % of per capita income	% of GDP 2001	% of GDP 2001/02[a]	Per student % of GDP per capita 2001/02[a]
Honduras	1994	0.6	..	..	3.2	*4.0*	..
Hungary	1996	9.7	1996	33.6	5.1	*4.9*	*20.5*
India	..	..	..	..	0.9	*4.1*	*20.8*
Indonesia	..	..	..	..	0.6	1.3	6.0
Iran, Islamic Rep.	1994	1.5	..	..	2.7	5.0	15.7
Iraq	..	..	..	..	1.0	..	..
Ireland	1997	4.6	1993	77.9	4.9	*4.3*	..
Israel	1996	5.9	1992	48.1	6.0	*7.3*	*23.0*
Italy	1997	17.6	..	..	6.3	*4.6*	..
Jamaica	1996	..	1989	25.9	2.9	6.3	23.1
Japan	1997	6.9	1989	33.9	6.2	*3.6*	*20.4*
Jordan	1995	4.2	1995	144.0	4.5	4.6	15.5
Kazakhstan	2001	3.8	2001	23.0	1.9	*4.4*	..
Kenya	1993	0.5	..	..	1.7	*6.3*	*4.7*
Korea, Dem. Rep.		..	..	..	1.9	..	..
Korea, Rep.	1997	1.3	..	..	2.6	3.6	*15.0*
Kuwait	1990	3.5	..	..	3.5	6.1	..
Kyrgyz Republic	1997	6.4	2001	45.0	1.9	3.1	*12.8*
Lao PDR	..	..	..	..	1.7	3.2	11.0
Latvia	1995	10.2	1994	47.6	3.4	*5.9*	*23.7*
Lebanon	..	..	..	..	*2.2*	2.9	..
Lesotho	..	..	..	..	4.3	*10.0*	..
Liberia	..	..	..	..	3.3	..	..
Libya	..	..	..	..	1.6	*2.7*	..
Lithuania	2002	7.1	1995	21.3	4.2	..	..
Macedonia, FYR	1998	8.7	1996	91.6	5.8	*3.7[d]*	*19.7[d]*
Madagascar	1990	0.2	..	..	1.3	2.5	..
Malawi	..	..	..	..	2.7	*4.1*	..
Malaysia	1999	6.5	..	..	2.0	7.9	*23.2*
Mali	1991	0.4	..	..	2.2	*2.8*	26.7
Mauritania	1992	0.2	..	..	2.6	*3.6*	22.5
Mauritius	1999	4.4	..	..	2.0	3.3	13.0
Mexico	2000	0.3[b]	..	..	2.7	*4.4*	*15.0*
Moldova	1996	7.5	..	..	2.8	*4.0*	..
Mongolia	2002	5.8	..	..	4.6	*6.2*	..
Morocco	1994	1.8	1994	118.0	2.0	*5.0*	..
Mozambique	1996	0.0	..	..	4.0	2.4	..
Myanmar		..	..	..	0.4	*1.3*	*7.8*
Namibia		..	..	..	4.7	*8.1*	28.2
Nepal		..	..	..	1.5	3.4	13.8
Netherlands	1997	11.1	1989	48.5	5.7	*4.8*	..
New Zealand	1997	6.5	..	..	6.4	6.6	*21.6*
Nicaragua	1996	2.5	..	..	3.8	*5.0*	..
Niger	1992	0.1	..	..	1.4	2.3	26.3
Nigeria	1991	0.1	1991	40.5	0.8	..	..
Norway	1997	8.2	1994	49.9	6.8	*6.8*	25.9
Oman	..	..	..	..	2.4	3.9	17.5
Pakistan	1993	0.9	..	..	1.0	*1.8*	..
Panama	1996	4.3	..	..	4.8	4.3	*19.1*
Papua New Guinea		..	..	..	3.9	*2.3*	*13.3*
Paraguay	2000	0.8[c]	..	..	3.0	4.7	15.8
Peru	2000	2.6	..	..	2.6	*3.3*	..
Philippines	1993	1.0	..	..	1.5	3.2	11.4
Poland	1997	15.5	1995	61.2	4.6	*5.0*	*18.8*
Portugal	1997	10.0	1989	44.6	6.3	*5.8*	..
Puerto Rico		..	..	..	..	..	..

		Public expenditure on pensions			Public expenditure on health	Public expenditure on education	
	Year	% of GDP	Year	Average pension % of per capita income	% of GDP **2001**	% of GDP **2001/02**[a]	Per student % of GDP per capita **2001/02**[a]
Romania	1996	5.1	1994	34.1	5.2	*3.5*	..
Russian Federation	1996	5.7	1995	18.3	3.7	3.1	..
Rwanda	..	..	..	3.1	*2.8*	12.8	
Saudi Arabia	..	..	..	3.4	*8.3*	..	
Senegal	1998	1.5	1997	85.0[c]	2.8	6.5[d]	*21.0*
Serbia and Montenegro	..	..	..	6.5	..	..	
Sierra Leone	..	..	..	2.6	*1.0*	..	
Singapore	1996	1.4	..	..	1.3	..	..
Slovak Republic	1994	9.1	1994	44.5	5.1	*4.1*	*16.8*
Slovenia	1996	13.6	1996	49.3	6.3	..	..
Somalia	..	..	..	1.2	..	..	
South Africa	..	..	..	3.6	*5.7*	*17.7*	
Spain	1997	10.9	1995	54.1	5.4	*4.5*	..
Sri Lanka	1996	2.4	..	..	1.8	1.3	*6.1*
Sudan	..	..	..	0.6	..	..	
Swaziland	..	..	..	2.3	5.5	19.2	
Sweden	1997	11.1	1994	78.0	7.4	*7.7*	*30.7*
Switzerland	1997	13.4	1993	44.4	6.4	*5.5*	*28.9*
Syrian Arab Republic	1991	0.5	..	..	2.4	4.1	..
Tajikistan	1996	3.0	..	..	1.0	2.4	..
Tanzania	..	..	..	2.0	*2.2*	..	
Thailand	..	..	..	2.1	5.0	*17.7*	
Togo	1997	0.6	1993	178.8	1.5	*4.8*	*16.0*
Trinidad and Tobago	1996	0.6	..	..	1.7	4.0	18.4
Tunisia	2000	4.2	1991	89.5	4.9	*6.8*	*23.9*
Turkey	1997	4.5	1993	56.0	*4.4*	3.7	16.4
Turkmenistan	1996	2.3	..	..	3.0	..	..
Uganda	1997	0.8	..	..	3.4	*2.5*	..
Ukraine	1996	8.6	1995	30.9	2.9	*4.2*	*17.0*
United Arab Emirates	..	..	..	2.6	*1.9*	*10.0*	
United Kingdom	1997	10.3	..	..	6.3	*4.4*	*15.8*
United States	1997	7.5	1989	33.0	6.2	*4.9*	*20.8*
Uruguay	1996	15.0	1996	64.1	5.1	2.5	*9.9*
Uzbekistan	1995	5.3	1995	45.8	2.7	..	..
Venezuela, RB	2001	2.7	..	..	3.7	..	..
Vietnam	1998	1.6	..	..	1.5	*2.8*	..
West Bank and Gaza	..	..	..	..	..	..	
Yemen, Rep.	1994	0.1	..	..	1.5	10.0	..
Zambia	1993	0.1	..	..	3.0	*2.3*	..
Zimbabwe	..	..	..	2.8	*10.4*	18.0	
World					**5.6 w**	**4.1 m**	**.. m**
Low income					1.1	*3.1*	..
Middle income					3.1	*4.5*	..
Lower middle income					2.7	*4.0*	..
Upper middle income					3.7	*4.4*	*15.0*
Low & middle income					2.7	*3.8*	..
East Asia & Pacific					1.9	*3.2*	*10.2*
Europe & Central Asia					4.3	*4.3*	..
Latin America & Carib.					3.4	*4.5*	*15.0*
Middle East & N. Africa					2.8	*4.3*	..
South Asia					1.0	*2.3*	*11.2*
Sub-Saharan Africa					2.5	*3.4*	..
High income					6.3	*5.2*	..
Europe EMU					6.8	*5.2*	..

a. Data are preliminary. b. Refers only to the scheme for civil servants. c. Refers to system covering private sector workers. d. Data are for 2002/03.

About the data

Enhancing security for poor people means reducing their vulnerability to such risks as ill health, providing them the means to manage risk themselves, and strengthening market or public institutions for managing risk. The tools include microfinance programs, old age assistance and pensions, and public provision of basic health care and education.

Public interventions and institutions can provide services directly to poor people, although whether these work well for the poor is debated. State action is often ineffective, in part because governments can influence only a few of the many sources of well-being and in part because of difficulties in delivering goods and services. The effectiveness of public provision is further constrained by the fiscal resources at governments' disposal and the fact that state institutions may not be responsive to the needs of poor people.

The data on public pension spending are from national sources and cover all government expenditures, including the administrative costs of pension programs. They cover noncontributory pensions or social assistance targeted to the elderly and disabled and spending by social insurance schemes for which contributions had previously been made. The pattern of spending in a country is correlated with its demographic structure—spending increases as the population ages.

The lack of consistent national health accounting systems in most developing countries makes cross-country comparisons of health spending difficult. Compiling estimates of public health expenditures is complicated in countries where state or provincial and local governments are involved in financing and delivering health care because the data on public spending often are not aggregated. The data in the table are the product of an effort to collect all available information on health expenditures from national and local government budgets, national accounts, household surveys, insurance publications, international donors, and existing tabulations.

The data on education spending in the table refer solely to public spending—government spending on public education plus subsidies for private education. The data generally exclude foreign aid for education. They may also exclude spending by religious schools, which play a significant role in many developing countries. Data for some countries and for some years refer to spending by the ministry of education only (excluding education expenditures by other ministries and departments and local authorities). The share of gross domestic product (GDP) devoted to education

can be interpreted as reflecting a country's effort in education. It often bears a weak relationship to the output of the education system as reflected in educational attainment. The pattern in this relationship suggests wide variations across countries in the efficiency with which the government's resources are translated into education outcomes. Data for education expenditure are reported for school years.

Definitions

• **Public expenditure on pensions** includes all government expenditures on cash transfers to the elderly, the disabled, and survivors and the administrative costs of these programs. • **Average pension** is estimated by dividing total pension expenditure by the number of pensioners. • **Public expenditure on health** consists of recurrent and capital spending from government (central and local) budgets, external borrowings and grants (including donations from international agencies and nongovernmental organizations), and social (or compulsory) health insurance funds. • **Public expenditure on education** consists of public spending on public education plus subsidies to private education at the primary, secondary, and tertiary levels.

Data sources

The data on pension spending are drawn from Robert Palacios and Montserrat Pallares-Miralles's "International Patterns of Pension Provision" (2000) and updates. For further updates, notes, and sources, go to "Knowledge and information" on the World Bank's Web site on pensions (http://www.worldbank.org/pensions). The estimates of health expenditure come from the World Health Organization's *World Health Report 2003* and updates, from the Organisation for Economic Co-operation and Development for its member countries, and from countries' national health accounts, supplemented by World Bank country and sector studies. The data on education expenditure are from the UNESCO Institute for Statistics.

	Public expenditure per student [a]						Public expenditure on education	Trained teachers in primary education	Primary pupil-teacher ratio
			% of GDP per capita				% of total government expenditure	% of total	pupils per teacher
	Primary		Secondary		Tertiary				
	1990/91	2001/02 [b]	1990/91	2001/02 [b]	1990/91	2001/02 [b]	2001/02 [b]	2001/02 [b]	2001/02 [b]
Afghanistan	..	..	..	..	..	..	..	..	43
Albania	..	..	..	..	..	..	..	..	22
Algeria	..	..	..	..	..	..	..	97.1	28
Angola	..	..	..	..	..	..	..	..	..
Argentina	..	12.4	..	15.8	..	17.8	13.7	67.0	20
Armenia	..	..	..	14.8	..	38.9	..	..	19
Australia	15.9	16.0	34.6	14.3	50.7	23.5	13.8	..	..
Austria	18.0	..	23.6	..	35.1	..	15.1	..	13
Azerbaijan	..	..	..	20.1	..	14.0	23.1	100.0	16
Bangladesh	..	8.3	15.2	13.4	26.0	42.5	15.8	65.6	55
Belarus	25.7	..	6.9	..	17.8	..	..	97.9	17
Belgium	..	..	27.1	..	29.0	..	11.6	..	12
Benin	..	10.1	..	18.5	..	..	..	65.0	53
Bolivia	..	12.0	..	10.2	..	45.0	18.4	74.1	25
Bosnia and Herzegovina	..	..	..	..	..	..	..	..	..
Botswana	7.4	6.0	44.2	5.5	161.5	88.6	..	89.5	27
Brazil	..	10.7	..	10.0	..	48.5	10.4	91.9	23
Bulgaria	22.1	..	..	..	..	30.9	..	..	17
Burkina Faso	..	..	..	..	..	..	..	80.4	47
Burundi	..	11.6	117.8	61.7	..	691.5	21.8	..	49
Cambodia	..	7.4	..	6.2	..	42.0	10.1	96.0	56
Cameroon	..	..	..	..	302.0	..	12.5	..	61
Canada	..	..	..	..	27.5	47.2	..	..	17
Central African Republic	..	..	17.7	..	347.1	..	..	..	..
Chad	7.0	9.5	..	28.4	..	422.7	..	..	71
Chile	8.4	14.3	7.7	14.7	27.1	19.2	17.5	94.9	32
China	5.4	..	12.5	..	102.4	..	..	96.8	20
Hong Kong, China	8.0	..	..	..	51.3	..	..	..	..
Colombia	..	16.4	10.4	18.5	33.0	38.5	18.0	..	26
Congo, Dem. Rep.	..	..	..	..	..	..	..	..	..
Congo, Rep.	..	0.4	..	..	..	8.8	12.6	64.6	56
Costa Rica	7.8	14.6	15.8	20.2	45.8	45.8	21.1	89.5	24
Côte d'Ivoire	..	14.9	..	49.4	328.5	..	21.5	99.1	44
Croatia	..	..	..	..	..	36.4	..	100.0	18
Cuba	..	32.7	..	43.3	..	96.5	16.8	100.0	14
Czech Republic	..	13.0	..	22.3	45.9	32.8	9.7	..	18
Denmark	21.9	23.4	31.2	37.7	40.4	69.0	15.3	..	10
Dominican Republic	2.5	6.6	..	5.0	..	..	13.2	..	33
Ecuador	..	..	9.5	..	23.9	..	8.0	68.6	24
Egypt, Arab Rep.	..	..	..	..	50.4	..	..	99.9	22
El Salvador	..	..	..	..	..	9.3	19.4	..	26
Eritrea	..	..	..	..	..	17.4	..	72.6	44
Estonia	..	23.6	38.7	29.7	55.9	31.8	..	..	14
Ethiopia	31.1	..	46.1	..	506.6	..	13.8	69.3	57
Finland	21.8	..	25.8	..	40.3	..	12.2	..	16
France	11.9	..	20.7	..	22.9	..	11.5	..	19
Gabon	..	4.7	..	18.9	..	..	..	95.3	63
Gambia, The	13.1	..	28.2	..	..	..	14.2	73.1	38
Georgia	..	..	..	..	..	..	13.1	87.6	14
Germany	..	..	..	..	..	..	9.9	..	15
Ghana	..	..	..	..	..	..	..	64.9	32
Greece	8.1	..	12.4	..	16.0	..	7.0	..	13
Guatemala	2.7	7.7	4.4	4.8	34.7	..	11.4	100.0	30
Guinea	10.8	9.2	34.9	..	572.0	..	25.6	..	47
Guinea-Bissau	..	..	..	..	..	..	4.8	35.1	44
Haiti	5.7	..	..	..	..	..	..	..	..

	Public expenditure per student[a]						Public expenditure on education	Trained teachers in primary education	Primary pupil-teacher ratio
	% of GDP per capita						% of total government expenditure	% of total	pupils per teacher
	Primary		Secondary		Tertiary				
	1990/91	2001/02[b]	1990/91	2001/02[b]	1990/91	2001/02[b]	2001/02[b]	2001/02[b]	2001/02[b]
Honduras	..	..	16.5	..	76.6	..	..	..	34
Hungary	20.3	19.2	25.4	18.8	81.3	31.4	14.1	..	11
India	..	13.7	13.6	23.0	92.0	85.8	12.7	..	40
Indonesia	..	3.7	..	7.3	..	21.0	9.6	93.5	21
Iran, Islamic Rep.	6.2	11.6	14.1	13.6	79.7	81.5	21.7	97.9	24
Iraq	..	..	..	..	..	..	..	..	21
Ireland	11.1	..	18.5	..	36.1	..	10.7	..	22
Israel	12.7	21.0	27.6	22.4	32.7	29.9	..	..	12
Italy	15.1	..	21.4	..	..	..	9.5	..	11
Jamaica	10.8	15.7	14.0	24.5	132.3	70.5	12.3	79.5	34
Japan	18.6	21.4	18.4	21.0	..	17.2	10.5	..	20
Jordan	..	16.0	..	19.0	78.9	..	20.6	..	20
Kazakhstan	..	..	..	..	..	..	..	..	19
Kenya	13.0	0.9	..	2.2	..	256.7	22.5	..	32
Korea, Dem. Rep.	..	..	..	..	..	..	..	..	..
Korea, Rep.	12.0	18.4	9.9	16.8	5.8	7.4	17.4	..	32
Kuwait	35.4	..	13.6	..	353.8	..	..	..	14
Kyrgyz Republic	..	..	28.4	..	53.5	..	18.6	49.3	24
Lao PDR	5.0	9.1	25.3	10.2	52.2	94.5	10.6	76.1	30
Latvia	..	23.1	19.4	24.7	18.6	22.0	..	..	15
Lebanon	..	8.3	..	..	..	9.8	11.1	14.9	17
Lesotho	16.7	21.4	61.8	52.9	609.1	..	18.4	74.8	47
Liberia	..	..	..	..	..	..	..	..	38
Libya	..	..	..	..	..	24.9	..	..	..
Lithuania	..	..	26.9	..	54.1	..	..	..	16
Macedonia, FYR	..	16.6[c]	30.9	17.1[c]	62.5	20.8[c]	..	..	18[c]
Madagascar	..	10.7	..	..	167.9	191.6	..	..	54[c]
Malawi	6.5	..	44.0	..	851.2	..	..	51.2	..
Malaysia	12.4	17.0	16.9	27.5	116.6	83.5	25.2	..	20
Mali	..	14.4	..	..	..	..	..	..	56
Mauritania	16.9	14.0	85.2	44.0	396.3	..	..	..	39
Mauritius	10.1	9.0	17.1	13.9	177.1	48.7	13.3	100.0	25
Mexico	3.5	11.8	8.3	13.8	23.6	45.2	22.6	..	27
Moldova	..	..	..	..	..	..	15.0	..	20
Mongolia	..	..	..	..	119.4	..	..	92.9	32
Morocco	..	17.9	47.1	47.5	73.1	..	..	..	28
Mozambique	11.0	..	27.4	..	..	..	..	59.9	66
Myanmar	..	5.8	..	7.0	..	28.5	18.1	85.4	33
Namibia	..	..	50.1	..	259.5	..	21.0	36.0	32
Nepal	..	12.5	8.1	11.8	90.8	82.3	13.9	51.8	40
Netherlands	12.1	..	21.7	..	54.1	..	10.4	..	10
New Zealand	17.1	19.6	15.0	21.9	67.8	25.1	..	..	15
Nicaragua	10.0	..	9.7	..	..	..	13.0	72.9	37
Niger	..	16.8	105.4	56.7	..	304.5	..	72.7	41
Nigeria	..	..	..	..	..	..	..	..	40
Norway	..	26.8	17.2	17.1	27.7	40.9	16.2	..	..
Oman	..	12.6	17.2	20.8	56.3	50.2	..	99.8	23
Pakistan	..	..	14.7	..	155.1	..	7.8	..	44
Panama	..	10.5	12.9	13.8	43.5	41.2	7.3	75.7	24
Papua New Guinea	..	12.4	..	19.2	..	..	..	100.0	36
Paraguay	3.1	12.9	6.7	15.4	38.0	47.1	9.7	..	..
Peru	..	..	..	..	..	..	21.1	78.2	29
Philippines	..	11.8	..	9.4	..	13.9	..	..	35
Poland	..	28.8	..	11.8	..	16.1	12.2	..	11
Portugal	15.4	..	18.0	..	32.5	..	12.8	..	13
Puerto Rico	..	..	..	..	..	..	..	..	..

	Public expenditure per student [a]						Public expenditure on education	Trained teachers in primary education	Primary pupil-teacher ratio
	% of GDP per capita						% of total government expenditure	% of total	pupils per teacher
	Primary		Secondary		Tertiary				
	1990/91	2001/02 [b]	1990/91	2001/02 [b]	1990/91	2001/02 [b]	2001/02 [b]	2001/02 [b]	2001/02 [b]
Romania	23.2	..	5.0	..	32.3	..	..	..	20
Russian Federation	..	..	..	..	..	9.6	10.6	..	17
Rwanda	..	6.9	..	22.0	..	575.0	..	81.2	51
Saudi Arabia	..	..	..	..	133.2	..	..	93.3	12
Senegal	17.3	13.8	..	..	..	..	..	100.0	49
Serbia and Montenegro	..	..	..	..	..	..	..	100.0	20
Sierra Leone	..	..	..	..	..	..	..	60.7	31
Singapore	..	..	13.6	..	43.4	..	..	..	..
Slovak Republic	22.8	11.4	7.9	16.8	63.7	27.9	13.8	..	19
Slovenia	17.5	..	15.4	..	38.7	..	..	..	13
Somalia	..	..	..	..	..	..	..	..	..
South Africa	..	14.3	..	18.3	90.9	56.8	18.1	67.6	37
Spain	11.8	..	13.6	..	18.0	..	11.3	..	14
Sri Lanka	..	10.0	..	..	78.6	..	..	..	..
Sudan	..	..	..	..	..	..	..	..	..
Swaziland	7.0	10.4	..	29.7	305.1	253.2	..	90.4	32
Sweden	46.5	24.3	18.8	27.8	38.6	52.0	13.6	..	11
Switzerland	34.9	22.8	13.5	27.8	43.7	53.2	15.2	..	14
Syrian Arab Republic	..	12.8	15.0	23.1	46.6	..	..	..	24
Tajikistan	..	..	..	..	..	..	..	81.6	22
Tanzania	..	..	..	..	..	..	..	..	47
Thailand	13.3	15.9	15.9	13.0	..	31.1	28.3	..	19
Togo	8.3	11.0	36.4	26.0	572.8	297.7	23.2	80.5	35
Trinidad and Tobago	4.5	14.2	15.5	20.1	67.4	68.5	13.4	78.1	19
Tunisia	..	15.8	27.6	25.7	115.5	68.0	17.4	94.1	22
Turkey	..	11.6	8.4	13.8	..	48.5	..	..	..
Turkmenistan	..	..	..	..	..	..	..	..	..
Uganda	..	..	..	..	..	..	..	..	59
Ukraine	20.9	..	9.5	16.9	19.5	35.3	15.0	99.7	19
United Arab Emirates	..	..	..	..	..	..	..	..	15
United Kingdom	15.1	13.6	26.5	14.5	40.9	25.7	11.4	..	18
United States	20.2	18.0	22.1	22.5	20.2	23.0	15.5	..	15
Uruguay	..	7.2	8.6	8.3	24.0	24.6	10.0	..	21
Uzbekistan	..	..	..	..	..	..	..	..	..
Venezuela, RB	2.4	..	7.8	..	36.3	..	..	..	..
Vietnam	..	..	..	..	..	..	..	87.0	26
West Bank and Gaza	..	..	..	..	..	..	..	..	..
Yemen, Rep.	..	..	..	..	..	..	32.8	..	..
Zambia	5.6	..	..	..	..	..	..	100.0	45
Zimbabwe	20.1	16.2	34.0	24.2	195.9	..	..	95.3	38
World	.. m	.. m	.. m	.. m	.. m	.. m	.. m	86.2 m	28 m
Low income	..	..	..	..	..	..	..	76.1	40
Middle income	..	..	..	..	..	..	..	90.4	22
Lower middle income	..	..	..	..	..	..	..	93.0	22
Upper middle income	..	12.4	16.9	..	61.8	30.6	13.7	77.7	21
Low & middle income	..	..	..	..	..	..	..	84.9	30
East Asia & Pacific	..	5.7	..	10.4	..	..	..	93.5	22
Europe & Central Asia	..	..	..	..	49.9	..	..	..	17
Latin America & Carib.	..	13.1	9.9	..	..	44.9	13.2	76.7	26
Middle East & N. Africa	..	..	..	..	76.0	..	..	96.8	24
South Asia	..	8.7	14.7	10.4	90.8	60.4	13.0	66.9	42
Sub-Saharan Africa	..	..	..	..	..	..	..	80.4	45
High income	40.2	26.2	31.0	..	47.1	66.5	11.5	..	17
Europe EMU								..	14

a. Break in series between 1997 and 1998 due to change from International Standard Classification of Education 1976 (ISCED76) to ISCED97. For information on ISCED, see *About the data.*
b. Data are preliminary. c. Data are for 2002/03.

About the data

Data on education are compiled by the UNESCO Institute for Statistics from official responses to surveys and from reports provided by education authorities in each country. Such data are used for monitoring, policymaking, and resource allocation. For a variety of reasons, however, education statistics generally fail to provide a complete and accurate picture of a country's education system. Statistics often lag by two to three years, though an effort is being made to shorten the delay. Moreover, coverage and data collection methods vary across countries and over time within countries, so the results of comparisons should be interpreted with caution.

The data on education spending in the table refer solely to public spending—government spending on public education plus subsidies for private education. The data generally exclude foreign aid for education. They may also exclude spending by religious schools, which play a significant role in many developing countries. Data for some countries and for some years refer to spending by the ministry of education only (excluding education expenditures by other ministries and departments and local authorities).

Many developing countries have sought to supplement public funds for education. Some countries have adopted tuition fees to recover part of the cost of providing education services or to encourage development of private schools. Charging fees raises difficult questions relating to equity, efficiency, access, and taxation, however, and some governments have used scholarships, vouchers, and other methods of public finance to counter criticism. Data for a few countries include private spending, although national

practices vary with respect to whether parents or schools pay for books, uniforms, and other supplies. For greater detail, see the country- and indicator-specific notes in the source.

The share of public expenditure devoted to education allows an assessment of the priority a government assigns to education relative to other public investments. It also reflects a government's commitment to investing in human capital development.

The share of trained teachers in primary schools measures the quality of the teaching staff. It does not take account of competencies acquired by teachers through their professional experience or self-instruction, or of such factors as work experience, teaching methods and materials, or classroom conditions, all of which may affect the quality of teaching. Since the training teachers receive varies greatly, care should be taken in comparing across countries.

The comparability of pupil-teacher ratios across countries is affected by the definition of teachers and by differences in class size by grade and in the number of hours taught. Moreover, the underlying enrollment levels are subject to a variety of reporting errors (for further discussion of enrollment data, see *About the data* for table 2.11). While the pupil-teacher ratio is often used to compare the quality of schooling across countries, it is often weakly related to the value added of schooling systems (Behrman and Rosenzweig 1994).

Data for education are reported for school years. For two decades the International Standard Classification of Education, 1976 (ISCED76), was used to assemble, compile, and present education

statistics. In 1998 UNESCO introduced ISCED97 and adjusted its data collection program and country reporting of education statistics to this new classification. The adjustments were made to ease the international compilation and comparison of education statistics and to take into account new types of learning opportunities and activities for both children and adults. Thus the time-series data for the years through 1997 are not consistent with those for 1998 and later. Any time-series analysis should therefore be undertaken with extreme caution.

Definitions

• **Public expenditure per student** is public current spending on education divided by the number of students by level, as a percentage of gross domestic product (GDP) per capita. • **Public expenditure on education** is current and capital public expenditure on education expressed as a percentage of total government expenditure. • **Trained teachers in primary education** are the percentage of primary school teachers who have received the minimum organized teacher training (preservice or in service) required for teaching. • **Primary pupil-teacher ratio** is the number of pupils enrolled in primary school divided by the number of primary school teachers (regardless of their teaching assignment).

2.10a

Education suffers in primary schools with high teacher absence rates

Teacher absence rate, 2000–03 (%)

The primary school teacher absence rate is the percentage of full-time teachers who were absent from a random sample of primary schools during a surprise visit, regardless of the reasons for their absence. Many teachers were absent for valid reasons, but even authorized absences reduce the quantity and quality of primary education.

Source: Chaudhury and others 2004; NRI and World Bank 2003; Habyarimana and others 2003.

Data sources

The data are from the UNESCO Institute for Statistics, which compiles international data on education in cooperation with national commissions and national statistical services.

	Gross enrollment ratio [a]							Net enrollment ratio [a]			
	% of relevant age group							% of relevant age group			
	Preprimary	Primary		Secondary		Tertiary		Primary		Secondary	
	2001/02 [b]	1990/91	2001/02 [b]	1990/91	2001/02 [b]	1990/91	2001/02 [b]	1990/91	2001/02 [b]	1990/91	2001/02 [b]
Afghanistan	..	27	23	9	12	2	..	..	..	..	..
Albania	44	100	107	78	78	7	15	..	97	..	74
Algeria	4	100	108	61	72	11	..	93	95	54	62
Angola	..	92	..	12	19	1	1	..	..	..	..
Argentina	61	106	120	71	100	39	57	..	100	..	81
Armenia	30	104	96	93	87	20	26	..	85	..	85
Australia	104	108	102	82	154	35	65	99	96	79	88
Austria	82	102	103	104	99	35	57	90	91	91	88
Azerbaijan	23	114	93	90	80	24	23	..	80	..	76
Bangladesh	19	72	98	19	47	4	6	64	87	18	44
Belarus	99	95	110	93	84	48	62	..	94	..	78
Belgium	112	101	105	103	154	40	58 d	97	100	88	..
Benin	6	58	104	12	26	3	4	49	71	..	20
Bolivia	47	95	114	37	84	21	39	91	94	29	67
Bosnia and Herzegovina	..	70	..	65	..	15	..	..	..	..	..
Botswana	..	113	103	43	73	3	5	93	81	34	55
Brazil	67	106	148	38	108	11	18	86	97	15	72
Bulgaria	70	98	99	75	94	31	40	86	90	63	87
Burkina Faso	1	33	48 c	7	10	1	..	27	35	7	8
Burundi	1	73	71	6	11	1	2	52	53	5	8
Cambodia	7	121	123	32	22	1	3	..	86	..	21
Cameroon	14	101	107	28	33	3	5	..	..	..	..
Canada	65	103	100	101	106	95	59	97	100	89	98
Central African Republic	..	65	66	12	..	2	2	53	..	..	..
Chad	..	54	73	8	12	1	1	..	58	..	8
Chile	77	100	103	73	85	21	37	88	89	55	75
China	27	125	114	49	68	3	13	97	93	..	..
Hong Kong, China	..	102	..	80	..	19	..	..	..	..	..
Colombia	37	102	110	50	65	13	24	69	87	34	54
Congo, Dem. Rep.	1	70	..	22	..	2	..	54	..	15	..
Congo, Rep.	4	133	86	53	32	5	4	..	..	..	..
Costa Rica	115	101	108	42	67	27	21	86	91	36	51
Côte d'Ivoire	3	67	80	22	23	3	..	47	63	..	..
Croatia	38	85	96	76	88	24	36	79	88	63	86
Cuba	111	98	100	89	89	21	27	92	96	69	83
Czech Republic	92	96	104	91	95	16	30	..	90	..	88
Denmark	90	98	102	109	128	36	59	98	99	87	89
Dominican Republic	35	97	126	40	67	20	..	..	97	..	41
Ecuador	73	116	117	55	59	20	..	..	99	..	50
Egypt, Arab Rep.	12	94	97	76	85	16	..	..	90	..	78
El Salvador	46	81	112	26	56	16	17	75	89	..	46
Eritrea	5	46	61	15	28	..	2	24	43	..	21
Estonia	102	111	103	102	110	26	59	94	98	82	92
Ethiopia	2 c	33	62 c	14	17 c	1	2	..	46	..	15
Finland	54	99	102	116	126	49	85 d	99	100	93	95
France	114	108	105	99	108	40	54	100	100	86	92
Gabon	13	..	134	..	51	..	..	..	78	..	..
Gambia, The	20	64	79	19	34	..	..	51	73	18	28
Georgia	41	97	92	95	79	37	36	..	91	..	..
Germany	101	101	103	98	99	34	..	84	86	89	88
Ghana	41	75	81	36	38	1	3	..	60	..	30
Greece	70	98	97	93	96	36	61	94	95	83	85
Guatemala	55	78	103	23	33	8	..	..	85	..	28
Guinea	..	37	77	10	..	1	..	..	61	..	..
Guinea-Bissau	3	56	70	9	18	1	0 d	..	45	..	..
Haiti	..	74	..	21	..	1	..	22	..	..	..

	Gross enrollment ratio [a]							Net enrollment ratio [a]			
				% of relevant age group					% of relevant age group		
	Preprimary	Primary		Secondary		Tertiary		Primary		Secondary	
	2001/02 [b]	1990/91	2001/02 [b]	1990/91	2001/02 [b]	1990/91	2001/02 [b]	1990/91	2001/02 [b]	1990/91	2001/02 [b]
Honduras	21	109	106	33	..	9	14	89	87	21	..
Hungary	79	95	102	79	98	14	40	91	90	75	87
India	26	97	99	44	48	6	11	..	83	..	..
Indonesia	20	115	111	44	58	9	15	97	92	38	47
Iran, Islamic Rep.	23	112	92	55	81	10	19	97	87	..	..
Iraq	5	111	99	47	38	13	14	79	91	37	33
Ireland	3	103	119	101	..	29	47	91	90	80	..
Israel	112	95	114	85	93	34	53	..	100	..	88
Italy	96	103	101	83	96	32	50	..	100	..	88
Jamaica	87	101	101	65	84	7	17	96	95	64	75
Japan	84	100	101	97	102	30	48	100	100	97	100
Jordan	31	71	99	45	86	16	31	66	91	33	80
Kazakhstan	13	87	99	98	89	40	39	..	90	..	84
Kenya	44	95	96	24	32	2	4	..	70	..	24
Korea, Dem. Rep.	..	..	..	..	..	..	..	..	..	..	..
Korea, Rep.	79	105	100	90	94	39	82	100	99	86	91
Kuwait	73	60	94	43	85	12	..	45	85	45	77
Kyrgyz Republic	14	111	102	100	85	14	44	..	82	..	..
Lao PDR	8	105	115	25	41	1	4	61	83	15	31
Latvia	57	94	99	93	93	25	64	83	91	..	89
Lebanon	74	120	103	73	77	29	45	..	90	..	..
Lesotho	21	112	124	25	34	1	2	73	84	15	22
Liberia	56	29	105	14	..	3	..	..	70	..	..
Libya	8	105	114	86	105	15	58	96	..	..	..
Lithuania	53	91	104	92	98	34	59	..	97	..	92
Macedonia, FYR	29	99	99	56	85	17	24	94	93	..	82
Madagascar	3	103	104	18	..	3	2	..	69	..	..
Malawi	..	68	..	8	..	1	..	50	..	..	..
Malaysia	89	94	95	56	70	7	26	..	95	..	69
Mali	2	26	57	7	..	1	2	21	..	5	..
Mauritania	..	49	86	14	22	3	3	..	67	..	15
Mauritius	87	109	106	53	80	4	11	95	93	..	62
Mexico	75	114	110	53	73	15	20	100	99	45	58
Moldova	39	93	85	80	72	36	29	..	78	..	68
Mongolia	32	97	99	82	76	14	35	..	87	..	71
Morocco	60	67	107	35	41	11	10	58	88	..	31
Mozambique	..	67	99	8	13	0 [d]	1	47	60	7	11
Myanmar	2	106	90	23	39	4	11	..	82	..	35
Namibia	23	129	106	44	61	3	7	89	78	31	38
Nepal	13	108	122	33	44	5	5	..	70	..	..
Netherlands	96	102	108	120	124	40	55	95	99	84	90
New Zealand	87	106	99	89	113	40	72	100	98	85	92
Nicaragua	26	94	105	40	57	8	..	72	82	..	37
Niger	1	29	40	7	6	1	1	25	34	6	5
Nigeria	..	91	96	25	..	4	..	..	..	..	..
Norway	79	100	101	103	115	42	70	100	100	88	95
Oman	5	86	83	46	79	4	7	70	75	49	68
Pakistan	55	61	73	23	..	3	..	..	67	..	..
Panama	51	106	110	63	69	21	34	91	99	51	62
Papua New Guinea	39	72	77	12	23	3	..	..	77	..	23
Paraguay	30	105	112	31	64	8	18	93	92	26	50
Peru	60	118	121	67	..	30	..	..	100	..	..
Philippines	33	111	112	73	82	28	30	97	93	57	56
Poland	49	98	100	81	101	22	55	97	98	76	91
Portugal	70	123	121	67	114	23	50	100	..	70	85
Puerto Rico	..	121	..	61	..	45	..	..	..	..	..

2.11 | Participation in education

	Gross enrollment ratio [a]						Net enrollment ratio [a]			
	% of relevant age group						% of relevant age group			
	Preprimary	Primary		Secondary		Tertiary		Primary		Secondary	
	2001/02 [b]	1990/91	2001/02 [b]	1990/91	2001/02 [b]	1990/91	2001/02 [b]	1990/91	2001/02 [b]	1990/91	2001/02 [b]
Romania	73	91	99	92	82	10	27	77	93	..	80
Russian Federation	92	109	114	93	92	52	68	..	..	..	..
Rwanda	3	70	117	8	14	1	2	66	96	7	..
Saudi Arabia	5	73	67	44	69	12	22	59	59	31	53
Senegal	3 [c]	59	75	16	19	3	..	48	58	..	..
Serbia and Montenegro	44	72	99	63	89	18	36	69	75	62	..
Sierra Leone	4	50	76	17	..	1	2	..	..	..	..
Singapore	..	104	..	68	..	19	..	..	..	..	..
Slovak Republic	81	98	103	87	87	19	30	..	89	..	75
Slovenia	75	108	100	91	106	24	61	..	93	..	96
Somalia	..	11	..	6	..	3	..	..	..	..	..
South Africa	35	122	105	74	86	13	15	99	90	51	62
Spain	102	109	107	104	114	37	57	100	100	..	93
Sri Lanka	..	106	110	74	81	5	..	..	..	..	..
Sudan	20	53	59	24	32	3	..	..	46	..	..
Swaziland	..	111	100	44	45	4	5	88	77	33	32
Sweden	74	100	110	90	149	32	70	100	100	85	96
Switzerland	95	90	107	99	100	26	42	84	99	80	88
Syrian Arab Republic	10	108	112	52	45	18	..	95	98	46	39
Tajikistan	10	91	107	102	82	22	15	..	98	..	79
Tanzania	..	70	70	5	6	0 [d]	1	51	54	..	5
Thailand	86	99	98	30	83	17	37	..	86	..	..
Togo	3	109	124	24	36	3	4	75	92	18	27
Trinidad and Tobago	63	97	105	80	70	7	7	91	94	65	65
Tunisia	20	113	112	45	79	9	23	94	97	43	68
Turkey	7	99	94	47	76	13	25	89	88	41	..
Turkmenistan	..	91	..	107	..	22	..	..	..	..	..
Uganda	4	71	136	13	..	1	3	..	..	..	..
Ukraine	72	89	90	93	97	47	57	..	82	..	91
United Arab Emirates	71	104	92	67	79	9	..	94	81	59	72
United Kingdom	82	104	101	85	158	30	59	97	100	79	95
United States	58	102	100	93	94	75	71	96	94	86	87
Uruguay	63	109	108	81	101	30	38	91	90	..	72
Uzbekistan	21	81	103	99	99	30	9	..	..	..	..
Venezuela, RB	52	96	106	35	69	29	18	88	92	19	57
Vietnam	43	103	103	32	70	2	10	..	94	..	65
West Bank and Gaza	..	..	..	..	..	..	..	..	..	..	..
Yemen, Rep.	0 [d]	58	81	58	46	4	..	..	67	..	35
Zambia	..	99	79	24	..	2	2	..	66	..	..
Zimbabwe	39	116	99	50	43	5	4	..	83	..	40
World	**40 w**	**102 w**	**103 w**	**55 w**	**70 w**	**16 w**	**24 w**	**.. w**	**88 w**	**.. w**	**.. w**
Low income	24	88	94	35	46	5	10	..	80	..	..
Middle income	40	113	111	56	75	13	22	95	92	..	..
Lower middle income	36	115	112	55	75	12	20	95	91	..	..
Upper middle income	63	102	104	64	81	20	33	92	93	50	69
Low & middle income	33	102	103	47	63	10	17	..	86	..	..
East Asia & Pacific	29	121	111	47	66	5	14	97	92	..	..
Europe & Central Asia	58	98	103	85	89	34	48	..	..	..	..
Latin America & Carib.	60	106	129	49	89	17	23	89	94	29	65
Middle East & N. Africa	21	96	96	57	70	12	..	..	83	..	54
South Asia	28	90	95	39	48	5	10	..	82	..	..
Sub-Saharan Africa	..	74	87	23	..	3	..	..	..	..	..
High income	90	103	102	94	106	47	61	98	97	87	91
Europe EMU	98	105	104	97	106	35	54	93	99	87	90

a. Break in series between 1997 and 1998 due to change from ISCED76 to ISCED97. For information on ISCED, see *About the data* for table 2.10. b. Data are preliminary. c. Data are for 2002/03. d. Less than 0.5.

About the data

School enrollment data are reported to the UNESCO Institute for Statistics by national education authorities. Enrollment ratios help to monitor two important issues for universal primary education: whether the Millennium Development Goal that implies achieving a net primary enrollment ratio of 100 percent is on track, and whether an education system has sufficient capacity to meet the needs of universal primary education, as indicated in part by its gross enrollment ratios. The gross enrollment ratio shows the share of children in the population who are enrolled in school regardless of their age. Net enrollment ratios show the share of children of primary school age who are enrolled in school and thus also the share who are not.

Enrollment ratios, while a useful measure of participation in education, also have significant limitations. They are based on data collected during annual school surveys, which are typically conducted at the beginning of the school year. They do not reflect actual rates of attendance or dropouts during the school year. And school administrators may report exaggerated enrollments, especially if there is a financial incentive to do so. Often the number of teachers paid by the government is related to the number of pupils enrolled.

Overage or underage enrollments frequently occur, particularly when parents prefer, for cultural or economic reasons, to have children start school at other than the official age. Children's age at enrollment may be inaccurately estimated or misstated, especially in communities where registration of births is not strictly enforced. Parents who want to enroll their underage children in primary school may do so by overstating the age of the children. And in some education systems ages for children repeating a grade may be deliberately or inadvertently underreported. As an international indicator, the gross primary enrollment ratio has been used to indicate broad levels of participation as well as school capacity. It has an inherent weakness: the length of primary education differs significantly across countries. A short duration tends to increase the ratio, and a long duration to decrease it (in part because there are more dropouts among older children).

Other problems affecting cross-country comparisons of enrollment data stem from errors in estimates of school-age populations. Age-gender structures from censuses or vital registration systems, the primary sources of data on school-age populations, are commonly subject to underenumeration (especially of young children) aimed at circumventing laws or regulations; errors are also introduced when parents round up children's ages. While census data are often adjusted for age bias, adjustments are rarely made for inadequate vital registration systems. Compounding these problems, pre- and post-census estimates of school-age children are interpolations or projections based on models that may miss important demographic events (see the discussion of demographic data in *About the data* for table 2.1).

In using enrollment data, it is also important to consider repetition rates. These rates are quite high in some developing countries, leading to a substantial number of overage children enrolled in each grade and raising the gross enrollment ratio. A common error that may also distort enrollment ratios is the lack of distinction between new entrants and repeaters, which, other things equal, leads to underreporting of repeaters and overestimation of dropouts.

Thus gross enrollment ratios indicate the capacity of each level of the education system, but a high ratio does not necessarily mean a successful education system. The net enrollment ratio excludes overage students in an attempt to capture more accurately the system's coverage and internal efficiency. It does not solve the problem completely, however, because some children fall outside the official school age because of late or early entry rather than because of grade repetition. The difference between gross and net enrollment ratios shows the incidence of overage and underage enrollments.

Definitions

• **Gross enrollment ratio** is the ratio of total enrollment, regardless of age, to the population of the age group that officially corresponds to the level of education shown. • **Net enrollment ratio** is the ratio of children of official school age (as defined by the national education system) who are enrolled in school to the population of the corresponding official school age. Based on the International Standard Classification of Education 1997 (ISCED97). • **Preprimary education** refers to the initial stage of organized instruction, designed primarily to introduce very young children to a school-type environment. • **Primary education** provides children with basic reading, writing, and mathematics skills along with an elementary understanding of such subjects as history, geography, natural science, social science, art, and music. • **Secondary education** completes the provision of basic education that began at the primary level and aims at laying the foundations for life-long learning and human development by offering more subject- or skill-oriented instruction using more specialized teachers. • **Tertiary education,** whether or not leading to an advanced research qualification, normally requires, as a minimum condition of admission, the successful completion of education at the secondary level.

2.11a

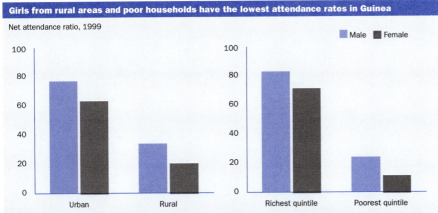

Girls from rural areas and poor households have the lowest attendance rates in Guinea

Net attendance ratio, 1999

■ Male ■ Female

Household surveys can provide data on attendance at school that cannot usually be derived from administrative data. In Guinea more children attend school in urban areas than in rural areas, and more than four times as many rich children attend school as poor children. Regardless of location and wealth, more boys than girls attend school.

Source: *Global Education Report 2003*, UNESCO Institute for Statistics 2003.

Data source

The data are from the UNESCO Institute for Statistics.

	Apparent intake rate in grade 1		Share of cohort reaching grade 5				Primary completion rate			Repeaters in primary school		
	% of relevant age group		% of grade 1 students				% of relevant age group			% of enrollment		
	Male	Female	Male		Female		Total	Male	Female	Total	Male	Female
	2001/02[a]	2001/02[a]	1990/91	2000/01[a]	1990/91	2000/01[a]	2000/01–2002/03[a,b]	2000/01–2002/03[a,b]	2000/01–2002/03[a,b]	2001/02[a]	2001/02[a]	2001/02[a]
Afghanistan	..	..	..	..	..	..	..	..	..	..	..	..
Albania	103	101	..	..	..	..	100	101	99	4.1	4.6	3.4
Algeria	102	100	95	95	93	97	96	96	95	11.7	14.2	9.0
Angola	..	..					..	..	..	29.0	29.0	29.0
Argentina	112	112	..	91	..	95	100	98	102	6.2	7.3	5.0
Armenia	97	95	..	..	..	..	74	74	74	0.1	0.1	0.1
Australia	..	..	..	..	..	..	..	..	..	..	..	..
Austria	108	105	..	..	..	..	..	..	..	..	..	..
Azerbaijan	91	88	..	..	..	..	100	101	99	0.3	0.3	0.3
Bangladesh	106	108	..	63	..	68	77	76	78	6.3	6.7	6.0
Belarus	..	..	..	..	..	..	131	..	..	0.3	0.6	0.6
Belgium	..	..	..	..	..	..	..	..	..	..	..	..
Benin	127	96	55	89	56	78	45	58	32	20.1	20.1	20.1
Bolivia	119	121	..	79	..	77	89	91	87	2.7	2.9	2.5
Bosnia and Herzegovina	..	..	..	..	..	..	77			..	..	..
Botswana	114	110	94	87	98	92	91	87	95	3.2	4.0	2.5
Brazil	130	119	..	..	..	..	82	..	..	21.5	25.0	25.0
Bulgaria	98	98	91	..	90	..	94	95	92	2.4	2.8	2.0
Burkina Faso	53	39	71	68	68	71	29	34	24	14.0[c]	17.5	17.7
Burundi	92	73	65	68	58	59	27	30	24	26.3	25.6	27.2
Cambodia	174	161	..	71	..	70	71	75	66	9.6	10.2	8.9
Cameroon	115	99	..	63	..	60	57	58	56	25.2	25.9	24.4
Canada	..	..	..	..	..	..	..	..	..	..	..	..
Central African Republic	76	53	25	..	22	..	..	..	..	..	..	..
Chad	94	70	58	58	43	48	22	31	13	25.5	25.3	25.9
Chile	97	96	..	101	..	101	96	95	97	2.0	2.4	1.6
China	..	..	..	..	..	..	102	..	..	0.6	..	..
Hong Kong, China	..	..	..	..	..	..	..	..	..	..	..	..
Colombia	130	125	71	59	50	63	90	87	92	6.6	7.3	5.9
Congo, Dem. Rep.	..	..	58	..	50	..	..	..	..	..	..	..
Congo, Rep.	67	61	58	..	67	..	58	59	56	24.8	25.1	24.4
Costa Rica	101	101	81	93	84	95	90	89	92	8.2	9.5	6.9
Côte d'Ivoire	82	62	75	73	70	65	48	57	38	23.3	23.1	23.6
Croatia	97	98					90	90	89	0.4	0.5	0.3
Cuba	95	96	..	95	..	96	100	101	99	1.2	1.7	0.6
Czech Republic	102	101	..	98	..	99	..	..	..	1.1	1.3	0.9
Denmark	100	100	94	..	94	..	..	..	..	..	..	..
Dominican Republic	148	137	..	71	..	79	95	91	100	5.9	7.1	4.6
Ecuador	139	138	40	77	41	79	99	99	99	2.0	2.3	1.8
Egypt, Arab Rep.	95	92	..	99	..	99	91	92	89	5.2	6.4	3.9
El Salvador	135	128	56	67	60	73	86	86	86	6.5	7.3	5.6
Eritrea	70	59	85	89	80	74	33	38	29	17.5	17.1	17.9
Estonia	98	94	92	100	94	99	103	108	98	2.3	3.2	1.3
Ethiopia	96	74	61	63	54	59	18	..	..	9.9[c]	8.6[c]	11.7[c]
Finland	98	98	100	99	100	101	..	..	..	0.5	0.7	0.3
France	..	..	..	98	..	97	..	..	..	4.2	4.2	4.2
Gabon	97	97	..	102	..	102	92	92	92	34.4	35.1	33.7
Gambia, The	88	88	85	75	89	63	69	77	60	10.6	10.7	10.5
Georgia	93	92					92	92	91	0.3	0.5	0.2
Germany	100	99	..	..	..	..	..	..	..	1.8	2.0	1.6
Ghana	86	84	81	67	79	65	59	61	57	5.2	5.3	5.0
Greece	..	..	99	..	100	..	..	..	..	..	..	..
Guatemala	126	123	..	57	..	54	59	63	55	14.2	14.8	13.5
Guinea	77	67	64	90	48	77	..	..	..	20.8	19.7	22.4
Guinea-Bissau	106	79	..	41	..	34	..	..	..	24.0	23.6	24.5
Haiti	..	..	..	..	..	..	..	..	..	..	..	..

	Apparent intake rate in grade 1		Share of cohort reaching grade 5				Primary completion rate			Repeaters in primary school		
	% of relevant age group		% of grade 1 students				% of relevant age group			% of enrollment		
			Male		Female		Total	Male	Female			
	Male	Female					2000/01–	2000/01 –	2000/01 –	Total	Male	Female
	2001/02[a]	2001/02[a]	1990/91	2000/01[a]	1990/91	2000/01[a]	2002/03[a,b]	2002/03[a,b]	2002/03[a,b]	2001/02[a]	2001/02[a]	2001/02[a]
Honduras	138	138	..	..	..	..	70	69	70	..	..	..
Hungary	99	97	..	..	..	..	..	..	..	2.5	3.0	2.0
India	136	114	..	59	..	59	77	85	69	3.7	3.7	3.7
Indonesia	119	113	..	87	..	92	107	106	108	5.3	5.5	5.1
Iran, Islamic Rep.	86	86	91	94	89	94	123	125	120	4.3	5.2	3.3
Iraq	118	104	..	..	..	..	..	..	..	12.3	14.1	10.0
Ireland	101	100	100	98	100	99	..	..	..	1.6	1.7	1.4
Israel	..	..	..	..	..	..	..	..	..	..	..	..
Italy	96	95	100	95	100	98	..	..	..	0.3	0.4	0.2
Jamaica	99	99	..	88	..	93	90	88	92	3.5	4.3	2.6
Japan	..	..	100	..	100	..	..	..	..	..	..	..
Jordan	103	103	100	98	100	97	98	97	99	0.5	0.5	0.5
Kazakhstan	107	106	..	..	..	..	99	99	99	0.2	0.2	0.1
Kenya	105	101	..	..	..	..	56	54	58	..	..	..
Korea, Dem. Rep.	..	..	..	..	..	..	..	..	..	..	..	..
Korea, Rep.	102	100	99	100	100	100	..	..	..	..	..	..
Kuwait	96	95	..	..	..	..	..	..	..	2.8	2.9	2.7
Kyrgyz Republic	111	108	..	..	..	..	94	96	92	0.2	0.2	0.1
Lao PDR	133	117	56	62	50	63	73	78	69	20.0	21.2	18.5
Latvia	94	93	..	..	..	..	90	..	..	2.0	2.7	1.2
Lebanon	98	96	..	92	..	96	68	65	71	8.7	10.1	7.2
Lesotho	158	139	58	60	83	74	65	55	75	19.7	22.1	17.3
Liberia	204	174	..	44	..	21	..	..	..	2.7	2.4	3.0
Libya	..	..	..	..	..	..	..	..	..	..	..	..
Lithuania	102	100	..	..	..	..	106	106	106	0.7	0.9	0.5
Macedonia, FYR	98	98	..	..	..	..	95	96	95	0.1	0.1	0.1
Madagascar	119	116	22	33	21	34	41	40	41	29.0[c]	31.5	29.4
Malawi	..	..	71	..	57	..	55	62	48	..	..	..
Malaysia	93	93	98	96	98	96	..	..	..	..	..	..
Mali	65	54	73	88	70	79	39	48	31	19.3	19.0	19.7
Mauritania	114	110	75	54	75	56	46	48	43	14.1	13.8	14.4
Mauritius	90	93	98	99	98	99	108	108	107	4.3	4.9	3.7
Mexico	110	110	81	88	82	89	96	96	97	5.5	6.5	4.4
Moldova	95	92	..	..	..	..	80	80	80	..	..	..
Mongolia	100	103	..	..	..	..	107	106	109	0.6	0.7	0.6
Morocco	119	115	75	84	76	83	68	72	64	12.6	14.1	10.8
Mozambique	126	112	37	56	28	47	22	27	17	22.9	22.5	23.4
Myanmar	116	117	..	59	..	61	71	71	71	0.7	0.7	0.7
Namibia	96	98	61	94	65	94	95	91	100	13.0	14.7	11.3
Nepal	128	117	52	57	52	69	73	78	67	21.6	21.8	21.4
Netherlands	99	98	..	..	..	..	..	..	..	..	..	..
New Zealand	99	98	90	..	91	..	..	..	..	..	..	..
Nicaragua	142	134	51	51	57	58	75	71	79	6.7	7.7	5.7
Niger	67	48	61	73	65	68	21	25	17	8.6	8.5	8.7
Nigeria	..	..	..	..	..	..	..	..	..	..	..	..
Norway	..	..	100	..	100	..	..	..	..	..	..	..
Oman	74	74	95	96	96	96	72	75	69	4.3	5.2	3.3
Pakistan	107	80	..	..	..	..	..	..	..	..	..	..
Panama	120	117	..	88	..	89	86	85	87	5.6	6.6	4.6
Papua New Guinea	102	90	60	61	58	58	59	63	55	..	..	..
Paraguay	114	112	69	76	72	78	89	88	90	8.0	9.2	6.7
Peru	115	116	..	88	..	87	98	98	99	10.7	10.9	10.4
Philippines	137	127	..	76	..	83	90	87	94	2.3	2.9	1.6
Poland	98	97	..	99	..	99	95	94	95	0.6	1.0	0.2
Portugal	..	..	..	..	..	..	..	..	..	..	..	..
Puerto Rico	..	..	..	..	..	..	..	..	..	..	..	..

2.12 Education efficiency

	Apparent intake rate in grade 1		Share of cohort reaching grade 5				Primary completion rate			Repeaters in primary school		
	% of relevant age group		% of grade 1 students				% of relevant age group			% of enrollment		
	Male	Female	Male		Female		Total	Male	Female	Total	Male	Female
	2001/02 [a]	2001/02 [a]	1990/91	2000/01 [a]	1990/91	2000/01 [a]	2000/01– 2002/03 [a,b]	2000/01– 2002/03 [a,b]	2000/01– 2002/03 [a,b]	2001/02 [a]	2001/02 [a]	2001/02 [a]
Romania	102	102	..	..	..	..	94	95	94	3.2	3.8	2.5
Russian Federation	..	..	..	..	..	..	99	..	..	0.9	..	..
Rwanda	132	133	61	39	59	41	25	25	24	36.1	36.0	36.2
Saudi Arabia	68	67	82	94	84	94	66	66	66	5.2	6.3	3.9
Senegal	87	86	..	70	..	65	49	53	44	13.6	13.7	13.6
Serbia and Montenegro	98	99	..	..	..	..	..	..	..	1.0	1.0	1.0
Sierra Leone	..	..	..	..	..	..	..	..	..	..	..	..
Singapore	..	..	..	..	..	..	..	..	..	..	..	..
Slovak Republic	100	100	..	..	..	..	..	..	..	2.4	2.6	2.1
Slovenia	106	106	..	..	..	..	96	99	93	0.8	0.9	0.6
Somalia	..	..	..	..	..	..	..	..	..	..	..	..
South Africa	117	116	72	..	79	..	90	89	91	8.8	10.2	7.3
Spain	..	..	100	..	100	..	..	..	..	..	..	..
Sri Lanka	..	..	94	..	95	..	108	113	103	0.8	..	..
Sudan	58	48	90	..	95	..	..	..	..	11.3	10.9	11.8
Swaziland	100	96	74	69	78	79	74	77	72	16.7	18.9	14.3
Sweden	..	..	100	..	100	..	..	..	..	..	..	..
Switzerland	92	96	76	101	75	101	..	..	..	1.7	1.8	1.5
Syrian Arab Republic	124	121	94	93	94	92	89	93	85	6.8	7.7	5.7
Tajikistan	117	112	..	..	..	..	101	104	98	0.4	0.3	0.4
Tanzania	107	100	77	79	81	83	58	57	59	2.5	2.5	2.5
Thailand	99	92	..	92	..	96	91	92	90	3.9	4.0	3.7
Togo	117	104	55	88	44	80	84	100	67	22.5	21.9	23.2
Trinidad and Tobago	100	96	96	98	96	101	108	107	110	8.0	8.4	7.5
Tunisia	98	99	92	95	78	96	98	99	98	9.8	11.5	8.0
Turkey	..	..	98	..	97	..	95	105	85	..	..	..
Turkmenistan	..	..	..	..	..	..	..	..	..	..	..	..
Uganda	..	..	..	..	..	..	67	73	62	..	..	..
Ukraine	119	118	..	..	..	..	98	98	97	0.2	0.2	0.2
United Arab Emirates	100	98	80	97	80	98	..	..	..	2.8	3.2	2.4
United Kingdom	..	..	..	..	..	..	..	..	..	..	..	..
United States	..	..	..	..	..	..	..	..	..	..	..	..
Uruguay	104	104	93	87	96	90	95	93	97	9.0	10.5	7.4
Uzbekistan	104	104	..	..	..	..	98	98	98	..	..	..
Venezuela, RB	107	104	83	82	90	88	58	51	65	7.7	9.3	5.9
Vietnam	103	97	..	90	..	88	104	106	101	2.4	2.8	1.9
West Bank and Gaza	..	..	..	..	..	..	66	61	72	..	..	..
Yemen, Rep.	104	79	..	80	..	98	68	90	45	9.0	11.1	5.5
Zambia	86	87	..	79	..	75	59	64	54	6.2	6.5	5.9
Zimbabwe	121	118	96	..	89	..	..	..	..	..	..	..
World	**116** w	**104** w	**..** w	**..** w	**..** w	**..** w	**..** w	**..** w	**..** w	**5.6** w	**..** w	**..** w
Low income	121	105	..	66	..	68	74	78	68	6.7	6.8	6.7
Middle income	98	98	..	..	..	..	98	98	97	4.8	..	..
Lower middle income	98	97	..	..	..	..	97	98	96	4.7	..	..
Upper middle income	101	101	..	90	..	92	89	88	90	5.2	6.2	4.2
Low & middle income	117	105	..	..	..	..	86	88	82	5.7	..	..
East Asia & Pacific	96	97	..	..	..	..	100	101	98	2.0	..	..
Europe & Central Asia	93	92	..	..	..	..	97	99	95	..	..	..
Latin America & Carib.	125	118	..	..	..	..	87	83	92	13.0	12.5	11.3
Middle East & N. Africa	96	95	..	93	..	95	91	94	87	7.8	9.3	6.1
South Asia	130	110	..	59	..	61	78	84	71	4.6	4.6	4.6
Sub-Saharan Africa	92	82	..	..	..	..	48 [d]	51 [d]	44 [d]	..	..	..
High income	..	..	..	..	..	..	..	..	..	..	..	..
Europe EMU	99	98	..	..	..	..	..	..	..	2.2	2.3	2.1

a. Data are preliminary. b. Data are for the most recent year available. c. Data are for 2002/03. d. Represent only 60% of the population.

About the data

Indicators of students' progress through school are estimated by the UNESCO Institute for Statistics and the World Bank. These indicators measure an education system's success in extending coverage to all students, maintaining the flow of students from one grade to the next, and, ultimately, imparting a particular level of education.

Apparent intake rate indicates the general level of access to primary education. It also indicates the capacity of the education system to provide access to primary education. Low apparent intake rates in grade 1 reflect the fact that many children do not enter primary school even though school attendance, at least through the primary level, is mandatory in all countries. Because the apparent intake rate includes all new entrants regardless of age, it can be more than 100 percent. Once enrolled, students drop out for a variety of reasons, including low quality of schooling, discouragement over poor performance, and the direct and indirect costs of schooling. Students' progress to higher grades may also be limited by the availability of teachers, classrooms, and educational materials.

The cohort survival rate is estimated as the proportion of an entering cohort of grade 1 students that eventually reaches grade 5. It measures the holding power and internal efficiency of an education system. Cohort survival rates approaching 100 percent indicate a high level of retention and a low level of dropout.

Cohort survival rates are typically estimated from data on enrollment and repetition by grade for two consecutive years, in a procedure called the reconstructed cohort method. This method makes three simplifying assumptions: dropouts never return to school; promotion, repetition, and dropout rates remain constant over the entire period in which the cohort is enrolled in school; and the same rates apply to all pupils enrolled in a given grade, regardless of whether they previously repeated a grade (Fredricksen 1993). Given these assumptions, cross-country comparisons should be made with caution, because other flows—caused by new entrants, reentrants, grade skipping, migration, or school transfers during the school year—are not considered.

The UNESCO Institute for Statistics measures cohort survival to grade 5 because research suggests that five to six years of schooling is a critical threshold for the achievement of sustainable basic literacy and numeracy skills. But the cohort survival rate only indirectly reflects the quality of schooling, and a high rate does not guarantee these learning outcomes. Measuring actual learning outcomes

requires setting curriculum standards and measuring students' learning progress against those standards through standardized assessments or tests.

The World Bank and the UNESCO Institute for Statistics are working jointly on development of the primary completion rate indicator. The primary completion rate is increasingly used as a core indicator of an education system's performance. It reflects both the coverage of the education system and the educational attainment of students. It is vital as a key measure of educational outcome at the primary level and of progress on the Millennium Development Goals and the Education for All initiative. However, because curricula and standards for school completion vary across countries, a high rate of primary completion does not necessarily mean high levels of student learning.

The primary completion rate reflects the primary cycle as nationally defined, ranging from three or four years of primary education (in a very small number of countries) to five or six years (in most countries) and seven or eight years (in a small number of countries).

The data shown in the table are for the proxy primary completion rate, calculated by subtracting the number of students who repeat the final primary grade from the number of students in that grade and dividing the result by the number of children of official graduation age in the population. Data limitations preclude adjusting this number for students who drop out during the final year of primary school. Thus proxy rates should be taken as an upper-bound estimate of the actual primary completion rate.

The numerator may include overage children who have repeated one or more grades of primary school but are now graduating successfully as well as children who entered school early. The denominator is the number of children of official graduation age, which could cause the primary completion rate to exceed 100 percent. There are other data limitations that contribute to completion rates exceeding 100 percent, such as the use of estimates for the population, the conduct of the school and population surveys at different times of year, and other discrepancies in the numbers used in the calculation.

Repeaters not only increase the cost of education for the family and for the school system, but also use up limited school resources. Countries have different policies on repetition and promotion of students; in some cases the number of repeaters is controlled because of limited capacity of the school system. Care should be taken in cross-country comparisons of this indicator.

Definitions

• **Apparent intake rate in grade 1** is the number of new entrants in the first grade of primary education regardless of age, expressed as a percentage of the population of the official primary school entrance age. • **Share of cohort reaching grade 5** is the percentage of children enrolled in the first grade of primary school who eventually reach grade 5. The estimate is based on the reconstructed cohort method (see *About the data*). • **Primary completion rate** is the percentage of students successfully completing the last year of primary school. It is calculated by taking the total number of students in the last grade of primary school, minus the number of repeaters in that grade, divided by the total number of children of official graduation age. • **Repeaters in primary school** refer to the total number of pupils who are enrolled in the same grade as in a previous year, expressed as a percentage of the total enrollment. It is calculated by taking the total number of students in the last grade of primary school, minus the number of repeaters in that grade, divided by the total number of children of official graduation age.

Data sources

The data on the apparent intake rate, the cohort reaching grade 5, and repeaters are from the UNESCO Institute for Statistics. The data on the primary completion rate are compiled by staff in the Development Data Group of the World Bank, in collaboration with the Education Anchor of the Human Development Network of the World Bank and the UNESCO Institute for Statistics.

	Adult literacy rate				Youth literacy rate				Expected years of schooling			
	% ages 15 and older				% ages 15–24							
	Male		Female		Male		Female		Male		Female	
	1990	2002[a]	1990	2002[a]	1990	2002[a]	1990	2002[a]	1990/91	2000/01	1990/91	2000/01
Afghanistan	..	..	..	..	..	..	..	..	..	..	..	..
Albania	87	99[b]	67	98[b]	97	99[b]	92	99[b]	..	11	..	11
Algeria	64	78	41	60	86	94	68	86	11	..	9	..
Angola	..	..	..	..	..	..	..	..	..	..	..	..
Argentina	96	97	96	97	98	98	98	99	..	14	..	15
Armenia	99	100[b]	96	99[b]	100	100[b]	99	100[b]	..	8	..	9
Australia	..	..	..	..	..	..	..	..	13	17	13	17
Austria	..	..	..	..	..	..	..	..	15	15	14	15
Azerbaijan	..	..	..	..	..	..	..	..	..	11	..	10
Bangladesh	44	50	24	31	51	58	33	41	6	8	4	8
Belarus	100	100	99	100	100	100	100	100	..	12	..	13
Belgium	..	..	..	..	..	..	..	..	14	16	14	16
Benin	38	55	15	26	57	73	25	38	..	9	..	5
Bolivia	87	93[b]	70	81[b]	96	99[b]	89	96[b]	..	..	..	..
Bosnia and Herzegovina	..	98	..	91	..	100	..	100	..	..	..	..
Botswana	66	76	70	82	79	85	87	93	10	12	11	12
Brazil	83	86[b]	81	87[b]	91	93[b]	93	96[b]	..	13	..	14
Bulgaria	98	99	96	98	100	100	99	100	12	13	12	13
Burkina Faso	25	19[b]	8	8[b]	36	26[b]	14	14[b]	3	..	2	..
Burundi	48	58	27	44	58	67	45	65	6	..	4	..
Cambodia	78	81	49	59	81	85	66	76	..	8	..	7
Cameroon	69	77[c]	48	60[c]	86	..	76	..	..	..	..	..
Canada	..	..	..	..	..	..	..	..	17	14	17	15
Central African Republic	47	65[c]	21	33[c]	66	70[c]	39	47[c]	..	..	..	..
Chad	37	55	19	38	58	76	38	64	..	7	..	4
Chile	94	96[b]	94	96[b]	98	99[b]	98	99[b]	..	14	..	13
China	87	95[b]	69	87[b]	97	99[b]	93	99[b]	..	..	..	..
Hong Kong, China	..	..	..	..	..	..	..	..	..	..	..	..
Colombia	89	92	88	92	94	97	96	98	..	11	..	11
Congo, Dem. Rep.	..	..	..	..	..	..	..	..	..	..	..	..
Congo, Rep.	77	89	58	77	95	98	90	97	..	..	..	..
Costa Rica	94	96	94	96	97	98	98	99	..	10	..	10
Côte d'Ivoire	51	..	26	..	65	70[c]	40	52[c]	..	..	..	..
Croatia	99	99[b]	95	97[b]	100	100[b]	100	100[b]	..	12	..	12
Cuba	95	97	95	97	99	100	99	100	12	12	13	12
Czech Republic	..	..	..	..	..	..	..	..	..	14	..	14
Denmark	..	..	..	..	..	..	..	..	14	15	14	16
Dominican Republic	80	84	79	84	87	91	88	92	..	..	..	..
Ecuador	90	92[b]	85	90[b]	96	96[b]	95	96[b]	..	..	..	..
Egypt, Arab Rep.	60	67[b]	34	44[b]	71	79[b]	51	67[b]	..	10	..	10
El Salvador	76	82	69	77	85	90	83	88	..	11	..	11
Eritrea	..	..	..	..	..	..	..	..	..	6	..	4
Estonia	100	100[b]	100	100[b]	100	100[b]	100	100[b]	12	14	12	15
Ethiopia	37	49	20	34	52	63	34	52	..	6	..	4
Finland	..	..	..	..	..	..	..	..	15	16	16	17
France	..	..	..	..	..	..	..	..	14	15	15	16
Gabon	..	..	..	..	..	..	..	..	..	..	..	..
Gambia, The	..	..	..	..	..	..	..	..	..	..	..	..
Georgia	..	..	..	..	..	..	..	..	..	6	..	6
Germany	..	..	..	..	..	..	..	..	15	15	14	15
Ghana	70	82	47	66	88	94	75	90	..	8	..	7
Greece	98	99	92	96	99	100	100	100	13	15	13	15
Guatemala	69	77	53	62	80	86	66	74	..	..	..	..
Guinea	..	..	..	..	..	..	..	..	..	..	..	..
Guinea-Bissau	..	..	..	..	..	..	..	..	..	..	..	..
Haiti	43	54	37	50	56	66	54	67	..	..	..	..

Education outcomes

	Adult literacy rate				Youth literacy rate				Expected years of schooling			
	% ages 15 and older				% ages 15–24							
	Male		Female		Male		Female		Male		Female	
	1990	2002 a	1990	2002 a	1990	2002 a	1990	2002 a	1990/91	2000/01	1990/91	2000/01
Honduras	69	80 b	67	80 b	78	87 b	81	91 b	..	..	..	..
Hungary	99	99	99	99	100	100	100	100	11	13	11	14
India	62	..	36	..	73	..	54	..	..	..	..	..
Indonesia	87	92	73	83	97	99	93	98	10	..	9	..
Iran, Islamic Rep.	72	84 c	54	70 c	92	..	81	..	..	..	..	..
Iraq	..	..	..	..	..	..	..	..	..	10	..	8
Ireland	..	..	..	..	..	..	..	..	12	14	13	15
Israel	95	97	88	93	99	100	98	99	..	14	..	15
Italy	98	99	97	98	100	100	100	100	..	15	..	15
Jamaica	78	84	86	91	87	91	95	98	11	11	11	11
Japan	..	..	..	..	..	..	..	..	..	14	..	14
Jordan	90	96	72	86	98	99	95	100	9	12	9	13
Kazakhstan	99	100	98	99	100	100	100	100	..	12	..	12
Kenya	81	90	61	79	93	96	87	95	..	8	..	8
Korea, Dem. Rep.	..	..	..	..	..	..	..	..	..	..	..	..
Korea, Rep.	..	..	..	..	..	..	..	..	14	16	13	14
Kuwait	79	85	73	81	88	92	87	94	7	8	7	9
Kyrgyz Republic	..	..	..	..	..	..	..	..	..	..	..	..
Lao PDR	70	77	43	55	79	86	61	73	9	9	6	7
Latvia	100	100 b	100	100 b	100	100 b	100	100 b	..	12	..	14
Lebanon	..	..	..	..	..	..	..	..	..	13	..	13
Lesotho	65	74 c	89	90 c	77	..	97	..	9	10	11	10
Liberia	55	72	23	39	75	86	39	55	..	11	..	8
Libya	83	92	51	71	99	100	83	94	..	..	..	..
Lithuania	100	100 b	99	100 b	100	100 b	100	100 b	..	14	..	15
Macedonia, FYR	..	..	..	..	..	..	..	..	..	12	..	12
Madagascar	..	..	..	..	..	..	..	..	..	6	..	6
Malawi	69	76	36	49	76	82	51	63	..	..	..	..
Malaysia	87	92 b	74	85 b	95	97 b	94	97 b	..	12	..	12
Mali	28	27 b	10	12 b	38	32 b	17	17 b	3	..	1	..
Mauritania	46	51	24	31	56	57	36	42	..	7	..	6
Mauritius	85	88 b	75	81 b	91	94 b	91	95 b	..	12	..	12
Mexico	91	93 b	84	89 b	96	97 b	94	96 b	..	12	..	11
Moldova	99	100	96	99	100	100	100	100	..	9	..	10
Mongolia	98	98 b	97	98 b	99	97 b	99	98 b	..	9	..	11
Morocco	53	63	25	38	68	77	42	61	..	9	..	7
Mozambique	49	62	18	31	66	77	32	49	4	7	3	5
Myanmar	87	89	74	81	90	92	86	91	..	7	..	7
Namibia	77	84	72	83	86	91	89	94	..	12	..	12
Nepal	47	62	14	26	67	78	27	46	..	..	..	..
Netherlands	..	..	..	..	..	..	..	..	15	16	15	16
New Zealand	..	..	..	..	..	..	..	..	14	16	15	17
Nicaragua	63	77 c	63	77 c	68	84 c	69	89 c	..	..	..	..
Niger	18	25	5	9	25	34	9	15	..	3	..	2
Nigeria	59	74	38	59	81	91	66	87	..	..	..	..
Norway	..	..	..	..	..	..	..	..	14	16	14	18
Oman	67	82	38	65	95	100	75	97	10	9	9	9
Pakistan	49	53 b	20	29 b	63	65 b	31	42 b	..	..	..	..
Panama	90	93	88	92	96	97	95	97	..	12	..	13
Papua New Guinea	..	..	..	..	..	..	..	..	..	6	..	6
Paraguay	92	93 c	88	90 c	96	96 c	95	96 c	9	10	8	10
Peru	92	91 c	79	80 c	97	98 c	92	96 c	..	13	..	11
Philippines	92	93 b	91	93 b	97	94 b	97	96 b	..	11	..	12
Poland	..	..	..	..	..	..	..	..	12	14	12	15
Portugal	91	95	84	91	99	100	100	100	13	15	14	16
Puerto Rico	92	94	91	94	95	97	97	98	..	..	..	..

2.13 Education outcomes

	Adult literacy rate				Youth literacy rate				Expected years of schooling			
	% ages 15 and older				% ages 15–24							
	Male		Female		Male		Female		Male		Female	
	1990	2002[a]	1990	2002[a]	1990	2002[a]	1990	2002[a]	1990/91	2000/01	1990/91	2000/01
Romania	99	98[b]	96	96[b]	99	98[b]	99	98[b]	*11*	12	*11*	12
Russian Federation	100	100	99	99	100	100	100	100	..	..	..	..
Rwanda	63	75	44	63	78	86	67	84	..	..	..	..
Saudi Arabia	76	84	50	69	91	95	79	92	9	..	7	*9*
Senegal	38	49	19	30	50	61	30	44	..	..	..	..
Serbia and Montenegro	..	..	..	..	..	..	..	..	..	10	..	11
Sierra Leone	..	..	..	..	..	..	..	..	..	7	..	5
Singapore	94	*97*[b]	83	*89*[b]	99	*99*[b]	99	*100*[b]	..	..	..	..
Slovak Republic	..	*100*[b]	..	*100*[b]	..	*100*[b]	..	*100*[b]	..	13	..	13
Slovenia	100	100	100	100	100	100	100	100	..	*14*	..	15
Somalia	..	..	..	..	..	..	..	..	..	..	..	..
South Africa	82	87	80	85	89	92	88	92	*13*	13	*13*	13
Spain	98	99	95	97	100	100	100	100	..	15	..	16
Sri Lanka	93	95	85	90	96	97	94	97	..	..	..	..
Sudan	60	71	32	49	76	84	54	74	..	..	..	..
Swaziland	74	82	70	80	85	90	85	92	*11*	13	*10*	*12*
Sweden	..	..	..	..	..	..	..	..	13	15	13	17
Switzerland	..	..	..	..	..	..	..	..	14	16	13	15
Syrian Arab Republic	82	91	48	74	92	97	67	93	11	..	9	..
Tajikistan	99	*100*[b]	97	*99*[b]	100	*100*[b]	100	*100*[b]	..	11	..	9
Tanzania	76	85	51	69	89	94	77	89	..	5	..	5
Thailand	95	*95*[b]	89	*91*[b]	99	*98*[b]	98	*98*[b]	..	*11*	..	*11*
Togo	60	74	29	45	79	88	48	67	11	*12*	6	*8*
Trinidad and Tobago	98	99	96	98	100	100	100	100	*11*	11	*11*	12
Tunisia	72	83	47	63	93	98	75	91	*11*	14	*10*	14
Turkey	89	*93*[b]	66	*75*[b]	97	*98*[b]	88	*93*[b]	..	..	..	..
Turkmenistan	..	*99*[b]	..	*98*[b]	..	*100*[b]	..	*100*[b]	..	..	..	..
Uganda	69	79	43	59	80	86	60	74	..	..	..	..
Ukraine	100	100	99	100	100	100	100	100	..	*11*	..	*12*
United Arab Emirates	71	76	71	81	82	88	89	95	10	..	11	..
United Kingdom	..	..	..	..	..	..	..	..	14	16	14	17
United States	..	..	..	..	..	..	..	..	15	15	16	16
Uruguay	96	97	97	98	98	99	99	99	..	*13*	..	*14*
Uzbekistan	99	100	98	99	100	100	100	100	..	..	..	..
Venezuela, RB	90	94	88	93	95	98	97	99	..	*10*	..	11
Vietnam	94	*94*[b]	87	*87*[b]	94	..	94	..	..	..	..	..
West Bank and Gaza	..	..	..	..	..	..	..	..	..	..	..	..
Yemen, Rep.	55	69	13	29	74	84	25	51	..	*11*	..	5
Zambia	79	86	59	74	86	91	76	87	..	7	..	7
Zimbabwe	87	94	75	86	97	99	91	96	..	10	..	9
World	**79 w**	**84 w**	**63 w**	**71 w**	**87 w**	**89 w**	**78 w**	**83 w**	**.. w**	**.. w**	**.. w**	**.. w**
Low income	64	72	42	53	75	82	59	70	..	..	..	..
Middle income	88	92	75	83	95	97	91	94	..	..	..	..
Lower middle income	87	92	74	82	95	96	91	94	..	..	..	..
Upper middle income	92	95	88	92	97	98	95	98	..	..	..	..
Low & middle income	78	83	62	70	86	89	77	82	..	..	..	..
East Asia & Pacific	88	93	71	82	97	98	93	97	..	..	..	..
Europe & Central Asia	98	99	95	96	99	100	98	99	..	..	..	..
Latin America & Carib.	87	90	83	89	93	95	93	96	..	..	..	..
Middle East & N. Africa	66	76	40	55	81	87	61	75	..	..	..	..
South Asia	59	67	34	44	70	77	50	61	..	..	..	..
Sub-Saharan Africa	60	71	40	56	75	83	60	74	..	..	..	..
High income	..	..	..	..	..	..	..	..	15	..	15	..
Europe EMU	..	..	..	..	..	..	..	..	15	..	15	..

a. Data are preliminary. b. National estimates based on census data. c. National estimates based on survey data.

About the data

Many governments collect and publish statistics that indicate how their education systems are working and developing—statistics on enrollment and on such efficiency indicators as repetition rates, pupil-teacher ratios, and cohort progression through school. But until recently, despite an obvious interest in what education achieves, few systems in high-income or developing countries had systematically collected information on outcomes of education.

Basic student outcomes include achievements in reading and mathematics judged against established standards. In many countries national learning assessments are enabling ministries of education to monitor progress in these outcomes. Internationally, the United Nations Educational, Scientific, and Cultural Organization (UNESCO) Institute for Statistics has established literacy as an outcome indicator based on an internationally agreed definition.

The literacy rate is defined as the percentage of people who can, with understanding, both read and write a short, simple statement about their everyday life. In practice, literacy is difficult to measure. To estimate literacy using such a definition requires census or survey measurements under controlled conditions. Many countries estimate the number of literate people from self-reported data. Some use educational attainment data as a proxy but apply different lengths of school attendance or level of completion. Because definition and methodologies of data collection differ across countries, data need to be used with caution.

The reported literacy data are national estimates or UNESCO Institute for Statistics estimates. The national estimates are received from countries and are based on national censuses or household surveys during 1995–2004. The UNESCO Institute for Statistics estimates were assessed in July 2002. The estimation methodology can be reviewed at www.uis.unesco.org.

Literacy statistics for most countries cover the population ages 15 and older, by five-year age groups, but some include younger ages or are confined to age ranges that tend to inflate literacy rates. As an alternative, the UNESCO Institute for Statistics has proposed the narrower age range of 15–24, which better captures the ability of participants in the formal education system. The youth illiteracy rate reported in the table measures the accumulated outcomes of primary education over the previous 10 years or so by indicating the proportion of people who have passed through the primary education system without acquiring basic literacy and numeracy skills (or never entered the system). Reasons for this may include difficulties in attending school or dropping out before reaching grade 5 (see *About the data* for table 2.12) and thereby failing to achieve basic learning competencies.

Expected years of schooling is an estimate of the total years of schooling that a typical child at the age of school entry will receive, including years spent on repetition, given the current patterns of enrollment across cycles of education. It may also be interpreted as an indicator of the total education resources, measured in school years, that a child will acquire over his or her "lifetime" in school—or as an indicator of an education system's overall level of development.

Because the calculation of this indicator assumes that the probability of a child's being enrolled in school at any future age is equal to the current enrollment ratio for that age, it does not account for changes and trends in future enrollment ratios. The expected number of years and the expected number of grades completed are not necessarily consistent, because the first includes years spent in repetition. Comparability across countries and over time may be affected by differences in the length of the school year or changes in policies on automatic promotions and grade repetition.

Definitions

• **Adult literacy rate** is the percentage of people ages 15 and older who can, with understanding, both read and write a short, simple statement about their everyday life. • **Youth literacy rate** is the literacy rate among people ages 15–24. • **Expected years of schooling** are the average number of years of formal schooling that children are expected to receive, including university education and years spent in repetition. They reflect the underlying age-specific enrollment ratios for primary, secondary, and tertiary education.

2.13a

There is a strong positive relationship between primary school enrollment ratios and literacy among youth

Children learn basic reading and writing along with other subjects in primary school. The primary school enrollment ratio and the literacy rate among young people (15–24) have a strong positive relationship, suggesting the push to achieve universal primary education will increase the number of literate young people.

Source: UNESCO Institute for Statistics.

Data sources

The data on literacy are national estimates collected by the UNESCO Institute for Statistics and estimates and projections by the UNESCO Institute for Statistics, assessed in July 2002. The data on expected years of schooling are from the UNESCO Institute for Statistics.

Health expenditure, services, and use

	Health expenditure			Health expenditure per capita	Physicians		Hospital beds		Inpatient admission rate	Average length of stay	Outpatient visits per capita
	Total % of GDP 2001	Public % of GDP 2001	Public % of total 2001	$ 2001	per 1,000 people 1980	1995–2002[a]	per 1,000 people 1980	1995–2002[a]	% of population 1995–2002[a]	days 1995–2002[a]	1995–2002[a]
Afghanistan	5.2	2.7	52.6	8	..	0.1	..	..	..	..	..
Albania	3.7	2.4	64.6	48	1.4	1.4	4.3	3.3	..	..	..
Algeria	4.1	3.1	75.0	73	..	1.0	..	2.1	..	..	..
Angola	4.4	2.8	63.1	31	..	0.1	..	..	..	..	..
Argentina	9.5	5.1	53.4	679	..	2.7	..	3.3	..	..	..
Armenia	7.8	3.2	41.2	28	3.2	2.9	8.4	4.3	8	15	2
Australia	9.2	6.2	67.9	1,741	..	2.5	12.3	7.9	16	16	6
Austria	8.0	5.5	69.3	1,866	1.6	3.2	11.2	8.6	30	9	7
Azerbaijan	0.9	*0.6*	*75.1*	*8*	3.4	3.6	9.7	8.5	6	..	1
Bangladesh	3.5	1.5	44.2	12	0.1	0.2	0.2	..	..	..	..
Belarus	5.6	4.8	86.7	68	3.0	4.5	12.5	12.6	26	18	11
Belgium	8.9	6.4	71.7	1,983	2.3	3.9	9.4	7.3	20	12	7
Benin	4.4	2.1	46.9	16	0.1	0.1	1.5	..	..	..	..
Bolivia	5.3	3.5	66.3	49	..	1.3	..	1.7	..	..	..
Bosnia and Herzegovina	7.5	2.8	36.8	85	1.0	1.4	4.8	3.2	..	15	..
Botswana	6.6	4.4	66.2	190	0.1	..	2.4	..	..	..	..
Brazil	7.6	3.2	41.6	222	..	1.3	..	3.1	0[b]	..	2
Bulgaria	4.8	3.9	82.1	81	2.5	3.4	8.9	7.2	..	12	..
Burkina Faso	..	2.0	..	..	0.0[c]	0.0[c]	..	1.4	2	3	0[b]
Burundi	3.6	2.1	59.0	4	..	..	..	..	..	..	..
Cambodia	11.8	1.7	14.9	30	..	0.3	..	..	..	..	..
Cameroon	3.3	1.2	37.1	20	..	0.1	..	..	..	..	..
Canada	9.5	6.8	70.8	2,163	1.8	2.1	6.8	3.9	10	9	6
Central African Republic	4.5	2.3	51.2	12	0.0[c]	0.0[c]	1.6	..	..	..	..
Chad	2.6	2.0	76.0	5	..	..	..	..	..	..	..
Chile	7.0	3.1	44.0	296	..	1.1	3.4	2.7	..	..	..
China	5.5	2.0	37.2	49	1.2	1.4	2.2	2.5	4	12	..
Hong Kong, China	..	..	..	..	0.8	1.3	4.0	..	..	..	..
Colombia	5.5	3.6	65.7	105	..	1.2	1.6	1.5	..	..	..
Congo, Dem. Rep.	3.5	1.5	44.4	5	..	0.1	..	..	..	..	..
Congo, Rep.	2.1	1.4	63.8	18	..	0.3	..	..	..	..	..
Costa Rica	7.2	4.9	68.5	293	..	0.9	3.3	1.7	9	6	1
Côte d'Ivoire	6.2	1.0	16.0	41	..	0.1	..	..	..	..	..
Croatia	9.0	7.3	81.8	394	1.7	2.4	7.2	6.0	..	..	..
Cuba	7.2	6.2	86.2	185	..	5.3	..	5.1	..	..	..
Czech Republic	7.4	6.7	91.4	407	2.3	3.4	11.3	8.8	21	11	13
Denmark	8.4	7.0	82.4	2,545	2.2	3.4	8.1	4.5	20	6	6
Dominican Republic	6.1	2.2	36.1	153	..	2.2	..	1.5	..	..	..
Ecuador	4.5	2.3	50.3	76	..	1.7	1.9	1.6	..	..	..
Egypt, Arab Rep.	3.9	1.9	48.9	46	1.1	1.6	2.0	2.1	3	6	4
El Salvador	8.0	3.7	46.7	174	0.3	1.1	..	1.6	..	..	..
Eritrea	5.7	3.7	65.1	10	..	0.0[c]	..	..	..	..	..
Estonia	5.5	4.3	77.8	226	2.9	3.1	12.2	6.7	18	9	5
Ethiopia	3.6	1.4	40.5	3	0.0[c]	..	0.3	..	..	..	..
Finland	7.0	5.3	75.6	1,631	1.7	3.1	15.6	7.5	27	11	4
France	9.6	7.3	76.0	2,109	2.0	3.3	11.1	8.2	23	13	7
Gabon	3.6	1.7	47.9	127	..	..	..	..	..	..	..
Gambia, The	6.4	3.2	49.4	19	..	0.0[c]	..	..	..	..	..
Georgia	3.6	1.4	37.8	22	4.1	3.9	10.2	4.3	5	11	1
Germany	10.8	8.1	74.9	2,412	2.3	3.3	11.5	9.1	24	12	7
Ghana	4.7	2.8	59.6	12	..	0.1	..	..	..	..	..
Greece	9.4	5.2	56.0	1,001	2.4	4.4	6.2	4.9	15	8	3
Guatemala	4.8	2.3	48.3	86	..	0.9	..	1.0	..	..	..
Guinea	3.5	1.9	54.1	13	..	0.1	..	..	..	..	..
Guinea-Bissau	5.9	3.2	53.8	8	0.1	0.2	1.9	..	..	..	..
Haiti	5.0	2.7	53.4	22	..	0.2	0.7	0.7	..	..	..

Health expenditure, services, and use

	Health expenditure			Health expenditure per capita	Physicians		Hospital beds		Inpatient admission rate	Average length of stay	Outpatient visits per capita
	Total % of GDP 2001	Public % of GDP 2001	Public % of total 2001	$ 2001	per 1,000 people 1980	1995–2002[a]	per 1,000 people 1980	1995–2002[a]	% of population 1995–2002[a]	days 1995–2002[a]	1995–2002[a]
Honduras	6.1	3.2	53.1	59	..	0.8	1.3	1.1	..	..	..
Hungary	6.8	5.1	75.0	345	2.3	2.9	9.1	8.2	24	9	12
India	5.1	0.9	17.9	24	0.4	..	0.8	..	..	..	..
Indonesia	2.4	0.6	25.1	16	..	..	..	..	..	..	..
Iran, Islamic Rep.	6.6	2.7	41.9	363	..	0.9	1.5	1.6	..	..	..
Iraq	3.2	1.0	31.8	225	0.6	0.6	1.9	1.5	..	..	..
Ireland	6.5	4.9	76.0	1,711	..	2.4	13.0	9.7	15	8	..
Israel	8.7	6.0	69.2	1,641	3.1	3.7	6.8	6.2	..	..	..
Italy	8.4	6.3	75.3	1,584	2.6	4.3	9.6	4.9	18	8	6
Jamaica	6.8	2.9	42.1	191	..	1.4	..	2.1	..	..	..
Japan	8.0	6.2	77.9	2,627	1.3	1.9	13.7	16.5	10	40	14
Jordan	9.5	4.5	47.0	163	0.8	1.7	1.3	1.8	11	4	..
Kazakhstan	3.1	1.9	60.4	44	3.0	3.6	13.1	7.0	15	16	0[b]
Kenya	7.8	1.7	21.4	29	..	0.1	..	..	..	..	..
Korea, Dem. Rep.	2.5	1.9	73.4	22	..	3.0	..	..	..	..	..
Korea, Rep.	6.0	2.6	44.4	532	..	1.4	1.7	6.1	6	13	9
Kuwait	4.3	3.5	81.0	630	1.7	1.9	4.1	2.8	..	..	..
Kyrgyz Republic	4.0	1.9	48.7	12	2.6	2.6	12.0	5.5	21	13	1
Lao PDR	3.1	1.7	55.5	10	..	0.2	..	..	..	..	..
Latvia	6.4	3.4	52.5	210	3.6	2.9	13.9	8.2	21	14	4
Lebanon	12.4	2.2	18.0	..	..	2.1	..	2.7	17	4	..
Lesotho	5.5	4.3	78.9	23	..	0.1	..	..	..	..	..
Liberia	4.3	3.3	75.9	1	..	0.0	c	..	..	..	.. ..
Libya	2.9	1.6	56.0	143	1.3	1.3	..	4.3	..	..	..
Lithuania	6.0	4.2	70.5	206	..	4.0	12.1	9.2	24	11	7
Macedonia, FYR	6.8	5.8	84.9	115	1.3	2.2	5.2	4.8	9	12	3
Madagascar	2.0	1.3	65.9	6	..	0.1	..	0.4	1	5	1
Malawi	7.8	2.7	35.0	13	..	..	..	1.3	..	..	2
Malaysia	3.8	2.0	53.7	143	0.3	0.7	..	2.0	..	..	..
Mali	4.3	1.7	38.6	11	0.0[c]	0.1	..	0.2	1	7	0[b]
Mauritania	3.6	2.6	72.4	12	..	0.1	..	..	..	..	..
Mauritius	3.4	2.0	59.5	128	0.5	0.9	3.1	..	..	..	..
Mexico	6.1	2.7	44.3	370	..	1.5	0.7	1.1	6	4	3
Moldova	5.1	2.8	55.8	18	2.8	2.7	12.1	5.9	19	18	8
Mongolia	6.4	4.6	72.3	25	..	2.4	11.2	..	..	..	..
Morocco	5.1	2.0	39.3	59	..	0.5	..	1.0	3	7	..
Mozambique	5.9	4.0	67.4	11	0.0[c]	..	..	1.1	..	..	..
Myanmar	2.1	0.4	17.8	197	..	0.3	0.9	..	..	..	..
Namibia	7.0	4.7	67.8	110	..	0.3	..	..	..	..	..
Nepal	5.2	1.5	29.7	12	0.0[c]	0.0[c]	0.2	0.2	..	..	..
Netherlands	8.9	5.7	63.3	2,138	1.9	3.3	12.3	10.8	10	33	6
New Zealand	8.3	6.4	76.8	1,073	1.6	2.2	10.2	6.2	13	8	4
Nicaragua	7.8	3.8	48.5	60	0.4	0.9	..	1.5	..	..	..
Niger	3.7	1.4	39.1	6	..	0.0[c]	..	0.1	28	5	0[b]
Nigeria	3.4	0.8	23.2	15	0.1	..	0.9	..	..	..	..
Norway	8.0	6.8	85.5	2,981	2.0	3.0	16.5	14.6	17	9	..
Oman	3.0	2.4	80.7	225	0.5	1.3	1.6	2.2	9	4	4
Pakistan	3.9	1.0	24.4	16	0.3	0.6	0.6	..	..	..	..
Panama	7.0	4.8	69.0	258	..	1.7	..	2.2	..	..	..
Papua New Guinea	4.4	3.9	89.0	24	0.1	0.1	5.5	..	..	..	..
Paraguay	8.0	3.0	38.3	97	..	1.1	..	1.3	..	..	..
Peru	4.7	2.6	55.0	97	0.7	0.9	..	1.5	1	6	..
Philippines	3.3	1.5	45.2	30	0.1	1.2	1.7	..	..	..	..
Poland	6.1	4.6	71.9	289	1.8	2.2	5.6	4.9	16	8	6
Portugal	9.2	6.3	69.0	982	2.0	3.2	5.2	4.0	12	9	3
Puerto Rico	..	..	..	..	..	1.8	..	3.3	..	..	..

2.14 Health expenditure, services, and use

	Health expenditure			Health expenditure per capita	Physicians		Hospital beds		Inpatient admission rate	Average length of stay	Outpatient visits per capita
	Total % of GDP	Public % of GDP	Public % of total	$	per 1,000 people		per 1,000 people		% of population	days	
	2001	**2001**	**2001**	**2001**	**1980**	**1995–2002**[a]	**1980**	**1995–2002**[a]	**1995–2002**[a]	**1995–2002**[a]	**1995–2002**[a]
Romania	6.5	5.2	79.2	117	1.5	1.9	8.8	7.5	18	10	4
Russian Federation	5.4	3.7	68.2	115	..	4.2	..	10.8	22	17	8
Rwanda	5.5	3.1	55.5	11	0.0[c]	..	1.5	..	..	..	..
Saudi Arabia	4.6	3.4	74.6	375	..	1.7	..	2.3	11	4	1
Senegal	4.8	2.8	58.8	22	..	0.1	..	0.4	..	10	1
Serbia and Montenegro	8.2	6.5	79.2	103	..	2.1	..	5.3	..	12	2
Sierra Leone	4.3	2.6	61.0	7	0.1	0.1	1.2	..	..	..	..
Singapore	3.9	1.3	33.5	816	0.9	1.6	4.0	..	..	..	..
Slovak Republic	5.7	5.1	89.3	216	..	3.6	..	7.8	19	10	..
Slovenia	8.4	6.3	74.9	821	1.8	2.2	7.0	5.2	..	..	..
Somalia	2.6	1.2	44.6	6	0.0[c]	0.0[c]	..	..	..	..	..
South Africa	8.6	3.6	41.4	222	..	0.6	..	..	..	..	..
Spain	7.5	5.4	71.4	1,088	..	3.3	5.4	4.1	12	9	9
Sri Lanka	3.6	1.8	48.9	30	0.1	0.4	2.9	..	..	..	..
Sudan	3.5	0.6	18.7	14	0.1	0.1	0.9	..	..	..	..
Swaziland	3.3	2.3	68.5	41	..	0.2	..	..	..	..	..
Sweden	8.7	7.4	85.2	2,150	2.2	3.0	15.1	3.6	18	6	3
Switzerland	11.1	6.4	57.1	3,779	2.4	3.5	..	17.9	15	13	..
Syrian Arab Republic	5.4	2.4	43.9	65	0.4	1.3	1.1	1.4	..	..	..
Tajikistan	3.4	1.0	28.9	6	..	2.1	..	6.4	..	..	..
Tanzania	4.4	2.0	46.7	12	..	0.0[c]	1.4	..	..	..	..
Thailand	3.7	2.1	57.1	69	0.1	0.4	1.5	2.0	..	..	1
Togo	2.8	1.5	48.6	8	0.1	0.1	..	..	..	..	..
Trinidad and Tobago	4.0	1.7	43.3	279	0.7	0.8	..	5.1	..	..	..
Tunisia	6.4	4.9	75.7	134	0.3	0.7	2.1	1.7	..	..	..
Turkey	*6.9*	*4.4*	*63.0*	..	0.6	1.3	2.2	2.6	8	6	3
Turkmenistan	4.1	3.0	73.3	57	2.8	3.0	10.5	7.1	..	..	..
Uganda	5.9	3.4	57.5	14	..	..	..	..	..	..	..
Ukraine	4.3	2.9	67.8	33	3.5	3.0	12.1	8.7	20	..	10
United Arab Emirates	3.5	2.6	75.8	849	1.1	1.8	2.8	2.6	..	..	..
United Kingdom	7.6	6.3	82.2	1,835	1.3	2.0	8.1	4.1	15	10	5
United States	13.9	6.2	44.4	4,887	2.0	2.7	6.0	3.6	12	7	9
Uruguay	10.9	5.1	46.3	603	..	3.7	..	4.4	..	..	..
Uzbekistan	3.6	2.7	74.5	17	2.7	2.9	9.2	5.3	..	..	..
Venezuela, RB	6.0	3.7	62.1	307	0.8	2.4	0.3	1.5	..	..	..
Vietnam	5.1	1.5	28.5	21	0.2	0.5	3.5	1.7	8	7	..
West Bank and Gaza	..	..	..	..	..	0.5	..	1.2	9	3	4
Yemen, Rep.	4.5	1.5	34.1	20	..	0.2	..	0.6	..	..	..
Zambia	5.7	3.0	53.1	19	0.1	0.1	..	..	..	..	..
Zimbabwe	6.2	2.8	45.3	45	0.2	0.1	3.0	..	..	..	..
World	**9.8 w**	**5.6 w**	**59.2 w**	**500 w**	**1.1 w**	**.. w**	**3.7 w**	**.. w**	**9 w**	**.. w**	**.. w**
Low income	4.4	1.1	26.3	23	0.4	..	1.2	..	..	..	..
Middle income	6.0	3.1	51.1	118	1.2	1.9	3.0	3.7	7	11	..
Lower middle income	5.8	2.7	47.2	85	1.2	2.0	2.9	3.7	6	12	..
Upper middle income	6.4	3.7	57.7	357	..	1.8	3.8	3.4	11	6	5
Low & middle income	5.8	2.7	47.0	72	0.8	..	2.2	..	..	..	..
East Asia & Pacific	4.9	1.9	38.8	48	1.0	1.4	2.2	2.5	4	12	..
Europe & Central Asia	5.8	4.3	72.4	123	..	3.1	..	8.9	18	13	6
Latin America & Carib.	7.0	3.4	48.0	255	..	1.4	..	2.2	2	..	2
Middle East & N. Africa	4.9	2.8	59.3	166	..	..	..	..	..	..	..
South Asia	4.8	1.0	21.6	22	0.3	..	0.7	..	..	..	..
Sub-Saharan Africa	6.0	2.5	41.3	29	..	..	..	..	..	..	..
High income	10.8	6.3	62.1	2,841	1.9	2.8	8.6	7.4	14	14	8
Europe EMU	9.3	6.8	73.5	1,856	2.2	3.5	9.9	8.0	20	12	7

a. Data are for the most recent year available. b. Less than 0.5. c. Less than 0.05.

About the data

National health accounts track financial flows in the health sector, including public and private expenditures, by source of funding. In contrast with high-income countries, few developing countries have health accounts that are methodologically consistent with national accounting approaches. The difficulties in creating national health accounts go beyond data collection. To establish a national health accounting system, a country needs to define the boundaries of the health care system and to define a taxonomy of health care delivery institutions. The accounting system should be comprehensive and standardized, providing not only accurate measures of financial flows but also information on the equity and efficiency of health financing to inform health policy.

The absence of consistent national health accounting systems in most developing countries makes cross-country comparisons of health spending difficult. Records of private out-of-pocket spending are often lacking. And compiling estimates of public health expenditures is complicated in countries where state or provincial and local governments are involved in financing and delivering health care, because the data on public spending often are not aggregated. The data in the table are the product of an effort by the World Health Organization (WHO), the Organisation for Economic Co-operation and Development (OECD), and the World Bank to collect all available information on health expenditures from national and local government budgets, national accounts, household surveys, insurance publications, international donors, and existing tabulations.

Indicators on health services (physicians and hospital beds per 1,000 people) and health care utilization (inpatient admission rates, average length of stay, and outpatient visits) come from a variety of sources (see *Data sources*). Data are lacking for many countries, and for others comparability is limited by differences in definitions. In estimates of health personnel, for example, some countries incorrectly include retired physicians (because deletions to physician rosters are made only periodically) or those working outside the health sector. There is no universally accepted definition of hospital beds. Moreover, figures on physicians and hospital beds are indicators of availability, not of quality or use. They do not show how well trained the physicians are or how well equipped the hospitals or medical centers are. And physicians and hospital beds tend to be concentrated in urban areas, so these indicators give only a partial view of health services available to the entire population.

The average length of stay in hospitals is an indicator of the efficiency of resource use. Longer stays may reflect a waste of resources if patients are kept in hospitals beyond the time medically required, inflating demand for hospital beds and increasing hospital costs. Aside from differences in cases and financing methods, cross-country variations in average length of stay may result from differences in the role of hospitals. Many developing countries do not have separate extended care facilities, so hospitals become the source of both long-term and acute care. Other factors may also explain the variations. Data for some countries may not include all public and private hospitals. Admission rates may be overstated in some countries if outpatient surgeries are counted as hospital admissions. And in many countries outpatient visits, especially emergency visits, may result in double counting if a patient receives treatment in more than one department.

Definitions

• **Total health expenditure** is the sum of public and private health expenditure. It covers the provision of health services (preventive and curative), family planning activities, nutrition activities, and emergency aid designated for health but does not include provision of water and sanitation. • **Public health expenditure** consists of recurrent and capital spending from government (central and local) budgets, external borrowings and grants (including donations from international agencies and nongovernmental organizations), and social (or compulsory) health insurance funds. • **Physicians** are graduates of any faculty or school of medicine who are working in the country in any medical field (practice, teaching, research). • **Hospital beds** include inpatient beds available in public, private, general, and specialized hospitals and rehabilitation centers. In most cases beds for both acute and chronic care are included. • **Inpatient admission rate** is the percentage of the population admitted to hospitals during a year. • **Average length of stay** is the average duration of inpatient hospital admissions. • **Outpatient visits per capita** are the number of visits to health care facilities per capita, including repeat visits.

2.14a

High health personnel absence rates lower the quality of health care

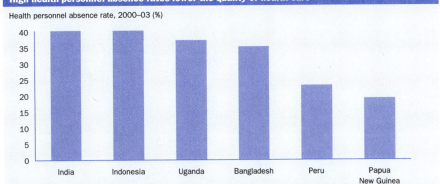

Health personnel absence rate, 2000–03 (%)

Health personnel absence rate is the percentage of full-time medical personnel who were absent from a random sample of primary health centers during surprise visits. Some personnel were absent for valid reasons, but even authorized absences reduce the quantity and quality of primary health care. Absence rates tend to be higher in remote areas, affecting the quality of health care available in these areas.

Source: Chaudhury and others 2004; NRI and World Bank 2003; Habyarimana and others 2003.

Data sources

The estimates of health expenditure come mostly from the WHO's *World Health Report 2003* and updates and from the OECD for its member countries, supplemented by World Bank poverty assessments and country and sector studies. Data are also drawn from World Bank public expenditure reviews, the International Monetary Fund's *Government Finance Statistics* database, and other studies. The data on private expenditure in developing countries are drawn largely from household surveys conducted by governments or by statistical or international organizations. The data on physicians, hospital beds, and utilization of health services are from the WHO, OECD, and TransMONEE, supplemented by country data.

Disease prevention: coverage and quality

	Access to an improved water source		Access to improved sanitation facilities		Tetanus vaccinations	Child immunization rate		Children sleeping under treated bednets[b]	Tuberculosis treatment success rate	DOTS detection rate
	% of population		% of population		% of pregnant women	% of children ages 12–23 months[a]		% of children under age 5	% of registered cases	% of estimated cases
	1990	2000	1990	2000	2002	Measles 2002	DPT 2002	1999–2001[c]	2001	2002
Afghanistan	..	13	..	12	34	44	47	..	84	19
Albania	..	97	..	91	..	96	98	..	98	24
Algeria	..	89	..	92	..	81	86	..	84	114
Angola	..	38	..	44	62	74	47	2.3	66	91
Argentina	94	..	82	..	..	97	88	..	64	51
Armenia	..	..	..	..	..	91	94	..	90	28
Australia	100	100	100	100	..	94	93	..	66	25
Austria	100	100	100	100	..	78	83	..	64	41
Azerbaijan	..	78	..	81	..	97	97	1.4	66	43
Bangladesh	94	97	41	48	89	77	85	..	84	32
Belarus	..	100	..	..	..	99	99	..	..	..
Belgium	..	..	..	..	..	75	90	..	64	64
Benin	..	63	20	23	66	78	79	7.4	79	98
Bolivia	71	83	52	70	..	79	81	..	82	75
Bosnia and Herzegovina	..	..	..	..	..	89	80	..	98	47
Botswana	93	95	60	66	..	90	97	..	78	73
Brazil	83	87	71	76	..	93	96	..	67	10
Bulgaria	..	100	..	100	..	90	94	..	87	43
Burkina Faso	..	42	..	29	44	46	41	..	65	18
Burundi	69	78	87	88	42	75	74	1.3	80	28
Cambodia	..	30	..	17	36	52	54	..	92	52
Cameroon	51	58	77	79	65	62	48	1.3	62	60
Canada	100	100	100	100	..	96	97	..	67	52
Central African Republic	48	70	24	25	63	35	40	1.5	61	49
Chad	..	27	18	29	39	55	40	0.6	..	42
Chile	90	93	97	96	..	95	94	..	83	112
China	71	75	29	40	..	65	79	..	96	27
Hong Kong, China	..	..	..	..	..	..	..	..	78	51
Colombia	94	91	83	86	..	89	85	0.7	85	9
Congo, Dem. Rep.	..	45	..	21	44	45	43	0.7	77	52
Congo, Rep.	..	51	..	..	41	37	41	..	66	69
Costa Rica	..	95	..	93	..	94	94	..	72	79
Côte d'Ivoire	80	81	46	52	80	56	54	1.1	73	25
Croatia	..	..	..	..	..	95	95	..	..	..
Cuba	..	91	..	98	..	98	99	..	93	91
Czech Republic	..	..	..	..	..	97	98	..	73	57
Denmark	..	100	..	..	..	99	98	..	..	..
Dominican Republic	83	86	66	67	..	92	72	..	85	43
Ecuador	71	85	70	86	..	80	89	..	82	31
Egypt, Arab Rep.	94	97	87	98	70	97	97	..	82	53
El Salvador	66	77	73	82	..	93	81	..	88	57
Eritrea	..	46	..	13	50	84	83	..	80	14
Estonia	..	..	..	..	..	95	97	..	64	61
Ethiopia	25	24	8	12	24	52	56	..	76	33
Finland	100	100	100	100	..	96	98	..	..	..
France	..	..	..	..	..	85	98	..	..	..
Gabon	..	86	..	53	50	55	38	..	49	73
Gambia, The	..	62	..	37	..	90	90	14.7	71	73
Georgia	..	79	..	100	..	73	84	..	67	50
Germany	..	..	..	..	..	89	97	..	67	52
Ghana	53	73	61	72	73	81	80	..	42	41
Greece	..	..	..	..	..	88	88	..	..	..
Guatemala	76	92	70	81	..	92	84	1.2	85	45
Guinea	45	48	55	58	43	54	47	..	74	54
Guinea-Bissau	..	56	44	56	41	47	50	7.4	51	43
Haiti	53	46	23	28	52	53	43	..	75	41

	Access to an improved water source		Access to improved sanitation facilities		Tetanus vaccinations	Child immunization rate		Children sleeping under treated bednets [b]	Tuberculosis treatment success rate	DOTS detection rate
	% of population		% of population		% of pregnant women	% of children ages 12–23 months [a]		% of children under age 5	% of registered cases	% of estimated cases
						Measles	DPT			
	1990	2000	1990	2000	2002	2002	2002	1999–2001 [c]	2001	2002
Honduras	83	88	61	75	..	97	95	..	86	114
Hungary	99	99	99	99	..	99	99	..	46	39
India	68	84	16	28	78	67	70	..	85	31
Indonesia	71	78	47	55	81	76	75	0.1	86	30
Iran, Islamic Rep.	..	92	..	83	..	99	99	..	84	60
Iraq	..	85	..	79	70	90	81	..	89	21
Ireland	..	..	..	..	..	73	84	..	..	..
Israel	..	..	..	..	..	95	97	..	79	58
Italy	..	..	..	..	..	70	95	..	40	63
Jamaica	93	92	99	99	..	86	87	..	78	68
Japan	..	..	..	..	..	98	95	..	75	33
Jordan	97	96	98	99	..	95	95	..	86	72
Kazakhstan	..	91	..	99	..	95	95	..	78	93
Kenya	45	57	80	87	60	78	84	2.9	80	49
Korea, Dem. Rep.	..	100	..	99	..	..	..	..	91	88
Korea, Rep.	..	92	..	63	..	97	97	..	..	..
Kuwait	..	..	..	..	..	99	98	..	..	..
Kyrgyz Republic	..	77	..	100	..	98	98	..	81	45
Lao PDR	..	37	..	30	35	55	55	..	77	43
Latvia	..	..	..	..	..	98	97	..	73	78
Lebanon	..	100	..	99	..	96	92	..	91	68
Lesotho	..	78	..	49	..	70	79	..	71	61
Liberia	..	..	..	..	41	57	51	..	..	..
Libya	71	72	97	97	..	91	93	..	..	106
Lithuania	..	..	..	..	..	98	95	..	75	62
Macedonia, FYR	..	..	..	..	..	98	96	..	88	37
Madagascar	44	47	36	42	35	61	62	0.2	69	62
Malawi	49	57	73	76	82	69	64	2.9	70	36
Malaysia	..	..	..	..	..	92	96	..	79	78
Mali	55	65	70	69	32	33	57	..	50	15
Mauritania	37	37	30	33	40	81	83	..	..	..
Mauritius	100	100	100	99	..	84	88	..	93	25
Mexico	80	88	70	74	..	96	91	..	83	73
Moldova	..	92	..	99	..	94	97	..	66	19
Mongolia	..	60	..	30	..	98	98	..	87	69
Morocco	75	80	58	68	..	96	94	..	87	83
Mozambique	..	57	..	43	67	58	60	..	77	45
Myanmar	..	72	..	64	71	75	77	..	81	73
Namibia	72	77	33	41	85	68	77	..	68	76
Nepal	67	88	20	28	69	71	72	..	88	64
Netherlands	100	100	100	100	..	96	98	..	76	54
New Zealand	..	..	..	..	..	85	90	..	9	48
Nicaragua	70	77	76	85	..	98	84	..	83	85
Niger	53	59	15	20	36	48	23	1.0	..	22
Nigeria	53	62	53	54	44	40	26	..	79	12
Norway	100	100	..	..	..	88	91	..	87	26
Oman	37	39	84	92	..	99	99	..	90	106
Pakistan	83	90	36	62	56	57	63	..	77	13
Panama	..	90	..	92	..	79	89	..	65	88
Papua New Guinea	40	42	82	82	34	71	57	..	67	15
Paraguay	63	78	93	94	..	82	77	..	86	8
Peru	74	80	60	71	..	95	89	..	90	84
Philippines	87	86	74	83	87	73	70	..	88	58
Poland	..	..	..	..	..	98	99	..	77	55
Portugal	..	..	..	..	..	87	96	..	78	94
Puerto Rico	..	..	..	..	..	..	..	..	80	65

	Access to an improved water source		Access to improved sanitation facilities		Tetanus vaccinations	Child immunization rate		Children sleeping under treated bednets [b]	Tuberculosis treatment success rate	DOTS detection rate
	% of population		% of population		% of pregnant women	% of children ages 12–23 months [a]		% of children under age 5	% of registered cases	% of estimated cases
	1990	2000	1990	2000	2002	Measles 2002	DPT 2002	1999–2001 [c]	2001	2002
Romania	..	58	..	53	..	98	99	..	78	41
Russian Federation	..	99	..	..	..	98	96	..	67	6
Rwanda	..	41	..	8	83	69	88	5.0	61	29
Saudi Arabia	..	95	..	100	..	97	95	..	77	37
Senegal	72	78	57	70	75	54	60	1.7	53	54
Serbia and Montenegro	..	98	..	100	..	92	95	..	88	22
Sierra Leone	..	57	..	66	60	60	50	1.5	80	36
Singapore	100	100	100	100	..	91	92	..	88	39
Slovak Republic	..	100	..	100	..	99	99	..	87	35
Slovenia	100	100	..	..	..	94	92	..	82	68
Somalia	..	..	..	..	60	45	40	0.3	86	28
South Africa	86	86	86	87	52	78	82	..	65	96
Spain	..	..	..	..	..	97	96	..	..	..
Sri Lanka	68	77	85	94	..	99	98	..	80	79
Sudan	67	75	58	62	35	49	40	0.4	80	33
Swaziland	..	..	..	..	..	72	77	0.1	36	31
Sweden	100	100	100	100	..	94	99	..	62	59
Switzerland	100	100	100	100	..	79	95	..	..	..
Syrian Arab Republic	..	80	..	90	..	98	99	..	81	42
Tajikistan	..	60	..	90	..	84	84	1.9	..	3
Tanzania	38	68	84	90	86	89	89	2.1	81	43
Thailand	80	84	79	96	..	94	96	..	75	73
Togo	51	54	37	34	38	58	64	2.0	55	6
Trinidad and Tobago	91	90	99	99	..	88	89	..	..	..
Tunisia	75	80	76	84	..	94	96	..	90	92
Turkey	79	82	87	90	37	82	78	..	..	..
Turkmenistan	..	..	..	..	..	88	98	..	75	36
Uganda	45	52	..	79	50	77	72	0.2	56	47
Ukraine	..	98	..	99	..	99	99	..	..	..
United Arab Emirates	..	..	..	..	..	94	94	..	62	25
United Kingdom	100	100	100	100	..	83	91	..	..	..
United States	100	100	100	100	..	..	..	..	70	87
Uruguay	..	98	..	94	..	92	93	..	85	70
Uzbekistan	..	85	..	89	..	97	98	..	76	24
Venezuela, RB	..	83	..	68	..	78	63	..	80	65
Vietnam	55	77	29	47	89	96	75	15.8	93	82
West Bank and Gaza	..	..	..	..	..	..	..	..	..	..
Yemen, Rep.	..	69	32	38	39	65	69	..	80	49
Zambia	52	64	63	78	60	85	78	1.1	75	40
Zimbabwe	78	83	56	62	77	58	58	..	71	46
World	**74 w**	**81 w**	**45 w**	**55 w**		**72 w**	**75 w**			
Low income	66	76	30	43		65	65			
Middle income	76	82	47	60		80	85			
Lower middle income	75	81	45	58		78	84			
Upper middle income	..	..	..	..		94	90			
Low & middle income	71	79	39	51		71	73			
East Asia & Pacific	71	76	35	46		70	78			
Europe & Central Asia	..	91	..	..		93	92			
Latin America & Carib.	82	86	72	77		91	88			
Middle East & N. Africa	..	88	..	85		92	92			
South Asia	72	84	22	34		66	70			
Sub-Saharan Africa	53	58	54	53		58	54			
High income	..	..	..	..		90	95			
Europe EMU	..	..	..	..		85	96			

a. Refers to children who were immunized before 12 months or, in some cases, at any time before the survey (between 12–23 months). b. For malaria prevention only. c. Data are for the most recent year available.

The indicators in the table are based on data provided to the World Health Organization (WHO) by member states as part of their efforts to monitor and evaluate progress in implementing national health strategies. Because reliable, observation-based statistical data for these indicators do not exist in some developing countries, some of the data are estimated.

People's health is influenced by the environment in which they live. Lack of clean water and basic sanitation is the main reason diseases transmitted by feces are so common in developing countries. The data on access to an improved water source measure the share of the population with ready access to water for domestic purposes. The data are based on surveys and estimates provided by governments to the Joint Monitoring Programme of the WHO and United Nations Children's Fund (UNICEF). The coverage rates for water and sanitation are based on information from service users on the facilities their households actually use rather than on information from service providers, who may include nonfunctioning systems. Access to drinking water from an improved source does not ensure that the water is safe or adequate, as these characteristics are not tested at the time of the surveys.

Neonatal tetanus is an important cause of infant mortality in some developing countries. It can be prevented through immunization of the mother during pregnancy. Recommended doses for full protection are generally two tetanus shots during the first pregnancy

2.15a

Children in rural households are less likely to use bednets

Children under five sleeping under bednets, 2000 (%)

■ Untreated bednets ■ Insecticide-treated bednets

Even though malaria is often more prevalent in rural areas, fewer children under age five sleep under a bednet in rural areas than in urban ones. The ratio of urban-rural difference is even greater for insecticide-treated bednets because they are more expensive than untreated bednets, and retreatment of insecticide-treated nets is still uncommon, especially in rural areas.

Source: WHO and UNICEF 2003.

and one booster shot during each subsequent pregnancy, with five doses considered adequate for lifetime protection. Information on tetanus shots during pregnancy is collected through surveys in which pregnant respondents are asked to show antenatal cards on which tetanus shots have been recorded. Because not all women have antenatal cards, respondents are also asked about their receipt of these injections. Poor recall may result in a downward bias in estimates of the share of births protected. But in settings where receiving injections is common, respondents may erroneously report having received tetanus shots.

Governments in developing countries usually finance immunization against measles and diphtheria, pertussis (whooping cough), and tetanus (DPT) as part of the basic public health package. In many developing countries, however, lack of precise information on the size of the cohort of children under one year of age makes immunization coverage difficult to estimate. The data shown here are based on an assessment of national immunization coverage rates by the WHO and UNICEF. The assessment considered both administrative data from service providers and household survey data on children's immunization histories. Based on the data available, consideration of potential biases, and contributions of local experts, the most likely true level of immunization coverage was determined for each year.

Sleeping under treated bednets, if properly used and maintained, is one of the most important malaria preventive strategies to limit human-mosquito contact. Studies have emphasized that mortality rates could be reduced by about 25–30 percent if every child under five in malaria-risk areas such as Africa slept under a treated bednet every night.

Data on the success rate of tuberculosis treatment are provided for countries that have implemented the recommended control strategy: directly observed treatment, short course (DOTS). Countries that have not adopted DOTS or have only recently done so are omitted because of lack of data or poor comparability or reliability of reported results. The treatment success rate for tuberculosis provides a useful indicator of the quality of health services. A low rate or no success suggests that infectious patients may not be receiving adequate treatment. An essential complement to the tuberculosis treatment success rate is the DOTS detection rate, which indicates whether there is adequate coverage by the recommended case detection and treatment strategy. A country with a high treatment success rate may still face big challenges if its DOTS detection rate remains low.

• **Access to an improved water source** refers to the percentage of the population with reasonable access to an adequate amount of water from an improved source, such as a household connection, public standpipe, borehole, protected well or spring, or rainwater collection. Unimproved sources include vendors, tanker trucks, and unprotected wells and springs. Reasonable access is defined as the availability of at least 20 liters a person a day from a source within 1 kilometer of the dwelling. • **Access to improved sanitation facilities** refers to the percentage of the population with at least adequate access to excreta disposal facilities (private or shared but not public) that can effectively prevent human, animal, and insect contact with excreta. Improved facilities range from simple but protected pit latrines to flush toilets with a sewerage connection. To be effective, facilities must be correctly constructed and properly maintained. • **Tetanus vaccinations** refer to the percentage of pregnant women who receive two tetanus toxoid injections during their first pregnancy and one booster shot during each subsequent pregnancy, with five doses considered adequate for a lifetime. • **Child immunization rate** is the percentage of children ages 12–23 months who received vaccinations before 12 months or at any time before the survey for four diseases—measles and diphtheria, pertussis (whooping cough), and tetanus (DPT). A child is considered adequately immunized against measles after receiving one dose of vaccine and against DPT after receiving three doses. • **Children sleeping under treated bednets** refer to the percentage of children under age five who slept under an insecticide-impregnated bednet to prevent malaria. • **Tuberculosis treatment success rate** is the percentage of new, registered smear-positive (infectious) cases that were cured or in which a full course of treatment was completed. • **DOTS detection rate** is the percentage of estimated new infectious tuberculosis cases detected under the directly observed treatment, short course case detection and treatment strategy.

Data sources

Data are drawn from a variety of sources, including WHO and UNICEF estimates of National Immunization Coverage, the WHO's *Global Tuberculosis Control Report 2003;* UNICEF's *State of the World's Children 2004;* and the WHO and UNICEF's *Global Water Supply and Sanitation Assessment 2000 Report.*

	Total fertility rate		Adolescent fertility rate	Women at risk of unintended pregnancy	Contraceptive prevalence rate	Births attended by skilled health staff		Maternal mortality ratio	
	births per woman		births per 1,000 women ages 15–19	% of married women ages 15–49	% of women ages 15–49	% of total		per 100,000 live births National estimates	Modeled estimates
	1980	**2002**	**2002**	**1990–2002**[a]	**1990–2002**[a]	**1985**	**1995–2002**[a]	**1985–2002**[a]	**2000**
Afghanistan	7.0	6.8	151	..	..	..	12	..	1,900
Albania	3.6	2.2	11	..	..	..	99	20	55
Algeria	6.7	2.8	17	..	51	..	92	140	140
Angola	6.9	7.0	225	..	..	..	45	..	1,700
Argentina	3.3	2.4	60	..	..	..	98	41	82
Armenia	2.3	1.1	35	12	61	..	97	22	55
Australia	1.9	1.8	18	..	..	..	100	..	8
Austria	1.6	1.3	20	..	..	..	100[b]	..	4
Azerbaijan	3.2	2.1	44	..	55	..	84	25	94
Bangladesh	6.1	3.0	129	15	54	..	12	380	380
Belarus	2.0	1.3	21	..	..	100	100	14	35
Belgium	1.7	1.6	11	..	..	100	100[b]	..	10
Benin	7.0	5.3	103	27	19	..	66	500	850
Bolivia	5.5	3.8	75	26	49	..	69	390	420
Bosnia and Herzegovina	2.1	1.3	23	..	..	..	100	10	31
Botswana	6.1	3.8	68	..	..	..	94	330	100
Brazil	3.9	2.1	68	7	77	81	88	160	260
Bulgaria	2.0	1.3	49	..	..	..	..	15	32
Burkina Faso	7.5	6.3	133	26	12	..	31	480	1,000
Burundi	6.8	5.8	50	..	..	19	25	..	1,000
Cambodia	5.7	3.8	57	30	24	..	32	440	450
Cameroon	6.4	4.6	127	20	19	..	60	430	730
Canada	1.7	1.5	20	..	..	100	98	..	6
Central African Republic	5.8	4.6	124	16	15	..	44	1,100	1,100
Chad	6.9	6.2	182	10	4	..	16	830	1,100
Chile	2.8	2.2	43	..	..	..	100	23	31
China	2.5	1.9	15	..	83	..	76	53	56
Hong Kong, China	2.0	1.0	6	..	..	..	..	..	..
Colombia	3.9	2.5	75	6	77	..	86	78	130
Congo, Dem. Rep.	6.6	6.7	226	..	..	..	61	950	990
Congo, Rep.	6.3	6.3	146	..	..	..	..	..	510
Costa Rica	3.6	2.3	69	..	..	97	98	29	43
Côte d'Ivoire	7.4	4.6	118	28	15	..	63	600	690
Croatia	1.9	1.5	18	..	..	..	100	2	8
Cuba	2.0	1.6	67	..	..	..	100	30	33
Czech Republic	2.1	1.2	23	..	69	..	99	3	9
Denmark	1.5	1.7	8	..	..	100	100[b]	10	5
Dominican Republic	4.2	2.6	89	12	70	..	98	230[b]	150
Ecuador	5.0	2.8	64	..	66	..	69	160	130
Egypt, Arab Rep.	5.1	3.0	46	11	56	..	61	84	84
El Salvador	4.9	2.9	87	..	60	..	90	120	150
Eritrea	7.5	4.8	101	28	8	..	21	1,000	630
Estonia	2.0	1.3	26	..	..	..	..	46	63
Ethiopia	6.6	5.6	135	36	8	..	6	870	850
Finland	1.6	1.7	10	..	..	..	100[b]	6	6
France	1.9	1.9	10	..	71	..	99[b]	10	17
Gabon	4.5	4.1	156	28	33	..	86	520	420
Gambia, The	6.5	4.8	139	..	..	..	55	..	540
Georgia	2.3	1.1	27	..	41	..	96	67	32
Germany	1.4	1.4	14	..	..	100	100[b]	8	8
Ghana	6.5	4.1	81	23	22	..	44	210[b]	540
Greece	2.2	1.3	17	..	..	..	..	1	9
Guatemala	6.3	4.3	100	23	38	35	41	190	240
Guinea	6.1	5.0	153	24	6	..	35	530	740
Guinea-Bissau	7.1	6.6	215	..	..	..	35	910	1,100
Haiti	5.9	4.2	72	40	28	..	24	520	680

	Total fertility rate		Adolescent fertility rate	Women at risk of unintended pregnancy	Contraceptive prevalence rate	Births attended by skilled health staff		Maternal mortality ratio	
			births per 1,000 women ages 15–19	% of married women ages 15–49	% of women ages 15–49	% of total		per 100,000 live births National estimates	Modeled estimates
	births per woman								
	1980	2002	2002	1990–2002[a]	1990–2002[a]	1985	1995–2002[a]	1985–2002[a]	2000
Honduras	6.5	4.0	110	..	62	*41*	56	110	110
Hungary	1.9	1.3	21	..	73	..	..	5	16
India	5.0	2.9	98	16	52	..	43	540	540
Indonesia	4.3	2.3	52	9	57	*36*	64	380	230
Iran, Islamic Rep.	6.7	2.0	25	..	73	..	90	37	76
Iraq	6.4	4.1	35	..	..	..	72	290	250
Ireland	3.2	1.9	15	..	60	..	100	6	5
Israel	3.2	2.7	19	..	..	*99*	99[b]	5	17
Italy	1.6	1.3	8	..	..	..	..	7	5
Jamaica	3.7	2.3	84	..	65	..	95	97	87
Japan	1.8	1.3	3	..	..	..	100	8	10
Jordan	6.8	3.5	30	14	56	..	97	41	41
Kazakhstan	2.9	1.8	35	9	66	..	99	50	210
Kenya	7.8	4.2	100	24	39	..	44	590	1,000
Korea, Dem. Rep.	2.8	2.1	2	..	..	..	97	110	67
Korea, Rep.	2.6	1.5	4	..	..	..	100	20	20
Kuwait	5.3	2.5	30	..	..	*96*	98	5	5
Kyrgyz Republic	4.1	2.4	29	12	60	..	98	44	110
Lao PDR	6.7	4.8	91	..	25	..	19	530	650
Latvia	1.9	1.2	32	..	..	..	100	25	42
Lebanon	4.0	2.2	23	..	61	..	89	100[b]	150
Lesotho	5.5	4.3	77	..	23	..	60	..	550
Liberia	6.8	5.8	196	..	..	..	51	580	760
Libya	7.3	3.3	32	..	45	..	94	77	97
Lithuania	2.0	1.3	33	..	..	..	..	13	13
Macedonia, FYR	2.5	1.8	31	..	..	..	97	15	23
Madagascar	6.6	5.2	157	26	17	..	46	490	550
Malawi	7.6	6.1	137	30	31	..	56	1,100	1,800
Malaysia	4.2	2.8	23	..	..	..	97	30	41
Mali	7.1	6.4	176	29	8	*32*	41	580	1,200
Mauritania	6.4	4.6	113	32	8	..	57	750	1,000
Mauritius	2.7	2.0	39	..	75	..	99	21	24
Mexico	4.7	2.4	62	..	65	..	86	79	83
Moldova	2.4	1.4	44	..	74	..	99	44	36
Mongolia	5.3	2.4	45	..	60	..	97	160	110
Morocco	5.4	2.8	44	20	59	*26*	40	230	220
Mozambique	6.5	5.0	153	23	6	..	44	1,100	1,000
Myanmar	4.9	2.8	29	..	..	..	56	230	360
Namibia	5.9	4.8	103	22	29	..	78	270	300
Nepal	6.1	4.2	112	28	39	..	11	540	740
Netherlands	1.6	1.7	5	..	75	..	100	7	16
New Zealand	2.0	1.9	30	..	..	..	100	15	7
Nicaragua	6.3	3.4	122	15	60	..	67	120	230
Niger	8.0	7.1	205	17	8	..	16	590	1,600
Nigeria	6.9	5.1	111	17	15	..	42	..	800
Norway	1.7	1.8	10	..	..	..	100[b]	6	16
Oman	9.9	4.0	54	..	24	*87*	95	23	87
Pakistan	7.0	4.5	62	32	28	..	20	530	500
Panama	3.7	2.4	75	..	..	..	90	70	160
Papua New Guinea	5.8	4.3	68	..	26	..	53	370[b]	300
Paraguay	5.2	3.8	75	15	57	..	71	190	170
Peru	4.5	2.6	61	10	69	..	59	190	410
Philippines	4.8	3.2	33	19	47	..	58	170	200
Poland	2.3	1.3	15	..	..	*99*	99[b]	4	13
Portugal	2.2	1.5	23	..	..	..	100	8	5
Puerto Rico	2.6	1.9	64	..	78	..	..	..	25

	Total fertility rate		Adolescent fertility rate	Women at risk of unintended pregnancy	Contraceptive prevalence rate	Births attended by skilled health staff		Maternal mortality ratio	
	births per woman		births per 1,000 women ages 15–19	% of married women ages 15–49	% of women ages 15–49	% of total		per 100,000 live births National estimates	Modeled estimates
	1980	2002	2002	1990–2002[a]	1990–2002[a]	1985	1995–2002[a]	1985–2002[a]	2000
Romania	2.4	1.3	41	..	64	..	98	34	49
Russian Federation	1.9	1.3	46	..	34	..	99	37	67
Rwanda	8.3	5.7	52	36	13	..	31	1,100	1,400
Saudi Arabia	7.3	5.3	91	..	21	..	91	..	23
Senegal	6.8	4.9	89	35	11	41	58	560	690
Serbia and Montenegro	2.3	1.7	32	..	..	..	99	7	11
Sierra Leone	6.5	5.6	182	..	..	..	42	1,800	2,000
Singapore	1.7	1.4	8	..	..	..	100	6	30
Slovak Republic	2.3	1.3	25	..	..	..	..	16	3
Slovenia	2.1	1.1	9	..	..	..	100[b]	17	17
Somalia	7.3	6.9	204	..	..	..	34	..	1,100
South Africa	4.6	2.8	43	15	62	..	84	150	230
Spain	2.2	1.3	9	..	..	..	..	0	4
Sri Lanka	3.5	2.1	20	..	..	..	97	92	92
Sudan	6.1	4.4	56	..	10	..	86[b]	550	590
Swaziland	6.2	4.2	103	..	..	..	70	230	370
Sweden	1.7	1.6	9	..	..	100	100[b]	5	2
Switzerland	1.5	1.5	5	..	..	..	..	5	7
Syrian Arab Republic	7.4	3.4	38	..	45	..	76[b]	110[b]	160
Tajikistan	5.6	2.9	24	..	..	..	71	45	100
Tanzania	6.7	5.0	115	22	25	..	36	530	1,500
Thailand	3.5	1.8	72	..	72	..	99	36	44
Togo	6.8	4.9	82	32	24	..	49	480	570
Trinidad and Tobago	3.3	1.8	42	..	..	98	96	70	160
Tunisia	5.2	2.1	10	..	60	..	90	69	120
Turkey	4.3	2.2	55	10	64	..	81	130[b]	70
Turkmenistan	4.9	2.7	16	10	62	..	97	9	31
Uganda	7.2	6.0	182	35	23	..	39	510	880
Ukraine	2.0	1.2	31	..	72	..	100	18	35
United Arab Emirates	5.4	3.0	64	..	..	..	96	3	54
United Kingdom	1.9	1.7	27	..	..	..	99	7	13
United States	1.8	2.1	47	..	64	..	99	8	17
Uruguay	2.7	2.2	64	..	..	..	100	26	27
Uzbekistan	4.8	2.3	37	14	56	..	96	34	24
Venezuela, RB	4.2	2.7	90	..	..	..	94	60	96
Vietnam	5.0	1.9	28	7	79	..	70	95	130
West Bank and Gaza	..	4.9	81	..	42	..	..	..	..
Yemen, Rep.	7.9	6.0	97	39	21	..	22	350	570
Zambia	7.0	5.1	129	27	26	..	43	650	750
Zimbabwe	6.4	3.7	86	13	54	..	73	700	1,100
World	**3.7 w**	**2.6 w**	**63 w**	**.. w**	**.. w**	**.. w**	**60 w**		**403 w**
Low income	5.5	3.5	98		..	..	41		657
Middle income	3.2	2.1	36		..	..	80		106
Lower middle income	3.1	2.1	33		86	..	78		112
Upper middle income	3.6	2.4	54		..	..	92		67
Low & middle income	4.1	2.8	68		..	..	56		440
East Asia & Pacific	3.1	2.1	25		83	..	72		115
Europe & Central Asia	2.5	1.6	38		..	..	93		58
Latin America & Carib.	4.1	2.5	70		..	..	82		193
Middle East & N. Africa	6.2	3.1	41		53	..	70		165
South Asia	5.3	3.2	98		50	..	35		506
Sub-Saharan Africa	6.6	5.1	126		..	..	44		917
High income	1.9	1.7	24		..	..	99[b]		13
Europe EMU	1.8	1.5	11		..	..	..		10

a. Data are for most recent year available. b. Data refer to period other than specified, differ from the standard definition, or refer to only part of a country.

About the data

Reproductive health is a state of physical and mental well-being in relation to the reproductive system and its functions and processes. Means of achieving reproductive health include education and services during pregnancy and childbirth, provision of safe and effective contraception, and prevention and treatment of sexually transmitted diseases. The complications of pregnancy and childbirth are the leading cause of death and disability among women of reproductive age in developing countries. Reproductive health services will need to expand rapidly over the next two decades, when the number of women and men of reproductive age is projected to increase by more than 600 million.

Total and adolescent fertility rates are based on data on registered live births from vital registration systems or, in the absence of such systems, from censuses or sample surveys. As long as the surveys are fairly recent, the estimated rates are generally considered reliable measures of fertility in the recent past. Where no empirical information on age-specific fertility rates is available, a model is used to estimate the share of births to adolescents. For countries without vital registration systems, fertility rates are generally based on extrapolations from trends observed in censuses or surveys from earlier years.

An increasing number of couples in the developing world want to limit or postpone childbearing but are not using effective contraceptive methods. These couples face the risk of unintended pregnancy, shown in the table as the percentage of married women of reproductive age who do not want to become pregnant but are not using contraception (Bulatao 1998). Information on this indicator is collected through surveys and excludes women not exposed to the risk of unintended pregnancy

because of menopause, infertility, or postpartum anovulation. Common reasons for not using contraception are lack of knowledge about contraceptive methods and concerns about their possible health side-effects.

Contraceptive prevalence reflects all methods—ineffective traditional methods as well as highly effective modern methods. Contraceptive prevalence rates are obtained mainly from Demographic and Health Surveys and contraceptive prevalence surveys (see *Primary data documentation* for the most recent survey year). Unmarried women are often excluded from such surveys, which may bias the estimates.

The share of births attended by skilled health staff is an indicator of a health system's ability to provide adequate care for pregnant women. Good antenatal and postnatal care improve maternal health and reduce maternal and infant mortality. But data may not reflect such improvements because health information systems are often weak, maternal deaths are underreported, and rates of maternal mortality are difficult to measure.

Maternal mortality ratios are generally of unknown reliability, as are many other cause-specific mortality indicators. Household surveys such as the Demographic and Health Surveys attempt to measure maternal mortality by asking respondents about survivorship of sisters. The main disadvantage of this method is that the estimates of maternal mortality that it produces pertain to 12 years or so before the survey, making them unsuitable for monitoring recent changes or observing the impact of interventions. In addition, measurement of maternal mortality is subject to many types of errors. Even in high-income countries with vital registration systems, misclassification of maternal deaths has been found to lead to serious underestimation.

The maternal mortality ratios shown in the table as national estimates are based on national surveys, vital registration, or surveillance or are derived from community and hospital records. Those shown as modeled estimates are based on an exercise carried out by the World Health Organization (WHO), United Nations Children's Fund (UNICEF), and United Nations Population Fund (UNFPA). In this exercise maternal mortality was estimated with a regression model using information on fertility, birth attendants, and HIV prevalence. Neither set of ratios can be assumed to provide an accurate estimate of maternal mortality in any of the countries in the table.

Definitions

• **Total fertility rate** is the number of children that would be born to a woman if she were to live to the end of her childbearing years and bear children in accordance with current age-specific fertility rates. • **Adolescent fertility rate** is the number of births per 1,000 women ages 15–19. • **Women at risk of unintended pregnancy** are fertile, married women of reproductive age who do not want to become pregnant and are not using contraception. • **Contraceptive prevalence rate** is the percentage of women who are practicing, or whose sexual partners are practicing, any form of contraception. It is usually measured for married women ages 15–49 only. • **Births attended by skilled health staff** are the percentage of deliveries attended by personnel trained to give the necessary supervision, care, and advice to women during pregnancy, labor, and the postpartum period; to conduct deliveries on their own; and to care for newborns. • **Maternal mortality ratio** is the number of women who die from pregnancy-related causes during pregnancy and childbirth, per 100,000 live births.

2.16a

Does household wealth affect antenatal care?

Pregnant women attending antenatal clinics, by wealth quintile (%)

Across 22 countries in Sub-Saharan Africa rich women were about 1.5 times more likely to attend antenatal clinics than were poor women. The lack of care can contribute to women's death during pregnancy or childbirth and can also compromise the health and survival of their infants.

Source: WHO and UNICEF 2003.

Data sources

The data on reproductive health come from Demographic and Health Surveys, the WHO's *Coverage of Maternity Care* (1997) and other WHO sources, UNICEF, and national statistical offices. Modeled estimates for maternal mortality ratios are from Carla AbouZahr and Tessa Wardlaw's "Maternal Mortality in 2000: Estimates Developed by WHO, UNICEF, and UNFPA" (2003).

	Prevalence of undernourishment		Prevalence of child malnutrition		Prevalence of overweight		Low-birthweight babies	Exclusive breastfeeding	Consumption of iodized salt	Vitamin A supplemen-tation
	% of population		% of children under age 5			% of children under age 5	% of births	% of children under 6 months	% of households	% of children 6–59 months
	1990–92	1999–2001	Weight for age 1996–2002[a]	Height for age 1996–2002[a]	Year		1998–2002[a]	1995–2002[a]	1997–2002[a]	2001
Afghanistan	58	70[b]	49	48	1997	4.0	..	..	2	84
Albania	5[c]	4	14	32	2000	22.5	3	6	62	..
Algeria	5	6	6	18	2000	10.1	7	13	69	..
Angola	61	49	31	45	1996	0.5	12	11	35	75
Argentina	<3	<3	5	12	1995–96	9.2	7	..	90[e]	..
Armenia	55[c]	51	3	13	2000–01	10.4	7	30	84	..
Australia	..	..	0	0	1995–96	5.2	7	..	..	..
Austria	..	..	..	..		..	7	..	..	..
Azerbaijan	37[c]	21	17	20	2000	3.8	11	7	26	..
Bangladesh	35	32	48	45	1999–2000	0.4	30	46	70	90
Belarus	<3[c]	3	..	..		..	5	..	37	..
Belgium	..	..	..	..		..	8[e]	..	..	..
Benin	20	16	23	31	2001	1.8	16	38	72	95
Bolivia	26	22	8	27	1998	6.5	9	39	65	31
Bosnia and Herzegovina	13[c]	8	4	10	2000	13.2	4	6	77	..
Botswana	18	24	13	23	2000	6.9	10	34	66	85
Brazil	12	9	6	11	1996	4.9	10[e]	42[f]	95[e]	..
Bulgaria	8[c]	16	..	..		..	10	..	..	..
Burkina Faso	22	17	34	37	1998–99	1.0	19	6	23[e]	97
Burundi	49	70	45	57	1987	1.1	16	62	96	95
Cambodia	43	38	45	45	2000	2.0	11	12	14	57
Cameroon	33	27	22	29	1998	5.0	11	12	84	100
Canada	..	..	..	..		..	6	..	..	..
Central African Republic	50	44	..	..	1995	0.8	14	17	86	90
Chad	58	34	28	29	2000	1.5	17[e]	10	58	91
Chile	8	4	1	2	2002	8.0	5	73[f]	100	..
China	17[d]	11[d]	10	14	2000	2.6	6	67[f]	93	..
Hong Kong, China	<3	<3	..	..		..	..	..	..	..
Colombia	17	13	7	14	2000	3.7	9	32	92	..
Congo, Dem. Rep.	31	75	31	38	2001	3.9	12	24	72	98
Congo, Rep.	37	30	..	..	1987	0.7	..	4[f]	..	100
Costa Rica	7	6	5	6	1996	6.2	7	35[e,f]	97[e]	..
Côte d'Ivoire	18	15	21	25	1998–99	2.5	17	10	31	97
Croatia	18[c]	12	1	1	1995–96	5.9	6	23	90	..
Cuba	8	11	4	5		..	6	41	73	..
Czech Republic	<3[c]	<3	..	..	1991	4.1	7	..	..	..
Denmark	..	..	..	..		..	5	..	..	..
Dominican Republic	27	25	5	6	1996	4.9	14	11	18	35
Ecuador	8	4	14	26		..	16	29[f]	99	50
Egypt, Arab Rep.	5	3	4	19	1995–96	8.6	12	57	28	..
El Salvador	12	14	12	23	1998	2.6	13	16	91[e]	..
Eritrea	..	61	40	38	1995–96	0.9	21[e]	52	97	61
Estonia	10[c]	4	..	..		..	4	..	..	..
Ethiopia	..	42	47	52	2000	1.2	15	55	28	16
Finland	..	..	..	..		..	4	..	..	..
France	..	..	..	..		..	7	..	..	..
Gabon	11	7	12	21	2000–01	3.7	14	6	15	89
Gambia, The	22	27	17	19		..	17	26	8	91
Georgia	45[c]	26	3	12	1999	12.7	6	18[f]	8	..
Germany	..	..	..	..		..	7	..	..	..
Ghana	35	12	25	26	1998–99	1.7	11	31	28	100
Greece	..	..	..	..		..	8	..	..	..
Guatemala	16	25	24	46	1998–99	4.4	13	39	49	..
Guinea	40	28	33	41	1999	2.7	12	11	12	93
Guinea-Bissau	..	..	25	30		..	22	37	2	100
Haiti	65	49	17	23	2000	2.0	21	24	11	..

	Prevalence of undernourishment		Prevalence of child malnutrition		Prevalence of overweight		Low-birthweight babies	Exclusive breastfeeding	Consumption of iodized salt	Vitamin A supplementation
	% of population		% of children under age 5			% of children under age 5	% of births	% of children under 6 months	% of households	% of children 6–59 months
			Weight for age	Height for age						
	1990–92	1999–2001	1996–2002[a]	1996–2002[a]	Year		1998–2002[a]	1995–2002[a]	1997–2002[a]	2001
Honduras	23	20	17	29	2001	2.2	14	35	80	62
Hungary	<3[c]	<3	..	..	1980–88	2.0	9	..	..	..
India	25	21	47	45	1998–99	2.2	30	37[f]	50	25
Indonesia	9	6	25	..	1995	4.0	10[e]	42	65	61
Iran, Islamic Rep.	5	5	11	15	1998	4.3	7[e]	44	94	..
Iraq	7	27[b]	16	22		..	15	12	40	..
Ireland	..	..	..	..		..	6	..	..	..
Israel	..	..	..	..		..	8	..	..	..
Italy	..	..	..	..	1975–77	4.4	6	..	..	..
Jamaica	14	9	4	4	1999	3.8	9	..	100	..
Japan	..	..	..	..	1978–81	1.6	8	..	..	..
Jordan	4	6	5	8	1997	2.8	10[e]	34	88	..
Kazakhstan	<3[c]	22	4	10	1999	3.0	8	36	20	..
Kenya	44	37	22	33	1993	3.5	11	5	91	90
Korea, Dem. Rep.	18	34	28	45		..	7	97[f]	..	99
Korea, Rep.	<3	<3	..	..		..	4	..	..	..
Kuwait	22	4	2	3	1996–97	5.7	7	12[f]	..	..
Kyrgyz Republic	28[c]	7	6	25	1997	6.3	7[e]	24	27	..
Lao PDR	29	22	40	41		..	14	23	75	70
Latvia	3[c]	6	..	..		..	5	..	..	..
Lebanon	3	3	3	12		..	6	27[f]	87	..
Lesotho	27	25	18	45		..	14	15	69	..
Liberia	33	42	27	40	1999–2000	2.3	..	35	..	100
Libya	<3	<3	..	..		..	7[e]	..	90[e]	..
Lithuania	4[c]	<3	..	..		..	4	..	..	..
Macedonia, FYR	15[c]	10	6	7	1999	4.9	5	37	100	..
Madagascar	35	36	33	49	1997	2.0	14	41	52	73
Malawi	49	33	25	49	2000	4.3	16	44	49	63
Malaysia	3	<3	..	..		..	10	29[f]	..	..
Mali	25	21	33	38	2001	1.5	23	38	74	74
Mauritania	14	10	32	35		..	42	20	2	98
Mauritius	6	5	..	..	1995	4.0	13	16[e,f]	0[e]	..
Mexico	5	5	8	18	1998–99	5.3	9	38[e,f]	90	..
Moldova	5[c]	12	..	..		..	5	..	33	..
Mongolia	34	38	13	25	1999	4.8	8	51	45	93
Morocco	6	7	9	23	1992	6.8	11[e]	66[f]	41	..
Mozambique	69	53	26	36	1997	3.4	14[e]	30	62[e]	71
Myanmar	10	7	28	42	1997	7.7	15	11	48	97
Namibia	20	7	..	..	1992	3.3	16[e]	26[f]	63	84
Nepal	18	17	48	51	2001	0.2	21	69	63	98
Netherlands	..	..	..	..	1980	1.6	..	..	..	..
New Zealand	..	..	..	..		..	6	..	83	..
Nicaragua	30	29	10	20	1998	2.6	13	31	96	..
Niger	42	34	40	40	2000	0.8	17	1	15	89
Nigeria	13	8	31	34	1993	3.3	12	17	98	77
Norway	..	..	..	..		..	5	..	..	..
Oman	..	..	18	10	1998	1.0	8	..	61	..
Pakistan	26	19	..	..	1990–94	1.3	19[e]	16[f]	17	100
Panama	20	26	8	18	1997	4.2	10[e]	25	95	..
Papua New Guinea	25	27	..	..	1982–83	1.6	11[e]	59	..	..
Paraguay	18	13	..	..	1990	3.9	9[e]	7[f]	83	..
Peru	40	11	7	25	2000	7.6	11[e]	71	93	6
Philippines	26	22	32	32	1998	1.0	20	37	24	84
Poland	<3[c]	<3	..	..		..	6	..	..	..
Portugal	..	..	..	..		..	8	..	..	..
Puerto Rico	..	..	..	..		..	..	..	..	..

	Prevalence of undernourishment		Prevalence of child malnutrition		Prevalence of overweight		Low-birthweight babies	Exclusive breastfeeding	Consumption of iodized salt	Vitamin A supplementation
	% of population		% of children under age 5		% of children under age 5		% of births	% of children under 6 months	% of households	% of children 6–59 months
	1990–92	1999–2001	Weight for age 1996–2002[a]	Height for age 1996–2002[a]	Year	age 5	1998–2002[a]	1995–2002[a]	1997–2002[a]	2001
Romania	<3[c]	<3	3	10	2002	5.5	9	..	..	..
Russian Federation	4[c]	4	6	11		..	6	..	30[e]	..
Rwanda	43	41	24	43	2000	4.0	9	84	90	94
Saudi Arabia	4	3	..	..		..	11[e]	31[f]	..	..
Senegal	23	24	23	25	2000	2.2	18	24[f]	16	85
Serbia and Montenegro	5[c]	9	2	5	1996	12.9	4	11[f]	73	..
Sierra Leone	46	50	27	34		..	..	4	23	91
Singapore	..	..	..	..	1970–77	0.5	8	..	..	..
Slovak Republic	4[c]	5	..	..		..	7	..	..	..
Slovenia	3[c]	<3	..	..		..	6	..	..	..
Somalia	68	71[b]	26	23		..	..	9	..	62
South Africa	..	..	..	..	1995	6.7	15	7	62	..
Spain	..	..	..	..		..	6[e]	..	..	..
Sri Lanka	29	25	33	..	1987	0.1	22	54[f]	88	..
Sudan	31	25	11	..		..	31	16	1	92
Swaziland	10	12	10	30		..	9	24	59	..
Sweden	..	..	..	..		..	4	..	..	..
Switzerland	..	..	..	..		..	6	..	..	..
Syrian Arab Republic	5	4	7	19		..	6	81[f]	40	..
Tajikistan	22[c]	71	..	31		..	15	14	20	..
Tanzania	35	43	29	44	1999	1.7	13	32	67	93
Thailand	28	19	..	..	1995	2.8	9	4[f]	74	..
Togo	33	25	25	22	1998	1.5	15	18	67	77
Trinidad and Tobago	13	12	6	4	1987	3.0	23	2	1	..
Tunisia	<3	<3	4	12	1996–97	4.5	7	46	97	..
Turkey	<3	3	8	16	1998	2.2	16	7	64	..
Turkmenistan	15[c]	7	12	22		..	6	13	75	..
Uganda	23	19	23	39	1995	2.8	12	65	95	37
Ukraine	<3[c]	4	3	16	2000	20.1	5	22	5	..
United Arab Emirates	4	<3	7	..		..	15[e]	34[f]	..	..
United Kingdom	..	..	..	..		..	8	..	..	..
United States	..	..	..	..	1988–94	4.5	8	..	..	..
Uruguay	6	3	..	..	1992–93	6.2	8	..	..	..
Uzbekistan	10[c]	26	19	31	1996	14.4	7	16	19	..
Venezuela, RB	11	18	4	13	2000	3.2	7	7[f]	90	..
Vietnam	27	19	34	37	2000	2.7	9	31	40	59
West Bank and Gaza	..	..	4	7	1996	2.3	..	..	..	..
Yemen, Rep.	35	33	46	52	1996	4.3	32[e]	18	39	100
Zambia	45	50	28	47	2001–02	3.0	10	40	68	83
Zimbabwe	43	39	13	27	1999	7.0	11	33	93	..
World	**21 w**	**17 w**	**.. w**	**.. w**			**15 w**		**66 w**	**.. w**
Low income	26	24	42	..			21		52	55
Middle income	15	10	..	25			9		79	..
Lower middle income	16	11	9	17			9		78	..
Upper middle income	..	..	..	..			8		89	..
Low & middle income	21	17	..	..			16		66	*51*
East Asia & Pacific	17	12	15	14			8		82	..
Europe & Central Asia	..	9	..	..			9		36	..
Latin America & Carib.	14	11	9	19			10		88	..
Middle East & N. Africa	7	8	..	..			12		58	..
South Asia	27	23	48	47			28		48	42
Sub-Saharan Africa	31	32	..	..			14		62	76
High income	..	..	..	..			7		..	..
Europe EMU	..	..	..	..			7		..	..

a. Data are for the most recent year available. b. Data are for 1998–2000. c. Data are for 1993–95. d. Includes Taiwan, China. e. Data refer to period other than specified, differ from the standard definition, or refer to only part of a country. f. Refers to exclusive breastfeeding for less than four months.

Data on undernourishment are produced by the Food and Agriculture Organization (FAO) based on the calories available from local food production, trade, and stocks; the number of calories needed by different age and gender groups; the proportion of the population represented by each age group; and a coefficient of distribution to take account of inequality in access to food (FAO 2000). From a policy and program standpoint, however, this measure has its limits. First, food insecurity exists even where food availability is not a problem because of inadequate access of poor households to food. Second, food insecurity is an individual or household phenomenon, and the average food available to each person, even corrected for possible effects of low income, is not a good predictor of food insecurity among the population. And third, nutrition security is determined not only by food security but also by the quality of care of mothers and children and the quality of the household's health environment (Smith and Haddad 2000).

Estimates of child malnutrition, based on weight for age (underweight) and height for age (stunting), are from national survey data. The proportion of children who are underweight is the most common indicator of malnutrition. Being underweight, even mildly, increases the risk of death and inhibits cognitive development in children. Moreover, it perpetuates the problem from one generation to the next, as malnourished women are more likely to have low-birthweight babies. Height for age reflects linear growth achieved pre- and postnatally, and a deficit indicates long-term, cumulative effects of inadequacies of health, diet, or care. It is often argued that stunting is a proxy for multifaceted deprivation and is a better indicator of long term changes in malnutrition.

Estimates of children who are overweight are also from national survey data. Overweight in children has become a growing concern in developing countries. Researchers show an association between obesity in childhood and a high prevalence of diabetes, respiratory disease, high blood pressure, and psychosocial and orthopedic disorders (de Onis and Blossner 2000). The survey data were analyzed in a standardized way by the World Health Organization (WHO) to allow comparisons across countries.

Low birthweight, which is associated with maternal malnutrition, raises the risk of infant mortality and stunts growth in infancy and childhood. There is also emerging evidence that low-birthweight babies are more prone to noncommunicable diseases such as diabetes and cardiovascular heart diseases. Estimates of low-birthweight infants are drawn mostly from hospital records and household surveys. Many births in developing countries take place at home, and these births are seldom recorded. A hospital birth may indicate higher income and therefore better nutrition, or it could indicate a higher-risk birth, possibly skewing the data on birthweights downward. The data should therefore be treated with caution.

It is estimated that breastfeeding can save some 1.5 million children a year. Breast milk alone contains all the nutrients, antibodies, hormones, and antioxidants an infant needs to thrive. It protects babies from diarrhea and acute respiratory infections, stimulates their immune systems and response to vaccination, and according to some studies, confers cognitive benefits as well. The data on breastfeeding are derived from national surveys.

Iodine deficiency is the single most important cause of preventable mental retardation, and it contributes significantly to the risk of stillbirth and miscarriage. Iodized salt is the best source of iodine, and a global campaign to iodize edible salt is significantly reducing the risks (UNICEF, *The State of the World's Children 1999*).

Vitamin A is essential for the functioning of the immune system. A child deficient in vitamin A faces a 23 percent greater risk of dying from a range of childhood ailments such as measles, malaria, and diarrhea. Improving the vitamin A status of pregnant women helps reduce anemia, improves their resistance to infection, and may reduce their risk of dying during pregnancy and childbirth. Giving vitamin A to new mothers who are breastfeeding helps to protect their children during the first months of life.

• **Prevalence of undernourishment** is the percentage of the population that is undernourished.
• **Prevalence of child malnutrition** is the percentage of children under five whose weight for age or height for age is more than two standard deviations below the median for the international reference population ages 0–59 months. For children up to two years of age height is measured by recumbent length. For older children height is measured by stature while standing. The reference population, adopted by the WHO in 1983, is based on children from the United States, who are assumed to be well nourished.
• **Prevalence of overweight** is the percentage of children under five whose weight for height is more than two standard deviations above the median for the international reference population of the corresponding age, established by the U.S. National Center for Health Statistics and the WHO. • **Low-birthweight babies** are newborns weighing less than 2,500 grams, with the measurement taken within the first hours of life, before significant postnatal weight loss has occurred. • **Exclusive breastfeeding** refers to the percentage of children less than 6 months old who are fed breast milk alone (no other liquids). • **Consumption of iodized salt** refers to the percentage of households that use edible salt fortified with iodine. • **Vitamin A supplementation** refers to the percentage of children ages 6–59 months who received at least one high-dose vitamin A capsule in the previous six months.

Data sources

Data are drawn from a variety of sources, including the FAO's *State of Food Insecurity in the World 2003;* the United Nations Administrative Committee on Coordination, Subcommittee on Nutrition's *Update on the Nutrition Situation;* the WHO's *World Health Report 2003;* and the United Nations Children's Fund's (UNICEF) *State of the World's Children 2004.*

Health risk factors and future challenges

	Prevalence of smoking		Incidence of tuberculosis	Prevalence of HIV		
	% of adults		per 100,000	% of adults	% ages 15–24 [a]		
	Male	Female	people		Male	Female
	2000	**2000**	**2002**	**2001**	**2001**	**2001**
Afghanistan	..	..	333	*<0.01*	..	..
Albania	60	18	27	*<0.01*	..	..
Algeria	44	7	52	0.10	..	..
Angola	..	..	335	5.50	2.23	5.74
Argentina	47	34	46	0.70	0.86	0.34
Armenia	64	1	77	0.20	0.22	0.06
Australia	21	18	6	0.10	0.12	0.01
Austria	30	19	15	0.20	0.22	0.12
Azerbaijan	30	1	82	<0.10	0.06	0.01
Bangladesh	54	24	221	<0.10	0.01	0.01
Belarus	55	5	83	0.30	0.58	0.19
Belgium	30	26	14	0.20	0.12	0.12
Benin	..	..	86	3.60	1.17	3.71
Bolivia	43	18	234	<0.10	0.11	0.05
Bosnia and Herzegovina	..	..	60	0.10	..	..
Botswana	..	..	657	38.80	16.08	37.49
Brazil	38	29	62	0.70	0.64	0.48
Bulgaria	49	24	48	<0.10	..	..
Burkina Faso	..	..	157	6.50	3.97	9.73
Burundi	..	..	359	8.30	4.95	11.05
Cambodia	66	8	549	2.70	0.96	2.48
Cameroon	..	..	188	11.80	5.44	12.67
Canada	27	23	6	0.30	0.28	0.17
Central African Republic	..	..	338	12.90	5.82	13.54
Chad	24	..	222	3.60	2.38	4.28
Chile	26	18	18	0.30	0.35	0.13
China	67	4	113	0.10	0.16	0.09
Hong Kong, China	..	..	93	0.10	0.00	0.00
Colombia	24	21	45	0.40	0.85	0.19
Congo, Dem. Rep.	..	6	383	4.90	2.92	5.91
Congo, Rep.	..	..	395	7.20	3.28	7.80
Costa Rica	29	7	15	0.60	0.58	0.27
Côte d'Ivoire	42	2	412	9.70	2.91	8.31
Croatia	34	32	47	<0.10	0.00	0.00
Cuba	48	26	12	<0.10	0.09	0.05
Czech Republic	36	22	13	<0.10	0.00	0.00
Denmark	32	29	13	0.20	0.14	0.06
Dominican Republic	24	17	95	2.50	2.10	2.76
Ecuador	46	17	137	0.30	0.31	0.15
Egypt, Arab Rep.	35	2	29	<0.10	..	..
El Salvador	38	12	60	0.60	0.77	0.35
Eritrea	..	..	268	2.80	2.78	4.30
Estonia	44	20	55	1.00	2.48	0.62
Ethiopia	..	..	370	6.40	4.39	7.82
Finland	27	20	10	<0.10	0.04	0.03
France	39	30	14	0.30	0.26	0.17
Gabon	..	..	248	*4.16*	*2.32*	*4.72*
Gambia, The	34	2	230	1.60	0.52	1.35
Georgia	61	15	85	<0.10	0.08	0.02
Germany	39	31	10	0.10	0.10	0.05
Ghana	28	4	211	3.00	1.36	2.97
Greece	47	29	20	0.20	0.14	0.06
Guatemala	38	18	77	1.00	0.90	0.85
Guinea	60	44	215	*1.54*	*0.57*	*1.43*
Guinea-Bissau	..	..	196	2.80	1.06	2.98
Haiti	11	9	319	6.10	4.06	4.95

Health risk factors and future challenges

	Prevalence of smoking		Incidence of tuberculosis	Prevalence of HIV		
	% of adults		per 100,000	% of	% ages 15–24 [a]	
	Male	Female	people	adults	Male	Female
	2000	2000	2002	2001	2001	2001
Honduras	36	11	86	1.60	1.20	1.50
Hungary	44	27	32	0.10	0.09	0.02
India	29	3	168	0.80	0.34	0.71
Indonesia	59	4	256	0.10	0.06	0.06
Iran, Islamic Rep.	27	3	29	<0.10	0.05	0.01
Iraq	40	5	167	<0.10	..	..
Ireland	32	31	13	0.10	0.06	0.05
Israel	33	24	10	0.10	*0.06*	*0.06*
Italy	32	17	8	0.40	0.28	0.26
Jamaica	..	..	8	1.20	0.82	0.86
Japan	53	13	33	<0.10	0.01	0.04
Jordan	48	10	5	<0.10	..	..
Kazakhstan	60	7	146	0.10	0.13	0.03
Kenya	67	32	540	6.70 [b]	6.01	15.56
Korea, Dem. Rep.	..	..	160	*<0.01*	..	..
Korea, Rep.	65	5	91	<0.10	0.03	0.01
Kuwait	30	2	26	*0.12*	..	..
Kyrgyz Republic	60	16	142	<0.10	0.00	0.00
Lao PDR	41	15	170	<0.10	0.05	0.03
Latvia	49	13	78	0.40	0.94	0.24
Lebanon	46	35	14	*0.09*	..	..
Lesotho	39	1	726	31.00	17.40	38.08
Liberia	..	..	247	*2.80*	..	..
Libya	..	..	21	0.20	..	..
Lithuania	51	16	66	0.10	0.16	0.05
Macedonia, FYR	40	32	41	<0.10	0.00	0.00
Madagascar	..	..	234	0.30	0.06	0.23
Malawi	20	9	431	15.00	6.35	14.89
Malaysia	49	4	95	0.40	0.70	0.12
Mali	..	..	334	1.70 [c]	1.37	2.08
Mauritania	..	..	188	*0.52*	*0.38*	*0.59*
Mauritius	45	3	64	0.10	*0.04*	*0.04*
Mexico	51	18	33	0.30	0.37	0.09
Moldova	46	18	154	0.20	0.46	0.14
Mongolia	68	26	209	<0.10	..	..
Morocco	35	2	114	0.10	..	..
Mozambique	..	..	436	13.00	6.13	14.67
Myanmar	44	22	154	*1.99*	*1.04*	*1.72*
Namibia	65	35	751	22.50	11.10	24.29
Nepal	48	29	190	0.50	0.26	0.28
Netherlands	37	29	8	0.20	0.20	0.09
New Zealand	25	25	11	0.10	0.05	0.01
Nicaragua	..	..	64	0.20	0.23	0.08
Niger	..	..	193	*1.35*	*0.95*	*1.50*
Nigeria	15	2	304	5.80	2.99	5.82
Norway	31	32	6	0.10	0.08	0.04
Oman	16	2	11	0.10	..	..
Pakistan	36	9	181	0.10	0.06	0.05
Panama	56	20	47	1.50	1.88	1.25
Papua New Guinea	46	28	254	0.70	0.33	0.39
Paraguay	24	6	70	*0.11*	*0.13*	*0.04*
Peru	42	16	202	0.40	0.41	0.18
Philippines	54	11	320	<0.10	0.01	0.01
Poland	44	25	32	0.10	0.09	0.05
Portugal	30	7	47	0.50	0.41	0.19
Puerto Rico	..	..	7	..	..	..

Health risk factors and future challenges

	Prevalence of smoking		Incidence of tuberculosis	Prevalence of HIV		
	% of adults		per 100,000	% of	% ages 15–24 [a]		
	Male	Female	people	adults	Male	Female
	2000	2000	2002	2001	2001	2001
Romania	62	25	148	<0.10	*0.02*	*0.02*
Russian Federation	63	10	126	0.90	1.87	0.67
Rwanda	7	4	389	8.90	4.91	11.20
Saudi Arabia	22	1	42	*0.01*	..	..
Senegal	..	..	242	0.50	0.19	0.54
Serbia and Montenegro	52	42	38	0.20	..	..
Sierra Leone	..	..	405	7.00	2.48	7.53
Singapore	27	3	43	0.20	0.14	0.16
Slovak Republic	55	30	24	<0.10	0.00	0.00
Slovenia	30	20	21	<0.10	0.00	0.00
Somalia	..	..	405	1.00	..	..
South Africa	42	11	558	15.60 [d]	10.66	25.64
Spain	42	25	30	0.50	0.51	0.24
Sri Lanka	26	2	54	<0.10	0.03	0.04
Sudan	24	1	217	2.60	1.08	3.13
Swaziland	25	2	1,067	33.40	15.23	39.49
Sweden	19	19	5	0.10	0.06	0.05
Switzerland	39	28	8	0.50	0.46	0.40
Syrian Arab Republic	51	10	44	*0.01*	..	..
Tajikistan	..	..	109	<0.10	0.00	0.00
Tanzania	50	12	363	7.80	3.55	8.06
Thailand	44	3	128	1.80	1.11	1.66
Togo	..	..	361	6.00	2.05	5.93
Trinidad and Tobago	42	8	13	2.50	2.41	3.23
Tunisia	62	8	23	*0.04*	..	..
Turkey	65	24	32	<0.10	..	..
Turkmenistan	27	1	94	<0.10	0.00	0.00
Uganda	52	17	377	5.00	1.99	4.63
Ukraine	51	19	95	1.00	1.96	0.88
United Arab Emirates	18	1	18	*0.18*	..	..
United Kingdom	27	26	12	0.10	0.10	0.05
United States	26	22	5	0.60	0.47	0.22
Uruguay	32	14	29	0.30	0.52	0.20
Uzbekistan	49	9	101	<0.10	0.01	0.00
Venezuela, RB	42	39	42	0.50	*0.65*	*0.15*
Vietnam	51	4	192	0.30	0.31	0.17
West Bank and Gaza	..	..	27	..	..	..
Yemen, Rep.	60	29	92	0.10	..	..
Zambia	35	10	668	15.60 [e]	8.06	20.98
Zimbabwe	34	1	683	33.70	12.38	33.01
World	**46 w**	**11 w**	**142 w**	**1.27 w**	**0.83 w**	**1.57 w**
Low income	37	7	226	2.31	1.11	2.51
Middle income	56	10	108	0.69	0.68	0.91
Lower middle income	58	9	116	0.70	0.69	0.98
Upper middle income	44	21	43	0.57	0.56	0.44
Low & middle income	48	9	164	1.45	0.91	1.77
East Asia & Pacific	63	5	147	0.19	0.19	0.17
Europe & Central Asia	56	17	88	0.45	1.03	0.39
Latin America & Carib.	40	24	67	0.67	0.68	0.47
Middle East & N. Africa	37	6	57	0.10	..	..
South Asia	33	6	176	0.64	0.27	0.54
Sub-Saharan Africa	..	..	358	8.38	4.14	9.44
High income	36	21	18	0.33	0.26	0.14
Europe EMU	37	26	15	0.28	0.25	0.15

a. Average of high and low estimates. b. Demographic and Health Survey 2003. c. Demographic and Health Survey 2001. d. Demographic and Health Survey 2002. e. Demographic and Health Survey 2001/02.

The limited availability of data on health status is a major constraint in assessing the health situation in developing countries. Surveillance data are lacking for many major public health concerns. Estimates of prevalence and incidence are available for some diseases but are often unreliable and incomplete. National health authorities differ widely in their capacity and willingness to collect or report information. To compensate for the paucity of data and ensure reasonable reliability and international comparability, the World Health Organization (WHO) prepares estimates in accordance with epidemiological models and statistical standards.

Smoking is the most common form of tobacco use in many countries, and the prevalence of smoking is therefore a good measure of the extent of the tobacco epidemic (Corrao and others 2000). While the prevalence of smoking has been declining in some high-income countries, it has been increasing in many developing countries. Tobacco use causes heart and other vascular diseases and cancers of the lung and other organs. Given the long delay between starting to smoke and the onset of disease, the health impact of smoking in developing countries will increase rapidly in the next few decades. Because the data present a one-time estimate, with no information on the intensity or duration of smoking, they should be interpreted with caution.

Tuberculosis is one of the main causes of death from a single infectious agent among adults in developing countries. In high-income countries tuberculosis has reemerged largely as a result of cases among immigrants. The estimates of tuberculosis incidence in the table are based on a new approach in which reported cases are adjusted using the ratio of case notifications to the estimated share of cases detected by panels of 80 epidemiologists convened by the WHO.

Adult HIV prevalence rates reflect the rate of HIV infection in each country's population. Low national prevalence rates can be very misleading, however. They often disguise serious epidemics that are initially concentrated in certain localities or among specific population groups and threaten to spill over into the wider population. In many parts of the developing world most new infections occur in young adults, with young women especially vulnerable. The estimates of HIV prevalence are based on extrapolations from data collected through surveys and surveillance of small, nonrepresentative groups.

Estimates from recent Demographic and Health Surveys (DHS) that have collected data on HIV/AIDS differ from those of the Joint United Nations Programme on HIV/AIDS (UNAIDS) and WHO, which are based on surveillance systems that focus on pregnant women who attend sentinel antenatal clinics. There are reasons to be cautious about comparing the two sets of estimates. DHS is a household survey that uses a representative sample from the whole population, whereas surveillance data from antenatal clinics is limited to pregnant women. Representative household surveys also frequently provide better coverage of rural populations. However, the fact that some respondents refuse to participate or are absent from the household adds considerable uncertainty to survey-based HIV estimates, because the possible association of absence or refusal with higher HIV prevalence is unknown. UNAIDS and WHO estimates are generally based on surveillance systems that focus on pregnant women who attend sentinel antenatal clinics. UNAIDS and WHO use a methodology to estimate HIV prevalence for the adult population (ages 15–49) that assumes that prevalence among pregnant women is a good approximation of prevalence among men and women. However, this assumption might not apply to all countries or over time. There are also other potential biases associated with the use of antenatal clinic data, such as differences among women who attend antenatal clinics and those who do not.

2.18a

HIV prevalence rates vary by method of data collection

Prevalence rate (%)

Country	UNAIDS and WHO surveillance data	Demographic and Health Survey data
Zambia	21.5	15.6
South Africa	20.1	15.6
Kenya	15.0	6.7
Mali	1.7	1.7

Recent household survey data from Demographic and Health Surveys show significantly lower HIV prevalence rates than those from UNAIDS and WHO, which are based on surveillance. This indicates that different data collection methodologies, and their quality and coverage, record different prevalence rates.

Source: UNAIDS and WHO 2002; Demographic and Health Survey data.

2.18b

In some countries men know more about preventing HIV than women do

Population with correct knowledge of HIV prevention (%)

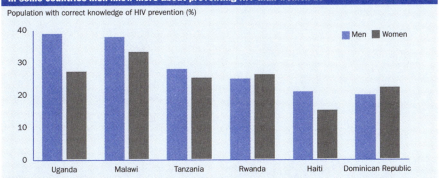

More men correctly identified the ways of preventing HIV transmission and had fewer misconceptions about it than did women. Countries where populations are more informed about HIV transmission do not necessarily have a low HIV prevalence rate, because it takes time to change people's behavior. However, there is no doubt that knowledge is an important prerequisite for behavior change.

Source: Demographic and Health Surveys, 1996–2000.

• **Prevalence of smoking** is the percentage of men and women who smoke cigarettes. The age range varies among countries but in most is 18 and older or 15 and older. • **Incidence of tuberculosis** is the estimated number of new tuberculosis cases (pulmonary, smear positive, extrapulmonary). • **Prevalence of HIV** is the percentage of people who are infected with HIV.

The data are drawn from a variety of sources, including the WHO's *World Health Report 2003*, *Tobacco Atlas 2002*, and *Global Tuberculosis Control Report 2003*; the National Tobacco Information Online System (NATIONS) database (http://apps.nccd.cdc.gov/nations/); and the Joint United Nations Programme on HIV/AIDS (UNAIDS) and WHO's *AIDS Epidemic Update 2002*.

2.19 Mortality

	Life expectancy at birth		Infant mortality rate		Under-five mortality rate		Child mortality rate		Adult mortality rate		Survival to age 65	
							per 1,000					
							Male	Female	per 1,000		% of cohort	
			per 1,000				1997–	1997–	Male	Female	Male	Female
	years		live births		per 1,000		2002 [a]	2002 [a]	2000–02 [a]	2000–02 [a]	2002	2002
	1980	2002	1980	2002	1980	2002						
Afghanistan	40	43	183	165	280	257	..	..	437	376	32	33
Albania	69	74	56	22	66	24	..	..	209	95	77	85
Algeria	59	71	94	39	134	49	..	..	155	119	73	79
Angola	41	47	158	154	265	260	..	..	492	386	34	39
Argentina	70	74	33	16	38	19	..	..	184	92	75	87
Armenia	73	75	22	30	80	35	5	3	223	106	70	83
Australia	74	79	11	6	13	6	..	..	100	52	84	92
Austria	73	79	14	5	17	5	..	..	122	58	83	91
Azerbaijan	68	65	91	76	117	96	..	..	261	150	58	72
Bangladesh	49	62	129	48	205	73	28	38	262	252	59	61
Belarus	71	68	21	17	26	20	..	..	381	133	54	81
Belgium	73	79	12	5	15	6	..	..	126	65	82	91
Benin	48	53	126	93	213	151	72	79	384	328	43	50
Bolivia	52	64	112	56	170	71	26	29	264	219	59	67
Bosnia and Herzegovina	70	74	31	15	39	18	..	..	200	93	75	86
Botswana	58	38	62	80	84	110	..	..	703	669	13	18
Brazil	63	69	67	33	86	37	..	..	259	136	62	79
Bulgaria	71	72	20	14	24	16	..	..	239	103	69	83
Burkina Faso	44	43	140	107	247	207	131	128	559	507	28	32
Burundi	47	42	114	123	190	208	..	..	648	603	26	29
Cambodia	39	54	110	96	190	138	34	30	386	334	42	48
Cameroon	50	48	105	95	173	166	69	75	488	440	35	41
Canada	75	79	11	5	13	7	..	..	101	57	83	92
Central African Republic	46	42	121	115	189	180	..	..	620	573	24	29
Chad	42	48	124	117	225	200	106	99	449	361	38	43
Chile	69	76	31	10	39	12	..	..	151	67	79	89
China	67	71	49	30	64	38	..	..	161	110	72	79
Hong Kong, China	74	80	..	..	..	..	..	..	97	50	85	92
Colombia	66	72	40	19	56	23	4	3	238	115	71	83
Congo, Dem. Rep.	49	45	130	129	210	205	..	..	571	493	31	35
Congo, Rep.	50	52	88	81	125	108	..	..	475	406	35	44
Costa Rica	73	78	24	9	26	11	..	..	131	78	82	90
Côte d'Ivoire	49	45	114	116	172	191	83	58	553	494	31	34
Croatia	70	74	20	7	23	8	..	..	150	110	71	87
Cuba	74	77	22	7	22	9	..	..	143	94	81	88
Czech Republic	70	75	17	4	19	5	..	..	160	75	75	88
Denmark	74	77	9	4	10	4	..	..	128	80	80	88
Dominican Republic	63	67	71	32	92	38	13	8	234	146	63	75
Ecuador	63	70	64	25	98	29	..	..	199	120	72	77
Egypt, Arab Rep.	56	69	118	33	173	39	15	16	210	147	69	75
El Salvador	57	70	84	33	118	39	..	..	250	148	68	81
Eritrea	44	51	141	59	210	80	55	50	493	441	37	42
Estonia	69	71	21	10	24	12	..	..	316	114	60	85
Ethiopia	42	42	143	114	220	171	83	86	594	535	26	30
Finland	73	78	8	4	9	5	..	..	144	61	80	91
France	74	79	10	4	13	6	..	..	130	57	82	92
Gabon	48	53	75	63	105	85	32	33	380	330	45	51
Gambia, The	40	53	144	91	231	126	..	..	373	320	40	47
Georgia	71	73	34	24	43	29	..	..	250	133	71	87
Germany	73	78	13	4	16	5	..	..	125	59	82	91
Ghana	53	55	96	60	157	97	53	51	379	326	47	51
Greece	74	78	20	5	23	5	..	..	114	47	83	91
Guatemala	57	65	97	36	139	49	15	18	286	182	58	72
Guinea	40	46	175	106	300	165	101	98	432	366	32	33
Guinea-Bissau	39	45	173	130	290	211	..	..	495	427	34	39
Haiti	51	52	132	79	195	123	52	54	524	373	38	47

	Life expectancy at birth		Infant mortality rate		Under-five mortality rate		Child mortality rate		Adult mortality rate		Survival to age 65	
							per 1,000				% of cohort	
							Male	Female	per 1,000			
			per 1,000				1997–	1997–	Male	Female	Male	Female
	years		live births		per 1,000		2002[a]	2002[a]	2000–02[a]	2000–02[a]	2002	2002
	1980	2002	1980	2002	1980	2002						
Honduras	60	66	75	32	103	42	..	..	221	157	59	72
Hungary	70	72	24	8	26	9	..	..	295	123	67	85
India	54	63	113	65	173	90	25	37	250	191	62	66
Indonesia	55	67	79	32	125	43	19	20	227	175	64	72
Iran, Islamic Rep.	58	69	92	34	130	41	..	..	170	139	71	75
Iraq	62	63	63	102	83	125	..	..	258	208	63	67
Ireland	73	77	12	6	14	6	..	..	108	62	80	89
Israel	73	79	16	6	19	6	..	..	99	56	84	90
Italy	74	78	15	4	17	6	..	..	110	53	81	91
Jamaica	71	76	28	17	34	20	..	..	169	127	80	87
Japan	76	82	8	3	11	5	..	..	98	44	86	94
Jordan	64	72	52	27	67	33	5	5	199	144	74	81
Kazakhstan	67	62	45	76	58	99	11	6	366	201	47	71
Kenya	55	46	73	78	115	122	36	38	578	529	28	33
Korea, Dem. Rep.	67	62	32	42	43	55	..	..	238	192	55	62
Korea, Rep.	67	74	16	5	18	5	..	..	186	71	72	86
Kuwait	71	77	29	9	35	10	..	..	100	68	82	88
Kyrgyz Republic	65	65	90	52	115	61	10	11	335	299	56	75
Lao PDR	45	55	135	87	200	100	..	..	355	299	45	50
Latvia	69	70	21	17	26	21	..	..	328	122	60	84
Lebanon	65	71	38	28	44	32	..	..	192	136	71	79
Lesotho	53	38	115	91	168	132	..	..	667	630	15	20
Liberia	51	47	157	157	235	235	..	..	448	385	33	37
Libya	60	72	55	16	70	19	..	..	210	157	73	83
Lithuania	71	73	21	8	22	9	..	..	286	106	66	87
Macedonia, FYR	..	73	53	22	69	26	..	..	160	89	75	84
Madagascar	51	55	106	84	175	135	75	68	385	322	49	55
Malawi	44	38	157	113	265	182	101	102	701	653	20	23
Malaysia	67	73	31	8	42	8	..	..	202	113	72	83
Mali	42	41	176	122	300	222	132	125	518	446	25	29
Mauritania	47	51	118	120	175	183	38	38	357	302	43	49
Mauritius	66	73	33	17	40	19	..	..	228	109	70	85
Mexico	67	74	56	24	74	29	..	..	180	101	75	85
Moldova	66	67	41	27	53	32	..	..	325	165	58	75
Mongolia	58	65	97	58	140	71	..	..	280	199	65	71
Morocco	58	68	99	39	144	43	..	..	174	113	68	76
Mozambique	44	41	140	128	233	205	85	82	674	612	25	30
Myanmar	51	57	94	77	134	108	..	..	343	245	46	58
Namibia	53	42	84	55	114	67	..	..	695	661	22	25
Nepal	48	60	124	62	183	83	28	40	314	314	58	56
Netherlands	76	78	9	5	11	5	..	..	95	64	83	90
New Zealand	73	78	13	6	16	6	..	..	108	69	83	90
Nicaragua	59	69	85	32	120	41	12	11	225	161	67	77
Niger	40	46	191	155	320	264	184	202	473	308	30	37
Nigeria	46	45	108	100	216	201	66	69	443	393	33	36
Norway	76	79	9	4	11	4	..	..	105	59	84	91
Oman	60	74	73	11	95	13	..	..	187	135	78	84
Pakistan	55	64	105	76	156	101	..	..	221	198	64	70
Panama	70	75	34	19	46	25	..	..	145	93	78	86
Papua New Guinea	51	57	79	70	108	94	..	..	359	329	49	53
Paraguay	67	71	46	26	61	30	..	..	173	129	70	80
Peru	60	70	89	30	126	39	19	17	190	139	69	78
Philippines	61	70	55	28	81	37	21	19	249	142	70	77
Poland	70	74	21	8	24	9	..	..	226	88	71	87
Portugal	71	76	25	5	31	6	..	..	164	66	77	89
Puerto Rico	74	77	..	..	..	..	..	..	148	55	76	91

	Life expectancy at birth (years)		Infant mortality rate (per 1,000 live births)		Under-five mortality rate (per 1,000)		Child mortality rate (per 1,000)		Adult mortality rate (per 1,000)		Survival to age 65 (% of cohort)	
							Male 1997–2002[a]	Female 1997–2002[a]	Male 2000–02[a]	Female 2000–02[a]	Male 2002	Female 2002
	1980	2002	1980	2002	1980	2002						
Romania	69	70	29	19	36	21	..	..	260	117	64	81
Russian Federation	67	66	28	18	35	21	..	..	420	149	48	77
Rwanda	46	40	130	118	219	203	105	97	667	599	23	25
Saudi Arabia	61	73	65	23	85	28	..	..	181	116	76	83
Senegal	45	52	128	79	218	138	76	74	355	303	38	47
Serbia and Montenegro	70	73	36	16	44	19	..	..	180	100	73	83
Sierra Leone	35	37	192	165	336	284	..	..	587	531	24	29
Singapore	71	78	11	3	13	4	..	..	114	61	83	89
Slovak Republic	70	73	20	8	23	9	..	..	204	82	70	86
Slovenia	70	76	16	4	18	5	..	..	170	76	76	89
Somalia	43	47	133	133	225	225	..	..	516	452	38	44
South Africa	57	46	64	52	91	65	18	13	621	583	27	33
Spain	76	78	13	5	16	6	..	..	122	49	83	92
Sri Lanka	68	74	34	16	46	19	..	..	244	124	76	84
Sudan	48	58	86	64	142	94	..	..	341	291	53	58
Swaziland	52	44	99	106	143	149	..	..	642	602	26	30
Sweden	76	80	7	3	9	3	..	..	87	55	85	92
Switzerland	76	80	9	5	11	6	..	..	99	58	85	93
Syrian Arab Republic	62	70	54	23	73	28	..	..	170	132	69	79
Tajikistan	66	67	..	90	..	116	..	..	293	204	62	75
Tanzania	50	43	106	104	175	165	61	58	569	520	27	31
Thailand	64	69	45	24	58	28	..	..	245	150	67	77
Togo	49	50	106	87	176	140	73	65	460	406	37	42
Trinidad and Tobago	68	72	35	17	40	20	..	..	209	133	74	82
Tunisia	62	73	72	21	100	26	..	..	169	99	75	83
Turkey	61	70	103	35	133	41	10	13	218	120	69	79
Turkmenistan	64	65	86	70	109	86	19	17	280	156	57	72
Uganda	48	43	107	83	185	141	78	70	617	567	25	28
Ukraine	69	68	22	16	27	20	..	..	365	135	56	80
United Arab Emirates	68	75	23	8	27	9	..	..	143	93	80	85
United Kingdom	74	77	12	5	14	7	..	..	108	65	81	89
United States	74	77	13	7	15	8	..	..	135	80	81	91
Uruguay	70	75	37	14	42	15	..	..	185	89	74	88
Uzbekistan	67	67	51	55	60	65	..	..	282	176	63	77
Venezuela, RB	68	74	34	19	42	22	..	..	178	99	75	85
Vietnam	60	70	44	20	66	26	10	13	203	139	68	78
West Bank and Gaza	..	73	..	..	..	..	..	..	154	97	74	83
Yemen, Rep.	49	57	135	83	205	114	33	36	278	226	50	53
Zambia	50	37	90	102	155	182	89	74	725	687	16	21
Zimbabwe	55	39	69	76	108	123	35	31	650	612	18	20
World	**63 w**	**67 w**	**79 w**	**55 w**	**119 w**	**81 w**	**.. w**	**.. w**	**234 w**	**166 w**	**69 w**	**78 w**
Low income	53	59	110	79	174	121	..	..	310	259	64	69
Middle income	66	70	57	30	76	37	..	..	211	128	63	80
Lower middle income	65	69	59	32	79	40	..	..	212	131	61	78
Upper middle income	68	73	42	19	54	22	..	..	197	103	68	82
Low & middle income	60	65	86	60	131	88	..	..	255	186	64	73
East Asia & Pacific	64	69	56	32	79	42	..	..	184	129	69	76
Europe & Central Asia	68	69	45	31	57	37	..	..	317	137	59	80
Latin America & Carib.	65	71	61	28	82	34	..	..	222	125	67	81
Middle East & N. Africa	58	69	94	44	134	54	..	..	193	143	68	73
South Asia	54	63	115	68	176	95	25	37	252	202	62	65
Sub-Saharan Africa	48	46	116	103	197	174	..	..	519	461	40	46
High income	74	78	12	5	15	7	..	..	128	66	81	90
Europe EMU	74	78	13	4	16	6	..	..	125	58	..	..

a. Data are for the most recent year available.

About the data

Mortality rates for different age groups—infants, children, or adults—and overall indicators of mortality—life expectancy at birth or survival to a given age—are important indicators of health status in a country. Because data on the incidence and prevalence of diseases (morbidity data) are frequently unavailable, mortality rates are often used to identify vulnerable populations. And they are among the indicators most frequently used to compare levels of socioeconomic development across countries.

The main sources of mortality data are vital registration systems and direct or indirect estimates based on sample surveys or censuses. A "complete" vital registration system—one covering at least 90 percent of vital events in the population—is the best source of age-specific mortality data. But such systems are fairly uncommon in developing countries. Thus estimates must be obtained from sample surveys or derived by applying indirect estimation techniques to registration, census, or survey data. Survey data are subject to recall error, and surveys estimating infant deaths require large samples because households in which a birth or an infant death has occurred during a given year cannot ordinarily be preselected for sampling. Indirect estimates rely on estimated actuarial ("life") tables that may be inappropriate for the population concerned. Because life expectancy at birth is constructed using infant mortality data and model life tables, similar reliability issues arise for this indicator.

Life expectancy at birth and age-specific mortality rates are generally estimates based on vital registration or the most recent census or survey available

(see *Primary data documentation*). Extrapolations based on outdated surveys may not be reliable for monitoring changes in health status or for comparative analytical work.

To produce harmonized estimates of infant and under-five mortality rates that make use of all available information in a transparent way, the United Nations Children's Fund (UNICEF) and the World Bank developed and adopted a methodology that fits a regression line to the relationship between mortality rates and their reference dates using weighted least squares. (For further discussion of methodology for childhood mortality estimates, see Hill and others 1999.) Some of the estimates shown in the table this year are World Bank estimates. Estimates may change after the harmonization process with UNICEF and the World Health Organization is completed.

Infant and child mortality rates are higher for boys than for girls in countries in which parental gender preferences are insignificant. Child mortality captures the effect of gender discrimination better than does infant mortality, as malnutrition and medical interventions are more important in this age group. Where female child mortality is higher, as in some countries in South Asia, girls probably have unequal access to resources.

Adult mortality rates have increased in many countries in Sub-Saharan Africa and Europe and Central Asia. In Sub-Saharan Africa the increase stems from AIDS-related mortality and affects both men and women. In Europe and Central Asia the causes are more diverse and affect men more. They include a

high prevalence of smoking, a high-fat diet, excessive alcohol use, and stressful conditions related to the economic transition.

The percentage of a cohort surviving to age 65 reflects both child and adult mortality rates. Like life expectancy, it is a synthetic measure based on current age-specific mortality rates and used in the construction of life tables. It shows that even in countries where mortality is high, a certain share of the current birth cohort will live well beyond the life expectancy at birth, while in low-mortality countries close to 90 percent will reach at least age 65.

Definitions

• **Life expectancy at birth** is the number of years a newborn infant would live if prevailing patterns of mortality at the time of its birth were to stay the same throughout its life. • **Infant mortality rate** is the number of infants dying before reaching one year of age, per 1,000 live births in a given year. • **Under-five mortality rate** is the probability that a newborn baby will die before reaching age five, if subject to current age-specific mortality rates. The probability is expressed as a rate per 1,000. • **Child mortality rate** is the probability of dying between the ages of one and five, if subject to current age-specific mortality rates. The probability is expressed as a rate per 1,000. • **Adult mortality rate** is the probability of dying between the ages of 15 and 60—that is, the probability of a 15-year-old dying before reaching age 60—if subject to current age-specific mortality rates between ages 15 and 60. • **Survival to age 65** refers to the percentage of a cohort of newborn infants that would survive to age 65, if subject to current age-specific mortality rates.

2.19a

Under-five mortality rates are higher in poor households than in rich ones

Under-five mortality per 1,000 people, by income quintile

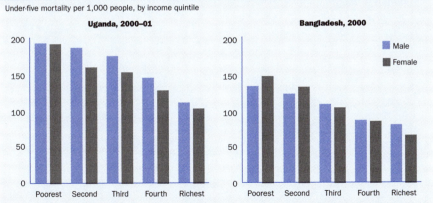

Higher under-five mortality rates for children from poor households than for those from wealthier households indicate the deprivation among the poor. Under-five mortality is usually higher for boys than for girls, except in cases of parental discrimination against girls.

Source: Demographic and Health Survey data.

Data sources

The data are from the United Nations Statistics Division's *Population and Vital Statistics Report,* publications and other releases from national statistical offices, Demographic and Health Surveys from national sources and Macro International, and UNICEF's *State of the World's Children 2004.*

3 | ENVIRONMENT

conomic development has led to dramatic improvements in the quality of life in developing countries, producing gains unparalleled in human history. But the picture is far from entirely positive. Gains have been unevenly distributed, and a large part of the world's population remains desperately poor. At the same time, natural resources—land, water, and forests—are being degraded at alarming rates in many countries, and environmental factors such as indoor and outdoor air pollution, waterborne diseases, and exposure to toxic chemicals threaten the health of millions of people. Addressing these concerns, successive international conferences, including the latest World Summit on Sustainable Development, have reaffirmed the commitment to eliminate poverty through environmentally sound and socially responsible economic development.

If the vision of a world without poverty is to be realized, sustainable development is the key. A healthy environment is central to the international development agenda and an integral part of meeting the Millennium Development Goals (see section 1, *World View*). The Millennium Development Goals call for integrating principles of environmental sustainability into country policies and programs and reversing environmental losses. This requires measuring and monitoring the state of the environment and its changes as well as the links between the economy and the environment.

Given such close links, there is a strong argument for developing indicators that integrate economic activity and environmental change. One approach that appears to hold much promise is environmental accounting. Aimed at deriving "greener" measures of national income, savings, and wealth, environmental accounting adds natural resources and pollutants to the assets and liabilities measured in the standard national accounts. But preparing full-fledged integrated environmental and economic accounts is costly, and not all countries are doing so. In the absence of such integrated accounts, physical indicators and descriptive statistics can provide useful information for monitoring the state of the environment.

Many such indicators are presented here, but despite greater awareness of the importance of environmental issues and efforts to improve environmental data, information on many aspects of the environment remains sparse. The available data are often of uneven quality, relate to different periods, and are sometimes out of date. The lack of adequate data hampers efforts to measure the state of the environment and design sound policies. Another problem is that many environmental indicators are not meaningful at the national level. Climate change has impacts that go beyond national boundaries. Other environmental factors such as air and water pollution may have relevance only to the locality where they are measured. So global, regional, or city (tables 3.11 and 3.13) indicators are often more meaningful than national aggregates.

Fragile land and increasing demand for food

Almost three of every five people in developing countries—some 3 billion—live in rural areas (table 3.1). In many of these countries agriculture is still the main source of employment. But most of the land available to meet current and future food requirements is already in production; any further expansion must necessarily involve fragile and marginal lands. This is particularly so in developing countries where population growth is high, poverty is endemic, and existing institutional capacities for land management are weak. Because land resources are finite, fragile, and nonrenewable, countries must meet their increased need for food and other agricultural products mainly by raising and sustaining crop and livestock yields and by using land more intensively. Low-income countries are increasing the land under cereal production, but their use of agricultural machinery lags far behind that in other countries (table 3.2). These countries, where current cereal yields are a third those in high-income countries, will have to expand their arable land—a strategy that cannot be sustained for long (table 3.3).

Shrinking forests and threatened biodiversity

A substantial number of the world's 1.2 billion extremely poor people—those living on less than $1 a day—depend for their livelihoods on forests and forest products . But the forests are shrinking, as is the diversity of the plants and animals they support. With growth and development, forests are being converted to agricultural land and urban areas. At the beginning of the 20th century the earth had about 5 billion hectares of forested area. Now it has less than 4 billion hectares. The loss has been concentrated in developing countries, driven by the growing demand for timber and agricultural land, exacerbated by weak monitoring institutions. Low-income countries lost some 73 million hectares—about 8 percent of their forest—in the 1990s. By contrast, high-income countries reforested about 8 million hectares of forest in the same period (table 3.4).

Closely linked to changes in land use is biodiversity, another important dimension of environmental sustainability. Many countries have designated a share of their land as protected areas (table 3.4). But even where protected areas are increased and environmental protections are effectively respected, losses of biologically diverse areas cannot be reversed. About 12 percent of the world's nearly 10,000 bird species are vulnerable or in immediate danger of extinction, as are 24 percent of the world's 4,800 mammal species and an estimated 30 percent of all fish species.

A thirsty planet—and getting thirstier

Water is crucial to economic growth and development—and to the survival of both terrestrial and aquatic systems. But more than 1 billion people lack access to safe water, and more than 430 million live in countries facing chronic and widespread water shortages—with water stress (less than 1,700 cubic meters of freshwater available per person a year) or water scarcity (less than 1,000 cubic meters; table 3.5).

Global per capita water supplies are declining, further growth in population and economic activity will add to the demand for water, and by 2050 the share of the world's population facing water stress could increase more than fivefold. These trends pose a significant challenge for meeting the Millennium Development Goal of halving the proportion of people without sustainable access to safe drinking water by 2015.

Energy use improves welfare, but has its consequences

The use of energy, especially electricity, is important in raising people's standard of living. High-income countries use more than five times as much energy as developing countries on a per capita basis, and with only 15 percent of the world's population they use more than half its energy (table 3.7 and figure 3a).

At the same time, energy use and electricity generation also have environmental consequences. Generating energy produces emissions of carbon dioxide, the main greenhouse gas contributing to global warming. Anthropogenic (human caused) carbon dioxide emissions result primarily from fossil fuel combustion and cement manufacturing, with high-income countries contributing half (table 3.8), Among countries in all income groups, per capita emissions vary widely (figure 3b). The extent of environmental damage depends largely on how energy is generated. For example, burning coal releases twice as much carbon dioxide as does burning an equivalent amount of natural gas (see *About the data* for table 3.8).

More urban—and more polluted

The world is become increasingly urban. Now urban areas are home to 48 percent of the world's population—two of five people in low- and middle-income countries and almost four of five in high-income countries. Most of Latin America is as urbanized as Europe, with 76 percent of the population living in urban areas. Asia is urbanizing rapidly. Even such traditionally rural countries as

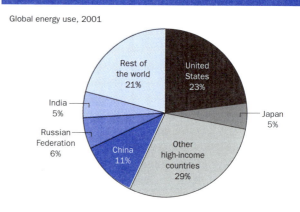

3a

High-income countries use more than half the world's energy

Global energy use, 2001

- Rest of the world 21%
- United States 23%
- India 5%
- Japan 5%
- Russian Federation 6%
- China 11%
- Other high-income countries 29%

Source: Table 3.7.

Emissions of carbon dioxide vary widely, even among the five largest producers of emissions

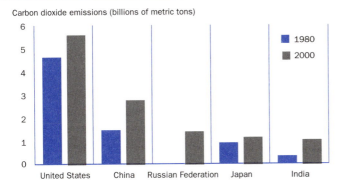

Carbon dioxide emissions (billions of metric tons)

- 1980
- 2000

United States / China / Russian Federation / Japan / India

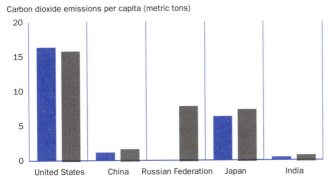

Carbon dioxide emissions per capita (metric tons)

United States / China / Russian Federation / Japan / India

Note: No data for 1980 are available for the Russian Federation.
Source: Table 3.8 and World Bank staff estimates.

China, India, and Indonesia now have hundreds of millions of people living in urban areas, with both the number of people and the share of the population in cities growing rapidly (table 3.10). Urbanization can yield important social benefits, improving access to public services such as education, health care, and cultural facilities (table 3.11).

Urbanization can also lead to adverse environmental effects that require policy responses. Greater urbanization usually means greater pollution, which can overwhelm the natural capacities of air and water to absorb pollutants. The costs of controlling pollution can be enormous. And pollution exposes people to severe health hazards. Several major urban air pollutants—lead, sulfur dioxide, suspended particulate matter—are known to harm human health (table 3.13). A big source of urban air pollution is motor vehicles, whose numbers are strongly linked to rising income. The number of passenger cars in developing countries has increased from 16 cars per 1,000 people in 1990 to 28 in 2001. At the same time, the number of passenger cars in high-income countries has increased from 400 per 1,000 people to 440 (table 3.12).

Commitment to change—necessary, but not sufficient

The strength of environmental policies in any country reflects the priority its government gives to problems of environmental degradation— and that priority reflects the benefits expected from using scarce resources that have competing uses. But measuring governments' commitment to these goals is difficult. The indicators of government commitment in table 3.14 are imperfect, measuring the existence of

policy instruments more than their effectiveness. Still, making a formal commitment is an essential first step toward taking action.

Beyond national environmental problems, governments are increasingly concerned about global environmental issues. To address these issues, countries have reached agreements and signed treaties on areas relating to the quality of life on earth (for example, figure 3c shows the decline in chlorofluorocarbons as a result of such agreements). Many of these agreements resulted from the 1992 United Nations Conference on Environment and Development in Rio de Janeiro, which produced Agenda 21—an array of actions to address environmental challenges. But 10 years after Rio the World Summit on Sustainable Development recognized that many of the proposed actions have yet to materialize.

Adjusted net savings—moving toward a measure of sustainability

The question of an economy's sustainability can be reduced to the question of whether welfare is expected to decline along the future development path as a result of decisions made today. Because flows of income and well-being are ultimately derived from the stocks of produced, natural, and human assets, a drop in the aggregate value of these stocks must eventually lead to a decline in welfare. One measure of change in total assets is provided by net adjusted savings—a measure of savings that accounts not only for a country's economic surplus but also for its depletion of natural resources, accumulation of pollutants and their damages, and investments in human capital. The data limitations and the approximations used in calculating net adjusted savings mean that these estimates still must be used with caution (for more details on the assumptions made, see *About the data* for table 3.15).

Many developing countries have low or negative adjusted net savings. Broadly speaking, the lowest adjusted savings rates are recorded for countries that depend heavily on resource rents, particularly those endowed with minerals and fossil fuels. These rents account for a sizable share of GDP in many countries, suggesting that managing natural resources and resource revenues should receive even more attention as these countries strive to ensure the sustainability of their economies and the welfare of future generations.

Emissions of some greenhouse and ozone-depleting gases have begun to fall or slow since Rio

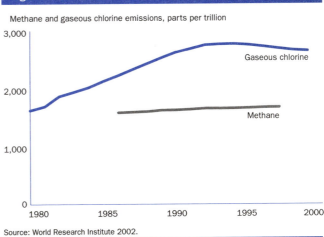

Methane and gaseous chlorine emissions, parts per trillion

Gaseous chlorine

Methane

Source: World Research Institute 2002.

3.1 Rural environment and land use

	Rural population			Rural population density	Land area	Land use					
	% of total		average annual % growth	people per sq. km of arable land	thousand sq. km	Arable land		Permanent cropland	% of land area	Other land	
	1980	2002	1980–2002	2001	2001	1980	2001	1980	2001	1980	2001
Afghanistan	84	77	2.2	268	652	12.1	12.1	0.2	0.2	87.7	87.6
Albania	66	56	0.0	309	27	21.4	21.1	4.3	4.4	74.4	74.5
Algeria	56	42	1.0	170	2,382	2.9	3.2	0.3	0.2	96.8	96.5
Angola	79	65	1.9	277	1,247	2.3	2.4	0.4	0.2	97.3	97.4
Argentina	17	12	−0.4	13	2,737	10.6	12.3	0.4	0.5	89.0	87.2
Armenia	34	33	−0.3	204	28	..	17.6	..	2.3	..	80.1
Australia	14	9	−1.0	3	7,682	5.7	6.5	0.0	0.0	94.2	93.4
Austria	33	32	0.2	187	83	18.6	16.9	1.2	0.9	80.2	82.2
Azerbaijan	47	48	1.4	230	87	..	19.6	..	2.7	..	77.7
Bangladesh	85	74	1.5	1,228	130	68.3	62.1	2.0	3.1	29.6	34.8
Belarus	43	30	−1.5	49	207	..	29.5	..	0.6	..	69.9
Belgium	5	3	−2.4	32	33 [a]	23.2 [a]	25.7 [a]	0.4 [a]	0.7 [a]	76.4 [a]	73.6 [a]
Benin	73	56	1.7	182	111	13.6	18.1	0.8	2.4	85.7	79.5
Bolivia	55	37	0.4	110	1,084	1.8	2.7	0.1	0.2	98.1	97.1
Bosnia and Herzegovina	64	56	−0.6	333	51	..	13.6	..	3.0	..	83.4
Botswana	82	50	0.7	232	567	0.7	0.7	0.0	0.0	99.3	99.3
Brazil	33	18	−1.2	54	8,457	5.3	7.0	0.9	0.9	93.7	92.1
Bulgaria	39	32	−1.3	59	111	34.6	40.0	3.2	1.9	62.2	58.1
Burkina Faso	92	83	2.0	243	274	10.0	14.4	0.1	0.2	89.8	85.4
Burundi	96	90	2.2	699	26	36.2	35.0	12.5	14.0	51.3	50.9
Cambodia	88	82	2.5	274	177	11.3	21.0	0.4	0.6	88.3	78.4
Cameroon	69	50	1.2	130	465	12.7	12.8	2.2	2.6	85.1	84.6
Canada	24	21	0.4	14	9,221	4.9	5.0	0.0	0.0	95.0	95.0
Central African Republic	65	58	1.8	114	623	3.0	3.1	0.1	0.1	96.9	96.8
Chad	81	75	2.5	171	1,259	2.5	2.9	0.0	0.0	97.5	97.1
Chile	19	14	0.1	108	749	5.1	2.6	0.3	0.4	94.6	96.9
China [b]	80	62	0.1	561	9,327	10.4	15.4	0.4	1.2	89.3	83.4
Hong Kong, China	9	0	..	..	..	7.0	..	1.0	..	92.0	..
Colombia	37	24	−0.1	420	1,039	3.6	2.4	1.4	1.7	95.0	95.9
Congo, Dem. Rep.	..	..	..	..	2,267	2.9	3.0	0.4	0.5	96.6	96.5
Congo, Rep.	58	33	0.7	690	342	0.4	0.5	0.1	0.1	99.5	99.4
Costa Rica	53	40	1.2	697	51	5.5	4.4	4.4	5.9	90.1	89.7
Côte d'Ivoire	65	56	2.5	292	318	6.1	9.7	7.2	13.8	86.6	76.4
Croatia	50	41	−1.0	128	56	..	26.1	..	2.3	..	71.6
Cuba	32	24	−0.6	76	110	23.9	33.1	6.4	7.6	69.7	59.3
Czech Republic	25	25	−0.0	85	77	..	39.8	..	3.1	..	57.1
Denmark	16	15	−0.2	35	42	62.3	54.0	0.3	0.2	37.4	45.8
Dominican Republic	49	33	0.1	263	48	22.1	22.7	7.2	10.3	70.6	67.0
Ecuador	53	36	0.4	285	277	5.6	5.9	3.3	4.9	91.1	89.2
Egypt, Arab Rep.	56	57	2.3	1,306	995	2.3	2.9	0.2	0.5	97.5	96.6
El Salvador	56	38	−0.3	370	21	26.9	31.9	11.7	12.1	61.4	56.1
Eritrea	86	80	2.4	679	101	..	5.0	..	0.0	..	95.0
Estonia	30	31	−0.3	62	42	..	16.0	..	0.4	..	83.5
Ethiopia	90	84	2.3	517	1,000	..	10.7	..	0.8	..	88.5
Finland	40	41	0.5	97	305	7.8	7.2	0.0	0.0	92.2	92.8
France	27	24	0.0	78	550	31.8	33.5	2.5	2.1	65.7	64.4
Gabon	50	17	−2.0	71	258	1.1	1.3	0.6	0.7	98.2	98.1
Gambia, The	80	68	2.8	372	10	15.5	25.0	0.4	0.5	84.1	74.5
Georgia	48	43	−0.4	286	69	..	11.4	..	3.9	..	84.7
Germany	17	12	−1.4	86	349	34.5	33.9	1.4	0.6	64.1	65.6
Ghana	69	63	2.4	343	228	8.4	16.3	7.5	9.7	84.2	74.1
Greece	42	39	0.1	154	129	22.5	21.1	7.9	8.8	69.6	70.1
Guatemala	63	60	2.3	516	108	11.7	12.5	4.4	5.0	83.9	82.4
Guinea	81	72	2.0	614	246	2.9	3.6	1.8	2.6	95.4	93.8
Guinea-Bissau	83	67	1.8	317	28	9.1	10.7	1.7	8.8	89.2	80.5
Haiti	76	63	1.1	664	28	28.3	28.3	11.6	11.6	60.1	60.1

	Rural population			Rural population density	Land area	Land use					
	% of total		average annual % growth	people per sq. km of arable land	thousand sq. km	Arable land		Permanent cropland		Other land	
						% of land area					
	1980	**2002**	**1980–2002**	**2001**	**2001**	**1980**	**2001**	**1980**	**2001**	**1980**	**2001**
Honduras	65	45	1.3	288	112	13.3	9.5	2.4	3.2	84.3	87.2
Hungary	43	35	–1.2	78	92	54.4	50.1	3.3	2.1	42.2	47.8
India	77	72	1.6	460	2,973	54.8	54.4	1.8	2.7	43.4	42.9
Indonesia	78	57	0.2	591	1,812	9.9	11.3	4.4	7.2	85.6	81.5
Iran, Islamic Rep.	50	35	0.6	160	1,636	7.9	8.7	0.4	1.4	91.6	89.9
Iraq	34	32	2.5	134	437	12.0	13.1	0.4	0.8	87.6	86.1
Ireland	45	40	0.2	150	69	16.1	15.2	0.0	0.0	83.9	84.8
Israel	11	8	0.8	157	21	15.8	16.4	4.3	4.2	80.0	79.4
Italy	33	33	0.0	232	294	32.2	27.8	10.0	9.5	57.7	62.7
Jamaica	53	43	–0.0	648	11	12.5	16.1	9.7	10.2	77.8	73.8
Japan	24	21	–0.2	603	365	13.3	12.2	1.6	1.0	85.1	86.8
Jordan	40	21	1.0	449	89	3.4	2.7	0.4	1.8	96.2	95.5
Kazakhstan	46	44	–0.2	31	2,700	..	8.0	..	0.1	..	92.0
Kenya	84	65	1.7	439	569	6.7	8.1	0.8	1.0	92.5	90.9
Korea, Dem. Rep.	43	39	0.8	353	120	19.0	20.8	2.4	2.5	78.6	76.7
Korea, Rep.	43	17	–3.2	491	99	20.9	17.2	1.4	2.0	77.8	80.9
Kuwait	9	4	–1.6	684	18	0.1	0.7	0.0	0.1	99.9	99.2
Kyrgyz Republic	62	66	1.7	232	192	..	7.3	..	0.3	..	92.4
Lao PDR	88	80	2.1	495	231	3.4	3.8	0.1	0.4	96.5	95.8
Latvia	32	40	0.6	51	62	..	29.7	..	0.5	..	69.9
Lebanon	26	10	–2.8	257	10	20.5	16.6	8.9	14.0	70.6	69.4
Lesotho	87	71	0.6	380	30	9.6	10.9	0.1	0.1	90.2	89.0
Liberia	65	54	1.7	461	96	3.9	3.9	2.1	2.3	94.0	93.8
Libya	31	12	–1.7	36	1,760	1.0	1.0	0.2	0.2	98.8	98.8
Lithuania	39	31	–0.9	37	65	..	45.2	..	0.9	..	53.9
Macedonia, FYR	47	40	–0.3	146	25	..	22.3	..	1.8	..	75.9
Madagascar	81	69	2.1	378	582	4.4	5.1	0.9	1.0	94.8	93.9
Malawi	91	85	2.2	406	94	16.1	23.4	0.9	1.5	83.0	75.1
Malaysia	58	41	1.0	554	329	3.0	5.5	11.6	17.6	85.4	76.9
Mali	82	68	1.7	165	1,220	1.6	3.8	0.0	0.0	98.3	96.1
Mauritania	72	40	–0.2	228	1,025	0.2	0.5	0.0	0.0	99.8	99.5
Mauritius	58	58	1.1	701	2	49.3	49.3	3.4	3.0	47.3	47.8
Mexico	34	25	0.5	102	1,909	12.1	13.0	0.8	1.3	87.1	85.7
Moldova	60	58	0.1	137	33	..	55.3	..	10.8	..	33.9
Mongolia	48	43	1.3	87	1,567	0.8	0.8	0.0	0.0	99.2	99.2
Morocco	59	43	0.5	146	446	16.9	19.6	1.1	2.2	82.0	78.2
Mozambique	87	66	0.6	302	784	3.7	5.1	0.3	0.3	96.0	94.6
Myanmar	76	71	1.4	346	658	14.6	15.2	0.7	1.0	84.8	83.8
Namibia	77	68	2.5	164	823	0.8	1.0	0.0	0.0	99.2	99.0
Nepal	93	87	2.0	668	143	16.0	21.7	0.2	0.6	83.8	77.7
Netherlands	12	10	0.1	184	34	23.3	26.7	0.9	1.0	75.7	72.3
New Zealand	17	14	0.3	36	268	9.8	5.6	3.4	7.0	86.8	87.4
Nicaragua	50	43	2.1	117	121	8.8	15.9	1.4	1.9	89.7	82.1
Niger	87	78	2.8	195	1,267	2.8	3.5	0.0	0.0	97.2	96.4
Nigeria	73	54	1.5	251	911	30.6	31.3	2.8	3.0	66.6	65.7
Norway	29	25	–0.3	128	307	2.7	2.9	..	..	..	..
Oman	68	23	–1.2	1,533	310	0.1	0.1	0.1	0.1	99.8	99.7
Pakistan	72	66	2.2	438	771	25.9	27.9	0.4	0.9	73.7	71.3
Panama	50	43	1.2	230	74	5.8	7.4	1.6	2.0	92.5	90.7
Papua New Guinea	87	82	2.3	2,060	453	0.4	0.5	1.1	1.4	98.5	98.1
Paraguay	58	43	1.2	77	397	4.1	7.6	0.3	0.2	95.6	92.2
Peru	35	27	0.7	191	1,280	2.5	2.9	0.3	0.4	97.2	96.7
Philippines	63	40	0.3	564	298	17.5	18.9	14.8	16.8	67.7	64.3
Poland	42	37	–0.2	104	304	48.0	45.9	1.1	1.1	50.9	53.0
Portugal	71	33	–3.2	176	92	26.5	21.7	7.8	7.8	65.7	70.4
Puerto Rico	33	24	–0.6	2,681	9	8.3	3.9	7.3	5.5	84.3	90.5

	Rural population			Rural population density	Land area	Land use					
	% of total		average annual % growth	people per sq. km of arable land	thousand sq. km	Arable land		Permanent cropland		Other land	
	1980	2002	1980–2002	2001	2001	1980	2001	1980	2001	1980	2001
Romania	51	45	−0.6	107	230	42.7	40.8	2.9	2.3	54.4	56.9
Russian Federation	30	27	−0.3	32	16,889	..	7.3	..	0.1	..	92.6
Rwanda	95	94	2.0	743	25	30.8	40.5	10.3	12.2	58.9	47.3
Saudi Arabia	34	13	−0.6	79	2,150	0.9	1.7	0.0	0.1	99.1	98.2
Senegal	64	51	1.6	203	193	12.2	12.8	0.0	0.2	87.8	87.0
Serbia and Montenegro	54	48	−1.3	..	..	28.0	..	2.9	..	69.1	..
Sierra Leone	76	62	1.3	644	72	6.3	7.0	0.7	0.9	93.0	92.1
Singapore	0	0	..	0	1	3.3	1.6	9.8	0.0	86.9	98.4
Slovak Republic	48	42	−0.3	158	48	..	30.4	..	2.8	..	66.8
Slovenia	52	51	0.0	581	20	..	8.6	..	1.5	..	89.9
Somalia	78	72	1.3	622	627	1.6	1.7	0.0	0.0	98.4	98.3
South Africa	52	42	1.3	129	1,221	10.2	12.1	0.7	0.8	89.1	87.1
Spain	27	22	−0.6	69	499	31.1	26.1	9.9	9.9	59.0	64.1
Sri Lanka	78	77	1.1	1,607	65	13.2	13.9	15.9	15.7	70.9	70.4
Sudan	80	62	1.2	125	2,376	5.2	6.8	0.0	0.2	94.8	93.0
Swaziland	82	73	2.4	440	17	10.8	10.3	0.2	0.7	89.0	89.0
Sweden	17	17	0.3	55	412	7.2	6.5	0.0	0.0	92.8	93.4
Switzerland	43	33	−0.6	571	40	9.9	10.4	0.5	0.6	89.6	89.0
Syrian Arab Republic	53	48	2.6	173	184	28.5	25.2	2.5	4.4	69.1	70.3
Tajikistan	66	72	2.5	485	141	..	6.6	..	0.9	..	92.5
Tanzania	85	66	1.7	575	884	3.5	4.5	1.0	1.1	95.5	94.4
Thailand	83	80	1.1	326	511	32.3	29.4	3.5	6.5	64.2	64.2
Togo	77	66	2.2	123	54	35.9	46.1	1.6	2.2	62.6	51.6
Trinidad and Tobago	37	25	−0.9	441	5	13.6	14.6	9.0	9.2	77.4	76.2
Tunisia	48	33	0.2	118	155	20.5	17.9	9.7	13.7	69.7	68.4
Turkey	56	33	−0.3	97	770	32.9	30.9	4.1	3.3	63.0	65.8
Turkmenistan	53	55	2.5	148	470	..	3.7	..	0.1	..	96.1
Uganda	91	85	2.7	401	197	20.7	25.9	8.1	10.7	71.2	63.5
Ukraine	38	32	−1.0	48	579	..	56.2	..	1.6	..	42.2
United Arab Emirates	29	12	1.3	773	84	0.2	0.6	0.1	2.2	99.7	97.2
United Kingdom	11	10	−0.1	109	241	28.7	23.5	0.3	0.2	71.0	76.3
United States	26	22	0.3	37	9,159	20.6	19.1	0.2	0.2	79.2	80.6
Uruguay	15	8	−2.3	20	175	8.0	7.4	0.3	0.2	91.7	92.3
Uzbekistan	59	63	2.4	352	414	..	10.8	..	0.8	..	88.3
Venezuela, RB	21	13	0.1	122	882	3.4	2.9	0.8	0.9	95.8	96.1
Vietnam	81	75	1.5	923	325	18.2	20.0	1.9	6.0	79.8	74.1
West Bank and Gaza	..	..	..	..	..	..	..	..	..	..	..
Yemen, Rep.	81	75	3.2	923	528	2.6	2.8	0.2	0.2	97.2	97.0
Zambia	60	60	2.6	115	743	6.9	7.1	0.0	0.0	93.1	92.9
Zimbabwe	78	63	1.8	255	387	6.5	8.3	0.3	0.3	93.3	91.3
World	**61 w**	**52 w**	**0.8 w**	**476 w**	**130,145 s**	**10.3 w**	**10.8 w**	**0.8 w**	**1.0 w**	**88.9 w**	**88.2 w**
Low income	78	69	1.6	510	32,424	11.7	12.5	1.0	1.5	87.3	86.0
Middle income	61	47	0.2	473	66,725	8.2	9.6	0.9	1.0	90.9	89.5
Lower middle income	65	51	0.2	492	54,034	8.6	9.9	1.0	0.9	90.3	89.2
Upper middle income	34	25	0.1	190	12,691	7.0	8.0	0.7	1.0	92.3	90.9
Low & middle income	68	58	0.9	494	99,149	9.6	10.5	1.0	1.1	89.4	88.3
East Asia & Pacific	79	62	0.3	568	15,885	10.1	13.3	1.5	2.7	88.5	84.0
Europe & Central Asia	41	36	−0.1	124	23,722	37.1	11.2	3.1	0.4	59.8	88.4
Latin America & Carib.	35	24	0.0	203	20,053	6.4	7.4	0.9	1.0	92.8	91.6
Middle East & N. Africa	52	42	1.5	601	11,105	4.4	4.9	0.4	0.8	95.2	94.4
South Asia	78	72	1.7	553	4,781	42.5	42.5	1.5	2.2	56.1	55.3
Sub-Saharan Africa	79	67	1.8	350	23,603	5.5	6.7	0.7	0.9	93.8	92.4
High income	27	22	−0.3	205	30,996	12.1	11.6	0.5	0.5	87.4	87.9
Europe EMU	27	22	−0.5	139	2,436	27.3	25.7	4.8	4.6	67.9	69.7

a. Includes Luxembourg. b. Includes Taiwan, China.

Rural environment and land use | **3.1**

Indicators of rural development are sparse, as few indicators are disaggregated between rural and urban areas (for some that are, see tables 2.5, 3.5, and 3.10). This table shows indicators of rural population and land use. Rural population is approximated as the midyear nonurban population.

The data in the table show that land use patterns are changing. They also indicate major differences in resource endowments and uses among countries.

True comparability of the data is limited, however, by variations in definitions, statistical methods, and the quality of data collection. Countries use different definitions of rural population and land use, for example. The Food and Agriculture Organization (FAO), the primary compiler of these data, occasionally adjusts its definitions of land use categories and sometimes revises earlier data. (In 1985, for example, the FAO began to exclude from cropland the land used for shifting cultivation but currently lying fallow.) And following FAO practice, this year's edition of *World Development Indicators,* like the previous five, breaks down the category *cropland,* used in the earliest editions, into *arable land* and *permanent cropland.* Because the data reflect changes in data reporting procedures as well as actual changes in land use, apparent trends should be interpreted with caution.

Satellite images show land use that differs from that given by ground-based measures in both area under cultivation and type of land use. Moreover, land use data in countries such as India are based on reporting systems that were designed for the collection of tax revenue. Because taxes on land are no longer a major source of government revenue, the quality and coverage of land use data (except for cropland) have declined. Data on forest area, aggregated

in the category *other,* may be particularly unreliable because of differences in definitions and irregular surveys (see *About the data* for table 3.4).

• **Rural population** is calculated as the difference between the total population and the urban population (see *Definitions* for tables 2.1 and 3.10). • **Rural population density** is the rural population divided by the arable land area. • **Land area** is a country's total area, excluding area under inland water bodies, national claims to the continental shelf, and exclusive economic zones. In most cases the definition of inland water bodies includes major rivers and lakes. (See table 1.1 for the total surface area of countries.) • **Land use** is broken into three categories. • **Arable land** includes land defined by the FAO as land under temporary crops (double-cropped areas are counted once), temporary meadows for mowing or for pasture, land under market or kitchen gardens, and land temporarily fallow. Land abandoned as a result of shifting cultivation is excluded. • **Permanent cropland** is land cultivated with crops that occupy the land for long periods and need not be replanted after each harvest, such as cocoa, coffee, and rubber. This category includes land under flowering shrubs, fruit trees, nut trees, and vines, but excludes land under trees grown for wood or timber. • **Other land** includes forest and woodland as well as logged-over areas to be forested in the near future. Also included are uncultivated land, grassland not used for pasture, wetlands, wastelands, and built-up areas—residential, recreational, and industrial lands and areas covered by roads and other fabricated infrastructure.

3.1a

All regions are becoming less rural

Rural population as a share of total population, by region (%)

Source: Table 3.1.

	Arable land		Irrigated land		Land under cereal production		Fertilizer consumption		Agricultural machinery			
	hectares per capita		% of cropland		thousands of hectares		hundreds of grams per hectare of arable land		tractors per 1,000 agricultural workers		tractors per 100 sq. km of arable land	
	1979–81	1999–2001	1979–81	1999–2001	1979–81	2000–02	1979–81	1999–2001	1979–81	1999–2001	1979–81	1999–2001
Afghanistan	0.50	0.30	31.1	29.6	3,037	2,302	62	12	0	0	1	1
Albania	0.22	0.19	53.0	48.6	367	183	1,556	277	15	11	173	140
Algeria	0.37	0.25	3.4	6.8	2,968	1,770	277	126	27	37	68	122
Angola	0.41	0.24	2.2	2.3	705	928	49	5	4	2	35	34
Argentina	1.03	0.91	5.2	4.5	11,154	10,714	39	253	132	205	63	89
Armenia	..	0.16	..	51.3	..	191	..	122	..	74	..	369
Australia	2.97	2.58	3.5	4.7	15,986	17,097	269	478	751	705	75	64
Austria	0.20	0.17	0.2	0.3	1,062	821	2,615	1,591	945	1,737	2,084	2,371
Azerbaijan	..	0.21	..	74.8	..	735	..	58	..	31	..	178
Bangladesh	0.10	0.06	17.1	49.6	10,823	11,712	459	1,662	0	0	5	7
Belarus	..	0.61	..	2.1	..	2,491	..	1,288	..	102	..	118
Belgium a	0.08	0.08	1.7	4.7	426	336	5,323	3,549	917	1,299	1,416	1,266
Benin	0.43	0.31	0.3	0.5	525	921	11	211	0	0	1	1
Bolivia	0.36	0.35	6.6	4.2	559	754	22	25	4	4	21	20
Bosnia and Herzegovina	..	0.17	..	0.4	..	381	..	581	..	304	..	433
Botswana	0.44	0.22	0.5	0.3	153	177	32	128	9	20	54	166
Brazil	0.37	0.34	3.0	4.4	20,612	17,799	777	1,103	31	61	118	139
Bulgaria	0.43	0.54	28.3	17.4	2,110	1,988	2,334	328	66	86	161	57
Burkina Faso	0.39	0.34	0.4	0.6	2,026	3,061	26	96	0	0	0	5
Burundi	0.23	0.13	4.2	5.9	203	205	11	41	0	0	1	2
Cambodia	0.29	0.31	5.8	7.1	1,264	2,014	45	0	0	0	6	5
Cameroon	0.67	0.39	0.2	0.5	1,021	747	56	83	0	0	1	1
Canada	1.86	1.48	1.3	1.6	19,561	17,106	416	550	827	1,870	144	160
Central African Republic	0.81	0.52	..	..	194	180	5	3	0	0	0	0
Chad	0.70	0.45	0.4	0.6	907	1,900	6	49	0	0	1	0
Chile	0.34	0.13	31.1	82.7	820	626	338	2,421	43	55	90	273
China	0.10	0.11	45.1	36.3	94,647	83,012	1,494	2,562	2	2	76	70
Hong Kong, China	0.00	..	37.5	..	0	..	..	..	0	..	10	..
Colombia	0.13	0.06	7.7	20.2	1,361	1,147	812	2,397	8	6	77	80
Congo, Dem. Rep.	0.24	0.14	0.1	0.1	1,115	2,043	12	2	0	0	3	4
Congo, Rep.	0.08	0.05	0.6	0.5	19	10	27	286	2	1	49	40
Costa Rica	0.12	0.06	12.1	20.6	136	68	2,650	7,096	22	21	210	311
Côte d'Ivoire	0.24	0.19	1.0	1.0	1,008	1,381	261	217	1	1	16	12
Croatia	..	0.33	..	0.2	..	710	..	1,445	..	13	..	16
Cuba	0.27	0.32	22.9	19.5	224	202	2,024	447	78	100	259	215
Czech Republic	..	0.30	..	0.7	..	1,615	..	1,075	..	192	..	293
Denmark	0.52	0.43	14.5	19.5	1,818	1,550	2,453	1,516	973	1,132	708	547
Dominican Republic	0.19	0.13	11.7	17.2	149	168	572	869	3	3	20	17
Ecuador	0.20	0.13	24.8	29.0	419	867	471	1,177	6	11	40	90
Egypt, Arab Rep.	0.06	0.04	100.0	100.0	2,007	2,700	2,864	4,401	4	10	158	307
El Salvador	0.12	0.10	4.6	5.0	422	363	1,376	1,189	5	4	61	53
Eritrea	..	0.12	..	4.2	..	293	..	212	..	0	..	10
Estonia	..	0.71	..	0.4	..	290	..	393	..	602	..	575
Ethiopia	..	0.16	..	1.7	..	7,440	..	150	..	0	..	3
Finland	0.49	0.42	2.5	2.9	1,190	1,170	2,024	1,384	721	1,355	893	889
France	0.32	0.31	7.2	13.4	9,804	9,106	3,260	2,367	737	1,411	836	687
Gabon	0.42	0.26	2.4	3.0	6	17	20	9	5	7	43	46
Gambia, The	0.26	0.18	0.6	0.8	54	137	136	40	0	0	3	2
Georgia	..	0.15	..	44.2	..	338	..	521	..	33	..	221
Germany	0.15	0.14	3.7	4.0	7,692	7,001	4,249	2,367	624	1,018	1,340	873
Ghana	0.17	0.19	0.2	0.2	902	1,425	104	34	1	1	19	10
Greece	0.30	0.26	24.2	37.3	1,600	1,287	1,927	1,635	120	323	485	912
Guatemala	0.19	0.12	5.0	6.8	716	660	726	1,449	3	2	32	32
Guinea	0.16	0.12	7.9	6.3	708	742	16	36	0	0	2	6
Guinea-Bissau	0.32	0.22	5.6	3.1	142	154	24	60	0	0	1	1
Haiti	0.15	0.10	6.4	6.8	416	448	43	158	0	0	2	2

	Arable land		Irrigated land		Land under cereal production		Fertilizer consumption		Agricultural machinery			
	hectares per capita		% of cropland		thousands of hectares		hundreds of grams per hectare of arable land		tractors per 1,000 agricultural workers		tractors per 100 sq. km of arable land	
	1979–81	1999–2001	1979–81	1999–2001	1979–81	2000–02	1979–81	1999–2001	1979–81	1999–2001	1979–81	1999–2001
Honduras	0.42	0.19	4.1	5.2	421	399	171	1,408	5	7	22	44
Hungary	0.47	0.46	3.6	4.6	2,878	2,936	2,906	835	59	209	111	228
India	0.24	0.16	22.8	32.2	104,350	97,956	345	1,074	2	6	24	94
Indonesia	0.12	0.10	16.2	14.4	11,825	15,004	645	1,243	0	1	5	35
Iran, Islamic Rep.	0.36	0.24	35.5	44.2	8,062	7,740	430	905	17	37	57	158
Iraq	0.40	0.24	32.1	60.8	2,159	2,526	172	668	23	91	44	107
Ireland	0.33	0.28	..	..	425	287	5,373	5,871	607	1,031	1,289	1,586
Israel	0.08	0.05	49.3	46.0	129	84	2,384	2,696	304	350	809	728
Italy	0.17	0.14	19.3	24.2	5,082	4,187	2,295	2,078	370	1,219	1,117	1,973
Jamaica	0.06	0.07	10.1	8.8	4	2	1,231	1,095	9	12	208	177
Japan	0.04	0.04	56.0	54.7	2,724	2,017	4,131	3,162	209	745	2,723	4,601
Jordan	0.14	0.05	11.0	19.3	158	52	404	913	47	32	153	234
Kazakhstan	..	1.44	..	10.8	..	13,082	..	19	..	36	..	24
Kenya	0.23	0.15	0.9	1.7	1,692	2,017	160	322	1	1	17	27
Korea, Dem. Rep.	0.13	0.11	44.0	52.1	1,625	1,278	3,346	1,061	12	20	196	280
Korea, Rep.	0.05	0.04	59.6	60.4	1,689	1,177	3,920	4,539	1	80	14	1,112
Kuwait	0.00	0.00	83.3	85.8	0	2	4,500	1,002	3	10	220	94
Kyrgyz Republic	..	0.28	..	74.2	..	618	..	157	..	46	..	186
Lao PDR	0.24	0.17	13.3	18.2	751	765	35	107	0	1	7	12
Latvia	..	0.78	..	1.1	..	440	..	305	..	350	..	302
Lebanon	0.07	0.04	28.3	32.0	34	53	1,663	3,105	28	177	141	453
Lesotho	0.23	0.19	0.3	0.3	203	236	150	247	6	6	47	61
Liberia	0.20	0.12	0.3	0.5	203	141	123	0	0	0	8	9
Libya	0.58	0.35	10.7	21.9	538	342	357	363	101	319	134	187
Lithuania	..	0.84	..	0.2	..	938	..	533	..	429	..	347
Macedonia, FYR	..	0.28	..	9.0	..	207	..	665	..	449	..	948
Madagascar	0.29	0.19	21.2	31.0	1,309	1,412	30	27	1	1	10	12
Malawi	0.25	0.21	1.1	1.3	1,155	1,602	203	195	0	0	8	7
Malaysia	0.07	0.08	6.7	4.8	729	705	4,273	6,695	4	25	77	239
Mali	0.31	0.43	4.5	3.0	1,346	2,769	61	95	0	1	5	6
Mauritania	0.13	0.18	22.8	9.8	125	185	57	30	1	1	13	8
Mauritius	0.10	0.08	15.0	19.5	0	0	2,547	3,667	4	6	33	37
Mexico	0.34	0.25	20.3	23.1	9,356	10,322	570	736	16	37	54	131
Moldova	..	0.42	..	14.1	..	989	..	25	..	84	..	230
Mongolia	0.71	0.50	3.0	7.1	559	196	83	26	32	16	82	42
Morocco	0.39	0.31	15.0	13.5	4,414	5,181	268	415	7	10	34	49
Mozambique	0.24	0.22	2.1	2.6	1,077	1,894	107	40	1	1	20	15
Myanmar	0.28	0.21	10.4	18.3	5,133	6,880	111	180	1	1	9	11
Namibia	0.64	0.43	0.6	0.9	195	292	0	4	11	11	39	39
Nepal	0.16	0.13	22.5	36.2	2,251	3,308	98	260	0	0	10	15
Netherlands	0.06	0.06	58.5	59.9	225	223	8,620	4,755	560	603	2,238	1,644
New Zealand	0.84	0.39	5.2	8.6	193	141	1,879	5,317	619	448	352	501
Nicaragua	0.38	0.37	6.2	4.5	266	464	415	159	6	7	20	15
Niger	0.62	0.42	0.7	1.5	3,872	7,693	10	10	0	0	0	0
Nigeria	0.39	0.22	0.7	0.8	6,048	19,783	59	68	1	2	3	11
Norway	0.20	0.20	..	..	311	326	3,146	2,196	824	1,263	1,603	1,511
Oman	0.02	0.02	74.5	78.2	2	2	475	1,690	1	1	43	40
Pakistan	0.24	0.15	72.7	81.6	10,693	12,300	525	1,362	5	13	50	150
Panama	0.22	0.19	5.0	5.1	166	123	692	584	27	20	122	93
Papua New Guinea	0.05	0.04	..	..	2	3	452	530	1	1	82	56
Paraguay	0.52	0.55	3.4	2.2	307	638	44	227	14	23	45	57
Peru	0.19	0.14	32.3	28.4	732	1,217	381	715	5	4	37	36
Philippines	0.11	0.07	12.8	14.6	6,790	6,514	636	1,337	1	1	20	20
Poland	0.41	0.36	0.7	0.7	7,875	8,643	2,393	1,110	112	302	425	933
Portugal	0.25	0.20	20.1	24.0	1,099	543	1,113	1,146	72	260	351	848
Puerto Rico	0.02	0.01	27.2	47.6	1	1	..	..	..	..	..	..

	Arable land		Irrigated land		Land under cereal production		Fertilizer consumption		Agricultural machinery			
	hectares per capita		% of cropland		thousands of hectares		hundreds of grams per hectare of arable land		tractors per 1,000 agricultural workers		tractors per 100 sq. km of arable land	
	1979–81	1999–2001	1979–81	1999–2001	1979–81	2000–02	1979–81	1999–2001	1979–81	1999–2001	1979–81	1999–2001
Romania	0.44	0.42	21.9	31.2	6,340	5,696	1,448	309	39	100	150	174
Russian Federation	..	0.85	..	3.6	..	41,919	..	117	..	96	..	63
Rwanda	0.15	0.12	0.4	0.4	239	298	3	3	0	0	1	1
Saudi Arabia	0.20	0.17	28.9	42.8	388	615	228	1,036	2	16	10	27
Senegal	0.42	0.25	2.6	2.9	1,216	1,174	104	162	0	0	2	3
Serbia and Montenegro	0.73	..	1.9	..	4,310	..	1,261	..	140	..	616	..
Sierra Leone	0.14	0.10	4.1	5.4	434	213	58	4	0	0	6	2
Singapore	0.00	0.00	..	..	..	..	22,333	30,423	3	22	220	650
Slovak Republic	..	0.27	..	11.2	..	..	..	610	..	..	..	164
Slovenia	..	0.09	..	1.3	..	102	..	4,384	..	..	..	..
Somalia	0.15	0.12	13.3	18.7	638	671	9	5	1	1	17	17
South Africa	0.45	0.34	8.4	9.2	6,760	4,633	874	510	92	43	140	50
Spain	0.42	0.33	14.8	20.1	7,391	6,658	1,012	1,674	200	686	335	668
Sri Lanka	0.06	0.05	28.3	33.6	864	809	1,800	2,768	4	2	141	90
Sudan	0.64	0.52	14.4	11.7	4,447	7,468	51	32	2	2	8	7
Swaziland	0.30	0.17	34.0	36.8	70	56	1,050	343	29	34	173	219
Sweden	0.36	0.31	2.4	4.2	1,505	1,163	1,654	1,055	715	1,108	623	616
Switzerland	0.06	0.06	6.2	5.7	172	177	4,623	2,277	494	700	2,428	2,710
Syrian Arab Republic	0.60	0.29	9.6	22.5	2,642	3,028	250	731	29	68	54	212
Tajikistan	..	0.15	..	68.3	..	376	..	114	..	37	..	325
Tanzania	0.16	0.12	3.1	3.3	2,834	2,980	110	56	1	1	35	19
Thailand	0.35	0.25	16.4	27.1	10,625	11,257	177	1,120	1	10	11	147
Togo	0.77	0.55	0.3	0.4	416	703	14	74	0	0	0	0
Trinidad and Tobago	0.06	0.06	2.9	3.3	4	3	1,064	1,163	50	54	337	360
Tunisia	0.51	0.30	4.8	7.7	1,416	782	212	389	30	37	79	123
Turkey	0.57	0.36	9.6	16.9	13,499	13,946	529	825	38	65	169	391
Turkmenistan	..	0.37	..	100.1	..	819	..	603	..	73	..	289
Uganda	0.32	0.22	0.1	0.1	752	1,395	1	11	0	1	6	9
Ukraine	..	0.66	..	7.2	..	13,436	..	136	..	90	..	101
United Arab Emirates	0.01	0.02	237.7	32.6	0	0	2,250	7,090	6	5	106	68
United Kingdom	0.12	0.10	2.0	1.8	3,930	3,203	3,191	3,251	726	931	744	860
United States	0.83	0.62	10.8	12.6	72,639	55,818	1,092	1,097	1,230	1,586	253	272
Uruguay	0.48	0.39	5.4	13.5	614	522	564	846	171	174	236	255
Uzbekistan	..	0.18	..	88.6	..	1,581	..	1,637	..	57	..	380
Venezuela, RB	0.19	0.11	10.1	16.9	814	928	696	1,012	50	61	131	189
Vietnam	0.11	0.08	25.6	37.6	5,962	8,301	302	3,407	1	6	38	254
West Bank and Gaza	..	..	..	..	..	..	..	..	..	..	..	..
Yemen, Rep.	0.16	0.09	19.9	30.2	865	654	93	102	3	2	33	41
Zambia	0.89	0.53	0.4	0.9	595	641	145	65	2	2	9	11
Zimbabwe	0.35	0.25	3.1	3.5	1,633	1,685	610	520	7	7	66	75
World	**0.25 w**	**0.23 w**	**17.5 w**	**19.6 w**	**588,621 s**	**666,427 s**	**860 w**	**988 w**	**19 w**	**20 w**	**173 w**	**189 w**
Low income	0.23	0.17	19.8	26.4	199,719	244,864	289	717	2	4	20	66
Middle income	0.18	0.24	22.6	19.4	232,191	289,922	941	1,020	8	12	110	127
Lower middle income	0.16	0.22	25.8	20.5	196,509	249,113	962	1,063	6	9	104	103
Upper middle income	0.36	0.32	11.5	13.4	35,682	40,809	871	804	50	117	133	253
Low & middle income	0.20	0.20	21.2	22.1	431,910	534,786	625	903	5	8	66	103
East Asia & Pacific	0.12	0.11	36.3	35.5	139,927	135,938	1,113	2,145	2	2	55	76
Europe & Central Asia	..	0.56	..	10.9	..	114,548	..	335	..	102	..	171
Latin America & Carib.	0.36	0.29	10.8	12.5	49,845	48,623	536	815	25	40	87	119
Middle East & N. Africa	0.29	0.19	25.8	37.9	25,653	25,446	421	808	12	25	61	131
South Asia	0.23	0.15	28.7	39.9	132,128	128,481	360	1,081	2	5	25	92
Sub-Saharan Africa	0.32	0.24	4.0	4.2	46,978	81,750	158	128	3	1	23	15
High income	0.44	0.37	10.2	12.1	156,711	131,641	1,327	1,238	430	895	385	439
Europe EMU	0.23	0.21	14.1	19.4	35,996	31,617	2,703	2,170	427	911	879	984

a. Includes Luxembourg.

About the data

Agricultural activities provide developing countries with food and revenue, but they also can degrade natural resources. Poor farming practices can cause soil erosion and loss of soil fertility. Efforts to increase productivity through the use of chemical fertilizers, pesticides, and intensive irrigation have environmental costs and health impacts. Excessive use of chemical fertilizers can alter the chemistry of soil. Pesticide poisoning is common in developing countries. And salinization of irrigated land diminishes soil fertility. Thus inappropriate use of inputs for agricultural production has far-reaching effects.

This table provides indicators of major inputs to agricultural production: land, fertilizer, and agricultural machinery. There is no single correct mix of inputs: appropriate levels and application rates vary by country and over time, depending on the type of crops, the climate and soils, and the production process used.

The data shown here and in table 3.3 are collected by the Food and Agriculture Organization (FAO) through annual questionnaires. The FAO tries to impose standard definitions and reporting methods, but exact consistency across countries and over time is not possible. Data on agricultural employment, in particular, should be used with caution. In many countries much agricultural employment is informal and unrecorded, including substantial work performed by women and children.

Fertilizer consumption measures the quantity of plant nutrients. Consumption is calculated as production plus imports minus exports. Because some chemical compounds used for fertilizers have other industrial applications, the consumption data may overstate the quantity available for crops.

To smooth annual fluctuations in agricultural activity, the indicators in the table have been averaged over three years.

Definitions

- **Arable land** includes land defined by the FAO as land under temporary crops (double-cropped areas are counted once), temporary meadows for mowing or for pasture, land under market or kitchen gardens, and land temporarily fallow. Land abandoned as a result of shifting cultivation is excluded. • **Irrigated land** refers to areas purposely provided with water, including land irrigated by controlled flooding. • **Cropland** refers to arable land and permanent cropland (see table 3.1). • **Land under cereal production** refers to harvested areas, although some countries report only sown or cultivated area. • **Fertilizer consumption** is the quantity of plant nutrients used per unit of arable land. Fertilizer products cover nitrogenous, potash, and phosphate fertilizers (including ground rock phosphate). Traditional nutrients—animal and plant manures—are not included. The time reference for fertilizer consumption is the crop year (July through June). • **Agricultural machinery** refers to wheel and crawler tractors (excluding garden tractors) in use in agriculture at the end of the calendar year specified or during the first quarter of the following year. • **Agricultural workers** refer to all economically active people engaged principally in agriculture, forestry, hunting, or fishing.

3.2a

The 10 countries with the most arable land per person in 1999–2001—and the 10 with the least

Ares per capita

Country	Arable land	Country	Arable land
Australia	258.1	Singapore	0.0
Canada	148.2	Kuwait	0.5
Kazakhstan	143.6	Puerto Rico	0.9
Argentina	90.6	Oman	1.6
Russian Federation	85.5	United Arab Emirates	1.8
Lithuania	83.7	Japan	3.5
Latvia	77.8	Korea, Rep.	3.6
Estonia	71.0	Papua New Guinea	4.0
Ukraine	65.9	Lebanon	4.2
United States	62.5	Egypt, Arab Rep.	4.4

Note: An are equals 100 square meters or 0.01 hectare.
Source: Table 3.2.

3.3 Agricultural output and productivity

	Crop production index		Food production index		Livestock production index		Cereal yield		Agricultural productivity	
							kilograms per hectare		Agriculture value added per worker 1995 $	
	1989–91 = 100		1989–91 = 100		1989–91 = 100					
	1979–81	**2000–02**	**1979–81**	**2000–02**	**1979–81**	**2000–02**	**1979–81**	**2000–02**	**1979–81**	**2000–02**
Afghanistan	..	..	..	..	..	..	1,337	1,533	..	..
Albania	..	..	..	..	..	..	2,500	3,154	1,184	1,868
Algeria	77.4	128.0	68.8	136.2	54.6	128.9	656	1,343	1,357	1,919
Angola	101.9	195.7	89.9	172.5	83.8	137.2	526	606	..	137
Argentina	83.6	165.2	91.7	142.5	100.9	108.8	2,184	3,374	7,148	10,317
Armenia	..	99.8	..	79.3	..	67.9	..	2,049	..	2,827
Australia	79.9	152.2	91.3	138.8	85.6	116.1	1,321	1,758	20,872	36,327
Austria	92.8	103.6	92.2	104.7	94.5	103.2	4,131	5,589	11,082	33,828
Azerbaijan	..	63.4	..	83.7	..	81.8	..	2,583	..	1,029
Bangladesh	80.2	135.6	79.3	138.3	81.3	142.1	1,938	3,312	232	318
Belarus	..	90.3	..	62.1	..	58.4	..	2,369	..	3,038
Belgium [a]	84.9	143.9	88.5	113.5	88.8	109.8	4,861	8,002	21,861	57,462
Benin	53.8	195.6	66.8	173.9	93.2	116.7	698	1,077	311	621
Bolivia	71.9	177.2	71.5	151.6	75.5	129.7	1,183	1,786	693	754
Bosnia and Herzegovina	..	..	..	..	..	..	..	3,186	..	*7,634*
Botswana	86.4	89.8	87.3	89.8	87.6	89.7	203	156	657	575
Brazil	75.4	135.8	69.5	153.2	67.9	169.8	1,496	3,081	2,049	4,899
Bulgaria	107.7	66.9	105.5	68.2	96.3	62.9	3,853	2,961	2,754	8,282
Burkina Faso	59.3	166.8	62.7	157.9	59.9	147.8	575	968	133	185
Burundi	79.9	92.7	79.9	93.2	82.3	76.1	1,081	1,325	177	151
Cambodia	55.0	147.2	48.9	152.0	27.3	166.9	1,006	1,978	..	422
Cameroon	87.3	141.6	80.6	138.3	61.3	121.8	849	1,696	826	1,213
Canada	77.6	106.7	79.7	123.5	88.3	142.2	2,173	2,521	16,002	43,064
Central African Republic	102.9	136.6	79.7	146.5	48.9	147.4	529	1,069	380	502
Chad	66.8	160.8	79.8	151.2	89.2	122.2	587	697	160	211
Chile	70.7	132.6	71.5	140.2	75.8	151.4	2,124	5,235	3,488	6,226
China	67.1	155.6	60.8	185.9	45.4	226.7	3,027	4,845	161	338
Hong Kong, China	133.6	..	99.8	..	194.3	..	1,712	..	..	..
Colombia	84.1	106.4	75.5	120.3	72.6	122.4	2,452	3,411	3,034	3,619
Congo, Dem. Rep.	73.0	83.2	72.8	86.3	83.5	98.3	807	774	241	212
Congo, Rep.	86.4	127.9	83.8	130.3	81.6	135.5	838	779	385	469
Costa Rica	66.2	147.0	69.5	150.0	77.1	136.6	2,498	3,968	3,139	5,270
Côte d'Ivoire	73.7	133.8	70.6	136.5	73.9	139.3	867	1,213	945	1,046
Croatia	..	90.6	..	68.5	..	55.2	..	4,748	..	9,741
Cuba	84.1	66.3	90.1	70.9	96.0	71.6	2,458	2,519	..	..
Czech Republic	..	88.6	..	78.0	..	70.8	..	4,297	..	6,382
Denmark	65.2	89.9	83.3	106.0	95.0	118.6	4,040	5,912	19,350	63,131
Dominican Republic	96.5	89.6	85.2	107.8	68.8	138.2	3,024	4,525	2,129	3,458
Ecuador	78.2	143.2	77.4	153.8	73.0	170.1	1,633	2,122	3,839	3,310
Egypt, Arab Rep.	75.5	154.9	68.5	158.2	67.0	165.9	4,053	7,244	721	1,316
El Salvador	120.4	98.9	88.9	111.7	86.5	116.3	1,702	2,264	1,925	1,678
Eritrea	..	121.9	..	116.3	..	112.0	..	351	..	68
Estonia	..	76.8	..	39.8	..	33.8	..	2,028	..	3,650
Ethiopia	..	160.6	..	152.6	..	129.8	..	1,293	..	154
Finland	76.3	99.7	93.8	93.7	107.5	91.8	2,511	3,219	17,885	42,306
France	87.4	107.0	93.6	104.3	97.8	105.5	4,700	6,796	19,318	59,243
Gabon	76.2	121.4	79.0	116.7	86.6	118.9	1,718	1,652	1,814	2,102
Gambia, The	79.2	132.8	82.4	127.2	93.7	102.7	1,284	1,231	325	307
Georgia	..	43.7	..	74.9	..	93.8	..	2,004	..	..
Germany	90.0	118.2	91.4	97.1	98.7	87.7	4,166	6,355	9,119	33,686
Ghana	67.0	190.0	68.5	181.2	78.7	127.3	807	1,191	671	571
Greece	86.8	110.6	91.2	101.3	99.9	94.0	3,090	3,555	8,600	13,860
Guatemala	85.8	131.8	68.0	136.2	76.9	130.3	1,578	1,758	2,143	2,115
Guinea	89.7	158.7	93.1	161.8	91.7	188.8	958	1,403	..	286
Guinea-Bissau	64.9	147.2	68.3	142.2	78.0	127.2	711	972	237	324
Haiti	103.4	87.2	101.2	101.7	100.2	156.2	1,009	840	..	..

	Crop production index		Food production index		Livestock production index		Cereal yield		Agricultural productivity	
							kilograms per hectare		Agriculture value added per worker 1995 $	
	1989–91 = 100		1989–91 = 100		1989–91 = 100					
	1979–81	**2000–02**	**1979–81**	**2000–02**	**1979–81**	**2000–02**	**1979–81**	**2000–02**	**1979–81**	**2000–02**
Honduras	90.4	114.1	88.3	121.1	81.0	153.8	1,170	1,382	696	1,037
Hungary	93.3	79.7	90.7	79.5	94.1	73.3	4,519	4,026	3,390	5,625
India	70.9	124.2	68.2	131.8	62.6	149.8	1,324	2,390	269	401
Indonesia	65.9	122.9	63.1	123.6	51.0	124.7	2,837	4,141	604	748
Iran, Islamic Rep.	57.5	151.5	61.2	154.8	68.0	158.3	1,108	2,163	2,165	3,737
Iraq	74.7	76.7	77.3	77.5	81.2	67.9	832	945	..	..
Ireland	93.6	111.3	83.5	106.7	83.5	107.7	4,733	7,053	..	..
Israel	99.8	97.4	85.0	115.3	78.4	127.6	1,840	2,853	..	..
Italy	106.1	101.9	101.4	102.3	93.0	105.1	3,548	4,815	11,090	27,064
Jamaica	101.4	127.5	93.6	125.9	85.5	126.2	1,667	1,002	1,123	1,487
Japan	108.3	87.1	94.1	91.6	85.1	93.2	5,252	5,879	17,378	33,077
Jordan	54.6	132.6	57.4	147.4	51.5	167.7	521	1,301	1,141	1,145
Kazakhstan	..	89.5	..	73.5	..	46.7	..	1,149	..	1,753
Kenya	70.2	123.1	65.6	122.2	60.5	118.0	1,364	1,516	265	213
Korea, Dem. Rep.	..	..	..	..	..	..	3,694	3,189	..	..
Korea, Rep.	87.8	114.3	77.5	132.3	52.4	159.9	4,986	6,118	3,765	14,251
Kuwait	37.1	198.1	81.0	229.0	94.5	211.2	3,124	2,206	..	..
Kyrgyz Republic	..	153.2	..	132.5	..	80.7	..	2,742	..	1,861
Lao PDR	73.5	177.5	70.3	186.4	56.0	188.8	1,402	3,140	..	621
Latvia	..	78.7	..	42.4	..	31.1	..	2,189	..	2,773
Lebanon	49.9	100.4	60.6	108.9	95.0	157.0	1,307	2,575	..	29,874
Lesotho	98.2	147.9	96.6	111.6	96.6	87.2	977	926	611	575
Liberia	..	..	..	..	..	..	1,251	983	..	..
Libya	76.3	129.4	78.7	134.1	68.4	134.9	430	631	..	..
Lithuania	..	76.5	..	64.7	..	52.6	..	2,807	..	3,431
Macedonia, FYR	..	94.9	..	89.5	..	89.9	..	2,642	..	4,243
Madagascar	83.1	108.5	83.8	115.8	87.7	114.2	1,664	2,007	158	155
Malawi	85.7	156.0	93.1	174.0	78.4	125.4	1,161	1,134	96	124
Malaysia	75.3	119.4	55.6	142.1	41.0	142.1	2,828	3,132	3,939	6,912
Mali	54.5	143.9	77.2	128.6	95.6	123.2	804	943	242	274
Mauritania	62.1	126.2	86.5	108.3	89.4	107.0	384	860	289	447
Mauritius	93.3	98.1	89.6	109.0	64.0	145.3	2,536	7,577	2,891	5,494
Mexico	86.5	123.6	85.3	135.7	86.2	150.1	2,164	2,870	1,482	1,813
Moldova	..	61.9	..	51.1	..	32.9	..	2,345	..	971
Mongolia	44.6	29.7	88.1	91.9	93.2	97.4	573	751	*994*	1,444
Morocco	54.8	91.8	55.8	103.6	59.8	124.6	811	1,129	1,146	1,513
Mozambique	109.9	141.1	100.7	127.5	85.8	103.9	603	848	..	136
Myanmar	89.0	178.5	88.2	176.5	89.1	169.4	2,521	3,453	..	..
Namibia	80.1	126.9	107.6	96.8	116.0	93.3	377	400	1,064	1,545
Nepal	61.9	137.9	65.4	135.8	77.3	129.3	1,615	2,178	156	203
Netherlands	79.8	111.7	86.5	98.4	88.3	96.5	5,696	7,531	24,360	59,476
New Zealand	74.4	142.9	90.7	135.2	95.5	123.9	4,089	6,230	16,637	28,740
Nicaragua	124.1	141.3	117.8	154.3	139.7	148.1	1,475	1,761	1,549	1,618
Niger	89.2	147.5	97.5	140.1	110.0	128.9	440	417	229	197
Nigeria	51.7	156.0	57.2	155.8	83.3	145.3	1,265	1,105	417	729
Norway	94.8	77.6	93.9	91.0	96.2	97.4	3,634	3,760	17,138	37,073
Oman	60.1	160.3	62.1	163.1	61.5	144.5	982	2,319	..	..
Pakistan	65.6	122.8	66.3	152.7	59.5	171.9	1,608	2,266	416	716
Panama	96.9	83.3	85.5	105.8	71.3	138.6	1,524	2,753	2,122	2,967
Papua New Guinea	86.5	120.7	86.1	124.3	84.9	146.0	2,087	3,919	692	823
Paraguay	58.7	115.5	60.8	141.0	62.1	136.9	1,535	2,034	2,641	3,318
Peru	82.1	180.3	77.3	175.0	78.0	159.1	1,946	3,302	1,299	1,863
Philippines	88.3	123.1	86.1	137.1	73.8	177.8	1,611	2,692	1,381	1,458
Poland	84.6	84.0	87.9	86.0	98.0	83.3	2,345	3,072	..	1,637
Portugal	85.0	91.7	72.2	102.2	71.8	122.3	1,102	2,702	3,796	7,567
Puerto Rico	131.3	67.9	99.8	84.0	90.3	89.4	7,970	1,731	..	..

	Crop production index		Food production index		Livestock production index		Cereal yield		Agricultural productivity	
									Agriculture value added per worker	
							kilograms per hectare		1995 $	
	1989–91 = 100		1989–91 = 100		1989–91 = 100					
	1979–81	**2000–02**	**1979–81**	**2000–02**	**1979–81**	**2000–02**	**1979–81**	**2000–02**	**1979–81**	**2000–02**
Romania	114.1	91.0	113.0	87.1	110.0	80.7	2,854	2,562	1,397	3,588
Russian Federation	..	86.1	..	66.6	..	52.6	..	1,846	..	3,822
Rwanda	84.9	115.4	85.8	117.3	80.3	112.3	1,134	1,011	271	254
Saudi Arabia	27.2	84.2	26.7	98.5	32.7	152.6	820	3,818	2,152	15,796
Senegal	77.2	111.0	74.1	122.4	65.7	147.0	690	755	345	354
Serbia and Montenegro	96.3	..	94.3	..	94.2	..	3,601	..	..	..
Sierra Leone	80.3	75.4	84.5	84.0	84.1	126.6	1,249	1,234	674	359
Singapore	595.0	48.2	154.3	31.9	173.7	31.8	..	..	16,664	42,920
Slovak Republic	..	..	..	..	..	..	..	..	..	..
Slovenia	..	81.9	..	100.9	..	108.7	..	5,452	..	37,671
Somalia	..	..	..	..	..	..	474	547	..	..
South Africa	94.9	110.1	90.5	111.1	86.0	104.3	2,105	2,633	2,857	4,072
Spain	83.0	115.8	81.9	120.1	83.9	134.2	1,986	3,091	7,556	22,412
Sri Lanka	99.3	114.8	98.1	117.2	92.0	147.7	2,462	3,520	642	725
Sudan	127.1	165.9	105.2	167.5	89.3	161.1	645	600	..	..
Swaziland	72.5	85.2	81.1	99.9	99.9	126.4	1,345	1,512	1,752	1,936
Sweden	93.1	89.3	100.6	96.0	103.8	100.2	3,595	4,878	20,865	40,368
Switzerland	95.5	89.6	95.8	95.6	98.8	94.9	4,883	6,466	..	..
Syrian Arab Republic	100.7	177.2	93.6	163.6	72.1	136.1	1,156	2,114	2,206	2,636
Tajikistan	..	62.2	..	60.5	..	41.6	..	1,561	..	728
Tanzania	80.5	107.7	75.4	112.8	69.2	126.9	1,063	1,438	..	187
Thailand	79.1	124.3	79.7	123.5	64.5	135.3	1,911	2,654	616	863
Togo	70.6	138.0	78.3	131.4	56.2	115.2	729	1,008	365	503
Trinidad and Tobago	121.5	87.9	111.1	127.8	96.9	157.3	3,167	2,807	3,536	3,034
Tunisia	68.1	98.4	66.3	115.0	60.3	164.4	828	2,218	1,743	3,115
Turkey	76.6	118.8	75.8	114.6	80.4	103.9	1,869	2,176	1,872	1,848
Turkmenistan	..	77.7	..	131.6	..	138.0	..	2,621	..	690
Uganda	67.5	138.9	69.7	136.7	81.9	130.6	1,555	1,651	..	346
Ukraine	..	71.3	..	52.4	..	45.7	..	2,399	..	1,576
United Arab Emirates	38.9	659.7	42.7	549.9	42.2	200.6	2,224	414	..	..
United Kingdom	80.1	97.2	92.2	92.4	98.1	93.1	4,792	6,841	20,326	32,918
United States	98.6	118.3	94.5	122.5	89.0	123.6	4,151	5,830	20,672	53,907
Uruguay	86.8	135.3	87.1	124.8	85.9	110.4	1,644	3,243	6,563	8,177
Uzbekistan	..	89.0	..	122.3	..	114.8	..	3,644	..	1,449
Venezuela, RB	76.3	119.3	80.2	135.0	84.9	138.8	1,904	3,278	3,935	5,399
Vietnam	65.8	180.3	62.5	171.4	50.1	193.8	2,049	4,375	..	256
West Bank and Gaza	..	..	..	..	..	..	..	..	..	..
Yemen, Rep.	82.3	133.6	74.8	142.6	68.9	160.4	1,038	966	..	412
Zambia	64.6	96.2	73.0	107.2	86.2	130.2	1,676	1,481	186	194
Zimbabwe	77.8	113.9	83.3	108.6	89.7	121.5	1,359	872	310	355
World	**79.1 w**	**131.5 w**	**78.8 w**	**133.1 w**	**79.6 w**	**136.4 w**	**1,605 w**	**2,233 w**	**.. w**	**.. w**
Low income	71.7	134.0	70.7	135.1	68.4	146.8	1,090	1,321	..	415
Middle income	74.3	147.0	71.8	150.3	69.6	164.4	1,759	2,497	..	820
Lower middle income	72.5	154.2	68.8	158.0	60.8	181.9	1,682	2,181	..	713
Upper middle income	79.4	116.2	78.8	118.6	82.8	114.0	1,842	2,926	..	3,937
Low & middle income	73.3	142.7	71.5	145.2	69.3	159.9	1,397	1,966	..	626
East Asia & Pacific	68.5	166.1	63.4	170.6	47.9	214.6	2,034	3,147	..	..
Europe & Central Asia	..	..	..	..	..	..	2,854	2,640	..	2,353
Latin America & Carib.	80.3	138.6	78.3	141.9	79.8	144.8	1,786	2,804	2,239	3,570
Middle East & N. Africa	66.0	136.4	64.8	137.1	64.1	145.3	925	1,726	..	2,340
South Asia	71.9	131.6	69.6	133.3	64.0	154.3	1,510	2,222	285	412
Sub-Saharan Africa	75.4	132.3	78.3	133.5	84.1	124.4	895	1,064	419	360
High income	93.4	112.5	91.9	113.2	90.6	112.5	3,274	3,746	..	..
Europe EMU	90.7	105.3	91.4	105.2	93.9	101.9	4,035	5,517	..	30,154

a. Includes Luxembourg.

The agricultural production indexes in the table are prepared by the Food and Agriculture Organization (FAO). The FAO obtains data from official and semi-official reports of crop yields, area under production, and livestock numbers. If data are not available, the FAO makes estimates. The indexes are calculated using the Laspeyres formula: production quantities of each commodity are weighted by average international commodity prices in the base period and summed for each year. Because the FAO's indexes are based on the concept of agriculture as a single enterprise, estimates of the amounts retained for seed and feed are subtracted from the production data to avoid double counting. The resulting aggregate represents production available for any use except as seed and feed. The FAO's indexes may differ from other sources because of differences in coverage, weights, concepts, time periods, calculation methods, and use of international prices.

To ease cross-country comparisons, the FAO uses international commodity prices to value production. These prices, expressed in international dollars (equivalent in purchasing power to the U.S. dollar), are derived using a Geary-Khamis formula applied to agricultural outputs (see Inter-Secretariat Working Group on National Accounts 1993, sections 16.93–96). This method assigns a single price to each commodity so that, for example, one metric ton of wheat has the same price regardless of where it was produced. The use of international prices eliminates fluctuations in the value of output due to transitory movements of nominal exchange rates unrelated to the purchasing power of the domestic currency.

Data on cereal yield may be affected by a variety of reporting and timing differences. The FAO allocates production data to the calendar year in which the bulk of the harvest took place. But most of a crop harvested near the end of a year will be used in the following year. Cereal crops harvested for hay or harvested green for food, feed, or silage, and those used for grazing, are generally excluded. But millet and sorghum, which are grown as feed for livestock and poultry in Europe and North America, are used as food in Africa, Asia, and countries of the former Soviet Union. So some cereal crops are excluded from the data for some countries and included elsewhere, depending on their use.

Agricultural productivity is measured by value added per unit of input. (For further discussion of the calculation of value added in national accounts, see *About the data* for tables 4.1 and 4.2.) Agricultural value added includes that from forestry and fishing. Thus interpretations of land productivity should be made with caution. To smooth annual fluctuations in agricultural activity, the indicators in the table have been averaged over three years.

- **Crop production index** shows agricultural production for each period relative to the base period 1989–91. It includes all crops except fodder crops. The regional and income group aggregates for the FAO's production indexes are calculated from the underlying values in international dollars, normalized to the base period 1989–91. The data in this table are three-year averages. • **Food production index** covers food crops that are considered edible and that contain nutrients. Coffee and tea are excluded because, although edible, they have no nutritive value. • **Livestock production index** includes meat and milk from all sources, dairy products such as cheese, and eggs, honey, raw silk, wool, and hides and skins. • **Cereal yield,** measured in kilograms per hectare of harvested land, includes wheat, rice, maize, barley, oats, rye, millet, sorghum, buckwheat, and mixed grains. Production data on cereals refer to crops harvested for dry grain only. Cereal crops harvested for hay or harvested green for food, feed, or silage, and those used for grazing, are excluded. • **Agricultural productivity** refers to the ratio of agricultural value added, measured in constant 1995 U.S. dollars, to the number of workers in agriculture.

3.3a

The 15 countries with the highest cereal yield in 2001–03—and the 15 with the lowest

Kilograms per hectare of arable land

Country	Cereal yield	Country	Cereal yield
Belgium [a]	8,002	Botswana	156
Mauritius	7,577	Eritrea	351
Netherlands	7,531	Namibia	400
Egypt, Arab Rep.	7,244	United Arab Emirates	414
Ireland	7,053	Niger	417
United Kingdom	6,841	Somalia	547
France	6,796	Sudan	600
Switzerland	6,466	Angola	606
Germany	6,355	Libya	631
New Zealand	6,230	Chad	697
Korea, Rep.	6,118	Mongolia	751
Denmark	5,912	Senegal	755
Japan	5,879	Congo, Dem. Rep.	774
United States	5,830	Congo, Rep.	779
Austria	5,589	Haiti	840

a. Includes Luxembourg.
Source: Table 3.3.

3.4 Deforestation and biodiversity

	Forest area		Average annual deforestation		Mammals		Birds		Higher plants [a]		Nationally protected areas	
	thousand sq. km 2000	% of total land area 2000	sq. km 1990–2000	% 1990–2000	Species 2002	Threatened species 2002	Species 2002	Threatened species 2002	Species 2002	Threatened species 2002	thousand sq. km 2003 [b]	% of total land area 2003 [b]
Afghanistan	14	2.1	..	..	119	13	181	11	4,000	1	2.0	0.3
Albania	10	36.2	78	0.8	68	3	193	3	3,031	0	1.0	3.8
Algeria	21	0.9	−266	−1.3	92	13	183	6	3,164	2	119.1	5.0
Angola	698	56.0	1,242	0.2	276	19	265	15	5,185	19	82.3	6.6
Argentina	346	12.7	2,851	0.8	320	34	362	39	9,372	42	180.6	6.6
Armenia	4	12.4	−42	−1.3	84	11	236	4	3,553	1	2.1	7.6
Australia	1,581	20.6	0	0.0	252	63	497	37	15,638	38	1,029.4	13.4
Austria	39	47.0	−77	−0.2	83	7	230	3	3,100	3	27.3	33.0
Azerbaijan	11	12.6	−130	−1.3	99	13	229	8	4,300	0	5.3	6.1
Bangladesh	13	10.2	−165	−1.3	125	23	166	23	5,000	12	1.0	0.8
Belarus	94	45.3	−2,562	−3.2	74	7	194	3	2,100	0	13.1	6.3
Belgium	7 [c]	22.2 [c]	−10 [c]	−0.2 [c]	58	11	191	2	1,550	0	*0.9*	*2.6*
Benin	27	24.0	699	2.3	188	8	112	2	2,500	11	12.6	11.4
Bolivia	531	48.9	1,611	0.3	316	24	504	28	17,367	70	145.3	13.4
Bosnia and Herzegovina	23	44.8	0	0.0	72	10	205	3	..	1	0.3	0.5
Botswana	124	21.9	1,184	0.9	164	6	184	7	2,151	0	104.8	18.5
Brazil	5,325	63.0	22,264	0.4	394	81	686	114	56,215	..	566.6	6.7
Bulgaria	37	33.4	−204	−0.6	81	14	248	10	3,572	0	5.0	4.5
Burkina Faso	71	25.9	152	0.2	147	7	138	2	1,100	2	31.5	11.5
Burundi	1	3.7	147	9.0	107	6	145	7	2,500	2	1.5	5.7
Cambodia	93	52.9	561	0.6	123	24	183	19	..	29	32.7	18.5
Cameroon	239	51.3	2,218	0.9	409	40	165	15	8,260	155	20.9	4.5
Canada	2,446	26.5	0	0.0	193	14	310	8	3,270	1	1,023.5	11.1
Central African Republic	229	36.8	300	0.1	209	14	168	3	3,602	10	54.2	8.7
Chad	127	10.1	817	0.6	134	17	141	5	1,600	2	114.6	9.1
Chile	155	20.7	203	0.1	91	21	157	22	5,284	40	141.5	18.9
China	1,589	17.0	−13,483	−0.9	394	79	618	74	32,200	168	727.5	7.8
Hong Kong, China	..	..	..	..	..	1	..	11	..	..	*0.5*	..
Colombia	496	47.8	1,905	0.4	359	41	708	78	51,220	213	105.9	10.2
Congo, Dem. Rep.	1,352	59.6	5,324	0.4	200	15	130	3	6,000	33	113.4	5.0
Congo, Rep.	221	64.6	175	0.1	450	40	345	28	11,007	55	22.2	6.5
Costa Rica	20	38.5	158	0.8	205	14	279	13	12,119	109	11.7	23.0
Côte d'Ivoire	71	22.4	2,649	3.1	230	19	252	12	3,660	101	19.1	6.0
Croatia	18	31.9	−20	−0.1	76	9	224	4	4,288	0	4.2	7.5
Cuba	23	21.4	−277	−1.3	31	11	86	18	6,522	160	75.9	69.1
Czech Republic	26	34.1	−5	−0.0	81	8	205	2	1,900	4	12.4	16.1
Denmark	5	10.7	−10	−0.2	43	5	196	1	1,450	3	14.4	34.0
Dominican Republic	14	28.4	0	0.0	20	5	79	15	5,657	29	25.1	51.9
Ecuador	106	38.1	1,372	1.2	302	33	640	62	19,362	197	50.7	18.3
Egypt, Arab Rep.	1	0.1	−20	−3.4	98	13	123	7	2,076	2	96.6	9.7
El Salvador	1	5.8	72	4.6	135	2	141	0	2,911	23	0.1	0.4
Eritrea	16	15.7	54	0.3	112	12	138	7	..	3	4.3	4.3
Estonia	21	48.7	−125	−0.6	65	4	204	3	1,630	0	5.0	11.8
Ethiopia	46	4.6	403	0.8	277	35	262	16	6,603	22	169.0	16.9
Finland	219	72.0	−80	−0.0	60	5	243	3	1,102	1	28.3	9.3
France	153	27.9	−616	−0.4	93	18	283	5	4,630	2	73.2	13.3
Gabon	218	84.7	101	0.0	190	15	156	5	6,651	71	1.8	0.7
Gambia, The	5	48.1	−45	−1.0	117	3	154	2	974	3	0.2	2.3
Georgia	30	43.0	0	0.0	107	13	208	3	4,350	..	1.6	2.3
Germany	107	30.8	0	0.0	76	11	247	5	2,682	12	113.8	31.9
Ghana	63	27.8	1,200	1.7	222	14	206	8	3,725	115	12.7	5.6
Greece	36	27.9	−300	−0.9	95	13	255	7	4,992	2	4.6	3.6
Guatemala	29	26.3	537	1.7	250	6	221	6	8,681	77	21.7	20.0
Guinea	69	28.2	347	0.5	190	12	109	10	3,000	21	1.7	0.7
Guinea-Bissau	22	77.8	216	0.9	108	3	235	0	1,000	4	..	..
Haiti	1	3.2	70	5.7	20	4	62	14	5,242	27	0.1	0.4

	Forest area		Average annual deforestation		Mammals		Birds		Higher plants [a]		Nationally protected areas	
	thousand sq. km 2000	% of total land area 2000	sq. km 1990–2000	% 1990–2000	Species 2002	Threatened species 2002	Species 2002	Threatened species 2002	Species 2002	Threatened species 2002	thousand sq. km 2003 [b]	% of total land area 2003 [b]
Honduras	54	48.1	590	1.0	173	10	232	5	5,680	108	7.2	6.4
Hungary	18	19.9	−72	−0.4	83	9	208	8	2,214	1	6.5	7.0
India	641	21.6	−381	−0.1	390	88	458	72	18,664	244	154.6	5.2
Indonesia	1,050	58.0	13,124	1.2	515	147	929	114	29,375	384	373.2	20.6
Iran, Islamic Rep.	73	4.5	0	0.0	140	22	293	13	8,000	1	78.5	4.8
Iraq	8	1.8	0	0.0	81	11	140	11	..	0	0.0	0.0
Ireland	7	9.6	−170	−3.0	25	5	143	1	950	1	1.2	1.7
Israel	1	6.4	−50	−4.9	116	14	162	12	2,317	0	3.3	15.8
Italy	100	34.0	−295	−0.3	90	14	250	5	5,599	3	23.2	7.9
Jamaica	3	30.0	54	1.5	24	5	75	12	3,308	206	..	..
Japan	241	66.1	−34	−0.0	188	37	210	34	5,565	11	24.8	6.8
Jordan	1	1.0	0	0.0	71	10	117	8	2,100	0	3.0	3.4
Kazakhstan	121	4.5	−2,390	−2.2	178	16	379	15	6,000	1	72.9	2.7
Kenya	171	30.0	931	0.5	359	51	344	24	6,506	98	45.5	8.0
Korea, Dem. Rep.	82	68.2	0	0.0	..	13	150	19	2,898	3	3.1	2.6
Korea, Rep.	63	63.3	49	0.1	49	13	138	25	2,898	0	6.8	6.9
Kuwait	0	0.3	−2	−5.2	21	1	35	7	234	0	0.3	1.5
Kyrgyz Republic	10	5.2	−228	−2.6	83	7	168	4	4,500	1	28.9	12.5
Lao PDR	126	54.4	527	0.4	172	31	212	20	8,286	18	6.9	3.6
Latvia	29	47.1	−127	−0.4	83	4	216	3	1,153	0	8.3	13.4
Lebanon	0	3.5	1	0.3	57	5	116	7	3,000	0	0.1	0.5
Lesotho	0	0.5	0	0.0	33	3	123	7	1,591	0	0.1	0.2
Liberia	35	36.1	760	2.0	193	17	146	11	2,200	46	1.6	1.7
Libya	4	0.2	−47	−1.4	76	8	76	1	1,825	1	1.8	0.1
Lithuania	20	30.8	−48	−0.2	68	5	201	4	1,796	0	6.7	10.3
Macedonia, FYR	9	35.6	0	0.0	78	11	199	3	3,500	0	1.8	7.1
Madagascar	117	20.2	1,174	0.9	141	50	172	27	9,505	162	25.0	4.3
Malawi	26	27.6	707	2.4	195	8	219	11	3,765	14	10.5	11.2
Malaysia	193	58.7	2,377	1.2	300	50	254	37	15,500	681	18.7	5.7
Mali	132	10.8	993	0.7	137	13	191	4	1,741	6	45.1	3.7
Mauritania	3	0.3	98	2.7	61	10	172	2	1,100	0	17.4	1.7
Mauritius	0	7.9	1	0.6	..	3	..	9	..	..	0.2	7.8
Mexico	552	28.9	6,306	1.1	491	70	440	39	26,071	..	194.7	10.2
Moldova	3	9.9	−7	−0.2	68	6	175	5	1,752	0	0.5	1.4
Mongolia	106	6.8	600	0.5	133	14	274	16	2,823	0	180.1	11.5
Morocco	30	6.8	12	0.0	105	16	206	9	3,675	2	3.1	0.7
Mozambique	306	39.0	637	0.2	179	14	144	16	5,692	36	65.9	8.4
Myanmar	344	52.3	5,169	1.4	300	39	310	35	7,000	37	2.0	0.3
Namibia	80	9.8	734	0.9	250	15	201	11	3,174	5	112.0	13.6
Nepal	39	27.3	783	1.8	181	31	274	25	6,973	6	12.7	8.9
Netherlands	4	11.1	−10	−0.3	55	10	192	4	1,221	0	4.8	14.2
New Zealand	79	29.7	−390	−0.5	..	8	..	63		..	79.3	29.6
Nicaragua	33	27.0	1,172	3.0	200	6	215	5	7,590	39	21.6	17.8
Niger	13	1.0	617	3.7	131	11	125	3	1,460	2	97.5	7.7
Nigeria	135	14.8	3,984	2.6	274	27	286	9	4,715	119	30.1	3.3
Norway	89	28.9	−310	−0.4	54	10	241	2	1,715	2	20.9	6.8
Oman	0	0.0	0	0.0	56	9	109	10	1,204	6	43.3	14.0
Pakistan	25	3.2	304	1.1	188	19	237	17	4,950	2	37.8	4.9
Panama	29	38.6	519	1.6	218	20	302	16	9,915	193	16.2	21.7
Papua New Guinea	306	67.6	1,129	0.4	214	58	414	32	11,544	142	10.4	2.3
Paraguay	234	58.8	1,230	0.5	305	10	233	26	7,851	10	13.9	3.5
Peru	652	50.9	2,688	0.4	460	49	695	76	17,144	269	78.1	6.1
Philippines	58	19.4	887	1.4	153	50	404	67	8,931	193	17.0	5.7
Poland	93	30.6	−110	−0.1	84	15	233	4	2,450	4	37.7	12.4
Portugal	37	40.1	−570	−1.7	63	17	235	7	5,050	15	6.0	6.6
Puerto Rico	2	25.8	5	0.2	..	2	..	8	..	..	0.3	3.5

	Forest area		Average annual deforestation		Mammals		Birds		Higher plants [a]		Nationally protected areas	
	thousand sq. km 2000	% of total land area 2000	sq. km 1990–2000	% 1990–2000	Species 2002	Threatened species 2002	Species 2002	Threatened species 2002	Species 2002	Threatened species 2002	thousand sq. km 2003[b]	% of total land area 2003[b]
Romania	64	28.0	−147	−0.2	84	17	257	8	3,400	1	10.8	4.7
Russian Federation	8,514	50.4	−1,353	−0.0	269	45	528	38	11,400	7	1,317.3	7.8
Rwanda	3	12.4	150	3.9	151	9	200	9	2,288	3	1.5	6.2
Saudi Arabia	15	0.7	0	0.0	77	8	125	15	2,028	3	823.3	38.3
Senegal	62	32.2	450	0.7	192	12	175	4	2,086	7	22.3	11.6
Serbia and Montenegro	29	..	14	0.0	96	12	238	5	4,082	1	..	3.3
Sierra Leone	11	14.7	361	2.9	147	12	172	10	2,090	43	1.5	2.1
Singapore	0	3.3	0	0.0	85	3	142	7	2,282	54	0.0	4.9
Slovak Republic	20	42.5	−69	−0.3	85	9	199	4	3,124	2	11.0	22.8
Slovenia	11	55.0	−22	−0.2	75	9	201	1	3,200	0	1.2	6.0
Somalia	75	12.0	769	1.0	171	19	179	10	3,028	17	5.0	0.8
South Africa	89	7.3	80	0.1	247	42	304	28	23,420	45	67.2	5.5
Spain	144	28.8	−860	−0.6	82	24	281	7	5,050	14	42.5	8.5
Sri Lanka	19	30.0	348	1.6	88	22	126	14	3,314	280	8.7	13.5
Sudan	616	25.9	9,589	1.4	267	23	280	6	3,137	17	123.6	5.2
Swaziland	5	30.3	−58	−1.2	..	4	..	5	..	..	0.6	3.5
Sweden	271	65.9	−6	−0.0	60	7	259	2	1,750	3	37.5	9.1
Switzerland	12	30.3	−43	−0.4	75	5	199	2	3,030	2	11.9	30.0
Syrian Arab Republic	5	2.5	0	0.0	63	4	145	8	3,000	0	..	..
Tajikistan	4	2.8	−20	−0.5	84	9	210	7	5,000	2	5.9	4.2
Tanzania	388	43.9	913	0.2	316	42	229	33	10,008	236	263.3	29.8
Thailand	148	28.9	1,124	0.7	265	37	285	37	11,625	78	71.0	13.9
Togo	5	9.4	209	3.4	196	9	117	0	3,085	9	4.3	7.9
Trinidad and Tobago	3	50.5	22	0.8	100	1	131	1	2,259	1	0.3	6.0
Tunisia	5	3.3	−11	−0.2	78	11	165	5	2,196	0	0.5	0.3
Turkey	102	13.3	−220	−0.2	116	17	278	11	8,650	3	12.3	1.6
Turkmenistan	38	8.0	0	0.0	103	13	204	6	..	0	19.7	4.2
Uganda	42	21.3	913	2.0	345	20	243	13	4,900	33	48.5	24.6
Ukraine	96	16.5	−310	−0.3	108	16	245	8	5,100	1	22.6	3.9
United Arab Emirates	3	3.8	−78	−2.8	25	3	34	8	..	0	0.0	0.0
United Kingdom	26	10.7	−200	−0.8	50	12	229	2	1,623	13	50.3	20.9
United States	2,260	24.7	−3,880	−0.2	428	37	508	55	19,473	..	2,372.2	25.9
Uruguay	13	7.4	−501	−5.0	81	6	115	11	2,278	1	0.5	0.3
Uzbekistan	20	4.8	−46	−0.2	97	9	203	9	4,800	1	8.3	2.0
Venezuela, RB	495	56.1	2,175	0.4	323	26	547	24	21,073	67	562.7	63.8
Vietnam	98	30.2	−516	−0.5	213	40	262	37	10,500	126	12.0	3.7
West Bank and Gaza	..	..	..	..	..	1	..	1	..	..	..	..
Yemen, Rep.	4	0.9	92	1.8	66	5	93	12	1,650	52	..	..
Zambia	312	42.0	8,509	2.4	233	12	252	11	4,747	8	237.1	31.9
Zimbabwe	190	49.2	3,199	1.5	270	12	229	10	4,440	14	46.8	12.1
World	**38,480 s**	**29.7 w**	**95,009 s**	**0.2 w**							**13,750.0 s**	**10.7 w**
Low income	9,031	27.1	73,087	0.8							2,665.5	8.4
Middle income	21,493	32.7	29,869	0.1							6,073.9	9.1
Lower middle income	19,065	31.8	14,730	−0.1							3,891.0	7.2
Upper middle income	2,428	34.5	15,139	0.5							2,183.0	17.3
Low & middle income	30,525	30.9	102,956	0.3							8,739.5	8.9
East Asia & Pacific	4,238	27.2	11,613	0.2							1,454.8	9.2
Europe & Central Asia	9,464	39.7	−8,143	−0.1							1,610.2	6.8
Latin America & Carib.	9,438	47.1	45,873	0.5							2,237.8	11.2
Middle East & N. Africa	168	1.5	−239	−0.1							1,169.3	11.3
South Asia	782	16.3	889	0.1							228.6	4.8
Sub-Saharan Africa	6,436	27.3	52,963	0.8							2,038.8	8.7
High income	7,955	26.1	−7,947	−0.1							5,010.5	19.5
Europe EMU	846	37.0	−2,978	−0.3							324.9	13.5

a. Flowering plants only. b. Data may refer to earlier years. They are the most recent reported by the World Conservation Monitoring Center in 2003. c. Includes Luxembourg.

About the data

The estimates of forest area are from the Food and Agriculture Organization's (FAO) *State of the World's Forests 2003,* which provides information on forest cover in 2000 and an estimate of forest cover in 1990. The current survey is the latest global forest assessment and the first to use a uniform global definition of forest. According to this assessment, the global rate of net deforestation has slowed to 9.5 million hectares a year, a rate 20 percent lower than that previously reported. No breakdown of forest cover between natural forest and plantation is shown in the table because of space limitations. (This breakdown is provided by the FAO only for developing countries.) For this reason the deforestation data in the table may underestimate the rate at which natural forest is disappearing in some countries.

Deforestation is a major cause of loss of biodiversity, and habitat conservation is vital for stemming this loss. Conservation efforts traditionally have focused on protected areas, which have grown substantially in recent decades. Measures of species richness are among the most straightforward ways to indicate the importance of an area for biodiversity. The number of small plants and animals is usually estimated by sampling plots. It is also important to know which aspects are under the most immediate threat. This, however, requires a large amount of data and time-consuming analysis. For this reason global analyses of the status of threatened species have been carried out for few groups of organisms. Only for birds has the status of all species been assessed. An estimated 45 percent of mammal species remain to be assessed. For plants the World Conservation Union's (IUCN) *1997 IUCN Red List of Threatened Plants* provides the first-ever comprehensive listing of threatened species on a global scale, the result of more than 20 years' work by botanists from around the world. Nearly 34,000 plant species, 12.5 percent of the total, are threatened with extinction.

The table shows information on protected areas, numbers of certain species, and numbers of those species under threat. The World Conservation Monitoring Centre (WCMC) compiles these data from a variety of sources. Because of differences in definitions and reporting practices, cross-country comparability is limited. Compounding these problems, available data cover different periods.

Nationally protected areas are areas of at least 1,000 hectares that fall into one of five management categories defined by the WCMC:

- Scientific reserves and strict nature reserves with limited public access.
- National parks of national or international significance (not materially affected by human activity).
- Natural monuments and natural landscapes with unique aspects.
- Managed nature reserves and wildlife sanctuaries.
- Protected landscapes and seascapes (which may include cultural landscapes).

Designating land as a protected area does not necessarily mean that protection is in force. For small countries that may only have protected areas smaller than 1,000 hectares, this size limit in the definition will result in an underestimate of the extent and number of protected areas.

Threatened species are defined according to the IUCN's classification categories: endangered (in danger of extinction and unlikely to survive if causal factors continue operating), vulnerable (likely to move into the endangered category in the near future if causal factors continue operating), rare (not endangered or vulnerable but at risk), indeterminate (known to be endangered, vulnerable, or rare but not enough information is available to say which), out of danger (formerly included in one of the above categories but now considered relatively secure because appropriate conservation measures are in effect), and insufficiently known (suspected but not definitely known to belong to one of the above categories).

Figures on species are not necessarily comparable across countries because taxonomic concepts and coverage vary. And while the number of birds and mammals is fairly well known, it is difficult to make an accurate count of plants. Although the data in the table should be interpreted with caution, especially for numbers of threatened species (where knowledge is very incomplete), they do identify countries that are major sources of global biodiversity and show national commitments to habitat protection.

The dataset on protected areas is tentative and is being revised. Due to variations in consistency and methodology of collection, the quality of the data are highly variable across countries. Some countries update their information more frequently than others, some may have more accurate data on extent of coverage, and many underreport the number or extent of protected areas.

Definitions

- **Forest area** is land under natural or planted stands of trees, whether productive or not. • **Average annual deforestation** refers to the permanent conversion of natural forest area to other uses, including shifting cultivation, permanent agriculture, ranching, settlements, and infrastructure development. Deforested areas do not include areas logged but intended for regeneration or areas degraded by fuelwood gathering, acid precipitation, or forest fires. Negative numbers indicate an increase in forest area. • **Mammals** exclude whales and porpoises. • **Birds** refer to breeding species and are listed for countries included within their breeding ranges. • **Higher plants** refer to native vascular plant species. • **Threatened species** are the number of species classified by the IUCN as endangered, vulnerable, rare, indeterminate, out of danger, or insufficiently known. • **Nationally protected areas** are totally or partially protected areas of at least 1,000 hectares that are designated as scientific reserves with limited public access, national parks, natural monuments, nature reserves or wildlife sanctuaries, and protected landscapes and seascapes. The data do not include sites protected under local or provincial law. Total land area is used to calculate the percentage of total area protected (see table 3.1).

Data sources

The forestry data are from the FAO's *State of the World's Forests 2003.* The data on species are from the WCMC's electronic files and the IUCN's *2002 IUCN Red List of Threatened Animals* and *1997 IUCN Red List of Threatened Plants.* The data on protected areas are from the United Nations Environment Programme and WCMC.

3.5 | Freshwater

	Renewable freshwater resources			Annual freshwater withdrawals					Access to improved water source			
	Internal flows	Net flows from other countries	Total resources per capita	billion cu. m	% of total resources	% for agriculture	% for industry	% for domestic	% of urban population		% of rural population	
	billion cu. m 2000	billion cu. m 2000	cu. m[a] 2000	1980–2000[b]	1980–2000[a,b]	1987	1987	1987	1990	2000	1990	2000
Afghanistan	55	10.0	2,322	26.1	40.2	99[c]	0[c]	1[c]	..	19	..	11
Albania	27	15.7	13,524	1.4	3.3	71	0	29	..	99	..	95
Algeria	14	0.4	457	5.0	35.0	52[c]	14[c]	34[c]	..	94	..	82
Angola	184	..	14,023	0.5	0.3	76[c]	10[c]	14[c]	..	34	..	40
Argentina	276	623.0	23,693	28.6	3.2	75	9	16	..	97	..	73
Armenia	9	1.5	3,455	2.9	27.4	66	4	30	..	87	..	45
Australia	492	0.0	25,022	14.6	3.0	33	2	65	100	100	100	100
Austria	55	29.0	10,437	2.4	2.9	9	58	33	100	100	100	100
Azerbaijan	8	21.0	3,561	16.5	56.7	70	25	5	..	93	..	58
Bangladesh	105	1,105.6	8,922	14.6	1.2	86	2	12	99	99	93	97
Belarus	37	20.8	5,844	2.7	4.7	35	43	22	..	100	..	100
Belgium	12	4.0	1,548	..	..	..	..	..	..	..	..	..
Benin	10	15.5	3,938	0.1	0.4	67[c]	10[c]	23[c]	..	74	..	55
Bolivia	304	7.2	35,271	1.2	0.4	87	3	10	91	95	47	64
Bosnia and Herzegovina	36	2.0	9,120	1.0	2.7	60	10	30	..	..	..	..
Botswana	3	11.8	8,586	0.1	0.7	48[c]	20[c]	32[c]	100	100	88	90
Brazil	5,418	1,900.0	41,941	54.9	0.8	61	18	21	93	95	54	53
Bulgaria	21	0.2	2,662	13.9	65.6	22	75	3	..	100	..	100
Burkina Faso	13	2.0	1,226	0.4	2.8	81[c]	0[c]	19[c]	..	66	..	37
Burundi	4	..	509	0.1	2.8	64[c]	0[c]	36[c]	96	91	67	77
Cambodia	121	355.6	38,136	0.5	0.1	94	1	5	..	54	..	26
Cameroon	273	0.0	17,312	0.4	0.1	35[c]	19[c]	46[c]	78	78	32	39
Canada	2,850	52.0	92,532	45.1	1.6	12	70	18	100	100	99	99
Central African Republic	141	..	36,911	0.1	0.1	74[c]	5[c]	21[c]	71	89	35	57
Chad	15	28.0	5,155	0.2	0.5	82[c]	2[c]	16[c]	..	31	..	26
Chile	884	0.0	56,707	20.3	2.3	84	11	5	98	99	49	58
China	2,812	17.2	2,210	525.5	18.6	78	18	5	99	94	60	66
Hong Kong, China	..	..	..	..	..	..	..	..	..	..	..	..
Colombia	2,112	0.0	48,293	8.9	0.4	37	4	59	98	99	84	70
Congo, Dem. Rep.	900	313.0	23,517	0.4	0.0	23[c]	16[c]	61[c]	..	89	..	26
Congo, Rep.	222	610.0	227,509	0.0	0.0	11[c]	27[c]	62[c]	..	71	..	17
Costa Rica	112	..	28,513	5.8	5.2	80	7	13	..	99	..	92
Côte d'Ivoire	77	..	4,645	0.7	0.9	67[c]	11[c]	22[c]	97	92	69	72
Croatia	38	33.7	15,991	0.8	1.1	0	50	50	..	..	..	..
Cuba	38	0.0	3,383	5.2	13.6	51	0	49	..	95	..	77
Czech Republic	13	1.0	1,391	2.7	19.0	2	57	41	..	..	..	..
Denmark	6	..	1,116	1.2	20.0	43	27	30	..	100	..	100
Dominican Republic	21	..	2,438	8.3	39.5	89	0	11	92	90	71	78
Ecuador	432	0.0	33,703	17.0	3.9	82	6	12	82	90	58	75
Egypt, Arab Rep.	2	66.7	1,032	66.0	96.4	82[c]	11[c]	7[c]	97	99	92	96
El Salvador	18	..	2,774	0.7	3.9	46	20	34	88	91	48	64
Eritrea	3	6.0	2,048	..	..	..	..	..	..	63	..	42
Estonia	13	0.1	9,426	0.2	1.6	5	39	56	..	..	..	..
Ethiopia	110	0.0	1,636	2.2	2.0	86[c]	3[c]	11[c]	80	81	17	12
Finland	107	3.0	21,158	2.2	2.0	3	85	12	100	100	100	100
France	179	11.0	3,186	32.3	17.0	10	72	18	..	..	..	..
Gabon	164	0.0	124,715	0.1	0.1	6[c]	22[c]	72[c]	..	95	..	47
Gambia, The	3	5.0	5,760	0.0	0.0	91[c]	2[c]	7[c]	..	80	..	53
Georgia	58	8.4	12,845	3.5	5.3	59	20	21	..	90	..	61
Germany	107	71.0	2,158	46.3	26.0	20	69	11	..	..	..	..
Ghana	30	22.9	2,624	0.3	0.6	52[c]	13[c]	35[c]	85	91	36	62
Greece	58	15.0	6,867	8.7	11.9	87	3	10	..	..	..	..
Guatemala	109	0.0	9,106	1.2	1.1	74	17	9	88	98	69	88
Guinea	226	0.0	29,184	0.7	0.3	87[c]	3[c]	10[c]	72	72	36	36
Guinea-Bissau	16	11.0	18,659	0.0	0.0	36[c]	4[c]	60[c]	..	79	..	49
Haiti	13	..	1,569	1.0	7.7	94	1	5	59	49	50	45

	Renewable freshwater resources			Annual freshwater withdrawals					Access to improved water source			
	Internal flows billion cu. m 2000	Net flows from other countries billion cu. m 2000	Total resources per capita cu. m[a] 2000	billion cu. m 1980–2000[b]	% of total resources 1980–2000[a,b]	% for agriculture 1987	% for industry 1987	% for domestic 1987	% of urban population 1990	% of urban population 2000	% of rural population 1990	% of rural population 2000
Honduras	96	0.0	14,109	1.5	1.6	91	5	4	89	95	78	81
Hungary	6	114.0	11,812	6.8	5.7	36	55	9	100	100	98	98
India	1,261	647.2	1,819	500.0	26.2	92	3	5	88	95	61	79
Indonesia	2,838	..	13,405	74.3	2.6	93	1	6	92	90	62	69
Iran, Islamic Rep.	129	..	1,961	70.0	54.5	92	2	6	..	98	..	83
Iraq	35	75.9	4,596	42.8	38.5	92	5	3	..	96	..	48
Ireland	49	3.0	13,265	0.8	1.5	10	74	16	..	..	..	..
Israel	1	0.9	259	1.6	94.1	54[c]	7[c]	39[c]	..	..	..	..
Italy	183	6.8	3,281	42.0	22.2	48	34	19	..	..	..	..
Jamaica	9	..	3,592	0.9	9.6	77	7	15	98	98	87	85
Japan	430	0.0	3,382	91.4	21.3	64	17	19	..	..	..	..
Jordan	1	..	135	1.0	..	75	3	22	99	100	92	84
Kazakhstan	75	34.2	7,368	33.7	30.7	81	17	2	..	98	..	82
Kenya	20	10.0	963	2.0	6.6	76[c]	4[c]	20[c]	91	88	31	42
Korea, Dem. Rep.	67	10.1	3,428	14.2	18.4	73	16	11	..	100	..	100
Korea, Rep.	65	4.9	1,465	23.7	34.0	63	11	26	..	97	..	71
Kuwait	0	0.0	..	0.5	..	60	2	37	..	..	..	..
Kyrgyz Republic	47	0.0	9,293	10.1	21.7	94	3	3	..	98	..	66
Lao PDR	190	143.1	60,307	1.0	0.3	82	10	8	..	61	..	29
Latvia	17	18.7	15,141	0.3	0.8	13	32	55	..	..	..	..
Lebanon	5	0.0	1,081	1.3	27.1	68	6	27	..	100	..	100
Lesotho	5	0.0	2,926	0.1	1.9	56[c]	22	22[c]	..	88	..	74
Liberia	200	32.0	70,410	0.1	0.0	60[c]	13[c]	27[c]	..	..	..	..
Libya	1	..	110	4.5	..	84[c]	3[c]	13[c]	72	72	68	68
Lithuania	16	9.3	7,178	0.3	1.2	3	16	81	..	..	..	..
Macedonia, FYR	5	1.0	3,140	1.9	29.7	74	15	12	..	..	..	..
Madagascar	337	0.0	20,503	16.3	4.8	99[c]	..[c]	1[c]	85	85	31	31
Malawi	16	1.1	1,601	0.9	5.2	86[c]	3[c]	10[c]	90	95	43	44
Malaysia	580	..	23,863	12.7	2.2	77	13	11	..	..	..	94
Mali	60	40.0	8,792	1.4	1.4	97[c]	1[c]	2[c]	65	74	52	61
Mauritania	0	11.0	4,093	1.6	14.0	92	2	6	34	34	40	40
Mauritius	2	0.0	1,815	..	..	77[c]	7[c]	16[c]	100	100	100	100
Mexico	409	49.0	4,543	77.8	17.0	78	5	17	90	95	52	69
Moldova	1	10.7	2,750	3.0	25.6	26	65	9	..	97	..	88
Mongolia	35	..	14,210	0.4	1.1	53	27	20	..	77	..	30
Morocco	29	0.0	978	11.5	39.7	89[c]	2[c]	10[c]	94	98	58	56
Mozambique	99	111.0	11,390	0.6	0.3	89[c]	2[c]	9[c]	..	81	..	41
Myanmar	881	165.0	21,432	4.0	0.4	90	3	7	..	89	..	66
Namibia	6	39.3	22,922	0.2	0.4	68[c]	3[c]	29[c]	98	100	63	67
Nepal	198	12.0	8,713	29.0	13.8	99	0	1	93	94	64	87
Netherlands	11	80.0	5,637	7.8	8.6	34	61	5	100	100	100	100
New Zealand	327	0.0	83,016	2.0	0.6	44	10	46	100	100	..	..
Nicaragua	190	0.0	35,511	1.3	0.7	84	2	14	93	91	44	59
Niger	4	29.0	2,845	0.5	1.5	82[c]	2[c]	16[c]	65	70	51	56
Nigeria	221	59.0	2,109	3.6	1.3	54[c]	15[c]	31[c]	83	78	37	49
Norway	382	11.0	86,602	2.0	0.5	8	72	20	100	100	100	100
Oman	1	..	394	1.2	..	94	2	5	41	41	30	30
Pakistan	52	170.3	1,534	155.6	70.0	97	2	2	96	95	77	87
Panama	147	..	50,136	1.6	1.1	70	2	28	..	99	..	79
Papua New Guinea	801	..	148,940	0.1	0.0	49	22	29	88	88	32	32
Paraguay	94	..	17,060	0.4	0.4	78	7	15	80	93	46	59
Peru	1,616	144.0	65,797	19.0	1.1	86	7	7	88	87	42	62
Philippines	479	0.0	5,992	55.4	11.6	88	4	8	93	91	82	79
Poland	54	8.0	1,595	12.3	20.0	11	76	13	..	..	..	..
Portugal	38	35.0	7,173	7.3	10.0	48	37	15	..	..	..	..
Puerto Rico	..	..	..	..	..	..	..	..	..	..	..	..

	Renewable freshwater resources			Annual freshwater withdrawals					Access to improved water source			
	Internal flows billion cu. m 2000	Net flows from other countries billion cu. m 2000	Total resources per capita cu. m[a] 2000	billion cu. m 1980–2000[b]	% of total resources 1980–2000[a,b]	% for agriculture 1987	% for industry 1987	% for domestic 1987	% of urban population 1990	% of urban population 2000	% of rural population 1990	% of rural population 2000
Romania	42	170.0	9,520	26.0	12.2	59	33	8	..	91	..	16
Russian Federation	4,313	185.5	31,222	77.1	1.7	20	62	19	..	100	..	96
Rwanda	5	..	637	0.8	15.4	94[c]	2[c]	5[c]	..	60	..	40
Saudi Arabia	2	..	110	17.0	..	90	1	9	..	100	..	64
Senegal	26	13.0	4,009	1.4	3.6	92[c]	3[c]	5[c]	90	92	60	65
Serbia and Montenegro	44	144.0	23,039	13.0	6.9	8[c]	86[c]	6[c]	..	99	..	97
Sierra Leone	160	0.0	30,564	0.4	0.3	89	4	7	..	75	..	46
Singapore	..	..	..	..	..	4	51	45	100	100	100	..
Slovak Republic	13	70.0	15,356	1.8	2.2	..	..	..	..	100	..	100
Slovenia	19	0.0	9,521	1.3	7.0	1[c]	80[c]	20[c]	100	100	100	100
Somalia	6	9.7	1,685	0.8	5.1	97[c]	0[c]	3[c]	..	..	..	..
South Africa	45	5.2	1,103	13.3	26.6	72	11	17	99	99	73	73
Spain	111	0.3	2,725	35.2	31.6	68	19	13	..	..	..	..
Sri Lanka	50	0.0	2,636	9.8	19.6	96[c]	2[c]	2[c]	91	98	62	70
Sudan	30	119.0	4,544	17.8	11.9	94[c]	1[c]	4[c]	86	86	60	69
Swaziland	3	1.9	4,136	..	..	96	2	2	..	..	..	..
Sweden	171	12.2	20,529	2.9	1.6	9	55	36	100	100	100	100
Switzerland	40	13.0	7,325	1.2	2.2	4	73	23	100	100	100	100
Syrian Arab Republic	7	37.7	2,632	12.0	26.8	90	2	8	..	94	..	64
Tajikistan	66	13.3	12,706	11.9	14.9	92[c]	4[c]	3[c]	..	93	..	47
Tanzania	82	9.0	2,587	1.2	1.3	89	2	9	76	90	28	57
Thailand	210	199.9	6,653	33.1	8.1	91[c]	4[c]	5[c]	87	95	78	81
Togo	12	0.5	2,521	0.1	0.8	25	13	62	82	85	38	38
Trinidad and Tobago	4	..	2,914	0.3	7.9	6[c]	26[c]	68[c]	..	..	..	..
Tunisia	4	0.4	470	2.8	60.9	86[c]	1[c]	13[c]	91	92	54	58
Turkey	227	7.6	3,369	35.5	15.1	73	12	16	83	81	72	86
Turkmenistan	1	59.5	12,706	23.8	39.1	98	1	1	..	..	..	..
Uganda	39	27.0	2,683	0.2	0.3	60	8	32	81	80	40	47
Ukraine	53	86.5	2,866	26.0	18.6	30	52	18	..	100	..	94
United Arab Emirates	0	..	62	2.1	..	67	9	24	..	..	..	..
United Kingdom	145	2.0	2,482	11.8	8.0	3[c]	77[c]	20[c]	100	100	100	100
United States	2,800	18.0	9,772	467.3	16.6	42	45	13	100	100	100	100
Uruguay	59	74.0	39,572	0.7	0.5	91	3	6	..	98	..	93
Uzbekistan	16	98.1	4,527	58.1	50.8	94	2	4	..	94	..	79
Venezuela, RB	723	..	28,796	4.1	0.6	46	10	44	..	85	..	70
Vietnam	367	524.7	11,081	54.3	6.1	87	10	4	86	95	48	72
West Bank and Gaza	..	..	..	..	..	..	..	..	..	..	..	..
Yemen, Rep.	4	..	220	2.9	70.7	92	1	7	..	74	..	68
Zambia	80	35.8	11,324	1.7	1.5	77[c]	7[c]	16[c]	88	88	28	48
Zimbabwe	14	..	1,085	1.2	8.5	79[c]	7[c]	14[c]	99	100	69	73
World	**42,900 s**	**9,463.8 s**	**8,513 w**	**3,325 s**	**6 w**	**71 w**	**20 w**	**10 w**	**94 w**	**94 w**	**62**	**71 w**
Low income	11,185	4,815.6	6,416	1,041	7	92	4	5	88	90	59	70
Middle income	22,898	4,275.4	9,938	1,430	5	73	18	9	95	95	63	70
Lower middle income	19,341	3,260.3	9,401	1,229	5	73	19	9	96	95	63	70
Upper middle income	3,556	1,015.2	13,848	201	4	71	14	15	..	..	..	77
Low & middle income	34,082	9,091.0	8,258	2,471	6	81	12	7	93	93	61	70
East Asia & Pacific	9,454	1,415.6	6,020	776	7	81	14	5	97	93	61	67
Europe & Central Asia	5,255	1,134.8	13,511	387	6	57	33	10	..	96	..	83
Latin America & Carib.	13,429	2,833.8	30,925	263	2	74	9	18	92	94	58	65
Middle East & N. Africa	234	183.1	1,377	238	57	88	5	7	..	96	..	78
South Asia	1,816	1,945.1	2,684	735	20	94	3	4	90	94	66	80
Sub-Saharan Africa	3,895	1,578.7	7,951	73	1	85	6	10	86	83	40	46
High income	8,818	372.8	..	854	9	42	42	16	..	..	..	..
Europe EMU	910	258.8	3,826	185	16	38	47	15	..	..	..	..

a. River flows from other countries and river outflows are included when available. b. Data are for the most recent year available. c. Data refer to a year other than 1987 (see *Primary data documentation*).

About the data

The data on freshwater resources are based on estimates of runoff into rivers and recharge of groundwater. These estimates are based on different sources and refer to different years, so cross-country comparisons should be made with caution. Because the data are collected intermittently, they may hide significant variations in total renewable water resources from one year to the next. The data also fail to distinguish between seasonal and geographic variations in water availability within countries. Data for small countries and countries in arid and semiarid zones are less reliable than those for larger countries and countries with greater rainfall. Finally, caution is also needed in comparing data on annual freshwater withdrawals, which are subject to variations in collection and estimation methods.

The table shows both internal freshwater resources and river flows arising outside countries. River outflows are also taken into account. However, because inflows and outflows may be estimated at different times and with different levels of quality and precision, these data must be used with caution, particularly in case of water-short countries, notably in the Middle East.

The data on access to an improved water source measure the share of the population with reasonable and ready access to an adequate amount of safe water for domestic purposes. An improved source can be any form of collection or piping used to make water regularly available. While information on access to an improved water source is widely used, it is extremely subjective, and such terms as *safe, improved, adequate,* and *reasonable* may have very different meanings in different countries despite official World Health Organization definitions (see *Definitions*). Even in high-income countries treated water may not always be safe to drink. While access to an improved water source is equated with connection to a public supply system, this does not take into account variations in the quality and cost (broadly defined) of the service once connected. Thus cross-country comparisons must be made cautiously. Changes over time within countries may result from changes in definitions or measurements. The definition in this table and in table 2.15 differs from that used for the city-level data shown in table 3.11, which is more stringent.

Definitions

• **Renewable freshwater resources** refer to total renewable resources, broken down between internal flows (internal river flows and groundwater from rainfall) in the country and net river flows from other countries. • **Net flows from other countries** refer to river flows arising outside countries minus river outflows, when these data are available. • **Freshwater resources per capita** are calculated using the World Bank's population estimates (see table 2.1). • **Annual freshwater withdrawals** refer to total water withdrawals, not counting evaporation losses from storage basins. Withdrawals also include water from desalination plants in countries where they are a significant source. Withdrawals can exceed 100 percent of total renewable resources where extraction from nonrenewable aquifers or desalination plants is considerable or where there is significant water reuse. Withdrawals for agriculture and industry are total withdrawals for irrigation and livestock production and for direct industrial use (including withdrawals for cooling thermoelectric plants). Withdrawals for domestic uses include drinking water, municipal use or supply, and use for public services, commercial establishments, and homes. • **Access to an improved water source** refers to the percentage of the population with reasonable access to an adequate amount of water from an improved source, such as a household connection, public standpipe, borehole, protected well or spring, or rainwater collection. Unimproved sources include vendors, tanker trucks, and unprotected wells and springs. Reasonable access is defined as the availability of at least 20 liters a person a day from a source within 1 kilometer of the dwelling.

3.5a

The distribution of freshwater resources is uneven

Internal freshwater flows, 2000

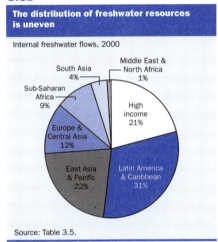

Source: Table 3.5.

3.5b

Latin America and the Caribbean has more than 20 times the freshwater resources per capita as the Middle East and North Africa

Total freshwater resources per capita, 2000 (thousands of cubic meters)

Source: Table 3.5.

Data sources

The data on freshwater resources and withdrawals are compiled by the World Resources Institute from various sources and published in *World Resources 2000–01* and *World Resources 2002–03* (produced in collaboration with the United Nations Environment Programme, United Nations Development Programme, and World Bank). These are supplemented by the Food and Agriculture Organization's AQUASTAT data. The data on access to an improved water source come from the World Health Organization.

	Emissions of organic water pollutants				Industry shares of emissions of organic water pollutants							
	kilograms per day		kilograms per worker		Primary metals	Paper and pulp	Chemicals	Food and beverages	Stone, ceramics, and glass	Textiles	Wood	Other
	1980	2000ª	1980	2000ª	2000ª	2000ª	2000ª	2000ª	2000ª	2000ª	2000ª	2000ª
Afghanistan	6,680	..	0.17	..	..	..	..	..	..	..	..	..
Albania	..	6,512	..	0.29	14.3	0.9	5.5	73.5	0.3	4.6	0.0	0.8
Algeria	60,290	45,645	0.19	0.24	23.4	2.0	3.3	59.5	0.7	7.6	0.8	−0.0
Angola	..	1,472	..	0.20	7.6	3.0	9.1	65.9	0.3	5.5	4.4	4.1
Argentina	244,711	177,882	0.18	0.21	6.5	12.5	8.0	59.4	0.1	7.4	1.5	4.5
Armenia	..	10,014	..	..	..	3.9	..	72.5	..	..	..	..
Australia	204,333	95,369	0.18	0.21	..	..	6.5	81.7	0.1	2.8	3.1	..
Austria	108,416	80,789	0.16	0.13	14.9	18.2	11.1	32.8	0.4	5.1	5.3	12.1
Azerbaijan	..	45,025	..	0.17	11.6	2.5	12.0	49.0	0.2	18.1	1.0	5.6
Bangladesh	66,713	273,082	0.16	0.14	1.8	6.8	6.6	23.2	0.1	64.1	0.5	..
Belarus	..	..	..	..	..	..	..	..	..	..	..	..
Belgium	136,452	102,460	0.16	0.17	13.7	18.0	10.5	40.4	0.2	6.0	2.0	7.5
Benin	1,646		0.28	..	..	..	1.2	..	..	..	..	..
Bolivia	9,343	12,759	0.22	0.25	0.9	20.5	6.6	61.4	0.3	7.1	2.4	0.9
Bosnia and Herzegovina	..	8,903	..	0.18	20.5	13.1	6.6	33.3	0.2	17.6	5.8	2.8
Botswana	1,307	4,635	0.24	0.20	1.7	15.8	0.8	56.4	0.2	17.2	1.4	1.8
Brazil	866,790	629,406	0.16	0.20	17.7	12.9	7.6	44.4	0.1	9.8	1.4	4.5
Bulgaria	152,125	107,945	0.13	0.17	11.7	7.9	8.2	48.1	0.1	17.0	2.0	6.6
Burkina Faso	2,385	2,598	0.29	0.22	3.5	1.1	5.8	73.8	0.1	4.1	10.1	1.9
Burundi	769	1,644	0.22	0.24	0.0	8.3	5.1	67.8	0.1	16.7	1.6	0.8
Cambodia	..	12,078	..	0.16	0.0	3.4	3.3	59.2	0.6	24.7	5.8	3.1
Cameroon	14,569	10,714	0.29	0.20	3.1	6.3	3.6	52.7	0.0	3.6	5.6	0.4
Canada	330,241	307,325	0.18	0.15	10.8	23.9	9.8	34.8	0.1	5.4	5.1	10.0
Central African Republic	861	670	0.26	0.17	0.0	..	4.0	62.0	0.0	13.8	19.6	..
Chad	..	..	..	..	..	..	..	..	..	..	..	..
Chile	44,371	72,850	0.21	0.24	6.9	11.3	8.9	62.7	0.1	5.0	2.6	2.5
China	3,377,105	6,204,237	0.14	0.14	20.6	10.8	15.3	28.4	0.5	14.8	0.8	8.9
Hong Kong, China	102,002	35,649	0.11	0.18	0.9	43.6	4.2	27.4	0.1	17.9	0.1	6.0
Colombia	96,055	93,879	0.19	0.21	3.1	16.2	10.3	53.2	0.2	14.2	1.0	2.4
Congo, Dem. Rep.	..	..	..	..	..	..	..	..	..	..	..	..
Congo, Rep.	1,039	..	0.21	..	..	..	..	..	..	..	..	..
Costa Rica	..	32,914	..	0.21	1.8	10.0	7.1	62.2	0.1	13.9	1.7	2.9
Côte d'Ivoire	15,414	12,401	0.23	0.24	..	5.5	5.0	71.9	0.0	8.6	5.9	..
Croatia	..	48,447	..	0.17	7.2	14.4	8.6	45.2	0.2	14.6	3.8	6.0
Cuba	120,703	..	0.24	..	..	..	..	..	..	..	..	..
Czech Republic	316,429	258,413	0.13	0.13	23.2	9.5	7.9	31.5	0.4	12.2	2.0	12.8
Denmark	65,465	83,591	0.17	0.17	4.4	29.1	7.0	44.2	0.2	2.2	3.5	8.6
Dominican Republic	54,935	..	0.38	..	..	..	1.9	..	..	..	..	..
Ecuador	25,297	32,266	0.23	0.27	2.3	10.8	7.1	71.8	0.1	6.0	1.5	1.3
Egypt, Arab Rep.	169,146	203,633	0.19	0.20	11.8	7.9	8.3	49.8	0.3	18.9	0.4	2.9
El Salvador	9,390	22,760	0.24	0.18	2.1	10.2	7.1	43.5	0.1	34.1	0.5	1.4
Eritrea	..	..	..	..	..	..	..	..	..	..	..	..
Estonia	..	..	..	..	..	..	..	..	..	..	..	..
Ethiopia	16,754	21,533	0.22	0.23	1.9	10.8	..	61.5	0.2	18.7	1.6	0.8
Finland	92,275	62,610	0.17	0.19	9.8	43.3	2.2	30.2	0.2	2.8	4.4	7.0
France	729,776	278,878	0.14	0.10	14.9	30.9	10.3	37.7	0.3	9.7	2.7	..
Gabon	2,661	1,886	0.15	0.26	0.0	6.0	5.0	79.7	0.1	1.2	6.9	1.2
Gambia, The	549	832	0.30	0.34	..	..	1.7	..	..	..	..	..
Georgia	..	..	..	..	..	..	..	..	..	..	..	..
Germany	..	792,194	..	0.13	11.2	22.3	9.8	34.4	0.2	3.2	2.3	16.5
Ghana	15,868	14,449	0.20	0.17	9.8	16.9	10.5	39.5	0.2	9.1	12.4	1.7
Greece	65,304	57,178	0.17	0.20	6.3	11.8	9.1	54.0	0.2	13.2	1.5	3.8
Guatemala	20,856	19,253	0.25	0.28	4.9	7.2	8.1	72.8	0.1	6.9	0.8	..
Guinea	..	..	..	..	..	..	..	..	..	..	..	..
Guinea-Bissau	..	..	..	..	..	..	..	..	..	..	..	..
Haiti	4,734	..	0.19	..	..	..	..	..	..	..	..	..

	Emissions of organic water pollutants				Industry shares of emissions of organic water pollutants % of total							
	kilograms per day		kilograms per day per worker		Primary metals	Paper and pulp	Chemicals	Food and beverages	Stone, ceramics, and glass	Textiles	Wood	Other
	1980	2000 [a]	1980	2000 [a]	2000 [a]	2000 [a]	2000 [a]	2000 [a]	2000 [a]	2000 [a]	2000 [a]	2000 [a]
Honduras	13,067	34,036	0.23	0.20	1.1	7.8	3.9	55.5	0.1	26.8	4.0	0.8
Hungary	201,888	152,531	0.15	0.17	8.0	12.1	7.9	48.0	0.2	14.1	2.4	7.3
India	1,422,564	1,582,285	0.21	0.20	13.9	6.6	9.6	52.2	0.2	13.1	0.3	4.2
Indonesia	214,010	752,834	0.22	0.18	2.8	8.6	8.6	50.1	0.1	22.0	5.3	4.5
Iran, Islamic Rep.	72,334	101,900	0.15	0.17	20.6	8.0	8.0	39.7	0.5	17.3	0.7	5.4
Iraq	32,986	19,617	0.19	0.16	8.8	14.1	15.1	39.4	0.7	16.7	0.3	4.8
Ireland	43,544	49,144	0.19	0.15	1.3	14.2	11.4	56.4	0.2	3.1	1.6	11.8
Israel	39,113	54,149	0.15	0.16	3.7	19.7	9.4	43.9	0.2	12.1	1.8	9.3
Italy	442,712	495,411	0.13	0.13	9.5	16.9	10.8	30.3	0.3	16.0	3.7	12.5
Jamaica	11,123	17,507	0.25	0.29	6.9	7.2	3.8	70.8	0.1	9.8	1.3	0.0
Japan	1,456,016	1,332,302	0.14	0.15	7.4	21.8	8.9	41.7	0.2	5.4	1.7	12.7
Jordan	4,146	16,142	0.17	0.18	3.9	16.2	14.5	51.4	0.5	7.2	3.3	3.0
Kazakhstan	..	..	..	..	..	..	..	..	..	..	..	..
Kenya	26,834	53,029	0.19	0.25	4.1	11.9	5.8	70.0	0.1	8.5	1.8	..
Korea, Dem. Rep.	..	..	..	..	..	..	..	..	..	..	..	..
Korea, Rep.	281,900	303,091	0.14	0.12	12.2	17.0	12.4	26.0	0.2	15.7	1.3	15.3
Kuwait	6,921	11,412	0.16	0.17	2.5	16.4	10.9	49.4	0.4	12.1	2.9	5.8
Kyrgyz Republic	..	20,700	..	0.16	13.7	0.2	0.9	54.8	0.4	21.0	1.0	8.0
Lao PDR	..	..	..	..	..	..	..	..	..	..	..	..
Latvia	..	25,106	..	0.19	2.8	8.7	0.8	64.5	0.1	11.5	9.7	..
Lebanon	14,586	14,899	0.20	0.19	0.9	15.6	3.3	60.7	0.5	10.2	4.6	3.4
Lesotho	993	3,123	0.24	0.16	1.2	4.0	0.7	39.7	0.1	51.3	0.6	2.3
Liberia	..	..	..	..	..	..	..	..	..	..	..	..
Libya	3,532	..	0.21	..	..	..	11.0	..	..	..	6.0	..
Lithuania	..	35,689	..	0.18	1.2	11.2	5.0	55.6	0.2	17.6	0.4	..
Macedonia, FYR	..	23,490	..	0.18	11.7	9.6	6.2	45.0	0.1	20.9	..	..
Madagascar	9,131	..	0.23	..	..	..	2.5	..	..	..	1.7	..
Malawi	12,224	11,805	0.32	0.29	0.0	16.0	3.7	70.0	0.0	7.8	7.0	..
Malaysia	77,215	158,761	0.15	0.12	6.5	14.5	16.5	34.1	0.2	7.5	3.2	19.7
Mali	..	..	..	..	..	..	..	..	..	..	..	..
Mauritania	..	..	..	..	..	..	..	..	..	..	..	..
Mauritius	9,224	17,700	0.21	0.15	0.9	6.6	2.6	32.8	0.1	55.4	0.9	0.8
Mexico	130,993	296,093	0.22	0.20	7.8	12.5	10.4	55.6	0.2	7.5	1.3	3.7
Moldova	..	34,234	..	0.29	0.2	4.0	1.4	81.7	0.2	10.8	4.9	..
Mongolia	9,254	7,939	0.19	0.18	1.8	4.3	2.9	64.2	0.3	24.6	0.9	..
Morocco	26,598	88,779	0.15	0.18	0.7	7.0	9.7	54.4	0.4	27.2	1.4	..
Mozambique	..	10,230	..	0.31	1.1	7.1	4.1	81.2	0.1	5.8	2.9	..
Myanmar	..	3,356	..	0.13	14.0	9.0	40.5	27.0	0.5	4.9	0.9	..
Namibia	..	7,350	..	0.35	0.0	5.0	1.6	90.4	0.1	1.2	1.7	0.4
Nepal	18,692	26,550	0.25	0.14	1.5	8.1	3.9	43.3	1.2	39.3	1.2	1.6
Netherlands	165,416	124,182	0.18	0.18	7.3	26.7	11.3	43.0	0.2	2.3	2.1	7.4
New Zealand	59,012	46,099	0.21	0.22	3.2	21.7	5.2	57.3	0.1	4.6	..	..
Nicaragua	9,647	..	0.28	..	..	..	5.1	..	..	..	..	..
Niger	372	..	0.19	..	..	..	..	..	..	..	4.7	..
Nigeria	72,082	82,477	0.17	0.17	1.4	15.4	11.3	40.2	0.1	23.5	3.0	5.1
Norway	67,897	55,439	0.19	0.20	8.7	31.7	4.9	42.9	0.1	1.4	3.8	6.5
Oman	..	5,789	..	0.16	6.1	13.1	6.9	50.4	0.8	14.1	0.3	5.9
Pakistan	75,125	100,821	0.17	0.18	11.6	7.0	8.1	39.9	0.2	30.3	0.5	2.1
Panama	8,121	11,462	0.26	0.31	1.6	13.7	3.8	74.6	0.2	4.2	..	..
Papua New Guinea	4,365	..	0.22	..	..	..	0.9	..	..	..	0.3	..
Paraguay	..	3,250	..	0.28	2.3	9.9	6.0	73.6	0.3	6.7	2.0	..
Peru	50,367	52,644	0.18	0.21	8.1	13.5	10.5	52.8	0.2	11.7	2.0	2.8
Philippines	182,052	201,952	0.19	0.18	5.2	9.8	7.3	54.5	0.2	16.4	2.6	4.3
Poland	580,869	388,153	0.14	0.16	13.8	6.2	6.8	48.8	0.4	13.6	5.4	5.1
Portugal	105,441	121,013	0.15	0.14	4.0	17.4	4.5	33.6	0.4	27.4	1.4	11.1
Puerto Rico	24,034	15,367	0.16	0.14	1.9	14.9	19.5	34.4	0.2	15.5	..	..

3.6 Water pollution

	Emissions of organic water pollutants				Industry shares of emissions of organic water pollutants							
					% of total							
	kilograms per day		kilograms per day per worker		Primary metals	Paper and pulp	Chemicals	Food and beverages	Stone, ceramics, and glass	Textiles	Wood	Other
	1980	2000 [a]	1980	2000 [a]	2000 [a]	2000 [a]	2000 [a]	2000 [a]	2000 [a]	2000 [a]	2000 [a]	2000 [a]
Romania	343,145	333,168	0.12	0.14	17.1	6.7	8.3	34.3	0.3	18.5	4.8	9.4
Russian Federation	..	1,485,833	..	0.16	17.7	7.4	9.3	46.8	0.3	6.9	2.1	9.5
Rwanda	..	..	..	..	..	..	..	..	..	..	..	..
Saudi Arabia	18,181	24,436	0.12	0.14	4.4	15.9	5.8	45.1	1.0	3.8	2.0	6.8
Senegal	9,865	6,643	0.31	0.36	0.0	6.6	4.0	87.0	0.1	1.8	0.2	0.7
Serbia and Montenegro	..	101,535	..	0.16	9.5	12.0	8.0	46.9	0.3	13.3	2.2	7.7
Sierra Leone	1,612	4,170	0.24	0.32	..	9.6	5.5	82.3	0.1	2.0	2.2	..
Singapore	28,558	32,119	0.10	0.09	1.4	26.2	16.0	21.6	0.1	4.0	1.4	28.6
Slovak Republic	..	57,970	..	0.15	17.2	12.7	7.9	37.5	0.3	11.9	2.7	9.9
Slovenia	..	38,601	..	0.17	32.3	15.6	8.5	24.4	0.2	11.1	2.1	5.9
Somalia	..	..	..	..	..	..	..	..	..	..	..	..
South Africa	237,599	234,012	0.17	0.17	13.7	16.3	9.1	40.3	0.2	10.2	3.4	6.8
Spain	376,253	374,589	0.16	0.15	6.7	19.8	8.9	42.5	0.3	9.3	4.0	8.6
Sri Lanka	30,086	83,058	0.18	0.18	0.6	7.4	9.8	52.6	0.2	29.8	1.1	..
Sudan	..	..	..	..	..	..	..	..	..	..	..	..
Swaziland	2,826	2,009	0.26	0.23	..	79.8	0.3	..	0.2	16.5	2.0	..
Sweden	130,439	103,913	0.15	0.14	11.3	35.0	7.8	26.6	0.1	1.3	3.0	14.9
Switzerland	..	123,752	..	0.17	24.9	23.6	10.4	25.0	0.2	3.2	4.2	8.7
Syrian Arab Republic	36,262	15,115	0.19	0.20	4.1	1.5	8.3	69.8	0.9	19.4	0.2	..
Tajikistan	..	..	..	..	..	..	..	..	..	..	..	..
Tanzania	21,084	35,155	0.21	0.25	1.5	9.4	4.9	69.3	0.1	14.0	1.5	1.4
Thailand	213,271	355,819	0.22	0.16	6.1	5.3	5.3	42.2	0.2	35.4	1.5	3.9
Togo	963	..	0.27	..	..	..	2.3	..	..	..	..	..
Trinidad and Tobago	7,835	11,787	0.18	0.28	4.4	10.9	18.3	72.6	0.1	2.9	1.3	..
Tunisia	20,294	46,052	0.16	0.16	5.8	8.0	6.5	41.1	0.4	33.5	1.5	3.3
Turkey	160,173	170,685	0.20	0.17	11.0	7.1	7.6	44.5	0.3	23.6	1.1	5.0
Turkmenistan	..	..	..	..	..	..	..	..	..	..	..	..
Uganda	..	..	..	..	..	..	..	..	..	..	..	..
Ukraine	..	499,886	..	0.18	22.8	3.4	6.6	51.6	0.3	5.8	1.6	7.9
United Arab Emirates	4,524	..	0.15	..	..	..	..	..	..	..	..	..
United Kingdom	964,510	569,736	0.15	0.15	7.2	30.4	10.0	32.1	0.2	5.6	2.5	12.0
United States	2,742,993	1,968,196	0.14	0.12	10.5	11.0	13.8	38.4	0.2	7.1	4.1	14.9
Uruguay	34,270	17,972	0.21	0.28	1.2	11.1	6.7	71.2	0.1	8.5	0.7	1.8
Uzbekistan	..	..	..	..	..	..	..	..	..	..	..	..
Venezuela, RB	84,797	94,175	0.20	0.21	13.7	10.4	9.8	53.1	0.3	7.5	1.5	3.3
Vietnam	..	..	..	..	..	..	..	..	..	..	..	..
West Bank and Gaza	..	..	..	..	..	..	..	..	..	..	..	..
Yemen, Rep.	..	7,823	..	0.25	0.0	9.1	12.9	71.1	0.3	4.9	1.0	0.9
Zambia	13,605	11,433	0.23	0.22	3.4	10.8	6.9	63.6	0.2	9.3	2.9	2.4
Zimbabwe	32,681	26,810	0.20	0.19	5.2	10.2	4.6	54.2	0.3	16.3	2.8	3.1

Note: Industry shares may not sum to 100 percent because data may be from different years.
a. Data refer to any year from 1993 to 2000.

Water pollution | 3.6

About the data

Emissions of organic pollutants from industrial activities are a major cause of degradation of water quality. Water quality and pollution levels are generally measured in terms of concentration or load—the rate of occurrence of a substance in an aqueous solution. Polluting substances include organic matter, metals, minerals, sediment, bacteria, and toxic chemicals. This table focuses on organic water pollution resulting from industrial activities. Because water pollution tends to be sensitive to local conditions, the national-level data in the table may not reflect the quality of water in specific locations.

The data in the table come from an international study of industrial emissions that may be the first to include data from developing countries (Hettige, Mani, and Wheeler 1998). These data were updated through 2000 by the World Bank's Development Research Group. Unlike estimates from earlier studies based on engineering or economic models, these estimates are based on actual measurements of plant-level water pollution. The focus is on organic water pollution caused by organic waste, measured in terms of biochemical oxygen demand (BOD), because the data for this indicator are the most plentiful and the most reliable for cross-country comparisons of emissions. BOD measures the strength of an organic waste in terms of the amount of oxygen consumed in breaking it down. A sewage overload in natural waters exhausts the water's dissolved oxygen content. Wastewater treatment, by contrast, reduces BOD.

Data on water pollution are more readily available than other emissions data because most industrial pollution control programs start by regulating emissions of organic water pollutants. Such data are fairly reliable because sampling techniques for measuring water pollution are more widely understood and much less expensive than those for air pollution.

Hettige, Mani, and Wheeler (1998) used plant- and sector-level information on emissions and employment from 13 national environmental protection agencies and sector-level information on output and employment from the United Nations Industrial Development Organization (UNIDO). Their econometric analysis found that the ratio of BOD to employment in each industrial sector is about the same across countries. This finding allowed the authors to estimate BOD loads across countries and over time. The estimated BOD intensities per unit of employment were multiplied by sectoral employment numbers from UNIDO's industry database for 1980–98. The estimates of sectoral emissions were then totaled to get daily emissions of organic water pollutants in kilograms per day for each country and year. The data in the table were derived by updating these estimates through 2000.

Definitions

• **Emissions of organic water pollutants** are measured in terms of biochemical oxygen demand, which refers to the amount of oxygen that bacteria in water will consume in breaking down waste. This is a standard water treatment test for the presence of organic pollutants. Emissions per worker are total emissions divided by the number of industrial workers.
• **Industry shares of emissions of organic water pollutants** refer to emissions from manufacturing activities as defined by two-digit divisions of the International Standard Industrial Classification (ISIC) revision 2: primary metals (ISIC division 37), paper and pulp (34), chemicals (35), food and beverages (31), stone, ceramics, and glass (36), textiles (32), wood (33), and other (38 and 39).

3.6a

High- and middle-income countries account for most water pollution from organic waste

Emissions of organic water pollutants, 1998

Source: World Bank staff estimates.

Data sources

The data come from a 1998 study by Hemamala Hettige, Muthukumara Mani, and David Wheeler, "Industrial Pollution in Economic Development: Kuznets Revisited" (available at http://www.worldbank.org/nipr). These data were updated through 2000 by the World Bank's Development Research Group using the same methodology as the initial study. Sectoral employment numbers are from UNIDO's industry database.

3.7 | Energy production and use

	Total energy production		Energy use					Energy use per capita		
	thousands of metric tons of oil equivalent		Total thousands of metric tons of oil equivalent		Combustible renewables and waste % of total		average annual % growth	kg of oil equivalent		average annual % growth
	1990	**2001**	**1990**	**2001**	**1990**	**2001**	**1990–2001**	**1990**	**2001**	**1990–2001**
Afghanistan	..	..	..	..	..	..	..	..	..	..
Albania	2,449	673	2,662	1,715	13.6	7.5	−1.6	812	548	−1.0
Algeria	104,559	144,330	23,926	29,438	0.1	0.3	1.6	956	955	−0.3
Angola	28,652	43,559	6,280	8,454	68.8	68.7	2.7	672	663	−0.1
Argentina	47,384	82,862	45,039	57,601	3.8	5.2	2.9	1,395	1,593	1.6
Armenia	263	602	4,298	2,297	0.0	0.0	−2.3	1,231	744	−0.9
Australia	157,712	250,436	87,536	115,627	4.5	4.5	2.7	5,130	5,956	1.5
Austria	8,080	9,717	25,042	30,721	9.8	10.4	1.6	3,241	3,825	1.3
Azerbaijan	18,150	19,581	16,675	11,582	0.0	0.0	−4.0	2,259	1,428	−5.0
Bangladesh	10,747	16,200	12,937	20,410	53.0	37.9	4.3	118	153	2.5
Belarus	4,103	3,533	39,703	24,415	1.5	4.3	−3.9	3,886	2,449	−3.6
Belgium	12,490	12,967	48,685	59,001	1.4	1.6	1.8	4,885	5,735	1.6
Benin	1,774	1,483	1,678	2,028	93.2	71.2	1.5	356	318	−1.2
Bolivia	4,923	6,938	2,774	4,271	27.2	16.8	5.7	422	496	3.1
Bosnia and Herzegovina	3,642	3,277	4,474	4,359	3.6	4.1	5.1	1,086	1,074	4.7
Botswana	..	..	..	..	..	..	..	..	..	..
Brazil	97,069	145,933	132,985	185,083	31.0	23.4	3.6	899	1,074	2.1
Bulgaria	9,613	10,297	28,820	19,476	0.6	2.8	−2.6	3,306	2,428	−2.0
Burkina Faso	..	..	..	..	..	..	..	..	..	..
Burundi	..	..	..	..	..	..	..	..	..	..
Cambodia	..	..	..	..	..	..	..	..	..	..
Cameroon	12,090	12,485	5,031	6,445	75.9	79.0	2.4	431	417	−0.2
Canada	273,680	379,207	209,090	248,184	3.9	4.2	1.8	7,524	7,985	0.8
Central African Republic	..	..	..	..	..	..	..	..	..	..
Chad	..	..	..	..	..	..	..	..	..	..
Chile	7,641	8,673	13,630	23,801	19.6	17.7	6.1	1,041	1,545	4.6
China	902,689	1,138,617	870,441	1,139,369	23.0	19.0	2.8	767	896	1.8
Hong Kong, China	43	48	10,662	16,278	0.5	0.3	3.9	1,869	2,421	2.1
Colombia	48,445	73,920	25,014	29,245	23.3	17.9	1.5	715	680	−0.4
Congo, Dem. Rep.	12,027	15,707	11,911	15,039	83.9	93.0	2.2	319	300	−0.5
Congo, Rep.	9,005	13,668	1,056	931	69.4	64.9	−2.8	423	262	−5.8
Costa Rica	1,032	1,733	2,025	3,481	36.6	11.0	4.8	664	899	2.6
Côte d'Ivoire	3,395	6,177	4,420	6,497	71.9	66.6	4.1	375	402	1.1
Croatia	4,346	3,720	6,714	7,904	3.8	3.7	2.1	1,405	1,771	3.1
Cuba	6,271	6,656	16,524	13,651	33.7	24.4	−0.5	1,555	1,216	−1.0
Czech Republic	38,474	30,489	47,401	41,396	1.2	1.7	−1.0	4,574	4,049	−0.9
Denmark	9,835	27,171	17,609	19,783	6.6	9.2	0.7	3,426	3,692	0.3
Dominican Republic	1,031	1,485	4,139	7,810	24.2	18.4	6.5	586	921	4.7
Ecuador	16,400	22,872	6,054	8,727	13.6	8.4	3.4	590	692	1.4
Egypt, Arab Rep.	54,869	59,301	32,024	48,012	3.3	2.8	3.9	611	737	1.9
El Salvador	1,722	2,329	2,535	4,269	48.2	32.9	4.5	496	677	2.4
Eritrea	..	..	..	..	..	..	..	..	..	..
Estonia	4,118	2,989	6,271	4,697	2.9	11.5	−2.2	4,091	3,444	−1.0
Ethiopia	14,158	18,000	15,151	19,161	92.8	93.1	2.4	296	291	0.1
Finland	12,081	15,156	29,171	33,815	15.6	19.7	1.7	5,851	6,518	1.3
France	111,278	132,709	227,114	265,570	4.8	4.5	1.2	4,003	4,487	0.8
Gabon	14,630	14,788	1,287	1,702	57.7	55.7	2.4	1,350	1,322	−0.4
Gambia, The	..	..	..	..	..	..	..	..	..	..
Georgia	1,470	1,265	8,762	2,413	7.7	..	−11.7	1,612	462	−11.4
Germany	186,157	133,745	356,218	351,092	1.3	2.3	−0.0	4,485	4,264	−0.3
Ghana	4,392	5,995	5,337	8,180	73.1	66.3	4.1	349	410	1.6
Greece	9,200	9,965	22,181	28,704	4.0	3.5	2.4	2,183	2,710	2.1
Guatemala	3,390	5,230	4,477	7,313	67.9	53.3	4.8	512	626	2.1
Guinea	..	..	..	..	..	..	..	..	..	..
Guinea-Bissau	..	..	..	..	..	..	..	..	..	..
Haiti	1,253	1,542	1,585	2,088	76.5	72.7	3.5	245	257	1.3

	Total energy production		Energy use				Energy use per capita		
	thousands of metric tons of oil equivalent		Total thousands of metric tons of oil equivalent		Combustible renewables and waste % of total		average annual % growth	kg of oil equivalent		average annual % growth
	1990	**2001**	**1990**	**2001**	**1990**	**2001**	**1990–2001**	**1990**	**2001**	**1990–2001**
Honduras	1,694	1,535	2,416	3,236	62.0	41.1	2.6	496	488	−0.2
Hungary	14,239	10,824	28,467	25,340	1.3	1.6	−0.7	2,746	2,487	−0.4
India	333,978	438,099	363,153	531,453	48.4	38.5	3.6	427	515	1.8
Indonesia	161,518	234,314	92,815	152,304	43.9	31.5	4.4	521	729	2.9
Iran, Islamic Rep.	179,738	246,644	68,775	120,000	1.0	0.7	5.2	1,264	1,860	3.6
Iraq	106,715	123,296	20,841	28,476	0.1	0.1	4.2	1,153	1,202	1.6
Ireland	3,467	1,729	10,575	14,981	1.0	1.2	3.6	3,016	3,876	2.7
Israel	433	685	12,112	21,193	0.0	0.0	5.3	2,599	3,291	2.4
Italy	25,547	26,264	152,552	171,998	0.6	1.4	1.2	2,690	2,981	1.0
Jamaica	485	487	2,943	4,009	16.2	11.9	3.0	1,231	1,545	2.2
Japan	73,209	104,006	436,523	520,729	1.0	1.0	1.8	3,534	4,099	1.5
Jordan	162	280	3,499	5,116	0.1	0.1	3.7	1,104	1,017	−0.1
Kazakhstan	*89,007*	83,752	*79,661*	40,324	*0.1*	0.2	−7.7	*4,823*	2,705	−6.6
Kenya	10,272	12,644	12,479	15,377	78.4	78.2	2.2	534	500	−0.4
Korea, Dem. Rep.	28,725	19,251	32,874	20,440	2.9	4.9	−5.1	1,647	914	−6.1
Korea, Rep.	21,908	34,207	92,578	194,780	*0.3*	1.2	7.1	2,160	4,114	6.1
Kuwait	48,519	108,851	8,413	16,368	0.1	..	9.9	3,959	7,195	6.3
Kyrgyz Republic	*1,818*	1,353	*5,066*	2,235	*0.1*	0.2	−6.4	*1,114*	451	−7.5
Lao PDR	..	..	..	..	..	..	..	..	..	..
Latvia	*794*	1,717	*5,979*	4,297	*8.1*	..	−3.4	*2,272*	1,822	−2.2
Lebanon	143	161	2,309	5,434	4.5	2.3	8.0	635	1,239	6.1
Lesotho	..	..	..	..	..	..	..	..	..	..
Liberia	..	..	..	..	..	..	..	..	..	..
Libya	73,173	74,363	11,541	15,992	1.1	0.9	2.1	2,680	2,994	0.1
Lithuania	*4,189*	4,144	*11,077*	8,023	*1.5*	8.2	−2.5	*2,994*	2,304	−1.9
Macedonia, FYR	..	..	..	..	..	..	..	..	..	..
Madagascar	..	..	..	..	..	..	..	..	..	..
Malawi	..	..	..	..	..	..	..	..	..	..
Malaysia	48,727	77,623	22,455	51,608	9.5	4.6	7.2	1,234	2,168	4.6
Mali	..	..	..	..	..	..	..	..	..	..
Mauritania	..	..	..	..	..	..	..	..	..	..
Mauritius	..	..	..	..	..	..	..	..	..	..
Mexico	194,454	230,236	124,028	152,273	5.9	5.4	1.8	1,490	1,532	0.2
Moldova	*58*	62	*6,884*	3,140	*0.5*	1.9	−8.3	*1,582*	735	−8.1
Mongolia	..	..	..	..	..	..	..	..	..	..
Morocco	773	583	6,725	11,006	4.7	4.0	4.4	280	377	2.6
Mozambique	6,846	7,560	7,203	7,687	94.4	88.3	0.0	509	425	−2.2
Myanmar	10,651	15,275	10,683	12,159	84.4	77.4	1.7	264	252	0.1
Namibia	*218*	294	*652*	1,159	*16.0*	15.2	5.3	*445*	596	2.5
Nepal	5,501	7,338	5,806	8,416	93.4	85.2	3.4	320	357	0.9
Netherlands	60,316	60,437	66,491	77,214	1.1	1.6	1.1	4,447	4,814	0.5
New Zealand	12,256	14,932	14,016	18,294	4.9	6.4	2.8	4,065	4,714	1.6
Nicaragua	1,495	1,540	2,118	2,792	53.3	48.2	2.6	554	536	−0.2
Niger	..	..	..	..	..	..	..	..	..	..
Nigeria	150,453	207,024	70,905	95,444	79.8	77.5	2.5	737	735	−0.3
Norway	120,304	226,570	21,492	26,607	4.8	5.6	1.9	5,066	5,896	1.3
Oman	38,312	64,534	4,562	9,984	..	..	5.4	2,804	4,029	1.8
Pakistan	34,360	48,606	43,424	64,506	43.2	37.2	3.8	402	456	1.3
Panama	612	678	1,490	3,180	28.3	14.6	6.1	621	1,098	4.3
Papua New Guinea	..	..	..	..	..	..	..	..	..	..
Paraguay	4,578	6,077	3,089	3,756	72.1	58.0	2.8	744	697	0.4
Peru	10,596	9,363	9,952	12,113	26.9	18.7	2.6	461	460	0.8
Philippines	15,901	20,006	28,292	42,151	34.8	23.1	4.2	463	538	1.9
Poland	99,228	79,861	99,847	90,570	2.2	4.8	−0.7	2,619	2,344	−0.8
Portugal	2,805	3,396	17,158	24,732	11.0	8.3	3.7	1,734	2,435	3.4
Puerto Rico	..	..	..	..	..	..	..	..	..	..

	Total energy production		Energy use				Energy use per capita		
	thousands of metric tons of oil equivalent		Total thousands of metric tons of oil equivalent		Combustible renewables and waste % of total		average annual % growth	kg of oil equivalent		average annual % growth
	1990	2001	1990	2001	1990	2001	1990–2001	1990	2001	1990–2001
Romania	40,834	28,222	62,403	36,841	1.0	6.4	–3.8	2,689	1,644	–3.5
Russian Federation	1,118,707	996,161	774,823	621,349	1.6	1.1	–2.4	5,211	4,293	–2.1
Rwanda	..	..	..	..	..	..	..	..	..	..
Saudi Arabia	368,753	476,831	60,834	110,586	0.0	0.0	4.3	3,850	5,195	1.6
Senegal	1,362	1,765	2,238	3,179	60.6	55.5	3.4	305	325	0.8
Serbia and Montenegro	11,835	10,774	15,002	16,061	5.0	5.0	1.8	1,435	1,508	1.6
Sierra Leone	..	..	..	..	..	..	..	..	..	..
Singapore	..	64	13,357	29,158	..	..	5.8	4,384	7,058	2.8
Slovak Republic	5,273	6,550	21,426	18,717	0.8	1.9	–0.9	4,056	3,480	–1.1
Slovenia	2,765	3,161	5,008	6,838	5.3	6.6	3.3	2,508	3,459	3.3
Somalia	..	..	..	..	..	..	..	..	..	..
South Africa	114,534	145,287	91,229	107,738	11.4	11.7	1.9	2,592	2,404	–0.3
Spain	34,648	33,022	91,209	127,381	4.5	3.2	3.1	2,349	3,127	2.7
Sri Lanka	4,191	4,462	5,516	7,923	71.0	52.9	3.8	339	423	2.5
Sudan	8,775	21,551	10,627	13,525	81.8	80.3	4.2	426	421	1.7
Swaziland	..	..	..	..	..	..	..	..	..	..
Sweden	29,754	34,377	46,667	51,054	11.8	16.0	0.7	5,452	5,740	0.4
Switzerland	9,831	12,367	25,106	28,019	4.1	6.0	0.8	3,740	3,875	0.2
Syrian Arab Republic	22,570	34,377	11,928	13,955	0.0	0.0	2.6	984	841	–0.3
Tajikistan	1,553	1,267	9,087	3,036	..	..	–8.9	1,631	487	–10.1
Tanzania	9,063	13,001	9,808	13,917	91.0	91.5	3.2	385	404	0.4
Thailand	25,908	40,059	43,215	75,542	33.9	17.1	5.2	777	1,235	4.4
Togo	778	1,056	1,001	1,422	77.7	74.3	4.5	290	305	1.6
Trinidad and Tobago	12,612	18,385	5,795	8,693	0.8	0.3	3.8	4,770	6,708	3.2
Tunisia	6,127	6,886	5,536	8,243	18.7	15.2	3.9	679	852	2.3
Turkey	25,857	26,154	53,005	72,458	13.6	8.7	3.8	944	1,057	2.0
Turkmenistan	48,822	50,443	11,307	15,309	..	..	2.4	2,912	3,244	0.3
Uganda	..	..	..	..	..	..	..	..	..	..
Ukraine	110,170	83,428	218,376	141,577	0.1	0.2	–4.5	4,187	2,884	–3.8
United Arab Emirates	108,472	144,566	17,611	32,624	0.2	0.1	5.3	9,550	10,860	1.2
United Kingdom	207,007	261,939	212,176	235,158	0.3	1.0	0.8	3,686	3,982	0.6
United States	1,650,408	1,711,814	1,927,572	2,281,414	3.2	3.1	1.7	7,728	7,996	0.4
Uruguay	1,149	1,211	2,251	2,703	24.3	15.6	2.4	725	809	1.7
Uzbekistan	40,461	55,630	44,994	50,650	..	..	1.7	2,098	2,029	–0.0
Venezuela, RB	148,854	216,020	43,918	54,856	1.2	1.0	2.2	2,252	2,227	0.1
Vietnam	24,988	50,346	24,690	39,356	76.5	58.3	4.5	373	495	2.8
West Bank and Gaza	..	..	..	..	..	..	..	..	..	..
Yemen, Rep.	9,792	22,687	2,626	3,560	2.9	2.2	2.2	221	197	–1.1
Zambia	4,923	6,052	5,469	6,423	73.5	81.5	1.3	703	638	–1.0
Zimbabwe	8,250	8,531	9,084	9,882	52.0	57.4	0.7	887	769	–1.3
World	**8,711,744 t**	**10,140,706 t**	**8,572,434 t**	**10,009,627 t**	**10.9 w**	**10.6 w**	**1.5 w**	**1,677 w**	**1,686 w**	**0.1 w**
Low income	980,692	1,330,614	923,451	1,233,424	52.0	46.2	2.7	480	518	0.7
Middle income	4,481,928	4,952,955	3,400,356	3,641,578	10.8	10.4	0.7	1,417	1,339	–0.4
Lower middle income	3,356,996	3,544,563	2,825,424	2,929,430	12.0	11.9	0.4	1,337	1,226	–0.7
Upper middle income	1,124,932	1,408,392	572,246	709,943	4.1	4.2	1.9	2,027	2,176	0.6
Low & middle income	5,462,620	6,283,569	4,311,187	4,850,856	18.9	18.9	1.1	1,012	966	–0.4
East Asia & Pacific	1,219,107	1,595,491	1,138,460	1,550,628	26.4	21.0	3.1	715	854	1.9
Europe & Central Asia	1,860,581	1,516,768	1,716,074	1,273,037	1.9	2.3	–3.0	3,681	2,684	–3.1
Latin America & Carib.	613,090	845,705	455,450	595,827	18.2	14.5	2.8	1,051	1,151	1.2
Middle East & N. Africa	965,686	1,254,273	257,289	413,276	1.4	1.1	4.1	1,087	1,383	2.0
South Asia	388,777	514,705	437,361	642,291	48.9	39.2	3.6	391	469	1.7
Sub-Saharan Africa	415,379	556,627	321,164	405,176	56.7	57.6	2.3	693	661	–0.3
High income	3,249,124	3,857,137	4,287,850	5,187,992	2.9	3.0	1.8	4,847	5,423	1.1
Europe EMU	466,100	439,167	1,049,967	1,189,043	3.1	3.5	1.1	3,580	3,904	0.8

Energy production and use | **3.7**

Definitions

About the data

In developing countries growth in energy use is closely related to growth in the modern sectors—industry, motorized transport, and urban areas—but energy use also reflects climatic, geographic, and economic factors (such as the relative price of energy). Energy use has been growing rapidly in low- and middle-income countries, but high-income countries still use more than five times as much on a per capita basis.

Energy data are compiled by the International Energy Agency (IEA). IEA data for countries that are not members of the Organisation for Economic Co-operation and Development (OECD) are based on national energy data adjusted to conform to annual questionnaires completed by OECD member governments.

Total energy use refers to the use of domestic primary energy before transformation to other end-use fuels (such as electricity and refined petroleum products). It includes energy from combustible renewables and waste—solid biomass and animal products, gas and liquid from biomass, and industrial and municipal waste. Biomass is defined as any plant matter used directly as fuel or converted into fuel, heat, or electricity. (The data series published in *World Development Indicators 1998* and earlier editions did not include energy from combustible renewables and waste.) Data for combustible renewables and waste are often based on small surveys or other incomplete information. Thus the data give only a broad impression of developments and are not strictly comparable between countries. The IEA reports (see *Data sources*) include country notes that explain some of these differences. All forms of energy—primary energy and primary electricity—are converted into oil equivalents. To convert nuclear electricity into oil equivalents, a notional thermal efficiency of 33 percent is assumed; for hydroelectric power 100 percent efficiency is assumed.

3.7a

Energy use varies by country, even among the five largest energy users

Total energy use (millions of metric tons of oil equivalent)

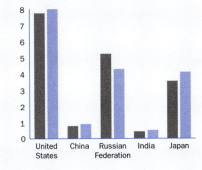

Energy use per capita (thousands of kg of oil equivalent)

Source: Table 3.7.

3.7b

People in high-income countries use more than five times as much energy as do people in low-income countries

Energy use per capita (thousands of kg of oil equivalent)

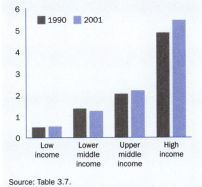

Source: Table 3.7.

Definitions

• **Total energy production** refers to forms of primary energy—petroleum (crude oil, natural gas liquids, and oil from nonconventional sources), natural gas, solid fuels (coal, lignite, and other derived fuels), and combustible renewables and waste—and primary electricity, all converted into oil equivalents (see *About the data*). • **Energy use** refers to apparent consumption, which is equal to indigenous production plus imports and stock changes, minus exports and fuels supplied to ships and aircraft engaged in international transport (see *About the data*). • **Combustible renewables and waste** comprise solid biomass, liquid biomass, biogas, industrial waste, and municipal waste, measured as a percentage of total energy use.

Data sources

The data on energy production and use come from IEA electronic files. The IEA's data are published in its annual publications, *Energy Statistics and Balances of Non-OECD Countries*, *Energy Statistics of OECD Countries*, and *Energy Balances of OECD Countries*.

3.8 Energy efficiency, dependency, and emissions

| | GDP per unit of energy use | | Net energy imports [a] | | Carbon dioxide emissions | | | | | |
| | 1995 PPP $ per kg oil equivalent | | % of energy use | | Total million metric tons | | Per capita metric tons | | kg per 1995 PPP $ of GDP | |
	1990	2001	1990	2001	1990	2000	1990	2000	1990	2000
Afghanistan	..	..	..	..	2.6	0.9	0.1	0.0	..	..
Albania	3.5	6.4	8	61	7.3	2.9	2.2	0.9	0.8	0.3
Algeria	5.1	5.0	−337	−390	80.4	89.4	3.2	2.9	0.7	0.6
Angola	2.7	2.2	−356	−415	4.6	6.4	0.5	0.5	0.3	0.4
Argentina	5.8	6.8	−5	−44	109.7	138.2	3.4	3.9	0.4	0.3
Armenia	1.2	3.3	94	74	3.7	3.5	1.1	1.1	0.7	0.5
Australia	3.7	4.2	−80	−117	266.0	344.8	15.6	18.0	0.8	0.7
Austria	6.6	6.8	68	68	57.5	60.8	7.4	7.6	0.4	0.3
Azerbaijan	1.4	1.7	−9	−69	47.1	29.0	6.4	3.6	2.0	1.6
Bangladesh	9.1	9.7	17	21	15.4	29.3	0.1	0.2	0.1	0.2
Belarus	1.1	1.9	90	86	94.6	59.2	9.3	5.9	2.1	1.3
Belgium	4.1	4.3	74	78	100.5	102.2	10.1	10.0	0.5	0.4
Benin	2.1	2.9	−6	27	0.6	1.6	0.1	0.3	0.2	0.3
Bolivia	4.5	4.3	−77	−62	5.5	11.1	0.8	1.3	0.4	0.6
Bosnia and Herzegovina	..	4.8	19	25	4.7	19.3	1.1	4.8	..	1.0
Botswana	..	..	..	..	2.2	3.9	1.7	2.3	0.3	0.3
Brazil	6.6	6.2	27	21	202.6	307.5	1.4	1.8	0.2	0.3
Bulgaria	1.9	2.5	67	47	75.3	42.3	8.6	5.2	1.3	0.9
Burkina Faso	..	..	..	..	1.0	1.0	0.1	0.1	0.2	0.1
Burundi	..	..	..	..	0.2	0.2	0.0	0.0	0.0	0.1
Cambodia	..	..	..	..	0.5	0.5	0.0	0.0	0.0	0.0
Cameroon	4.4	4.2	−140	−94	1.5	6.5	0.1	0.4	0.1	0.3
Canada	2.9	3.2	−31	−53	428.8	435.9	15.4	14.2	0.7	0.5
Central African Republic	..	..	..	..	0.2	0.3	0.1	0.1	0.1	0.1
Chad	..	..	..	..	0.1	0.1	0.0	0.0	0.0	0.0
Chile	5.0	5.6	44	64	35.3	59.5	2.7	3.9	0.5	0.5
China	2.0	4.2	−4	0	2,401.7	2,790.5	2.1	2.2	1.4	0.6
Hong Kong, China	9.7	9.9	100	100	26.2	33.1	4.6	5.0	0.3	0.2
Colombia	7.0	7.9	−94	−153	55.9	58.5	1.6	1.4	0.3	0.3
Congo, Dem. Rep.	4.2	1.9	−1	−4	4.1	2.7	0.1	0.1	0.1	0.1
Congo, Rep.	2.4	3.3	−753	−1,368	2.0	1.8	0.8	0.5	0.8	0.6
Costa Rica	8.5	8.3	49	50	2.9	5.4	1.0	1.4	0.2	0.2
Côte d'Ivoire	4.1	3.7	23	5	11.9	10.5	1.0	0.7	0.7	0.4
Croatia	4.3	4.7	35	53	16.8	19.6	3.5	4.4	0.6	0.5
Cuba	..	..	62	51	32.0	30.9	3.0	2.8	..	..
Czech Republic	2.7	3.2	19	26	137.9	118.8	13.4	11.6	1.2	0.9
Denmark	6.4	7.3	44	−37	50.7	44.6	9.9	8.4	0.4	0.3
Dominican Republic	5.9	5.7	75	81	9.4	25.1	1.3	3.0	0.4	0.6
Ecuador	2.8	4.4	−171	−162	16.6	25.5	1.6	2.0	1.0	0.7
Egypt, Arab Rep.	4.3	4.5	−71	−24	75.4	142.2	1.4	2.2	0.6	0.7
El Salvador	6.6	6.2	32	45	2.6	6.7	0.5	1.1	0.2	0.3
Eritrea	..	..	..	..	..	0.6	..	0.1	..	0.2
Estonia	1.7	2.8	34	36	24.9	16.0	16.2	11.7	2.4	1.3
Ethiopia	1.8	2.2	7	6	3.0	5.6	0.1	0.1	0.1	0.1
Finland	3.4	3.6	59	55	52.9	53.4	10.6	10.3	0.5	0.4
France	5.0	5.3	51	50	357.5	362.4	6.3	6.2	0.3	0.3
Gabon	4.3	4.2	−1,037	−769	6.7	3.5	7.0	2.8	1.2	0.5
Gambia, The	..	..	..	..	0.2	0.3	0.2	0.2	0.1	0.1
Georgia	1.3	4.2	83	48	15.1	6.2	2.8	1.2	1.4	0.6
Germany	4.7	5.6	48	62	890.2	785.5	11.1	9.6	0.5	0.4
Ghana	4.1	4.3	18	27	3.5	5.9	0.2	0.3	0.2	0.2
Greece	5.7	5.8	59	65	72.2	89.6	7.1	8.5	0.6	0.6
Guatemala	6.1	5.7	24	28	5.1	9.9	0.6	0.9	0.2	0.2
Guinea	..	..	..	..	1.0	1.3	0.2	0.2	0.1	0.1
Guinea-Bissau	..	..	..	..	0.8	0.3	0.8	0.2	1.0	0.3
Haiti	8.3	5.8	21	26	1.0	1.4	0.2	0.2	0.1	0.1

Energy efficiency, dependency, and emissions

3.8

	GDP per unit of energy use		Net energy imports [a]		Carbon dioxide emissions					
	1995 PPP $ per kg oil equivalent		% of energy use		Total million metric tons		Per capita metric tons		kg per 1995 PPP $ of GDP	
	1990	2001	1990	2001	1990	2000	1990	2000	1990	2000
Honduras	4.3	4.6	30	53	2.6	4.8	0.5	0.7	0.2	0.3
Hungary	3.7	4.7	50	57	58.5	54.2	5.6	5.4	0.6	0.5
India	3.6	4.4	8	18	675.3	1,070.9	0.8	1.1	0.5	0.5
Indonesia	3.9	3.7	−74	−54	165.2	269.6	0.9	1.3	0.5	0.5
Iran, Islamic Rep.	3.3	3.0	−161	−106	212.4	310.3	3.9	4.9	0.9	0.9
Iraq	..	..	−412	−333	49.3	76.3	2.7	3.3	..	..
Ireland	4.6	7.0	67	88	29.8	42.2	8.5	11.1	0.6	0.4
Israel	5.7	5.6	96	97	34.6	63.1	7.4	10.0	0.5	0.6
Italy	7.4	7.8	83	85	398.9	428.2	7.0	7.4	0.4	0.3
Jamaica	2.8	2.1	84	88	8.0	10.8	3.3	4.2	1.0	1.3
Japan	6.0	5.8	83	80	1,070.7	1,184.5	8.7	9.3	0.4	0.4
Jordan	3.2	3.7	95	95	10.2	15.6	3.2	3.2	0.9	0.8
Kazakhstan	0.9	1.7	−12	−108	252.7	121.3	15.3	8.1	3.5	2.0
Kenya	1.9	1.8	18	18	5.8	9.4	0.2	0.3	0.2	0.3
Korea, Dem. Rep.	..	..	13	6	244.6	188.9	12.3	8.5	..	..
Korea, Rep.	3.9	3.5	76	82	241.2	427.0	5.6	9.1	0.7	0.7
Kuwait	2.5	2.2	−477	−565	42.2	47.9	19.9	21.9	0.9	1.3
Kyrgyz Republic	1.6	3.2	64	39	11.0	4.6	2.4	0.9	1.4	0.7
Lao PDR	..	..	..	..	0.2	0.4	0.1	0.1	0.1	0.1
Latvia	2.5	4.1	87	60	12.7	6.0	4.8	2.5	0.8	0.4
Lebanon	3.7	3.2	94	97	9.1	15.2	2.5	3.5	1.1	0.9
Lesotho	..	..	..	..	..	..	..	..	..	..
Liberia	..	..	..	..	0.5	0.4	0.2	0.1	..	..
Libya	..	..	−534	−365	37.8	57.1	8.8	10.9	..	..
Lithuania	2.6	3.7	62	48	21.4	11.9	5.8	3.4	0.8	0.4
Macedonia, FYR	..	..	..	..	10.6	11.2	5.5	5.5	0.9	0.9
Madagascar	..	..	..	..	0.9	2.3	0.1	0.1	0.1	0.2
Malawi	..	..	..	..	0.6	0.8	0.1	0.1	0.1	0.1
Malaysia	4.1	3.6	−117	−50	55.3	144.4	3.0	6.2	0.6	0.8
Mali	..	..	..	..	0.4	0.6	0.0	0.1	0.1	0.1
Mauritania	..	..	..	..	2.6	3.1	1.3	1.2	1.0	0.8
Mauritius	..	..	..	..	1.2	2.9	1.1	2.4	0.2	0.3
Mexico	4.7	5.3	−57	−51	305.4	424.0	3.7	4.3	0.5	0.5
Moldova	1.3	1.7	99	98	20.9	6.6	4.8	1.5	2.4	1.3
Mongolia	..	..	..	..	10.0	7.5	4.7	3.1	2.9	2.2
Morocco	11.0	9.0	89	95	23.5	36.5	1.0	1.3	0.3	0.4
Mozambique	..	..	5	2	1.0	1.2	0.1	0.1	..	..
Myanmar	..	..	0	−26	4.1	9.1	0.1	0.2	..	..
Namibia	10.4	9.3	67	75	0.0	1.8	0.0	1.0	0.0	0.2
Nepal	3.0	3.5	5	13	0.6	3.4	0.0	0.1	0.0	0.1
Netherlands	4.5	5.2	9	22	150.0	138.9	10.0	8.7	0.5	0.3
New Zealand	3.9	4.0	13	18	23.6	32.1	6.8	8.3	0.4	0.5
Nicaragua	3.4	..	29	45	2.6	3.7	0.7	0.7	0.4	0.4
Niger	..	..	..	..	1.1	1.2	0.1	0.1	0.2	0.2
Nigeria	1.1	1.1	−112	−117	88.7	36.1	0.9	0.3	1.2	0.4
Norway	4.8	5.5	−460	−752	31.7	49.9	7.5	11.1	0.3	0.3
Oman	3.8	3.0	−740	−546	11.5	19.8	7.1	8.2	0.7	0.7
Pakistan	3.7	3.8	21	25	67.9	104.8	0.6	0.8	0.4	0.4
Panama	6.6	5.1	59	79	3.1	6.3	1.3	2.2	0.3	0.4
Papua New Guinea	..	..	..	..	2.4	2.4	0.6	0.5	0.4	0.2
Paraguay	5.9	6.1	−48	−62	2.3	3.7	0.5	0.7	0.1	0.2
Peru	7.7	9.4	−6	23	21.7	29.5	1.0	1.1	0.3	0.3
Philippines	7.4	6.8	44	53	44.3	77.5	0.7	1.0	0.2	0.3
Poland	2.5	3.9	1	12	347.6	301.3	9.1	7.8	1.4	0.9
Portugal	7.0	6.4	84	86	42.3	59.8	4.3	5.9	0.4	0.4
Puerto Rico	..	..	..	..	11.8	8.7	3.3	2.3	0.3	0.2

	GDP per unit of energy use		Net energy imports[a]		Carbon dioxide emissions					
	1995 PPP $ per kg oil equivalent		% of energy use		Total million metric tons		Per capita metric tons		kg per 1995 PPP $ of GDP	
	1990	2001	1990	2001	1990	2000	1990	2000	1990	2000
Romania	2.3	3.4	35	23	155.1	86.3	6.7	3.8	1.1	0.7
Russian Federation	1.5	1.6	–44	–60	1,984.0	1,435.1	13.3	9.9	1.7	1.5
Rwanda	..	..	..	..	0.5	0.6	0.1	0.1	0.1	0.1
Saudi Arabia	2.9	2.0	–506	–331	177.9	374.3	11.3	18.1	1.0	1.7
Senegal	4.1	4.3	39	44	2.9	4.2	0.4	0.4	0.3	0.3
Serbia and Montenegro	..	..	21	33	130.5	39.5	12.4	3.7	..	..
Sierra Leone	..	..	..	..	0.3	0.6	0.1	0.1	0.1	0.3
Singapore	3.1	2.9	..	100	41.9	59.0	13.8	14.7	1.0	0.7
Slovak Republic	2.5	3.1	75	65	44.7	35.4	8.4	6.6	1.0	0.6
Slovenia	4.3	4.5	45	54	12.3	14.6	6.2	7.3	0.6	0.5
Somalia	..	..	..	..	0.0	..	0.0	..	..	..
South Africa	3.4	3.5	–26	–35	291.1	327.3	8.3	7.4	0.9	0.9
Spain	6.2	6.0	62	74	211.8	282.9	5.5	7.0	0.4	0.4
Sri Lanka	6.4	7.3	24	44	3.9	10.2	0.2	0.6	0.1	0.2
Sudan	2.3	3.3	17	–59	3.5	5.2	0.1	0.2	0.1	0.1
Swaziland	..	..	..	..	0.4	0.4	0.6	0.4	0.1	0.1
Sweden	3.7	4.0	36	33	48.5	46.9	5.7	5.3	0.3	0.2
Switzerland	7.1	7.0	61	56	42.7	39.1	6.4	5.4	0.2	0.2
Syrian Arab Republic	2.4	3.5	–89	–146	35.8	54.2	3.0	3.3	1.2	1.1
Tajikistan	0.9	1.7	83	58	20.6	4.0	3.7	0.6	2.6	0.9
Tanzania	1.2	1.2	8	7	2.3	4.3	0.1	0.1	0.2	0.3
Thailand	5.3	4.8	40	47	95.7	198.6	1.7	3.3	0.4	0.6
Togo	5.2	4.2	22	26	0.7	1.8	0.2	0.4	0.1	0.3
Trinidad and Tobago	1.4	1.3	–118	–111	16.9	26.4	13.9	20.5	2.1	2.4
Tunisia	6.3	7.0	–11	16	13.3	18.4	1.6	1.9	0.4	0.3
Turkey	5.1	4.9	51	64	143.8	221.6	2.6	3.3	0.5	0.6
Turkmenistan	1.7	1.3	–332	–229	28.0	34.6	7.2	7.5	1.4	2.1
Uganda	..	..	..	..	0.8	1.5	0.0	0.1	0.1	0.1
Ukraine	1.6	1.4	50	41	600.0	342.8	11.5	6.9	1.7	1.9
United Arab Emirates	..	..	–516	–343	60.9	58.9	33.0	21.0	..	..
United Kingdom	5.0	5.8	2	–11	569.3	567.8	9.9	9.6	0.5	0.4
United States	3.4	4.0	14	25	4,815.9	5,601.5	19.3	19.8	0.7	0.6
Uruguay	8.9	9.7	49	55	3.9	5.4	1.3	1.6	0.2	0.2
Uzbekistan	0.7	0.7	10	–10	113.3	118.6	5.3	4.8	3.7	3.5
Venezuela, RB	2.4	2.4	–239	–294	113.8	157.7	5.8	6.5	1.1	1.2
Vietnam	2.8	4.0	–1	–28	22.5	57.5	0.3	0.7	0.3	0.4
West Bank and Gaza	..	..	..	..	..	..	..	..	..	..
Yemen, Rep.	3.0	3.8	–273	–537	9.4	8.4	0.7	0.5	1.2	0.6
Zambia	1.2	1.2	10	6	2.4	1.8	0.3	0.2	0.4	0.3
Zimbabwe	2.8	2.8	9	14	16.6	14.8	1.6	1.2	0.6	0.5
World	**3.5 w**	**4.2 w**	**0 w**	**0 w**	**21,297.5 t**	**22,994.5 t**	**4.1 w**	**3.8 w**	**0.7 w**	**0.6 w**
Low income	3.1	3.6	–6	–8	1,653.2	2,066.7	0.8	0.9	0.5	0.5
Middle income	2.7	3.7	–32	–36	9,169.8	9,129.1	3.8	3.4	1.0	0.7
Lower middle income	2.5	3.7	–19	–21	7,561.2	7,116.3	3.6	3.0	1.1	0.7
Upper middle income	3.7	4.0	–97	–98	1,608.5	2,012.0	5.7	6.2	0.8	0.7
Low & middle income	2.8	3.7	–27	–30	10,823.2	11,196.2	2.5	2.2	0.9	0.6
East Asia & Pacific	..	..	–7	–3	3,051.3	3,752.3	1.9	2.1	1.0	0.6
Europe & Central Asia	1.9	2.2	–8	–19	4,818.2	3,162.6	10.3	6.7	1.4	1.2
Latin America & Carib.	5.4	5.7	–35	–42	962.7	1,357.4	2.2	2.7	0.4	0.4
Middle East & N. Africa	3.8	3.4	–275	–203	751.1	1,227.2	3.3	4.2	0.8	0.9
South Asia	3.8	4.6	11	20	765.9	1,220.3	0.7	0.9	0.5	0.4
Sub-Saharan Africa	2.5	2.5	–29	–37	471.8	478.8	0.9	0.7	0.6	0.5
High income	4.3	4.7	24	26	10,480.8	11,804.3	11.8	12.4	0.6	0.5
Europe EMU	5.3	5.8	56	63	2,463.9	2,414.6	8.4	8.0	0.4	0.4

a. A negative value indicates that a country is a net exporter.

Energy efficiency, dependency, and emissions

3.8

About the data

The ratio of GDP to energy use provides a measure of energy efficiency. To produce comparable and consistent estimates of real GDP across countries relative to physical inputs to GDP—that is, units of energy use—GDP is converted to 1995 constant international dollars using purchasing power parity (PPP) rates. Differences in this ratio over time and across countries reflect in part structural changes in the economy, changes in the energy efficiency of particular sectors, and differences in fuel mixes.

Because commercial energy is widely traded, it is necessary to distinguish between its production and its use. Net energy imports show the extent to which an economy's use exceeds its domestic production. High-income countries are net energy importers; middle-income countries have been their main suppliers.

Carbon dioxide emissions, largely a by-product of energy production and use (see table 3.7), account for the largest share of greenhouse gases, which are associated with global warming. Anthropogenic carbon dioxide emissions result primarily from fossil fuel combustion and cement manufacturing. In combustion, different fossil fuels release different amounts of carbon dioxide for the same level of energy use. Burning oil releases about 50 percent more carbon dioxide than burning natural gas, and burning coal releases about twice as much. Cement manu-

facturing releases about half a metric ton of carbon dioxide for each metric ton of cement produced.

The Carbon Dioxide Information Analysis Center (CDIAC), sponsored by the U.S. Department of Energy, calculates annual anthropogenic emissions of carbon dioxide. These calculations are based on data on fossil fuel consumption (from the World Energy Data Set maintained by the United Nations Statistics Division) and data on world cement manufacturing (from the Cement Manufacturing Data Set maintained by the U.S. Bureau of Mines). Emissions of carbon dioxide are often calculated and reported in terms of their content of elemental carbon. For this table these values were converted to the actual mass of carbon dioxide by multiplying the carbon mass by 3.664 (the ratio of the mass of carbon to that of carbon dioxide).

Although the estimates of global carbon dioxide emissions are probably within 10 percent of actual emissions (as calculated from global average fuel chemistry and use), country estimates may have larger error bounds. Trends estimated from a consistent time series tend to be more accurate than individual values. Each year the CDIAC recalculates the entire time series from 1950 to the present, incorporating its most recent findings and the latest corrections to its database. Estimates do not include fuels supplied to ships and aircraft engaged in international transport

because of the difficulty of apportioning these fuels among the countries benefiting from that transport.

Definitions

• **GDP per unit of energy use** is the PPP GDP per kilogram of oil equivalent of energy use. PPP GDP is gross domestic product converted to 1995 constant international dollars using purchasing power parity rates. An international dollar has the same purchasing power over GDP as a U.S. dollar has in the United States. • **Net energy imports** are estimated as energy use less production, both measured in oil equivalents. A negative value indicates that the country is a net exporter. • **Carbon dioxide emissions** are those stemming from the burning of fossil fuels and the manufacture of cement. They include carbon dioxide produced during consumption of solid, liquid, and gas fuels and gas flaring.

3.8a

Per capita emissions of carbon dioxide vary, even among the five largest producers of emissions

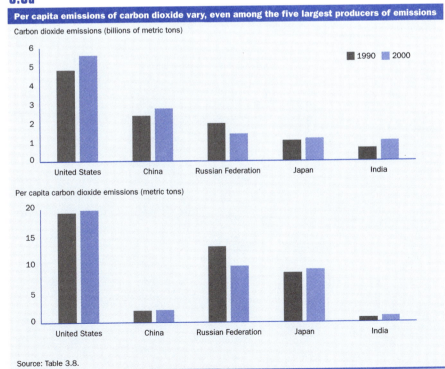

Carbon dioxide emissions (billions of metric tons)

Per capita carbon dioxide emissions (metric tons)

Source: Table 3.8.

Data sources

The underlying data on energy production and use are from electronic files of the International Energy Agency. The data on carbon dioxide emissions are from the CDIAC, Environmental Sciences Division, Oak Ridge National Laboratory, in the U.S. state of Tennessee.

3.9 | Sources of electricity

	Electricity production (billion kwh)		Access to electricity (% of population)	Sources of electricity[a] (% of total)									
				Hydropower		Coal		Oil		Gas		Nuclear power	
	1990	2001	2000	1990	2001	1990	2001	1990	2001	1990	2001	1990	2001
Afghanistan	..	..	2.0	..	..	..	..	..	..	..	..	..	..
Albania	3.2	3.7	..	89.1	96.3	..	..	10.9	3.7	..	..	..	..
Algeria	16.1	26.6	98.0	0.8	0.3	..	..	5.4	2.9	93.7	96.8	..	..
Angola	0.8	1.6	12.0	86.2	63.2	..	..	13.8	36.8	..	..	..	..
Argentina	51.0	90.2	94.6	35.6	41.1	1.3	1.7	9.7	2.0	39.0	46.7	14.3	7.8
Armenia	9.0	5.7	..	33.8	16.8	..	..	43.3	..	22.9	48.6	..	34.6
Australia	154.3	216.9	..	9.2	7.6	77.1	78.3	2.7	1.3	10.6	12.1	..	..
Austria	49.3	62.4	..	63.9	67.0	14.2	12.7	3.8	3.2	15.7	13.6	..	..
Azerbaijan	19.7	19.0	..	8.9	6.9	..	..	91.1	28.4	..	64.8	..	..
Bangladesh	7.7	16.3	20.4	11.4	6.0	..	..	4.3	9.4	84.3	84.6	..	..
Belarus	37.6	25.0	..	0.0	0.1	..	..	52.1	7.7	47.9	92.2	..	..
Belgium	70.3	78.6	..	0.4	0.6	28.2	16.2	1.9	2.1	7.7	20.1	60.8	59.0
Benin	0.0	0.1	22.0	..	2.3	..	..	100.0	97.7	..	..	..	..
Bolivia	2.1	4.0	60.4	55.3	54.6	..	..	5.3	17.4	37.6	26.1	..	..
Bosnia and Herzegovina	6.5	10.4	..	52.2	48.8	47.8	50.7	..	0.5	..	..	..	..
Botswana	..	..	22.0	..	..	..	..	..	..	..	..	..	..
Brazil	222.8	327.9	94.9	92.8	81.7	2.1	3.1	2.5	5.4	0.0	2.6	1.0	4.4
Bulgaria	42.1	43.5	..	4.5	4.0	35.4	45.4	4.7	1.3	20.6	4.4	34.8	44.9
Burkina Faso	..	..	13.0	..	..	..	..	..	..	..	..	..	..
Burundi	..	..	..	..	..	..	..	..	..	..	..	..	..
Cambodia	..	..	15.8	..	..	..	..	..	..	..	..	..	..
Cameroon	2.7	3.5	20.0	98.5	98.1	..	..	1.5	1.9	..	..	..	..
Canada	481.9	587.9	..	61.6	56.7	17.1	20.1	3.4	2.9	2.0	6.1	15.1	13.0
Central African Republic	..	..	..	..	..	..	..	..	..	..	..	..	..
Chad	..	..	..	..	..	..	..	..	..	..	..	..	..
Chile	18.4	43.9	99.0	55.3	49.4	34.3	16.5	7.6	1.6	1.3	28.7	..	..
China	621.2	1471.7	98.6	20.4	18.9	71.2	76.2	7.9	3.2	0.5	0.4	..	1.2
Hong Kong, China	28.9	32.4		..	..	98.3	61.5	1.7	0.4	..	38.1	..	..
Colombia	36.2	43.5	81.0	76.0	73.2	9.8	7.3	1.1	0.2	12.4	18.0	..	..
Congo, Dem. Rep.	5.6	5.7	6.7	99.6	99.7	..	..	0.4	0.3	..	..	..	..
Congo, Rep.	0.5	0.3	20.9	99.4	99.7	..	..	0.6	0.3	..	..	..	..
Costa Rica	3.5	6.9	95.7	97.5	81.5	..	..	2.5	1.4	..	..	..	..
Côte d'Ivoire	2.0	4.9	50.0	72.4	36.7	..	..	27.6	0.3	..	63.0	..	..
Croatia	8.9	11.8	..	48.8	52.7	..	13.9	35.8	18.0	15.4	15.4	..	..
Cuba	15.0	15.3	97.0	0.6	0.5	..	..	91.5	93.9	0.2	0.0	..	..
Czech Republic	62.6	74.2	..	2.3	2.8	71.8	71.7	4.8	0.5	1.0	4.2	20.1	19.9
Denmark	26.0	37.7	..	0.1	0.1	90.3	47.3	3.7	11.1	2.7	24.6	..	..
Dominican Republic	3.7	10.3	66.8	9.4	5.4	1.2	5.3	88.6	88.9	..	..	..	..
Ecuador	6.3	11.1	80.0	78.5	64.0	..	..	21.5	36.0	..	..	..	..
Egypt, Arab Rep.	42.3	82.7	93.8	23.5	17.1	..	..	36.9	14.7	39.6	68.2	..	..
El Salvador	2.2	3.9	70.8	73.5	29.8	..	..	6.8	45.0	..	..	..	..
Eritrea	..	..	17.0	..	..	..	..	..	..	..	..	..	..
Estonia	11.8	8.5	..	0.0	0.1	90.0	90.2	4.5	0.5	5.5	9.1	..	..
Ethiopia	1.2	1.8	4.7	88.4	98.7	..	..	11.6	1.0	..	..	..	..
Finland	54.4	74.5	..	20.0	17.7	33.0	23.5	3.1	0.9	8.6	15.5	35.3	30.6
France	416.8	546.0	..	12.8	13.6	8.5	4.5	2.1	1.0	0.7	3.1	75.4	77.1
Gabon	1.0	1.4	31.0	72.1	63.1	..	..	11.2	20.6	16.4	15.8	..	..
Gambia, The	..	..	..	..	..	..	..	..	..	..	..	..	..
Georgia	11.2	6.9	..	58.3	79.9	..	..	5.0	0.4	36.6	19.7	..	..
Germany	547.6	579.8	..	3.2	3.5	58.8	51.9	1.9	1.1	7.4	9.9	27.8	29.5
Ghana	5.7	7.9	45.0	100.0	84.1	..	..	..	15.9	..	..	..	..
Greece	34.8	53.1	..	5.1	4.0	72.4	66.8	22.3	16.0	0.3	11.6	..	..
Guatemala	2.3	5.9	66.7	76.0	32.9	..	8.5	9.0	44.1	..	..	..	..
Guinea	..	..	..	..	..	..	..	..	..	..	..	..	..
Guinea-Bissau	..	..	..	..	..	..	..	..	..	..	..	..	..
Haiti	0.6	0.5	34.0	76.5	51.7	..	..	20.6	48.3	..	..	..	..

	Electricity production (billion kwh)		Access to electricity (% of population)	Sources of electricity [a] (% of total)									
				Hydropower		Coal		Oil		Gas		Nuclear power	
	1990	2001	2000	1990	2001	1990	2001	1990	2001	1990	2001	1990	2001
Honduras	2.3	4.0	54.5	98.3	59.5	..	..	1.7	38.6	..	..	..	..
Hungary	28.4	36.4	..	0.6	0.5	30.5	24.5	4.8	11.5	15.7	24.3	48.3	38.8
India	289.4	576.5	43.0	24.8	12.8	67.5	78.3	2.7	1.2	2.9	3.6	2.1	3.4
Indonesia	37.0	101.7	53.4	17.6	10.5	28.8	28.9	46.8	23.6	3.8	34.2	..	..
Iran, Islamic Rep.	59.1	130.1	97.9	10.3	3.9	..	..	37.3	21.2	52.5	74.9	..	..
Iraq	24.0	34.9	95.0	10.8	1.8	..	..	89.2	98.2	..	..	..	..
Ireland	14.2	24.6	..	4.9	2.4	57.4	37.6	10.0	21.1	27.7	37.1	..	..
Israel	20.9	43.8	100.0	0.0	0.0	50.1	75.1	49.9	24.8	..	0.0	..	..
Italy	213.2	271.9	..	14.8	17.2	16.8	13.5	48.2	27.6	18.6	38.3	..	..
Jamaica	2.5	6.7	90.0	3.6	1.7	..	..	92.4	96.7	..	..	..	..
Japan	850.8	1,033.2	..	10.5	8.1	14.5	23.1	29.7	11.3	19.4	24.9	23.8	31.0
Jordan	3.6	7.5	95.0	0.3	0.6	..	..	87.8	89.2	11.9	10.2	..	..
Kazakhstan	82.7	55.4	..	8.3	14.6	72.3	69.9	8.8	4.9	10.6	10.6	..	..
Kenya	3.0	4.4	7.9	81.6	54.7	..	..	7.6	34.4	..	..	..	..
Korea, Dem. Rep.	27.7	20.2	20.0	56.3	52.5	40.1	42.5	3.6	5.0	..	..	..	..
Korea, Rep.	105.4	281.5	..	6.0	1.5	16.8	39.2	17.9	8.5	9.1	10.8	50.2	39.8
Kuwait	18.5	33.5	100.0	..	..	..	..	17.1	76.6	82.9	23.4	..	..
Kyrgyz Republic	11.9	13.7	..	77.4	90.9	9.1	4.5	..	..	13.6	4.5	..	..
Lao PDR	..	..	..	..	..	..	..	..	..	..	..	..	..
Latvia	3.8	4.3	..	65.8	66.2	..	1.0	7.9	2.2	26.3	30.5	..	..
Lebanon	1.5	8.2	95.0	33.3	4.1	..	..	66.7	95.9	..	..	..	..
Lesotho	..	..	5.0	..	..	..	..	..	..	..	..	..	..
Liberia	..	..	..	..	..	..	..	100.0	100.0	..	..	..	..
Libya	16.8	21.5	99.8	..	..	..	..	100.0	100.0	..	..	..	..
Lithuania	16.5	14.4	..	1.9	2.3	..	..	7.4	5.0	2.2	13.0	88.5	79.1
Macedonia, FYR	..	..	..	..	..	..	..	..	..	..	..	..	..
Madagascar	..	..	8.0	..	..	..	..	..	..	..	..	..	..
Malawi	..	..	5.0	..	..	..	..	..	..	..	..	..	..
Malaysia	23.0	71.4	96.9	17.3	9.9	4.7	3.4	55.9	8.6	22.0	78.1	..	..
Mali	..	..	..	..	..	..	..	..	..	..	..	..	..
Mauritania	..	..	..	..	..	..	..	..	..	..	..	..	..
Mauritius	..	..	100.0	..	..	..	..	..	..	..	..	..	..
Mexico	122.7	209.6	..	19.1	13.6	6.3	11.1	57.3	44.2	10.6	24.0	2.4	4.2
Moldova	11.2	3.6	..	2.3	2.0	34.4	3.3	26.4	0.9	36.9	93.7	..	..
Mongolia	..	..	90.0	..	..	..	..	..	..	..	..	..	..
Morocco	9.6	16.1	71.1	12.7	5.4	23.0	72.2	64.4	21.1	..	..	..	..
Mozambique	0.5	8.8	7.2	62.6	99.5	13.9	..	23.6	0.5	0.2	0.0	..	..
Myanmar	2.5	5.7	5.0	48.1	32.1	1.6	..	10.9	10.9	39.3	57.0	..	..
Namibia	1.4	1.4	34.0	95.2	96.7	1.5	0.4	3.3	2.9	..	..	..	..
Nepal	0.9	1.9	15.4	99.9	99.0	..	..	0.1	1.0	..	..	..	..
Netherlands	71.9	93.7	..	0.1	0.1	38.3	28.5	4.3	3.3	50.9	58.9	4.9	4.2
New Zealand	32.3	39.9	..	72.3	53.8	1.5	3.7	0.0	..	17.6	31.2	..	..
Nicaragua	1.4	2.5	48.0	28.8	8.0	..	..	39.8	82.0	..	..	..	..
Niger	..	..	..	..	..	..	..	..	..	..	..	..	..
Nigeria	12.6	18.1	40.0	34.9	38.2	0.2	..	36.5	8.2	28.5	53.6	..	..
Norway	121.6	121.3	..	99.6	99.3	0.2	0.2	0.0	0.0	..	0.2	..	..
Oman	4.5	9.7	94.0	..	..	..	..	18.4	17.7	81.6	82.3	..	..
Pakistan	37.7	72.4	52.9	44.9	26.2	0.1	0.4	20.6	36.0	33.6	34.3	0.8	3.2
Panama	2.7	5.1	76.1	83.2	48.8	..	..	14.7	50.8	..	..	..	..
Papua New Guinea	..	..	..	..	..	..	..	..	..	..	..	..	..
Paraguay	27.2	45.4	74.7	99.9	99.9	..	..	0.0	0.0	..	..	..	..
Peru	13.8	20.8	73.0	75.8	84.7	..	0.9	21.5	9.7	1.7	3.8	..	..
Philippines	25.2	46.2	87.4	24.0	15.4	7.7	40.6	46.7	21.3	..	0.1	..	..
Poland	134.4	143.7	..	1.1	1.6	97.5	95.2	1.2	1.7	0.1	0.9	..	..
Portugal	28.4	46.2	..	32.3	30.4	32.1	29.5	33.1	20.2	..	15.6	..	..
Puerto Rico	..	..	..	..	..	..	..	..	..	..	..	..	..

| | Electricity production (billion kwh) | | Access to electricity % of population | Sources of electricity [a] % of total | | | | | | | | | |
| | | | | Hydropower | | Coal | | Oil | | Gas | | Nuclear power | |
	1990	2001	2000	1990	2001	1990	2001	1990	2001	1990	2001	1990	2001
Romania	64.3	53.9	..	17.7	27.7	28.8	37.2	18.4	10.0	35.1	15.0	..	10.1
Russian Federation	1008.5	889.3	..	17.0	19.6	15.3	19.0	9.9	3.4	45.7	42.4	11.9	15.4
Rwanda	..	..	..	..	..	..	..	..	..	..	..	..	..
Saudi Arabia	64.9	137.4	97.7					61.5	63.5	38.5	36.5	..	..
Senegal	0.9	1.7	30.1	..	..	..	..	98.0	100.0	2.0	0.1	..	..
Serbia and Montenegro	36.5	31.8	..	31.1	36.5	65.4	60.9	1.9	1.0	1.6	1.6	..	..
Sierra Leone	..	..	..	..	..	..	..	..	..	..	..	..	..
Singapore	15.7	33.1	100.0	..	..	..	..	100.0	52.7	..	45.1	..	..
Slovak Republic	23.4	31.9	..	8.0	15.5	32.2	19.5	3.4	2.2	4.9	8.5	51.4	53.7
Slovenia	12.1	14.5	..	28.2	26.2	36.2	34.0	2.5	0.9	0.2	2.0	32.9	36.3
Somalia	..	..	..	..	..	..	..	..	..	..	..	..	..
South Africa	165.4	211.5	66.1	0.6	1.0	94.3	94.0	..	..	..	..	5.1	5.1
Spain	151.2	234.7	..	16.8	17.5	40.1	30.6	5.7	10.5	1.0	10.0	35.9	27.1
Sri Lanka	3.2	6.6	62.0	99.8	47.0	..	..	0.2	53.0	..	..	..	..
Sudan	1.5	2.6	30.0	63.2	48.3	..	..	36.8	51.7	..	..	..	..
Swaziland	..	..	..	..	..	..	..	..	..	..	..	..	..
Sweden	146.0	161.7	..	49.7	49.0	1.2	2.1	0.8	1.7	0.3	0.2	46.7	44.6
Switzerland	54.6	70.5	..	54.6	58.6	0.1	..	0.5	0.1	0.6	1.2	43.3	38.0
Syrian Arab Republic	11.6	25.5	85.9	48.6	39.0	..	..	32.4	19.9	18.9	41.1	..	..
Tajikistan	16.8	14.4	..	94.7	97.7	..	..	..	..	5.3	2.3	..	..
Tanzania	1.6	2.8	10.5	95.1	91.7	..	3.2	4.9	5.1	..	..	..	..
Thailand	44.2	102.4	82.1	11.3	6.2	25.0	19.2	23.5	2.9	40.2	70.5	..	..
Togo	0.1	0.0	9.0	4.6	6.3	..	..	95.4	93.8	..	..	..	..
Trinidad and Tobago	3.6	5.6	99.0	..	..	..	..	0.1	0.1	99.0	99.4	..	..
Tunisia	5.8	11.2	94.6	0.8	0.5	..	..	35.5	9.8	63.7	89.4	..	..
Turkey	57.5	122.7	..	40.2	19.6	35.1	31.3	6.9	8.5	17.7	40.4	..	..
Turkmenistan	13.2	10.8	..	0.0	0.0	..	..	..	..	100.0	100.0	..	..
Uganda	..	..	3.7	..	..	..	..	..	..	..	..	..	..
Ukraine	252.5	172.8	..	3.2	7.0	26.2	27.5	10.1	4.0	31.2	17.4	29.2	44.1
United Arab Emirates	17.1	40.2	96.0	..	..	..	..	3.7	7.9	96.3	92.1	..	..
United Kingdom	317.8	383.5	..	1.6	1.1	65.0	34.8	10.9	1.9	1.6	37.2	20.7	23.5
United States	3,181.5	3,863.8	..	8.6	5.2	53.4	51.3	4.1	3.5	12.0	16.7	19.2	20.9
Uruguay	7.4	9.3	98.0	94.2	99.4	..	..	5.1	0.2	..	..	..	..
Uzbekistan	50.9	47.9	..	12.3	12.5	4.9	4.2	6.9	11.4	75.9	71.8	..	..
Venezuela, RB	59.3	90.0	94.0	62.3	67.2	..	..	11.5	10.4	26.2	22.4	..	..
Vietnam	8.7	30.6	75.8	61.7	59.5	23.0	10.5	15.2	15.5	0.1	14.5	..	..
West Bank and Gaza	..	..	..	..	..	..	..	..	..	..	..	..	..
Yemen, Rep.	1.7	3.1	50.0	..	..	..	..	100.0	100.0	..	..	..	..
Zambia	8.0	8.2	12.0	99.2	99.4	0.5	0.2	0.3	0.4	..	..	..	..
Zimbabwe	9.4	7.9	39.7	40.5	37.8	59.5	61.8	..	0.4	..	..	..	..
World	**11,696.7 s**	**15,442.7 s**	**.. w**	**18.1 w**	**16.6 w**	**38.0 w**	**38.8 w**	**11.3 w**	**7.4 w**	**13.9 w**	**18.3 w**	**17.2 w**	**17.2 w**
Low income	606.4	1,017.2	37.4	32.8	22.7	38.9	49.2	13.0	8.8	13.1	16.4	1.1	2.1
Middle income	3,756.1	5,133.7	94.0	21.2	22.5	34.7	38.8	15.2	10.1	20.4	20.9	7.6	6.9
Lower middle income	3,091.3	4,098.3	93.9	22.0	23.5	34.9	42.5	13.1	6.7	21.8	19.7	7.2	6.9
Upper middle income	664.8	1,035.4	..	17.2	18.6	33.6	24.0	24.9	23.4	14.2	25.8	9.5	7.1
Low & middle income	4,362.5	6,150.9	65.1	22.8	22.5	35.3	40.5	14.9	9.8	19.4	20.2	6.7	6.1
East Asia & Pacific	789.5	1,849.8	87.3	21.6	18.3	60.8	65.1	13.2	5.2	3.6	9.5	..	0.9
Europe & Central Asia	2,143.0	1,855.8	..	12.9	16.9	31.6	31.0	12.7	4.3	29.5	31.4	12.3	16.0
Latin America & Carib.	607.0	962.2	86.6	63.7	56.5	3.8	4.8	19.0	17.7	9.5	15.5	2.1	3.1
Middle East & N. Africa	261.5	514.6	90.4	10.0	6.1	0.8	2.3	51.7	41.3	37.4	50.3	..	..
South Asia	338.9	673.7	40.8	27.6	14.7	57.7	67.1	4.7	5.6	8.1	8.8	1.9	3.2
Sub-Saharan Africa	222.5	294.8	24.7	18.4	19.7	72.6	69.1	3.4	2.9	1.7	4.4	3.8	3.6
High income	7,334.2	9,291.8	..	15.4	12.7	39.7	37.6	9.2	5.9	10.6	17.1	23.4	24.5
Europe EMU	1,652.7	2,066.1	..	11.0	12.4	34.4	27.0	9.5	6.9	8.7	15.3	35.5	35.3

a. Shares may not sum to 100 percent because some sources of generated electricity are not shown.

Sources of electricity | 3.9

About the data

Use of energy in general, and access to electricity in particular, are important in improving people's standard of living. But electricity generation also can damage the environment. Whether such damage occurs depends largely on how electricity is generated. For example, burning coal releases twice as much carbon dioxide—a major contributor to global warming—as does burning an equivalent amount of natural gas (see *About the data* for table 3.8). Nuclear energy does not generate carbon dioxide emissions, but it produces other dangerous waste products. The table provides information on electricity production by source. Shares may not sum to 100 percent because some sources of generated electricity (such as wind, solar, and geothermal) are not shown.

The International Energy Agency (IEA) compiles data on energy inputs used to generate electricity. IEA data for countries that are not members of the Organisation for Economic Co-operation and Development (OECD) are based on national energy data adjusted to conform to annual questionnaires completed by OECD member governments. In addition, estimates are sometimes made to complete major aggregates from which key data are missing, and adjustments are made to compensate for differences in definitions.

The IEA makes these estimates in consultation with national statistical offices, oil companies, electricity utilities, and national energy experts. The IEA occasionally revises its time series to reflect political changes. Since 1990, for example, it has constructed energy statistics for countries of the former Soviet Union. In addition, energy statistics for other countries have undergone continuous changes in coverage or methodology as more detailed energy accounts have become available in recent years. Breaks in series are therefore unavoidable.

There is no single internationally accepted definition for access to electricity. The definition used here covers access at the household level—that is, the number of people who have electricity in their home. It includes commercially sold electricity, both on-grid and off-grid. For countries where access to electricity has been assessed through surveys by government agencies, the definition also includes self-generated electricity. The data do not capture unauthorized connections.

3.9a

Sources of electricity generation have shifted differently in different income groups

Sources of electricity generation, by income group (% of total production)

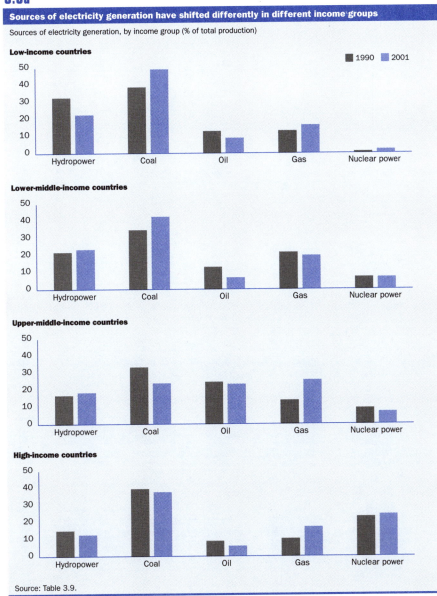

Definitions

- **Electricity production** is measured at the terminals of all alternator sets in a station. In addition to hydropower, coal, oil, gas, and nuclear power generation, it covers generation by geothermal, solar, wind, and tide and wave energy as well as that from combustible renewables and waste. Production includes the output of electricity plants designed to produce electricity only, as well as that of combined heat and power plants. • **Access to electricity** refers to the number of people with access to electricity (both on-grid and off-grid) as a percentage of the total population (see table 2.1). • **Sources of electricity** refer to the inputs used to generate electricity: hydropower, coal, oil, gas, and nuclear power. • **Hydropower** refers to electricity produced by hydroelectric power plants. • **Oil** refers to crude oil and petroleum products. • **Gas** refers to natural gas but not natural gas liquids. • **Nuclear power** refers to electricity produced by nuclear power plants.

Data sources

The data on electricity production are from the IEA's electronic files and its annual publications *Energy Statistics and Balances of Non-OECD Countries, Energy Statistics of OECD Countries,* and *Energy Balances of OECD Countries.* Data on access to electricity are from the IEA's *World Energy Outlook 2002: Energy and Poverty.*

Source: Table 3.9.

	Urban population				Population in urban agglomerations of more than 1 million			Population in largest city		Access to improved sanitation facilities			
	millions		% of total population		% of total population			% of urban population		% of urban population		% of rural population	
	1980	2002	1980	2002	1980	2000	2015	1980	2001	1990	2000	1990	2000
Afghanistan	2.5	6.4	16	23	6	10	14	39	45	..	25	..	8
Albania	0.9	1.4	34	44	..	..	..	..	22	..	99	..	85
Algeria	8.1	18.2	44	58	8	6	7	20	16	..	99	..	81
Angola	1.5	4.7	21	35	13	20	25	62	60	..	70	..	30
Argentina	23.3	33.6	83	88	42	41	40	43	37	..	87	..	47
Armenia	2.0	2.1	66	67	34	34	35	51	55	..	..	..	..
Australia	12.6	18.0	86	91	61	56	55	26	22	100	100	100	100
Austria	5.1	5.4	67	68	27	26	26	40	38	100	100	100	100
Azerbaijan	3.3	4.2	53	52	26	24	26	48	47	..	90	..	70
Bangladesh	12.7	35.5	15	26	6	13	18	26	38	81	71	31	41
Belarus	5.4	6.9	57	70	14	18	20	24	24	..	..	..	..
Belgium	9.4	10.1	95	97	12	11	11	13	11	..	..	..	..
Benin	0.9	2.9	27	44	..	..	..	..	8	46	46	6	6
Bolivia	2.4	5.6	45	63	14	18	20	33	28	73	86	26	42
Bosnia and Herzegovina	1.5	1.8	36	44	..	..	..	..	31	..	..	..	..
Botswana	0.2	0.9	18	50	..	..	..	..	27	87	88	41	43
Brazil	81.2	143.5	67	82	32	34	34	16	13	82	84	38	43
Bulgaria	5.4	5.4	61	68	12	15	16	20	22	..	100	..	100
Burkina Faso	0.6	2.0	8	17	..	..	..	45	45	..	39	..	27
Burundi	0.2	0.7	4	10	..	..	..	..	54	65	68	89	90
Cambodia	0.8	2.2	12	18	..	..	..	44	53	..	56	..	10
Cameroon	2.8	7.9	31	50	11	21	27	19	23	97	92	64	66
Canada	18.6	24.8	76	79	32	37	38	16	20	100	100	99	99
Central African Republic	0.8	1.6	35	42	..	..	..	..	42	38	38	16	16
Chad	0.8	2.0	19	25	..	..	..	..	38	70	81	4	13
Chile	9.1	13.5	81	86	33	36	37	41	42	98	96	92	97
China	192.8	481.8	20	38	13	14	17	6	3	57	69	18	27
Hong Kong, China	4.6	6.8	91	100	91	100	100	100	100	..	..	..	..
Colombia	17.8	33.2	63	76	26	32	35	21	21	96	96	55	56
Congo, Dem. Rep.	..	..	..	..	8	10	12	..	..	..	54	..	6
Congo, Rep.	0.8	2.4	42	67	27	41	44	263	158	..	..	..	..
Costa Rica	1.1	2.4	47	60	..	..	..	56	43	..	89	..	97
Côte d'Ivoire	2.8	7.3	35	44	15	21	25	44	54	70	71	29	35
Croatia	2.3	2.6	50	59	..	..	..	28	42	..	..	..	..
Cuba	6.6	8.5	68	76	20	20	20	29	27	..	99	..	95
Czech Republic	7.6	7.6	75	75	12	12	12	15	16	..	..	..	..
Denmark	4.3	4.6	84	85	27	26	26	32	29	..	..	..	..
Dominican Republic	2.9	5.7	51	67	34	61	67	50	47	70	70	60	60
Ecuador	3.7	8.2	47	64	23	32	37	29	27	88	92	49	74
Egypt, Arab Rep.	17.9	28.4	44	43	23	23	24	38	35	96	100	79	96
El Salvador	2.0	4.0	44	62	16	22	25	35	35	87	89	62	76
Eritrea	0.3	0.8	14	20	..	..	..	..	63	..	66	..	1
Estonia	1.0	0.9	70	69	..	..	..	..	42	..	93	..	..
Ethiopia	4.0	10.9	10	16	3	4	6	30	27	24	33	6	7
Finland	2.9	3.1	60	59	13	23	25	24	31	100	100	100	100
France	39.5	45.0	73	76	21	21	20	23	22	..	..	..	..
Gabon	0.3	1.1	50	83	..	..	..	..	55	..	55	..	43
Gambia, The	0.1	0.4	20	32	..	..	..	..	100	..	41	..	35
Georgia	2.6	2.9	52	57	22	24	29	42	..	..	100	..	99
Germany	64.7	72.5	83	88	39	41	43	10	9	..	..	..	..
Ghana	3.4	7.4	31	37	9	10	14	30	27	56	74	64	70
Greece	5.6	6.4	58	61	31	30	29	54	49	..	..	..	..
Guatemala	2.6	4.8	37	40	11	28	32	29	72	82	83	62	79
Guinea	0.9	2.2	19	28	12	25	32	75	60	94	94	41	41
Guinea-Bissau	0.1	0.5	17	33	..	..	..	..	74	87	95	33	44
Haiti	1.3	3.1	24	37	13	22	28	55	62	33	50	19	16

	Urban population				Population in urban agglomerations of more than 1 million			Population in largest city		Access to improved sanitation facilities			
	millions		% of total population		% of total population			% of urban population		% of urban population		% of rural population	
	1980	2002	1980	2002	1980	2000	2015	1980	2001	1990	2000	1990	2000
Honduras	1.2	3.7	35	55	..	..	..	33	28	88	93	41	55
Hungary	6.1	6.6	57	65	19	18	19	34	28	100	100	98	98
India	158.5	294.5	23	28	8	10	12	5	6	44	61	6	15
Indonesia	32.9	91.0	22	43	8	10	13	18	13	66	69	38	46
Iran, Islamic Rep.	19.4	42.9	50	65	21	23	24	26	17	..	86	..	79
Iraq	8.5	16.3	66	68	29	31	34	39	31	..	93	..	31
Ireland	1.9	2.3	55	60	..	..	..	48	44	..	..	..	..
Israel	3.4	6.0	89	92	37	35	33	41	35	..	..	..	..
Italy	37.6	38.8	67	67	24	19	20	14	11	..	..	..	..
Jamaica	1.0	1.5	47	57	..	..	..	..	46	99	99	99	99
Japan	89.0	100.5	76	79	34	38	39	25	26	..	..	..	..
Jordan	1.3	4.1	60	79	29	29	32	49	30	100	100	95	98
Kazakhstan	8.0	8.3	54	56	6	8	9	12	13	..	100	..	98
Kenya	2.7	11.0	16	35	5	8	10	32	22	91	96	77	82
Korea, Dem. Rep.	9.8	13.7	57	61	11	14	16	19	24	..	99	..	100
Korea, Rep.	21.7	39.5	57	83	40	47	45	38	26	..	76	..	4
Kuwait	1.2	2.2	91	96	60	60	55	67	46	..	..	..	..
Kyrgyz Republic	1.4	1.7	38	34	..	..	..	..	43	..	100	..	100
Lao PDR	0.4	1.1	12	20	..	..	..	..	62	..	67	..	19
Latvia	1.7	1.4	68	60	..	..	..	49	53	..	..	..	..
Lebanon	2.2	4.0	74	90	40	47	48	55	53	..	100	..	87
Lesotho	0.2	0.5	13	29	..	..	..	..	46	..	72	..	40
Liberia	0.7	1.5	35	46	..	..	..	..	34	..	..	..	..
Libya	2.1	4.8	69	88	26	34	34	38	37	97	97	96	96
Lithuania	2.1	2.4	61	69	..	..	..	..	24	..	..	..	..
Macedonia, FYR	1.0	1.2	53	60	..	..	..	..	36	..	..	..	..
Madagascar	1.6	5.1	19	31	6	10	13	33	35	70	70	25	30
Malawi	0.6	1.7	9	15	..	..	..	..	33	96	96	70	70
Malaysia	5.8	14.3	42	59	7	6	6	16	10	..	..	..	98
Mali	1.2	3.6	18	32	..	..	..	40	34	95	93	62	58
Mauritania	0.4	1.7	28	60	..	..	..	..	39	44	44	19	19
Mauritius	0.4	0.5	42	42	..	..	..	..	35	100	100	100	99
Mexico	44.8	75.4	66	75	28	28	25	29	25	87	88	26	34
Moldova	1.6	1.8	40	42	..	..	..	..	37	..	100	..	98
Mongolia	0.9	1.4	52	57	..	..	..	49	56	..	46	..	2
Morocco	8.0	16.8	41	57	15	18	20	26	21	88	86	31	44
Mozambique	1.6	6.3	13	34	6	17	21	35	19	..	68	..	26
Myanmar	8.1	14.0	24	29	7	9	11	27	33	..	84	..	57
Namibia	0.2	0.6	23	32	..	..	..	..	38	84	96	14	17
Nepal	1.0	3.0	7	13	..	..	..	..	26	69	73	15	22
Netherlands	12.5	14.5	88	90	14	14	14	8	8	100	100	100	100
New Zealand	2.6	3.4	83	86	..	..	..	30	34	..	..	..	..
Nicaragua	1.5	3.0	50	57	..	..	..	36	35	97	95	53	72
Niger	0.7	2.5	13	22	..	..	..	37	35	71	79	4	5
Nigeria	19.1	60.7	27	46	8	12	15	13	15	69	66	44	45
Norway	2.9	3.4	71	75	..	..	..	22	23	100	..	..	..
Oman	0.3	2.0	32	77	..	..	..	..	28	98	98	61	61
Pakistan	23.2	48.9	28	34	15	21	25	22	22	77	95	17	43
Panama	1.0	1.7	50	57	..	..	..	62	73	..	99	..	83
Papua New Guinea	0.4	1.0	13	18	..	..	..	..	28	92	92	80	80
Paraguay	1.3	3.2	42	57	22	23	26	52	41	96	94	91	93
Peru	11.2	19.7	65	73	25	29	30	39	39	77	79	21	49
Philippines	18.0	48.1	37	60	14	16	17	33	22	85	93	63	69
Poland	20.6	24.2	58	63	18	18	19	16	14	..	..	..	..
Portugal	2.9	6.8	29	67	19	57	68	46	60	..	..	..	..
Puerto Rico	2.1	2.9	67	76	34	36	37	51	48	..	..	..	..

	Urban population				Population in urban agglomerations of more than 1 million			Population in largest city		Access to improved sanitation facilities			
	millions		% of total population		% of total population			% of urban population		% of urban population		% of rural population	
	1980	2002	1980	2002	1980	2000	2015	1980	2001	1990	2000	1990	2000
Romania	10.9	12.4	49	55	9	9	10	18	16	..	86	..	10
Russian Federation	97.0	105.0	70	73	18	19	21	8	8	..	..	..	..
Rwanda	0.2	0.5	5	6	..	..	..	..	76	..	12	..	8
Saudi Arabia	6.2	19.1	66	87	19	25	24	17	25	..	100	..	100
Senegal	2.0	4.8	36	49	17	22	27	48	46	86	94	38	48
Serbia and Montenegro	4.5	4.2	46	52	11	14	15	25	30	..	100	..	99
Sierra Leone	0.8	2.0	24	38	..	..	..	47	43	..	88	..	53
Singapore	2.4	4.2	100	100	100	89	83	100	100	..	100	..	..
Slovak Republic	2.6	3.1	52	58	..	..	..	..	15	..	100	..	100
Slovenia	0.9	1.0	48	49	..	..	..	..	26	100	..	..	..
Somalia	1.4	2.6	22	28	..	..	..	27	48	..	..	..	..
South Africa	13.3	26.5	48	58	27	32	36	13	12	93	93	80	80
Spain	27.2	31.9	73	78	20	17	17	16	13	..	..	..	..
Sri Lanka	3.1	4.4	22	23	..	..	..	..	16	94	97	82	93
Sudan	3.9	12.4	20	38	6	9	11	30	24	87	87	48	48
Swaziland	0.1	0.3	18	27	..	..	..	..	28	..	..	..	..
Sweden	6.9	7.4	83	83	17	18	18	20	22	100	100	100	100
Switzerland	3.6	4.9	57	67	..	..	..	20	19	100	100	100	100
Syrian Arab Republic	4.1	8.9	47	52	28	28	31	26	27	..	98	..	81
Tajikistan	1.4	1.7	34	28	..	..	..	..	30	..	97	..	88
Tanzania	2.7	12.0	15	34	5	12	18	30	19	84	99	84	86
Thailand	8.0	12.5	17	20	10	12	15	59	61	95	96	75	96
Togo	0.6	1.6	23	34	..	..	..	..	46	71	69	24	17
Trinidad and Tobago	0.7	1.0	63	75	..	..	..	..	6	..	..	..	..
Tunisia	3.3	6.5	52	67	18	20	21	35	30	96	96	48	62
Turkey	19.5	46.4	44	67	19	27	30	23	21	97	97	70	70
Turkmenistan	1.3	2.2	47	45	..	..	..	..	23	..	..	..	..
Uganda	1.1	3.7	9	15	..	..	..	42	39	..	93	..	77
Ukraine	30.9	33.2	62	68	14	15	17	7	7	..	100	..	98
United Arab Emirates	0.7	2.8	71	88	..	..	..	34	35	..	..	..	..
United Kingdom	50.0	53.1	89	90	25	23	23	15	15	100	100	100	100
United States	167.6	224.0	74	78	38	38	37	9	8	100	100	100	100
Uruguay	2.5	3.1	85	92	42	37	35	49	43	..	95	..	85
Uzbekistan	6.5	9.3	41	37	11	9	8	28	24	..	97	..	85
Venezuela, RB	12.0	21.9	79	87	28	29	30	21	15	..	71	..	48
Vietnam	10.3	20.1	19	25	14	13	14	33	24	52	82	23	38
West Bank and Gaza	..	..	..	..	..	..	..	..	..	..	..	..	..
Yemen, Rep.	1.6	4.7	19	25	..	..	..	15	31	69	89	21	21
Zambia	2.3	4.1	40	40	9	16	22	23	41	86	99	48	64
Zimbabwe	1.6	4.8	22	37	9	14	19	39	40	70	71	50	57
World	**1,741.3 s**	**2,953.1 s**	**39 w**	**48 w**	**.. w**	**.. w**	**.. w**	**18 w**	**16 w**	**75 w**	**81 w**	**27 w**	**38 w**
Low income	348.3	763.1	22	31	..	..	..	17	18	58	71	20	31
Middle income	785.9	1,438.9	39	53	..	..	..	18	15	75	82	29	43
Lower middle income	629.7	1,190.5	35	49	16	18	21	16	13	72	81	28	42
Upper middle income	156.2	248.4	66	75	..	..	..	29	26	..	..	..	64
Low & middle income	1,134.2	2,202.0	32	42	..	..	..	18	16	68	78	24	36
East Asia & Pacific	288.6	701.8	21	38	..	..	..	13	9	61	72	24	36
Europe & Central Asia	249.2	301.0	59	64	16	18	20	15	15	..	..	..	..
Latin America & Carib.	231.8	401.1	65	76	29	32	32	27	24	85	86	41	52
Middle East & N. Africa	83.4	177.2	48	58	21	22	24	30	26	..	94	..	72
South Asia	201.1	392.9	22	28	8	12	14	9	11	52	66	11	21
Sub-Saharan Africa	80.2	227.8	21	33	..	..	..	27	26	75	76	45	46
High income	607.1	751.1	73	78	..	..	..	18	18	..	..	..	..
Europe EMU	209.5	237.3	73	78	26	27	27	17	16	..	..	..	..

About the data

The population of a city or metropolitan area depends on the boundaries chosen. For example, in 1990 Beijing, China, contained 2.3 million people in 87 square kilometers of "inner city" and 5.4 million in 158 square kilometers of "core city." The population of "inner city and inner suburban districts" was 6.3 million, and that of "inner city, inner and outer suburban districts, and inner and outer counties" was 10.8 million. (For most countries the last definition is used.)

Estimates of the world's urban population would change significantly if China, India, and a few other populous nations were to change their definition of urban centers. According to China's State Statistical Bureau, by the end of 1996 urban residents accounted for about 43 percent of China's population, while in 1994 only 20 percent of the population was considered urban. In addition to the continuous migration of people from rural to urban areas, one of the main reasons for this shift was the rapid growth in the hun-

dreds of towns reclassified as cities in recent years. Because the estimates in the table are based on national definitions of what constitutes a city or metropolitan area, cross-country comparisons should be made with caution. To estimate urban populations, the United Nations' ratios of urban to total population were applied to the World Bank's estimates of total population (see table 2.1).

The urban population with access to improved sanitation facilities is defined as people with access to at least adequate excreta disposal facilities that can effectively prevent human, animal, and insect contact with excreta. The rural population with access is included to allow comparison of rural and urban access. This definition and the definition of urban areas vary, however, so comparisons between countries can be misleading.

Definitions

• **Urban population** is the midyear population of areas defined as urban in each country and reported to the United Nations (see *About the data*).
• **Population in urban agglomerations of more than 1 million** is the percentage of a country's population living in metropolitan areas that in 1990 had a population of more than 1 million. • **Population in largest city** is the percentage of a country's urban population living in that country's largest metropolitan area.
• **Access to improved sanitation facilities** refers to the percentage of the urban or rural population with access to at least adequate excreta disposal facilities (private or shared but not public) that can effectively prevent human, animal, and insect contact with excreta. Improved facilities range from simple but protected pit latrines to flush toilets with a sewerage connection. To be effective, facilities must be correctly constructed and properly maintained.

3.10a

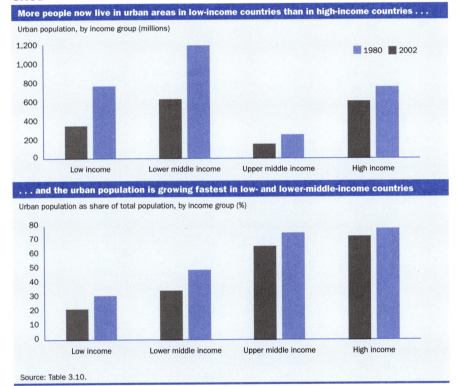

More people now live in urban areas in low-income countries than in high-income countries . . .

Urban population, by income group (millions)

. . . and the urban population is growing fastest in low- and lower-middle-income countries

Urban population as share of total population, by income group (%)

Source: Table 3.10.

3.10b

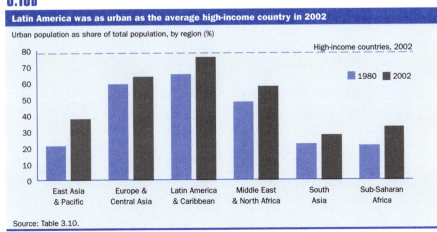

Latin America was as urban as the average high-income country in 2002

Urban population as share of total population, by region (%)

Source: Table 3.10.

Data sources

The data on urban population and the population in urban agglomerations and in the largest city come from the United Nations Population Division's *World Urbanization Prospects: The 2001 Revision.* The total population figures are World Bank estimates. The data on access to sanitation in urban and rural areas are from the World Health Organization.

City		Urban population	Secure tenure	House price to annual income ratio	Work trips by public trans-portation	Travel time to work	Households with access to services				Wastewater treated
							Potable water	Sewerage connection	Electricity	Telephone	
		thousands	% of population		%	minutes	%	%	%	%	%
		2000	1998[a]	1998[a]	1998[a]	1998[a]	1998[a]	1998[a]	1998[a]	1998[a]	1998[a]
Algeria	Algiers	2,562[b]	93.2	..	..	75	..	..	..	..	80
Argentina	Buenos Aires	2,996[b]	92.1	5.10	59	42	100	98	100	70	..
	Córdoba	1,322[b]	85.0	6.80	44	32	99	40	99	80	49
	Rosario	1,248[b]	..	5.7	..	22	98	67	93	76	1
Armenia	Yerevan	1,250[b]	100.0	4.0	84	30	98	98	100	88	36
Bangladesh	Chittagong	2,301[b]	..	8.1	27	45	44	..	95	..	..
	Dhaka	10,000[b]	..	16.7	9	45	60	22	90	7	..
	Sylhet	242[b]	..	6.0	10	50	29	0	93	40	..
	Tangail	152[b]	85.7	13.9	..	30	12	0	90	12	..
Barbados	Bridgetown	..	99.7	4.4	..	..	98	5	99	78	7
Belize	Belize City	55[b]	..	..	..	..	..	..	..	..	..
Bolivia	Santa Cruz de la Sierra	1,065[c]	87.0	29.3	..	29	53	33	98	59	53
Bosnia and Herzegovina	Sarajevo	522[c]	..	..	100	12	95	90	100	..	..
Brazil	Belém	1,638[c]	..	..	..	..	..	..	..	..	..
	Icapui	..	91.7	4.5	..	30	88	..	90	33	..
	Maranguape	..	..	..	30	20	73	..	..	..	..
	Porto Alegre	3[b]	..	..	..	..	99	87	100	..	..
	Recife	3,088[b]	..	12.5	46	35	89	41	100	29	33
	Rio de Janeiro	10,192[b]	..	..	..	..	88	80	10	..	..
	Santo Andre	1,658[b]	80.3	23.4	43	40	98	95	100	79	..
Bulgaria	Bourgas	..	..	5.1	61	32	100	93	100	..	93
	Sofia	1,200[b]	100.0	13.2	79	32	95	91	100	89	94
	Troyan	24[b]	100.0	3.7	44	22	99	82	100	45	..
	Veliko Tarnovo	..	100.0	5.4	46	30	98	98	100	96	50
Burkina Faso	Bobo-Dioulasso	..	100.0	..	..	..	24	..	29	6	..
	Koudougou	..	..	..	..	..	30	..	26	7	..
	Ouagadougou	1,130[c]	100.0	..	2	..	30	..	47	11	19
Burundi	Bujumbura	373[b]	97.0	..	48	25	26	62	57	19	21
Cambodia	Phnom Penh	1,000[b]	..	8.9	0	45	45	75	76	40	..
Cameroon	Douala	1,148[b]	..	13.4	..	40	34	1	95	9	5
	Yaoundé	968[b]	..	..	42	45	34	1	95	9	24
Canada	Hull	254[b]	100.0	..	16	..	100	100	100	100	100
Central African Republic	Bangui	..	94.0	..	66	60	31	..	18	11	0
Chad	N'Djamena	998[c]	..	..	35	..	42	0	13	6	21
Chile	Gran Concepción	..	..	..	57	35	100	91	95	69	6
	Santiago de Chile	5,737[b]	..	..	60	38	100	99	99	73	3
	Tome	..	..	..	..	..	92	52	98	58	57
	Valparaiso	851[b]	91.8	..	55	..	98	92	97	63	100
	Viña del mar	851[b]	92.7	..	..	..	97	97	98	65	93
Colombia	Armenia	..	94.1	5.0	42	60	90	50	99	97	..
	Marinilla	170[b]	94.5	8.5	18	15	98	93	100	65	..
	Medellin	2,901[b]	..	..	38	35	100	99	100	87	..
Congo	Brazzaville	989[b]	87.9	..	55	20	56	0	52	18	..
Côte d'Ivoire	Abidjan	3,201[b]	..	14.5	..	45	26	15	41	5	45
Croatia	Zagreb	2,497[b]	96.5	7.8	56	31	98	97	100	94	..
Cuba	Baracoa	..	96.2	..	..	..	83	3	93	32	..
	Camaguey	..	84.7	..	2	60	72	47	97	..	..
	Cienfuegos	..	96.3	4.0	..	80	100	73	100	9	2
	Ciudad Habana	..	..	8.5	58	83	100	85	100	14	..
	Pinar Del Rio	..	96.4	..	..	80	97	48	100	..	..
	Santa Clara	..	98.8	..	7	48	95	42	100	43	..
Czech Republic	Brno	..	..	..	50	25	100	96	100	69	100
	Prague	1,193[b]	99.3	..	55	22	99	100	100	100	..
Dem. Rep. of Congo	Kinshasa	5,398[b]	94.9	..	72	57	72	0	66	1	..
Dominican Republic	Santiago de los Caballeros	691[b]	..	..	..	30	75	80	..	71	80
Ecuador	Ambato	286[b]	..	..	..	..	90	81	91	87	..

	City	Urban population	Secure tenure	House price to annual income ratio	Work trips by public trans-portation	Travel time to work	Households with access to services				Wastewater treated
							Potable water	Sewerage connection	Electricity	Telephone	
		thousands **2000**	% of population **1998**[a]	**1998**[a]	% **1998**[a]	minutes **1998**[a]	% **1998**[a]	% **1998**[a]	% **1998**[a]	% **1998**[a]	% **1998**[a]
Ecuador	Cuenca	..	91.0	4.6	..	25	97	92	97	48	82
	Guayaquil	2,317[b]	45.8	3.4	89	45	70	42	..	44	9
	Manta	126[b]	..	..	..	30	70	52	98	40	..
	Puyo	40[b]	..	2.1	..	15	80	30	90	60	..
	Quito	1,531[b]	93.8	2.4	..	33	85	70	96	55	..
	Tena	..	..	6.3	..	5	80	60	..	..	..
El Salvador	San Salvador	1,863[b]	90.5	3.5	..	..	82	80	98	70	..
Estonia	Riik	..	99.5	..	..	..	92	90	98	55	..
	Tallin	397[c]	98.8	6.4	..	35	98	98	100	86	10
Gabon	Libreville	523[c]	..	..	80	30	55	0	95	45	44
Gambia	Banjul	50[b]	91.8	11.4	55	22	23	12	24	..	..
Georgia	Tbilisi	1,310[c]	100.0	9.4	..	..	..	98	100	58	..
Ghana	Accra	1,500[b]	..	14.0	54	21	..	..	..	..	..
	Kumasi	780[b]	77.7	13.7	51	21	65	..	95	51	..
Guatemala	Quetzaltenango	333[b]	..	4.3	..	15	60	55	80	40	..
Guinea	Conakry	1,824[c]	..	..	26	45	30	32	54	6	..
Indonesia	Jakarta	9,489[b]	95.5	14.6	..	..	50	65	99	..	16
	Semarang	1,076[b]	80.2	..	..	..	34	..	85	..	..
	Surabaya	2,373[b]	97.6	3.4	18	35	41	56	89	71	..
Iraq	Baghdad	4,797[c]	..	..	..	..	..	..	..	..	..
Italy	Aversa	..	..	..	..	..	..	..	..	..	90
Jamaica	Kingston	655[c]	..	..	..	..	97	..	88	..	20
	Montego Bay	..	..	..	..	..	78	..	86	..	15
Jordan	Amman	1,621[b]	97.3	6.1	21	25	98	81	99	62	54
Kenya	Kisumu	134[b]	97.3	8.5	43	24	38	31	49	..	65
	Mombasa	..	..	..	47	20	..	..	..	..	50
	Nairobi	2,310[c]	..	..	71	57	89	..	..	..	52
Korea, Rep	Hanam	124[b]	..	3.7	..	..	81	68	100	100	81
	Pusan	3,843[b]	100.0	4.0	39	42	98	69	100	100	69
	Seoul	10,389[b]	98.6	5.7	71	60	100	99	100	..	99
Kuwait	Kuwait City	1,165[c]	..	6.5	21	10	100	98	100	98	..
Kyrgyz Republic	Bishkek	60[b]	94.8	..	95	35	30	23	100	20	15
Lao	Vientiane	562[b]	92.2	23.2	2	27	87	..	100	87	20
Latvia	Riga	775[c]	97.4	15.6	..	..	95	93	100	70	..
Lebanon	Sin El Fil	..[b]	..	8.3	50	10	80	30	98	80	..
Liberia	Monrovia	651[b]	57.6	28.0	80	60	..	..	..	..	..
Libya	Tripoli	1,773[b]	..	0.8	18	20	97	90	99	6	40
Lithuania	Vilnius	578[b]	100.0	20.0	52	37	89	89	100	77	54
Madagascar	Antananarivo	1,507[c]	..	..	..	..	..	..	..	..	..
Malawi	Lilongwe	765[c]	..	..	27	5	65	12	50	10	..
Malaysia	Penang	..	..	7.2	55	40	99	..	100	98	20
Mauritania	Nouakchott	881[c]	89.9	5.4	45	50	..	..	..	..	..
Mexico	Ciudad Juárez	1,018[b]	..	..	24	23	89	77	96	45	..
Moldova	Chisinau	..	..	..	80	23	100	95	100	83	71
Mongolia	Ulaanbaatar	627[b]	51.6	7.8	80	30	60	60	100	90	96
Morocco	Casablanca	3,292[b]	..	..	..	30	83	93	91	..	..
	Rabat	646[b]	..	..	40	20	93	97	52	..	..
Myanmar	Yangon	3,692[b]	..	8.3	69	45	78	81	85	17	..
Nicaragua	Leon	..	98.8	..	..	15	78	..	84	21	..
Niger	Niamey	731[c]	87.4	..	..	30	33	0	51	4	..
Nigeria	Ibadan	1,731[c]	85.8	..	46	45	26	12	41	..	..
	Lagos	13,427[c]	93.0	..	48	60	..	..	41	..	..
Oman	Muscat	887[b]	..	..	..	20	80	90	89	53	..
Panama	Colón	132[b]	..	14.2	..	15	..	..	..	..	..
Paraguay	Asunción	1,262[c]	90.2	10.7	..	25	46	8	86	17	..
Peru	Cajamarca	..	90.0	3.9	..	20	86	69	81	38	62

3.11 Urban environment

	City	Urban population	Secure tenure	House price to annual income ratio	Work trips by public transportation	Travel time to work	Households with access to services				Wastewater treated
							Potable water	Sewerage connection	Electricity	Telephone	
		thousands	% of population		%	minutes	%	%	%	%	%
		2000	1998[a]	1998[a]	1998[a]	1998[a]	1998[a]	1998[a]	1998[a]	1998[a]	1998[a]
Peru	Huanuco	747[b]	..	30.0	..	20	57	28	80	32	..
	Huaras	54[b]	..	6.7	..	15	..	..	71	..	..
	Iquitos	347[b]	97.3	5.6	25	10	73	60	82	62	..
	Lima	7,431[b]	80.6	10.4	82	..	75	71	99	..	4
	Tacna	..	..	4.0	..	25	65	58	74	16	64
	Tumbes	..	..	..	..	20	60	35	80	25	..
Philippines	Cebu	2,189[b]	95.0	13.3	..	35	41	92	80	25	..
Poland	Bydgoszcz	..	60.5	4.3	35	18	95	87	100	85	28
	Gdansk	893[c]	..	4.4	56	20	99	94	100	56	100
	Katowice	3,487[c]	27.8	1.7	29	36	99	94	100	75	67
	Poznan	..	65.5	5.8	51	25	95	96	100	86	78
Qatar	Doha	391[c]	..	..	..	..	..	..	..	..	..
Russian Federation	Astrakhan	..	100.0	5.0	66	35	81	79	100	51	92
	Belgorod	..	100.0	4.0	..	25	90	89	100	51	96
	Kostroma	..	100.0	6.9	68	20	88	84	100	46	96
	Moscow	9,321[c]	100.0	5.1	85	62	100	100	100	102	98
	Nizhny Novgorod	1,458[c]	100.0	6.9	79	35	98	98	100	64	98
	Novomoscowsk	..	100.0	4.2	61	25	99	93	100	62	97
	Omsk	1,216[c]	99.7	3.9	86	43	87	87	100	41	89
	Pushkin	..	100.0	9.6	60	15	99	99	100	89	100
	Surgut	..	100.0	4.5	81	57	98	98	100	50	93
	Veliky Novgorod	..	100.0	3.4	75	30	97	97	100	51	95
Rwanda	Kigali	358[b]	..	11.4	32	45	36	20	57	6	20
Samoa	Apia	34[b]	..	10.0	..	..	60	0	98	96	..
Serbia and Montenegro	Belgrad	1,182[b]	96.5	13.5	72	40	95	86	100	86	20
Singapore	Singapore	3,164[b]	100.0	3.1	53	30	100	100	100	100	100
Slovenia	Ljubljana	273[b]	98.9	7.8	20	30	100	100	100	97	98
Spain	Madrid	4,577[b]	..	..	16	32	..	..	..	..	100
	Pamplona	..	..	..	..	..	100	..	100	..	79
Sweden	Amal	13[b]	..	2.9	..	..	100	100	100	..	100
	Stockholm	736[b]	..	6.0	48	28	100	100	100	..	100
	Umea	104[b]	..	5.3	..	16	100	100	100	..	100
Switzerland	Basel	170[b]	..	12.3	..	..	100	100	100	99	100
Syria	Damascus	2,335[b]	..	10.3	33	40	98	71	95	10	3
Thailand	Bangkok	5,647[b]	77.2	8.8	28	60	99	100	100	60	..
	Chiang Mai	499[b]	96.5	6.8	5	30	95	60	100	75	70
Togo	Lomé	663[b]	64.0	..	40	30	..	70	51	18	..
Trinidad and Tobago	Port of Spain	..	78.6	..	44	..	..	..	..	..	..
Tunisia	Tunis	2,023[b]	..	5.0	..	..	75	47	95	27	83
Turkey	Ankara	2,837[b]	91.3	4.5	..	32	97	98	100	..	80
Uganda	Entebbe	65[b]	74.0	10.4	65	20	48	13	42	0	30
	Jinja	92[b]	82.0	15.4	49	12	65	43	55	5	30
Uruguay	Montevideo	1,670[b]	88.0	5.6	60	45	98	79	100	75	34
West Bank and Gaza	Gaza	367[b]	87.3	5.4	..	..	85	38	99	38	..
Yemen	Aden	1,200[b]	..	..	78	20	..	..	96	..	30
	Sana'a	1,200[b]	..	..	78	20	30	9	96	..	30
Zimbabwe	Bulawayo	900[b]	99.4	..	75	15	100	100	98	..	80
	Chegutu	..	51.5	3.4	20	22	100	68	9	3	69
	Gweru	..	94.0	..	..	15	100	100	90	61	95
	Harare	1,634[b]	99.9	..	32	45	100	100	88	42	..
	Mutare	149[b]	..	..	70	20	88	88	74	4	100

a. Data are preliminary. b. Data are for 1998 and are from United Nations Centre for Human Settlements. c. Data are for 2000 and are from the United Nations Population Division's *World Urbanization Prospects: The 2001 Revision.*

Despite the importance of cities and urban agglomerations as home to almost half the world's people, data on many aspects of urban life are sparse. The available data have been scattered among international agencies with different mandates, and compiling comparable data has been difficult. Even within cities it is difficult to assemble an integrated data set. Urban areas are often spread across many jurisdictions with no single agency responsible for collecting and reporting data for the entire area. Adding to the difficulties of data collection are gaps and overlaps in the data collection and reporting responsibilities of different administrative units. Creating a comprehensive, comparable international data set is further complicated by differences in the definition of an urban area and by uneven data quality.

The United Nations Global Plan of Action calls for monitoring the changing role of the world's cities and human settlements. The international agency with the mandate to assemble information on urban areas is the United Nations Centre for Human Settlements (UNCHS, or Habitat). Its Urban Indicators Programme is intended to provide data for monitoring and evaluating the performance of urban areas and for developing government policies and strategies. These data are collected through questionnaires completed by city officials in more than a hundred countries.

The table shows selected indicators for more than 160 cities from the UNCHS data set. A few more indicators are included on the *World Development Indicators* CD-ROM. The selection of cities in the UNCHS database does not reflect population weights or the economic importance of cities and is therefore biased toward smaller cities. Moreover, it is based on demand for participation in the Urban Indicators Programme. As a result, the database excludes a large number of major cities. The table reflects this bias as well as the criterion of data availability for the indicators shown.

The data should be used with care. Because different data collection methods and definitions may have been used, comparisons can be misleading. In addition, the definitions used here for access to potable water and urban population are more stringent than those used for tables 3.5 and 3.10 (see *Definitions*).

• **Urban population** refers to the population of the urban agglomeration, a contiguous inhabited territory without regard to administrative boundaries. • **Secure tenure** refers to the percentage of the population protected from involuntary removal from land or residence—including subtenancy, residence in social housing, and residences owned, purchased, or privately rented—except through due legal process. • **House price to annual income ratio** is the average house price divided by the average household income. • **Work trips by public transportation** are the percentage of trips to work made by bus or minibus, tram, or train. Buses or minibuses are road vehicles other than cars taking passengers on a farepaying basis. Other means of transport commonly used in developing countries, such as taxi, ferry, rickshaw, or animal, are not included. • **Travel time to work** is the average time in minutes, for all modes, for a one-way trip to work. Train and bus times include average walking and waiting times, and car times include parking and walking to the workplace. • **Households with access to services** are the percentage of households in formal settlements with access to potable water and connections to sewerage, electricity, and telephone service. Households with access to potable water are those with access to safe or potable drinking water within 200 meters of the dwelling. • **Potable water** is water that is free from contamination and safe to drink without further treatment. • **Wastewater treated** is the percentage of all wastewater undergoing some form of treatment.

3.11a

		Share of total			Share of total
Country	**City**	**work trips (%)**	**Country**	**City**	**work trips (%)**
Lao PDR	Vientiane	2	Kyrgyz Republic	Bishkek	95
Spain	Madrid	16	Russian Federation	Moscow	85
Canada	Hull	16	Armenia	Yerevan	84
Libya	Tripoli	18	Peru	Lima	82
Slovenia	Ljubljana	20	Gabon	Libreville	80
Kuwait	Kuwait City	21	Liberia	Monrovia	80
Jordan	Amman	21	Mongolia	Ulaanbaatar	80
Mexico	Ciudad Juarez	24	Moldova	Chisinau	80
Guinea	Conakry	26	Bulgaria	Sofia	79
Malawi	Lilongwe	27	Yemen, Rep.	Aden	78

The use of public transportation for work trips varied widely across cities in 1998

Source: Table 3.11.

3.12 Traffic and congestion

	Motor vehicles				Passenger cars		Two-wheelers		Road traffic		Fuel prices	
	per 1,000 people		per kilometer of road		per 1,000 people		per 1,000 people		million vehicle kilometers		$ per liter	
											Super	Diesel
	1990	1999–2001	1990	1999–2001	1990	1999–2001	1990	1999–2001	1990	1999–2001	2002	2002
Afghanistan	..	..	..	..	..	..	..	..	..	..	0.34	0.27
Albania	11	66	3	11	2	43	3	1	..	29	0.80	0.51
Algeria	..	..	..	..	..	..	..	..	..	..	0.22	0.10
Angola	19	..	..	..	14	..	..	..	..	..	0.19	0.13
Argentina	181	181	27	37	134	140	1	..	43,119	27,458	0.63	0.46
Armenia	5	..	2	..	1	..	..	..	..	..	0.42	0.29
Australia	530	..	11	..	450	..	18	18	138,501	..	0.50	0.48
Austria	421	536	30	22	387	495	71	77	..	..	0.84	0.73
Azerbaijan	52	52	7	17	36	42	5	1	..	..	0.37	0.16
Bangladesh	1	1	0	..	0	0	1	1	..	..	0.52	0.29
Belarus	61	112	13	..	59	145	..	52	10,026	4,964	0.50	0.36
Belgium	423	515	30	35	385	462	14	29	..	156,633	1.04	0.80
Benin	3	..	2	..	2	..	34	..	..	..	0.54	0.41
Bolivia	41	53	6	8	25	..	9	3	1,139	..	0.69	0.42
Bosnia and Herzegovina	114	..	24	..	101	..	..	..	..	..	0.74	0.74
Botswana	18	69	3	11	10	30	..	1	..	..	0.41	0.38
Brazil	88	..	8	..	..	..	..	28	..	..	0.55	0.31
Bulgaria	163	273	39	60	146	234	55	64	..	213	0.68	0.59
Burkina Faso	4	..	3	..	2	..	9	..	..	..	0.83	0.62
Burundi	..	..	..	..	..	..	..	..	..	..	0.58	0.54
Cambodia	1	6	0	49	0	..	9	134	314	7,210	0.63	0.44
Cameroon	10	..	3	..	6	..	..	..	..	..	0.68	0.57
Canada	605	580	20	20	468	458	12	11	..	73,500	0.51	0.43
Central African Republic	1	1	0	0	1	0	0	..	1,494	..	1.00	0.87
Chad	2	..	0	..	1	..	0	..	..	..	0.79	0.77
Chile	81	133	13	25	52	87	2	2	..	..	0.58	0.39
China	5	12	4	11	1	7	3	26	..	840,960	0.42	0.37
Hong Kong, China	66	77	253	279	42	57	4	5	8,192	10,781	1.47	0.77
Colombia	..	51	..	19	..	43	8	12	50,945	41,587	0.44	0.24
Congo, Dem. Rep.	..	..	..	..	..	..	..	..	..	..	0.70	0.69
Congo, Rep.	18	..	3	..	12	..	..	..	..	..	0.69	0.48
Costa Rica	87	..	7	13	55	..	14	22	..	551,139	0.64	0.44
Côte d'Ivoire	24	..	6	..	15	..	..	..	..	..	0.85	0.60
Croatia	..	274	..	44	..	247	..	14	..	15,168	0.89	0.74
Cuba	37	32	16	6	18	16	19	16	..	..	0.90	0.45
Czech Republic	246	364	46	67	228	335	113	73	..	7,753	0.81	0.71
Denmark	368	420	27	31	320	359	9	13	36,304	45,165	1.09	0.94
Dominican Republic	75	..	48	0	21	..	..	..	..	..	0.49	0.27
Ecuador	35	48	8	14	31	43	2	2	10,306	17,528	0.55	0.27
Egypt, Arab Rep.	29	..	33	..	21	..	6	..	..	..	0.19	0.80
El Salvador	33	61	14	36	17	30	0	5	2,002	4,244	0.46	0.33
Eritrea	1	..	1	..	1	..	..	..	..	..	0.36	0.25
Estonia	211	404	22	11	154	339	66	5	..	6,539	0.58	0.56
Ethiopia	1	2	2	3	1	1	0	0	..	26,450	0.52	0.32
Finland	441	461	29	31	386	403	12	35	39,750	46,010	1.12	0.80
France	494	575	32	38	405	477	55	40	422,000	519,400	1.05	0.80
Gabon	32	..	4	..	19	..	..	..	..	..	0.69	0.53
Gambia, The	13	..	5	..	6	..	..	..	..	..	0.46	0.40
Georgia	107	70	27	15	89	55	5	1	4,620	..	0.48	0.41
Germany	405	..	53	..	386	516	18	56	446,000	589,500	1.03	0.82
Ghana	..	..	..	..	..	..	..	..	..	15,320	0.28	0.23
Greece	248	328	22	..	171	254	120	220	..	79,377	0.78	0.68
Guatemala	..	52	..	119	..	1	..	12	..	4,547	0.48	0.32
Guinea	4	..	1	..	2	..	..	..	..	..	0.66	0.56
Guinea-Bissau	7	..	2	..	4	..	..	..	..	..	..	..
Haiti	..	..	..	..	..	..	..	..	..	..	0.54	0.30

	Motor vehicles				Passenger cars		Two-wheelers		Road traffic		Fuel prices	
	per 1,000 people		per kilometer of road		per 1,000 people		per 1,000 people		million vehicle kilometers		$ per liter	
	1990	1999–2001	1990	1999–2001	1990	1999–2001	1990	1999–2001	1990	1999–2001	Super 2002	Diesel 2002
Honduras	22	60	10	28	..	51	..	14	3,288	..	0.63	0.46
Hungary	212	271	21	16	188	237	16	14	22,898	23,670	0.94	0.85
India	4	10	2	..	2	6	15	29	..	..	0.66	0.41
Indonesia	16	25	10	..	7	..	34	59	..	..	0.27	0.19
Iran, Islamic Rep.	34	..	14	..	25	..	36	..	..	..	0.07	0.02
Iraq	14	..	6	..	1	..	..	..	..	..	0.02	0.01
Ireland	270	408	10	..	227	349	6	8	24,205	..	0.90	0.80
Israel	210	275	74	108	174	233	8	12	18,212	37,010	0.90	0.62
Italy	529	606	99	74	476	542	45	125	344,726	67,916	1.05	0.86
Jamaica	..	..	..	..	..	..	..	..	..	..	0.52	0.44
Japan	469	572	52	62	283	413	146	110	628,581	775,723	0.91	0.66
Jordan	60	..	26	..	..	..	0	..	1,098	490,248	0.52	0.17
Kazakhstan	76	86	8	16	50	67	..	8	18,248	..	0.35	0.29
Kenya	12	11	5	4	10	8	1	1	5,170	..	0.70	0.56
Korea, Dem. Rep.	..	..	..	..	..	..	..	..	..	..	0.55	0.41
Korea, Rep.	79	255	60	120	48	171	32	59	30,464	67,266	1.09	0.51
Kuwait	..	..	..	..	..	..	..	..	..	4,450	0.20	0.18
Kyrgyz Republic	44	..	10	..	44	38	..	4	5,220	1,933	0.39	0.25
Lao PDR	9	..	3	..	6	..	18	..	..	..	0.36	0.30
Latvia	135	281	6	11	106	235	76	9	3,932	..	0.70	0.65
Lebanon	321	..	183	..	300	..	13	..	..	..	0.65	0.25
Lesotho	11	..	4	..	3	..	..	..	..	..	0.50	0.47
Liberia	14	..	4	..	7	..	..	..	..	..	..	..
Libya	..	..	..	..	..	..	..	..	..	..	0.10	0.08
Lithuania	160	345	12	17	133	317	52	5	..	872	0.69	0.59
Macedonia, FYR	132	170	30	27	121	..	1	..	3,102	..	0.85	0.63
Madagascar	6	..	2	..	4	..	..	..	41,500	..	1.08	0.65
Malawi	4	..	4	0	2	..	..	..	..	..	0.66	0.62
Malaysia	124	..	26	..	101	..	167	233	..	..	0.35	0.19
Mali	3	..	2	..	2	..	..	..	..	..	0.69	0.55
Mauritania	10	..	3	..	7	..	..	..	..	..	0.63	0.39
Mauritius	59	106	35	64	44	78	54	101	..	78	..	..
Mexico	119	159	41	44	82	107	3	..	55,095	..	0.62	0.47
Moldova	53	82	17	24	48	64	45	..	..	557	0.45	0.31
Mongolia	21	31	1	2	6	18	22	10	340	2,093	0.38	0.37
Morocco	37	51	15	26	28	41	1	1	..	16,834	0.87	0.55
Mozambique	4	..	2	..	3	..	..	..	1,889	..	0.46	0.43
Myanmar	..	..	..	..	..	..	..	..	..	..	0.36	0.28
Namibia	71	82	1	2	39	38	1	2	1,896	2,317	0.45	0.43
Nepal	..	..	..	..	..	..	..	..	..	..	0.66	0.34
Netherlands	405	428	58	58	368	384	44	25	90,150	109,955	1.12	0.81
New Zealand	524	696	19	..	436	578	24	20	..	35,200	0.55	0.33
Nicaragua	19	30	5	8	10	12	3	5	108	440	0.54	0.41
Niger	6	..	4	..	5	..	..	..	178	..	0.77	0.55
Nigeria	30	..	21	..	12	..	5	..	..	..	0.20	0.19
Norway	458	511	22	25	380	411	48	55	..	32,589	1.23	1.18
Oman	130	..	9	..	83	..	3	..	..	..	0.31	0.26
Pakistan	6	9	4	5	4	5	8	15	..	234,515	0.52	0.35
Panama	75	..	18	..	60	..	2	3	..	..	0.51	0.36
Papua New Guinea	..	..	..	..	..	..	..	..	..	..	0.53	0.34
Paraguay	..	..	..	..	..	..	..	..	..	..	0.56	0.34
Peru	..	43	..	13	..	27	..	..	..	..	0.74	0.48
Philippines	10	32	4	12	7	10	6	16	6,189	9,548	0.35	0.27
Poland	168	307	18	32	138	259	36	21	59,608	138,100	0.83	0.68
Portugal	222	347	34	..	162	321	5	77	28,623	47,943	0.97	0.71
Puerto Rico	..	..	..	..	..	..	..	..	..	..	..	..

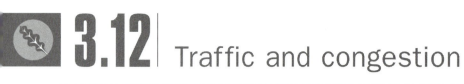

	Motor vehicles				Passenger cars		Two-wheelers		Road traffic		Fuel prices	
	per 1,000 people		per kilometer of road		per 1,000 people		per 1,000 people		million vehicle kilometers		$ per liter	
											Super	Diesel
	1990	1999–2001	1990	1999–2001	1990	1999–2001	1990	1999–2001	1990	1999–2001	2002	2002
Romania	72	160	11	18	56	139	13	14	23,907	39,184	0.64	0.57
Russian Federation	87	176	14	48	65	132	..	43	..	59,522	0.35	0.25
Rwanda	2	..	1	..	1	..	..	..	..	..	0.84	0.84
Saudi Arabia	165	..	19	..	98	..	0	..	..	..	0.24	0.10
Senegal	11	14	6	2	8	11	0	0	..	4,013	0.75	0.53
Serbia and Montenegro	137	163	31	39	133	150	3	3	..	1,428	0.74	0.66
Sierra Leone	10	0	4	..	7	0	2	0	996	..	0.51	0.50
Singapore	130	168	142	..	89	122	40	32	..	..	0.85	0.38
Slovak Republic	194	266	57	34	163	236	61	8	..	543	0.74	0.70
Slovenia	306	465	42	46	289	426	8	6	5,620	9,449	0.76	0.67
Somalia	2	..	1	..	1	..	..	..	..	..	0.35	0.29
South Africa	139	..	26	..	97	..	8	4	..	..	0.43	0.40
Spain	360	467	43	54	309	408	79	92	100,981	201,896	0.83	0.72
Sri Lanka	21	37	4	7	7	12	24	42	3,468	15,630	0.54	0.31
Sudan	9	..	22	..	8	..	..	..	..	..	0.30	0.24
Swaziland	66	71	18	21	35	35	3	3	..	..	0.47	0.44
Sweden	464	494	29	21	426	450	11	31	61,040	128,200	1.06	0.96
Switzerland	491	534	46	54	449	493	114	102	48,660	54,707	0.89	0.93
Syrian Arab Republic	26	29	10	..	10	9	..	..	..	..	0.53	0.18
Tajikistan	3	..	1	..	0	..	..	..	..	1,730	0.36	0.24
Tanzania	5	..	2	..	1	..	..	..	..	..	0.67	0.61
Thailand	46	..	36	..	14	..	86	..	45,769	..	0.36	0.32
Togo	24	..	11	..	16	..	8	..	..	..	0.56	0.46
Trinidad and Tobago	..	..	..	..	..	..	..	..	..	..	0.40	0.21
Tunisia	48	79	19	..	23	53	..	1	..	14,635	0.29	0.19
Turkey	50	85	8	14	34	63	10	15	27,041	52,631	1.02	0.78
Turkmenistan	..	..	..	..	..	..	..	..	..	..	0.02	0.01
Uganda	2	..	..	..	1	..	0	3	..	..	0.83	0.70
Ukraine	63	..	20	..	63	104	..	46	59,500	..	0.47	0.34
United Arab Emirates	121	..	52	..	97	..	..	..	..	..	0.29	0.30
United Kingdom	400	391	64	62	341	384	14	3	399,000	462,400	1.18	1.20
United States	758	779	30	34	573	481	17	15	2,527,441	2,653,043	0.40	0.39
Uruguay	138	..	45	..	122	..	74	..	..	..	0.46	0.20
Uzbekistan	..	..	..	..	..	..	..	..	..	..	0.38	0.26
Venezuela, RB	..	..	..	..	..	..	..	..	..	..	0.05	0.05
Vietnam	..	..	..	..	..	..	45	..	..	..	0.34	0.27
West Bank and Gaza	..	..	..	..	..	..	..	..	..	..	0.99	0.52
Yemen, Rep.	34	..	8	..	14	..	..	..	8,681	..	0.21	0.10
Zambia	14	..	3	..	8	..	..	..	..	..	0.72	0.60
Zimbabwe	..	..	..	..	..	..	..	..	..	..	0.85	0.72
World	**118 w**	**.. w**	**..**	**..**	**91 w**	**.. w**	**..**	**..**	**..**	**..**	**0.58 m**	**0.44 m**
Low income	7	11	..	..	4	8	..	..	..	..	0.54	0.41
Middle income	40	52	..	..	26	40	..	..	..	..	0.54	0.39
Lower middle income	25	34	..	..	13	26	..	..	..	..	0.52	0.36
Upper middle income	149	213	..	..	114	166	..	..	..	..	0.60	0.43
Low & middle income	26	37	..	..	16	28	..	..	..	..	0.54	0.40
East Asia & Pacific	9	17	..	..	4	10	..	..	..	..	0.36	0.31
Europe & Central Asia	97	199	..	..	82	152	..	..	..	..	0.64	0.56
Latin America & Carib.	100	108	..	..	..	72	..	..	..	..	0.54	0.36
Middle East & N. Africa	48	..	..	..	31	..	..	..	..	..	0.29	0.18
South Asia	4	10	..	..	2	6	..	..	..	..	0.54	0.34
Sub-Saharan Africa	21	..	..	..	14	..	..	..	..	..	0.64	0.51
High income	505	668	..	..	396	436	..	..	..	..	0.87	0.66
Europe EMU	429	553	..	..	379	494	..	..	..	..	1.00	0.80

About the data

Traffic congestion in urban areas constrains economic productivity, damages people's health, and degrades the quality of their lives. The particulate air pollution emitted by motor vehicles—the dust and soot in exhaust—is proving to be far more damaging to human health than was once believed. (For information on particulate matter and other air pollutants, see table 3.13.)

In recent years ownership of passenger cars has increased, and the expansion of economic activity has led to the transport by road of more goods and services over greater distances (see table 5.9). These developments have increased demand for roads and vehicles, adding to urban congestion, air pollution, health hazards, traffic accidents, and injuries.

Congestion, the most visible cost of expanding vehicle ownership, is reflected in the indicators in the table. Other relevant indicators—such as average vehicle speed in major cities or the cost of traffic congestion, which takes a heavy toll on economic productivity—are not included because data are incomplete or difficult to compare. The data in the table—except for those on fuel prices—are compiled by the International Road Federation (IRF) through questionnaires sent to national organizations. The IRF uses a hierarchy of sources to gather as much information as possible. The primary sources are national road associations. Where such an association lacks data or does not respond, other agencies are contacted, including road directorates, ministries of transport or public works, and central statistical offices. As a result, the compiled data are of uneven quality. The coverage of each indicator may differ across countries because of differences in defini-

tions. Comparability also is limited when time-series data are reported. Moreover, the data do not capture the quality or age of vehicles or the condition or width of roads. Thus comparisons over time and between countries should be made with caution.

The data on fuel prices are compiled by the German Agency for Technical Cooperation (GTZ) from its global network of regional offices and representatives as well as other sources, including the Allgemeiner Deutscher Automobil Club (for Europe) and a project of the Latin American Energy Organization (OLADE, for Latin America). Local prices have been converted to U.S. dollars using the exchange rate on the survey date as listed in the international monetary table of the *Financial Times*. For countries with multiple exchange rates, the market, parallel, or black market rate was used rather than the official exchange rate.

Definitions

• **Motor vehicles** include cars, buses, and freight vehicles but not two-wheelers. Population figures refer to the midyear population in the year for which data are available. Roads refer to motorways, highways, main or national roads, and secondary or regional roads. A motorway is a road specially designed and built for motor traffic that separates the traffic flowing in opposite directions. • **Passenger cars** refer to road motor vehicles, other than two-wheelers, intended for the carriage of passengers and designed to seat no more than nine people (including the driver). • **Two-wheelers** refer to mopeds and motorcycles. • **Road traffic** is the number of vehicles multiplied by the average distances they travel. • **Fuel prices** refer to the pump prices of the most widely sold grade of gasoline and of diesel fuel. Prices have been converted from the local currency to U.S. dollars (see *About the data*).

3.12a

The 10 countries with the most vehicles per 1,000 people in 2001—and the 10 with the fewest

Vehicles per 1,000 people

Country	Motor vehicles	Country	Motor vehicles
United States	779	Mongolia	31
New Zealand	696	Nicaragua	30
Italy	606	Syrian Arab Republic	29
Canada	580	Indonesia	25
France	575	India	10
Japan	572	Pakistan	9
Austria	536	Cambodia	6
Switzerland	534	Uganda	5
Belgium	515	Ethiopia	2
Norway	511	Bangladesh	1

Note: Data are for the most recent year available between 1999 and 2001.
Source: Table 3.12.

Data sources

The data on vehicles and traffic are from the IRF's electronic files and its annual *World Road Statistics*. The data on fuel prices are from the GTZ's electronic files.

3.13 Air pollution

	City	City population	Particulate matter	Sulfur dioxide	Nitrogen dioxide
		thousands **2000**	micrograms per cubic meter **1999**	micrograms per cubic meter **1995–2001**[a]	microgram per cubic meter **1995–2001**[a]
Argentina	Córdoba	1,370	52	..	97
Australia	Melbourne	3,293	15	..	30
	Perth	1,245	15	5	19
	Sydney	3,855	22	28	81
Austria	Vienna	1,904	39	14	42
Belgium	Brussels	983	31	20	48
Brazil	Rio de Janeiro	5,902	40	129	..
	São Paulo	9,984	46	43	83
Bulgaria	Sofia	1,177	83	39	122
Canada	Montreal	3,519	22	10	42
	Toronto	4,535	26	17	43
	Vancouver	1,880	15	14	37
Chile	Santiago	4,522	73	29	81
China	Anshan	3,132	99	115	88
	Beijing	9,302	106	90	122
	Changchun	3,766	88	21	64
	Chengdu	4,401	103	77	74
	Chongqing	3,945	147	340	70
	Dalian	4,389	60	61	100
	Guangzhu	495	74	57	136
	Guiyang	2,103	84	424	53
	Harbin	4,545	91	23	30
	Jinan	3,037	112	132	45
	Kunming	2,037	84	19	33
	Lanzhou	2,044	109	102	104
	Liupanshui	2,330	70	102	..
	Nanchang	1,594	94	69	29
	Pinxiang	1,754	80	75	..
	Quingdao	2,316	..	190	64
	Shanghai	10,367	87	53	73
	Shenyang	5,881	120	99	73
	Taiyuan	2,811	105	211	55
	Tianjin	7,333	149	82	50
	Urumqi	1,467	61	60	70
	Wuhan	4,842	94	40	43
	Zhengzhou	2,214	116	63	95
	Zibo	3,139	88	198	43
Colombia	Bogota	5,442	33	..	..
Croatia	Zagreb	908	39	31	..
Cuba	Havana	2,270	28	1	5
Czech Republic	Prague	1,211	27	14	33
Denmark	Copenhagen	1,371	24	7	54
Ecuador	Guayaquil	2,120	26	15	..
	Quito	1,598	34	22	..
Egypt, Arab Rep.	Cairo	7,941	178	69	..
Finland	Helsinki	1,095	22	4	35
France	Paris	9,851	15	14	57
Germany	Berlin	3,555	25	18	26
	Frankfurt	668	22	11	45
	Munich	1,275	22	8	53
Ghana	Accra	1,938	31	..	..
Greece	Athens	3,229	50	34	64
Hungary	Budapest	1,958	26	39	51
Iceland	Reykjavik	164	21	5	42
India	Ahmedabad	4,154	104	30	21
	Bangalore	5,180	56	..	..

About the data

In many towns and cities exposure to air pollution is the main environmental threat to human health. Long-term exposure to high levels of soot and small particles in the air contributes to a wide range of health effects, including respiratory diseases, lung cancer, and heart disease. Particulate pollution, on its own or in combination with sulfur dioxide, leads to an enormous burden of ill health.

Emissions of sulfur dioxide and nitrogen oxides lead to the deposition of acid rain and other acidic compounds over long distances. Acid deposition changes the chemical balance of soils and can lead to the leaching of trace minerals and nutrients critical to trees and plants.

Where coal is the primary fuel for power plants, steel mills, industrial boilers, and domestic heating, the result is usually high levels of urban air pollution—especially particulates and sometimes sulfur dioxide—and, if the sulfur content of the coal is high, widespread acid deposition. Where coal is not an important primary fuel or is used in plants with effective dust control, the worst emissions of air pollutants stem from the combustion of petroleum products.

The data on sulfur dioxide and nitrogen dioxide concentrations are based on reports from urban monitoring sites. Annual means (measured in micrograms per cubic meter) are average concentrations observed at these sites. Coverage is not comprehensive because not all cities have monitoring systems.

The data on particulate matter concentrations are estimates, for selected cities, of average annual concentrations in residential areas away from air pollution "hotspots," such as industrial districts and transport corridors. The data have been extracted from a complete set of estimates developed by the World Bank's Development Research Group and Environment Department in a study of annual ambient concentrations of particulate matter in world cities with populations exceeding 100,000 (Pandey and others 2003).

Pollutant concentrations are sensitive to local conditions, and even in the same city different monitoring sites may register different concentrations. Thus these data should be considered only a general indication of air quality in each city, and cross-country comparisons should be made with caution. The current World Health Organization (WHO) air quality guidelines for annual mean concentrations are 50 micrograms per cubic meter for sulfur dioxide and 40 micrograms for nitrogen dioxide. The WHO has set no guidelines for particulate matter concentrations below which there are no appreciable health effects.

City		City population	Particulate matter	Sulfur dioxide	Nitrogen dioxide
		thousands	micrograms per cubic meter	micrograms per cubic meter	microgram per cubic meter
		2000	**1999**	**1995–2001**[a]	**1995–2001**[a]
India	Calcutta	13,822	153	49	34
	Chennai	6,002	..	15	17
	Delhi	10,558	187	24	41
	Hyderabad	5,448	51	12	17
	Kanpur	2,546	136	15	14
	Lucknow	2,093	136	26	25
	Mumbai	15,797	79	33	39
	Nagpur	2,087	69	6	13
	Pune	3,128	58		
Indonesia	Jakarta	10,845	103	..	..
Iran, Islamic Rep.	Tehran	7,689	71	209	..
Ireland	Dublin	991	23	20	..
Italy	Milan	1,381	36	31	248
	Rome	2,713	35	..	..
	Torino	969	53	..	..
Japan	Osaka	2,626	39	19	63
	Tokyo	12,483	43	18	68
	Yokohama	3,366	32	100	13
Kenya	Nairobi	2,383	49	..	..
Korea, Rep	Pusan	4,075	43	60	51
	Seoul	11,548	45	44	60
	Taegu	2,417	49	81	62
Malaysia	Kuala Lumpur	1,530	24	24	..
Mexico	Mexico City	18,017	69	74	130
Netherlands	Amsterdam	1,131	37	10	58
New Zealand	Auckland	989	15	3	20
Norway	Oslo	805	23	8	43
Philippines	Manila	10,432	60	33	..
Poland	Lodz	873	45	21	43
	Warsaw	1,716	49	16	32
Portugal	Lisbon	3,318	30	8	52
Romania	Bucharest	2,070	25	10	71
Russian Federation	Moscow	8,811	27	109	..
	Omsk	1,206	28	20	34
Singapore	Singapore	3,163	41	20	30
Slovak Republic	Bratislava	456	22	21	27
South Africa	Capetown	2,942	15	21	72
	Durban	1,364	29	31	..
	Johannesburg	2,344	30	19	31
Spain	Barcelona	1,645	43	11	43
	Madrid	3,068	37	24	66
Sweden	Stockholm	916	15	3	20
Switzerland	Zurich	980	24	11	39
Thailand	Bangkok	7,296	82	11	23
Turkey	Ankara	3,702	53	55	46
	Istanbul	9,286	62	120	..
Ukraine	Kiev	2,622	45	14	51
United Kingdom	Birmingham	2,344	17	9	45
	London	7,812	23	25	77
	Manchester	2,325	19	26	49
United States	Chicago	9,024	27	14	57
	Los Angeles	16,195	38	9	74
	New York	20,951	23	26	79
Venezuela, RB	Caracas	3,488	18	33	57

a. Data are for the most recent year available.

Definitions

• **City population** is the number of residents of the city or metropolitan area as defined by national authorities and reported to the United Nations.
• **Particulate matter** refers to fine suspended particulates less than 10 microns in diameter that are capable of penetrating deep into the respiratory tract and causing significant health damage. The state of a country's technology and pollution controls is an important determinant of particulate matter concentrations. • **Sulfur dioxide** is an air pollutant produced when fossil fuels containing sulfur are burned. It contributes to acid rain and can damage human health, particularly that of the young and the elderly.
• **Nitrogen dioxide** is a poisonous, pungent gas formed when nitric oxide combines with hydrocarbons and sunlight, producing a photochemical reaction. These conditions occur in both natural and anthropogenic activities. Nitrogen dioxide is emitted by bacteria, motor vehicles, industrial activities, nitrogenous fertilizers, combustion of fuels and biomass, and aerobic decomposition of organic matter in soils and oceans.

Data sources

City population data are from the United Nations Population Division. The data on sulfur dioxide and nitrogen dioxide concentrations are from the WHO's Healthy Cities Air Management Information System and the World Resources Institute, which relies on various national sources as well as, among others, the Organisation for Economic Co-operation and Development's (OECD) *OECD Environmental Data Compendium 1999*, the U.S. Environmental Protection Agency's *National Air Quality and Emissions Trends Report 1995*, the Aerometric Information Retrieval System (AIRS) Executive International database, and the United Nations Centre for Human Settlements' (UNCHS) Urban Indicators database. The data on particulate matter concentrations are from a recent World Bank study by Kiran D. Pandey, Katharine Bolt, Uwe Deichman, Kirk Hamilton, Bart Ostro, and David Wheeler, "The Human Cost of Air Pollution: New Estimates for Developing Countries" (2003).

Government commitment

	Environmental strategies or action plans	Biodiversity assessments, strategies or action plans	Participation in treaties[a]					
			Climate change[b]	Ozone layer	CFC control	Law of the Sea[c]	Biological diversity[b]	Kyoto Protocol
Afghanistan	..	..	2002	..	..	..	2002	..
Albania	1993	..	1995	1999	1999	2003[f]	1994[f]	..
Algeria	2001	..	1994	1992	1992	1996	1995	..
Angola	..	..	2000	2000	2000	1994	1998	..
Argentina	1992	..	1994	1990	1990	1996	1995	2001
Armenia	..	..	1994	1999	1999	2002[f]	1993[d]	2003[f]
Australia	1992	1994	1994	1987	1989	1995	1993	..
Austria	..	..	1994	1987	1989	1995	1994	2002
Azerbaijan	1998	..	1995	1996	1996	..	2000[e]	2000[f]
Bangladesh	1991	1990	1994	1990	1990	2001	1994	2001[f]
Belarus	..	..	2000	1986	1988	..	1993	..
Belgium	..	..	1996	1988	1988	1998	1997	2002
Benin	1993	..	1994	1993	1993	1997	1994	2002[f]
Bolivia	1994	1988	1995	1994	1994	1995	1995	1999
Bosnia and Herzegovina	..	..	2000	1992	1992	1994[g]	2002[f]	..
Botswana	1990	1991	1994	1991	1991	1994	1996	2003[f]
Brazil	..	1988	1994	1990	1990	1994	1994	2002
Bulgaria	..	1994	1995	1990	1990	1996	1996	2002
Burkina Faso	1993	..	1994	1989	1989	..	1993	..
Burundi	1994	1989	1997	1997	1997	..	1997	2001[f]
Cambodia	1999	..	1996	2001	2001	..	1995[f]	2002[f]
Cameroon	..	1989	1995	1989	1989	1994	1995	2002[f]
Canada	1990	1994	1994	1986	1988	2003	1993	2002
Central African Republic	..	..	1995	1993	1993	..	1995	..
Chad	1990	..	1994	1989	1994	..	1994	..
Chile	..	1993	1995	1990	1990	1997	1994	2002
China	1994	1994	1994	1989	1991	1996	1993	2002[e]
Hong Kong, China	..	..	..	..	..	..	..	..
Colombia	1998	1988	1995	1990	1993	..	1995	2001[f]
Congo, Dem. Rep.	..	1990	1995	1994	1994	1994	1995	..
Congo, Rep.	..	1990	1997	1994	1994	..	1996	..
Costa Rica	1990	1992	1994	1991	1991	1994	1994	2002
Côte d'Ivoire	1994	1991	1995	1993	1993	1994	1995	..
Croatia	2001	2000	1996	1991	1991	1994[g]	1997	..
Cuba	..	..	1994	1992	1992	1994	1994	..
Czech Republic	1994	..	1994	1993	1993	1996	1994[e]	2001[e]
Denmark	1994	..	1994	1988	1988	..	1994	2002
Dominican Republic	..	1995	1999	1993	1993	..	1996	2002[f]
Ecuador	1993	1995	1994	1990	1990	..	1993	2000
Egypt, Arab Rep.	1992	1988	1995	1988	1988	1994	1994	..
El Salvador	1994	1988	1996	1992	1992	..	1994	1998
Eritrea	1995	..	1995	..	..	..	1996[f]	..
Estonia	1998	..	1994	1996	1996	..	1994	2002
Ethiopia	1994	1991	1994	1994	1994	..	1994	..
Finland	1995	..	1994	1986	1988	1996	1994[d]	2002
France	1990	..	1994	1987	1988	1996	1994	2002[e]
Gabon	..	1990	1998	1994	1994	1998	2000	..
Gambia, The	1992	1989	1994	1990	1990	1998	1994	2001[f]
Georgia	1998	..	1994	1996	1996	1996[f]	1994[f]	1999[f]
Germany	..	..	1994	1988	1988	1994[f]	1994	2002
Ghana	1992	1988	1995	1989	1989	1994	1994	2003[f]
Greece	..	..	1994	1988	1988	1995	1994	2002
Guatemala	1994	1988	1996	1987	1989	1997	1995	1999
Guinea	1994	1988	1994	1992	1992	1994	1993	2000[f]
Guinea-Bissau	1993	1991	1996	2002	2002	1994	1996	..
Haiti	1999	..	1996	2000	2000	1996	1996	..

3.14a

The Kyoto Protocol on climate change

The Kyoto Protocol was adopted at the third conference of the parties to the United Nations Framework Convention on Climate Change, held in Kyoto, Japan, in December 1997 and was open for signature from March 1998 onward.

At the heart of the protocol are its legally binding greenhouse gas emissions targets for industrial and transition economies (known as "Annex I Parties"), which accounted for at least 55 percent of carbon dioxide emissions in 1990. The emissions targets amount to an aggregate reduction of greenhouse gas emissions by all Annex I Parties of at least 5 percent from 1990 levels during the commitment period, 2008–12. All Annex I Parties have individual emissions targets, which were decided in Kyoto after intensive negotiation and are listed in the protocol's Annex B.

The protocol's rules focus on:
- Commitments, including legally binding emissions targets and general commitments.
- Implementation, including domestic steps and three novel implementing mechanisms.
- Minimization of impacts on developing countries, including use of an Adaptation Fund.
- Accounting, reporting, and review, including in-depth review of national reporting.
- Compliance, including a Compliance Committee to assess and deal with problem cases.

In addition to emissions targets for Annex I Parties, the Kyoto Protocol also contains a set of general commitments that apply to all parties, such as:
- Improving the quality of emissions data.
- Mounting national mitigation and adaptation programs.
- Promoting environmentally friendly technology transfer.
- Cooperating in scientific research and international climate observation networks.
- Supporting education, training, public awareness, and capacity building initiatives.

The Protocol is subject to ratification, acceptance, approval, or accession by Parties to the Convention, which bind the parties to the protocol's commitments, once the protocol comes into force.

The table contains the latest information on dates of signature and ratification from the Secretary-General of the United Nations, the depository of the Kyoto Protocol. The dates are those of the receipt of the instrument of ratification, acceptance, approval, or accession. As of November 2003, 84 parties had signed the Kyoto Protocol and 120 parties had ratified or accepted it.

	Environ-mental strategies or action plans	Biodiversity assessments, strategies or action plans	Participation in treaties[a]					
			Climate change[b]	Ozone layer	CFC control	Law of the Sea[c]	Biological diversity[b]	Kyoto Protocol
Honduras	1993	..	1996	1993	1993	1994	1995	2000
Hungary	1995	..	1994	1988	1989	2002	1994	2002[f]
India	1993	1994	1994	1991	1992	1995	1994	2002[f]
Indonesia	1993	1993	1994	1992	1992	1994	1994	..
Iran, Islamic Rep.	..	..	1996	1990	1990	..	1996	..
Iraq	..	..	..	..	..	1994	..	..
Ireland	..	..	1994	1988	1988	1996	1996	2002
Israel	..	..	1996	1992	1992	..	1995	..
Italy	..	..	1994	1988	1988	1995	1994	2002
Jamaica	1994	..	1995	1993	1993	1994	1995	1999[f]
Japan	..	..	1994	1988	1988	1996	1993[d]	2002[d]
Jordan	1991	..	1994	1989	1989	1995[f]	1994	2003[f]
Kazakhstan	..	..	1995	1998	1998	..	1994	..
Kenya	1994	1992	1994	1988	1988	1994	1994	..
Korea, Dem. Rep.	..	..	1995	1995	1995	..	1995[e]	..
Korea, Rep.	..	..	1994	1992	1992	1996	1995	2002
Kuwait	..	..	1995	1992	1992	1994	2002	..
Kyrgyz Republic	1995	..	2000	2000	2000	..	1996[e]	2003[f]
Lao PDR	1995	..	1995	1998	1998	1998	1996[e]	2003[f]
Latvia	..	..	1995	1995	1995	..	1996	2002
Lebanon	..	..	1995	1993	1993	1995	1995	..
Lesotho	1989	..	1995	1994	1994	..	1995	2000[f]
Liberia	..	..	2003	1996	1996	..	2000	2002[f]
Libya	..	..	1999	1990	1990	..	2001	..
Lithuania	..	..	1995	1995	1995	2003[f]	1996	2003
Macedonia, FYR	..	..	1998	1994	1994	1994[g]	1997[f]	..
Madagascar	1988	1991	1999	1996	1996	2001	1996	2003[f]
Malawi	1994	..	1994	1991	1991	..	1994	2001[f]
Malaysia	1991	1988	1994	1989	1989	1997	1994	2002
Mali	..	1989	1995	1994	1994	1994	1995	2002
Mauritania	1988	..	1994	1994	1994	1996	1996	..
Mauritius	1990	..	1994	1992	1992	1994	1993	2001[f]
Mexico	..	1988	1994	1987	1988	1994	1993	2000
Moldova	2002	..	1995	1996	1996	..	1996	2003[f]
Mongolia	1995	..	1994	1996	1996	1997	1993	1999[f]
Morocco	..	1988	1996	1995	1995	..	1995	2002[f]
Mozambique	1994	..	1995	1994	1994	1997	1995	..
Myanmar	..	1989	1995	1993	1993	1996	1995	2003[f]
Namibia	1992	..	1995	1993	1993	1994	1997	2003[f]
Nepal	1993	..	1994	1994	1994	1998	1994	..
Netherlands	1994	..	1994	1988	1988	1996	1994[d]	2002[f]
New Zealand	1994	..	1994	1987	1988	1996	1993	2002
Nicaragua	1994	..	1996	1993	1993	2000	1996	1999
Niger	..	1991	1995	1992	1992	..	1995	..
Nigeria	1990	1992	1994	1988	1988	1994	1994	..
Norway	..	1994	1994	1986	1988	1996	1993	2002
Oman	..	..	1995	1999	1999	1994	1995	..
Pakistan	1994	1991	1994	1992	1992	1997	1994	..
Panama	1990	..	1995	1989	1989	1996	1995	1999
Papua New Guinea	1992	1993	1994	1992	1992	1997	1993	2002
Paraguay	..	..	1994	1992	1992	1994	1994	1999
Peru	..	1988	1994	1989	1993	..	1993	2002
Philippines	1989	1989	1994	1991	1991	1994	1994	2003
Poland	1993	1991	1994	1990	1990	1998	1996	2002
Portugal	1995	..	1994	1988	1988	1997	1994	2002[e]
Puerto Rico	..	..	..	..	..	..	..	..

3.14b

Global atmospheric concentrations of chlorofluorocarbons have leveled off

Parts per trillion

Chlorofluorocarbon-12

Chlorofluorocarbon-11

Chlorofluorocarbon-113

Note: Chlorofluorocarbon-11, chlorofluorocarbon-12, and chlorofluorocarbon-113 are potent depletors of strato-spheric ozone.
Source: World Resources Institute and others 2002.

	Environ-mental strategies or action plans	Biodiversity assessments, strategies or action plans	Participation in treaties [a]					
			Climate change [b]	Ozone layer	CFC control	Law of the Sea [c]	Biological diversity [b]	Kyoto Protocol
Romania	1995	..	1994	1993	1993	1997	1994	2001
Russian Federation	1999	1994	1995	1986	1988	1997	1995	..
Rwanda	1991	..	1998	2001	2001	..	1996	..
Saudi Arabia	..	..	1995	1993	1993	1996	2001 [e]	..
Senegal	1984	1991	1995	1993	1993	1994	1995	2001 [f]
Serbia and Montenegro	..	..	2001	1992	1992	2001 [g]	2002	..
Sierra Leone	1994	..	1995	2001	2001	1995	1995 [e]	..
Singapore	1993	1995	1997	1989	1989	1994	1996	..
Slovak Republic	..	..	1994	1993	1993	1996	1994 [e]	2002
Slovenia	1994	..	1996	1992	1992	1994 [g]	1996	2002
Somalia	..	..	..	2001	2001	1994	..	..
South Africa	1993	..	1997	1990	1990	1997	2000	2002 [f]
Spain	..	..	1994	1988	1988	1997	1994	2002
Sri Lanka	1994	1991	1994	1989	1989	1994	1994	2002 [f]
Sudan	..	..	1994	1993	1993	1994	1996	..
Swaziland	..	..	1997	1992	1992	..	1995	..
Sweden	..	..	1994	1986	1988	1996	1994	2002
Switzerland	..	..	1994	1987	1988	..	1995	2003
Syrian Arab Republic	1999	..	1996	1989	1989	..	1996	..
Tajikistan	..	..	1998	1996	1998	..	1997 [e]	..
Tanzania	1994	1988	1996	1993	1993	1994	1996	2002 [f]
Thailand	..	..	1995	1989	1989	..	..	2002
Togo	1991	..	1995	1991	1991	1994	1996 [d]	..
Trinidad and Tobago	..	..	1994	1989	1989	1994 [f]	1996	1999
Tunisia	1994	1988	1994	1989	1989	1994	1993	2003 [f]
Turkey	1998	..	..	1991	1991	..	1997	..
Turkmenistan	..	..	1995	1993	1993	..	1996 [e]	1999
Uganda	1994	1988	1994	1988	1988	1994	1993	2002 [f]
Ukraine	1999	..	1997	1986	1988	1999	1995	..
United Arab Emirates	..	..	1996	1989	1989	..	2000	..
United Kingdom	1995	1994	1994	1987	1988	1997 [f]	1994	2002
United States	1995	1995	1994	1986	1988	..	..	..
Uruguay	..	..	1994	1989	1991	1994	1994	2001
Uzbekistan	..	..	1994	1993	1993	..	1995 [e]	1999
Venezuela	..	..	1995	1988	1989	..	1994	..
Vietnam	..	1993	1995	1994	1994	1994	1995	2002
West Bank and Gaza	..	..	..	..	..	..	..	..
Yemen, Rep.	1996	1992	1996	1996	1996	1994	1996	..
Zambia	1994	..	1994	1990	1990	1994	1993	..
Zimbabwe	1987	..	1994	1992	1992	1994	1995	..

a. Ratification of the treaty. b. The years shown refer to the year the treaty entered into force in that country. c. Convention became effective November 16, 1994. d. Acceptance. e. Approval. f. Accession. g. Succession.

3.14c

Global focus on biodiversity and climate change

Allocation of funds for Global Environment Facility programs, February 1991–January 2004
Total allocation: $19,944 million

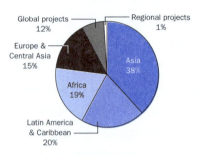

By region

- Global projects 12%
- Regional projects 1%
- Europe & Central Asia 15%
- Asia 38%
- Africa 19%
- Latin America & Caribbean 20%

By focal area

- Multiple areas 6%
- Ozone depletion 2%
- Persistent organic pollutants 1%
- International waters 11%
- Climate change 54%
- Biodiversity 26%

Source: Global Environment Facility data.

About the data

National environmental strategies and participation in international treaties on environmental issues provide some evidence of government commitment to sound environmental management. But the signing of these treaties does not always imply ratification, nor does it guarantee that governments will comply with treaty obligations.

In many countries efforts to halt environmental degradation have failed, primarily because governments have neglected to make this issue a priority, a reflection of competing claims on scarce resources. To address this problem, many countries are preparing national environmental strategies—some focusing narrowly on environmental issues, and others integrating environmental, economic, and social concerns. Among such initiatives are conservation strategies and environmental action plans. Some countries have also prepared country environmental profiles and biodiversity strategies and profiles.

National conservation strategies—promoted by the World Conservation Union (IUCN)—provide a comprehensive, cross-sectoral analysis of conservation and resource management issues to help integrate environmental concerns with the development process. Such strategies discuss current and future needs, institutional capabilities, prevailing technical conditions, and the status of natural resources in a country.

National environmental action plans, supported by the World Bank and other development agencies, describe a country's main environmental concerns, identify the principal causes of environmental problems, and formulate policies and actions to deal with them (table 3.14a). These plans are a continuing process in which governments develop comprehensive environmental policies, recommend specific actions, and outline the investment strategies, legislation, and institutional arrangements required to implement them.

Biodiversity profiles—prepared by the World Conservation Monitoring Centre and the IUCN—provide basic background on species diversity, protected areas, major ecosystems and habitat types, and legislative and administrative support. In an effort to establish a scientific baseline for measuring progress in biodiversity conservation, the United Nations Environment Programme (UNEP) coordinates global biodiversity assessments.

To address global issues, many governments have also signed international treaties and agreements launched in the wake of the 1972 United Nations Conference on Human Environment in Stockholm and the 1992 United Nations Conference on Environment and Development (the Earth Summit) in Rio de Janeiro, which produced Agenda 21—an array of actions to address environmental challenges:

- The Framework Convention on Climate Change aims to stabilize atmospheric concentrations of greenhouse gases at levels that will prevent human activities from interfering dangerously with the global climate.
- The Vienna Convention for the Protection of the Ozone Layer aims to protect human health and the environment by promoting research on the effects of changes in the ozone layer and on alternative substances (such as substitutes for chlorofluorocarbons) and technologies, monitoring the ozone layer, and taking measures to control the activities that produce adverse effects.
- The Montreal Protocol for CFC Control requires that countries help protect the earth from excessive ultraviolet radiation by cutting chlorofluorocarbon consumption by 20 percent over their 1986 level by 1994 and by 50 percent over their 1986 level by 1999, with allowances for increases in consumption by developing countries.
- The United Nations Convention on the Law of the Sea, which became effective in November 1994, establishes a comprehensive legal regime for seas and oceans, establishes rules for environmental standards and enforcement provisions, and develops international rules and national legislation to prevent and control marine pollution.
- The Convention on Biological Diversity promotes conservation of biodiversity among nations through scientific and technological cooperation, access to financial and genetic resources, and transfer of ecologically sound technologies.

But 10 years after Rio the World Summit on Sustainable Development recognized that many of the proposed actions have yet to materialize. To help developing countries comply with their obligations under these agreements, the Global Environment Facility (GEF) was created to focus on global improvement in biodiversity, climate change, international waters, and ozone layer depletion. The UNEP, United Nations Development Programme (UNDP), and the World Bank manage the GEF according to the policies of its governing body of country representatives. The World Bank is responsible for the GEF Trust Fund and is chair of the GEF.

Definitions

- **Environmental strategies and action plans** provide a comprehensive, cross-sectoral analysis of conservation and resource management issues to help integrate environmental concerns with the development process. They include national conservation strategies, national environmental action plans, national environmental management strategies, and national sustainable development strategies. The year shown for a country refers to the year in which a strategy or action plan was adopted. • **Biodiversity assessments, strategies, and action plans** include biodiversity profiles (see *About the data*). • **Participation in treaties** covers five international treaties (see *About the data*). • **Climate change** refers to the Framework Convention on Climate Change (signed in New York in 1992). • **Ozone layer** refers to the Vienna Convention for the Protection of the Ozone Layer (signed in 1985). • **CFC control** refers to the Montreal Protocol for Chlorofluorocarbon Control (formally, the Protocol on Substances That Deplete the Ozone Layer, signed in 1987). • **Law of the Sea** refers to the United Nations Convention on the Law of the Sea (signed in Montego Bay, Jamaica, in 1982). • **Biological diversity** refers to the Convention on Biological Diversity (signed at the Earth Summit in Rio de Janeiro in 1992). The year shown for a country refers to the year in which a treaty entered into force in that country. • **Kyoto Protocol** refers to the protocol on climate change adopted at the third conference of the parties to the United Nations Framework Convention on Climate Change, held in Kyoto, Japan, in December 1997 (for more details see box 3.14a).

Data sources

The data are from the Secretariat of the United Nations Framework Convention on Climate Change, the Ozone Secretariat of the UNEP, the World Resources Institute, the UNEP, the U.S. National Aeronautics and Space Administration's Socioeconomic Data and Applications Center, and Center for International Earth Science Information Network.

3.15 Toward a broader measure of savings

	Gross national savings [a]	Consumption of fixed capital	Net national savings	Education expenditure	Energy depletion	Mineral depletion	Net forest depletion	Carbon dioxide damage	Particulate emissions damage	Adjusted net savings
	% of GNI	% of GNI	% of GNI	% of GNI	% of GNI	% of GNI	% of GNI	% of GNI	% of GNI	% of GNI
	2002	2002	2002	2002	2002	2002	2002	2002	2002	2002
Afghanistan	..	..	..	..	..	..	..	..	..	..
Albania	13.8	9.1	4.7	2.8	1.0	0.0	0.0	0.3	0.1	6.1
Algeria	..	11.1	..	4.5	33.4	0.1	0.1	1.3	0.7	..
Angola	23.3	10.4	12.9	4.4	36.3	0.0	0.0	0.5	..	−19.6 [b]
Argentina	22.3	11.1	11.2	3.2	5.4	0.2	0.0	0.8	1.6	6.5
Armenia	13.9	8.5	5.3	1.8	0.0	0.1	0.0	1.1	2.0	4.0
Australia	19.7	16.2	3.5	5.2	1.2	1.4	0.0	0.6	0.1	5.4
Austria	21.4	14.4	7.0	5.0	0.1	0.0	0.0	0.2	0.2	11.5
Azerbaijan	21.5	15.0	6.5	3.0	38.7	0.0	0.0	5.2	1.0	−35.3
Bangladesh	28.5	5.8	22.7	1.3	0.8	0.0	0.8	0.4	0.3	21.7
Belarus	18.6	9.3	9.3	5.4	2.2	0.0	0.0	3.4	0.0	9.2
Belgium	23.4	14.5	8.9	3.0	0.0	0.0	0.0	0.3	0.2	11.4
Benin	9.2	8.1	1.1	2.7	0.1	0.0	1.3	0.4	0.3	1.8
Bolivia	12.2	9.1	3.1	4.8	5.9	0.8	0.0	1.1	0.7	−0.5
Bosnia and Herzegovina	7.5	8.5	−1.0	..	0.1	0.0	0.0	2.4	0.4	..
Botswana	..	11.8	..	5.6	0.0	0.2	0.0	0.6	..	..
Brazil	19.7	10.8	8.9	4.7	2.9	1.1	0.0	0.5	0.2	9.0
Bulgaria	15.4	10.3	5.1	3.0	0.2	0.4	0.0	2.2	2.1	3.3
Burkina Faso	8.0	6.7	1.3	2.4	0.0	0.0	1.2	0.3	0.5	1.8
Burundi	11.0	6.4	4.6	3.9	0.0	0.1	10.4	0.2	0.1	−2.3
Cambodia	18.5	7.3	11.2	1.8	0.0	0.0	0.9	0.1	0.1	11.9
Cameroon	..	8.9	..	2.3	6.2	0.0	0.0	0.6	0.7	..
Canada	23.2	13.0	10.2	6.9	4.0	0.1	0.0	0.5	0.2	12.3
Central African Republic	..	7.8	..	1.6	0.0	0.0	0.0	0.2	0.4	..
Chad	..	7.2	..	1.4	0.0	0.0	0.0	0.1	..	..
Chile	24.5	10.0	14.4	3.4	0.2	4.7	0.0	0.7	1.0	11.2
China	43.7	9.0	34.7	2.0	2.7	0.2	0.0	2.2	1.0	30.7
Hong Kong, China	32.1	12.9	19.2	2.8	0.0	0.0	0.0	0.2	0.0	21.8
Colombia	13.7	10.5	3.2	3.1	6.5	0.2	0.0	0.5	0.1	−1.0
Congo, Dem. Rep.	..	6.8	..	0.9	1.8	0.0	0.0	0.3	0.0	..
Congo, Rep.	34.6	12.5	22.2	5.9	47.4	0.2	0.0	0.8	..	..
Costa Rica	15.1	5.9	9.2	5.2	0.0	0.0	0.3	0.2	0.3	13.5
Côte d'Ivoire	20.5	9.2	11.3	4.5	0.0	0.0	0.6	0.5	0.6	14.1
Croatia	21.2	11.5	9.7	..	0.6	0.0	0.0	0.6	0.3	..
Cuba	..	..	..	6.1	..	..	..	..	..	..
Czech Republic	23.0	12.2	10.7	4.4	0.1	0.0	0.0	1.2	0.1	13.8
Denmark	23.4	15.4	8.0	7.7	0.3	0.0	0.0	0.2	0.1	15.0
Dominican Republic	20.4	5.3	15.1	1.7	0.0	0.3	0.0	0.9	0.2	15.4
Ecuador	..	10.6	..	3.2	13.8	0.0	0.0	1.2	0.1	..
Egypt, Arab Rep.	15.1	9.5	5.6	4.4	4.6	0.1	0.2	1.0	1.4	2.7
El Salvador	14.2	10.4	3.8	2.2	0.0	0.0	0.6	0.3	0.2	4.9
Eritrea	21.7	5.2	16.6	1.4	0.0	0.0	0.0	0.5	0.5	16.9
Estonia	20.2	14.2	6.0	6.3	0.5	0.0	0.0	2.2	0.2	9.4
Ethiopia	15.4	6.1	9.3	4.0	0.0	0.1	12.8	0.6	0.3	−0.5
Finland	27.0	16.1	11.0	7.0	0.0	0.0	0.0	0.3	0.1	17.5
France	21.1	12.4	8.7	5.6	0.0	0.0	0.0	0.2	0.0	14.0
Gabon	40.7	12.9	27.8	2.2	27.8	0.0	0.0	0.6	0.1	1.5
Gambia, The	..	8.4	..	3.4	0.0	0.0	0.6	0.5	0.7	..
Georgia	15.0	15.7	−0.7	4.3	0.5	0.0	0.0	1.0	2.5	−0.5
Germany	20.4	14.8	5.5	4.4	0.1	0.0	0.0	0.3	0.1	9.5
Ghana	20.4	7.1	13.3	2.8	0.0	1.2	2.7	0.8	0.2	11.3
Greece	19.7	8.7	11.0	3.1	0.1	0.0	0.0	0.5	0.7	12.8
Guatemala	14.8	10.1	4.7	1.6	0.7	0.0	0.9	0.3	0.2	4.2
Guinea	17.1	8.1	9.0	2.0	0.0	1.7	1.9	0.3	0.6	6.5
Guinea-Bissau	..	7.7	..	..	0.0	0.0	0.0	0.7	0.9	..
Haiti	..	1.9	..	1.5	0.0	0.0	0.9	0.3	0.2	..

Toward a broader measure of savings

	Gross national savings [a]	Consumption of fixed capital	Net national savings	Education expenditure	Energy depletion	Mineral depletion	Net forest depletion	Carbon dioxide damage	Particulate emissions damage	Adjusted net savings
	% of GNI 2002	% of GNI 2002	% of GNI 2002	% of GNI 2002	% of GNI 2002	% of GNI 2002	% of GNI 2002	% of GNI 2002	% of GNI 2002	% of GNI 2002
Honduras	23.3	5.6	17.7	3.5	0.0	0.2	0.0	0.5	0.2	20.4
Hungary	23.5	11.8	11.7	4.3	0.3	0.0	0.0	0.7	0.4	14.6
India	22.3	9.7	12.6	3.2	2.3	0.3	1.0	1.7	0.7	9.8
Indonesia	18.2	5.4	12.7	0.6	8.6	1.2	0.0	0.9	0.5	2.1
Iran, Islamic Rep.	38.9	9.7	29.2	3.5	29.7	0.2	0.0	2.1	0.7	0.1
Iraq	..	..	..	..	..	..	..	..	..	..
Ireland	28.0	12.5	15.5	5.7	0.0	0.1	0.0	0.4	0.1	20.6
Israel	13.4	13.2	0.2	6.9	0.0	0.1	0.0	0.4	0.0	6.7
Italy	19.8	13.6	6.1	4.7	0.1	0.0	0.0	0.2	0.2	10.3
Jamaica	20.7	11.6	9.1	5.8	0.0	1.2	0.0	0.9	0.3	12.4
Japan	27.2	15.8	11.4	3.6	0.0	0.0	0.0	0.2	0.4	14.4
Jordan	26.2	10.6	15.6	5.6	0.0	1.1	0.0	1.2	0.7	18.2
Kazakhstan	25.5	10.0	15.5	4.4	33.4	0.0	0.0	4.4	0.4	–18.3
Kenya	13.7	7.9	5.7	6.1	0.0	0.0	0.1	0.4	0.2	11.0
Korea, Dem. Rep.	..	..	..	..	..	..	..	..	..	..
Korea, Rep.	27.3	12.0	15.3	3.7	0.0	0.0	0.0	0.7	0.8	17.5
Kuwait	19.4	6.7	12.7	5.0	42.2	0.0	0.0	0.8	2.0	–27.3
Kyrgyz Republic	17.4	8.2	9.2	5.1	1.0	0.0	0.0	2.6	0.2	10.5
Lao PDR	..	8.0	..	1.8	0.0	0.0	0.0	0.2	0.2	..
Latvia	19.6	10.8	8.9	6.1	0.0	0.0	0.0	0.7	0.3	13.9
Lebanon	2.1	10.3	–8.2	2.5	0.0	0.0	0.0	0.6	0.6	–6.8
Lesotho	22.0	6.5	15.4	6.4	0.0	0.0	2.5	0.0	0.4	18.9
Liberia	..	8.2	..	..	0.0	0.2	3.3	1.1	0.0	..
Libya	..	..	..	..	..	..	..	..	..	..
Lithuania	17.4	10.1	7.2	5.2	0.3	0.0	0.0	0.9	0.7	10.5
Macedonia, FYR	12.9	9.8	3.1	4.9	0.0	0.0	0.0	2.0	0.3	5.8
Madagascar	8.5	7.9	0.6	1.9	0.0	0.0	0.0	0.3	0.2	2.0
Malawi	0.8	7.0	–6.3	4.4	0.0	0.0	1.4	0.3	0.2	–3.7
Malaysia	34.5	11.7	22.8	4.1	8.9	0.0	0.0	1.0	0.1	16.8
Mali	3.2	8.4	–5.2	2.1	0.0	0.0	0.0	0.2	0.5	–3.8
Mauritania	..	8.1	..	3.7	0.0	20.5	0.9	2.4	..	..
Mauritius	27.7	10.8	16.9	3.3	0.0	0.0	0.0	0.4	..	..
Mexico	18.3	10.5	7.8	4.6	4.9	0.1	0.0	0.5	0.5	6.5
Moldova	14.4	7.3	7.2	10.3	0.0	0.0	0.0	3.3	0.5	13.6
Mongolia	26.7	12.1	14.6	5.7	0.0	2.3	0.0	4.8	0.5	12.7
Morocco	26.1	10.0	16.1	4.9	0.0	0.2	0.0	0.7	0.2	19.9
Mozambique	27.7	8.3	19.4	3.8	0.0	0.0	0.0	0.3	0.4	22.4
Myanmar	12.4	..	..	0.9	..	..	..	..	..	..
Namibia	39.6	11.5	28.1	8.5	0.0	0.4	0.0	0.4	0.2	35.6
Nepal	22.1	2.4	19.8	3.2	0.0	0.0	4.2	0.4	0.1	18.2
Netherlands	22.2	15.0	7.2	4.9	0.1	0.0	0.0	0.3	0.4	11.3
New Zealand	19.4	10.8	8.6	6.9	0.9	0.1	0.0	0.4	0.0	14.2
Nicaragua	11.2	..	..	3.7	0.0	0.1	0.9	0.6	0.0	..
Niger	..	7.1	..	2.3	0.0	0.0	3.6	0.4	0.4	..
Nigeria	13.1	8.3	4.8	0.5	38.7	0.0	0.0	0.5	0.8	–34.7
Norway	32.0	15.9	16.1	6.9	4.2	0.0	0.0	0.3	0.1	18.4
Oman	..	11.5	..	4.1	40.3	0.0	0.0	0.6	..	..
Pakistan	25.6	7.7	17.9	2.3	3.6	0.0	1.0	1.2	1.0	13.4
Panama	24.2	7.6	16.6	4.8	0.0	0.0	0.0	0.6	0.3	20.4
Papua New Guinea	..	8.6	..	..	10.0	4.2	0.0	0.5	0.0	..
Paraguay	14.2	9.0	5.2	3.9	0.0	0.0	0.0	0.5	0.4	8.3
Peru	17.2	10.4	6.7	2.6	0.9	1.4	0.0	0.3	0.6	6.0
Philippines	24.5	7.9	16.5	2.9	0.0	0.1	0.2	0.7	0.4	18.0
Poland	16.6	11.2	5.4	7.5	0.3	0.1	0.0	1.3	0.7	10.5
Portugal	19.3	15.3	4.0	5.3	0.0	0.0	0.0	0.3	0.4	8.6
Puerto Rico	..	7.4	..	..	0.0	0.0	0.0	0.2	..	..

3.15 Toward a broader measure of savings

	Gross national savings[a]	Consumption of fixed capital	Net national savings	Education expenditure	Energy depletion	Mineral depletion	Net forest depletion	Carbon dioxide damage	Particulate emissions damage	Adjusted net savings
	% of GNI 2002	% of GNI 2002	% of GNI 2002	% of GNI 2002	% of GNI 2002	% of GNI 2002	% of GNI 2002	% of GNI 2002	% of GNI 2002	% of GNI 2002
Romania	19.9	9.8	10.0	3.6	2.3	0.0	0.0	1.4	0.2	9.7
Russian Federation	30.6	10.4	20.1	3.6	25.5	0.3	0.0	3.1	0.6	−5.7
Rwanda	12.2	7.3	4.9	3.5	0.0	0.0	3.9	0.3	0.0	4.2
Saudi Arabia	28.9	10.0	18.9	7.2	42.2	0.0	0.0	0.8	1.0	−17.9
Senegal	11.5	8.4	3.2	3.7	0.0	0.2	0.3	0.6	..	..
Serbia and Montenegro	..	9.6	..	..	0.9	0.1	0.0	1.7	0.2	..
Sierra Leone	..	7.1	..	0.9	0.0	0.0	5.2	0.4	0.4	..
Singapore	42.7	14.4	28.3	2.3	0.0	0.0	0.0	0.6	0.4	29.6
Slovak Republic	23.2	11.2	12.0	4.6	0.0	0.0	0.0	1.2	0.1	15.2
Slovenia	25.2	11.7	13.5	5.3	0.0	0.0	0.0	0.5	0.2	18.2
Somalia	..	..	..	..	..	..	..	..	..	..
South Africa	16.5	13.3	3.2	7.6	1.6	1.2	0.3	2.3	0.2	5.2
Spain	24.0	12.8	11.1	4.6	0.0	0.0	0.0	0.3	0.4	15.0
Sri Lanka	19.9	5.1	14.8	2.9	0.0	0.0	0.6	0.3	0.3	16.3
Sudan	13.1	8.3	4.8	0.9	0.0	0.1	0.0	0.2	0.6	4.8
Swaziland	7.2	8.9	−1.7	5.1	0.0	0.0	0.0	0.2	0.1	3.1
Sweden	21.4	13.4	8.0	8.3	0.1	0.1	0.0	0.1	0.0	16.0
Switzerland	26.8	14.9	12.0	4.9	0.0	0.0	0.0	0.1	0.2	16.6
Syrian Arab Republic	24.3	10.4	13.9	2.6	27.5	0.1	0.0	1.7	0.8	−13.6
Tajikistan	5.0	7.4	−2.5	2.0	0.4	0.0	0.0	3.8	0.2	−4.8
Tanzania	14.5	7.5	7.0	2.4	0.0	0.4	0.0	0.3	0.2	8.5
Thailand	30.4	14.9	15.5	3.6	0.8	0.0	0.3	1.1	0.4	16.5
Togo	8.0	7.8	0.2	4.2	0.0	0.6	3.9	1.0	0.3	−1.4
Trinidad and Tobago	28.9	11.9	17.0	3.3	21.9	0.0	0.0	1.9	0.0	−3.4
Tunisia	22.7	10.1	12.6	6.6	3.6	0.5	0.1	0.7	0.3	13.9
Turkey	16.7	7.0	9.8	2.2	0.3	0.0	0.0	0.7	1.2	9.8
Turkmenistan	36.3	9.7	26.6	..	53.6	0.0	0.0	4.8	0.3	..
Uganda	15.8	7.6	8.2	1.9	0.0	0.0	5.6	0.2	0.0	4.3
Ukraine	27.1	19.0	8.1	6.4	7.6	0.0	0.0	6.3	1.0	−0.5
United Arab Emirates	..	..	..	..	..	..	..	..	..	..
United Kingdom	14.4	11.3	3.1	5.3	0.6	0.0	0.0	0.2	0.1	7.5
United States	14.4	11.8	2.6	5.4	0.9	0.0	0.0	0.4	0.3	6.4
Uruguay	13.5	11.1	2.4	3.0	0.0	0.0	0.3	0.3	1.9	3.0
Uzbekistan	17.2	9.9	7.3	9.4	51.7	0.0	0.0	10.9	0.6	−46.6
Venezuela, RB	26.6	7.4	19.2	4.3	27.0	0.3	0.0	1.0	0.0	−4.8
Vietnam	33.6	8.1	25.4	2.8	6.7	0.0	0.7	1.0	0.4	19.3
West Bank and Gaza	..	7.3	..	..	0.0	0.0	0.0	0.0	..	..
Yemen, Rep.	24.1	9.5	14.6	..	36.0	0.0	0.0	1.1	0.5	..
Zambia	..	8.2	..	2.0	0.0	1.1	0.0	0.4	..	..
Zimbabwe	..	9.0	..	6.9	0.3	0.3	0.0	1.1	0.5	..
World	**19.5 w**	**12.5 w**	**7.0 w**	**4.7 w**	**1.9 w**	**0.1 w**	**0.0 w**	**0.5 w**	**0.3 w**	**8.8 w**
Low income	21.5	8.4	13.1	2.6	5.9	0.4	0.8	1.3	0.6	6.7
Middle income	27.7	10.1	17.6	3.8	7.7	0.3	0.0	1.4	0.7	11.3
Lower middle income	30.8	9.9	20.9	3.2	6.6	0.3	0.1	1.7	0.7	14.6
Upper middle income	21.4	10.6	10.8	5.0	9.7	0.2	0.0	0.7	0.6	4.5
Low & middle income	26.6	9.8	16.8	3.6	7.4	0.3	0.2	1.4	0.6	10.5
East Asia & Pacific	38.8	9.2	29.6	2.2	3.4	0.3	0.1	1.8	0.8	25.5
Europe & Central Asia	22.7	10.5	12.2	4.8	9.7	0.1	..	2.1	0.6	..
Latin America & Carib.	19.3	10.3	9.0	4.2	5.2	0.6	0.0	0.5	0.5	6.3
Middle East & N. Africa	23.4	10.0	13.4	5.2	26.3	0.1	0.0	1.3	0.9	−10.0
South Asia	23.1	9.0	14.0	2.9	2.2	0.3	1.0	1.5	0.7	11.3
Sub-Saharan Africa	15.9	10.2	5.8	5.1	8.1	0.5	0.7	1.1	0.4	0.0
High income	17.4	13.1	4.3	5.0	0.7	0.0	..	0.3	0.3	..
Europe EMU	21.1	13.8	7.4	4.8	0.0	0.0	..	0.3	0.2	..

a. The cutoff date for these data is February 2004; later revisions are not captured in this table. b. Adjusted net savings do not include particulate emission damage.

Adjusted net savings measure the change in value of a specified set of assets, excluding capital gains. If a country's net savings are positive and the accounting includes a sufficiently broad range of assets, economic theory suggests that the present value of social welfare is increasing. Conversely, persistently negative adjusted net savings indicate that an economy is on an unsustainable path.

Adjusted net savings are derived from standard national accounting measures of gross national savings by making four adjustments. First, estimates of capital consumption of produced assets are deducted to obtain net national savings. Second, current expenditures on education are added to net national savings (in standard national accounting these expenditures are treated as consumption). Third, estimates of the depletion of a variety of natural resources are deducted to reflect the decline in asset values associated with their extraction and harvest. And fourth, deductions are made for damage from carbon dioxide and particulate emissions.

The exercise treats education expenditures as an addition to savings effort. But because of the wide variability in the effectiveness of government education expenditures, these figures cannot be construed as the value of investments in human capital. The accounting for human capital is also incomplete because depreciation of human capital is not estimated.

There are also gaps in the accounting of natural resource depletion and pollution costs. Key estimates missing on the resource side include the value of fossil water extracted from aquifers, net depletion of fish stocks, and depletion and degradation of soils. Important pollutants affecting human health and economic assets are excluded because no internationally comparable data are widely available on damage from ground-level ozone or from sulfur oxides.

Estimates of resource depletion are based on the calculation of unit resource rents. An economic rent represents an excess return to a given factor of production—in this case the returns from resource extraction or harvest are higher than the normal rate of return on capital. Natural resources give rise to rents because they are not produced; in contrast, for produced goods and services competitive forces will expand supply until economic profits are driven to zero. For each type of resource and each country, unit resource rents are derived by taking the difference between world prices and the average unit extraction or harvest costs (including a "normal"

return on capital). Unit rents are then multiplied by the physical quantity extracted or harvested in order to arrive at a depletion figure. This figure is one of a range of depletion estimates that are possible, depending on the assumptions made about future quantities, prices, and costs, and there is reason to believe that it is at the high end of the range. Some of the largest depletion estimates in the table should therefore be viewed with caution.

A positive net depletion figure for forest resources implies that the harvest rate exceeds the rate of natural growth; this is not the same as deforestation, which represents a change in land use (see *Definitions* for table 3.4). In principle, there should be an addition to savings in countries where growth exceeds harvest, but empirical estimates suggest that most of this net growth is in forested areas that cannot be exploited economically at present. Because the depletion estimates reflect only timber values, they ignore all the external and nontimber benefits associated with standing forests.

Pollution damage from emissions of carbon dioxide is calculated as the marginal social cost per unit multiplied by the increase in the stock of carbon dioxide. The unit damage figure represents the present value of global damage to economic assets and to human welfare over the time the unit of pollution remains in the atmosphere.

Pollution damage from particulate emissions is estimated by valuing the human health effects from exposure to particulate matter less than 10 microns in diameter. The estimates are calculated as willingness to pay to avoid mortality attributable to particulate emissions (in particular, mortality relating to cardiopulmonary disease in adults, lung cancer in adults, and acute respiratory infections in children).

• **Gross national savings** are calculated as the difference between gross national income and public and private consumption, plus net current transfers. • **Consumption of fixed capital** represents the replacement value of capital used up in the process of production. • **Net national savings** are equal to gross national savings less the value of consumption of fixed capital. • **Education expenditure** refers to public current operating expenditures in education, including wages and salaries and excluding capital investments in buildings and equipment. • **Energy depletion** is equal to the product of unit resource rents and the physical quantities of energy extracted. It covers coal, crude oil, and natural gas. • **Mineral depletion** is equal to the product of unit resource rents and the physical quantities of minerals extracted. It refers to tin, gold, lead, zinc, iron, copper, nickel, silver, bauxite, and phosphate. • **Net forest depletion** is calculated as the product of unit resource rents and the excess of roundwood harvest over natural growth. • **Carbon dioxide emissions damage** is estimated to be $20 per ton of carbon (the unit damage in 1995 U.S. dollars) times the number of tons of carbon emitted. • **Particulate emissions damage** is calculated as the willingness to pay to avoid mortality attributable to particulate emissions. • **Adjusted net savings** are equal to net national savings plus education expenditure and minus energy depletion, mineral depletion, net forest depletion, and carbon dioxide and particulate emissions damage.

Gross national savings are derived from the World Bank's national accounts data files, described in the *Economy* section. Consumption of fixed capital is from the United Nations Statistics Division's *National Accounts Statistics: Main Aggregates and Detailed Tables, 1997,* extrapolated to 2002. The education expenditure data are from the United Nations Statistics Division's *Statistical Yearbook 1997,* extrapolated to 2002. The wide range of data sources and estimation methods used to arrive at resource depletion estimates are described in a World Bank working paper, "Estimating National Wealth" (Kunte and others 1998). The unit damage figure for carbon dioxide emissions is from Fankhauser (1995). The estimates of damage from particulate emissions are from Pandey and others (2003). The conceptual underpinnings of the savings measure appear in Hamilton and Clemens (1999).

4|ECONOMY

In 2002 the world economy grew by 1.9 percent, a slight increase from 1.3 percent in 2001, but below the 2.7 percent annual average in the 1990s. The world's recorded output—and income—grew by more than $1.1 trillion. Lower-middle-income economies saw the fastest growth, followed by low-income economies. Upper-middle-income economies, affected by slowing investment and widespread uncertainty in financial markets, experienced negative growth. High-income economies, accounting for 81 percent of the world's gross domestic product (GDP), almost doubled their growth over 2001, from 0.9 percent to 1.6 percent (figure 4a).

Over the past decade economic growth was fastest in East Asia and Pacific (averaging 7.3 percent a year) and South Asia (5.4 percent). Leading this growth were China and India, each accounting for more than 70 percent of its region's output. These two regions even did comparatively well in 2002, with East Asia registering 6.7 percent growth—demonstrating its continuing recovery from the financial crisis in 1998, when annual growth fell to 0.7 percent—and South Asia recording 4.3 percent growth, a slight decline over 2001.

Output declined in the transition economies of Europe and Central Asia in the 1990s, but recovered in the early 2000s, averaging 3.5 percent growth for 2001–02. Several countries of the former Soviet Union, such as Armenia, Azerbaijan, Kazakhstan, Moldova, Tajikistan, and Turkmenistan, have been registering growth rates of more than 7 percent, buoyed by increased exports of natural gas and petroleum products. But in Russia growth declined from 5 percent in 2001 to 4.3 percent in 2002.

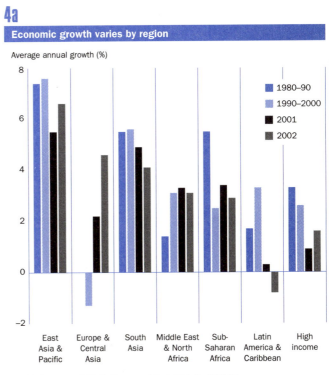

4a

Economic growth varies by region

Average annual growth (%)

- 1980–90
- 1990–2000
- 2001
- 2002

East Asia & Pacific · Europe & Central Asia · South Asia · Middle East & North Africa · Sub-Saharan Africa · Latin America & Caribbean · High income

Note: No data are available for Europe and Central Asia for 1980–90.
Source: World Bank data files.

In Latin America and the Caribbean and the Middle East and North Africa growth was faster in the 1990s than in the 1980s. But in Latin America growth decelerated sharply in 2001 and turned negative in 2002, with Argentina, Uruguay, and Venezuela experiencing large declines in growth and with Mexico growing only 0.9 percent and Brazil only 1.5 percent. However, the heavily indebted poor countries, many in Sub-Saharan Africa, registered 4.1 percent growth in 2002, following 4.7 percent growth in 2001. As a result, Sub-Saharan Africa did better in 2001 and 2002 than in the 1990s, when growth declined sharply.

With two decades of high growth, the East Asia and Pacific region has nearly reached the GDP level of the Latin America and Caribbean region (figure 4b). By contrast GDP in the Europe and Central Asia region, almost equal to that of Latin America and the Caribbean in 1990, is now only about half its size after half a decade of negative growth. Steady growth has also moved South Asia ahead of the Middle East and North Africa, but GDP per capita lags far behind in this populous region.

Patterns of change

Most developing economies are following familiar patterns of growth, with agriculture giving way first to manufacturing and later to services as the main source of income. But some, such as Jordan and Panama, have moved directly from agriculture to service-based economies. For most economies services have been the fastest growing sector. In 1990–2002 the service sector grew by 3.6 percent a year in developing and transition economies and by 3 percent in high-income economies. Among developing regions South Asia had the fastest growth in services in the 1990s, at 7 percent a year, and Europe and Central Asia the slowest, at 0.8 percent (table 4.1).

With two decades of rapid growth, East Asia and Pacific has caught up with Latin America and the Caribbean

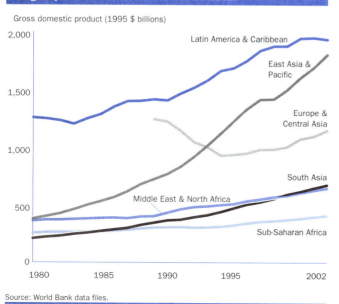

Source: World Bank data files.

In developing economies services generated more than half of GDP in 2002, compared with 71 percent in high-income economies (table 4.2). But in East Asia and Pacific services produced only 38 percent of GDP in 2002, and from 1990 to 2002 growth in manufacturing, at 9.8 percent a year, outpaced growth in services, at 6.4 percent. This trend reflects the rapid growth of manufacturing in China (11.9 percent a year), which also had rapid expansion in services (8.8 percent a year).

The contribution of trade

After expanding by 6.7 percent a year in 1990–2001, global trade (exports plus imports) grew by only 3.7 percent in 2002. High-income economies, which account for more than 75 percent of global trade, grew by only 2.3 percent in 2002, recovering from a slowdown in 2001. But trade by low-income economies grew by 5.6 percent.

Trade in services has grown rapidly, but trade in merchandise—primary commodities and manufactured goods—continues to dominate. In 2002 merchandise accounted for 81 percent of all exports of goods and commercial services, and manufactured goods for 78 percent of merchandise exports (tables 4.5 and 4.7). Exporters of primary nonfuel commodities saw their trade volumes increase, but a continuing decline in their terms of trade left them with less income (table 4.4). The economies of Sub-Saharan Africa were hit particularly hard.

The structure of trade in services is also changing. Transport services are being replaced in importance by travel services. In the 1990s high-income countries were the main exporters of financial services. Now, many developing countries are emerging as exporters of these new services along with computer, information, and business services. The share of low- and middle-income economies in these new service exports is increasing slowly, rising by 1.1 percentage points between 1990 and 2002 (table 4.7).

Increased globalization has enabled greater labor mobility, and worker remittances have been steadily growing in countries like India, resulting in favorable current account balances and increased reserves. India has the ninth largest reserves, ahead of many high-income countries. Japan has the largest reserves, followed by China. The increase in the price of gold from $277 in 2001 to $343 in 2002 resulted in a considerable increase in the reserves of many countries (table 4.15).

Steady trends in consumption, investment, and saving

Most of the world's output goes to final consumption by households (including individuals) and governments. The share of final consumption in world output has remained fairly constant over time, averaging about 80 percent in 1990–2002 (table 4.9). Growth of per capita household consumption expenditure provides an important indicator of the potential for reducing poverty. In 1990–2002 per capita consumption grew by 5.5 percent a year in East Asia and Pacific but rose by only 0.1 percent in Sub-Saharan Africa. It rose by 1.7 in Europe and Central Asia and by 2.7 percent in South Asia (table 4.10).

Output that is not consumed goes to exports (less imports) and gross capital formation (investment). Investment is financed out of domestic and foreign savings. In 2002 the global savings rate averaged 20 percent of total output. But global averages disguise large differences between countries. Savings rates are consistently lower in Sub-Saharan Africa. And they tend to be volatile in countries dependent on commodity exports. Gross domestic savings in the Middle East and North Africa rose from 23 percent of GDP in 1999 to 30 percent in 2000 and 29 percent in 2002, buoyed by higher oil prices. The highest savings rate was in East Asia and Pacific, where gross domestic savings averaged above 35 percent during most of the past decade and was 37 percent in 2002 (table 4.9).

In 1990–2002 the rate of gross capital formation increased by about 6.9 percent a year in East Asia and Pacific and 6.5 percent in South Asia, but declined by 6.6 percent in Europe and Central Asia. East Asia and Pacific continued to have the highest investment rate in the world, at 32 percent of GDP in 2002. By contrast, investment averaged only 18 percent of GDP in Sub-Saharan Africa (tables 4.9 and 4.10).

Fiscal affairs

Developing countries have had larger overall central government deficits than high-income countries. But with the exception of East Asia and Pacific and Latin America and the Caribbean, deficits have been falling. The South Asia region has the largest deficit among the developing regions. Central governments of developing economies had expenditures averaging 21 percent of GDP in 1999 and revenues (mainly from taxes on goods and services) averaging 17 percent of GDP, leaving a fiscal deficit of about 3 percent of GDP after taking grants into account (table 4.11).

Government expenditures go mostly to the purchase of goods and services (including the wages and salaries of public employees) and to subsidies and current transfers to private and public enterprises and local governments. The rest go to interest payments and capital expenditures. In 2000 subsidies and current transfers accounted for 59 percent of government spending in high-income economies and 51 percent in Europe and Central Asia, but only 14 percent in the Middle East and North Africa (table 4.12).

The sources of government revenue have been changing. Taxes on income, profits, and capital gains generated 23 percent of current revenues in 1990, but their share fell to 18 percent in 2000, whereas taxes on goods and services rose from 27 percent to 34 percent. High-income economies depended more on income taxes (26 percent) than did low- and middle-income economies, which derived 35 percent of their revenue from taxes on goods and services and 9 percent from taxes on trade (table 4.13).

Governments, because of their size, have a large effect on economic performance. High taxes and subsidies can distort economic behavior, and large fiscal deficits make it harder to manage the growth of the money supply and thus increase the likelihood of inflation. As governments have adopted policies

leading to greater fiscal stability, inflation rates and interest rates have tended to decline (table 4.14).

External debt increases

In 2002 the external debt of low- and middle-income economies increased by $74 billion, or about 3 percent of their total debt stock, reversing the decline in 2001. Middle-income economies accounted for 75 percent of the increase. The increase was $47 billion in Europe and Central Asia, $12 billion in South Asia, $11 billion in the Middle East and North Africa, and $8 billion in Sub-Saharan Africa. By contrast, debt stocks fell by $2 billion in East Asia, and $1 billion in Latin America and the Caribbean (table 4.16). Debt management indicators are shown in table 4.17.

Data on the economy

The indicators in this section measure changes in the size and structure of the global economy and the varying effects of these changes on national economies. They include measures of macroeconomic performance (gross domestic product, consumption, investment, and international trade) and of stability (central government budgets, prices, the money supply, the balance of payments, and external debt). Other important economic indicators appear throughout the book, especially in the *States and markets* section (credit, investment, financial markets, tax policies, exchange rates) and the *Global links* section (trade and tariffs, foreign investment, and aid flows).

Most of the indicators in this section remain the same as last year, with a few exceptions. Tables 4.7 and 4.8 now break out insurance and financial services and computer, information, and communications services. Balance of payments data (table 4.15) are presented in calendar years for all countries except Bhutan and Myanmar, which are still in fiscal years. Thus for countries whose data were previously reported in fiscal years, such as Egypt, India, and Pakistan, this year's data will not be comparable with previous data. The switch from fiscal year to calendar year was made so that data will be consistent among countries and with the calendar year data in tables 4.5 and 4.6.

In table 4.17 the gross national income (GNI) and export values used as denominators for calculating the ratio of the present value of debt are three-year averages instead of single year values. The switch, made to even out fluctuations in GNI and exports, is consistent with the methodology followed in other World Bank publications. Workers' remittances are not included as part of exports. And because the level of public and publicly guaranteed debt is the primary concern of the Heavily Indebted Poor Countries (HIPC) Debt Initiative and of the Millennium Development Goals, public and publicly guaranteed debt service replaces total debt service as a ratio of GNI and as a ratio of exports, and multilateral debt service as a ratio of public and publicly guaranteed debt replaces public and publicly guaranteed debt service as a ratio of central government current revenue. The indicators dropped are still available on the *World Development Indicators* CD-ROM.

4.a

	Gross domestic product		Exports of goods and services		Imports of goods and services		GDP deflator		Current account balance		Total reserves[a]	
	annual % growth		annual % growth		annual % growth		% growth		% of GDP		$ millions	months of import coverage
	2002	2003	2002	2003	2002	2003	2002	2003	2002	2003	2003	2003
Algeria	4.1	6.8	4.7	6.8	17.8	4.6	1.0	7.3	..	10.9	..	..
Argentina	−10.9	7.0	3.1	3.7	−50.1	39.1	30.6	10.7	9.4	6.1	1,313	0.6
Armenia	12.9	12.0	29.0	40.2	14.2	33.8	2.3	4.0	−6.3	−7.1	550	4.3
Azerbaijan	10.6	9.3	16.6	8.1	49.8	39.2	0.7	5.9	−12.6	−26.9	732	1.8
Bangladesh	4.4	5.3	−2.3	−0.4	−11.2	0.8	3.2	4.4	1.6	0.6	2,454	2.8
Bolivia	2.8	2.4	12.4	14.6	7.7	−7.1	2.7	3.7	−4.4	−0.9	843	4.4
Bosnia and Herzegovina	3.9	3.5	5.3	11.5	−1.9	10.6	2.1	1.1	−38.2	−17.7	1,418	4.1
Botswana	3.1	3.7	−4.8	6.9	3.8	6.9	5.5	5.6	..	9.0	5,853	29.0
Brazil	1.5	−0.2	7.8	14.2	−12.8	−1.9	8.5	10.1	−1.7	0.4	35,869	5.1
Bulgaria	4.8	4.7	6.2	14.3	4.7	21.2	3.9	2.5	−4.4	−7.0	5,774	5.4
Cameroon	4.4	4.2	1.6	3.8	3.4	−2.6	0.7	1.1	..	−3.1	114	0.4
Chile	2.1	4.0	5.6	5.7	0.4	7.1	2.6	3.0	−0.9	−1.4	18,707	9.1
China	8.0	8.2	29.4	22.7	27.5	31.0	−0.3	1.1	2.8	1.1	410,049	10.7
Colombia	1.6	2.5	−4.4	5.4	0.6	3.3	6.1	7.4	−2.0	−2.5	10,586	6.1
Costa Rica	3.0	5.0	5.1	8.5	7.0	4.5	9.1	9.3	−5.6	−5.9	1,300	1.7
Dominican Republic	4.1	−1.3	13.0	8.0	13.9	−7.0	6.4	28.0	−4.0	4.5	665	0.9
Ecuador	3.4	2.5	0.9	1.8	17.2	1.7	11.8	8.8	−5.0	−3.3	1,072	1.4
Egypt, Arab Rep.	3.0	3.1	−10.4	14.0	−10.8	0.2	4.0	3.9	0.7	1.9	..	..
El Salvador	2.1	2.2	5.7	3.4	0.5	5.2	1.3	2.8	−2.7	..	1,607	..
Estonia	6.0	4.5	6.0	3.8	10.2	7.9	4.1	4.4	−12.3	−12.9	1,386	2.4
Ghana	4.5	4.7	−1.7	2.7	−4.4	7.7	22.8	27.6	−0.5	−0.5	811	2.4
Guatemala	2.2	2.4	−3.2	5.2	4.2	2.9	8.0	5.5	−5.1	−4.3	2,667	4.3
Honduras	2.5	1.5	2.1	−2.5	2.1	1.3	6.2	9.8	−4.1	−7.6	1,492	4.5
India	4.3	6.8	9.9	6.9	17.9	14.2	3.0	4.3	0.9	−0.3	78,222	8.8
Indonesia	3.7	4.1	−1.2	4.0	−8.3	2.0	7.2	6.6	4.3	3.9	36,246	7.0
Iran, Islamic Rep.	6.7	6.2	2.5	2.5	16.1	13.1	21.5	23.4	..	−1.5	23,706	7.6
Jamaica	1.1	3.0	−5.3	..	3.6	..	8.0	10.0	−14.2	−11.6	1,037	2.2
Jordan	4.9	3.0	11.6	4.1	0.7	6.6	0.5	0.8	5.0	4.4	3,940	6.5
Kazakhstan	9.8	9.0	22.6	26.7	4.3	42.4	5.8	6.6	−2.8	−1.7	4,852	4.0
Kenya	1.0	1.3	−18.5	5.7	−16.7	8.8	8.7	7.2	..	−1.4	1,564	4.1
Latvia	6.1	7.0	6.3	8.2	4.5	5.1	1.8	3.0	−7.7	−8.3	..	..
Lesotho	4.5	3.9	43.0	0.0	15.0	0.7	9.0	9.8	−15.1	−12.2	417	4.5
Lithuania	6.7	6.3	19.4	23.1	16.1	21.9	0.0	0.0	−5.2	−5.9	..	..

continues on page 180

4.b

	Nominal exchange rate			Real effective exchange rate		Money and quasi money		Gross domestic credit		Real interest rate		Short-term debt [a]
	local currency units per $	% change		1995 = 100		annual % growth		annual % growth		%		% of exports
	2003	2002	2003	2002	2003	2002	2003	2002	2003	2002	2003	2002
Algeria	72.6	2.4	−8.9	101.7	91.1	..	..	..	..	7.4	8.2	..
Argentina	2.9	232.2	−12.5	..	..	19.7	26.8	97.1	−4.0	16.2	7.6	46.6
Armenia	566.0	4.1	−3.2	95.9	85.8	34.0	13.7	−8.1	−15.0	18.5	13.9	1.6
Azerbaijan	4,923.0	2.5	0.6	..	..	14.6	30.8	84.2	27.1	16.5	16.7	2.9
Bangladesh	58.8	1.6	1.5	..	..	13.3	14.7	12.2	6.7	12.4	5.7	5.3
Bolivia	7.8	9.8	4.5	115.4	97.7	−6.9	6.4	4.9	3.4	17.5	9.7	21.5
Bosnia and Herzegovina	1.5	−16.0	−17.0	..	..	9.4	8.0	27.7	21.3	10.4	7.1	3.2
Botswana	4.4	−21.7	−18.7	..	..	−1.1	..	−55.8	..	9.9	5.9	0.5
Brazil	2.9	52.2	−18.2	..	..	23.0	2.3	21.5	7.3	50.1	44.9	31.2
Bulgaria	1.5	−15.1	−17.8	135.6	143.2	12.2	19.6	27.4	37.3	5.3	1.9	9.6
Cameroon	519.4	−16.0	−17.0	102.1	106.5	15.9	3.7	4.4	2.1	17.2	14.9	..
Chile	599.4	8.6	−15.9	90.7	85.3	−0.3	9.8	6.5	2.5	5.0	0.4	16.0
China	8.3	0.0	0.0	121.4	111.8	19.4	20.4	29.3	19.5	5.6	1.7	12.8
Colombia	2,780.8	24.5	−2.9	90.4	77.2	13.6	10.2	14.2	11.5	9.7	5.9	22.1
Costa Rica	418.5	10.8	10.5	109.4	98.1	20.9	17.3	26.5	19.2	15.8	4.1	20.0
Dominican Republic	37.3	23.6	75.8	112.1	73.0	10.3	72.6	22.6	57.3	18.4	3.9	19.3
Ecuador	1.0	0.0	0.0	113.8	111.7	..	..	..	..	2.9	4.9	30.3
Egypt, Arab Rep.	6.2	0.2	36.7	..	..	12.6	..	13.1	..	9.4	−0.8	17.3
El Salvador	8.8	0.0	0.0	..	..	−3.1	2.0	−1.4	10.5	..	..	16.9
Estonia	12.4	−15.6	−16.9	..	..	11.2	10.9	27.6	28.7	2.5	−1.6	27.9
Ghana	8,753.9	15.3	5.8	81.0	81.6	48.9	..	22.8	..	..	..	22.6
Guatemala	8.0	−2.4	3.0	..	..	11.8	21.3	16.1	7.2	8.2	1.8	16.9
Honduras	17.7	6.3	4.9	..	..	13.7	17.3	7.0	30.3	15.5	5.4	16.3
India	45.6	−0.3	−5.0	..	..	16.8	11.9	16.0	9.8	8.2	1.7	5.2
Indonesia	8,465.0	−14.0	−5.3	..	..	4.5	8.4	5.4	3.3	11.0	3.7	34.1
Iran, Islamic Rep.	8,272.1	354.2	4.0	198.1	187.3	27.5	23.0	29.4	42.5	..	..	6.5
Jamaica	60.5	7.4	19.2	..	..	12.0	12.6	30.0	68.3	9.7	4.3	16.9
Jordan	0.7	0.0	0.0	..	..	8.6	16.2	6.2	4.4	9.7	4.7	8.0
Kazakhstan	144.2	2.9	−6.7	..	..	30.1	43.0	30.2	35.8	..	..	9.9
Kenya	76.1	−1.9	−1.2	..	..	11.7	12.2	9.2	9.3	9.0	..	22.7
Latvia	0.5	−6.9	−8.9	..	..	19.9	20.6	38.3	38.4	6.1	−0.5	101.1
Lesotho	6.6	−28.8	−23.1	60.8	68.6	8.8	1.5	120.5	−67.9	6.7	0.9	0.7
Lithuania	2.8	−17.2	−16.6	..	..	16.9	18.3	22.3	44.1	6.9	0.8	27.5

continues on page 181

4.a

	Gross domestic product		Exports of goods and services		Imports of goods and services		GDP deflator		Current account balance		Total reserves [a]	
	annual % growth		annual % growth		annual % growth		% growth		% of GDP		$ millions	months of import coverage
	2002	2003	2002	2003	2002	2003	2002	2003	2002	2003	2003	2003
Macedonia, FYR	0.7	3.0	−4.4	9.3	10.7	3.5	3.6	0.4	−8.6	−5.5	861	4.2
Malawi	1.8	5.9	−3.8	−0.6	17.6	−16.6	17.5	6.9	−10.6	−12.5	..	..
Malaysia	4.1	4.6	3.6	5.3	6.2	10.6	3.6	3.0	7.6	8.3	..	..
Mauritius	4.4	4.5	9.4	2.6	5.2	4.1	5.1	5.3	5.7	3.3	1,151	5.1
Mexico	0.9	1.5	1.4	−0.3	1.6	−0.9	4.6	3.5	−2.2	−1.8	52,705	3.1
Moldova	7.2	6.0	14.6	11.8	13.9	13.3	8.1	11.9	−6.4	−8.2	258	1.9
Morocco	3.2	5.5	6.3	0.6	5.6	7.4	0.6	1.5	4.1	0.7	..	..
Nicaragua	1.0	2.3	−3.3	−5.1	−0.5	−7.1	5.3	6.1	−22.2	−17.6	447	2.5
Pakistan	2.8	5.8	10.3	18.8	4.5	20.2	3.1	4.0	6.6	5.9	9,630	7.0
Panama	0.8	2.5	−4.2	2.3	5.3	8.1	1.2	1.2	−1.3	−3.8	1,269	2.9
Paraguay	−2.3	1.5	−9.3	5.1	−15.0	6.3	14.6	8.8	5.3	0.3	859	3.1
Peru	4.9	4.0	6.8	9.7	2.4	8.8	0.6	3.1	−2.1	−2.1	11,026	10.1
Philippines	4.4	4.2	3.6	3.5	4.7	6.2	4.9	3.3	5.4	2.6	16,115	3.9
Poland	1.0	3.5	3.1	13.6	−5.3	8.3	1.7	1.0	−2.6	−0.1	31,747	6.4
Romania	4.3	4.8	16.9	8.2	12.1	6.4	24.2	16.0	−3.3	−4.9	7,794	4.3
Russian Federation	4.3	6.5	10.2	3.7	19.1	2.7	15.2	14.0	8.6	9.9	74,098	8.9
Senegal	1.1	6.3	1.7	1.5	1.9	−0.1	2.7	0.8	−9.5	−6.6	555	2.9
Serbia and Montenegro	4.0	3.0	12.3	27.7	26.3	22.9	25.5	16.5	−8.8	−8.3	3,325	4.5
Slovak Republic	4.4	3.9	5.9	8.5	5.3	7.1	3.9	5.0	..	−5.6	12,126	7.0
South Africa	3.0	3.0	−1.4	−0.9	3.1	−0.7	8.5	4.1	0.3	0.5	7,495	2.4
Sri Lanka	4.0	5.5	5.6	5.5	11.2	7.9	8.3	5.1	−1.6	−2.2	2,200	3.2
Swaziland	1.6	2.2	1.6	−6.0	1.6	−4.0	13.5	9.0	−3.8	−6.3	272	1.8
Syrian Arab Republic	2.7	0.9	2.1	−17.8	−2.4	5.4	4.4	1.5	..	0.1	4,450	6.8
Thailand	5.3	6.4	10.9	6.8	11.3	6.9	0.8	1.4	6.0	9.6	42,100	6.8
Trinidad and Tobago	2.7	4.0	−9.6	10.2	2.5	6.9	0.8	2.7	..	5.9	3,401	8.2
Tunisia	1.7	6.0	−2.1	4.0	−2.4	3.0	2.3	2.3	−3.5	−3.5	..	..
Turkey	7.8	4.8	4.8	4.2	20.0	11.6	43.8	25.2	−0.8	−3.2	36,832	5.8
Ukraine	4.8	7.5	9.1	5.0	3.7	10.4	3.2	5.1	7.7	6.5	6,874	3.4
Uruguay	−10.8	−1.0	−10.9	10.0	−28.3	−3.0	18.8	22.9	2.2	2.7	1,486	5.8
Uzbekistan	4.2	1.0	−8.8	2.8	−12.6	−1.7	45.5	30.0	3.0	6.7	1,743	6.9
Venezuela, RB	−8.9	−12.0	−7.8	−10.9	−26.7	−37.5	31.6	30.0	8.0	8.6	15,844	12.2
Zambia	3.3	4.2	11.4	11.1	3.5	4.1	19.9	20.1	..	−14.8	245	1.5
Zimbabwe	−5.6	−13.6	−0.8	−10.0	−4.8	−5.0	107.5	..	..	0.6	..	..

Note: Data for 2003 are the latest preliminary estimates and may differ from those in earlier World Bank publications.
a. International reserves including gold valued at London gold price.
Source: World Bank staff estimates.

4.b

Key macroeconomic indicators

	Nominal exchange rate			Real effective exchange rate		Money and quasi money		Gross domestic credit		Real interest rate		Short-term debt [a]
	local currency units per $	% change		1995 = 100		annual % growth		annual % growth		%		% of exports
	2003	2002	2003	2002	2003	2002	2003	2002	2003	2002	2003	2002
Macedonia, FYR	52.2	−15.3	−16.0	72.6	71.6	15.7	11.1	−14.7	12.5	14.3	8.0	5.0
Malawi	108.4	29.5	34.6	115.0	85.4	20.7	30.8	75.8	44.9	28.1	35.8	27.1
Malaysia	3.8	0.0	0.0	91.3	81.7	3.1	8.2	7.5	9.1	2.7	0.0	7.6
Mauritius	26.1	−3.9	−10.6	..	..	12.5	11.2	7.0	9.4	15.1	10.9	29.4
Mexico	11.2	12.8	9.0	..	..	4.6	5.1	18.1	2.1	3.4	0.8	5.3
Moldova	13.2	5.6	−4.4	100.2	97.5	38.6	30.4	25.2	23.6	14.3	0.2	6.2
Morocco	8.7	−12.1	−13.9	103.4	103.4	6.4	8.5	4.7	3.2	12.5	..	10.9
Nicaragua	15.6	6.0	6.0	111.6	95.3	13.3	..	4.7	..	17.0	..	42.8
Pakistan	57.2	−3.8	−2.3	90.0	83.9	16.8	18.4	1.6	11.0	..	..	9.7
Panama	1.0	0.0	0.0	..	..	−0.3	..	−4.5	..	9.7	7.8	4.4
Paraguay	6,115.0	51.7	−13.9	75.6	68.2	3.1	7.5	13.8	−25.9	21.0	25.8	15.6
Peru	3.5	2.0	−1.5	..	..	5.1	−3.7	−3.1	−8.8	14.1	8.7	22.8
Philippines	55.6	3.3	4.7	85.6	74.4	10.4	5.1	5.5	7.6	4.1	1.3	12.2
Poland	3.7	−3.7	−2.6	133.4	115.9	−2.8	4.0	2.6	7.9	10.7	..	14.8
Romania	32,595.0	6.0	−2.7	110.2	133.6	38.2	27.2	39.9	48.5	..	..	2.9
Russian Federation	29.5	5.5	−7.3	109.0	117.7	33.9	39.0	26.5	28.8	0.4	−9.9	12.9
Senegal	519.4	−16.0	−17.0	..	..	8.2	..	−5.2	..	..	..	16.8
Serbia and Montenegro	..	..	..	..	..	..	..	..	..	..	..	61.7
Slovak Republic	33.0	−17.4	−17.6	105.8	106.2	4.1	10.0	−7.0	−9.9	6.1	−2.2	24.2
South Africa	6.6	−28.8	−23.1	62.6	84.8	14.5	7.7	7.8	29.3	6.6	5.1	19.8
Sri Lanka	96.7	3.8	0.0	..	..	13.4	..	8.1	..	4.5	..	6.8
Swaziland	6.6	−28.8	−23.1	..	.	13.1	7.8	−206.4	164.7	4.0	−0.9	5.6
Syrian Arab Republic	11.2	0.0	0.0	..	.	18.5	..	0.1	..	4.4	..	66.7
Thailand	39.6	−2.4	−8.3	..	..	1.4	6.6	7.8	2.0	6.1	2.6	13.9
Trinidad and Tobago	6.3	0.2	−0.4	126.6	118.8	5.7	..	11.0	..	11.6	..	18.5
Tunisia	1.2	−9.1	−9.4	96.2	91.9	4.4	7.6	4.6	5.9	..	..	5.6
Turkey	1,396,638.0	13.3	−15.0	..	..	29.1	11.6	28.3	15.4	..	..	25.7
Ukraine	5.3	0.6	0.0	112.4	96.5	42.3	47.4	28.9	39.3	21.4	3.4	2.4
Uruguay	29.3	84.2	7.7	87.9	66.3	28.2	−1.6	71.6	4.0	91.4	..	50.0
Uzbekistan	..	..	..	..	..	..	..	..	..	..	..	11.0
Venezuela, RB	1,596.0	83.7	13.9	132.9	114.0	15.8	54.2	19.6	−3.2	3.8	−31.9	12.7
Zambia	4,770.7	13.2	10.1	115.8	114.3	31.1	16.8	12.1	−6.2	21.1	5.0	9.5
Zimbabwe	826.4	0.0	1,401.7	..	..	191.7	472.6	128.7	485.0	−34.2	49.7	..

Note: Data for 2003 are preliminary and may not cover the entire year.

a. More recent data on short-term debt are available on a Web site maintained by the Bank for International Settlements, the International Monetary Fund, the Organisation for Economic Co-operation and Development, and the World Bank: www.oecd.org/dac/debt.

Source: International Monetary Fund, *International Financial Statistics*; World Bank, Debtor Reporting System.

4.1 Growth of output

	Gross domestic product		Agriculture		Industry				Services	
					Total		Manufacturing			
	average annual % growth		average annual % growth		average annual % growth		average annual % growth		average annual % growth	
	1980–90	1990–2002	1980–90	1990–2002	1980–90	1990–2002	1980–90	1990–2002	1980–90	1990–2002
Afghanistan	..	..	..	..	..	..	..	..	..	..
Albania [a]	1.5	5.4	1.9	3.7	2.1	2.5	..	8.7	–0.4	9.2
Algeria [a]	2.7	2.2	4.1	3.6	2.6	2.0	4.1	–1.9	3.0	2.3
Angola	*3.6*	2.7	*0.5*	1.4	*6.3*	5.2	*–11.1*	1.6	*1.4*	–1.4
Argentina [a]	–0.7	2.7	0.7	2.9	–1.3	1.8	–0.8	0.9	0.0	3.1
Armenia [a]	..	0.4	..	1.4	..	–4.2	..	–2.0	..	–2.5
Australia [a]	3.4	3.8	3.2	*3.8*	3.1	*2.8*	1.9	*2.2*	3.8	*4.3*
Austria [a]	2.3	2.2	1.4	4.0	1.8	2.7	2.5	*2.8*	2.8	1.9
Azerbaijan [a]	..	*1.2*	..	0.8	..	1.8	..	–14.1	..	*1.8*
Bangladesh [a]	3.7	4.9	2.1	3.1	6.0	7.1	5.2	6.9	3.8	4.6
Belarus [a]	..	–0.1	..	–3.5	..	–0.7	..	0.4	..	0.5
Belgium [a]	2.1	2.1	2.2	2.6	2.4	2.0	..	2.8	1.8	1.9
Benin	2.5	4.9	5.1	5.7	3.4	4.5	5.1	6.0	0.7	4.4
Bolivia [a]	–0.2	3.6	1.5	2.7	–2.3	3.8	–1.1	3.5	–0.2	3.8
Bosnia and Herzegovina	..	..	..	..	..	..	..	..	..	..
Botswana	11.0	5.1	2.5	–1.2	11.4	4.3	11.4	4.0	14.3	7.2
Brazil [a]	2.7	2.7	2.8	3.4	2.0	2.2	1.6	1.6	3.3	2.8
Bulgaria [a]	3.4	–0.7	–2.1	3.0	5.2	–3.3	..	..	4.7	–3.3
Burkina Faso	3.6	4.0	3.1	3.7	3.8	2.8	2.0	1.6	3.8	4.6
Burundi [a]	4.4	–1.8	3.1	–0.7	4.5	–2.6	5.7	–8.0	5.6	–1.0
Cambodia [a]	..	6.6	..	3.2	..	14.8	..	17.8	..	5.8
Cameroon [a]	3.4	2.4	2.2	5.6	5.9	0.7	5.0	2.7	2.1	0.6
Canada [a]	3.2	3.2	2.3	0.8	2.9	*3.0*	*3.8*	*4.0*	3.2	*3.2*
Central African Republic [a]	1.4	2.1	1.6	4.0	1.4	1.4	5.0	0.7	1.0	–1.1
Chad [a]	6.1	2.5	2.3	3.8	8.1	4.6	..	..	6.7	1.7
Chile [a]	4.2	5.9	5.9	2.1	3.5	5.4	3.4	3.8	2.9	4.5
China	10.3	9.7	5.9	3.9	11.1	12.6	10.8	11.9	13.5	8.8
Hong Kong, China [a]	6.8	3.8	..	..	..	..	..	..	..	..
Colombia [a]	3.7	2.3	2.9	–1.5	5.0	1.4	3.5	–1.5	3.1	3.7
Congo, Dem. Rep.	1.6	–4.4	2.5	0.3	0.9	–6.8	1.6	..	1.3	–10.5
Congo, Rep.	3.3	1.6	3.4	1.3	5.2	2.9	6.8	–0.7	2.2	0.5
Costa Rica [a]	3.0	4.9	3.1	3.6	2.8	5.5	3.0	5.8	3.3	4.6
Côte d'Ivoire	0.7	2.8	0.3	3.4	4.4	4.2	3.0	3.4	–0.1	2.0
Croatia [a]	..	1.3	..	–1.3	..	–1.0	..	–1.5	..	2.5
Cuba	..	3.9	..	3.5	..	5.0	..	4.7	..	3.2
Czech Republic [a]	..	1.3	..	3.7	..	–0.3	..	..	..	2.1
Denmark [a]	2.0	2.5	2.6	2.8	2.0	2.4	1.3	*2.2*	1.9	2.5
Dominican Republic	3.1	6.0	–1.0	3.9	3.0	6.7	2.3	4.6	4.2	6.0
Ecuador	2.1	1.9	4.5	–0.4	1.3	2.0	0.1	1.1	1.8	2.5
Egypt, Arab Rep. [a]	5.4	4.5	2.7	3.2	3.3	4.6	..	6.5	7.8	4.6
El Salvador	0.2	4.3	–1.1	0.9	0.2	4.9	–0.1	5.0	0.7	4.8
Eritrea [a]	..	4.3	..	–1.4	..	11.5	..	8.1	..	*4.6*
Estonia [a]	2.2	1.0	..	–2.5	..	–0.7	..	7.1	..	2.7
Ethiopia [a]	*2.3*	4.6	*0.6*	2.2	*3.1*	4.0	2.7	4.0	*4.9*	6.9
Finland [a]	3.3	2.9	–0.4	1.5	3.2	4.4	..	*6.9*	3.6	2.5
France [a]	2.4	1.9	1.3	*1.9*	1.4	*1.5*	1.3	*2.4*	3.0	*2.1*
Gabon	0.9	2.5	1.2	–0.5	1.5	2.4	1.8	*0.6*	0.1	3.2
Gambia, The [a]	3.6	3.3	0.9	4.3	4.7	2.9	7.8	1.7	2.7	4.1
Georgia [a]	0.4	–4.3	..	–0.9	..	7.8	..	..	..	15.5
Germany [a]	2.3	1.6	1.6	1.6	1.4	–0.1	..	*0.2*	3.0	2.6
Ghana	3.0	4.3	1.0	3.5	3.3	3.2	3.9	–1.4	5.7	5.4
Greece [a]	0.9	2.6	–0.1	0.3	1.3	1.9	..	*1.9*	0.9	3.0
Guatemala	0.8	4.0	1.2	2.7	–0.2	3.9	0.0	2.6	0.9	4.5
Guinea [a]	..	4.3	..	4.6	..	4.8	..	4.4	..	3.3
Guinea-Bissau [a]	4.0	0.7	4.7	3.1	2.2	–2.5	..	–1.8	3.5	–0.0
Haiti [a]	–0.2	–1.0	–0.1	–4.4	–1.7	–2.6	–1.7	–8.1	0.9	0.8

	Gross domestic product		Agriculture		Industry				Services	
					Total average annual % growth		Manufacturing average annual % growth			
	average annual % growth		average annual % growth						average annual % growth	
	1980–90	1990–2002	1980–90	1990–2002	1980–90	1990–2002	1980–90	1990–2002	1980–90	1990–2002
Honduras [a]	2.7	3.1	2.7	2.1	3.3	3.5	3.7	4.1	2.5	3.9
Hungary [a]	1.3	2.2	1.7	–0.8	0.2	3.9	..	7.6	2.1	2.1
India [a]	5.7	5.8	3.1	2.7	6.9	6.0	7.4	6.6	6.5	7.9
Indonesia	6.1	3.6	3.6	1.9	7.3	4.5	12.8	5.9	6.5	3.4
Iran, Islamic Rep. [a]	1.7	3.8	4.5	4.2	3.3	–2.0	4.5	5.5	–1.0	8.1
Iraq	–6.8	..	..	..	..	..	..	..	..	..
Ireland [a]	3.2	7.8	..	..	..	..	..	..	..	..
Israel	3.5	4.6	..	..	..	..	..	..	..	..
Italy [a]	2.5	1.7	–0.5	1.2	1.8	1.2	2.1	1.4	3.0	1.9
Jamaica	2.0	0.7	0.9	–0.1	2.4	–0.8	2.7	–2.0	1.6	1.7
Japan [a]	4.1	1.3	1.3	–2.9	4.2	–0.0	..	0.7	4.2	2.2
Jordan [a]	2.5	4.7	6.8	–2.4	1.7	4.9	0.5	5.6	2.3	4.8
Kazakhstan [a]	..	–1.6	..	–5.4	..	–5.4	..	5.3	..	–1.4
Kenya [a]	4.2	1.9	3.3	1.2	3.9	1.5	4.9	1.8	4.9	2.9
Korea, Dem. Rep.	..	..	..	..	..	..	..	..	..	..
Korea, Rep.	8.9	5.6	3.0	1.8	11.4	6.2	12.1	7.6	8.4	5.6
Kuwait	1.3	2.9	14.7	..	1.0	..	2.3	..	2.1	..
Kyrgyz Republic [a]	..	–2.2	..	2.5	..	–7.6	..	–13.4	..	–3.0
Lao PDR [a]	3.7	6.3	3.5	4.9	6.1	10.9	8.9	12.6	3.3	6.5
Latvia [a]	3.5	–1.0	2.3	–4.0	4.3	–5.1	4.4	–4.6	3.2	3.6
Lebanon [a]	..	4.9	..	1.7	..	–0.8	..	–2.4	..	3.0
Lesotho [a]	4.5	3.5	2.8	2.0	5.3	4.8	9.8	6.0	4.0	3.8
Liberia [a]	–7.0	7.4	..	6.5	..	–11.2	..	..	..	–12.5
Libya [a]	–7.0	..	..	..	..	..	..	..	..	..
Lithuania [a]	..	–0.9	..	–1.0	..	4.2	..	6.7	..	5.5
Macedonia, FYR [a]	..	–0.1	..	–0.2	..	–2.1	..	–4.0	..	1.3
Madagascar [a]	1.1	2.1	2.5	1.9	0.9	2.1	2.1	2.2	0.3	2.4
Malawi [a]	2.5	3.1	2.0	6.8	2.9	0.7	3.6	–1.0	3.3	2.1
Malaysia	5.3	6.2	3.4	0.3	6.8	7.5	9.3	8.8	4.9	6.4
Mali [a]	0.8	4.2	3.3	2.5	4.3	8.2	6.8	–2.2	1.9	3.5
Mauritania [a]	1.8	4.4	1.7	3.7	4.9	2.4	–2.1	–1.0	0.4	5.9
Mauritius [a]	6.0	5.2	2.6	0.4	9.2	5.4	10.4	5.3	5.1	6.3
Mexico [a]	1.1	3.0	0.8	1.6	1.1	3.5	1.5	4.0	1.4	3.0
Moldova [a]	2.8	–7.1	..	–8.1	..	–9.5	..	–1.1	..	0.4
Mongolia	5.4	1.5	1.4	3.2	6.6	0.1	..	..	8.4	0.8
Morocco	4.2	2.6	6.7	0.1	3.0	3.3	4.1	2.8	4.2	2.9
Mozambique [a]	–0.1	6.9	6.6	5.1	–4.5	14.1	..	18.9	9.1	3.4
Myanmar	0.6	7.4	0.5	5.7	0.5	10.5	–0.2	7.9	0.8	7.2
Namibia [a]	1.3	3.7	1.9	2.8	0.0	2.7	3.7	3.3	3.6	4.2
Nepal [a]	4.6	4.7	4.0	2.7	8.8	6.4	9.3	7.5	3.9	5.8
Netherlands [a]	2.4	2.9	3.6	1.7	1.6	1.7	..	2.4	2.6	3.2
New Zealand [a]	1.9	3.2	4.1	3.0	1.0	2.2	..	2.0	–1.5	5.5
Nicaragua	–1.9	4.3	–2.2	3.1	–2.3	3.0	–3.2	1.7	–0.7	2.3
Niger	–0.1	2.6	1.7	3.2	–1.7	2.2	–2.7	2.8	3.7	2.8
Nigeria [a]	1.6	2.4	3.3	3.5	–1.1	0.9	0.7	1.2	2.8	3.8
Norway [a]	3.0	3.6	0.1	1.8	4.0	3.2	0.2	2.3	2.8	3.8
Oman	8.4	4.3	7.9	..	10.3	..	20.6	..	5.9	..
Pakistan [a]	6.3	3.6	4.0	3.8	7.7	3.9	8.1	4.0	6.8	4.3
Panama [a]	0.5	4.2	2.5	2.7	–1.3	4.3	0.4	2.9	0.7	4.4
Papua New Guinea	1.9	3.1	1.8	3.2	1.9	3.7	0.1	3.8	2.0	2.6
Paraguay	2.5	1.8	3.6	2.1	0.3	3.0	4.0	0.8	3.1	1.0
Peru [a]	–0.1	4.1	3.0	5.3	0.1	4.4	–0.2	3.3	–0.4	3.7
Philippines	1.0	3.5	1.0	2.0	–0.9	3.5	0.2	3.1	2.8	4.2
Poland [a]	..	4.3	..	1.1	..	5.8	..	8.3	..	4.4
Portugal [a]	3.2	2.8	1.5	–0.2	3.4	2.9	..	2.3	2.5	2.3
Puerto Rico	4.0	4.3	1.8	..	3.6	..	3.6	..	4.6	..

4.1 Growth of output

	Gross domestic product		Agriculture		Industry				Services	
					Total		Manufacturing			
	average annual % growth		average annual % growth		average annual % growth		average annual % growth		average annual % growth	
	1980–90	1990–2002	1980–90	1990–2002	1980–90	1990–2002	1980–90	1990–2002	1980–90	1990–2002
Romania [a]	1.3	–0.2	1.9	–1.4	–1.0	–0.3	..	..	..	1.0
Russian Federation [a]	..	–2.7	..	–1.9	..	–4.5	..	..	..	–0.6
Rwanda	2.2	1.7	0.5	4.3	2.5	–1.0	2.6	–3.7	3.6	0.5
Saudi Arabia	–1.3	2.1	12.5	1.7	–3.8	1.8	6.2	5.4	0.6	2.4
Senegal	3.1	3.9	2.8	1.8	4.3	5.3	4.6	4.6	2.8	4.1
Serbia and Montenegro	..	0.1	..	..	..	..	..	..	..	..
Sierra Leone [a]	0.5	–3.8	3.1	–3.6	1.7	–4.0	..	5.0	–0.9	–2.9
Singapore	6.7	6.7	–5.3	–3.1	5.2	7.3	6.6	6.9	7.6	6.8
Slovak Republic [a]	2.0	2.3	1.6	2.5	2.0	–3.4	..	4.3	0.6	7.7
Slovenia [a]	..	4.1	..	–0.1	..	4.7	..	4.7	..	4.0
Somalia [a]	2.1	..	3.3	..	1.0	..	–1.7	..	0.9	..
South Africa [a]	1.0	2.2	2.9	1.2	0.7	1.3	1.1	1.6	2.4	2.8
Spain [a]	3.1	2.8	3.1	0.7	2.7	2.5	..	3.9	3.3	3.0
Sri Lanka [a]	4.0	4.8	2.2	1.6	4.6	6.1	6.3	7.0	4.7	5.3
Sudan	2.3	5.5	1.8	9.0	1.6	6.1	4.8	2.0	4.5	3.1
Swaziland [a]	6.7	3.2	2.3	1.9	12.0	3.3	15.7	2.6	4.8	3.5
Sweden [a]	2.5	2.3	1.4	–0.7	2.8	4.5	..	8.6	2.4	1.8
Switzerland [a]	2.0	1.0	..	..	..	..	..	..	..	..
Syrian Arab Republic	1.5	4.7	–0.6	4.5	6.6	8.7	..	9.6	1.6	3.3
Tajikistan [a]	2.0	–6.8	–2.8	–4.6	5.5	–11.7	5.6	–10.8	3.4	–0.3
Tanzania [b]	..	3.5	..	3.4	..	4.1	..	3.3	..	3.3
Thailand	7.6	3.7	3.9	1.5	9.8	4.9	9.5	6.1	7.3	3.1
Togo	1.7	2.0	5.6	3.3	1.1	2.8	1.7	4.2	–0.3	0.4
Trinidad and Tobago	–0.8	3.5	–5.9	3.3	–5.5	3.8	–10.1	5.5	6.7	3.3
Tunisia	3.3	4.6	2.8	1.8	3.1	4.7	3.7	5.5	3.5	5.3
Turkey [a]	5.3	3.1	1.2	1.1	7.7	3.1	7.9	3.8	4.5	3.4
Turkmenistan [a]	..	–1.0	..	–3.2	..	–1.6	..	..	..	–3.2
Uganda [a]	2.9	6.9	2.1	3.9	5.0	11.2	3.9	13.0	2.8	7.9
Ukraine [a]	..	–6.6	..	–4.0	..	–7.9	..	–7.2	..	–8.0
United Arab Emirates [a]	–2.1	4.2	9.6	..	–4.2	..	3.1	..	3.6	..
United Kingdom [a]	3.2	2.6	2.4	–1.1	3.3	1.2	..	..	3.1	3.4
United States [a]	3.5	3.3	3.2	3.8	3.0	3.4	..	3.9	3.3	3.7
Uruguay [a]	0.5	2.0	0.1	1.6	–0.2	–0.0	0.4	–1.3	1.0	3.1
Uzbekistan	..	0.8	..	1.3	..	–2.1	..	..	..	1.9
Venezuela, RB	1.1	1.1	3.1	1.3	1.7	1.8	4.4	1.3	0.5	0.5
Vietnam	4.6	7.6	2.8	4.2	4.4	11.4	1.9	11.2	7.1	7.1
West Bank and Gaza [a]	..	–0.8	..	–4.2	..	–6.7	..	–0.5	..	2.4
Yemen, Rep.	..	5.9	..	5.6	..	6.5	..	3.0	..	5.8
Zambia [a]	1.0	1.1	3.6	3.5	1.0	–2.8	4.1	1.5	–0.2	3.0
Zimbabwe [a]	3.6	1.1	3.1	2.9	3.2	–1.1	2.8	–2.0	3.0	2.0
World	**3.3 w**	**2.7 w**	**2.6 w**	**1.8 w**	**3.1 w**	**2.1 w**	**.. w**	**2.9 w**	**3.5 w**	**3.1 w**
Low income	4.7	4.3	3.0	2.7	5.6	4.7	7.9	5.7	5.4	5.4
Middle income	2.9	3.2	3.5	2.1	2.7	3.4	3.7	5.3	3.1	3.3
Lower middle income	4.0	3.2	3.7	2.2	4.0	3.6	4.4	5.7	4.4	3.3
Upper middle income	0.8	3.0	2.8	1.4	–0.1	2.9	1.9	4.0	1.1	3.3
Low & middle income	3.2	3.4	3.4	2.3	3.1	3.6	4.2	5.3	3.4	3.6
East Asia & Pacific	7.5	7.3	4.6	3.1	8.5	9.7	9.5	9.8	8.6	6.4
Europe & Central Asia	..	–0.5	..	–0.8	..	–2.2	..	..	..	0.8
Latin America & Carib.	1.7	2.9	2.3	2.3	1.4	2.6	1.4	2.0	1.9	3.0
Middle East & N. Africa	1.4	3.2	5.0	2.9	–0.4	1.8	4.9	4.6	1.9	4.2
South Asia	5.5	5.4	3.1	2.9	6.9	5.9	7.3	6.3	6.4	7.0
Sub-Saharan Africa	1.6	2.6	2.3	2.8	1.3	1.9	1.7	1.9	2.4	2.8
High income	3.3	2.5	1.9	1.2	3.1	1.8	..	2.3	3.5	3.0
Europe EMU	2.4	2.0	1.3	1.4	1.7	1.1	..	1.5	2.9	2.4

a. Components are at basic prices. b. Data cover mainland Tanzania only.

ECONOMY

About the data

An economy's growth is measured by the change in the volume of its output or in the real incomes of persons resident in the economy. The 1993 United Nations System of National Accounts (1993 SNA) offers three plausible indicators from which to calculate growth: the volume of gross domestic product (GDP), real gross domestic income, and real gross national income. The volume of GDP is the sum of value added, measured at constant prices, by households, government, and the industries operating in the economy. This year's edition of *World Development Indicators* continues to follow the practice of past editions, measuring the growth of the economy by the change in GDP measured at constant prices.

Each industry's contribution to the growth in the economy's output is measured by the growth in value added by the industry. In principle, value added in constant prices can be estimated by measuring the quantity of goods and services produced in a period, valuing them at an agreed set of base year prices, and subtracting the cost of intermediate inputs, also in constant prices. This double-deflation method, recommended by the 1993 SNA and its predecessors, requires detailed information on the structure of prices of inputs and outputs.

In many industries, however, value added is extrapolated from the base year using single volume indexes of outputs or, more rarely, inputs. Particularly in the service industries, including most of government, value added in constant prices is often imputed from labor inputs, such as real wages or the number of employees. In the absence of well-defined measures of output, measuring the growth of services remains difficult.

Moreover, technical progress can lead to improvements in production processes and in the quality of goods and services that, if not properly accounted for, can distort measures of value added and thus of growth. When inputs are used to estimate output, as is the case for nonmarket services, unmeasured technical progress leads to underestimates of the volume of output. Similarly, unmeasured changes in the quality of goods and services produced lead to underestimates of the value of output and value added. The result can be underestimates of growth and productivity improvement, and overestimates of inflation. These issues are highly complex, and only a few high-income countries have attempted to introduce any GDP adjustments for these factors.

Informal economic activities pose a particular measurement problem, especially in developing countries, where much economic activity may go unrecorded. Obtaining a complete picture of the economy requires estimating household outputs produced for home use, sales in informal markets, barter exchanges, and illicit or deliberately unreported activities. The consistency and completeness of such estimates depend on the skill and methods of the compiling statisticians and the resources available to them.

Rebasing national accounts

When countries rebase their national accounts, they update the weights assigned to various components to better reflect the current pattern of production or uses of output. The new base year should represent normal operation of the economy—that is, it should be a year without major shocks or distortions—but the choice of base year is often constrained by lack of data. Some developing countries have not rebased their national accounts for many years. Using an old base year can be misleading because implicit price and volume weights become progressively less relevant and useful.

To obtain comparable series of constant price data, the World Bank rescales GDP and value added by industrial origin to a common reference year, currently 1995. This process gives rise to a discrepancy between the rescaled GDP and the sum of the rescaled components. Because allocating the discrepancy would give rise to distortions in the growth rates, the discrepancy is left unallocated. As a result, the weighted average of the growth rates of the components generally will not equal the GDP growth rate.

Growth rates of GDP and its components are calculated using constant price data in the local currency. Regional and income group growth rates are calculated after converting local currencies to constant price U.S. dollars using an exchange rate in the common reference year. The growth rates in the table are average annual compound growth rates. Methods of computing growth rates and the alternative conversion factor are described in *Statistical methods*.

Changes in the System of National Accounts

World Development Indicators adopted the terminology of the 1993 SNA in 2001. Although most countries continue to compile their national accounts according to the SNA version 3 (referred to as the 1968 SNA), more and more are adopting the 1993 SNA. Some low-income countries still use concepts from the even older 1953 SNA guidelines, including valuations such as factor cost, in describing major economic aggregates. Countries that use the 1993 SNA are identified in *Primary data documentation*.

- **Gross domestic product** (GDP) at purchaser prices is the sum of gross value added by all resident producers in the economy plus any product taxes (less subsidies) not included in the valuation of output. It is calculated without making deductions for depreciation of fabricated capital assets or for depletion and degradation of natural resources. Value added is the net output of an industry after adding up all outputs and subtracting intermediate inputs. The industrial origin of value added is determined by the International Standard Industrial Classification (ISIC) revision 3. • **Agriculture** corresponds to ISIC divisions 1–5 and includes forestry and fishing. • **Industry** covers mining, manufacturing (also reported as a separate subgroup), construction, electricity, water, and gas (ISIC divisions 10–45). • **Manufacturing** corresponds to industries belonging to ISIC divisions 15–37. • **Services** correspond to ISIC divisions 50–99. This sector is derived as a residual (from GDP less agriculture and industry) and may not properly reflect the sum of service output, including banking and financial services. For some countries it includes product taxes (minus subsidies) and may also include statistical discrepancies.

Data sources

The national accounts data for most developing countries are collected from national statistical organizations and central banks by visiting and resident World Bank missions. The data for high-income economies come from data files of the Organisation for Economic Co-operation and Development (for information on the OECD's national accounts series, see its monthly *Main Economic Indicators*). The World Bank rescales constant price data to a common reference year. The complete national accounts time series is available on the *World Development Indicators 2004* CD-ROM. The United Nations Statistics Division publishes detailed national accounts for United Nations member countries in *National Accounts Statistics: Main Aggregates and Detailed Tables* and publishes updates in the *Monthly Bulletin of Statistics*.

	Gross domestic product		Agriculture		Industry				Services	
					Total		Manufacturing			
	$ millions		% of GDP		% of GDP		% of GDP		% of GDP	
	1990	2002	1990	2002	1990	2002	1990	2002	1990	2002
Afghanistan	..	..	..	52	..	24	..	18	..	24
Albania [a]	2,102	4,835	36	25	48	19	..	10	16	56
Algeria [a]	62,045	55,914	11	10	48	53	11	8	40	37
Angola	10,260	11,248	18	8	41	68	5	4	41	24
Argentina [a]	141,352	102,042	8	11	36	32	27	21	56	57
Armenia [a]	2,257	2,367	17	26	52	37	33	23	31	37
Australia [a]	310,588	409,420	4	4	29	26	14	12	67	71
Austria [a]	161,692	204,066	4	2	34	32	23	22	62	66
Azerbaijan [a]	4,991	6,090	30	16	33	52	19	20	37	32
Bangladesh [a]	30,129	47,563	30	23	21	26	13	16	48	51
Belarus [a]	17,370	14,304	24	11	47	37	39	31	29	52
Belgium [a]	197,174	245,395	2	1	33	27	..	19	65	72
Benin	1,845	2,695	36	36	13	14	8	9	51	50
Bolivia [a]	4,868	7,801	17	15	39	33	18	15	44	52
Bosnia and Herzegovina	..	5,599	..	18	..	37	..	23	..	45
Botswana	3,791	5,273	5	2	57	48	5	4	39	50
Brazil [a]	461,952	452,387	8	6	39	21	25	13	53	73
Bulgaria [a]	20,726	15,486	17	13	49	28	..	17	34	59
Burkina Faso	3,120	3,127	28	32	20	18	15	13	52	50
Burundi [a]	1,132	719	56	49	19	19	13	..	25	31
Cambodia [a]	1,115	4,005	..	36	..	28	..	20	..	36
Cameroon [a]	11,152	9,060	25	43	29	20	15	11	46	38
Canada [a]	574,204	714,327	3	..	32	..	17	..	65	..
Central African Republic [a]	1,488	1,046	48	57	20	22	11	9	33	21
Chad [a]	1,739	2,002	29	38	18	17	14	15	53	45
Chile [a]	30,323	64,153	9	9	41	34	20	16	50	57
China	354,644	1,266,052	27	15	42	51	33	35	31	34
Hong Kong, China [a]	75,433	161,531	0	0	25	13	17	5	74	87
Colombia [a]	40,274	80,925	17	14	38	30	21	16	45	56
Congo, Dem. Rep.	9,348	5,707	30	56	28	19	11	4	42	25
Congo, Rep.	2,799	3,017	13	6	41	63	8	5	46	30
Costa Rica [a]	5,713	16,837	18	8	29	29	22	22	53	62
Côte d'Ivoire	10,796	11,682	32	26	23	20	21	13	44	53
Croatia [a]	18,156	22,436	10	8	34	30	28	21	56	62
Cuba	..	..	..	7	..	46	..	37	..	47
Czech Republic [a]	34,880	69,514	6	4	49	40	..	..	45	57
Denmark [a]	133,361	172,928	4	3	27	27	18	17	69	71
Dominican Republic	7,074	21,651	13	12	31	33	18	16	55	55
Ecuador	10,356	24,311	13	9	38	28	19	11	49	63
Egypt, Arab Rep. [a]	43,130	89,854	19	17	29	33	18	19	52	50
El Salvador	4,807	14,284	17	9	27	30	22	23	56	61
Eritrea [a]	477	642	31	12	12	25	8	12	57	63
Estonia [a]	4,649	6,507	17	5	50	30	42	19	34	65
Ethiopia [a]	8,609	6,059	49	40	13	12	8	..	38	48
Finland [a]	137,224	131,508	6	3	35	33	..	26	59	64
France [a]	1,215,893	1,431,278	4	3	30	25	21	18	66	72
Gabon	5,952	4,971	7	8	43	46	6	5	50	46
Gambia, The [a]	317	357	29	26	13	14	7	5	58	60
Georgia [a]	7,738	3,396	32	21	33	23	24	..	35	56
Germany [a]	1,671,312	1,984,095	2	1	39	30	28	23	59	69
Ghana	5,886	6,160	45	34	17	24	10	9	38	42
Greece [a]	84,075	132,824	11	7	28	22	..	12	61	70
Guatemala	7,650	23,277	26	22	20	19	15	13	54	58
Guinea [a]	2,818	3,213	24	24	33	37	5	4	43	39
Guinea-Bissau [a]	244	203	61	62	19	13	8	10	21	25
Haiti [a]	2,864	3,435	..	..	..	17	..	..	..	..

	Gross domestic product ($ millions)		Agriculture (% of GDP)		Industry				Services (% of GDP)	
					Total (% of GDP)		Manufacturing (% of GDP)			
	1990	2002	1990	2002	1990	2002	1990	2002	1990	2002
Honduras [a]	3,049	6,564	22	13	26	31	16	20	51	56
Hungary [a]	33,056	65,843	15	4	39	31	23	23	46	65
India [a]	316,937	510,177	31	23	28	27	17	16	41	51
Indonesia	114,426	172,911	19	17	39	44	21	25	48	38
Iran, Islamic Rep. [a]	120,404	108,243	24	12	29	39	12	14	48	49
Iraq	48,657	..	..	..	..	..	..	..	..	..
Ireland [a]	47,301	121,449	9	3	35	42	28	33	56	54
Israel	52,490	103,689	..	..	..	..	..	..	..	..
Italy [a]	1,102,437	1,184,273	4	3	34	29	25	21	63	69
Jamaica	4,592	7,871	7	6	40	31	19	14	52	63
Japan [a]	3,053,143	3,993,433	2	1	39	31	27	21	58	68
Jordan [a]	4,020	9,301	8	2	28	26	15	16	64	72
Kazakhstan [a]	26,931	24,637	27	9	45	39	9	16	29	53
Kenya [a]	8,551	12,330	29	16	19	19	12	13	52	65
Korea, Dem. Rep.	..	..	..	..	..	..	..	..	..	..
Korea, Rep.	252,622	476,690	9	4	43	41	29	29	48	55
Kuwait	18,428	35,369	1	..	52	..	12	..	47	..
Kyrgyz Republic [a]	2,659	1,603	34	39	36	26	28	11	30	35
Lao PDR [a]	866	1,680	61	51	15	23	10	18	24	26
Latvia [a]	7,279	8,406	22	5	46	25	34	15	32	71
Lebanon [a]	2,838	17,294	..	12	..	21	..	10	..	67
Lesotho [a]	615	714	24	16	33	43	14	20	43	41
Liberia [a]	384	562	..	..	..	..	..	..	..	..
Libya [a]	28,905	19,131	..	..	..	..	..	..	..	..
Lithuania [a]	10,259	13,796	27	7	31	31	21	20	42	62
Macedonia, FYR [a]	4,472	3,791	9	12	46	30	36	19	46	57
Madagascar [a]	3,081	4,400	29	32	13	13	11	11	59	55
Malawi [a]	1,881	1,901	45	37	29	15	19	10	26	49
Malaysia	44,024	94,900	15	9	42	47	24	31	43	44
Mali [a]	2,421	3,364	46	34	16	30	9	3	39	36
Mauritania [a]	1,020	969	30	21	29	29	10	9	42	50
Mauritius [a]	2,383	4,533	13	7	33	31	25	23	54	62
Mexico [a]	262,710	637,203	8	4	28	27	21	19	64	69
Moldova [a]	3,549	1,624	43	24	33	25	..	17	24	51
Mongolia	..	1,119	17	30	30	16	..	5	52	54
Morocco	25,821	36,093	18	16	32	30	18	17	50	54
Mozambique [a]	2,463	3,599	37	23	18	34	10	13	44	43
Myanmar	..	..	57	57	11	10	8	7	32	33
Namibia [a]	2,350	2,904	12	11	38	31	14	11	50	58
Nepal [a]	3,628	5,549	52	41	16	22	6	8	32	38
Netherlands [a]	294,290	417,910	4	3	30	26	19	16	65	71
New Zealand [a]	43,618	58,581	7	..	28	..	19	..	65	..
Nicaragua	1,009	4,003	31	18	21	25	17	14	48	57
Niger	2,481	2,171	35	40	16	17	7	7	49	43
Nigeria [a]	28,472	43,540	33	37	41	29	6	4	26	34
Norway [a]	116,107	190,477	4	2	36	38	13	..	61	60
Oman	10,535	20,309	3	..	58	..	4	..	39	..
Pakistan [a]	40,010	59,071	26	23	25	23	17	16	49	53
Panama [a]	5,313	12,296	9	6	15	14	9	6	76	80
Papua New Guinea	3,221	2,814	29	27	30	42	9	9	41	32
Paraguay	5,265	5,508	28	22	25	29	17	15	47	49
Peru [a]	26,294	56,517	9	8	27	28	18	16	64	64
Philippines	44,331	77,954	22	15	34	33	25	23	44	53
Poland [a]	58,976	189,021	8	3	50	30	..	18	42	66
Portugal [a]	71,466	121,595	9	4	32	30	22	..	60	66
Puerto Rico	30,604	67,897	1	1	42	43	40	40	57	56

	Gross domestic product		Agriculture		Industry				Services	
					Total		Manufacturing			
	$ millions		% of GDP		% of GDP		% of GDP		% of GDP	
	1990	2002	1990	2002	1990	2002	1990	2002	1990	2002
Romania [a]	38,299	45,749	24	13	50	38	*34*	*17*	26	49
Russian Federation [a]	516,814	346,520	17	6	48	34	..	..	35	60
Rwanda	2,584	1,732	33	41	25	21	18	11	43	37
Saudi Arabia	116,778	188,479	6	5	49	51	9	10	45	44
Senegal	5,699	5,037	20	15	19	22	13	14	61	63
Serbia and Montenegro	..	15,681	..	*15*	..	*32*	..	..	..	*53*
Sierra Leone [a]	650	783	32	53	13	32	5	5	55	16
Singapore	36,902	86,969	..	0	..	36	..	28	..	64
Slovak Republic [a]	15,485	23,682	7	4	59	29	..	21	33	67
Slovenia [a]	*12,673*	21,960	*6*	3	*46*	36	*35*	27	*49*	61
Somalia [a]	917	..	65	..	..	..	5	..	..	..
South Africa [a]	112,014	104,242	5	4	40	32	24	19	55	64
Spain [a]	509,968	653,075	6	3	35	30	..	*18*	59	66
Sri Lanka [a]	8,032	16,567	26	20	26	26	15	16	48	54
Sudan	13,167	13,516	..	39	..	18	..	9	..	43
Swaziland [a]	882	1,186	13	16	42	50	35	38	45	35
Sweden [a]	245,941	240,313	4	2	32	28	..	*23*	64	70
Switzerland [a]	228,415	267,445	..	*1*	..	*27*	..	..	..	*72*
Syrian Arab Republic	12,309	20,783	28	23	24	28	20	25	48	49
Tajikistan [a]	2,629	1,212	33	24	38	24	25	21	29	52
Tanzania [b]	4,259	9,382	46	44	18	16	9	8	36	39
Thailand	85,345	126,905	12	9	37	43	27	34	50	48
Togo	1,628	1,384	34	40	23	22	10	9	44	38
Trinidad and Tobago	5,068	9,628	3	2	46	42	9	7	51	56
Tunisia	12,291	21,024	16	10	30	29	17	19	54	60
Turkey [a]	150,642	183,665	18	13	30	27	20	17	52	60
Turkmenistan [a]	3,232	7,672	32	*29*	30	*51*	..	..	38	*20*
Uganda [a]	4,304	5,803	57	32	11	22	6	10	32	46
Ukraine [a]	81,456	41,477	26	15	45	38	*44*	23	30	47
United Arab Emirates [a]	34,132	70,960	2	..	64	..	8	..	35	..
United Kingdom [a]	989,564	1,566,283	2	1	35	26	23	*17*	63	73
United States [a]	5,750,800	10,383,100	2	*2*	28	*23*	19	*15*	70	75
Uruguay [a]	9,286	12,129	9	9	35	27	28	17	56	64
Uzbekistan	13,361	7,932	33	35	33	22	..	9	34	44
Venezuela, RB	48,592	94,340	5	3	50	43	20	6	44	54
Vietnam	6,472	35,086	39	23	23	39	12	21	39	38
West Bank and Gaza [a]	..	3,396	..	6	..	13	..	11	..	80
Yemen, Rep.	4,828	9,984	24	15	27	40	9	5	49	44
Zambia [a]	3,288	3,697	21	22	51	26	36	12	28	52
Zimbabwe [a]	8,784	8,304	16	17	33	24	23	13	50	59
World	**21,676,054 t**	**32,312,146 t**	**5 w**	**4 w**	**34 w**	**29 w**	**22 w**	**19 w**	**60 w**	**68 w**
Low income	765,007	1,123,865	29	24	30	30	17	17	41	46
Middle income	3,229,351	5,139,306	14	9	39	34	*24*	21	47	57
Lower middle income	2,326,049	3,426,319	16	10	39	34	*26*	22	44	56
Upper middle income	905,385	1,708,823	9	6	39	34	21	18	53	60
Low & middle income	3,991,257	6,259,154	16	11	38	33	*23*	20	46	55
East Asia & Pacific	674,196	1,833,073	24	15	40	47	29	32	37	38
Europe & Central Asia	1,099,616	1,132,845	17	9	44	32	..	..	39	59
Latin America & Carib.	1,098,727	1,668,800	9	7	36	26	*23*	15	55	67
Middle East & N. Africa	424,126	670,722	15	11	38	41	13	13	47	48
South Asia	404,808	649,079	31	23	27	26	17	16	43	51
Sub-Saharan Africa	298,443	319,288	18	18	34	29	17	15	48	54
High income	17,683,764	26,052,812	3	*2*	33	*27*	22	*19*	64	71
Europe EMU	5,503,913	6,648,492	3	2	34	28	*24*	21	62	70

a. Components are at basic prices. b. Data cover mainland Tanzania only.

Structure of output | 4.2

About the data

An economy's gross domestic product (GDP) represents the sum of value added by all producers in that economy. Value added is the value of the gross output of producers less the value of intermediate goods and services consumed in production, before taking account of the consumption of fixed capital in the production process. Since 1968 the United Nations System of National Accounts has called for estimates of value added to be valued at either basic prices (excluding net taxes on products) or producer prices (including net taxes on products paid by producers but excluding sales or value added taxes). Both valuations exclude transport charges that are invoiced separately by producers. Some countries, however, report such data at purchaser prices—the prices at which final sales are made (including transport charges)—which may affect estimates of the distribution of output. Total GDP as shown in the table and elsewhere in this book is measured at purchaser prices. Value added by industry is normally measured at basic prices. When value added is measured at producer prices, this is noted in *Primary data documentation*.

While GDP estimates based on the production approach are generally more reliable than estimates compiled from the income or expenditure side, different countries use different definitions, methods, and reporting standards. World Bank staff review the quality of national accounts data and sometimes make adjustments to increase consistency with international guidelines. Nevertheless, significant discrepancies remain between international standards and actual practice. Many statistical offices, especially those in developing countries, face severe limitations in the resources, time, training, and budgets required to produce reliable and comprehensive series of national accounts statistics.

Data problems in measuring output

Among the difficulties faced by compilers of national accounts is the extent of unreported economic activity in the informal or secondary economy. In developing countries a large share of agricultural output is either not exchanged (because it is consumed within the household) or not exchanged for money.

Agricultural production often must be estimated indirectly, using a combination of methods involving estimates of inputs, yields, and area under cultivation. This approach sometimes leads to crude approximations that can differ from the true values over time and across crops for reasons other than climatic conditions or farming techniques. Similarly,

agricultural inputs that cannot easily be allocated to specific outputs are frequently "netted out" using equally crude and ad hoc approximations. For further discussion of the measurement of agricultural production, see *About the data* for table 3.3.

Ideally, industrial output should be measured through regular censuses and surveys of firms. But in most developing countries such surveys are infrequent, so earlier survey results must be extrapolated using an appropriate indicator. The choice of sampling unit, which may be the enterprise (where responses may be based on financial records) or the establishment (where production units may be recorded separately), also affects the quality of the data. Moreover, much industrial production is organized in unincorporated or owner-operated ventures that are not captured by surveys aimed at the formal sector. Even in large industries, where regular surveys are more likely, evasion of excise and other taxes and nondisclosure of income lower the estimates of value added. Such problems become more acute as countries move from state control of industry to private enterprise, because new firms enter business and growing numbers of established firms fail to report. In accordance with the System of National Accounts, output should include all such unreported activity as well as the value of illegal activities and other unrecorded, informal, or small-scale operations. Data on these activities need to be collected using techniques other than conventional surveys of firms.

In industries dominated by large organizations and enterprises, such as public utilities, data on output, employment, and wages are usually readily available and reasonably reliable. But in the service industry the many self-employed workers and one-person businesses are sometimes difficult to locate, and they have little incentive to respond to surveys, let alone report their full earnings. Compounding these problems are the many forms of economic activity that go unrecorded, including the work that women and children do for little or no pay. For further discussion of the problems of using national accounts data, see Srinivasan (1994) and Heston (1994).

Dollar conversion

To produce national accounts aggregates that are measured in the same standard monetary units, the value of output must be converted to a single common currency. The World Bank conventionally uses the U.S. dollar and applies the average official exchange rate reported by the International

Monetary Fund for the year shown. An alternative conversion factor is applied if the official exchange rate is judged to diverge by an exceptionally large margin from the rate effectively applied to transactions in foreign currencies and traded products.

- **Gross domestic product** (GDP) at purchaser prices is the sum of gross value added by all resident producers in the economy plus any product taxes (less subsidies) not included in the valuation of output. It is calculated without making deductions for depreciation of fabricated assets or for depletion and degradation of natural resources. Value added is the net output of an industry after adding up all outputs and subtracting intermediate inputs. The industrial origin of value added is determined by the International Standard Industrial Classification (ISIC) revision 3. • **Agriculture** corresponds to ISIC divisions 1–5 and includes forestry and fishing. • **Industry** covers mining, manufacturing (also reported as a separate subgroup), construction, electricity, water, and gas (ISIC divisions 10–45). • **Manufacturing** corresponds to industries belonging to ISIC divisions 15–37. • **Services** correspond to ISIC divisions 50–99. This sector is derived as a residual (from GDP less agriculture and industry) and may not properly reflect the sum of service output, including banking and financial services. For some countries it includes product taxes (minus subsidies) and may also include statistical discrepancies.

The national accounts data for most developing countries are collected from national statistical organizations and central banks by visiting and resident World Bank missions. The data for high-income economies come from data files of the Organisation for Economic Co-operation and Development (for information on the OECD's national accounts series, see its monthly *Main Economic Indicators*). The complete national accounts time series is available on the *World Development Indicators 2004* CD-ROM. The United Nations Statistics Division publishes detailed national accounts for United Nations member countries in *National Accounts Statistics: Main Aggregates and Detailed Tables* and publishes updates in the *Monthly Bulletin of Statistics*.

Structure of manufacturing

	Manufacturing value added		Food, beverages, and tobacco		Textiles and clothing		Machinery and transport equipment		Chemicals		Other manufacturing [a]	
	$ millions		% of total		% of total		% of total		% of total		% of total	
	1990	2000	1990	2000	1990	2000	1990	2000	1990	2000	1990	2000
Afghanistan	..	..	..	..	..	..	..	..	..	..	..	..
Albania	..	376	24	..	33	..	..	..	..	..	44	..
Algeria	6,452	3,897	13	33	17	8	..	..	..	..	70	59
Angola	513	264	..	..	..	..	..	..	..	..	..	..
Argentina	37,868	46,877	20	30	10	7	13	15	12	12	46	36
Armenia	681	418	..	..	..	..	..	..	..	..	..	..
Australia	38,868	42,528	18	..	6	..	20	..	7	..	48	..
Austria	33,386	37,189	15	12	7	3	28	41	7	6	43	38
Azerbaijan	1,092	675	..	..	..	..	..	..	..	..	..	..
Bangladesh	3,839	6,933	24	22	38	33	7	16	17	10	15	19
Belarus	6,630	3,444	..	..	..	..	..	..	..	..	..	..
Belgium	..	39,986	17	19	7	6	..	..	13	16	62	59
Benin	145	198	..	..	..	..	..	..	..	..	..	..
Bolivia	826	1,121	28	31	5	4	1	1	3	3	63	60
Bosnia and Herzegovina	..	480	12	..	15	..	18	..	7	..	49	..
Botswana	181	253	51	..	12	..	..	..	..	..	36	..
Brazil	89,966	80,280	14	..	12	..	27	..	..	..	48	..
Bulgaria	..	1,985	22	20	9	10	19	5	5	..	45	65
Burkina Faso	460	281	..	..	..	..	..	..	..	..	..	..
Burundi	134	60	83	..	9	..	..	..	2	..	7	..
Cambodia	58	583	..	..	..	..	..	..	..	..	..	..
Cameroon	1,581	940	61	47	−13	15	1	1	5	4	46	32
Canada	91,674	117,240	15	13	6	3	26	36	10	8	44	39
Central African Republic	154	81	57	..	6	..	2	..	6	..	28	..
Chad	239	152	..	..	..	..	..	..	..	..	..	..
Chile	5,613	10,663	25	32	7	4	5	5	10	14	52	45
China	116,573	375,455	15	14	15	11	24	30	13	12	34	33
Hong Kong, China	12,639	9,197	8	7	36	20	21	33	2	4	33	37
Colombia	8,034	12,207	31	33	15	9	9	5	14	17	31	35
Congo, Dem. Rep.	1,029	205	..	..	..	..	..	..	..	..	..	..
Congo, Rep.	234	112	..	..	..	..	..	..	..	..	..	..
Costa Rica	1,107	3,677	47	46	8	6	7	6	9	12	30	29
Côte d'Ivoire	2,257	1,591	..	42	..	10	..	3	..	12	..	33
Croatia	4,770	3,219	22	..	15	..	20	..	8	..	36	..
Cuba	..	..	..	..	..	..	..	..	..	..	..	..
Czech Republic	..	..	..	..	..	..	..	..	..	..	..	..
Denmark	20,757	23,156	22	4	..	..	24	..	12	..	39	..
Dominican Republic	1,270	3,325	..	..	..	..	..	..	..	..	..	..
Ecuador	1,988	2,171	22	38	10	6	5	3	8	4	56	50
Egypt, Arab Rep.	7,296	17,969	19	18	15	12	9	12	14	16	43	42
El Salvador	1,044	3,031	36	29	14	28	4	3	24	16	23	24
Eritrea	35	67	..	..	..	..	..	..	..	..	..	..
Estonia	1,632	830	..	..	..	..	..	..	..	..	..	..
Ethiopia	624	..	62	54	21	12	1	7	2	5	14	22
Finland	..	27,771	13	7	4	2	24	24	8	2	52	64
France	228,263	215,860	13	..	6	..	31	..	9	..	41	..
Gabon	332	205	45	..	2	..	1	..	7	..	45	..
Gambia, The	18	18	..	..	..	..	..	..	..	..	..	..
Georgia	1,773	..	..	..	..	..	..	..	..	..	..	..
Germany	456,400	385,839	..	..	..	..	..	..	..	..	..	..
Ghana	575	449	..	..	..	..	..	..	..	..	..	..
Greece	..	11,441	22	28	20	11	12	11	10	11	36	38
Guatemala	1,151	2,542	..	..	..	..	..	..	..	..	..	..
Guinea	126	121	..	..	..	..	..	..	..	..	..	..
Guinea-Bissau	19	21	..	..	..	..	..	..	..	..	..	..
Haiti	..	..	51	46	9	19	..	..	..	..	40	34

	Manufacturing value added		Food, beverages, and tobacco		Textiles and clothing		Machinery and transport equipment		Chemicals		Other manufacturing[a]	
	$ millions		% of total		% of total		% of total		% of total		% of total	
	1990	2000	1990	2000	1990	2000	1990	2000	1990	2000	1990	2000
Honduras	443	1,025	45	42	10	22	3	2	5	5	36	29
Hungary	6,613	9,534	14	19	9	8	26	26	12	7	39	40
India	48,808	66,024	12	13	15	12	25	20	14	22	34	33
Indonesia	23,643	37,393	27	19	15	17	12	25	9	11	37	28
Iran, Islamic Rep.	14,503	15,456	12	..	20	..	20	..	8	..	40	..
Iraq	..	..	20	..	16	..	4	..	11	..	49	..
Ireland	11,982	28,130	27	16	4	1	29	31	16	36	24	16
Israel	..	..	14	12	9	9	32	32	9	5	37	42
Italy	247,930	203,247	8	10	13	12	34	26	7	8	37	44
Jamaica	853	1,018	41	48	5	7	..	..	..	..	54	46
Japan	810,232	1,040,351	9	11	5	3	40	39	10	10	37	36
Jordan	520	1,125	28	28	7	6	4	5	15	17	47	45
Kazakhstan	1,941	3,139	..	..	..	..	..	..	..	..	..	..
Kenya	864	1,163	38	48	10	8	10	9	9	8	33	28
Korea, Dem. Rep.	..	..	..	..	..	..	..	..	..	..	..	..
Korea, Rep.	72,837	144,376	11	8	12	8	32	45	9	9	36	30
Kuwait	2,142	..	4	7	3	4	2	4	3	2	88	83
Kyrgyz Republic	703	105	..	..	..	..	..	..	..	..	..	..
Lao PDR	85	292	..	..	..	..	..	..	..	..	..	..
Latvia	2,524	926	..	39	..	12	..	15	..	6	..	29
Lebanon	..	1,560	..	..	..	..	..	..	..	..	..	..
Lesotho	71	131	..	..	..	..	..	..	..	..	..	..
Liberia	..	..	..	..	..	..	..	..	..	..	..	..
Libya	..	..	..	..	..	..	..	..	..	..	..	..
Lithuania	2,113	1,995	..	..	..	..	..	..	..	..	..	..
Macedonia, FYR	1,411	621	20	32	26	18	14	15	9	11	31	24
Madagascar	314	430	..	..	..	..	..	..	..	..	..	..
Malawi	313	197	38	44	10	8	1	5	18	16	33	28
Malaysia	10,665	29,447	13	10	6	4	31	46	11	11	39	30
Mali	200	86	..	..	..	..	..	..	..	..	..	..
Mauritania	94	78	..	..	..	..	..	..	..	..	..	..
Mauritius	491	918	30	31	46	48	2	2	4	5	17	15
Mexico	49,992	107,195	22	25	5	4	24	28	18	15	32	28
Moldova	..	183	..	..	..	..	..	..	..	..	..	..
Mongolia	..	58	33	..	37	..	1	..	1	..	27	..
Morocco	4,753	5,858	22	36	17	16	8	8	12	13	41	27
Mozambique	230	442	..	..	..	..	..	..	..	..	..	..
Myanmar	..	..	..	..	..	..	..	..	..	..	..	..
Namibia	292	342	..	..	..	..	..	..	..	..	..	..
Nepal	209	486	37	35	31	34	1	3	5	6	25	23
Netherlands	51,978	55,742	21	23	3	2	25	25	16	14	35	35
New Zealand	7,574	8,479	28	31	8	..	13	14	7	13	44	43
Nicaragua	170	553	..	..	..	..	..	..	..	..	..	..
Niger	163	122	37	20	29	9	..	..	..	..	34	71
Nigeria	1,562	1,635	15	30	46	11	13	8	4	26	22	25
Norway	13,450	17,076	18	16	2	2	25	29	9	8	46	46
Oman	396	..	..	12	..	5	..	4	..	5	..	74
Pakistan	6,184	8,637	24	23	27	26	9	13	15	16	25	22
Panama	502	713	51	51	8	5	2	..	8	6	31	37
Papua New Guinea	289	286	..	..	..	..	..	..	..	..	..	..
Paraguay	883	1,033	55	..	16	..	..	..	..	..	29	..
Peru	3,926	7,707	23	26	11	10	8	6	9	10	49	49
Philippines	11,008	16,878	39	33	11	9	13	15	12	13	26	29
Poland	..	28,625	21	26	9	6	26	23	7	6	37	38
Portugal	13,631	18,926	15	..	21	..	13	..	6	..	45	..
Puerto Rico	12,126	23,375	16	8	5	3	18	15	44	58	17	15

	Manufacturing value added		Food, beverages, and tobacco		Textiles and clothing		Machinery and transport equipment		Chemicals		Other manufacturing [a]	
	$ millions		% of total		% of total		% of total		% of total		% of total	
	1990	2000	1990	2000	1990	2000	1990	2000	1990	2000	1990	2000
Romania	9,152	4,768	19	..	18	..	14	..	4	..	45	..
Russian Federation	..	..	..	16	..	2	..	19	..	9	..	54
Rwanda	473	205	..	..	..	..	..	..	..	..	..	..
Saudi Arabia	10,049	18,235	..	..	..	..	..	..	..	..	..	..
Senegal	747	566	60	44	3	5	5	3	9	26	23	21
Serbia and Montenegro	..	..	..	28	..	8	..	13	..	11	..	40
Sierra Leone	31	28	..	..	..	..	..	..	..	..	..	..
Singapore	..	24,407	4	2	3	1	53	62	10	14	29	20
Slovak Republic	..	4,075	..	..	..	..	..	..	..	..	..	..
Slovenia	4,008	4,468	12	11	15	9	16	16	9	11	48	52
Somalia	41	..	..	..	..	..	..	..	..	..	..	..
South Africa	24,043	21,643	14	14	8	7	18	20	9	9	50	50
Spain	..	95,110	18	14	8	7	25	23	10	10	39	47
Sri Lanka	1,077	2,459	51	42	24	26	4	8	4	4	17	19
Sudan	..	1,059	..	..	..	..	..	..	..	..	..	..
Swaziland	250	348	69	..	8	..	1	..	0	..	22	..
Sweden	..	47,689	10	7	2	1	32	39	9	11	47	42
Switzerland	..	..	10	9	4	3	34	27	..	..	53	60
Syrian Arab Republic	2,508	4,579	35	27	29	24	..	..	..	..	36	49
Tajikistan	653	237	..	..	..	..	..	..	..	..	..	..
Tanzania [b]	361	624	51	45	3	0	6	5	11	7	28	43
Thailand	23,217	41,212	24	..	30	..	19	..	2	..	26	..
Togo	162	118	..	..	..	..	..	..	..	..	..	..
Trinidad and Tobago	438	599	30	..	3	..	3	..	19	..	44	..
Tunisia	2,075	3,537	19	18	20	33	5	9	4	9	52	31
Turkey	26,882	26,994	16	13	15	18	16	17	10	11	43	41
Turkmenistan	..	643	..	..	..	..	..	..	..	..	..	..
Uganda	230	527	..	..	..	..	..	..	..	..	..	..
Ukraine	32,977	5,099	..	..	..	..	..	..	..	..	..	..
United Arab Emirates	2,643	..	..	..	..	..	..	..	..	..	..	..
United Kingdom	206,727	232,507	13	..	5	..	32	..	11	..	38	..
United States	1,040,600	1,520,300	12	..	5	..	31	..	12	..	40	..
Uruguay	2,597	3,392	31	37	18	12	9	3	10	8	32	39
Uzbekistan	..	645	..	..	..	..	..	..	..	..	..	..
Venezuela, RB	9,809	15,621	17	22	5	2	5	..	9	..	64	76
Vietnam	793	5,786	..	..	..	..	..	..	..	..	..	..
West Bank and Gaza	..	591	..	..	..	..	..	..	..	..	..	..
Yemen, Rep.	449	493	..	..	..	..	..	..	..	..	..	..
Zambia	1,048	329	44	..	11	..	7	..	9	..	29	..
Zimbabwe	1,799	1,003	28	30	19	7	9	29	6	6	38	28
World	**4,475,773 t**	**5,826,313 t**										
Low income	112,968	149,818										
Middle income	698,289	1,114,738										
Lower middle income	490,903	806,107										
Upper middle income	170,285	302,007										
Low & middle income	755,166	1,263,141										
East Asia & Pacific	188,907	514,058										
Europe & Central Asia	..	..										
Latin America & Carib.	243,987	307,798										
Middle East & N. Africa	47,699	81,370										
South Asia	61,101	85,928										
Sub-Saharan Africa	42,805	37,493										
High income	3,708,270	4,573,059										
Europe EMU	1,221,575	1,119,610										

a. Includes unallocated data. b. Data cover mainland Tanzania only.

The data on the distribution of manufacturing value added by industry are provided by the United Nations Industrial Development Organization (UNIDO). UNIDO obtains data on manufacturing value added from a variety of national and international sources, including the United Nations Statistics Division, the World Bank, the Organisation for Economic Co-operation and Development, and the International Monetary Fund. To improve comparability over time and across countries, UNIDO supplements these data with information from industrial censuses, statistics supplied by national and international organizations, unpublished data that it collects in the field, and estimates by the UNIDO Secretariat. Nevertheless, coverage may be less than complete, particularly for the informal sector. To the extent that direct information on inputs and outputs is not available, estimates may be used that may result in errors in industry totals. Moreover, countries use different reference periods (calendar or fiscal year) and valuation methods (basic, producer, or purchaser prices) to estimate value added. (See also *About the data* for table 4.2.)

The data on manufacturing value added in U.S. dollars are from the World Bank's national accounts files. These figures may differ from those used by UNIDO to calculate the shares of value added by industry, in part because of differences in exchange rates. Thus estimates of value added in a particular industry calculated by applying the shares to total manufacturing value added will not match those from UNIDO sources. The classification of manufacturing industries in the table accords with the United Nations International Standard Industrial Classification (ISIC) revision 2. First published in 1948, the ISIC has its roots in the work of the League of Nations Committee of Statistical Experts. The committee's efforts, interrupted by the Second World War, were taken up by the United Nations Statistical Commission, which at its first session appointed a committee on industrial classification. The latest revision, ISIC revision 3, was completed in 1989, and many countries have now switched to it. But revision 2 is still widely used for compiling cross-country data. Concordances matching ISIC categories to national systems of classification and to related systems such as the Standard International Trade Classification (SITC) are readily available.

In establishing a classification system, compilers must define both the types of activities to be described and the organizational units whose activities are to be reported. There are many possibilities, and the choices made affect how the resulting statistics can be interpreted and how useful they are in analyzing economic behavior. The ISIC emphasizes commonalities in the production process and is explicitly not intended to measure outputs (for which there is a newly developed Central Product Classification). Nevertheless, the ISIC views an activity as defined by "a process resulting in a homogeneous set of products" (United Nations 1990 [ISIC, series M, no. 4, rev. 3], p. 9).

Firms typically use a multitude of processes to produce a final product. For example, an automobile manufacturer engages in forging, welding, and painting as well as advertising, accounting, and many other service activities. In some cases the processes may be carried out by different technical units within the larger enterprise, but collecting data at such a detailed level is not practical. Nor would it be useful to record production data at the very highest level of a large, multiplant, multiproduct firm. The ISIC has therefore adopted as the definition of an establishment "an enterprise or part of an enterprise which independently engages in one, or predominantly one, kind of economic activity at or from one location...for which data are available..." (United Nations 1990, p. 25). By design, this definition matches the reporting unit required for the production accounts of the United Nations System of National Accounts.

• **Manufacturing value added** is the sum of gross output less the value of intermediate inputs used in production for industries classified in ISIC major division 3. • **Food, beverages, and tobacco** correspond to ISIC division 31. • **Textiles and clothing** correspond to ISIC division 32. • **Machinery and transport equipment** comprise ISIC groups 382–84. • **Chemicals** correspond to ISIC groups 351 and 352. • **Other manufacturing** covers wood and related products (ISIC division 33), paper and related products (ISIC division 34), petroleum and related products (ISIC groups 353–56), basic metals and mineral products (ISIC divisions 36 and 37), fabricated metal products and professional goods (ISIC groups 381 and 385), and other industries (ISIC group 390). When data for textiles and clothing, machinery and transport equipment, or chemicals are shown in the table as not available, they are included in "other manufacturing."

4.3a

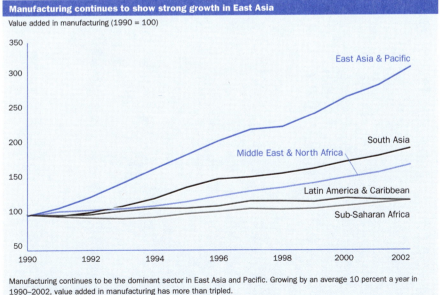

Manufacturing continues to show strong growth in East Asia

Value added in manufacturing (1990 = 100)

East Asia & Pacific

South Asia

Middle East & North Africa

Latin America & Caribbean

Sub-Saharan Africa

Manufacturing continues to be the dominant sector in East Asia and Pacific. Growing by an average 10 percent a year in 1990–2002, value added in manufacturing has more than tripled.

Source: World Bank data files.

	Export volume		Import volume		Export value		Import value		Net barter terms of trade	
	average annual % growth		average annual % growth		average annual % growth		average annual % growth		1995 = 100	
	1980–90	1990–2001	1980–90	1990–2001	1980–90	1990–2001	1980–90	1990–2001	1990	2001
Afghanistan	–9.7	–3.9	–1.8	–0.2	–10.5	–4.7	–0.1	–1.1	99	100
Albania [a]	..	..	..	..	..	13.3	..	17.2	..	..
Algeria	3.3	2.3	–8.0	2.0	–4.4	3.0	–2.7	1.2	128	174
Angola	10.0	5.6	–1.8	7.3	16.5	6.6	3.7	8.0	118	109
Argentina	4.9	8.8	–6.8	13.6	2.2	9.2	–6.6	13.4	97	108
Armenia [a]	..	..	..	..	..	–6.8	..	0.5	..	..
Australia [a]	6.3	7.1	6.0	8.7	6.6	4.7	6.4	5.4	117	105
Austria [a]	6.6	..	..	..	10.2	5.3	8.7	3.8	..	..
Azerbaijan [a]	..	..	..	..	..	–6.4	..	4.0	..	..
Bangladesh	8.4	28.2	3.0	23.3	8.0	14.2	3.5	9.6	100	92
Belarus [a]	..	..	..	..	..	13.9	..	14.1	..	..
Belgium [a, b]	4.5	6.2	4.0	5.4	7.8	6.3	6.4	4.5	100	..
Benin	11.9	2.3	–10.0	6.6	18.7	2.4	–4.8	6.9	100	82
Bolivia	3.1	3.2	–1.3	8.1	–1.9	4.4	–0.4	8.4	115	111
Bosnia and Herzegovina	..	..	..	..	..	..	..	..	..	..
Botswana	14.9	9.3	9.3	5.3	18.7	8.5	9.1	1.7	109	130
Brazil	6.2	5.4	0.8	14.7	5.2	5.6	–1.8	10.9	60	91
Bulgaria [a]	..	..	..	..	–12.3	2.2	–14.0	5.6	..	..
Burkina Faso	–0.3	11.4	3.8	1.6	7.8	10.4	4.4	1.5	91	83
Burundi	3.4	10.3	0.9	6.0	2.5	–5.6	2.2	–6.3	79	44
Cambodia	..	..	..	..	..	..	..	..	..	..
Cameroon	8.4	2.3	4.8	5.5	2.4	–0.3	0.1	2.1	90	95
Canada [a]	6.4	8.7	7.4	8.7	6.8	7.8	7.9	7.0	100	103
Central African Republic	–0.0	18.8	4.2	3.2	3.5	3.0	7.8	–0.7	124	54
Chad	8.7	1.5	10.7	3.6	9.4	1.8	12.5	6.2	116	110
Chile	9.1	10.7	–2.9	9.3	8.1	8.6	2.8	8.9	84	69
China [†]	..	13.4	..	8.1	..	12.8	..	10.3	..	81
Hong Kong, China	15.3	7.7	13.8	8.2	16.7	7.3	14.7	7.7	101	102
Colombia	7.9	4.3	–2.1	7.6	7.7	6.7	–0.2	8.5	95	109
Congo, Dem. Rep.	14.8	–10.0	37.8	–6.1	7.7	–6.7	26.7	–0.5	108	125
Congo, Rep.	7.3	5.7	–2.5	1.8	2.1	7.5	–0.7	1.4	122	156
Costa Rica	3.7	12.6	5.2	13.8	4.7	14.8	4.4	12.8	72	95
Côte d'Ivoire	2.6	3.0	–2.1	3.5	1.8	5.0	–1.5	3.6	82	103
Croatia [a]	..	..	..	..	..	1.6	..	7.7	..	..
Cuba	–1.1	–1.0	–0.5	3.1	–0.9	–1.5	1.5	2.3	96	92
Czech Republic [a]	..	..	..	..	..	9.9	..	10.0	..	..
Denmark [a]	4.1	5.2	3.1	6.0	8.4	3.6	6.3	3.8	100	102
Dominican Republic	–0.9	3.3	0.8	12.8	–2.1	3.9	3.3	12.9	97	104
Ecuador	7.1	5.6	–1.9	6.5	–0.5	6.0	–1.3	7.9	141	114
Egypt, Arab Rep.	2.1	2.8	8.0	1.1	–3.3	3.7	12.6	3.8	86	85
El Salvador	–4.6	3.0	4.5	7.5	–4.7	8.9	2.4	10.6	69	80
Eritrea	..	26.0	..	7.1	..	24.4	..	5.8	91	97
Estonia [a]	..	..	..	..	..	17.4	..	18.9	..	..
Ethiopia	–0.4	6.8	3.6	3.1	–1.0	9.2	3.9	7.7	90	79
Finland [a]	2.3	9.3	4.4	4.3	7.4	6.9	6.9	4.4	100	88
France [a]	3.6	6.4	3.7	5.6	7.5	3.8	6.5	3.2	97	96
Gabon	2.6	3.4	–3.5	2.8	–3.9	0.7	1.1	2.4	126	113
Gambia, The	–4.2	–13.2	–6.0	0.1	–0.0	–13.7	2.4	–0.4	100	100
Georgia	..	..	..	..	..	..	..	..	..	..
Germany [a, c]	4.5	5.9	4.9	4.3	9.2	3.7	7.1	3.2	102	95
Ghana	–17.2	10.0	–20.1	9.7	–2.6	10.6	–0.4	9.0	94	101
Greece [a]	5.0	8.9	6.4	8.9	5.8	2.1	6.6	4.2	108	107
Guatemala	–1.1	8.2	0.1	10.2	–2.3	8.9	0.5	11.0	98	83
Guinea	..	4.7	..	–1.9	..	0.8	..	–2.3	135	100
Guinea-Bissau	–2.1	17.1	–0.3	–5.5	4.2	13.3	5.3	–3.2	143	70
Haiti	–0.4	12.2	–4.6	12.7	–1.2	11.8	–2.9	13.7	116	89
[†] Data for Taiwan, China	..	5.3	..	6.8	..	6.6	..	7.2	102	117

Growth of merchandise trade

	Export volume		Import volume		Export value		Import value		Net barter terms of trade	
	average annual % growth		average annual % growth		average annual % growth		average annual % growth		1995 = 100	
	1980–90	1990–2001	1980–90	1990–2001	1980–90	1990–2001	1980–90	1990–2001	1990	2001
Honduras	4.1	2.5	1.6	12.3	1.6	6.3	0.5	13.2	81	102
Hungary [a]	3.4	10.9	1.3	12.0	1.4	12.8	0.1	13.2	106	96
India	4.2	11.2	4.7	12.6	7.3	9.1	4.2	9.5	79	91
Indonesia	8.1	8.6	..	..	–0.8	7.1	..	..	..	..
Iran, Islamic Rep.	17.1	–0.9	–2.4	–7.5	7.2	1.2	0.2	–6.5	170	225
Iraq	2.3	29.5	–4.5	9.8	–4.0	29.4	–2.2	10.3	132	162
Ireland [a]	9.3	15.1	4.8	11.2	12.8	13.4	7.0	10.4	107	99
Israel [a]	6.9	9.6	5.8	8.2	8.3	10.5	5.9	7.3	97	106
Italy [a]	4.3	5.4	5.3	4.7	8.7	4.2	6.9	3.2	98	102
Jamaica	1.6	4.6	3.0	7.3	1.1	2.2	2.8	6.8	105	87
Japan [a]	5.1	2.3	6.6	5.1	8.9	3.3	5.1	4.3	91	88
Jordan	7.8	5.3	1.1	3.9	6.0	6.7	–1.9	5.2	80	85
Kazakhstan [a]	..	..	..	..	..	12.4	..	5.1	..	..
Kenya	1.7	4.1	2.5	6.6	–1.1	5.6	1.7	5.6	68	88
Korea, Dem. Rep.	..	..	..	..	..	..	..	..	..	..
Korea, Rep.	12.3	15.4	11.7	9.3	15.0	9.1	12.0	6.5	96	69
Kuwait	..	20.0	..	..	..	16.3	..	..	..	..
Kyrgyz Republic [a]	..	..	..	..	..	4.9	..	4.7	..	..
Lao PDR [a]	..	..	..	..	11.0	13.2	6.6	10.5	..	..
Latvia [a]	..	7.2	..	..	..	10.7	..	17.4	..	..
Lebanon	–5.6	2.4	–7.5	8.6	–5.6	4.1	–5.5	8.9	105	112
Lesotho	6.3	13.9	3.5	1.6	3.8	12.2	3.4	–0.4	97	100
Liberia	–3.5	7.4	–7.6	9.7	–3.1	4.6	–7.2	8.8	112	89
Libya	0.1	–4.1	–6.6	0.3	–7.3	–2.2	–4.4	1.8	145	200
Lithuania [a]	..	..	..	..	..	9.5	..	13.2	..	..
Macedonia, FYR [a]	..	..	..	..	..	1.8	..	4.4	..	..
Madagascar	–2.2	4.7	–4.4	6.2	–1.0	9.7	–2.4	7.4	102	148
Malawi	2.3	3.0	–0.1	–2.3	2.0	1.1	3.2	–0.9	141	96
Malaysia	14.6	10.7	..	..	8.6	14.0	..	..	..	..
Mali	4.4	11.5	3.0	5.3	6.1	7.5	2.7	3.8	122	95
Mauritania	4.1	2.1	–2.9	4.3	8.2	–2.4	–1.8	0.2	96	96
Mauritius	11.5	2.4	11.8	3.1	14.3	3.1	12.8	3.1	104	113
Mexico	15.4	14.8	0.8	12.3	5.8	15.4	6.3	13.0	109	107
Moldova [a]	..	..	..	..	..	–0.2	..	2.6	..	..
Mongolia	3.1	..	..	..	5.0	–1.7	5.0	0.8	..	..
Morocco	5.6	6.7	3.1	7.2	6.1	6.6	3.6	5.2	95	115
Mozambique	–9.5	18.8	–2.7	3.0	–9.6	12.9	0.1	1.6	115	79
Myanmar	–5.9	16.7	–10.0	13.7	–7.2	16.0	–5.1	21.3	117	65
Namibia [a]	..	2.1	..	4.8	..	0.3	..	3.6	115	98
Nepal [a]	..	..	..	..	8.1	10.8	6.9	8.2	..	..
Netherlands [a]	4.5	6.8	4.5	6.7	4.6	5.2	4.4	5.0	98	99
New Zealand [a]	3.5	4.4	4.3	5.5	6.2	3.5	5.4	4.8	103	106
Nicaragua	–4.8	10.1	–3.5	8.8	–5.8	9.5	–3.1	11.0	119	71
Niger	–5.2	3.7	–5.2	–2.2	–5.4	0.2	–3.5	0.9	136	77
Nigeria	–4.4	2.6	–21.4	2.8	–8.4	3.7	–15.6	3.5	162	157
Norway [a]	4.2	6.3	3.5	7.4	5.3	5.5	6.2	3.5	111	157
Oman	11.0	11.0	..	..	–2.2	14.8	..	..	..	..
Pakistan	7.9	3.0	2.6	1.9	8.0	4.0	2.9	2.5	91	83
Panama	–0.6	6.1	–6.6	6.4	–0.6	9.1	–3.6	7.3	69	100
Papua New Guinea	4.6	2.5	..	..	4.8	5.9	..	..	..	..
Paraguay	12.6	1.2	10.1	2.3	11.5	2.7	4.2	3.6	87	84
Peru	2.7	9.6	–2.0	9.3	–1.5	8.3	1.3	9.2	93	78
Philippines	17.3	21.9	18.3	16.5	3.9	17.1	2.9	10.3	109	118
Poland [a]	4.8	9.8	1.5	17.2	1.4	9.9	–3.2	16.7	86	95
Portugal [a]	11.9	..	..	..	15.1	4.7	10.3	4.7	..	..
Puerto Rico	..	..	..	..	..	..	..	..	..	..

	Export volume		Import volume		Export value		Import value		Net barter terms of trade	
	average annual % growth		average annual % growth		average annual % growth		average annual % growth		1995 = 100	
	1980–90	1990–2001	1980–90	1990–2001	1980–90	1990–2001	1980–90	1990–2001	1990	2001
Romania [a]	..	..	..	..	–4.0	8.7	–3.8	7.4	..	..
Russian Federation [a]	..	..	..	..	..	9.1	..	2.5	..	..
Rwanda	3.3	–4.2	2.3	1.2	–0.3	–1.4	3.3	–0.8	36	72
Saudi Arabia	–6.3	1.6	..	..	–13.3	3.5	..	..	..	..
Senegal	1.2	6.8	0.4	5.5	3.6	3.7	1.4	3.3	109	91
Serbia and Montenegro	..	..	..	..	..	..	..	..	..	..
Sierra Leone	–2.7	–36.3	–3.0	–8.0	–2.4	–24.8	–8.7	–2.7	73	..
Singapore	12.2	10.8	8.5	7.1	9.9	8.6	8.1	6.6	111	92
Slovak Republic [a]	..	..	..	..	..	9.8	..	10.7	..	..
Slovenia [a]	..	..	..	..	..	7.5	..	8.3	..	..
Somalia	–1.5	–0.5	–11.1	2.3	–1.1	–2.4	–9.2	1.7	99	82
South Africa [a, d]	1.6	5.0	–0.9	7.7	0.7	2.3	–1.4	5.0	99	100
Spain [a]	2.7	10.9	10.5	9.2	10.8	7.9	10.6	6.0	96	99
Sri Lanka	4.6	6.9	1.7	10.2	5.4	10.1	2.2	12.3	83	..
Sudan	–3.0	17.1	–7.7	11.2	–2.5	14.0	–6.4	9.9	123	141
Swaziland	7.7	1.2	2.3	3.8	4.6	2.2	–0.5	4.8	100	100
Sweden [a]	4.4	8.4	5.0	6.2	8.0	4.9	6.7	3.7	99	89
Switzerland [a]	3.7	..	..	..	9.5	2.5	8.8	1.9	..	..
Syrian Arab Republic	19.4	1.2	–1.0	8.2	2.4	0.8	–8.5	10.2	131	..
Tajikistan	..	..	..	..	..	..	..	..	..	..
Tanzania	..	6.5	..	–0.8	..	7.1	..	0.7	110	95
Thailand	13.7	9.1	11.3	2.2	13.8	9.6	12.6	4.7	102	78
Togo	–1.2	9.3	0.6	5.7	1.1	7.1	2.0	5.0	134	107
Trinidad and Tobago	–10.9	3.6	–20.4	10.2	–9.4	7.3	–12.3	11.3	117	172
Tunisia	4.9	5.8	1.6	4.8	3.4	5.9	2.7	5.1	103	99
Turkey	19.4	10.8	15.4	9.6	14.1	8.8	9.3	8.8	104	93
Turkmenistan	..	..	..	..	..	..	..	..	..	..
Uganda	–13.5	15.6	–6.7	24.1	–8.3	13.0	3.4	19.0	74	78
Ukraine [a]	..	..	..	..	..	7.0	..	6.3	..	..
United Arab Emirates	8.9	2.1	–1.3	9.2	–0.8	4.0	0.7	11.2	174	213
United Kingdom [a]	4.5	6.2	6.7	6.8	5.9	4.7	8.5	4.9	101	104
United States [a]	3.6	6.2	7.2	8.8	5.7	6.6	8.2	9.1	98	99
Uruguay	4.4	5.3	1.2	8.8	4.5	4.0	–1.3	8.3	100	87
Uzbekistan	..	..	..	..	..	..	..	..	..	..
Venezuela, RB	3.4	5.1	–4.0	5.3	–4.4	5.7	–3.3	5.6	142	132
Vietnam	..	..	..	..	..	..	..	..	..	..
West Bank and Gaza	..	..	..	..	..	..	..	..	..	..
Yemen, Rep. [a]	..	..	..	..	..	..	..	..	..	..
Zambia	–0.5	6.2	2.1	4.3	0.9	–1.4	–0.0	1.9	109	56
Zimbabwe	4.1	8.7	3.4	9.6	2.9	2.4	–0.4	3.1	100	104

a. Data are from the International Monetary Fund's *International Financial Statistics* database. b. Includes Luxembourg. c. Data prior to 1990 refer to the Federal Republic of Germany before unification. d. Data refer to the South African Customs Union (Botswana, Lesotho, Namibia, South Africa, and Swaziland).

About the data

Data on international trade in goods are available from each country's balance of payments and customs records. While the balance of payments focuses on the financial transactions that accompany trade, customs data record the direction of trade and the physical quantities and value of goods entering or leaving the customs area. Customs data may differ from data recorded in the balance of payments because of differences in valuation and the time of recording. The 1993 System of National Accounts and the fifth edition of the International Monetary Fund's (IMF) *Balance of Payments Manual* (1993) attempted to reconcile the definitions and reporting standards for international trade statistics, but differences in sources, timing, and national practices limit comparability. Real growth rates derived from trade volume indexes and terms of trade based on unit price indexes may therefore differ from those derived from national accounts aggregates.

Trade in goods, or merchandise trade, includes all goods that add to or subtract from an economy's material resources. Thus the total supply of goods in an economy is made up of gross output plus imports less exports (currency in circulation, titles of ownership, and securities are excluded, but nonmonetary gold is included). Trade data are collected on the basis of a country's customs area, which in most cases is the same as its geographic area. Goods provided as part of foreign aid are included, but goods destined for extraterritorial agencies (such as embassies) are not.

Collecting and tabulating trade statistics are difficult. Some developing countries lack the capacity to report timely data; this is a problem especially for countries that are landlocked and those whose territorial boundaries are porous. As a result, it is necessary to estimate their trade from the data reported by their partners. (For further discussion of the use of partner country reports, see *About the data* for table 6.2.) Countries that belong to common customs unions may need to collect data through direct inquiry of companies. In some cases economic or political concerns may lead national authorities to suppress or misrepresent data on certain trade flows, such as oil, military equipment, or the exports of a dominant producer. In other cases reported trade data may be distorted by deliberate under- or over-invoicing to effect capital transfers or avoid taxes. And in some regions smuggling and black market trading result in unreported trade flows.

By international agreement customs data are reported to the United Nations Statistics Division, which maintains the Commodity Trade (COMTRADE) database. The United Nations Conference on Trade and Development (UNCTAD) compiles a variety of international trade statistics, including price and volume indexes, based on the COMTRADE data. The IMF and the World Trade Organization also compile data on trade prices and volumes. The growth rates and terms of trade for low- and middle-income economies shown in the table were calculated from index numbers compiled by UNCTAD. Volume measures for high-income economies were derived by deflating the value of trade using deflators from the IMF's *International Financial Statistics*. In some cases price and volume indexes from different sources may vary significantly as a result of differences in estimation procedures. All indexes are rescaled to a 1995 base year. Terms of trade were computed from the same indicators.

The terms of trade measures the relative prices of a country's exports and imports. There are a number of ways to calculate terms of trade. The most common is the net barter (or commodity) terms of trade, constructed as the ratio of the export price index to the import price index. When a country's net barter terms of trade increase, its exports are becoming more valuable or its imports cheaper.

Definitions

• **Export and import volumes** are average annual growth rates calculated for low- and middle-income economies from UNCTAD's quantum index series and for high-income economies from export and import data deflated by the IMF's trade price deflators. • **Export and import values** are average annual growth rates calculated from UNCTAD's value indexes or from current values of merchandise exports and imports. • **Net barter terms of trade** are calculated as the ratio of the export price index to the corresponding import price index measured relative to the base year 1995.

Data sources

The main source of trade data for developing countries is UNCTAD's annual *Handbook of International Trade and Development Statistics*. The IMF's *International Financial Statistics* includes data on the export and import values and deflators for high-income and selected developing economies.

Structure of merchandise exports

	Merchandise exports		Food		Agricultural raw materials		Fuels		Ores and metals		Manufactures	
	$ millions		% of total		% of total		% of total		% of total		% of total	
	1990	**2002**	**1990**	**2002**	**1990**	**2002**	**1990**	**2002**	**1990**	**2002**	**1990**	**2002**
Afghanistan	235	101	..	..	..	..	..	..	..	..	..	..
Albania	230	330	..	4	..	7	..	1	..	3	..	86
Algeria	12,930	19,130	0	0	0	0	96	97	0	0	3	2
Angola	3,910	7,600	0	..	0	..	93	..	6	..	0	..
Argentina	12,353	25,352	56	46	4	2	8	17	2	4	29	31
Armenia	..	508	..	16	..	2	..	4	..	18	..	61
Australia	39,752	65,034	22	22	10	5	21	22	20	16	24	29
Austria	41,265	78,694	3	6	4	2	1	2	3	3	88	82
Azerbaijan	..	2,168	..	3	..	1	..	89	..	0	..	6
Bangladesh	1,671	6,093	14	7	7	1	1	0	..	0	77	92
Belarus	..	8,100	..	8	..	4	..	20	..	1	..	64
Belgium [a]	117,703	224,185	..	9	..	1	..	4	..	3	..	79
Benin	288	365	15	23	56	71	15	0	0	0	13	6
Bolivia	926	1,310	19	34	8	3	25	27	44	20	5	17
Bosnia and Herzegovina	276	950	..	..	..	..	..	..	..	..	..	..
Botswana	1,784	2,510	..	3	..	0	..	0	..	5	..	91
Brazil	31,414	60,362	28	28	3	4	2	4	14	8	52	54
Bulgaria	5,030	5,745	..	10	..	3	..	9	..	11	..	61
Burkina Faso	152	166	..	22	..	56	..	3	..	0	..	19
Burundi	75	30	..	88	..	1	..	..	..	10	..	1
Cambodia	86	1,500	..	..	..	..	..	..	..	..	..	..
Cameroon	2,002	1,700	20	21	14	20	50	47	7	4	9	7
Canada	127,629	252,394	9	7	9	5	10	13	9	4	59	63
Central African Republic	120	160	..	..	..	..	..	..	..	..	..	..
Chad	188	180	..	..	..	..	..	..	..	..	..	..
Chile	8,372	18,340	24	26	9	10	1	1	55	41	11	18
China [†]	62,091	325,565	13	5	3	1	8	3	2	2	72	90
Hong Kong, China [b]	82,390	201,150	3	2	0	0	0	1	1	2	95	95
Colombia	6,766	12,001	33	19	4	6	37	36	0	1	25	38
Congo, Dem. Rep.	2,326	1,210	..	..	..	..	..	..	..	..	..	..
Congo, Rep.	981	2,215	..	..	..	..	..	..	..	..	..	..
Costa Rica	1,448	5,258	58	31	5	3	1	1	1	1	27	63
Côte d'Ivoire	3,072	4,390	..	59	..	14	..	11	..	0	..	21
Croatia	4,597	4,899	13	11	6	4	9	9	5	3	68	73
Cuba	5,100	1,500	..	59	..	0	..	1	..	29	..	10
Czech Republic	12,170	38,403	..	3	..	2	..	4	..	1	..	89
Denmark	36,870	57,045	27	19	3	3	3	6	1	1	60	66
Dominican Republic	2,170	5,183	21	41	0	..	0	16	0	2	78	34
Ecuador	2,714	5,030	44	43	1	7	52	40	0	0	2	10
Egypt, Arab Rep.	3,477	4,381	10	9	10	0	29	34	9	5	42	35
El Salvador	582	2,992	57	33	1	1	2	5	3	3	38	58
Eritrea	15	14	..	..	..	..	..	..	..	..	..	..
Estonia	..	4,336	..	12	..	8	..	5	..	2	..	72
Ethiopia	298	415	..	69	..	15	..	0	..	1	..	14
Finland	26,571	44,836	2	2	10	6	1	3	4	3	83	85
France	216,588	331,780	16	11	2	1	2	2	3	2	77	81
Gabon	2,204	2,560	..	1	..	12	..	83	..	2	..	2
Gambia, The	31	15	..	81	..	1	..	0	..	0	..	17
Georgia	..	326	..	26	..	2	..	9	..	27	..	35
Germany	421,100	613,093	5	4	1	1	1	1	3	2	89	86
Ghana	897	1,840	51	45	15	10	9	11	17	17	8	16
Greece	8,105	10,353	30	24	3	3	7	11	7	8	54	52
Guatemala	1,163	2,232	67	53	6	4	2	7	0	1	24	35
Guinea	671	750	..	2	..	0	..	1	..	68	..	28
Guinea-Bissau	19	51	..	..	..	..	..	..	..	..	..	..
Haiti	160	280	14	..	1	..	0	..	0	..	85	..
[†] Data for Taiwan, China	67,245	135,065	4	1	2	1	1	1	1	1	93	94

Structure of merchandise exports | 4.5

	Merchandise exports		Food		Agricultural raw materials		Fuels		Ores and metals		Manufactures	
	$ millions		% of total		% of total		% of total		% of total		% of total	
	1990	2002	1990	2002	1990	2002	1990	2002	1990	2002	1990	2002
Honduras	831	1,270	82	64	4	5	1	0	4	6	9	26
Hungary	10,000	34,337	23	7	3	1	3	1	6	2	63	86
India	17,969	49,251	16	12	4	1	3	5	5	4	71	75
Indonesia	25,675	57,130	11	12	5	4	44	24	4	5	35	54
Iran, Islamic Rep.	19,305	24,440	..	4	..	0	..	86	..	1	..	9
Iraq	12,380	13,520	..	..	..	..	..	..	..	..	..	..
Ireland	23,743	88,224	22	7	2	0	1	0	1	0	70	88
Israel	12,080	29,513	8	4	3	1	1	0	2	1	87	93
Italy	170,304	250,975	6	7	1	1	2	2	1	1	88	88
Jamaica	1,158	1,105	19	23	0	0	1	3	10	10	69	64
Japan	287,581	416,726	1	1	1	1	0	0	1	1	96	93
Jordan	1,064	2,743	11	15	0	0	0	0	38	17	51	68
Kazakhstan	..	9,709	..	5	..	1	..	56	..	18	..	19
Kenya	1,031	2,094	49	32	6	11	13	31	3	2	29	24
Korea, Dem. Rep.	1,857	724	..	..	..	..	..	..	..	..	..	..
Korea, Rep.	65,016	162,470	3	2	1	1	1	4	1	1	94	92
Kuwait	7,042	15,426	1	..	0	..	93	..	0	..	6	..
Kyrgyz Republic	..	486	..	18	..	23	..	20	..	6	..	33
Lao PDR	79	298	..	..	..	..	..	..	..	..	..	..
Latvia	..	2,284	..	10	..	24	..	1	..	6	..	59
Lebanon	494	1,046	..	19	..	6	..	0	..	6	..	69
Lesotho	62	395	..	..	..	..	..	..	..	..	..	..
Liberia	868	220	..	..	..	..	..	..	..	..	..	..
Libya	13,225	10,970	0	..	0	..	94	..	0	..	5	..
Lithuania	..	5,560	..	12	..	4	..	23	..	2	..	58
Macedonia, FYR	1,199	1,112	..	16	..	1	..	4	..	8	..	70
Madagascar	319	785	73	..	4	..	1	..	8	..	14	..
Malawi	417	478	93	87	2	2	0	0	0	0	5	10
Malaysia	29,452	93,265	12	8	14	2	18	9	2	1	54	79
Mali	359	947	36	..	62	..	..	..	0	..	2	..
Mauritania	469	315	..	..	..	..	..	..	..	..	..	..
Mauritius	1,194	1,755	32	26	1	0	1	0	0	0	66	73
Mexico	40,711	160,682	12	5	2	1	38	9	6	1	43	84
Moldova	..	667	..	64	..	3	..	0	..	2	..	31
Mongolia	661	501	..	6	..	15	..	1	..	43	..	36
Morocco	4,265	7,930	26	21	3	1	4	3	15	8	52	66
Mozambique	126	682	..	23	..	4	..	10	..	55	..	8
Myanmar	325	3,015	51	..	36	..	0	..	2	..	10	..
Namibia	1,085	1,096	..	36	..	1	..	1	..	9	..	52
Nepal	204	568	13	10	3	0	..	..	0	0	83	67
Netherlands	131,775	244,304	20	19	4	4	10	1	3	2	59	74
New Zealand	9,394	14,363	47	49	18	13	4	2	6	4	23	28
Nicaragua	330	596	77	72	14	4	0	2	1	3	8	19
Niger	282	303	..	38	..	1	..	0	..	56	..	3
Nigeria	13,596	15,107	1	0	1	0	97	100	0	0	1	0
Norway	34,047	60,971	7	7	2	1	48	61	10	6	33	22
Oman	5,508	11,172	1	6	0	0	92	77	1	1	5	15
Pakistan	5,615	9,913	9	11	10	1	1	2	0	0	79	85
Panama	340	846	75	79	1	1	0	6	1	1	21	12
Papua New Guinea	1,177	1,550	22	15	9	2	0	29	58	51	10	2
Paraguay	959	1,030	52	75	38	14	0	0	0	1	10	15
Peru	3,230	7,688	21	30	3	3	10	8	47	38	18	21
Philippines	8,117	36,265	19	5	2	0	2	1	8	1	38	50
Poland	14,320	41,010	13	8	3	1	11	5	9	4	59	82
Portugal	16,417	25,621	7	7	6	3	3	2	3	2	80	86
Puerto Rico	..	..	..	..	..	..	..	..	..	..	..	..

	Merchandise exports		Food		Agricultural raw materials		Fuels		Ores and metals		Manufactures	
	$ millions		% of total		% of total		% of total		% of total		% of total	
	1990	2002	1990	2002	1990	2002	1990	2002	1990	2002	1990	2002
Romania	4,960	13,869	1	3	3	3	18	8	4	4	73	81
Russian Federation	40,000	106,858	..	2	..	4	..	56	..	8	..	22
Rwanda	110	56	..	56	..	5	..	0	..	36	..	3
Saudi Arabia	44,417	73,940	1	1	0	0	92	89	0	0	7	10
Senegal	761	1,055	53	16	3	3	12	23	9	6	23	51
Serbia and Montenegro	2,929	2,275	7	..	..	..	2	..	7	..	79	..
Sierra Leone	138	49	..	..	..	..	..	..	..	..	..	..
Singapore[b]	52,730	125,177	5	2	3	0	18	8	2	1	72	85
Slovak Republic	6,355	14,367	..	4	..	2	..	6	..	3	..	85
Slovenia	6,681	9,471	7	4	2	1	3	1	3	4	86	90
Somalia	150	145	..	..	..	..	..	..	..	..	..	..
South Africa[c]	23,549	29,723	7	11	3	3	6	12	9	11	36	63
Spain	55,642	119,131	15	15	2	1	5	3	2	2	75	78
Sri Lanka	1,912	4,699	34	21	6	2	1	0	2	2	54	74
Sudan	374	1,850	61	18	38	6	..	72	0	0	1	3
Swaziland	556	820	..	15	..	12	..	1	..	0	..	76
Sweden	57,540	81,137	2	3	7	5	3	3	3	3	83	81
Switzerland	63,784	87,876	3	3	1	0	0	0	3	4	94	93
Syrian Arab Republic	4,212	5,540	14	13	4	5	45	72	1	1	36	7
Tajikistan	..	738	..	4	..	13	..	14	..	56	..	13
Tanzania	331	875	..	61	..	13	..	0	..	9	..	17
Thailand	23,068	68,853	29	15	5	3	1	3	1	1	63	74
Togo	268	429	23	23	21	11	0	1	45	17	9	43
Trinidad and Tobago	2,080	4,594	5	5	0	0	67	49	1	0	27	46
Tunisia	3,526	6,799	11	7	1	1	17	9	2	1	69	82
Turkey	12,959	34,561	22	10	3	1	2	2	4	2	68	84
Turkmenistan	..	2,950	..	0	..	10	..	81	..	0	..	7
Uganda	152	442	..	73	..	11	..	7	..	2	..	8
Ukraine	..	17,954	..	13	..	2	..	9	..	8	..	67
United Arab Emirates	23,544	47,275	8	1	1	..	5	92	39	4	46	4
United Kingdom	185,172	279,647	7	5	1	0	8	8	3	2	79	79
United States	393,592	693,860	11	8	4	2	3	2	3	2	74	81
Uruguay	1,693	1,861	40	49	21	13	0	1	0	0	39	37
Uzbekistan	..	3,184	..	..	..	..	..	..	..	..	..	..
Venezuela, RB	17,497	26,890	2	2	0	0	80	82	7	4	10	13
Vietnam	2,404	16,530	..	..	..	..	..	..	..	..	..	..
West Bank and Gaza	..	..	..	..	..	..	..	..	..	..	..	..
Yemen, Rep.	692	3,240	75	..	10	..	8	..	7	..	1	..
Zambia	1,309	970	..	10	..	3	..	2	..	72	..	14
Zimbabwe	1,726	1,760	44	26	7	12	1	1	16	22	31	38
World	**3,452,501 t**	**6,454,929 t**	**10 w**	**7 w**	**3 w**	**2 w**	**8 w**	**7 w**	**4 w**	**2 w**	**74 w**	**78 w**
Low income	101,140	211,197	16	16	6	4	23	16	6	5	49	58
Middle income	550,042	1,447,025	17	8	4	2	23	24	6	3	48	60
Lower middle income	317,249	859,842	20	8	4	2	10	21	5	5	59	60
Upper middle income	232,440	587,183	14	9	5	2	39	27	6	2	35	60
Low & middle income	651,141	1,658,222	17	9	5	2	23	23	6	4	48	60
East Asia & Pacific	155,939	606,270	15	7	6	2	14	8	3	2	59	79
Europe & Central Asia[d]	136,412	357,686	..	6	..	3	..	25	..	5	..	57
Latin America & Carib.	143,154	347,667	26	22	4	3	24	17	12	8	34	48
Middle East & N. Africa	125,520	184,863	4	4	1	1	79	75	2	1	15	19
South Asia	27,728	70,831	16	13	5	1	2	4	4	3	71	77
Sub-Saharan Africa	68,415	90,905	..	17	..	6	..	29	..	8	..	35
High income	2,800,647	4,796,707	8	7	3	2	5	4	3	2	79	82
Europe EMU	1,229,213	2,031,196	10	9	2	1	3	2	2	2	81	83

Note: Components may not sum to 100 percent because of unclassified trade.
a. Includes Luxembourg. b. Includes re-exports. c. Data on total merchandise exports for 1990 refer to the South African Customs Union (Botswana, Lesotho, Namibia, South Africa, and Swaziland); those for 2002 refer to South Africa only. Data on export commodity shares refer to the South African Customs Union. d. Data for 2002 include the intratrade of the Baltic states and the Commonwealth of Independent States.

Structure of merchandise exports | 4.5

About the data

Data on merchandise trade come from customs reports of goods movement into or out of an economy or from reports of the financial transactions related to merchandise trade recorded in the balance of payments. Because of differences in timing and definitions, estimates of trade flows from customs reports are likely to differ from those based on the balance of payments. Moreover, several international agencies process trade data, each making estimates to correct for unreported or misreported data, and this leads to other differences in the available data.

The most detailed source of data on international trade in goods is the Commodity Trade (COMTRADE) database maintained by the United Nations Statistics Division. In addition, the International Monetary Fund (IMF) collects customs-based data on exports and imports of goods. The value of exports is recorded as the cost of the goods delivered to the frontier of the exporting country for shipment—the free on board (f.o.b.) value. Many countries report trade data in U.S. dollars. When countries report in local currency, the United Nations Statistics Division applies the average official exchange rate for the period shown.

Countries may report trade according to the general or special system of trade (see *Primary data documentation*). Under the general system exports comprise outward-moving goods that are (a) goods wholly or partly produced in the country; (b) foreign goods, neither transformed nor declared for domestic consumption in the country, that move outward from customs storage; and (c) goods previously included as imports for domestic consumption but subsequently exported without transformation. Under the special system exports comprise categories a and c. In some compilations categories b and c are classified as re-exports. Because of differences in reporting practices, data on exports may not be fully comparable across economies.

The data on total exports of goods (merchandise) in this table come from the World Trade Organization (WTO). The WTO uses two main sources, national statistical offices and the IMF's *International Financial Statistics*. It supplements these with the COMTRADE database and publications or databases of regional organizations, specialized agencies, and economic groups (such as the Commonwealth of Independent States, the Economic Commission for Latin America and the Caribbean, Eurostat, the Food and Agriculture Organization, the Organisation for Economic Co-operation and Development, and the Organization of Petroleum Exporting Countries). It also consults private sources, such as country reports of the Economist Intelligence Unit and press clippings. In recent years country Web sites and direct contacts through email have helped to improve the collection of up-to-date statistics for many countries, reducing the proportion of estimated figures. The WTO database now covers most of the major traders in Africa, Asia, and Latin America, which together with the high-income countries account for nearly 90 percent of total world trade. There has also been a remarkable improvement in the availability of recent, reliable, and standardized figures for countries in Europe and Central Asia.

The shares of exports by major commodity group were estimated by World Bank staff from the COMTRADE database. The values of total exports reported here have not been fully reconciled with the estimates of exports of goods and services from the national accounts (shown in table 4.9) or those from the balance of payments (table 4.15).

The classification of commodity groups is based on the Standard International Trade Classification (SITC) revision 1. Most countries now report using later revisions of the SITC or the Harmonized System. Concordance tables are used to convert data reported in one system of nomenclature to another. The conversion process may introduce some errors of classification, but conversions from later to early systems are generally reliable. Shares may not sum to 100 percent because of unclassified trade.

Definitions

• **Merchandise exports** are the f.o.b. value of goods provided to the rest of the world, valued in U.S. dollars. • **Food** corresponds to the commodities in SITC sections 0 (food and live animals), 1 (beverages and tobacco), and 4 (animal and vegetable oils and fats) and SITC division 22 (oil seeds, oil nuts, and oil kernels). • **Agricultural raw materials** correspond to SITC section 2 (crude materials except fuels) excluding divisions 22, 27 (crude fertilizers and minerals excluding coal, petroleum, and precious stones), and 28 (metalliferous ores and scrap). • **Fuels** correspond to SITC section 3 (mineral fuels). • **Ores and metals** correspond to the commodities in SITC divisions 27, 28, and 68 (nonferrous metals). • **Manufactures** correspond to the commodities in SITC sections 5 (chemicals), 6 (basic manufactures), 7 (machinery and transport equipment), and 8 (miscellaneous manufactured goods), excluding division 68.

4.5a

Some developing country regions are increasing their share of merchandise exports

Merchandise exports

1990
- East Asia & Pacific 5%
- Europe & Central Asia 4%
- Latin America & Caribbean 4%
- Middle East & North Africa 4%
- Sub-Saharan Africa 2%
- South Asia 1%
- High income 80%

2002
- East Asia & Pacific 9%
- Europe & Central Asia 6%
- Latin America & Caribbean 5%
- Middle East & North Africa 3%
- Sub-Saharan Africa 1%
- South Asia 1%
- High income 75%

The share of developing economies in world merchandise exports increased by 5 percentage points between 1990 and 2002. East Asia and Pacific was the biggest gainer, capturing an additional 4 percentage points.

Source: International Monetary Fund data files.

Data sources

The WTO publishes data on world trade in its *Annual Report*. The IMF publishes estimates of total exports of goods in its *International Financial Statistics* and *Direction of Trade Statistics*, as does the United Nations Statistics Division in its *Monthly Bulletin of Statistics*. And the United Nations Conference on Trade and Development (UNCTAD) publishes data on the structure of exports and imports in its *Handbook of International Trade and Development Statistics*. Tariff line records of exports and imports are compiled in the United Nations Statistics Division's COMTRADE database.

4.6 Structure of merchandise imports

	Merchandise imports $ millions		Food % of total		Agricultural raw materials % of total		Fuels % of total		Ores and metals % of total		Manufactures % of total	
	1990	**2002**	**1990**	**2002**	**1990**	**2002**	**1990**	**2002**	**1990**	**2002**	**1990**	**2002**
Afghanistan	936	950	..	..	..	..	..	..	..	..	..	..
Albania	380	1,516	..	20	..	1	..	9	..	2	..	68
Algeria	9,780	10,791	24	*28*	5	*3*	1	*1*	2	*1*	68	*67*
Angola	1,578	3,795	..	..	..	..	..	..	..	..	..	..
Argentina	4,076	8,988	4	5	4	2	8	5	6	3	78	84
Armenia	..	991	..	21	..	1	..	18	..	3	..	57
Australia	41,985	72,689	5	5	2	1	6	8	1	1	84	84
Austria	49,146	77,984	5	7	3	3	6	6	4	3	81	81
Azerbaijan	..	1,665	..	14	..	1	..	18	..	2	..	65
Bangladesh	3,618	7,914	19	*16*	5	*7*	16	*5*	3	*2*	56	*69*
Belarus	..	8,980	..	11	..	2	..	26	..	4	..	51
Belgium[a]	119,702	210,548	..	*9*	..	*2*	..	*9*	..	*3*	..	*77*
Benin	265	653	*38*	20	*4*	5	*1*	17	*1*	1	*56*	56
Bolivia	687	1,770	12	13	2	1	1	5	1	1	85	80
Bosnia and Herzegovina	*360*	3,425	..	..	..	..	..	..	..	..	..	..
Botswana	1,946	1,950	..	*14*	..	*1*	..	*7*	..	*2*	..	*72*
Brazil	22,524	49,720	9	7	3	2	27	15	5	3	56	73
Bulgaria	5,100	7,897	*8*	5	*3*	1	*36*	5	*4*	6	*49*	65
Burkina Faso	536	577	..	*15*	..	*1*	..	*25*	..	*1*	..	*58*
Burundi	231	129	..	*13*	..	*3*	..	*12*	..	*2*	..	*70*
Cambodia	164	1,989	..	..	..	..	..	..	..	..	..	..
Cameroon	1,400	1,796	19	18	0	1	2	13	1	1	78	66
Canada	123,244	227,463	6	6	2	1	6	5	3	2	81	84
Central African Republic	154	110	..	..	..	..	..	..	..	..	..	..
Chad	285	780	..	..	..	..	..	..	..	..	..	..
Chile	7,742	17,093	4	8	2	1	16	16	1	1	75	73
China[†]	53,345	295,203	9	3	6	4	2	7	3	5	80	80
Hong Kong, China	84,725	207,168	8	4	2	1	2	2	2	2	85	91
Colombia	5,590	12,738	7	12	4	2	6	2	3	2	77	81
Congo, Dem. Rep.	1,739	980	..	..	..	..	..	..	..	..	..	..
Congo, Rep.	621	850	..	..	..	..	..	..	..	..	..	..
Costa Rica	1,990	7,175	8	8	2	1	10	7	2	1	66	83
Côte d'Ivoire	2,097	3,075	..	23	..	1	..	21	..	2	..	54
Croatia	*4,500*	10,714	*12*	9	*4*	2	*10*	12	*4*	2	*64*	75
Cuba	4,600	4,161	..	*18*	..	*1*	..	*20*	..	*1*	..	*60*
Czech Republic	*12,880*	40,756	..	4	..	2	..	14	..	3	..	77
Denmark	33,333	49,381	12	12	3	3	7	4	2	2	73	77
Dominican Republic	3,006	8,882	..	*12*	..	*2*	..	*23*	..	*1*	..	*62*
Ecuador	1,861	6,431	9	9	3	1	2	4	2	1	84	84
Egypt, Arab Rep.	12,412	12,552	32	28	7	4	3	4	2	3	56	51
El Salvador	1,263	5,190	14	18	3	2	15	13	4	1	63	65
Eritrea	*278*	375	..	*..*	..	*..*	..	*..*	..	*..*	..	*..*
Estonia	..	5,863	..	12	..	3	..	7	..	2	..	76
Ethiopia	1,081	1,594	..	11	..	1	..	12	..	1	..	74
Finland	27,001	33,577	5	6	2	3	12	12	4	5	76	73
France	234,436	329,322	10	9	3	2	10	9	4	3	74	78
Gabon	918	1,080	..	*18*	..	*1*	..	*4*	..	*1*	..	*75*
Gambia, The	188	225	..	*35*	..	*1*	..	*12*	..	*1*	..	*51*
Georgia	..	725	..	*19*	..	*1*	..	*23*	..	*1*	..	*57*
Germany	355,686	493,712	10	7	3	2	8	8	4	3	72	71
Ghana	1,205	2,790	*11*	20	*1*	2	*17*	9	*0*	2	*70*	68
Greece	19,777	31,273	15	*12*	3	*1*	8	*15*	3	*3*	70	*68*
Guatemala	1,649	6,078	10	13	2	1	17	13	2	1	69	71
Guinea	723	620	..	*23*	..	*1*	..	*19*	..	*0*	..	*56*
Guinea-Bissau	86	82	..	..	..	..	..	..	..	..	..	..
Haiti	332	1,130	..	..	..	..	..	..	..	..	..	..
[†]Data for Taiwan, China	54,782	112,602	7	*4*	5	*2*	11	*11*	6	*5*	69	*76*

	Merchandise imports		Food		Agricultural raw materials		Fuels		Ores and metals		Manufactures	
	$ millions		% of total		% of total		% of total		% of total		% of total	
	1990	2002	1990	2002	1990	2002	1990	2002	1990	2002	1990	2002
Honduras	935	2,940	10	16	1	1	16	13	1	1	71	69
Hungary	10,340	37,612	8	3	4	1	14	7	4	2	70	84
India	23,580	56,595	3	6	4	3	27	33	8	5	51	52
Indonesia	21,837	31,288	5	11	5	6	9	21	4	3	77	59
Iran, Islamic Rep.	20,322	22,190	..	11	..	2	..	3	..	2	..	82
Iraq	7,660	12,000	..	..	..	..	..	..	..	..	..	..
Ireland	20,669	51,906	11	7	2	1	6	3	2	1	76	81
Israel	16,793	35,517	8	6	2	1	9	9	3	2	77	82
Italy	181,968	242,957	12	9	6	3	11	9	5	4	64	70
Jamaica	1,928	3,500	15	15	1	1	20	18	1	1	61	63
Japan	235,368	337,194	15	13	7	3	25	19	9	5	44	58
Jordan	2,600	4,962	26	17	2	2	18	15	1	2	51	62
Kazakhstan	..	6,491	..	8	..	1	..	13	..	3	..	75
Kenya	2,223	3,277	9	12	3	2	20	17	2	1	66	67
Korea, Dem. Rep.	2,930	1,718	..	..	..	..	..	..	..	..	..	..
Korea, Rep.	69,844	152,126	6	6	8	3	16	21	7	6	63	64
Kuwait	3,972	8,960	17	..	1	..	1	..	2	..	79	..
Kyrgyz Republic	..	589	..	13	..	2	..	26	..	4	..	55
Lao PDR	185	431	..	..	..	..	..	..	..	..	..	..
Latvia	..	4,053	..	13	..	2	..	9	..	2	..	74
Lebanon	2,529	6,447	..	18	..	2	..	18	..	2	..	60
Lesotho	672	779	..	..	..	..	..	..	..	..	..	..
Liberia	570	675	..	..	..	..	..	..	..	..	..	..
Libya	5,336	5,700	23	..	2	..	0	..	1	..	74	..
Lithuania	..	7,739	..	9	..	3	..	20	..	1	..	64
Macedonia, FYR	1,206	1,921	..	14	..	2	..	14	..	2	..	44
Madagascar	651	1,150	11	..	1	..	17	..	1	..	69	..
Malawi	575	674	9	12	1	2	11	17	1	1	78	69
Malaysia	29,258	79,869	7	5	1	1	5	5	4	3	82	83
Mali	602	928	26	..	1	..	19	..	1	..	53	..
Mauritania	388	440	..	..	..	..	..	..	..	..	..	..
Mauritius	1,618	2,168	12	19	3	2	8	10	1	1	76	67
Mexico	43,548	173,087	15	6	4	1	4	3	3	2	75	87
Moldova	..	1,052	..	13	..	3	..	22	..	1	..	61
Mongolia	924	659	..	18	..	1	..	22	..	1	..	59
Morocco	6,922	11,644	10	14	6	3	17	16	6	2	61	65
Mozambique	878	1,340	..	14	..	1	..	16	..	0	..	47
Myanmar	270	2,324	13	..	1	..	5	..	0	..	81	..
Namibia	1,163	1,450	..	13	..	1	..	10	..	2	..	74
Nepal	672	1,419	15	13	7	4	9	16	2	3	67	49
Netherlands	126,098	219,788	13	12	2	2	10	9	3	3	71	74
New Zealand	9,501	15,077	7	9	1	1	8	9	3	2	81	79
Nicaragua	638	1,795	19	15	1	1	19	13	1	0	59	68
Niger	388	430	..	44	..	1	..	13	..	2	..	40
Nigeria	5,627	7,547	6	20	1	1	0	1	2	2	67	76
Norway	27,231	34,812	6	7	2	2	4	4	6	5	82	81
Oman	2,681	6,005	19	21	1	1	4	2	1	3	69	69
Pakistan	7,411	11,233	17	12	4	5	21	27	4	3	54	53
Panama	1,539	2,982	12	13	1	1	16	17	1	1	70	68
Papua New Guinea	1,193	1,100	18	18	0	1	7	22	1	1	73	58
Paraguay	1,352	1,770	8	12	0	1	14	17	1	1	77	69
Peru	2,634	7,523	24	13	2	2	12	14	1	1	61	70
Philippines	13,042	35,229	10	8	2	1	15	9	3	2	53	56
Poland	11,570	55,113	8	6	3	2	22	9	4	3	63	80
Portugal	25,263	38,451	12	13	4	2	11	10	2	2	71	73
Puerto Rico	..	..	..	..	..	..	..	..	..	..	..	..

	Merchandise imports		Food		Agricultural raw materials		Fuels		Ores and metals		Manufactures	
	$ millions		% of total		% of total		% of total		% of total		% of total	
	1990	**2002**	**1990**	**2002**	**1990**	**2002**	**1990**	**2002**	**1990**	**2002**	**1990**	**2002**
Romania	7,600	17,857	12	6	4	1	38	11	6	3	39	78
Russian Federation	*33,100*	60,520	..	23	..	1	..	2	..	2	..	70
Rwanda	288	203	..	16	..	4	..	16	..	2	..	62
Saudi Arabia	24,069	32,310	15	16	1	1	0	0	3	3	81	79
Senegal	1,219	1,560	29	26	2	2	16	15	2	2	51	55
Serbia and Montenegro	*4,634*	6,320	12	..	5	..	17	..	3	..	63	..
Sierra Leone	149	264	..	..	..	..	..	..	..	..	..	..
Singapore	60,774	116,441	6	4	2	0	16	13	2	2	73	80
Slovak Republic	*6,670*	16,492	..	5	..	2	..	13	..	3	..	76
Slovenia	*6,142*	10,937	*9*	6	*4*	3	*11*	7	*4*	4	*67*	79
Somalia	95	195	..	..	..	..	..	..	..	..	..	..
South Africa[b]	18,399	29,267	*8*	5	*2*	1	*1*	13	*1*	2	*75*	70
Spain	87,715	154,701	11	10	3	2	12	11	4	3	71	74
Sri Lanka	2,688	6,104	19	14	2	1	13	14	1	2	65	68
Sudan	618	1,790	*13*	19	*1*	1	*20*	5	*0*	1	*66*	74
Swaziland	663	925	..	20	..	2	..	2	..	1	..	72
Sweden	54,264	66,219	6	8	2	2	9	9	3	3	79	75
Switzerland	69,681	83,672	6	6	2	1	5	4	3	5	84	84
Syrian Arab Republic	2,400	5,220	31	16	2	4	3	3	1	3	62	64
Tajikistan	..	715	..	*10*	..	1	..	37	..	0	..	51
Tanzania	1,027	1,687	..	*15*	..	2	..	13	..	1	..	69
Thailand	33,045	64,721	5	*5*	5	*3*	9	12	4	*3*	75	*76*
Togo	581	650	22	22	1	1	8	15	1	2	67	60
Trinidad and Tobago	1,262	4,040	19	*9*	1	*1*	11	23	6	*1*	62	*65*
Tunisia	5,513	9,527	11	10	4	3	9	9	4	2	72	75
Turkey	22,302	49,663	8	4	4	4	21	14	5	5	61	68
Turkmenistan	..	2,453	..	*12*	..	*0*	..	1	..	1	..	*80*
Uganda	288	1,710	..	14	..	3	..	16	..	1	..	66
Ukraine	..	16,993	..	6	..	1	..	39	..	3	..	48
United Arab Emirates	11,199	32,180	14	*11*	1	*1*	3	*1*	4	*2*	77	*86*
United Kingdom	222,977	345,321	10	8	3	2	6	4	4	2	75	79
United States	516,987	1,202,430	6	5	2	1	13	10	3	2	73	78
Uruguay	1,343	1,964	7	14	4	4	18	15	2	1	69	65
Uzbekistan	..	3,160	..	..	..	..	..	..	..	..	..	..
Venezuela, RB	7,335	11,834	11	13	4	1	3	2	4	2	77	82
Vietnam	2,752	19,000	..	..	..	..	..	..	..	..	..	..
West Bank and Gaza	..	..	..	..	..	..	..	..	..	..	..	..
Yemen, Rep.	1,571	2,590	*27*	..	*1*	..	*40*	..	*1*	..	*31*	..
Zambia	1,220	1,270	..	14	..	2	..	7	..	2	..	75
Zimbabwe	1,847	1,440	4	11	3	2	16	8	2	2	73	76
World	**3,532,918 t**	**6,590,272 t**	**9 w**	**8 w**	**3 w**	**2 w**	**11 w**	**10 w**	**4 w**	**3 w**	**71 w**	**75 w**
Low income	106,125	197,606	8	11	4	4	17	24	5	3	64	57
Middle income	502,597	1,364,003	10	9	4	2	10	9	3	3	71	75
Lower middle income	323,769	821,000	10	9	4	3	11	10	3	3	69	72
Upper middle income	179,974	543,003	10	7	2	1	8	7	3	2	76	81
Low & middle income	609,669	1,561,609	10	9	4	2	11	11	4	3	70	73
East Asia & Pacific	160,493	535,235	7	6	4	3	6	9	3	4	77	76
Europe & Central Asia[c]	*150,809*	371,275	..	10	..	2	..	12	..	3	..	72
Latin America & Carib.	119,568	343,449	11	9	3	2	13	9	3	2	69	78
Middle East & N. Africa	104,010	142,093	19	16	3	2	4	5	3	3	70	72
South Asia	39,124	84,787	9	8	4	3	23	30	6	4	54	54
Sub-Saharan Africa	57,515	84,770	..	*10*	..	*2*	..	*16*	..	*1*	..	*66*
High income	2,913,452	5,028,663	9	8	3	2	11	10	4	3	71	75
Europe EMU	1,247,461	1,884,219	11	9	3	2	9	9	4	3	72	74

Note: Components may not sum to 100 percent because of unclassified trade.
a. Includes Luxembourg. b. Data on total merchandise imports for 1990 refer to the South African Customs Union (Botswana, Lesotho, Namibia, South Africa, and Swaziland); those for 2002 refer to South Africa only. Data on import commodity shares refer to the South African Customs Union. c. Data for 2002 include the intratrade of the Baltic states and the Commonwealth of Independent States.

Structure of merchandise imports | 4.6

Data on imports of goods are derived from the same sources as data on exports. In principle, world exports and imports should be identical. Similarly, exports from an economy should equal the sum of imports by the rest of the world from that economy. But differences in timing and definitions result in discrepancies in reported values at all levels. For further discussion of indicators of merchandise trade, see *About the data* for tables 4.4 and 4.5.

The value of imports is generally recorded as the cost of the goods when purchased by the importer plus the cost of transport and insurance to the frontier of the importing country—the cost, insurance, and freight (c.i.f.) value, corresponding to the landed cost at the point of entry of foreign goods into the country. A few countries, including Australia, Canada, and the United States, collect import data on a free on board (f.o.b.) basis and adjust them for freight and insurance costs. Many countries collect and report trade data in U.S. dollars. When countries report in local currency, the United Nations Statistics Division applies the average official exchange rate for the period shown.

Countries may report trade according to the general or special system of trade (see *Primary data documentation*). Under the general system imports include goods imported for domestic consumption and imports into bonded warehouses and free trade zones. Under the special system imports comprise goods imported for domestic consumption (including transformation and repair) and withdrawals for domestic consumption from bonded warehouses and free trade zones. Goods transported through a country en route to another are excluded.

The data on total imports of goods (merchandise) in this table come from the World Trade Organization (WTO). For further discussion of the WTO's sources and methodology, see *About the data* for table 4.5. The shares of imports by major commodity group were estimated by World Bank staff from the United Nations Statistics Division's Commodity Trade (COMTRADE) database. The values of total imports reported here have not been fully reconciled with the estimates of imports of goods and services from the national accounts (shown in table 4.9) or those from the balance of payments (table 4.15).

The classification of commodity groups is based on the Standard International Trade Classification (SITC) revision 1. Most countries now report using later revisions of the SITC or the Harmonized System. Concordance tables are used to convert data reported in one system of nomenclature to another. The conversion process may introduce some errors of classification, but conversions from later to early systems are generally reliable. Shares may not sum to 100 percent because of unclassified trade.

• **Merchandise imports** are the c.i.f. value of goods purchased from the rest of the world valued in U.S. dollars. • **Food** corresponds to the commodities in SITC sections 0 (food and live animals), 1 (beverages and tobacco), and 4 (animal and vegetable oils and fats) and SITC division 22 (oil seeds, oil nuts, and oil kernels). • **Agricultural raw materials** correspond to SITC section 2 (crude materials except fuels) excluding divisions 22, 27 (crude fertilizers and minerals excluding coal, petroleum, and precious stones), and 28 (metalliferous ores and scrap). • **Fuels** correspond to SITC section 3 (mineral fuels). • **Ores and metals** correspond to the commodities in SITC divisions 27, 28, and 68 (nonferrous metals). • **Manufactures** correspond to the commodities in SITC sections 5 (chemicals), 6 (basic manufactures), 7 (machinery and transport equipment), and 8 (miscellaneous manufactured goods), excluding division 68.

4.6a

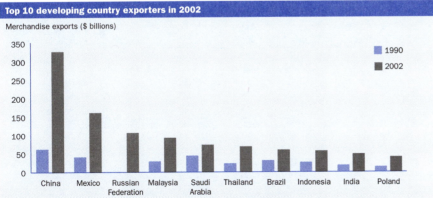

Top 10 developing country exporters in 2002

Merchandise exports ($ billions)

China led the developing economies in merchandise exports in 2002, followed by Mexico. The top 10 economies accounted for 63 percent of exports of developing economies and 16 percent of world exports.

Note: No data are available for the Russian Federation for 1990.
Source: World Trade Organization data files.

4.7 Structure of service exports

| | Commercial service exports | | Transport | | Travel | | Insurance and financial services | | Computer, information, communications, and other commercial services | |
| | $ millions | | % of total services | | % of total services | | % of total services | | % of total services | |
	1990	2002	1990	2002	1990	2002	1990	2002	1990	2002
Afghanistan	..	..	..	..	..	..	..	..	..	..
Albania	32	552	20.0	3.4	11.1	88.2	2.2	2.0	66.7	6.4
Algeria	479	..	41.7	..	13.4	..	5.9	..	39.0	..
Angola	65	*203*	48.8	*6.6*	20.6	..	4.6	*13.7*	26.1	*79.7*
Argentina	2,264	2,878	51.1	24.3	39.9	53.3	0.0	0.2	9.0	22.1
Armenia	..	176	..	36.5	..	35.9	..	3.8	..	23.8
Australia	9,833	17,443	35.5	23.9	43.2	49.2	4.2	5.1	17.2	21.8
Austria	22,755	34,647	6.4	16.7	59.0	32.1	2.9	6.4	31.7	44.8
Azerbaijan	..	321	..	66.1	..	15.9	..	..	..	18.0
Bangladesh	296	305	12.9	30.4	6.4	18.6	0.1	4.7	80.6	46.3
Belarus	..	1,276	..	55.7	..	15.1	..	0.5	..	28.7
Belgium[a]	26,646	*48,970*	27.5	*20.8*	14.0	*15.5*	18.2	*27.8*	40.3	*35.9*
Benin	109	*133*	33.4	*14.7*	50.2	*63.4*	6.9	*2.3*	9.5	*19.6*
Bolivia	133	220	35.8	27.3	43.6	37.1	10.0	16.8	10.6	18.8
Bosnia and Herzegovina	..	300	..	10.0	..	37.3	..	13.8	..	38.9
Botswana	183	..	20.4	..	64.1	..	8.2	..	7.3	..
Brazil	3,706	8,844	36.4	18.0	37.3	22.6	3.1	6.7	23.2	52.7
Bulgaria	837	2,553	27.5	30.2	38.2	52.3	3.1	1.1	31.2	16.5
Burkina Faso	34	*32*	37.1	*14.6*	34.1	*61.6*	..	*0.4*	28.9	*23.4*
Burundi	7	4	38.7	23.1	51.4	30.6	1.6	28.7	8.3	17.6
Cambodia	*50*	593	..	15.0	..	76.5	..	..	..	8.4
Cameroon	369	..	42.6	..	14.4	..	9.4	..	33.6	..
Canada	18,350	36,272	23.0	19.0	34.7	29.4	..	8.4	42.3	43.1
Central African Republic	17	..	50.9	..	16.0	..	18.8	..	14.3	..
Chad	23	..	18.4	..	34.1	..	0.2	..	47.3	..
Chile	1,786	3,878	40.0	55.7	29.8	18.9	4.9	2.4	25.3	23.0
China	5,748	39,381	47.1	14.5	30.2	51.8	3.9	0.7	18.7	33.1
Hong Kong, China	..	43,333	..	*30.5*	..	*15.1*	..	*8.3*	..	*46.1*
Colombia	1,548	1,789	31.3	30.1	26.2	53.8	17.1	2.0	25.5	14.1
Congo, Dem. Rep.	..	..	..	..	..	..	..	..	..	..
Congo, Rep.	65	158	53.9	23.6	12.9	16.1	..	2.5	33.1	57.8
Costa Rica	583	1,854	16.3	13.2	48.9	62.6	*1.5*	1.2	34.8	23.0
Côte d'Ivoire	425	506	62.4	19.0	12.1	10.0	8.3	13.3	17.2	57.7
Croatia	..	5,549	..	10.6	..	68.7	..	1.9	..	18.8
Cuba	..	..	..	..	..	..	..	..	..	..
Czech Republic	..	7,024	..	24.7	..	42.2	..	2.8	..	30.4
Denmark	12,731	27,182	32.5	54.5	26.2	21.6	2.3	..	39.0	23.9
Dominican Republic	1,086	2,966	5.6	2.4	66.8	92.2	0.2	..	27.3	5.4
Ecuador	508	917	47.6	36.9	37.0	48.8	9.3	0.2	6.1	14.1
Egypt, Arab Rep.	4,812	9,127	50.1	30.6	22.9	41.2	1.0	1.2	26.1	26.9
El Salvador	301	749	26.2	41.6	25.2	32.8	7.5	4.2	41.1	21.3
Eritrea	*73*	*54*	*85.7*	*18.2*	*1.0*	*64.2*	..	*1.0*	*13.3*	*16.6*
Estonia	*200*	1,979	*74.7*	54.4	*13.7*	28.0	*0.1*	1.0	*11.5*	16.6
Ethiopia	261	450	80.6	55.6	2.1	16.0	0.7	1.6	16.6	26.8
Finland	4,562	6,400	38.4	24.2	25.8	24.7	0.1	0.2	35.6	51.0
France	74,948	85,912	21.7	21.9	27.0	38.1	14.8	2.5	36.4	37.5
Gabon	214	..	33.4	..	1.4	..	5.7	..	59.4	..
Gambia, The	53	..	8.8	..	87.9	..	0.1	..	3.3	..
Georgia	..	354	..	52.0	..	35.5	..	4.9	..	7.6
Germany	51,545	99,622	28.6	25.8	27.8	19.3	1.0	11.8	42.6	43.2
Ghana	79	539	49.2	21.3	5.6	66.5	2.7	1.1	42.6	11.1
Greece	6,514	20,125	4.9	40.0	39.7	49.6	0.1	1.1	55.2	9.3
Guatemala	313	1,048	7.4	8.8	37.6	58.6	1.9	5.3	53.0	27.3
Guinea	91	43	14.2	20.4	32.6	..	0.1	1.7	53.1	77.9
Guinea-Bissau	4	..	5.4	..	..	..	..	..	94.6	..
Haiti	43	..	19.8	..	78.9	..	1.3	..	0.0	..

Structure of service exports

	Commercial service exports		Transport		Travel		Insurance and financial services		Computer, information, communications, and other commercial services	
	$ millions		% of total services		% of total services		% of total services		% of total services	
	1990	**2002**	**1990**	**2002**	**1990**	**2002**	**1990**	**2002**	**1990**	**2002**
Honduras	121	463	35.1	11.7	24.0	62.9	12.9	3.9	28.0	21.4
Hungary	2,677	7,726	1.6	8.9	36.8	42.4	0.2	2.1	61.4	46.7
India	4,610	24,553	20.8	10.3	33.8	12.3	2.7	1.5	42.7	75.9
Indonesia	2,488	6,517	2.8	16.2	86.5	81.1	..	0.0	10.7	2.7
Iran, Islamic Rep.	343	*1,357*	10.5	*49.4*	8.2	*36.9*	6.4	*10.7*	74.9	*2.9*
Iraq	..	..	..	..	..	..	..	..	..	..
Ireland	3,286	28,134	31.1	5.7	44.4	11.0	..	22.3	24.5	61.0
Israel	4,546	10,825	30.8	19.6	30.7	19.4	..	0.1	38.8	60.8
Italy	48,579	59,374	21.0	15.4	33.9	45.3	5.5	3.3	39.6	36.1
Jamaica	976	1,888	18.0	19.5	77.0	64.0	1.4	2.0	3.6	14.4
Japan	41,384	64,909	..	37.0	..	5.4	..	4.2	..	53.4
Jordan	1,430	1,473	26.0	19.6	35.7	53.4	..	..	38.3	27.1
Kazakhstan	..	1,432	..	47.6	..	43.4	..	0.8	..	8.2
Kenya	774	*791*	32.0	*54.1*	60.2	*39.0*	0.7	*0.5*	7.1	*6.4*
Korea, Dem. Rep.	..	..	..	..	..	..	..	..	..	..
Korea, Rep.	9,155	27,080	34.7	48.3	34.5	19.5	0.1	3.3	30.7	28.8
Kuwait	1,054	1,372	87.5	82.3	12.5	8.6	..	7.9	–0.0	1.2
Kyrgyz Republic	..	118	..	31.7	..	30.2	..	3.3	..	34.8
Lao PDR	11	*127*	74.8	*18.0*	24.3	*82.0*	0.9	..	..	..
Latvia	*290*	1,235	*94.9*	62.5	*2.5*	13.1	*0.0*	5.5	*2.6*	18.9
Lebanon	..	..	..	..	..	..	..	..	..	..
Lesotho	34	31	14.1	1.3	51.2	64.0	..	–0.0	34.7	34.7
Liberia	..	..	..	..	..	..	..	..	..	..
Libya	83	..	83.8	..	7.7	..	..	..	8.5	..
Lithuania	..	1,451	..	45.1	..	34.8	..	0.7	..	19.4
Macedonia, FYR	..	220	..	36.3	..	17.7	..	2.2	..	43.8
Madagascar	129	158	32.1	26.8	31.3	22.9	0.3	0.7	36.3	49.6
Malawi	37	49	46.1	32.7	42.6	67.3	0.1	..	11.2	0.0
Malaysia	3,769	14,753	31.8	19.3	44.7	48.2	0.1	1.4	23.5	31.0
Mali	71	*140*	31.0	*17.0*	54.3	*62.9*	4.9	*2.9*	9.8	*17.3*
Mauritania	14	..	35.3	..	64.7	..	..	..	–0.0	..
Mauritius	478	1,132	32.9	24.1	51.1	54.0	0.1	1.8	15.8	20.0
Mexico	7,222	12,474	12.4	9.2	76.5	71.0	4.6	9.7	6.5	10.1
Moldova	..	201	..	54.4	..	23.2	..	1.9	..	20.6
Mongolia	48	179	41.8	21.8	10.4	72.7	4.6	0.8	43.2	4.7
Morocco	1,871	4,098	9.6	19.0	68.4	64.6	0.8	0.7	21.2	15.7
Mozambique	103	*249*	61.3	*22.4*	..	*25.6*	..	..	38.7	*52.1*
Myanmar	94	*405*	10.3	*19.8*	20.9	*31.0*	0.5	..	68.3	*49.2*
Namibia	106	230	..	..	81.0	95.2	5.9	0.6	13.1	4.2
Nepal	166	*303*	3.6	*15.6*	65.6	*47.5*	..	..	30.8	*36.9*
Netherlands	28,478	54,573	45.4	32.4	14.6	14.1	0.8	2.0	39.2	51.4
New Zealand	2,415	5,041	43.4	23.8	42.7	57.6	–0.3	0.9	14.2	17.7
Nicaragua	34	270	19.2	9.5	35.5	42.0	..	0.9	45.3	47.7
Niger	22	..	5.2	..	59.5	..	13.5	..	21.8	..
Nigeria	965	..	3.9	..	2.5	..	0.3	..	93.3	..
Norway	12,452	19,116	68.7	56.8	12.6	11.4	0.4	4.7	18.3	27.1
Oman	68	*349*	15.3	*45.5*	84.7	*41.0*	..	*4.5*	–0.0	*9.0*
Pakistan	1,218	1,536	59.3	54.1	12.0	6.3	1.4	2.3	27.3	37.3
Panama	907	2,254	64.9	55.7	18.9	23.4	3.8	12.6	12.4	8.2
Papua New Guinea	198	*285*	11.2	*7.5*	12.0	*1.8*	0.5	*1.8*	76.3	*88.9*
Paraguay	404	506	18.3	13.8	21.1	11.6	..	5.3	60.5	69.3
Peru	714	1,430	43.4	19.9	30.4	56.1	11.2	6.8	15.0	17.2
Philippines	2,897	3,029	8.5	20.8	16.1	57.4	0.5	2.2	74.9	19.5
Poland	3,200	10,030	57.3	32.6	11.2	43.0	4.0	3.5	27.6	20.9
Portugal	5,054	9,720	15.6	18.7	70.4	61.4	0.7	2.3	13.3	17.7
Puerto Rico	..	..	..	..	..	..	..	..	..	..

4.7 Structure of service exports

	Commercial service exports		Transport		Travel		Insurance and financial services		Computer, information, communications, and other commercial services	
	$ millions		% of total services		% of total services		% of total services		% of total services	
	1990	**2002**	**1990**	**2002**	**1990**	**2002**	**1990**	**2002**	**1990**	**2002**
Romania	610	2,326	50.5	41.4	17.4	14.4	5.6	4.4	26.6	39.7
Russian Federation	..	13,453	..	40.8	..	31.1	..	1.7	..	26.3
Rwanda	31	48	56.1	25.7	32.8	65.3	1.0	..	10.0	9.0
Saudi Arabia	3,031	5,184	..	..	..	..	..	..	..	..
Senegal	356	..	19.1	..	42.7	..	0.5	..	37.6	..
Serbia and Montenegro	..	..	..	..	..	..	..	..	..	..
Sierra Leone	45	..	9.7	..	76.2	..	0.1	..	14.1	..
Singapore	12,719	29,599	17.5	38.6	36.6	14.8	0.7	2.5	45.3	44.0
Slovak Republic	..	2,218	..	44.9	..	19.5	..	2.2	..	33.4
Slovenia	1,219	2,286	22.6	26.2	55.0	47.4	1.2	2.0	21.2	24.4
Somalia	..	..	..	..	..	..	..	..	..	..
South Africa	3,290	4,391	21.6	23.3	55.8	62.1	10.8	5.4	11.9	9.1
Spain	27,649	62,109	17.2	15.1	67.2	54.4	4.3	4.2	11.3	26.4
Sri Lanka	425	1,247	39.7	41.2	30.2	29.1	4.2	3.6	25.9	26.0
Sudan	134	45	14.1	36.7	15.7	50.9	0.5	0.9	69.7	11.5
Swaziland	102	113	24.5	9.4	29.2	23.3	..	..	46.3	67.3
Sweden	13,453	23,508	35.8	22.0	21.7	19.1	9.1	4.3	33.5	54.5
Switzerland	18,233	27,856	16.3	11.6	40.6	28.2	23.3	34.7	19.7	25.5
Syrian Arab Republic	740	1,481	29.7	16.6	43.3	73.1	..	..	27.0	10.3
Tajikistan	..	60	..	75.7	..	2.7	..	1.9	..	19.6
Tanzania	131	609	19.9	10.1	36.4	71.8	0.5	3.9	43.1	14.3
Thailand	6,292	15,232	21.1	21.4	68.7	51.9	0.2	0.6	10.0	26.1
Togo	114	53	26.9	23.1	50.7	20.4	13.7	2.8	8.6	53.6
Trinidad and Tobago	322	563	50.7	36.8	29.4	35.7	..	14.0	19.9	13.6
Tunisia	1,575	2,603	23.0	23.5	64.8	58.5	1.5	2.4	10.7	15.6
Turkey	7,882	14,738	11.7	19.0	40.9	57.5	1.7	1.7	47.4	21.8
Turkmenistan	..	..	..	..	..	..	..	..	..	..
Uganda	..	230	..	16.2	..	76.0	..	1.6	..	6.2
Ukraine	..	4,583	..	73.8	..	17.2	..	0.5	..	8.4
United Arab Emirates	..	..	..	..	..	..	..	..	..	..
United Kingdom	53,830	123,130	25.2	14.5	29.0	17.2	16.4	23.7	29.4	44.6
United States	132,880	272,630	28.1	17.0	37.9	31.3	3.5	6.9	30.5	44.9
Uruguay	460	752	36.9	34.6	51.8	46.7	1.0	10.0	10.3	8.7
Uzbekistan	..	..	..	..	..	..	..	..	..	..
Venezuela, RB	1,121	960	40.9	36.0	44.2	45.7	0.2	0.1	14.7	18.1
Vietnam	..	2,948	..	..	..	..	..	..	..	..
West Bank and Gaza	..	..	..	..	..	..	..	..	..	..
Yemen, Rep.	82	129	27.2	15.7	48.8	29.3	..	..	24.0	55.0
Zambia	94	114	68.9	37.2	13.5	58.3	4.1	4.5	13.4	0.1
Zimbabwe	253	..	44.3	..	25.3	..	1.2	..	29.2	..
World	**750,300 s**	**1,511,226 s**	**25.0 w**	**22.4 w**	**32.9 w**	**30.5 w**	**6.6 w**	**8.3 w**	**36.3 w**	**39.2 w**
Low income	14,230	40,966	24.6	15.7	38.3	28.2	2.5	1.5	35.1	54.6
Middle income	78,877	225,630	26.9	23.3	42.0	46.9	3.2	2.5	28.5	27.3
Lower middle income	49,966	144,059	27.0	24.0	42.1	47.6	3.6	1.9	28.1	26.6
Upper middle income	28,911	81,571	26.7	22.2	41.8	45.6	2.6	3.7	29.2	28.7
Low & middle income	93,107	266,596	26.6	22.2	41.4	44.2	3.1	2.4	29.5	31.3
East Asia & Pacific	22,049	82,632	26.1	17.1	48.5	54.0	1.3	0.8	24.2	28.1
Europe & Central Asia	15,237	77,656	21.9	31.4	32.8	41.8	1.7	2.1	44.0	24.7
Latin America & Carib.	25,004	46,516	28.7	21.4	50.5	50.2	4.5	6.2	16.5	22.6
Middle East & N. Africa	14,513	22,615	26.7	19.9	30.5	38.7	..	1.2	41.8	40.5
South Asia	6,816	27,994	27.9	14.2	30.1	13.8	2.4	1.7	39.7	70.3
Sub-Saharan Africa	9,487	10,833	28.1	26.3	39.7	48.9	5.8	4.2	26.8	19.5
High income	657,193	1,244,630	24.8	22.5	31.7	27.4	7.1	9.5	37.2	40.9
Europe EMU	300,015	480,820	23.9	21.0	33.2	32.1	7.2	8.6	35.8	38.3

a. Includes Luxembourg.

Structure of service exports |4.7

About the data

Balance of payments statistics, the main source of information on international trade in services, have many weaknesses. Some large economies—such as the former Soviet Union—did not report data on trade in services until recently. Disaggregation of important components may be limited, and it varies significantly across countries. There are inconsistencies in the methods used to report items. And the recording of major flows as net items is common (for example, insurance transactions are often recorded as premiums less claims). These factors contribute to a downward bias in the value of the service trade reported in the balance of payments.

Efforts are being made to improve the coverage, quality, and consistency of these data. Eurostat and the Organisation for Economic Co-operation and Development, for example, are working together to improve the collection of statistics on trade in services in member countries. In addition, the International Monetary Fund (IMF) has implemented the new classification of trade in services introduced in the fifth edition of its Balance of Payments Manual (1993).

Still, difficulties in capturing all the dimensions of international trade in services mean that the record is likely to remain incomplete. Cross-border intrafirm service transactions, which are usually not captured in the balance of payments, have increased in recent years. One example of such transactions is transnational corporations' use of mainframe computers around the clock for data processing, exploiting time zone differences between their home country and the host countries of their affiliates. Another important dimension of service trade not captured by conventional balance of payments statistics is establishment trade—sales in the host country by foreign affiliates. By contrast, cross-border intrafirm transactions in merchandise may be reported as exports or imports in the balance of payments.

The data on exports of services in this table and on imports of services in table 4.8, unlike those in editions before 2000, include only commercial services and exclude the category "government services not included elsewhere." The data are compiled by the IMF based on returns from national sources. Data on total trade in goods and services from IMF's Balance of Payments database are shown in table 4.15.

Definitions

• **Commercial service exports** are total service exports minus exports of government services not included elsewhere. International transactions in services are defined by the IMF's Balance of Payments Manual (1993) as the economic output of intangible commodities that may be produced, transferred, and consumed at the same time. Definitions may vary among reporting economies. • **Transport** covers all transport services (sea, air, land, internal waterway, space, and pipeline) performed by residents of one economy for those of another and involving the carriage of passengers, movement of goods (freight), rental of carriers with crew, and related support and auxiliary services. Excluded are freight insurance, which is included in insurance services; goods procured in ports by nonresident carriers and repairs of transport equipment, which are included in goods; repairs of harbors, railway facilities, and airfield facilities, which are included in construction services; and rental of carriers without crew, which is included in other services. • **Travel** covers goods and services acquired from an economy by travelers in that economy for their own use during visits of less than one year for business or personal purposes. Travel services include the goods and services consumed by travelers, such as meals, lodging, and transport (within the economy visited), including car rental. • **Insurance and financial services** cover freight insurance on goods exported and other direct insurance such as life insurance, financial intermediation services such as commissions, foreign exchange transactions, and brokerage services; and auxiliary services such as financial market operational and regulatory services. • **Computer, information, communications, and other commercial services** include such activities as international telecommunications and postal and courier services; computer data; news-related service transactions between residents and nonresidents; construction services; royalties and license fees; miscellaneous business, professional, and technical services; and personal, cultural, and recreational services.

4.7a

Top 10 developing country exporters of commercial services in 2002

Major exporters of merchandise trade also tend to be major exporters of commercial services. The exceptions are the fuel exporters—Saudi Arabia and Indonesia. These top 10 developing country exporters accounted for 61 percent of commercial services exports of developing economies and 11 percent of world commercial services exports in 2002.

Note: No data are available for the Russian Federation for 1990.
Source: International Monetary Fund data files.

Data sources

The data on exports of commercial services are from the IMF. The IMF publishes balance of payments data in its International Financial Statistics and Balance of Payments Statistics Yearbook.

4.8 Structure of service imports

	Commercial service imports		Transport		Travel		Insurance and financial services		Computer, information, communications, and other commercial services	
	$ millions		% of total services		% of total services		% of total services		% of total services	
	1990	2002	1990	2002	1990	2002	1990	2002	1990	2002
Afghanistan	..	..	..	..	..	..	..	..	..	..
Albania	29	561	26.3	22.8	..	65.1	2.9	9.0	70.8	3.1
Algeria	1,155	..	58.1	..	12.9	..	9.8	..	19.2	..
Angola	1,288	3,176	38.3	12.4	3.0	2.1	2.6	2.9	56.1	82.6
Argentina	2,876	4,360	32.6	21.8	40.7	53.4	1.7	2.0	26.7	22.9
Armenia	..	217	..	60.0	..	24.9	..	5.2	..	9.9
Australia	13,388	17,740	33.9	33.8	31.5	34.4	4.8	4.5	29.8	27.4
Austria	14,104	34,416	8.4	10.4	54.9	27.5	4.6	6.5	32.1	55.6
Azerbaijan	..	1,283	..	13.5	..	8.2	..	1.0	..	77.2
Bangladesh	554	1,391	71.1	71.2	14.1	14.5	6.6	7.4	8.3	6.8
Belarus	..	892	..	15.3	..	62.6	..	1.7	..	20.5
Belgium[a]	25,924	42,856	23.3	19.5	21.1	24.7	14.7	19.1	40.8	36.7
Benin	113	186	46.9	67.9	12.8	9.3	5.7	10.2	34.6	12.6
Bolivia	291	500	61.7	58.4	20.6	14.8	10.0	18.7	7.6	8.1
Bosnia and Herzegovina	..	228	..	59.4	..	21.3	..	12.5	..	6.7
Botswana	371	..	57.5	..	15.0	..	5.5	..	22.0	..
Brazil	6,733	13,631	44.4	26.6	22.4	17.6	2.7	9.2	30.5	46.6
Bulgaria	600	1,986	40.5	44.1	31.5	31.0	4.5	4.0	23.5	20.9
Burkina Faso	196	135	64.7	65.1	16.6	16.1	5.1	14.7	13.6	4.2
Burundi	59	33	62.6	55.2	29.0	42.1	6.3	1.4	2.2	1.3
Cambodia	64	372	24.5	57.4	..	10.3	..	4.7	75.5	27.7
Cameroon	1,018	..	45.3	..	27.5	..	7.2	..	20.1	..
Canada	27,479	41,932	21.1	21.6	39.8	28.2	..	11.3	39.2	38.9
Central African Republic	166	..	49.7	..	30.6	..	8.9	..	10.7	..
Chad	223	..	45.1	..	31.2	..	4.4	..	19.2	..
Chile	1,982	4,771	47.4	45.0	21.5	16.5	3.3	8.0	27.9	30.5
China	4,113	46,080	78.9	29.5	11.4	33.4	2.3	7.2	7.4	29.8
Hong Kong, China	..	24,800	..	26.6	..	50.1	..	4.8	..	18.5
Colombia	1,683	3,249	34.9	37.0	27.0	33.0	13.7	13.1	24.4	17.0
Congo, Dem. Rep.	..	..	..	..	..	..	..	..	..	..
Congo, Rep.	748	917	18.4	13.1	15.2	7.7	1.6	3.9	64.9	75.4
Costa Rica	540	1,188	41.2	38.6	28.8	29.0	6.0	7.4	24.0	24.9
Côte d'Ivoire	1,518	1,341	32.1	39.6	11.1	21.6	4.7	11.1	52.0	27.7
Croatia	..	2,399	..	18.7	..	32.6	..	5.5	..	43.2
Cuba	..	..	..	..	..	..	..	..	..	..
Czech Republic	..	6,372	..	14.0	..	25.1	..	12.4	..	48.5
Denmark	10,106	25,116	38.3	47.4	36.5	27.6	1.6	..	23.6	25.0
Dominican Republic	435	1,241	40.0	60.3	33.1	23.8	4.1	9.1	22.8	6.8
Ecuador	755	1,505	41.6	43.2	23.2	24.2	8.1	5.1	27.2	27.5
Egypt, Arab Rep.	3,327	6,013	44.0	29.6	3.9	21.1	4.6	7.1	47.5	42.2
El Salvador	296	960	45.9	43.4	20.5	19.9	12.0	13.0	21.5	23.7
Eritrea	..	24	..	27.6	..	49.5	..	1.9	..	21.0
Estonia	123	1,404	76.3	54.3	15.4	16.4	0.3	1.1	8.0	28.2
Ethiopia	348	558	76.5	57.2	3.3	8.1	3.4	5.4	16.8	29.3
Finland	7,432	8,130	26.1	30.4	37.2	24.2	1.8	1.2	34.8	44.2
France	59,560	68,171	29.4	26.2	20.7	28.9	19.2	4.5	30.7	40.5
Gabon	984	..	23.2	..	13.9	..	5.3	..	57.6	..
Gambia, The	35	..	65.1	..	23.1	..	9.0	..	2.8	..
Georgia	..	316	..	33.0	..	47.1	..	5.8	..	14.1
Germany	84,336	149,107	20.3	20.4	46.3	35.8	1.0	3.4	32.4	40.4
Ghana	226	546	55.1	48.8	5.9	22.0	11.2	5.4	27.8	23.9
Greece	2,756	10,306	34.0	46.0	39.5	32.0	5.4	4.2	21.0	17.8
Guatemala	363	996	41.0	51.5	27.4	26.8	3.4	11.3	28.2	10.4
Guinea	243	156	57.5	30.1	12.2	19.7	5.5	5.8	24.8	44.4
Guinea-Bissau	17	..	54.5	..	19.8	..	5.6	..	20.0	..
Haiti	71	..	47.9	..	52.1	..	..	..	..	..

	Commercial service imports		Transport		Travel		Insurance and financial services		Computer, information, communications, and other commercial services	
	$ millions		% of total services		% of total services		% of total services		% of total services	
	1990	2002	1990	2002	1990	2002	1990	2002	1990	2002
Honduras	213	601	45.4	51.3	17.6	21.7	15.0	..	22.0	26.9
Hungary	2,264	7,093	8.8	14.6	25.9	24.3	1.0	4.4	64.3	56.8
India	5,943	18,464	57.5	13.7	6.6	18.7	5.8	1.7	30.1	65.9
Indonesia	5,898	16,779	47.4	30.7	14.2	19.6	4.0	1.1	34.5	48.6
Iran, Islamic Rep.	3,703	1,577	47.3	72.4	9.2	13.0	10.8	13.5	32.8	1.1
Iraq	..	..	..	..	..	..	..	..	..	..
Ireland	5,145	40,393	24.3	4.4	22.6	9.3	1.9	11.3	51.2	75.0
Israel	4,825	11,269	39.6	37.3	29.7	22.6	4.4	3.4	26.2	36.8
Italy	46,602	61,485	23.7	22.2	22.1	27.5	10.4	3.9	43.8	46.4
Jamaica	667	1,603	47.9	38.3	17.0	16.1	6.7	8.5	28.4	37.1
Japan	84,281	106,612	..	29.6	..	25.0	..	4.6	..	40.9
Jordan	1,118	1,480	52.0	48.3	30.1	28.2	5.2	6.8	12.7	16.7
Kazakhstan	..	3,635	..	19.1	..	20.8	..	2.5	..	57.5
Kenya	598	764	66.2	48.8	6.4	18.7	8.9	10.0	18.5	22.4
Korea, Dem. Rep.	..	..	..	..	..	..	..	..	..	..
Korea, Rep.	10,050	35,145	39.8	30.4	27.5	25.8	0.3	1.7	32.4	42.1
Kuwait	2,805	4,880	31.9	35.8	65.5	61.9	1.2	1.5	1.4	0.8
Kyrgyz Republic	..	142	..	38.0	..	6.9	..	15.1	..	40.0
Lao PDR	25	5	73.0	99.0	..	1.0	6.3	..	20.6	..
Latvia	120	698	82.3	33.3	10.9	32.9	4.8	8.7	2.1	25.1
Lebanon	..	..	..	..	..	..	..	..	..	..
Lesotho	48	45	67.9	68.0	24.7	30.7	5.6	1.1	1.7	0.1
Liberia	..	..	..	..	..	..	..	..	..	..
Libya	926	..	41.9	..	45.7	..	4.1	..	8.3	..
Lithuania	..	878	..	33.8	..	37.1	..	4.3	..	24.7
Macedonia, FYR	..	270	..	37.2	..	16.5	..	3.4	..	42.9
Madagascar	172	317	43.5	45.4	23.4	28.6	3.5	1.5	29.5	24.5
Malawi	268	222	81.8	50.1	5.9	35.2	8.7	0.0	3.7	14.7
Malaysia	5,394	16,248	46.9	36.3	26.9	16.1	..	3.3	26.2	44.3
Mali	352	414	57.4	64.0	15.8	8.6	1.9	3.5	24.9	23.9
Mauritania	126	..	76.9	..	18.3	..	3.1	..	1.7	..
Mauritius	407	779	51.6	36.6	23.0	26.2	5.5	4.8	19.9	32.4
Mexico	10,063	17,031	25.0	11.7	54.9	35.6	6.2	39.5	14.0	13.3
Moldova	..	231	..	33.0	..	37.3	..	2.3	..	27.3
Mongolia	155	260	56.2	38.3	0.8	45.8	6.3	2.7	36.8	13.2
Morocco	940	1,903	58.3	45.0	19.9	23.4	6.0	2.4	15.9	29.2
Mozambique	206	607	57.7	26.0	..	18.8	4.3	3.2	38.1	52.0
Myanmar	73	364	35.4	82.1	22.6	7.6	2.5	..	39.5	10.3
Namibia	341	226	46.9	37.1	17.9	24.6	6.8	5.8	28.5	32.5
Nepal	159	205	40.8	34.9	28.5	38.8	3.2	..	27.5	26.3
Netherlands	28,995	56,478	37.7	22.8	25.4	23.0	1.0	4.1	35.9	50.1
New Zealand	3,251	4,682	40.6	35.2	29.5	31.8	2.5	4.0	27.5	29.0
Nicaragua	73	315	70.7	55.1	20.1	22.1	7.9	4.0	1.4	18.8
Niger	209	..	68.3	..	10.4	..	4.3	..	17.1	..
Nigeria	1,901	..	33.6	..	30.3	..	3.1	..	32.9	..
Norway	12,247	16,459	44.6	34.2	30.0	30.8	1.7	4.4	23.6	30.6
Oman	719	1,678	36.6	37.1	6.5	21.9	4.1	7.1	52.8	34.0
Pakistan	1,863	2,093	67.0	66.4	23.1	12.2	1.3	5.7	8.6	15.8
Panama	666	1,204	66.6	51.1	14.8	14.8	10.2	20.6	8.4	13.5
Papua New Guinea	393	662	35.6	26.1	12.8	5.8	4.0	7.3	47.6	60.8
Paraguay	361	294	61.6	59.4	19.8	22.0	11.4	17.4	7.3	1.1
Peru	1,070	2,371	43.5	39.7	27.6	26.0	10.9	10.3	18.0	23.9
Philippines	1,721	4,311	56.9	51.9	6.4	20.2	3.4	7.9	33.2	20.1
Poland	2,847	9,089	52.4	20.0	14.9	35.2	1.0	6.1	31.8	38.6
Portugal	3,772	6,578	48.4	33.1	23.0	34.6	5.1	5.0	23.5	27.3
Puerto Rico	..	..	..	..	..	..	..	..	..	..

4.8 Structure of service imports

	Commercial service imports		Transport		Travel		Insurance and financial services		Computer, information, communications, and other commercial services	
	$ millions		% of total services		% of total services		% of total services		% of total services	
	1990	2002	1990	2002	1990	2002	1990	2002	1990	2002
Romania	787	2,304	65.5	36.2	13.1	17.2	7.3	7.0	14.1	39.5
Russian Federation	..	23,577	..	12.1	..	50.9	..	2.9	..	34.0
Rwanda	94	124	69.0	71.9	23.7	19.2	0.0	..	7.3	8.9
Saudi Arabia	12,694	7,159	18.1	33.5	..	..	2.2	3.7	79.7	62.7
Senegal	368	..	60.1	..	12.4	..	8.8	..	18.7	..
Serbia and Montenegro	..	..	..	..	..	..	..	..	..	..
Sierra Leone	67	..	29.5	..	32.7	..	4.8	..	33.0	..
Singapore	8,575	27,155	41.0	42.6	21.0	19.2	9.1	4.3	29.0	33.9
Slovak Republic	..	1,779	..	24.4	..	16.6	..	4.9	..	54.1
Slovenia	1,034	1,719	42.5	21.3	27.3	35.7	2.5	2.3	27.8	40.7
Somalia	..	..	..	..	..	..	..	..	..	..
South Africa	3,593	5,221	40.2	45.6	31.5	34.6	11.6	9.7	16.7	10.1
Spain	15,197	37,620	30.8	24.6	28.0	17.7	6.3	6.9	34.9	50.8
Sri Lanka	620	966	64.2	34.2	11.9	27.3	6.8	2.8	17.1	35.7
Sudan	202	784	31.9	87.5	25.4	11.7	4.9	0.1	37.8	0.8
Swaziland	171	134	6.1	15.4	20.6	24.6	..	8.7	73.4	51.2
Sweden	16,959	23,732	23.2	14.8	37.1	30.4	7.9	3.6	31.7	51.1
Switzerland	11,093	16,980	33.7	25.6	53.0	38.9	1.4	4.8	12.0	30.6
Syrian Arab Republic	702	1,468	54.5	47.5	35.5	45.6	4.4	..	5.7	6.9
Tajikistan	..	103	..	79.0	..	1.7	..	6.3	..	13.0
Tanzania	288	647	58.0	27.3	7.9	52.2	6.2	4.8	27.9	15.7
Thailand	6,160	16,573	58.0	43.0	23.3	19.9	5.5	5.9	13.2	31.2
Togo	217	129	56.9	71.8	18.4	3.7	9.1	15.3	15.5	9.2
Trinidad and Tobago	460	339	51.7	34.4	26.6	44.5	9.9	2.4	11.9	18.7
Tunisia	682	1,353	51.4	48.3	26.2	19.2	7.3	7.5	15.0	25.0
Turkey	2,794	6,283	32.2	30.7	18.6	29.9	9.6	15.8	49.2	23.6
Turkmenistan	..	..	..	..	..	..	..	..	..	..
Uganda	195	530	58.3	..	..	..	6.5	..	35.2	..
Ukraine	..	3,143	..	15.5	..	20.9	..	8.1	..	55.5
United Arab Emirates	..	..	..	..	..	..	..	..	..	..
United Kingdom	44,713	101,408	33.2	24.2	41.0	41.4	2.4	6.3	23.4	28.1
United States	97,950	205,580	36.3	28.5	38.9	29.6	4.5	9.2	20.4	32.7
Uruguay	363	619	48.2	41.7	30.7	28.7	1.5	7.0	19.6	22.6
Uzbekistan	..	..	..	..	..	..	..	..	..	..
Venezuela, RB	2,390	3,767	33.5	41.1	42.8	26.0	4.3	7.6	19.4	25.2
Vietnam	..	3,698	..	..	..	..	..	..	..	..
West Bank and Gaza	..	..	..	..	..	..	..	..	..	..
Yemen, Rep.	639	883	27.6	44.2	9.9	8.8	5.4	7.6	57.1	39.4
Zambia	370	328	76.8	67.7	14.6	13.3	5.3	1.7	3.3	17.3
Zimbabwe	460	..	51.8	..	14.4	..	3.4	..	30.4	..
World	**779,679 s**	**1,475,405 s**	**28.3 w**	**26.1 w**	**28.6 w**	**28.7 w**	**6.0 w**	**6.8 w**	**38.2 w**	**38.6 w**
Low income	28,313	52,561	50.4	28.9	13.9	18.7	4.6	2.4	31.1	49.9
Middle income	92,233	240,279	40.6	29.1	22.5	28.8	5.2	9.0	32.4	33.1
Lower middle income	45,983	154,902	50.4	30.9	19.1	30.6	6.4	7.1	24.5	31.5
Upper middle income	46,250	85,376	30.8	25.9	25.8	25.6	3.8	12.4	40.3	36.0
Low & middle income	120,546	292,840	42.9	29.1	20.5	27.1	5.1	7.9	32.1	35.9
East Asia & Pacific	24,308	104,321	56.0	34.1	18.2	25.5	4.1	5.4	22.6	35.1
Europe & Central Asia	9,321	73,106	36.0	19.5	19.5	35.3	2.1	6.0	43.0	39.2
Latin America & Carib.	32,757	60,676	37.2	29.3	35.9	27.6	6.0	17.7	21.5	25.7
Middle East & N. Africa	26,605	18,791	33.3	36.2	7.9	13.1	4.7	5.4	54.1	45.3
South Asia	9,176	23,023	60.4	23.0	11.3	18.3	4.9	2.5	23.4	56.2
Sub-Saharan Africa	18,379	17,855	44.1	38.0	19.2	21.0	6.3	6.0	30.6	35.0
High income	659,133	1,182,565	25.7	25.4	30.1	29.1	6.1	6.5	39.3	39.3
Europe EMU	293,822	486,299	25.4	20.5	31.5	27.2	8.0	6.4	35.2	45.9

a. Includes Luxembourg.

Trade in services differs from trade in goods because services are produced and consumed at the same time. Thus services to a traveler may be consumed in the producing country (for example, use of a hotel room) but are classified as imports of the traveler's country. In other cases services may be supplied from a remote location; for example, insurance services may be supplied from one location and consumed in another. For further discussion of the problems of measuring trade in services, see *About the data* for table 4.7.

The data on exports of services in table 4.7 and on imports of services in this table, unlike those in editions before 2000, include only commercial services and exclude the category "government services not included elsewhere." The data are compiled by the International Monetary Fund (IMF) based on returns from national sources.

• **Commercial service imports** are total service imports minus imports of government services not included elsewhere. International transactions in services are defined by the IMF's *Balance of Payments Manual* (1993) as the economic output of intangible commodities that may be produced, transferred, and consumed at the same time. Definitions may vary among reporting economies. • **Transport** covers all transport services (sea, air, land, internal waterway, space, and pipeline) performed by residents of one economy for those of another and involving the carriage of passengers, movement of goods (freight), rental of carriers with crew, and related support and auxiliary services. Excluded are freight insurance, which is included in insurance services; goods procured in ports by nonresident carriers and repairs of transport equipment, which are included in goods; repairs of harbors, railway facilities, and airfield facilities, which are included in construction services; and rental of carriers without crew, which is included in other services. • **Travel** covers goods and services acquired from an economy by travelers in that economy for their own use during visits of less than one year for business or personal purposes. Travel services include the goods and services consumed by travelers, such as meals, lodging, and transport (within the economy visited), including car rental. • **Insurance and financial services** cover freight insurance on goods imported and other direct insurance such as life insurance, financial intermediation services such as commissions, foreign exchange transactions, and brokerage services; and auxiliary services such as financial market operational and regulatory services. • **Computer, information, communications, and other commercial services** include such activities as international telecommunications, and postal and courier services; computer data; news-related service transactions between residents and nonresidents; construction services; royalties and license fees; miscellaneous business, professional, and technical services; and personal, cultural, and recreational services.

4.8a

Commercial service imports (% of total)

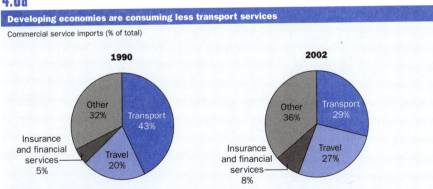

Between 1990 and 2002 travel, insurance and finance, and other services displaced transport as the most important categories of service imports for developing economies.

Source: International Monetary Fund data files.

The data on imports of commercial services are from the IMF. The IMF publishes balance of payments data in its *International Financial Statistics* and *Balance of Payments Statistics Yearbook*.

4.9 Structure of demand

	Household final consumption expenditure		General government final consumption expenditure		Gross capital formation		Exports of goods and services		Imports of goods and services		Gross domestic savings	
	% of GDP		% of GDP		% of GDP		% of GDP		% of GDP		% of GDP	
	1990	2002	1990	2002	1990	2002	1990	2002	1990	2002	1990	2002
Afghanistan	..	108	..	9	..	16	..	57	..	89	..	−16
Albania	61	93	19	8	29	23	15	19	23	43	21	−1
Algeria	57	44	16	15	29	31	23	36	25	26	27	40
Angola	36	61	34	..ᵃ	12	32	39	77	21	70	30	39
Argentina	77	61	3	12	14	12	10	28	5	13	20	27
Armenia	46	87	18	10	47	21	35	30	46	47	36	3
Australia	59	60	19	18	22	24	17	20	17	22	22	22
Austria	55	58	19	19	25	22	40	52	38	51	26	23
Azerbaijan	51	60	18	15	27	33	44	44	39	51	31	25
Bangladesh	86	77	4	5	17	23	6	14	14	19	10	18
Belarus	47	61	24	21	27	22	46	70	44	74	29	18
Belgium	55	55	20	21	22	19	71	82	69	78	24	23
Benin	87	81	11	13	14	18	14	14	26	26	2	6
Bolivia	77	75	12	15	13	15	23	22	24	27	11	10
Bosnia and Herzegovina	..	113	..	..ᵃ	..	20	..	26	..	59	..	−13
Botswana	33	28	24	33	37	25	55	51	50	37	43	38
Brazil	59	58	19	19	20	20	8	16	7	14	21	22
Bulgaria	60	69	18	18	26	20	33	53	37	60	22	13
Burkina Faso	82	82	13	13	18	18	11	9	24	22	5	5
Burundi	95	92	11	13	15	8	8	7	28	19	−5	−4
Cambodia	91	80	7	6	8	22	6	59	13	67	2	14
Cameroon	67	71	13	12	18	19	20	27	17	28	21	18
Canada	56	*56*	23	*19*	21	*20*	26	*44*	26	*39*	21	*25*
Central African Republic	86	78	15	12	12	15	15	12	28	17	−1	10
Chad	88	86	10	8	16	59	13	12	28	65	2	6
Chile	62	61	10	12	25	23	35	36	31	32	28	27
China	50	43	12	13	35	40	18	29	14	26	38	43
Hong Kong, China	57	58	7	10	28	23	133	151	124	142	36	32
Colombia	66	66	9	21	19	15	21	20	15	21	24	14
Congo, Dem. Rep.	79	92	12	4	9	7	30	18	29	21	9	4
Congo, Rep.	62	32	14	18	16	23	54	81	46	54	24	50
Costa Rica	61	68	18	15	27	22	35	42	41	47	21	17
Côte d'Ivoire	72	60	17	11	7	10	32	48	27	30	11	28
Croatia	*74*	60	*24*	22	*10*	27	*78*	46	*86*	55	*2*	18
Cuba	..	70	..	23	..	10	..	16	..	18	..	7
Czech Republic	49	53	23	21	25	28	45	65	43	67	28	26
Denmark	49	48	26	26	20	20	36	45	31	39	25	26
Dominican Republic	80	76	5	10	25	23	34	26	44	35	15	15
Ecuador	67	69	11	10	21	28	33	24	32	31	22	20
Egypt, Arab Rep.	73	79	11	10	29	17	20	16	33	23	16	10
El Salvador	89	90	10	8	14	16	19	27	31	41	1	2
Eritrea	*104*	92	*22*	38	*8*	26	*11*	29	*45*	85	*−26*	−30
Estonia	62	58	16	20	30	31	*60*	84	*54*	94	22	22
Ethiopia	74	78	18	19	12	21	8	16	12	34	7	2
Finland	50	51	22	22	30	20	23	38	24	30	29	28
France	55	55	22	24	23	19	21	27	22	25	22	21
Gabon	50	52	13	..ᵃ	22	28	46	59	31	39	37	48
Gambia, The	76	83	14	13	22	21	60	54	72	72	11	4
Georgia	65	81	10	10	31	21	40	27	46	39	25	9
Germany	57	59	20	19	24	18	25	35	25	32	24	22
Ghana	85	83	9	10	14	20	17	43	26	55	5	7
Greece	72	67	15	16	23	23	18	21	28	27	13	17
Guatemala	84	85	7	8	14	19	21	16	25	28	10	7
Guinea	73	82	9	7	18	17	31	24	31	30	18	11
Guinea-Bissau	87	105	10	13	30	15	10	45	37	77	3	−17
Haiti	81	103	8	..ᵃ	13	21	18	13	20	36	11	−3

	Household final consumption expenditure		General government final consumption expenditure		Gross capital formation		Exports of goods and services		Imports of goods and services		Gross domestic savings	
	% of GDP		% of GDP		% of GDP		% of GDP		% of GDP		% of GDP	
	1990	2002	1990	2002	1990	2002	1990	2002	1990	2002	1990	2002
Honduras	66	74	14	14	23	28	36	37	40	53	20	12
Hungary	61	67	11	11	25	24	31	64	29	67	28	22
India	66	65	12	13	24	23	7	15	9	16	23	22
Indonesia	59	71	9	8	31	14	25	35	24	29	32	21
Iran, Islamic Rep.	62	50	11	13	29	35	22	31	24	29	27	37
Iraq	..	..	..	..	..	..	..	..	..	..	..	..
Ireland	58	*47*	16	*15*	21	*24*	57	*98*	52	*83*	26	*38*
Israel	56	59	30	31	25	18	35	37	45	46	14	9
Italy	58	60	20	19	22	20	20	27	20	26	22	21
Jamaica	65	67	13	20	26	34	48	39	52	60	22	13
Japan	53	*56*	13	*17*	33	*26*	10	*10*	9	*10*	34	*26*
Jordan	74	75	25	23	32	23	62	46	93	67	1	3
Kazakhstan	*52*	60	*18*	12	*32*	27	*74*	47	*75*	46	*30*	28
Kenya	67	71	19	19	20	14	26	27	31	30	14	10
Korea, Dem. Rep.	..	..	..	..	..	..	..	..	..	..	..	..
Korea, Rep.	53	62	10	11	38	26	29	40	30	39	37	27
Kuwait	57	56	39	26	18	9	45	48	58	40	4	18
Kyrgyz Republic	71	67	25	18	24	19	29	39	50	43	4	15
Lao PDR	..	..	9	..	..	22	11	..	25	..	..	..
Latvia	53	63	9	21	40	27	48	45	49	56	39	17
Lebanon	140	95	25	14	18	18	18	14	100	41	−64	−9
Lesotho	121	82	23	33	49	40	16	51	109	107	−44	−15
Liberia	..	..	..	..	..	..	..	..	..	..	..	..
Libya	48	58	24	17	19	14	40	48	31	36	27	26
Lithuania	57	62	19	21	33	22	52	54	61	60	24	17
Macedonia, FYR	72	77	19	22	19	20	26	38	36	57	9	0
Madagascar	86	84	8	8	17	14	17	16	28	23	6	8
Malawi	72	88	15	18	23	12	24	25	33	43	13	−6
Malaysia	52	44	14	14	32	24	75	114	72	97	34	42
Mali	80	77	14	11	23	20	17	32	34	41	6	12
Mauritania	69	79	26	19	20	31	46	39	61	68	5	2
Mauritius	64	66	13	9	31	22	64	61	71	57	23	26
Mexico	70	70	8	12	23	20	19	27	20	29	22	18
Moldova	77	86	..[a]	17	25	23	49	54	51	79	23	−3
Mongolia	58	64	32	19	38	31	24	67	53	81	9	16
Morocco	65	62	15	20	25	23	26	32	32	37	19	18
Mozambique	101	59	12	11	16	45	8	24	36	38	−12	30
Myanmar	89	*88*	..[a]	..[a]	13	*12*	3	..	5	..	11	*12*
Namibia	51	48	31	28	34	24	52	48	67	49	18	23
Nepal	84	78	9	10	18	25	11	16	22	29	7	12
Netherlands	50	50	23	24	24	20	54	62	51	56	27	26
New Zealand	61	60	19	19	20	20	27	33	27	32	20	22
Nicaragua	59	78	43	16	19	32	25	23	46	49	−2	6
Niger	84	84	15	12	8	13	15	16	22	25	1	4
Nigeria	56	55	15	27	15	23	43	38	29	44	29	17
Norway	49	*67*	21	..[a]	23	19	40	41	34	27	30	33
Oman	27	43	38	23	13	13	53	57	31	35	35	34
Pakistan	74	74	15	11	19	15	16	19	23	19	11	14
Panama	60	63	18	13	17	25	38	28	34	29	21	24
Papua New Guinea	59	..	25	..	24	..	41	..	49	..	16	..
Paraguay	77	84	6	8	23	20	33	31	39	43	17	8
Peru	74	72	8	10	16	18	16	16	14	17	18	18
Philippines	72	69	10	12	24	19	28	49	33	49	18	19
Poland	48	65	19	19	26	19	29	28	22	31	33	16
Portugal	63	*61*	16	*21*	28	*28*	33	*31*	39	*41*	21	*18*
Puerto Rico	65	..	14	..	17	..	*77*	*81*	*101*	*100*	21	..

	Household final consumption expenditure		General government final consumption expenditure		Gross capital formation		Exports of goods and services		Imports of goods and services		Gross domestic savings	
	% of GDP		% of GDP		% of GDP		% of GDP		% of GDP		% of GDP	
	1990	2002	1990	2002	1990	2002	1990	2002	1990	2002	1990	2002
Romania	66	76	13	7	30	23	17	35	26	41	21	17
Russian Federation	49	51	21	17	30	21	18	35	18	24	30	32
Rwanda	84	87	10	12	15	19	6	8	14	25	6	1
Saudi Arabia	47	37	29	26	15	20	41	41	32	23	24	37
Senegal	76	76	15	14	14	20	25	31	30	41	9	10
Serbia and Montenegro	..	89	..	18	..	16	..	21	..	44	..	–7
Sierra Leone	83	93	8	21	10	9	22	18	24	40	9	–14
Singapore	47	42	10	13	36	21	..	..	..	..	43	45
Slovak Republic	54	55	22	21	33	31	27	73	36	80	24	24
Slovenia	55	55	19	21	17	23	84	58	74	56	26	25
Somalia	112	..	..a	..	16	..	10	..	38	..	–12	..
South Africa	57	62	20	19	17	16	24	34	19	31	23	19
Spain	60	58	17	18	27	26	16	28	20	30	23	24
Sri Lanka	76	77	10	9	23	21	29	36	38	43	14	14
Sudan	..	79	..	..a	..	20	..	15	..	13	..	21
Swaziland	62	74	18	17	19	18	75	91	74	100	20	9
Sweden	47	49	29	28	24	17	29	43	28	37	25	23
Switzerland	57	76	14	..a	28	17	36	44	36	38	29	24
Syrian Arab Republic	69	59	14	11	17	22	28	37	28	28	17	30
Tajikistan	74	82	9	9	25	23	28	58	35	72	17	10
Tanzaniab	81	77	18	13	26	17	13	17	37	24	1	10
Thailand	57	58	9	11	41	24	34	65	42	57	34	31
Togo	71	86	14	10	27	22	33	33	45	50	15	5
Trinidad and Tobago	59	69	12	10	13	16	45	47	29	43	29	20
Tunisia	58	63	16	16	32	25	44	45	51	49	25	21
Turkey	69	71	11	13	24	16	13	30	18	30	20	16
Turkmenistan	49	49	23	15	40	37	..	47	..	47	28	36
Uganda	92	78	8	16	13	22	7	12	19	27	1	6
Ukraine	57	56	17	20	27	19	28	56	29	52	26	24
United Arab Emirates	39	..	16	..	20	..	65	..	40	..	45	..
United Kingdom	63	66	20	20	20	16	24	26	27	28	18	14
United States	67	70	17	16	18	18	10	10	11	14	16	14
Uruguay	70	73	12	13	12	12	24	22	18	20	18	14
Uzbekistan	61	58	25	19	32	20	29	38	48	34	13	24
Venezuela, RB	62	65	8	6	10	17	39	29	20	17	29	29
Vietnam	84	66	12	6	13	32	36	56	45	60	3	28
West Bank and Gaza	..	79	..	52	..	4	..	12	..	47	..	–31
Yemen, Rep.	74	70	17	14	15	17	14	38	20	39	9	16
Zambia	64	84	19	12	17	17	36	29	37	42	17	4
Zimbabwe	63	72	19	17	17	8	23	24	23	22	17	11
World	**59 w**	**63 w**	**17 w**	**17 w**	**24 w**	**20 w**	**19 w**	**24 w**	**19 w**	**23 w**	**24 w**	**20 w**
Low income	67	69	12	12	23	20	17	25	19	25	21	19
Middle income	59	58	15	16	25	23	20	32	19	28	26	27
Lower middle income	58	57	15	16	27	25	17	29	17	26	27	28
Upper middle income	63	61	12	15	21	19	28	39	25	33	24	25
Low & middle income	61	59	14	15	25	23	20	31	19	28	25	26
East Asia & Pacific	54	51	11	12	34	32	25	41	24	37	34	37
Europe & Central Asia	55	61	18	16	28	21	23	40	24	38	26	23
Latin America & Carib.	65	63	13	16	19	19	14	21	12	19	21	22
Middle East & N. Africa	59	53	20	18	23	23	31	34	33	29	21	29
South Asia	69	68	12	12	23	22	9	17	12	18	20	20
Sub-Saharan Africa	63	66	18	18	17	18	27	33	26	34	19	17
High income	59	64	17	18	24	19	19	22	19	22	24	19
Europe EMU	56	57	20	20	24	20	27	36	27	33	23	22

a. Data on general government final consumption expenditure are not available separately; they are included in household final consumption expenditure. b. Data cover mainland Tanzania only.

About the data

Gross domestic product (GDP) from the expenditure side is made up of household final consumption expenditure, general government final consumption expenditure, gross capital formation (private and public investment in fixed assets, changes in inventories, and net acquisitions of valuables), and net exports (exports minus imports) of goods and services. Such expenditures are recorded in purchaser prices and include net taxes on products.

Because policymakers have tended to focus on fostering the growth of output, and because data on production are easier to collect than data on spending, many countries generate their primary estimate of GDP using the production approach. Moreover, many countries do not estimate all the separate components of national expenditures but instead derive some of the main aggregates indirectly using GDP (based on the production approach) as the control total.

Household final consumption expenditure (private consumption in the 1968 System of National Accounts, or SNA) is often estimated as a residual, by subtracting from GDP all other known expenditures. The resulting aggregate may incorporate fairly large discrepancies. When household consumption is calculated separately, many of the estimates are based on household surveys, which tend to be one-year studies with limited coverage. Thus the estimates quickly become outdated and must be supplemented by estimates using price- and quantity-based statistical procedures. Complicating the issue, in many developing countries the distinction between cash outlays for personal business and those for household use may be blurred. *World Development Indicators* includes in household consumption the expenditures of nonprofit institutions serving households.

General government final consumption expenditure (general government consumption in the 1968 SNA) includes expenditures on goods and services for individual consumption as well as those on services for collective consumption. Defense expenditures, including those on capital outlays (with certain exceptions), are treated as current spending.

Gross capital formation (gross domestic investment in the 1968 SNA) consists of outlays on additions to the economy's fixed assets plus net changes in the level of inventories. It is generally obtained from reports by industry of acquisition and distinguishes only the broad categories of capital formation. The 1993 SNA recognizes a third category of capital formation: net acquisitions of valuables. Included in gross capital formation under the 1993 SNA guidelines are capital outlays on defense establishments that may be used by the general public, such as schools, airfields, and hospitals, and intangibles such as computer software and mineral exploration outlays. Data on capital formation may be estimated from direct surveys of enterprises and administrative records or based on the commodity flow method using data from production, trade, and construction activities. The quality of data on fixed capital formation by government depends on the quality of government accounting systems (which tend to be weak in developing countries). Measures of fixed capital formation by households and corporations—particularly capital outlays by small, unincorporated enterprises—are usually unreliable.

Estimates of changes in inventories are rarely complete but usually include the most important activities or commodities. In some countries these estimates are derived as a composite residual along with household final consumption expenditure. According to national accounts conventions, adjustments should be made for appreciation of the value of inventory holdings due to price changes, but this is not always done. In highly inflationary economies this element can be substantial.

Data on exports and imports are compiled from customs reports and balance of payments data. Although the data from the payments side provide reasonably reliable records of cross-border transactions, they may not adhere strictly to the appropriate definitions of valuation and timing used in the balance of payments or correspond to the change-of-ownership criterion. This issue has assumed greater significance with the increasing globalization of international business. Neither customs nor balance of payments data usually capture the illegal transactions that occur in many countries. Goods carried by travelers across borders in legal but unreported shuttle trade may further distort trade statistics.

Domestic savings, a concept used by the World Bank, represent the difference between GDP and total consumption. Domestic savings also satisfy the fundamental identity: exports minus imports equal domestic savings minus capital formation. Domestic savings differ from savings as defined in the national accounts; the SNA concept of savings represents the difference between disposable income and consumption. For further discussion of the problems in compiling national accounts, see Srinivasan (1994), Heston (1994), and Ruggles (1994). For a classic analysis of the reliability of foreign trade and national income statistics, see Morgenstern (1963).

Definitions

• **Household final consumption expenditure** is the market value of all goods and services, including durable products (such as cars, washing machines, and home computers), purchased by households. It excludes purchases of dwellings but includes imputed rent for owner-occupied dwellings. It also includes payments and fees to governments to obtain permits and licenses. *World Development Indicators* includes in household consumption expenditure the expenditures of nonprofit institutions serving households, even when reported separately by the country. In practice, household consumption expenditure may include any statistical discrepancy in the use of resources relative to the supply of resources. • **General government final consumption expenditure** includes all government current expenditures for purchases of goods and services (including compensation of employees). It also includes most expenditures on national defense and security but excludes government military expenditures that potentially have wider public use and are part of government capital formation. • **Gross capital formation** consists of outlays on additions to the fixed assets of the economy, net changes in the level of inventories, and net acquisitions of valuables. Fixed assets include land improvements (fences, ditches, drains, and so on); plant, machinery, and equipment purchases; and the construction of roads, railways, and the like, including schools, offices, hospitals, private residential dwellings, and commercial and industrial buildings. Inventories are stocks of goods held by firms to meet temporary or unexpected fluctuations in production or sales, and "work in progress." • **Exports** and **imports of goods and services** represent the value of all goods and other market services provided to, or received from, the rest of the world. They include the value of merchandise, freight, insurance, transport, travel, royalties, license fees, and other services, such as communication, construction, financial, information, business, personal, and government services. They exclude labor and property income (factor services in the 1968 SNA) as well as transfer payments. • **Gross domestic savings** are calculated as GDP less total consumption.

Data sources

The national accounts indicators for most developing countries are collected from national statistical organizations and central banks by visiting and resident World Bank missions. The data for high-income economies come from Organisation for Economic Co-operation and Development data files (see the OECD's *National Accounts of OECD Countries, Detailed Tables 1970–2001*, volumes 1 and 2). The United Nations Statistics Division publishes detailed national accounts for United Nations member countries in *National Accounts Statistics: Main Aggregates and Detailed Tables* and updates in the *Monthly Bulletin of Statistics*.

4.10 Growth of consumption and investment

	Household final consumption expenditure						General government final consumption expenditure		Gross capital formation	
	$ millions		average annual % growth		Per capita average annual % growth		average annual % growth		average annual % growth	
	1990	2002	1980–90	1990–2002	1980–90	1990–2002	1980–90	1990–2002	1980–90	1990–2002
Afghanistan	..	..	..	..	..	..	..	..	..	..
Albania	1,271	4,496	..	4.2	..	4.8	..	1.6	−0.3	20.5
Algeria	35,265	24,745	1.5	0.9	−1.4	−0.9	0.7	3.4	−1.8	0.3
Angola	3,674	..	−3.6	..	..	..	8.4	..	−5.6	..
Argentina	109,038	62,158	..	0.5	..	−0.7	..	1.3	−5.2	2.5
Armenia	1,097	2,121	..	1.1	..	2.5	..	−1.0	..	−6.2
Australia	182,448	247,950	2.9	3.7	1.4	2.5	3.5	3.0	3.7	6.4
Austria	89,789	117,605	2.4	2.3	2.2	2.0	1.4	1.6	2.4	2.0
Azerbaijan	3,186	3,587	..	11.3	..	10.3	..	7.0	..	8.0
Bangladesh	24,988	36,548	3.0	2.8	0.4	1.0	2.9	4.9	6.9	9.0
Belarus	8,223	8,781	..	0.9	..	1.2	..	−1.0	..	−6.3
Belgium	109,154	135,445	2.0	1.9	1.9	1.6	1.1	1.6	2.9	1.9
Benin	1,602	2,183	1.9	3.4	−1.2	0.7	0.5	5.8	−5.3	12.8
Bolivia	3,741	5,835	1.2	3.4	−0.9	0.9	−3.8	3.4	0.8	5.1
Bosnia and Herzegovina	..	..	..	..	..	..	..	..	..	..
Botswana	1,260	1,537	6.3	4.1	2.7	1.5	14.9	7.6	7.6	2.6
Brazil[a]	273,952	263,710	1.2	4.7	−0.7	3.2	7.3	0.2	3.3	0.6
Bulgaria	12,401	10,742	3.1	−1.0	3.2	−0.3	5.1	−5.8	..	..
Burkina Faso	2,284	2,556	2.6	3.9	0.1	1.4	6.2	−0.5	8.6	7.9
Burundi	1,070	655	3.4	−1.7	0.5	−3.7	3.2	−1.6	6.9	1.2
Cambodia[a]	1,016	3,287	..	4.7	..	2.2	..	7.7	..	12.2
Cameroon	7,423	6,394	3.5	3.5	0.6	0.9	6.8	2.8	−2.6	2.3
Canada	322,564	391,155	3.2	2.7	2.0	1.7	2.4	0.5	5.0	4.6
Central African Republic[a]	1,274	815	1.5	..	..	..	−1.7	..	10.0	..
Chad[a]	1,538	1,719	2.9	2.0	0.2	−1.1	17.0	−0.8	22.0	18.0
Chile	18,759	39,211	2.0	6.2	0.3	4.7	0.4	3.6	6.4	6.2
China	174,249	586,381	8.8	8.7	7.2	7.6	9.8	9.0	10.8	10.7
Hong Kong, China	42,723	93,401	6.6	3.5	5.2	1.8	5.3	3.3	3.9	4.3
Colombia	26,357	53,046	2.6	1.8	0.5	−0.1	4.2	8.9	1.4	0.8
Congo, Dem. Rep.[a]	7,398	5,269	3.4	−2.9	0.4	−5.4	0.0	−15.9	−5.1	0.3
Congo, Rep.[a]	1,746	955	2.3	1.7	−0.9	−1.5	4.3	−2.6	−11.6	2.3
Costa Rica[a]	3,502	11,521	3.6	4.4	0.6	2.2	1.1	2.0	4.6	5.5
Côte d'Ivoire	7,766	7,048	1.5	3.1	−2.1	0.2	−0.1	0.8	−10.4	4.5
Croatia	13,527	13,483	..	3.0	..	3.5	..	0.1	..	5.7
Cuba	..	..	..	..	..	..	..	..	..	..
Czech Republic	17,195	36,165	..	2.7	..	2.8	..	−1.0	..	4.8
Denmark	65,430	82,827	1.4	1.8	1.4	1.4	0.9	2.2	4.7	5.2
Dominican Republic[a]	5,633	16,408	3.9	5.6	1.7	3.8	−3.2	13.6	4.5	6.2
Ecuador[a]	6,988	16,837	1.1	2.2	−1.5	0.3	−0.7	−1.0	−1.3	1.3
Egypt, Arab Rep.	30,933	71,236	4.6	4.3	2.0	2.3	3.1	2.5	0.0	5.5
El Salvador	4,273	12,847	0.8	4.8	−0.2	2.8	0.1	2.4	2.2	6.0
Eritrea	496	592	..	−0.3	..	−2.9	..	14.2	..	10.7
Estonia	2,539	3,727	..	1.2	..	2.5	..	4.4	..	1.8
Ethiopia	6,382	4,756	0.7	5.6	−2.4	3.2	4.0	9.5	4.9	5.8
Finland	68,341	66,204	3.9	2.1	3.4	1.8	3.2	1.1	3.3	1.8
France	672,960	784,209	2.2	1.6	1.7	1.2	2.6	1.9	3.3	2.0
Gabon[a]	2,961	3,040	1.5	2.1	−1.6	−0.6	−0.6	4.0	−5.7	3.2
Gambia, The	240	296	−2.4	5.3	−5.9	1.8	1.7	0.5	0.0	2.6
Georgia	5,231	2,799	..	4.6	..	5.0	..	4.3	..	−8.3
Germany	950,047	1,168,773	2.3	1.6	2.2	1.3	1.5	1.5	1.8	0.4
Ghana	5,016	5,093	2.8	1.3	−0.6	−1.1	2.4	4.7	3.3	1.1
Greece	60,164	89,446	2.0	2.4	1.5	2.0	1.1	1.6	−0.7	4.5
Guatemala[a]	6,398	19,794	1.1	4.1	−1.4	1.4	2.6	5.3	−1.8	6.3
Guinea	2,068	2,625	..	3.6	..	1.1	..	4.3	..	2.3
Guinea-Bissau	212	213	0.8	1.5	−1.9	−1.4	7.2	2.1	12.9	−12.3
Haiti	2,332	3,334	0.9	..	..	..	−4.4	..	−0.6	8.7

	Household final consumption expenditure						General government final consumption expenditure		Gross capital formation	
	$ millions		average annual % growth		Per capita average annual % growth		average annual % growth		average annual % growth	
	1990	2002	1980–90	1990–2002	1980–90	1990–2002	1980–90	1990–2002	1980–90	1990–2002
Honduras [a]	2,026	4,858	2.7	3.1	–0.5	0.3	3.3	3.7	2.9	5.2
Hungary	20,290	42,860	1.3	0.9	1.7	1.1	1.9	1.5	–0.9	7.6
India	215,762	328,706	4.2	4.9	2.0	3.1	7.3	6.4	6.2	6.9
Indonesia	65,010	122,193	5.3	5.8	3.4	4.3	4.6	0.9	7.7	–2.1
Iran, Islamic Rep.	74,476	54,403	2.8	3.3	–0.6	1.7	–5.0	4.3	–2.5	4.6
Iraq	..	..	..	..	..	..	..	..	..	..
Ireland	27,957	*47,973*	2.2	*5.7*	1.9	*4.8*	–0.3	*4.6*	–0.4	*9.8*
Israel	32,112	61,552	..	*4.2*	..	*1.7*	..	*3.0*	..	*–1.5*
Italy	634,194	713,186	2.9	1.7	2.8	1.5	2.9	0.4	2.1	1.8
Jamaica	2,980	5,859	..	..	..	..	..	..	..	..
Japan	1,618,040	2,282,911	3.6	1.5	3.0	1.2	3.6	3.0	5.5	*–0.1*
Jordan	2,978	7,622	1.9	5.2	–1.9	1.4	1.9	4.1	–1.9	0.3
Kazakhstan [a]	*12,856*	14,392	..	–5.5	..	–4.6	..	–4.5	..	–11.8
Kenya	5,320	8,819	4.7	2.2	1.2	–0.3	2.6	7.5	0.4	2.9
Korea, Dem. Rep.	..	..	..	..	..	..	..	..	..	..
Korea, Rep.	132,113	286,818	7.9	4.9	6.7	4.0	5.2	2.6	12.0	1.3
Kuwait	10,459	19,720	–1.4	..	..	..	2.2	..	–4.5	..
Kyrgyz Republic	1,896	1,083	..	–4.7	..	–5.6	..	–6.5	..	–2.2
Lao PDR	..	..	..	..	..	..	..	..	..	..
Latvia	*3,365*	5,274	2.3	–1.6	1.8	–0.4	5.0	1.8	3.4	–6.5
Lebanon	3,961	16,921	..	2.4	..	0.7	..	5.7	..	4.1
Lesotho	746	585	1.3	–0.4	–0.8	–1.5	3.6	6.7	5.0	1.0
Liberia	..	..	..	..	..	..	..	..	..	..
Libya	13,999	10,970	..	..	..	..	..	..	..	..
Lithuania [a]	5,826	8,577	..	*4.9*	..	*5.6*	..	*1.6*	..	*9.3*
Macedonia, FYR	3,021	2,924	..	2.1	..	1.4	..	1.5	..	1.5
Madagascar	2,663	3,703	–0.7	2.3	–3.4	–0.6	0.5	0.6	4.9	4.0
Malawi	1,345	1,665	1.5	4.9	–1.7	2.9	6.3	–1.5	–2.8	–13.7
Malaysia	22,806	41,971	3.3	4.9	0.4	2.4	2.7	5.6	3.1	3.5
Mali	1,943	2,230	0.6	3.2	–1.9	0.7	7.9	5.5	3.6	3.5
Mauritania	705	762	1.4	3.9	–0.9	1.1	–3.8	2.0	6.9	9.1
Mauritius	1,519	2,983	6.2	4.8	5.3	3.6	3.3	4.8	10.3	4.0
Mexico	182,791	445,791	1.1	2.8	–1.0	1.1	2.4	1.6	–3.3	4.6
Moldova [a]	*1,780*	1,403	..	*8.6*	..	*8.9*	..	*–9.2*	..	*–12.0*
Mongolia [a]	..	744	..	..	..	..	..	..	..	..
Morocco	16,833	23,952	4.3	2.7	2.0	0.9	2.1	3.6	1.2	3.9
Mozambique [a]	2,481	2,124	–1.6	1.5	–3.1	–0.7	–1.1	6.2	3.8	14.0
Myanmar	..	..	0.6	*3.9*	..	..	..	..	–4.1	*15.3*
Namibia	1,204	1,377	1.3	5.1	–1.9	2.2	3.7	3.0	–3.2	6.5
Nepal	3,060	4,336	..	..	..	..	..	..	..	..
Netherlands	145,871	209,068	1.7	2.8	1.1	2.2	2.2	2.1	3.3	2.8
New Zealand	26,632	34,955	2.1	3.1	1.2	2.0	1.6	2.6	3.0	5.1
Nicaragua [a]	592	3,123	–3.6	6.1	–6.2	3.2	3.4	–2.6	–4.8	12.6
Niger	2,079	1,814	0.0	*1.8*	–3.1	–1.7	4.4	*0.8*	–7.1	*4.0*
Nigeria	15,816	24,135	–2.6	*0.2*	–5.5	–2.7	–3.5	*–1.8*	–8.5	*5.4*
Norway	57,047	*73,067*	2.2	*3.5*	1.9	*2.9*	2.4	*2.7*	0.9	4.5
Oman	2,810	8,752	..	..	..	..	..	..	25.5	..
Pakistan	29,512	43,936	4.3	4.4	1.6	1.8	10.3	0.8	5.8	1.4
Panama [a]	3,022	5,673	2.1	4.1	–0.0	2.4	1.2	2.6	–8.9	8.0
Papua New Guinea	1,902	..	0.4	*5.2*	–2.1	*2.6*	–0.1	*2.2*	–0.9	*1.3*
Paraguay	4,063	4,649	2.4	3.2	–0.5	0.8	1.5	4.0	–0.8	–1.6
Peru [a]	19,376	40,717	0.7	3.6	–1.5	1.7	–0.9	4.6	–3.8	4.9
Philippines	31,566	53,307	2.6	3.7	0.2	1.4	0.6	3.3	–2.1	3.7
Poland [a]	28,281	123,535	..	4.8	..	4.7	..	3.1	..	8.5
Portugal	44,679	*67,078*	2.6	*2.8*	2.4	*2.5*	5.0	*2.9*	3.0	*5.4*
Puerto Rico	19,827	..	3.5	..	..	..	5.1	..	6.9	..

4.10 Growth of consumption and investment

	$ millions		Household final consumption expenditure average annual % growth		Per capita average annual % growth		General government final consumption expenditure average annual % growth		Gross capital formation average annual % growth	
	1990	2002	1980–90	1990–2002	1980–90	1990–2002	1980–90	1990–2002	1980–90	1990–2002
Romania [a]	25,232	34,785	..	1.9	..	2.2	..	0.7	..	–2.7
Russian Federation	252,561	177,362	..	0.3	..	0.5	..	–1.5	..	–13.6
Rwanda [a]	2,162	1,503	1.2	2.2	–1.8	0.8	5.2	0.7	4.3	2.7
Saudi Arabia	54,508	69,666	..	..	..	..	..	..	..	..
Senegal	4,353	3,820	2.1	2.9	–0.8	0.2	3.3	4.1	5.2	8.0
Serbia and Montenegro	..	13,915	..	..	..	..	..	..	..	..
Sierra Leone	546	728	–2.7	–5.2	–4.7	–7.3	–4.7	3.2	44.9	2.7
Singapore	17,019	37,360	5.8	5.5	3.9	2.6	6.6	9.3	3.1	4.5
Slovak Republic	8,350	13,133	3.8	1.8	3.5	1.6	4.8	1.4	0.0	5.8
Slovenia	6,917	11,697	..	3.5	..	3.5	..	3.9	..	9.3
Somalia	..	..	1.3	..	..	..	7.0	..	–2.6	..
South Africa	64,251	64,741	2.4	2.7	–0.2	0.5	3.5	0.7	–5.3	3.1
Spain	306,953	378,319	2.6	2.5	2.3	2.0	4.9	3.0	5.9	3.4
Sri Lanka [a]	6,143	12,736	4.0	4.7	2.9	3.4	7.3	10.9	0.6	5.3
Sudan	..	8,339	0.0	..	..	..	–0.5	..	–1.8	10.8
Swaziland [a]	547	883	5.3	3.5	2.1	0.4	1.4	3.4	–0.4	1.5
Sweden	116,475	116,993	2.2	1.6	1.9	1.3	1.6	0.5	4.7	2.0
Switzerland	130,900	149,886	1.6	1.1	1.1	0.5	3.1	1.0	3.9	1.0
Syrian Arab Republic	8,458	12,289	3.6	2.0	0.2	–0.8	–3.6	0.3	–5.3	2.1
Tajikistan	1,940	932	..	0.9	..	–0.3	4.1	–11.2	–4.3	–10.1
Tanzania [b]	3,526	7,365	..	3.5	..	0.7	..	1.2	..	–0.3
Thailand	48,270	71,743	5.9	3.3	4.1	2.5	4.2	4.5	9.5	–4.1
Togo	1,158	1,184	4.7	3.6	1.3	0.8	–1.2	–2.1	2.7	1.3
Trinidad and Tobago	2,975	6,424	–1.3	2.0	–2.5	1.5	–1.7	1.3	–6.3	8.4
Tunisia	7,152	13,152	2.9	4.5	0.3	2.9	3.8	4.2	–1.8	3.7
Turkey	103,324	130,631	..	3.1	..	1.2	..	4.4	..	1.4
Turkmenistan	1,616	2,918	..	..	..	..	..	..	..	4.3
Uganda	4,002	4,528	2.6	6.0	–0.6	3.0	2.0	7.1	8.0	8.1
Ukraine	46,497	23,251	..	–4.7	..	–4.1	..	–3.1	..	–13.9
United Arab Emirates	12,726	..	4.6	..	..	..	–3.9	..	–8.7	..
United Kingdom	619,782	1,034,301	4.0	3.3	3.8	3.1	0.8	1.4	6.4	3.7
United States	3,831,500	7,303,700	3.8	3.5	2.9	2.3	3.3	1.3	4.0	6.2
Uruguay [a]	6,525	8,836	0.7	3.2	0.1	2.5	1.8	1.5	–6.6	2.3
Uzbekistan	8,204	4,569	..	..	..	..	..	..	..	0.1
Venezuela, RB	30,170	60,977	1.3	0.4	–1.2	–1.7	2.0	0.4	–5.3	2.3
Vietnam	5,485	22,780	..	5.0	..	3.6	..	3.4	..	17.2
West Bank and Gaza	..	2,756	..	–1.0	..	–5.1	..	13.6	..	–22.7
Yemen, Rep.	3,561	6,882	..	3.6	..	0.3	..	2.2	..	7.5
Zambia	2,078	3,110	1.8	–2.3	–1.3	–4.5	–3.4	–6.5	–4.3	6.4
Zimbabwe	5,543	6,020	3.7	0.4	–0.0	–1.5	4.7	–2.9	3.6	–6.2
World	**12,863,243 t**	**20,040,617 t**	**3.3 w**	**2.8 w**	**1.5 w**	**1.4 w**	**3.0 w**	**1.9 w**	**3.9 w**	**2.5 w**
Low income	513,634	757,325	3.4	4.4	1.0	2.4	5.2	3.8	4.7	4.2
Middle income	1,879,875	2,964,278	2.4	3.5	0.8	2.3	..	2.1	1.6	1.3
Lower middle income	1,323,786	1,913,292	3.3	3.8	1.6	2.7	5.5	2.2	3.4	0.3
Upper middle income	558,438	1,046,796	..	2.6	..	1.3	..	2.0	–2.5	4.5
Low & middle income	2,389,174	3,715,003	2.9	3.7	0.9	2.1	5.3	2.3	2.1	1.7
East Asia & Pacific	361,814	932,055	6.4	6.7	4.7	5.5	6.3	6.8	8.4	6.9
Europe & Central Asia	604,731	689,168	..	1.2	..	1.1	..	–0.3	..	–6.6
Latin America & Carib.	722,234	1,098,409	1.3	3.4	–0.7	1.7	5.6	1.1	–0.3	2.6
Middle East & N. Africa	238,847	361,722	..	..	..	..	..	..	..	..
South Asia	283,645	432,695	4.1	4.6	1.8	2.7	7.6	5.8	6.0	6.5
Sub-Saharan Africa	186,935	203,372	1.5	2.6	–1.3	0.1	2.7	1.4	–3.8	3.4
High income	10,474,011	16,329,652	3.3	2.6	2.7	1.9	2.8	1.8	4.2	2.7
Europe EMU	3,115,871	3,795,770	2.4	1.9	2.1	1.5	2.3	1.7	2.6	1.8

a. Household final consumption expenditure includes statistical discrepancy. b. Data cover mainland Tanzania only.

About the data

Measures of growth in consumption and capital formation are subject to two kinds of inaccuracy. The first stems from the difficulty of measuring expenditures at current price levels, as described in *About the data* for table 4.9. The second arises in deflating current price data to measure volume growth, where results depend on the relevance and reliability of the price indexes and weights used. Measuring price changes is more difficult for investment goods than for consumption goods because of the one-time nature of many investments and because the rate of technological progress in capital goods makes capturing change in quality difficult. (An example is computers—prices have fallen as quality has improved.) Several countries estimate capital formation from the supply side, identifying capital goods entering an economy directly from detailed production and international trade statistics. This means that the price indexes used in deflating production and international trade, reflecting delivered or offered prices, will determine the deflator for capital formation expenditures on the demand side.

The data in the table on household final consumption expenditure (private consumption in the 1968 System of National Accounts), in current U.S. dollars, are converted from national currencies using official exchange rates or an alternative conversion factor as noted in *Primary data documentation*. (For a discussion of alternative conversion factors, see *Statistical methods*.) Growth rates of household final consumption expenditure, household final consumption expenditure per capita, general government final consumption expenditure, and gross capital formation are estimated using constant price data. (Consumption and capital formation as shares of GDP are shown in table 4.9.)

To obtain government consumption in constant prices, countries may deflate current values by applying a wage (price) index or extrapolate from the change in government employment. Neither technique captures improvements in productivity or changes in the quality of government services. Deflators for household consumption are usually calculated on the basis of the consumer price index. Many countries estimate household consumption as a residual that includes statistical discrepancies associated with the estimation of other expenditure items, including changes in inventories; thus these estimates lack detailed breakdowns of household consumption expenditures.

4.10a

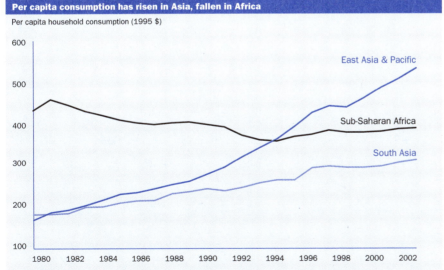

Per capita consumption has risen in Asia, fallen in Africa

Per capita household consumption (1995 $)

Starting from slightly lower per capita household consumption in 1980 than South Asia, East Asia and Pacific has raised consumption dramatically and lowered poverty. In Sub-Saharan Africa, by contrast, which had per capita household consumption of well more than twice that in East and South Asia in 1980, per capita household consumption has fallen below that of East Asia and Pacific.

Source: World Bank data files.

Data sources

The national accounts indicators for most developing countries are collected from national statistical organizations and central banks by visiting and resident World Bank missions. Data for high-income economies come from data files of the Organisation for Economic Co-operation and Development (see the OECD's *National Accounts of OECD Countries, Detailed Tables, 1970–2001*, volumes 1 and 2). The United Nations Statistics Division publishes detailed national accounts for United Nations member countries in *National Accounts Statistics: Main Aggregates and Detailed Tables* and updates in the *Monthly Bulletin of Statistics*.

	Current revenue[a] % of GDP		Total expenditure % of GDP		Overall budget balance (including grants) % of GDP		Financing from abroad % of GDP		Domestic financing % of GDP		Debt and interest payments	
											Total debt % of GDP	Interest % of current revenue
	1990	2001	1990	2001	1990	2001	1990	2001	1990	2001	2001	2001
Afghanistan	..	..	..	..	..	..	..	..	..	..	..	..
Albania	..	..	..	..	..	..	..	..	..	..	..	..
Algeria	..	35.5	..	31.2	..	4.0	..	−2.6	..	−1.4	50.4	9.8
Angola	..	..	..	..	..	..	..	..	..	..	..	..
Argentina	10.4	13.8	10.6	17.1	−0.4	−3.3	0.2	4.2	0.2	−0.9	..	27.5
Armenia	..	..	..	..	..	..	..	..	..	..	..	..
Australia	24.9	23.9	23.2	23.5	2.0	1.4	0.2	−0.5	−2.2	−0.9	15.4	5.3
Austria	34.0	37.2	37.6	40.3	−4.4	..	0.5	..	3.9	..	62.3	8.9
Azerbaijan	..	17.6	..	22.6	..	−2.5	..	..	..	..	..	2.5
Bangladesh	..	9.3	..	12.7	..	−2.8	..	0.1	..	2.7	40.1	15.7
Belarus	30.9	28.5	37.3	29.6	−4.8	−1.4	2.7	−0.1	2.4	1.5	11.4	2.5
Belgium	42.7	..	47.9	..	−5.5	..	−0.3	..	5.8	..	..	..
Benin	..	..	..	..	..	..	..	..	..	..	..	..
Bolivia	13.7	17.1	16.4	26.6	−1.7	−6.7	0.7	2.0	1.0	4.7	69.3	12.2
Bosnia and Herzegovina	..	..	..	..	..	..	..	..	..	..	..	..
Botswana	50.8	..	33.6	..	11.2	..	0.0	..	−11.3	..	..	..
Brazil	22.8	..	34.9	..	−5.8	..	..	..	..	..	..	..
Bulgaria	47.1	33.0	55.1	34.4	−8.3	1.9	−0.8	−0.2	9.1	−1.7	..	11.2
Burkina Faso	9.7	..	13.3	..	−1.2	..	..	..	..	..	..	..
Burundi	18.2	17.9	28.7	26.1	−3.3	−4.7	4.9	3.3	−1.6	1.5	183.9	13.2
Cambodia	..	..	..	..	..	..	..	..	..	..	..	..
Cameroon	15.4	15.7	21.2	15.5	−5.9	0.1	5.2	0.2	1.2	−0.3	102.3	19.2
Canada	21.5	21.1	26.1	19.8	−4.8	1.3	0.2	0.6	4.6	−1.9	58.5	12.4
Central African Republic	..	..	..	..	..	..	..	..	..	..	..	..
Chad	6.7	..	21.8	..	−4.7	..	5.0	..	−0.3	..	..	..
Chile	20.6	22.8	20.4	23.1	0.8	−0.3	..	0.7	..	−0.4	15.6	2.1
China	6.3	7.2	10.1	10.9	−1.9	−2.9	0.8	−0.1	1.1	3.0	12.7	..
Hong Kong, China	..	..	..	..	..	..	..	..	..	..	..	..
Colombia	12.6	12.4	11.6	18.8	3.9	−7.0	..	2.1	..	4.9	29.3	26.8
Congo, Dem. Rep.	10.1	0.0	18.8	0.1	−6.5	−0.0	0.0	0.0	6.5	0.0	..	..
Congo, Rep.	22.5	31.2	35.6	25.7	−14.1	5.8	..	2.0	..	−3.1	160.6	19.3
Costa Rica	23.0	22.2	25.6	23.6	−3.1	−1.2	0.3	1.4	2.8	−0.2	38.4	17.9
Côte d'Ivoire	22.0	17.0	24.5	16.5	−2.9	0.9	4.0	0.2	0.4	−1.1	102.5	19.5
Croatia	33.0	40.2	37.6	45.3	−4.6	−2.5	0.0	1.4	4.7	1.1	..	5.0
Cuba	..	..	..	..	..	..	..	..	..	..	..	..
Czech Republic	..	33.5	..	38.2	..	−1.9	..	−0.2	..	2.1	16.7	2.7
Denmark	37.8	36.6	39.0	35.4	−0.7	1.6	..	..	..	..	..	10.8
Dominican Republic	12.0	16.9	11.7	16.0	0.6	1.0	−0.0	−1.0	−0.6	−0.0	20.7	4.5
Ecuador	18.7	..	15.0	..	3.8	..	..	..	..	..	..	..
Egypt, Arab Rep.	23.0	..	27.8	..	−5.7	..	−0.7	..	6.4	..	..	..
El Salvador	..	2.0	..	2.5	..	−0.3	..	0.4	..	−0.1	3.6	8.0
Eritrea	..	..	..	..	..	..	..	..	..	..	..	..
Estonia	26.2	29.9	23.7	29.9	0.4	2.5	0.0	−0.3	−0.4	−2.2	2.6	0.6
Ethiopia	17.3	19.0	27.1	26.6	−9.8	−5.0	2.8	2.8	7.0	2.2	101.4	10.8
Finland	30.5	..	30.2	..	0.2	..	0.7	..	−0.8	..	..	..
France	39.7	..	41.8	..	−2.1	..	1.1	..	1.0	..	..	..
Gabon	20.6	..	20.2	..	3.2	..	2.7	..	−5.8	..	..	..
Gambia, The	19.4	..	23.6	..	−0.8	..	..	..	..	..	..	..
Georgia	..	10.4	..	10.9	..	0.1	..	−0.2	..	0.0	67.0	16.6
Germany	25.9	..	26.5	..	−1.5	..	0.5	0.6	1.0	−0.1	20.0	..
Ghana	12.5	..	13.2	..	0.2	..	1.3	..	−1.5	..	..	..
Greece	27.8	..	52.2	..	−22.9	..	1.6	..	21.3	..	..	..
Guatemala	..	..	..	..	..	..	..	..	..	..	..	..
Guinea	16.0	11.7	22.9	21.0	−3.3	−2.4	4.1	2.3	−0.8	0.2	..	37.1
Guinea-Bissau	..	..	..	..	..	..	..	..	..	..	..	..
Haiti	..	7.9	..	10.5	..	−2.3	..	−0.2	..	2.5	..	6.1

	Current revenue [a] (% of GDP)		Total expenditure (% of GDP)		Overall budget balance (including grants) (% of GDP)		Financing from abroad (% of GDP)		Domestic financing (% of GDP)		Debt and interest payments	
											Total debt % of GDP	Interest % of current revenue
	1990	2001	1990	2001	1990	2001	1990	2001	1990	2001	2001	2001
Honduras	..	..	..	..	..	..	..	..	..	..	..	..
Hungary	52.9	37.1	52.1	41.5	0.8	–3.8	–0.5	3.3	–0.3	0.5	53.1	12.9
India	12.6	13.0	16.3	17.3	–7.6	–4.7	0.6	0.1	7.1	4.6	57.7	37.1
Indonesia	18.8	21.2	18.4	24.8	0.4	–1.2	0.7	0.5	–1.1	0.7	45.2	21.6
Iran, Islamic Rep.	18.1	21.0	19.9	21.9	–1.8	–0.6	–0.0	0.1	1.8	0.5	..	0.7
Iraq	..	..	..	..	..	..	..	..	..	..	..	..
Ireland	33.6	..	37.7	..	–2.4	..	..	..	..	..	..	..
Israel	39.4	41.2	50.7	47.3	–5.3	–3.6	0.8	–0.1	4.6	3.7	99.1	12.9
Italy	38.2	41.3	47.4	41.9	–10.2	–1.6	..	..	..	..	..	15.5
Jamaica	26.6	33.9	24.3	38.8	3.6	–2.7	..	..	..	..	142.5	43.5
Japan	14.0	..	15.3	..	–1.5	..	..	..	..	..	..	..
Jordan	26.1	25.1	35.8	32.4	–3.5	–2.5	3.0	0.2	0.5	2.3	91.9	13.3
Kazakhstan	..	11.4	..	14.6	..	–0.4	..	0.3	..	0.1	17.7	10.0
Kenya	22.4	..	27.5	..	–3.8	..	1.3	..	4.5	..	..	..
Korea, Dem. Rep.	..	..	..	..	..	..	..	..	..	..	..	..
Korea, Rep.	17.5	..	16.2	..	–0.7	..	–0.2	..	0.9	..	..	..
Kuwait	58.7	34.5	55.3	44.2	..	–9.7	..	..	..	..	..	4.0
Kyrgyz Republic	..	16.1	..	17.7	..	0.4	..	..	..	..	99.3	8.8
Lao PDR	..	..	..	..	..	..	..	..	..	..	..	..
Latvia	..	25.8	..	29.1	..	–1.4	..	2.2	..	–0.8	14.8	3.9
Lebanon	..	19.5	..	35.7	..	–16.2	..	8.1	..	8.1	135.2	74.4
Lesotho	39.4	..	51.7	..	–1.1	..	8.0	..	–6.9	..	..	..
Liberia	..	..	..	..	..	..	..	..	..	..	..	..
Libya	..	..	..	..	..	..	..	..	..	..	..	..
Lithuania	31.9	24.7	28.9	26.6	1.4	–0.4	..	1.0	..	–0.6	23.2	6.3
Macedonia, FYR	..	..	..	..	..	..	..	..	..	..	..	..
Madagascar	11.6	11.7	16.0	17.1	–1.1	–2.4	2.1	1.7	–1.2	0.5	..	12.1
Malawi	19.8	..	25.4	..	–1.6	..	..	..	..	..	..	..
Malaysia	26.4	..	29.3	..	–2.0	..	–0.7	..	2.8	..	..	..
Mali	..	..	..	..	..	..	..	..	..	..	..	..
Mauritania	..	..	..	..	..	..	..	..	..	..	..	..
Mauritius	24.3	20.3	24.3	24.5	–0.4	0.9	–0.5	–2.9	0.9	1.9	32.5	13.6
Mexico	15.3	14.8	17.9	15.9	–2.5	–1.3	0.3	–0.9	2.3	2.1	23.2	14.0
Moldova	..	21.3	..	22.8	..	1.1	..	–2.7	..	1.6	60.9	19.7
Mongolia	19.6	30.7	23.1	30.7	–6.4	–4.0	7.5	6.3	–1.1	–2.3	83.5	4.6
Morocco	26.4	29.6	28.8	32.5	–2.2	–2.5	3.9	–1.5	–1.6	4.0	72.8	16.5
Mozambique	..	..	..	..	..	..	..	..	..	..	..	..
Myanmar	10.5	5.3	16.0	8.7	–5.1	–3.4	0.0	–0.0	5.1	3.4	..	..
Namibia	31.3	32.4	33.3	35.9	–1.2	–3.5	..	..	..	..	..	7.0
Nepal	8.4	11.2	17.2	18.0	–6.8	–4.5	5.4	1.8	1.4	2.7	63.8	10.2
Netherlands	45.3	..	49.8	..	–4.3	..	–0.3	..	4.6	..	..	..
New Zealand	42.1	29.7	43.4	29.1	4.0	0.3	..	..	..	..	30.4	6.9
Nicaragua	33.5	18.0	72.0	27.3	–35.6	–6.3	12.7	3.3	22.9	0.5	..	13.4
Niger	..	..	..	..	..	..	..	..	..	..	..	..
Nigeria	..	..	..	..	..	..	..	..	..	..	..	..
Norway	42.2	40.1	41.1	35.4	0.5	–3.8	–0.6	3.7	0.0	0.1	19.9	3.8
Oman	38.9	27.0	39.5	29.9	–0.8	–4.2	–3.9	3.1	4.7	1.1	19.9	4.6
Pakistan	19.1	15.6	22.4	21.6	–5.4	–4.7	2.3	2.2	3.1	2.5	90.0	58.4
Panama	25.6	22.5	23.7	23.5	3.0	0.3	–3.4	1.4	0.4	–1.7	..	20.7
Papua New Guinea	25.2	23.0	34.7	31.4	–3.5	–2.8	0.4	1.7	3.0	1.0	63.9	19.0
Paraguay	12.3	17.2	9.4	18.5	2.9	–0.8	–0.9	..	–2.1	..	..	7.5
Peru	12.5	15.8	20.6	18.5	–8.1	–1.8	5.4	1.1	2.7	0.8	44.3	13.6
Philippines	16.2	15.3	19.6	19.2	–3.5	–4.0	0.4	0.6	3.1	3.4	64.9	31.2
Poland	..	29.6	..	35.1	..	–4.3	..	–1.5	..	5.7	38.8	9.5
Portugal	31.3	..	37.6	..	–4.4	..	–1.3	..	5.7	..	..	..
Puerto Rico	..	..	..	..	..	..	..	..	..	..	..	..

4.11 Central government finances

	Current revenue[a] (% of GDP)		Total expenditure (% of GDP)		Overall budget balance (including grants) (% of GDP)		Financing from abroad (% of GDP)		Domestic financing (% of GDP)		Debt and interest payments	
											Total debt % of GDP	Interest % of current revenue
	1990	2001	1990	2001	1990	2001	1990	2001	1990	2001	2001	2001
Romania	34.4	26.7	33.8	30.4	0.9	–3.0	0.0	0.8	–0.9	2.2	..	11.5
Russian Federation	..	26.8	..	24.4	..	3.4	..	–2.6	..	–0.9	48.8	9.5
Rwanda	10.8	..	18.9	..	–5.3	..	2.5	..	2.8	..	..	..
Saudi Arabia	..	..	..	..	..	..	..	..	..	..	..	..
Senegal	..	17.8	..	21.8	..	–2.0	..	1.6	..	0.4	72.8	5.0
Serbia and Montenegro	..	..	..	..	..	..	..	..	..	..	..	..
Sierra Leone	5.6	*7.1*	8.3	*20.9*	–2.5	*–8.5*	0.5	*1.1*	2.0	*7.4*	*247.4*	*81.8*
Singapore	26.7	24.9	21.3	22.2	10.8	5.2	–0.1	0.0	–10.6	–5.2	99.4	1.3
Slovak Republic	..	33.3	..	39.1	..	–3.2	..	0.8	..	2.4	42.2	9.3
Slovenia	*39.8*	37.4	*38.6*	38.9	*0.3*	–1.0	*0.1*	0.4	*–0.4*	0.6	26.4	4.1
Somalia	..	..	..	..	..	..	..	..	..	..	..	..
South Africa	26.3	27.7	30.1	28.8	–4.1	–1.0	–0.0	3.4	4.1	–2.4	46.8	17.5
Spain	29.3	..	32.6	..	–3.1	..	0.7	..	2.4	..	..	..
Sri Lanka	21.0	16.4	28.4	26.1	–7.8	–9.8	3.6	1.0	4.2	8.8	103.1	40.8
Sudan	..	*8.0*	..	*8.5*	..	*–0.9*	..	*0.1*	..	*0.8*	*8.7*	*9.4*
Swaziland	32.7	28.1	25.5	30.1	0.0	–0.9	–0.2	–0.6	0.2	*1.5*	*28.7*	*2.0*
Sweden	41.3	38.0	38.1	37.9	0.9	0.1	–0.3	–5.3	–0.7	5.2	..	11.4
Switzerland	*20.8*	*25.3*	*23.3*	*26.6*	*–0.9*	*2.9*	*0.0*	*0.0*	*0.9*	*–2.9*	*26.7*	*3.6*
Syrian Arab Republic	21.9	*23.9*	21.8	*23.2*	0.3	*0.7*	..	*2.1*	..	*–2.8*	..	..
Tajikistan	..	11.5	..	11.6	..	0.1	..	0.2	..	–0.2	81.4	4.8
Tanzania	..	..	..	..	..	..	..	..	..	..	..	..
Thailand	18.5	17.5	14.1	19.7	4.6	–2.8	–1.5	0.4	–3.1	2.4	29.8	7.1
Togo	..	..	..	..	..	..	..	..	..	..	..	..
Trinidad and Tobago	..	..	..	..	..	..	..	..	..	..	..	..
Tunisia	30.7	*28.6*	34.6	*32.0*	–5.4	*–2.6*	1.8	*0.7*	3.6	*1.8*	*62.6*	*11.4*
Turkey	13.7	29.1	17.4	49.5	–3.0	–19.6	–0.0	–1.9	3.0	21.5	99.9	85.1
Turkmenistan	..	..	..	..	..	..	..	..	..	..	..	..
Uganda	..	10.9	..	21.4	..	–2.2	..	3.3	..	–1.2	39.6	10.7
Ukraine	..	26.6	..	28.9	..	–0.9	..	0.2	..	0.7	36.5	7.2
United Arab Emirates	1.6	*3.4*	11.5	*9.9*	0.4	*0.0*	0.0	*0.0*	–0.4	*–0.0*	..	..
United Kingdom	36.0	*36.0*	37.5	*35.9*	0.6	*0.0*	0.2	*–0.4*	–0.8	*0.3*	..	*7.7*
United States	18.9	20.8	22.7	19.5	–3.8	1.3	0.2	–0.5	3.6	–0.8	32.6	10.8
Uruguay	23.8	25.1	23.3	31.2	0.3	–4.6	1.4	3.0	–1.7	1.6	..	9.7
Uzbekistan	..	..	..	..	..	..	..	..	..	..	..	..
Venezuela, RB	23.7	21.2	20.7	25.1	0.0	–4.3	1.0	0.3	–1.0	4.0	..	13.4
Vietnam	..	20.1	..	24.3	..	–2.9	..	1.0	..	1.9	..	4.3
West Bank and Gaza	..	..	..	..	..	..	..	..	..	..	..	..
Yemen, Rep.	18.9	*23.9*	27.8	*26.7*	–8.8	*–3.5*	3.2	*1.3*	5.6	*2.2*	..	*9.8*
Zambia	..	..	..	..	..	..	..	..	..	..	..	..
Zimbabwe	24.1	..	27.3	..	–5.3	..	0.9	..	4.4	..	..	..
World	**22.3 w**	**.. w**	**25.3 w**	**.. w**	**–2.8 w**	**.. w**	**0.2 m**	**1.1 m**	**0.9 m**	**0.8 m**	**.. m**	**11.3 m**
Low income	14.4	16.0	17.1	20.1	–4.8	–3.3	..	..	..	..	..	..
Middle income	16.8	*17.7*	21.4	*21.3*	–2.7	*–3.2*	..	*0.1*	0.5	*1.0*	34.7	9.8
Lower middle income	16.9	..	23.0	..	–3.2	..	..	*0.4*	1.1	*1.2*	53.9	11.4
Upper middle income	16.3	*20.0*	17.1	*22.3*	–1.1	*–1.6*	..	1.0	0.2	1.1	23.4	9.3
Low & middle income	16.4	*17.1*	20.7	*20.6*	–3.0	*–3.3*	0.3	*1.3*	0.7	*0.9*	..	11.8
East Asia & Pacific	11.7	*10.8*	13.8	*15.0*	–0.9	*–3.7*	0.4	*1.4*	2.8	*1.4*	52.3	13.9
Europe & Central Asia	..	28.3	..	33.0	..	–3.4	..	..	..	0.6	40.5	9.3
Latin America & Carib.	18.6	..	25.3	..	–3.5	..	0.2	..	0.1	*0.5*	..	13.4
Middle East & N. Africa	..	..	..	..	..	..	0.9	*1.3*	2.7	*1.7*	..	*12.2*
South Asia	12.9	13.5	16.4	18.3	–7.3	–4.9	2.3	1.4	3.1	3.7	63.8	38.9
Sub-Saharan Africa	21.9	*23.6*	25.3	*25.9*	–3.5	*–1.6*	0.9	..	..	..	..	..
High income	23.5	..	26.2	..	–2.8	..	0.2	..	1.0	..	..	*7.5*
Europe EMU	33.6	..	37.2	..	–4.0	..	0.5	..	3.1	..	..	..

a. Excluding grants.

Tables 4.11–4.13 present an overview of the size and role of central governments relative to national economies. The International Monetary Fund's (IMF) *Manual on Government Finance Statistics* describes the government as the sector of the economy responsible for "implementation of public policy through the provision of primarily nonmarket services and the transfer of income, supported mainly by compulsory levies on other sectors" (1986, p. 3). The definition of government generally excludes nonfinancial public enterprises and public financial institutions (such as the central bank).

A second edition of the *Manual on Government Finance Statistics,* harmonized with the 1993 System of National Accounts, was released in 2001. The new manual recommends an accrual accounting method instead of the earlier cash-based method. However, most countries still follow the previous manual.

Units of government meeting this definition exist at many levels, from local administrative units to the highest level of national government. Inadequate statistical coverage precludes the presentation of subnational data, however, making cross-country comparisons potentially misleading.

Central government can refer to one of two accounting concepts: consolidated or budgetary. For most countries central government finance data have been consolidated into one account, but for others only budgetary central government accounts are available. Countries reporting budgetary data are noted in *Primary data documentation.* Because budgetary accounts do not necessarily include all central government units, the picture they provide of central

government activities is usually incomplete. A key issue is the failure to include the quasi-fiscal operations of the central bank. Central bank losses arising from monetary operations and subsidized financing can result in sizable quasi-fiscal deficits. Such deficits may also result from the operations of other financial intermediaries, such as public development finance institutions. Also missing from the data are governments' contingent liabilities for unfunded pension and national insurance plans.

Data on government revenues and expenditures are collected by the IMF through questionnaires distributed to member governments and by the Organisation for Economic Co-operation and Development. Despite the IMF's efforts to systematize and standardize the collection of public finance data, statistics on public finance are often incomplete, untimely, and not comparable across countries.

Government finance statistics are reported in local currency. The indicators here are shown as percentages of GDP. Many countries report government finance data according to fiscal years; see *Primary data documentation* for the timing of these years. For further discussion of government finance statistics, see *About the data* for tables 4.12 and 4.13.

• **Current revenue** includes all revenue from taxes and current nontax revenues (other than grants), such as fines, fees, recoveries, and income from property or sales. • **Total expenditure** includes nonrepayable current and capital expenditures. It does not include government lending or repayments to the government or government acquisition of equity for public policy purposes. • **Overall budget balance** is current and capital revenue and official grants received, less total expenditure and lending minus repayments. • **Financing from abroad** (obtained from nonresidents) and **domestic financing** (obtained from residents) refer to the means by which a government provides financial resources to cover a budget deficit or allocates financial resources arising from a budget surplus. The data include all government liabilities—other than those for currency issues or demand, time, or savings deposits with government—or claims on others held by government, and changes in government holdings of cash and deposits. They exclude government guarantees of the debt of others. • **Debt** is the entire stock of direct government fixed-term contractual obligations to others outstanding on a particular date. It includes domestic debt (such as debt held by monetary authorities, deposit money banks, nonfinancial public enterprises, and households) and foreign debt (such as debt to international development institutions and foreign governments). It is the gross amount of government liabilities not reduced by the amount of government claims against others. Because debt is a stock rather than a flow, it is measured as of a given date, usually the last day of the fiscal year. • **Interest payments** include interest payments on government debt—including long-term bonds, long-term loans, and other debt instruments—to both domestic and foreign residents.

4.11a

Some developing economies spend a large part of their current revenue on interest payments

Central government interest payments as share of current revenue (%)

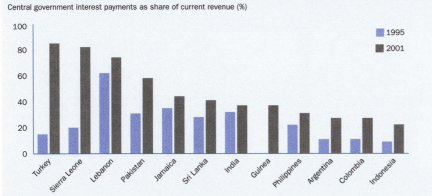

Note: 2001 data refer to the most recent year for which data are available in 1998–2001. No data are available for Guinea for 1995.

Source: International Monetary Fund, Government Finance Statistics data files.

Central government expenditures

	Goods and services		Wages and salaries [a]		Interest payments		Subsidies and other current transfers		Capital expenditure	
	% of total expenditure		% of total expenditure		% of total expenditure		% of total expenditure		% of total expenditure	
	1990	2001	1990	2001	1990	2001	1990	2001	1990	2001
Afghanistan	..	..	..	..	..	..	..	..	..	..
Albania	..	..	..	..	..	..	..	..	..	..
Algeria	..	28	..	20	..	11	..	34	..	27
Angola	..	..	..	..	..	..	..	..	..	..
Argentina	30	18	23	14	8	22	57	54	5	5
Armenia	..	..	..	..	..	..	..	..	..	..
Australia	27	..	2	..	8	5	56	..	9	..
Austria	25	25	10	10	9	8	57	61	9	5
Azerbaijan	..	31	..	11	..	2	..	50	..	17
Bangladesh	..	27	..	18	..	11	..	25	..	23
Belarus	37	24	2	11	2	2	46	61	16	13
Belgium	19	..	14	..	21	..	56	..	5	..
Benin	..	..	..	..	..	..	..	..	..	..
Bolivia	63	41	36	24	6	8	16	37	15	14
Bosnia and Herzegovina	..	..	..	..	..	..	..	..	..	..
Botswana	51	..	23	..	2	..	25	..	21	..
Brazil	16	..	9	..	78	..	39	..	2	..
Bulgaria	35	28	3	8	10	11	52	51	3	11
Burkina Faso	60	..	51	..	6	..	11	..	23	..
Burundi	34	50	22	30	5	9	10	11	51	23
Cambodia	..	..	..	..	..	..	..	..	..	..
Cameroon	51	52	39	32	5	19	13	15	26	14
Canada	21	19	9	9	20	13	57	66	2	2
Central African Republic	..	..	..	..	..	..	..	..	..	..
Chad	41	..	28	..	2	..	3	..	56	..
Chile	28	27	18	19	10	2	51	56	11	15
China	..	..	..	..	..	..	..	..	..	..
Hong Kong, China	..	..	..	..	..	..	..	..	..	..
Colombia	26	19	18	14	10	18	42	41	22	22
Congo, Dem. Rep.	73	47	23	17	7	0	4	35	16	18
Congo, Rep.	56	32	49	20	22	23	20	8	2	37
Costa Rica	57	48	43	37	12	17	20	27	11	8
Côte d'Ivoire	..	56	..	35	..	20	..	12	..	11
Croatia	54	44	22	24	0	4	42	46	3	6
Cuba	..	..	..	..	..	..	..	..	..	..
Czech Republic	..	14	..	7	..	2	..	75	..	9
Denmark	20	22	12	13	15	11	61	64	3	3
Dominican Republic	39	53	29	41	4	5	13	16	44	22
Ecuador	42	..	38	..	23	..	16	..	18	..
Egypt, Arab Rep.	42	..	23	..	14	..	26	..	17	..
El Salvador	..	62	..	37	..	6	..	15	..	22
Eritrea	..	..	..	..	..	..	..	..	..	..
Estonia	25	40	8	9	0	1	73	54	8	6
Ethiopia	77	52	40	18	5	8	9	31	16	19
Finland	20	..	10	..	3	..	70	..	7	..
France	26	..	17	..	5	..	63	..	6	..
Gabon	63	..	37	..	0	..	6	..	32	..
Gambia, The	41	..	21	..	16	..	9	..	34	..
Georgia	..	36	..	11	..	16	..	48	..	1
Germany	32	..	8	..	5	..	58	..	5	..
Ghana	50	..	32	..	11	..	20	..	19	..
Greece	31	..	21	..	20	..	41	..	8	..
Guatemala	..	..	..	..	..	..	..	..	..	..
Guinea	37	29	18	19	7	21	4	8	53	36
Guinea-Bissau	..	..	..	..	..	..	..	..	..	..
Haiti	..	65	..	42	..	5	..	8	..	22

Central government expenditures

	Goods and services		Wages and salaries [a]		Interest payments		Subsidies and other current transfers		Capital expenditure	
	% of total expenditure		% of total expenditure		% of total expenditure		% of total expenditure		% of total expenditure	
	1990	2001	1990	2001	1990	2001	1990	2001	1990	2001
Honduras	..	..	..	..	..	..	..	..	..	..
Hungary	27	18	6	9	6	12	64	57	4	13
India	24	22	11	9	22	28	43	41	11	9
Indonesia	23	18	16	8	13	19	21	39	43	24
Iran, Islamic Rep.	53	68	40	52	0	1	22	10	25	21
Iraq	..	..	..	..	..	..	..	..	..	..
Ireland	19	..	14	..	21	..	54	..	7	..
Israel	38	34	14	15	18	11	37	50	6	6
Italy	17	20	13	16	21	15	54	59	8	6
Jamaica	47	51	21	32	29	38	1	0	23	11
Japan	14	..	..	..	19	..	54	..	13	..
Jordan	55	64	44	45	18	10	11	8	16	18
Kazakhstan	..	38	..	8	..	8	..	42	..	12
Kenya	51	..	31	..	19	..	10	..	20	..
Korea, Dem. Rep.	..	..	..	..	..	..	..	..	..	..
Korea, Rep.	35	..	13	..	4	..	46	..	15	..
Kuwait	62	58	31	35	0	3	20	26	18	13
Kyrgyz Republic	..	66	..	29	..	8	..	15	..	11
Lao PDR	..	..	..	..	..	..	..	..	..	..
Latvia	..	25	..	12	..	3	..	65	..	6
Lebanon	..	30	..	23	..	41	..	12	..	17
Lesotho	40	..	22	..	11	..	5	..	45	..
Liberia	..	..	..	..	..	..	..	..	..	..
Libya	..	..	..	..	..	..	..	..	..	..
Lithuania	12	46	6	16	..	6	67	39	20	9
Macedonia, FYR	..	..	..	..	..	..	..	..	..	..
Madagascar	37	36	25	23	9	8	9	6	43	38
Malawi	54	..	23	..	14	..	8	..	24	..
Malaysia	41	..	26	..	20	..	16	..	24	..
Mali	..	..	..	..	..	..	..	..	..	..
Mauritania	..	..	..	..	..	..	..	..	..	..
Mauritius	47	44	37	32	15	11	22	28	17	17
Mexico	25	24	18	17	45	13	17	52	14	10
Moldova	..	25	..	12	..	18	..	54	..	3
Mongolia	30	35	7	10	1	5	56	46	13	14
Morocco	48	46	35	36	16	15	8	16	28	22
Mozambique	..	..	..	..	..	..	..	..	..	..
Myanmar	..	..	..	..	..	..	..	..	29	39
Namibia	73	63	46	44	1	6	10	17	15	14
Nepal	..	..	..	..	..	6	..	..	..	..
Netherlands	15	..	9	..	9	..	70	..	6	..
New Zealand	19	53	12	..	15	7	64	37	2	3
Nicaragua	43	33	23	16	0	9	14	24	4	34
Niger	..	..	..	..	..	..	..	..	..	..
Nigeria	..	..	..	..	..	..	..	..	..	..
Norway	19	21	8	8	6	4	69	70	5	5
Oman	76	77	22	27	6	4	7	6	11	13
Pakistan	44	23	..	4	25	42	20	27	12	7
Panama	64	47	49	34	8	20	26	24	2	9
Papua New Guinea	61	56	34	29	11	14	18	24	11	6
Paraguay	54	52	36	46	10	7	19	25	17	16
Peru	30	41	17	19	37	12	25	36	8	12
Philippines	44	49	29	28	34	25	7	18	16	8
Poland	..	16	..	8	..	8	..	72	..	4
Portugal	38	..	27	..	18	..	33	..	12	..
Puerto Rico	..	..	..	..	..	..	..	..	..	..

4.12 Central government expenditures

	Goods and services		Wages and salaries [a]		Interest payments		Subsidies and other current transfers		Capital expenditure	
	% of total expenditure		% of total expenditure		% of total expenditure		% of total expenditure		% of total expenditure	
	1990	2001	1990	2001	1990	2001	1990	2001	1990	2001
Romania	26	33	12	12	0	10	57	45	17	12
Russian Federation	..	37	..	11	..	10	..	44	..	9
Rwanda	53	..	29	..	5	..	16	..	33	..
Saudi Arabia	..	..	..	..	..	..	..	..	..	..
Senegal	..	42	..	24	..	4	..	24	..	29
Serbia and Montenegro	..	..	..	..	..	..	..	..	..	..
Sierra Leone	77	*60*	35	*46*	18	*28*	1	*6*	8	*11*
Singapore	51	50	27	24	14	1	12	22	24	26
Slovak Republic	..	25	..	14	..	8	..	55	..	12
Slovenia	*40*	41	*20*	23	*1*	4	*52*	49	*7*	7
Somalia	..	..	..	..	..	..	..	..	..	..
South Africa	53	28	23	13	14	17	23	50	10	5
Spain	19	..	13	..	9	..	63	..	9	..
Sri Lanka	33	38	17	21	23	26	23	18	21	18
Sudan	..	74	..	34	..	9	..	7	..	10
Swaziland	62	57	42	32	3	2	11	22	24	19
Sweden	15	*18*	6	*6*	11	*11*	72	69	2	*2*
Switzerland	*31*	28	*5*	4	*3*	3	*61*	64	*5*	5
Syrian Arab Republic	..	..	..	..	..	..	..	..	27	36
Tajikistan	..	44	..	13	..	5	..	35	..	17
Tanzania	..	..	..	..	..	..	..	..	..	..
Thailand	60	55	35	30	13	6	9	17	18	22
Togo	..	..	..	..	..	..	..	..	..	..
Trinidad and Tobago	..	..	..	..	..	..	..	..	..	..
Tunisia	34	*41*	28	*34*	10	*10*	35	*25*	22	*23*
Turkey	52	24	38	18	18	50	16	20	13	7
Turkmenistan	..	..	..	..	..	..	..	..	..	..
Uganda	..	30	..	9	..	5	..	17	..	47
Ukraine	..	30	..	13	..	7	..	57	..	6
United Arab Emirates	88	*78*	33	*35*	0	*0*	10	*18*	1	*4*
United Kingdom	30	*29*	13	*6*	9	*8*	52	*59*	10	*4*
United States	28	21	10	8	15	11	49	63	8	5
Uruguay	35	26	20	15	8	8	50	62	7	4
Uzbekistan	..	..	..	..	..	..	..	..	..	..
Venezuela, RB	31	26	23	19	16	11	37	42	16	21
Vietnam	..	..	..	..	..	4	..	..	..	34
West Bank and Gaza	..	..	..	..	..	..	..	..	..	..
Yemen, Rep.	64	*54*	55	*39*	8	*9*	6	*18*	33	*17*
Zambia	..	..	..	..	..	..	..	..	..	..
Zimbabwe	56	..	37	..	16	..	18	..	10	..
World	**39** m	**37** m	**23** m	**18** m	**10** m	**9** m	**23** m	**31** m	**13** m	**13** m
Low income	..	..	..	..	..	..	..	..	..	..
Middle income	42	37	25	18	11	8	23	42	16	12
Lower middle income	43	*41*	29	*24*	13	*10*	21	*23*	17	*15*
Upper middle income	38	26	23	15	9	8	26	54	11	9
Low & middle income	..	39	..	21	..	9	..	26	..	16
East Asia & Pacific	*42*	..	*27*	..	*10*	11	*16*	..	21	24
Europe & Central Asia	..	30	..	12	..	8	..	51	..	9
Latin America & Carib.	35	41	23	19	10	9	25	36	11	14
Middle East & N. Africa	53	*50*	35	*35*	10	*11*	11	*14*	23	*19*
South Asia	33	23	..	9	23	27	23	27	12	9
Sub-Saharan Africa	..	..	..	..	..	..	..	..	..	..
High income	25	*29*	13	..	11	*7*	56	*59*	7	*5*
Europe EMU	20	..	13	..	9	..	57	..	7	..

Note: Components include expenditures financed by grants in kind and other cash adjustments to total expenditure.
a. Part of goods and services.

About the data

Government expenditures include all nonrepayable payments, whether current or capital, requited or unrequited. Total central government expenditure as presented in the International Monetary Fund's (IMF) *Government Finance Statistics Yearbook* is a more limited measure of general government consumption than that shown in the national accounts (see table 4.10) because it excludes consumption expenditures by state and local governments. At the same time, the IMF's concept of central government expenditure is broader than the national accounts definition because it includes government gross capital formation and transfer payments.

Expenditures can be measured either by function (health, defense, education) or by economic type (interest payments, wages and salaries, purchases of goods and services). Functional data are often incomplete, and coverage varies by country because functional responsibilities stretch across levels of government for which no data are available. Defense expenditures, usually the central government's responsibility, are shown in table 5.8. For more information on education expenditures, see table 2.10; for more on health expenditures, see table 2.14.

The classification of expenditures by economic type can also be problematic. For example, the distinction between current and capital expenditure may be arbitrary, and subsidies to state-owned enterprises or banks may be disguised as capital financing. Subsidies may also be hidden in special contractual pricing for goods and services.

Expenditure shares may not sum to 100 percent because adjustments to total expenditures financed by grants in kind and other cash adjustments (which may be positive or negative) are not shown separately. For further discussion of government finance statistics, see *About the data* for tables 4.11 and 4.13.

Definitions

• **Goods and services** include all government payments in exchange for goods and services, whether in the form of wages and salaries to employees or other purchases of goods and services. • **Wages and salaries** consist of all payments in cash, but not in kind (such as food and housing), to employees in return for services rendered, before deduction of withholding taxes and employee contributions to social security and pension funds. • **Interest payments** are payments made to domestic sectors and to nonresidents for the use of borrowed money. (Repayment of principal is shown as a financing item, and commission charges are shown as purchases of services.) Interest payments do not include payments by government as guarantor or surety of interest on the defaulted debts of others, which are classified as government lending. • **Subsidies and other current transfers** include all unrequited, nonrepayable transfers on current account to private and public enterprises and the cost to the public of covering the cash operating deficits on sales to the public by departmental enterprises. • **Capital expenditure** is spending to acquire fixed capital assets, land, intangible assets, government stocks, and nonmilitary, nonfinancial assets. Also included are capital grants.

4.12a

Interest payments are a large part of government expenditure for some developing economies

Central government interest payments as share of total expenditure (%)

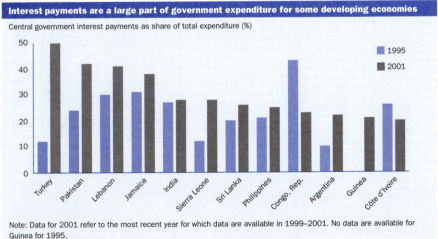

Note: Data for 2001 refer to the most recent year for which data are available in 1999–2001. No data are available for Guinea for 1995.
Source: International Monetary Fund, Government Finance Statistics data files.

Data sources

The data on central government expenditures are from the IMF's *Government Finance Statistics Yearbook, 2003* and IMF data files. Each country's accounts are reported using the system of common definitions and classifications in the IMF's *Manual on Government Finance Statistics* (1986). See these sources for complete and authoritative explanations of concepts, definitions, and data sources.

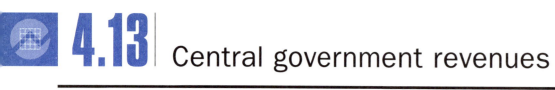

	Taxes on income, profits, and capital gains % of total current revenue		Social security taxes % of total current revenue		Taxes on goods and services % of total current revenue		Taxes on international trade % of total current revenue		Other taxes % of total current revenue		Nontax revenue % of total current revenue	
	1990	2001	1990	2001	1990	2001	1990	2001	1990	2001	1990	2001
Afghanistan	..	..	..	..	..	..	..	..	..	..	..	..
Albania	..	..	..	..	..	..	..	..	..	..	..	..
Algeria	..	70	..	0	..	8	..	11	..	1	..	10
Angola	..	..	..	..	..	..	..	..	..	..	..	..
Argentina	2	18	44	23	20	36	14	4	10	9	10	9
Armenia	..	..	..	..	..	..	..	..	..	..	..	..
Australia	65	..	0	..	21	..	4	..	2	..	8	8
Austria	19	25	37	40	25	25	1	0	9	4	9	6
Azerbaijan	..	22	..	22	..	40	..	9	..	2	..	5
Bangladesh	..	11	..	0	..	40	..	23	..	1	..	25
Belarus	12	10	32	38	40	36	5	6	9	3	2	7
Belgium	35	..	35	..	24	..	0	..	3	..	3	..
Benin	..	..	..	..	..	..	..	..	..	..	..	..
Bolivia	5	7	9	11	31	48	7	5	11	9	38	19
Bosnia and Herzegovina	..	..	..	..	..	..	..	..	..	..	..	..
Botswana	39	..	0	..	2	..	13	..	0	..	46	..
Brazil	20	..	31	..	24	..	2	..	6	..	16	..
Bulgaria	30	13	23	24	18	37	2	2	1	1	27	24
Burkina Faso	23	..	0	..	30	..	33	..	7	..	8	..
Burundi	21	21	6	7	37	44	24	20	1	1	10	6
Cambodia	..	..	..	..	..	..	..	..	..	..	..	..
Cameroon	18	21	6	0	21	26	14	28	4	4	28	20
Canada	51	52	16	21	17	17	3	1	0	0	13	9
Central African Republic	..	..	..	..	..	..	..	..	..	..	..	..
Chad	19	..	0	..	39	..	24	..	10	..	8	..
Chile	12	20	8	7	43	46	12	5	3	4	21	18
China	31	6	0	0	18	75	14	10	0	4	37	6
Hong Kong, China	..	..	..	..	..	..	..	..	..	..	..	..
Colombia	29	34	0	0	30	39	20	7	1	5	19	14
Congo, Dem. Rep.	27	15	1	0	18	22	46	32	1	23	7	8
Congo, Rep.	26	5	0	0	16	20	21	8	2	1	35	66
Costa Rica	10	14	29	32	27	40	23	5	1	0	14	10
Côte d'Ivoire	16	20	7	9	27	21	29	42	11	5	9	4
Croatia	17	8	52	33	24	46	3	6	0	1	3	5
Cuba	..	..	..	..	..	..	..	..	..	..	..	..
Czech Republic	..	20	..	44	..	29	..	1	..	1	..	4
Denmark	37	35	4	4	41	45	0	0	3	4	15	12
Dominican Republic	21	18	4	4	23	25	40	43	1	2	10	8
Ecuador	62	..	0	..	22	..	13	..	1	..	2	..
Egypt, Arab Rep.	19	..	15	..	14	..	14	..	11	..	27	..
El Salvador	..	15	..	14	..	36	..	6	..	11	..	18
Eritrea	..	..	..	..	..	..	..	..	..	..	..	..
Estonia	27	13	28	36	41	42	1	0	1	0	2	9
Ethiopia	29	22	0	0	25	17	15	26	2	3	30	32
Finland	31	..	9	..	47	..	1	..	3	..	9	..
France	17	..	44	..	28	..	0	..	3	..	7	..
Gabon	24	..	1	..	23	..	18	..	2	..	32	..
Gambia, The	13	..	0	..	37	..	43	..	1	..	6	..
Georgia	..	4	..	20	..	62	..	6	..	0	..	9
Germany	16	..	53	..	24	..	0	..	0	..	6	..
Ghana	23	..	0	..	30	..	39	..	0	..	8	..
Greece	22	..	29	..	43	..	0	..	8	..	8	..
Guatemala	..	..	..	..	..	..	..	..	..	..	..	..
Guinea	9	10	0	1	15	5	47	77	0	4	28	4
Guinea-Bissau	..	..	..	..	..	..	..	..	..	..	..	..
Haiti	..	..	..	..	..	..	..	..	..	..	..	..

	Taxes on income, profits, and capital gains		Social security taxes		Taxes on goods and services		Taxes on international trade		Other taxes		Nontax revenue	
	% of total current revenue		% of total current revenue		% of total current revenue		% of total current revenue		% of total current revenue		% of total current revenue	
	1990	2001	1990	2001	1990	2001	1990	2001	1990	2001	1990	2001
Honduras	..	..	..	..	..	..	..	..	..	..	..	..
Hungary	18	21	29	31	31	34	6	2	0	2	16	10
India	15	29	0	0	36	29	29	18	0	0	20	24
Indonesia	62	31	0	2	24	25	6	3	3	3	5	36
Iran, Islamic Rep.	10	17	8	9	4	6	13	7	4	1	60	60
Iraq	..	..	..	..	..	..	..	..	..	..	..	..
Ireland	37	..	15	..	38	..	0	..	3	..	7	..
Israel	36	40	9	15	33	29	2	1	4	3	14	12
Italy	37	36	29	30	29	24	0	0	2	3	3	7
Jamaica	36	30	0	0	30	33	12	7	9	7	13	23
Japan	69	..	0	..	17	..	1	..	7	..	5	..
Jordan	16	12	0	0	21	36	27	17	7	10	29	24
Kazakhstan	..	24	..	0	..	53	..	7	..	0	..	16
Kenya	30	..	0	..	43	..	16	..	1	..	10	..
Korea, Dem. Rep.	..	..	..	..	..	..	..	..	..	..	..	..
Korea, Rep.	34	..	5	..	35	..	12	..	5	..	9	..
Kuwait	1	1	0	6	0	0	2	3	0	0	97	90
Kyrgyz Republic	..	17	..	0	..	58	..	3	..	0	..	23
Lao PDR	..	..	..	..	..	..	..	..	..	..	..	..
Latvia	..	14	..	35	..	42	..	1	..	0	..	7
Lebanon	..	11	..	0	..	20	..	28	..	13	..	28
Lesotho	11	..	0	..	21	..	57	..	0	..	11	..
Liberia	..	..	..	..	..	..	..	..	..	..	..	..
Libya	..	..	..	..	..	..	..	..	..	..	..	..
Lithuania	20	11	28	31	40	48	1	1	3	0	8	9
Macedonia, FYR	..	..	..	..	..	..	..	..	..	..	..	..
Madagascar	13	15	0	0	19	28	48	52	2	2	18	3
Malawi	37	..	0	..	33	..	16	..	1	..	13	..
Malaysia	31	..	1	..	20	..	18	..	3	..	28	..
Mali	..	..	..	..	..	..	..	..	..	..	..	..
Mauritania	..	..	..	..	..	..	..	..	..	..	..	..
Mauritius	14	12	4	5	21	37	46	25	6	6	9	15
Mexico	31	34	13	10	56	62	6	4	2	1	11	10
Moldova	..	3	..	32	..	49	..	6	..	0	..	10
Mongolia	24	8	14	17	31	41	17	8	0	1	15	25
Morocco	24	24	4	5	38	36	18	16	4	3	13	16
Mozambique	..	..	..	..	..	..	..	..	..	..	..	..
Myanmar	18	20	0	0	28	33	14	4	0	0	41	44
Namibia	34	32	0	0	25	21	27	37	1	1	13	8
Nepal	11	18	0	0	36	36	31	27	5	3	17	16
Netherlands	31	..	35	..	22	..	0	..	3	..	9	..
New Zealand	53	64	0	0	27	27	2	2	3	1	15	6
Nicaragua	17	13	9	19	35	52	19	8	8	..	13	8
Niger	..	..	..	..	..	..	..	..	..	..	..	..
Nigeria	..	..	..	..	..	..	..	..	..	..	..	..
Norway	16	20	24	23	34	36	1	0	1	1	24	20
Oman	23	21	0	0	1	1	2	3	1	2	73	73
Pakistan	9	23	0	0	30	38	31	12	0	6	30	21
Panama	17	18	20	19	17	..	12	..	3	4	31	37
Papua New Guinea	37	54	0	0	14	11	25	27	3	4	20	5
Paraguay	9	9	0	0	21	37	20	10	24	2	25	41
Peru	5	22	7	8	50	52	17	9	19	5	7	14
Philippines	28	40	0	0	31	26	25	17	3	4	13	13
Poland	..	17	..	31	..	37	..	2	..	1	..	12
Portugal	23	..	25	..	34	..	2	..	4	..	12	..
Puerto Rico	..	..	..	..	..	..	..	..	..	..	..	..

	Taxes on income, profits, and capital gains		Social security taxes		Taxes on goods and services		Taxes on international trade		Other taxes		Nontax revenue	
	% of total current revenue		% of total current revenue		% of total current revenue		% of total current revenue		% of total current revenue		% of total current revenue	
	1990	2001	1990	2001	1990	2001	1990	2001	1990	2001	1990	2001
Romania	19	10	23	41	33	30	1	3	15	1	10	14
Russian Federation	..	9	..	26	..	35	..	14	..	0	..	16
Rwanda	18	..	7	..	34	..	26	..	4	..	12	..
Saudi Arabia	..	..	..	..	..	..	..	..	..	..	..	..
Senegal	..	22	..	0	..	33	..	37	..	4	..	4
Serbia and Montenegro	..	..	..	..	..	..	..	..	..	..	..	..
Sierra Leone	31	26	0	0	23	22	40	49	0	0	5	4
Singapore	26	33	0	0	16	19	2	2	14	9	43	38
Slovak Republic	..	17	..	38	..	31	..	1	..	1	..	11
Slovenia	12	14	47	35	27	37	8	2	0	5	5	6
Somalia	..	..	..	..	..	..	..	..	..	..	..	..
South Africa	51	54	2	2	34	33	4	3	2	3	8	5
Spain	32	..	38	..	22	..	2	..	0	..	5	..
Sri Lanka	11	15	0	0	46	59	29	11	5	4	10	12
Sudan	..	15	..	0	..	35	..	29	..	1	..	20
Swaziland	30	25	0	0	11	14	47	52	2	4	10	5
Sweden	18	14	31	33	29	27	1	0	9	15	13	11
Switzerland	15	16	51	47	23	25	1	1	3	4	7	7
Syrian Arab Republic	31	38	0	0	31	19	7	10	7	6	24	27
Tajikistan	..	3	..	18	..	53	..	16	..	1	..	9
Tanzania	..	..	..	..	..	..	..	..	..	..	..	..
Thailand	24	28	0	3	41	40	22	10	4	0	8	18
Togo	..	..	..	..	..	..	..	..	..	..	..	..
Trinidad and Tobago	..	..	..	..	..	..	..	..	..	..	..	..
Tunisia	13	20	13	17	19	38	28	11	5	4	22	9
Turkey	43	35	0	0	32	40	6	1	3	7	15	17
Turkmenistan	..	..	..	..	..	..	..	..	..	..	..	..
Uganda	..	20	..	0	..	29	..	50	..	1	..	1
Ukraine	..	12	..	36	..	29	..	4	..	0	..	18
United Arab Emirates	0	0	2	1	36	51	0	0	0	0	62	48
United Kingdom	39	40	17	17	28	31	0	0	7	7	9	5
United States	52	55	35	33	3	3	2	1	1	1	8	6
Uruguay	7	15	27	23	36	39	10	3	12	8	5	7
Uzbekistan	..	..	..	..	..	..	..	..	..	..	..	..
Venezuela, RB	64	20	4	3	3	25	7	7	0	3	22	42
Vietnam	..	27	..	0	..	34	..	18	..	5	..	16
West Bank and Gaza	..	..	..	..	..	..	..	..	..	..	..	..
Yemen, Rep.	26	18	0	0	10	9	17	10	5	2	43	61
Zambia	..	..	..	..	..	..	..	..	..	..	..	..
Zimbabwe	45	..	0	..	26	..	17	..	1	..	10	..
World	**23 m**	**18 m**	**4 m**	**5 m**	**27 m**	**34 m**	**13 m**	**7 m**	**3 m**	**2 m**	**13 m**	**12 m**
Low income	..	..	..	..	..	..	..	..	..	..	..	..
Middle income	21	15	4	14	25	37	14	5	3	2	16	14
Lower middle income	23	20	1	3	28	36	15	9	4	3	16	14
Upper middle income	17	17	10	31	21	37	12	3	2	1	18	10
Low & middle income	19	17	0	2	28	35	17	9	3	2	13	12
East Asia & Pacific	31	25	0	0	24	32	18	9	3	2	20	11
Europe & Central Asia	..	13	..	31	..	40	..	3	..	1	..	10
Latin America & Carib.	17	15	9	11	27	39	13	6	3	3	14	18
Middle East & N. Africa	21	19	2	0	17	19	15	14	5	3	28	28
South Asia	11	21	0	0	36	37	30	15	3	3	18	18
Sub-Saharan Africa	..	..	..	..	..	..	..	..	..	..	..	..
High income	32	26	17	19	28	27	1	1	3	3	9	9
Europe EMU	31	..	35	..	28	..	0	..	3	..	7	..

Note: Components may not sum to 100 percent as a result of adjustments to tax revenue.

About the data

The International Monetary Fund (IMF) classifies government transactions as receipts or payments and according to whether they are repayable or nonrepayable. If nonrepayable, they are classified as capital (meant to be used in production for more than a year) or current and as requited (involving payment in return for a benefit or service) or unrequited. Revenues include all nonrepayable receipts (other than grants), the most important of which are taxes. Grants are unrequited, nonrepayable, noncompulsory receipts from other governments or from international organizations. Transactions are generally recorded on a cash rather than an accrual basis. Measuring the accumulation of arrears on revenues or payments on an accrual basis would typically result in a higher deficit. Transactions within a level of government are not included, but transactions between levels are included. In some cases the government budget may include transfers used to finance the deficits of autonomous, extrabudgetary agencies.

The IMF's *Manual on Government Finance Statistics* (1986) describes taxes as compulsory, unrequited payments made to governments by individuals, businesses, or institutions. Taxes traditionally have been classified as either direct (those levied directly on the income or profits of individuals and corporations) or indirect (sales and excise taxes and duties levied on goods and services). This distinction may be a useful simplification, but it has no particular analytical significance except with respect to the capacity to fix tax rates.

Social security taxes do not reflect compulsory payments made by employers to provident funds or other agencies with a like purpose. Similarly, expenditures from such funds are not reflected in government expenditure (see table 4.12). The revenue shares shown in this table may not sum to 100 percent because adjustments to tax revenues are not shown.

For further discussion of taxes and tax policies, see *About the data* for table 5.6. For further discussion of government revenues and expenditures, see *About the data* for tables 4.11 and 4.12.

Definitions

• **Taxes on income, profits, and capital gains** are levied on the actual or presumptive net income of individuals, on the profits of enterprises, and on capital gains, whether realized or not, on land, securities, or other assets. Intragovernmental payments are eliminated in consolidation. • **Social security taxes** include employer and employee social security contributions and those of self-employed and unemployed people. • **Taxes on goods and services** include general sales and turnover or value added taxes, selective excises on goods, selective taxes on services, taxes on the use of goods or property, and profits of fiscal monopolies. • **Taxes on international trade** include import duties, export duties, profits of export or import monopolies, exchange profits, and exchange taxes. • **Other taxes** include employer payroll or labor taxes, taxes on property, and taxes not allocable to other categories. They may include negative values that are adjustments (for example, for taxes collected on behalf of state and local governments and not allocable to individual tax categories). • **Nontax revenue** includes requited, nonrepayable receipts for public purposes—such as fines, administrative fees, or entrepreneurial income from government ownership of property—and voluntary, unrequited, nonrepayable receipts other than from government sources. It does not include proceeds of grants and borrowing, funds arising from the repayment of previous lending by governments, incurrence of liabilities, and proceeds from the sale of capital assets.

4.13a

Poor countries rely more on indirect taxes

Indirect taxes as share of current revenue, 2000–01 (%)

Low-income countries tend to rely on indirect taxes on international trade and on goods and services, while high-income countries prefer to tax income, property, and social security contributions. But in all groups there are exceptions.

Source: International Monetary Fund, Government Finance Statistics data files.

Data sources

The data on central government revenues are from the IMF's *Government Finance Statistics Yearbook, 2003* and IMF data files. Each country's accounts are reported using the system of common definitions and classifications in the IMF's *Manual on Government Finance Statistics* (1986). The IMF receives additional information from the Organisation for Economic Co-operation and Development on the tax revenues of some of its members. See the IMF sources for complete and authoritative explanations of concepts, definitions, and data sources.

4.14 Monetary indicators and prices

	Money and quasi money		Claims on private sector		Claims on governments and other public entities		GDP implicit deflator		Consumer price index		Food price index	
	M2 annual % growth		annual growth as % of M2		annual growth as % of M2		average annual % growth		average annual % growth		average annual % growth	
	1990	2002	1990	2002	1990	2002	1980–90	1990–2002	1980–90	1990–2002	1980–90	1990–2002
Afghanistan	..	..	..	..	..	..	..	..	..	..	..	..
Albania	..	5.9	..	2.9	..	2.4	–0.4	28.6	..	21.6	..	31.2
Algeria	11.4	24.8	12.2	2.6	3.2	–5.6	8.3	15.7	9.1	14.0	9.7	14.7
Angola	..	158.6	..	37.8	..	28.8	5.9	584.3	..	562.9	..	223.1
Argentina	1,113.3	19.7	1,444.7	–9.5	1,573.2	143.2	391.1	4.5	390.6	7.2	486.5	6.5
Armenia	..	34.0	..	1.0	..	–6.0	..	142.2	..	44.7	..	81.5
Australia	12.8	13.2	15.3	10.8	–2.2	1.0	7.2	1.8	7.9	2.3	7.4	2.9
Austria [a]	..	..	..	..	..	..	3.3	1.8	3.2	2.1	2.7	1.5
Azerbaijan	..	14.6	..	9.7	..	24.6	..	78.6	..	109.1	..	109.8
Bangladesh	10.4	13.3	9.2	12.0	–0.2	0.8	9.8	3.8	..	5.1	10.8	4.8
Belarus	..	53.5	..	35.7	..	28.8	..	283.6	..	258.0	2.4	141.1
Belgium [a]	..	..	..	..	..	..	4.1	1.9	4.2	1.9	4.0	1.2
Benin	28.6	–7.0	–1.3	5.5	12.4	0.1	1.7	7.5	..	7.2	–3.5	10.5
Bolivia	52.8	–6.9	40.8	–1.6	18.0	8.1	326.9	7.5	322.5	7.5	321.8	6.8
Bosnia and Herzegovina	..	9.4	..	18.6	..	–0.6	..	3.4	..	..	..	..
Botswana	–14.0	–1.1	12.6	12.9	–51.9	117.2	13.6	9.0	10.0	9.8	10.1	9.6
Brazil	1,289.2	23.0	1,566.4	11.8	3,093.6	29.9	284.0	139.8	285.6	134.1	314.0	–15.7
Bulgaria	53.8	12.2	1.9	14.7	83.1	–1.7	1.8	83.8	6.3	94.0	1.8	89.9
Burkina Faso	–0.5	0.6	3.6	11.7	–1.5	–12.1	3.3	4.8	3.4	4.9	0.7	5.0
Burundi	9.6	29.5	15.4	29.0	–6.9	7.9	4.4	12.8	7.1	15.3	6.1	..
Cambodia	..	31.1	..	5.6	..	–2.2	..	3.7	..	4.7	..	4.8
Cameroon	–1.7	15.9	0.9	6.1	–3.0	–2.4	5.6	4.5	8.7	5.5	..	4.1
Canada	7.8	5.6	9.2	5.9	0.6	1.6	4.6	1.5	5.3	1.8	4.6	1.7
Central African Republic	–3.7	–4.3	–1.6	6.2	2.3	2.6	7.9	4.1	3.2	4.6	2.0	5.5
Chad	–2.4	26.6	1.3	8.9	–17.3	–3.7	1.4	7.1	0.6	7.7	–5.3	–0.7
Chile	24.2	–0.3	21.7	14.8	16.3	0.2	20.7	7.1	20.6	7.7	20.7	6.8
China	28.9	19.4	26.5	13.4	1.5	1.4	5.7	5.5	..	6.7	8.8	11.3
Hong Kong, China	8.5	0.5	7.9	–2.6	–1.0	3.3	7.8	2.5	..	4.1	6.3	3.5
Colombia	33.0	13.6	107.1	8.2	23.9	8.1	24.7	19.0	22.7	18.0	24.6	16.4
Congo, Dem. Rep.	195.4	40.0	18.0	3.8	429.7	–36.2	62.9	731.4	57.1	691.7	..	..
Congo, Rep.	18.5	13.1	5.1	–15.7	–12.6	3.0	0.5	8.5	0.9	7.9	4.3	8.1
Costa Rica	27.5	20.9	7.3	16.6	8.2	6.8	23.6	15.6	23.0	14.6	16.0	4.5
Côte d'Ivoire	–2.6	30.0	–3.9	–0.3	–3.0	1.3	2.8	7.8	5.4	6.3	..	..
Croatia	..	9.6	..	19.9	..	3.1	..	61.3	304.1	61.3	124.6	58.7
Cuba	..	..	..	..	..	..	..	1.1	..	..	..	..
Czech Republic	..	6.9	..	–12.3	..	11.6	..	9.9	..	6.7	..	0.8
Denmark	6.5	4.2	3.0	13.9	–3.1	1.6	5.8	2.0	5.6	2.1	4.8	2.1
Dominican Republic	42.5	10.3	19.1	15.9	1.1	3.6	21.6	8.9	22.4	8.3	25.4	7.8
Ecuador	48.9	21.4	17.2	26.0	–27.4	–20.3	–5.4	3.8	35.8	38.6	40.7	37.8
Egypt, Arab Rep.	28.7	12.6	6.3	3.4	25.3	11.5	13.7	7.4	17.4	7.5	22.0	6.5
El Salvador	–17.5	–3.1	–24.2	3.0	10.2	–4.5	16.3	6.3	19.6	7.2	21.5	7.9
Eritrea	..	20.3	..	3.8	..	17.8	..	9.6	..	..	..	..
Estonia	76.5	11.2	27.6	12.7	–6.8	1.2	2.3	40.3	..	16.7	..	–20.1
Ethiopia	18.5	13.3	0.3	–0.6	21.7	1.3	3.5	5.6	4.0	4.0	3.8	–3.6
Finland [a]	..	..	..	..	..	..	6.7	2.0	6.2	1.6	5.8	–0.3
France [a]	..	..	..	..	..	..	5.8	1.5	5.8	1.6	5.7	1.5
Gabon	3.3	5.7	0.7	7.2	–20.6	–9.6	1.8	5.3	5.1	4.6	4.9	4.3
Gambia, The	8.4	35.3	7.8	13.9	–35.4	0.2	17.9	4.6	20.0	4.0	20.3	3.7
Georgia	..	17.9	..	14.4	..	2.7	1.9	225.2	..	17.7	..	15.9
Germany [a]	..	..	..	..	..	..	2.7	1.7	2.2 [b]	2.1	..	0.5
Ghana	13.3	48.9	4.9	13.6	9.9	10.6	42.1	26.4	39.1	27.4	33.1	25.0
Greece [a]	..	..	..	..	..	..	19.3	8.0	18.7	7.7	18.0	6.7
Guatemala	25.8	11.8	15.0	4.7	0.5	3.8	14.6	9.6	14.0	9.4	22.1	9.2
Guinea	–17.4	19.7	13.1	2.7	2.9	36.0	..	5.0	..	..	..	9.2
Guinea-Bissau	574.6	22.8	90.5	–0.3	460.7	4.5	57.4	25.6	..	27.3	..	..
Haiti	2.5	22.8	–0.6	11.8	0.4	11.7	7.3	20.1	5.2	19.8	4.1	..

	Money and quasi money		Claims on private sector		Claims on governments and other public entities		GDP implicit deflator		Consumer price index		Food price index	
	M2 annual % growth		annual growth as % of M2		annual growth as % of M2		average annual % growth		average annual % growth		average annual % growth	
	1990	2002	1990	2002	1990	2002	1980–90	1990–2002	1980–90	1990–2002	1980–90	1990–2002
Honduras	21.4	13.7	13.0	4.9	−10.5	−0.5	5.7	17.1	6.3	17.2	5.2	16.7
Hungary	29.2	14.9	23.0	13.8	69.7	9.3	8.9	17.4	9.6	18.1	9.5	17.4
India	15.1	16.8	5.9	10.7	10.5	4.9	8.2	7.2	8.6	8.3	8.8	7.9
Indonesia	44.6	4.5	66.9	6.3	−6.7	−0.8	8.5	15.6	8.3	14.1	8.7	16.7
Iran, Islamic Rep.	18.0	27.5	14.7	19.2	5.8	7.8	14.4	25.0	18.2	23.6	16.2	24.3
Iraq	..	..	..	..	..	..	10.3	..	..	..	..	..
Ireland [a]	..	..	..	..	..	..	6.6	3.8	6.8	2.6	6.0	2.9
Israel	19.4	6.9	18.5	8.6	4.9	−3.2	101.1	8.9	101.7	8.3	102.4	7.4
Italy [a]	..	..	..	..	..	..	10.0	3.5	9.1	3.4	8.2	2.8
Jamaica	21.5	12.0	12.5	8.5	−16.0	5.6	19.9	19.7	15.1	19.7	16.1	18.6
Japan	8.2	3.4	9.7	−4.4	1.5	1.7	1.8	−0.3	1.7	0.5	1.5	0.3
Jordan	8.3	8.6	4.7	1.7	1.0	3.1	4.3	2.7	5.7	3.1	4.7	3.4
Kazakhstan	..	30.1	..	33.0	..	−14.6	..	141.0	..	45.6	..	106.1
Kenya	20.1	11.7	8.0	1.6	21.5	5.0	9.1	12.8	11.2	13.3	10.0	12.3
Korea, Dem. Rep.	..	..	..	..	..	..	..	..	..	..	..	..
Korea, Rep.	17.2	11.0	36.1	22.4	−1.2	−1.1	6.5	4.2	4.9	4.7	5.0	4.9
Kuwait	−100.0	4.8	−89.7	9.0	−23.0	1.5	−2.8	2.6	2.9	1.9	1.6	1.5
Kyrgyz Republic	..	33.9	..	3.9	..	12.6	..	82.5	..	18.7	..	45.9
Lao PDR	7.8	37.6	3.6	−0.0	7.0	−5.6	37.6	28.8	..	30.0	..	..
Latvia	..	19.9	..	25.7	..	5.7	−0.0	36.1	..	21.7	..	18.2
Lebanon	55.1	7.3	27.6	1.5	18.5	−1.0	..	13.4	..	..	..	19.8
Lesotho	8.4	8.8	6.8	6.8	−14.9	15.2	12.1	9.6	13.6	8.9	13.5	9.8
Liberia	−100.0	2.0	−39.8	7.7	−271.0	535.8	2.9	53.8	..	..	..	..
Libya	19.0	1.1	2.0	−0.3	15.0	10.2	1.2	..	7.5	6.3	..	..
Lithuania	..	16.9	..	13.3	..	−1.2	..	53.1	..	22.7	2.7	39.5
Macedonia, FYR	..	15.7	..	3.2	..	−14.3	..	56.4	..	6.5	..	..
Madagascar	4.5	8.0	23.8	0.3	−14.8	9.8	17.1	17.0	16.6	16.8	15.7	19.1
Malawi	11.1	20.7	15.5	3.7	−12.9	42.2	15.1	32.2	16.9	32.6	16.4	33.2
Malaysia	10.6	3.1	20.8	5.8	−1.2	3.2	1.7	3.5	2.6	3.3	2.2	4.6
Mali	−4.9	27.9	0.1	14.1	−13.4	−2.8	4.5	6.7	..	4.6	2.7	4.8
Mauritania	11.5	8.9	20.2	35.2	1.5	−95.2	8.4	5.6	7.1	5.7	..	6.3
Mauritius	21.2	12.5	10.8	5.8	0.8	1.2	9.4	6.0	6.9	6.6	7.8	7.5
Mexico	81.9	4.6	48.5	5.8	13.6	9.6	71.5	17.3	73.8	17.7	73.1	17.3
Moldova	358.0	38.6	53.3	21.9	469.1	6.9	..	89.4	..	18.5	..	110.5
Mongolia	31.6	42.0	40.2	28.0	38.5	−7.2	−1.6	45.4	..	39.0	..	..
Morocco	21.5	6.4	44.2	2.3	−4.9	1.1	7.1	2.5	7.0	3.3	6.7	3.1
Mozambique	37.2	21.6	22.0	−0.5	−5.1	7.0	38.3	26.8	..	26.6	..	..
Myanmar	37.7	34.6	12.8	16.7	24.2	18.8	12.2	24.6	11.5	25.4	11.9	27.5
Namibia	30.3	6.9	15.4	20.4	−4.2	−5.4	13.7	10.3	12.6	9.5	13.9	8.8
Nepal	18.5	3.8	5.7	10.7	7.3	8.1	11.1	7.2	10.2	7.2	10.5	8.4
Netherlands [a]	..	..	..	..	..	..	1.5	2.3	2.0	2.5	1.3	1.3
New Zealand	12.5	7.7	4.2	9.8	−1.7	1.0	10.5	1.7	11.0	1.9	9.8	1.7
Nicaragua	7,677.8	13.3	4,932.9	9.8	12,679.2	2.0	422.3	30.7	535.7	24.6	69.2	22.6
Niger	−4.1	−0.5	−5.1	7.2	1.4	3.5	1.9	5.5	0.7	5.4	−1.5	6.3
Nigeria	32.7	21.6	7.8	8.5	27.1	28.8	16.7	25.0	18.9	27.8	22.5	25.9
Norway	5.6	7.6	5.0	8.8	−0.6	4.4	5.4	3.2	7.4	2.2	7.8	1.8
Oman	10.0	5.2	9.6	0.4	−10.9	−3.6	−3.6	2.0	..	−0.1	0.9	0.1
Pakistan	11.6	16.8	5.9	2.5	7.7	−1.0	6.7	9.1	6.3	8.6	6.6	8.8
Panama	36.6	−0.3	0.8	−8.7	−25.7	3.1	1.9	3.2	1.4	1.1	1.5	0.7
Papua New Guinea	4.3	4.0	−0.9	−3.1	8.8	18.1	5.3	7.4	5.6	10.0	4.6	9.6
Paraguay	54.4	3.1	32.0	0.2	−9.2	9.8	24.4	11.3	21.9	12.0	24.9	10.5
Peru	6,384.9	5.1	2,123.7	−0.4	2,129.5	−2.2	220.2	20.4	246.1	20.9	221.8	18.7
Philippines	22.4	10.4	15.6	0.5	3.4	4.7	14.9	8.0	13.4	7.7	14.1	6.7
Poland	160.1	−2.8	158.7	2.7	−20.6	−0.7	..	19.8	50.9	21.0	52.4	17.9
Portugal [a]	..	..	..	..	..	..	17.9	4.9	17.1	4.1	16.7	3.4
Puerto Rico	..	..	..	..	..	..	3.5	3.1	..	..	2.7	9.8

	Money and quasi money		Claims on private sector		Claims on governments and other public entities		GDP implicit deflator		Consumer price index		Food price index	
	M2 annual % growth		annual growth as % of M2		annual growth as % of M2		average annual % growth		average annual % growth		average annual % growth	
	1990	2002	1990	2002	1990	2002	1980–90	1990–2002	1980–90	1990–2002	1980–90	1990–2002
Romania	26.4	38.2	..	13.3	0.0	1.1	*1.5*	84.3	..	85.5	4.3	69.1
Russian Federation	..	33.9	..	20.9	..	7.2	..	121.1	..	*75.2*	..	*122.1*
Rwanda	5.6	12.6	–10.0	6.3	26.8	–8.8	4.0	11.7	3.9	*13.4*	*6.4*	12.7
Saudi Arabia	4.6	15.2	–4.5	5.7	4.2	0.2	–3.8	1.7	–0.8	0.7	–0.2	0.7
Senegal	–4.8	8.2	–8.4	3.5	–5.3	–8.3	6.5	4.0	6.2	4.6	5.3	5.1
Serbia and Montenegro	..	..	..	..	..	..	..	57.1	..	..	..	*4.1*
Sierra Leone	74.0	29.6	4.9	7.5	228.7	–1.8	60.3	26.7	72.4	24.5	..	..
Singapore	20.0	–0.3	13.7	–8.8	–4.9	–4.0	2.0	0.7	1.6	1.5	1.0	1.5
Slovak Republic	..	4.1	..	8.2	..	–14.1	*1.8*	9.7	..	*8.3*	*1.6*	14.7
Slovenia	*123.0*	12.3	*96.1*	9.1	–10.4	–3.7	..	10.2	..	10.8	129.5	21.3
Somalia	..	..	..	..	..	..	49.7	..	..	..	..	..
South Africa	11.4	14.5	13.7	6.7	1.8	4.1	15.5	9.1	14.8	8.2	15.2	9.4
Spain[a]	..	..	..	..	..	..	9.3	3.8	9.0	3.6	9.3	3.1
Sri Lanka	19.9	13.4	16.2	10.3	4.4	–1.2	11.0	9.1	10.9	9.8	11.0	10.3
Sudan	48.8	30.3	12.6	17.9	29.4	6.4	38.4	51.9	37.6	*66.8*	..	..
Swaziland	0.6	13.1	20.5	16.7	–13.1	42.1	10.7	12.1	14.6	9.2	13.3	11.9
Sweden	0.8	*1.9*	13.4	*12.4*	–12.1	*2.1*	7.3	1.9	7.0	1.8	8.2	–0.0
Switzerland	0.8	5.7	11.7	0.4	1.0	0.2	3.4	1.1	2.9	1.4	3.1	0.8
Syrian Arab Republic	26.1	18.5	3.4	0.7	11.4	–0.7	15.3	6.9	23.2	4.9	25.0	3.8
Tajikistan	..	40.5	..	26.1	..	17.8	*2.5*	175.2	..	..	..	*477.3*
Tanzania	41.9	25.1	22.6	10.2	80.6	–4.0	..	18.6	31.0	17.8	32.0	*20.1*
Thailand	26.7	1.4	30.0	11.9	–4.0	–0.1	3.9	3.6	3.5	4.3	2.7	4.9
Togo	9.5	–2.2	1.8	–4.0	6.9	–6.4	4.8	6.3	2.5	7.2	1.1	1.7
Trinidad and Tobago	6.2	5.7	2.7	2.9	–1.9	2.5	2.4	5.9	10.7	5.4	14.6	*12.7*
Tunisia	7.6	4.4	5.9	5.4	1.8	–0.0	7.4	4.1	*7.4*	4.0	8.3	4.2
Turkey	53.2	29.1	42.9	3.3	0.4	29.3	45.3	71.8	44.9	75.5	18.3	*31.8*
Turkmenistan	..	*83.3*	..	*10.8*	..	*59.0*	..	266.6	..	..	..	..
Uganda	60.2	25.0	0.0	5.5	–0.9	28.1	*113.8*	9.5	102.5	8.5	..	8.5
Ukraine	..	42.3	..	29.2	..	1.5	..	183.4	..	*102.6*	*2.0*	99.5
United Arab Emirates	–8.2	11.0	1.3	9.6	–4.8	–1.6	0.8	2.8	..	..	..	..
United Kingdom	10.5	5.1	13.1	10.1	1.0	1.1	5.8	2.8	5.8	2.7	4.5	1.7
United States	4.9	4.3	1.1	5.7	0.6	2.1	3.8	2.0	4.2	2.6	3.9	2.4
Uruguay	118.5	28.2	56.2	27.1	25.8	41.5	62.7	25.5	61.1	27.5	62.0	25.1
Uzbekistan	..	..	..	..	..	..	..	184.2	..	..	..	..
Venezuela, RB	64.9	15.8	17.6	0.6	45.3	14.5	19.3	40.8	20.9	43.2	35.1	39.5
Vietnam	..	13.3	..	16.7	..	2.7	*222.2*	12.5	..	*2.9*	..	..
West Bank and Gaza	..	..	..	..	..	..	..	8.8	..	..	..	..
Yemen, Rep.	*11.3*	17.5	*1.4*	2.4	*10.2*	–12.4	..	19.8	..	*32.6*	..	..
Zambia	47.9	31.1	22.8	2.3	195.2	27.0	42.2	44.7	48.5	42.8	48.7	..
Zimbabwe	15.1	191.7	13.5	106.2	5.0	45.4	11.6	32.3	13.8	36.1	15.1	40.1

Note: The inconsistencies in the growth rates of the GDP deflator and consumer and food price indexes are mainly due to uneven coverage of the time period.

a. As members of the European Monetary Union, these countries share a single currency, the euro. b. Data prior to 1990 refer to the Federal Republic of Germany before unification.

Monetary indicators and prices

4.14

ECONOMY

About the data

Money and the financial accounts that record the supply of money lie at the heart of a country's financial system. There are several commonly used definitions of the money supply. The narrowest, M1, encompasses currency held by the public and demand deposits with banks. M2 includes M1 plus time and savings deposits with banks that require a notice for withdrawal. M3 includes M2 as well as various money market instruments, such as certificates of deposit issued by banks, bank deposits denominated in foreign currency, and deposits with financial institutions other than banks. However defined, money is a liability of the banking system, distinguished from other bank liabilities by the special role it plays as a medium of exchange, a unit of account, and a store of value.

The banking system's assets include its net foreign assets and net domestic credit. Net domestic credit includes credit extended to the private sector and general government and credit extended to the nonfinancial public sector in the form of investments in short- and long-term government securities and loans to state enterprises; liabilities to the public and private sectors in the form of deposits with the banking system are netted out. Net domestic credit also includes credit to banking and nonbank financial institutions.

Domestic credit is the main vehicle through which changes in the money supply are regulated, with central bank lending to the government often playing the most important role. The central bank can regulate lending to the private sector in several ways—for example, by adjusting the cost of the refinancing facilities it provides to banks, by changing market interest rates through open market operations, or by controlling the availability of credit through changes in the reserve requirements imposed on banks and ceilings on the credit provided by banks to the private sector.

Monetary accounts are derived from the balance sheets of financial institutions—the central bank, commercial banks, and nonbank financial intermediaries. Although these balance sheets are usually reliable, they are subject to errors of classification, valuation, and timing and to differences in accounting practices. For example, whether interest income is recorded on an accrual or a cash basis can make a substantial difference, as can the treatment of nonperforming assets. Valuation errors typically arise with respect to foreign exchange transactions, particularly in countries with flexible exchange rates or in those that have undergone a currency devaluation during the reporting period. The valuation of financial derivatives and the net liabilities of the banking system can also be difficult. The quality of commercial bank reporting also may be adversely affected by delays in reports from bank branches, especially in countries where branch accounts are not computerized. Thus the data in the balance sheets of commercial banks may be based on preliminary estimates subject to constant revision. This problem is likely to be even more serious for nonbank financial intermediaries.

Controlling inflation is one of the primary goals of monetary policy and is intimately linked to the growth in money supply. Inflation is measured by the rate of increase in a price index, but actual price change can also be negative. Which index is used depends on which set of prices in the economy is being examined. The GDP deflator reflects changes in prices for total gross domestic product. The most general measure of the overall price level, it takes into account changes in government consumption, capital formation (including inventory appreciation), international trade, and the main component, household final consumption expenditure. The GDP deflator is usually derived implicitly as the ratio of current to constant price GDP, resulting in a Paasche index. It is defective as a general measure of inflation for use in policy because of the long lags in deriving estimates and because it is often only an annual measure.

Consumer price indexes are more current and produced more frequently. They are also constructed explicitly, based on surveys of the cost of a defined basket of consumer goods and services. Nevertheless, consumer price indexes should be interpreted with caution. The definition of a household, the basket of goods chosen, and the geographic (urban or rural) and income group coverage of consumer price surveys can all vary widely across countries. In addition, the weights are derived from household expenditure surveys, which, for budgetary reasons, tend to be conducted infrequently in developing countries, leading to poor comparability over time. Although useful for measuring consumer price inflation within a country, consumer price indexes are of less value in making comparisons across countries. Food price indexes, like consumer price indexes, should be interpreted with caution because of the high variability across countries in the items covered.

The least-squares method is used to calculate the growth rates of the GDP implicit deflator, consumer price index, and food price index.

Definitions

• **Money and quasi money** comprise the sum of currency outside banks, demand deposits other than those of the central government, and the time, savings, and foreign currency deposits of resident sectors other than the central government. This definition of the money supply, often called M2, corresponds to lines 34 and 35 in the International Monetary Fund's (IMF) *International Financial Statistics* (IFS). The change in money supply is measured as the difference in end-of-year totals relative to M2 in the preceding year. • **Claims on private sector** (IFS line 32d) include gross credit from the financial system to individuals, enterprises, nonfinancial public entities not included under net domestic credit, and financial institutions not included elsewhere. • **Claims on governments and other public entities** (IFS line 32an + 32b + 32bx + 32c) usually comprise direct credit for specific purposes, such as financing the government budget deficit; loans to state enterprises; advances against future credit authorizations; and purchases of treasury bills and bonds, net of deposits by the public sector. Public sector deposits with the banking system also include sinking funds for the service of debt and temporary deposits of government revenues. • **GDP implicit deflator** measures the average annual rate of price change in the economy as a whole for the periods shown. • **Consumer price index** reflects changes in the cost to the average consumer of acquiring a basket of goods and services that may be fixed or may change at specified intervals, such as yearly. The Laspeyres formula is generally used. • **Food price index** is a subindex of the consumer price index.

Data sources

The monetary, financial, and consumer price index data are published by the IMF in its monthly *International Financial Statistics* and annual *International Financial Statistics Yearbook*. The IMF collects data on the financial systems of its member countries. The World Bank receives data from the IMF in electronic files that may contain more recent revisions than the published sources. The GDP deflator data are from the World Bank's national accounts files. The food price index data are from the United Nations Statistics Division's *Statistical Yearbook* and *Monthly Bulletin of Statistics*. The discussion of monetary indicators draws from an IMF publication by Marcello Caiola, *A Manual for Country Economists* (1995). Also see the IMF's *Monetary and Financial Statistics Manual* (2000) for guidelines for the presentation of monetary and financial statistics.

	Goods and services ($ millions)				Net income ($ millions)		Net current transfers ($ millions)		Current account balance ($ millions)		Total reserves[a] ($ millions)	
	Exports		Imports									
	1990	2002	1990	2002	1990	2002	1990	2002	1990	2002	1990	2002
Afghanistan	..	..	..	..	..	..	..	..	..	..	638	..
Albania	354	915	485	2,076	−2	128	15	625	−118	−408	..	866
Algeria	13,462	..	10,106	..	−2,268	..	333	..	1,420	..	2,703	25,151
Angola	3,992	8,573	3,385	7,796	−765	−1,531	−77	*91*	−236	*−1,431*	..	376
Argentina	14,800	28,654	6,846	13,011	−4,400	−6,465	998	413	4,552	9,592	6,222	10,492
Armenia	..	698	..	1,107	..	88	..	173	..	−148	*1*	440
Australia	49,843	82,975	53,056	88,635	−13,176	−11,541	439	−64	−15,950	−17,264	19,319	21,567
Austria	63,694	108,865	61,580	104,594	−942	−2,082	−6	−1,615	1,166	575	17,228	13,182
Azerbaijan	..	2,667	..	3,121	..	−385	..	70	..	−768	*0*	722
Bangladesh	2,064	6,972	3,960	9,192	−116	−281	1,613	3,242	−398	742	660	1,722
Belarus	..	9,264	..	9,787	..	−29	..	174	..	−378	..	619
Belgium[b]	138,605	*213,811*	135,098	*203,106*	2,316	*2,907*	−2,197	*−4,220*	3,627	*9,392*	23,789[c]	14,698[c]
Benin	364	555	454	790	−25	−17	97	126	−18	−126	69	616
Bolivia	977	1,534	1,086	2,049	−249	−201	159	369	−199	−347	511	893
Bosnia and Herzegovina	..	1,417	..	4,751	..	256	..	939	..	−2,139	..	1,321
Botswana	2,005	2,651	1,987	2,229	−106	−279	69	−47,313	−19	−47,169	3,331	5,474
Brazil	35,170	69,967	28,184	61,863	−11,608	−18,191	799	2,390	−3,823	−7,696	9,200	37,835
Bulgaria	6,950	8,286	8,027	9,287	−758	−228	125	549	−1,710	−679	*670*	4,846
Burkina Faso	349	273	758	687	0	−26	332	116	−77	−324	305	313
Burundi	89	39	318	147	−15	−12	174	118	−69	−3	112	59
Cambodia	*314*	2,350	*507*	2,693	*−21*	−168	*120*	447	*−93*	−64	..	913
Cameroon	2,508	..	2,475	..	−558	..	−26	..	−551	..	37	640
Canada	149,538	301,274	149,118	269,721	−19,388	−17,514	−796	871	−19,764	14,909	23,530	37,189
Central African Republic	220	..	410	..	−22	..	123	..	−89	..	123	127
Chad	271	..	488	..	−21	..	192	..	−46	..	132	223
Chile	10,221	22,300	9,166	20,744	−1,737	−2,536	198	426	−485	−553	6,784	15,344
China[†]	57,374	365,395	46,706	328,012	1,055	−14,946	274	12,984	11,997	35,422	34,476	297,739
Hong Kong, China	..	243,633	..	230,153	..	2,806	..	−1,896	..	14,390	24,656	111,919
Colombia	8,679	14,160	6,858	15,392	−2,305	−2,812	1,026	2,406	542	−1,639	4,869	10,844
Congo, Dem. Rep.	..	..	..	..	..	..	..	..	..	..	261	..
Congo, Rep.	1,488	2,454	1,282	1,618	−460	−860	3	−10	−251	−34	10	35
Costa Rica	1,963	7,141	2,346	7,724	−233	−532	192	169	−424	−946	525	1,497
Côte d'Ivoire	3,503	5,747	3,445	3,869	−1,091	−629	−181	−482	−1,214	767	21	1,863
Croatia	..	10,545	..	12,709	..	−518	..	1,076	..	−1,606	*167*	5,885
Cuba	..	..	..	..	..	..	..	..	..	..	..	..
Czech Republic	..	45,562	..	47,159	..	−3,800	..	912	..	−4,485	..	23,707
Denmark	48,902	82,768	41,415	72,394	−5,708	−2,771	−408	−2,612	1,372	4,991	11,226	27,719
Dominican Republic	1,832	8,238	2,233	10,166	−249	−1,135	371	2,188	−280	−875	69	475
Ecuador	3,262	6,173	2,519	7,742	−1,210	−1,306	107	1,654	−360	−1,222	1,009	1,004
Egypt, Arab Rep.	9,895	16,438	14,091	19,508	−1,022	−267	7,545	3,960	2,327	622	3,620	14,076
El Salvador	973	3,799	1,624	5,898	−132	−287	631	2,003	−152	−384	595	1,784
Eritrea	..	187	..	552	..	−6	*450*	286	*188*	−85	..	30
Estonia	*664*	5,504	*711*	6,119	*−13*	−331	*97*	144	*36*	−802	*198*	1,003
Ethiopia	597	1,066	1,271	2,038	−69	−23	449	845	−294	−150	55	966
Finland	31,180	51,347	33,456	39,952	−3,735	−542	−952	−648	−6,962	10,205	10,415	9,825
France	285,389	392,362	283,238	365,576	−3,896	12,823	−8,199	−13,865	−9,944	25,744	68,291	61,697
Gabon	2,730	3,399	1,812	2,022	−617	−718	−134	−75	168	584	279	144
Gambia, The	168	..	192	..	−11	..	59	..	23	..	55	107
Georgia	..	975	..	1,398	..	19	..	174	..	−230	..	198
Germany	474,654	721,017	428,619	643,327	20,593	−5,997	−21,954	−25,108	44,674	46,586	104,547	89,143
Ghana	983	2,570	1,506	3,325	−111	−176	411	900	−223	−31	309	636
Greece	13,018	30,091	19,564	41,997	−1,709	−1,957	4,718	3,458	−3,537	−10,405	4,721	9,432
Guatemala	1,568	3,769	1,812	6,622	−196	−298	227	1,958	−213	−1,193	362	2,373
Guinea	829	976	953	999	−149	−69	70	46	−203	−46	*80*	171
Guinea-Bissau	26	..	88	..	−22	..	39	..	−45	..	18	103
Haiti	318	..	515	..	−18	..	193	..	−22	..	10	82
[†]Data for Taiwan, China	74,172	151,058	67,015	130,241	4,362	7,353	−596	−2,492	10,923	25,678	77,653	166,304

Balance of payments current account

	Goods and services ($ millions)				Net income ($ millions)		Net current transfers ($ millions)		Current account balance ($ millions)		Total reserves[a] ($ millions)	
	Exports		Imports									
	1990	2002	1990	2002	1990	2002	1990	2002	1990	2002	1990	2002
Honduras	1,032	2,451	1,127	3,420	−237	−159	280	862	−51	−266	47	1,531
Hungary	12,035	42,599	11,017	44,104	−1,427	−1,586	787	447	379	−2,644	1,185	10,383
India	22,911	77,602	29,527	83,850	−3,257	−3,886	2,837	14,790	−7,036	4,656	5,637	71,608
Indonesia	29,295	65,826	27,511	52,706	−5,190	−7,048	418	1,751	−2,988	7,823	8,657	32,032
Iran, Islamic Rep.	19,741	35,554	22,292	31,228	378	−217	2,500	457	327	12,645	..	..
Iraq	..	..	..	..	..	..	..	..	..	..	..	..
Ireland	26,786	114,169	24,576	91,385	−4,955	−24,514	2,384	805	−361	−925	5,362	5,475
Israel	17,312	38,505	20,228	42,682	−1,981	−3,599	5,060	6,549	163	−1,226	6,598	24,083
Italy	219,971	313,931	218,573	300,688	−14,712	−14,550	−3,164	−5,434	−16,479	−6,741	88,595	55,622
Jamaica	2,217	3,229	2,390	4,828	−430	−606	291	1,086	−312	−1,119	168	1,645
Japan	323,692	461,293	297,306	409,691	22,492	65,769	−4,800	−4,923	44,078	112,447	87,828	469,618
Jordan	2,511	4,283	3,569	6,186	−214	111	1,045	2,260	−227	468	1,139	4,116
Kazakhstan	..	11,615	..	11,394	..	−1,031	..	113	..	−696	..	3,136
Kenya	2,228	3,295	2,705	3,670	−418	−122	368	580	−527	84	236	1,068
Korea, Dem. Rep.	..	..	..	..	..	..	..	..	..	..	..	..
Korea, Rep.	73,295	190,696	76,360	183,977	−87	451	1,150	−1,078	−2,003	6,092	14,916	121,498
Kuwait	8,268	17,015	7,169	14,037	7,738	3,360	−4,951	−2,145	3,886	4,192	2,929	10,078
Kyrgyz Republic	..	636	..	697	..	−60	..	86	..	−35	..	317
Lao PDR	102	477	212	560	−1	−34	56	..	−55	−82	8	216
Latvia	1,090	3,828	997	4,728	2	−7	96	260	191	−647	..	1,327
Lebanon	511	2,399	2,836	7,065	622	817	1,818	1,000	115	−2,848	4,210	10,405
Lesotho	100	390	754	792	433	161	286	121	65	−119	72	406
Liberia	..	163	..	173	..	−85	..	43	..	−52	0	3
Libya	11,468	..	8,960	..	174	..	−481	..	2,201	..	7,225	15,892
Lithuania	..	7,492	..	8,258	..	−183	..	229	..	−721	107	2,420
Macedonia, FYR	..	1,364	..	2,156	..	−31	..	498	..	−325	..	790
Madagascar	471	710	809	1,001	−161	−75	234	96	−265	−270	92	363
Malawi	443	472	549	795	−80	−38	99	161	−86	−201	142	170
Malaysia	32,665	108,261	31,765	91,696	−1,872	−6,595	102	−2,780	−870	7,190	10,659	34,623
Mali	420	1,157	830	1,211	−37	−241	225	136	−221	−310	198	594
Mauritania	471	..	520	..	−46	..	86	..	−10	..	59	400
Mauritius	1,722	2,965	1,916	2,805	−23	10	97	89	−119	259	761	1,249
Mexico	48,805	173,503	51,915	186,339	−8,316	−11,436	3,975	10,268	−7,451	−14,004	10,217	50,671
Moldova	..	871	..	1,283	..	165	..	155	..	−92	0	269
Mongolia	493	708	1,096	946	−44	−5	7	138	−640	−105	23	398
Morocco	6,239	12,199	7,783	13,314	−988	−738	2,336	3,330	−196	1,477	2,338	10,375
Mozambique	229	1,153	996	1,782	−97	−113	448	217	−415	−657	233	841
Myanmar[d]	319	2,741	603	2,968	−192	−367	39	286	−436	−309	410	549
Namibia	1,220	1,309	1,584	1,485	37	28	354	278	28	130	50	323
Nepal	422	884	834	1,446	14	−4	109	390	−289	−165	354	1,070
Netherlands	159,304	262,898	147,652	244,133	−620	−2,441	−2,943	−6,208	8,089	10,116	34,401	18,948
New Zealand	11,683	19,625	11,699	18,770	−1,576	−3,181	138	57	−1,453	−2,269	4,129	3,739
Nicaragua	392	909	682	1,970	−217	−203	202	377	−305	−888	166	453
Niger	533	..	728	..	−54	..	14	..	−236	..	226	134
Nigeria	14,550	17,151	6,909	15,526	−2,738	−2,090	85	1,466	4,988	1,001	4,129	7,567
Norway	47,078	79,358	38,910	52,290	−2,700	465	−1,476	−2,385	3,992	25,148	15,788	21,088
Oman	5,577	11,423	3,342	6,988	−254	−588	−874	..	1,106	2,315	1,784	3,174
Pakistan	6,835	12,261	10,205	12,645	−1,084	−2,190	2,794	6,445	−1,661	3,871	1,046	8,796
Panama	4,438	7,574	4,193	7,724	−255	−217	219	213	209	−154	344	1,183
Papua New Guinea	1,381	2,098	1,509	1,594	−103	−230	156	13	−76	286	427	343
Paraguay	2,514	2,859	2,169	2,715	2	34	43	116	390	294	675	641
Peru	4,120	9,192	4,087	9,932	−1,733	−1,509	281	1,043	−1,419	−1,206	1,891	9,721
Philippines	11,430	37,439	13,967	38,295	−872	4,550	714	503	−2,695	4,197	2,036	16,136
Poland	19,037	56,777	15,095	63,177	−3,386	−1,887	2,511	3,280	3,067	−5,007	4,674	29,784
Portugal	21,554	36,864	27,146	45,857	−96	−3,135	5,507	3,315	−181	−8,813	20,579	17,701
Puerto Rico	..	..	..	..	..	..	..	..	..	..	..	..

Balance of payments current account

	Goods and services $ millions				Net income $ millions		Net current transfers $ millions		Current account balance $ millions		Total reserves [a] $ millions	
	Exports		Imports									
	1990	2002	1990	2002	1990	2002	1990	2002	1990	2002	1990	2002
Romania	6,380	16,223	9,901	18,825	161	−459	106	1,536	−3,254	−1,525	1,374	8,372
Russian Federation	..	121,214	..	85,188	..	−6,117	..	−5	..	29,905	..	48,326
Rwanda	143	132	354	435	−16	−19	143	195	−85	−126	44	244
Saudi Arabia	47,445	76,862	43,939	49,287	7,979	96	−15,637	−15,975	−4,152	11,696	13,437	22,186
Senegal	1,453	1,549	1,840	2,066	−129	−168	153	207	−363	−478	22	637
Serbia and Montenegro	..	3,241	..	6,857	..	−111	..	2,343	..	−1,384	..	..
Sierra Leone	210	..	215	..	−71	..	7	..	−69	..	5	85
Singapore	67,489	158,075	64,953	137,122	1,006	−1,145	−421	−1,104	3,122	18,704	27,748	82,021
Slovak Republic	..	17,174	..	18,843	..	−459	..	120	..	−694	..	9,196
Slovenia	7,900	12,764	6,930	12,452	−38	−71	46	134	978	375	112	7,063
Somalia	..	..	..	..	..	..	..	..	..	..	..	..
South Africa	27,742	35,571	21,016	32,034	−4,271	−2,691	−321	−556	2,134	290	2,583	7,817
Spain	83,595	188,552	100,870	196,780	−3,533	−9,890	2,799	2,176	−18,009	−15,942	57,238	40,303
Sri Lanka	2,293	5,967	2,965	7,103	−167	−251	541	1,123	−298	−264	447	1,652
Sudan	499	1,996	877	2,971	−136	−617	141	666	−372	−926	11	441
Swaziland	658	1,072	768	1,177	59	48	102	10	51	−46	216	276
Sweden	70,560	105,298	70,490	89,903	−4,473	−1,907	−1,936	−2,864	−6,339	10,624	20,324	19,171
Switzerland	96,927	129,854	96,388	111,148	8,746	11,485	−2,329	−4,179	6,955	26,011	61,284	61,276
Syrian Arab Republic	5,030	8,228	2,955	6,341	−401	−925	88	485	1,762	1,062	..	..
Tajikistan	185	708	238	868	0	−58	..	184	−53	−34	..	90
Tanzania	538	1,568	1,474	2,224	−185	−16	562	420	−559	−251	193	1,529
Thailand	29,229	82,114	35,870	73,741	−853	−1,340	213	618	−7,281	7,650	14,258	38,903
Togo	663	457	847	683	−32	−33	132	77	−84	−169	358	205
Trinidad and Tobago	2,289	4,521	1,427	4,183	−397	−510	−6	33	459	416	513	2,049
Tunisia	5,203	9,538	6,039	10,431	−455	−984	828	1,131	−463	−746	867	2,365
Turkey	21,042	54,617	25,652	55,046	−2,508	−4,549	4,493	3,496	−2,625	−1,482	7,626	28,348
Turkmenistan	1,238	3,138	857	2,703	0	−111	66	68	447	−74	..	..
Uganda	178	720	686	1,643	−48	−136	293	707	−263	−353	44	934
Ukraine	..	23,351	..	21,494	..	−604	..	1,921	..	3,174	469	4,414
United Arab Emirates	..	..	..	..	..	..	..	..	..	..	4,891	15,355
United Kingdom	239,226	404,794	264,090	436,634	−5,154	31,255	−8,794	−13,828	−38,811	−14,414	43,146	42,819
United States	535,260	974,107	616,120	1,392,145	28,560	−3,968	−26,660	−58,852	−78,960	−480,859	173,094	157,763
Uruguay	2,158	2,708	1,659	2,525	−321	10	8	69	186	262	1,446	772
Uzbekistan	..	2,985	..	2,721	..	−145	..	120	..	239	..	..
Venezuela, RB	18,806	27,716	9,451	17,474	−774	−2,654	−302	−165	8,279	7,423	12,733	12,107
Vietnam	..	19,654	..	21,458	..	−721	..	1,921	..	−604	..	4,121
West Bank and Gaza	..	..	..	..	..	..	..	..	..	..	..	..
Yemen, Rep.	1,490	3,787	2,170	3,867	−372	−766	1,790	1,384	739	538	441	4,428
Zambia	1,360	1,080	1,897	1,585	−437	−108	380	32	−594	−553	201	535
Zimbabwe	2,012	..	2,001	..	−263	..	112	..	−140	..	295	132
World	**4,301,369 t**	**7,985,963 t**	**4,330,919 t**	**7,986,659 t**								
Low income	118,587	273,925	135,542	279,942								
Middle income	632,588	1,702,940	593,980	1,591,324								
Lower middle income	356,798	1,017,575	356,720	952,348								
Upper middle income	272,381	683,839	236,047	636,247								
Low & middle income	752,042	1,976,803	730,892	1,871,332								
East Asia & Pacific	166,647	691,152	165,402	620,489								
Europe & Central Asia	..	452,206	..	443,440								
Latin America & Carib.	168,326	403,563	145,500	399,939								
Middle East & N. Africa	127,663	210,917	134,989	178,855								
South Asia	34,818	104,364	47,813	115,016								
Sub-Saharan Africa	79,306	111,723	72,835	110,384								
High income	3,542,141	6,007,813	3,583,425	6,113,233								
Europe EMU	1,517,749	2,447,680	1,480,370	2,284,894								

a. International reserves Including gold valued at London gold price. b. Includes Luxembourg. c. Excludes Luxembourg. d. Data are in fiscal years.

The balance of payments records an economy's transactions with the rest of the world. Balance of payments accounts are divided into two groups: the current account, which records transactions in goods, services, income, and current transfers, and the capital and financial account, which records capital transfers, acquisition or disposal of nonproduced, nonfinancial assets, and transactions in financial assets and liabilities. The table presents data from the current account with the addition of gross international reserves.

The balance of payments is a double-entry accounting system that shows all flows of goods and services into and out of an economy; all transfers that are the counterpart of real resources or financial claims provided to or by the rest of the world without a quid pro quo, such as donations and grants; and all changes in residents' claims on and liabilities to nonresidents that arise from economic transactions. All transactions are recorded twice—once as a credit and once as a debit. In principle the net balance should be zero, but in practice the accounts often do not balance. In these cases a balancing item, net errors and omissions, is included.

Discrepancies may arise in the balance of payments because there is no single source for balance of payments data and therefore no way to ensure that the data are fully consistent. Sources include customs data, monetary accounts of the banking system, external debt records, information provided by enterprises, surveys to estimate service transactions, and foreign exchange records. Differences in collection methods—such as in timing, definitions of residence and ownership, and the exchange rate used to value transactions—contribute to net errors and omissions. In addition, smuggling and other illegal or quasi-legal transactions may be unrecorded or misrecorded. For further discussion of issues relating to the recording of data on trade in goods and services, see *About the data* for tables 4.4–4.8.

The concepts and definitions underlying the data in the table are based on the fifth edition of the International Monetary Fund's (IMF) *Balance of Payments Manual* (1993). The fifth edition redefined as capital transfers some transactions previously included in the current account, such as debt forgiveness, migrants' capital transfers, and foreign aid to acquire capital goods. Thus the current account balance now reflects more accurately net current transfer receipts in addition to transactions in goods, services (previously nonfactor services), and income (previously factor income). Many countries maintain their data collection systems according to the fourth edition. Where necessary, the IMF converts data reported in such systems to conform to the fifth edition (see *Primary data documentation*). Values are in U.S. dollars converted at market exchange rates.

The data in this table come from the IMF's Balance of Payments and International Financial Statistics databases, supplemented by estimates by World Bank staff for countries for which the IMF does not collect balance of payments statistics. In addition, World Bank staff make estimates of missing data for up to three years prior to the current year.

• **Exports and imports of goods and services** comprise all transactions between residents of an economy and the rest of the world involving a change in ownership of general merchandise, goods sent for processing and repairs, nonmonetary gold, and services. • **Net income** refers to receipts and payments of employee compensation for nonresident workers, and investment income (receipts and payments on direct investment, portfolio investment, and other investments and receipts on reserve assets). Income derived from the use of intangible assets is recorded under business services. • **Net current transfers** are recorded in the balance of payments whenever an economy provides or receives goods, services, income, or financial items without a quid pro quo. All transfers not considered to be capital are current. • **Current account balance** is the sum of net exports of goods and services, net income, and net current transfers. • **Total reserves** comprise holdings of monetary gold, special drawing rights, reserves of IMF members held by the IMF, and holdings of foreign exchange under the control of monetary authorities. The gold component of these reserves is valued at year-end (31 December) London prices ($385.00 an ounce in 1990, and $342.75 an ounce in 2002).

4.15a

Workers' remittances, 2002

Country	$ billions	% of merchandise trade	Country	$ billions	% of merchandise trade
Mexico	10	6	Jordan	2	70
India	8	17	Brazil	2	3
Spain	4	3	China	2	1
Pakistan	4	36	Guatemala	2	71
Portugal	3	13	Ecuador	1	28
Egypt, Arab Rep.	3	66	Yemen, Rep.	1	40
Morocco	3	36	Sri Lanka	1	27
Bangladesh	3	47	Indonesia	1	2
Colombia	2	20	Greece	1	11
Serbia and Montenegro	2	92	Jamaica	1	102
Dominican Republic	2	37	Poland	1	3
Turkey	2	6	Tunisia	1	16
El Salvador	2	65	**World total**	**76**	

Remittances accounted for $76 billion in 2002, and 25 countries received more than $1 billion in remittances.

Source: International Monetary Fund, Balance of Payments data files.

More information about the design and compilation of the balance of payments can be found in the IMF's *Balance of Payments Manual*, fifth edition (1993), *Balance of Payments Textbook* (1996a), and *Balance of Payments Compilation Guide* (1995). The balance of payments data are published in the IMF's *Balance of Payments Statistics Yearbook* and *International Financial Statistics*. The World Bank exchanges data with the IMF through electronic files that in most cases are more timely and cover a longer period than the published sources. The IMF's International Financial Statistics and Balance of Payments databases are available on CD-ROM.

	Total external debt $ millions		Long-term debt $ millions		Public and publicly guaranteed debt $ millions				Private nonguaranteed external debt $ millions		Use of IMF credit $ millions	
					Total		IBRD loans and IDA credits					
	1990	2002	1990	2002	1990	2002	1990	2002	1990	2002	1990	2002
Afghanistan	..	..	..	..	..	..	..	..	..	..	..	..
Albania	..	1,312	..	1,200	..	1,187	..	476	..	13	..	81
Algeria	28,149	22,800	26,688	21,362	26,688	21,255	1,208	1,203	0	107	670	1,330
Angola	8,594	10,134	7,605	8,883	7,605	8,883	0	265	0	0	0	0
Argentina	62,233	132,314	48,676	103,140	46,876	74,661	2,609	8,513	1,800	28,479	3,083	14,340
Armenia	..	1,149	..	941	..	920	..	538	..	21	..	195
Australia	..	..	..	..	..	..	..	..	..	..	..	..
Austria	..	..	..	..	..	..	..	..	..	..	..	..
Azerbaijan	..	1,398	..	1,037	..	964	..	314	..	73	..	279
Bangladesh	12,439	17,037	11,657	16,445	11,657	16,445	4,159	7,076	0	0	626	71
Belarus	..	908	..	711	..	710	..	89	..	1	..	56
Belgium	..	..	..	..	..	..	..	..	..	..	..	..
Benin	1,292	1,843	1,218	1,690	1,218	1,690	326	654	0	0	18	73
Bolivia	4,275	4,867	3,864	4,302	3,687	3,378	587	1,320	177	923	257	195
Bosnia and Herzegovina	..	2,515	..	2,303	..	2,282	..	1,115	..	21	..	139
Botswana	553	480	547	464	547	464	169	16	0	0	0	0
Brazil	119,964	227,932	94,427	183,710	87,756	96,565	8,427	8,585	6,671	87,145	1,821	20,827
Bulgaria	..	10,462	..	8,585	..	7,474	..	958	..	1,111	..	1,049
Burkina Faso	834	1,580	750	1,399	750	1,399	282	745	0	0	0	127
Burundi	907	1,204	851	1,095	851	1,095	398	648	0	0	43	13
Cambodia	1,845	2,907	1,683	2,594	1,683	2,594	0	306	0	0	27	96
Cameroon	6,657	8,502	5,577	7,417	5,347	7,240	871	988	230	177	121	307
Canada	..	..	..	..	..	..	..	..	..	..	..	..
Central African Republic	698	1,066	624	980	624	980	265	399	0	0	37	33
Chad	524	1,281	464	1,148	464	1,148	186	632	0	0	31	107
Chile	19,226	41,945	14,687	38,188	10,425	6,792	1,874	562	4,263	31,396	1,156	0
China	55,301	168,255	45,515	120,370	45,515	88,531	5,881	20,677	0	31,839	469	0
Hong Kong, China	..	..	..	..	..	..	..	..	..	..	..	..
Colombia	17,222	33,853	15,784	30,052	14,671	21,177	3,874	2,355	1,113	8,876	0	0
Congo, Dem. Rep.	10,259	8,726	8,994	7,391	8,994	7,391	1,161	1,504	0	0	521	571
Congo, Rep.	4,947	5,152	4,200	3,974	4,200	3,974	239	207	0	0	11	33
Costa Rica	3,756	4,834	3,367	3,335	3,063	3,139	412	93	304	196	11	0
Côte d'Ivoire	17,251	11,816	13,223	10,369	10,665	9,110	1,920	2,068	2,558	1,259	431	491
Croatia	..	15,347	..	14,984	..	7,679	..	588	..	7,305	..	0
Cuba	..	..	..	..	..	..	..	..	..	..	..	..
Czech Republic	..	26,419	..	15,661	..	6,903	..	185	..	8,757	..	0
Denmark	..	..	..	..	..	..	..	..	..	..	..	..
Dominican Republic	4,372	6,256	3,518	4,206	3,419	4,035	258	363	99	171	72	27
Ecuador	12,107	16,452	10,029	13,828	9,865	11,243	848	847	164	2,586	265	308
Egypt, Arab Rep.	33,017	30,750	28,438	27,282	27,438	26,624	2,401	1,859	1,000	658	125	0
El Salvador	2,149	5,828	1,938	4,837	1,913	4,712	164	385	26	126	0	0
Eritrea	..	528	..	496	..	496	..	219	..	0	..	0
Estonia	..	4,741	..	3,151	..	482	..	39	..	2,669	..	0
Ethiopia	8,630	6,523	8,479	6,313	8,479	6,313	851	2,756	0	0	6	143
Finland	..	..	..	..	..	..	..	..	..	..	..	..
France	..	..	..	..	..	..	..	..	..	..	..	..
Gabon	3,983	3,533	3,150	3,231	3,150	3,231	69	50	0	0	140	67
Gambia, The	369	573	308	504	308	504	102	195	0	0	45	32
Georgia	..	1,838	..	1,495	..	1,444	..	491	..	51	..	310
Germany	..	..	..	..	..	..	..	..	..	..	..	..
Ghana	3,837	7,338	2,772	6,382	2,740	6,129	1,423	3,476	33	253	745	363
Greece	..	..	..	..	..	..	..	..	..	..	..	..
Guatemala	3,080	4,676	2,605	3,744	2,478	3,641	293	400	127	102	67	0
Guinea	2,476	3,401	2,253	2,972	2,253	2,972	420	1,096	0	0	52	139
Guinea-Bissau	692	699	630	662	630	662	146	237	0	0	5	23
Haiti	910	1,248	772	1,063	772	1,063	324	501	0	0	38	31

External debt | 4.16

	Total external debt $ millions		Long-term debt $ millions		Public and publicly guaranteed debt $ millions				Private nonguaranteed external debt $ millions		Use of IMF credit $ millions	
					Total		IBRD loans and IDA credits					
	1990	2002	1990	2002	1990	2002	1990	2002	1990	2002	1990	2002
Honduras	3,718	5,395	3,487	4,675	3,420	4,212	635	1,119	66	463	32	197
Hungary	21,202	34,958	17,931	29,289	17,931	13,551	1,512	517	0	15,738	330	0
India	83,628	104,429	72,462	99,860	70,974	88,271	20,996	26,093	1,488	11,589	2,623	0
Indonesia	69,872	132,208	58,242	100,037	47,982	70,011	10,385	11,523	10,261	30,026	494	8,862
Iran, Islamic Rep.	9,020	9,154	1,797	6,797	1,797	6,578	86	400	0	219	0	0
Iraq	..	..	..	..	..	..	..	..	..	..	..	..
Ireland	..	..	..	..	..	..	..	..	..	..	..	..
Israel	..	..	..	..	..	..	..	..	..	..	..	..
Italy	..	..	..	..	..	..	..	..	..	..	..	..
Jamaica	4,748	5,477	4,045	4,678	4,011	4,593	672	495	34	86	357	24
Japan	..	..	..	..	..	..	..	..	..	..	94	483
Jordan	8,333	8,094	7,202	7,076	7,202	7,076	593	1,072	0	0	94	483
Kazakhstan	..	17,538	..	16,355	..	3,209	..	1,178	..	13,146	..	0
Kenya	7,058	6,031	5,641	5,188	4,761	5,139	2,056	2,460	880	49	482	88
Korea, Dem. Rep.	..	..	..	..	..	..	..	..	..	..	..	..
Korea, Rep.	..	..	..	..	..	..	..	..	..	..	..	..
Kuwait	..	..	..	..	..	..	..	..	..	..	..	..
Kyrgyz Republic	..	1,797	..	1,593	..	1,394	..	454	..	199	..	185
Lao PDR	1,768	2,664	1,758	2,620	1,758	2,620	131	474	0	0	8	43
Latvia	..	6,690	..	2,512	..	1,124	..	263	..	1,388	..	16
Lebanon	1,779	17,077	358	14,530	358	13,829	34	313	0	701	0	0
Lesotho	396	637	378	611	378	611	112	255	0	0	15	22
Liberia	1,849	2,324	1,116	1,065	1,116	1,065	248	240	0	0	322	304
Libya	..	..	..	..	..	..	..	..	..	..	..	..
Lithuania	..	6,199	..	3,955	..	2,486	..	279	..	1,469	..	121
Macedonia, FYR	..	1,619	..	1,476	..	1,262	..	432	..	214	..	67
Madagascar	3,704	4,518	3,335	4,137	3,335	4,137	797	1,652	0	0	144	150
Malawi	1,558	2,912	1,385	2,688	1,382	2,688	854	1,773	3	0	115	95
Malaysia	15,328	48,557	13,422	40,188	11,592	26,200	1,102	719	1,830	13,988	0	0
Mali	2,468	2,803	2,337	2,487	2,337	2,487	498	1,134	0	0	69	166
Mauritania	2,113	2,309	1,806	1,984	1,806	1,984	264	547	0	0	70	113
Mauritius	984	1,803	910	911	762	832	195	107	148	79	22	0
Mexico	104,442	141,264	81,809	131,364	75,974	76,327	11,030	10,797	5,835	55,038	6,551	0
Moldova	..	1,349	..	1,126	..	846	..	331	..	280	..	152
Mongolia	..	1,037	..	950	..	950	..	181	..	0	..	43
Morocco	25,017	18,601	23,860	16,913	23,660	15,001	3,138	2,573	200	1,912	750	0
Mozambique	4,650	4,609	4,231	4,039	4,211	2,526	268	985	19	1,513	74	200
Myanmar	4,695	6,556	4,466	5,391	4,466	5,391	716	729	0	0	0	0
Namibia	..	..	..	..	..	..	..	..	..	..	..	..
Nepal	1,640	2,953	1,572	2,913	1,572	2,913	668	1,210	0	0	44	4
Netherlands	..	..	..	..	..	..	..	..	..	..	..	..
New Zealand	..	..	..	..	..	..	..	..	..	..	..	..
Nicaragua	10,745	6,485	8,313	5,756	8,313	5,576	299	811	0	181	0	174
Niger	1,726	1,797	1,487	1,658	1,226	1,604	461	867	261	54	85	106
Nigeria	33,439	30,476	31,935	28,206	31,545	28,057	3,321	1,951	391	149	0	0
Norway	..	..	..	..	..	..	..	..	..	..	..	..
Oman	2,736	4,639	2,400	3,451	2,400	1,979	52	0	0	1,471	0	0
Pakistan	20,663	33,672	16,643	30,100	16,506	28,102	3,922	8,143	138	1,998	836	2,032
Panama	6,506	8,298	3,855	7,877	3,855	6,408	462	287	0	1,469	272	50
Papua New Guinea	2,594	2,485	2,461	2,305	1,523	1,488	349	358	938	818	61	116
Paraguay	2,105	2,967	1,732	2,481	1,713	2,064	320	241	19	417	0	0
Peru	20,064	28,167	13,959	25,596	13,629	20,477	1,188	2,609	330	5,118	755	237
Philippines	30,580	61,121	25,241	53,877	24,040	39,575	4,044	3,533	1,201	14,303	912	1,686
Poland	49,364	69,521	39,261	60,637	39,261	29,374	55	2,385	0	31,263	509	0
Portugal	..	..	..	..	..	..	..	..	..	..	..	..
Puerto Rico	..	..	..	..	..	..	..	..	..	..	..	..

	Total external debt $ millions		Long-term debt $ millions		Public and publicly guaranteed debt $ millions		IBRD loans and IDA credits		Private nonguaranteed external debt $ millions		Use of IMF credit $ millions	
					Total							
	1990	2002	1990	2002	1990	2002	1990	2002	1990	2002	1990	2002
Romania	1,140	14,683	230	13,780	223	8,112	0	2,173	7	5,668	0	428
Russian Federation	..	147,541	..	124,738	..	96,223	..	6,599	..	28,514	..	6,481
Rwanda	712	1,435	664	1,305	664	1,305	340	826	0	0	0	85
Saudi Arabia	..	..	..	..	..	..	..	..	..	..	..	..
Senegal	3,736	3,918	3,000	3,372	2,940	3,339	835	1,578	60	33	314	253
Serbia and Montenegro [a]	..	12,688	..	8,793	..	8,514	..	2,419	..	280	..	567
Sierra Leone	1,196	1,448	940	1,262	940	1,262	92	479	0	0	108	169
Singapore	..	..	..	..	..	..	..	..	..	..	..	..
Slovak Republic	..	13,013	..	8,776	..	4,295	..	204	..	4,481	..	0
Slovenia	..	..	..	..	..	..	..	..	..	..	..	..
Somalia	2,370	2,688	1,926	1,860	1,926	1,860	419	405	0	0	159	152
South Africa	..	25,041	..	17,640	..	9,427	0	13	..	8,213	0	0
Spain	..	..	..	..	..	..	..	..	..	..	..	..
Sri Lanka	5,863	9,611	5,049	8,805	4,947	8,455	946	1,738	102	351	410	310
Sudan	14,762	16,389	9,651	9,539	9,155	9,043	1,048	1,192	496	496	956	573
Swaziland	243	342	238	274	238	274	44	13	0	0	0	0
Sweden	..	..	..	..	..	..	..	..	..	..	..	..
Switzerland	..	..	..	..	..	..	..	..	..	..	..	..
Syrian Arab Republic	17,259	21,504	15,108	15,849	15,108	15,849	523	38	0	0	0	0
Tajikistan	..	1,153	..	999	..	912	..	195	..	87	..	94
Tanzania	6,459	7,244	5,799	6,201	5,787	6,182	1,493	2,874	12	20	140	400
Thailand	28,095	59,212	19,771	46,902	12,460	22,628	2,530	2,428	7,311	24,274	1	391
Togo	1,281	1,581	1,081	1,338	1,081	1,338	398	632	0	0	87	52
Trinidad and Tobago	2,512	2,672	2,055	1,807	1,782	1,697	41	87	273	110	329	0
Tunisia	7,690	12,625	6,880	12,027	6,662	10,641	1,406	1,498	218	1,386	176	0
Turkey	49,424	131,556	39,924	94,278	38,870	61,823	6,429	5,456	1,054	32,455	0	22,086
Turkmenistan	..	..	..	..	..	..	..	31	..	..	..	0
Uganda	2,583	4,100	2,160	3,690	2,160	3,690	969	2,576	0	0	282	257
Ukraine	..	13,555	..	11,100	..	8,348	..	2,233	..	2,752	..	1,876
United Arab Emirates	..	..	..	..	..	..	..	..	..	..	..	..
United Kingdom	..	..	..	..	..	..	..	..	..	..	..	..
United States	..	..	..	..	..	..	..	..	..	..	..	..
Uruguay	4,415	10,736	3,114	7,343	3,045	6,851	359	703	69	493	101	1,793
Uzbekistan	..	4,568	..	4,175	..	3,901	..	275	..	274	..	62
Venezuela, RB	33,171	32,563	28,159	28,843	24,509	23,264	974	670	3,650	5,578	3,012	0
Vietnam	23,270	13,349	21,378	12,181	21,378	12,181	59	1,715	0	0	112	381
West Bank and Gaza	..	..	..	..	..	..	..	..	..	..	..	..
Yemen, Rep.	6,352	5,290	5,160	4,563	5,160	4,563	602	1,384	0	0	0	386
Zambia	6,916	5,969	4,554	4,846	4,552	4,737	813	2,155	2	108	949	1,015
Zimbabwe	3,247	4,066	2,649	3,269	2,464	3,123	449	871	185	146	7	280
World	.. s	.. s	.. s	.. s	.. s	.. s	.. s	.. s	.. s	.. s	.. s	.. s
Low income	411,419	523,464	351,318	448,932	333,366	399,076	67,061	104,388	17,953	49,857	11,317	20,258
Middle income [b]	940,479	1,817,163	749,931	1,469,476	707,793	983,880	70,222	107,517	42,138	485,596	23,334	75,550
Lower middle income	583,682	1,149,118	477,625	925,294	453,753	651,767	49,234	80,019	23,872	273,527	7,811	59,160
Upper middle income [b]	356,797	668,045	272,306	544,182	254,040	332,112	20,988	27,498	18,266	212,069	15,523	16,390
Low & middle income [b]	1,351,898	2,340,627	1,101,250	1,918,408	1,041,159	1,382,955	137,283	211,905	60,091	535,453	34,651	95,809
East Asia & Pacific	234,092	499,133	194,633	388,064	172,998	272,783	25,306	42,764	21,635	115,281	2,085	11,618
Europe & Central Asia	217,224	545,842	176,378	434,625	171,457	276,350	10,429	30,214	4,921	158,275	1,305	34,245
Latin America & Carib.	444,227	727,944	352,476	613,916	327,447	384,961	35,841	42,072	25,029	228,956	18,297	38,302
Middle East & N. Africa	155,134	189,010	120,603	148,851	119,101	142,396	10,074	10,417	1,502	6,455	1,815	2,219
South Asia	124,395	168,349	107,527	158,723	105,799	144,785	30,717	44,349	1,727	13,938	4,537	2,416
Sub-Saharan Africa	176,826	210,350	149,632	174,229	144,355	161,681	24,916	42,089	5,276	12,548	6,612	7,009
High income												
Europe EMU												

a. Data for 1990 refer to the former Socialist Federal Republic of Yugoslavia. Data for 2002 are estimates and reflect borrowings by the former Socialist Federal Republic of of Yugoslavia that are not yet allocated to the successor republics. b. Includes data for Gibraltar not included in other tables.

Data on the external debt of developing countries are gathered by the World Bank through its Debtor Reporting System. World Bank staff calculate the indebtedness of these countries using loan-by-loan reports submitted by them on long-term public and publicly guaranteed borrowing, along with information on short-term debt collected by the countries or collected from creditors through the reporting systems of the Bank for International Settlements and the Organisation for Economic Co-operation and Development. These data are supplemented by information on loans and credits from major multilateral banks, loan statements from official lending agencies in major creditor countries, and estimates by World Bank and International Monetary Fund (IMF) staff. In addition, the table includes data on private nonguaranteed debt for 80 countries either reported to the World Bank or estimated by its staff.

The coverage, quality, and timeliness of debt data vary across countries. Coverage varies for both debt instruments and borrowers. With the widening spectrum of debt instruments and investors and the expansion of private nonguaranteed borrowing, comprehensive coverage of long-term external debt becomes more complex. Reporting countries differ in their capacity to monitor debt, especially private nonguaranteed debt. Even data on public and publicly guaranteed debt are affected by coverage and accuracy in reporting—again because of monitoring capacity and sometimes because of unwillingness to provide information. A key part often underreported is military debt.

Because debt data are normally reported in the currency of repayment, they have to be converted into U.S. dollars to produce summary tables. Stock figures (amount of debt outstanding) are converted using end-of-period exchange rates, as published in

the IMF's *International Financial Statistics* (line ae). Flow figures are converted at annual average exchange rates (line rf). Projected debt service is converted using end-of-period exchange rates. Debt repayable in multiple currencies, goods, or services and debt with a provision for maintenance of the value of the currency of repayment are shown at book value.

Because flow data are converted at annual average exchange rates and stock data at end-of-period exchange rates, year-to-year changes in debt outstanding and disbursed are sometimes not equal to net flows (disbursements less principal repayments); similarly, changes in debt outstanding, including undisbursed debt, differ from commitments less repayments. Discrepancies are particularly significant when exchange rates have moved sharply during the year. Cancellations and reschedulings of other liabilities into long-term public debt also contribute to the differences.

Variations in reporting rescheduled debt also affect cross-country comparability. For example, rescheduling under the auspices of the Paris Club of official creditors may be subject to lags between the completion of the general rescheduling agreement and the completion of the specific, bilateral agreements that define the terms of the rescheduled debt. Other areas of inconsistency include country treatment of arrears and of nonresident national deposits denominated in foreign currency.

• **Total external debt** is debt owed to nonresidents repayable in foreign currency, goods, or services. It is the sum of public, publicly guaranteed, and private nonguaranteed long-term debt, use of IMF credit, and short-term debt. Short-term debt includes all debt having an original maturity of one year or less and interest in arrears on long-term debt. • **Long-term debt** is debt that has an original or extended maturity of more than one year. It has three components: public, publicly guaranteed, and private nonguaranteed debt. • **Public and publicly guaranteed debt** comprises the long-term external obligations of public debtors, including the national government and political subdivisions (or an agency of either) and autonomous public bodies, and the external obligations of private debtors that are guaranteed for repayment by a public entity. • **IBRD loans and IDA credits** are extended by the World Bank. The International Bank for Reconstruction and Development (IBRD) lends at market rates. The International Development Association (IDA) provides credits at concessional rates. • **Private nonguaranteed external debt** consists of the long-term external obligations of private debtors that are not guaranteed for repayment by a public entity. • **Use of IMF credit** denotes repurchase obligations to the IMF for all uses of IMF resources (excluding those resulting from drawings on the reserve tranche). These obligations, shown for the end of the year specified, comprise purchases outstanding under the credit tranches (including enlarged access resources) and all special facilities (the buffer stock, compensatory financing, extended fund, and oil facilities), trust fund loans, and operations under the structural adjustment and enhanced structural adjustment facilities.

4.16a

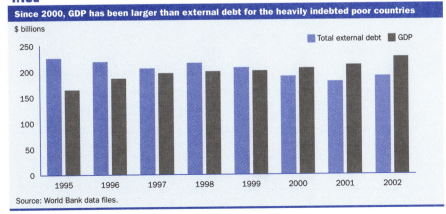

Source: World Bank data files.

The main sources of external debt information are reports to the World Bank through its Debtor Reporting System from member countries that have received IBRD loans or IDA credits. Additional information has been drawn from the files of the World Bank and the IMF. Summary tables of the external debt of developing countries are published annually in the World Bank's *Global Development Finance* and on its *Global Development Finance* CD-ROM.

External debt management

	Indebtedness classification [a]	Present value of debt		Public and publicly guaranteed debt service				Multilateral debt service		Short-term debt	
		% of GNI	% of exports of goods, services, and income	% of GNI		% of exports of goods, services, and income		% of public and publicly guaranteed		% of total debt	
	2002	**2002**	**2002**	**1990**	**2002**	**1990**	**2002**	**1990**	**2002**	**1990**	**2002**
Afghanistan	..	..	..	..	..	..	..	..	..	..	..
Albania	L	20	91	..	0.7	..	3.4	..	37.5	..	2.4
Algeria	L	42	..	14.3	7.0	63.3	..	5.0	25.2	2.8	0.5
Angola	S	118	125	3.4	8.7	7.1	9.8	2.2	1.0	11.5	12.4
Argentina	S	66	393	3.6	4.3	28.9	12.8	16.2	80.1	16.8	11.2
Armenia	L	34	111	..	2.1	..	6.3	..	54.6	..	1.2
Australia	..	..	..	..	..	..	..	..	..	..	..
Austria	..	..	..	..	..	..	..	..	..	..	..
Azerbaijan	L	21	46	..	1.6	..	3.4	..	18.0	..	5.9
Bangladesh	L	22	155	1.6	1.3	23.3	8.9	22.8	48.7	1.3	3.1
Belarus	L	7	10	..	1.1	..	1.7	..	31.6	..	15.6
Belgium	..	..	..	..	..	..	..	..	..	..	..
Benin	M	36 [b]	155 [b]	1.8	1.9	8.6	8.5	95.7	60.0	4.3	4.4
Bolivia	L	23 [b]	111 [b]	5.9	2.8	27.6	13.1	67.6	89.7	3.6	7.6
Bosnia and Herzegovina	L	34	98	..	2.0	..	6.6	..	57.2	..	2.9
Botswana	L	8	13	2.9	1.2	4.3	2.0	61.3	69.5	1.0	3.3
Brazil	S	48	342	1.3	5.0	15.7	29.4	43.5	15.5	19.8	10.3
Bulgaria	M	79	136	..	3.8	..	6.8	..	26.6	..	7.9
Burkina Faso	M	16 [b]	171 [b]	0.9	1.4	7.7	14.8	73.0	85.5	10.1	3.4
Burundi	S	110	1,553	3.6	2.6	40.7	47.1	51.1	87.6	1.5	8.0
Cambodia	M	68	114	2.6	0.2	..	0.3	..	60.3	7.3	7.4
Cameroon	M	58 [b]	.. [b]	3.0	3.2	12.6	..	43.5	46.3	14.4	9.2
Canada	..	..	..	..	..	..	..	..	..	..	..
Central African Republic	S	78	..	1.1	0.0	7.5	..	50.0	100.0	5.4	4.9
Chad	S	37 [b]	.. [b]	0.4	1.2	2.4	..	72.3	77.0	5.7	2.0
Chile	M	63	173	5.6	2.4	15.1	6.3	35.7	31.3	17.6	9.0
China	L	14	50	1.6	1.0	9.7	3.5	7.6	32.8	16.8	28.5
Hong Kong, China	..	..	..	..	..	..	..	..	..	..	..
Colombia	M	46	229	8.2	6.4	34.5	33.4	32.2	26.0	8.4	11.2
Congo, Dem. Rep.	S	171	..	1.6	7.5	..	..	49.6	100.0	7.2	8.8
Congo, Rep.	S	228	200	20.4	0.5	31.6	0.5	12.7	100.0	14.9	22.2
Costa Rica	L	33	69	7.9	3.7	20.7	8.2	36.1	53.2	10.0	31.0
Côte d'Ivoire	S	91	188	5.7	4.5	14.7	8.6	77.5	73.6	20.8	8.1
Croatia	M	76	150	..	7	..	14	..	6	..	2.4
Cuba	..	..	..	..	..	..	..	..	..	..	..
Czech Republic	L	46	62	..	2.2	..	3.0	..	10.7	..	40.7
Denmark	..	..	..	..	..	..	..	..	..	..	..
Dominican Republic	L	..	68	2.1	2.8	7.2	6.6	50.3	24.1	17.9	32.3
Ecuador	S	95	300	9.6	5.7	26.6	20.9	34.8	40.5	15.0	14.1
Egypt, Arab Rep.	L	28	150	5.9	2.0	23.2	10.6	18.7	25.5	13.5	11.3
El Salvador	L	46	162	3.7	2.7	17.7	9.5	60.2	54.5	9.8	17.0
Eritrea	M	40	200	..	1.2	..	4.5	..	58.6	..	5.9
Estonia	S	86	89	..	1.6	..	1.7	..	54.1	..	33.5
Ethiopia	S	66 [b, c]	386 [b, c]	2.3	1.6	33.1	8.9	14.5	79.0	1.7	1.0
Finland	..	..	..	..	..	..	..	..	..	..	..
France	..	..	..	..	..	..	..	..	..	..	..
Gabon	S	87	107	1.9	9.2	3.8	11.0	32.6	11.3	17.4	6.7
Gambia, The	M	77 [b]	.. [b]	10.4	5.3	17.9	..	25.4	51.9	4.3	6.5
Georgia	M	42	144	..	2.0	..	6.2	..	24.4	..	1.8
Germany	..	..	..	..	..	..	..	..	..	..	..
Ghana	M	73 [b]	157 [b]	3.3	2.8	19.3	6.6	30.7	47.9	8.3	8.1
Greece	..	..	..	..	..	..	..	..	..	..	..
Guatemala	L	21	110	2.2	1.5	10.4	9.0	36.8	61.3	13.3	19.9
Guinea	M	47 [b]	166 [b]	5.6	3.9	17.7	12.4	22.1	57.0	6.9	8.5
Guinea-Bissau	S	235 [b]	..	2.4	6.1	21.8	..	70.2	46.5	8.2	2.0
Haiti	L	23	..	0.5	0.4	4.4	..	69.2	41.4	11.1	12.3

External debt management

	Indebtedness classification [a]	Present value of debt		Public and publicly guaranteed debt service				Multilateral debt service		Short-term debt	
		% of GNI	% of exports of goods, services, and income	% of GNI		% of exports of goods, services, and income		% of public and publicly guaranteed		% of total debt	
	2002	2002	2002	1990	2002	1990	2002	1990	2002	1990	2002
Honduras	M	49	121	10.8	2.6	29.1	6.5	90.7	76.1	5.4	9.7
Hungary	M	62	82	11.9	3.4	30.4	4.9	8.0	9.2	13.9	16.2
India	L	17	115	..	..	..	..	..	..	10.2	4.4
Indonesia	S	89	191	6.8	4.0	24.9	9.8	22.5	42.1	15.9	17.6
Iran, Islamic Rep.	L	7	25	0.2	1.2	1.3	3.6	30.4	8.1	80.1	25.7
Iraq	..	..	..	..	..	..	..	..	..	..	..
Ireland	..	..	..	..	..	..	..	..	..	..	..
Israel	..	..	..	..	..	..	..	..	..	..	..
Italy	..	..	..	..	..	..	..	..	..	..	..
Jamaica	S	82	163	11.6	10.9	20.7	22.9	38.6	22.1	7.3	14.2
Japan	..	..	..	..	..	..	..	..	..	..	..
Jordan	S	84	165	14.5	5.2	21.4	10.1	26.8	47.7	12.4	6.6
Kazakhstan	M	80	151	..	3.7	..	7.4	..	18.2	..	6.7
Kenya	M	40	147	6.3	2.8	22.7	10.4	44.7	31.8	13.2	12.5
Korea, Dem. Rep.	..	..	..	..	..	..	..	..	..	..	..
Korea, Rep.	..	..	..	..	..	..	..	..	..	..	..
Kuwait	..	..	..	..	..	..	..	..	..	..	..
Kyrgyz Republic	S	93	221	..	2.9	..	7.0	..	39.9	..	1.0
Lao PDR	S	87	..	1.0	2.2	8.0	..	53.6	62.8	0.1	0.0
Latvia	S	85	176	..	1.2	..	2.4	..	70.9	..	62.2
Lebanon	S	102	557	1.1	9.5	3.2	51.8	27.8	5.4	79.9	14.9
Lesotho	L	45	78	2	7	4	11	45	68	1	0.6
Liberia	S	559	1,686	..	..	..	..	100.0	..	22.2	41.1
Libya	..	..	..	..	..	3.8	..	..	..	..	..
Lithuania	M	50	95	..	4.2	..	7.4	..	18.7	..	34.2
Macedonia, FYR	L	37	87	..	3.9	..	10.5	..	38.5	..	4.7
Madagascar	L	33 [b]	129 [b]	5.2	1.5	31.9	9.1	23.7	61.0	6.1	5.1
Malawi	M	51 [b]	183 [b]	5.5	1.5	22.4	5.7	38.2	100.0	3.7	4.5
Malaysia	M	57	44	8.7	6.4	10.6	5.1	9.9	4.4	12.4	17.2
Mali	M	47 [b]	134 [b]	1.8	2.4	9.7	5.8	54.3	64.0	2.5	5.4
Mauritania	M	66 [b]	.. [b]	10.9	5.8	24.8	..	73.8	69.8	11.2	9.2
Mauritius	L	39	60	3.4	4.2	4.5	6.3	51.6	21.8	5.3	49.5
Mexico	L	26	86	3.1	3.0	15.1	10.7	26.0	15.0	15.4	7.0
Moldova	M	79	126	..	6.1	..	9.4	..	40.1	..	5.3
Mongolia	M	69	107	..	3.9	..	6.1	..	13.4	..	4.3
Morocco	M	51	147	5.9	8.5	23.1	23.9	39.8	37.4	1.6	9.1
Mozambique	L	27 [b]	88 [b]	2.2	1.1	17.2	2.9	30.6	61.9	7.4	8.0
Myanmar	S	..	..	..	..	17.7	..	43.6	0.7	4.9	17.8
Namibia	..	..	..	..	..	0.1	..	..	..	..	..
Nepal	M	31	147	1.5	1.7	12.1	9.8	36.8	72.7	1.5	1.2
Netherlands	..	..	..	..	..	..	..	..	..	..	..
New Zealand	..	..	..	..	..	..	..	..	..	..	..
Nicaragua	S	77	301	..	2.6	2.4	10.7	21.1	26.0	22.6	8.5
Niger	M	26 [b]	.. [b]	0.7	0.7	3.1	..	71.3	89.9	8.9	1.8
Nigeria	S	80	152	12.8	3.6	22.3	8.2	15.5	31.3	4.5	7.4
Norway	..	..	..	..	..	..	..	..	..	..	..
Oman	L	23	..	6.9	4.4	12.0	..	5.1	7.6	12.3	25.6
Pakistan	M	45	238	3.5	3.5	19.8	16.8	40.3	56.4	15.4	4.6
Panama	S	84	107	2.8	11.5	2.5	16.4	90.7	9.5	36.6	4.5
Papua New Guinea	S	82	..	8.7	5.2	18.2	..	23.0	53.6	2.8	2.6
Paraguay	L	42	96	5.6	3.4	11.5	6.2	35.9	68.1	17.7	16.4
Peru	S	56	319	0.7	5.5	4.1	31.7	28.8	24.1	26.7	8.3
Philippines	M	77	135	6.6	6.7	22.2	12.3	28.7	16.1	14.5	9.1
Poland	L	38	124	1.5	2.0	4.3	6.3	9.2	8.4	19.4	12.8
Portugal	..	..	..	..	..	..	..	..	..	..	..
Puerto Rico	..	..	..	..	..	..	..	..	..	..	..

	Indebtedness classification [a]	Present value of debt		Public and publicly guaranteed debt service				Multilateral debt service		Short-term debt	
		% of GNI	% of exports of goods, services, and income	% of GNI		% of exports of goods, services, and income		% of public and publicly guaranteed		% of total debt	
	2002	2002	2002	1990	2002	1990	2002	1990	2002	1990	2002
Romania	L	37	106	..	4.0	..	11.0	..	27.1	79.8	3.2
Russian Federation	M	50	122	..	2.6	..	7.1	..	8.9	..	11.1
Rwanda	S	40 [b]	453 [b]	0.6	1.1	10.2	13.2	60.7	61.8	6.6	3.2
Saudi Arabia	..	..	..	..	..	1.2	..	..	..	..	..
Senegal	M	53 [b]	165 [b]	3.8	3.6	13.8	11.4	39.8	42.9	11.3	7.5
Serbia and Montenegro	S	102	421	..	0.7	..	3.1	..	86.0	..	26.2
Sierra Leone	S	103 [b]	.. [b]	2.8	2.8	7.8	..	26.1	43.5	12.4	1.1
Singapore	..	..	..	..	..	..	..	..	..	..	..
Slovak Republic	M	62	82	..	3.8	..	5.0	..	10.4	..	32.6
Slovenia	..	..	..	..	..	..	..	..	..	..	..
Somalia	S	..	..	0.8	..	..	..	100.0	..	12.0	25.1
South Africa	L	22	66	..	1.6	..	4.2	..	0.4	..	29.6
Spain	..	..	..	..	..	..	..	..	..	..	..
Sri Lanka	M	48	122	3.6	3.2	11.9	8.7	13.8	18.7	6.9	5.2
Sudan	S	136	851	0.1	0.0	4.5	0.0	100.0	100.0	28.1	38.3
Swaziland	L	25	26	4.8	1.5	5.6	1.6	73.0	75.7	1.9	19.9
Sweden	..	..	..	..	..	..	..	..	..	..	..
Switzerland	..	..	..	..	..	..	..	..	..	..	..
Syrian Arab Republic	S	114	270	9.3	0.8	20.3	1.9	3.5	55.9	12.5	26.3
Tajikistan	S	88	124	..	1.5	..	2.5	..	62.5	..	5.2
Tanzania	L	19 [b, d]	117 [b, d]	3.4	1.4	25.1	7.8	52.7	39.6	8.0	8.9
Thailand	M	49	69	3.9	6.1	10.4	8.9	22.1	33.7	29.6	20.1
Togo	S	92	251	3.8	0.1	8.6	0.2	40.8	100.0	8.8	12.1
Trinidad and Tobago	L	35	61	7.3	2.4	14.6	4.7	4.7	44.5	5.1	32.4
Tunisia	M	65	135	10.3	6.8	23.0	14.1	26.0	49.4	8.2	4.7
Turkey	S	77	246	4.3	5.6	29.6	17.7	23.3	10.0	19.2	11.5
Turkmenistan	M	..	..	..	..	..	..	..	..	..	..
Uganda	L	22 [b]	175 [b]	2.0	1.0	47.1	7.6	37.4	83.1	5.4	3.7
Ukraine	L	35	59	..	2.8	..	4.9	..	29.8	..	4.3
United Arab Emirates	..	..	..	..	..	..	..	..	..	..	..
United Kingdom	..	..	..	..	..	..	..	..	..	..	..
United States	..	..	..	..	..	..	..	..	..	..	..
Uruguay	S	65	279	7.9	8.9	29.4	33.7	16.2	26.2	27.2	14.9
Uzbekistan	M	57	136	..	7.8	..	20.2	..	11.6	..	7.2
Venezuela, RB	..	33	112	8.8	6.6	19.4	20.5	1.6	10.2	6.0	11.4
Vietnam	L	35	61	2.4	3.1	..	5.5	3.4	2.6	7.7	5.9
West Bank and Gaza	..	..	..	..	..	..	..	..	..	..	..
Yemen, Rep.	L	40	90	2.3	1.5	7.1	3.5	51.0	60.0	18.8	6.5
Zambia	S	127	406	5.7	6.4	12.7	19.9	41.6	26.9	20.4	1.8
Zimbabwe	M	..	..	4.3	..	18.2	..	24.0	16.9	18.2	12.7
World				.. w	.. w	.. w	.. w	.. w	..	.. w	.. w
Low income				3.5	2.8	21.4	10.9	25.4	44.3	11.9	10.4
Middle income				3.4	3.2	14.6	8.9	19.2	20.8	17.8	15.0
Lower middle income				3.1	3.0	17.3	9.1	21.2	22.3	16.8	14.3
Upper middle income				3.9	3.7	11.8	8.6	15.8	18.1	19.3	16.1
Low & middle income				3.4	3.1	15.9	9.2	20.6	24.7	16.0	13.9
East Asia & Pacific				3.6	2.3	13.7	5.5	17.5	27.4	16.0	19.9
Europe & Central Asia				..	3.2	18.3	7.6	17.1	12.7	18.2	14.1
Latin America & Carib.				3.0	4.2	17.7	16.1	26.6	22.4	16.5	10.4
Middle East & N. Africa				4.2	..	13.3	..	10.8	26.5	21.1	20.1
South Asia				2.1	2.4	23.1	14.5	25.0	49.2	9.9	4.3
Sub-Saharan Africa				..	2.6	..	6.5	30.0	32.7	11.6	13.8
High income											
Europe EMU											

a. S = severely indebted, M = moderately indebted, L = less indebted. b. Data are from debt sustainability analyses undertaken as part of the Debt Initiative for Heavily Indebted Poor Countries (HIPCs). Present value estimates for these countries are for public and publicly guaranteed debt only. c. As of December 31, 2002, Ethiopia had yet to reach the completion point under the HIPC Debt Initiative. d. Data refer to mainland Tanzania only.

External debt management

The indicators in the table measure the relative burden on developing countries of servicing external debt. The present value of external debt provides a measure of future debt service obligations that can be compared with the current value of such indicators as gross national income (GNI) and exports of goods and services. The table shows the present value of total debt service both as a percentage of GNI in 2002 and as a percentage of exports in 2002. The ratios compare total debt service obligations with the size of the economy and its ability to obtain foreign exchange through exports. The ratios shown here may differ from those published elsewhere because estimates of exports and GNI have been revised to incorporate data available as of February 1, 2004. Exports refer to exports of goods, services, and income. Workers' remittances are not included here, though they are included with income receipts in other World Bank publications such as *Global Development Finance.*

The present value of external debt is calculated by discounting the debt service (interest plus amortization) due on long-term external debt over the life of existing loans. Short-term debt is included at its face value. The data on debt are in U.S. dollars converted at official exchange rates (see *About the data* for table 4.16). The discount rate applied to long-term debt is determined by the currency of repayment of the loan and is based on reference rates for commercial interest established by the Organisation for Economic Co-operation and Development. Loans from the International Bank for Reconstruction and Development (IBRD) and credits from the International Development Association (IDA) are discounted using a special drawing rights (SDR) reference rate, as are obligations to the International

Monetary Fund (IMF). When the discount rate is greater than the interest rate of the loan, the present value is less than the nominal sum of future debt service obligations.

The ratios in the table are used to assess the sustainability of a country's debt service obligations, but there are no absolute rules that determine what values are too high. Empirical analysis of the experience of developing countries and their debt service performance has shown that debt service difficulties become increasingly likely when the ratio of the present value of debt to exports reaches 200 percent. Still, what constitutes a sustainable debt burden varies from one country to another. Countries with fast-growing economies and exports are likely to be able to sustain higher debt levels.

The World Bank classifies countries by their level of indebtedness for the purpose of developing debt management strategies. The most severely indebted countries may be eligible for debt relief under special programs, such as the HIPC Debt Initiative. Indebted countries may also apply to the Paris and London Clubs for renegotiation of obligations to public and private creditors. In 2002, countries with a present value of debt service greater than 220 percent of exports or 80 percent of GNI were classified as severely indebted, countries that were not severely indebted but whose present value of debt service exceeded 132 percent of exports or 48 percent of GNI were classified as moderately indebted, and countries that did not fall into either group were classified as less indebted.

• **Indebtedness classification** refers to assessment on a three-point scale: severely indebted (S), moderately indebted (M), and less indebted (L). • **Present value of debt** is the sum of short-term external debt plus the discounted sum of total debt service payments due on public, publicly guaranteed, and private nonguaranteed long-term external debt over the life of existing loans. • **Public and publicly guaranteed debt service** is the sum of principal repayments and interest actually paid in foreign currency, goods, or services on long-term obligations of public debtors and long-term private obligations guaranteed by a public entity. • **Multilateral debt service** is the repayment of principal and interest to the World Bank, regional development banks, and other multilateral and intergovernmental agencies. • **Short-term debt** includes all debt having an original maturity of one year or less and interest in arrears on long-term debt.

4.17a

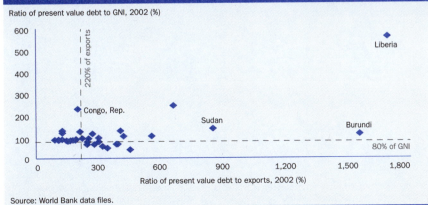

When the present value of a country's external debt exceeds 220 percent of exports or 80 percent of GNI the World Bank classifies it as severely indebted

Ratio of present value debt to GNI, 2002 (%)

Source: World Bank data files.

The main sources of external debt information are reports to the World Bank through its Debtor Reporting System from member countries that have received IBRD loans or IDA credits. Additional information has been drawn from the files of the World Bank and the IMF. The data on GNI and exports of goods and services are from the World Bank's national accounts files and the IMF's Balance of Payments database. Summary tables of the external debt of developing countries are published annually in the World Bank's *Global Development Finance* and on its *Global Development Finance* CD-ROM.

5 | STATES AND MARKETS

Successful development requires that states complement markets, not substitute for them. States should focus on providing a good business environment—in which contracts are enforced, markets function, basic infrastructure is provided, and people (especially poor people) are empowered to participate. Government institutions can support the development of markets in many ways—by providing information, fostering competition, enforcing contracts, and helping to make credit available to entrepreneurs. By leveling the playing field, governments create opportunities for poor people to participate in markets and improve their standards of living and give them hope for a better future for their children.

Good governance matters for long-term growth, but good policies and effective government spending also have immediate effects on people. Many governments are working with service providers and beneficiaries to improve public service delivery. For example, in Bangalore, India, a civil society group introduced report cards in 1994 rating user experiences with public services. The reports of poor quality and corruption were widely publicized, leading to improvements in service delivery and public governance.

This section covers a broad range of indicators showing how effective and accountable government, together with energetic private initiative, produces employment opportunities and services that empower poor people. Its 12 tables cover three cross-cutting development themes: private sector development, public sector policies, and infrastructure, information, and telecommunications.

Creating the conditions for private sector development

Investment is the foundation of growth, and most investment comes from the private sector. But governments play an important role in providing a predictable environment in which people, ideas, and money work together productively and efficiently. This allows private firms operating in competitive markets to be the engines of growth and job creation, providing opportunities to escape poverty.

Governments around the world are expanding opportunities for improved investment and business climates. State-owned enterprises are being privatized, trade barriers are being reduced, and improvements in regulations that enhance business activity are contributing to greater business opportunities and growth.

Investment in infrastructure—whether in power, transport, housing, telecommunications, or water and sanitation—enables businesses to grow. And when private firms participate in infrastructure, bringing with them capital and know-how, they can improve access to basic infrastructure services, a key to reducing poverty.

In developing countries private firms participate mainly in telecommunications and energy, and in many countries investment has been robust. In Chile in 1990–95 investment in telecommunications projects with private participation totaled about $150 million, but in 1996–2002 it increased tenfold, to almost $1,600 million. India also saw a dramatic increase in private participation in energy investment, which soared from $2,888 million in 1990–95 to $9,680 million in 1996–2002. Substantial increases in investment with private participation have also occurred in water and sanitation. In China these investments rose from $68 million in 1990–95 to $3,886 million in 1996–2002 (table 5.1).

The case for creating a good investment climate (sound macroeconomic framework, and legal and regulatory framework, good governance to overcome bureaucratic inefficiencies, and access to key financial and infrastructure services) is simple: an economy needs a predictable environment in which people, ideas, and money can work together productively and efficiently. In the context of a sound macroeconomic framework, a good investment climate strengthens governance and overcomes bureaucratic inefficiencies, improves access to key financial and infrastructure services, and provides a sound legal and regulatory framework for enterprises that promotes competition. Countries should focus on improving the investment climate for domestic entrepreneurs, but a better investment climate will also attract foreign investors. And countries that receive more foreign investment—an important conduit for new technologies, management experience, and access to markets—enjoy faster growth and greater poverty reduction.

External perceptions of the investment climate are reflected in risk ratings, and changes in sovereign risk ratings may affect country risk and stock returns. One example is the Euromoney creditworthiness ratings, which rank the risk of investing in an economy from 0 (high risk) to 100 (low risk). Although many factors determine the level of foreign investment, countries with high risk, such as the Democratic Republic of Congo, at 18, and Haiti, at 24, have very low foreign direct investment—0.6 percent of gross domestic product (GDP) for the Democratic Republic of Congo and 0.2 percent for Haiti. Countries with low perceived risk, such as the Czech Republic, at 66, and Slovenia, at 76, have much higher levels of foreign direct investment—13.4 percent for the Czech Republic and about 8.5 percent for Slovenia (see table 5.1 for data on foreign direct investment and table 5.2 for credit and risk ratings). Countries with low perceived risk also have large stock markets relative to their GDP. Market capitalization is about 74 percent of GDP in Chile, 93 percent in Australia, and 131 percent in Malaysia (table 5.4).

The World Bank's *Doing Business* database identifies regulations that enhance or constrain business investment, productivity, and growth, providing indicators of the cost of doing business (see http://rru.worldbank.org/DoingBusiness/default.aspx). The business environment in a country is determined by many factors, including regulation of new entry, access to credit markets, contract enforcement, insolvency procedures and cost, and labor regulations (several indicators for these areas are included in table 5.3). A new business environment indicator from the *Doing Business* database is the employment laws index, constructed by examining the detailed provisions of labor laws (table 5.3).

Public sector policies and institutions can improve service delivery—and private sector business activities

Improving people's standard of living by ensuring access to essential services such as health, education, safety, water, sanitation, and electricity is widely viewed as government's responsibility. An efficient and accountable public sector has institutions that are responsive to citizens, provide information, deliver services efficiently and equitably, and help to enforce people's rights. Making services work better, especially for poor people who often do not get their fair share of public spending on services, is a challenge that can be met by governments, citizens, and private service providers working together.

Measuring the quality of public sector governance is difficult. For example, for public goods, including public service delivery, it is difficult to exclude anyone from benefiting from them, so individuals adopt a "free rider" position, resulting in fewer resources being allocated to public goods. Another example is measurement of some dimensions of governance, such as corruption. Corruption is almost impossible to measure directly because of its illegal and clandestine nature. And although no international benchmarks of good governance have been established, and *World Development Indicators* does not report on national governance measures, research shows a strong positive correlation between the quality of institutions and economic growth. A related finding is that as countries become richer, institutions and governance do not necessarily improve. But there is a strong positive causal effect going from better governance to higher per capita incomes (Kaufmann and Kraay 2002).

Despite the difficulty of measuring the quality of institutions and governance, several international and regional initiatives are under way to identify trends and the links to development:

- **Country Policy and Institutional Assessments** by the World Bank include ratings covering economic management, structural policies, policies for social inclusion and equity, and public sector management and institutions. Public sector management and institutions include measures of property rights and rule-based governance, quality of budgetary and financial management, efficiency of revenue mobilization, quality of public administration, and transparency, accountability, and corruption of the public sector. These assessments are calculated for World Bank member countries that are eligible for lending by the International Development Association (IDA) (see www.worldbank.org/ida). The African Development Bank conducts similar assessments.

- **Worldwide Governance Indicators** from the World Bank Institute measure broad dimensions of governance such as voice and accountability, political instability and violence, government effectiveness, regulatory burden, rule of law, and control of corruption. The database covers 199 countries and territories and draws on 25 sources. Aggregating data from many sources reduces the measurement error from any single source. The database

5a

Employment laws index, range 0 (less rigid) to 100 (very rigid)

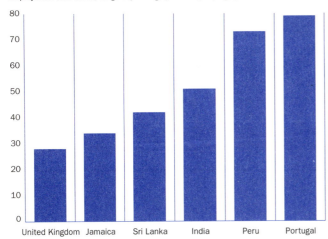

Factors such as the legal tradition (common law, French legal origin) and other political and efficiency considerations determine every country's labor regulations.
Source: *Doing Business* database.

includes point estimates and margins of error, to help interpret the estimates (see www.worldbank.org/wbi/governance/govdata2002/).

- *Business Environment and Enterprise Performance Surveys* are a joint European Bank for Reconstruction and Development and World Bank survey covering 22 countries. Survey questions cover issues related to bureaucratic red tape and corruption (see http://info.worldbank.org/governance/beeps/).
- *African Peer Review Mechanism (APRM),* launched by the New Partnership for Africa's Development, addresses four dimensions of governance: democracy and political governance, economic governance and management, corporate governance, and socioeconomic development. Sixteen countries have formally joined the APRM (see http://www.touchtech.biz/nepad/).
- *Code of Good Practices on Fiscal Transparency* was adopted by the International Monetary Fund (IMF) in 1998 and updated in 2001. Countries volunteer to prepare a Fiscal Report on Standards and Codes. Key requirements of transparency covered in the reports include roles and responsibilities in government; full information disclosure to the public on fiscal activities; open procedures for budget preparation, execution, and reporting; and fiscal information prepared according to internationally accepted standards of data quality and integrity (see http://www.imf.org/external/np/rosc/rosc.asp).

Government functions and policies affect many areas of social and economic life: health and education, natural resources and environmental protection, fiscal and monetary stability, and flows of trade. Data related to these topics are presented in the respective sections. This section provides data on key public sector activities: tax policies, exchange rates, and defense expenditures (tables 5.6–5.8).

Taxes are the principle source of revenue for most governments. They are levied mainly on income, profits, capital gains, goods and services, and exports and imports. (Nontax revenue is also important in some economies; see table 4.13.) A comparison of tax levels across countries provides an overview of the fiscal obligations and incentives facing the private sector. Central government tax revenues range from 2–3 percent of GDP in Myanmar to more than 35 percent in Croatia, Israel, and Slovenia (table 5.6).

The level and progressivity of taxes on personal and corporate income influence incentives to work and invest. Marginal tax rates on individual income range from 0 percent to 50 percent or more. Most marginal tax rates on corporate income are in the 20–30 percent range (table 5.6).

Tapping the benefits of infrastructure, information, and telecommunications

Infrastructure has become an increasingly important part of the World Bank Group's development agenda and is central to the Bank's efforts to help achieve the Millennium Development Goals (tables 1.2–1.4 and *World view*). There is widespread recognition of the key role that infrastructure plays in helping to achieve these goals. Better quality infrastructure—and better access to it—contribute to the success of manufacturing and agricultural businesses by strengthening employment prospects, productivity, and growth. Roads, rails, power, communication, and water and sanitation systems deliver services that promote better health and education. Better housing increases people's earning capacity and assets. And good transportation and schooling advance gender equality and the empowerment of women (table 1.5). New information and communications technologies offer vast opportunities for economic growth, improved health, better service delivery, learning through distance education, and social and cultural advances.

Efficient transport is critical to the development of competitive economies (table 5.9). But measuring progress in transport is difficult. Data for most transport sectors are often not strictly comparable across countries that do not consistently follow common definitions and specifications. Moreover, the data do not indicate the quality and level of service, which depend on such factors as maintenance budgets, the availability of trained personnel, geographic and climatic conditions, and incentives and competition to provide the best service at the lowest cost. Recognizing the need for better data on infrastructure for analysis and project planning, World Bank staff are developing a new database on infrastructure. *World Development Indicators* will report these data as they become available.

New information and communications technologies are helping people everywhere improve their quality of life by creating, using, and sharing information and knowledge (tables 5.10 and 5.11). Successful e-government applications such as Citizen Service Centers in Brazil; income tax on line in Brazil, Jordan, Mexico, and Singapore; and new business registration in China, Jamaica, and Jordan have resulted in more convenience, less corruption, lower costs, and greater transparency. The Internet has spread to every corner of the world, starting with only 8 countries online in 1988 to 209 countries by 2003. But many countries still have a long way to go. In some countries, such as Bangladesh, Chad, Ethiopia, Myanmar, and Tajikistan, only 1–2 people per 1,000 have access to the Internet (table 5.11).

5.1 Private sector investment

	Domestic credit to private sector		Foreign direct investment		Investment in infrastructure projects with private participation[a]							
									$ millions			
	% of GDP		% of GDP		Telecommunications		Energy		Transport		Water and sanitation	
	1990	2002	1990	2002	1990–95	1996–2002	1990–95	1996–2002	1990–95	1996–2002	1990–95	1996–2002
Afghanistan	..	..	..	..	..	70.0	..	..	..	..	..	..
Albania	..	6.8	0.0	2.8	..	283.2	..	8.0	..	..	..	..
Algeria	44.4	6.8	0.0	1.9	..	501.5	2,300.0	..	..	..	..	..
Angola	..	4.7	–3.3	11.7	..	75.3	..	..	..	..	..	..
Argentina	15.6	15.3	1.3	0.8	11,907.0	13,452.2	12,035.1	13,470.3	5,991.7	8,385.5	5,166.0	3,071.5
Armenia	40.4	6.9	..	4.7	..	468.4	..	12.0	..	50.0	..	..
Australia	64.2	89.8	2.6	4.1	..	..	..	..	..	..	..	..
Austria	91.6	106.4	0.4	0.4	..	..	..	..	..	..	..	..
Azerbaijan	10.8	5.6	..	22.9	14.0	144.6	..	375.2	..	..	..	..
Bangladesh	16.7	28.9	0.0	0.1	146.0	594.4	..	1,040.2	..	25.0	..	..
Belarus	..	9.1	..	1.7	10.0	180.3	..	500.0	..	..	..	..
Belgium	37.0	76.3	4.1	..	..	..	..	..	..	..	..	..
Benin	20.3	11.8	3.4	1.5	..	90.4	..	..	..	..	..	..
Bolivia	24.0	51.4	0.6	8.7	38.0	808.9	252.4	2,718.2	..	185.3	..	682.0
Bosnia and Herzegovina	..	36.3	..	5.2	..	..	..	..	..	..	..	..
Botswana	9.4	18.4	2.5	0.7	..	80.0	..	..	..	..	..	..
Brazil	38.9	35.5	0.2	3.7	..	70,824.6	613.6	48,631.8	1,349.4	19,577.8	155.3	3,019.0
Bulgaria	7.2	18.4	0.5	3.9	64.0	547.3	..	..	..	..	..	152.0
Burkina Faso	16.8	13.5	0.0	0.3	..	36.6	..	5.6	..	..	..	..
Burundi	13.7	26.1	0.1	0.0	0.5	15.6	..	..	..	..	..	..
Cambodia	..	6.8	0.0	1.3	31.6	155.7	..	123.2	120.0	72.2	..	..
Cameroon	26.7	10.2	–1.0	1.0	..	266.1	..	91.9	30.8	95.0	..	..
Canada	75.9	82.2	1.3	2.9	..	..	..	..	..	..	..	..
Central African Republic	7.2	5.7	0.0	0.4	1.1	..	..	..	..	..	0.7	..
Chad	7.3	4.1	0.5	45.0	..	13.0	..	..	..	..	..	..
Chile	47.2	68.1	2.2	2.7	148.9	1,574.8	2,260.0	6,457.3	539.9	6,709.6	67.5	3,886.1
China	87.7	136.5	1.0	3.9	..	13,024.7	6,113.5	14,301.6	6,219.8	15,849.8	104.0	1,992.4
Hong Kong, China	163.7	150.1	..	7.9	..	..	..	..	..	..	..	..
Colombia	30.8	25.1	1.2	2.5	1,551.2	1,551.0	1,813.2	5,762.2	1,008.8	1,597.4	..	330.0
Congo, Dem. Rep.	1.8	0.7	–0.2	0.6	..	369.7	..	..	..	..	..	..
Congo, Rep.	15.7	2.9	0.0	11.0	4.6	111.9	..	325.0	..	..	..	..
Costa Rica	15.8	30.1	2.8	3.9	..	..	76.3	243.1	..	161.0	..	..
Côte d'Ivoire	36.5	14.8	0.4	2.0	..	827.4	147.2	223.0	..	178.0	..	..
Croatia	..	51.6	..	4.4	..	1,425.5	..	375.6	..	672.2	..	298.7
Cuba	..	..	..	..	371.0	60.0	..	165.0	..	..	..	600.0
Czech Republic	..	33.4	..	13.4	876.0	7,960.9	356.0	4,718.9	263.7	126.7	36.5	314.6
Denmark	52.2	146.4	0.8	3.7	..	..	..	..	..	..	..	..
Dominican Republic	27.5	40.2	1.9	4.4	10.0	433.2	372.5	1,936.3	..	833.9	..	..
Ecuador	13.6	27.9	1.2	5.2	51.2	728.8	..	310.0	12.5	886.8	..	550.0
Egypt, Arab Rep.	30.6	60.6	1.7	0.7	..	2,895.4	..	1,378.0	..	1,057.2	6.0	..
El Salvador	20.1	40.3	0.0	1.5	..	910.7	106.0	879.2	..	..	..	..
Eritrea	..	32.4	..	3.3	..	40.0	..	..	..	..	..	..
Estonia	20.2	29.2	2.1	4.4	211.7	629.0	..	26.5	..	299.4	..	81.0
Ethiopia	19.5	26.7	0.1	1.2	..	..	..	..	..	..	..	..
Finland	86.5	60.0	0.6	6.2	..	..	..	..	..	..	..	..
France	96.1	87.2	1.1	3.6	..	..	..	..	..	..	..	..
Gabon	13.0	12.0	1.2	2.5	..	35.0	..	624.8	..	46.7	..	..
Gambia, The	11.0	17.3	0.0	12.0	..	6.6	..	..	..	..	..	..
Georgia	..	8.1	0.0	4.9	21.6	43.8	..	36.0	..	..	..	..
Germany	90.6	118.9	0.2	1.9	..	..	..	..	..	..	..	..
Ghana	4.9	12.0	0.3	0.8	25.0	436.1	..	132.8	..	10.0	..	..
Greece	36.3	67.1	1.2	0.0	..	..	..	..	..	..	..	..
Guatemala	14.2	19.1	0.6	0.5	20.0	1,673.3	134.8	1,298.4	..	33.8	..	..
Guinea	3.5	3.8	0.6	0.0	45.0	75.3	36.4	..	..	..	..	..
Guinea-Bissau	22.0	3.0	0.8	0.5	..	..	23.2	..	..	..	..	..
Haiti	12.6	18.0	0.0	0.2	..	19.5	4.7	..	..	..	..	..

Private sector investment

	Domestic credit to private sector		Foreign direct investment		Investment in infrastructure projects with private participation [a]							
									$ millions			
	% of GDP		% of GDP		Telecommunications		Energy		Transport		Water and sanitation	
	1990	2002	1990	2002	1990–95	1996–2002	1990–95	1996–2002	1990–95	1996–2002	1990–95	1996–2002
Honduras	31.1	40.7	1.4	2.2	..	71.1	95.3	86.8	..	130.5	..	220.0
Hungary	46.6	35.3	0.9	1.3	3,510.9	5,298.9	2,156.7	1,906.1	1,004.0	135.0	10.9	167.6
India	25.2	32.6	0.1	0.6	720.5	14,950.0	2,888.5	9,680.5	126.9	1,969.1	..	216.0
Indonesia	46.9	22.3	1.0	–0.9	3,549.0	9,215.5	3,202.5	7,534.7	1,204.9	2,314.6	3.8	919.5
Iran, Islamic Rep.	32.5	34.3	–0.3	0.0	5.0	28.0	..	..	..	..	..	..
Iraq	..	..	..	..	..	..	..	..	..	..	..	..
Ireland	47.6	110.3	1.3	20.3	..	..	..	..	..	..	..	..
Israel	57.6	97.8	0.3	1.6	..	..	..	..	..	..	..	..
Italy	56.5	82.3	0.6	1.2	..	..	..	..	..	..	..	..
Jamaica	36.1	15.7	3.0	6.1	..	494.0	289.0	201.0	30.0	390.0	..	..
Japan	195.1	175.3	0.1	0.2	..	..	..	..	..	..	..	..
Jordan	72.3	73.5	0.9	0.6	43.0	967.9	..	..	..	182.0	..	209.0
Kazakhstan	..	18.6	0.4	10.5	30.0	1,849.5	..	2,125.0	..	..	..	40.0
Kenya	32.8	23.4	0.7	0.4	..	107.0	..	171.5	..	53.4	..	..
Korea, Dem. Rep.	..	..	..	..	..	..	..	..	..	..	..	..
Korea, Rep.	65.5	115.6	0.3	0.4	2,650.0	17,600.0	..	2,690.0	2,280.0	5,950.0	..	..
Kuwait	52.1	73.8	0.0	0.0	..	..	..	..	..	..	..	..
Kyrgyz Republic	..	4.2	0.0	0.3	..	94.0	..	..	..	..	..	..
Lao PDR	1.0	8.4	0.7	1.5	..	185.5	..	535.5	..	100.0	..	..
Latvia	..	29.0	0.6	4.5	230.0	894.9	..	177.1	..	75.0	..	..
Lebanon	79.4	90.8	0.2	1.5	100.0	550.9	..	..	..	200.0	..	..
Lesotho	15.8	14.3	2.8	11.3	..	33.5	..	..	..	..	..	..
Liberia	30.9	3.2	0.0	–11.6	..	..	..	..	..	..	..	..
Libya	31.0	18.0	..	..	..	..	..	..	..	..	..	..
Lithuania	..	14.2	0.0	5.2	74.0	1,345.0	..	20.0	..	..	..	..
Macedonia, FYR	..	17.7	..	2.0	..	607.3	..	..	..	..	..	..
Madagascar	16.9	9.3	0.7	0.2	5.0	10.1	..	..	..	20.3	..	..
Malawi	10.9	4.1	1.2	0.3	8.0	25.5	..	..	..	6.0	..	..
Malaysia	108.5	146.1	5.3	3.4	2,630.0	3,241.6	6,909.5	2,131.6	4,657.6	7,919.0	3,986.7	1,105.5
Mali	12.8	17.6	0.2	3.0	..	42.7	0.1	747.0	..	..	..	..
Mauritania	43.5	31.7	0.7	1.2	..	99.6	..	..	..	..	..	..
Mauritius	35.6	61.3	1.7	0.6	..	365.6	..	109.3	..	42.6	..	..
Mexico	17.5	12.6	1.0	2.3	18,031.0	17,426.2	1.0	5,759.1	7,910.3	5,432.5	312.1	331.5
Moldova	5.9	17.6	0.0	6.8	..	84.6	..	85.3	..	..	..	..
Mongolia	19.0	18.8	..	7.0	13.1	20.4	..	..	..	..	..	..
Morocco	34.0	54.4	0.6	1.2	..	3,643.0	2,300.0	4,819.9	..	..	..	1,000.0
Mozambique	17.6	2.1	0.4	11.3	..	44.0	..	1,200.0	..	959.7	..	0.6
Myanmar	4.7	12.1	..	..	4.0	..	394.0	..	..	50.0	..	..
Namibia	22.6	48.4	..	..	18.0	4.0	..	5.0	..	450.0	..	..
Nepal	12.8	30.7	0.0	0.2	..	45.6	131.4	137.2	..	..	..	..
Netherlands	80.0	147.9	3.6	6.8	..	..	..	..	..	..	..	..
New Zealand	76.0	118.1	4.0	1.4	..	..	..	..	..	..	..	..
Nicaragua	112.6	30.8	0.0	4.3	9.9	162.2	..	347.4	..	104.0	..	..
Niger	12.3	5.0	1.6	0.4	..	52.7	..	..	..	..	..	4.9
Nigeria	9.4	17.8	2.1	2.9	..	982.7	..	225.0	..	22.8	..	..
Norway	81.7	86.3	0.9	0.5	..	..	..	..	..	..	..	..
Oman	22.9	38.6	1.4	0.2	..	..	204.5	998.3	..	546.1	..	..
Pakistan	27.7	27.9	0.6	1.4	602.0	343.0	3,417.3	2,519.7	299.6	118.7	..	..
Panama	46.7	97.6	2.6	0.5	..	1,429.2	..	1,064.9	409.9	806.0	..	25.0
Papua New Guinea	28.6	13.7	4.8	1.8	..	..	..	65.0	..	..	..	175.0
Paraguay	15.8	24.2	1.5	–0.4	48.1	204.4	..	..	..	58.0	..	..
Peru	11.8	23.1	0.2	4.2	2,568.7	5,412.0	1,207.8	3,095.7	6.6	315.8	..	56.0
Philippines	22.3	36.4	1.2	1.4	1,279.0	6,700.0	6,831.3	7,013.1	300.0	2,007.5	..	5,867.7
Poland	21.1	28.8	0.2	2.2	479.0	11,070.3	145.0	2,154.8	3.1	705.9	..	22.1
Portugal	49.1	147.9	3.7	3.5	..	..	..	..	..	..	..	..
Puerto Rico	..	..	..	..	..	..	..	..	..	..	..	..

	Domestic credit to private sector		Foreign direct investment		Investment in infrastructure projects with private participation[a]							
	% of GDP		% of GDP		$ millions							
					Telecommunications		Energy		Transport		Water and sanitation	
	1990	2002	1990	2002	1990–95	1996–2002	1990–95	1996–2002	1990–95	1996–2002	1990–95	1996–2002
Romania	..	8.3	0.0	2.5	5.0	2,735.0	..	100.0	..	23.4	..	1,040.0
Russian Federation	..	17.6	*0.0*	0.9	918.0	6,467.2	1,100.0	2,295.3	..	515.4	..	108.0
Rwanda	6.9	10.3	0.3	0.2	..	15.6	..	..	..	..	..	..
Saudi Arabia	54.7	58.2	..	..	..	..	..	..	..	..	..	..
Senegal	26.5	19.6	1.0	1.9	..	406.8	..	124.0	..	..	..	6.3
Serbia and Montenegro	..	..	..	3.0	..	1,929.5	..	..	..	..	..	..
Sierra Leone	3.2	3.5	5.0	0.6	..	23.5	..	..	..	..	..	..
Singapore	96.8	115.5	15.1	7.0	..	..	..	..	..	..	..	..
Slovak Republic	..	40.6	..	16.9	118.6	1,754.1	..	3,184.6	..	..	..	..
Slovenia	*34.9*	39.2	*0.9*	8.5	..	..	..	..	..	..	..	..
Somalia	..	..	0.6	..	..	2.0	..	..	..	..	..	..
South Africa	81.0	131.7	..	0.7	1,072.8	10,654.8	3.0	1,244.3	..	1,874.1	..	212.5
Spain	80.2	111.1	2.7	3.3	..	..	..	..	..	..	..	..
Sri Lanka	19.6	28.5	0.5	1.5	43.6	849.6	21.7	286.6	..	240.0	..	..
Sudan	4.8	5.0	0.0	4.7	..	6.0	..	..	..	..	..	..
Swaziland	20.7	14.3	3.4	3.8	..	33.6	..	..	..	..	..	..
Sweden	124.4	*43.6*	0.8	4.9	..	..	..	..	..	..	..	..
Switzerland	167.9	159.0	2.6	1.3	..	..	..	..	..	..	..	..
Syrian Arab Republic	7.5	8.0	0.6	1.1	..	130.0	..	..	..	..	..	..
Tajikistan	..	18.8	*0.5*	0.7	..	1.0	..	..	..	..	..	..
Tanzania	13.9	6.3	0.0	2.6	30.1	321.0	6.0	490.0	..	23.0	..	..
Thailand	83.4	102.5	2.9	0.7	4,814.0	5,116.2	2,059.6	6,981.0	2,395.9	546.4	153.0	347.5
Togo	22.6	13.3	1.1	5.4	..	5.0	..	..	..	..	..	..
Trinidad and Tobago	44.7	40.7	2.2	7.6	47.0	146.7	..	207.0	..	..	..	120.0
Tunisia	*66.2*	68.6	0.6	3.8	..	277.0	627.0	265.0	..	..	..	..
Turkey	16.7	14.9	0.5	0.6	190.3	7,875.4	2,478.0	5,167.2	..	724.8	..	942.0
Turkmenistan	..	*2.3*	..	1.3	..	..	..	..	..	..	..	..
Uganda	*4.0*	6.7	0.0	2.6	8.8	204.1	..	..	..	..	..	..
Ukraine	*2.6*	18.0	*0.3*	1.7	100.6	1,299.9	..	160.0	..	..	..	..
United Arab Emirates	37.4	55.9	..	..	..	..	..	..	..	..	..	..
United Kingdom	115.8	142.6	3.4	1.8	..	..	..	..	..	..	..	..
United States	93.5	140.6	0.8	0.4	..	..	..	..	..	..	..	..
Uruguay	32.4	66.4	0.0	1.5	19.0	57.7	86.0	330.0	96.0	621.2	10.0	351.0
Uzbekistan	..	..	*0.1*	0.8	2.5	367.4	..	..	..	..	..	..
Venezuela, RB	25.4	9.8	0.9	0.7	4,603.3	6,446.7	..	133.0	100.0	268.0	..	44.0
Vietnam	*2.5*	43.1	2.8	4.0	128.0	18.0	..	2,215.5	10.0	115.0	..	212.8
West Bank and Gaza	..	..	..	..	65.0	410.6	..	150.0	..	..	..	9.5
Yemen, Rep.	6.1	6.2	−2.7	1.1	25.0	340.0	..	..	..	190.0	..	..
Zambia	8.9	6.2	6.2	5.3	..	56.9	..	289.4	..	..	..	..
Zimbabwe	23.0	37.0	−0.1	0.3	..	46.0	..	603.0	18.0	70.0	..	..
World	**97.5 w**	**118.1 w**	**1.0 w**	**2.0 w**	.. s	.. s	.. s	.. s	.. s	.. s	.. s	.. s
Low income	26.5	*26.5*	0.4	1.2	5,395.3	31,713.9	10,251.3	29,334.5	1,810.2	6,518.8	4.5	1,535.1
Middle income	42.9	62.2	0.9	2.8	56,414.0	228,094.2	53,083.3	156,285.5	32,299.2	80,769.9	10,008.0	27,245.8
Lower middle income	50.3	76.7	0.6	2.7	13,427.6	152,884.0	28,718.7	112,141.9	11,323.0	47,579.9	418.3	17,377.6
Upper middle income	27.3	*34.5*	1.4	2.9	42,986.4	75,210.2	24,364.6	44,143.6	20,976.2	33,190.0	9,589.7	9,868.2
Low & middle income	39.3	*55.9*	0.8	2.5	61,809.3	259,808.1	63,334.6	185,620.0	34,109.4	87,288.7	10,012.5	28,780.9
East Asia & Pacific	74.0	*116.5*	1.6	3.1	12,481.7	37,827.2	25,510.4	40,901.2	14,908.2	28,974.5	4,247.5	10,620.4
Europe & Central Asia	..	21.9	*0.4*	2.9	6,856.2	55,357.0	6,235.7	23,427.6	1,270.8	3,327.8	47.4	3,166.0
Latin America & Carib.	28.4	*24.4*	0.7	2.7	39,482.4	123,980.3	19,482.2	93,198.0	17,455.1	46,534.7	5,710.9	13,335.7
Middle East & N. Africa	39.5	50.2	0.6	*0.9*	238.0	9,744.3	5,431.5	7,611.2	..	2,225.3	6.0	1,218.5
South Asia	24.6	*31.8*	0.1	0.7	1,512.1	16,852.6	6,458.9	13,664.2	426.5	2,352.8	..	216.0
Sub-Saharan Africa	42.4	53.5	..	2.5	1,238.9	16,046.7	215.9	6,817.8	48.8	3,873.6	0.7	224.3
High income	107.7	133.1	1.0	1.9	..	..	..	..	..	..	..	..
Europe EMU	79.8	102.8	1.1	5.0	..	..	..	..	..	..	..	..

a. Data refer to total for the period shown.

About the data

Private sector development and investment—that is, tapping private sector initiative and investment for socially useful purposes—are critical for poverty reduction. In parallel with public sector efforts, private investment, especially in competitive markets, has tremendous potential to contribute to growth. Private markets serve as the engine of productivity growth, creating productive jobs and higher incomes. And with government playing a complementary role of regulation, funding, and provision of services, private initiative and investment can help provide the basic services and conditions that empower the poor—by improving health, education, and infrastructure.

Credit is an important link in the money transmission process; it finances production, consumption, and capital formation, which in turn affect the level of economic activity. The data on domestic credit to the private sector are taken from the banking survey of the International Monetary Fund's (IMF) *International Financial Statistics* or, when data are unavailable, from its monetary survey. The monetary survey includes monetary authorities (the central bank), deposit money banks, and other banking institutions, such as finance companies, development banks, and savings and loan institutions. In some cases credit to the private sector may include credit to state-owned or partially state-owned enterprises.

The statistics on foreign direct investment are based on balance of payments data reported by the IMF, supplemented by data on net foreign direct investment reported by the Organisation for Economic Co-operation and Development and official national sources. (For a detailed discussion of data on foreign direct investment, see *About the data* for table 6.7).

Private participation in infrastructure has made important contributions to easing fiscal constraints, improving the efficiency of infrastructure services,

and extending their delivery to poor people. The privatization trend in infrastructure that began in the 1970s and 1980s took off in the 1990s. Developing countries have been at the head of this wave, pioneering better approaches to providing infrastructure services and reaping the benefits of greater competition and customer focus. In 1990–2002 more than 130 developing countries introduced private participation in at least one infrastructure sector, awarding almost 2,500 projects attracting investment commitments of $750 billion.

The data on investment in infrastructure projects with private participation refer to all investment (public and private) in projects in which a private company assumes operating risk during the operating period or assumes development and operating risk during the contract period. Foreign state-owned companies are considered private entities for the purposes of this measure. The data are from the World Bank's Private Participation in Infrastructure (PPI) Project Database, which tracks almost 2,500 projects, newly owned or managed by private companies, that reached financial closure in low- and middle-income economies in 1990–2002. For more information, see http://www.worldbank.org/privatesector/ppi/ppi_database.htm.

Definitions

• **Domestic credit to private sector** refers to financial resources provided to the private sector—such as through loans, purchases of nonequity securities, and trade credits and other accounts receivable—that establish a claim for repayment. For some countries these claims include credit to public enterprises. • **Foreign direct investment** is net inflows of investment to acquire a lasting management interest (10 percent or more of voting stock) in an enterprise operating in an economy other than that of the investor. It is the sum of equity capital, reinvestment of earnings, other long-term capital, and short-term capital as shown in the balance of payments. • **Investment in infrastructure projects with private participation** covers infrastructure projects in telecommunications, energy (electricity and natural gas transmission and distribution), transport, and water and sanitation that have reached financial closure and directly or indirectly serve the public. Incinerators, movable assets, stand-alone solid waste projects, and small projects such as windmills are excluded. The types of projects included are operation and management contracts, operation and management contracts with major capital expenditure, greenfield projects (in which a private entity or a public-private joint venture builds and operates a new facility), and divestiture.

5.1a

Foreign direct investment has expanded rapidly in many developing countries, contributing to increased productivity

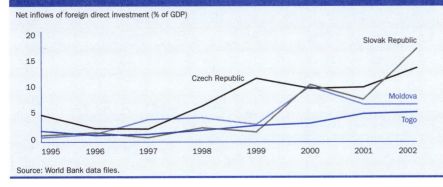

Net inflows of foreign direct investment (% of GDP)

Source: World Bank data files.

Data sources

The data on domestic credit are from the IMF's *International Financial Statistics.* The data on foreign direct investment are based on estimates compiled by the IMF in its *Balance of Payments Statistics Yearbook,* supplemented by World Bank staff estimates. The data on investment in infrastructure projects with private participation are from the World Bank's Private Participation in Infrastructure (PPI) Project Database (http://www.worldbank.org/privatesector/ppi/ppi_database.htm).

	Credit markets			Composite ICRG risk rating [a]	Institutional Investor credit rating [a]	Euromoney country credit-worthiness rating [a]	Moody's sovereign long-term debt rating [a]		Standard & Poor's sovereign long-term debt rating [a]	
	Creditor rights index range 0 (weak) to 4 (strong)	Public registry coverage borrowers per 1,000 adults	Private bureau coverage borrowers per 1,000 adults				Foreign currency	Domestic currency	Foreign currency	Domestic currency
	January 2003	January 2003	January 2003	December 2003	September 2003	September 2003	January 2004	January 2004	January 2004	January 2004
Afghanistan	..	..	..	..	7.6	7.8	..	..	..	..
Albania	3	0	0	66.8	17.0	34.5	..	..	..	..
Algeria	1	0	0	66.3	41.6	41.3	..	..	..	..
Angola	3	19	0	53.3	17.0	26.9	..	..	..	..
Argentina	1	202	645	64.0	18.4	25.8	Caa1	B3	SD	SD
Armenia	2	0	0	62.3	17.9	33.8	..	..	..	..
Australia	3	0	897	81.8	84.3	91.7	Aaa	Aaa	AAA	AAA
Austria	3	10	366	86.0	90.3	92.4	Aaa	Aaa	AAA	AAA
Azerbaijan	3	0	0	69.0	30.4	43.3	..	..	..	..
Bangladesh	2	2	0	63.0	28.6	38.3	..	..	..	..
Belarus	2	..	0	65.3	17.5	32.0	..	..	..	..
Belgium	2	82	50	85.3	87.2	90.9	Aa1	Aa1	AA+	AA+
Benin	1	2	0	..	20.2	30.9	..	..	B+	B+
Bolivia	2	88	213	65.8	27.5	37.5	B3	B3	B–	B–
Bosnia and Herzegovina	3	0	80	..	26.0	35.6	..	..	..	..
Botswana	3	0	615	79.8	62.2	60.3	A2	A1	A	A+
Brazil	1	60	602	65.5	37.1	47.6	B2	B2	B+	BB
Bulgaria	3	6	0	71.8	47.0	50.7	Ba2	Ba2	BB+	BBB
Burkina Faso	1	2	0	57.8	17.8	31.0	..	..	..	..
Burundi	1	1	0	..	10.5	25.0	..	..	..	..
Cambodia	2	0	0	..	18.7	35.0	..	..	..	..
Cameroon	1	1	0	62.0	19.9	31.3	..	..	B	B
Canada	1	0	976	85.8	90.3	92.1	Aaa	Aaa	AAA	AAA
Central African Republic	2	1	0	..	12.8	26.2	..	..	..	..
Chad	1	0	0	..	14.4	27.7	..	..	..	..
Chile	2	284	1,000	77.0	65.2	66.3	Baa1	A1	A	AA
China	2	4	0	77.3	59.9	61.5	A2	..	BBB	..
Hong Kong, China	4	0	242	82.0	67.8	80.6	A1	Aa3	A+	AA–
Colombia	0	0	269	63.5	37.2	47.2	Ba2	Baa2	BB	BBB
Congo, Dem. Rep.	2	0	0	47.0	7.3	18.4	..	..	..	..
Congo, Rep.	0	0	0	48.8	12.6	26.7	..	..	..	..
Costa Rica	1	10	78	72.0	44.4	54.8	Ba1	Ba1	BB	BB+
Côte d'Ivoire	1	2	0	55.8	15.7	26.6	..	..	..	..
Croatia	3	0	0	72.0	50.9	57.1	Baa3	Baa1	BBB–	BBB+
Cuba	..	..	..	60.3	12.3	12.0	Caa1	..	..	..
Czech Republic	3	12	163	77.8	65.6	66.1	A1	A1	A–	A+
Denmark	3	0	71	85.5	91.0	95.3	Aaa	Aaa	AAA	AAA
Dominican Republic	2	..	617	60.3	36.6	43.4	B2	B2	CCC	CCC
Ecuador	1	121	0	62.5	24.2	36.2	Caa2	Caa1	CCC+	CCC+
Egypt, Arab Rep.	1	..	0	66.0	41.1	49.2	Ba1	Baa1	BB+	BBB–
El Salvador	3	197	192	69.8	46.4	49.3	Baa3	Baa2	BB+	BB+
Eritrea	..	..	..	..	12.0	26.0	..	..	..	..
Estonia	..	..	..	75.0	61.5	64.5	A1	A1	A–	A–
Ethiopia	3	0	0	59.3	16.1	29.4	..	..	..	..
Finland	1	0	842	86.8	90.6	93.8	Aaa	Aaa	AAA	AAA
France	0	15	0	79.0	91.7	91.1	Aaa	Aaa	AAA	AAA
Gabon	..	..	..	65.3	22.7	34.1	..	..	..	..
Gambia, The	..	..	..	67.0	17.8	32.2	..	..	..	..
Georgia	..	0	0	..	18.4	26.5	..	..	..	..
Germany	3	6	813	81.8	86.8	90.3	Aaa	Aaa	AAA	AAA
Ghana	1	0	1	62.8	25.8	35.0	..	..	B+	B+
Greece	1	0	100	76.0	73.1	80.7	A1	A1	A+	A+
Guatemala	1	0	65	67.0	32.3	44.6	Ba2	Ba1	BB–	BB
Guinea	1	0	0	62.0	16.5	27.2	..	..	..	..
Guinea-Bissau	..	..	..	46.5	10.6	23.0	..	..	..	..
Haiti	2	2	0	52.0	15.8	24.4	..	..	..	..

	Credit markets			Composite ICRG risk rating[a]	Institutional Investor credit rating[a]	Euromoney country credit-worthiness rating[a]	Moody's sovereign long-term debt rating[a]		Standard & Poor's sovereign long-term debt rating[a]	
	Creditor rights index range 0 (weak) to 4 (strong)	Public registry coverage borrowers per 1,000 adults	Private bureau coverage borrowers per 1,000 adults				Foreign currency	Domestic currency	Foreign currency	Domestic currency
	January 2003	January 2003	January 2003	December 2003	September 2003	September 2003	January 2004	January 2004	January 2004	January 2004
Honduras	2	74	0	62.3	25.3	39.2	B2	B2	..	..
Hungary	2	0	17	76.5	65.4	68.8	A1	A1	A–	A
India	3	0	0	69.0	48.0	54.9	Ba1	Ba2	BB	BB+
Indonesia	2	4	0	60.8	30.3	40.0	B2	B2	B	B+
Iran, Islamic Rep.	2	..	0	70.5	36.6	45.1	..	..	..	..
Iraq	..	..	..	42.0	8.4	4.3	..	..	..	..
Ireland	1	0	917	87.3	87.5	92.3	Aaa	Aaa	AAA	AAA
Israel	3	0	64	72.5	53.4	68.0	A2	A2	A–	A+
Italy	1	63	482	80.0	83.1	86.9	Aa2	Aa2	AA	AA
Jamaica	2	0	0	69.5	27.8	43.3	B1	Ba2	B	B+
Japan	2	0	907	86.5	77.2	90.0	Aa1	A2	AA–	AA–
Jordan	1	30	0	71.0	38.5	44.1	Ba2	Baa3	BB	BBB
Kazakhstan	..	0	0	72.3	41.4	50.3	Baa3	Baa1	BB+	BBB
Kenya	4	0	526	65.8	24.6	36.1	..	..	..	..
Korea, Dem. Rep.	..	..	..	53.5	7.5	3.3	..	..	..	..
Korea, Rep.	3	0	672	80.8	68.5	67.7	A3	A3	A–	A+
Kuwait	2	0	207	86.3	79.2	73.9	A2	A2	A+	A+
Kyrgyz Republic	..	0	0	..	16.7	28.1	..	..	..	..
Lao PDR	0	0	0	..	19.8	33.0	..	..	..	..
Latvia	..	0	0	78.3	51.5	62.1	A2	A2	BBB+	A–
Lebanon	4	0	0	55.5	25.2	38.1	B2	B3	B–	B–
Lesotho	2	0	0	..	29.5	33.7	..	..	..	..
Liberia	..	..	..	36.0	6.6	11.6	..	..	..	..
Libya	..	..	..	74.0	34.2	21.9	..	..	..	..
Lithuania	..	9	0	76.5	55.6	62.0	A3	A3	BBB+	A–
Macedonia, FYR	3	3	0	..	25.3	36.1	..	..	..	..
Madagascar	2	3	0	60.0	15.8	28.0	..	..	..	..
Malawi	2	0	0	54.0	18.8	31.3	..	..	..	..
Malaysia	2	154	676	75.3	61.7	62.1	Baa1	A3	A–	A+
Mali	1	1	0	58.5	18.4	30.4	..	..	..	..
Mauritania	3	0	0	..	18.6	26.7	..	..	..	..
Mauritius	..	..	..	..	53.9	54.9	Baa2	A2	..	..
Mexico	0	0	562	71.5	54.8	61.1	Baa2	Baa1	BBB–	A–
Moldova	..	0	0	64.5	18.7	31.5	Caa1	Caa1	..	..
Mongolia	1	23	0	63.8	22.9	37.3	..	..	B	B
Morocco	1	..	0	75.0	49.4	53.8	Ba1	Ba1	BB	BBB
Mozambique	2	1	0	61.3	20.6	32.5	..	..	..	..
Myanmar	..	..	..	59.5	13.5	20.4	..	..	..	..
Namibia	..	0	..	76.5	39.8	24.5	..	..	..	..
Nepal	2	0	0	..	23.8	37.2	..	..	..	..
Netherlands	3	0	645	85.0	92.2	93.5	Aaa	Aaa	AAA	AAA
New Zealand	4	0	1,000	81.8	81.1	87.1	Aaa	Aaa	AA+	AAA
Nicaragua	4	83	0	54.3	18.0	24.2	Caa1	B3	..	..
Niger	1	1	0	57.5	14.7	30.5	..	..	..	..
Nigeria	4	0	0	57.0	20.2	33.5	..	..	..	..
Norway	2	0	1,000	90.5	92.9	97.8	Aaa	Aaa	AAA	AAA
Oman	0	0	0	81.0	56.5	61.3	Baa2	Baa2	BBB	BBB+
Pakistan	1	1	0	63.5	26.2	32.0	B2	B2	B	BB–
Panama	4	0	428	71.5	45.0	49.8	Ba1	..	BB	BB
Papua New Guinea	2	0	0	59.0	28.9	37.3	B1	B1	B	B+
Paraguay	2	0	..	62.5	22.4	34.7	Caa1	Caa1	SD	CCC
Peru	0	133	267	68.3	38.3	45.5	Ba3	Baa3	BB–	BB+
Philippines	1	0	33	69.3	43.8	51.3	Ba1	Baa3	BB	BBB
Poland	2	0	665	75.0	61.1	64.0	A2	A2	BBB+	A–
Portugal	1	610	30	78.5	80.4	84.3	Aa2	Aa2	AA	AA
Puerto Rico	1	0	643	..	..	..	..	..	..	..

	Credit markets			Composite ICRG risk rating[a]	Institutional Investor credit rating[a]	Euromoney country credit-worthiness rating[a]	Moody's sovereign long-term debt rating[a]		Standard & Poor's sovereign long-term debt rating[a]	
	Creditor rights index range 0 (weak) to 4 (strong)	Public registry coverage borrowers per 1,000 adults	Private bureau coverage borrowers per 1,000 adults				Foreign currency	Domestic currency	Foreign currency	Domestic currency
	January 2003	January 2003	January 2003	December 2003	September 2003	September 2003	January 2004	January 2004	January 2004	January 2004
Romania	0	1	0	70.5	41.3	49.8	Ba3	Ba3	BB	BB+
Russian Federation	2	0	0	75.0	45.1	49.0	Baa3	Baa3	BB	BB+
Rwanda	1	1	0	..	8.2	24.2	..	..	..	..
Saudi Arabia	2	0	0	76.5	52.4	65.7	Baa2	Baa1	A+	A+
Senegal	1	3	0	64.8	29.2	39.6	..	..	B+	B+
Serbia and Montenegro	2	0	0	55.3	16.1	31.5	..	..	..	..
Sierra Leone	2	0	0	51.3	8.5	22.2	..	..		
Singapore	3	0	640	87.5	84.2	89.1	Aaa	Aaa	AAA	AAA
Slovak Republic	..	3	0	74.3	57.8	59.1	A3	A3	BBB	A–
Slovenia	3	16	0	79.5	69.2	76.1	Aa3	Aa3	A+	AA
Somalia	..	..	..	45.5	6.5	13.2	..	..	..	..
South Africa	3	0	684	68.8	54.6	60.4	Baa2	A2	BBB	A
Spain	2	344	55	80.0	85.7	87.2	Aaa	Aaa	AA+	AA+
Sri Lanka	2	12	0	63.5	34.1	44.3	..	..	..	..
Sudan	..	..	..	54.3	10.5	26.4	..	..	..	..
Swaziland	..	..	..	..	30.7	33.1	..	..	..	..
Sweden	1	0	592	86.5	89.3	93.8	Aaa	Aaa	AA+	AAA
Switzerland	1	0	213	91.0	94.0	97.5	Aaa	Aaa	AAA	AAA
Syrian Arab Republic	..	0	0	70.3	22.7	33.5	..	..	..	..
Tajikistan	..	..	..	..	14.3	29.9	..	..	..	..
Tanzania	2	0	0	57.8	21.8	37.0	..	..	..	..
Thailand	3	0	127	76.5	56.9	59.5	Baa1	Baa1	BBB	A
Togo	2	..	0	58.3	17.3	28.1	..	..	..	..
Trinidad and Tobago	..	..	..	76.5	54.2	61.0	Baa3	Baa1	BBB	A–
Tunisia	0	6	0	72.8	52.6	57.7	Baa2	Baa2	BBB	A
Turkey	2	10	266	62.8	32.4	45.2	B1	B3	B+	B+
Turkmenistan	..	..	..	..	20.8	32.2	B2	B2	..	..
Uganda	..	0	0	62.3	20.1	37.8	..	..	..	..
Ukraine	2	0	0	68.8	32.5	39.0	B1	B1	B	B
United Arab Emirates	2	15	0	84.5	64.7	72.3	A2	..	..	..
United Kingdom	4	0	813	83.8	92.3	93.9	Aaa	Aaa	AAA	AAA
United States	1	0	1,000	75.8	92.8	96.6	Aaa	Aaa	AAA	AAA
Uruguay	..	65	630	64.5	27.3	39.8	B3	B3	B–	B–
Uzbekistan	2	0	0	..	20.5	33.9	..	..	..	..
Venezuela, RB	2	141	0	58.3	27.1	34.6	Caa1	Caa1	B–	B–
Vietnam	0	3	0	69.8	37.7	47.8	B1	..	BB–	BB
West Bank and Gaza	..	..	..	..	..	..	..	..	..	..
Yemen, Rep.	0	12	0	67.0	24.3	33.0	..	..	..	..
Zambia	1	0	0	53.0	15.3	26.3	..	..	..	..
Zimbabwe	4	0	0	34.3	11.0	22.6	..	..	..	..
World	**2 u**	**24 u**	**182 u**	**68.9 m**	**30.4 m**	**39.6 m**				
Low income	2	4	11	58.8	17.9	30.1				
Middle income	2	32	168	70.4	39.8	47.2				
Lower middle income	2	24	100	68.3	36.6	44.1				
Upper middle income	2	46	288	75.0	54.0	60.6				
Low & middle income	2	18	93	65.1	25.3	35.6				
East Asia & Pacific	2	19	84	66.6	29.6	38.7				
Europe & Central Asia	2	2	50	72.0	32.5	44.3				
Latin America & Carib.	2	77	293	65.0	30.0	43.3				
Middle East & N. Africa	1	6	0	70.5	38.5	44.1				
South Asia	2	3	0	63.5	27.4	37.8				
Sub-Saharan Africa	2	1	57	58.0	17.5	28.7				
High income	2	40	491	83.4	86.3	90.6				
Europe EMU	2	103	391	81.8	87.2	90.9				

a. This copyrighted material is reprinted with permission from the following data providers: PRS Group, Inc., 6320 Fly Road, Suite 102, East Syracuse, NY 13057; Institutional Investor Inc., 225 Park Ave. South, New York, NY 10003; Euromoney Publications PLC, Nestor House, Playhouse Yard, London EC4V 5EX, UK; Moody's Investors Service, 99 Church Street, New York, NY 10007; and Standard & Poor's Rating Services, The McGraw-Hill Companies, Inc., 1221 Avenue of the Americas, New York, NY 10020. Prior written consent from the original data providers cited must be obtained for third-party use of these data.

This year the table includes newly developed measures of the credit market: a creditor rights index, public credit registry coverage, and private credit bureau coverage. The data are from the World Bank's *Doing Business* database.

As investment portfolios become increasingly global, investors as well as governments seeking to attract investment must have a good understanding of the investment climate. This table includes data on credit market risks and indicators of creditworthiness ratings from several major international rating services.

Lack of access to credit is one of the biggest barriers entrepreneurs face in starting and operating a business. And this in turn affects growth in the economy and opportunities for improved livelihoods. Information on credit histories made available in credit registries is one way for creditors to assess risk and allocate credit more efficiently. Information on creditor rights and how well collateral systems facilitate access to credit offers an additional institutional solution to expanding credit. The creditor rights index is an indicator of the powers of secured lenders in liquidation and reorganization. This composite index captures information on issues related to reorganization of insolvent companies, the ability of secured creditors to seize collateral if there is a reorganization, whether secured creditors are paid first from proceeds from liquidating a bankrupt firm, and whether management remains in power during a reorganization. The index ranges from 0 for weak creditor rights to 4 for strong creditor rights. A public credit registry is a database owned by public authorities (usually the central bank or banking supervisory) that collect information on the standing of borrowers in the financial system and make it available to financial institutions. A private credit bureau is a private firm or nonprofit organization that maintains a database on the standing of borrowers in the financial system. Its primary role is to facilitate exchange of information among banks and financial institutions. Coverage of public credit registries and private credit bureaus provides an indication of how many borrowers, as a percentage of the adult population, have information on their payment histories available in credit registries. A score of 0 indicates that a public registry or private bureau does not operate in the country. The maximum score is 1,000.

Most risk ratings are numerical or alphabetical indexes, with a higher number or a letter closer to the beginning of the alphabet meaning lower risk (a good prospect). (For more on the rating processes of the rating agencies, see *Data sources*.) Risk ratings may

be highly subjective, reflecting external perceptions that do not always capture the actual situation in a country. But these subjective perceptions are the reality that policymakers face. Countries not rated by credit risk rating agencies typically do not attract registered flows of private capital. The risk ratings presented here are included for their analytical usefulness and are not endorsed by the World Bank.

The PRS Group's *International Country Risk Guide* (ICRG) collects information on 22 components of risk, groups it into three major categories (political, financial, and economic), and converts it into a single numerical risk assessment ranging from 0 to 100. Ratings below 50 indicate very high risk, and those above 80 very low risk. Ratings are updated monthly.

Institutional Investor country credit ratings are based on information provided by leading international banks. Responses are weighted using a formula that gives more importance to responses from banks with greater worldwide exposure and more sophisticated country analysis systems. Countries are rated on a scale of 0 to 100 (highest risk to lowest), and ratings are updated every six months.

Euromoney country creditworthiness ratings are based on nine weighted categories (covering debt, economic performance, political risk, and access to financial and capital markets) that assess country risk. The ratings, also on a scale of 0 to 100 (highest risk to lowest), are based on polls of economists and political analysts supplemented by quantitative data such as debt ratios and access to capital markets.

Moody's sovereign long-term debt ratings are opinions of the capacity of entities to honor senior unsecured financial obligations and contracts denominated in foreign currency (foreign currency issuer ratings) or in domestic currency (domestic currency issuer ratings).

Standard & Poor's ratings of sovereign long-term foreign and domestic currency debt are based on current information furnished by obligors or obtained by Standard & Poor's from other sources it considers reliable. A Standard & Poor's issuer credit rating (one form of which is a sovereign credit rating) is a current opinion of an obligor's capacity and willingness to pay its financial obligations as they come due (its creditworthiness). This opinion does not apply to any specific financial obligation, as it does not take into account the nature and provisions of obligations, their standing in bankruptcy or liquidation, statutory preferences, or the legality and enforceability of obligations.

• **Creditor rights index** measures four powers of secured lenders in liquidation and reorganization: there are restrictions on entering reorganization, there is no automatic stay (or asset freeze), secured creditors are paid first, and management does not stay in reorganization. • **Public registry coverage and private bureau coverage** measure the number of borrowers with records contained in either the public credit registry or private credit bureau, expressed as a percentage of the adult population. A score of 0 indicates that a public registry or private bureau does not operate in the country. The maximum score is 1,000. • **Composite International Country Risk Guide (ICRG) risk rating** is an overall index, ranging from 0 to 100 (highest risk to lowest), based on 22 components of risk. • **Institutional Investor credit rating** ranks, from 0 to 100 (highest risk to lowest), the chances of a country's default. • **Euromoney country creditworthiness rating** ranks, from 0 to 100 (highest risk to lowest), the risk of investing in an economy. • **Moody's sovereign foreign or domestic currency long-term debt rating** assesses the risk of lending to governments. An entity's capacity to meet its senior financial obligations is rated from AAA (offering exceptional financial security) to C (usually in default, with potential recovery values low). Modifiers 1–3 are applied to ratings from AA to B, with 1 indicating a high ranking in the rating category. • **Standard & Poor's sovereign foreign or domestic currency long-term debt rating** ranges from AAA (extremely strong capacity to meet financial commitments) to CCC (currently highly vulnerable). Ratings from AA to CCC may be modified by a plus or minus sign to show relative standing in the category. An obligor rated SD (selective default) has failed to pay one or more financial obligations when due.

Data sources

The data on credit markets are from the World Bank's Doing Business project (http://rru. worldbank.org/DoingBusiness/). The country risk and creditworthiness ratings are from the PRS Group's monthly *International Country Risk Guide* (http://www.ICRGonline.com); the monthly *Institutional Investor;* the monthly *Euromoney;* Moody's Investors Service's *Sovereign, Subnational and Sovereign-Guaranteed Issuers;* and Standard & Poor's Sovereign List in *Credit Week.*

5.3 | Business environment

	Entry regulations				Contract enforcement			Insolvency		Labor regulations
	Number of start-up procedures **January 2003**	Time to start a business days **January 2003**	% of GNI per capita Cost to register a business **January 2003**	Minimum capital requirement **January 2003**	Procedures to enforce a contract **January 2003**	Time to enforce a contract days **January 2003**	Cost to enforce a contract % of GNI per capita **January 2003**	Time to resolve insolvency years **January 2003**	Cost to resolve insolvency % of insolvency estate **January 2003**	Employment laws index range 0 (less rigid) to 100 (very rigid) **January 2003**
Afghanistan	..	..	..	..	..	..	..	..	..	..
Albania	11	47	65	52	37	220	73	*2.0*	*38*	41
Algeria	18	29	32	73	20	387	13	3.5	4	46
Angola	14	146	838	174	46	865	16	..	..	78
Argentina	15	68	8	0	32	300	9	2.8	18	66
Armenia	10	25	9	11	22	65	15	1.9	4	57
Australia	2	2	2	0	11	320	8	1.0	18	36
Austria	9	29	7	141	20	434	1	1.3	18	30
Azerbaijan	14	106	17	0	25	115	3	2.7	8	63
Bangladesh	7	30	76	0	15	270	270	..	..	50
Belarus	19	118	27	111	19	135	44	2.2	4	77
Belgium	7	56	11	75	22	365	9	0.9	4	48
Benin	9	63	189	378	44	248	31	3.2	18	52
Bolivia	18	67	167	0	44	464	5	2.0	18	66
Bosnia and Herzegovina	12	59	52	379	31	630	21	1.9	8	49
Botswana	10	97	36	0	22	56	0	2.2	18	35
Brazil	15	152	12	0	16	380	2	10.0	8	78
Bulgaria	10	30	8	134	26	410	6	3.8	18	53
Burkina Faso	15	136	325	652	24	376	173	4.0	8	53
Burundi	11	17	253	0	62	367	28	..	..	62
Cambodia	11	94	554	1,826	18	210	269	..	..	54
Cameroon	12	37	191	244	46	548	63	2.0	18	44
Canada	2	3	1	0	17	425	28	0.8	4	34
Central African Republic	..	..	..	..	..	..	0	..	..	62
Chad	19	73	395	652	50	604	58	10.0	38	66
Chile	10	28	12	0	21	200	15	5.8	18	50
China	11	46	14	3,856	20	180	32	2.6	18	47
Hong Kong, China	5	11	2	0	17	180	7	1.0	18	27
Colombia	19	60	27	0	37	527	6	3.0	1	59
Congo, Dem. Rep.	13	215	872	321	55	414	92	..	..	60
Congo, Rep.	8	67	271	205	44	500	51	3.0	18	60
Costa Rica	11	80	21	0	21	370	23	2.5	18	63
Côte d'Ivoire	10	77	143	235	18	150	83	2.2	18	53
Croatia	13	50	18	51	20	330	7	3.1	18	65
Cuba	..	..	..	..	..	..	..	..	..	..
Czech Republic	10	88	12	110	16	270	19	9.2	38	36
Denmark	4	4	0	52	14	83	4	4.2	8	25
Dominican Republic	12	78	48	23	19	495	441	3.5	4	49
Ecuador	14	90	63	28	33	332	11	3.5	18	55
Egypt, Arab Rep.	13	43	61	789	19	202	31	4.3	18	59
El Salvador	12	115	130	550	42	240	7	..	..	69
Eritrea	..	..	..	..	..	..	..	..	..	..
Estonia	..	..	..	..	..	..	..	..	..	..
Ethiopia	8	44	422	1,756	24	895	35	2.2	8	51
Finland	4	33	3	32	19	240	16	0.9	1	55
France	10	53	3	32	21	210	4	2.4	18	50
Gabon	..	..	..	..	..	..	..	..	..	..
Gambia, The	..	..	..	..	..	..	..	..	..	..
Georgia	9	30	26	140	17	180	63	3.2	1	55
Germany	9	45	6	104	22	154	6	1.2	8	51
Ghana	10	84	112	1	21	90	24	*1.6*	*18*	35
Greece	16	45	70	145	15	315	8	2.2	8	67
Guatemala	13	39	67	37	19	1,460	20	4.0	18	65
Guinea	13	71	229	397	41	150	40	..	..	60
Guinea-Bissau	..	..	..	..	..	..	..	..	..	..
Haiti	12	203	199	210	41	76	18	..	..	60

	Entry regulations				Contract enforcement			Insolvency		Labor regulations
	Number of start-up procedures	Time to start a business days	% of GNI per capita Cost to register a business	% of GNI per capita Minimum capital requirement	Procedures to enforce a contract	Time to enforce a contract days	Cost to enforce a contract % of GNI per capita	Time to resolve insolvency years	Cost to resolve insolvency % of insolvency estate	Employment laws index range 0 (less rigid) to 100 (very rigid)
	January 2003	January 2003	January 2003	January 2003	January 2003	January 2003	January 2003	January 2003	January 2003	January 2003
Honduras	14	80	73	165	32	225	7	..	..	56
Hungary	5	65	64	220	17	365	5	2.0	38	54
India	10	88	50	430	11	365	95	11.3	8	51
Indonesia	11	168	15	303	0	225	269	6.0	18	57
Iran, Islamic Rep.	9	48	7	7	23	150	6	1.8	8	52
Iraq	..	..	..	..	..	..	..	..	..	..
Ireland	3	12	10	0	16	183	7	0.4	8	49
Israel	5	34	5	0	19	315	34	4.0	38	38
Italy	9	23	24	50	16	645	4	1.3	18	59
Jamaica	7	31	16	0	14	202	42	1.1	18	34
Japan	11	31	11	71	16	60	6	0.6	4	37
Jordan	14	98	50	2,404	32	147	0	4.3	8	60
Kazakhstan	10	25	10	35	41	120	8	3.3	18	55
Kenya	11	61	54	0	25	255	50	4.6	18	34
Korea, Dem. Rep.	..	..	..	..	..	..	..	..	..	..
Korea, Rep.	12	33	18	403	23	75	5	1.5	4	51
Kuwait	12	33	2	911	17	195	4	4.2	1	41
Kyrgyz Republic	9	26	13	75	44	365	255	4.0	4	64
Lao PDR	9	198	20	151	..	..	0	..	..	54
Latvia	7	11	15	93	19	189	8	1.2	4	62
Lebanon	6	46	130	83	27	721	54	4.0	18	46
Lesotho	9	92	68	20	..	..	0	..	..	45
Liberia	..	..	..	..	..	..	..	..	..	..
Libya	..	..	..	..	..	..	..	..	..	..
Lithuania	9	26	6	74	17	74	13	1.2	18	64
Macedonia, FYR	13	48	13	138	27	509	43	3.6	38	50
Madagascar	15	67	63	31	29	166	120	2.2	18	61
Malawi	11	45	125	0	16	108	521	2.8	8	52
Malaysia	8	31	27	0	22	270	19	2.2	18	25
Mali	13	61	232	598	27	150	7	3.5	18	54
Mauritania	11	73	110	897	..	..	0	8.0	8	59
Mauritius	..	..	..	..	..	..	..	..	..	..
Mexico	7	51	19	88	47	325	10	2.0	18	77
Moldova	11	42	26	86	36	210	14	2.8	8	67
Mongolia	8	31	12	2,047	26	224	2	4.0	8	50
Morocco	11	36	19	763	17	192	9	1.9	18	51
Mozambique	15	153	100	30	18	540	9	..	..	74
Myanmar	..	..	..	..	..	..	..	..	..	..
Namibia	10	85	19	0	..	..	0	..	..	43
Nepal	8	25	191	0	24	350	44	5.0	8	45
Netherlands	7	11	14	71	21	39	1	2.6	1	54
New Zealand	3	3	0	0	19	50	12	2.0	4	32
Nicaragua	12	71	338	0	17	125	18	2.3	8	61
Niger	11	27	447	844	29	365	57	5.0	18	59
Nigeria	10	44	92	29	23	730	7	1.6	18	43
Norway	4	24	4	33	12	87	10	0.9	1	41
Oman	9	34	5	721	17	250	5	7.0	4	54
Pakistan	10	22	47	0	30	365	46	2.8	4	58
Panama	7	19	26	0	44	197	20	6.5	38	79
Papua New Guinea	7	69	26	0	22	270	41	..	..	26
Paraguay	18	73	156	0	46	188	34	3.9	8	73
Peru	9	100	25	0	35	441	30	2.1	8	73
Philippines	11	59	24	10	28	164	104	5.7	38	60
Poland	12	31	20	21	18	1,000	11	1.5	18	55
Portugal	11	95	13	43	22	420	5	2.6	8	79
Puerto Rico	6	6	3	0	55	365	21	3.8	8	41

5.3 Business environment

	Entry regulations				Contract enforcement			Insolvency		Labor regulations
	Number of start-up procedures	Time to start a business days	% of GNI per capita Cost to register a business	Minimum capital requirement	Procedures to enforce a contract	Time to enforce a contract days	Cost to enforce a contract % of GNI per capita	Time to resolve insolvency years	Cost to resolve insolvency % of insolvency estate	Employment laws index range 0 (less rigid) to 100 (very rigid)
	January 2003	January 2003	January 2003	January 2003	January 2003	January 2003	January 2003	January 2003	January 2003	January 2003
Romania	6	27	12	3	28	225	13	3.2	8	54
Russian Federation	12	29	9	30	16	160	20	1.5	4	61
Rwanda	9	43	232	457	0	..	87	..	..	60
Saudi Arabia	14	95	131	1,611	19	195	0	3.0	18	36
Senegal	9	58	124	296	30	335	49	3.0	8	54
Serbia and Montenegro	10	44	13	357	40	1,028	20	7.3	38	56
Sierra Leone	9	26	1,298	0	48	114	8	2.5	38	67
Singapore	7	8	1	0	23	50	14	0.7	1	20
Slovak Republic	10	98	10	112	26	420	13	4.8	18	61
Slovenia	10	61	16	89	22	1,003	4	3.7	18	59
Somalia	..	..	..	..	..	..	..	..	..	..
South Africa	9	38	9	0	26	207	17	2.0	18	36
Spain	11	115	19	20	20	147	11	1.5	8	70
Sri Lanka	8	58	18	0	17	440	8	2.3	18	42
Sudan	..	..	..	..	..	..	..	..	..	..
Swaziland	..	..	..	..	..	..	..	..	..	..
Sweden	3	16	1	41	19	190	8	2.0	8	42
Switzerland	6	20	9	34	14	224	4	4.6	4	36
Syrian Arab Republic	10	42	17	5,627	36	596	31	4.1	8	45
Tajikistan	..	..	..	..	..	..	..	..	..	..
Tanzania	13	35	199	0	14	127	4	3.0	8	61
Thailand	9	42	7	0	19	210	30	2.6	38	61
Togo	14	63	281	531	43	503	21	..	..	57
Trinidad and Tobago	..	..	..	..	..	..	..	..	..	..
Tunisia	10	46	16	352	14	7	4	2.5	8	57
Turkey	13	38	37	13	18	105	5	1.8	8	55
Turkmenistan	..	..	..	..	..	..	..	..	..	..
Uganda	17	36	135	0	16	99	10	2.0	38	42
Ukraine	14	40	27	451	20	224	11	3.0	18	73
United Arab Emirates	10	29	25	404	27	559	11	5.0	38	45
United Kingdom	6	18	1	0	12	101	1	1.0	8	28
United States	5	4	1	0	17	365	0	3.0	4	22
Uruguay	10	27	47	699	38	360	14	4.0	8	39
Uzbekistan	9	33	16	64	34	258	2	3.3	4	55
Venezuela, RB	14	119	19	0	41	360	47	4.0	38	75
Vietnam	11	63	30	0	28	120	9	2.0	18	56
West Bank and Gaza	..	..	..	..	..	..	..	..	..	..
Yemen, Rep.	13	96	264	1,717	27	240	1	2.4	4	43
Zambia	6	40	24	138	16	188	16	3.7	8	46
Zimbabwe	10	122	285	0	13	197	40	2.3	18	27
World	**10 u**	**57 u**	**93 u**	**297 u**	**25 u**	**307 u**	**36 u**	**3.2 u**	**14 u**	**53 u**
Low income	11	74	213	339	28	304	65	3.8	13	54
Middle income	11	57	36	369	26	332	27	3.4	17	56
Lower middle income	12	58	38	455	27	333	32	3.3	15	56
Upper middle income	10	56	33	204	25	329	15	3.6	20	55
Low & middle income	11	65	118	355	27	319	44	3.6	15	55
East Asia & Pacific	10	80	73	819	20	208	77	3.8	23	49
Europe & Central Asia	11	47	22	115	26	317	29	3.2	15	58
Latin America & Carib.	12	78	74	90	32	363	39	3.7	16	62
Middle East & N. Africa	12	56	67	1,286	23	281	14	3.5	11	50
South Asia	9	45	76	86	19	358	93	5.3	10	49
Sub-Saharan Africa	11	72	255	278	30	334	52	3.5	18	53
High income	7	30	9	99	19	267	8	2.1	10	44
Europe EMU	9	47	16	65	19	287	6	1.6	9	56

About the data

The table presents key indicators on the environment for doing business. The indicators, covering entry regulations, contract enforcement, insolvency, and labor regulations, identify regulations that enhance or constrain business investment, productivity, and growth. The data are from the World Bank's *Doing Business* database.

A vibrant private sector is central to promoting growth and expanding opportunities for poor people. But encouraging firms to invest, improve productivity, and create jobs requires a legal and regulatory environment that fosters access to credit, protection of property rights, and efficient judicial, taxation, and customs systems. The indicators in the table point to the administrative and regulatory reforms and institutions needed to create a favorable environment for doing business.

When entrepreneurs start a business, the first obstacles they face are the administrative and legal procedures required to register the new firm. Countries differ widely in how they regulate the entry of new businesses. In some countries the process is straightforward and affordable. But in others the procedures are so burdensome that entrepreneurs may opt to run their business informally.

The data on entry regulations are derived from a survey of the procedures that a typical domestic limited-liability company must complete before legally starting operation. The data cover the number and duration of start-up procedures, the cost to register a business, and the minimum capital requirement.

Contract enforcement is critical to enable businesses to engage with new borrowers or customers. Without good contract enforcement, trade and credit will be restricted to a small community of people who have developed relationships through repeated dealings or through the security of assets. The institution that enforces contracts between debtors and creditors, and suppliers and customers, is the court.

The efficiency of contract enforcement is reflected in three indicators: the number of judicial procedures to resolve a dispute, the time it takes to enforce a commercial contract, and the associated costs. The data are derived from structured surveys answered by attorneys at private law firms. The questionnaires cover the step-by-step evolution of a commercial case before local courts in the country's largest city.

The continuing existence of unviable competitors is consistently rated by firms as one of the greatest potential barriers to operation and growth. The institution that deals with the exit of unviable companies and the rehabilitation of viable but financially distressed companies is the insolvency system. Two indicators measure the time it takes to resolve insolvency and the associated costs. With effective insolvency systems, one may expect greater access and better allocation of credit.

All economies have labor regulations intended to protect the interests of workers and to guarantee a minimum standard of living. These laws and institutions encompass four bodies of law: employment laws, industrial relations laws, occupational health and safety laws, and social security laws. The employment laws index is a simple average of the flexibility of hiring index, the conditions of employment index, and the flexibility of firing index; each index has values between 0 and 100, with higher values indicating more rigid regulation. Flexibility of hiring covers the availability of part-time, fixed-term, and family members' contracts. Conditions of employment cover working time requirements, including mandatory minimum daily rest, maximum number of hours in a normal work week, premium for overtime work, and restrictions on weekly holidays; mandatory payment for nonworking days, which includes days of annual leave with pay and paid time off for holidays; and minimum wage legislation. Flexibility of firing covers workers' legal protections against dismissal, including the grounds for dismissal; procedures for dismissal (individual and collective); notice period; and severance payment.

To ensure cross-country comparability, several standard characteristics of a company are defined in all surveys, such as size, ownership, location, legal status, and type of activities undertaken. The data were collected through a study of laws and regulations in each country, surveys of regulators or private sector professionals on each topic, and cooperative arrangements with private consulting firms and business and law associations.

Definitions

• **Start-up procedures** are those required to start a business. Procedures are interactions of a company with external parties (government agencies, lawyers, auditors, notaries, and the like), including interactions required to obtain necessary permits and licenses and to complete all inscriptions, verifications, and notifications to start operations. Data are for businesses with specific characteristics of ownership, size, and type of production. • **Time to start a business** is the time, measured in calendar days, needed to complete the required procedures for legally operating a business. If a procedure can be speeded up at additional cost, the fastest procedure, independent of cost, is chosen. Time spent gathering information about the registration process is excluded. • **Cost to register a business** is normalized by presenting it as a percentage of gross national income (GNI) per capita. • **Minimum capital requirement** is the amount that an entrepreneur needs to deposit in a bank to obtain a company registration number. The amount is typically specified in the commercial code or company law and is often returned to the entrepreneur only when the company is dissolved. • **Procedures to enforce a contract** are independent actions, each defined as a procedure (mandated by law or court regulation) that demands interaction between the parties or between them and the judge or court officer. • **Time to enforce a contract** is the number of calendar days from the time the plaintiff files the lawsuit in court until the time of final determination and, in appropriate cases, payment. • **Cost to enforce a contract** includes filing fees, court costs, and estimated attorney fees. • **Time to resolve insolvency** is the number of years from the time of filing for insolvency in court until the time of resolution of distressed assets. • **Cost to resolve insolvency** includes filing fees, court costs, attorney fees, and payments to other professionals (accountants, assessors), out of the insolvency estate. The costs are averages of the estimates of survey respondents, who chose among six options: 0–2 percent, 3–5 percent, 6–10 percent, 11–25 percent, 26–50 percent, and more than 50 percent. • **Employment laws index** is a composite index of three aspects of labor regulations: flexibility of hiring, conditions of employment, and flexibility of firing. The index ranges from 0 (less rigid) to 100 (more rigid).

Data source

All data are from the World Bank's Doing Business project (http://rru.worldbank.org/DoingBusiness/).

5.4 Stock markets

	Market capitalization				Market liquidity		Turnover ratio		Listed domestic companies		S&P/IFC Investable index	
	$ millions		% of GDP		value traded as % of GDP		value of shares traded as % of market capitalization		number		% change in price index	
	1990	**2003**	**1990**	**2002**	**1990**	**2002**	**1990**	**2003**	**1990**	**2003**	**2002**	**2003**
Afghanistan	..	..	..	..	..	..	..	..	..	..	..	..
Albania	..	..	..	..	..	..	..	..	..	..	..	..
Algeria	..	..	..	..	..	..	..	..	..	..	..	..
Angola	..	..	..	..	..	..	..	..	..	..	..	..
Argentina	3,270	38,927	2.3	100.9	0.6	1.3	33.6	1.7	179	107	–51.4	131.4
Armenia	..	..	..	..	..	..	..	..	..	..	..	..
Australia	109,000	*380,969*	35.1	93.1	12.9	72.0	31.6	*77.2*	1,089	*1,355*	..	..
Austria	11,500	*31,664*	7.1	15.5	11.5	2.9	110.3	*21.3*	97	*91*	..	..
Azerbaijan	..	..	..	..	..	..	..	..	..	..	..	..
Bangladesh	321	1,622	1.1	2.5	0.0	1.4	1.5	3.5	134	247	–4.2 [a]	15.4 [a]
Belarus	..	..	..	..	..	..	..	..	..	..	..	..
Belgium	65,400	*127,556*	33.2	52.0	3.3	13.8	..	*247.9*	182	*143*	..	..
Benin	..	..	..	..	..	..	..	..	..	..	..	..
Bolivia	..	*1,560*	..	19.4	..	*0.0*	..	0.1	..	29	..	..
Bosnia and Herzegovina	..	..	..	..	..	..	..	..	..	..	..	..
Botswana	*261*	2,131	*6.6*	32.6	*0.2*	1.0	6.1	1.1	*9*	19	31.1 [a]	25.6 [a]
Brazil	16,400	234,560	3.6	27.4	1.2	10.7	23.6	3.4	581	367	–33.0	105.4
Bulgaria	..	1,755	..	4.7	..	1.1	..	2.0	..	356	62.5 [a]	189.2 [a]
Burkina Faso	..	..	..	..	..	..	..	..	..	..	..	..
Burundi	..	..	..	..	..	..	..	..	..	..	..	..
Cambodia	..	..	..	..	..	..	..	..	..	..	..	..
Cameroon	..	..	..	..	..	..	..	..	..	..	..	..
Canada	242,000	*575,316*	42.1	80.5	12.4	56.8	26.7	*68.2*	1,144	*3,756*	..	..
Central African Republic	..	..	..	..	..	..	..	..	..	..	..	..
Chad	..	..	..	..	..	..	..	..	..	..	..	..
Chile	13,600	86,291	44.9	74.2	2.6	4.9	6.3	0.9	215	240	–14.8	79.5
China	*2,030*	681,204	*0.5*	36.6	*0.2*	26.3	*158.9*	11.5	*14*	1,296	–14.5	77.7
Hong Kong, China	83,400	*463,108*	110.6	286.7	45.9	130.4	43.1	*43.5*	284	*968*	..	..
Colombia	1,420	14,258	3.5	11.9	0.2	0.3	5.6	0.6	80	114	9.7 [a]	27.3 [a]
Congo, Dem. Rep.	..	..	..	..	..	..	..	..	..	..	..	..
Congo, Rep.	..	..	..	..	..	..	..	..	..	..	..	..
Costa Rica	*475*	..	*5.5*	..	..	..	*5.8*	..	*82*	..	..	..
Côte d'Ivoire	549	1,650	5.1	11.4	0.2	0.1	3.4	0.6	23	38	17.4 [a]	27.4 [a]
Croatia	..	6,126	..	17.7	..	0.7	..	0.7	*2*	66	44.2 [a]	12.8 [a]
Cuba	..	..	..	..	..	..	..	..	..	..	..	..
Czech Republic	..	17,663	..	22.9	..	8.8	..	6.0	..	63	38.9	54.4
Denmark	39,100	*76,788*	29.3	44.4	8.3	29.8	28.0	*60.3*	258	*201*	..	..
Dominican Republic	..	..	..	..	..	..	..	..	..	..	..	..
Ecuador	*69*	2,153	*0.6*	7.2	..	0.1	..	0.2	*65*	30	23.4 [a]	14.6 [a]
Egypt, Arab Rep.	1,760	27,073	4.1	29.0	0.3	2.8	..	1.6	573	967	–5.8	79.3
El Salvador	..	*1,520*	..	*11.0*	..	*0.2*	..	*1.5*	..	32	..	..
Eritrea	..	..	..	..	..	..	..	..	..	..	..	..
Estonia	..	3,790	..	37.3	..	3.7	..	1.6	..	14	66.3 [a]	41.5 [a]
Ethiopia	..	..	..	..	..	..	..	..	..	..	..	..
Finland	22,700	*138,833*	16.5	105.6	2.9	134.2	..	*106.8*	73	*147*	..	..
France	314,000	*966,962*	25.8	67.6	9.6	65.3	..	*88.0*	578	*772*	..	..
Gabon	..	..	..	..	..	..	..	..	..	..	..	..
Gambia, The	..	..	..	..	..	..	..	..	..	..	..	..
Georgia	..	..	..	..	..	..	..	..	..	..	..	..
Germany	355,000	*685,970*	21.2	34.6	30.0	62.1	139.3	*140.5*	413	*715*	..	..
Ghana	*76*	1,426	*1.2*	12.0	..	0.2	..	0.2	*13*	25	27.6 [a]	65.4 [a]
Greece	15,200	*68,741*	18.1	51.8	4.7	18.7	36.3	*26.0*	145	*341*	–31.2	..
Guatemala	..	*232*	..	*1.1*	..	*0.0*	..	*3.1*	..	10	..	..
Guinea	..	..	..	..	..	..	..	..	..	..	..	..
Guinea-Bissau	..	..	..	..	..	..	..	..	..	..	..	..
Haiti	..	..	..	..	..	..	..	..	..	..	..	..

	Market capitalization				Market liquidity		Turnover ratio		Listed domestic companies		S&P/IFC Investable index	
	$ millions		% of GDP		value traded as % of GDP		value of shares traded as % of market capitalization		number		% change in price index	
	1990	2003	1990	2002	1990	2002	1990	2003	1990	2003	2002	2003
Honduras	40	..	1.3	..	..	..	..	..	26	..	..	..
Hungary	505	16,729	1.5	19.9	0.3	9.0	6.3	4.6	21	49	34.6	28.6
India	38,600	279,093	12.2	25.7	6.9	38.6	65.9	14.1	2,435	5,644	6.8	76.5
Indonesia	8,080	54,659	7.1	17.3	3.5	7.5	75.8	3.8	125	333	33.3	69.7
Iran, Islamic Rep.	34,300	9,700	..	8.5	..	1.0	30.4	11.3	97	316	..	..
Iraq	..	..	..	..	..	..	..	..	..	..	..	..
Ireland	..	59,938	..	49.4	..	27.1	..	50.5	..	62	..	..
Israel	3,320	75,719	6.3	43.8	10.5	53.3	95.8	5.9	216	576	–26.6	59.5
Italy	149,000	477,075	13.5	40.3	3.9	45.6	26.8	109.1	220	295	40.0 [a]	–3.4 [a]
Jamaica	911	8,500	19.8	74.2	0.7	1.8	3.4	0.3	44	39	40.0 [a]	–3.4 [a]
Japan	2,920,000	2,126,075	95.6	53.2	52.5	39.4	43.8	71.0	2,071	3,058	–10.1 [b]	37.8 [b]
Jordan	2,000	10,963	49.7	76.2	10.1	14.4	20.0	3.6	105	161	–2.1 [a]	65.4 [a]
Kazakhstan	..	1,200	..	5.4	..	1.4	..	26.5	..	31	..	..
Kenya	453	4,178	5.3	11.5	0.1	0.3	2.2	0.7	54	51	42.2 [a]	186.2 [a]
Korea, Dem. Rep.	..	..	..	..	..	..	..	..	..	..	..	..
Korea, Rep.	111,000	329,616	43.9	52.2	30.1	166.2	61.3	17.8	669	1,563	5.8	33.3
Kuwait	..	..	..	56.1	..	11.4	..	..	..	..	..	..
Kyrgyz Republic	..	..	..	..	..	..	..	..	..	..	..	..
Lao PDR	..	..	..	..	..	..	..	..	..	..	..	..
Latvia	..	1,141	..	8.5	..	1.5	..	5.0	..	56	–14.1 [a]	62.6 [a]
Lebanon	..	1,497	..	8.1	..	0.7	..	0.6	..	13	5.7	0.9 [a]
Lesotho	..	..	..	..	..	..	..	..	..	..	..	..
Liberia	..	..	..	..	..	..	..	..	..	..	..	..
Libya	..	..	..	..	..	..	..	..	..	..	..	..
Lithuania	..	3,510	..	10.6	..	1.3	..	0.8	..	48	25.7 [a]	117.9 [a]
Macedonia, FYR	..	46	..	1.3	..	0.1	..	4.3	..	2	..	..
Madagascar	..	..	..	..	..	..	..	..	..	..	..	..
Malawi	..	156	..	9.2	..	1.3	..	13.8	..	8	..	..
Malaysia	48,600	168,376	110.4	130.7	24.7	29.1	24.6	3.3	282	897	–2.6	25.5
Mali	..	..	..	..	..	..	..	..	..	..	..	..
Mauritania	..	1,090	..	113.3	..	..	..	..	..	40	..	..
Mauritius	268	1,955	11.2	29.3	0.3	1.3	1.9	0.3	13	40	22.9 [a]	43.7 [a]
Mexico	32,700	122,532	12.4	16.2	4.6	4.4	44.0	1.5	199	159	–16.4	30.4
Moldova	..	350	..	23.7	..	14.2	..	60.1	..	22	..	..
Mongolia	..	..	..	..	..	..	..	..	..	..	..	..
Morocco	966	13,152	3.7	23.8	0.2	1.6	..	0.9	71	53	–8.1	44.0
Mozambique	..	..	..	..	..	..	..	..	..	..	..	..
Myanmar	..	..	..	..	..	..	..	..	..	..	..	..
Namibia	21	308	0.7	5.9	..	0.0	..	0.0	3	13	22.5	37.1 [a]
Nepal	..	..	..	14.6	..	0.6	..	..	..	..	..	..
Netherlands	120,000	401,465	40.8	96.1	13.7	110.6	29.0	123.7	260	180	..	..
New Zealand	8,840	21,745	20.3	37.1	4.4	12.8	17.3	38.3	171	149	..	..
Nicaragua	..	..	..	..	..	..	..	..	..	..	..	..
Niger	..	..	..	..	..	..	..	..	..	..	..	..
Nigeria	1,370	9,494	4.8	13.2	0.0	1.1	0.9	0.9	131	200	–0.3 [a]	57.5 [a]
Norway	26,100	67,300	22.5	35.3	12.1	25.7	54.4	67.8	112	179	..	..
Oman	1,060	5,014	9.4	19.7	0.9	2.6	12.3	2.1	55	96	31.8	47.0 [a]
Pakistan	2,850	16,579	7.1	17.3	0.6	44.1	8.7	40.1	487	701	112.0 [a]	50.4 [a]
Panama	226	2,600	3.4	21.6	0.0	0.4	0.9	1.7	13	29	..	..
Papua New Guinea	..	..	..	..	..	..	..	..	..	..	..	..
Paraguay	..	..	..	..	..	..	..	..	..	..	..	..
Peru	812	16,055	3.1	23.7	0.4	2.0	19.3	0.5	294	197	33.5	88.1
Philippines	5,930	23,565	13.4	50.0	2.7	4.0	13.6	0.9	153	234	–19.7	41.4
Poland	144	37,165	0.2	15.2	0.0	3.1	89.7	2.2	9	203	2.2	29.5
Portugal	9,200	42,846	12.9	35.2	2.4	16.7	16.9	52.4	181	63	..	..
Puerto Rico	..	..	..	..	..	..	..	..	..	..	..	..

	Market capitalization				Market liquidity		Turnover ratio		Listed domestic companies		S&P/IFC Investable index	
	$ millions		% of GDP		value traded as % of GDP		value of shares traded as % of market capitalization		number		% change in price index	
	1990	2003	1990	2002	1990	2002	1990	2003	1990	2003	2002	2003
Romania	..	5,584	..	10.0	..	0.9	..	0.5	..	4,484	96.7 [a]	42.5 [a]
Russian Federation	244	230,786	0.0	35.8	..	10.4	..	3.0	13	214	34.8	68.5
Rwanda	..	..	..	..	..	..	..	..	..	..	..	..
Saudi Arabia	48,200	157,302	36.7	39.7	1.7	18.9	..	10.3	59	70	3.8 [a]	49.5 [a]
Senegal	..	..	..	..	..	..	..	..	..	..	..	..
Serbia and Montenegro	..	..	..	..	..	..	..	..	..	..	..	..
Sierra Leone	..	..	..	..	..	..	..	..	..	..	..	..
Singapore	34,300	101,900	92.9	117.2	55.0	64.5	..	39.3	150	434	..	..
Slovak Republic	..	2,779	..	8.0	..	3.3	..	1.9	..	306	23.6 [a]	57.2 [a]
Slovenia	..	5,209	..	21.0	..	0.5	..	1.4	24	32	78.3 [a]	42.1 [a]
Somalia	..	..	..	..	..	..	..	..	..	..	..	..
South Africa	138,000	267,745	123.2	177.5	7.3	75.6	..	3.6	732	426	44.9	37.6
Spain	111,000	461,559	21.8	70.7	8.0	155.3	..	211.1	427	2,986	..	..
Sri Lanka	917	2,711	11.4	10.1	0.5	1.9	5.8	1.2	175	244	28.4 [a]	35.6 [a]
Sudan	..	..	..	..	..	..	..	..	..	..	..	..
Swaziland	17	127	1.9	10.0	..	0.6	..	6.7	1	5	..	..
Sweden	97,900	177,065	39.8	73.7	7.1	90.9	14.9	96.2	258	278	..	..
Switzerland	160,000	553,758	70.0	207.1	29.6	245.6	..	100.5	182	258	..	..
Syrian Arab Republic	..	..	..	..	..	..	..	..	..	..	..	..
Tajikistan	..	..	..	..	..	..	..	..	..	..	..	..
Tanzania	..	398	..	4.3	..	0.1	..	1.9	..	4	..	..
Thailand	23,900	120,887	28.0	36.3	26.8	37.5	92.6	18.2	214	405	18.3	147.2
Togo	..	..	..	..	..	..	..	..	..	..	..	..
Trinidad and Tobago	696	10,605	13.7	67.6	1.1	1.8	10.0	0.6	30	35	33.2 [a]	46.7 [a]
Tunisia	533	2,464	4.3	10.1	0.2	1.1	3.3	0.9	13	46	−2.5 [a]	14.9 [a]
Turkey	19,100	68,379	12.7	18.5	3.9	38.5	42.5	28.5	110	284	−33.5	113.2
Turkmenistan	..	..	..	..	..	..	..	..	..	..	..	..
Uganda	..	36	..	0.6	..	..	..	..	..	2	..	..
Ukraine	..	4,303	..	7.5	..	0.3	..	0.5	..	149	26.7 [a]	40.3 [a]
United Arab Emirates	..	7,881	..	11.4	..	0.0	..	3.4	..	12	..	..
United Kingdom	849,000	1,864,134	85.8	119.0	28.2	173.7	33.4	135.4	1,701	1,701	−16.5 [c]	26.3 [c]
United States	3,060,000	11,052,403	53.2	106.4	30.5	244.4	53.4	202.5	6,599	5,685	−23.4 [d]	26.4 [d]
Uruguay	..	153	..	0.8	..	0.0	..	0.5	36	15	..	..
Uzbekistan	..	..	..	0.6	..	0.2	..	..	..	..	..	..
Venezuela, RB	8,360	3,820	17.2	4.2	4.6	0.1	43.0	0.6	76	54	−35.1 [a]	14.3 [a]
Vietnam	..	..	..	..	..	..	..	..	..	..	..	..
West Bank and Gaza	..	723	..	17.9	..	1.9	..	10.3	..	24	..	..
Yemen, Rep.	..	..	..	..	..	..	..	..	..	..	..	..
Zambia	..	217	..	6.0	..	1.3	..	22.5	..	9	..	..
Zimbabwe	2,400	4,975	27.3	187.9	0.6	29.9	2.9	1.2	57	81	97.9 [a]	−74.8 [a]
World	**9,403,525** s	**23,359,484** s	**48.0** w	**74.6** w	**28.5** w	**122.8** w	**57.1** w	**123.0** w	**25,424** s	**47,576** s		
Low income	54,623	197,220	9.8	22.6	4.7	27.5	53.8	139.6	3,446	7,322		
Middle income	320,160	1,639,528	20.0	35.3	5.2	16.0	..	44.1	4,231	13,307		
Lower middle income	212,666	1,099,924	15.5	36.6	9.0	20.8	..	56.3	3,146	10,725		
Upper middle income	107,494	539,604	29.6	33.0	6.1	7.1	50.3	23.2	1,085	2,582		
Low & middle income	374,783	1,836,748	18.8	33.3	5.2	17.8	..	57.8	7,677	20,629		
East Asia & Pacific	86,510	702,100	16.4	40.4	6.6	24.4	118.1	72.7	774	3,132		
Europe & Central Asia	19,100	234,597	2.2	22.7	..	12.3	..	53.6	110	6,781		
Latin America & Carib.	78,169	418,720	7.7	27.4	2.1	5.4	29.8	21.7	1,734	1,381		
Middle East & N. Africa	5,259	124,210	27.4	26.1	2.2	6.0	..	19.6	817	1,585		
South Asia	42,688	144,070	10.8	22.7	5.6	35.4	54.0	180.3	3,231	6,839		
Sub-Saharan Africa	143,057	213,051	52.2	47.3	..	32.4	..	23.7	1,011	911		
High income	9,028,742	21,522,735	51.6	83.4	31.4	145.2	59.4	137.9	17,747	26,947		
Europe EMU	1,183,500	3,485,194	21.7	52.4	14.2	67.4	..	106.1	2,630	5,843		

Note: Aggregates for market capitalization are unavailable for 2003; those shown refer to 2002.
a. Data refer to the S&P/IFC Global index. b. Data refer to the Nikkei 225 index. c. Data refer to the FT 100 index. d. Data refer to the S&P 500 index.

About the data

The development of an economy's financial markets is closely related to its overall development. Well functioning financial systems provide good and easily accessible information. That lowers transaction costs, which in turn improves resource allocation and boosts economic growth. Both banking systems and stock markets enhance growth, the main factor in poverty reduction. At low levels of economic development commercial banks tend to dominate the financial system, while at higher levels domestic stock markets tend to become more active and efficient relative to domestic banks.

Open economies with sound macroeconomic policies, good legal systems, and shareholder protection attract capital and therefore have larger financial markets. Recent research on stock market development shows that new communications technology and increased financial integration have resulted in more cross-border capital flows, a stronger presence of financial firms around the world, and the migration of stock exchange activities to international exchanges. Many firms in emerging markets now cross-list on international exchanges, which provides them with lower cost capital and more liquidity-traded shares. However, this also means that exchanges in emerging markets may not have enough financial activity to sustain them, putting pressure on them to rethink their operations.

The stock market indicators in the table include measures of size (market capitalization, number of listed domestic companies) and liquidity (value traded as a percentage of gross domestic product, value of shares traded as a percentage of market capitalization). The comparability of such indicators between countries may be limited by conceptual and statistical weaknesses, such as inaccurate reporting and differences in accounting standards. The percentage change in stock market prices in U.S. dollars, from the Standard & Poor's Investable (S&P/IFCI) and Global (S&P/IFCG) country indexes, is an important measure of overall performance. Regulatory and institutional factors that can affect investor confidence, such as entry and exit restrictions, the existence of a securities and exchange commission, and the quality of laws to protect investors, may influence the functioning of stock markets but are not included in the table.

Stock market size can be measured in a number of ways, and each may produce a different ranking of countries. Market capitalization shows the overall size of the stock market in U.S. dollars and as a percentage of GDP. The number of listed domestic companies is another measure of market size. Market size is positively correlated with the ability to mobilize capital and diversify risk.

Market liquidity, the ability to easily buy and sell securities, is measured by dividing the total value traded by GDP. This indicator complements the market capitalization ratio by showing whether market size is matched by trading. The turnover ratio—the value of shares traded as a percentage of market capitalization—is also a measure of liquidity as well as of transaction costs. (High turnover indicates low transaction costs.) The turnover ratio complements the ratio of value traded to GDP, because the turnover ratio is related to the size of the market and the value traded ratio to the size of the economy. A small, liquid market will have a high turnover ratio but a low value traded ratio. Liquidity is an important attribute of stock markets because, in theory, liquid markets improve the allocation of capital and enhance prospects for long-term economic growth. A more comprehensive measure of liquidity would include trading costs and the time and uncertainty in finding a counterpart in settling trades.

Standard & Poor's maintains a series of indexes for investors interested in investing in stock markets in developing countries. At the core of the Standard & Poor's family of emerging market indexes, the S&P/IFCG index is intended to represent the most active stocks in the markets it covers and to be the broadest possible indicator of market movements. The S&P/IFCI index, which applies the same calculation methodology as the S&P/IFCG index, is designed to measure the returns foreign portfolio investors might receive from investing in emerging market stocks that are legally and practically open to foreign portfolio investment.

Standard & Poor's Emerging Markets Data Base, the source for all the data in the table, provides regular updates on 54 emerging stock markets encompassing more than 2,200 stocks. The S&P/IFCG index includes 34 markets and more than 1,900 stocks, and the S&P/IFCI index covers 30 markets and close to 1,200 stocks. These indexes are widely used benchmarks for international portfolio management. See Standard & Poor's (2001b) for further information on the indexes.

Because markets included in Standard & Poor's emerging markets category vary widely in level of development, it is best to look at the entire category to identify the most significant market trends. And it is useful to remember that stock market trends may be distorted by currency conversions, especially when a currency has registered a significant devaluation.

About the data is based on Demirgüç-Kunt and Levine (1996a), Beck and Levine (2001), and Claessens, Klingebiel, and Schmukler (2002).

Definitions

• **Market capitalization** (also known as market value) is the share price times the number of shares outstanding. • **Market liquidity** is the total value traded divided by GDP. Value traded is the total value of shares traded during the period. • **Turnover ratio** is the total value of shares traded during the period divided by the average market capitalization for the period. Average market capitalization is calculated as the average of the end-of-period values for the current period and the previous period. • **Listed domestic companies** are the domestically incorporated companies listed on the country's stock exchanges at the end of the year. This indicator does not include investment companies, mutual funds, or other collective investment vehicles. • **S&P/IFC Investable index** price change is the U.S. dollar price change in the stock markets covered by the S&P/IFCI country index, supplemented by the S&P/IFCG country index.

Data sources

The data on stock markets are from Standard & Poor's *Emerging Stock Markets Factbook 2003*, which draws on the Emerging Markets Data Base, supplemented by other data from Standard & Poor's. The firm collects data through an annual survey of the world's stock exchanges, supplemented by information provided by its network of correspondents and by Reuters. The GDP data are from the World Bank's national accounts data files.

5.5 Financial depth and efficiency

	Domestic credit provided by banking sector		Liquid liabilities		Quasi-liquid liabilities		Ratio of bank liquid reserves to bank assets		Interest rate spread		Risk premium on lending	
									Lending minus deposit rate percentage points		Prime lending rate minus treasury bill rate percentage points	
	% of GDP		% of GDP		% of GDP		%					
	1990	2002	1990	2002	1990	2002	1990	2002	1990	2002	1990	2002
Afghanistan	..	..	..	..	..	..	..	..	..	..	..	..
Albania	..	43.6	..	61.5	..	38.9	..	10.5	2.1	6.8	..	5.8
Algeria	74.5	29.1	73.5	49.0	24.8	19.7	1.3	12.5	..	3.3	..	6.7
Angola	..	5.5	..	22.2	..	15.3	..	14.5	..	48.6	..	..
Argentina	32.4	62.4	11.5	27.9	7.1	18.9	7.4	9.5	..	12.4	..	..
Armenia	58.7	7.3	79.9	15.6	42.9	7.1	13.6	11.4	..	11.5	..	6.4
Australia	71.4	93.9	55.0	71.0	43.2	47.6	1.5	1.2	4.5	5.0	4.0	3.3
Austria	121.4	124.3	..	..	..	..	2.1	..	..	..	..	..
Azerbaijan	65.9	8.7	38.6	13.3	13.4	6.7	4.5	10.2	..	8.7	..	3.3
Bangladesh	23.9	40.2	23.4	39.1	16.8	29.8	12.8	8.6	4.0	7.8	..	..
Belarus	..	17.5	..	15.4	..	10.1	..	7.7	..	10.0	..	..
Belgium	73.1	115.4	..	..	..	..	0.2	..	6.9	5.1	3.4	4.5
Benin	22.4	5.8	26.7	26.6	5.9	7.1	29.3	20.9	9.0	..	..	..
Bolivia	30.7	62.3	24.5	49.1	18.0	40.7	18.8	5.8	18.0	11.1	..	8.2
Bosnia and Herzegovina	..	35.8	..	46.3	..	19.1	..	10.5	..	8.2	..	..
Botswana	−46.0	−29.6	21.9	28.5	13.6	20.9	11.0	3.8	1.8	5.7	..	..
Brazil	89.8	64.8	26.4	33.1	18.5	25.0	7.6	23.6	..	43.7	..	43.4
Bulgaria	118.5	23.7	71.9	41.9	53.6	24.8	10.2	8.9	8.9	6.6	8.6	6.5
Burkina Faso	12.1	12.7	18.8	18.2	6.6	7.0	12.7	6.8	9.0	..	..	..
Burundi	23.2	35.1	18.2	22.3	6.5	7.3	2.8	3.9	..	..	..	..
Cambodia	..	6.0	..	18.4	..	13.2	..	71.3	..	13.7	..	..
Cameroon	31.2	16.3	22.6	20.2	10.1	8.0	3.4	28.0	11.0	13.0	..	..
Canada	82.3	92.6	74.3	78.4	59.8	54.4	1.6	0.6	4.2	3.4	1.3	1.6
Central African Republic	12.9	13.2	15.3	14.4	1.8	1.4	2.8	2.5	11.0	13.0	..	..
Chad	11.5	10.9	14.6	13.5	0.6	0.8	3.3	25.2	11.0	13.0	..	..
Chile	73.0	77.6	40.8	40.0	32.8	30.0	3.6	3.0	8.5	4.0	..	..
China	90.0	166.4	79.2	178.3	41.4	108.9	15.7	12.1	0.7	3.3	..	..
Hong Kong, China	154.9	144.5	179.4	238.9	164.7	219.8	0.1	0.2	3.3	4.7	2.7	3.7
Colombia	35.9	36.5	29.8	31.8	19.3	21.2	27.4	6.7	8.8	7.4	..	..
Congo, Dem. Rep.	25.3	0.2	12.9	4.8	2.1	1.8	49.0	6.2	..	..	..	..
Congo, Rep.	29.1	11.4	22.0	13.9	6.1	1.0	2.0	17.0	11.0	13.0	..	..
Costa Rica	29.9	36.9	42.7	39.8	30.0	25.9	68.5	12.3	11.4	15.0	..	..
Côte d'Ivoire	44.5	20.7	28.8	29.4	10.9	7.9	2.1	6.2	9.0	..	..	..
Croatia	..	63.8	..	65.7	..	48.2	..	14.3	499.3	11.0	..	..
Cuba	..	..	..	..	..	..	..	..	..	..	..	..
Czech Republic	..	45.8	..	75.5	..	39.2	..	3.8	..	4.0	..	3.5
Denmark	63.0	156.6	59.0	51.0	29.4	19.4	1.1	1.2	6.2	4.7	..	..
Dominican Republic	31.5	44.8	28.6	39.5	13.3	28.5	31.2	18.8	15.2	9.5	..	..
Ecuador	15.5	28.0	21.1	24.8	11.6	15.6	22.6	3.3	−6.0	9.6	..	..
Egypt, Arab Rep.	106.8	109.9	87.9	94.1	60.7	74.5	17.1	17.1	7.0	4.5	..	8.3
El Salvador	32.0	49.4	30.6	42.7	19.6	35.1	27.3	9.5	3.2	4.6	..	..
Eritrea	..	148.9	..	152.5	..	86.0	..	24.1	..	..	..	..
Estonia	66.7	49.6	136.0	42.0	95.2	16.8	43.1	9.6	..	4.0	..	..
Ethiopia	66.8	58.0	42.2	52.9	12.6	26.5	24.0	13.6	3.6	4.6	3.0	7.4
Finland	82.8	64.7	54.3	..	..	..	4.1	..	4.1	3.3	..	..
France	104.4	105.0	..	..	..	..	1.0	..	6.1	3.6	0.4	2.7
Gabon	20.0	18.8	17.8	17.3	6.6	7.3	2.0	8.9	11.0	13.0	..	..
Gambia, The	3.4	26.3	20.7	45.1	8.8	20.4	8.8	13.7	15.2	11.3	..	..
Georgia	..	19.6	..	11.7	..	5.6	..	14.4	..	22.0	..	−11.6
Germany	104.4	144.7	69.6	..	..	..	3.2	..	4.5	7.0	3.5	6.7
Ghana	17.5	31.9	14.1	30.7	3.4	14.2	20.2	11.2	..	..	..	..
Greece	99.3	109.5	..	..	..	..	13.9	17.2	8.1	4.7	3.6	3.9
Guatemala	17.4	15.7	21.2	30.6	11.8	18.1	31.8	22.0	5.1	9.9	..	..
Guinea	6.0	12.5	9.2	13.0	1.1	2.3	6.2	27.5	0.2	11.9	..	4.7
Guinea-Bissau	77.5	16.1	68.9	60.9	4.4	0.9	10.8	17.2	13.1	..	..	..
Haiti	34.3	37.3	32.6	42.8	16.6	28.8	74.9	40.0	..	17.4	..	18.1

	Domestic credit provided by banking sector		Liquid liabilities		Quasi-liquid liabilities		Ratio of bank liquid reserves to bank assets		Interest rate spread		Risk premium on lending	
									Lending minus deposit rate percentage points		Prime lending rate minus treasury bill rate percentage points	
	% of GDP		% of GDP		% of GDP		%					
	1990	2002	1990	2002	1990	2002	1990	2002	1990	2002	1990	2002
Honduras	40.9	34.2	33.6	56.8	18.8	43.6	6.7	23.0	8.3	8.9	..	..
Hungary	105.5	53.0	43.8	47.2	19.0	27.8	11.2	5.2	4.1	2.8	–1.4	1.3
India	51.5	58.5	43.1	63.2	28.1	45.7	14.8	5.6	..	..	..	..
Indonesia	45.5	59.5	40.4	54.9	29.1	43.2	4.2	11.1	3.3	3.4	..	..
Iran, Islamic Rep.	70.8	47.6	57.6	44.5	31.1	25.6	66.0	26.8	..	..	..	..
Iraq	..	..	..	..	..	..	..	..	..	..	..	..
Ireland	55.2	110.6	44.5	..	..	..	4.8	..	5.0	3.7	0.4	..
Israel	106.2	93.6	70.2	104.6	63.6	96.7	11.9	8.9	12.0	3.9	11.4	2.5
Italy	89.4	99.6	70.5	..	..	..	12.0	..	7.3	4.3	1.7	2.5
Jamaica	32.2	27.6	47.2	49.3	35.0	33.7	37.4	22.3	6.6	9.9	4.3	3.0
Japan	259.6	312.5	182.3	201.5	155.3	132.0	1.6	3.7	3.4	1.8	..	..
Jordan	117.9	90.4	131.2	120.2	77.8	85.7	20.5	27.1	2.2	5.8	..	..
Kazakhstan	..	13.0	..	19.2	..	9.1	..	4.4	..	..	..	..
Kenya	52.9	43.2	43.3	42.6	29.3	27.2	9.9	8.2	5.1	13.0	4.0	9.5
Korea, Dem. Rep.	..	..	..	..	..	..	..	..	..	..	..	..
Korea, Rep.	65.7	116.9	54.6	103.7	45.7	93.1	6.3	2.6	0.0	1.8	..	..
Kuwait	243.0	105.8	192.2	89.8	153.9	70.6	1.2	1.1	0.0	3.3	0.0	..
Kyrgyz Republic	..	11.4	..	14.7	..	4.4	..	11.3	..	18.9	..	14.7
Lao PDR	5.1	12.6	7.2	19.6	3.1	16.4	3.4	26.5	2.5	23.3	..	7.9
Latvia	..	39.6	..	36.5	..	16.3	..	5.9	..	4.7	..	4.5
Lebanon	132.6	196.1	193.7	217.9	170.9	208.1	3.9	18.8	23.1	5.5	21.1	5.7
Lesotho	32.8	10.7	39.2	28.8	22.6	9.7	23.0	6.2	7.4	11.9	4.1	5.8
Liberia	319.5	168.7	101.9	8.4	20.8	1.5	67.3	56.3	0.0	14.0	..	..
Libya	104.1	50.3	68.1	41.3	13.7	9.0	26.4	24.0	1.5	4.0	1.5	1.5
Lithuania	..	18.3	..	29.3	..	12.8	..	10.9	..	5.1	..	3.1
Macedonia, FYR	..	15.9	..	28.6	..	17.3	..	7.5	..	8.8	..	..
Madagascar	26.2	18.4	17.8	24.3	5.3	5.5	8.5	23.3	5.3	13.3	..	15.0
Malawi	19.7	14.3	20.2	16.2	10.8	7.4	32.9	23.0	8.9	22.5	8.1	8.8
Malaysia	75.7	154.2	118.0	128.5	97.8	103.0	5.9	12.5	1.3	3.2	1.1	3.7
Mali	13.7	16.4	20.5	26.6	5.5	5.8	50.8	18.0	9.0	..	..	..
Mauritania	54.7	–8.3	28.5	16.0	7.0	5.0	6.1	4.0	5.0	..	..	..
Mauritius	48.4	77.1	67.9	87.2	52.7	73.9	8.8	5.1	5.4	11.1	..	..
Mexico	36.6	26.6	22.8	24.5	16.4	14.5	4.3	11.1	..	4.4	..	1.1
Moldova	62.8	29.7	70.3	30.5	35.4	14.4	8.3	16.5	..	9.3	..	17.6
Mongolia	73.4	17.1	56.2	37.8	14.7	22.7	2.0	15.8	..	15.2	..	..
Morocco	60.1	84.5	61.0	89.4	18.4	21.0	11.3	8.1	0.5	8.6	..	..
Mozambique	15.6	13.2	26.5	32.7	5.2	19.0	61.5	14.2	..	8.7	..	–2.0
Myanmar	32.8	35.1	27.9	33.5	7.8	13.1	286.7	16.8	2.1	5.5	..	..
Namibia	20.3	49.0	24.3	40.2	14.2	18.3	4.4	2.9	10.6	6.0	6.3	2.8
Nepal	28.9	43.2	32.2	51.5	18.5	34.9	12.7	22.2	2.5	2.9	6.5	2.7
Netherlands	103.6	160.4	..	..	..	..	0.3	..	8.4	1.2	..	..
New Zealand	80.6	118.2	77.0	89.2	64.0	74.4	0.8	0.5	4.4	4.5	2.2	4.3
Nicaragua	206.6	93.0	56.9	40.3	23.1	34.4	20.2	30.9	12.5	15.8	..	..
Niger	16.2	8.5	19.8	9.0	8.3	2.7	42.9	19.0	9.0	..	..	..
Nigeria	23.7	25.3	23.6	30.5	10.3	12.4	11.9	17.9	5.5	8.1	6.9	5.7
Norway	89.0	54.0	59.5	55.7	26.8	8.8	0.5	4.7	4.6	2.1	..	..
Oman	16.6	40.3	28.9	35.4	19.3	25.5	6.9	4.2	1.4	5.7	..	..
Pakistan	50.9	43.5	39.8	54.8	10.0	23.9	8.9	9.0	..	..	..	..
Panama	52.7	90.7	41.1	76.4	33.0	65.6	..	..	3.6	5.6	..	..
Papua New Guinea	35.7	26.3	35.2	30.2	24.0	15.3	3.2	9.6	6.9	8.1	4.1	3.0
Paraguay	14.9	29.3	22.3	36.7	13.7	28.0	31.0	24.1	8.1	15.8	..	..
Peru	20.2	23.9	24.8	32.4	11.8	21.3	22.0	25.4	2,335.0	10.5	..	..
Philippines	26.9	60.5	37.0	63.0	28.4	51.1	20.9	8.5	4.6	4.5	0.4	3.6
Poland	19.5	36.2	34.0	42.7	17.2	28.1	20.6	5.6	462.5	5.9	–5.0	3.4
Portugal	69.4	149.9	..	..	..	..	29.0	..	7.8	..	8.3	..
Puerto Rico	..	..	..	..	..	..	..	..	..	..	..	..

5.5 Financial depth and efficiency

	Domestic credit provided by banking sector		Liquid liabilities		Quasi-liquid liabilities		Ratio of bank liquid reserves to bank assets		Interest rate spread		Risk premium on lending	
	% of GDP		% of GDP		% of GDP		%		Lending minus deposit rate percentage points		Prime lending rate minus treasury bill rate percentage points	
	1990	2002	1990	2002	1990	2002	1990	2002	1990	2002	1990	2002
Romania	79.7	13.2	60.4	24.7	32.7	19.2	1.2	61.7	..	..	..	..
Russian Federation	..	26.6	..	26.2	..	12.4	..	13.9	..	10.8	..	3.0
Rwanda	17.1	11.1	14.9	17.3	7.0	8.8	4.3	9.9	6.3	..	..	..
Saudi Arabia	52.7	70.1	42.9	54.0	19.6	25.3	5.6	10.0	..	..	..	..
Senegal	33.8	22.6	22.9	27.6	9.7	11.6	14.1	15.9	9.0	..	..	..
Serbia and Montenegro	..	..	..	..	..	..	..	..	..	..	..	..
Sierra Leone	36.3	48.4	18.1	22.9	3.6	7.9	64.1	9.0	12.0	13.9	5.0	7.0
Singapore	75.2	84.8	122.7	115.8	99.9	92.8	3.7	2.5	2.7	4.5	3.7	4.6
Slovak Republic	..	52.8	..	65.3	..	42.5	..	5.2	..	3.6	..	..
Slovenia	36.8	46.0	34.2	55.6	25.8	42.7	2.7	4.0	142.0	4.9	..	4.4
Somalia	..	..	..	..	..	..	..	..	..	..	..	..
South Africa	97.8	150.9	44.6	50.1	27.2	18.3	3.3	2.7	2.1	5.0	3.2	4.6
Spain	107.0	129.6	..	..	..	..	8.7	..	5.4	1.8	1.8	1.0
Sri Lanka	38.0	43.6	34.9	39.3	22.6	30.5	9.9	8.1	−6.4	4.0	−1.1	0.7
Sudan	20.4	11.7	20.1	15.8	2.9	5.9	79.5	19.9	..	..	..	..
Swaziland	7.5	5.6	28.3	20.9	19.8	14.3	21.5	7.1	5.8	7.2	3.4	6.7
Sweden	135.9	75.2	50.7	..	..	..	1.9	0.4	6.8	3.7	3.0	1.9
Switzerland	179.0	174.4	145.2	157.9	118.6	112.0	1.1	0.9	−0.9	3.5	−0.9	3.0
Syrian Arab Republic	56.6	26.7	54.7	79.2	10.5	31.7	46.0	9.1	5.0	5.0	..	..
Tajikistan	..	21.3	..	8.4	..	3.2	..	11.0	..	5.0	..	..
Tanzania	34.6	10.0	19.9	23.0	6.3	12.4	5.3	13.0	0.0	13.1	..	12.9
Thailand	91.1	116.0	74.9	114.5	66.0	102.1	3.1	3.4	2.2	4.9	..	..
Togo	21.3	17.0	36.1	24.3	19.1	8.9	59.0	16.9	9.0	..	..	..
Trinidad and Tobago	58.5	41.5	54.6	51.8	42.7	38.7	13.5	13.4	6.9	7.7	5.4	7.7
Tunisia	62.5	74.4	51.5	60.0	26.7	37.0	1.6	3.4	..	..	..	..
Turkey	19.5	59.3	24.1	49.8	16.4	44.5	16.4	9.0	..	..	..	..
Turkmenistan	..	30.7	..	20.4	..	8.9	..	6.7	..	..	..	..
Uganda	17.8	15.4	7.6	20.2	1.4	9.4	15.2	9.8	7.4	13.5	−2.3	13.2
Ukraine	83.2	28.1	50.1	29.1	9.0	10.9	49.0	9.0	..	17.4	..	..
United Arab Emirates	34.7	47.6	46.3	66.6	37.7	48.6	4.4	9.3	..	..	..	..
United Kingdom	121.2	145.3	..	..	..	..	0.5	0.3	2.2	..	0.7	0.1
United States	110.8	159.4	65.5	70.0	49.4	54.2	2.4	1.1	..	..	2.5	3.1
Uruguay	46.7	93.0	58.1	72.5	51.5	67.0	31.2	12.4	76.6	37.4	..	..
Uzbekistan	..	..	..	..	..	..	..	..	..	..	..	..
Venezuela, RB	37.4	15.0	38.8	17.8	29.4	7.8	21.9	23.2	7.7	7.6	..	..
Vietnam	4.7	44.8	22.7	53.0	9.3	29.6	25.3	6.3	..	2.6	..	3.1
West Bank and Gaza	..	..	..	..	..	..	..	..	..	..	..	..
Yemen, Rep.	60.6	−0.5	55.1	37.4	10.4	19.9	121.2	16.5	..	4.7	..	6.2
Zambia	67.8	46.7	21.8	22.3	10.6	14.0	33.7	22.8	9.4	21.9	9.2	10.7
Zimbabwe	41.7	58.7	41.8	61.3	30.3	24.8	12.2	18.8	2.9	18.1	3.3	8.0
World	**121.2 w**	**150.7 w**	**83.3 w**	**97.5 w**	**.. w**	**68.6 w**	**10.3 m**	**10.3 m**	**5.4 m**	**7.0 m**	**.. m**	**.. m**
Low income	44.7	48.6	36.9	52.1	22.0	35.6	12.8	15.1	7.4	13.0	..	..
Middle income	65.3	82.9	42.3	79.0	24.5	50.3	14.6	9.5	5.0	6.7	..	..
Lower middle income	75.0	100.7	48.8	97.4	28.7	61.9	17.9	9.3	5.6	8.4	..	..
Upper middle income	45.5	49.1	29.1	43.8	16.1	28.2	9.9	9.6	6.2	5.6	..	..
Low & middle income	60.9	76.9	41.2	74.2	24.0	47.7	13.2	11.3	6.6	8.7	..	..
East Asia & Pacific	76.4	143.8	63.1	150.6	37.2	97.0	5.1	12.1	2.2	4.9	..	..
Europe & Central Asia	..	36.9	..	39.3	..	24.9	..	9.9	..	8.2	..	..
Latin America & Carib.	59.1	42.7	25.2	29.8	17.6	20.2	22.3	18.8	8.2	9.9	..	..
Middle East & N. Africa	70.4	72.9	59.0	67.3	26.9	40.2	14.2	16.5	2.2	5.0	..	..
South Asia	48.8	55.3	41.0	59.8	25.2	42.0	12.7	8.6	2.5	7.3	..	..
Sub-Saharan Africa	56.9	65.5	32.1	36.2	16.8	15.4	11.9	13.7	8.2	13.0	..	..
High income	132.1	168.5	92.9	105.6	..	78.7	2.0	1.2	4.6	3.8	2.4	3.5
Europe EMU	99.5	123.0	..	..	..	..	4.1	..	6.5	3.7	2.6	3.5

About the data

The organization and performance of financial activities in a country affect economic growth through their impact on how businesses raise and manage funds. These funds come from savings: savers accumulate claims on financial institutions, which pass the funds to their final users. But even if a country has savings, growth may not materialize—because the financial system may fail to direct the savings to where they can be invested most efficiently. Enabling it to do so requires established payments systems, the availability of price information, a way to manage uncertainty and control risk, and mechanisms to deal with problems of asymmetric information between parties to a financial transaction.

As an economy develops, the indirect lending by savers to investors becomes more efficient and gradually increases financial assets relative to gross domestic product (GDP). More specialized savings and financial institutions emerge and more financing instruments become available, spreading risks and reducing costs to liability holders. Securities markets mature, allowing savers to invest their resources directly in financial assets issued by firms. Financial systems vary widely across countries: banks, nonbank financial institutions, and stock markets are larger, more active, and more efficient in richer countries.

The ratio of domestic credit provided by the banking sector to GDP is used to measure the growth of the banking system because it reflects the extent to which savings are financial. In a few countries governments may hold international reserves as deposits in the banking system rather than in the central bank. Since the claims on the central government are a net item (claims on the central government minus central government deposits), this net figure may be negative, resulting in a negative figure for domestic credit provided by the banking sector.

Liquid liabilities are a general indicator of the size of financial intermediaries relative to the size of the economy, or an overall measure of financial sector development. Quasi-liquid liabilities are long-term deposits and assets—such as bonds, commercial paper, and certificates of deposit—that can be converted into currency or demand deposits, but at a cost. The ratio of bank liquid reserves to bank assets captures the banking system's liquidity. In countries whose banking system is liquid, adverse macroeconomic conditions should be less likely to lead to banking and financial crises. Data on domestic credit and liquid and quasi-liquid liabilities are cited on an end-of-year basis.

No less important than the size and structure of the financial sector is its efficiency, as indicated by the margin between the cost of mobilizing liabilities and the earnings on assets—or the interest rate spread. A narrowing of the interest rate spread reduces transaction costs, which lowers the overall cost of investment and is therefore crucial to economic growth. Interest rates reflect the responsiveness of financial institutions to competition and price incentives. The interest rate spread, also known as the intermediation margin, is a summary measure of a banking system's efficiency (although if governments set interest rates, the spreads become less reliable measures of efficiency). The risk premium on lending can be approximated by the spread between the lending rate to the private sector (line 60p in the International Monetary Fund's International Financial Statistics, or IFS) and the "risk free" treasury bill interest rate (IFS line 60c). A small spread indicates that the market considers its best corporate customers to be low risk. Interest rates are expressed as annual averages.

In some countries financial markets are distorted by restrictions on foreign investment, selective credit controls, and controls on deposit and lending rates. Interest rates may reflect the diversion of resources to finance the public sector deficit through statutory reserve requirements and direct borrowing from the banking system. And where state-owned banks dominate the financial sector, noncommercial considerations may unduly influence credit allocation. The indicators in the table provide quantitative assessments of each country's financial sector, but qualitative assessments of policies, laws, and regulations are needed to analyze overall financial conditions. Recent international financial crises highlight the risks of weak financial intermediation, poor corporate governance, and deficient government policies.

The accuracy of financial data depends on the quality of accounting systems, which are weak in some developing countries. Some indicators in the table are highly correlated, particularly the ratios of domestic credit, liquid liabilities, and quasi-liquid liabilities to GDP, because changes in liquid and quasi-liquid liabilities flow directly from changes in domestic credit. Moreover, the precise definition of the financial aggregates presented varies by country.

The indicators reported here do not capture the activities of the informal sector, which remains an important source of finance in developing economies. Personal credit or credit extended through community-based pooling of assets may be the only source of credit for small farmers, small businesses, and home-based producers. And in financially repressed economies the rationing of formal credit forces many borrowers and lenders to turn to the informal market, which is very expensive, or to self-financing and family savings.

Definitions

- **Domestic credit provided by banking sector** includes all credit to various sectors on a gross basis, with the exception of credit to the central government, which is net. The banking sector includes monetary authorities, deposit money banks, and other banking institutions for which data are available (including institutions that do not accept transferable deposits but do incur such liabilities as time and savings deposits). Examples of other banking institutions include savings and mortgage loan institutions and building and loan associations. • **Liquid liabilities** are also known as broad money, or M3. They include bank deposits of generally less than one year plus currency. Liquid liabilities are the sum of currency and deposits in the central bank (M0); plus transferable deposits and electronic currency (M1); plus time and savings deposits, foreign currency transferable deposits, certificates of deposit, and securities repurchase agreements (M2); plus travelers' checks, foreign currency time deposits, commercial paper, and shares of mutual funds or market funds held by residents. The ratio of liquid liabilities to GDP indicates the relative size of these readily available forms of money—money that the owners can use to buy goods and services without incurring any cost. • **Quasi-liquid liabilities** are the M3 money supply less M1. • **Ratio of bank liquid reserves to bank assets** is the ratio of domestic currency holdings and deposits with the monetary authorities to claims on other governments, nonfinancial public enterprises, the private sector, and other banking institutions. • **Interest rate spread** is the interest rate charged by banks on loans to prime customers minus the interest rate paid by commercial or similar banks for demand, time, or savings deposits. • **Risk premium on lending** is the interest rate charged by banks on loans to prime private sector customers minus the "risk free" treasury bill interest rate at which short-term government securities are issued or traded in the market. In some countries this spread may be negative, indicating that the market considers its best corporate clients to be lower risk than the government.

Data sources

The data on credit, liabilities, bank reserves, and interest rates are collected from central banks and finance ministries and reported in the print and electronic editions of the International Monetary Fund's *International Financial Statistics*.

	Tax revenue	Taxes on income, profits, and capital gains		Domestic taxes on goods and services		Export duties		Import duties		Highest marginal tax rate [a]		
	% of GDP	% of total taxes		% of value added in industry and services		% of tax revenue		% of tax revenue		Individual %	Individual on income over $	Corporate %
	2002	1990	2002	1990	2002	1990	2002	1990	2002	2003	2003	2003
Afghanistan	..	..	..	..	..	..	..	..	..	..	..	..
Albania	..	..	..	..	..	..	..	..	..	..	..	..
Algeria	32.0	..	77.9	..	3.4	..	0.0	..	12.1	..	..	..
Angola	..	..	..	..	..	..	..	..	..	..	..	..
Argentina	12.5	2.7	19.9	2.2	5.5	9.3	0.2	2.6	4.5	35	36,697	35
Armenia	14.6	..	18.3	..	5.7	..	0.0	..	4.9	20	..	20
Australia	..	70.9	..	5.9	..	0.1	..	4.4	..	47	35,149	30
Austria	..	20.8	..	10.0	..	0.0	..	1.6	..	50	48,698	34
Azerbaijan	..	..	..	..	..	..	..	..	..	35	12,257	25
Bangladesh	..	..	..	0.0	..	..	..	..	..	..	..	..
Belarus	26.6	12.1	10.3	17.1	13.5	3.6	..	0.4	..	..	..	..
Belgium	..	36.1	..	11.5	..	0.0	..	0.0	..	50	28,596	39
Benin	..	..	..	..	..	..	..	..	..	..	..	..
Bolivia	13.8	7.9	8.7	5.6	11.2	0.0	0.0	11.1	6.4	13	..	25
Bosnia and Herzegovina	..	..	..	..	..	..	..	..	..	..	..	..
Botswana	..	71.7	..	1.0	..	0.0	..	24.7	..	25	18,560	15
Brazil	..	24.5	..	7.1	..	0.0	..	2.5	..	28	7,251	15
Bulgaria	25.2	40.6	17.0	9.9	16.2	0.0	0.0	2.5	2.6	29	3,982	24
Burkina Faso	..	24.7	..	4.0	..	1.1	..	33.1	..	..	..	..
Burundi	..	23.4	..	0.0	..	3.1	..	23.2	..	..	..	..
Cambodia	..	..	..	..	..	..	..	..	..	20	38,462	20
Cameroon	..	25.1	..	4.3	..	1.7	..	18.9	..	..	..	..
Canada	19.3	59.1	57.3	4.0	..	0.0	0.0	3.2	1.4	29	65,206	38
Central African Republic	..	..	..	..	..	..	..	..	..	..	..	..
Chad	7.2	20.3	..	3.9	..	..	..	..	..	..	..	..
Chile	18.7	15.8	24.7	10.4	13.0	..	..	..	..	40	6,127	17
China	..	49.8	..	1.5	..	0.0	..	22.1	..	45	12,048	..
Hong Kong, China	..	..	..	..	..	..	..	..	..	17	13,462	18
Colombia	..	36.4	..	4.8	..	2.0	..	22.5	..	35	29,426	39
Congo, Dem. Rep.	3.9	28.5	16.7	2.6	1.5	4.1	1.0	45.1	33.7	50	6,056	40
Congo, Rep.	10.5	40.2	16.0	0.0	6.5	0.0	0.0	32.3	23.2	..	..	..
Costa Rica	20.0	11.5	15.1	8.7	10.8	8.0	0.2	18.2	4.2	30	16,860	30
Côte d'Ivoire	16.3	18.1	21.0	8.9	4.8	3.7	15.3	28.4	27.6	10	3,837	35
Croatia	38.2	17.4	8.7	9.6	24.9	0.0	0.0	3.6	6.8	45	35,171	..
Cuba	..	..	..	..	..	..	..	..	..	..	..	..
Czech Republic	32.1	..	21.1	..	11.3	..	0.0	..	1.4	32	10,988	31
Denmark	32.3	43.5	40.2	18.9	19.8	0.0	0.0	0.1	0.0	59	..	30
Dominican Republic	15.6	23.8	19.6	3.1	4.8	0.1	0.0	41.4	44.1	25	16,637	25
Ecuador	..	62.9	..	4.7	..	0.3	..	12.1	..	25	54,400	25
Egypt, Arab Rep.	..	26.4	..	4.1	..	0.0	..	18.9	..	32	10,823	40
El Salvador	10.0	..	18.6	0.0	0.8	..	0.0	..	7.3	..	..	..
Eritrea	..	..	..	..	..	..	..	..	..	..	..	..
Estonia	27.2	27.5	14.7	14.8	15.0	0.0	0.0	0.8	0.2	26	803	35
Ethiopia	15.3	40.9	39.4	9.1	5.4	2.8	0.4	18.0	41.4	35	..	30
Finland	..	34.5	..	17.5	..	0.0	..	1.0	..	36	52,843	29
France	..	18.7	..	13.1	..	0.0	..	0.0	..	..	..	33
Gabon	..	35.9	..	5.0	..	2.8	..	23.4	..	50	..	..
Gambia, The	..	13.7	..	12.2	..	0.2	..	45.6	..	..	..	..
Georgia	10.4	..	3.8	..	9.4	..	0.0	..	7.7	..	..	..
Germany	..	17.5	..	6.9	..	0.0	..	0.0	..	49	52,659	27
Ghana	..	25.1	..	6.8	..	12.4	..	28.7	..	30	5,647	33
Greece	..	23.3	..	14.5	..	0.0	..	0.1	..	40	22,402	35
Guatemala	..	..	..	..	..	..	..	..	..	31	38,028	31
Guinea	..	12.6	..	3.2	..	51.7	..	11.2	..	..	..	..
Guinea-Bissau	..	..	..	..	..	..	..	..	..	..	..	..
Haiti	..	..	..	..	..	..	..	..	..	..	..	..

	Tax revenue	Taxes on income, profits, and capital gains		Domestic taxes on goods and services		Export duties		Import duties		Highest marginal tax rate[a]		Corporate
	% of GDP	% of total taxes		% of value added in industry and services		% of tax revenue		% of tax revenue		Individual on income		%
	2002	1990	2002	1990	2002	1990	2002	1990	2002	% 2003	over $ 2003	2003
Honduras	..	..	..	..	..	..	..	..	..	..	..	..
Hungary	33.6	21.2	23.7	22.6	15.2	1.3	0.0	5.6	2.5	40	5,999	18
India	9.9	18.6	37.4	7.4	5.5	0.1	0.1	35.8	24.1	30	3,139	37
Indonesia	13.6	65.4	48.0	5.5	6.5	0.1	0.3	6.6	4.6	35	22,371	30
Iran, Islamic Rep.	8.5	24.7	41.7	1.0	1.6	0.0	0.0	18.6	14.4	35	125,345	25
Iraq	..	..	..	..	..	..	..	..	..	..	..	..
Ireland	..	39.7	..	15.5	..	0.0	..	0.0	..	42	26,805	16
Israel	36.2	42.4	45.2	..	..	0.0	0.0	1.4	0.7	50	50,886	36
Italy	..	37.7	..	12.7	..	0.0	..	0.0	..	45	67,011	34
Jamaica	26.1	41.5	39.0	0.0	11.8	0.0	0.0	14.0	9.3	25	2,363	33
Japan	..	73.0	..	2.4	..	0.0	..	1.4	..	37	148,478	30
Jordan	19.0	22.9	16.4	6.8	10.6	0.0	0.0	34.7	20.4	..	..	..
Kazakhstan	9.6	..	28.9	..	7.1	..	0.3	..	5.7	30	39,185	30
Kenya	..	32.9	..	15.9	..	0.0	..	17.8	..	30	5,720	30
Korea, Dem. Rep.	..	..	..	..	..	..	..	..	..	..	..	..
Korea, Rep.	..	37.5	..	6.7	..	0.0	..	13.0	..	36	66,644	27
Kuwait	..	19.5	..	0.0	..	0.0	..	76.8	..	0	..	..
Kyrgyz Republic	12.4	..	21.9	..	16.0	..	..	..	..	..	..	..
Lao PDR	..	..	..	..	..	..	..	..	..	..	..	..
Latvia	24.0	..	15.4	..	12.9	..	0.0	..	1.3	25	..	19
Lebanon	..	..	..	..	..	..	..	..	..	..	..	..
Lesotho	..	12.7	..	13.0	..	0.2	..	63.6	..	..	..	..
Liberia	..	..	..	..	..	..	..	..	..	..	..	..
Libya	..	..	..	..	..	..	..	..	..	..	..	..
Lithuania	22.5	22.2	11.9	16.4	14.3	..	0.0	..	1.3	33	..	15
Macedonia, FYR	33.0	..	12.8	..	18.3	..	..	..	7.9	18	..	15
Madagascar	11.3	15.7	15.7	3.4	5.2	8.5	0.0	50.1	53.5	..	..	..
Malawi	..	42.5	..	13.9	..	0.0	..	18.7	..	..	..	..
Malaysia	..	42.5	..	6.3	..	9.7	..	15.1	..	28	65,789	28
Mali	..	..	..	..	..	..	..	..	..	..	..	..
Mauritania	..	..	..	..	..	..	..	..	..	..	..	..
Mauritius	17.3	15.2	14.0	7.0	9.2	4.6	0.0	45.7	29.3	25	862	25
Mexico	13.2	34.2	38.1	10.2	10.5	0.1	0.0	6.9	4.5	35	61,689	34
Moldova	20.5	..	2.6	..	18.2	..	0.0	..	5.6	..	..	..
Mongolia	23.0	28.2	10.5	9.3	18.2	0.0	0.4	19.6	9.8	..	..	..
Morocco	..	27.3	..	12.1	..	0.3	..	20.3	..	44	5,243	35
Mozambique	..	..	..	..	..	..	..	..	..	32	42,583	32
Myanmar	3.0	29.8	34.5	6.8	4.0	0.0	0.0	23.3	7.2	..	..	..
Namibia	29.7	39.4	35.3	9.9	8.6	3.6	..	26.9	..	36	17,241	35
Nepal	9.6	13.0	20.8	6.6	7.1	0.4	2.4	37.0	31.3	..	..	..
Netherlands	..	33.6	..	11.5	..	0.0	..	0.0	..	52	47,352	35
New Zealand	27.9	62.2	68.3	13.2	..	0.0	0.0	2.5	1.8	39	31,561	33
Nicaragua	16.5	20.0	14.7	16.9	11.3	0.0	0.0	21.3	8.4	..	..	..
Niger	..	..	..	..	..	..	..	..	..	..	..	..
Nigeria	..	..	..	..	..	..	..	..	..	..	..	..
Norway	..	21.7	..	16.8	..	0.1	..	0.6	..	..	..	28
Oman	7.4	87.6	77.1	0.3	..	0.0	0.0	7.8	10.3	0	..	12
Pakistan	12.9	12.8	31.1	8.6	8.4	0.0	0.0	44.4	10.8	35	11,111	45
Panama	14.1	24.4	29.4	4.8	..	1.3	0.0	15.8	..	30	200,000	30
Papua New Guinea	..	47.0	..	5.0	..	2.1	..	29.3	..	47	24,842	25
Paraguay	10.1	12.4	16.1	3.6	8.1	0.0	0.0	18.8	17.5	0	..	30
Peru	13.6	5.8	25.1	8.2	9.7	7.6	0.0	9.9	10.5	30	45,863	27
Philippines	13.3	32.5	45.6	6.4	4.7	0.0	0.0	28.4	19.6	32	9,320	32
Poland	26.2	..	18.8	0.0	13.1	..	0.0	..	2.1	40	18,278	27
Portugal	..	25.7	..	13.0	..	0.0	..	2.6	..	40	50,045	30
Puerto Rico	..	..	..	..	..	..	..	..	..	33	50,000	20

5.6 Tax policies

	Tax revenue	Taxes on income, profits, and capital gains		Domestic taxes on goods and services		Export duties		Import duties		Highest marginal tax rate[a]		
	% of GDP	% of total taxes		% of value added in industry and services		% of tax revenue		% of tax revenue		Individual on income		Corporate
										%	over $	%
	2002	1990	2002	1990	2002	1990	2002	1990	2002	2003	2003	2003
Romania	22.8	21.0	12.0	16.0	10.6	0.0	0.0	0.6	3.4	40	3,743	25
Russian Federation	22.5	..	10.8	..	11.3	..	11.2	..	5.1	13	..	24
Rwanda	..	20.0	..	5.5	..	7.4	..	20.7	..	..	..	..
Saudi Arabia	..	..	..	..	..	..	..	..	..	0	..	0
Senegal	17.9	..	22.8	0.0	7.4	..	..	..	..	..	..	..
Serbia and Montenegro	..	..	..	..	..	..	..	..	..	..	..	..
Sierra Leone	..	33.0	..	2.1	..	0.4	..	41.3	..	..	..	..
Singapore	15.4	44.6	52.7	..	5.1	0.0	0.0	3.5	2.6	22	184,438	22
Slovak Republic	29.6	..	19.7	..	10.9	..	0.0	..	1.3	38	14,087	25
Slovenia	35.0	12.3	15.5	12.7	16.6	..	0.0	..	1.8	50	..	25
Somalia	..	..	..	..	..	..	..	..	..	..	..	..
South Africa	26.3	55.0	57.0	10.3	10.3	0.0	0.0	3.9	2.9	40	30,380	30
Spain	..	34.0	..	7.5	..	0.0	..	1.7	..	29	44,794	35
Sri Lanka	14.5	12.0	16.9	14.7	13.6	4.2	0.0	27.4	12.7	30	3,708	30
Sudan	..	..	..	..	..	..	..	..	..	..	..	..
Swaziland	26.7	33.2	26.4	5.2	6.6	2.0	0.0	50.5	54.7	33	4,215	30
Sweden	..	20.6	..	14.5	..	0.0	..	0.6	..	25	50,767	28
Switzerland	23.5	17.0	17.7	..	6.7	0.0	0.0	6.9	1.1	..	..	9
Syrian Arab Republic	..	40.2	..	9.6	..	1.3	..	8.2	..	..	..	..
Tajikistan	10.5	..	3.0	..	9.4	..	0.0	..	17.1	..	..	..
Tanzania	..	..	..	..	..	..	..	..	..	30	7,074	30
Thailand	14.4	26.2	34.3	8.8	7.8	0.2	0.3	23.7	12.3	37	92,379	30
Togo	..	..	..	..	..	..	..	..	..	..	..	..
Trinidad and Tobago	..	..	..	0.0	..	..	..	..	..	30	7,937	30
Tunisia	26.0	16.0	22.3	7.1	12.5	0.4	0.1	35.1	12.5	..	..	..
Turkey	24.2	51.2	42.2	5.9	15.4	0.0	0.0	7.3	1.1	40	73,417	30
Turkmenistan	..	..	..	..	..	..	..	..	..	..	..	..
Uganda	10.8	..	20.1	0.0	5.3	..	0.0	..	50.3	30	2,860	30
Ukraine	21.7	..	14.3	..	10.5	..	0.0	..	4.4	40	3,826	30
United Arab Emirates	..	0.0	..	0.6	..	..	..	..	..	0	..	0
United Kingdom	..	43.2	..	11.3	..	0.0	..	0.0	..	40	48,413	30
United States	17.7	56.1	55.5	0.7	0.7	0.0	0.0	1.7	1.0	39	311,950	35
Uruguay	23.3	7.1	16.5	9.4	10.4	0.6	0.1	8.1	3.0	0	..	35
Uzbekistan	..	..	..	..	..	..	..	..	..	32	561	20
Venezuela, RB	12.2	82.2	34.0	0.8	5.9	0.0	0.0	7.1	12.1	34	72,000	34
Vietnam	16.4	..	32.0	..	9.0	..	0.0	..	22.8	..	..	32
West Bank and Gaza	..	..	..	..	..	..	..	..	..	..	..	..
Yemen, Rep.	..	44.9	..	2.5	..	0.0	..	29.2	..	..	..	..
Zambia	..	..	..	..	..	..	..	..	..	30	368	35
Zimbabwe	..	49.7	..	8.4	..	0.0	..	18.8	..	45	26,249	30

a. These data are from PricewaterhouseCoopers's *Individual Taxes: Worldwide Summaries 2003–2004* and *Corporate Taxes: Worldwide Summaries 2003–2004*, copyright 2003 by PricewaterhouseCoopers by permission of John Wiley and Sons, Inc.

About the data

Taxes are the main source of revenue for many governments. The sources of the tax revenue received by governments and the relative contributions of these sources are determined by policy choices about where and how to impose taxes and by changes in the structure of the economy. Tax policy may reflect concerns about distributional effects, economic efficiency (including corrections for externalities), and the practical problems of administering a tax system. There is no ideal level of taxation. But taxes influence incentives and thus the behavior of economic actors and the economy's competitiveness.

Taxes are compulsory transfers to governments from individuals, businesses, or institutions. They include service fees that are clearly out of proportion to the costs of providing the services but exclude fines, penalties, and compulsory social security contributions. Taxes are considered unrequited because governments provide nothing specifically in return for them, although taxes typically are used to provide goods or services to individuals or communities on a collective basis.

The level of taxation is typically measured by tax revenue as a share of gross domestic product (GDP). Comparing levels of taxation across countries provides a quick overview of the fiscal obligations and incentives facing the private sector. In this table tax data in local currencies are normalized by scaling values in the same units to ease cross-country comparisons. The table shows only central government data, which may significantly understate the total tax burden, particularly in countries where provincial and municipal governments are large or have considerable tax authority.

Low ratios of tax revenue to GDP may reflect weak administration and large-scale tax avoidance or evasion. Low ratios may also reflect the presence of a sizable parallel economy with unrecorded and undisclosed incomes. Tax revenue ratios tend to rise with income, with higher income countries relying on taxes to finance a much broader range of social services and social security than lower income countries are able to provide.

As economies develop, their capacity to tax residents directly typically expands and indirect taxes become less important as a source of revenue. Thus the share of taxes on income, profits, and capital gains is one measure of an economy's (and tax system's) level of development. In the early stages of development governments tend to rely on indirect taxes because the administrative costs of collecting them are relatively low. The two main indirect taxes are international trade taxes (including customs revenues) and domestic taxes on goods and services. The table shows these domestic taxes as a percentage of value added in industry and services. Agriculture and mining are excluded from the denominator

because indirect taxes on goods originating from these sectors are usually negligible. What is missing here is a measure of the uniformity of these taxes across industries and along the value added chain of production. Without such data, no clear inferences can be drawn about how neutral a tax system is between subsectors. "Surplus" revenues raised by some governments by charging higher prices for goods produced under monopoly by state-owned enterprises are not counted as tax revenues. Similarly, losses from charging below-market prices for products are rarely identified as subsidies.

Export and import duties are shown separately because the burden they impose on the economy (and thus growth) is likely to be large. Export duties, typically levied on primary (particularly agricultural) products, often take the place of direct taxes on income and profits, but they reduce the incentive to export and encourage a shift to other products. High import duties penalize consumers, create protective barriers—which promote higher priced output and inefficient production—and implicitly tax exports. By contrast, lower trade taxes enhance openness—to foreign competition, knowledge, technologies, and resources—energizing development in many ways. Seeing this pattern, some of the fastest growing economies have lowered import tariffs in recent years. The simple mean import tariff in India, for example, declined from almost 80 percent in 1990 to about 30 percent in 2001. In some countries, such as members of the European Union, most customs duties are collected by a supranational authority; these revenues are not reported in the individual countries' accounts.

The tax revenues collected by governments are the outcomes of systems that are often complex, containing many exceptions, exemptions, penalties, and other inducements that affect the incidence of taxes and thus influence the decisions of workers, managers, and entrepreneurs. A potentially important influence on both domestic and international investors is a tax system's progressivity, as reflected in the highest marginal tax rate levied at the national level on individual and corporate income. Figures for individual marginal tax rates generally refer to employment income. In some countries the highest marginal tax rate is also the basic or flat rate, and other surtaxes, deductions, and the like may apply. And in many countries several different corporate tax rates may be levied, depending on the type of business (mining, banking, insurance, agriculture, manufacturing), ownership (domestic or foreign), volume of sales, or whether surtaxes or exemptions are included. The corporate tax rates in the table are mainly general rates applied to domestic companies. For more detailed information, see the country's laws, regulations, and tax treaties.

Definitions

• **Tax revenue** comprises compulsory transfers to the central government for public purposes. Compulsory transfers such as fines, penalties, and most social security contributions are excluded. Refunds and corrections of erroneously collected tax revenue are treated as negative revenue. • **Taxes on income, profits, and capital gains** are levied on wages, salaries, tips, fees, commissions, and other compensation for labor services; interest, dividends, rent, and royalties; profits of businesses, estates, and trusts; and capital gains and losses. Social security contributions based on gross pay, payroll, or number of employees are not included, but taxable portions of social security, pension, and other retirement account distributions are included. • **Domestic taxes on goods and services** are all taxes and duties levied by central governments on the production, extraction, sale, transfer, leasing, or delivery of goods and rendering of services, or on the use of goods or permission to use goods or perform activities. These include value added taxes, general sales taxes, single-stage and multistage taxes (where *stage* refers to stage of production or distribution), excise taxes, motor vehicle taxes, and taxes on the extraction, processing, or production of minerals or other products. • **Export duties** are all levies collected on goods at the point of export. Rebates on exported goods that are repayments of previously paid general consumption taxes, excise taxes, or import duties are deducted from the gross amounts receivable from these taxes, not from amounts receivable from export duties. • **Import duties** are all levies collected on goods at the point of entry into the country. They include levies imposed for revenue or protection purposes and determined on a specific or ad valorem basis as long as they are restricted to imported products. • **Highest marginal tax rate** is the highest rate shown on the national level schedule of tax rates applied to the annual taxable income of individuals and corporations. Also presented are the income levels for individuals above which the highest marginal tax rates levied at the national level apply.

Data sources

The definitions used here are from the International Monetary Fund's (IMF) *Manual on Government Finance Statistics* (2002). The data on tax revenues are from print and electronic editions of the IMF's *Government Finance Statistics Yearbook*. The data on individual and corporate tax rates are from PricewaterhouseCoopers's *Individual Taxes: Worldwide Summaries 2003–2004* and *Corporate Taxes: Worldwide Summaries 2003–2004*.

	Exchange rate arrangements[a]		Official exchange rate	Purchasing power parity (PPP) conversion factor		Ratio of PPP conversion factor to official exchange rate	Real effective exchange rate	Interest rate		
			local currency units to $	local currency units to international $			index 1995 = 100	Deposit	% Lending	Real
	Classification 2002	Structure 2002	2002	1990	2002	2002	2002	2002	2002	2002
Afghanistan	MF	U	3,000.00	..	..	..	..	..	..	..
Albania	IF	U	140.15	2.0	44.5	0.3	..	8.5	15.3	8.7
Algeria	MF	U	79.68	5.0	24.7	0.3	101.7	5.3	8.5	7.4
Angola	MF	U	43.53	0.0	17.5	0.4	..	48.7	97.3	−2.9
Argentina	MF	U	3.06	0.3	0.8	0.2	..	39.2	51.7	16.2
Armenia	IF	U	573.35	..	141.9	0.2	95.9	9.6	21.1	18.5
Australia	IF	U	1.84	1.4	1.4	0.7	96.1	3.0	8.0	5.5
Austria	Euro	U	1.06	0.9	0.9	0.9	92.1	..	..	..
Azerbaijan	MF	U	4,860.82	1.1	1,127.8	0.2	..	8.7	17.4	16.5
Bangladesh	P	U	57.89	9.6	11.9	0.2	..	8.2	16.0	12.4
Belarus	P	U	1,790.92	..	465.9	0.3	..	26.9	36.9	−3.6
Belgium	Euro	U	1.06	0.9	0.9	0.9	90.2	2.6	7.7	5.8
Benin	EA/Euro	U	696.99	160.7	267.2	0.4	..	3.5	..	..
Bolivia	P	U	7.17	1.3	2.6	0.4	115.4	9.6	20.6	17.5
Bosnia and Herzegovina	CB/Euro	U	2.08	..	..	..	..	4.5	12.7	10.4
Botswana	P/Euro	D	6.33	1.2	2.4	0.4	..	10.3	16.0	9.9
Brazil	IF	U	2.92	0.0	1.0	0.3	..	19.1	62.9	50.1
Bulgaria	CB/Euro	U	2.08	0.0	0.6	0.3	135.6	2.8	9.3	5.3
Burkina Faso	EA/Euro	U	696.99	136.3	168.0	0.2	..	3.5	..	..
Burundi	MF	U	930.75	49.6	149.3	0.2	79.1	..	19.5	5.8
Cambodia	MF	D	3,912.08	..	610.5	0.2	..	2.5	16.2	12.8
Cameroon	EA/Euro	U	696.99	171.8	210.9	0.3	102.1	5.0	18.0	17.2
Canada	IF	U	1.57	1.3	1.2	0.8	97.7	0.8	4.2	3.2
Central African Republic	EA/Euro	U	696.99	136.0	162.6	0.2	95.4	5.0	18.0	16.3
Chad	EA/Euro	U	696.99	106.1	163.6	0.2	..	5.0	18.0	13.8
Chile	IF	U	688.94	149.5	288.7	0.4	90.7	3.8	7.8	5.0
China	P	U	8.28	1.2	1.8	0.2	121.4	2.0	5.3	5.6
Hong Kong, China	CB	U	7.80	6.4	6.9	0.9	..	0.3	5.0	8.2
Colombia	IF	U	2,504.24	120.6	727.5	0.3	90.4	8.9	16.3	9.7
Congo, Dem. Rep.	IF	U	346.48	0.0	58.7	0.2	109.2	..	66.8	35.3
Congo, Rep.	EA/Euro	U	696.99	387.9	587.7	0.8	..	5.0	18.0	18.8
Costa Rica	P	U	359.82	32.8	173.8	0.5	109.4	11.5	26.4	15.8
Côte d'Ivoire	EA/Euro	U	696.99	168.0	324.3	0.5	103.7	3.5	..	..
Croatia	MF	U	7.87	..	3.9	0.5	103.7	1.9	12.8	9.6
Cuba	..	..	..	..	..	..	..	..	..	..
Czech Republic	MF	U	32.74	8.1	14.1	0.4	133.6	2.2	6.2	3.5
Denmark	P	U	7.89	8.1	8.2	1.0	96.7	2.4	7.1	6.2
Dominican Republic	MF	D	18.61	2.6	7.0	0.4	112.1	16.5	26.1	18.4
Ecuador	EA/Other	U	1.00	0.4	0.5	0.5	113.8	5.5	15.1	2.9
Egypt, Arab Rep.	MF	U	4.50	0.8	1.5	0.3	..	9.3	13.8	9.4
El Salvador	EA/Other	U	8.75	2.4	4.0	0.5	..	9.3	14.0	10.5
Eritrea	P	U	13.96	1.2	2.3	0.2	..	..	..	..
Estonia	CB/Euro	U	16.61	0.1	6.5	0.4	..	2.7	6.7	2.5
Ethiopia	MF	U	8.57	0.7	1.0	0.1	79.4	4.1	8.7	16.9
Finland	Euro	U	1.06	1.0	1.0	1.0	90.2	1.5	4.8	3.5
France	Euro	U	1.06	1.0	0.9	0.9	89.8	3.0	6.6	4.7
Gabon	EA/Euro	U	696.99	341.2	399.5	0.6	91.4	5.0	18.0	11.4
Gambia, The	MF	U	19.92	1.8	3.0	0.2	68.4	12.7	24.0	3.6
Georgia	IF	U	2.20	..	0.6	0.3	..	9.8	31.8	23.9
Germany	Euro	U	1.06	1.0	0.9	0.9	86.6	2.7	9.7	8.0
Ghana	MF	U	7,932.70	94.9	1,134.2	0.1	81.0	16.2	..	..
Greece	Euro	U	1.06	0.4	0.7	0.7	100.0	2.8	7.4	3.6
Guatemala	MF	U	7.82	1.4	3.7	0.5	..	6.9	16.9	8.2
Guinea	P	U	1,975.84	225.0	390.8	0.2	..	7.4	19.4	7.4
Guinea-Bissau	EA/Euro	U	696.99	11.0	137.8	0.2	..	3.5	..	..
Haiti	MF	U	29.25	1.2	7.2	0.2	..	8.2	25.7	15.3

	Exchange rate arrangements[a]		Official exchange rate	Purchasing power parity (PPP) conversion factor		Ratio of PPP conversion factor to official exchange rate	Real effective exchange rate	Interest rate		
			local currency units to $	local currency units to international $			index 1995 = 100	Deposit	% Lending	Real
	Classification 2002	Structure 2002	2002	1990	2002	2002	2002	2002	2002	2002
Honduras	P	U	16.43	1.3	6.1	0.4	..	13.7	22.7	15.5
Hungary	P	U	257.89	22.3	124.8	0.5	130.8	7.4	10.2	–0.5
India	MF	U	48.61	4.9	8.8	0.2	..	..	11.9	8.7
Indonesia	MF	U	9,311.19	642.6	2,357.7	0.3	..	15.5	18.9	11.0
Iran, Islamic Rep.	MF	D	6,906.96	180.4	1,963.4	0.3	198.1	..	..	..
Iraq	MF	U	0.31	..	..	..	..	..	..	..
Ireland	Euro	U	1.06	0.8	0.9	0.9	99.0	0.1	3.8	–2.7
Israel	P	U	4.74	1.8	3.8	0.8	102.5	6.0	9.9	5.2
Italy	Euro	U	1.06	0.7	0.8	0.8	110.0	1.4	5.8	2.9
Jamaica	MF	U	48.42	4.4	36.6	0.8	..	8.6	18.5	9.7
Japan	IF	U	125.39	190.2	146.2	1.2	78.9	0.0	1.9	3.6
Jordan	P	U	0.71	0.3	0.3	0.4	..	4.4	10.2	9.7
Kazakhstan	MF	U	153.28	..	43.2	0.3	..	..	..	..
Kenya	MF	U	78.75	9.1	30.4	0.4	..	5.5	18.5	9.0
Korea, Dem. Rep.	..	..	..	..	..	..	..	..	..	..
Korea, Rep.	IF	U	1,251.09	563.7	738.7	0.6	..	4.9	6.8	5.0
Kuwait	P	U	0.30	0.3	0.3	0.9	..	3.2	6.5	3.0
Kyrgyz Republic	MF	U	46.94	..	9.3	0.2	..	5.9	24.8	22.0
Lao PDR	MF	D	10,056.33	174.9	1,884.2	0.2	..	6.0	29.3	18.4
Latvia	p	U	0.62	..	0.2	0.4	..	3.2	8.0	6.1
Lebanon	P	U	1,507.50	307.0	1,346.0	0.9	..	11.0	16.6	13.8
Lesotho	P	U	10.54	1.0	1.7	0.2	60.8	5.2	17.1	7.4
Liberia	IF	U	61.75	..	..	..	..	6.2	20.2	–7.1
Libya	P	U	1.27	..	..	..	..	3.0	7.0	..
Lithuania	CB/Euro	U	3.68	..	1.4	0.4	..	1.7	6.8	6.9
Macedonia, FYR	P	U	64.35	..	18.5	0.3	72.6	9.6	18.4	14.3
Madagascar	IF	U	6,831.96	516.0	2,456.7	0.4	..	12.0	25.3	8.6
Malawi	IF	U	76.69	1.4	23.3	0.3	115.0	28.1	50.5	28.1
Malaysia	P	U	3.80	1.5	1.6	0.4	91.3	3.2	6.4	2.7
Mali	EA/Euro	U	696.99	141.4	222.8	0.3	..	3.5	..	..
Mauritania	MF	U	271.74	36.5	42.7	0.2	..	..	..	..
Mauritius	MF	U	29.96	6.5	10.5	0.3	..	9.9	21.0	15.1
Mexico	IF	U	9.66	1.5	6.8	0.7	..	3.8	8.2	3.4
Moldova	MF	U	13.57	..	3.5	0.3	100.2	14.2	23.5	14.3
Mongolia	MF	U	1,110.31	2.9	296.8	0.3	..	13.2	28.4	21.1
Morocco	P	U	11.02	3.2	3.5	0.3	103.4	4.5	13.1	12.5
Mozambique	IF	U	23,677.96	321.5	4,406.7	0.2	..	18.0	26.7	13.9
Myanmar	MF	D	6.57	..	..	..	..	9.5	15.0	–6.2
Namibia	P	U	10.54	0.9	2.5	0.2	..	7.8	13.8	4.0
Nepal	P	U	77.88	6.8	12.7	0.2	..	4.8	7.7	4.3
Netherlands	Euro	U	1.06	0.9	0.9	0.9	95.8	2.8	4.0	0.7
New Zealand	IF	U	2.16	1.6	1.5	0.7	88.9	5.3	9.8	8.0
Nicaragua	P	U	14.25	0.0	4.3	0.3	111.6	7.3	23.2	17.0
Niger	EA/Euro	U	696.99	122.3	165.4	0.2	..	3.5	..	..
Nigeria	MF	M	120.58	3.8	46.2	0.4	90.3	16.7	24.8	11.8
Norway	IF	U	7.98	8.0	9.2	1.1	107.9	6.5	8.5	10.0
Oman	P	U	0.38	0.3	0.2	0.6	..	2.9	8.5	6.6
Pakistan	MF	U	59.72	5.8	12.9	0.2	90.0	..	..	..
Panama	EA/Other	U	1.00	0.6	0.7	0.7	..	5.0	10.6	9.3
Papua New Guinea	IF	U	3.90	0.5	0.9	0.2	81.2	5.8	13.9	1.5
Paraguay	MF	U	5,716.26	408.1	1,240.2	0.2	75.6	22.9	38.7	21.0
Peru	IF	U	3.52	0.1	1.5	0.4	..	4.2	14.7	14.1
Philippines	IF	U	51.60	5.6	12.1	0.2	85.6	4.6	9.1	4.1
Poland	IF	U	4.08	0.2	1.9	0.5	133.4	6.2	12.1	10.3
Portugal	Euro	U	1.06	0.5	0.7	0.7	100.6	..	..	..
Puerto Rico	..	..	..	0.7	0.7	..	..	..	..	..

	Exchange rate arrangements[a]		Official exchange rate	Purchasing power parity (PPP) conversion factor		Ratio of PPP conversion factor to official exchange rate	Real effective exchange rate	Interest rate		
			local currency units to $	local currency units to international $			index 1995 = 100	Deposit	% Lending	Real
	Classification 2002	Structure 2002	2002	1990	2002	2002	2002	2002	2002	2002
Romania	P	U	33,055.43	6.9	10,344.3	0.3	110.2	..	..	..
Russian Federation	MF	U	31.35		9.2	0.3	109.0	5.0	15.7	0.4
Rwanda	MF	U	476.33	31.4	79.5	0.2	..	8.0	..	..
Saudi Arabia	P	U	3.74	2.9	2.5	0.7	107.2	2.2	..	..
Senegal	EA/Euro	U	696.99	185.8	222.2	0.3	..	3.5	..	..
Serbia and Montenegro	MF	U	..	..	..	..	..	..	..	..
Sierra Leone	IF	D	2,099.03	30.0	599.7	0.3	94.1	8.2	22.2	17.6
Singapore	MF	U	1.79	1.9	1.6	0.9	93.7	0.9	5.4	5.2
Slovak Republic	MF	U	45.33	5.9	15.5	0.3	105.8	6.6	10.2	6.1
Slovenia	P	U	240.25	..	144.9	0.6	..	8.2	13.2	4.7
Somalia	IF	D	..	..	..	..	..	..	..	..
South Africa	IF	U	10.54	1.0	2.4	0.2	62.6	10.8	15.8	6.6
Spain	Euro	U	1.06	0.6	0.8	0.7	98.3	2.5	4.3	−0.1
Sri Lanka	MF	U	95.66	10.3	23.4	0.2	..	9.2	13.2	4.5
Sudan	P	U	263.31	0.7	59.8	0.2	..	..	..	..
Swaziland	P	U	10.54	0.9	2.5	0.2	..	8.0	15.3	1.5
Sweden	IF	U	9.74	9.9	10.1	1.0	89.8	*2.2*	*5.8*	*4.5*
Switzerland	IF	U	1.56	2.0	1.9	1.2	93.1	0.4	3.9	3.5
Syrian Arab Republic	P	M	11.23	10.3	16.9	1.5	..	4.0	9.0	4.4
Tajikistan	MF	U	2.76	..	0.5	0.2	..	9.2	14.2	−6.4
Tanzania	IF	U	966.58	76.0	444.9	0.5	..	3.3	16.4	11.8
Thailand	MF	U	42.96	10.8	12.6	0.3	..	2.0	6.9	6.1
Togo	EA/Euro	U	696.99	94.5	137.1	0.2	105.4	3.5	..	..
Trinidad and Tobago	MF	U	6.25	3.1	4.9	0.8	126.6	4.8	12.5	11.6
Tunisia	P	U	1.42	0.4	0.5	0.3	96.2	..	..	..
Turkey	IF	U	1,507,226.38	1,643.1	621,572.8	0.4	..	50.5	..	..
Turkmenistan	P	D	*5,200.00*	..	*1,544.1*	0.3	..	..	..	..
Uganda	IF	U	1,797.55	111.4	298.4	0.2	76.7	5.6	19.1	23.1
Ukraine	P	U	5.33	..	0.9	0.2	112.4	7.9	25.3	21.4
United Arab Emirates	P	U	3.67	3.4	..	..	..	..	*8.1*	..
United Kingdom	IF	U	0.67	0.6	0.7	1.0	130.4	..	4.0	0.8
United States	IF	U	1.00	1.0	1.0	1.0	133.6	..	4.7	3.5
Uruguay	IF	U	21.26	0.6	10.0	0.5	87.9	*14.3*	126.1	90.3
Uzbekistan	MF	M	*236.61*	..	177.4	*0.4*	..	..	..	..
Venezuela, RB	P	U	1,160.95	24.7	810.6	0.7	132.9	29.0	36.6	3.8
Vietnam	MF	U	15,279.50	644.4	2,892.2	0.2	..	6.4	9.1	4.8
West Bank and Gaza	..	..	..	..	..	..	..	..	..	..
Yemen, Rep.	IF	U	175.63	20.4	108.3	0.6	..	13.0	17.7	11.9
Zambia	MF	U	4,398.60	18.7	1,893.0	0.4	115.8	23.3	45.2	21.1
Zimbabwe	P	U	55.04	1.0	*16.4*	*0.3*	..	18.4	36.5	−34.2

a. Exchange rate arrangements are given for the end of the year in 2002. Exchange rate classifications include independent floating (IF), managed floating (MF), pegged (P), currency board (CB), and several exchange arrangements (EA): Euro that the currency is pegged to the euro, and other that the currency of another country is used as legal tender. Exchange rate structures include dual exchange rates (D), multiple exchange rates (M), and unitary rate (U).

About the data

In a market-based economy the choices households, producers, and governments make about the allocation of resources are influenced by relative prices, including the real exchange rate, real wages, real interest rates, and a host of other prices in the economy. Relative prices also reflect, to a large extent, the choices of these agents. Thus relative prices convey vital information about the interaction of economic agents in an economy and with the rest of the world.

The exchange rate is the price of one currency in terms of another. Official exchange rates and exchange rate arrangements are established by governments. (Other exchange rates fully recognized by governments include market rates, which are determined largely by legal market forces, and for countries maintaining multiple exchange arrangements, principal rates, secondary rates, and tertiary rates.) Also see *Statistical methods* for information on alternative conversion factors used in the Atlas method of calculating gross national income (GNI) per capita in U.S. dollars.

The official or market exchange rate is often used to compare prices in different currencies. Since exchange rates reflect at best the relative prices of tradable goods, the volume of goods and services that a U.S. dollar buys in the United States may not correspond to what a U.S. dollar converted to another country's currency at the official exchange rate would buy in that country. Since identical volumes of goods and services in different countries correspond to different values (and vice versa) when official exchange rates are used, an alternative method of comparing prices across countries has been developed. In this method national currency estimates of GNI are converted to a common unit of account by using conversion factors that reflect equivalent purchasing power. Purchasing power parity (PPP) conversion factors are based on price and expenditure surveys conducted by the International Comparison Program and represent the conversion factors applied to equalize price levels across countries. See *About the data* for table 1.1 for further discussion of the PPP conversion factor.

The ratio of the PPP conversion factor to the official exchange rate (also referred to as the national price level) makes it possible to compare the cost of the bundle of goods that make up gross domestic product (GDP) across countries. These national price levels vary systematically, rising with GNI per capita.

Real effective exchange rates are derived by deflating a trade-weighted average of the nominal exchange rates that apply between trading partners.

For most high-income countries the weights are based on trade in manufactured goods with other high-income countries in 1989–91, and an index of relative, normalized unit labor costs is used as the deflator. (Normalization smooths a time series by removing short-term fluctuations while retaining changes of a large amplitude over the longer economic cycle.) For other countries the weights before 1990 take into account trade in manufactured and primary products in 1980–82, the weights from January 1990 onward take into account trade in 1988–90, and an index of relative changes in consumer prices is used as the deflator. An increase in the real effective exchange rate represents an appreciation of the local currency. Because of conceptual and data limitations, changes in real effective exchange rates should be interpreted with caution.

Many interest rates coexist in an economy, reflecting competitive conditions, the terms governing loans and deposits, and differences in the position and status of creditors and debtors. In some economies interest rates are set by regulation or administrative fiat. In economies with imperfect markets, or where reported nominal rates are not indicative of effective rates, it may be difficult to obtain data on interest rates that reflect actual market transactions. Deposit and lending rates are collected by the International Monetary Fund (IMF) as representative interest rates offered by banks to resident customers. The terms and conditions attached to these rates differ by country, however, limiting their comparability. Real interest rates are calculated by adjusting nominal rates by an estimate of the inflation rate in the economy. A negative real interest rate indicates a loss in the purchasing power of the principal. The real interest rates in the table are calculated as $(i - P) / (1 + P)$, where i is the nominal interest rate and P is the inflation rate (as measured by the GDP deflator).

Data sources

The information on exchange rate arrangements is from the IMF's *Exchange Arrangements and Exchange Restrictions Annual Report, 2003*. The official and real effective exchange rates and deposit and lending rates are from the IMF's *International Financial Statistics*. PPP conversion factors are from the World Bank. The real interest rates are calculated using World Bank data on the GDP deflator.

	Military expenditures				Armed forces personnel				Arms transfers			
	% of GDP		% of central government expenditure		Total thousands		% of labor force		$ millions 1990 prices			
									Exports		Imports	
	1992	2002	1992	2002	1992	1999	1992	1999	1992	2002	1992	2002
Afghanistan	..	..	..	..	45	..	0.6	..	..	..	..	31
Albania	4.6	1.2	..	3.7	65	18	4.1	1.2	..	..	..	0
Algeria	2.2	3.7	9.5	0.0	126	120	1.6	1.2	..	..	16	464
Angola	12.0	3.7	..	..	128	100	2.8	1.8	20	1	106	5
Argentina	1.4	1.2	12.0	8.1	65	73	0.5	0.5	15	3	16	210
Armenia	2.2	2.7	..	..	20	50	1.2	3.2	..	..	8	2
Australia	2.3	1.7	8.9	7.5	68	55	0.8	0.6	4	30	250	614
Austria	1.0	0.8	2.4	2.0	44	49	1.2	1.3	13	124	2	79
Azerbaijan	3.3	2.1	12.4	10.2	43	75	1.4	2.1	..	..	64	3
Bangladesh	1.1	1.1	..	11.2	107	110	0.2	0.2	..	..	63	21
Belarus	1.5	1.4	4.1	4.5	102	65	1.9	1.2	8	333	..	41
Belgium	1.8	1.3	3.7	3.2	79	42	1.9	1.0	20	14	64	29
Benin	..	..	..	..	7	8	0.3	0.3	..	..	..	..
Bolivia	2.1	1.7	10.6	6.1	32	33	1.2	1.0	..	..	24	1
Bosnia and Herzegovina	..	9.5	..	..	60	30	3.2	1.7	..	..	0	25
Botswana	4.3	4.0	11.7	..	7	8	1.2	1.1	..	..	3	12
Brazil	1.1	1.6	3.7	5.2	296	300	0.4	0.4	61	18	66	154
Bulgaria	2.7	2.7	6.6	7.9	99	70	2.3	1.7	18	20	44	6
Burkina Faso	2.3	1.7	14.0	..	9	9	0.2	0.2	..	..	..	..
Burundi	3.6	7.6	10.7	27.1	13	40	0.4	1.1	..	..	..	1
Cambodia	4.7	2.7	..	..	135	60	2.7	1.0	0	..	2	22
Cameroon	1.5	1.4	8.4	10.4	12	15	0.2	0.2	..	..	3	1
Canada	1.9	1.1	6.9	6.2	82	60	0.5	0.4	210	318	344	359
Central African Republic	1.6	..	..	..	4	3	0.3	0.2	..	..	1	..
Chad	2.7	1.4	..	..	38	30	1.3	0.8	..	..	8	15
Chile	3.4	2.9	16.2	12.4	92	88	1.8	1.4	1	1	182	56
China	2.7	2.5	32.5	19.2	3,160	2,400	0.5	0.3	642	818	1,163	2,307
Hong Kong, China	..	..	..	..	..	..	..	..	..	..	..	..
Colombia	2.4	3.7	15.8	18.8	139	155	0.9	0.9	..	..	32	119
Congo, Dem. Rep.	..	..	..	..	45	55	0.3	0.3	..	..	2	14
Congo, Rep.	..	..	..	..	10	10	0.9	0.7	..	..	..	0
Costa Rica	..	..	..	..	8	10	0.6	0.7	..	..	3	..
Côte d'Ivoire	1.4	0.9	4.0	3.7	15	15	0.3	0.2	..	..	1	7
Croatia	7.6	2.5	19.1	5.9	103	60	4.6	2.9	..	2	24	2
Cuba	..	..	..	..	175	50	3.5	0.9	..	..	..	..
Czech Republic	2.3	2.1	6.2	5.4	107	54	1.9	0.9	265	85	..	53
Denmark	1.9	1.6	4.8	4.3	28	27	1.0	0.9	190	9	42	7
Dominican Republic	..	..	..	..	22	30	0.7	0.8	..	..	..	13
Ecuador	2.7	2.1	16.9	..	57	58	1.5	1.2	..	..	14	1
Egypt, Arab Rep.	3.6	2.7	10.5	10.2	424	430	2.2	1.8	10	25	995	638
El Salvador	2.0	0.8	..	31.2	49	15	2.4	0.6	..	..	3	3
Eritrea	21.4	27.5	..	..	55	215	3.2	10.8	..	..	14	180
Estonia	0.5	1.9	2.2	5.6	3	7	0.4	0.9	..	..	1	1
Ethiopia	2.7	5.2	19.3	43.0	120	300	0.5	1.1	..	..	..	20
Finland	1.9	1.2	4.6	4.4	33	35	1.3	1.3	3	12	441	24
France	3.4	2.5	7.6	6.4	522	421	2.1	1.6	845	1,617	387	22
Gabon	..	0.3	..	..	7	7	1.4	1.2	..	..	..	..
Gambia, The	1.0	0.9	..	..	1	1	0.2	0.2	..	..	..	..
Georgia	..	0.6	..	4.9	25	14	0.9	0.5	..	108	4	80
Germany	2.1	1.5	6.3	4.7	442	331	1.1	0.8	1,134	745	969	16
Ghana	0.6	0.6	3.6	..	7	7	0.1	0.1	..	..	10	9
Greece	4.5	4.3	15.5	15.6	208	204	4.8	4.5	15	11	1,994	567
Guatemala	1.3	0.6	..	..	44	30	1.4	0.7	..	..	10	1
Guinea	1.9	1.7	9.0	8.5	15	12	0.5	0.3	..	..	..	5
Guinea-Bissau	0.3	3.1	..	..	11	7	2.1	1.1	..	..	1	..
Haiti	..	..	..	..	8	0	0.3	0.0	..	..	..	..

Defense expenditures and arms transfers

	Military expenditures				Armed forces personnel				Arms transfers $ millions 1990 prices			
	% of GDP		% of central government expenditure		Total thousands		% of labor force		Exports		Imports	
	1992	2002	1992	2002	1992	1999	1992	1999	1992	2002	1992	2002
Honduras	..	..	..	..	17	8	0.9	0.3	..	..	..	..
Hungary	2.4	1.8	4.3	4.4	78	51	1.6	1.1	21	24	1,021	14
India	2.3	2.6	..	..	1,270	1,300	0.3	0.3	0	0	871	1,668
Indonesia	1.7	1.1	9.4	4.6	283	296	0.3	0.3	20	70	47	51
Iran, Islamic Rep.	1.9	4.8	11.2	17.2	528	460	3.2	2.4	1	0	386	298
Iraq	..	..	..	..	407	420	8.2	6.7	..	..	..	..
Ireland	1.2	0.7	3.0	2.8	13	14	1.0	0.9	..	0	48	20
Israel	10.5	8.6	21.6	16.6	181	173	8.8	6.6	68	178	1,330	226
Italy	2.0	1.9	3.9	4.8	471	391	1.9	1.5	368	490	42	308
Jamaica	..	..	..	..	3	3	0.2	0.2	..	..	..	5
Japan	0.9	1.0	4.5	..	242	240	0.4	0.4	13	3	1,523	154
Jordan	8.2	8.4	27.8	26.5	100	102	9.8	7.3	73	5	1	149
Kazakhstan	1.0	0.9	..	6.8	15	33	0.2	0.4	..	9	..	69
Kenya	1.9	1.6	7.9	5.8	24	24	0.2	0.2	..	..	3	61
Korea, Dem. Rep.	..	..	..	..	1,200	1,000	11.3	8.6	225	32	45	3
Korea, Rep.	3.4	2.7	20.6	16.6	750	665	3.6	2.8	21	22	497	229
Kuwait	31.8	11.2	31.5	18.8	12	21	2.1	2.5	..	82	897	27
Kyrgyz Republic	0.7	1.7	3.2	9.7	12	12	0.6	0.6	..	..	..	..
Lao PDR	..	2.1	..	..	37	50	1.7	2.0	..	..	..	34
Latvia	0.8	1.8	3.4	3.9	5	5	0.3	0.4	8	..	0	3
Lebanon	8.0	4.7	25.7	14.0	37	58	3.1	3.9	..	45	38	4
Lesotho	2.6	3.1	5.7	6.4	2	2	0.3	0.3	..	..	..	6
Liberia	10.6	..	..	..	2	..	0.2	..	..	..	..	8
Libya	..	..	..	..	85	85	6.6	5.8	8	11	..	145
Lithuania	0.7	2.0	3.5	6.8	10	12	0.5	0.7	..	3	74	7
Macedonia, FYR	..	2.8	..	..	10	16	1.1	1.7	..	..	27	133
Madagascar	1.2	1.2	6.6	7.1	21	20	0.4	0.3	..	..	..	..
Malawi	1.4	0.8	..	..	10	5	0.2	0.1	..	1	1	..
Malaysia	3.0	2.1	10.5	10.6	128	95	1.7	1.0	..	8	16	213
Mali	2.4	2.0	..	..	12	10	0.3	0.2	..	..	..	7
Mauritania	3.5	1.9	..	..	16	11	1.6	0.9	..	..	27	9
Mauritius	0.4	0.2	1.5	0.8	1	2	0.2	0.4	..	..	6	1
Mexico	0.5	0.5	3.3	3.2	175	255	0.5	0.6	..	..	12	19
Moldova	0.5	0.3	..	1.2	9	11	0.4	0.5	12	5	6	..
Mongolia	2.5	2.3	11.6	7.5	21	20	2.1	1.7	..	..	..	..
Morocco	4.3	4.1	14.4	12.4	195	195	2.1	1.7	..	..	30	169
Mozambique	5.1	2.5	..	..	50	8	0.6	0.1	..	..	..	0
Myanmar	3.4	2.3	30.1	26.6	286	345	1.3	1.4	..	..	52	208
Namibia	4.3	2.9	10.6	9.1	8	3	1.3	0.4	..	..	14	11
Nepal	0.9	1.4	6.4	8.6	35	35	0.4	0.3	..	..	..	8
Netherlands	2.4	1.6	4.7	4.0	90	54	1.3	0.7	285	260	143	236
New Zealand	1.6	1.1	4.3	4.0	11	10	0.6	0.5	4	13	61	17
Nicaragua	2.4	1.4	7.6	2.6	15	12	1.0	0.6	87	..	..	..
Niger	1.2	1.1	..	..	5	6	0.1	0.1	..	..	11	3
Nigeria	0.5	1.1	..	..	76	77	0.2	0.2	..	..	56	2
Norway	3.0	1.8	7.0	5.9	36	33	1.7	1.4	5	203	317	82
Oman	16.2	13.0	40.9	40.7	35	38	6.7	6.1	1	..	20	48
Pakistan	6.1	4.5	27.7	21.6	580	590	1.4	1.2	1	8	..	..
Panama	1.2	1.2	4.8	4.2	11	13	1.1	1.1	..	..	2	12
Papua New Guinea	1.3	0.8	4.2	3.3	4	4	0.2	0.2	..	..	10	12
Paraguay	1.6	0.9	11.8	5.0	16	17	1.0	0.9	..	..	1	6
Peru	..	1.3	..	9.2	112	115	1.4	1.2	..	5	132	4
Philippines	1.3	1.0	6.5	5.1	107	107	0.4	0.3	..	..	59	17
Poland	2.3	1.8	5.5	5.3	270	187	1.4	0.9	49	43	20	258
Portugal	2.7	2.3	6.2	5.4	80	71	1.6	1.4	1	..	6	103
Puerto Rico	..	..	..	..	..	..	..	..	..	..	..	..

5.8 | Defense expenditures and arms transfers

	Military expenditures				Armed forces personnel				Arms transfers			
	% of GDP		% of central government expenditure		Total thousands		% of labor force		$ millions 1990 prices Exports		Imports	
	1992	2002	1992	2002	1992	1999	1992	1999	1992	2002	1992	2002
Romania	4.3	2.3	10.7	*8.1*	172	170	1.6	1.6	12	*3*	160	186
Russian Federation	5.5	4.0	*21.1*	*15.4*	1,900	900	2.5	1.2	2,384	5,941	86	170
Rwanda	4.4	3.6	21.6	..	30	40	0.8	1.0	..	..	2	*14*
Saudi Arabia	11.7	11.3	..	..	172	190	3.1	2.9	*13*	..	1,198	478
Senegal	1.8	1.5	..	*6.8*	18	13	0.5	0.3	..	..	1	..
Serbia and Montenegro	..	4.9	..	..	137	105	2.8	2.1	24	*7*	0	*0*
Sierra Leone	2.5	2.2	17.7	..	8	3	0.5	0.2	..	..	1	*13*
Singapore	4.8	5.2	24.0	*22.8*	56	60	3.4	3.0	8	2	100	227
Slovak Republic	*2.1*	*1.9*	..	*4.9*	*33*	36	*1.2*	1.2	*157*	40	*181*	27
Slovenia	*2.2*	1.5	5.8	*3.5*	15	10	1.5	1.0	..	..	*30*	0
Somalia	..	..	..	..	..	..	..	..	..	..	..	..
South Africa	2.9	*1.6*	8.8	*5.4*	75	68	0.5	0.4	83	34	140	*17*
Spain	1.6	1.2	4.4	*4.2*	198	155	1.2	0.9	88	65	187	132
Sri Lanka	3.0	*3.9*	11.3	*14.7*	110	110	1.6	1.4	..	..	21	9
Sudan	2.5	*3.0*	..	*27.4*	82	105	0.8	0.9	..	..	5	*134*
Swaziland	1.9	*1.5*	..	*5.2*	3	3	1.1	0.8	..	..	..	1
Sweden	2.6	1.9	5.6	*5.4*	70	52	1.5	1.1	182	120	47	45
Switzerland	1.8	1.1	7.0	*4.2*	31	39	0.8	1.0	283	11	170	36
Syrian Arab Republic	9.0	6.1	39.0	*24.2*	408	310	11.0	6.2	38	*0*	317	162
Tajikistan	0.4	*1.2*	..	*10.1*	3	7	0.1	0.3	..	..	*24*	..
Tanzania	1.9	*1.3*	..	..	46	35	0.3	0.2	..	..	20	..
Thailand	2.3	1.4	15.3	*7.1*	283	300	0.9	0.8	..	..	395	150
Togo	2.9	..	..	..	8	11	0.5	0.6	..	..	3	7
Trinidad and Tobago	..	..	..	..	2	2	0.4	0.4	..	..	..	1
Tunisia	1.9	*1.6*	5.8	*5.2*	35	35	1.1	0.9	..	..	32	7
Turkey	3.7	5.0	18.8	*10.0*	704	789	2.7	2.5	..	29	1,347	721
Turkmenistan	*1.8*	*3.8*	..	..	28	15	1.8	0.8	..	..	..	..
Uganda	1.6	2.4	..	*10.1*	70	50	0.7	0.5	..	..	..	6
Ukraine	*0.5*	2.8	..	*9.8*	430	340	1.6	1.3	232	270	..	..
United Arab Emirates	4.5	*2.5*	37.4	*30.1*	55	65	5.2	4.9	..	*28*	204	452
United Kingdom	3.8	2.4	8.7	*7.0*	293	218	1.0	0.7	693	719	1,166	575
United States	4.8	3.4	21.1	*16.0*	1,920	1,490	1.5	1.0	12,108	3,941	198	346
Uruguay	2.1	*1.3*	8.0	*4.2*	25	24	1.8	1.6	..	*1*	37	2
Uzbekistan	*1.5*	*1.1*	..	..	40	60	0.5	0.6	..	170	..	5
Venezuela, RB	1.6	1.2	8.2	*6.1*	75	75	1.0	0.8	..	..	48	50
Vietnam	3.4	..	10.6	..	857	485	2.4	1.2	..	..	..	69
West Bank and Gaza	..	..	..	..	..	..	..	..	..	..	..	..
Yemen, Rep.	9.1	4.5	30.7	*18.8*	64	69	1.5	1.3	..	..	..	496
Zambia	3.0	*0.6*	..	..	16	17	0.5	0.4	..	..	..	27
Zimbabwe	3.7	3.2	11.3	*9.4*	48	40	1.0	0.7	..	..	57	*8*
World	**3.0 w**	**2.4 w**	**11.3 w**	***11.0* w**	**24,533 t**	**21,198 t**	**0.9 w**	**0.7 w**				
Low income	2.4	2.7	14.5	13.0	6,040	5,869	0.7	0.6				
Middle income	3.1	2.6	13.4	11.9	12,071	9,931	1.0	0.7				
Lower middle income	3.1	2.7	15.1	14.7	10,676	8,495	1.0	0.7				
Upper middle income	3.0	2.6	8.5	6.1	1,395	1,436	1.3	1.1				
Low & middle income	3.0	2.6	13.6	*12.3*	18,111	15,800	0.9	0.7				
East Asia & Pacific	2.4	2.3	23.7	16.4	6,506	5,166	0.7	0.5				
Europe & Central Asia	4.5	3.2	*15.8*	9.6	4,303	3,192	2.1	1.3				
Latin America & Carib.	1.2	1.2	5.3	6.9	1,443	1,371	0.8	0.6				
Middle East & N. Africa	7.9	*6.9*	..	..	2,624	2,520	3.3	2.6				
South Asia	2.7	2.7	16.8	14.7	2,152	2,153	0.4	0.4				
Sub-Saharan Africa	2.5	*1.8*	8.4	..	1,083	1,398	0.5	0.5				
High income	3.0	2.4	11.1	*11.0*	6,422	5,398	1.4	1.1				
Europe EMU	2.3	1.8	5.7	*4.9*	2,181	1,768	1.6	1.3				

Note: Data for some countries are based on partial or uncertain data or rough estimates; see SIPRI (2003) and U.S. Department of State (2002).

About the data

Although national defense is an important function of government and security from external threats contributes to economic development, high levels of defense spending burden the economy and may impede growth. Comparisons of defense spending between countries should take into account the many factors that influence perceptions of vulnerability and risk, including historical and cultural traditions, the length of borders that need defending, the quality of relations with neighbors, and the role of the armed forces in the body politic.

Data on military expenditures as a share of gross domestic product (GDP) are a rough indicator of the portion of national resources used for military activities and of the burden on the national economy. As an "input" measure, military spending is not directly related to the "output" of military activities, capabilities, or military security. Data on defense spending from governments are often incomplete and unreliable. Even in countries where the parliament vigilantly reviews government budgets and spending, defense spending and arms transfers often do not receive close scrutiny. For a detailed critique of the quality of such data, see Ball (1984) and Happe and Wakeman-Linn (1994).

This and the previous edition of *World Development Indicators* use data on military expenditures and arms transfers from the Stockholm International Peace Research Institute (SIPRI). The data on military expenditures as a percentage of GDP are from SIPRI, and military expenditures as a percentage of central government expenditure are calculated from SIPRI data on military expenditures and IMF data on central government expenditures.

SIPRI's primary source of military expenditure data is official data provided by national governments. These data are derived from national budget documents, defense white papers, and other public documents from official government agencies, including governments' responses to questionnaires sent by SIPRI, the United Nations, or the Organization for Security and Co-operation in Europe. Secondary sources include international statistics, such as those of the North Atlantic Treaty Organization (NATO) and the International Monetary Fund's (IMF) *Government Finance Statistics Yearbook*. Other secondary sources include country reports of the Economist Intelligence Unit, country reports by IMF staff, and specialist journals and newspapers. Data on military expenditures presented in the table may therefore differ from national source data.

Lack of sufficiently detailed data makes it difficult to apply a common definition of military expenditure globally, so SIPRI has adopted a definition (derived from the NATO definition) as a guideline (see *Definitions*). This definition cannot be applied for all countries, however, since that would require much more detailed information than is available about what is included in military budgets and off-budget military expenditure items. In the many cases where SIPRI cannot make independent estimates, it uses the national data provided. Because of the differences in definitions and the difficulty in verifying the accuracy and completeness of data, the data on military spending are not strictly comparable across countries.

The data on armed forces are from the U.S. Department of State's Bureau of Verification and Compliance, which attributes its data to unspecified U.S. government sources. These data refer to military personnel on active duty, including paramilitary forces. These data exclude civilians in the defense establishment and so are not consistent with the data on military spending on personnel. Moreover, because they exclude personnel not on active duty, they underestimate the share of the labor force working for the defense establishment. Because governments rarely report the size of their armed forces, such data typically come from intelligence sources.

The data on arms transfers are from SIPRI's Arms Transfers Project, which reports on international flows of conventional weapons. Data are collected from open sources, and since publicly available information is inadequate for tracking all weapons and other military equipment, SIPRI covers only what it terms *major conventional weapons.*

SIPRI's data on arms transfers cover sales of weapons, manufacturing licenses, and aid and gifts; therefore the term *arms transfers* rather than *arms trade* is used. The transferred weapons must be transferred voluntarily by the supplier, must have a military purpose, and must be destined for the armed forces, paramilitary forces, or intelligence agencies of another country. SIPRI data also cover weapons supplied to or from rebel forces in an armed conflict as well as arms deliveries for which neither the supplier nor the recipient can be identified with an acceptable degree of certainty; these data are available in SIPRI's database.

SIPRI's estimates of arms transfers, presented in 1990 constant price US dollars, are designed as a *trend-measuring device* in which similar weapons have similar values, reflecting both the value and quality of weapons transferred. The trends presented in the tables are based on actual deliveries only. SIPRI cautions that these estimated values do not reflect financial value (payments for weapons transferred) for three reasons: reliable data on the value of the transfer are not available; even when the value of a transfer is known, it usually includes more than the actual conventional weapons such as spares, support systems, and training; and even when the value of the transfer is known, details of the financial arrangements such as credit and loan conditions and discounts are usually not known.

Given these measurement issues, SIPRI's method of estimating the transfer of military resources includes an evaluation of the technical parameters of the weapons. Weapons for which a price is not known are compared with the same weapons for which actual acquisition prices are available ("core weapons") or for the closet match. These weapons are assigned a value in an index that reflects the military resource value of the weapons in relation to the "core weapons." These matches are based on such characteristics as size, performance, and type of electronics, and adjustments are made for second-hand weapons. More information on SIPRI's estimation methods and sources of arms transfers is available at http://projects.sipri.se/armstrade/atmethods.html.

Definitions

• **Military expenditures** data from SIPRI are derived from the NATO definition, which includes all current and capital expenditures on the armed forces, including peacekeeping forces; defense ministries and other government agencies engaged in defense projects; paramilitary forces, if these are judged to be trained and equipped for military operations; and military space activities. Such expenditures include military and civil personnel, including retirement pensions of military personnel and social services for personnel; operation and maintenance; procurement; military research and development; and military aid (in the military expenditures of the donor country). Excluded are civil defense and current expenditures for previous military activities, such as for veterans' benefits, demobilization, conversion, and destruction of weapons. This definition cannot be applied for all countries, however, since that would require much more detailed information than is available about what is included in military budgets and off-budget military expenditure items. (For example, military budgets might or might not cover civil defense, reserves and auxiliary forces, police and paramilitary forces, dual-purpose forces such as military and civilian police, military grants in kind, pensions for military personnel, and social security contributions paid by one part of government to another.) • **Armed forces personnel** are active duty military personnel, including paramilitary forces if these forces resemble regular units in their organization, equipment, training, or mission. • **Arms transfers** cover the supply of military weapons through sales, aid, gifts, and those made through manufacturing licenses. Data cover major conventional weapons such as aircraft, armored vehicles, artillery, radar systems, missiles, and ships designed for military use. Excluded are transfers of other military equipment such as small arms and light weapons, trucks, small artillery, ammunition, support equipment, technology transfers, and other services. See *About the data* for more detail.

Data sources

The data on military expenditures and arms transfers are from SIPRI's *Yearbook 2003: Armaments, Disarmament and International Security.* The data on armed forces personnel are from the Bureau of Verification and Compliance's *World Military Expenditures and Arms Transfers 2000* (U.S. Department of State 2002).

5.9 Transport infrastructure

	Roads			Railways					Ports	Air		
	Total road network km 1995–2001[a]	Paved roads % 1995–2001[a]	Goods hauled million ton-km 1995–2001[a]	Rail lines Total km 1996–2001[a]	Electric km 1996–2001[a]	Traffic density traffic units per km 1996–2001[a]	Employee productivity traffic units per employee 1996–2001[a]	Ratio of passenger tariffs to freight tariffs 1996–2001[a]	Container traffic TEU thousands 2001	Aircraft departures thousands 2002	Passengers carried thousands 2002	Air freight millions ton-km 2002
Afghanistan	21,000	13.3	..	..	..	..	..	..	..	3	150	8
Albania	18,000	39.0	1,830	440	..	334	39	..	..	4	138	..
Algeria	104,000	68.9	..	3,793	283	419	230	..	338.2	48	3,027	18
Angola	51,429	10.4	..	..	..	..	..	..	..	4	190	51
Argentina	215,471	29.4	..	28,291	179	318	1,209	1.28	500.2	94	5,257	76
Armenia	15,918	96.3	39	842	784	465	80	0.30	..	3	408	5
Australia	811,603	38.7	..	..	..	..	..	..	4,272.0	356	32,483	1,497
Austria	200,000	100.0	16,100	5,780	3,493	4,261	482	1.14	..	136	7,070	396
Azerbaijan	25,013	92.3	4,836							8	575	76
Bangladesh	207,486	9.5	..	2,768	..	1,704	126	0.24	486.3	7	1,544	172
Belarus	75,302	89.0	8,982	5,512	874	7,857	630	..	..	6	205	1
Belgium	149,028	78.3	17,487	3,471	2,705	4,445	373	1.07	5,757.6	134	2,342	655
Benin	6,787	20.0	..	..	..	..	..	..	..	1	46	7
Bolivia	53,790	6.5	..	3,163	..	336	1,381	0.31	..	21	1,509	15
Bosnia and Herzegovina	21,846	52.3	..	..	..	..	..	..	..	4	66	1
Botswana	10,217	55.0	..	..	..	..	..	..	..	7	175	0
Brazil	1,724,929	5.5	..	25,652	1,220	1,805	3,970	..	2,923.1	628	35,890	1,540
Bulgaria	37,286	94.0	168	4,290	2,708	1,846	216	0.89	..	2	63	2
Burkina Faso	12,506	16.0	..	..	..	..	..	..	..	1	53	7
Burundi	14,480	7.1	..	..	..	..	..	..	..	..	..	..
Cambodia	12,323	16.2	412	601	..	228	69	0.39	..	5	125	4
Cameroon	34,300	12.5	..	1,006	..	1,333	496	0.34	..	5	243	43
Canada	901,903	35.3	84,752	39,400	..	7,479	7,600	6.63	3,299.7	264	23,323	1,578
Central African Republic	23,810	2.7	60	..	..	..	..	..	..	1	46	7
Chad	33,400	0.8	..	..	..	..	..	..	..	1	46	7
Chile	79,605	20.2	..	4,814	850	370	2,162	..	1,147.2	78	4,987	1,098
China	1,698,012	91.0	633,040	58,656	14,864	30,262	1,155	1.19	55,717.5[b]	932	83,672	5,014
Hong Kong, China	1,831	100.0	..	..	..	..	..	..	..	91	15,636	5,715
Colombia	112,988	14.4	31	3,154	..	..	1,795	..	603.1	178	9,395	540
Congo, Dem. Rep.	157,000	..	..	3,641	858	169	40	..	..	5	47	7
Congo, Rep.	12,800	9.7	..	900	..	188	55	..	..	5	128	7
Costa Rica	35,881	22.0	3,070	424	109	..	..	..	563.8	26	620	13
Côte d'Ivoire	50,400	9.7	..	639	..	986	540	0.67	579.1	1	46	7
Croatia	28,275	84.6	6,783	2,726	983	1,280	163	0.80	..	19	1,127	3
Cuba	60,858	49.0	..	4,667	132	468	81	..	..	10	589	40
Czech Republic	127,728	100.0	40,260	9,365	2,843	2,615	284	..	..	47	2,801	27
Denmark	71,622	100.0	11,696	2,047	625	3,648	770	..	457.3	98	6,322	185
Dominican Republic	12,600	49.4	..	..	..	..	..	..	430.6	..	..	..
Ecuador	43,197	18.9	4,405	..	..	..	..	..	462.5	15	1,292	6
Egypt, Arab Rep.	64,000	78.1	31,500	5,024	59	14,308	753	0.20	1,223.1	42	4,478	248
El Salvador	10,029	19.8	..	1,202	503	..	367	..	..	19	1,804	12
Eritrea	4,010	21.8	..	..	..	..	..	..	..	..	..	..
Estonia	52,038	19.7	4,677	968	132	7,999	1,358	2.36	..	7	254	1
Ethiopia	31,663	12.0	..	781	..	..	..	..	..	28	1,103	84
Finland	77,900	64.5	26,500	5,854	2,372	2,308	1,056	2.47	1,091.8	109	6,414	213
France	894,000	100.0	245,400	32,515	14,104	3,854	715	1.54	3,278.0	733	49,096	4,997
Gabon	8,464	9.9	..	814	..	2,087	894	..	..	8	366	49
Gambia, The	2,700	35.4	..	..	..	..	..	..	..	..	..	..
Georgia	20,229	93.5	520	1,562	1,544	2,794	276	0.37	..	2	112	2
Germany	230,735	99.1	226,982	36,652	19,079	4,128	681	2.77	9,122.3	782	61,043	7,196
Ghana	46,179	18.4	..	953	..	1,778	376	..	..	4	256	19
Greece	117,000	91.8	13,909	2,299	..	830	182	..	1,660.5	113	7,579	81
Guatemala	14,118	34.5	..	..	..	..	..	..	360.2	..	..	..
Guinea	30,500	16.5	..	..	..	..	..	..	..	..	..	..
Guinea-Bissau	4,400	10.3	..	..	..	..	..	..	..	..	..	..
Haiti	4,160	24.3	..	..	..	..	..	..	..	..	..	..

	Roads			Railways					Ports	Air		
	Total road network km	Paved roads %	Goods hauled million ton-km	Rail lines		Traffic density traffic units per km	Employee productivity traffic units per employee	Ratio of passenger tariffs to freight tariffs	Container traffic TEU	Aircraft departures	Passengers carried	Air freight millions ton-km
				Total km	Electric km							
	1995– 2001[a]	1995– 2001[a]	1995– 2001[a]	1996– 2001[a]	1996– 2001[a]	1996– 2001[a]	1996– 2001[a]	1996– 2001[a]	thousands 2001	thousands 2002	thousands 2002	ton-km 2002
Honduras	13,603	20.4	..	..	..	..	..	..	406.4	..	..	..
Hungary	167,839	43.7	11,398	7,729	2,628	2,242	319	..	..	33	2,134	27
India	3,319,644	45.7	958	62,759	14,261	11,725	467	0.31	3,243.0	242	18,225	550
Indonesia	342,700	46.3	..	5,324	131	3,974	610	0.95	4,539.9	152	12,114	406
Iran, Islamic Rep.	167,157	56.3	..	6,688	148	3,185	758	..	..	90	10,085	82
Iraq	45,550	84.3	..	..	..	..	..	..	..	..	..	..
Ireland	92,500	94.1	5,900	1,915	37	982	171	..	775.3	177	19,729	116
Israel	16,521	100.0	..	925	..	2,112	1,628	..	1,461.0	39	3,731	1,058
Italy	479,688	100.0	219,800	16,499	10,937	4,102	618	1.42	7,918.3	351	28,245	1,394
Jamaica	18,700	70.1	..	..	..	..	..	..	1,065.0	23	2,016	57
Japan	1,166,340	76.6	313,118	20,165	12,080	13,048	1,528	..	13,501.4	648	109,247	8,102
Jordan	7,245	100.0	..	293	..	2,123	518	..	..	16	1,300	197
Kazakhstan	82,638	93.9	5,497	13,545	3,725	9,981	1,069	..	..	13	593	15
Kenya	63,942	12.1	..	2,634	..	699	184	..	..	26	1,600	118
Korea, Dem. Rep.	31,200	6.4	..	..	..	..	..	..	..	1	84	2
Korea, Rep.	86,990	74.5	74,504	3,123	668	12,456	1,323	1.43	11,542.7	243	34,512	7,913
Kuwait	4,450	80.6	..	..	..	..	..	..	..	19	2,299	254
Kyrgyz Republic	18,500	91.1	1,220	..	..	..	..	..	..	4	177	6
Lao PDR	21,716	44.5	..	..	..	..	..	..	..	7	220	2
Latvia	69,732	38.6	5,359	2,331	258	5,834	917	..	..	9	265	1
Lebanon	7,300	84.9	..	..	..	..	..	..	298.9	11	874	81
Lesotho	5,940	18.3	..	..	..	..	..	..	..	..	..	..
Liberia	10,600	6.2	..	..	..	..	..	..	..	..	..	..
Libya	83,200	57.2	..	..	..	..	..	..	..	6	559	0
Lithuania	76,573	91.3	8,274	1,905	122	4,171	611	..	..	10	304	2
Macedonia, FYR	8,684	62.0	2,693	699	233	972	162	0.39	..	2	166	0
Madagascar	49,827	11.6	..	..	..	..	..	..	..	19	549	29
Malawi	28,400	18.5	..	710	..	159	176	0.25	..	5	105	1
Malaysia	65,877	75.8	..	1,622	152	1,368	370	0.87	7,541.7	186	16,208	1,924
Mali	15,100	12.1	..	734	..	658	322	..	..	1	46	7
Mauritania	7,660	11.3	..	..	..	..	..	..	..	2	106	0
Mauritius	2,000	98.0	..	..	..	..	..	..	..	14	1,025	189
Mexico	329,532	32.8	197,958	17,697	250	2,660	3,925	..	1,561.9	271	19,282	311
Moldova	12,691	86.1	964	..	..	..	..	..	..	4	129	0
Mongolia	49,250	3.5	129	1,810	..	2,963	394	..	..	6	270	8
Morocco	57,698	56.0	2,952	1,907	1,003	3,425	610	0.86	375.8	38	3,146	51
Mozambique	30,400	18.7	110	..	..	..	..	..	..	8	282	7
Myanmar	28,200	12.2	..	..	..	..	..	..	..	21	1,186	2
Namibia	62,237	12.9	..	2,382	..	474	..	..	..	5	222	21
Nepal	13,223	30.8	..	..	..	..	..	..	..	13	681	18
Netherlands	116,500	90.0	32,700	2,802	2,061	6,631	752	2.56	6,741.7	250	22,931	4,204
New Zealand	92,207	63.1	..	3,913	519	938	1,120	1.46	1,413.6	265	12,240	688
Nicaragua	19,032	11.0	..	..	..	..	..	..	..	1	61	1
Niger	10,100	7.9	..	..	..	..	..	..	..	1	46	7
Nigeria	194,394	30.9	..	3,557	..	287	65	0.10	..	11	512	9
Norway	91,443	77.0	12,796					..	..	271	13,706	185
Oman	32,800	30.0	..	..	..	..	..	..	1,415.5	23	2,104	130
Pakistan	257,683	59.0	111,323	7,791	293	2,838	232	0.28	965.6	42	4,141	347
Panama	11,643	34.6	..	..	..	..	..	..	1,248.4	22	1,048	22
Papua New Guinea	19,600	3.5	..	..	..	..	..	..	..	31	1,235	24
Paraguay	29,500	50.8	..	..	..	..	..	..	..	9	269	..
Peru	72,900	12.8	..	1,691	..	406	363	..	537.6	31	1,879	102
Philippines	201,994	21.0	..	491	..	505	112	0.09	3,270.8	43	5,660	267
Poland	364,697	68.3	74,403	22,560	11,826	3,537	415	0.79	287.4	70	2,846	67
Portugal	68,732	86.0	14,200	2,814	904	2,066	465	..	970.1	114	6,894	198
Puerto Rico	24,023	94.0	..	..	..	..	..	..	1,426.2	..	..	..

	Roads			Railways					Ports	Air		
	Total road network km	Paved roads %	Goods hauled million ton-km	Rail lines		Traffic density traffic units per km	Employee productivity traffic units per employee	Ratio of passenger tariffs to freight tariffs	Container traffic TEU	Aircraft departures	Passengers carried	Air freight millions ton-km
				Total km	Electric km							
	1995–2001 a	1995–2001 a	1995–2001 a	1996–2001 a	1996–2001 a	1996–2001 a	1996–2001 a	1996–2001 a	thousands 2001	thousands 2002	thousands 2002	2002
Romania	198,603	49.5	14,288	11,364	3,929	2,467	267	1.24	..	18	961	9
Russian Federation	537,289	67.4	139	86,075	40,962	15,854	1,054	0.97	795.7	345	20,892	1,039
Rwanda	12,000	8.3	..	..	..	..	..	..	..	..	..	..
Saudi Arabia	152,044	29.9	..	1,390	..	799	555	..	1,930.1	109	13,564	862
Senegal	14,576	29.3	..	906	..	562	339	..	..	3	245	7
Serbia and Montenegro	44,993	62.3	630	4,058	1,103	522	94	..	..	20	1,186	4
Sierra Leone	11,330	7.9	..	..	..	..	..	..	..	0	14	6
Singapore	3,066	100.0	..	..	..	..	..	..	16,986.0	72	17,257	6,772
Slovak Republic	42,956	87.3	20,233	3,662	1,536	3,851	302	1.11	..	2	39	1
Slovenia	20,236	100.0	5,695	..	..	2,746	..	..	..	15	721	5
Somalia	22,100	11.8	..	..	..	..	..	..	..	..	..	..
South Africa	362,099	20.3	..	22,657	10,430	5,018	2,933	..	1,801.6	122	8,167	783
Spain	663,795	99.0	98,145	13,866	7,523	2,295	842	..	6,669.2	500	40,585	807
Sri Lanka	11,547	95.0	30	1,447	..	2,271	189	0.11	1,764.7	11	1,741	203
Sudan	11,900	36.3	..	4,599	..	298	98	..	..	8	409	33
Swaziland	3,107	..	..	..	..	..	..	..	..	2	90	0
Sweden	212,961	78.6	32,000	10,068	7,405	2,492	2,144	2.34	914.9	201	12,696	267
Switzerland	71,176	..	23,500	..	..	..	..	..	..	243	13,292	1,028
Syrian Arab Republic	44,575	21.1	..	1,771	..	996	160	..	..	13	824	25
Tajikistan	27,767	82.7	..	..	..	..	..	..	..	6	397	4
Tanzania	88,200	4.2	..	2,722	..	598	181	0.41	..	5	138	2
Thailand	57,403	98.5	..	4,044	..	3,342	660	0.75	3,800.9	98	18,112	1,824
Togo	7,520	31.6	..	..	..	..	..	..	..	1	46	7
Trinidad and Tobago	8,320	51.1	..	..	..	..	..	..	385.2	23	1,269	36
Tunisia	18,997	65.4	..	2,260	60	1,010	341	1.87	..	19	1,789	19
Turkey	354,373	35.5	151,421	8,671	1,752	1,798	330	1.20	1,777.1	106	10,640	381
Turkmenistan	24,000	81.2	..	..	..	..	..	..	..	25	1,464	14
Uganda	27,000	6.7	..	261	..	805	131	..	..	0	41	21
Ukraine	169,630	96.7	16,811	22,302	9,170	9,535	598	..	..	34	1,512	12
United Arab Emirates	1,088	100.0	..	..	..	..	..	..	5,872.2	55	9,667	2,079
United Kingdom	371,913	100.0	150,700	17,067	5,225	3,500	2,678	..	7,059.6	906	71,892	4,941
United States	6,304,193	58.8	1,534,430	160,000	484	13,800	13,476	9.28	29,676.9	7,878 c	593,246 c	29,070 c
Uruguay	8,983	90.0	..	3,003	..	127	191	..	293.0	8	525	12
Uzbekistan	81,600	87.3	..	..	619	4,830	304	..	..	23	1,451	69
Venezuela, RB	96,155	33.6	..	336	..	161	180	0.21	1,078.0	167	6,370	33
Vietnam	93,300	25.1	..	3,142	..	1,624	154	0.88	1,290.6	43	4,082	151
West Bank and Gaza	..	..	..	..	..	..	..	..	..	..	..	..
Yemen, Rep.	67,000	11.5	..	..	..	..	..	..	388.4	16	869	37
Zambia	91,440	22.0	..	1,273	..	144	610	0.27	..	5	47	1
Zimbabwe	18,338	47.4	..	2,759	311	1,977	454	0.60	..	5	251	26
World	**44.0 m**			**.. s**	**.. s**	**.. m**	**.. m**	**.. m**	**259,736 s**	**20,481 s**	**1,615,074 s**	**116,626 s**
Low income	16.0			..	..	..	..	..	..	791	53,966	2,330
Middle income	52.3			..	..	..	610	..	94,397	4,365	321,221	17,661
Lower middle income	52.7			..	..	..	610	..	76,710	3,094	236,701	12,669
Upper middle income	51.1			..	..	..	583	..	17,687	1,272	84,520	4,993
Low & middle income	30.9			..	..	..	..	..	104,113	5,156	375,186	19,992
East Asia & Pacific	25.1			..	..	2,293	382	..	74,871	1,626	144,068	9,726
Europe & Central Asia	89.0			..	..	..	304	..	..	825	50,903	1,767
Latin America & Carib.	26.9			..	..	..	..	..	12,058	1,626	94,234	3,938
Middle East & N. Africa	63.8			..	..	..	555	..	..	429	42,619	1,750
South Asia	36.9			..	..	..	..	0.24	5,973	319	26,431	1,290
Sub-Saharan Africa	12.9			..	..	..	..	..	..	331	16,931	1,520
High income	92.9			..	..	3,648	770	..	155,622	15,325	1,239,888	96,634
Europe EMU	92.9			124,467	63,215	3,854	618	..	43,985	3,440	252,823	24,415

a. Data are for the latest year available in the period shown. b. Includes Hong Kong, China. c. Data cover only the carriers designated by the U.S. Department of Transportation as major and national air carriers.

Transport infrastructure—highways, railways, ports and waterways, and airports and air traffic control systems—and the services that flow from it are crucial to the activities of households, producers, and governments. Because performance indicators vary significantly by transport mode and focus (whether physical infrastructure or the services flowing from that infrastructure), highly specialized and carefully specified indicators are required. The table provides selected indicators of the size, extent, and productivity of roads, railways, and air transport systems and of the volume of traffic in these modes as well as in ports.

Data for transport sectors are not always internationally comparable. Unlike for demographic statistics, national income accounts, and international trade data, the collection of infrastructure data has not been "internationalized." But data on roads are collected by the International Road Federation (IRF), and data on air transport by the International Civil Aviation Organization (ICAO).

National road associations are the primary source of IRF data. In countries where such an association is lacking or does not respond, other agencies are contacted, such as road directorates, ministries of transport or public works, or central statistical offices. As a result, the compiled data are of uneven quality. Even when data are available, they are often of limited value because of incompatible definitions (for example, in some countries a path used mainly by animals may be considered a road, while in others a road must be registered with a state agency responsible for its maintenance), inappropriate geographic units, lack of timeliness, and variations in the nature of the terrain.

Moreover, the quality of transport service (reliability, transit time, and condition of goods delivered) is rarely measured, though it may be as important as quantity in assessing an economy's transport system. A new initiative is under way in the World Bank to improve data availability and consistency. Information covering access, affordability, efficiency, quality, and fiscal and institutional aspects of the transport sector will help to measure progress and improve performance.

The railways indicators focus on efficiency and productivity. Traffic density is an indication of the intensity of use of a railway's largest investment—its track. Traffic densities for branch lines tend to range around 500,000 traffic units per kilometer (see *Definitions*), while those for mainlines range from more than 5 million traffic units per kilometer to 100

million. (Note that kilometers of track may exceed kilometers of line because of double and triple tracking, yard tracks, and the like.) Railways whose traffic density averages less than 500,000 traffic units per kilometer need to operate at low costs and very high labor productivity to survive. Labor is the most expensive factor of production for a railway, and most railways have found that improving labor productivity is the most important factor in establishing economic viability. Employee productivity is heavily influenced by the balance of passenger and freight service, with productivity far lower in passenger service. In developing countries a ratio of passenger tariffs to freight tariffs greater than 1 indicates an absence of significant cross-subsidies and a potential to provide higher quality service. This ratio, like the other railway indicators, has no normative value and is intended for relative analysis only.

Measures of port container traffic, much of it commodities of medium to high value added, give some indication of economic growth in a country. But when traffic is merely transshipment, much of the economic benefit goes to the terminal operator and ancillary services for ships and containers rather than to the country more broadly. In transshipment centers empty containers may account for as much as 40 percent of traffic.

The air transport data represent the total (international and domestic) scheduled traffic carried by the air carriers registered in a country. Countries submit air transport data to ICAO on the basis of standard instructions and definitions issued by ICAO. In many cases, however, the data include estimates by ICAO for nonreporting carriers. Where possible, these estimates are based on previous submissions supplemented by information published by the air carriers, such as flight schedules.

The data represent the air traffic carried on scheduled services, but changes in air transport regulations in Europe have made it more difficult to classify traffic as scheduled or nonscheduled. Thus recent increases shown for some European countries may be due to changes in the classification of air traffic rather than actual growth. For countries with few air carriers or only one, the addition or discontinuation of a home-based air carrier may cause significant changes in air traffic.

• **Total road network** covers motorways, highways, main or national roads, secondary or regional roads, and all other roads in a country. • **Paved roads** are roads surfaced with crushed stone (macadam) and hydrocarbon binder or bituminized agents, with concrete, or with cobblestones. • **Goods hauled by road** are the volume of goods transported by road vehicles, measured in millions of metric tons times kilometers traveled. • **Total rail lines** refer to the track length of the railway lines. • **Electric rail lines** refer to the length of line with electric traction. This line can include overhead catenary at various direct current or alternating current voltages and third-rail direct current systems. • **Railway traffic density** is total traffic units divided by total rail lines; total traffic units are the sum of passenger-kilometers (passengers times kilometers traveled) and freight ton-kilometers (metric tons of freight times kilometers traveled) divided by kilometers of line. • **Railway employee productivity** is annual output (in traffic units) per employee. • **Ratio of railway passenger tariffs to freight tariffs** is the average passenger fare (total passenger revenue divided by total passenger-kilometers) divided by the average freight rate (total freight revenue divided by total ton-kilometers). A ratio of very much less than 1 indicates a likelihood of passengers being cross-subsidized by freight tariffs. • **Port container traffic** measures the flow of containers from land to sea transport modes and vice versa in twenty-foot-equivalent units (TEUs), a standard-size container. Data refer to coastal shipping as well as international journeys. Transshipment traffic is counted as two lifts at the intermediate port (once to off-load and again as an outbound lift) and includes empty units. • **Aircraft departures** are domestic and international takeoffs of air carriers registered in the country. • **Air passengers carried** include both domestic and international passengers of air carriers registered in the country. • **Air freight** is the sum of the metric tons of freight, express, and diplomatic bags carried on each flight stage (the operation of an aircraft from takeoff to its next landing), multiplied by the stage distance, by air carriers registered in the country.

The data on roads are from the IRF's *World Road Statistics*. The data on railways are from a database maintained by the World Bank's Transport and Urban Development Department, Transport Division. The data on port container traffic are from Containerisation International's *Containerisation International Yearbook*. And the data on air transport are from the ICAO's *Civil Aviation Statistics of the World* and ICAO staff estimates.

5.10 Power and communications

	Electric power		Telephone mainlines [a]							Mobile phones [a]	International telecommunications [a]	
	Consumption per capita kwh	Transmission and distribution losses % of output	per 1,000 people	In largest city per 1,000 people	Waiting list thousands	Faults per 100 mainlines	per employee	Revenue per line $	Cost of local call $ per 3 minutes	per 1,000 people	Outgoing traffic minutes per subscriber	Cost of call to U.S. $ per 3 minutes
	2001	2001	2002	2002	2002	2002	2002	2002	2002	2002	2002	2002
Afghanistan	..	..	1	8	..	..	..	..	..	1	..	..
Albania	1,123	51	71	94	98.5	57.2	65	1,139	0.02	276	282	2.47
Algeria	638	16	61	124	727.0	6.0	105	192	0.02	13	111	..
Angola	100	15	6	21	240.3	..	38	1,633	0.09	9	404	3.11
Argentina	2,107	14	219	..	93.1	..	337	931	0.03	178	53	..
Armenia	1,127	26	143	212	64.1	60.0	92	151	0.02	19	67	..
Australia	9,292	7	539	..	0.0	8.0	136	1,276	0.12	640	215	0.68
Austria	7,031	5	489	..	0.0	5.7	228	1,315	0.19	786	312	..
Azerbaijan	1,846	13	113	270	55.4	48.0	113	93	0.10	107	35	5.52
Bangladesh	94	18	5	30	199.1	..	29	593	0.03	8	77	2.47
Belarus	2,676	14	299	397	341.5	26.8	112	72	0.01	47	81	2.25
Belgium	7,596	5	494	..	..	5.9	197	1,343	0.14	786	353	..
Benin	66	70	9	..	23.0	6.0	48	1,044	0.28	32	294	5.76
Bolivia	403	12	68	109	..	..	174	742	0.09	105	69	..
Bosnia and Herzegovina	1,444	17	237	502	..	..	130	247	0.03	196	106	3.01
Botswana	..	..	87	..	..	..	83	1,238	0.02	241	425	..
Brazil	1,729	17	223	311	200.0	3.0	400	546	0.03	201	21	..
Bulgaria	3,066	14	368	..	145.8	3.5	104	318	0.02	333	48	1.45
Burkina Faso	..	..	5	42	12.4	19.7	51	984	0.10	8	307	2.58
Burundi	..	..	3	..	4.7	..	27	737	0.02	7	127	3.71
Cambodia	..	..	3	19	..	..	61	705	0.03	28	278	..
Cameroon	170	26	7	..	..	..	50	..	0.06	43	208	..
Canada	15,385	8	635	..	0.0	..	237	1,053	..	377	254	..
Central African Republic	..	..	2	..	1.2	..	23	1,196	0.43	3	466	12.93
Chad	..	..	2	8	..	60.8	16	..	0.11	4	363	9.11
Chile	2,557	7	230	333	32.3	25.0	179	698	0.10	428	79	2.18
China	893	7	167	584	..	..	..	238	0.03	161	7	..
Hong Kong, China	5,541	12	565	577	0.0	..	216	1,700	0.00	942	1,039	2.62
Colombia	818	22	179	327	1,174.7	45.5	229	499	0.03	106	40	..
Congo, Dem. Rep.	47	4	0	..	..	..	..	..	..	11	..	..
Congo, Rep.	75	65	7	..	..	..	..	..	..	67	..	..
Costa Rica	1,557	7	251	..	15.8	4.2	213	351	0.03	111	125	1.93
Côte d'Ivoire	..	..	20	68	24.2	81.0	91	1,186	0.22	62	204	6.38
Croatia	2,683	21	417	..	0.0	12.0	171	679	0.09	535	198	..
Cuba	1,069	15	51	121	..	9.6	34	1,370	0.09	2	65	7.35
Czech Republic	4,977	7	362	666	25.1	8.3	153	890	0.13	849	107	0.83
Denmark	6,160	5	689	..	0.0	8.0	173	1,091	0.08	833	214	..
Dominican Republic	822	26	110	..	..	..	55	..	0.06	207	245	..
Ecuador	631	25	110	133	14.5	35.3	275	336	0.03	121	48	1.75
Egypt, Arab Rep.	1,046	12	110	..	206.1	0.5	140	335	0.02	67	36	2.57
El Salvador	595	13	103	..	38.2	14.5	168	903	0.07	138	243	1.23
Eritrea	..	..	9	43	38.5	53.3	56	458	0.03	0	125	3.55
Estonia	3,764	16	351	422	4.1	16.3	136	881	0.09	650	217	0.74
Ethiopia	22	10	5	60	145.9	..	47	295	0.02	1	36	7.05
Finland	14,899	4	523	..	0.0	..	124	1,735	0.13	867	172	1.06
France	6,682	6	569	..	0.0	..	232	944	0.12	647	139	..
Gabon	814	18	25	..	..	..	32	2,771	0.22	215	854	..
Gambia, The	..	..	28	97	10.6	..	34	760	0.03	73	352	3.46
Georgia	718	12	131	233	138.8	17.2	39	208	0.03	102	108	0.68
Germany	6,093	4	651	696	0.0	..	232	1,084	0.09	727	190	0.35
Ghana	341	15	13	83	154.8	67.4	57	460	0.03	21	213	1.13
Greece	4,205	9	491	731	7.6	12.1	302	864	0.07	845	158	0.67
Guatemala	358	23	71	..	..	..	236	593	0.08	131	172	..
Guinea	..	..	3	..	1.4	..	33	1,119	0.08	12	734	4.61
Guinea-Bissau	..	..	9	..	5.1	70.5	46	..	..	0	271	..
Haiti	36	53	16	..	..	..	18	..	..	17	..	..

	Electric power		Telephone mainlines[a]							Mobile phones[a]	International telecommunications[a]	
	Consumption per capita kwh	Transmission and distribution losses % of output	per 1,000 people	In largest city per 1,000 people	Waiting list thousands	Faults per 100 mainlines	per employee	Revenue per line $	Cost of local call $ per 3 minutes	per 1,000 people	Outgoing traffic minutes per subscriber	Cost of call to U.S. $ per 3 minutes
	2001	2001	2002	2002	2002	2002	2002	2002	2002	2002	2002	2002
Honduras	508	21	48	..	342.2	3.6	62	1,210	0.06	49	144	2.85
Hungary	2,998	13	361	588	7.8	..	176	1,015	0.13	676	66	0.79
India	365	27	40	136	1,648.8	126.0	92	198	0.02	12	16	3.20
Indonesia	404	13	37	261	..	20.0	181	300	0.03	55	37	..
Iran, Islamic Rep.	1,570	16	187	381	1,480.5	..	258	104	0.01	33	21	7.70
Iraq	1,475	..	28	..	..	..	..	..	..	1	..	..
Ireland	5,415	8	502	..	..	7.6	133	1,643	0.14	763	706	..
Israel	5,841	3	467	..	..	..	249	1,190	0.02	955	385	..
Italy	4,813	7	481	..	0.0	..	358	1,288	0.11	939	169	..
Jamaica	2,343	8	170	..	168.6	39.7	192	1,050	0.07	535	310	..
Japan	7,237	4	558	554	0.0	..	490	1,609	0.07	637	37	1.67
Jordan	1,252	12	127	183	1.4	10.7	108	1,128	0.04	229	294	1.96
Kazakhstan	2,850	17	130	..	168.3	..	65	289	0.00	64	63	..
Kenya	117	21	10	77	134.0	220.9	17	1,482	0.07	42	75	5.84
Korea, Dem. Rep.	..	..	21	..	..	..	..	..	..	0	..	..
Korea, Rep.	5,288	6	489	632	0.0	1.5	437	935	0.03	679	45	1.74
Kuwait	10,251	3	204	46	0.0	..	66	1,778	0.00	519	394	1.50
Kyrgyz Republic	1,351	34	77	168	37.7	..	50	110	0.09	10	46	8.92
Lao PDR	..	..	11	65	5.9	..	45	437	0.02	10	138	6.37
Latvia	1,943	23	301	500	14.3	22.7	180	338	0.11	394	65	2.02
Lebanon	1,824	18	199	..	..	..	..	..	0.07	227	149	..
Lesotho	..	..	13	64	21.1	72.8	80	415	0.11	42	64	2.31
Liberia	..	..	2	..	..	..	..	..	..	1	868	..
Libya	4,020	..	118	..	..	..	43	..	..	13	68	..
Lithuania	1,851	10	270	427	3.9	17.0	217	472	0.14	475	36	2.31
Macedonia, FYR	..	..	271	..	..	..	143	406	0.01	177	116	..
Madagascar	..	..	4	9	1.8	42.5	25	1,614	0.07	10	111	7.41
Malawi	..	..	7	41	17.4	..	17	625	0.06	8	435	0.06
Malaysia	2,731	6	190	..	65.9	40.0	222	948	0.03	377	144	2.37
Mali	..	..	5	24	..	177.6	37	1,159	0.07	5	300	12.28
Mauritania	..	..	12	..	..	..	26	1,330	0.13	92	394	..
Mauritius	..	..	270	376	13.5	56.8	181	499	0.04	289	113	2.50
Mexico	1,643	14	147	156	..	1.9	139	1,134	0.16	255	134	3.04
Moldova	785	47	161	350	107.3	4.9	95	136	0.02	77	75	2.21
Mongolia	..	..	53	99	37.8	28.4	30	443	0.02	89	37	4.92
Morocco	461	7	38	..	5.0	24.8	74	1,465	0.15	209	226	1.63
Mozambique	266	3	5	..	12.7	70.0	39	1,533	0.08	14	274	..
Myanmar	88	20	7	32	93.5	169.0	43	..	0.05	1	27	0.36
Namibia	..	..	65	157	2.6	42.2	81	700	0.03	80	499	4.28
Nepal	61	21	14	315	317.3	88.1	70	257	0.01	1	102	..
Netherlands	6,199	4	618	..	0.0	..	169	1,313	0.11	745	260	..
New Zealand	8,792	11	448	..	0.0	30.7	325	1,127	0.00	622	547	..
Nicaragua	268	30	32	..	..	4.6	82	591	0.08	38	108	3.20
Niger	..	..	2	24	..	104.6	16	848	0.10	1	292	8.77
Nigeria	82	38	6	12	..	..	58	715	..	13	124	..
Norway	24,881	7	734	..	0.0	..	221	1,549	0.15	844	165	0.31
Oman	3,078	17	84	..	2.1	..	105	2,238	0.07	171	729	0.79
Pakistan	358	26	25	..	214.0	..	58	395	0.02	8	35	3.60
Panama	1,340	22	122	284	..	30.8	78	1,018	0.12	189	120	4.36
Papua New Guinea	..	..	12	115	0.2	..	36	1,221	0.08	3	402	4.32
Paraguay	833	3	47	91	..	3.4	25	1,069	0.09	288	104	0.82
Peru	692	11	66	..	33.0	..	372	690	0.08	86	82	..
Philippines	489	12	42	265	..	..	273	824	0.00	191	52	..
Poland	2,490	10	295	..	501.6	17.2	159	646	0.08	363	73	1.79
Portugal	3,932	9	421	..	..	10.2	240	1,485	0.11	825	124	0.93
Puerto Rico	..	..	346	..	..	..	261	1,534	..	316	..	..

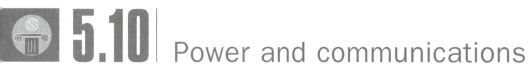

5.10 | Power and communications

	Electric power		Telephone mainlines [a]							Mobile phones [a]	International telecommunications [a]	
	Consumption per capita kwh	Transmission and distribution losses % of output	per 1,000 people	In largest city per 1,000 people	Waiting list thousands	Faults per 100 mainlines	per employee	Revenue per line $	Cost of local call $ per 3 minutes	per 1,000 people	Outgoing traffic minutes per subscriber	Cost of call to U.S. $ per 3 minutes
	2001	2001	2002	2002	2002	2002	2002	2002	2002	2002	2002	2002
Romania	1,620	13	194	..	542.1	23.0	114	410	0.11	236	50	1.82
Russian Federation	4,270	12	242	..	5,809.6	..	75	209	..	120	34	..
Rwanda	..	..	3	..	..	..	61	934	0.09	14	245	..
Saudi Arabia	5,117	8	144	214	73.6	26.2	155	1,893	0.04	217	578	2.40
Senegal	130	19	22	71	9.8	17.3	152	852	0.10	55	294	1.81
Serbia and Montenegro	..	..	233	424	143.0	..	178	146	0.01	257	123	2.08
Sierra Leone	..	..	5	..	..	..	19	..	0.03	13	336	..
Singapore	7,178	4	463	463	0.0	2.4	221	1,738	0.02	796	1,020	0.68
Slovak Republic	4,360	4	268	665	7.0	27.0	106	604	0.12	544	134	0.79
Slovenia	5,535	5	506	..	0.5	22.5	227	671	0.07	835	106	0.52
Somalia	..	..	10	..	..	..	..	..	..	3	..	..
South Africa	3,793	8	107	..	50.0	48.2	116	1,102	0.09	304	117	0.58
Spain	4,933	9	506	..	..	..	273	1,447	0.07	824	210	..
Sri Lanka	285	18	47	299	257.7	99.6	72	379	0.03	49	58	2.33
Sudan	67	15	21	80	444.0	..	150	364	0.03	6	80	3.92
Swaziland	..	..	34	131	15.6	160.0	67	826	0.04	61	657	2.42
Sweden	14,916	7	736	..	0.0	..	304	1,189	0.11	889	188	0.32
Switzerland	7,474	5	744	..	0.0	..	231	1,771	0.15	789	481	..
Syrian Arab Republic	973	..	123	156	2,805.9	50.0	84	238	0.01	23	90	4.81
Tajikistan	2,151	15	37	133	6.1	126.0	48	32	0.01	2	42	6.96
Tanzania	58	25	5	20	8.0	24.0	46	1,471	0.12	19	73	5.28
Thailand	1,508	9	105	452	710.2	19.8	222	637	0.07	260	52	1.54
Togo	..	..	10	35	27.5	6.2	57	823	0.10	35	349	2.15
Trinidad and Tobago	3,829	8	250	..	..	..	100	958	0.04	278	218	2.22
Tunisia	987	11	117	..	108.7	29.0	143	450	0.02	52	164	..
Turkey	1,391	19	281	388	142.9	37.4	297	275	0.13	347	34	2.09
Turkmenistan	1,231	13	77	..	36.8	86.4	52	145	..	2	64	..
Uganda	..	..	2	..	..	..	23	..	0.21	16	125	3.51
Ukraine	2,217	20	216	..	2,158.7	..	86	146	..	84	36	..
United Arab Emirates	10,787	9	314	348	0.4	0.3	115	1,994	0.00	696	1,732	1.73
United Kingdom	5,653	8	591	..	0.0	11.0	148	2,087	0.18	841	258	..
United States	11,714	6	646	..	..	12.4	170	1,579	0.00	488	217	..
Uruguay	1,918	16	280	335	0.0	..	168	751	0.17	193	87	4.88
Uzbekistan	1,634	9	66	248	38.9	87.4	69	118	0.01	7	36	13.95
Venezuela, RB	2,605	25	113	..	..	2.0	192	1,033	0.04	256	104	..
Vietnam	325	14	48	..	..	..	49	356	0.02	23	17	..
West Bank and Gaza	..	..	87	..	0.7	97.0	188	353	0.05	93	132	1.03
Yemen, Rep.	109	26	28	80	704.8	..	100	266	0.02	21	81	4.10
Zambia	585	3	8	22	11.6	90.8	28	808	0.09	13	178	6.45
Zimbabwe	810	21	25	76	158.9	..	63	817	0.04	30	309	4.36
World	**2,159 w**	**9 w**	**176 w**	**296 w**	**.. s**	**26.4 m**	**105 m**	**890 m**	**0.06 m**	**110 m**	**155 m**	**2.09 m**
Low income	317	23	28	130	4,517.4	62.5	49	437	0.07	13	108	3.63
Middle income	1,447	11	167	406	..	28.3	133	700	0.05	149	124	2.08
Lower middle income	1,304	11	164	524	..	35.3	110	637	0.04	99	110	2.09
Upper middle income	2,505	12	190	..	..	17.2	173	885	0.09	241	166	2.20
Low & middle income	938	13	100	270	..	40.0	80	545	0.06	62	117	2.40
East Asia & Pacific	816	8	131	502	..	..	45	440	0.03	24	44	4.62
Europe & Central Asia	2,774	13	228	..	10,859.2	22.8	113	318	0.06	196	65	2.08
Latin America & Carib.	1,493	16	168	..	..	9.6	161	709	0.06	126	172	2.22
Middle East & N. Africa	1,409	12	107	..	6,099.3	10.1	140	1,128	0.04	52	213	2.18
South Asia	331	27	34	127	2,623.8	88.1	55	387	0.02	8	68	2.33
Sub-Saharan Africa	456	11	15	..	..	56.8	56	984	0.09	16	208	3.55
High income	8,421	6	585	..	..	8.3	197	1,343	0.07	698	285	0.93
Europe EMU	5,904	6	555	..	14.1	6.8	215	1,395	0.13	805	181	0.77

a. Data are from the International Telecommunication Union's (ITU) *World Telecommunication Development Report 2003*. Please cite the ITU for third-party use of these data.

About the data

The quality of an economy's infrastructure, including power and communications, is an important element in investment decisions for both domestic and foreign investors. Government effort alone will not suffice to meet the need for investments in modern infrastructure; public-private partnerships, especially those involving local providers and financiers, will be critical in lowering costs and delivering value for money. In telecommunications, competition in the marketplace, along with sound regulation, is lowering costs and improving the quality of and access to services around the globe.

An economy's production and consumption of electricity is a basic indicator of its size and level of development. Although a few countries export electric power, most production is for domestic consumption. Expanding the supply of electricity to meet the growing demand of increasingly urbanized and industrialized economies without incurring unacceptable social, economic, and environmental costs is one of the great challenges facing developing countries.

Data on electric power production and consumption are collected from national energy agencies by the International Energy Agency (IEA) and adjusted by the IEA to meet international definitions (for data on electricity production, see table 3.9). Electricity consumption is equivalent to production less power plants' own use and transmission, distribution, and transformation losses. It includes consumption by auxiliary stations, losses in transformers that are considered integral parts of those stations, and electricity produced by pumping installations. It covers electricity generated by primary sources of energy—coal, oil, gas, nuclear, hydro, geothermal, wind, tide and wave, and combustible renewables—where data are available. Neither production nor consumption data capture the reliability of supplies, including breakdowns, load factors, and frequency of outages.

Over the past decade new financing and technology, along with privatization and liberalization, have spurred dramatic growth in telecommunications in many countries. The table presents some common performance indicators for telecommunications, including measures of supply and demand, service quality, productivity, economic and financial performance, and tariffs. The quality of data varies among reporting countries as a result of differences in regulatory obligations for the provision of data.

Demand for telecommunications is often measured by the sum of telephone mainlines and registered applicants for new connections. (A mainline is normally identified by a unique number that is the one billed.) In some countries the list of registered applicants does not reflect real current pending demand, which is often hidden or suppressed, reflecting an extremely short supply that has discouraged potential applicants from applying for telephone service. And in some countries the waiting list may overstate demand because applicants have placed their names on the list several times to improve their chances. Telephone mainline faults refer to the number of reported faults per 100 main telephone lines. It is calculated by the total number of reported faults for the year divided by the number of telephone mainlines and multiplied by 100. The definition of fault varies among countries: some operators define faults as including malfunctioning customer equipment while others include only technical faults. The number of mainlines no longer reflects a telephone system's full capacity because mobile telephones—whose use has been expanding rapidly in most countries, rich and poor—provide an alternative point of access.

In addition to waiting list and mainline faults, the table includes two other measures of efficiency in telecommunications: mainlines per employee and revenue per mainline. Caution should be used in interpreting the estimates of mainlines per employee because firms often subcontract part of their work. The cross-country comparability of revenue per mainline may also be limited because, for example, some countries do not require telecommunications providers to submit financial information; the data usually do not include revenues from mobile phones or radio, paging, and data services; and there are definitional and accounting differences between countries.

5.10a

Mobile phone subscribers are approaching (or surpassing) 500 per 1,000 people in some developing and transition economies

Source: World Bank data files, based on International Telecommunication Union data.

Definitions

• **Electric power consumption** measures the production of power plants and combined heat and power plants less transmission, distribution, and transformation losses and own use by heat and power plants. • **Electric power transmission and distribution losses** are losses in transmission between sources of supply and points of distribution and in distribution to consumers, including pilferage. • **Telephone mainlines** are telephone lines connecting a customer's equipment to the public switched telephone network. Data are presented for the entire country and for the largest city. • **Waiting list** shows the number of applications for a connection to a mainline that have been held up by a lack of technical capacity. • **Telephone mainline faults** is the number of reported faults per 100 telephone mainlines. • **Telephone mainlines per employee** are calculated by dividing the number of mainlines by the number of telecommunications staff (with part-time staff converted to full-time equivalents) employed by enterprises providing public telecommunications services. • **Revenue per line** is the revenue received by firms per mainline for providing telecommunications services. • **Cost of local call** is the cost of a three-minute, peak rate, fixed line call within the same exchange area using the subscriber's equipment (that is, not from a public phone). • **Mobile phones** refer to portable telephone subscribers to an automatic public mobile telephone service using cellular technology that provides access to the public switched telephone network, per 1,000 people. • **International telecommunications outgoing traffic** is the telephone traffic, measured in minutes per subscriber, that originates in the country and has a destination outside the country. • **Cost of call to U.S.** is the cost of a three-minute, peak rate, fixed line call from the country to the United States.

Data sources

The data on electricity consumption and losses are from the IEA's *Energy Statistics and Balances of Non-OECD Countries 2000–2001,* the IEA's *Energy Statistics of OECD Countries 2000–2001,* and the United Nations Statistics Division's *Energy Statistics Yearbook.* The telecommunications data are from the International Telecommunication Union's *World Telecommunication Development Report 2003.*

	Daily newspapers	Radios	Television[a]		Personal computers		Internet				Information and communications technology expenditures	
			Sets	Cable subscribers		In education	Users	Total monthly price[a] 20 hours of use	% of monthly	Secure servers	% of GDP	Per capita
	per 1,000 people	per 1,000 people	per 1,000 people	per 1,000 people	per 1,000 people[a]	number	per 1,000 people[a]	$	GNI per capita	number		$
	2000	2001	2002	2002	2002	2002	2002	2003	2003	2003	2002	2002
Afghanistan	5	114	14	0.0	..	..	0	..	..	1	..	..
Albania	35	260	318	2.3	11.7	..	4	29	24.8	1	..	..
Algeria	27	244	114	0.0	7.7	..	16	18	12.4	4	..	..
Angola	11	78	52	0.9	1.9	..	3	79	143.3	1	..	..
Argentina	37	681	326	162.9	82.0	98,635	112	13	3.9	274	3.9	95
Armenia	5	264	229	1.2	15.8	..	16	45	68.0	2	..	..
Australia	293	1,996	731	76.3	565.1	672,471	482	18	1.1	5,749	6.4	1,298
Austria	296	763	637	132.0	369.3	196,210	409	33	1.7	1,156	5.3	1,322
Azerbaijan	27	22	332	0.6	..	..	37	108	183.0	1	..	..
Bangladesh	53	49	59	27.0	3.4	..	2	20	66.8	1	..	..
Belarus	152	199	362	77.2	..	..	82	13	11.3	6	..	..
Belgium	160	793	541	374.7	241.4	285,395	328	29	1.5	576	5.5	1,324
Benin	5	445	12	..	2.2	..	7	46	146.5	1	..	..
Bolivia	55	667	121	9.7	22.8	..	32	22	29.8	10	..	..
Bosnia and Herzegovina	152	243	116	19.4	..	..	26	7	6.9	4	..	..
Botswana	27	150	44	..	40.7	..	30	27	10.9	..	..	..
Brazil	43	433	349	13.8	74.8	774,363	82	28	11.8	1,580	8.3	205
Bulgaria	116	543	453	93.5	51.9	22,078	81	12	8.3	24	6.9	146
Burkina Faso	1	433	79	0.0	1.6	..	2	45	247.5	..	..	..
Burundi	2	220	31	0.0	0.7	..	1	81	971.3	..	..	..
Cambodia	2	119	8	..	2.0	..	2	57	245.8	1	..	..
Cameroon	7	161	75	..	5.7	..	4	52	110.7	1	..	..
Canada	159	1,047	691	252.9	487.0	1,306,715	513	13	0.7	10,785	5.9	1,352
Central African Republic	2	80	6	..	2.0	..	1	175	807.9	..	..	..
Chad	0	233	2	..	1.7	..	2	69	375.6	..	..	..
Chile	98	759	523	57.4	119.3	131,024	238	22	6.1	233	5.7	246
China	..	339	350	75.0	27.6	3,555,157	46	10	13.0	182	5.8	58
Hong Kong, China	792	686	504	90.6	422.0	173,161	430	4	0.2	768	4.6	1,025
Colombia	46	549	303	13.6	49.3	167,461	46	19	12.2	105	6.7	114
Congo, Dem. Rep.	3	385	2	..	..	..	1	74	986.7	..	..	..
Congo, Rep.	8	109	13	..	3.9	..	2	121	207.8	..	..	..
Costa Rica	91	816	231	..	197.2	12,320	193	26	7.6	144	..	..
Côte d'Ivoire	16	185	61	0.0	9.3	..	5	67	132.1	1	..	..
Croatia	114	339	293	8.1	173.8	..	180	17	4.4	107	7.5	364
Cuba	118	185	251	..	31.8	..	11	58	32.2	1	..	..
Czech Republic	254	803	538	94.4	177.4	62,900	256	21	4.5	229	7.2	489
Denmark	283	1,400	859	201.4	576.8	276,813	513	18	0.7	998	5.8	1,852
Dominican Republic	27	181	..	..	..	44,792	36	33	17.1	22	..	..
Ecuador	96	422	237	33.8	31.1	99,334	42	32	26.3	23	..	..
Egypt, Arab Rep.	31	339	229	0.0	16.6	48,816	28	5	4.5	17	3.3	38
El Salvador	28	481	233	49.7	25.2	..	46	48	27.8	23	..	..
Eritrea	..	464	50	0.0	2.5	..	2	27	200.9	..	..	..
Estonia	176	1,136	502	107.0	210.3	..	328	14	3.9	89	..	..
Ethiopia	0	189	6	0.0	1.5	..	1	27	329.1	2	..	..
Finland	445	1,624	670	199.7	441.7	210,163	509	23	1.2	932	5.8	1,464
France	201	950	632	57.5	347.1	1,682,650	314	14	0.8	2,860	5.2	1,246
Gabon	30	488	308	11.5	19.2	..	19	122	46.9	3	..	..
Gambia, The	2	394	15	..	13.8	..	18	27	116.2	..	..	..
Georgia	5	568	357	12.4	31.6	..	15	26	48.4	4	..	..
Germany	305	570	661	249.9	431.3	2,379,660	412	14	0.7	8,451	5.2	1,252
Ghana	14	695	53	0.3	3.8	..	8	44	194.8	5	..	..
Greece	23	478	519	0.0	81.7	117,911	155	38	3.9	205	4.8	604
Guatemala	33	79	145	..	14.4	8,310	33	31	21.4	36	..	..
Guinea	..	52	47	0.0	5.5	..	5	63	185.2	..	..	..
Guinea-Bissau	5	178	36	..	..	..	4	105	840.7	..	..	..
Haiti	3	18	6	4.8	..	..	10	130	354.5	3	..	..

	Daily newspapers	Radios	Television [a]		Personal computers		Internet				Information and communications technology expenditures	
			Sets	Cable subscribers		In	Users	Total monthly price [a]		Secure		
								20 hours of use	% of monthly	servers		Per capita
	per 1,000 people	per 1,000 people	per 1,000 people	per 1,000 people	per 1,000 people [a]	education number	per 1,000 people [a]	$	GNI per capita	number	% of GDP	$
	2000	2001	2002	2002	2002	2002	2002	2003	2003	2003	2002	2002
Honduras	55	411	119	21.6	13.6	..	25	41	52.9	16	..	..
Hungary	465	690	475	170.1	108.4	52,452	158	10	2.3	139	6.4	420
India	60	120	83	38.9	7.2	347,801	16	9	21.9	281	2.8	13
Indonesia	23	159	153	0.3	11.9	58,593	38	22	37.6	60	1.5	11
Iran, Islamic Rep.	28	281	173	..	75.0	..	48	6	4.2	1	..	..
Iraq	19	222	83	..	8.3	..	1	..	..	..	..	..
Ireland	150	695	694	143.0	420.8	141,360	271	28	1.4	784	4.0	1,256
Israel	290	526	330	184.0	242.6	..	301	30	2.1	562	6.9	1,173
Italy	104	878	494	1.4	230.7	1,109,182	352	17	1.0	1,430	4.4	898
Jamaica	62	795	374	..	53.9	..	229	44	18.5	12	..	..
Japan	578	956	785	183.1	382.2	2,292,417	449	21	0.8	11,878	5.3	1,671
Jordan	75	372	177	0.3	37.5	..	58	26	18.0	9	..	..
Kazakhstan	..	411	338	6.6	..	..	16	34	27.4	3	..	..
Kenya	10	221	26	0.5	6.4	..	13	46	152.4	4	..	..
Korea, Dem. Rep.	208	154	162	0.0	..	..	0	..	..	..	..	..
Korea, Rep.	393	1,034	363	132.0	555.8	857,233	552	10	1.2	688	6.5	645
Kuwait	374	570	418	..	120.6	..	106	25	2.0	38	..	..
Kyrgyz Republic	27	110	49	3.1	12.7	..	30	15	62.1	1	..	..
Lao PDR	4	148	52	0.0	3.3	..	3	32	123.4	..	..	..
Latvia	135	700	850	132.2	171.7	..	133	58	20.0	53	..	..
Lebanon	107	182	357	29.9	80.5	..	117	37	11.1	16	..	..
Lesotho	8	61	35	..	..	..	10	43	110.7	..	..	..
Liberia	12	274	25	..	..	..	0	..	..	..	..	..
Libya	15	273	137	..	23.4	..	23	19	3.8	..	..	..
Lithuania	29	524	487	75.1	109.7	..	144	34	11.2	29	..	..
Macedonia, FYR	21	205	282	..	..	..	48	19	13.3	..	..	..
Madagascar	5	216	25	..	4.4	..	3	67	336.7	1	..	..
Malawi	3	499	4	0.0	1.3	..	3	62	465.0	..	..	..
Malaysia	158	420	210	0.0	146.8	241,392	320	8	2.9	174	7.3	304
Mali	1	180	33	..	1.4	..	2	58	289.8	1	..	..
Mauritania	0	148	99	..	10.8	..	4	39	113.1	1	..	..
Mauritius	119	379	299	..	116.5	..	99	15	4.7	17	..	..
Mexico	94	330	282	24.3	82.0	302,325	98	23	4.6	416	4.4	2,097
Moldova	13	758	296	13.3	17.5	..	34	19	49.6	7	..	..
Mongolia	30	50	79	18.5	28.4	..	21	18	48.6	3	..	..
Morocco	28	243	167	..	23.6	..	24	25	25.5	15	..	..
Mozambique	2	44	14	..	4.5	..	2	51	290.2	2	..	..
Myanmar	9	66	8	..	5.1	..	1	43	180.9	..	..	..
Namibia	19	134	269	16.0	70.9	..	27	33	22.5	9	..	..
Nepal	12	39	8	..	3.7	..	3	13	70.3	2	..	..
Netherlands	306	980	648	401.4	466.6	652,319	506	24	1.2	58	5.8	1,505
New Zealand	362	992	557	7.1	413.8	196,364	484	13	1.1	1,276	7.4	1,096
Nicaragua	30	270	123	10.8	27.9	..	17	51	138.6	8	..	..
Niger	0	122	10	..	0.6	..	1	97	683.6	..	..	..
Nigeria	24	200	103	0.5	7.1	..	3	85	353.7	3	..	..
Norway	569	3,324	884	184.5	528.3	268,861	503	26	0.8	726	4.1	1,703
Oman	29	621	553	0.0	35.0	..	66	24	3.8	1	..	..
Pakistan	40	105	150	0.2	4.2	..	10	16	45.7	25	..	..
Panama	62	300	191	..	38.3	15,253	41	36	10.7	85	..	..
Papua New Guinea	14	86	21	4.2	58.7	..	14	20	45.3	..	..	..
Paraguay	43	188	218	21.3	34.6	..	17	36	37.3	4	..	..
Peru	0	269	172	16.6	43.0	32,308	93	33	19.2	73	..	..
Philippines	82	161	182	37.0	27.7	125,055	44	17	20.1	97	4.2	40
Poland	102	523	422	91.4	105.6	109,598	230	16	4.1	389	5.2	256
Portugal	32	301	413	122.1	134.9	169,230	194	21	2.3	319	5.8	697
Puerto Rico	126	761	339	91.2	..	302,941	156	..	..	63	..	..

5.11 The information age

	Daily newspapers	Radios	Television[a]		Personal computers		Internet				Information and communications technology expenditures	
			Sets	Cable subscribers		In	Users	Total monthly price[a]		Secure		Per capita
								20 hours of use	% of monthly	servers		
	per 1,000 people	per 1,000 people	per 1,000 people	per 1,000 people	per 1,000 people[a]	education number	per 1,000 people[a]	$	GNI per capita	number	% of GDP	$
	2000	**2001**	**2002**	**2002**	**2002**	**2002**	**2002**	**2003**	**2003**	**2003**	**2002**	**2002**
Romania	300	358	697	152.2	69.2	36,754	83	26	17.1	30	4.3	88
Russian Federation	105	418	538	43.6	88.7	229,630	41	10	5.6	233	3.7	88
Rwanda	0	85	..	..	..	..	3	67	348.3	1	..	..
Saudi Arabia	326	326	265	0.3	130.2	..	62	35	4.9	26	4.6	369
Senegal	5	128	78	0.1	19.8	..	10	41	103.7	3	..	..
Serbia and Montenegro	107	297	282	..	27.1	..	60	13	11.3	6	..	..
Sierra Leone	4	259	13	..	..	..	2	12	102.9	1	..	..
Singapore	298	672	303	84.5	622.0	136,000	504	11	0.6	732	6.5	1,268
Slovak Republic	131	965	409	127.3	180.4	27,729	160	21	6.3	48	5.8	251
Slovenia	169	405	366	160.3	300.6	28,842	376	25	3.1	96	4.9	556
Somalia	1	60	14	..	..	..	9	..	..	..	..	..
South Africa	32	336	177	0.0	72.6	364,722	68	33	15.4	648	9.2	225
Spain	100	330	564	19.9	196.0	636,590	156	21	1.7	1,964	4.5	734
Sri Lanka	29	215	117	0.3	13.2	..	11	15	21.5	23	..	..
Sudan	26	461	386	0.0	6.1	..	3	161	550.8	..	..	..
Swaziland	26	161	34	..	24.2	..	19	21	21.0	2	..	..
Sweden	410	2,811	965	246.0	621.3	541,805	573	22	1.1	1,595	6.5	1,765
Switzerland	373	1,002	552	376.2	708.7	405,134	351	22	0.7	1,931	6.2	2,259
Syrian Arab Republic	20	276	182	0.0	19.4	..	13	55	58.6	1	..	..
Tajikistan	20	141	357	0.1	..	..	1	54	362.3	..	..	..
Tanzania	4	406	45	0.2	4.2	..	2	117	501.4	..	..	..
Thailand	64	235	300	12.9	39.8	230,000	78	7	4.2	179	4.7	94
Togo	2	263	123	..	30.8	..	41	30	134.9	..	..	..
Trinidad and Tobago	123	534	345	..	79.5	..	106	13	2.5	13	..	..
Tunisia	19	158	207	..	30.7	..	52	17	10.4	13	..	..
Turkey	111	470	423	14.2	44.6	123,907	73	20	9.5	496	4.6	122
Turkmenistan	7	279	182	..	..	..	2	20	20.2	..	..	..
Uganda	2	122	18	0.3	3.3	..	4	97	464.4	2	..	..
Ukraine	175	889	456	38.6	19.0	..	18	17	26.0	28	..	..
United Arab Emirates	156	330	252	..	129.0	..	337	13	0.8	83	..	..
United Kingdom	329	1,445	950	57.2	405.7	2,099,346	423	24	1.1	13,540	6.1	1,600
United States	213	2,117	938	255.0	658.9	19,787,772	551	15	0.5	138,514	6.5	2,358
Uruguay	293	603	530	125.9	110.1	..	119	26	7.3	39	..	..
Uzbekistan	3	456	280	3.7	..	..	11	20	53.8	1	..	..
Venezuela, RB	206	294	186	36.3	60.9	104,297	51	19	5.7	106	4.4	147
Vietnam	4	109	197	..	9.8	29,516	18	20	55.4	3	2.4	10
West Bank and Gaza	..	..	148	0.0	36.2	..	30	25	32.8	..	..	..
Yemen, Rep.	15	65	308	..	7.4	..	5	31	75.3	1	..	..
Zambia	12	179	51	1.2	7.5	..	5	33	118.7	..	..	..
Zimbabwe	18	362	56	2.1	51.6	..	43	23	58.3	7	..	..
World	.. w	**419** w	**275** w	**65.5** w	**100.8** w		**131** u	**37** u	**88.7** u	**217,255** s		
Low income	40	139	91	23.7	7.5		10	57	246.4	435		
Middle income	..	360	326	57.6	45.4		80	29	18.9	6,686		
Lower middle income	..	346	326	58.9	37.7		46	29	24.9	3,965		
Upper middle income	123	466	326	47.1	100.5		149	30	8.6	2,721		
Low & middle income	..	257	190	40.2	28.4		50	41	114.8	7,121		
East Asia & Pacific	..	287	317	70.1	26.3		44	31	66.1	720		
Europe & Central Asia	102	447	407	47.6	73.4		87	26	39.5	1,930		
Latin America & Carib.	70	410	289	33.9	67.4		92	33	31.8	3,309		
Middle East & N. Africa	33	277	200	..	38.2		37	31	29.9	103		
South Asia	60	112	84	37.3	6.8		14	30	58.6	333		
Sub-Saharan Africa	12	198	69	0.3	11.9		16	64	268.8	726		
High income	284	1,266	735	191.0	466.9		364	23	1.6	210,134		
Europe EMU	209	813	597	158.1	317.5		331	24	1.5	18,846		

a. Data are from the International Telecommunication Union's (ITU) *World Telecommunication Development Report 2003*. Please cite the ITU for third-party use of these data.

The digital and information revolution has changed the way the world learns, communicates, does business, and treats illnesses. New information and communications technologies offer vast opportunities for progress in all walks of life in all countries—opportunities for economic growth, improved health, better service delivery, learning through distance education, and social and cultural advances. This table presents indicators of the penetration of the information economy—newspapers, radios, televisions, personal computers, and Internet use—as well as some of the economics of the information age—Internet access charges, the number of secure servers, and spending on information and communications technology.

The data on the number of daily newspapers in circulation and radio receivers in use are from statistical surveys by the United Nations Educational, Scientific, and Cultural Organization (UNESCO). In some countries definitions, classifications, and methods of enumeration do not entirely conform to UNESCO standards. For example, newspaper circulation data should refer to the number of copies distributed, but in some cases the figures reported are the number of copies printed. In addition, many countries impose radio and television license fees to help pay for public broadcasting, discouraging radio and television owners from declaring ownership. Because of these and other data collection problems, estimates of the number of newspapers and radios vary widely in reliability and should be interpreted with caution.

The data for other electronic communications and information technology are from the International Telecommunication Union (ITU), the Internet Software Consortium, Netcraft, the World Information Technology and Services Alliance, and the International Data Corporation. The ITU collects data on television sets and cable television subscribers through annual questionnaires sent to national broadcasting authorities and industry associations. Some countries require that television sets be registered. To the extent that households do not register their televisions or do not register all of them, the data on licensed sets may understate the true number.

The estimates of personal computers are derived from an annual ITU questionnaire, supplemented by other sources. In many countries mainframe computers are used extensively. Since thousands of users can be connected to a single mainframe computer, the number of personal computers understates the total use of computers.

The data on Internet users are based on estimates derived from reported counts of Internet service subscribers or calculated by multiplying the number of Internet hosts by an estimated multiplier. Internet hosts are computers connected directly to the worldwide network, each allowing many computer users to access the Internet. This method may undercount the number of people actually using the Internet, particularly in developing countries, where many commercial subscribers rent out computers connected to the Internet or pre-paid cards are used to access the Internet. Although survey methods used to estimate the number of Internet hosts have improved in recent years, some measurement problems remain (see Zook 2000). For detailed analysis of Internet trends by country, it is best to use the original source data.

The table shows the total monthly Internet price, which refers to the sum of Internet service provider (ISP) charges and telephone usage charges. The Internet price is also calculated as a percentage of monthly GNI per capita. Data are generally derived from the prices listed by the largest ISP and incumbent telephone company. The number of secure servers, from the Netcraft Secure Server Survey, gives an indication of how many companies are conducting encrypted transactions over the Internet.

The data on information and communications technology expenditures cover the world's 55 largest buyers of such technology among countries and regions. These account for 98 percent of global spending.

Because of different regulatory requirements for the provision of data, complete measurement of the telecommunications sector is not possible. Telecommunications data are compiled through annual questionnaires sent to telecommunications authorities and operating companies by the ITU. The data are supplemented by annual reports and statistical yearbooks of telecommunications ministries, regulators, operators, and industry associations. In some cases estimates are derived from ITU documents or other references.

• **Daily newspapers** refer to those published at least four times a week and calculated as average circulation (or copies printed) per 1,000 people. • **Radios** refer to radio receivers in use for broadcasts to the general public. • **Television sets** refer to those in use. • **Cable television subscribers** are households that subscribe to a multichannel television service delivered by a fixed line connection. Some countries also report subscribers to pay-television using wireless technology or those cabled to community antenna systems. • **Personal computers** are self-contained computers designed to be used by a single individual. • **Personal computers in education** are those installed in primary and secondary schools and universities. • **Internet users** are people with access to the worldwide network. • **Total monthly price** refers to the sum of ISP and telephone usage charges for 20 hours of use and as a percentage of monthly GNI per capita. • **Secure servers** are servers using encryption technology in Internet transactions. • **Information and communications technology expenditures** cover external spending on information technology ("tangible" spending on information technology products purchased by businesses, households, governments, and education institutions from vendors or organizations outside the purchasing entity), internal spending on information technology ("intangible" spending on internally customized software, capital depreciation, and the like), and spending on telecommunications and other office equipment.

The data on newspapers and radios are compiled by the UNESCO Institute for Statistics. The data on television sets, cable television subscribers, personal computers, Internet users, and Internet access charges are from the ITU and are reported in the ITU's *World Telecommunication Development Report 2003* and the *World Telecommunications Indicators Database* (2003). The data on personal computers in education and on information and communications technology expenditures are from *Digital Planet 2002: The Global Information Economy* by the World Information Technology and Services Alliance (WITSA), and the International Data Corporation. The data on secure servers are from Netcraft (http://www.netcraft.com/).

	Researchers in R&D	Technicians in R&D	Scientific and technical journal articles	Expenditures for R&D	High-technology exports		Royalty and license fees		Patent applications filed[a]		Trademark applications filed[b]	
	per million people 1990–2001[c]	per million people 1990–2001[c]	1999	% of GDP 1996–2002[c]	$ millions 2002	% of manufactured exports 2002	Receipts $ millions 2002	Payments $ millions 2002	Residents 2001	Non-residents 2001	Residents 2001	Non-residents 2001
Afghanistan	..	..	0	..	..	..	..	..	..	..	..	..
Albania	..	..	17	..	2	1	..	..	0	129,865	0	2,070
Algeria	..	..	162	..	21	4	..	..	52	72,257	1,418	3,284
Angola	..	..	3	..	..	..	4	0	..	..	..	..
Argentina	684	149	2,361	0.42	583	7	17	225	0	6,634	..	..
Armenia	1,534	223	142	0.2	3	2	..	..	155	75,502	510	2,696
Australia	3,439	792	12,525	1.53	2,945	16	304	1,012	10,244	84,929	25,159	13,893
Austria	2,313	979	3,580	1.93	8,433	15	111	1,053	3,358	229,823	7,544	11,818
Azerbaijan	2,799	160	66	0.37	10	8	..	2	0	75,462	0	2,055
Bangladesh	51	32	148	..	10	0	0	3	..	..	..	..
Belarus	1,893	273	564	..	212	4	1	3	945	75,750	1,885	4,846
Belgium	2,953	1,157	4,896	1.98	15,736	11	887	1,246	1,953	154,676	21,382[d]	12,510[d]
Benin	174	53	20	..	0	0	0	1	..	..	..	..
Bolivia	123	6	33	0.34	15	7	2	6	..	..	..	..
Bosnia and Herzegovina	..	..	9	..	..	..	..	..	52	76,362	152	4,298
Botswana	..	..	41	..	6	0	..	..	2	56	..	..
Brazil	323	129	5,144	1.05	6,007	19	100	1,229	6,706	87,301	85,098	16,415
Bulgaria	1,167	472	801	0.55	85	3	4	23	291	77,331	3,508	5,894
Burkina Faso	16	15	23	0.19	2	7	..	0	..	..	..	..
Burundi	21	32	3	..	0	2	0	0	..	..	..	..
Cambodia	..	..	5	..	..	..	..	6	..	..	231	1,268
Cameroon	3	4	61	..	1	1	..	..	..	..	..	..
Canada	2,978	1,035	19,685	1.94	22,662	14	1,689	3,651	5,737	92,752	17,314	21,778
Central African Republic	47	27	4	..	..	..	..	..	..	..	..	..
Chad	..	..	2	..	..	..	..	..	..	..	..	..
Chile	419	307	879	0.54	107	3	6	345	241	2,879	..	..
China	584	202	11,675	1.09	68,182	23	133	3,114	30,324	118,970	229,775	30,149
Hong Kong, China	1,998	100	1,817	0.44	2,688	17	196	491	74	8,840	5,458	15,487
Colombia	101	48	207	0.17	319	7	4	87	63	44,882	7,265	7,096
Congo, Dem. Rep.	..	..	6	..	..	..	..	..	..	..	..	..
Congo, Rep.	33	37	13	..	..	..	..	..	..	..	..	..
Costa Rica	530	..	69	0.20	1,146	37	2	51	0	74,360	..	..
Côte d'Ivoire	..	..	40	..	27	3	0	10	..	..	..	..
Croatia	1,187	347	545	0.98	432	12	85	77	456	76,035	992	6,111
Cuba	489	2,393	192	0.65	48	29	..	..	4	75,687	0	2,090
Czech Republic	1,466	712	2,005	1.31	4,494	14	45	119	605	78,648	8,100	10,949
Denmark	3,476	2,594	4,131	2.15	8,089	22	..	..	3,770	229,151	3,646	8,351
Dominican Republic	..	..	6	..	..	1	..	24	..	..	..	..
Ecuador	83	72	20	0.09	34	7	..	44	0	28,909	4,832	5,011
Egypt, Arab Rep.	493	366	1,198	0.19	13	1	38	171	464	923	0	3,216
El Salvador	47	303	0	0.01	44	6	2	20	..	..	..	..
Eritrea	..	..	2	..	..	..	0	0	..	..	..	..
Estonia	1,947	387	261	0.66	375	12	5	14	25	77,142	910	5,617
Ethiopia	..	..	95	..	0	..	0	0	3	4	..	..
Finland	7,110	..	4,025	3.42	9,139	24	559	604	3,405	227,036	2,879	7,365
France	2,718	2,878	27,374	2.20	52,582	21	3,241	1,956	21,790	153,332	60,513	14,324
Gabon	..	..	20	..	4	7	..	..	..	..	..	..
Gambia, The	..	..	17	..	0	3	..	..	1	150,081	..	..
Georgia	2,421	97	112	0.33	41	38	6	11	257	76,207	218	3,114
Germany	3,153	1,345	37,308	2.50	86,861	17	3,765	5,064	80,222	212,176	63,645	14,235
Ghana	..	..	73	..	3	3	..	0	2	150,194	..	..
Greece	1,400	554	2,241	0.68	524	10	13	288	78	155,268	5,879	6,240
Guatemala	103	111	14	..	55	7	0	0	5	260	3,048	5,040
Guinea	..	..	2	..	0	0	0	1	..	..	..	..
Guinea-Bissau	..	..	6	..	..	..	..	..	0	..	..	..
Haiti	..	..	1	..	..	..	..	..	1	5	..	..

	Researchers in R&D	Technicians in R&D	Scientific and technical journal articles	Expenditures for R&D	High-technology exports		Royalty and license fees		Patent applications filed [a]		Trademark applications filed [b]	
	per million people 1990–2001[c]	per million people 1990–2001[c]	1999	% of GDP 1996–2002[c]	$ millions 2002	% of manufactured exports 2002	Receipts $ millions 2002	Payments $ millions 2002	Residents 2001	Non-residents 2001	Residents 2001	Non-residents 2001
Honduras	73	256	11	..	5	2	0	11	7	155	..	..
Hungary	1,440	510	1,958	0.95	7,364	25	350	399	1,019	78,181	4,755	10,673
India	157	115	9,217	..	1,788	5	12	350	234	78,288	..	..
Indonesia	..	..	142	..	5,070	16	..	..	0	77,407	..	..
Iran, Islamic Rep.	590	174	624	..	64	3	0	0	691	302	9,858	1,224
Iraq	..	..	21	..	..	..	..	..	..	..	..	..
Ireland	2,190	588	1,237	1.16	31,624	41	249	10,347	1,334	155,155	918	3,038
Israel	1,563	516	5,025	4.96	5,414	20	389	450	2,378	82,027	2,468	6,468
Italy	1,128	808	17,149	1.07	19,872	9	539	1,273	3,819	153,039	0	11,005
Jamaica	..	..	44	..	1	0	6	32	3	66	599	2,394
Japan	5,321	667	47,826	3.09	94,730	24	10,422	11,021	388,390	108,231	104,655	19,133
Jordan	1,948	717	204	6.33	48	3	..	..	..	..	..	..
Kazakhstan	716	293	104	0.29	157	10	0	19	1,610	75,560	1,796	3,300
Kenya	..	..	252	..	35	10	5	62	2	150,443	0	1,442
Korea, Dem. Rep.	..	..	1	..	..	..	..	..	0	74,672	0	2,587
Korea, Rep.	2,880	564	6,675	2.96	46,438	32	826	2,979	74,001	116,021	86,408	20,729
Kuwait	212	53	260	0.20	..	..	0	0	..	..	..	..
Kyrgyz Republic	581	49	10	0.19	6	6	3	3	84	75,489	59	2,382
Lao PDR	..	..	2	..	..	..	..	..	..	..	14	563
Latvia	1,078	298	153	0.40	51	4	3	6	124	130,315	1,062	6,133
Lebanon	..	..	100	..	16	3	..	..	0	104	..	..
Lesotho	..	..	1	..	..	..	11	0	1	150,361	0	1,009
Liberia	..	..	1	..	..	..	..	..	0	76,005	0	1,018
Libya	361	493	19	..	..	..	..	..	..	..	..	..
Lithuania	2,303	492	214	0.63	130	5	0	11	70	130,287	1,323	5,994
Macedonia, FYR	387	29	36	..	9	1	3	10	66	129,995	440	3,962
Madagascar	15	46	..	0.13	..	..	0	13	0	76,048	236	336
Malawi	..	..	36	..	1	3	0	0	2	150,687	146	515
Malaysia	160	45	416	0.40	40,912	58	12	628	..	..	..	..
Mali	..	..	11	..	..	..	0	1	..	..	..	..
Mauritania	..	..	2	..	..	..	..	..	..	..	..	..
Mauritius	360	157	16	0.28	29	2	0	2	..	..	..	..
Mexico	225	183	2,291	0.43	28,939	21	48	720	594	81,876	43,788	21,147
Moldova	329	1,641	92	0.62	8	4	1	1	437	75,549	..	..
Mongolia	531	116	8	..	1	0	0	..	106	76,133	206	3,189
Morocco	..	..	386	..	439	11	11	41	0	74,468	0	3,499
Mozambique	..	..	14	..	2	3	0	0	1	146,278	0	1,162
Myanmar	..	..	10	..	..	..	0	0	..	..	..	..
Namibia	..	..	13	..	6	1	4	2	..	..	..	..
Nepal	..	..	39	..	0	0	..	..	..	..	..	..
Netherlands	2,572	..	10,441	1.95	33,667	28	1,962	2,612	8,107	150,825	..	..
New Zealand	2,197	776	2,375	1.03	388	10	89	347	920	82,362	8,382	12,232
Nicaragua	73	33	8	0.15	6	5	..	..	9	136	..	..
Niger	..	..	21	..	0	8	..	..	..	..	..	..
Nigeria	..	..	397	..	0	0	..	..	..	..	..	..
Norway	4,377	1,836	2,598	1.64	2,863	22	171	325	1,780	82,593	3,316	11,767
Oman	4	0	73	..	36	2	..	..	0	2,174	..	..
Pakistan	69	12	277	..	59	1	2	18	58	1,168	4,852	2,392
Panama	95	213	37	0.44	1	1	0	41	7	153	..	..
Papua New Guinea	..	..	36	..	11	19	..	..	..	..	..	..
Paraguay	166	231	4	0.00	7	3	184	1	..	..	..	..
Peru	229	1	56	0.11	24	2	2	56	48	944	6,940	6,983
Philippines	156	22	164	..	11,488	65	1	230	0	13,598	..	..
Poland	1,473	507	4,523	0.67	915	3	34	557	2,218	78,856	12,434	13,358
Portugal	1,754	506	1,508	0.78	1,628	7	32	294	189	230,719	7,191	9,682
Puerto Rico	..	..	..	..	..	..	..	..	..	..	..	..

	Researchers in R&D per million people 1990–2001 [c]	Technicians in R&D per million people 1990–2001 [c]	Scientific and technical journal articles 1999	Expenditures for R&D % of GDP 1996–2002 [c]	High-technology exports $ millions 2002	High-technology exports % of manufactured exports 2002	Royalty and license fees Receipts $ millions 2002	Royalty and license fees Payments $ millions 2002	Patent applications filed [a] Residents 2001	Patent applications filed [a] Non-residents 2001	Trademark applications filed [b] Residents 2001	Trademark applications filed [b] Non-residents 2001
Romania	879	584	785	0.40	390	3	3	85	1,148	130,602	5,374	7,208
Russian Federation	3,494	551	15,654	1.16	2,897	13	147	338	25,046	82,632	39,801	13,295
Rwanda	..	6	4	..	0	1	0	0	0	4	..	..
Saudi Arabia	..	..	528	..	30	0	0	0	46	683	..	..
Senegal	2	3	66	0.01	15	4	..	..	..	..	..	..
Serbia and Montenegro	2,389	515	546	..	..	..	..	..	470	77,043	971	6,022
Sierra Leone	..	..	3	..	..	..	..	..	1	150,465	0	1,038
Singapore	4,052	335	1,653	2.11	63,792	60	..	..	0	79,026	0	3,079
Slovak Republic	1,774	790	871	0.62	386	3	16	58	260	77,131	2,158	8,958
Slovenia	2,258	877	599	1.63	488	5	7	78	344	130,599	1,009	7,481
Somalia	..	..	0	..	..	..	..	..	..	..	..	..
South Africa	992	303	2,018	..	740	5	43	94	175	76,571	..	..
Spain	1,948	1,019	12,289	0.96	6,777	7	370	1,810	3,814	230,729	73,937	15,263
Sri Lanka	191	46	84	0.18	19	1	..	..	0	76,095	..	..
Sudan	..	..	43	..	4	7	0	0	5	150,388	0	1,063
Swaziland	..	..	6	..	3	1	0	46	1	75,091	0	1,054
Sweden	5,186	3,164	8,326	4.61	10,760	16	1,505	888	7,133	224,350	6,603	8,552
Switzerland	3,592	1,399	6,993	2.64	17,077	21	..	..	7,323	226,329	7,665	17,053
Syrian Arab Republic	29	24	55	0.18	2	1	..	..	0	0	0	0
Tajikistan	660	..	20	..	37	42	0	1	0	75,462	0	1,965
Tanzania	..	..	92	..	1	2	0	0	2	148,738	0	16
Thailand	74	74	470	0.10	15,234	31	7	1,104	1,117	4,548	..	..
Togo	102	65	11	..	1	1	0	1	..	..	..	..
Trinidad and Tobago	456	882	37	0.14	75	3	..	..	1	76,045	..	..
Tunisia	336	32	237	0.45	177	4	16	6	0	195	..	..
Turkey	306	26	2,761	0.64	568	2	0	107	425	228,914	19,885	8,544
Turkmenistan	..	..	0	..	8	5	..	..	0	75,440	0	1,803
Uganda	24	14	59	0.75	4	12	0	..	2	150,406	0	14
Ukraine	2,118	594	2,194	0.95	572	5	4	110	7,234	77,196	6,854	7,320
United Arab Emirates	..	..	118	..	17	2	..	..	0	75,414	..	..
United Kingdom	2,666	1,014	39,711	1.90	71,481	31	7,701	5,993	34,500	230,206	50,601	20,490
United States	4,099	..	163,526	2.80	162,345	32	44,142	19,258	190,907	184,750	181,713	34,861
Uruguay	276	52	144	0.24	19	3	0	10	44	572	..	..
Uzbekistan	1,754	312	236	..	..	..	..	..	803	76,432	690	2,723
Venezuela, RB	193	32	448	0.44	94	3	0	58	56	2,292	..	..
Vietnam	274	..	98	..	..	..	..	..	0	76,542	0	2,422
West Bank and Gaza	..	..	..	..	..	..	..	..	..	..	..	..
Yemen, Rep.	..	..	10	..	..	..	..	..	..	..	..	..
Zambia	..	..	26	..	2	2	..	0	8	3,178	213	617
Zimbabwe	..	..	85	..	21	3	..	..	2	150,320	1	17
World	.. w	.. w	528,627 s	2.46 w	1,149,146 s	21 w	79,611 s	82,187 s	939,267 s	10,814,596 s	1,263,071 s	630,592 s
Low income	..	..	12,040	..	..	9	36	420	2,008	2,642,403	6,866	33,611
Middle income	818	..	64,710	0.66	182,644	19	1,361	10,299	81,357	3,317,058	505,531	247,653
Lower middle income	810	..	46,694	0.89	97,450	17	753	7,034	75,937	2,057,922	430,009	158,713
Upper middle income	662	..	18,016	0.53	84,405	21	608	3,265	5,420	1,259,136	75,522	88,940
Low & middle income	..	..	76,750	0.57	..	17	1,397	10,718	83,365	5,959,461	512,397	281,264
East Asia & Pacific	584	202	13,055	1.09	..	32	153	5,082	30,430	437,322	230,226	40,178
Europe & Central Asia	2,069	..	34,679	0.96	16,726	10	695	1,898	43,800	2,493,388	113,877	151,290
Latin America & Carib.	..	..	12,018	0.52	38,457	16	407	2,980	7,383	766,888	151,570	66,176
Middle East & N. Africa	..	..	3,617	..	880	2	65	218	1,253	151,002	11,276	11,223
South Asia	158	113	9,769	..	..	4	18	371	292	155,551	4,852	3,096
Sub-Saharan Africa	..	..	3,612	..	..	4	59	169	207	1,955,310	596	9,301
High income	3,284	..	451,877	2.64	853,545	23	78,214	71,469	855,902	4,855,135	750,674	349,328
Europe EMU	2,302	996	122,077	2.13	278,406	17	10,963	25,404	128,297	2,283,274	243,888	105,480

Note: The original information on patent and trademark applications was provided by the World Intellectual Property Organization (WIPO). The International Bureau of WIPO assumes no responsibility with respect to the transformation of these data.

a. Other patent applications filed in 2001 include those filed under the auspices of the African Regional Industrial Property Organization (ARIPO) (5 by residents, 75,101 by nonresidents), European Patent Office (67,330 by residents, 90,960 by nonresidents), and the Eurasian Patent Organization (491 by residents, 75,355 by nonresidents). b. Other trademark applications filed in 2001 include those filed under the auspices of the Office for Harmonization in the Internal Market (30,543 by residents, 18,342 by nonresidents) and ARIPO (6 by residents, 18 by nonresidents). c. Data are for the latest year available. d. Includes Luxembourg and the netherlands.

The best opportunities to improve living standards, including new ways of reducing poverty, will come from science and technology. Science, advancing rapidly in virtually all fields—particularly in biotechnology—is playing a growing economic role: countries able to access, generate, and apply relevant scientific knowledge will have a competitive edge over those that cannot. And there is greater appreciation of the need for high-quality scientific input into public policy issues such as regional and global environmental concerns. Technological innovation, often fueled by government-led research and development (R&D), has been the driving force for industrial growth around the world.

Science and technology cover a range of issues too complex and too broad to be quantified by any single set of indicators, but those in the table shed light on countries' "technological base"—the availability of skilled human resources, the number of scientific and technical articles published, the competitive edge countries enjoy in high-technology exports, sales and purchases of technology through royalties and licenses, and the number of patent and trademark applications filed.

The United Nations Educational, Scientific, and Cultural Organization (UNESCO) collects data on scientific researchers and technical workers and R&D expenditures from member states, mainly through questionnaires and special surveys as well as from official reports and publications, supplemented by information from other national and international sources. UNESCO reports either the stock of researchers and technicians or the number of economically active people qualified as such. UNESCO supplements these data with estimates of qualified researchers by counting people who have completed education at International Standard Classification of Education (ISCED) levels 6 and 7; qualified technicians are estimated using the number of people who have completed education at ISCED level 5. The data are normally calculated in terms of full-time-equivalent staff. The information does not reflect the quality of training and education, which varies widely. Similarly, R&D expenditures are no guarantee of progress; governments need to pay close attention to the practices that make them effective.

The counts of scientific and technical journal articles include those published in a stable set of about 5,000 of the world's most influential scientific and technical journals, tracked since 1985 by the Institute of Scientific Information's Science Citation Index (SCI) and Social Science Citation Index (SSCI). (See *Definitions* for the fields covered.) The SCI and SSCI databases cover the core set of scientific journals but may exclude some of regional or local importance. They may also reflect some bias toward English-language journals.

The method used for determining a country's high technology exports was developed by the Organisation for Economic Co-operation and Development in collaboration with Eurostat. Termed the "product approach" to distinguish it from a "sectoral approach," the method is based on the calculation of R&D intensity (R&D expenditure divided by total sales) for groups of products from six countries (Germany, Italy, Japan, the Netherlands, Sweden, and the United States). Because industrial sectors characterized by a few high-technology products may also produce many low-technology products, the product approach is more appropriate for analyzing international trade than is the sectoral approach. To construct a list of high-technology manufactured products (services are excluded), the R&D intensity was calculated for products classified at the three-digit level of the Standard International Trade Classification revision 3. The final list was determined at the four- and five-digit levels. At these levels, since no R&D data were available, final selection was based on patent data and expert opinion. This method takes only R&D intensity into account. Other characteristics of high technology are also important, such as know-how, scientific and technical personnel, and technology embodied in patents; considering these characteristics would result in a different list. (See Hatzichronoglou 1997 for further details.) Moreover, the R&D for high-technology exports may not have occurred in the reporting country.

Most countries have adopted systems that protect patentable inventions. Under most patent legislation an idea, to be protected by law (patentable), must be new in the sense that it has not already been published or publicly used; it must be nonobvious (involve an inventive step) in the sense that it would not have occurred to any specialist in the industrial field had such a specialist been asked to find a solution to the problem; and it must be capable of industrial application in the sense that it can be industrially manufactured or used. Information on patent applications filed is shown separately for residents and nonresidents of the country.

A trademark provides protection to its owner by ensuring the exclusive right to use it to identify goods or services or to authorize another to use it in return for payment. The period of protection varies, but a trademark can be renewed indefinitely by paying additional fees. The trademark system helps consumers identify and purchase a product or service whose nature and quality, indicated by its unique trademark, meet their needs.

- **Researchers in R&D** are people engaged in professional R&D activity who have received tertiary level training to work in any field of science. • **Technicians in R&D** are people engaged in professional R&D activity who have received vocational or technical training in any branch of knowledge or technology. Most such jobs require three years beyond the first stage of secondary education. • **Scientific and technical journal articles** refer to scientific and engineering articles published in the following fields: physics, biology, chemistry, mathematics, clinical medicine, biomedical research, engineering and technology, and earth and space sciences. • **Expenditures for R&D** are current and capital expenditures on creative, systematic activity that increases the stock of knowledge. Included are fundamental and applied research and experimental development work leading to new devices, products, or processes. • **High-technology exports** are products with high R&D intensity, such as in aerospace, computers, pharmaceuticals, scientific instruments, and electrical machinery. • **Royalty and license fees** are payments and receipts between residents and nonresidents for the authorized use of intangible, nonproduced, nonfinancial assets and proprietary rights (such as patents, copyrights, trademarks, franchises, and industrial processes) and for the use, through licensing agreements, of produced originals of prototypes (such as films and manuscripts). • **Patent applications filed** are applications filed with a national patent office for exclusive rights to an invention—a product or process that provides a new way of doing something or offers a new technical solution to a problem. A patent provides protection for the invention to the owner of the patent for a limited period, generally 20 years. • **Trademark applications filed** are applications for registration of a trademark with a national or regional trademark office. Trademarks are distinctive signs that identify goods or services as those produced or provided by a specific person or enterprise. A trademark provides protection to the owner of the mark by ensuring the exclusive right to use it to identify goods or services or to authorize another to use it in return for payment.

The data on technical personnel and R&D expenditures are from UNESCO's *Statistical Yearbook*. The data on scientific and technical journal articles are from the National Science Foundation's *Science and Engineering Indicators 2002*. The information on high-technology exports is from the United Nations Statistics Division's Commodity Trade (COMTRADE) database. The data on royalty and license fees are from the International Monetary Fund's *Balance of Payments Statistics Yearbook*, and the data on patents and trademarks are from the World Intellectual Property Organization's *Industrial Property Statistics*.

6 GLOBAL LINKS

In the past 20 years the global economy has become increasingly integrated. International financial flows have grown. More people are on the move. And countries are exchanging more goods and services. In 2002 trade in goods and services as a share of world output reached 54 percent, up from 31 percent in 1980 (figure 6a). Several rounds of tariff reductions and expanding trade in services have spurred growth in trade among high-income economies. Developing economies' trade has recovered from a slowdown in the 1980s. Since 1992 the share of trade in their output, measured in constant dollars, has been growing as fast or faster than that of the high-income economies.

Still, there are many obstacles to global integration. National policies that protect home industries from competition or subsidize their output distort patterns of trade and prevent developing countries from reaching their full potential. The movement of people, an important mode of trade in services, remains particularly restricted. Risk and uncertainty also inhibit the flow of finance, while development assistance may be directed more by political considerations than by development opportunities. Table 6.1 highlights additional trends in global integration.

Movement of goods

High-income countries continue to dominate the global scene. They account for more than three-quarters of the world's gross domestic product (GDP) and for three-quarters of world trade. They also remain the most important markets for low- and middle-income economies. In 2002, 17 percent of world trade moved from high-income countries to low- and middle-income economies. Trade between developing economies is still relatively small, but it is

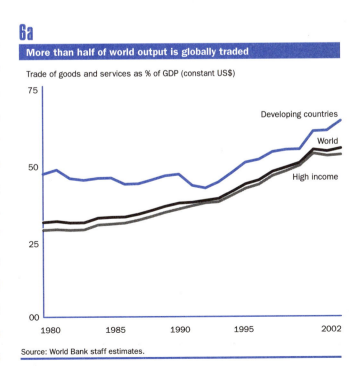

6a

More than half of world output is globally traded

Trade of goods and services as % of GDP (constant US$)

Source: World Bank staff estimates.

growing in importance. In 2002 the movement of goods between low- and middle-income economies accounted for 6 percent of world trade, but in the period 1992–2002 the nominal value of trade between developing economies grew faster than that between high-income countries and between high-income and developing economies (table 6.2).

The types of goods traded by developing economies have been shifting. Exports of manufactures have grown at nearly twice the rate of agricultural exports and account for more than half of exports from developing economies. In 2002, 68 percent of imports to high-income Organisation for Economic Co-operation and Development (OECD) countries from middle-income countries were manufactured goods, up from 46 percent in 1992. Low-income economies also saw significant increases, with shares rising from 38 percent in 1992 to 54 percent in 2002. Both middle- and low-income economies experienced declines in the value of exports of agricultural raw materials (table 6.3), during a period when many commodity prices were falling (table 6.4).

Yet trade barriers continue to be a significant problem. The World Trade Organization's Fifth Ministerial Meeting in Cancun in September 2003, which was supposed to move the Doha Round development agenda forward, produced disappointing results. Some 70 percent of the world's poor live in rural areas and earn incomes from agriculture, while two-thirds of the world's agricultural trade originates in OECD countries. This occurs in part because rich countries subsidize their producers. Subsidies in OECD countries amount to $330 billion—with some $250 billion going directly to producers.

In addition, agricultural exports from developing countries to high-income economies are four to seven times greater than manufacturing exports. Reduced protection in agriculture would account for two-thirds of the gains from full global liberalization of all merchandise trade. Although tariffs on manufactured goods are lower on average in high-income countries than in developing economies, rich countries place substantially lower tariffs on products from other industrial countries than on those from developing economies. But both high-income and developing economies distort trade through tariffs. Latin American exporters of manufactures face tariffs in other markets in the region that are seven times higher than in high-income countries. Tariffs are six times higher in Sub-Saharan Africa than in high-income countries and twice as high in South Asia. Protection also comes through nontariff barriers. Table 6.6 includes new estimates of the ad valorem equivalents of nontariff barriers.

Financial flows and aid

The downturn in foreign direct investment (FDI) that began in 2000 continued through 2002. World FDI grew from $202 billion in 1990 to a peak of $1.5 trillion in 2000 and then dropped off to $631 billion in 2002. Middle-income economies, which

6b

Aid after Monterrey

Official development assistance (ODA) declined from 0.34 percent of donor countries' gross national income (GNI) in 1990 to 0.22 percent in 2001 (table 6.9). At the United Nations Conference on Financing for Development in Monterrey, Mexico, in March 2002, donor countries agreed to scale up their commitment on aid to developing economies to help them achieve the Millennium Development Goals. Between 2001 and 2002, ODA flows began to increase, reaching 0.23 percent of donors' GNI in 2002. In coming years aid flows will continue to rise and by 2006, if countries keep their commitments, aid is expected to reach 0.29 percent of donor GNI.

Will aid flows be enough to reach the Monterrey goals?

Country	Net ODA 2002 ($ millions)	ODA as % of GNI 2002	ODA as % of GNI 2006
Austria	520	0.26	0.33
Belgium	1,072	0.43	0.46
Denmark	1,643	0.96	0.83
Finland	462	0.35	0.42
France[a]	5,486	0.38	0.47
Germany	5,324	0.27	0.33
Greece	276	0.21	0.33
Ireland[a]	398	0.40	0.63
Italy	2,332	0.20	0.33
Luxembourg	147	0.77	1.00
Netherlands	3,338	0.81	0.80
Portugal	323	0.27	0.33
Spain	1,712	0.26	0.33
Sweden	1,991	0.83	0.87
United Kingdom	4,924	0.31	0.40
EU members, total	**29,949**	**0.35**	**0.42**
Australia[b]	989	0.26	0.26
Canada	2,006	0.28	0.34
Japan	9,283	0.23	0.26
New Zealand	122	0.22	0.26
Norway	1,696	0.89	1.00
Switzerland[a]	939	0.32	0.36
United States[c]	13,290	0.13	0.17
DAC members, total	**58,274**	**0.23**	**0.29**

Estimates are based on commitments made by donor countries at the United Nations International Conference on Financing for Development in March 2002.

a. ODA/GNI ratio for 2006 interpolated between 2002 and year target scheduled to be attained. b. Estimated ODA/GNI of 0.26 percent in 2003/04. Since aid volumes are determined in annual budgets, the same ratio is assumed in forward years. c. For 2006, assumes additional $5 billion from the Millennium Challenge Account, $2 billion from the Emergency Plan for AIDS Relief, phased spending from Iraq and Afghanistan reconstruction supplements, and 2 percent annual inflation to deflate from 2006 to 2002 prices.

Source: Organisation for Economic Co-operation and Development, Development Assistance Committee.

receive the largest share of FDI flows to developing countries, were hit hardest. FDI fell from $164 billion in 2001 to $134 billion. Flows to low-income economies increased slightly from $11 billion to $13 billion. The largest drops occurred in Latin America and the Caribbean, Middle East and North Africa, and Sub-Saharan Africa. China's growth led to an increase in FDI flows in East Asia and Pacific, as did India's strength in South Asia (table 6.7).

Aid—which consists of official development assistance (ODA) and official aid to transition and certain high-income countries—continues to be a major source of financing for developing economies. Net aid flows reached $70 billion in 2002, up from $54 billion in 1997. More than a quarter of net aid flows went to Sub-Saharan Africa, which was equivalent to 32 percent of the region's gross capital formation, compared with an average of 4.4 percent for all developing economies (table 6.10).

The poorest countries are not the only recipients of aid. In 2002, excluding unallocated aid, middle-income countries received almost half of total net aid. In dollar terms the largest aid recipients in 2002 were Pakistan ($2.1 billion), Mozambique ($2.1 billion), Serbia and Montenegro ($1.9 billion), West Bank and Gaza ($1.6 billion), and China ($1.5 billion). The largest recipients of aid per capita were several small island states, as well as West Bank and Gaza ($500), Serbia and Montenegro ($237), Bosnia and Herzegovina ($143), Macedonia, FYR ($136), and Mauritania ($128). Only Mauritania is classified by the World Bank as a low-income economy.

Movement of people

The movement of people across borders can be important to both high-income and developing economies. Rich countries benefit from access to a larger labor force. And poor countries gain from higher salaries and remittances. In 2001 remittances—current transfers by migrants who are employed or intend to remain employed for more than a year in a country in which they are considered residents—totaled $70 billion, roughly equivalent to net aid flows. The total is even higher when net income flows are included. In addition, workers often bring back skills to their country of origin.

Not all migrant flows are well recorded. Records are especially weak for illegal immigration, movements within countries, and flows between developing countries. But migration to OECD

6c

Immigrant labor plays an important role in some high-income economies

Foreign labor as share of total labor force (%)

Recent inflows have pushed up the share of the foreign labor force in the United States and Italy. In Japan foreign workers make up less than a quarter of a percent of the labor force.

Source: Table 6.13.

countries, seen in table 6.13, has become an important feature of the global labor market. In 2001 some 1 million migrants entered the United States and 350,000 entered Japan. Foreign and foreign-born persons now make up about 38 percent of the population in Luxembourg and 9 percent each in Austria and Germany.

International tourism also plays a key role in movements of people. Although most travelers still come from high-income countries, there has been rapid growth in travelers from the developing world. While global tourism receipts have grown at an average annual rate of 5 percent since 1990, in the developing world these have grown more than 9 percent. Global tourism receipts reached $473 billion in 2002, up from $265 billion in 1990. During the same period receipts in the developing world grew from $48 billion to $138 billion (table 6.14). Tourism is a significant export earner and an important factor in the balance of payments of most nations. And it has become an important source of employment.

	Trade in goods				Ratio of commercial service exports to merchandise exports		Growth in real trade less growth in real GDP	Gross private capital flows		Gross foreign direct investment	
	% of GDP		% of goods GDP		%		percentage points	% of GDP		% of GDP	
	1990	**2002**	**1990**	**2002**	**1990**	**2002**	**1990–2002**	**1990**	**2002**	**1990**	**2002**
Afghanistan	..	..	..	..	..	..	..	..	..	..	..
Albania	29.0	38.2	34.5	*69.4*	13.7	167.3	5.5	18.0	6.3	0.0	2.8
Algeria	36.6	53.5	55.0	82.2	3.7	..	–0.5	2.6	..	0.0	..
Angola	53.5	101.3	91.0	133.4	1.7	2.7	..	10.1	*30.7*	3.3	*22.7*
Argentina	11.6	33.7	27.0	74.4	18.3	11.4	5.1	8.2	39.4	1.3	9.0
Armenia	..	63.3	..	94.9	..	34.7	–10.4	..	12.3	..	4.7
Australia	26.3	33.5	68.7	*96.5*	24.7	25.8	3.4	9.3	20.0	3.7	6.3
Austria	55.9	76.8	140.5	209.0	55.1	44.0	4.1	9.8	41.9	1.5	3.8
Azerbaijan	..	62.9	..	..	..	14.8	18.3	..	54.3	..	49.0
Bangladesh	17.6	29.4	..	..	17.7	5.0	5.3	0.9	2.6	0.0	0.1
Belarus	..	119.4	..	*232.0*	..	15.7	–3.4	..	7.1	..	3.2
Belgium	120.4	177.2	321.7	542.2	22.6	21.8	2.3	5.1	49.3	5.1	10.7
Benin	30.0	37.8	60.8	65.1	38.0	36.5	–2.0	10.7	*11.4*	3.7	*3.9*
Bolivia	33.1	39.5	57.0	77.6	14.3	16.8	1.3	3.1	17.2	0.7	8.7
Bosnia and Herzegovina	..	78.1	..	..	..	31.6	–4.0	..	29.5	..	5.2
Botswana	98.4	84.6	..	..	10.3	..	–1.1	9.0	..	4.4	..
Brazil	11.7	24.3	..	..	11.8	14.7	4.8	1.9	13.2	0.4	4.4
Bulgaria	48.9	88.1	70.8	185.9	16.6	44.4	5.6	39.2	16.5	0.0	4.1
Burkina Faso	22.0	23.8	43.3	46.4	22.1	19.5	–2.7	1.0	*4.3*	0.0	*0.4*
Burundi	27.0	22.1	35.1	..	8.7	12.5	8.1	3.7	3.2	0.1	0.0
Cambodia	22.4	94.9	33.6	..	57.8	39.5	8.5	*3.2*	5.5	*1.7*	1.6
Cameroon	30.5	38.6	..	..	18.4	..	2.4	15.5	..	1.1	..
Canada	43.7	67.1	115.1	..	14.4	14.4	4.2	8.1	13.4	2.7	7.3
Central African Republic	18.4	25.1	26.4	*37.7*	14.5	..	..	2.2	..	0.5	..
Chad	27.2	48.0	54.9	84.7	12.5	..	4.6	5.6	..	0.0	..
Chile	53.1	55.2	100.5	111.2	21.3	21.1	3.2	15.0	23.6	2.2	5.5
China	32.5	49.0	47.4	73.8	9.3	12.1	4.5	2.5	8.0	1.2	4.7
Hong Kong, China	221.5	252.8	772.3	2,020.6	..	22.5	3.5	..	92.4	..	29.6
Colombia	30.7	30.6	..	..	22.9	14.9	3.3	3.1	10.8	1.3	3.6
Congo, Dem. Rep.	43.5	38.4	74.5	50.6	..	..	7.1	..	..	..	..
Congo, Rep.	57.2	101.7	107.0	141.9	6.7	7.1	1.6	6.6	37.4	0.0	19.4
Costa Rica	60.2	73.8	..	..	40.3	35.3	3.8	7.0	10.5	2.9	4.8
Côte d'Ivoire	47.9	63.9	86.0	137.1	13.8	11.5	0.4	3.5	9.8	0.4	2.3
Croatia	*88.8*	69.6	*164.8*	140.3	..	113.3	4.1	..	31.4	..	6.7
Cuba	..	..	..	..	..	..	..	..	..	..	..
Czech Republic	*83.6*	113.9	..	232.4	..	18.3	9.4	..	28.6	..	13.8
Denmark	52.6	61.9	144.1	171.2	34.5	47.7	3.0	15.1	12.1	2.0	6.7
Dominican Republic	73.2	65.0	163.2	146.0	50.1	57.2	–0.3	5.0	6.9	1.9	4.6
Ecuador	44.2	47.1	..	..	18.7	18.2	2.0	11.0	21.1	1.2	5.2
Egypt, Arab Rep.	36.8	18.8	72.9	35.6	138.4	208.3	–2.1	6.8	6.6	1.7	0.8
El Salvador	38.4	57.3	87.6	146.9	51.7	25.0	6.9	2.0	15.3	0.8	1.6
Eritrea	*37.6*	60.4	*65.0*	*104.4*	484.7	386.6	1.0	*32.5*	*9.8*	..	*4.4*
Estonia	..	156.7	..	361.6	..	45.6	10.0	*3.7*	30.1	*2.0*	8.1
Ethiopia	16.0	33.2	25.5	62.0	87.4	108.5	2.2	1.6	3.1	0.0	..
Finland	39.0	59.6	86.3	141.0	17.2	14.3	5.0	17.3	38.8	3.6	13.4
France	37.1	46.2	101.6	*148.5*	34.6	25.9	4.0	20.6	20.2	3.9	8.0
Gabon	52.5	73.2	97.7	..	9.7	..	–1.8	18.0	..	8.4	..
Gambia, The	69.1	67.3	134.4	116.3	170.6	..	–1.2	0.9	..	0.0	..
Georgia	..	30.9	..	66.7	..	108.5	13.9	..	9.6	..	5.0
Germany	46.5	55.8	108.8	161.3	12.2	16.2	4.0	9.8	21.7	1.8	5.4
Ghana	35.7	75.2	58.0	129.3	8.8	29.3	4.4	2.7	4.4	0.3	0.8
Greece	33.2	31.3	83.5	89.1	80.4	194.4	3.8	3.9	22.6	1.2	1.0
Guatemala	36.8	35.7	..	..	26.9	47.0	3.2	2.9	24.6	0.6	9.8
Guinea	49.5	42.7	85.5	63.6	13.6	5.8	–1.0	3.9	2.1	0.6	0.0
Guinea-Bissau	43.0	61.6	53.3	86.1	19.4	..	3.8	23.0	..	0.0	..
Haiti	17.2	41.0	..	..	26.7	..	5.4	1.1	..	0.3	..

	Trade in goods				Ratio of commercial service exports to merchandise exports		Growth in real trade less growth in real GDP	Gross private capital flows		Gross foreign direct investment	
	% of GDP		% of goods GDP		%		percentage points	% of GDP		% of GDP	
	1990	2002	1990	2002	1990	2002	1990–2002	1990	2002	1990	2002
Honduras	57.9	64.1	106.4	126.7	14.5	36.4	−0.4	7.2	5.6	1.4	2.2
Hungary	61.5	109.3	102.4	..	26.8	22.5	8.8	4.6	19.3	0.0	3.9
India	..	..	..	..	25.7	49.9	..	..	..	..	..
Indonesia	41.5	51.1	68.1	82.6	9.7	11.3	0.8	4.1	5.4	1.0	2.1
Iran, Islamic Rep.	32.9	43.1	61.8	86.0	1.8	5.6	−7.9	2.6	2.4	0.0	0.0
Iraq	41.2	..	..	..	..	..	..	..	..	..	..
Ireland	93.9	114.1	186.7	255.2	13.8	31.9	7.1	22.2	278.2	2.2	47.1
Israel	55.0	62.7	..	..	37.6	36.7	1.4	6.5	10.8	0.7	3.0
Italy	32.0	41.7	83.3	121.1	28.5	23.7	3.5	10.6	13.7	1.3	2.7
Jamaica	67.2	58.5	162.2	174.2	84.2	170.9	−1.1	8.4	27.1	3.0	7.1
Japan	17.1	18.9	44.1	64.2	14.4	15.6	2.6	5.4	15.3	1.7	1.4
Jordan	91.1	82.8	205.2	221.3	134.4	53.7	−2.6	6.3	7.8	1.7	0.9
Kazakhstan	..	65.8	..	128.9	..	14.8	−3.0	..	34.2	..	12.3
Kenya	38.1	43.6	68.5	100.6	75.0	37.8	1.4	3.6	5.4	0.7	0.0
Korea, Dem. Rep.	..	..	..	..	..	..	..	..	..	..	..
Korea, Rep.	53.4	66.0	102.7	152.0	14.1	16.7	6.9	5.6	7.4	0.7	1.0
Kuwait	59.8	68.9	112.9	..	15.0	8.9	..	19.3	18.9	1.3	0.5
Kyrgyz Republic	..	67.1	..	99.3	..	24.3	−2.1	..	11.6	..	1.4
Lao PDR	30.5	43.4	40.2	..	13.5	42.5	..	3.7	1.4	0.7	1.4
Latvia	..	75.4	..	202.6	..	54.1	7.3	1.7	29.5	0.5	5.0
Lebanon	106.5	43.3	..	..	..	..	−2.5	..	..	..	..
Lesotho	119.3	149.8	..	..	54.9	7.7	0.6	9.6	10.5	2.8	10.3
Liberia	374.1	159.3	..	..	..	..	..	..	..	..	..
Libya	64.2	87.1	..	..	0.6	..	..	7.3	..	0.9	..
Lithuania	..	96.4	..	212.0	..	26.1	8.8	..	13.3	..	5.3
Macedonia, FYR	103.8	80.0	168.9	150.4	..	19.8	5.4	..	14.6	..	2.0
Madagascar	31.5	44.0	53.7	91.2	40.5	20.1	1.5	1.8	1.2	0.7	0.2
Malawi	52.7	60.6	70.6	108.9	8.8	10.3	−2.1	3.2	3.2	0.0	0.3
Malaysia	133.4	182.4	232.3	347.4	12.8	15.8	3.3	10.3	19.9	5.3	5.8
Mali	39.7	60.7	63.4	87.4	19.7	14.8	2.7	2.0	22.9	0.2	12.2
Mauritania	84.1	76.8	134.0	133.9	3.0	..	−1.2	48.8	..	0.7	..
Mauritius	118.0	86.6	219.8	193.5	40.0	64.5	0.1	8.0	26.9	1.7	0.6
Mexico	32.1	52.4	78.9	148.7	17.7	7.8	9.2	9.2	6.3	1.0	2.4
Moldova	..	105.9	..	191.0	..	29.9	11.7	..	17.8	..	6.8
Mongolia	..	101.5	..	227.6	7.3	35.7	..	..	13.4	..	6.8
Morocco	43.3	54.2	86.5	116.8	43.9	51.7	2.7	5.5	3.3	0.6	1.4
Mozambique	40.8	56.2	68.9	93.3	81.7	36.5	0.6	0.4	10.0	0.4	7.4
Myanmar	..	..	..	..	29.0	13.4	..	..	..	..	..
Namibia	95.6	87.7	190.3	182.7	9.7	21.0	−0.6	16.5	26.8	5.0	4.8
Nepal	24.1	35.8	..	..	81.5	53.3	..	3.5	3.2	0.0	0.0
Netherlands	87.6	111.1	230.9	332.6	21.6	22.3	3.6	29.8	69.1	8.3	15.0
New Zealand	43.3	49.0	121.0	..	25.7	35.1	2.3	17.8	9.2	11.5	4.0
Nicaragua	..	59.7	..	138.9	10.4	45.2	..	..	9.8	..	4.3
Niger	27.0	33.8	49.9	57.2	7.8	..	−2.6	2.8	..	1.6	..
Nigeria	67.5	52.0	90.8	95.0	7.1	..	2.1	5.9	..	2.1	..
Norway	52.8	50.3	126.6	112.9	36.6	31.4	1.5	11.9	38.3	2.1	5.2
Oman	77.7	84.6	127.4	..	1.2	3.1	..	3.8	5.0	1.4	0.2
Pakistan	32.6	35.8	..	..	21.7	15.5	−1.5	4.2	5.3	0.6	1.4
Panama	35.4	31.1	..	..	266.7	266.4	−2.0	106.6	69.4	2.6	7.4
Papua New Guinea	73.6	94.2	123.9	147.6	16.8	18.4	0.7	5.7	15.8	4.8	2.2
Paraguay	43.9	50.8	82.8	106.6	42.1	49.1	−3.8	5.4	19.1	1.5	8.3
Peru	22.3	26.9	..	..	22.1	18.6	3.6	3.2	10.8	0.2	4.2
Philippines	47.7	91.7	84.7	194.1	35.7	8.4	3.1	4.4	41.2	1.2	1.5
Poland	43.9	50.9	75.2	121.0	22.3	24.5	9.9	11.0	10.2	0.2	3.7
Portugal	58.3	52.7	140.8	151.0	30.8	37.9	3.7	11.4	37.6	3.9	7.1
Puerto Rico	..	..	..	..	..	..	−0.4	..	..	..	..

	Trade in goods				Ratio of commercial service exports to merchandise exports		Growth in real trade less growth in real GDP	Gross private capital flows		Gross foreign direct investment	
	% of GDP		% of goods GDP		%		percentage points	% of GDP		% of GDP	
	1990	2002	1990	2002	1990	2002	1990–2002	1990	2002	1990	2002
Romania	32.8	69.3	45.2	*117.7*	12.3	16.8	8.5	2.9	8.5	0.0	2.5
Russian Federation	*16.5*	48.3	*35.0*	105.1	..	12.6	2.6	..	12.2	..	1.9
Rwanda	15.4	14.9	26.9	23.6	28.0	84.9	0.6	2.8	0.9	0.3	0.2
Saudi Arabia	58.6	56.4	107.5	99.8	6.8	7.0	..	8.8	13.9	1.6	0.5
Senegal	34.7	51.9	90.0	141.8	46.8	..	0.1	4.8	..	1.3	..
Serbia and Montenegro	..	54.8	..	..	..	..	..	..	..	..	..
Sierra Leone	44.2	39.7	..	..	32.8	..	–13.4	11.0	..	5.0	..
Singapore	307.6	277.8	..	921.3	24.1	23.6	..	54.2	47.8	20.6	11.7
Slovak Republic	*110.8*	130.2	*192.1*	*302.5*		15.4	8.4	..	*29.6*	..	*11.8*
Slovenia	*102.4*	92.9	*196.5*	206.2	18.3	24.1	3.1	*3.4*	21.2	*0.9*	10.2
Somalia	26.7	..	33.2		..	..	..	..	..	..	..
South Africa	37.4[a]	56.6[a]	73.6[a]	136.6[a]	14.0	14.8	3.2	2.2	10.1	0.2	1.4
Spain	28.1	41.9	70.6	117.3	49.7	52.1	6.5	11.4	26.9	3.4	6.2
Sri Lanka	57.3	65.2	..	..	22.2	26.5	2.6	13.1	3.6	0.5	1.5
Sudan	4.1	26.5	..	..	35.9	2.5	5.8	0.2	7.5	0.0	4.6
Swaziland	138.2	144.6	217.1	195.5	18.3	13.8	–0.6	10.7	19.6	5.0	8.5
Sweden	45.5	61.3	112.0	167.8	23.4	29.0	4.6	33.1	29.3	6.8	14.5
Switzerland	58.4	64.1	..	*246.7*	28.6	31.7	3.1	15.9	59.9	5.8	9.2
Syrian Arab Republic	53.7	51.8	102.4	90.0	17.6	26.7	3.6	18.0	*16.8*	0.0	*1.5*
Tajikistan	..	119.9	..	152.7	..	8.2	..	..	10.6	..	3.0
Tanzania	31.9	27.3	47.8	43.0	39.5	69.6	0.5	0.2	3.4	0.0	2.6
Thailand	65.7	105.6	132.2	205.0	27.3	22.1	2.9	13.5	13.6	3.0	0.8
Togo	52.1	78.0	92.6	126.4	42.6	12.4	–0.5	9.6	*14.4*	1.1	*6.2*
Trinidad and Tobago	65.9	89.7	*149.7*	214.8	15.5	12.3	2.5	11.4	*20.5*	3.1	*11.6*
Tunisia	73.5	77.7	161.6	196.2	44.7	38.3	0.3	9.5	10.6	0.6	3.8
Turkey	23.4	45.9	44.5	*105.5*	60.8	42.6	6.8	4.3	7.7	0.5	0.7
Turkmenistan	..	70.4	..	..	..	..	3.8	..	..	..	..
Uganda	10.2	36.7	..	..	0.0	52.1	6.8	1.1	4.5	0.0	2.6
Ukraine	..	84.3	..	145.7	..	25.5	3.8	..	11.8	..	1.7
United Arab Emirates	101.8	..	159.6	..	..	..	..	..	..	..	..
United Kingdom	41.2	39.9	102.6	123.9	29.1	44.0	3.9	35.3	60.3	7.4	23.8
United States	15.8	18.3	44.8	*66.8*	33.8	39.3	4.5	5.7	9.2	2.8	2.4
Uruguay	32.7	31.5	85.0	104.6	27.2	40.4	2.9	12.7	81.7	0.0	1.7
Uzbekistan	..	80.0	..	130.5	..	..	–1.2	..	..	..	..
Venezuela, RB	51.1	41.0	90.8	86.3	6.4	3.5	3.1	49.9	15.4	1.7	3.1
Vietnam	79.7	101.3	129.7	..	..	17.8	..	..	5.8	..	4.0
West Bank and Gaza	..	..	..	..	..	..	–3.2	..	..	..	..
Yemen, Rep.	46.9	58.4	90.0	*97.1*	11.8	4.0	3.1	16.2	3.6	2.7	1.1
Zambia	76.9	60.6	102.3	113.2	7.2	11.8	2.0	64.7	*9.3*	6.2	*3.8*
Zimbabwe	40.7	38.5	74.5	*97.5*	14.7	..	4.8	1.7	..	0.1	..
World	**32.5 w**	**40.3 w**	**80.2 w**	***116.0* w**	**21.5**	**23.1 w**		**10.1 w**	**20.8 w**	**2.7 w**	**6.0 w**
Low income	26.9	37.3	..	..	14.6	19.4		3.0	4.4	0.5	1.7
Middle income	35.2	54.9	74.6	116.8	16.5	15.6		6.8	12.4	1.0	3.7
Lower middle income	30.6	49.2	*63.2*	98.0	18.7	16.8		4.1	11.0	0.8	3.6
Upper middle income	45.0	66.2	86.4	146.8	13.7	13.9		12.2	15.1	1.5	3.9
Low & middle income	33.4	51.8	74.5	115.0	16.2	16.1		6.0	11.1	0.9	3.3
East Asia & Pacific	47.0	63.4	78.5	104.6	14.1	13.6		5.0	10.2	1.7	4.1
Europe & Central Asia	*28.8*	64.3	*53.3*	132.1	29.6	21.7		..	13.9	..	3.7
Latin America & Carib.	23.1	41.2	*66.4*	132.0	17.5	13.4		7.9	13.7	0.9	4.0
Middle East & N. Africa	46.6	50.5	84.0	90.9	11.6	12.2		6.0	10.3	0.8	0.9
South Asia	16.5	24.2	..	..	24.6	39.5		1.4	3.2	0.1	0.7
Sub-Saharan Africa	40.8	55.3	77.1	119.7	13.9	10.1		4.9	9.6	1.0	2.2
High income	32.3	37.6	80.9	*117.2*	23.2	25.5		10.9	22.9	3.0	6.6
Europe EMU	44.9	*56.3*	112.6	*141.9*	24.4	23.7		14.1	*49.3*	2.9	*14.8*

a. Data refer to the South African Customs Union (Botswana, Lesotho, Namibia, South Africa, and Swaziland).

About the data

The growing integration of societies and economies has helped reduce poverty in many countries. Between 1990 and 2000 the number of people living on less than $1 a day declined by about 137 million. Although global integration is a powerful force in reducing poverty, more needs to be done—2 billion people are in danger of becoming marginal to the world economy. All countries have a stake in helping developing countries integrate with the global economy and gain better access to rich country markets.

One indication of increasing global economic integration is the growing importance of trade in the world economy. Another is the increased size and importance of private capital flows to developing countries that have liberalized their financial markets. This table presents standardized measures of the size of trade and capital flows relative to gross domestic product (GDP). The numerators are based on gross flows that capture the two-way flow of goods and capital. In conventional balance of payments accounting exports are recorded as a credit and imports as a debit. And in the financial account inward investment is a credit and outward investment a debit. Thus net flows, the sum of credits and debits, represent a balance in which many transactions are canceled out. Gross flows are a better measure of integration because they show the total value of financial transactions during a given period.

Trade in goods (exports and imports) is shown relative to both total GDP and goods GDP (GDP less services such as storage, transport, communications, retail trade, business services, public administration, restaurants and hotels, and social, community, and personal services). As a result of the growing share of services in GDP, trade as a share of total GDP appears to be declining for some economies. Comparing merchandise trade with GDP after deducting value added in services thus provides a better measure of its relative size than does comparing it with total GDP, although this neglects the growing service component of most goods output.

Trade in services (such as transport, travel, finance, insurance, royalties, construction, communications, and cultural services) is an increasingly important element of global integration. The difference between the growth of real trade in goods and services and the growth of GDP helps to identify economies that have integrated with the global economy by liberalizing trade, lowering barriers to foreign investment, and harnessing their abundant labor to gain a competitive advantage in labor-intensive manufactures and services.

Trade and capital flows are converted to U.S. dollars at the International Monetary Fund's average official exchange rate for the year shown. An alternative conversion factor is applied if the official exchange rate diverges by an exceptionally large margin from the rate effectively applied to transactions in foreign currencies and traded products.

Definitions

• **Trade in goods as a share of GDP** is the sum of merchandise exports and imports divided by the value of GDP, all in current U.S. dollars. • **Trade in goods as a share of goods GDP** is the sum of merchandise exports and imports divided by the value of GDP after subtracting value added in services, all in current U.S. dollars. • **Ratio of commercial service exports to merchandise exports** is total service exports minus exports of government services not included elsewhere over the f.o.b. value of goods provided to the rest of the world, all in current U.S. dollars. • **Growth in real trade less growth in real GDP** is the difference between annual growth in trade of goods and services and annual growth in GDP. Growth rates are calculated using constant price series taken from national accounts and are expressed as a percentage. • **Gross private capital flows** are the sum of the absolute values of direct, portfolio, and other investment inflows and outflows recorded in the balance of payments financial account, excluding changes in the assets and liabilities of monetary authorities and general government. The indicator is calculated as a ratio to GDP in U.S. dollars. • **Gross foreign direct investment** is the sum of the absolute values of inflows and outflows of foreign direct investment recorded in the balance of payments financial account. It includes equity capital, reinvestment of earnings, other long-term capital, and short-term capital. This indicator differs from the standard measure of foreign direct investment, which captures only inward investment (see table 6.7). The indicator is calculated as a ratio to GDP in U.S. dollars.

Data sources

The data on merchandise trade are from the World Trade Organization. The data on GDP come from the World Bank's national accounts files, converted from national currencies to U.S. dollars using the official exchange rate, supplemented by an alternative conversion factor if the official exchange rate is judged to diverge by an exceptionally large margin from the rate effectively applied to transactions in foreign currencies and traded products. The data on real trade and GDP growth come from the World Bank's national accounts files. Gross private capital flows and foreign direct investment were calculated using the International Monetary Fund's Balance of Payments database.

Direction of trade, 2002

High-income importers
% of world trade

Source of exports	European Union	Japan	United States	Other industrial	All industrial	Other high income	All high income
High-income economies	29.9	2.9	11.5	5.9	50.2	7.2	57.4
Industrial economies	28.4	1.8	9.3	5.5	45.0	5.1	50.1
European Union	23.3	0.6	3.6	2.1	29.6	1.7	31.3
Japan	1.0		1.9	0.3	3.2	1.6	4.8
United States	2.3	0.8		2.9	6.0	1.3	7.3
Other industrial economies	1.8	0.4	3.9	0.2	6.3	0.4	6.7
Other high-income economies	1.6	1.1	2.2	0.4	5.2	2.0	7.3
Low- and middle-income economies	6.4	1.9	6.3	0.8	15.5	3.6	19.1
East Asia & Pacific	1.4	1.4	1.9	0.4	5.1	2.5	7.6
Europe & Central Asia	2.7	0.0	0.2	0.2	3.2	0.2	3.4
Latin America & Caribbean	0.6	0.1	3.2	0.1	4.1	0.2	4.3
Middle East & N. Africa	0.9	0.3	0.3	0.1	1.6	0.4	2.0
South Asia	0.3	0.0	0.3	0.0	0.6	0.2	0.8
Sub-Saharan Africa	0.5	0.1	0.3	0.0	0.9	0.1	1.0
World	36.3	4.8	17.8	6.8	65.7	10.8	76.5

Low- and middle-income importers
% of world trade

Source of exports	East Asia & Pacific	Europe & Central Asia	Latin America & Caribbean	Middle East & N. Africa	South Asia	Sub-Saharan Africa	All low- & middle-income	World
High-income economies	6.3	3.4	1.7	1.6	0.7	0.8	17.2	74.6
Industrial economies	3.2	3.3	1.5	1.4	0.5	0.7	12.9	63.0
European Union	0.9	3.0	0.5	1.0	0.3	0.5	6.8	38.1
Japan	1.3	0.1	0.2	0.1	0.1	0.1	1.8	6.5
United States	0.8	0.2	0.8	0.2	0.1	0.1	3.6	10.9
Other industrial economies	0.3	0.1	0.1	0.1	0.1	0.0	0.7	7.5
Other high-income economies	3.1	0.1	0.1	0.1	0.2	0.1	4.3	11.6
Low- and middle-income economies	1.7	1.6	1.0	0.6	0.4	0.4	6.3	25.4
East Asia & Pacific	0.9	0.2	0.1	0.2	0.2	0.1	1.9	9.5
Europe & Central Asia	0.2	1.1	0.0	0.2	0.0	0.0	1.6	5.1
Latin America & Caribbean	0.1	0.0	0.7	0.1	0.0	0.0	1.3	5.6
Middle East & N. Africa	0.2	0.1	0.0	0.1	0.1	0.0	0.7	2.7
South Asia	0.1	0.0	0.0	0.1	0.1	0.0	0.3	1.1
Sub-Saharan Africa	0.1	0.0	0.0	0.0	0.0	0.2	0.4	1.4
World	8.0	4.9	2.7	2.2	1.1	1.3	23.5	100.0

Direction and growth of merchandise trade

Nominal growth of trade, 1992–2002

High-income importers
annual % growth

Source of exports	European Union	Japan	United States	Other industrial	All industrial	Other high income	All high income
High-income economies	3.3	2.4	6.1	4.2	3.9	4.8	4.0
Industrial economies	3.2	1.6	6.5	4.3	3.9	3.9	3.9
European Union	3.5	3.3	8.3	3.3	4.0	5.6	4.0
Japan	–0.9		2.2	–0.1	0.9	2.5	1.4
United States	2.9	0.7		5.7	3.8	3.8	3.8
Other industrial economies	2.9	0.8	7.7	4.2	5.4	3.5	5.3
Other high-income economies	4.5	3.8	4.6	3.7	4.3	7.5	5.1
Low- and middle-income economies	7.0	6.9	11.7	9.3	8.7	8.0	8.6
East Asia & Pacific	12.1	9.3	14.4	13.0	12.0	8.0	10.5
Europe & Central Asia	11.2	0.2	12.7	11.7	11.0	10.9	11.0
Latin America & Caribbean	2.4	–0.5	12.3	10.0	9.4	9.7	9.4
Middle East & N. Africa	2.7	3.0	3.7	4.0	3.0	4.4	3.3
South Asia	6.1	0.0	10.9	7.3	7.4	9.5	7.8
Sub-Saharan Africa	6.6	17.6	5.6	4.9	6.7	16.8	7.3
World	3.9	3.9	7.7	4.7	4.9	5.7	5.0

Low- and middle-income importers
annual % growth

Source of exports	East Asia & Pacific	Europe & Central Asia	Latin America & Caribbean	Middle East & N. Africa	South Asia	Sub-Saharan Africa	All low- & middle-income	World
High-income economies	8.7	7.5	2.9	0.9	5.1	1.3	6.5	4.5
Industrial economies	7.3	7.8	3.0	0.7	4.0	1.0	5.8	4.2
European Union	7.2	8.6	3.1	1.5	4.6	1.5	6.5	4.4
Japan	7.1	4.0	–0.1	–3.2	–0.4	–3.5	4.0	2.1
United States	8.2	1.8	3.9	–2.0	5.4	1.1	6.0	4.5
Other industrial economies	6.0	2.4	1.5	4.3	4.5	3.1	4.2	5.2
Other high-income economies	10.5	–1.0	2.8	1.7	7.5	1.2	8.7	6.3
Low- and middle-income economies	14.9	3.2	7.1	6.3	10.2	9.0	9.2	8.7
East Asia & Pacific	16.5	10.7	16.7	10.0	14.7	15.8	14.3	11.2
Europe & Central Asia	6.3	8.7	7.0	5.7	8.3	10.9	7.8	9.9
Latin America & Caribbean	12.9	6.1	7.0	4.8	14.8	5.3	8.1	9.1
Middle East & N. Africa	16.1	2.9	–2.1	6.0	4.6	8.7	6.7	4.1
South Asia	15.5	5.2	19.0	4.6	9.8	11.5	9.7	8.3
Sub-Saharan Africa	27.6	17.5	10.0	5.7	8.7	11.4	13.5	8.8
World	9.7	6.0	4.2	2.1	6.7	3.3	7.1	5.4

About the data

The table provides estimates of the flow of trade in goods between groups of economies. The data are from the International Monetary Fund's (IMF) Direction of Trade database. All high-income countries and 22 of the 156 developing countries report trade on a timely basis, covering about 80 percent of trade for recent years. Trade by less timely reporters and by countries that do not report is estimated using reports of partner countries. Because the largest exporting and importing countries are reliable reporters, a large portion of the missing trade flows can be estimated from partner reports. Partner country data may introduce discrepancies due to smuggling, confidentiality, different exchange rates, overreporting of transit trade, inclusion or exclusion of freight rates, and different points of valuation and times of recording.

In addition, estimates of trade within the European Union (EU) have been significantly affected by changes in reporting methods following the creation of a customs union. The new system for collecting data on trade between EU members—Intrastat, introduced in 1993—has less exhaustive coverage than the previous customs-based system and has resulted in some problems of asymmetry (estimated imports are about 5 percent less than exports). Despite these issues, only a small portion of world trade is estimated to be omitted from the IMF's *Direction of Trade Statistics Yearbook* and Direction of Trade database.

Most countries report their trade data in national currencies, which are converted using the IMF's published period average exchange rates (series rf or rh, monthly averages of the market or official rates) for the reporting country or, if those are not available, monthly average rates in New York. Because imports are reported at cost, insurance, and freight (c.i.f.) valuations, and exports at free on board (f.o.b.) valuations, the IMF adjusts country reports of import values by dividing them by 1.10 to estimate equivalent export values. This approximation is more or less accurate, depending on the set of partners and the items traded. Other factors affecting the accuracy of trade data include lags in reporting, recording differences across countries, and whether the country reports trade according to the general or special system of trade. (For further discussion of the measurement of exports and imports, see *About the data* for tables 4.5 and 4.6.)

The regional trade flows shown in the table were calculated from current price values. The growth rates presented are in nominal terms; that is, they include the effects of changes in both volumes and prices.

Definitions

• **Merchandise trade** includes all trade in goods; trade in services is excluded. • **High-income economies** are those classified as such by the World Bank (see inside front cover). • **Industrial economies** are those classified as such in the IMF's *Direction of Trade Statistics Yearbook*. They include the countries of the European Union, Japan, the United States, and the other industrial economies listed below. • **European Union** comprises Austria, Belgium, Denmark, Finland, France, Germany, Greece, Ireland, Italy, Luxembourg, the Netherlands, Portugal, Spain, Sweden, and the United Kingdom. • **Other industrial economies** include Australia, Canada, Iceland, New Zealand, Norway, and Switzerland. • **Other high-income economies** include Antigua and Barbuda, Aruba, The Bahamas, Bahrain, Barbados, Bermuda, Brunei, Cyprus, Faeroe Islands, French Polynesia, Greenland, Guam, Hong Kong (China), Israel, the Republic of Korea, Kuwait, Macao (China), Malta, Netherlands Antilles, New Caledonia, Qatar, Singapore, Slovenia, Taiwan (China), and the United Arab Emirates. • **Low- and middle-income regional groupings** are based on World Bank classifications and may differ from those used by other organizations.

6.2a

Rich markets for developing country exports

Developing economy exports as % of world trade, 2002

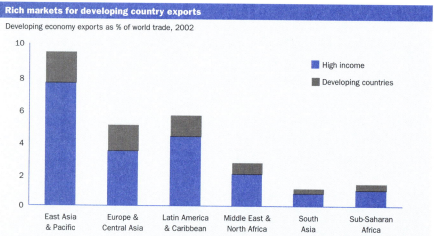

High-income countries continue to be the principal trading partners of developing countries. Yet trade between and within developing countries continues to grow. At 9.5 percent, East Asia and Pacific is the developing region with the largest exports as a share of world trade. Sub-Saharan Africa's share, although small, has been growing.

Source: International Monetary Fund, Direction of Trade database.

Data sources

Intercountry trade flows are published in the IMF's *Direction of Trade Statistics Yearbook* and *Direction of Trade Statistics Quarterly*; the data in the table were calculated using the IMF's Direction of Trade database.

OECD trade with low- and middle-income economies

6.3 GLOBAL LINKS

Exports to low-income economies

	High-income OECD countries		European Union		Japan		United States	
	1992	2002	1992	2002 [a]	1992	2002	1992	2002
$ billions								
Food	6.1	8.2	3.4	4.2	0.1	0.1	1.7	2.2
Cereals	2.7	2.2	1.0	0.9	0.0	0.0	1.2	1.0
Agricultural raw materials	1.9	2.9	0.4	0.7	0.2	0.2	0.6	0.9
Ores and nonferrous metals	1.4	2.1	0.6	0.8	0.1	0.2	0.3	0.2
Fuels	1.9	2.1	0.8	0.8	0.1	0.1	0.2	0.2
Crude petroleum	0.3	0.0	0.0	0.0	0.0	0.0	0.0	0.0
Petroleum products	1.3	1.4	0.8	0.7	0.1	0.1	0.2	0.2
Manufactured goods	57.4	69.6	30.0	34.4	12.9	13.1	6.3	8.7
Chemical products	8.1	10.3	4.5	5.6	1.0	1.1	1.3	1.5
Mach. and transport equip.	33.6	38.2	16.4	17.5	9.0	8.5	4.2	5.6
Other	15.7	21.1	9.1	11.3	2.9	3.4	0.9	1.7
Miscellaneous goods	1.5	3.3	0.6	1.2	0.1	0.3	0.3	0.7
Total	**70.3**	**88.2**	**35.8**	**42.1**	**13.4**	**14.1**	**9.3**	**12.9**
% of total exports								
Food	8.7	9.3	9.5	10.0	0.6	0.4	18.0	17.0
Cereals	3.8	2.5	2.7	2.2	0.1	0.2	13.3	7.5
Agricultural raw materials	2.8	3.2	1.2	1.7	1.6	1.7	6.7	7.3
Ores and nonferrous metals	2.0	2.4	1.6	2.0	0.7	1.8	2.8	1.3
Fuels	2.7	2.4	2.4	1.8	0.6	0.9	1.7	1.3
Crude petroleum	0.4	0.0	0.0	0.0	0.0	0.0	0.0	0.0
Petroleum products	1.8	1.6	2.3	1.8	0.6	0.7	1.7	1.3
Manufactured goods	81.7	78.9	83.6	81.7	95.9	93.0	67.9	67.8
Chemical products	11.6	11.7	12.5	13.2	7.2	8.1	13.5	11.3
Mach. and transport equip.	47.8	43.3	45.7	41.6	67.0	60.4	45.3	43.4
Other	22.3	23.9	25.4	26.9	21.7	24.4	9.1	13.1
Miscellaneous goods	2.2	3.8	1.7	2.8	0.6	2.2	2.8	5.3
Total	**100.0**	**100.0**	**100.0**	**100.0**	**100.0**	**100.0**	**100.0**	**100.0**

Imports from low-income economies

	High-income OECD countries		European Union		Japan		United States	
	1992	2002	1992	2002	1992	2002	1992	2002
$ billions								
Food	11.5	17.5	7.1	9.5	2.1	2.8	1.6	3.9
Cereals	0.1	0.4	0.1	0.2	0.0	0.0	0.0	0.1
Agricultural raw materials	4.4	5.0	2.5	2.8	0.8	0.6	0.7	0.8
Ores and nonferrous metals	5.1	5.6	2.0	2.4	2.1	2.3	0.4	0.2
Fuels	29.4	37.0	8.4	9.0	8.8	8.6	9.2	11.8
Crude petroleum	22.2	26.8	7.9	7.7	3.6	3.0	8.8	10.8
Petroleum products	2.3	3.0	0.3	0.5	0.9	0.7	0.5	1.0
Manufactured goods	31.6	76.0	16.0	32.8	3.9	7.6	8.8	28.9
Chemical products	1.3	4.1	0.7	1.6	0.1	0.6	0.2	1.2
Mach. and transport equip.	1.9	9.3	1.0	3.9	0.1	1.9	0.4	2.6
Other	28.5	62.5	14.3	27.4	3.6	5.1	8.2	25.1
Miscellaneous goods	0.4	1.0	0.2	0.4	0.1	0.1	0.1	0.3
Total	**82.4**	**142.0**	**36.2**	**56.8**	**17.8**	**22.1**	**20.9**	**45.9**
% of total imports								
Food	13.9	12.3	19.6	16.7	11.9	12.6	7.6	8.5
Cereals	0.2	0.3	0.3	0.3	0.0	0.1	0.1	0.2
Agricultural raw materials	5.4	3.5	6.9	4.9	4.6	2.8	3.5	1.8
Ores and nonferrous metals	6.2	3.9	5.6	4.2	11.9	10.4	2.0	0.5
Fuels	35.7	26.1	23.2	15.9	49.5	39.2	44.2	25.7
Crude petroleum	26.9	18.9	21.9	13.6	20.4	13.7	41.9	23.4
Petroleum products	2.7	2.1	0.9	0.9	5.3	3.2	2.2	2.2
Manufactured goods	38.4	53.5	44.1	57.7	21.7	34.4	42.3	62.8
Chemical products	1.5	2.9	1.8	2.8	0.8	2.6	1.0	2.5
Mach. and transport equip.	2.3	6.6	2.9	6.8	0.6	8.8	1.9	5.6
Other	34.6	44.0	39.4	48.2	20.3	23.0	39.3	54.6
Miscellaneous goods	0.5	0.7	0.6	0.7	0.4	0.7	0.4	0.7
Total	**100.0**	**100.0**	**100.0**	**100.0**	**100.0**	**100.0**	**100.0**	**100.0**

6.3 OECD trade with low- and middle-income economies

Exports to middle-income economies

	High-income OECD countries		European Union		Japan		United States	
	1992	2002	1992	2002 [a]	1992	2002	1992	2002
$ billions								
Food	35.8	44.7	16.7	19.9	0.3	0.3	13.0	16.7
Cereals	13.8	10.6	4.7	3.4	0.1	0.0	5.8	5.5
Agricultural raw materials	7.4	14.1	2.3	4.9	0.5	1.0	3.0	5.1
Ores and nonferrous metals	6.4	15.0	2.2	5.8	0.6	2.0	2.0	3.5
Fuels	8.1	14.5	2.8	4.7	0.5	0.5	3.3	5.1
Crude petroleum	0.9	1.2	0.5	0.4	0.0	0.0	0.0	0.0
Petroleum products	5.4	9.8	2.2	3.7	0.4	0.5	2.2	3.9
Manufactured goods	311.1	619.2	139.4	307.9	60.7	92.5	85.3	153.8
Chemical products	38.5	86.5	20.5	45.4	3.4	8.1	10.6	20.0
Mach. and transport equip.	185.0	361.1	77.3	169.9	41.7	62.6	53.9	93.8
Other	87.5	171.6	41.6	92.6	15.6	21.8	20.8	39.9
Miscellaneous goods	10.3	22.6	3.2	6.6	0.6	3.3	5.2	9.1
Total	**379.0**	**730.0**	**166.6**	**349.8**	**63.2**	**99.6**	**111.8**	**193.2**
% of total exports								
Food	9.5	6.1	10.0	5.7	0.5	0.3	11.6	8.6
Cereals	3.6	1.5	2.8	1.0	0.1	0.0	5.2	2.8
Agricultural raw materials	2.0	1.9	1.4	1.4	0.8	1.0	2.7	2.6
Ores and nonferrous metals	1.7	2.1	1.3	1.7	1.0	2.0	1.8	1.8
Fuels	2.1	2.0	1.7	1.4	0.7	0.5	3.0	2.6
Crude petroleum	0.2	0.2	0.3	0.1	0.0	0.0	0.0	0.0
Petroleum products	1.4	1.3	1.3	1.0	0.6	0.5	2.0	2.0
Manufactured goods	82.1	84.8	83.7	88.0	96.1	92.9	76.3	79.6
Chemical products	10.2	11.9	12.3	13.0	5.3	8.1	9.5	10.4
Mach. and transport equip.	48.8	49.5	46.4	48.6	66.0	62.9	48.2	48.5
Other	23.1	23.5	25.0	26.5	24.7	21.9	18.6	20.7
Miscellaneous goods	2.7	3.1	1.9	1.9	0.9	3.3	4.7	4.7
Total	**100.0**	**100.0**	**100.0**	**100.0**	**100.0**	**100.0**	**100.0**	**100.0**

Imports from middle-income economies

	High-income OECD countries		European Union		Japan		United States	
	1992	2002	1992	2002 [a]	1992	2002	1992	2002
$ billions								
Food	59.5	81.8	30.0	36.5	10.0	14.5	14.2	22.4
Cereals	2.1	4.4	0.4	1.9	0.6	0.5	0.2	0.6
Agricultural raw materials	15.2	17.9	7.3	9.6	4.2	2.9	1.9	3.8
Ores and nonferrous metals	24.8	39.6	12.4	17.3	6.0	7.0	4.2	8.9
Fuels	122.7	182.3	61.1	76.4	20.5	24.1	30.6	61.2
Crude petroleum	87.9	134.7	41.6	52.7	14.5	17.4	23.4	49.7
Petroleum products	19.6	24.9	9.2	11.6	2.4	1.2	6.8	9.8
Manufactured goods	196.1	730.2	75.6	254.1	19.0	75.6	85.1	335.6
Chemical products	13.9	34.7	7.2	15.0	1.8	3.5	3.3	11.3
Mach. and transport equip.	59.6	333.8	17.5	107.5	3.7	32.1	33.6	164.8
Other	122.6	361.6	50.9	131.6	13.5	39.9	48.2	159.5
Miscellaneous goods	7.4	15.7	3.3	2.2	0.6	1.6	3.2	11.5
Total	**425.7**	**1,067.4**	**189.7**	**396.1**	**60.4**	**125.7**	**139.2**	**443.3**
% of total imports								
Food	14.0	7.7	15.8	9.2	16.6	11.5	10.2	5.1
Cereals	0.5	0.4	0.2	0.5	1.1	0.4	0.2	0.1
Agricultural raw materials	3.6	1.7	3.9	2.4	7.0	2.3	1.3	0.9
Ores and nonferrous metals	5.8	3.7	6.5	4.4	10.0	5.6	3.0	2.0
Fuels	28.8	17.1	32.2	19.3	33.9	19.2	22.0	13.8
Crude petroleum	20.6	12.6	21.9	13.3	24.0	13.8	16.8	11.2
Petroleum products	4.6	2.3	4.8	2.9	4.0	1.0	4.9	2.2
Manufactured goods	46.1	68.4	39.9	64.1	31.4	60.2	61.1	75.7
Chemical products	3.3	3.3	3.8	3.8	3.0	2.8	2.3	2.5
Mach. and transport equip.	14.0	31.3	9.2	27.1	6.1	25.6	24.2	37.2
Other	28.8	33.9	26.8	33.2	22.4	31.8	34.6	36.0
Miscellaneous goods	1.7	1.5	1.7	0.6	1.0	1.3	2.3	2.6
Total	**100.0**	**100.0**	**100.0**	**100.0**	**100.0**	**100.0**	**100.0**	**100.0**

a. Data for Belgium, Greece, and Luxembourg are for 2001.

Developing countries are becoming increasingly important in the global trading system. Since the early 1990s trade between high-income members of the Organisation for Economic Co-operation and Development (OECD) and low- and middle-income economies has grown faster than trade between OECD members. The increased trade benefits consumers and producers. But as the World Trade Organization's (WTO) Ministerial Conference in Doha, Qatar, in October 2001 showed, achieving a more prodevelopment outcome from trade remains a major challenge. Meeting this challenge will require strengthening international consultation. Negotiations after the Doha meetings have been launched on services, agriculture, manufactures, WTO rules, the environment, dispute settlement, intellectual property rights protection, and disciplines on regional integration. These negotiations are scheduled to be concluded by 2005.

Trade flows between high-income OECD members and low- and middle-income economies reflect the changing mix of exports to and imports from developing economies. While food imports from middle-income countries have continued to fall as a share of OECD imports, food imports from low-income countries to high-income countries have increased as a share of U.S. and Japanese imports. The share of manufactures in total goods imports to high-income countries has grown dramatically for both low- and middle-income countries. Moreover, trade between developing countries has grown substantially over the past decade. This growth has resulted from many factors, including developing countries' increasing share of world output and the liberalization of their trade. Yet trade barriers remain high (more than 70 percent of the tariff burden faced by manufactured

goods from developing countries is imposed by other developing countries). The growing trade between developing countries strengthens the case for reducing these barriers. Despite the growth in trade between developing countries, high-income OECD countries remain the developing world's most important partners.

The aggregate flows in the table were compiled from intercountry flows recorded in the United Nations Statistics Division's Commodity Trade (COMTRADE) database. Partner country reports by high-income OECD countries were used for both exports and imports. Exports are recorded free on board (f.o.b.); imports include insurance and freight charges (c.i.f.). Because of differences in sources of data, timing, and treatment of missing data, the data in this table may not be fully comparable with those used to calculate the direction of trade statistics in table 6.2 or the aggregate flows in tables 4.4–4.6. For further discussion of merchandise trade statistics, see *About the data* for tables 4.4–4.6 and 6.2.

The product groups in the table are defined in accordance with the Standard International Trade Classification (SITC) revision 1: food (0, 1, 22, and 4) and cereals (04); agricultural raw materials (2 excluding 22, 27, and 28); ores and nonferrous metals (27, 28, and 68); fuels (3), crude petroleum (331), and petroleum products (332); manufactured goods (5–8 excluding 68), chemical products (5), machinery and transport equipment (7), and other manufactured goods (6 and 8 excluding 68); and miscellaneous goods (9). • **Exports** are all merchandise exports by high-income OECD countries to low-income and middle-income economies as recorded in the United Nations Statistics Division's COMTRADE database. • **Imports** are all merchandise imports by high-income OECD countries from low-income and middle-income economies as recorded in the United Nations Statistics Division's COMTRADE database. • **High-income OECD countries** in 2002 were Australia, Austria, Belgium, Canada, Denmark, Finland, France, Germany, Greece, Iceland, Ireland, Italy, Japan, the Republic of Korea, Luxembourg, the Netherlands, New Zealand, Norway, Portugal, Spain, Sweden, Switzerland, the United Kingdom, and the United States. • **European Union** comprises Austria, Belgium, Denmark, Finland, France, Germany, Greece, Ireland, Italy, Luxembourg, the Netherlands, Portugal, Spain, Sweden, and the United Kingdom.

6.3a

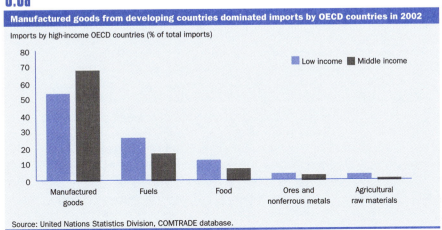

Manufactured goods from developing countries dominated imports by OECD countries in 2002

Imports by high-income OECD countries (% of total imports)

Source: United Nations Statistics Division, COMTRADE database.

COMTRADE data are available in electronic form from the United Nations Statistics Division. Although not as comprehensive as the underlying COMTRADE records, detailed statistics on international trade are published annually in the United Nations Conference on Trade and Development's (UNCTAD) *Handbook of International Trade and Development Statistics* and the United Nations Statistics Division's *International Trade Statistics Yearbook*.

6.4 Primary commodity prices

	1970	1980	1990	1995	1997	1998	1999	2000	2001	2002	2003
World Bank commodity price index											
(1990 = 100)											
Non-energy commodities	156	159	100	104	114	99	89	89	84	89	91
Agriculture	163	175	100	112	124	108	93	90	85	93	95
Beverages	203	230	100	129	165	141	108	91	76	91	87
Food	166	177	100	100	112	105	88	87	91	97	96
Raw materials	130	133	100	116	110	88	89	94	82	89	98
Fertilizers	108	164	100	88	116	123	115	109	105	108	106
Metals and minerals	144	120	100	87	87	76	74	85	80	78	82
Petroleum	19	204	100	64	81	57	80	127	113	117	126
Steel products [a]	111	100	100	91	86	75	69	79	71	73	79
MUV G-5 index	28	79	100	117	104	100	99	97	94	93	100
Commodity prices											
(1990 prices)											
Agricultural raw materials											
Cotton (cents/kg)	225	260	182	182	169	145	118	134	112	109	140
Logs, Cameroon ($/cu. m) [a]	153	319	343	290	275	287	271	283	282	..	..
Logs, Malaysian ($/cu. m)	154	248	177	218	230	163	188	195	169	175	187
Rubber (cents/kg)	145	181	86	135	98	72	63	71	64	83	106
Sawnwood, Malaysian ($/cu. m)	625	503	533	632	641	486	605	614	510	565	551
Tobacco ($/mt)	3,836	2,888	3,392	2,258	3,411	3,349	3,064	3,063	3,185	2,947	2,643
Beverages (cents/kg)											
Cocoa	240	330	127	122	156	168	114	93	113	191	175
Coffee, robustas	330	411	118	237	168	183	150	94	64	71	81
Coffee, Arabica	409	440	197	285	403	299	231	198	146	146	142
Tea, avg., 3 auctions	298	211	206	127	199	205	185	193	169	162	152
Energy											
Coal, Australian ($/mt)	..	49.67	39.67	33.63	33.90	29.34	26.08	27.01	34.26	29.05	27.83
Coal, U.S. ($/mt)	..	54.69	41.67	33.46	35.15	34.51	33.41	34.02	47.56	42.97	..
Natural gas, Europe ($/mmbtu)	..	4.31	2.55	2.33	2.65	2.43	2.15	3.97	4.30	3.28	3.91
Natural gas, U.S. ($/mmbtu)	0.59	1.97	1.70	1.47	2.40	2.09	2.28	4.44	4.19	3.60	5.49
Petroleum ($/bbl)	4.31	46.78	22.88	14.68	18.52	13.12	18.20	29.05	25.82	26.76	28.90

About the data

Primary commodities—raw or partially processed materials that will be transformed into finished goods—are often the most significant exports of developing countries, and revenues obtained from them have an important effect on living standards. Price data for primary commodities are collected from a variety of sources, including trade journals, international study groups, government market surveys, newspaper and wire service reports, and commodity exchange spot and near-term forward prices. This table is based on frequently updated price reports. When possible, the prices received by exporters are used; if export prices are unavailable,

the prices paid by importers are used. Annual price series are generally simple averages based on higher frequency data. The constant price series in the table is deflated using the manufactures unit value (MUV) index for the G-5 countries (see below).

The commodity price indexes are calculated as Laspeyres index numbers, in which the fixed weights are the 1987–89 export values for low- and middle-income economies, rebased to 1990. Each index represents a fixed basket of primary commodity exports. The non-energy commodity price index contains 37 price series for 31 non-energy commodities. Separate indexes are compiled for petroleum and for

steel products, which are not included in the non-energy commodity price index.

The MUV index is a composite index of prices for manufactured exports from the five major (G-5) industrial countries (France, Germany, Japan, the United Kingdom, and the United States) to low- and middle-income economies, valued in U.S. dollars. The index covers products in groups 5–8 of the Standard International Trade Classification (SITC) revision 1. To construct the MUV G-5 index, unit value indexes for each country are combined using weights determined by each country's export share.

	1970	1980	1990	1995	1997	1998	1999	2000	2001	2002	2003
Commodity prices (continued)											
(1990 prices)											
Fertilizers ($/mt)											
Phosphate rock	39	59	40	30	40	43	44	45	44	43	38
TSP	152	229	132	128	166	174	156	142	135	143	149
Food											
Fats and oils ($/mt)											
Coconut oil	1,417	855	336	572	634	660	742	463	337	452	467
Groundnut oil	1,350	1,090	964	847	976	913	793	734	721	738	1,242
Palm oil	927	740	290	536	527	674	439	319	303	419	443
Soybeans	417	376	247	221	285	244	203	218	208	228	264
Soybean meal	367	332	200	168	266	171	153	194	192	188	211
Soybean oil	1,021	758	447	534	545	628	430	348	375	488	554
Grains ($/mt)											
Grain sorghum	185	164	104	102	106	98	85	91	101	109	107
Maize	208	159	109	105	113	102	91	91	95	107	105
Rice	450	521	271	274	293	305	250	208	183	206	198
Wheat	196	219	136	151	154	127	113	117	134	159	146
Other food											
Bananas ($/mt)	590	481	541	380	499	491	376	436	618	568	375
Beef (cents/kg)	465	350	256	163	179	173	186	199	226	226	198
Oranges ($/mt)	599	496	531	454	443	444	434	374	631	606	682
Sugar, EU domestic (cents/kg)	40	62	58	59	61	60	60	57	56	59	60
Sugar, U.S. domestic (cents/kg)	59	84	51	43	47	49	47	44	50	50	47
Sugar, world (cents/kg)	29	80	28	25	24	20	14	19	20	16	16
Metals and minerals											
Aluminum ($/mt)	1,982	1,847	1,639	1,542	1,545	1,363	1,371	1,594	1,531	1,449	1,431
Copper ($/mt)	5,038	2,769	2,661	2,508	2,199	1,660	1,584	1,866	1,673	1,674	1,779
Iron ore (cents/dmtu)	35	36	32	24	29	31	28	30	32	31	31
Lead (cents/kg)	108	115	81	54	60	53	51	47	50	49	51
Nickel ($/mt)	10,148	8,271	8,864	7,028	6,691	4,647	6,055	8,888	6,303	7,271	9,627
Tin (cents/kg)	1,310	2,128	609	531	545	556	544	559	475	436	489
Zinc (cents/kg)	105	97	151	88	127	103	108	116	94	84	83

a. Series not included in the non-energy index.

Definitions

- **Non-energy commodity price index** covers the 31 non-energy primary commodities that make up the agriculture, fertilizer, and metals and minerals indexes. • **Agriculture** includes beverages, food, and agricultural raw material. • **Beverages** include cocoa, coffee, and tea. • **Food** includes rice, wheat, maize, sorghum, soybeans, soybean oil, soybean meal, palm oil, coconut oil, groundnut oil, bananas, beef, oranges, and sugar. • **Agricultural raw materials** include cotton, timber (logs and sawnwood), natural rubber, and tobacco. • **Fertilizers** include phosphate rock and triple superphosphate (TSP). • **Metals and minerals** include aluminum, copper, iron ore, lead, nickel, tin, and zinc. • **Petroleum price index** refers to the average spot price of Brent, Dubai, and West Texas Intermediate crude oils, equally weighted. • **Steel products price index** is the composite price index for eight steel products based on quotations free on board (f.o.b.) Japan excluding shipments to China and the United States, weighted by product shares of apparent combined consumption (volume of deliveries) for Germany, Japan, and the United States. • **MUV G-5 index** is the manufactures unit value index for G-5 country exports to low- and middle-income economies. • **Commodity prices**—for definitions and sources, see "Commodity Price Data" (also known as the "Pink Sheet") at the Global Prospects Web site (http://www.worldbank.org/prospects).

Data sources

Commodity price data and the G-5 MUV index are compiled by the World Bank's Development Prospects Group. Monthly updates of commodity prices are available on the Web at http://www.worldbank.org/prospects.

6.5 Regional trade blocs

$ millions

	1970	1980	1990	1995	1997	1998	1999	2000	2001	2002
High-income and low- and middle-income economies										
APEC [a]	58,633	357,697	901,560	1,688,708	1,869,192	1,734,386	1,896,213	2,262,159	2,070,710	2,166,764
CEFTA	1,157	7,766	4,235	12,118	13,169	14,234	13,226	15,123	17,054	19,180
European Union	76,451	456,857	981,260	1,259,699	1,159,112	1,223,801	1,396,574	1,407,525	1,396,252	1,473,375
NAFTA	22,078	102,218	226,273	394,472	496,423	521,649	581,161	676,440	639,138	626,985
Latin America and the Caribbean										
ACS	758	4,892	5,398	11,049	12,032	12,505	11,252	15,773	14,984	16,937
Andean Group	97	1,161	1,312	4,812	5,524	5,408	3,929	4,785	5,461	5,026
CACM	287	1,174	667	1,594	1,993	2,010	2,175	2,418	2,394	2,598
CARICOM	52	576	448	867	968	1,020	1,136	1,050	1,202	1,221
Central American Group of Four	176	692	399	1,026	1,302	1,230	1,369	1,582	1,546	1,678
Group of Three	59	706	1,046	3,460	3,944	3,921	2,912	3,544	4,178	3,647
LAIA	1,263	10,981	12,331	35,299	44,700	42,959	34,785	42,593	40,755	35,755
MERCOSUR	451	3,424	4,127	14,199	20,680	20,352	15,313	17,884	15,244	10,341
OECS	..	8	29	39	34	36	37	38	40	43
Africa										
CEMAC	22	75	139	120	161	153	127	102	120	131
CEPGL	3	2	7	8	6	8	9	10	11	12
COMESA	392	609	910	1,244	1,391	1,342	1,357	1,556	1,639	1,801
Cross-Border Initiative	209	447	613	1,002	1,144	1,156	964	1,066	947	1,019
ECCAS	162	89	163	163	211	198	179	196	217	236
ECOWAS	86	692	1,557	1,936	2,244	2,350	2,364	2,873	2,794	3,009
Indian Ocean Commission	23	39	73	127	75	95	91	105	135	136
MRU	1	7	0	1	7	2	4	5	4	5
SADC	483	617	1,630	3,373	4,471	3,865	4,224	4,452	4,132	4,268
UDEAC	22	75	139	120	160	152	126	101	119	130
UEMOA	52	460	621	560	707	752	805	741	776	875
Middle East and Asia										
Arab Common Market	102	661	911	1,368	1,146	978	951	1,312	1,728	1,857
ASEAN	1,456	13,350	28,648	81,911	88,773	72,352	80,415	101,848	90,105	95,473
Bangkok Agreement	132	1,464	4,476	12,066	13,684	12,851	14,463	16,844	16,733	18,299
EAEG	9,197	98,532	281,067	634,606	669,833	549,010	612,415	772,420	698,550	779,364
ECO	63	15,891	1,243	4,746	4,929	4,031	3,903	4,485	4,457	4,915
GCC	156	4,632	6,906	6,832	8,124	7,358	7,306	7,218	6,959	6,922
SAARC	99	613	863	2,024	2,174	2,466	2,180	2,614	2,828	2,999
UMA	60	109	958	1,109	924	881	919	1,104	1,136	1,178

Note: Regional bloc memberships are as follows: **Asia Pacific Economic Cooperation (APEC),** Australia, Brunei Darussalam, Canada, Chile, China, Hong Kong (China), Indonesia, Japan, the Republic of Korea, Malaysia, Mexico, New Zealand, Papua New Guinea, Peru, the Philippines, the Russian Federation, Singapore, Taiwan (China), Thailand, the United States, and Vietnam; **Central European Free Trade Area (CEFTA),** Bulgaria, the Czech Republic, Hungary, Poland, Romania, the Slovak Republic, and Slovenia; **European Union (EU; formerly European Economic Community and European Community),** Austria, Belgium, Denmark, Finland, France, Germany, Greece, Ireland, Italy, Luxembourg, the Netherlands, Portugal, Spain, Sweden, and the United Kingdom; **North American Free Trade Area (NAFTA),** Canada, Mexico, and the United States; **Association of Caribbean States (ACS),** Antigua and Barbuda, the Bahamas, Barbados, Belize, Colombia, Costa Rica, Cuba, Dominica, the Dominican Republic, El Salvador, Grenada, Guatemala, Guyana, Haiti, Honduras, Jamaica, Mexico, Nicaragua, Panama, St. Kitts and Nevis, St. Lucia, St. Vincent and the Grenadines, Suriname, Trinidad and Tobago, and República Bolivariana de Venezuela; **Andean Group,** Bolivia, Colombia, Ecuador, Peru, and República Bolivariana de Venezuela; **Central American Common Market (CACM),** Costa Rica, El Salvador, Guatemala, Honduras, and Nicaragua; **Caribbean Community and Common Market (CARICOM),** Antigua and Barbuda, the Bahamas (part of the Caribbean Community but not of the Common Market), Barbados, Belize, Dominica, Grenada, Guyana, Jamaica, Montserrat, St. Kitts and Nevis, St. Lucia, St. Vincent and the Grenadines, Suriname, and Trinidad and Tobago; **Central American Group of Four,** El Salvador, Guatemala, Honduras, and Nicaragua; **Group of Three,** Colombia, Mexico, and República Bolivariana de Venezuela; **Latin American Integration Association (LAIA; formerly Latin American Free Trade Area),** Argentina, Bolivia, Brazil, Chile, Colombia, Ecuador, Mexico, Paraguay, Peru, Uruguay, and República Bolivariana de Venezuela; **Southern Cone Common Market (MERCOSUR),** Argentina, Brazil, Paraguay, and Uruguay; **Organization of Eastern Caribbean States (OECS),** Antigua and Barbuda, Dominica, Grenada, Montserrat, St. Kitts and Nevis, St. Lucia, and St. Vincent and the Grenadines; **Economic and Monetary Community of Central Africa (CEMAC),** Cameroon, the Central African Republic, Chad, the Republic of Congo, Equatorial Guinea, Gabon, and São Tomé and Principe; **Economic Community of the Countries of the Great Lakes (CEPGL),** Burundi, the Democratic Republic of Congo, and Rwanda; **Common Market for Eastern and Southern Africa (COMESA),** Angola, Burundi, Comoros, the Democratic Republic of Congo, Djibouti, the Arab Republic of Egypt, Eritrea, Ethiopia, Kenya, Madagascar, Malawi, Mauritius, Namibia, Rwanda, Seychelles, Sudan, Swaziland, Uganda, Tanzania, Zambia,

Merchandise exports within bloc

% of total bloc exports

	1970	1980	1990	1995	1997	1998	1999	2000	2001	2002
High-income and low- and middle-income economies										
APEC [a]	57.8	57.9	68.3	71.8	71.6	69.7	71.8	73.1	72.6	73.3
CEFTA	12.9	14.8	9.9	14.6	13.4	13.0	12.1	12.2	12.4	12.2
European Union	59.5	60.8	65.9	62.4	55.4	56.8	62.9	61.6	60.8	60.6
NAFTA	36.0	33.6	41.4	46.2	49.1	51.7	54.6	55.7	55.5	56.7
Latin America and the Caribbean										
ACS	9.6	8.7	8.4	8.5	7.0	7.2	5.6	6.4	6.5	7.1
Andean Group	1.8	3.8	4.1	12.0	10.8	12.8	8.8	7.9	10.3	9.5
CACM	26.1	24.4	15.3	21.8	18.7	15.8	13.6	14.8	15.5	11.1
CARICOM	4.2	5.3	8.1	12.1	14.4	17.3	16.9	14.7	14.0	12.5
Central American Group of Four	20.1	18.1	13.7	22.2	20.2	17.1	14.6	15.1	14.8	12.8
Group of Three	1.1	1.8	2.0	3.2	2.7	2.6	1.7	1.7	2.1	1.8
LAIA	9.9	13.7	10.8	17.1	17.0	16.7	12.7	12.8	12.8	11.1
MERCOSUR	9.4	11.6	8.9	20.3	24.8	25.0	20.6	20.8	17.2	11.6
OECS	..	9.1	8.1	12.6	10.7	12.0	13.1	10.0	5.3	3.8
Africa										
CEMAC	4.8	1.6	2.3	2.1	2.0	2.3	1.7	1.0	1.3	1.5
CEPGL	0.4	0.1	0.5	0.5	0.4	0.6	0.8	0.8	0.8	0.7
COMESA	8.7	6.0	6.3	7.0	7.1	7.7	7.4	5.7	7.0	6.4
Cross-Border Initiative	9.3	8.8	10.3	11.9	12.7	13.9	12.1	10.6	10.0	10.2
ECCAS	9.6	1.4	1.4	1.5	1.5	1.8	1.3	1.1	1.3	1.3
ECOWAS	2.9	10.1	7.9	9.0	8.6	10.7	10.4	9.5	9.6	10.6
Indian Ocean Commission	8.4	3.9	4.1	6.0	3.9	4.7	4.8	4.2	5.5	5.3
MRU	0.2	0.8	0.0	0.1	0.5	0.1	0.4	0.4	0.3	0.2
SADC	8.0	2.0	4.8	8.7	10.4	10.4	11.9	11.9	10.2	9.3
COMESA	4.9	1.6	2.3	2.1	2.0	2.3	1.7	1.0	1.3	1.5
UDEAC	4.9	1.6	2.3	2.1	2.0	2.3	1.7	1.0	1.3	1.5
UEMOA	6.5	9.6	13.0	10.3	11.8	11.0	13.1	13.1	14.3	12.3
Middle East and Asia										
Arab Common Market	2.2	2.4	2.7	6.7	4.1	4.8	3.3	3.0	4.5	4.8
ASEAN	22.9	18.7	19.8	25.4	24.9	21.9	22.4	23.9	23.3	23.7
Bangkok Agreement	2.7	3.7	3.7	5.0	5.1	5.0	5.1	5.1	5.5	5.6
EAEG	28.9	35.6	39.7	47.9	47.8	42.0	43.8	46.6	46.6	48.2
ECO	1.5	73.2	3.2	7.9	7.5	6.8	5.8	5.6	5.5	5.9
GCC	2.9	3.0	8.0	6.8	6.5	8.0	6.7	4.5	4.5	4.6
SAARC	3.2	4.8	3.2	4.4	4.2	4.8	4.0	4.1	4.3	4.2
UMA	1.4	0.3	2.9	3.8	2.7	3.3	2.5	2.3	2.6	2.7

and Zimbabwe; **Cross-Border Initiative,** Burundi, Comoros, Kenya, Madagascar, Malawi, Mauritius, Namibia, Rwanda, Seychelles, Swaziland, Tanzania, Uganda, Zambia, and Zimbabwe; **Economic Community of Central African States (ECCAS),** Angola, Burundi, Cameroon, the Central African Republic, Chad, the Democratic Republic of the Congo, the Republic of Congo, Equatorial Guinea, Gabon, Rwanda, and São Tomé and Principe; **Economic Community of West African States (ECOWAS),** Benin, Burkina Faso, Cape Verde, Côte d'Ivoire, the Gambia, Ghana, Guinea, Guinea-Bissau, Liberia, Mali, Mauritania, Niger, Nigeria, Senegal, Sierra Leone, and Togo; **Indian Ocean Commission,** Comoros, Madagascar, Mauritius, Reunion, and Seychelles; **Mano River Union (MRU),** Guinea, Liberia, and Sierra Leone; **Southern African Development Community (SADC; formerly Southern African Development Coordination Conference),** Angola, Botswana, the Democratic Republic of the Congo, Lesotho, Malawi, Mauritius, Mozambique, Namibia, Seychelles, South Africa, Swaziland, Tanzania, Zambia, and Zimbabwe; **Central African Customs and Economic Union (UDEAC; formerly Union Douanière et Economique de l'Afrique Centrale),** Cameroon, the Central African Republic, Chad, the Republic of Congo, Equatorial Guinea, and Gabon; **West African Economic and Monetary Union (UEMOA),** Benin, Burkina Faso, Côte d'Ivoire, Guinea-Bissau, Mali, Niger, Senegal, and Togo; **Arab Common Market,** the Arab Republic of Egypt, Iraq, Jordan, Libya, Mauritania, the Syrian Arab Republic, and the Republic of Yemen; **Association of South-East Asian Nations (ASEAN),** Brunei, Cambodia, Indonesia, the Lao People's Democratic Republic, Malaysia, Myanmar, the Philippines, Singapore, Thailand, and Vietnam; **Bangkok Agreement,** Bangladesh, India, the Republic of Korea, the Lao People's Democratic Republic, the Philippines, Sri Lanka, and Thailand; **East Asian Economic Caucus (EAEC),** Brunei, China, Hong Kong (China), Indonesia, Japan, the Republic of Korea, Malaysia, the Philippines, Singapore, Taiwan (China), and Thailand; **Economic Cooperation Organization (ECO),** Afghanistan, Azerbaijan, the Islamic Republic of Iran, Kazakhstan, the Kyrgyz Republic, Pakistan, Tajikistan, Turkey, Turkmenistan, and Uzbekistan; **Gulf Cooperation Council (GCC),** Bahrain, Kuwait, Oman, Qatar, Saudi Arabia, and the United Arab Emirates; **South Asian Association for Regional Cooperation (SAARC),** Bangladesh, Bhutan, India, Maldives, Nepal, Pakistan, and Sri Lanka; and **Arab Maghreb Union (UMA),** Algeria, Libya, Mauritania, Morocco, and Tunisia.

a. No preferential trade agreement.

6.5 | Regional trade blocs

					% of world exports					
	1970	1980	1990	1995	1997	1998	1999	2000	2001	2002
High-income and low- and middle-income economies										
APEC [a]	36.0	33.7	39.0	46.3	47.3	46.1	46.6	48.6	46.5	46.0
CEFTA	3.2	2.9	1.3	1.6	1.8	2.0	1.9	2.0	2.2	2.4
European Union	45.6	41.0	44.0	39.7	37.9	39.9	39.2	35.9	37.4	37.9
NAFTA	21.7	16.6	16.2	16.8	18.3	18.7	18.8	19.1	18.8	17.2
Latin America and the Caribbean										
ACS	2.8	3.1	1.9	2.6	3.1	3.2	3.5	3.8	3.7	3.7
Andean Group	1.9	1.7	0.9	0.8	0.9	0.8	0.8	1.0	0.9	0.8
CACM	0.4	0.3	0.1	0.1	0.2	0.2	0.3	0.3	0.3	0.4
CARICOM	0.4	0.6	0.2	0.1	0.1	0.1	0.1	0.1	0.1	0.2
Central American Group of Four	0.3	0.2	0.1	0.1	0.1	0.1	0.2	0.2	0.2	0.2
Group of Three	1.8	2.1	1.5	2.1	2.7	2.8	3.0	3.3	3.2	3.1
LAIA	4.5	4.4	3.4	4.1	4.8	4.8	4.8	5.2	5.2	5.0
MERCOSUR	1.7	1.6	1.4	1.4	1.5	1.5	1.3	1.3	1.4	1.4
OECS	..	0.0	0.0	0.0	0.0	0.0	0.0	0.0	0.0	0.0
Africa										
CEMAC	0.2	0.3	0.2	0.1	0.1	0.1	0.1	0.2	0.2	0.1
CEPGL	0.3	0.1	0.0	0.0	0.0	0.0	0.0	0.0	0.0	0.0
COMESA	1.6	0.6	0.4	0.4	0.4	0.3	0.3	0.4	0.4	0.4
Cross-Border Initiative	0.8	0.3	0.2	0.2	0.2	0.2	0.1	0.2	0.2	0.2
ECCAS	0.6	0.3	0.3	0.2	0.3	0.2	0.2	0.3	0.3	0.3
ECOWAS	1.1	0.4	0.6	0.4	0.5	0.4	0.4	0.5	0.5	0.4
Indian Ocean Commission	0.1	0.1	0.1	0.0	0.0	0.0	0.0	0.0	0.0	0.0
MRU	0.1	0.0	0.1	0.0	0.0	0.0	0.0	0.0	0.0	0.0
SADC	2.2	1.6	1.0	0.8	0.8	0.7	0.6	0.6	0.7	0.7
UDEAC	0.2	0.3	0.2	0.1	0.1	0.1	0.1	0.2	0.2	0.1
UEMOA	0.3	0.3	0.1	0.1	0.1	0.1	0.1	0.1	0.1	0.1
Middle East and Asia										
Arab Common Market	1.6	1.5	1.0	0.4	0.5	0.4	0.5	0.7	0.6	0.6
ASEAN	2.0	3.7	4.1	6.1	6.6	5.8	5.6	6.9	6.0	6.3
Bangkok Agreement	1.6	2.1	3.5	4.6	5.0	4.6	4.5	5.4	4.7	5.1
EAEC	11.3	15.1	20.9	26.1	25.4	24.2	24.7	26.1	24.4	25.2
ECO	1.5	1.2	1.1	1.2	1.2	1.1	1.2	1.3	1.3	1.3
GCC	1.9	8.5	2.5	2.0	2.3	1.7	1.9	2.5	2.5	2.3
SAARC	1.1	0.7	0.8	0.9	0.9	0.9	1.0	1.0	1.1	1.1
UMA	1.5	2.3	1.0	0.6	0.6	0.5	0.6	0.8	0.7	0.7

About the data

Trade blocs are groups of countries that have established special preferential arrangements governing trade between members. Although in some cases the preferences—such as lower tariff duties or exemptions from quantitative restrictions—may be no greater than those available to other trading partners, the general purpose of such arrangements is to encourage exports by bloc members to one another—sometimes called intratrade.

Most countries are members of a regional trade bloc, and more than a third of the world's trade takes place within such arrangements. While trade blocs vary widely in structure, they all have the same main objective: to reduce trade barriers among member countries. But effective integration requires more than reducing tariffs and quotas. Economic gains from competition and scale may not be achieved unless other barriers that divide markets and impede the free flow of goods, services, and investments are lifted. For example, many regional trade blocs retain contingent protections or restrictions on intrabloc trade. These include antidumping, countervailing duties, and "emergency protection" to address balance of payments problems or to protect an industry from surges in imports. Other barriers include differing product standards, discrimination in public procurement, and cumbersome and costly border formalities.

Membership in a regional trade bloc may reduce the frictional costs of trade, increase the credibility of reform initiatives, and strengthen security among partners. But making it work effectively is a challenge for any government. All sectors of an economy may be affected, and some sectors may expand while others contract, so it is important to weigh the potential costs and benefits that membership may bring.

The table shows the value of merchandise intratrade for important regional trade blocs (service exports are excluded) as well as the size of intratrade relative to each bloc's total exports of goods and the share of the bloc's total exports in world exports. Although the Asia Pacific Economic Cooperation (APEC) has no preferential arrangements, it is included in the table because of the volume of trade between its members.

The data on country exports are drawn from the International Monetary Fund's (IMF) Direction of Trade database and should be broadly consistent with those from other sources, such as the United Nations Statistics Division's Commodity Trade (COMTRADE) database. However, trade flows between many developing countries, particularly in Africa, are not well recorded. Thus the value of intratrade for certain groups may be understated. Data on trade between developing and high-income countries are generally complete.

Membership in the trade blocs shown is based on the most recent information available, from the World Bank Policy Research Report *Trade Blocs* (2000a) and from consultation with the World Bank's international trade unit. Although bloc exports have been calculated back to 1970 on the basis of current membership, most of the blocs came into existence in later years and their membership may have changed over time. For this reason, and because systems of preferences also change over time, intratrade in earlier years may not have been affected by the same preferences as in recent years. In addition, some countries belong to more than one trade bloc, so shares of world exports exceed 100 percent. Exports of blocs include all commodity trade, which may include items not specified in trade bloc agreements. Differences from previously published estimates may be due to changes in bloc membership or to revisions in the underlying data.

Definitions

• **Merchandise exports within bloc** are the sum of merchandise exports by members of a trade bloc to other members of the bloc. They are shown both in U.S. dollars and as a percentage of total merchandise exports by the bloc. • **Total merchandise exports by bloc** as a share of world exports are the ratio of the bloc's total merchandise exports (within the bloc and to the rest of the world) to total merchandise exports by all economies in the world.

Data sources

Data on merchandise trade flows are published in the IMF's *Direction of Trade Statistics Yearbook* and *Direction of Trade Statistics Quarterly;* the data in the table were calculated using the IMF's Direction of Trade database. The United Nations Conference on Trade and Development (UNCTAD) publishes data on intratrade in its *Handbook of International Trade and Development Statistics.* The information on trade bloc membership is from the World Bank Policy Research Report *Trade Blocs* (2000a) and the World Bank's international trade unit.

	Year	Binding coverage	Simple mean bound rate	All products Simple mean tariff	All products Weighted mean tariff	All products Share of lines with international peaks	All products Share of lines with specific rates	All products Ad valorem equivalent of nontariff barriers [a]	Primary products Simple mean tariff	Primary products Weighted mean tariff	Manufactured products Simple mean tariff	Manufactured products Weighted mean tariff
Albania	1997	..	..	17.7	16.0	59.8	0.0	..	15.7	12.8	17.2	15.2
	2001	100.0	7.0	11.8	12.4	40.0	0.0	0.6	12.1	10.6	11.6	11.6
Algeria	1993	..	..	20.9	16.1	43.7	0.0	..	22.5	8.9	21.7	18.7
	2002	..	..	18.8	15.3	43.5	0.0	1.1	19.7	12.8	18.3	13.1
Argentina	1992	..	..	14.9	13.4	36.8	0.0	..	8.1	5.8	14.8	13.6
	2002	100.0	31.9	14.6	11.9	50.3	0.0	4.7	10.9	8.0	14.8	12.2
Australia	1991 [b]	..	..	14.4	10.3	36.3	0.7	..	3.0	1.7	14.1	10.5
	2002 [b]	97.0	9.9	5.9	3.9	8.4	0.7	0.6	1.5	0.8	5.6	4.3
Bangladesh	1989	..	..	110.5	131.0	98.9	1.0	..	79.8	53.6	108.6	109.6
	2002	16.1	163.8	19.3	23.0	45.9	0.0	1.7	22.4	20.1	19.3	21.1
Belarus	1996	..	..	11.8	7.8	30.2	0.0	..	9.4	6.5	12.6	10.5
	2002	..	..	11.1	8.0	19.4	1.1	0.0	11.1	7.0	11.6	10.3
Belize	1996	22.0	21.1	48.8	42.2	..	23.0	10.5	20.4	18.8		
	2001	98.0	58.2	12.6	13.3	41.7	0.0	..	19.7	9.9	11.6	11.2
Benin	2001	..	..	14.5	15.5	57.9	0.0	..	15.5	12.9	14.1	12.4
	2002	39.4	28.3	14.5	15.5	57.6	0.0	..	15.5	12.9	14.0	12.4
Bhutan	1996	..	..	16.1	14.4	52.2	2.7	..	21.2	9.7	17.0	16.8
	2002	..	..	16.3	14.3	45.4	0.0	..	24.4	14.3	16.4	15.0
Bolivia	1993	..	..	9.7	9.2	0.0	0.0	..	10.0	10.0	9.7	9.3
	2001	100.0	40.0	9.4	8.8	0.0	0.0	0.8	9.8	9.1	9.3	8.8
Brazil	1989	..	..	43.5	35.6	92.9	0.2	..	31.5	18.6	44.0	37.1
	2002	99.9	31.4	14.9	9.9	43.1	0.0	2.4	10.9	4.8	15.1	12.0
Burkina Faso	1993	..	..	25.9	23.5	75.3	0.0	..	27.5	23.1	25.5	20.3
	2002	39.2	41.9	13.1	11.2	48.1	0.0	..	15.0	15.2	12.8	9.2
Cameroon	1994	..	..	19.2	15.3	52.7	0.0	..	23.9	14.9	18.8	13.6
	2002	13.6	79.9	18.7	15.8	51.7	0.0	0.1	21.7	18.1	18.0	13.9
Canada	1989 [b]	..	..	10.8	6.4	18.4	2.4	..	4.3	2.6	10.5	6.6
	2002 [b]	100.0	5.1	5.1	1.1	13.0	3.3	1.5	1.9	0.5	4.7	1.0
Central African Republic	1995	..	..	17.1	14.3	50.0	0.7	..	19.1	13.7	16.8	13.1
	2002	62.5	36.2	18.3	20.0	51.3	0.0	..	24.3	25.5	17.7	13.4
Chad	1995 [b]	..	..	15.9	17.0	44.2	0.0	..	19.0	15.9	15.6	13.4
	2002	13.7	79.9	16.8	14.2	43.8	0.0	..	21.4	24.0	16.5	13.3
Chile	1992	..	..	11.0	11.0	0.0	0.0	..	11.0	11.0	11.0	10.9
	2002	100.0	25.1	7.0	7.0	0.0	0.0	1.0	7.0	7.0	7.0	6.9
China	1992	..	..	41.6	35.3	79.5	0.0	..	36.3	14.0	40.6	35.6
	2001	..	..	15.1	12.8	41.7	0.7	1.5	16.0	19.2	15.0	12.8
Colombia	1991	..	..	5.6	4.3	0.3	0.0	..	7.0	7.5	5.8	6.1
	2002	100.0	42.9	12.8	10.1	23.0	0.0	3.4	12.9	13.2	12.7	10.8
Congo, Rep.	1994	..	..	20.8	16.6	61.4	0.0	..	24.4	20.5	20.3	14.6
	2002	16.3	27.5	19.6	18.0	55.2	0.0	..	23.7	21.3	18.8	16.1
Costa Rica	1995 [b]	..	..	10.4	8.7	29.8	0.0	..	12.9	10.5	9.9	8.0
	2001	..	..	6.6	5.8	0.1	0.0	0.2	10.4	7.9	6.1	3.7
Côte d'Ivoire	1993	..	..	24.3	23.1	73.0	0.0	..	26.5	21.6	24.1	22.5
	2002	33.1	11.1	12.8	12.0	45.7	0.0	2.0	14.8	10.7	12.6	10.3
Cuba	1993	..	..	14.1	12.3	30.5	0.0	..	12.1	7.2	14.0	12.9
	2002	30.9	21.2	12.3	9.4	12.5	0.1	..	11.5	5.8	12.0	11.0
Czech Republic	1996	..	..	6.4	5.4	2.4	0.0	..	5.9	4.1	6.5	6.2
	2002	..	..	5.0	4.1	3.4	0.0	1.1	5.5	3.9	5.0	4.3
Dominican Republic	1997	..	..	15.7	17.4	33.1	0.0	..	18.0	10.4	15.2	17.7
	2001	100.0	34.9	9.7	10.1	29.1	0.1	..	13.1	8.0	9.4	9.8
Ecuador	1993	..	..	9.4	6.4	19.8	0.0	..	9.1	6.4	9.3	8.3
	2002	99.8	21.7	12.5	10.5	22.8	0.0	..	12.3	10.8	12.3	10.7
Egypt, Arab Rep.	1995	..	..	23.3	17.1	53.5	0.6	..	25.9	7.6	24.0	22.2
	2002	98.9	37.2	18.4	13.4	44.6	10.0	0.1	18.2	6.6	19.0	16.4
El Salvador	1995	..	..	10.4	8.8	28.0	0.0	..	12.8	10.2	9.8	8.7
	2001	100.0	36.6	7.5	6.1	12.1	0.0	6.9	10.6	8.0	6.9	6.0
Equatorial Guinea	1998	..	..	19.4	13.3	56.7	0.2	..	24.6	23.6	18.5	13.6
	2002	..	..	18.6	14.0	51.0	0.1	..	24.1	23.0	17.9	13.1
Ethiopia [c]	1995	..	..	35.2	16.9	75.8	0.2	..	36.9	18.4	32.3	18.0
	2001	..	..	21.3	16.5	57.8	0.3	0.0	22.0	6.3	20.3	15.2
European Union	1988 [b]	..	..	2.6	3.0	1.7	12.4	..	5.8	2.7	2.6	4.3
	2002 [b]	100.0	4.1	3.1	2.4	1.3	4.7	1.5	3.4	1.5	2.9	2.9
Gabon	1995	..	..	20.5	16.1	60.3	0.0	..	24.4	20.2	19.9	15.2
	2002	100.0	21.4	20.2	15.8	58.6	0.0	0.2	24.1	20.2	19.6	13.5
Ghana	1993	..	..	15.3	10.5	45.1	0.0	..	19.4	14.1	13.8	9.2
	2000	14.3	92.4	15.2	9.5	47.3	0.0	0.1	21.4	28.2	14.0	8.9
Guatemala	1995	..	..	10.0	8.4	25.8	0.0	..	12.6	10.2	9.4	8.0
	2001	34.6	36.6	7.8	5.8	14.3	0.0	0.0	9.8	7.9	7.2	5.8
Guinea-Bissau	2001	..	..	14.1	16.1	55.1	0.0	..	17.0	18.6	13.4	12.4
	2002	97.7	48.7	13.6	13.9	51.8	0.0	..	16.3	15.2	12.6	10.4
Guyana	1996	..	..	22.6	20.6	47.8	43.6	..	28.0	15.5	21.0	19.0
	2001	100.0	56.7	12.2	10.6	40.2	0.4	..	20.1	14.5	11.3	9.8

	Year	All products							Primary products		Manufactured products	
		Binding coverage	Simple mean bound rate	Simple mean tariff	% Weighted mean tariff	Share of lines with international peaks	Share of lines with specific rates	Ad valorem equivalent of nontariff barriers [a]	% Simple mean tariff	Weighted mean tariff	% Simple mean tariff	Weighted mean tariff
Honduras	1995	..	..	9.8	10.3	25.6	0.0	..	13.0	12.9	9.2	7.5
	2001	100.0	32.5	7.5	7.3	11.9	0.7	0.0	10.7	11.4	7.1	6.2
Hungary	1991 [b]	..	..	12.0	9.6	15.0	0.0	..	13.5	5.5	12.1	11.7
	2002	96.3	9.7	8.3	7.5	4.8	0.0	1.0	18.0	7.2	7.7	8.0
India	1990 [b]	..	..	76.6	49.8	98.4	0.5	..	69.8	25.4	79.9	70.8
	2001 [b]	73.8	49.8	31.0	21.0	94.9	0.2	3.2	32.8	22.7	30.8	28.4
Indonesia	1989 [b]	..	..	18.7	12.0	48.5	0.1	..	18.1	5.9	19.2	15.1
	2001 [b]	96.6	37.5	6.0	3.9	1.9	0.0	0.5	6.0	2.4	6.2	5.2
Jamaica	1996	..	..	21.7	21.8	46.0	45.7	..	23.7	14.2	20.7	20.9
	2001	100.0	49.8	9.1	7.8	38.9	0.2	..	15.3	9.5	8.5	10.1
Japan	1988 [b]	..	..	4.0	3.4	8.6	8.4	..	8.3	4.4	3.5	2.7
	2002 [b]	99.6	2.9	2.9	2.2	6.9	1.4	1.6	5.2	2.5	2.4	1.7
Jordan	2000	..	..	24.0	20.7	63.7	0.4	..	28.0	17.0	23.3	19.8
	2002	100.0	16.3	16.2	11.3	43.9	0.1	10.2	21.8	11.7	15.9	13.1
Kenya	1994 [b]	..	..	32.4	25.5	91.0	0.0	..	32.4	17.0	31.9	23.3
	2001	14.6	95.6	20.0	14.4	41.3	0.1	0.3	20.9	15.3	19.6	12.5
Korea, Rep.	1988	..	..	18.7	14.7	76.8	10.6	..	19.3	8.2	18.6	17.0
	2002	94.5	16.1	7.9	5.7	3.1	0.7	0.0	12.0	6.1	7.4	4.7
Kyrgyz Republic	1995	..	..	0.0	0.0	0.0	9.6	..	0.0	0.0	0.0	0.0
	2002	99.9	7.4	8.4	7.8	9.9	0.0	..	8.2	6.3	8.2	7.1
Lao PDR	2000	..	..	8.7	14.5	8.3	0.6	..	15.6	14.7	8.6	12.6
	2001 [b]	..	..	8.6	12.2	7.9	0.0	..	15.9	17.3	8.8	11.9
Latvia	1996	..	..	3.6	3.0	0.5	0.0	..	6.5	1.5	3.3	2.6
	2001	100.0	12.7	3.4	2.5	0.7	0.0	0.4	8.2	5.4	2.7	1.5
Lebanon	1999	..	..	15.3	13.1	31.2	0.1	..	13.1	11.2	14.4	12.7
	2002	..	..	6.4	8.0	9.8	0.0	3.7	13.7	10.2	5.9	6.6
Libya	1996	..	..	21.8	17.0	57.9	0.2	..	24.9	9.6	22.5	25.6
	2002	..	..	18.8	15.9	45.7	0.7	..	18.1	15.7	19.9	29.0
Lithuania	1995 [b]	..	..	3.0	2.1	4.3	0.0	..	6.2	3.7	2.6	1.8
	2002 [b]	100.0	9.3	0.7	0.5	1.3	0.0	0.4	3.5	1.5	0.5	0.3
Madagascar	1995	..	..	7.9	4.8	8.0	0.0	..	6.3	2.9	7.6	6.3
	2001	29.7	27.4	5.5	2.9	6.5	0.0	0.6	6.1	1.4	5.4	4.3
Malawi	1994	..	..	32.7	29.9	89.3	0.0	..	29.1	12.9	31.9	26.6
	2001 [b]	26.1	82.7	13.8	12.5	43.0	0.0	..	12.8	11.1	12.8	11.7
Malaysia	1988 [b]	..	..	14.4	11.5	50.7	5.5	..	10.8	4.6	14.9	10.8
	2001 [b]	83.7	14.5	7.5	4.6	19.5	0.4	1.7	4.4	2.4	8.1	4.7
Mali	1995	..	..	16.5	9.5	43.1	0.0	..	19.5	13.4	16.0	8.5
	2002	40.1	28.8	12.9	11.4	46.7	0.0	..	15.1	12.1	12.6	9.9
Mauritius	1995 [b]	..	..	35.7	22.5	63.7	0.0	..	26.0	25.7	37.2	22.9
	2002	14.9	114.8	25.1	15.8	40.2	0.1	0.0	20.1	9.0	25.8	14.4
Mexico	1991	..	..	14.7	12.7	20.9	0.0	..	13.4	8.3	14.6	13.0
	2002 [b]	99.9	34.9	16.2	4.9	43.7	0.4	1.8	14.5	7.0	15.8	4.7
Moldova	1996	..	..	6.4	3.3	19.7	0.0	..	11.3	1.5	4.7	2.3
	2001	..	..	5.3	3.9	0.0	0.2	..	8.9	2.6	4.5	2.9
Morocco	1993	..	..	64.6	47.0	97.9	0.0	..	55.0	30.2	65.0	55.2
	2002	100.0	41.2	27.7	28.2	76.9	0.0	0.5	35.7	27.7	28.0	26.2
Mozambique	1994	..	..	5.0	5.0	0.0	0.0	..	5.0	5.0	5.0	5.0
	2002 [b]	100.0	99.6	12.3	9.4	36.4	0.0	..	14.8	11.0	11.6	8.7
Nepal	1993	..	..	21.8	18.1	60.8	0.1	..	11.8	9.3	22.9	21.0
	2002	..	..	13.1	14.3	14.8	0.1	..	16.0	8.3	13.8	17.8
New Zealand	1992	..	..	10.5	8.5	37.5	1.5	..	5.5	4.0	10.7	9.4
	2002 [b]	99.9	10.3	4.3	2.8	9.8	7.1	2.2	1.7	0.5	4.2	3.6
Nicaragua	1995 [b]	..	..	7.9	4.0	20.5	0.0	..	7.7	7.1	7.4	4.6
	2002 [b]	100.0	41.7	4.4	2.3	0.0	0.0	..	6.2	3.6	4.1	2.5
Niger	2001	..	..	14.6	14.1	57.5	0.0	..	15.1	12.9	14.2	12.7
	2002	96.8	44.3	14.5	14.1	57.2	0.0	..	15.1	12.9	14.2	12.7
Nigeria	1988	..	..	25.5	20.0	63.8	0.1	..	33.3	32.4	25.3	21.4
	2002	19.0	118.8	26.6	15.8	56.3	0.7	0.4	40.1	20.6	24.9	15.5
Norway	1988 [b]	..	..	2.1	1.0	5.8	6.4	..	0.6	0.2	2.1	0.8
	2002 [b]	100.0	3.0	0.8	0.7	1.9	7.0	0.3	2.4	2.1	0.6	0.2
Oman	1992	..	..	5.2	5.1	0.8	0.0	..	7.2	14.2	5.1	5.4
	2002	100.0	13.8	7.7	6.7	0.2	2.3	0.9	9.5	31.6	7.6	6.5
Pakistan	1995	..	..	50.1	45.5	93.9	3.5	..	43.4	24.0	51.1	50.8
	2002	38.0	60.5	16.9	15.2	54.9	0.0	..	17.9	11.2	17.5	19.1
Panama	1997	..	..	12.1	9.7	35.3	0.2	..	17.8	9.6	11.8	11.0
	2001	100.0	23.5	7.9	5.7	0.1	0.2	..	11.4	5.9	7.7	7.4
Papua New Guinea	1997	..	..	19.1	13.4	32.2	0.4	..	33.2	21.8	18.5	13.7
	2002	100.0	31.7	6.3	2.7	21.9	0.3	..	17.5	6.7	5.8	3.2
Paraguay	1991	..	..	16.1	13.9	44.0	0.0	..	14.1	3.6	15.7	14.5
	2001	100.0	33.5	13.9	12.5	33.2	0.0	1.7	12.8	8.2	13.6	11.9
Peru	1993	..	..	18.2	16.8	25.6	0.0	..	18.3	15.8	18.0	16.6
	2000	100.0	30.1	13.4	12.6	14.6	0.0	1.7	15.6	13.9	13.0	12.3

6.6 Tariff barriers

	Year	All products %							Primary products %		Manufactured products %	
		Binding coverage	Simple mean bound rate	Simple mean tariff	Weighted mean tariff	Share of lines with international peaks	Share of lines with specific rates	Ad valorem equivalent of nontariff barriers[a]	Simple mean tariff	Weighted mean tariff	Simple mean tariff	Weighted mean tariff
Philippines	1988	..	..	27.7	21.1	74.7	0.1	..	29.9	18.5	27.9	23.4
	2002	66.8	25.6	4.8	2.8	0.3	0.0	0.4	6.7	5.4	5.0	2.6
Poland	1991	..	..	11.8	9.5	24.0	0.0	..	11.9	8.2	12.2	11.2
	2003[b]	..	..	4.0	2.0	7.1	4.7	1.2	12.4	4.0	3.1	1.4
Romania	1991	..	..	19.2	10.7	54.8	0.0	..	20.0	8.1	18.9	17.9
	2001[b]	100.0	40.4	11.3	7.3	26.2	0.0	2.5	18.0	11.2	10.6	7.2
Russian Federation	1993	..	..	8.9	7.2	2.3	0.0	..	3.1	3.9	9.5	7.4
	2002	..	..	9.9	8.4	10.0	16.8	..	9.7	8.3	10.5	8.9
Rwanda	1993	..	..	39.6	29.6	65.9	1.1	..	60.7	24.9	37.4	25.5
	2001[b]	100.0	89.3	10.0	6.6	12.1	0.0	1.4	13.2	6.8	9.5	5.9
Saudi Arabia	1994	..	..	12.3	11.1	9.6	0.1	..	12.0	9.1	12.4	11.5
	2000	..	..	12.3	11.4	8.6	3.5	0.9	11.7	7.9	12.2	11.4
Senegal	2001	..	..	14.0	8.6	53.6	0.0	..	14.5	8.3	13.8	10.4
	2002	100.0	30.0	13.9	8.4	52.9	0.0	0.0	14.4	8.2	13.7	9.9
Singapore	1989	..	..	0.4	0.2	0.0	0.3	..	0.2	2.5	0.4	0.6
	2002	69.2	6.9	0.0	0.0	0.0	0.0	0.5	0.0	0.0	0.0	0.0
Slovenia	1999	..	..	11.9	10.9	23.7	2.5	..	9.5	7.5	11.7	12.1
	2001	100.0	24.3	11.6	10.2	26.3	0.0	0.6	9.8	7.5	11.2	10.5
South Africa[d]	1988	..	..	11.4	7.7	31.9	19.9	..	4.8	3.6	11.8	12.3
	2001[b]	98.0	17.8	9.8	3.6	38.0	1.6	0.5	7.5	2.0	9.5	5.8
Sri Lanka	1990	..	..	27.1	31.5	53.6	0.8	..	32.4	32.3	26.6	24.2
	2001[b]	22.6	42.7	8.4	4.2	18.1	0.4	0.0	13.9	11.3	8.7	5.0
Switzerland[e]	1990	..	..	..	..	..	51.7	..	..	..	..	..
	2001	99.8	1.7	1.9	0.8	..	39.2	1.2	15.0	9.5	1.1	0.2
Taiwan, China	1989	..	..	11.1	9.7	13.7	0.6	..	14.5	8.6	10.8	10.5
	2002	..	..	6.9	3.3	7.5	2.1	..	9.7	4.1	6.4	3.0
Tanzania	1993	..	..	16.7	19.0	45.6	0.0	..	22.7	19.9	15.3	15.0
	2000	13.3	120.0	19.1	15.4	74.7	0.0	0.0	19.9	13.2	18.4	13.0
Thailand	1989	..	..	38.7	31.7	76.5	18.7	..	30.0	24.3	39.0	34.9
	2001[b]	74.7	25.7	14.7	8.7	49.4	0.4	0.3	16.2	4.7	14.6	9.7
Togo	2001	..	..	14.5	11.5	58.7	0.0	..	14.7	10.5	14.2	11.2
	2002	13.7	80.0	14.5	11.5	58.4	0.0	..	14.7	10.5	14.1	11.2
Trinidad and Tobago	1991	..	..	18.5	11.2	40.6	0.0	..	24.8	10.9	17.8	14.1
	2002	100.0	55.7	9.6	2.9	38.1	0.0	0.2	15.5	5.8	9.2	4.7
Tunisia	1990	..	..	28.6	29.9	98.1	0.0	..	25.1	17.4	28.3	28.5
	2002	57.4	57.7	30.2	27.4	86.4	0.0	0.8	44.7	26.7	28.7	25.5
Turkey	1993[b]	..	..	7.5	5.7	6.1	0.0	..	6.3	7.9	7.4	5.3
	1999	49.5	28.4	7.1	4.5	6.4	0.4	0.2	16.6	5.5	6.2	5.3
Turkmenistan	1998	..	..	0.0	0.0	0.0	0.0	..	0.0	0.0	0.0	0.0
	2002	..	..	5.5	1.7	12.2	3.3	..	16.0	13.2	3.7	1.1
Uganda	1994[b]	..	..	17.5	15.0	57.3	0.0	..	19.4	17.4	16.8	12.3
	2002[b]	15.7	73.3	8.0	6.8	0.0	0.0	0.1	10.0	8.8	7.7	6.1
Ukraine	1995	..	..	8.0	4.3	11.5	0.0	..	8.9	2.7	7.3	4.3
	2002	..	..	7.9	4.4	10.5	6.9	0.0	7.1	1.5	7.9	6.4
United States	1989[b]	..	..	5.9	5.2	9.6	13.2	..	2.5	2.0	5.5	4.1
	2002[b]	100.0	3.6	4.1	2.6	7.0	7.5	1.6	2.7	1.1	3.8	2.0
Uruguay	1992	..	..	6.7	6.7	0.0	0.0	..	7.9	5.8	7.0	5.8
	2001[b]	100.0	31.7	13.3	6.5	38.9	0.0	1.9	8.9	2.8	13.4	8.1
Venezuela, RB	1992	..	..	17.4	12.9	48.2	0.4	..	16.3	14.7	17.1	16.5
	2000	..	..	13.5	11.3	25.1	0.0	1.4	13.5	13.6	13.4	13.3
Vietnam	1994	..	..	14.1	13.0	36.7	0.8	..	20.9	46.7	13.9	13.1
	2001	..	..	15.0	17.4	37.9	0.0	..	19.6	20.7	14.7	16.3
Zambia	1993	..	..	26.2	18.1	94.1	0.0	..	30.0	12.4	25.2	20.0
	2002	17.1	106.4	13.9	8.4	36.5	2.3	0.2	17.3	12.6	13.3	8.3
Zimbabwe	1996[b]	..	..	41.2	37.3	95.9	0.4	..	34.2	40.4	41.3	38.8
	2001	21.4	94.3	20.4	12.0	45.7	1.4	..	20.7	7.0	20.6	14.2

a. Ad valorem equivalents of nontariff barriers are calculated for the year 2000 only. b. Rates are either partially or fully recorded applied rates. All other simple and weighted tariff rates are most favored nation rates. c. Excludes Eritrea. d. Data refer to South African Customs Union (Botswana, Lesotho, Namibia, South Africa, and Swaziland). e. Data for Switzerland include all specific rates converted to their ad valorem equivalents.

Poor people in developing countries work primarily in agriculture and labor-intensive manufactures, sectors that confront the greatest trade barriers. Removing barriers to merchandise trade could increase growth by about 0.5 percent a year in these countries—even more if trade in services (retailing, business, financial, and telecommunications services) were also liberalized.

In general, tariffs in high-income countries on imports from developing countries, though low, are four times those collected from other high-income countries. But protection is also an issue for developing countries, which maintain high tariffs on agricultural commodities, labor-intensive manufactures, and other products and services. In some developing regions new trade policies could make the difference between achieving important Millennium Development Goals—reducing poverty, lowering maternal and child mortality rates, improving educational attainment—and falling far short.

Countries use a combination of tariff and nontariff measures to regulate imports. The most common form of tariff is an ad valorem duty, based on the value of the import, but tariffs may also be levied on a specific, or per unit, basis or may combine ad valorem and specific rates. Tariffs may be used to raise fiscal revenues or to protect domestic industries from foreign competition—or both. Nontariff barriers, which limit the quantity of imports of a particular good, include quotas, prohibitions, licensing schemes, export restraint arrangements, and health and quarantine measures.

Nontariff barriers are generally considered less desirable than tariffs because changes in an exporting country's efficiency and costs no longer result in changes in market share in the importing country. Further, the quotas or licenses that regulate trade become very valuable, and resources are often wasted in attempts to acquire these assets. A high percentage of products subject to nontariff barriers suggests a protectionist trade regime, but the frequency of nontariff barriers does not measure how much they restrict trade. Moreover, a wide range of domestic policies and regulations (such as health regulations) may act as nontariff barriers.

Estimates of ad valorem equivalents of nontariff barriers are given at the six-digit level of the Harmonized System, which provides the simple averages of core nontariff barriers, including quantity control measures such as nonautomatic licensing, quotas, prohibitions, and export restraint arrangements but excluding tariff-quotas and enterprise-specific restrictions; financial measures, which include advance payment requirements, multiple exchange rates, and restrictive official foreign exchange allocation and exclude regulations on terms of payment, transfer delays, and queuing; and price control measures, which affect the cost of imports based on differences between domestic prices and foreign prices. They include administrative price fixing, voluntary export price restraints, variable charges, antidumping measures, and countervailing measures.

Countries typically maintain a hierarchy of trade preferences applicable to specific trading partners. The tariff rates used in calculating the indicators in the table are most favored nation rates unless they are specified as applied rates. Effectively applied rates are those in effect for partners in preferential trade agreements such as the North American Free Trade Agreement. The difference between most favored nation and applied rates can be substantial. For example, the weighted average of Slovenia's 2001 most favored nation rates is 10.2 percent, while the effectively applied rate in 2000 averaged less than 2 percent. As more countries report their free trade agreements, suspensions of tariffs, or other special preferences, *World Development Indicators* will include their effectively applied rates.

Three measures of average tariffs are shown: the simple and the weighted mean rates and simple bound rates. The most favored nation or applied rates are calculated using all traded items, while bound rates are based on all products in a country's tariff schedule. Weighted mean tariffs are weighted by the value of the country's trade with each trading partner. Simple averages are often a better indicator of tariff protection than weighted averages, which are biased downward because higher tariffs discourage trade and reduce the weights applied to these tariffs. Bound rates have resulted from trade negotiations that are incorporated into a country's schedule of concessions and are thus enforceable. If a contracting party raises a tariff to a higher level than its bound rate, beneficiaries of the earlier binding have a right to receive compensation, usually as reduced tariffs on other products they export to the country. If the beneficiaries are not compensated, they may retaliate by raising their own tariffs against an equivalent value of the original country's exports. Specific duties (not expressed as a proportion of declared value) are not included in the table, except for Switzerland. Work is under way to complete the estimations for ad valorem equivalents of specific duties for all countries.

Some countries set fairly uniform tariff rates across all imports. Others are more selective, setting high tariffs to protect favored domestic industries. The standard deviation of tariffs is a measure of the dispersion of tariff rates around their mean value. Highly dispersed rates increase the costs of protection substantially. But these nominal tariff rates tell only part of the story. The effective rate of protection—the degree to which the value added in an industry is protected—may exceed the nominal rate if the tariff system systematically differentiates among imports of raw materials, intermediate products, and finished goods.

Two other measures of tariff coverage are shown: the share of tariff lines with international peaks (those for which ad valorem tariff rates exceed 15 percent) and the share of tariff lines with specific duties (those not covered by ad valorem rates). Some countries—for example, Switzerland—apply only specific duties.

The indicators were calculated from data supplied by the United Nations Conference on Trade and Development (UNCTAD) and the World Trade Organization (WTO). Data are classified using the Harmonized System of trade at the six- or eight-digit level. Tariff line data were matched to Standard International Trade Classification (SITC) revision 2 codes to define commodity groups and import weights. Import weights were calculated using the United Nations Statistics Division's Commodity Trade (COMTRADE) database. Data are shown only for the first and last year for which complete data are available. To conserve space, data for the European Union are shown instead of data for individual members.

• **Primary products** are commodities classified in SITC revision 2 sections 0–4 plus division 68 (nonferrous metals). • **Manufactured products** are commodities classified in SITC revision 2 sections 5–8 excluding division 68. • **Binding coverage** is the percentage of product lines with an agreed bound rate. • **Simple mean bound rate** is the unweighted average of all the lines in the tariff schedule in which bound rates have been set. • **Simple mean tariff** is the unweighted average of effectively applied rates or most favored nation rates for all products subject to tariffs calculated for all traded goods. • **Weighted mean tariff** is the average of effectively applied rates or most favored nation rates weighted by the product import shares corresponding to each partner country. • **Share of lines with international peaks** is the share of lines in the tariff schedule with tariff rates that exceed 15 percent. • **Share of lines with specific rates** is the share of lines in the tariff schedule that are set on a per unit basis or that combine ad valorem and per unit rates. • **Ad valorem equivalent of nontariff barriers** are the simple average of core nontariff barriers transformed into a price effect using import demand elasticities; they are calculated for traded products only.

All indicators in the table were calculated by World Bank staff using the World Integrated Trade Solution (WITS) system. Tariff data were provided by UNCTAD and the WTO. Data on global imports come from the United Nations Statistics Division's COMTRADE database.

Global private financial flows

	Net private capital flows		Foreign direct investment		Portfolio investment flows				Bank and trade-related lending	
					Bonds		Equity			
	$ millions		$ millions		$ millions				$ millions	
	1990	**2002**	**1990**	**2002**	**1990**	**2002**	**1990**	**2002**	**1990**	**2002**
Afghanistan	..	..	..	..	..	..	..	..	..	..
Albania	..	136	..	135	..	0	..	0	..	1
Algeria	–424	1,023	0	1,065	–16	0	0	0	–409	–42
Angola	235	1,420	–335	1,312	0	0	0	0	570	108
Argentina	–216	681	1,836	785	–857	86	0	–99	–1,195	–91
Armenia	..	108	..	111	..	0	..	1	..	–4
Australia	..	..	8,111	16,622	..	..	..	..	..	..
Austria	..	..	653	886	..	..	..	..	..	..
Azerbaijan	..	1,313	..	1,392	..	0	..	0	..	–79
Bangladesh	59	132	3	47	0	0	0	0	55	85
Belarus	..	227	..	247	..	0	..	0	..	–21
Belgium	..	..	8,047	..	..	..	..	..	..	..
Benin	62	41	62	41	0	0	0	0	0	0
Bolivia	3	601	27	677	0	0	0	0	–24	–76
Bosnia and Herzegovina	..	299	0	293	..	0	..	0	..	6
Botswana	77	35	96	37	0	0	0	0	–19	–2
Brazil	666	9,861	989	16,566	129	1,519	103	1,981	–555	–10,205
Bulgaria	..	808	..	600	..	–79	..	–23	..	310
Burkina Faso	0	8	1	8	0	0	0	0	–1	0
Burundi	–5	–2	1	0	0	0	0	0	–6	–2
Cambodia	0	54	0	54	0	0	0	0	0	0
Cameroon	–124	38	–113	86	0	0	0	0	–12	–49
Canada	..	..	7,581	20,501	..	..	..	..	..	..
Central African Republic	0	4	1	4	0	0	0	0	–1	0
Chad	9	900	9	901	0	0	0	0	–1	–1
Chile	2,216	2,781	661	1,713	–7	1,614	367	–317	1,194	–230
China	8,107	47,107	3,487	49,308	–48	–1,289	0	2,249	4,668	–3,161
Hong Kong, China	..	..	..	12,794	..	..	..	..	..	..
Colombia	345	947	500	2,023	–4	68	0	17	–151	–1,161
Congo, Dem. Rep.	–27	32	–15	32	0	0	0	0	–12	0
Congo, Rep.	–100	331	0	331	0	0	0	0	–100	0
Costa Rica	22	602	163	662	–42	–44	0	0	–99	–16
Côte d'Ivoire	57	117	48	230	–1	0	0	1	10	–114
Croatia	..	3,604	..	980	..	–27	..	78	..	2,573
Cuba	..	..	..	..	..	..	..	..	..	..
Czech Republic	..	10,382	..	9,323	..	180	..	–265	..	1,143
Denmark	..	..	1,132	6,410	..	..	..	..	..	..
Dominican Republic	129	1,351	133	961	0	–20	0	0	–3	410
Ecuador	184	2,103	126	1,275	0	0	0	1	58	826
Egypt, Arab Rep.	668	437	734	647	–1	0	0	–212	–65	3
El Salvador	7	1,419	2	208	0	1,252	0	0	6	–40
Eritrea	..	21	..	21	..	0	..	0	..	0
Estonia	..	1,586	..	285	..	219	..	0	..	1,083
Ethiopia	–45	71	12	75	0	0	0	0	–57	–4
Finland	..	..	812	8,156	..	..	..	..	..	..
France	..	..	13,183	52,020	..	..	..	..	..	..
Gabon	103	139	74	123	0	0	0	0	29	16
Gambia, The	–8	42	0	43	0	0	0	0	–8	0
Georgia	..	149	..	165	..	0	..	0	..	–17
Germany	..	..	3,005	37,296	..	..	..	..	..	..
Ghana	–5	27	15	50	0	0	0	0	–20	–23
Greece	..	..	1,005	53	..	..	..	..	..	..
Guatemala	44	61	48	110	–11	–31	0	0	7	–19
Guinea	–1	0	18	0	0	0	0	0	–19	0
Guinea-Bissau	2	1	2	1	0	0	0	0	0	0
Haiti	0	6	0	6	0	0	0	0	0	0

	Net private capital flows		Foreign direct investment		Portfolio investment flows				Bank and trade-related lending	
						$ millions				
					Bonds		Equity			
	$ millions		$ millions						$ millions	
	1990	2002	1990	2002	1990	2002	1990	2002	1990	2002
Honduras	75	100	44	143	0	0	0	0	32	–43
Hungary	–147	221	311	854	921	–742	0	–137	–1,379	247
India	1,842	4,944	237	3,030	147	–272	0	967	1,458	1,219
Indonesia	2,923	–6,966	1,093	–1,513	26	–406	0	877	1,804	–5,924
Iran, Islamic Rep.	–392	816	–362	37	0	0	0	0	–30	779
Iraq	..	..	..	..	..	..	..	..	..	..
Ireland	..	..	627	24,697	..	..	..	..	..	..
Israel	..	..	151	1,649	..	..	..	..	..	..
Italy	..	..	6,411	14,699	..	..	..	..	..	..
Jamaica	92	540	138	481	0	70	0	0	–46	–11
Japan	..	..	1,777	9,087	..	..	..	..	..	..
Jordan	252	–31	38	56	0	–11	0	–52	214	–24
Kazakhstan	..	4,431	..	2,583	..	–50	..	39	..	1,859
Kenya	122	39	57	50	0	0	0	0	65	–12
Korea, Dem. Rep.	..	..	..	..	..	..	..	..	..	..
Korea, Rep.	..	..	788	1,972	..	..	..	..	..	..
Kuwait	..	..	0	7	..	..	..	..	..	..
Kyrgyz Republic	..	–54	..	5	..	0	..	0	..	–59
Lao PDR	6	25	6	25	0	0	0	0	0	0
Latvia	..	496	..	382	..	0	..	22	..	91
Lebanon	13	4,803	7	257	0	4,626	0	4	6	–84
Lesotho	17	73	17	81	0	0	0	0	0	–8
Liberia	0	–65	0	–65	0	0	0	0	0	0
Libya	..	..	..	..	..	..	..	..	..	..
Lithuania	..	760	..	712	..	–200	..	6	..	242
Macedonia, FYR	..	113	..	77	..	0	..	0	..	35
Madagascar	7	8	22	8	0	0	0	0	–15	0
Malawi	26	6	23	6	0	0	1	0	2	0
Malaysia	476	4,807	2,332	3,203	–1,239	1,962	0	–250	–617	–110
Mali	5	102	6	102	0	0	0	0	–1	0
Mauritania	5	16	7	12	0	0	0	0	–1	4
Mauritius	86	–43	41	28	0	0	0	0	45	–71
Mexico	9,600	10,261	2,549	14,622	661	–3,899	1,995	–104	4,396	–359
Moldova	..	77	..	111	..	–43	..	2	..	8
Mongolia	..	78	..	78	..	0	..	0	..	0
Morocco	483	15	165	428	0	–31	0	–14	318	–369
Mozambique	35	381	9	406	0	0	0	0	26	–25
Myanmar	155	69	163	129	0	0	0	0	–8	–60
Namibia	..	..	..	..	..	..	..	..	..	..
Nepal	–14	9	0	10	0	0	0	0	–14	0
Netherlands	..	..	10,676	28,534	..	..	..	..	..	..
New Zealand	..	..	1,735	823	..	..	..	..	..	..
Nicaragua	20	206	0	174	0	0	0	0	20	32
Niger	51	0	41	8	0	0	0	0	10	–8
Nigeria	467	639	588	1,281	0	–452	0	0	–121	–190
Norway	..	..	1,003	1,008	..	..	..	..	..	..
Oman	–257	–1,131	142	40	0	–225	0	–13	–400	–933
Pakistan	182	379	245	823	0	–178	0	79	–63	–345
Panama	129	180	136	57	–2	13	–1	0	–4	110
Papua New Guinea	204	–46	155	50	0	0	0	0	49	–96
Paraguay	68	34	77	–22	0	0	0	0	–9	56
Peru	59	3,131	41	2,391	0	720	0	–9	18	30
Philippines	639	3,549	530	1,111	395	1,540	0	410	–286	488
Poland	71	5,075	89	4,131	0	1,307	0	–830	–18	468
Portugal	..	..	2,610	4,235	..	..	..	..	..	..
Puerto Rico	..	..	..	..	..	..	..	..	..	..

	Net private capital flows		Foreign direct investment		Portfolio investment flows				Bank and trade-related lending	
						$ millions				
					Bonds		Equity			
	$ millions		$ millions						$ millions	
	1990	2002	1990	2002	1990	2002	1990	2002	1990	2002
Romania	4	3,173	0	1,144	0	−28	0	21	4	2,037
Russian Federation	..	8,011	..	3,009	..	2,745	..	2,626	..	−370
Rwanda	6	3	8	3	0	0	0	0	−2	0
Saudi Arabia	..	..	..	..	..	..	..	..	..	..
Senegal	43	94	57	93	0	0	1	0	−15	1
Serbia and Montenegro	..	507	..	475	..	0	..	0	..	32
Sierra Leone	36	5	32	5	0	0	0	0	4	0
Singapore	..	..	5,575	6,097	..	..	..	..	..	..
Slovak Republic	..	5,460	..	4,012	..	−189	..	0	..	1,637
Slovenia	..	..	..	1,865	..	..	..	..	..	..
Somalia	6	0	6	0	0	0	0	0	0	0
South Africa	..	783	..	739	..	3,187	..	−388	..	−2,754
Spain	..	..	13,984	21,284	..	..	..	..	..	..
Sri Lanka	54	206	43	242	0	0	0	0	10	−36
Sudan	0	633	0	633	0	0	0	0	0	0
Swaziland	26	45	30	45	0	0	−2	0	−2	0
Sweden	..	..	1,982	11,828	..	..	..	..	..	..
Switzerland	..	..	5,987	3,599	..	..	..	..	..	..
Syrian Arab Republic	63	224	72	225	0	0	0	0	−9	−1
Tajikistan	..	−10	..	9	..	0	..	2	..	−20
Tanzania	5	214	0	240	0	0	0	0	5	−26
Thailand	4,371	−1,992	2,444	900	−87	−1,010	440	207	1,574	−2,089
Togo	23	75	18	75	0	0	4	0	0	0
Trinidad and Tobago	−68	736	109	736	−52	0	0	0	−126	0
Tunisia	−116	1,625	76	795	−60	650	5	6	−137	174
Turkey	1,836	7,582	684	1,037	597	956	89	−16	466	5,605
Turkmenistan	..	..	..	100	..	..	..	0	..	..
Uganda	16	149	0	150	0	0	0	0	16	−1
Ukraine	..	−576	..	693	..	101	..	−1,958	..	588
United Arab Emirates	..	..	..	..	..	..	..	..	..	..
United Kingdom	..	..	33,504	28,180	..	..	..	..	..	..
United States	..	..	48,490	39,633	..	..	..	..	..	..
Uruguay	−192	107	0	177	−16	77	0	−39	−176	−108
Uzbekistan	..	−11	..	65	..	0	..	0	..	−76
Venezuela, RB	−126	−1,639	451	690	345	−1,066	0	75	−922	−1,337
Vietnam	180	759	180	1,400	0	0	0	0	0	−641
West Bank and Gaza	..	..	..	..	..	..	..	..	..	..
Yemen, Rep.	30	114	−131	114	0	0	0	0	161	0
Zambia	194	186	203	197	0	0	0	0	−9	−12
Zimbabwe	85	−3	−12	26	−30	0	0	0	127	−29
World	.. s	.. s	202,476 s	630,827 s	.. s	.. s	.. s	.. s	.. s	.. s
Low income	6,820	7,151	2,764	12,941	142	−1,351	6	1,927	3,908	−6,365
Middle income	36,872	146,679	21,269	134,145	933	14,090	2,997	3,018	11,673	−4,574
Lower middle income	21,964	98,852	10,180	91,104	1,270	10,259	636	4,887	9,878	−7,397
Upper middle income	14,908	47,828	11,089	43,041	−336	3,832	2,361	−1,869	1,795	2,824
Low & middle income	43,692	153,831	24,032	147,086	1,076	12,739	3,004	4,945	15,581	−10,939
East Asia & Pacific	17,179	47,524	10,512	54,834	−952	798	439	3,493	7,180	−11,601
Europe & Central Asia	7,490	53,739	1,227	32,931	1,893	4,149	89	−433	4,281	17,092
Latin America & Carib.	13,199	34,544	8,181	44,682	145	498	2,464	1,507	2,408	−12,143
Middle East & N. Africa	2,266	5,359	2,604	2,653	−126	5,010	5	−281	−217	−2,023
South Asia	2,129	5,697	536	4,164	147	−450	1	1,046	1,446	938
Sub-Saharan Africa	1,429	6,968	972	7,822	−31	2,735	6	−387	482	−3,202
High income	..	..	178,443	483,741	..	..	..	..	..	..
Europe EMU	..	..	60,540	320,893	..	..	..	..	..	..

About the data

The data on foreign direct investment are based on balance of payments data reported by the International Monetary Fund (IMF), supplemented by data on net foreign direct investment reported by the Organisation for Economic Co-operation and Development (OECD) and official national sources.

The internationally accepted definition of foreign direct investment is provided in the fifth edition of the IMF's *Balance of Payments Manual* (1993). Under this definition foreign direct investment has three components: equity investment, reinvested earnings, and short- and long-term intercompany loans between parent firms and foreign affiliates. But many countries fail to report reinvested earnings, and the definition of long-term loans differs among countries. Foreign direct investment, as distinguished from other kinds of international investment, is made to establish a lasting interest in or effective management control over an enterprise in another country. As a guideline, the IMF suggests that investments should account for at least 10 percent of voting stock to be counted as foreign direct investment. In practice, many countries set a higher threshold.

The OECD has also published a definition, in consultation with the IMF, Eurostat, and the United Nations. Because of the multiplicity of sources and differences in definitions and reporting methods, there may be more than one estimate of foreign direct investment for a country and data may not be comparable across countries.

Foreign direct investment data do not give a complete picture of international investment in an economy. Balance of payments data on foreign direct investment do not include capital raised locally, which has become an important source of financing for investment projects in some developing countries. In addition, foreign direct investment data capture only cross-border investment flows involving equity participation and thus omit nonequity cross-border transactions such as intrafirm flows of goods and services. For a detailed discussion of the data issues, see the World Bank's *World Debt Tables 1993–94* (volume 1, chapter 3).

Portfolio flow data are compiled from several market and official sources, including Euromoney databases and publications; Micropal; Lipper Analytical Services; published reports of private investment houses, central banks, national securities and exchange commissions, and national stock exchanges; and the World Bank's Debtor Reporting System.

Gross statistics on international bond and equity issues are produced by aggregating individual transactions reported by market sources. Transactions of public and publicly guaranteed bonds are reported through the Debtor Reporting System by World Bank member economies that have received either loans from the International Bank for Reconstruction and Development or credits from the International Development Association. Information on private nonguaranteed bonds is collected from market sources, because official national sources reporting to the Debtor Reporting System are not asked to report the breakdown between private nonguaranteed bonds and private nonguaranteed loans. Information on transactions by nonresidents in local equity markets is gathered from national authorities, investment positions of mutual funds, and market sources.

The volume of portfolio investment reported by the World Bank generally differs from that reported by other sources because of differences in the sources, in the classification of economies, and in the method used to adjust and disaggregate reported information. Differences in reporting arise particularly for foreign investments in local equity markets because clarity, adequate disaggregation, and comprehensive and periodic reporting are lacking in many developing economies. By contrast, capital flows through international debt and equity instruments are well recorded, and for these the differences in reporting lie primarily in the classification of economies, the exchange rates used, whether particular installments of the transactions are included, and the treatment of certain offshore issuances.

Definitions

• **Net private capital flows** consist of private debt and nondebt flows. Private debt flows include commercial bank lending, bonds, and other private credits, as well as foreign direct investment and portfolio equity investment. • **Foreign direct investment** is net inflows of investment to acquire a lasting management interest (10 percent or more of voting stock) in an enterprise operating in an economy other than that of the investor. It is the sum of equity capital, reinvestment of earnings, other long-term capital, and short-term capital, as shown in the balance of payments. • **Portfolio investment flows** are net and include non-debt-creating portfolio equity flows (the sum of country funds, depository receipts, and direct purchases of shares by foreign investors) and portfolio debt flows (bond issues purchased by foreign investors). • **Bank and trade-related lending** covers commercial bank lending and other private credits.

Data sources

The data are compiled from a variety of public and private sources, including the World Bank's Debtor Reporting System, the IMF's International Financial Statistics and Balance of Payments databases, and other sources mentioned in *About the data*. These data are also published in the World Bank's *Global Development Finance 2004*.

Net flows to part I countries

$ millions	Official development assistance Total 2002	Bilateral grants 2002	Bilateral loans 2002	Contributions to multilateral institutions 2002	Other official flows 2002	Private flows Total 2002	Foreign direct investment 2002	Bilateral portfolio investment 2002	Multilateral portfolio investment 2002	Private export credits 2002	Net grants by NGOs 2002	Total net flows 2002
Australia	989	774	..	215	31	−433	−103	−331	..	..	248	834
Austria	520	367	−2	156	−36	1,325	1,029	..	..	296	57	1,866
Belgium	1,072	736	−25	360	106	86	555	..	..	−469	74	1,337
Canada	2,006	1,527	−24	503	−424	188	829	−604	..	−37	276	2,046
Denmark	1,643	1,019	19	605	−3	−63	−63	..	..	..	..	1,577
Finland	462	248	4	211	3	−676	−5	−720	..	48	10	−200
France	5,486	3,874	−259	1,871	635	−1,392	2,915	−2,859	..	−1,448	..	4,729
Germany	5,324	3,904	−576	1,997	3,710	−1,124	1,760	−2,496	−676	287	823	8,733
Greece	276	107	..	169	..	40	40	..	..	..	6	322
Ireland	398	267	..	131	..	986	..	986	..	..	86	1,469
Italy	2,332	1,083	−77	1,326	−370	−563	639	−3,250	..	2,048	..	1,399
Japan	9,283	4,373	2,320	2,591	−4,208	−573	6,362	−3,077	−2,804	−1,054	157	4,659
Luxembourg	147	116	..	31	..	..	..	..	..	..	2	148
Netherlands	3,338	2,585	−136	889	229	−5,310	281	−7,395	946	859	257	−1,487
New Zealand	122	92	..	30	2	17	17	..	..	..	23	164
Norway	1,696	1,143	2	551	..	131	23	..	..	109	452	2,279
Portugal	323	183	3	137	−1	−150	−360	..	..	210	..	171
Spain	1,712	769	229	714	54	6,404	6,540	..	..	−136	..	8,171
Sweden	1,991	1,242	8	741	2	199	296	..	..	−97	19	2,211
Switzerland	939	750	15	174	3	1,089	1,222	..	..	−133	202	2,234
United Kingdom	4,924	3,384	121	1,419	−4	13,547	13,940	840	..	−1,233	353	18,820
United States	13,290	11,251	−681	2,720	227	5,173	12,928	−7,930	−590	765	5,720	24,410
Total	**58,274**	**39,793**	**941**	**17,540**	**−45**	**18,899**	**48,844**	**−26,835**	**−3,124**	**14**	**8,765**	**85,893**

Net flows to part II countries

$ millions	Official aid Total 2002	Bilateral grants 2002	Bilateral loans 2002	Contributions to multilateral institutions 2002	Other official flows 2002	Private flows Total 2002	Foreign direct investment 2002	Bilateral portfolio investment 2002	Private export credits 2002	Net grants by NGOs 2002	Total net flows 2002
Australia	7	4	..	4	13	1,747	572	1,174	..	248	2,015
Austria	196	142	0	55	..	3,215	3,215	..	..	8	3,420
Belgium	97	6	6	85	−24	−2,527	−2,497	0	−30	10	−2,443
Canada	104	104	..	..	−106	5,603	5,534	76	−7	..	5,602
Denmark	167	90	5	72	19	431	431	..	..	..	617
Finland	67	33	−1	35	−1	1,043	390	519	134	0	1,109
France	1,464	1,083	−20	401	21	4,352	1,925	2,626	−199	..	5,837
Germany	780	347	−81	514	−505	10,980	7,734	4,692	−1,446	78	11,333
Greece	16	16	..	..	..	216	216	..	..	1	234
Ireland	26	1	..	25	..	..	..	..	..	..	26
Italy	..	..	..	..	25	−199	197	−469	73	..	−173
Japan	99	123	−66	43	−896	6,150	6,182	−349	318	..	5,353
Luxembourg	10	3	..	7	..	..	..	..	..	..	10
Netherlands	211	138	−6	79	..	−1,061	2,775	−4,066	230	..	−850
New Zealand	1	0	..	0	..	..	..	..	..	..	1
Norway	45	43	..	2	0	1,084	1,082	..	1	..	1,129
Portugal	33	1	..	32	−2	71	57	..	14	..	102
Spain	11	11	..	..	..	206	206	..	..	..	218
Sweden	107	100	0	7	−2	−1,261	−1,288	0	27	..	−1,155
Switzerland	66	57	1	9	2	1,302	1,320	0	−17	9	1,379
United Kingdom	494	92	−4	407	..	8,121	5,350	2,880	−110	6	8,621
United States	2,313	2,418	−173	69	−52	4,182	21,372	−17,120	−70	3,146	9,589
Total	**6,317**	**4,813**	**−342**	**1,846**	**−1,508**	**43,655**	**54,774**	**−10,036**	**−1,083**	**3,508**	**51,972**

Note: Data may not sum to totals because of gaps in reporting.

About the data

The high-income members of the Development Assistance Committee (DAC) of the Organisation for Economic Co-operation and Development (OECD) are the main source of official external finance for developing countries. This table shows the flow of official and private financial resources from DAC members to official and private recipients in developing and transition economies.

DAC exists to help its members coordinate their development assistance and to encourage the expansion and improve the effectiveness of the aggregate resources flowing to recipient economies. In this capacity DAC monitors the flow of all financial resources, but its main concern is official development assistance (ODA). DAC has three criteria for ODA: It is undertaken by the official sector. It promotes the economic development and welfare of developing countries as a main objective. And it is provided on concessional terms, with a grant element of at least 25 percent on loans (calculated at a rate of discount of 10 percent).

This definition excludes nonconcessional flows from official creditors, which are classified as "other official flows," and military aid, which is not recorded in DAC statistics. The definition includes food aid, capital projects, emergency relief, technical cooperation, and post-conflict peacekeeping efforts. Also included are contributions to multilateral institutions, such as the United Nations and its specialized agencies, and concessional funding to the multilateral development banks. In 1999, to avoid double counting extrabudgetary expenditures reported by DAC countries

and flows reported by the United Nations, all United Nations agencies revised their data to include only regular budgetary expenditures since 1990 (except for the World Food Programme and the United Nations High Commissioner for Refugees, which revised their data from 1996 onward).

DAC maintains a list of countries and territories that are aid recipients. Part I of the list comprises developing countries and territories considered by DAC members to be eligible for ODA. Part II comprises economies in transition: more advanced countries of Central and Eastern Europe, the countries of the former Soviet Union, and certain advanced developing countries and territories. Flows to these recipients that meet the criteria for ODA are termed official aid.

The data in the table were compiled from replies by DAC member countries to questionnaires issued by the DAC Secretariat. Net flows of ODA, official aid, and other official resources are defined as gross disbursements of grants and loans minus repayments of principal on earlier loans. Because the data are based on donor country reports, they do not provide a complete picture of the resources received by developing and transition economies, for two reasons. First, flows from DAC members are only part of the aggregate resource flows to these economies. Second, the data that record contributions to multilateral institutions measure the flow of resources made available to those institutions by DAC members, not the flow of resources from those institutions to developing and transition economies.

Definitions

- **Official development assistance** comprises grants and loans (net of repayments of principal) that meet the DAC definition of ODA and are made to countries and territories in part I of the DAC list of aid recipients. • **Official aid** comprises grants and loans (net of repayments) that meet the criteria for ODA and are made to countries and territories in part II of the DAC list of aid recipients.
- **Bilateral grants** are transfers of money or in kind for which no repayment is required. • **Bilateral loans** are loans extended by governments or official agencies that have a grant element of at least 25 percent (calculated at a rate of discount of 10 percent). • **Contributions to multilateral institutions** are concessional funding received by multilateral institutions from DAC members in the form of grants or capital subscriptions. • **Other official flows** are transactions by the official sector whose main objective is other than development or whose grant element is less than 25 percent. • **Private flows** consist of flows at market terms financed from private sector resources in donor countries. They include changes in holdings of private long-term assets by residents of the reporting country. • **Foreign direct investment** is investment by residents of DAC member countries to acquire a lasting management interest (at least 10 percent of voting stock) in an enterprise operating in the recipient country. The data reflect changes in the net worth of subsidiaries in recipient countries whose parent company is in the DAC source country. • **Bilateral portfolio investment** covers bank lending and the purchase of bonds, shares, and real estate by residents of DAC member countries in recipient countries. • **Multilateral portfolio investment** records the transactions of private banks and nonbanks in DAC member countries in the securities issued by multilateral institutions. • **Private export credits** are loans extended to recipient countries by the private sector in DAC member countries to promote trade; they may be supported by an official guarantee. • **Net grants by NGOs** are private grants by nongovernmental organizations, net of subsidies from the official sector. • **Total net flows** comprise ODA or official aid flows, other official flows, private flows, and net grants by NGOs.

Data sources

The data on financial flows are compiled by DAC and published in its annual statistical report, *Geographical Distribution of Financial Flows to Aid Recipients*, and its annual *Development Cooperation Report*. Data are available electronically on the OECD's *International Development Statistics* CD-ROM and to registered users at http://www.oecd.org/dataoecd/50/17/5037721.htm.

6.8a

Who were the largest donors in 2002?

Official development assistance

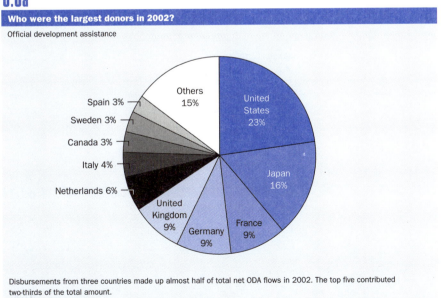

Disbursements from three countries made up almost half of total net ODA flows in 2002. The top five contributed two-thirds of the total amount.

Source: Organisation for Economic Co-operation and Development, Development Assistance Committee.

6.9 Aid flows from Development Assistance Committee members

| | Net official development assistance | | | | | | | | | | Untied aid[a] | |
| | $ millions | | % of GNI | | average annual % change in volume[b] 1996–97 to | Per capita of donor country[b] $ | | % of general government disbursement | | % of bilateral ODA commitments | |
	1997	2002	1997	2002	2001–02	1997	2002	1997	2002	1997	2002
Australia	1,061	989	0.27	0.26	2.4	43	47	0.70	0.68	63.1	56.7
Austria	495	520	0.24	0.26	5.2	51	61	0.44	0.49	60.6	69.0
Belgium	764	1,072	0.31	0.43	7.1	63	97	0.61	0.87	49.9	..
Canada	2,045	2,006	0.34	0.28	–0.6	65	64	0.72	0.67	33.4	61.4
Denmark	1,637	1,643	0.97	0.96	2.8	266	286	1.67	1.71	71.6	82.1
Finland	379	462	0.32	0.35	5.1	63	83	0.55	0.70	76.8	82.5
France	6,307	5,486	0.45	0.38	–2.6	89	86	0.82	0.72	65.1	91.5
Germany	5,857	5,324	0.28	0.27	–0.5	58	60	0.56	0.55	73.6	86.6
Greece	173	276	0.14	0.21	9.6	14	23	0.30	0.44	..	13.9
Ireland	187	398	0.31	0.40	14.3	47	93	0.63	0.97	..	100.0
Italy	1,266	2,332	0.11	0.20	4.6	19	37	0.21	0.41	45.6	..
Japan	9,358	9,283	0.21	0.23	3.0	70	76	0.61	0.60	99.6	82.8
Luxembourg	95	147	0.55	0.77	13.5	198	316	1.25	1.57	95.1	..
Netherlands	2,947	3,338	0.81	0.81	3.6	170	190	1.62	1.68	90.0	88.6
New Zealand	154	122	0.26	0.22	3.5	28	28	0.56	0.54	..	76.0
Norway	1,306	1,696	0.84	0.89	2.8	291	333	1.76	1.87	91.1	99.1
Portugal	250	323	0.25	0.27	6.7	23	28	0.53	0.57	99.0	33.0
Spain	1,234	1,712	0.24	0.26	9.5	28	38	0.53	0.66	0.0	59.9
Sweden	1,731	1,991	0.79	0.83	5.2	151	207	1.11	1.42	74.5	78.5
Switzerland	911	939	0.34	0.32	2.3	114	118	..	..	94.9	95.1
United Kingdom	3,433	4,924	0.26	0.31	6.5	56	78	0.63	0.77	71.7	100.0
United States	6,878	13,290	0.09	0.13	6.8	28	46	0.24	0.36	..	..
Total or average	**48,465**	**58,274**	**0.22**	**0.23**	**3.5**	**53**	**65**	**0.54**	**0.59**	**83.2**	**84.8**

| | Net official aid | | | | | | |
| | $ millions | | % of GNI | | average annual % change in volume[b] 1996–97 to | Per capita of donor country[b] $ | |
	1997	2002	1997	2002	2001–02	1997	2002
Australia	0	7	0.00	0.00	10.7	0	0
Austria	181	196	0.09	0.10	4.8	19	23
Belgium	59	97	0.02	0.04	12.0	5	9
Canada	157	104	0.03	0.01	–4.3	5	3
Denmark	133	167	0.08	0.10	10.3	22	29
Finland	71	67	0.06	0.05	3.3	12	12
France	574	1,464	0.04	0.10	22.2	8	23
Germany	660	780	0.03	0.04	–1.0	7	9
Greece	9	16	0.01	0.01	20.6	1	1
Ireland	1	26	0.00	0.03	94.4	0	6
Italy	241	..	0.02	..	..	4	..
Japan	84	99	0.00	0.00	–4.5	1	1
Luxembourg	2	10	0.01	0.05	38.1	5	22
Netherlands	7	211	0.00	0.05	88.8	0	12
New Zealand	0	1	0.00	0.00	86.8	0	0
Norway	55	45	0.04	0.02	–6.6	12	9
Portugal	18	33	0.02	0.03	13.5	2	3
Spain	3	11	0.00	0.00	–20.9	0	0
Sweden	148	107	0.07	0.04	–1.7	13	11
Switzerland	75	66	0.03	0.02	–2.5	9	8
United Kingdom	337	494	0.03	0.03	5.4	6	8
United States	2,516	2,313	0.03	0.02	–3.4	10	8
Total or average	**5,331**	**6,317**	**0.02**	**0.03**	**3.3**	**6**	**7**

a. Excluding administrative costs and technical cooperation. b. At 2001 exchange rates and prices.

About the data

Effective aid supports institutional development and policy reforms, which are at the heart of successful development. To be effective, especially in reducing global poverty, aid requires partnerships among recipient countries, aid agencies, and donor countries. It also requires improvements in economic policies and institutions. Where traditional methods of nurturing such reforms have failed, aid agencies need to find alternative approaches and new opportunities.

As part of its work, the Development Assistance Committee (DAC) of the Organisation for Economic Co-operation and Development (OECD) assesses the aid performance of member countries relative to the size of their economies. As measured here, aid comprises bilateral disbursements of concessional financing to recipient countries plus the provision by donor governments of concessional financing to multilateral institutions. Volume amounts, at constant prices and exchange rates, are used to measure the change in real resources provided over time. Aid flows to part I recipients—official development assistance (ODA)—are tabulated separately from those to part II recipients—official aid (see *About the data* for table 6.8 for more information on the distinction between the two types of aid flows).

Measures of aid flows from the perspective of donors differ from aid receipts from the perspective of recipients for two main reasons. First, aid flows include expenditure items about which recipients may have no precise information, such as development-oriented research, stipends and tuition costs for aid-financed students in donor countries, or payment of experts hired by donor countries. Second, donors record their concessional funding (usually grants) to multilateral agencies when they make payments, while the agencies make funds available to recipients with a time lag and in many cases in the form of soft loans where donors' grants have been used to reduce the interest burden over the life of the loan.

Aid as a share of gross national income (GNI), aid per capita, and ODA as a share of the general government disbursements of the donor are calculated by the OECD. The denominators used in calculating these ratios may differ from corresponding values elsewhere in this book because of differences in timing or definitions.

DAC members have progressively introduced the new United Nations System of National Accounts (adopted in 1993), which replaced gross national product (GNP) with GNI. Because GNI includes items not included in GNP, ratios of ODA to GNI are slightly smaller than previously reported ratios of ODA to GNP.

The proportion of untied aid is reported here because tying arrangements may prevent recipients from obtaining the best value for their money and so reduce the value of the aid received. Tying arrangements require recipients to purchase goods and services from the donor country or from a specified group of countries. They may be justified on the grounds that they prevent a recipient from misappropriating or mismanaging aid receipts, but they may also be motivated by a desire to benefit suppliers in the donor country. The same volume of aid may have different purchasing power depending on the relative costs of suppliers in countries to which the aid is tied and the degree to which each recipient's aid basket is untied.

Definitions

• **Net official development assistance** and **net official aid** record the actual international transfer by the donor of financial resources or of goods or services valued at the cost to the donor, less any repayments of loan principal during the same period. Data are shown at current prices and dollar exchange rates. • **Aid as a percentage of GNI** shows the donor's contributions of ODA or official aid as a share of its gross national income. • **Average annual percentage change in volume** and **aid per capita of donor country** are calculated using 2001 exchange rates and prices. • **Aid as a percentage of general government disbursements** shows the donor's contributions of ODA as a share of public spending. • **Untied aid** is the share of ODA that is not subject to restrictions by donors on procurement sources.

6.9a

Official development assistance from selected non-DAC donors, 1998–2002

Net disbursements ($ millions)

Donor	1998	1999	2000	2001	2002
OECD members (non-DAC)					
Czech Republic	16	15	16	26	45
Iceland	7	8	9	10	13
Korea, Rep.	183	317	212	265	279
Poland	19	20	29	36	14
Slovak Republic	..	7	6	8	7
Turkey	69	120	82	64	73
Arab countries					
Kuwait	278	147	165	73	20
Saudi Arabia	288	185	295	490	2,478
United Arab Emirates	63	92	150	127	156
Other donors					
Israel	87	114	164[a]	76[a]	114[a]
Other[b]	27	0	1	2	3
Total	**1,037**	**1,026**	**1,128**	**1,178**	**3,201**

Note: China also provides aid but does not disclose the amount.
a. These figures include $66.8 million in 2000, $50.1 million in 2001, and $87.8 million in 2002 for first-year sustenance expenses for people arriving from developing countries (many of which are experiencing civil war or severe unrest) or who have left their country for humanitarian or political reasons. b. Includes Estonia, Latvia, Lithuania, and Taiwan, China.
Source: Organisation for Economic Co-operation and Development.

Data sources

The data on financial flows are compiled by DAC and published in its annual statistical report, *Geographical Distribution of Financial Flows to Aid Recipients*, and its annual *Development Cooperation Report*. Data are available electronically on the OECD's *International Development Statistics* CD-ROM and to registered users at http://www.oecd.org/dataoecd/50/17/5037721.htm.

| | Net official development assistance or official aid ($ millions) | | Aid per capita ($) | | Aid dependency ratios | | | | | | | |
| | | | | | Aid as % of GNI | | Aid as % of gross capital formation | | Aid as % of imports of goods and services | | Aid as % of central government expenditure | |
	1997	2002	1997	2002	1997	2002	1997	2002	1997	2002	1997	2002
Afghanistan	230	1,285	10	46	..	..	..	..	..	..	..	..
Albania	166	317	53	101	7.5	6.4	75.8	28.8	20.2	15.1	25.3	..
Algeria	250	361	9	12	0.5	0.7	2.2	2.1	..	..	1.7	1.1
Angola	355	421	31	32	5.5	4.3	18.2	11.6	5.7	4.5	..	..
Argentina	105	0	3	0	0.0	0.0	0.2	0.0	0.2	0.0	0.2	0.3
Armenia	166	293	52	96	9.6	12.0	53.2	59.2	16.8	25.4	..	..
Australia												
Austria												
Azerbaijan	184	349	23	43	4.7	6.1	13.6	17.5	8.6	9.9	24.2	..
Bangladesh	1,011	913	8	7	2.3	1.8	11.5	8.3	12.6	9.6	..	..
Belarus	55	39	5	4	0.4	0.3	1.5	1.3	0.6	0.4	1.2	1.1
Belgium												
Benin	221	220	38	34	10.4	8.3	55.7	45.9	27.8	26.3	..	..
Bolivia	700	681	89	77	9.1	9.0	45.0	59.2	29.7	28.9	40.0	34.2
Bosnia and Herzegovina	862	587	236	143	26.1	10.0	59.2	53.4	..	12.1	..	..
Botswana	122	38	77	22	2.4	0.8	8.3	2.9	3.9	1.3	..	..
Brazil	288	376	2	2	0.0	0.1	0.2	0.4	0.3	0.5	0.1	..
Bulgaria	220	381	26	48	2.2	2.5	21.5	12.5	3.5	3.9	6.5	7.4
Burkina Faso	368	473	35	40	14.2	15.2	56.5	82.8	..	65.1	..	..
Burundi	56	172	9	24	6.0	24.2	72.9	303.8	35.5	107.7	24.5	..
Cambodia	335	487	30	39	10.1	12.7	66.0	54.7	25.6	16.7	..	..
Cameroon	499	632	35	40	5.9	7.3	33.9	37.6	..	..	..	..
Canada												
Central African Republic	91	60	26	16	9.2	5.8	92.6	38.6	..	..	..	..
Chad	228	233	32	28	14.5	11.8	102.0	19.8	..	..	..	..
Chile	129	−23	9	−1	0.2	−0.0	0.6	−0.2	0.5	−0.1	0.8	0.4
China	2,054	1,476	2	1	0.2	0.1	0.6	0.3	1.1	0.4	2.8	..
Hong Kong, China	8	4	1	1	0.0	0.0	0.0	0.0	..	0.0	..	..
Colombia	196	441	5	10	0.2	0.6	0.9	3.6	0.9	2.3	1.1	..
Congo, Dem. Rep.	158	807	3	16	5.5	14.7	102.8	199.5	..	..	26.2	..
Congo, Rep.	270	420	86	115	16.2	19.1	52.0	59.7	14.0	16.9	30.8	10.5
Costa Rica	−8	5	−2	1	−0.1	0.0	−0.3	0.1	−0.1	0.1	−0.3	0.1
Côte d'Ivoire	446	1,069	30	65	4.1	9.6	26.4	87.4	9.0	23.0	17.4	9.6
Croatia	40	166	9	37	0.2	0.8	0.7	2.7	0.3	1.2	0.5	1.3
Cuba	65	61	6	5	0.3	..	3.7	..	..	..	..	..
Czech Republic	117	393	11	38	0.2	0.6	0.7	2.0	0.3	0.7	0.6	1.4
Denmark												
Dominican Republic	71	157	9	18	0.5	0.8	2.3	3.1	0.8	1.4	2.8	..
Ecuador	155	216	13	17	0.7	1.0	3.0	3.2	2.1	2.4	..	..
Egypt, Arab Rep.	1,985	1,286	33	19	2.6	1.4	14.4	8.5	9.0	6.3	8.6	..
El Salvador	279	233	47	36	2.5	1.7	16.5	10.0	6.3	3.7	..	67.8
Eritrea	123	230	33	54	14.3	30.8	57.5	135.6	..	40.7	..	..
Estonia	66	69	47	51	1.5	1.1	4.6	3.4	1.5	1.0	4.5	4.1
Ethiopia	579	1,307	10	19	8.4	21.7	53.3	105.2	39.6	63.0	38.7	..
Finland												
France												
Gabon	39	72	33	55	0.8	1.7	2.4	5.1	1.4	2.5	..	..
Gambia, The	39	61	33	44	9.7	17.3	55.1	79.0	13.2	..	..	..
Georgia	242	313	45	60	6.5	9.2	58.0	43.6	16.4	20.5	39.8	74.6
Germany												
Ghana	494	653	27	32	7.3	10.8	28.9	53.8	17.7	18.6	..	..
Greece												
Guatemala	264	249	25	21	1.5	1.1	10.9	5.7	5.9	3.5	..	..
Guinea	381	250	55	32	10.4	7.9	42.7	46.4	39.9	23.2	..	..
Guinea-Bissau	124	59	99	41	48.9	30.5	212.4	198.7	120.8	..	..	..
Haiti	325	156	43	19	9.9	4.5	40.3	22.1	35.9	..	93.4	..

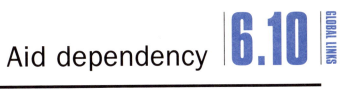
	Net official development assistance or official aid		Aid per capita		Aid dependency ratios							
					Aid as % of GNI		Aid as % of gross capital formation		Aid as % of imports of goods and services		Aid as % of central government expenditure	
	$ millions		$									
	1997	2002	1997	2002	1997	2002	1997	2002	1997	2002	1997	2002
Honduras	297	435	50	64	6.6	6.8	19.5	23.8	10.6	11.9	..	..
Hungary	180	471	18	46	0.4	0.7	1.5	3.0	0.7	1.0	0.9	1.9
India	1,648	1,463	2	1	0.4	0.3	1.8	1.3	2.6	1.6	2.6	2.1
Indonesia	810	1,308	4	6	0.4	0.8	1.2	5.3	1.1	2.1	2.1	4.3
Iran, Islamic Rep.	200	116	3	2	0.2	0.1	0.9	0.3	1.1	0.4	0.5	..
Iraq	220	116	10	5	..	..	..	..	..	..	..	..
Ireland												
Israel	1,196	754	205	115	1.2	0.7	4.8	4.0	2.8	1.5	2.5	0.3
Italy												
Jamaica	72	24	28	9	1.1	0.3	3.3	0.9	1.6	0.4	2.7	1.8
Japan												
Jordan	462	534	104	103	6.6	5.8	24.8	25.0	8.2	8.1	19.5	15.1
Kazakhstan	140	188	9	13	0.6	0.8	4.1	2.8	1.6	1.5	3.2	4.6
Kenya	448	393	16	13	4.3	3.2	27.1	23.5	11.1	10.3	17.2	..
Korea, Dem. Rep.	88	267	4	12	..	..	..	..	..	..	..	..
Korea, Rep.	−160	−82	−3	−2	−0.0	−0.0	−0.1	−0.1	−0.1	−0.0	−0.2	..
Kuwait	0	5	0	2	0.0	0.0	0.0	0.1	0.0	0.0	0.0	..
Kyrgyz Republic	240	186	51	37	14.1	12.0	62.5	62.7	27.0	24.4	60.6	70.0
Lao PDR	329	278	67	50	19.3	17.3	69.4	..	44.4	..	..	..
Latvia	81	86	33	37	1.4	1.0	6.3	3.8	2.3	1.7	4.6	4.8
Lebanon	251	456	61	103	1.6	2.5	6.4	14.7	3.1	5.9	4.0	..
Lesotho	92	76	54	43	6.8	8.7	17.1	26.7	7.6	9.5	18.1	..
Liberia	76	52	26	16	28.8	11.0	..	..	..	..	..	..
Libya	7	10	1	2	..	..	0.2	0.4	0.1	..	..	..
Lithuania	104	147	29	42	1.1	1.1	4.2	4.7	1.6	1.7	3.9	4.1
Macedonia, FYR	98	277	49	136	2.7	7.4	12.5	37.0	5.1	12.4	..	..
Madagascar	834	373	59	23	24.1	8.6	183.5	59.4	69.8	33.8	147.4	..
Malawi	344	377	36	35	13.8	20.2	111.3	160.0	35.9	44.9	..	..
Malaysia	−240	86	−11	4	−0.3	0.1	−0.6	0.4	−0.2	0.1	−1.2	..
Mali	429	472	43	42	17.7	15.1	84.1	69.1	44.4	31.8	..	..
Mauritania	238	355	98	128	22.8	45.4	123.5	116.5	42.8	..	..	..
Mauritius	43	24	38	20	1.0	0.5	3.6	2.4	1.6	0.8	4.5	2.1
Mexico	105	136	1	1	0.0	0.0	0.1	0.1	0.1	0.1	0.2	..
Moldova	65	142	15	33	3.3	8.0	14.2	38.4	4.3	10.2	8.1	33.4
Mongolia	251	208	108	85	28.1	18.6	96.8	60.8	43.6	21.6	112.4	65.7
Morocco	464	636	17	21	1.4	1.8	6.7	7.8	3.9	4.4	4.5	..
Mozambique	948	2,058	57	112	29.5	60.4	135.6	127.9	80.3	103.4	..	..
Myanmar	50	121	1	2	..	..	..	..	1.9	..	0.3	..
Namibia	166	135	96	68	4.1	4.2	22.6	19.3	7.1	8.3	12.6	..
Nepal	402	365	19	15	8.2	6.6	32.2	26.8	20.7	24.2	49.5	37.6
Netherlands												
New Zealand												
Nicaragua	411	517	88	97	24.1	13.6	66.0	40.3	21.8	23.7	60.4	84.9
Niger	333	298	34	26	18.3	13.8	166.1	107.7	..	..	..	..
Nigeria	200	314	2	2	0.6	0.8	3.2	3.1	1.1	1.8	..	..
Norway												
Oman	65	41	29	16	0.4	0.2	2.3	1.6	0.9	..	1.4	0.0
Pakistan	596	2,144	5	15	1.0	3.6	5.3	24.7	3.8	14.3	4.5	15.2
Panama	46	35	17	12	0.5	0.3	1.7	1.1	0.4	0.4	2.0	..
Papua New Guinea	346	203	73	38	7.4	7.5	33.5	..	12.6	..	24.0	..
Paraguay	108	57	22	10	1.1	1.0	4.8	3.8	2.1	2.0	6.8	4.8
Peru	395	491	16	18	0.7	0.9	2.8	4.7	2.9	4.2	3.9	4.6
Philippines	689	560	10	7	0.8	0.7	3.4	3.7	1.3	1.3	4.3	4.2
Poland	861	1,160	22	30	0.6	0.6	2.4	3.2	1.8	1.7	1.5	1.5
Portugal												
Puerto Rico												

6.10 Aid dependency

| | Net official development assistance or official aid ($ millions) | | Aid per capita ($) | | Aid dependency ratios | | | | | | | |
| | | | | | Aid as % of GNI | | Aid as % of gross capital formation | | Aid as % of imports of goods and services | | Aid as % of central government expenditure | |
	1997	2002	1997	2002	1997	2002	1997	2002	1997	2002	1997	2002
Romania	219	701	10	31	0.6	1.5	3.0	6.6	1.7	3.6	2.0	5.3
Russian Federation	793	1,301	5	9	0.2	0.4	0.9	1.8	0.8	1.3	..	1.5
Rwanda	230	356	32	44	12.5	20.8	89.8	109.2	45.8	77.1	..	..
Saudi Arabia	11	27	1	1	0.0	0.0	0.0	0.1	0.0	0.1	..	..
Senegal	423	449	48	46	9.8	9.2	54.2	45.3	24.8	19.9	50.5	41.0
Serbia and Montenegro	97	1,931	9	237	..	12.4	4.8	76.6	1.9	27.5	..	..
Sierra Leone	119	353	25	68	14.3	47.0	278.9	514.7	..	..	81.3	..
Singapore	3	7	1	2	0.0	0.0	0.0	0.0	0.0	0.0	0.0	0.0
Slovak Republic	71	189	13	35	0.3	0.8	1.0	2.6	0.5	1.0	0.8	2.1
Slovenia	99	171	50	87	0.5	0.8	2.3	3.3	0.9	1.3	1.4	1.7
Somalia	81	194	10	21	..	..	..	..	..	..	..	..
South Africa	496	657	12	14	0.3	0.6	2.0	4.0	1.3	1.8	1.1	1.3
Spain												
Sri Lanka	331	344	19	18	2.2	2.1	9.0	9.9	4.7	4.6	8.5	7.6
Sudan	139	351	5	11	1.3	2.7	6.6	13.3	8.7	9.7	..	..
Swaziland	28	25	29	23	1.8	2.0	9.6	11.6	2.1	1.9	..	..
Sweden												
Switzerland												
Syrian Arab Republic	197	81	13	5	1.4	0.4	6.4	1.8	3.2	1.1	1.2	..
Tajikistan	86	168	14	27	8.0	14.6	39.5	61.2	9.8	18.2	..	..
Tanzania	945	1,233	30	35	12.5	13.2	82.5	78.7	44.4	53.3	..	..
Thailand	626	296	11	5	0.4	0.2	1.2	1.0	0.8	0.4	2.1	1.2
Togo	125	51	31	11	8.5	3.8	51.3	17.0	16.4	6.9	..	..
Trinidad and Tobago	33	−7	26	−6	0.6	−0.1	1.6	−0.5	0.9	−0.1	..	..
Tunisia	194	475	21	49	1.1	2.4	3.9	9.0	2.0	4.1	3.2	..
Turkey	7	636	0	9	0.0	0.4	0.0	2.1	0.0	1.0	0.0	0.2
Turkmenistan	12	41	3	8	0.4	..	1.2	1.7	0.7	..	..	..
Uganda	813	638	38	26	13.0	11.2	77.2	50.7	46.0	35.4	..	65.5
Ukraine	268	484	5	10	0.5	1.2	2.5	6.1	1.2	2.2	..	4.7
United Arab Emirates	2	4	1	1	0.0	..	0.0	..	..	..	0.0	..
United Kingdom												
United States												
Uruguay	34	13	11	4	0.2	0.1	1.0	0.9	0.7	0.5	0.5	0.3
Uzbekistan	140	189	6	7	1.3	2.4	5.7	11.8	3.0	6.5	..	..
Venezuela, RB	9	57	0	2	0.0	0.1	0.0	0.4	0.0	0.3	0.0	0.1
Vietnam	998	1,277	13	16	3.8	3.6	13.1	11.3	7.0	5.7	16.5	16.2
West Bank and Gaza	603	1,616	230	500	13.1	42.9	35.9	1,349.0	..	..	..	..
Yemen, Rep.	356	584	22	31	5.6	6.3	20.8	35.1	9.5	12.2	16.1	..
Zambia	610	641	66	63	16.5	18.1	107.0	99.4	37.3	36.6	..	..
Zimbabwe	336	201	28	15	4.2	..	22.0	29.2	..	..	11.1	..
World	**54,482 s**	**69,814 s**	**9 w**	**11 w**	**0.2 w**	**0.2 w**	**0.8 w**	**1.0 w**	**0.7 w**	**0.7 w**	**..**	**..**
Low income	21,534	29,622	9	12	2.1	2.7	8.9	13.1	7.9	9.5	..	..
Middle income	18,914	25,382	7	9	0.4	0.5	1.4	1.9	1.3	1.4	..	..
Lower middle income	15,853	19,979	7	8	0.5	0.6	1.7	2.1	1.8	1.9	..	..
Upper middle income	2,578	4,018	8	12	0.2	0.2	0.7	1.2	0.4	0.6	..	..
Low & middle income	52,324	67,945	11	13	0.9	1.1	3.4	4.4	3.0	3.3	..	..
East Asia & Pacific	6,939	7,340	4	4	0.5	0.4	1.3	1.2	1.4	1.1	..	..
Europe & Central Asia	7,121	12,819	15	27	0.7	1.1	2.7	5.3	1.8	2.7	..	..
Latin America & Carib.	5,399	5,108	11	10	0.3	0.3	1.2	1.6	1.2	1.1	..	..
Middle East & N. Africa	5,440	6,527	20	21	0.9	1.0	4.5	4.3	3.2	3.4	..	..
South Asia	4,313	6,615	3	5	0.8	1.0	3.6	4.9	4.5	5.3	..	..
Sub-Saharan Africa	14,976	19,406	24	28	4.5	6.3	24.5	32.2	12.4	15.3	..	..
High income												
Europe EMU												

Note: Regional aggregates include data for economies not specified elsewhere. World and income group totals include aid not allocated by country or region.

6.10

About the data

Ratios of aid to gross national income (GNI), gross capital formation, imports, and government spending provide a measure of the recipient country's dependency on aid. But care must be taken in drawing policy conclusions. For foreign policy reasons some countries have traditionally received large amounts of aid. Thus aid dependency ratios may reveal as much about a donor's interest as they do about a recipient's needs. Ratios in Sub-Saharan Africa are generally much higher than those in other regions, and they increased in the 1980s. These high ratios are due only in part to aid flows. Many African countries saw severe erosion in their terms of trade in the 1980s, which, along with weak policies, contributed to falling incomes, imports, and investment. Thus the increase in aid dependency ratios reflects events affecting both the numerator and the denominator.

As defined here, aid includes official development assistance (ODA) and official aid (see *About the data* for table 6.8). The data cover loans and grants from Development Assistance Committee (DAC) member countries, multilateral organizations, and non-DAC donors. They do not reflect aid given by recipient countries to other developing countries. As a result, some countries that are net donors (such as Saudi Arabia) are shown in the table as aid recipients (see table 6.9a).

The data in the table do not distinguish among different types of aid (program, project, or food aid; emergency assistance; postconflict peacekeeping assistance; or technical cooperation), each of which may have very different effects on the economy.

Expenditures on technical cooperation do not always directly benefit the economy to the extent that they defray costs incurred outside the country on the salaries and benefits of technical experts and the overhead costs of firms supplying technical services.

In 1999, to avoid double counting extrabudgetary expenditures reported by DAC countries and flows reported by the United Nations, all United Nations agencies revised their data since 1990 to include only regular budgetary expenditures (except for the World Food Programme and the United Nations High Commissioner for Refugees, which revised their data from 1996 onward). These revisions have affected net ODA and official aid and, as a result, aid per capita and aid dependency ratios.

Because the table relies on information from donors, it is not consistent with information recorded by recipients in the balance of payments, which often excludes all or some technical assistance—particularly payments to expatriates made directly by the donor. Similarly, grant commodity aid may not always be recorded in trade data or in the balance of payments. Moreover, DAC statistics exclude purely military aid.

The nominal values used here may overstate the real value of aid to the recipient. Changes in international prices and in exchange rates can reduce the purchasing power of aid. The practice of tying aid, still prevalent though declining in importance, also tends to reduce its purchasing power (see *About the data* for table 6.9).

The values for population, GNI, gross capital formation, imports of goods and services, and central government expenditure used in computing the ratios are taken from World Bank and International Monetary Fund (IMF) databases. The aggregates also refer to World Bank definitions. Therefore the ratios shown may differ somewhat from those computed and published by the Organisation for Economic Co-operation and Development (OECD). Aid not allocated by country or region—including administrative costs, research on development issues, and aid to nongovernmental organizations—is included in the world total. Thus regional and income group totals do not sum to the world total.

Definitions

• **Net official development assistance** consists of disbursements of loans made on concessional terms (net of repayments of principal) and grants by official agencies of the members of DAC, by multilateral institutions, and by non-DAC countries to promote economic development and welfare in countries and territories in part I of the DAC list of aid recipients. It includes loans with a grant element of at least 25 percent (calculated at a rate of discount of 10 percent). • **Net official aid** refers to aid flows (net of repayments) from official donors to countries and territories in part II of the DAC list of aid recipients: more advanced countries of Central and Eastern Europe, the countries of the former Soviet Union, and certain advanced developing countries and territories. Official aid is provided under terms and conditions similar to those for ODA. • **Aid per capita** includes both ODA and official aid. • **Aid dependency ratios** are calculated using values in U.S. dollars converted at official exchange rates. For definitions of GNI, gross capital formation, imports of goods and services, and central government expenditure, see *Definitions* for tables 1.1, 4.9, and 4.12.

6.10a

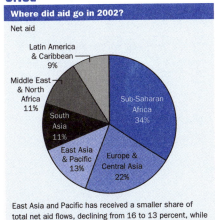

Where did aid go in 2002?

Net aid

East Asia and Pacific has received a smaller share of total net aid flows, declining from 16 to 13 percent, while flows to Europe and Central Asia increased from 16 to 22 percent.

Source: Organisation for Economic Co-operation and Development, Development Assistance Committee.

Data sources

The data on financial flows are compiled by DAC and published in its annual statistical report, *Geographical Distribution of Financial Flows to Aid Recipients,* and in its annual *Development Cooperation Report.* Data are available in electronic format on the OECD's *International Development Statistics* CD-ROM and to registered users at http://www.oecd.org/dataoecd/50/17/5037721.htm. The data on population, GNI, gross capital formation, imports of goods and services, and central government expenditure are from World Bank and IMF databases.

$ millions	Total 2002	United States 2002	Japan 2002	France 2002	Germany 2002	United Kingdom 2002	Netherlands 2002	Canada 2002	Sweden 2002	Norway 2002	Denmark 2002	Other DAC donors 2002
Afghanistan	985.9	367.6	31.7	11.9	92.6	130.8	88.3	35.8	27.5	60.9	7.8	131.2
Albania	177.2	61.8	4.0	3.0	24.7	4.9	11.6	1.3	4.0	5.8	3.3	52.9
Algeria	122.8	5.2	−2.2	89.6	−3.9	..	0.4	0.4	0.7	3.2	0.0	29.6
Angola	286.4	105.6	27.2	9.9	16.5	10.2	27.7	2.6	14.1	22.2	1.0	49.4
Argentina	51.9	1.6	12.9	11.7	13.1	..	0.3	2.1	0.2	0.1	0.0	10.0
Armenia	171.4	114.3	11.4	3.8	19.9	1.7	7.2	0.7	1.1	3.3	0.2	7.8
Australia												
Austria												
Azerbaijan	232.2	61.5	141.8	2.9	9.8	0.5	4.1	0.8	0.4	3.5	..	6.9
Bangladesh	520.8	72.1	122.7	7.3	30.0	101.8	44.3	30.9	15.0	16.6	37.3	42.7
Belarus	26.0	8.4	0.2	2.8	6.8	0.1	1.0	0.1	2.9	0.2	1.0	2.6
Belgium												
Benin	140.1	23.4	4.5	40.5	24.0	0.1	2.4	2.4	0.1	0.1	23.6	19.0
Bolivia	482.2	127.7	37.5	33.9	71.9	14.2	62.6	14.6	16.4	3.3	30.6	69.4
Bosnia and Herzegovina	292.3	75.8	14.7	2.4	19.4	7.3	37.3	6.9	27.0	23.8	0.4	77.2
Botswana	36.7	22.4	−0.1	0.6	4.5	2.2	1.9	0.2	0.6	3.2	0.8	0.6
Brazil	197.6	−37.1	117.6	20.5	31.9	16.6	14.7	6.0	2.0	2.9	0.4	22.1
Bulgaria	189.2	47.5	36.7	14.9	49.2	7.0	7.9	1.3	0.2	0.5	3.3	20.7
Burkina Faso	229.9	16.2	10.0	53.9	19.4	0.3	37.3	8.6	7.5	0.4	23.0	53.3
Burundi	84.7	21.2	0.1	7.1	2.7	1.2	9.6	1.8	3.6	10.2	..	27.2
Cambodia	272.8	44.4	98.6	24.6	18.4	13.2	9.3	4.9	14.5	3.1	6.6	35.0
Cameroon	436.2	13.1	7.5	119.0	67.0	43.5	7.5	80.3	0.0	5.7	17.0	75.5
Canada												
Central African Republic	39.6	0.8	12.9	16.5	7.1	0.4	0.4	0.1	0.2	..	..	1.2
Chad	67.0	7.0	0.1	34.8	13.0	..	0.8	0.5	0.0	..	..	10.8
Chile	−13.8	−18.4	−39.6	11.8	18.7	0.3	3.3	1.6	0.9	0.5	0.0	7.1
China	1,212.8	17.0	828.7	77.2	149.9	36.1	17.9	30.0	6.4	12.2	6.3	31.1
Hong Kong, China	4.0	..	2.2	1.6	0.0	..	0.1	..	..	..	..	0.1
Colombia	426.1	306.3	4.3	13.0	21.4	3.2	15.2	6.1	6.9	7.7	0.2	41.9
Congo, Dem. Rep.	351.0	80.0	0.9	0.8	21.1	14.9	135.0	9.8	7.7	12.5	..	68.4
Congo, Rep.	41.4	5.9	0.2	23.7	2.6	0.3	0.2	0.4	2.2	0.4	..	5.6
Costa Rica	4.5	−23.7	−2.8	4.8	3.1	−0.1	6.2	3.7	1.1	0.5	0.0	11.7
Côte d'Ivoire	831.1	53.1	5.2	531.3	31.1	11.7	24.3	78.7	0.2	0.5	0.7	94.2
Croatia	82.1	49.5	0.5	2.5	2.2	2.1	1.6	1.1	5.5	13.2	0.1	3.7
Cuba	49.6	4.6	3.7	2.8	4.3	0.6	1.7	5.4	1.9	1.2	..	23.5
Czech Republic	48.5	2.5	1.6	8.3	16.3	1.3	1.2	0.3	1.2	0.3	2.4	13.1
Denmark												
Dominican Republic	138.2	15.7	42.7	5.9	8.0	25.9	1.4	1.0	0.2	0.4	0.4	36.6
Ecuador	205.1	65.0	28.3	6.8	16.4	0.6	10.5	9.2	0.6	2.3	4.8	60.6
Egypt, Arab Rep.	1,124.2	845.8	12.9	100.1	61.9	12.2	17.1	10.3	2.2	0.6	16.1	44.9
El Salvador	217.9	62.0	32.9	3.0	15.2	11.1	8.4	3.3	5.3	1.7	1.3	73.8
Eritrea	120.7	44.9	4.3	4.3	3.7	1.2	12.6	1.1	4.2	13.5	10.2	20.8
Estonia	16.9	−7.7	0.6	1.3	2.4	0.2	0.6	0.3	3.4	0.7	12.2	3.1
Ethiopia	489.2	156.4	50.5	10.2	40.6	43.7	34.8	6.9	21.3	28.5	2.7	93.7
Finland												
France												
Gabon	49.5	2.3	3.8	41.0	0.5	0.2	0.3	0.9	..	..	..	0.5
Gambia, The	17.5	2.8	8.2	0.4	1.8	1.7	0.3	0.6	0.5	0.7	0.2	0.4
Georgia	209.6	133.3	18.6	1.9	21.0	3.9	8.9	0.7	2.0	4.4	0.3	14.4
Germany												
Ghana	406.2	68.9	23.6	10.2	34.0	123.7	59.6	12.4	1.4	0.7	51.5	20.4
Greece												
Guatemala	199.6	64.7	29.4	1.4	19.0	0.6	20.6	10.2	11.3	11.5	1.9	29.0
Guinea	125.6	47.7	18.6	22.6	15.4	2.7	4.0	4.3	0.5	0.6	..	9.4
Guinea-Bissau	25.8	3.8	0.1	4.0	1.4	..	3.6	0.3	1.8	0.0	0.3	10.5
Haiti	125.4	69.9	9.3	17.2	4.3	0.2	4.2	10.2	0.4	1.7	0.1	8.1

Distribution of net aid by Development Assistance Committee members

	Total	Ten major DAC donors										Other DAC donors
		United States	Japan	France	Germany	United Kingdom	Netherlands	Canada	Sweden	Norway	Denmark	
	2002	2002	2002	2002	2002	2002	2002	2002	2002	2002	2002	2002
Honduras	297.9	97.3	94.9	3.9	13.4	1.9	8.9	7.1	11.0	0.9	12.7	46.0
Hungary	40.3	1.9	6.9	7.5	11.5	2.4	1.2	0.4	0.2	0.3	0.3	7.8
India	785.3	–3.8	493.6	–135.9	–26.1	343.7	59.4	16.0	8.2	8.5	8.5	13.2
Indonesia	1,162.0	225.8	538.3	44.8	78.4	31.7	127.3	11.6	1.6	6.1	1.9	94.7
Iran, Islamic Rep.	81.5	0.2	17.5	7.9	31.8	2.8	3.8	..	0.0	5.3	..	12.1
Iraq	85.1	0.0	0.1	2.0	18.4	13.7	15.8	0.3	4.5	17.9	..	12.3
Ireland												
Israel	749.3	786.8	0.6	6.2	–50.4	..	2.0	..	1.5	..	..	2.6
Italy												
Jamaica	–3.6	–11.0	–6.6	–0.9	–0.8	7.4	1.6	7.1	0.1	0.6	..	–1.2
Japan												
Jordan	370.9	286.8	–0.2	3.2	51.1	5.0	0.3	3.7	4.2	2.3	0.1	14.5
Kazakhstan	143.9	74.0	30.1	2.3	13.1	1.1	2.0	0.7	0.5	1.8	0.4	18.0
Kenya	288.1	102.4	17.4	17.6	27.1	54.4	12.7	7.3	14.4	3.0	9.7	22.2
Korea, Dem. Rep.	187.8	131.2	..	0.5	33.2	3.0	0.6	0.2	4.3	3.6	..	11.4
Korea, Rep.	–79.8	–44.6	–47.2	11.5	–0.2	..	0.1	..	..	..	..	0.7
Kuwait	3.0	..	0.1	1.4	1.5	..	0.0	..	..	..	..	..
Kyrgyz Republic	95.2	51.7	8.1	0.4	11.0	4.5	1.7	0.7	0.8	1.3	0.6	14.4
Lao PDR	177.8	8.5	90.1	14.9	12.0	1.0	2.0	1.5	15.4	5.7	5.0	21.9
Latvia	26.2	0.8	0.4	1.4	3.8	0.1	0.4	0.5	5.7	0.8	9.8	2.5
Lebanon	102.4	36.2	10.1	33.2	7.2	0.2	0.4	1.3	1.1	5.3	..	7.4
Lesotho	29.7	6.0	3.9	–0.9	4.7	1.7	0.7	0.2	0.3	0.4	0.8	11.9
Liberia	27.0	15.1	0.0	1.7	–2.1	2.9	2.9	0.3	1.1	1.9	0.1	3.1
Libya	4.4	..	0.2	1.6	1.7	..	0.1	..	..	..	..	0.8
Lithuania	36.0	–1.5	1.5	2.0	6.9	0.1	0.7	0.8	13.3	1.0	8.9	2.3
Macedonia, FYR	179.8	50.5	3.8	2.0	16.8	7.6	17.6	2.0	6.2	11.7	1.0	60.6
Madagascar	125.9	41.7	7.6	46.3	8.6	0.7	0.4	1.2	0.1	5.7	0.0	13.5
Malawi	224.9	61.2	18.8	5.1	24.0	50.2	16.9	8.5	7.7	15.6	7.8	9.3
Malaysia	85.4	1.1	54.2	–2.7	4.5	–0.1	0.9	0.7	..	0.3	26.0	0.6
Mali	256.8	49.2	17.0	63.6	28.0	6.8	38.2	13.6	9.1	7.1	0.1	24.1
Mauritania	146.6	5.5	13.0	20.0	25.6	19.4	27.6	2.2	0.3	0.5	..	32.5
Mauritius	3.5	0.2	0.7	–0.2	1.4	0.2	0.1	0.2	..	0.3	..	0.6
Mexico	92.6	84.0	–6.6	–0.2	15.0	2.6	3.3	3.9	0.4	0.4	–0.2	–9.8
Moldova	86.3	56.9	5.9	2.3	2.4	3.3	3.5	0.3	4.6	1.1	1.5	4.6
Mongolia	141.3	20.4	79.0	1.0	23.2	0.6	2.6	0.9	2.4	2.6	–0.9	7.7
Morocco	218.7	–13.3	40.8	145.8	16.9	..	1.2	4.4	0.8	0.2	–0.9	22.8
Mozambique	1,661.0	159.7	69.7	431.6	156.9	48.0	52.0	9.0	45.3	38.7	51.9	598.2
Myanmar	79.1	4.8	49.4	1.5	1.7	6.5	4.2	1.3	0.9	3.9	0.9	4.1
Namibia	84.8	17.0	3.2	3.0	18.3	3.0	4.8	0.7	9.4	3.4	1.9	20.2
Nepal	279.4	32.6	97.5	–1.9	34.5	36.9	7.3	4.2	3.6	13.1	25.4	26.3
Netherlands												
New Zealand												
Nicaragua	287.2	66.7	31.4	0.9	34.5	0.4	26.0	7.7	38.7	9.1	25.0	47.0
Niger	114.5	16.3	13.3	34.4	14.9	0.6	1.8	5.3	0.1	2.4	6.8	18.7
Nigeria	215.0	76.1	19.1	8.8	37.7	41.7	2.8	18.1	1.5	3.1	0.0	6.2
Norway												
Oman	–0.4	–4.9	3.7	0.6	0.1	..	0.0	..	..	..	..	0.1
Pakistan	702.5	209.0	301.1	2.5	76.2	66.9	12.2	7.8	1.6	10.3	–1.2	16.2
Panama	23.3	6.0	5.3	0.8	1.7	0.2	0.5	0.8	..	..	2.0	6.0
Papua New Guinea	197.1	0.2	4.4	0.6	3.2	..	1.3	0.0	0.1	0.2	..	187.2
Paraguay	50.8	11.2	26.8	0.2	3.5	–0.2	1.4	0.9	1.3	0.6	..	5.1
Peru	463.0	143.6	119.6	4.9	24.3	84.4	12.9	7.9	3.9	1.4	2.1	57.9
Philippines	509.1	78.6	318.0	–2.4	14.5	1.3	25.9	15.6	1.6	1.0	2.2	52.9
Poland	388.6	3.1	–3.8	159.6	37.3	3.2	1.1	70.8	4.1	1.1	14.3	97.9
Portugal												
Puerto Rico												

6.11 Distribution of net aid by Development Assistance Committee members

	Total	Ten major DAC donors										Other DAC donors
		United States	Japan	France	Germany	United Kingdom	Netherlands	Canada	Sweden	Norway	Denmark	
	2002	2002	2002	2002	2002	2002	2002	2002	2002	2002	2002	2002
Romania	176.6	54.7	29.6	23.6	29.7	9.7	6.8	2.2	0.6	1.3	6.0	12.5
Russian Federation	1,109.3	858.8	5.3	23.8	54.1	41.5	8.2	12.8	31.7	22.7	13.2	37.2
Rwanda	199.1	46.4	0.4	6.6	10.8	52.6	19.6	5.6	15.6	6.1	0.5	35.0
Saudi Arabia	13.4	..	9.0	3.7	0.6	..	0.0	0.0	..	0.0	..	0.1
Senegal	242.8	37.1	37.8	104.5	13.2	0.6	10.4	9.8	0.3	1.4	0.9	26.9
Serbia and Montenegro	1,921.3	495.4	0.3	103.7	531.4	459.7	61.9	..	24.5	22.1	8.0	214.2
Sierra Leone	225.3	70.1	0.1	3.6	15.9	54.3	20.6	3.3	1.7	10.6	0.4	44.6
Singapore	7.1	..	2.0	3.2	1.5	0.1	0.0	0.2	..	..	..	0.1
Slovak Republic	39.2	4.9	3.6	4.1	6.7	4.3	1.5	0.7	0.2	0.3	3.9	9.0
Slovenia	2.4	0.3	0.3	1.4	−2.9	0.2	0.0	0.0	0.0	0.1	..	3.0
Somalia	102.4	35.4	..	0.4	2.8	3.1	13.1	0.2	5.5	25.4	1.4	15.2
South Africa	375.3	89.4	4.7	25.4	42.4	47.0	45.6	9.5	22.0	17.5	18.8	53.2
Spain												
Sri Lanka	188.5	−11.0	118.9	−2.5	7.8	7.7	18.6	3.5	15.0	21.5	0.2	8.8
Sudan	232.3	119.6	1.2	2.4	14.5	13.5	22.7	4.9	9.6	23.3	0.6	19.9
Swaziland	6.6	−0.2	4.5	0.0	−2.1	−1.4	1.1	0.2	0.2	0.2	−0.2	4.3
Sweden												
Switzerland												
Syrian Arab Republic	25.0	..	15.8	13.5	−12.8	0.1	2.3	0.2	0.2	0.8	..	4.9
Tajikistan	128.8	75.9	27.0	0.2	10.2	3.3	0.6	1.5	2.0	1.4	0.1	6.8
Tanzania	902.8	85.4	58.2	16.0	23.2	103.2	138.3	8.3	61.4	46.7	69.9	292.3
Thailand	280.4	36.4	222.4	−7.1	−4.2	0.3	2.4	2.5	3.6	1.6	8.5	14.1
Togo	39.2	6.7	0.3	18.7	8.1	0.5	0.5	1.0	0.1	0.2	0.1	3.1
Trinidad and Tobago	5.7	0.6	2.7	0.8	0.1	0.2	0.0	1.3	..	..	..	0.1
Tunisia	144.6	−20.8	63.3	96.6	−5.2	..	−3.2	0.8	0.1	0.1	..	12.9
Turkey	99.0	144.5	−15.9	9.1	−71.0	−0.7	0.3	1.1	1.7	4.2	0.0	25.7
Turkmenistan	26.0	12.1	11.4	0.4	0.8	0.2	0.0	0.4	..	0.2	..	0.4
Uganda	466.1	109.4	8.1	5.5	33.9	84.0	43.5	6.4	23.4	32.6	43.1	76.3
Ukraine	358.2	255.5	1.6	6.8	44.6	12.5	2.8	14.0	5.0	0.2	5.1	10.1
United Arab Emirates	3.7	0.4	0.1	2.6	0.5	0.1	..	..	..	..	..	0.0
United Kingdom												
United States												
Uruguay	6.8	−1.7	4.1	2.4	2.0	0.0	0.1	0.7	0.1	..	..	−0.9
Uzbekistan	152.9	74.3	40.2	1.6	21.6	1.4	0.7	0.5	0.1	2.6	..	10.0
Venezuela, RB	42.0	10.9	3.7	5.0	3.0	0.1	0.3	1.4	0.1	0.1	..	17.5
Vietnam	746.0	14.7	374.7	77.8	41.7	26.5	30.1	20.0	24.4	7.9	48.4	79.9
West Bank and Gaza	410.2	138.1	12.8	15.6	37.9	23.8	13.9	8.9	28.0	50.9	5.5	74.8
Yemen, Rep.	119.4	24.1	6.0	4.2	28.4	7.8	40.8	0.5	0.4	0.4	..	7.0
Zambia	359.5	48.3	68.4	10.1	44.2	28.1	35.5	12.2	19.4	29.1	32.2	32.1
Zimbabwe	177.8	47.0	23.6	3.2	10.3	28.7	22.3	6.5	8.3	7.2	5.6	15.0
World	**45,249.8 s**	**12,814.5 s**	**6,748.3 s**	**4,677.7 s**	**3,593.5 s**	**3,593.3 s**	**2,624.9 s**	**1,607.2 s**	**1,350.3 s**	**1,188.3 s**	**1,133.5 s**	**5,918.3 s**
Low income	17,698.7	3,559.1	3,141.6	1,788.8	1,368.2	1,648.9	1,325.7	496.4	463.6	533.4	541.3	2,831.6
Middle income	15,415.8	5,022.6	2,555.7	1,444.8	1,609.6	991.4	553.0	447.7	315.0	363.8	268.1	1,844.3
Lower middle income	13,328.4	4,744.1	2,421.5	952.0	1,390.9	885.7	502.7	218.5	264.9	272.3	156.1	1,519.7
Upper middle income	1,467.5	179.2	118.3	433.6	164.2	96.4	26.2	95.6	37.9	28.4	80.6	207.2
Low & middle income	43,667.3	12,042.3	6,780.0	3,904.1	3,637.0	3,592.8	2,528.2	1,606.5	1,348.8	1,187.7	1,133.5	5,906.4
East Asia & Pacific	5,742.1	778.1	2,755.2	317.8	378.7	138.3	226.5	96.4	79.8	56.0	107.0	808.3
Europe & Central Asia	7,112.1	3,004.4	401.6	422.8	902.6	593.2	196.1	233.6	183.9	184.6	143.1	846.1
Latin America & Carib.	3,891.7	1,207.3	583.2	174.6	355.2	292.4	218.8	143.1	126.0	60.1	89.5	641.5
Middle East & N. Africa	2,914.9	1,310.6	195.9	561.7	243.4	65.7	93.8	31.8	44.2	87.4	20.9	259.6
South Asia	3,518.0	667.2	1,190.0	−118.6	216.3	688.2	233.8	99.0	71.3	133.4	88.3	249.1
Sub-Saharan Africa	11,675.0	2,369.4	579.5	2,129.8	935.0	1,022.0	939.5	374.1	404.5	447.8	392.5	2,080.8
High income												
Europe EMU												

Note: Regional aggregates include data for economies not specified elsewhere. World and income group totals include aid not allocated by country or region.

Distribution of net aid by Development Assistance Committee members

About the data

The data in the table show net bilateral aid to low- and middle-income economies from members of the Development Assistance Committee (DAC) of the Organisation for Economic Co-operation and Development (OECD). The DAC compilation of the data includes aid to some countries and territories not shown in the table and small quantities of aid to unspecified economies that are recorded only at the regional or global level. Aid to countries and territories not shown in the table has been assigned to regional totals based on the World Bank's regional classification system. Aid to unspecified economies has been included in regional totals and, when possible, in income group totals. Aid not allocated by country or region—including administrative costs,

research on development issues, and aid to non-governmental organizations—is included in the world total; thus regional and income group totals do not sum to the world total.

In 1999 all United Nations agencies revised their data since 1990 to include only regular budgetary expenditures (except for the World Food Programme and the United Nations High Commissioner for Refugees, which revised their data from 1996 onward). They did so to avoid double counting extra-budgetary expenditures reported by DAC countries and flows reported by the United Nations.

The data in the table are based on donor country reports of bilateral programs, which may differ from reports by recipient countries. Recipients may lack

access to information on such aid expenditures as development-oriented research, stipends and tuition costs for aid-financed students in donor countries, or payment of experts hired by donor countries. Moreover, a full accounting would include donor country contributions to multilateral institutions, the flow of resources from multilateral institutions to recipient countries, and flows from countries that are not members of DAC.

The expenditures that countries report as official development assistance (ODA) have changed. For example, some DAC members have reported as ODA the aid provided to refugees during the first 12 months of their stay within the donor's borders.

Some of the aid recipients shown in the table are also aid donors. See table 6.9a for a summary of ODA from non-DAC countries.

6.11a

Top aid recipients from top DAC donors reflect historical alliances and geopolitical events

Total bilateral aid, 2002

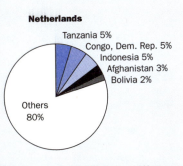

This figure shows the distribution of aid from the top six donors to their top five recipients in 2002. Serbia and Montenegro and Afghanistan drew a large share of aid from donors in 2002.

Source: Organisation for Economic Co-operation and Development, Development Assistance Committee.

Definitions

• **Net aid** comprises net bilateral official development assistance to part I recipients and net bilateral official aid to part II recipients (see *About the data* for table 6.8). • **Other DAC donors** are Australia, Austria, Belgium, Finland, Greece, Ireland, Italy, Luxembourg, New Zealand, Portugal, Spain, and Switzerland.

Data sources

Data on financial flows are compiled by DAC and published in its annual statistical report, *Geographical Distribution of Financial Flows to Aid Recipients*, and its annual *Development Cooperation Report*. Data are available electronically on the OECD's *International Development Statistics* CD-ROM and to registered users at http://www.oecd.org/dataoecd/50/17/5037721.htm.

	International financial institutions ($ millions)							United Nations					Total
	World Bank		IMF		Regional development banks					($ millions)			
	IDA	IBRD	Concessional	Non-concessional	Concessional	Non-concessional	Others	UNDP	UNFPA	UNICEF	WFP	Others	$ millions
	2002	2002	2002	2002	2002	2002	2002	2002	2002	2002	2002	2002	2002
Afghanistan	..	..	..	..	..	..	..	9.0	9.0	9.2	2.0	15.4	44.6
Albania	78.9	0.0	−2.9	−5.7	0.0	3.5	18.7	1.4	0.4	0.7	0.5	3.1	98.5
Algeria	0.0	−129.5	0.0	−297.5	0.0	−33.3	−155.5	0.8	1.3	0.9	4.6	6.2	−602.0
Angola	17.9	0.0	0.0	0.0	−0.3	−2.6	−0.1	1.7	2.4	5.3	30.3	15.8	70.4
Argentina	0.0	−928.3	0.0	−743.0	0.0	−502.3	0.0	0.3	0.3	0.6	..	2.8	−2,169.5
Armenia	66.5	−0.4	15.0	−7.3	0.0	−6.1	−9.4	0.8	0.3	0.6	1.3	3.5	64.8
Australia													
Austria													
Azerbaijan	56.9	0.0	7.8	−46.4	0.0	0.6	11.2	2.2	0.8	0.9	3.3	3.7	40.9
Bangladesh	195.0	−5.5	−22.9	−65.1	84.6	6.2	56.6	14.4	10.3	11.3	25.4	13.3	323.7
Belarus	0.0	−9.8	0.0	−30.3	0.0	−15.3	−5.7	0.2	0.2	..	..	1.5	−59.1
Belgium													
Benin	20.1	0.0	−4.6	0.0	1.1	−0.3	21.2	2.8	3.6	1.6	1.4	3.9	50.8
Bolivia	96.4	0.0	−17.1	0.0	89.2	−54.4	76.8	1.0	3.2	1.2	2.8	3.2	202.3
Bosnia and Herzegovina	96.8	−23.1	0.0	18.2	0.0	−7.5	0.5	1.1	0.1	0.5	..	20.1	106.7
Botswana	−0.5	−3.5	0.0	0.0	−1.5	−12.0	−12.4	0.5	1.3	1.3	..	3.1	−23.7
Brazil	0.0	337.6	0.0	11,246.8	0.0	853.1	−6.4	0.4	0.9	1.2	..	131.0	12,564.6
Bulgaria	0.0	2.1	0.0	−144.0	0.0	−13.7	31.4	0.7	0.2	..	..	2.0	−121.4
Burkina Faso	65.3	0.0	6.4	0.0	37.9	−1.8	1.8	5.0	1.9	4.0	2.2	4.3	126.9
Burundi	25.0	0.0	−2.5	12.5	0.0	0.0	−0.4	5.4	1.5	2.5	5.4	11.5	60.9
Cambodia	47.2	0.0	10.8	−1.4	69.9	0.0	7.0	3.1	3.6	3.5	3.2	5.4	152.4
Cameroon	41.8	−21.0	41.2	0.0	20.6	−40.2	−11.2	1.7	2.3	2.8	1.6	3.4	42.8
Canada													
Central African Republic	0.7	0.0	0.0	0.0	0.0	−0.2	0.0	3.3	1.0	2.0	2.7	4.6	14.1
Chad	70.3	0.3	12.7	0.0	11.2	0.0	5.7	3.7	2.7	2.4	1.7	3.8	114.4
Chile	−0.7	−172.0	0.0	0.0	−1.3	−76.2	−0.3	−4.6	0.2	0.6	..	1.6	−252.7
China	94.7	−576.9	0.0	0.0	0.0	2.2	−13.7	9.7	4.6	11.4	12.1	12.3	−443.7
Hong Kong, China	..	..	..	..	..	..	..	0.0	..	..	..	0.0	0.0
Colombia	−0.7	248.8	0.0	0.0	−13.2	−424.1	33.5	0.4	0.9	0.8	0.7	7.5	−145.5
Congo, Dem. Rep.	275.2	−81.5	358.8	−203.4	−32.0	0.0	0.0	6.2	1.7	18.8	10.3	42.8	397.0
Congo, Rep.	−0.3	−6.5	−3.6	−4.7	0.0	0.0	0.0	1.4	0.7	1.7	0.3	8.8	−2.2
Costa Rica	−0.2	−11.1	0.0	0.0	−10.9	−22.5	−44.7	0.2	0.4	0.6	..	2.2	−86.2
Côte d'Ivoire	161.2	−89.9	−10.6	0.0	34.3	−109.4	−1.9	2.5	2.0	3.1	1.6	8.6	1.5
Croatia	0.0	104.8	0.0	−125.9	0.0	11.5	40.6	0.1	..	..	..	9.9	41.0
Cuba	..	..	..	..	..	..	..	0.6	1.0	0.3	1.2	2.2	5.3
Czech Republic	0.0	−41.0	0.0	0.0	0.0	0.0	39.7	0.1	..	..	..	1.5	0.3
Denmark													
Dominican Republic	−0.7	32.6	0.0	−25.7	−16.1	80.2	−1.7	0.3	1.1	0.6	0.4	1.6	72.5
Ecuador	−1.1	−60.0	0.0	97.9	−21.8	−25.4	8.1	0.2	1.5	0.8	1.5	4.0	5.6
Egypt, Arab Rep.	20.5	−46.6	0.0	0.0	0.6	−65.0	14.4	1.5	1.1	2.7	3.2	7.3	−60.4
El Salvador	−0.8	36.0	0.0	0.0	−17.6	107.8	64.8	0.4	1.1	0.7	0.1	1.1	193.5
Eritrea	46.2	0.0	0.0	0.0	11.9	0.0	7.6	2.7	2.0	1.1	2.1	18.0	91.6
Estonia	0.0	−35.2	0.0	−13.8	0.0	−4.3	0.7	..	0.0	..	..	0.2	−52.3
Ethiopia	459.5	0.0	33.0	0.0	73.3	−19.7	27.3	13.3	3.8	14.0	23.5	32.2	660.4
Finland													
France													
Gabon	0.0	−5.9	0.0	−13.1	0.0	−12.5	8.9	..	0.3	0.6	0.0	3.2	−18.5
Gambia, The	14.3	0.0	3.7	0.0	4.7	−0.7	4.8	2.6	0.5	0.7	0.9	2.3	33.8
Georgia	61.3	0.0	11.2	−12.0	0.0	4.3	0.5	1.4	0.3	0.7	0.9	5.3	73.8
Germany													
Ghana	88.7	−1.2	63.4	0.0	36.1	−17.7	6.5	3.1	3.4	3.3	1.0	4.6	191.3
Greece													
Guatemala	0.0	69.5	0.0	0.0	−6.4	163.3	−12.5	0.8	13.5	0.8	3.2	1.8	233.9
Guinea	28.4	0.0	6.6	0.0	0.7	−12.4	−13.7	0.8	0.5	2.1	3.1	26.2	42.3
Guinea-Bissau	3.8	0.0	−1.2	−0.3	−0.8	−0.3	−1.0	2.3	0.7	1.1	1.7	1.9	7.9
Haiti	−0.1	0.0	−1.9	−7.3	1.3	0.0	−0.3	2.7	3.3	2.8	3.6	1.4	5.4

	International financial institutions ($ millions)							United Nations ($ millions)					Total ($ millions)
	World Bank		IMF		Regional development banks								
	IDA	IBRD	Conces-sional	Non-concessional	Conces-sional	Non-concessional	Others	UNDP	UNFPA	UNICEF	WFP	Others	
	2002	2002	2002	2002	2002	2002	2002	2002	2002	2002	2002	2002	2002
Honduras	45.6	−9.7	−4.2	−30.8	39.4	−19.2	7.8	1.1	2.0	1.1	2.1	1.6	36.8
Hungary	0.0	−62.9	0.0	0.0	0.0	−18.9	201.3	0.3	..	..	..	1.8	121.6
India	429.8	−2,383.4	0.0	0.0	0.0	−1,341.7	−24.5	21.2	13.2	30.4	9.4	35.5	−3,210.1
Indonesia	59.8	−706.0	0.0	−950.2	8.0	384.1	−37.6	4.1	6.2	5.1	0.4	20.3	−1,205.8
Iran, Islamic Rep.	0.0	−56.3	0.0	0.0	0.0	0.0	0.0	0.9	2.4	1.8	0.8	23.8	−26.6
Iraq	..	..	..	..	..	..	..	0.7	0.4	1.7	1.6	13.8	18.2
Ireland													
Israel	..	..	..	..	..	..						0.3	0.3
Italy													
Jamaica	0.0	39.9	0.0	−18.7	−4.6	92.2	−0.3	0.2	0.3	0.6	..	1.6	111.1
Japan													
Jordan	−2.6	110.7	0.0	13.6	0.0	0.0	−3.3	0.5	0.8	0.7	1.7	83.3	205.3
Kazakhstan	0.0	35.9	0.0	0.0	0.0	4.4	19.6	0.7	0.6	0.9	..	2.1	64.2
Kenya	23.6	−11.8	−18.2	0.0	−1.0	−8.1	−8.2	4.6	4.9	4.7	10.5	30.2	31.2
Korea, Dem. Rep.	..	..	..	..	..	..	..	0.7	1.1	2.1	0.1	4.1	7.9
Korea, Rep.	..	..	..	..	..	..	..	0.0	..	..	..	1.5	1.5
Kuwait	..	..	..	..	..	..	..	..	..	..	..	0.3	0.3
Kyrgyz Republic	33.4	0.0	−1.4	−7.0	27.2	−7.4	6.4	1.5	0.6	0.9	..	1.7	56.0
Lao PDR	27.2	0.0	2.6	0.0	43.7	0.0	1.8	1.1	1.8	1.5	2.7	2.0	84.5
Latvia	0.0	−2.8	0.0	−9.9	0.0	−12.7	18.3	0.1	0.1	..	..	0.5	−6.3
Lebanon	0.0	35.7	0.0	0.0	0.0	0.0	−23.0	0.5	0.6	0.6	..	53.5	67.8
Lesotho	18.5	−21.3	5.3	0.0	3.7	−1.5	−1.9	0.9	0.5	1.3	3.5	0.9	9.7
Liberia	0.0	0.0	0.0	−0.3	0.0	0.0	0.0	0.8	0.5	1.5	5.0	11.6	19.1
Libya	..	..	..	..	..	..	..	..	..	..	..	4.7	4.7
Lithuania	0.0	−9.7	0.0	−40.2	0.0	−7.8	−25.8	0.2	0.1	..	..	0.4	−82.8
Macedonia, FYR	18.2	9.6	−1.2	−7.6	0.0	−23.9	33.4	0.4	..	0.6	0.0	5.5	35.0
Madagascar	157.3	0.0	13.1	0.0	3.5	−5.8	5.7	5.5	1.7	5.1	4.2	4.7	195.0
Malawi	45.8	−1.6	−7.3	22.5	17.4	−2.3	0.0	2.8	2.9	4.9	7.0	4.4	96.5
Malaysia	0.0	−70.0	0.0	0.0	0.0	−30.3	−2.4	0.4	0.2	0.4	..	1.0	−100.8
Mali	87.5	0.0	−9.6	0.0	5.2	0.0	5.5	3.6	2.2	5.3	4.7	3.2	107.5
Mauritania	40.7	0.0	10.0	0.0	11.0	2.1	19.5	0.6	2.0	1.4	5.0	3.4	95.8
Mauritius	−0.6	19.6	0.0	0.0	−0.1	48.3	2.1	0.2	0.2	0.5	..	1.0	71.1
Mexico	0.0	−86.4	0.0	0.0	0.0	598.0	0.0	0.8	4.7	1.2	..	6.3	524.6
Moldova	21.9	−4.4	12.0	−17.8	0.0	−3.1	−9.6	0.8	0.2	0.6	..	1.3	1.9
Mongolia	13.3	0.0	−7.7	0.0	26.0	0.0	1.4	1.2	2.0	0.9	..	3.4	40.6
Morocco	−1.4	−222.3	0.0	0.0	2.7	−284.4	193.6	1.0	0.9	1.5	1.3	3.0	−304.1
Mozambique	146.9	0.0	5.9	0.0	68.1	−1.1	15.0	4.0	5.9	6.5	5.7	6.7	263.6
Myanmar	0.0	0.0	0.0	0.0	0.0	0.0	−0.9	6.5	1.5	7.4	0.8	11.0	26.3
Namibia	..	..	..	..	..	..	..	−0.2	1.2	1.2	0.9	7.3	10.4
Nepal	14.5	0.0	−4.5	0.0	1.9	0.0	2.9	6.5	3.3	3.3	7.5	14.2	49.6
Netherlands													
New Zealand													
Nicaragua	71.7	0.0	4.7	0.0	100.8	−1.1	20.3	2.2	2.0	0.7	2.1	1.4	204.8
Niger	68.3	0.0	19.6	0.0	17.0	0.0	22.7	3.4	2.9	6.1	4.0	4.3	148.3
Nigeria	7.6	−176.1	0.0	0.0	27.1	−80.6	−1.8	12.7	6.4	18.3	..	24.1	−162.3
Norway													
Oman	0.0	−1.4	0.0	0.0	0.0	0.0	−9.9	..	0.0	0.4	..	1.5	−9.4
Pakistan	851.3	−208.5	297.0	−222.0	153.4	106.3	−173.7	6.4	4.2	11.0	4.4	34.5	864.2
Panama	0.0	3.2	0.0	−8.1	−9.5	50.3	4.0	0.2	0.5	0.6	..	1.8	43.1
Papua New Guinea	−3.4	−14.2	0.0	0.0	−2.4	−2.5	−0.7	1.6	0.8	1.1	..	1.9	−17.8
Paraguay	−1.4	−1.9	0.0	0.0	−10.4	13.8	−13.9	0.2	0.6	0.6	..	0.9	−11.6
Peru	0.0	−16.8	0.0	−173.3	−5.0	168.8	307.0	0.7	6.4	1.0	2.1	9.6	300.4
Philippines	−5.2	−143.8	0.0	−405.3	−1.2	−18.6	−0.7	2.3	3.3	2.8	..	3.7	−562.7
Poland	0.0	−33.3	0.0	0.0	0.0	0.0	0.0	0.3	0.1	..	..	1.5	−31.5
Portugal													
Puerto Rico													

	International financial institutions $ millions							United Nations		$ millions			Total
	World Bank		IMF		Regional development banks								
	IDA	IBRD	Conces-sional	Non-concessional	Conces-sional	Non-concessional	Others	UNDP	UNFPA	UNICEF	WFP	Others	$ millions
	2002	2002	2002	2002	2002	2002	2002	2002	2002	2002	2002	2002	2002
Romania	0.0	214.3	0.0	9.0	0.0	9.9	−16.1	0.5	0.4	0.7	..	2.0	220.7
Russian Federation	0.0	−296.3	0.0	−1,486.0	0.0	−15.4	0.1	0.3	0.6	..	1.0	17.6	−1,778.0
Rwanda	73.2	0.0	0.7	−2.5	6.5	−0.1	−1.7	2.1	1.7	3.1	4.8	10.1	98.1
Saudi Arabia	..	..	..	..	..	..	..	..	0.0	0.6	..	12.8	13.4
Senegal	108.4	0.0	−10.8	0.0	18.2	−14.6	32.9	3.4	2.2	1.9	3.7	3.9	149.1
Serbia and Montenegro	159.4	0.0	0.0	0.0	0.0	0.0	84.2	..	2.0	0.5	−0.4	1.6	247.4
Sierra Leone	43.0	0.0	35.5	0.0	14.2	0.0	−0.5	2.8	1.1	3.0	6.5	24.8	130.3
Singapore	..	..	..	..	..	..	..	..	..	..	..	0.3	0.3
Slovak Republic	0.0	−21.9	0.0	0.0	0.0	−1.2	2.1	0.2	..	..	..	1.8	−19.0
Slovenia	..	..	..	..	..	..	..	0.1	..	..	..	0.8	0.9
Somalia	0.0	0.0	0.0	0.0	0.0	0.0	0.0	4.0	0.6	4.5	1.4	13.1	23.7
South Africa	0.0	5.1	0.0	0.0	0.0	−0.8	0.0	1.8	1.5	1.6	..	6.7	15.9
Spain													
Sri Lanka	58.9	−4.4	−50.8	125.2	70.0	37.2	4.1	1.7	1.2	0.7	4.2	10.2	258.2
Sudan	−0.3	0.0	0.0	−22.0	0.0	0.0	0.0	2.0	2.1	4.4	11.3	26.8	24.1
Swaziland	−0.3	0.1	0.0	0.0	2.7	−2.6	2.4	0.2	0.6	1.5	0.1	2.2	6.8
Sweden													
Switzerland													
Syrian Arab Republic	−1.5	−6.2	0.0	0.0	0.0	0.0	−49.6	1.1	4.0	0.8	0.9	33.6	−16.9
Tajikistan	9.6	0.0	−14.2	−9.7	14.1	0.0	−7.5	2.4	0.7	1.2	4.9	1.8	3.3
Tanzania	142.8	−2.4	47.0	0.0	14.2	−0.8	9.4	5.6	7.5	6.9	7.7	33.3	271.1
Thailand	−3.4	−695.8	0.0	−1,360.0	−2.6	−1,274.1	−74.9	0.3	0.3	0.9	..	9.3	−3,400.1
Togo	6.8	0.0	−9.4	0.0	0.0	0.0	2.4	1.6	1.1	1.6	..	1.7	5.7
Trinidad and Tobago	0.0	−3.1	0.0	0.0	−0.1	−19.7	6.3	0.1	0.0	..	..	2.0	−14.5
Tunisia	−2.1	−36.9	0.0	0.0	0.0	85.2	69.8	0.4	0.4	0.7	..	1.6	119.0
Turkey	−5.9	594.3	0.0	6,490.9	0.0	0.0	−103.3	0.9	0.9	0.8	..	6.3	6,984.8
Turkmenistan	0.0	0.7	..	..	..	..	..	0.5	0.6	0.9	..	0.8	3.5
Uganda	95.8	0.0	−17.0	0.0	14.7	−0.7	−4.1	4.0	5.4	5.0	14.9	20.2	138.0
Ukraine	0.0	−76.4	0.0	−182.3	0.0	−26.0	−61.8	1.4	0.6	..	..	4.4	−340.0
United Arab Emirates	..	..	..	..	..	..	..	−0.1	..	..	..	0.5	0.5
United Kingdom													
United States													
Uruguay	0.0	158.3	0.0	1,559.8	−1.7	488.2	−3.8	0.3	0.1	0.6	..	1.3	2,203.0
Uzbekistan	0.0	21.5	0.0	−21.5	6.8	5.2	0.0	1.2	0.6	1.9	..	1.4	16.9
Venezuela, RB	0.0	−169.1	0.0	0.0	0.0	45.7	271.0	0.3	0.7	0.7	..	3.7	152.9
Vietnam	258.9	0.0	−9.0	−5.2	175.1	20.0	6.6	4.1	2.9	4.0	..	6.6	464.0
West Bank and Gaza	..	..	..	..	..	..	..	3.5	1.3	1.6	5.4	238.1	249.9
Yemen, Rep.	63.9	0.0	0.0	−17.6	0.0	0.0	−1.3	5.1	2.8	3.0	3.5	7.0	66.4
Zambia	140.5	−6.4	109.8	0.0	22.8	−11.0	−15.9	2.8	2.4	3.7	11.0	20.0	279.8
Zimbabwe	0.0	0.0	−1.1	−1.9	0.0	−0.7	1.6	2.3	1.0	1.8	4.2	6.2	13.4
World	.. s	.. s	.. s	.. s	.. s	.. s	.. s	277.9 s	312.5 s	571.4 s	351.6 s	2,156.0 s	.. s
Low income	4,753.6	−3,720.2	959.7	−1,583.3	1,166.6	−1,159.7	−6.0	232.1	160.2	264.0	281.5	651.4	2,000.0
Middle income	771.0	−2,013.3	−53.9	14,691.3	118.3	−128.9	924.5	46.5	80.8	63.3	58.3	920.5	15,478.4
Lower middle income	758.1	−682.5	−53.9	14,083.9	143.4	−664.8	428.7	44.6	67.1	53.1	58.3	712.2	14,948.2
Upper middle income	12.8	−1,330.9	0.0	607.4	−25.2	535.9	495.8	1.8	9.8	9.8	0.0	123.1	440.3
Low & middle income	5,524.6	−5,733.5	905.8	13,108.0	1,284.9	−1,288.6	918.6	278.9	312.5	571.4	351.6	2,149.1	18,383.4
East Asia & Pacific	489.4	−2,210.6	−3.3	−2,722.1	320.6	−919.0	−119.8	38.6	32.6	44.3	19.2	92.7	−4,937.4
Europe & Central Asia	597.0	366.0	26.2	4,609.8	48.1	−95.9	231.0	19.8	10.3	16.3	11.4	147.1	5,987.0
Latin America & Carib.	230.1	−530.2	−20.4	11,899.2	134.3	1,526.4	767.1	11.2	47.7	21.8	19.9	231.0	14,338.1
Middle East & N. Africa	94.1	−352.8	5.9	−303.8	7.4	−297.5	37.5	16.6	17.3	18.6	25.6	543.8	−187.2
South Asia	1,557.4	−2,601.9	218.9	−161.9	327.6	−1,192.0	−121.1	60.7	42.3	67.3	55.3	126.4	−1,620.8
Sub-Saharan Africa	2,556.6	−404.1	678.4	−213.3	447.0	−310.5	123.8	131.8	98.2	168.2	213.8	616.1	4,106.0
High income													
Europe EMU													

Note: The aggregates for the regional development banks, United Nations, and total net financial flows include amounts for economies not specified elsewhere.

About the data

The table shows concessional and nonconcessional financial flows from the major multilateral institutions—the World Bank, the International Monetary Fund (IMF), regional development banks, United Nations agencies, and regional groups such as the Commission of the European Communities. Much of the data comes from the World Bank's Debtor Reporting System.

The multilateral development banks fund their nonconcessional lending operations primarily by selling low-interest, highly rated bonds (the World Bank, for example, has an AAA rating) backed by prudent lending and financial policies and the strong financial support of their members. These funds are then on-lent at slightly higher interest rates and with relatively long maturities (15–20 years) to developing countries. Lending terms vary with market conditions and the policies of the banks.

Concessional flows from bilateral donors are defined by the Development Assistance Committee (DAC) of the Organisation for Economic Co-operation and Development (OECD) as financial flows containing a grant element of at least 25 percent. The grant element of loans is evaluated assuming a nominal market interest rate of 10 percent. The grant element is nil for a loan carrying a 10 percent interest rate, and it is 100 percent for a grant, which requires no repayment. Concessional flows from multilateral development agencies are credits provided through their concessional lending facilities. The cost of these loans is reduced through subsidies provided by donors or drawn from other resources available to the agencies. Grants provided by multilateral agencies are not included in the net flows.

All concessional lending by the World Bank is carried out by the International Development Association (IDA). Eligibility for IDA resources is based on gross national income (GNI) per capita; countries must also meet performance standards assessed by World Bank staff. Since July 1, 2003, the GNI per capita cutoff has been set at $735, measured in 2002 using the *World Bank Atlas* method (see *Users guide*). In exceptional circumstances IDA extends eligibility temporarily to countries that are above the cutoff and are undertaking major adjustment efforts but are not creditworthy for lending by the International Bank for Reconstruction and Development (IBRD). An exception has also been made for small island economies. Lending by the International Finance Corporation is not included in this table.

The IMF makes concessional funds available through its Poverty Reduction and Growth Facility, which replaced the Enhanced Structural Adjustment Facility in 1999, and through the IMF Trust Fund.

Eligibility is based principally on a country's per capita income and eligibility under IDA, the World Bank's concessional window.

Regional development banks also maintain concessional windows for funds. Loans from the major regional development banks—the African Development Bank, Asian Development Bank, and Inter-American Development Bank—are recorded in the table according to each institution's classification.

In 1999 all United Nations agencies revised their data since 1990 to include only regular budgetary expenditures (except for the World Food Programme and the United Nations High Commissioner for Refugees, which revised their data from 1996 onward). They did so to avoid double counting extra-budgetary expenditures reported by DAC countries and flows reported by the United Nations.

Definitions

• **Net financial flows** in this table are disbursements of public or publicly guaranteed loans and credits, less repayments of principal. • **IDA** is the International Development Association, the concessional loan window of the World Bank. • **IBRD** is the International Bank for Reconstruction and Development, the founding and largest member of the World Bank Group. • **IMF** is the International Monetary Fund. Its nonconcessional lending consists of the credit it provides to its members, mainly to meet their balance of payments needs. It provides concessional assistance through the Poverty Reduction and Growth Facility and the IMF Trust Fund. • **Regional development banks** include the African Development Bank, in Abidjan, Côte d'Ivoire, which lends to all of Africa, including North Africa; the Asian Development Bank, in Manila, Philippines, which serves countries in South and Central Asia and East Asia and Pacific; the European Bank for Reconstruction and Development, in London, United Kingdom, which serves countries in Europe and Central Asia; the European Development Fund, in Brussels, Belgium, which serves countries in Africa, the Caribbean, and the Pacific; and the Inter-American Development Bank, in Washington, D.C., which is the principal development bank of the Americas. Concessional financial flows cover disbursements made through concessional lending facilities. Nonconcessional financial flows cover all other disbursements. • **Others** is a residual category in the World Bank's Debtor Reporting System. It includes such institutions as the Caribbean Development Bank and the European Investment Bank. • **United Nations** includes the United Nations Development Programme (UNDP), United Nations Population Fund (UNFPA), United Nations Children's Fund (UNICEF), World Food Programme (WFP), and other United Nations agencies, such as the United Nations High Commissioner for Refugees, United Nations Relief and Works Agency for Palestine Refugees in the Near East, and United Nations Regular Programme for Technical Assistance.

Data sources

The data on net financial flows from international financial institutions come from the World Bank's Debtor Reporting System. These data are published in the World Bank's *Global Development Finance 2004* and electronically as *GDF Online*. The data on aid from United Nations agencies come from the DAC annual *Development Cooperation Report*. Data are available in electronic format on the OECD's *International Development Statistics* CD-ROM and to registered users at http://www.oecd.org/dataoecd/50/17/5037721.htm.

	Foreign population[a]				Foreign labor force[b]		Inflows of foreign population			
	thousands		% of total population		% of total labor force		Total thousands[c]		Asylum seekers thousands	
	1990	**2001**	**1990**	**2001**	**1990**	**2001**	**1990**	**2001**	**1990**	**2001**
Austria	456	764	5.9	9.4	7.4	11.0	..	75	23	30
Belgium	905	847	9.1	8.2	7.1	8.9	50	66	13	25
Denmark	161	267	3.1	5.0	2.4	3.5	15	25	13	10
Finland	26	99	0.5	1.9	..	1.7	6	11	3	2
France	3,597	3,263	6.3	5.6	6.2	6.2	102[d]	141[d]	55	47
Germany	5,343	7,319	8.4	8.9	..	9.1[e]	842	685	193	88
Ireland	80	151	2.3	3.9	2.6	4.6	..	28[d]	0	10
Italy	781	1,363	1.4	2.4	1.4	3.8	..	233[d]	5	13
Japan	1,075	1,778	0.9	1.4	0.1	0.2	224	351	..	0
Luxembourg	113	167	29.4	37.5	45.2[e]	61.7[e]	9	11	0	1
Netherlands	692	690	4.6	4.3	3.1	..	81	95	21	33
Norway	143	186	3.4	4.1	2.3	4.9	16	25	4	15
Portugal	108	224	1.1	2.2	1.0	2.0	..	14[d]	0	0
Spain	279	1,109	0.7	2.7	0.6	3.4	..	..	9	9
Sweden	484	476	5.6	5.3	5.4	5.1	53	44	29	24
Switzerland	1,100	1,419	16.3	19.7	18.9	18.1	101	100	36	21
United Kingdom	1,723	2,587	3.2	4.4	3.3	4.4	175	373	38	92

	Foreign-born population[a]				Foreign-born labor force[b]		Inflows of foreign population			
	thousands		% of total population		% of total labor force		Total thousands[c, d]		Asylum seekers thousands	
	1990	**2001**	**1990**	**2001**	**1990**	**2001**	**1990**	**2001**	**1990**	**2001**
Australia	3,965	4,482	22.9	23.1	25.7	24.2	121	88.9	4	13
Canada	4,343	5,448	16.1	18.2	18.5	19.9	214	250	37	42
United States	19,767[f]	31,811[g]	7.9[f]	11.1[g]	9.4	13.9	1,536	1,064	74	63

a. Data are from population registers or from registers of foreigners, except for Australia (1991–2001); Canada (1991–2001); France (1990–99); and the United States (censuses); Italy, Portugal, and Spain (residence permits); and Ireland and the United Kingdom (labor force surveys) and refer to the population on December 31 of the year indicated. b. Data include the unemployed, except in Italy, Luxembourg, the Netherlands, Norway, and the United Kingdom. Cross-border and seasonal workers are excluded unless otherwise noted. c. Inflow data are based on population registers and are not fully comparable because the criteria governing who gets registered differ from country to country. Counts for the Netherlands, Norway, and (especially) Germany include substantial numbers of asylum seekers. d. Data are based on residence permits or other sources. e. Includes cross-border workers. f. From the U.S. Census Bureau, *1990 Census of Population*. g. From the U.S. Census Bureau, *Current Population Report* (March 2000).

The data in the table are based on national definitions and data collection practices and are not fully comparable across countries. Japan and the European members of the Organisation for Economic Co-operation and Development (OECD) have traditionally defined foreigners by nationality of descent. Australia, Canada, and the United States use place of birth, which is closer to the concept used in the United Nations' definition of the immigrant stock. Few countries, however, apply just one criterion in all circumstances. For this and other reasons, data based on the concept of foreign nationality and data based on the concept of foreign born cannot be completely reconciled. See the notes to the table for other breaks in comparability between countries and over time.

Data on the size of the foreign labor force are also problematic. Countries use different permit systems to gather information on immigrants. Some countries issue a single permit for residence and work, while others issue separate residence and work permits. Differences in immigration laws across countries, particularly with respect to immigrants' access to employment, greatly affect the recording and measurement of migration and reduce the international comparability of raw data. The data exclude temporary visitors and tourists (see table 6.14).

OECD countries are not the only ones that receive substantial migration flows. Migrant workers make up a significant share of the labor force in Gulf countries and in southern Africa, and people are displaced by wars and natural disasters throughout the world. Systematic recording of migration flows is difficult, however, especially in poor countries and those affected by civil disorder.

- **Foreign (or foreign-born) population** is the number of foreign or foreign-born residents in a country.
- **Foreign (or foreign-born) labor force as a percentage of total labor force** is the share of foreign or foreign-born workers in a country's workforce.
- **Inflows of foreign population** are the gross arrivals of immigrants in the country shown. The total does not include asylum seekers, except as noted. • **Asylum seekers** are immigrants who apply for permission to remain in a country for humanitarian reasons.

6.13a

Migration to OECD countries is growing

Foreign population (% of total population)

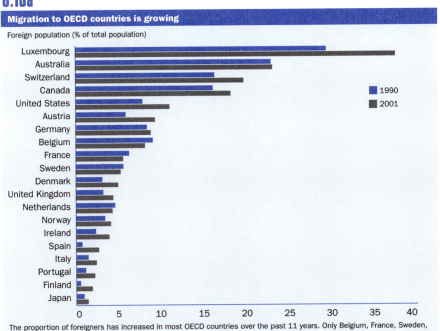

The proportion of foreigners has increased in most OECD countries over the past 11 years. Only Belgium, France, Sweden, and the Netherlands have shown small declines.

Note: Australia, Canada, and the United States refer to foreign born.
Source: Organisation for Economic Co-operation and Development, Development Assistance Committee.

International migration data are collected by the OECD through information provided by national correspondents to the Continuous Reporting System on Migration (SOPEMI) network, which provides an annual overview of trends and policies. The data appear in the OECD's *Trends in International Migration 2003*.

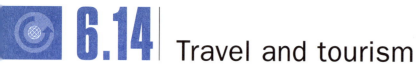
	International tourism				International tourism receipts				International tourism expenditures			
	thousands				$ millions		% of exports		$ millions		% of imports	
	Inbound tourists		Outbound tourists									
	1990	2002	1990	2002	1990	2002	1990	2002	1990	2002	1990	2002
Afghanistan	..	..	..	..	..	..	..	..	1	..	..	..
Albania	30	34	..	..	4	487	1.1	53.2	4	366	0.8	17.6
Algeria	1,137	988	3,828	1,257	64	133	0.5	..	149	193	1.5	..
Angola	67	91	..	..	13	22	0.3	0.3	38	66	1.1	1.0
Argentina	1,930	2,820	2,398	3,008	1,131	2,547	7.6	8.2	1,505	3,800	22.0	13.8
Armenia	15	123	..	110	..	63	..	9.0	..	54	..	4.9
Australia	2,215	4,841	2,170	3,461	4,088	8,087	8.2	9.7	4,535	6,116	8.5	6.9
Austria	19,011	18,611	2,572	3,907	13,417	11,237	21.1	10.3	7,748	9,391	12.6	9.0
Azerbaijan	77	834	..	1,130	42	51	..	1.9	..	106	..	3.4
Bangladesh	115	207	388	1,075	11	57	0.5	0.8	78	202	2.0	2.2
Belarus	..	61	..	1,386	..	193	..	2.1	..	559	..	5.7
Belgium	5,147	6,724	6,453	6,773	3,721	6,892	2.7	3.2	5,477	10,435	4.1	4.8
Benin	110	72	418	..	55	60	15.1	10.8	15	7	3.3	0.9
Bolivia	254	308	242	240	91	156	9.3	10.3	130	118	12.0	6.0
Bosnia and Herzegovina	..	160	..	..	..	112	..	7.9	..	49	..	1.0
Botswana	543	1,037	192	..	117	309	5.8	11.7	56	..	2.8	..
Brazil	1,091	3,783	1,188	1,861	1,444	3,120	4.1	4.5	1,559	2,380	5.5	3.8
Bulgaria	1,586	3,433	2,395	3,188	320	1,344	4.6	16.2	189	616	2.4	6.6
Burkina Faso	74	149	..	..	11	34	3.2	13.1	32	..	4.2	..
Burundi	109	36	24	35	4	1	4.5	2.6	17	14	5.3	9.5
Cambodia	17	787	..	..	50	379	15.9	16.1	..	38	..	1.4
Cameroon	89	221	..	..	53	39	2.1	..	279	..	11.3	..
Canada	15,209	20,057	20,415	17,705	6,339	9,700	4.2	3.2	10,931	9,929	7.3	3.7
Central African Republic	6	..	..	..	3	..	1.4	..	51	..	12.4	..
Chad	9	32	24	39	8	..	3.0	..	70	..	14.4	..
Chile	943	1,412	768	1,938	540	845	5.3	3.8	426	793	4.6	3.8
China	10,484	36,803	2,134	16,600	2,218	20,385	3.9	5.6	470	15,398	1.0	4.7
Hong Kong, China	6,581	16,566	2,043	4,709	5,032	10,117	..	4.2	..	12,417	..	5.4
Colombia	813	541	781	1,241	406	962	4.7	6.8	454	1,072	6.6	7.0
Congo, Dem. Rep.	55	103	..	..	7	..	..	..	16	..	..	..
Congo, Rep.	33	19	..	..	8	25	0.5	1.0	113	70	8.8	4.3
Costa Rica	435	1,113	191	..	275	1,078	14.0	15.1	148	367	6.3	4.8
Côte d'Ivoire	196	..	2	..	51	50	1.5	0.9	169	290	4.9	7.5
Croatia	7,049	6,944	..	..	1,704	3,811	..	36.1	729	781	..	6.1
Cuba	327	1,656	12	..	243	1,633	..	..	..	..	..	..
Czech Republic	7,278	4,579	13,380	..	419	2,941	..	6.5	455	1,575	..	3.3
Denmark	1,838	2,010	2,530	..	3,322	5,785	6.8	7.0	3,676	6,856	8.9	9.5
Dominican Republic	1,305	2,811	137	..	900	2,736	49.1	33.2	144	295	6.4	2.9
Ecuador	362	654	181	598	188	447	5.8	7.2	175	364	6.9	4.7
Egypt, Arab Rep.	2,411	4,906	2,012	3,074	1,100	3,764	11.1	22.9	129	1,278	0.9	6.6
El Salvador	194	951	525	1,001	18	342	1.8	9.0	61	229	3.8	3.9
Eritrea	169	101	..	..	..	73	..	39.1	..	..	..	..
Estonia	372	1,360	80	1,658	27	555	4.1	10.1	19	231	2.7	3.8
Ethiopia	79	148	89	..	25	75	4.2	7.7	11	45	0.9	2.2
Finland	1,572	2,875	1,169	5,824	1,167	1,573	3.7	3.1	2,791	1,966	8.3	4.9
France	52,497	77,012	19,430	17,404	20,184	32,329	7.1	8.2	12,423	19,460	4.4	5.3
Gabon	109	212	161	..	3	7	0.1	0.2	137	170	7.6	8.7
Gambia, The	100	75	..	..	26	..	15.5	..	8	..	4.2	..
Georgia	..	298	..	317	..	472	..	48.4	..	174	..	12.4
Germany	17,045	17,969	..	73,300	14,288	19,158	3.0	2.7	33,771	53,196	7.9	8.3
Ghana	146	483	..	..	81	358	8.2	13.9	13	120	0.9	3.6
Greece	8,873	14,180	1,651	..	2,587	9,741	19.9	32.4	1,090	2,450	5.6	5.8
Guatemala	509	884	289	629	185	612	11.8	16.2	100	267	5.5	4.0
Guinea	..	43	..	..	30	31	3.6	3.2	30	21	3.1	2.1
Guinea-Bissau	..	8	..	..	..	..	..	..	..	..	..	..
Haiti	144	142	..	..	46	54	14.5	..	37	..	7.2	..

Travel and tourism 6.14

	International tourism				International tourism receipts				International tourism expenditures			
	thousands				$ millions		% of exports		$ millions		% of imports	
	Inbound tourists		Outbound tourists									
	1990	2002	1990	2002	1990	2002	1990	2002	1990	2002	1990	2002
Honduras	290	550	196	285	29	342	2.8	14.0	38	185	3.4	5.4
Hungary	3,693	3,013	13,596	12,966	824	3,273	6.8	7.7	477	1,722	4.3	3.9
India	1,707	2,384	2,281	4,205	1,513	2,923	6.6	3.8	393	3,449	1.3	4.1
Indonesia	2,178	5,033	688	..	2,105	4,306	7.2	6.5	836	3,368	3.0	6.4
Iran, Islamic Rep.	154	1,402	788	2,400	61	1,122	0.3	3.9	340	238	1.5	1.1
Iraq	748	127	239	..	55	..	..	..	..	..	..	..
Ireland	3,666	6,476	1,798	4,634	1,459	3,089	5.4	2.7	1,163	3,741	4.7	4.1
Israel	1,063	862	883	3,273	1,396	1,197	8.1	3.1	1,442	2,547	7.1	6.0
Italy	26,679	39,799	..	25,126	16,458	26,915	7.5	8.6	10,304	16,935	4.7	5.6
Jamaica	989	1,266	..	..	740	1,209	33.4	37.4	114	258	4.8	5.3
Japan	3,236	5,239	10,997	16,523	3,578	3,499	1.1	0.8	24,928	26,681	8.4	6.5
Jordan	572	1,622	1,143	1,726	512	786	20.4	18.4	336	416	9.4	6.7
Kazakhstan	..	2,832	..	2,274	..	621	..	5.3	..	756	..	6.6
Kenya	814	838	210	..	443	297	19.9	9.0	38	143	1.4	3.6
Korea, Dem. Rep.	115	..	..	..	..	..	..	..	..	..	..	..
Korea, Rep.	2,959	5,347	1,561	7,123	3,559	5,277	4.9	2.8	3,166	7,642	4.1	4.2
Kuwait	15	73	..	..	132	119	1.6	0.7	1,837	3,021	25.6	21.5
Kyrgyz Republic	..	..	..	..	2	36	..	5.7	..	10	..	1.4
Lao PDR	14	215	..	..	3	113	2.9	21.8	1	8	0.5	1.4
Latvia	..	848	..	2,306	7	161	0.6	4.2	13	230	1.3	4.9
Lebanon	210	956	..	..	..	956	..	39.8	..	..	..	..
Lesotho	171	..	254	..	17	20	17.0	5.1	12	14	1.6	1.8
Liberia	..	..	..	..	..	..	..	..	..	..	..	..
Libya	96	174	425	..	6	..	0.1	..	424	..	4.7	..
Lithuania	780	1,271	..	3,584	..	383	..	6.3	..	218	..	3.3
Macedonia, FYR	562	99	..	..	45	23	..	1.6	..	..	..	..
Madagascar	53	170	34	..	40	115	8.5	9.0	40	115	4.9	7.8
Malawi	130	285	..	..	16	125	3.6	26.5	16	78	2.9	9.8
Malaysia	7,446	13,292	14,920	36,248	1,667	6,785	5.1	6.3	1,450	2,618	4.6	2.9
Mali	44	96	..	..	47	71	11.2	11.0	62	41	7.5	4.4
Mauritania	..	30	..	..	9	..	1.9	..	23	..	4.4	..
Mauritius	292	682	89	162	244	612	14.2	20.6	94	204	4.9	7.3
Mexico	17,176	19,667	7,357	11,948	5,467	8,858	11.2	5.1	5,519	6,060	10.6	3.3
Moldova	226	18	129	52	..	47	..	5.4	..	86	..	6.7
Mongolia	147	198	..	..	5	130	1.0	18.4	1	119	0.1	12.6
Morocco	4,024	4,193	1,202	1,533	1,259	2,152	20.2	17.6	184	444	2.4	3.3
Mozambique	..	..	..	..	..	144	..	12.5	..	296	..	16.6
Myanmar	21	217	..	..	9	45	2.8	1.6	16	27	2.7	0.9
Namibia	213	670	..	..	85	404	7.0	29.6	63	..	4.0	..
Nepal	255	275	82	200	64	107	15.2	12.1	45	80	5.4	4.7
Netherlands	5,795	9,595	9,000	16,760	4,155	7,706	2.6	2.9	7,376	12,919	5.0	5.3
New Zealand	976	2,045	717	1,293	1,030	2,918	8.8	14.9	958	1,480	8.2	7.9
Nicaragua	106	472	173	532	12	116	3.1	12.8	15	69	2.2	3.5
Niger	21	52	18	..	17	..	3.2	..	44	28	6.0	..
Nigeria	190	831	56	..	25	156	0.2	0.8	576	700	8.3	4.9
Norway	1,955	3,107	508	..	1,570	2,738	3.3	3.5	3,679	5,814	9.5	11.1
Oman	149	602	..	..	69	116	1.2	1.0	47	367	1.4	5.3
Pakistan	424	498	..	..	156	105	2.3	0.9	440	179	4.3	1.4
Panama	214	534	151	200	179	679	4.0	9.0	99	178	2.4	2.3
Papua New Guinea	41	54	66	92	41	101	3.0	4.8	50	..	3.3	..
Paraguay	280	250	264	141	128	62	5.1	2.2	103	65	4.7	2.4
Peru	317	862	329	859	217	801	5.3	8.7	295	616	7.2	6.2
Philippines	1,025	1,933	1,137	1,968	1,306	1,741	11.4	4.7	111	871	0.8	2.3
Poland	3,400	13,980	22,131	45,043	358	4,500	1.9	7.9	423	3,200	2.8	5.1
Portugal	8,020	11,666	192	..	3,555	5,919	16.5	16.1	867	2,274	3.2	5.0
Puerto Rico	2,560	3,087	996	1,227	1,366	2,486	..	..	630	928	..	..

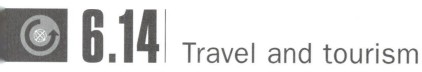

	International tourism				International tourism receipts				International tourism expenditures			
	thousands											
	Inbound tourists		Outbound tourists		$ millions		% of exports		$ millions		% of imports	
	1990	2002	1990	2002	1990	2002	1990	2002	1990	2002	1990	2002
Romania	3,009	3,204	11,247	5,757	106	612	1.7	3.8	103	396	1.0	2.1
Russian Federation	3,009	7,943	4,150	20,343	752	4,188	..	3.5	..	12,005	..	14.1
Rwanda	..	113	..	..	10	31	7.0	23.4	23	24	6.5	5.5
Saudi Arabia	2,209	7,511	..	7,896	1,884	3,420	4.0	4.7	..	7,356	..	14.9
Senegal	246	427	..	..	167	140	11.5	10.9	105	..	5.7	..
Serbia and Montenegro	1,186	448	..	..	419	77	..	2.4	..	..	..	..
Sierra Leone	98	28	..	27	19	12	9.1	..	4	6	1.9	..
Singapore	4,842	6,996	1,237	4,399	4,937	4,932	7.3	3.1	1,893	5,213	2.9	3.8
Slovak Republic	822	1,399	188	437	70	724	..	4.2	181	442	..	2.3
Slovenia	650	1,302	..	2,055	721	1,083	8.5	8.5	282	614	4.1	4.9
Somalia	..	..	..	..	..	..	..	..	..	..	..	..
South Africa	1,029	6,550	616	2,794	992	2,728	3.6	7.7	1,117	1,804	5.3	5.6
Spain	34,085	51,748	21,878	3,748	18,593	33,609	22.2	17.8	4,254	6,638	4.2	3.4
Sri Lanka	298	337	297	533	132	253	5.8	4.2	74	253	2.5	3.6
Sudan	33	52	219	..	21	56	4.2	3.3	51	91	5.8	3.1
Swaziland	263	256	..	..	30	26	4.6	2.4	35	33	4.6	2.8
Sweden	1,900	7,458	8,691	12,300	2,906	4,233	4.1	4.0	6,286	6,816	8.9	7.6
Switzerland	13,200	10,000	9,627	11,427	7,411	7,628	7.6	5.9	5,873	6,427	6.1	5.8
Syrian Arab Republic	562	1,658	1,041	4,362	320	1,366	6.4	16.6	249	610	8.4	10.2
Tajikistan	..	4	..	3	..	2	..	0.3	..	2	..	0.2
Tanzania	153	550	301	..	65	730	12.1	46.5	23	337	1.6	15.2
Thailand	5,299	10,873	883	2,044	4,326	7,902	14.8	9.6	854	3,303	2.4	4.5
Togo	103	57	..	..	58	11	8.7	2.6	40	5	4.7	0.8
Trinidad and Tobago	195	379	254	..	95	224	4.2	5.0	122	151	8.6	3.8
Tunisia	3,204	5,064	1,727	1,669	948	1,422	18.2	14.9	179	260	3.0	2.5
Turkey	4,799	12,782	2,917	5,130	3,225	9,010	15.3	16.5	520	1,881	2.0	3.4
Turkmenistan	..	..	..	..	..	..	..	..	..	..	..	..
Uganda	69	254	..	152	10	185	5.6	25.7	8	..	1.2	..
Ukraine	..	6,326	..	9,270	..	2,992	..	12.8	..	2,087	..	9.7
United Arab Emirates	633	5,445	..	..	169	1,328	..	..	..	..	..	..
United Kingdom	18,013	24,180	31,150	59,377	13,762	17,591	5.8	4.3	17,560	40,409	6.6	9.3
United States	39,362	41,892	44,623	56,359	43,007	66,547	8.0	6.8	37,349	58,044	6.1	4.2
Uruguay	1,267	1,258	..	530	262	318	12.1	11.7	111	178	6.7	7.0
Uzbekistan	..	332	..	264	..	68	..	2.3	..	..	..	..
Venezuela, RB	525	432	309	881	496	468	2.6	1.7	1,023	1,418	10.8	8.1
Vietnam	250	1,599	..	..	85	..	..	..	..	..	..	..
West Bank and Gaza	..	7	..	..	..	0	..	..	..	..	..	..
Yemen, Rep.	52	76	..	..	20	38	1.3	1.0	64	78	2.9	2.0
Zambia	141	565	..	..	41	117	3.0	11.1	54	44	2.8	3.3
Zimbabwe	605	2,068	352	..	60	76	3.0	..	66	..	3.3	..
World	**448,870 t**	**692,292 t**	**380,321 t**	**692,300 t**	**264,889 t**	**472,506 t**	**6.1 w**	**5.9 w**	**268,743 t**	**449,218 t**	**6.3 w**	**5.9 w**
Low income	10,477	23,235	..	..	5,892	12,570	5.0	5.5	4,551	10,718	3.8	4.8
Middle income	115,149	215,705	130,244	273,535	42,455	126,123	6.8	7.4	29,525	79,801	5.0	5.6
Lower middle income	55,932	130,729	49,323	98,526	25,307	77,080	7.5	7.7	..	51,214	3.1	5.8
Upper middle income	58,506	84,172	91,270	..	17,171	48,887	5.9	6.9	15,183	28,357	7.9	5.2
Low & middle income	127,339	242,033	157,717	..	48,376	138,458	6.5	7.2	34,183	92,314	4.8	5.5
East Asia & Pacific	28,191	73,291	21,595	61,131	12,577	43,448	7.3	6.3	3,947	26,658	2.4	4.4
Europe & Central Asia	42,782	75,225	124,053	183,289	9,756	36,977	7.4	8.2	..	28,911	2.6	7.2
Latin America & Carib.	30,253	43,682	16,209	27,174	13,500	28,249	7.9	6.4	12,349	19,019	9.1	4.1
Middle East & N. Africa	15,665	27,947	16,504	21,501	..	..	4.9	8.9	3,126	..	..	11.0
South Asia	3,054	4,254	3,503	6,964	1,968	3,774	5.7	3.6	1,048	4,265	2.1	3.6
Sub-Saharan Africa	7,217	19,836	..	..	3,106	7,557	3.9	6.7	3,641	5,489	5.6	5.4
High income	314,680	442,385	223,939	349,895	215,805	336,311	6.1	5.5	232,521	357,414	6.5	6.0
Europe EMU	183,210	257,531	..	..	100,855	160,354	6.6	6.8	88,022	141,301	6.0	6.3

About the data

Tourism is defined as the activities of people traveling to and staying in places outside their usual environment for no more than one consecutive year for leisure, business, and other purposes not related to an activity remunerated from within the place visited. The social and economic phenomenon of tourism has grown substantially over the past quarter of a century.

In the past, descriptions of tourism focused on the characteristics of visitors, such as the purpose of their visit and the conditions in which they traveled and stayed. Now, there is a growing awareness of the direct, indirect, and induced effects of tourism on employment, value added, personal income, government income, and the like.

Statistical information on tourism is based mainly on data on arrivals and overnight stays along with balance of payments information. But these do not completely capture the economic phenomenon of tourism. Thus governments, businesses, and citizens may not receive the information needed for effective public policies and efficient business operations. Although the World Tourism Organization reports that progress has been made in harmonizing definitions and measurement units, differences in national practices still prevent full international comparability. By 2005 the World Tourism Organization will improve coverage of tourism expenditure data by adding the balance of payments category "international passenger transportation" to "travel."

Credible data are needed on the scale and significance of tourism. Information on the role tourism plays in national economies throughout the world is particularly deficient.

The data in the table are from the World Tourism Organization. The data on international inbound and outbound tourists refer to the number of arrivals and departures of visitors within the reference period, not to the number of people traveling. Thus a person who makes several trips to a country during a given period is counted each time as a new arrival. International visitors include tourists (overnight visitors), same-day visitors, cruise passengers, and crew members.

Regional and income group aggregates are based on the World Bank's classification of countries and differ from those shown in the World Tourism Organization's publications. Countries not shown in the table but for which data are available are included in the regional and income group totals. World totals are no longer calculated by the World Tourism Organization. The aggregates in the table are calculated using the World Bank's weighted aggregation methodology (see *Statistical methods*) and differ from aggregates provided by the World Tourism Organization.

6.14a

Tourism is highest in high-income countries

$ billions, 2002

Tourism receipts are almost three times larger in high-income economies than in middle-income economies. Expenditures are more than five times the size.

Source: World Tourism Organization.

Definitions

• **International inbound tourists** (overnight visitors) are the number of tourists who travel to a country other than that in which they have their usual residence, but outside their usual environment, for a period not exceeding 12 months and whose main purpose in visiting is other than an activity remunerated from within the country visited. • **International outbound tourists** are the number of departures that people make from their country of usual residence to any other country for any purpose other than a remunerated activity in the country visited. • **International tourism receipts** are expenditures by international inbound visitors, including payments to national carriers for international transport. These receipts include any other prepayment made for goods or services received in the destination country. They also may include receipts from same-day visitors, except in cases where these are important enough to justify a separate classification. Their share in exports is calculated as a ratio to exports of goods and services (for definition of exports of goods and services see *Definitions* for table 4.9). • **International tourism expenditures** are expenditures of international outbound visitors in other countries, including payments to foreign carriers for international transport. These expenditures may include those by residents traveling abroad as same-day visitors, except in cases where these are so important as to justify a separate classification. Their share in imports is calculated as a ratio to imports of goods and services (for definition of imports of goods and services see *Definitions* for table 4.9).

Data sources

The visitor and expenditure data are available in the World Tourism Organization's *Yearbook of Tourism Statistics* and *Compendium of Tourism Statistics, 2002.* The data in the table were updated from electronic files provided by the World Tourism Organization. The data on exports and imports are from the International Monetary Fund's *International Financial Statistics* and World Bank staff estimates.

PRIMARY DATA DOCUMENTATION

The World Bank is not a primary data collection agency for most issues other than living standards surveys and debt. As a major user of socioeconomic data, however, the World Bank places particular emphasis on data documentation to inform users of data in economic analysis and policymaking. The tables in this section provide information on the sources, treatment, and currentness of the principal demographic, economic, and environmental indicators in *World Development Indicators*.

Differences in the methods and conventions used by the primary data collectors—usually national statistical agencies, central banks, and customs services—may give rise to significant discrepancies over time both among and within countries. Delays in reporting data and the use of old surveys as the base for current estimates may severely compromise the quality of national data.

Although data quality is improving in some countries, many developing countries lack the resources to train and maintain the skilled staff and obtain the equipment needed to measure and report demographic, economic, and environmental trends in an accurate and timely way. The World Bank recognizes the need for reliable data to measure living standards, track and evaluate economic trends, and plan and monitor development projects. Thus, working with bilateral and other multilateral agencies, it continues to fund and participate in technical assistance projects to improve statistical organization and basic data methods, collection, and dissemination.

The World Bank is working at several levels to meet the challenge of improving the quality of the data that it collates and disseminates. With a view to strengthening national capacity the Bank conducts technical assistance, training, and surveys at the country level in the following areas:

- Poverty assessments in most borrower member countries.
- Living standards measurement and other household and farm surveys with national statistical agency partners.
- National accounts and inflation.
- Price and expenditure surveys for the International Comparison Program.
- Projects to improve statistics in the countries of the former Soviet Union.
- External debt management.
- Environmental and economic accounting.

PRIMARY DATA DOCUMENTATION

	National currency	Fiscal year end	National accounts					Balance of payments and trade			Government finance	IMF data dissemination standard
			Reporting period	Base year	SNA price valuation	Alternative conversion factor[a]	PPP survey year	Balance of Payments Manual in use	External debt	System of trade	Accounting concept	
Afghanistan	Afghan afghani	Mar. 20	FY	1975	VAB							
Albania	Albanian lek	Dec. 31	CY	1990[b]	VAB		1996	BPM5	Actual	G	C	G
Algeria	Algerian dinar	Dec. 31	CY	1980	VAB			BPM5	Actual	S	B	
Angola	Angolan kwanza	Dec. 31	CY	1997	VAP	1991–96		BPM4	Estimate	S		G
Argentina	Argentine peso	Dec. 31	CY	1993	VAB	1971–84	1996	BPM5	Preliminary	S	C	S*
Armenia	Armenian dram	Dec. 31	CY	1996[b, c]	VAB	1990–95	2000	BPM5	Actual	S		S*
Australia	Australian dollar	Jun. 30	FY	1995[b, c]	VAB		2000	BPM5		G	C	S*
Austria	Euro	Dec. 31	CY	1995[b]	VAB		2000	BPM5		S	C	S*
Azerbaijan	Azeri manat	Dec. 31	CY	2000[b, c]	VAB	1992–95	2000	BPM5	Actual	G	C	G
Bangladesh	Bangladesh taka	Jun. 30	FY	1996[b]	VAB	1960–2002	1996	BPM5	Actual	G		G
Belarus	Belarussian rubel	Dec. 31	CY	1990[b, c]	VAB	1990–95	2000	BPM5	Actual	G	C	
Belgium	Euro	Dec. 31	CY	1995[b]	VAB		2000	BPM5		S	C	S*
Benin	CFA franc	Dec. 31	CY	1985	VAP	1992	1996	BPM5	Actual	S		G
Bolivia	Boliviano	Dec. 31	CY	1990[b]	VAB	1960–85	1996	BPM5	Actual	S	C	G
Bosnia and Herzegovina	Convertible mark	Dec. 31	CY	1996[c]	VAB			BPM5	Actual			
Botswana	Botswana pula	Dec. 31	CY	1994	VAP		1996	BPM5	Actual	G	B	G
Brazil	Brazilian real	Dec. 31	CY	1995	VAB		1996	BPM5	Preliminary	S	C	S*
Bulgaria	Bulgarian lev	Dec. 31	CY	2002[b, c]	VAB	1978–89, 1991–92	2000	BPM5	Actual	G	C	S*
Burkina Faso	CFA franc	Dec. 31	CY	1990	VAB	1992–93		BPM4	Actual	G	C	G
Burundi	Burundi franc	Dec. 31	CY	1980	VAB			BPM5	Preliminary	S	C	
Cambodia	Cambodian riel	Dec. 31	CY	2000	VAB			BPM5	Preliminary	G		G
Cameroon	CFA franc	Dec. 31	CY	1990	VAB	1965–2001	1996	BPM5	Preliminary	S	C	G
Canada	Canadian dollar	Mar. 31	CY	1995[b]	VAB		2000	BPM5		G	C	S*
Central African Republic	CFA franc	Dec. 31	CY	1987	VAB			BPM4	Estimate	S		
Chad	CFA franc	Dec. 31	CY	1995	VAB			BPM5	Preliminary	S	C	G
Chile	Chilean peso	Dec. 31	CY	1986	VAB		1996	BPM5	Actual	S	C	S*
China	Chinese yuan	Dec. 31	CY	1990	VAP	1978–93	1986	BPM5	Estimate	S	B	G
Hong Kong, China	Hong Kong dollar	Dec. 31	CY	2000	VAB		1996	BPM5		G		S*
Colombia	Colombian peso	Dec. 31	CY	1994	VAB	1992–94		BPM5	Actual	S	B	S*
Congo, Dem. Rep.	Congo franc	Dec. 31	CY	1987	VAP	1999–2001		BPM5	Preliminary	S	C	
Congo, Rep.	CFA franc	Dec. 31	CY	1978	VAP	1999–2001	1996	BPM5	Estimate	S	C	G
Costa Rica	Costa Rican colon	Dec. 31	CY	1991[b]	VAB			BPM5	Actual	S	C	S*
Côte d'Ivoire	CFA franc	Dec. 31	CY	1996	VAP		1996	BPM5	Estimate	S	C	G
Croatia	Croatian kuna	Dec. 31	CY	1997[b]	VAB		2000	BPM5	Actual	G	C	S*
Cuba	Cuban peso	Dec. 31	CY	1984	VAP					G		
Czech Republic	Czech koruna	Dec. 31	CY	1995[b]	VAB		2000	BPM5	Preliminary	G	C	S*
Denmark	Danish krone	Dec. 31	CY	1995[b]	VAB		2000	BPM5		G	C	S*
Dominican Republic	Dominican peso	Dec. 31	CY	1990	VAP			BPM5	Actual	G	C	
Ecuador	U.S. dollar	Dec. 31	CY	2000	VAP		1996	BPM5	Estimate	S	B	S*
Egypt, Arab Rep.	Egyptian pound	Jun. 30	FY	1992	VAB	1965–91	1996	BPM5	Actual	S	C	
El Salvador	Salvadoran colone	Dec. 31	CY	1990	VAP	1982–90		BPM5	Actual	S	B	S*
Eritrea	Eritrean nakfa	Dec. 31	CY	1992	VAB			BPM4	Actual			
Estonia	Estonian kroon	Dec. 31	CY	2000[b]	VAB	1991–95	2000	BPM5	Actual	G	C	S*
Ethiopia	Ethiopian birr	Jul. 7	FY	1981	VAB	1965–2002		BPM5	Preliminary	B	B	G
Finland	Euro	Dec. 31	CY	1995[b]	VAB		2000	BPM5		G	C	S*
France	Euro	Dec. 31	CY	1995[b, c]	VAB		2000	BPM5		S	C	S*
Gabon	CFA franc	Dec. 31	CY	1991	VAP	1993	1996	BPM5	Preliminary	S	B	G
Gambia, The	Gambian dalasi	Jun. 30	CY	1987	VAB			BPM5	Actual	G	B	G
Georgia	Georgian lari	Dec. 31	CY	1996[b]	VAB	1990–95	2000	BPM5	Actual	G	C	
Germany	Euro	Dec. 31	CY	1995[b]	VAB		2000	BPM5		S	C	S*
Ghana	Ghanaian cedi	Dec. 31	CY	1975	VAP	1973–87		BPM5	Actual	G	B	
Greece	Euro	Dec. 31	CY	1995[b, c]	VAB		2000	BPM5	Estimate	S	C	S*
Guatemala	Guatemalan quetzal	Dec. 31	CY	1958	VAP			BPM5	Actual	S	B	
Guinea	Guinean franc	Dec. 31	CY	1994	VAB		1996	BPM5	Estimate	S	C	G
Guinea-Bissau	CFA franc	Dec. 31	CY	1986	VAB	1970–86		BPM5	Estimate	G		G
Haiti	Haitian gourde	Sep. 30	FY	1976	VAB	1991		BPM5	Preliminary	G		

	Latest population census (including registration-based censuses)	Latest demographic, education, or health household survey	Source of most recent income and expenditure data	Vital registration complete	Latest agricultural census	Latest industrial data	Latest trade data	Latest water withdrawal data
Afghanistan		MICS, 2000						1987
Albania	1989	MICS, 2000	LSMS, 2002	Yes	1995	1990	2002	1995
Algeria	1998	MICS, 2000	HLSS, 1995		1973	1996	2000	1995
Angola	1970	MICS, 2000	Priority survey, 1995		1964–65		1991	1987
Argentina	2001		EPH, 2002	Yes	1988	1996	2002	1995
Armenia	2001	DHS, 2000	LSMS, 1996	Yes			2002	1994
Australia	2001			Yes	1990	1992	2002	1985
Austria	2001			Yes	1990	2000	2002	1991
Azerbaijan	1999	MICS, 2000	HBS, 2001	Yes			2002	1995
Bangladesh	2001	Special, 2001			1976	1997	2001	1990
Belarus	1999		IES, 2000	Yes	1994		2002	1990
Belgium	2001			Yes	1990	1997	2001	..
Benin	2002	DHS, 2001			1992–93	1981	2001	1994
Bolivia	2001	DHS, 2003	EH, 2002			1997	2002	1987
Bosnia and Herzegovina	1991	MICS, 2000	LSMS, 2001	Yes		1991		1995
Botswana	2001	MICS, 2000	HIES, 1993–94		1993	1995	2001	1992
Brazil	2000	DHS, 1996	PNAD, 2001		1996	1995	2002	1992
Bulgaria	2001		LSMS, 2001	Yes		1996	2001	1988
Burkina Faso	1996	DHS, 2003	Priority survey, 1998		1993		2001	1992
Burundi	1990	MICS, 2000	Priority survey, 1998			1991	2002	1987
Cambodia	1998	DHS, 2000	SES, 1997					1987
Cameroon	1987	DHS, 2004	Priority survey, 2001		1972–73	1999	2002	1987
Canada	2001			Yes	1991	2000	2002	1991
Central African Republic	1988	MICS, 2000	EPI, 1993			1993	1996	1987
Chad	1993	MICS, 2000						1987
Chile	2002		CASEN, 2000	Yes	1997	2000	2002	1987
China	2000	Population, 1995	HHS (Rural/Urban), 1998		1996	2000	2002	1993
Hong Kong, China	2001			Yes		2000		
Colombia	1993	DHS, 2000	ECV, 2003		1988	1999	2002	1996
Congo, Dem. Rep.	1984	MICS, 2000			1990			1990
Congo, Rep.	1996				1986	1988	1995	1987
Costa Rica	2000	CDC, 1993	EHPM, 2000	Yes	1973	2000	2002	1997
Côte d'Ivoire	1998	MICS, 2000	LSMS, 1998		1974–75	1997	2002	1987
Croatia	2001		HBS, 2001	Yes		1992	2002	1996
Cuba	2002	MICS, 2000		Yes		1989	2001	1995
Czech Republic	2001	CDC, 1993	Microcensus 1997	Yes	..		2002	1991
Denmark	2001			Yes	1989	1991	2002	1990
Dominican Republic	2002	DHS, 2002	ENFT, 1998		1971	1984	2001	1994
Ecuador	2001	CDC, 1999	LSMS, 1998		1997	1999	2002	1997
Egypt, Arab Rep.	1996	SPA, 2002	HECS, 1999	Yes	1989–90	1996	2002	1996
El Salvador	1992	CDC, 1994	EHPM, 2000	Yes	1970–71	1998	2002	1992
Eritrea	1984	DHS, 2002						
Estonia	2000			Yes	1994		2002	1995
Ethiopia	1994	DHS, 2000	ICES, 2000		1988–89	1996	2002	1987
Finland	2000			Yes	1990	1999	2002	1991
France	1999			Yes	1988	1995	2002	1999
Gabon	1993	DHS, 2000			1974–75	1995	2000	1987
Gambia, The	2003	MICS, 2000	HHS, 1998			1993	2000	1982
Georgia, Rep.	2002	MICS, 2000		Yes			2001	1990
Germany	1995			Yes	1993		2002	1991
Ghana	2000	SPA, 2002; DHS, 2003	LSMS, 1998/99		1984	1995	2001	1997
Greece	2001			Yes	1993	2000	2001	1980
Guatemala	2002	DHS, 1998–99	LSMS, 2000; ENCOVI, 2000	Yes	1979	1988	2002	1992
Guinea	1996	DHS, 1999	LSMS, 1994		1996		2001	1987
Guinea-Bissau	1991	MICS, 2000	IES, 1993		1988		1995	1991
Haiti	2003	DHS, 2000			1971	1996	1997	1991

	National currency	Fiscal year end	National accounts					Balance of payments and trade			Government finance	IMF data dissemination standard
			Reporting period	Base year	SNA price valuation	Alternative conversion factor[a]	PPP survey year	Balance of Payments Manual in use	External debt	System of trade	Accounting concept	
Honduras	Honduran lempira	Dec. 31	CY	1978	VAB	1988–89		BPM5	Actual	S		
Hungary	Hungarian forint	Dec. 31	CY	2000[b]	VAB		2000	BPM5	Actual	S	C	S*
India	Indian rupee	Mar. 31	FY	1993	VAB	1960–2002		BPM5	Actual	G	C	S*
Indonesia	Indonesian rupiah	Mar. 31	CY	1993	VAP		1996	BPM5	Preliminary	S	C	S*
Iran, Islamic Rep.	Iranian rial	Mar. 20	FY	1982	VAB	1980–90	1996	BPM5	Actual	G	C	
Iraq	Iraqi dinar	Dec. 31	CY	1969	VAB					S		
Ireland	Euro	Dec. 31	CY	1995[b]	VAB		2000	BPM5		G	C	S*
Israel	Israeli new shekel	Dec. 31	CY	2000[b]	VAP		2000	BPM5		S	C	S*
Italy	Euro	Dec. 31	CY	1995[b]	VAB		2000	BPM5		S	C	S*
Jamaica	Jamaica dollar	Dec. 31	CY	1996	VAP		1996	BPM5	Actual	G	C	G
Japan	Japanese yen	Mar. 31	CY	1995	VAB		2000	BPM5		G	C	S*
Jordan	Jordan dinar	Dec. 31	CY	1994	VAB		1996	BPM5	Actual	G	B	G
Kazakhstan	Kazakh tenge	Dec. 31	CY	1995[b,c]	VAB	1987–95	2000	BPM5	Actual	G	C	S*
Kenya	Kenya shilling	Jun. 30	CY	1982	VAB		1996	BPM5	Actual	G	B	G
Korea, Dem. Rep.	Democratic Republic of Korea won	Dec. 31	CY	..	..			BPM5				
Korea, Rep.	Korean won	Dec. 31	CY	1995[b]	VAP		2000	BPM5	Actual	S	C	S*
Kuwait	Kuwaiti dinar	Jun. 30	CY	1984	VAP			BPM5		S	C	G
Kyrgyz Republic	Kyrgyz som	Dec. 31	CY	1995[b,c]	VAB	1990–95	2000	BPM5	Actual	G	B	G
Lao PDR	Lao kip	Dec. 31	CY	1990	VAB		1993	BPM5	Preliminary	G		
Latvia	Latvian lat	Dec. 31	CY	2000[b]	VAB	1991–95	1996	BPM5	Actual	S	C	S*
Lebanon	Lebanese pound	Dec. 31	CY	1994	VAB			BPM4	Actual	G	C	G
Lesotho	Lesotho loti	Mar. 31	CY	1995	VAB			BPM5	Actual	G	C	G
Libya	Libyan dinar	Dec. 31	CY	1975	VAB	1986		BPM5		G		
Liberia	Liberian dollar	Dec. 31	CY	1992	VAB				Estimate			
Lithuania	Lithuanian litas	Dec. 31	CY	2000[b]	VAB	1990–95	2000	BPM5	Actual	G	C	S*
Macedonia, FYR	Macedonian denar	Dec. 31	CY	1997[b]	VAB		2000	BPM5	Actual	G		G
Madagascar	Malagasy franc	Dec. 31	CY	1984	VAB		1996	BPM5	Preliminary	S	C	
Malawi	Malawi kwacha	Mar. 31	CY	1994	VAB		1996	BPM5	Estimate	G	B	G
Malaysia	Malaysian ringgit	Dec. 31	CY	1987	VAP		1993	BPM5	Estimate	G	C	S*
Mali	CFA franc	Dec. 31	CY	1987	VAB		1996	BPM4	Actual	G		G
Mauritania	Mauritanian ouguiya	Dec. 31	CY	1985	VAB			BPM4	Actual	G		
Mauritius	Mauritian rupee	Jun. 30	FY	1998	VAB		1996	BPM5	Actual	G	C	G
Mexico	Mexican new peso	Dec. 31	CY	1993[b]	VAB		2000	BPM5	Actual	G	C	S*
Moldova	Moldovan leu	Dec. 31	CY	1996	VAB	1987–95	2000	BPM5	Actual	G	C	
Mongolia	Mongolian tugrik	Dec. 31	CY	1998	VAP		2000	BPM5	Actual	G	C	
Morocco	Moroccan dirham	Dec. 31	CY	1980	VAP		1996	BPM5	Preliminary	S	C	
Mozambique	Mozambican metical	Dec. 31	CY	1995	VAB	1992–95		BPM5	Estimate	S		G
Myanmar	Myanmar kyat	Mar. 31	FY	1985	VAP			BPM5	Estimate	G	C	
Namibia	Namibia dollar	Mar. 31	CY	1995	VAB			BPM5	Estimate		B	G
Nepal	Nepalese rupee	Jul. 14	FY	1985	VAB	1966–2002	1996	BPM5	Actual	S	C	G
Netherlands	Euro	Dec. 31	CY	1995[b,c]	VAB		2000	BPM5		S	C	S*
New Zealand	New Zealand dollar	Mar. 31	FY	1995	VAB		2000	BPM5		G	B	
Nicaragua	Nicaraguan gold cordoba	Dec. 31	CY	1998	VAP	1965–93		BPM5	Actual	S	C	
Niger	CFA franc	Dec. 31	CY	1987	VAP	1993		BPM5	Preliminary	S		G
Nigeria	Nigerian naira	Dec. 31	CY	1987	VAB	1971–98	1996	BPM5	Estimate	G		G
Norway	Norwegian krone	Dec. 31	CY	1995[b,c]	VAB		2000	BPM5		G	C	S*
Oman	Rial Omani	Dec. 31	CY	1978	VAP		1996	BPM5	Actual	G	B	G
Pakistan	Pakistan rupee	Jun. 30	FY	1981	VAB	1972–2002	1996	BPM5	Preliminary	G	C	G
Panama	Panamanian balboa	Dec. 31	CY	1982[c]	VAP		1996	BPM5	Actual	S	C	G
Papua New Guinea	Papua New Guinea kina	Dec. 31	CY	1983	VAP	1989		BPM5	Actual	G	B	
Paraguay	Paraguayan guarani	Dec. 31	CY	1982	VAP	1982–88		BPM5	Actual	G	C	G
Peru	Peruvian new sol	Dec. 31	CY	1994	VAB	1985–91	1996	BPM5	Actual	G	C	S*
Philippines	Philippine peso	Dec. 31	CY	1985	VAB		1996	BPM5	Actual	G	B	S*
Poland	Polish zloty	Dec. 31	CY	2002[b,c]	VAB		2000	BPM5	Actual	S	C	S*
Portugal	Euro	Dec. 31	CY	1995[b]	VAB		2000	BPM5		S	C	S*
Puerto Rico	U.S. dollar	Jun. 30	FY	1954	VAP					G		

PRIMARY DATA DOCUMENTATION

	Latest population census (including registration-based censuses)	Latest demographic, education, or health household survey	Source of most recent income and expenditure data	Vital registration complete	Latest agricultural census	Latest industrial data	Latest trade data	Latest water withdrawal data
Honduras	2001	CDC, 1994	EPHPM, 1999		1993	1996	2002	1992
Hungary	2001		FBS, 1998	Yes	1994	2000	2002	1991
India	2001	Benchmark, 1998–2002	LSMS, 1997–98 [d]		1986	2000	2002	1990
Indonesia	2000	DHS, 2002; Special, 2002	SUSENAS, 2002		1993	2000	2002	1990
Iran, Islamic Republic	1996	Demographic, 1995	SECH, 1998		1988	1993	2002	1993
Iraq	1997	MICS, 2000			1981	1992		1990
Ireland	2002			Yes	1991	1999	2002	1980
Israel	1995			Yes	1983	1996	2002	1997
Italy	2001			Yes	1990	2000	2002	1998
Jamaica	2001	CDC, 1997; MICS, 2000	LSMS, 2000		1979	1996	2002	1993
Japan	2000			Yes	1990	2000	2002	1992
Jordan	1994	DHS, 2002	HIES, 1997		1997	1997	2002	1993
Kazakhstan	1999	DHS, 1999	HBS, 2001	Yes			2001	1993
Kenya	1999	DHS, 2003	WMS II, 1997		1981	2000	2002	1990
Korea, Dem. Rep.	1993	MICS, 2000						1987
Korea, Rep.	2000				1991	2000	2002	1994
Kuwait	1995	FHS, 1996		Yes	1970	1999	1999	1994
Kyrgyz Rep.	1999	DHS, 1997	HBS, 2001	Yes			2002	1994
Lao PDR	1995	MICS, 2000	ECS I, 1997		1999			1987
Latvia, Rep.	2000		HBS, 1998	Yes	1994	1996	2002	1994
Lebanon	1970	MICS, 2000			1999		2001	1996
Lesotho	2001	MICS, 2000			1989–90	1985		1987
Libya	1995	MICS, 2000			1987		1998	1999
Liberia								1987
Lithuania	2001		LSMS, 2000	Yes	1994		2002	1995
Macedonia, FYR	2002			Yes	1994	1996	2001	1996
Madagascar	1993	MICS, 2000; DHS, 2003	Priority survey, 2001		1984	1988	1999	1984
Malawi	1998	EdData, 2002	HHS, 1997		1992–93	1998	2001	1994
Malaysia	2000		HIBAS, 1997	Yes		1999	2002	1995
Mali	1998	DHS, 2001	EMCES, 1994		1978		1997	1987
Mauritania	2000	Special, 2003	LSMS, 2000		1985		1996	1985
Mauritius	2000	CDC, 1991		Yes		1997	2002	..
Mexico	2000	Population, 1995	ENIGH, 2002	Yes	1991	2000	2002	1998
Moldova	1989	MICS, 2000	HBS, 2000	Yes			2002	1992
Mongolia	2000	MICS, 2000	LSMS/Integrated Survey, 1998			1995	2002	1993
Morocco	1994	DHS, 2003	LSMS, 1998/99		1997	2000	2002	1998
Mozambique	1997	Interim, 2003	NHS, 1996/97				2001	1992
Myanmar	1983	MICS, 2000			1993		1992	1987
Namibia	2001	DHS, 2000	NHIES, 1993		1995	1994	2001	1991
Nepal	2001	DHS, 2001	LSMS, 1996		1992	1996	2000	1994
Netherlands	2002			Yes	1989	2000	2002	1991
New Zealand	2001			Yes	1990	1996	2002	1991
Nicaragua	1995	DHS, 2001	LSMS, 2001		1963		2002	1998
Niger	2001	MICS, 2000	LSMS, 1995		1980	1998	2001	1988
Nigeria	1991	DHS, 2003	NCS, 1996		1960	1996	2000	1987
Norway	2001			Yes	1989	1999	2002	1985
Oman	2003	FHS, 1995			1979	2000	2002	1991
Pakistan	1998	RHS, 2000–01	PIHS, 1998/99		1990	1996	2002	1991
Panama	2000	LSMS, 1997	EH, 2000		1990	1999	2002	1990
Papua New Guinea	2000	DHS, 1996	HGS, 1997				2000	1987
Paraguay	2002	CDC, 1998	EPH, 2003		1991	1991	2002	1987
Peru	1993	DHS, 2000	ENAHO, 2003		1994	1996	2002	1992
Philippines	2000	DHS, 2003	FIES, 2000		1991	1997	2002	1995
Poland	2002		HBS, 1998	Yes	1990	2000	2002	1991
Portugal	2001			Yes	1989	1995	2002	1990
Puerto Rico	2000			Yes	1987	2000		

PRIMARY DATA DOCUMENTATION

	National currency	Fiscal year end	National accounts					Balance of payments and trade			Government finance	IMF data dissemi- nation stan- dard
			Reporting period	Base year	SNA price valuation	Alternative conversion factor[a]	PPP survey year	Balance of Payments Manual in use	External debt	System of trade	Accounting concept	
Romania	Romanian leu	Dec. 31	CY	1998[c]	VAB	1987–89, 1992	2000	BPM5	Actual	S	C	G
Russian Federation	Russian ruble	Dec. 31	CY	2000[b, c]	VAB	1987–95	2000	BPM5	Estimate	G	C	
Rwanda	Rwanda franc	Dec. 31	CY	1995	VAP			BPM5	Estimate	G	C	G
Saudi Arabia	Saudi Arabian riyal	Dec. 31	CY	1999	VAP			BPM4	Estimate	G		
Senegal	CFA franc	Dec. 31	CY	1987	VAP	.	1996	BPM5	Preliminary	S	B	G
Serbia and Montenegro	Yugoslav new dinar	Dec. 31	CY	1994	VAP				Preliminary			
Sierra Leone	Sierra Leonean leone	Jun. 30	CY	1990	VAB	1971–79, 1987	1996	BPM5	Actual	G	B	G
Singapore	Singapore dollar	Mar. 31	CY	1995	VAB		1996	BPM5		G	C	S*
Slovak Republic	Slovak koruna	Dec. 31	CY	1995[b]	VAP		2000	BPM5	Actual	G	C	S*
Slovenia	Slovenian tolar	Dec. 31	CY	2000[b]	VAB		2000	BPM5	Actual	S	C	S*
Somalia	Somali shilling	Dec. 31	CY	1985	VAB	1977–90			Estimate			
South Africa	South African rand	Mar. 31	CY	1995	VAB			BPM5	Preliminary	S	C	S*
Spain	Euro	Dec. 31	CY	1995[b]	VAB		2000	BPM5		S	C	S*
Sri Lanka	Sri Lankan rupee	Dec. 31	CY	1996	VAB		1996	BPM5	Actual	G	B	G
Sudan	Sudanese dinar	Dec. 31	CY	1982	VAB	1970–95		BPM5	Estimate	G	B	G
Swaziland	Lilangeni	Jun. 30	FY	1985	VAB				Actual		B	G
Sweden	Swedish krona	Jun. 30	CY	1995[c]	VAB		2000	BPM5		G	C	S*
Switzerland	Swiss franc	Dec. 31	CY	1995	VAB		2000	BPM5	Estimate	S	C	S*
Syrian Arab Republic	Syrian pound	Dec. 31	CY	1995	VAP	1970–2002	1996	BPM5	Estimate	S	C	
Tajikistan	Tajik somoni	Dec. 31	CY	1985[b]	VAB	1990–95	2000	BPM5	Actual	G	C	
Tanzania	Tanzania shilling	Dec. 31	CY	1992	VAB		1996	BPM5	Estimate	S		G
Thailand	Thai baht	Sep. 30	CY	1988	VAP		1996	BPM5	Preliminary	G	C	S*
Togo	CFA franc	Dec. 31	CY	1978	VAP			BPM5	Preliminary	S		G
Trinidad and Tobago	Trinidad and Tobago dollar	Dec. 31	CY	1985	VAP		1996	BPM5	Preliminary	S	C	
Tunisia	Tunisian dinar	Dec. 31	CY	1990	VAP		1996	BPM5	Actual	G	C	S*
Turkey	Turkish lira	Dec. 31	CY	1987	VAB		2000	BPM5	Actual	S	C	S*
Turkmenistan	Turkmen manat	Dec. 31	CY	1987[b]	VAB	1987–95	2000	BPM5		G		
Uganda	Uganda shilling	Jun. 30	FY	1998	VAB	1980–99		BPM5	Actual	G	B	G
Ukraine	Ukrainian hryvnia	Dec. 31	CY	1990[b, c]	VAB	1990–95	2000	BPM5	Actual	G	C	S*
United Arab Emirates	U.A.E. dirham	Dec. 31	CY	1985	VAB			BPM4		G	B	
United Kingdom	Pound sterling	Dec. 31	CY	1995[b]	VAB		2000	BPM5		G	C	S*
United States	U.S. dollar	Sep. 30	CY	1995[c]	VAB		2000	BPM5		G	C	S*
Uruguay	Uruguayan peso	Dec. 31	CY	1983	VAP		1996	BPM5	Actual	S	C	S*
Uzbekistan	Uzbek sum	Dec. 31	CY	1997[c]	VAB	1990–95	2000	BPM5	Actual	G		
Venezuela, R.B.	Venezuelan bolivar	Dec. 31	CY	1984	VAB		1996	BPM5	Actual	G	C	G
Vietnam	Vietnamese dong	Dec. 31	CY	1994	VAP	1991	1996	BPM4	Preliminary	G	B	G
West Bank and Gaza	Israeli new shekel	Dec. 31	CY	1998	VAB							
Yemen, Rep.	Yemen rial	Dec. 31	CY	1990	VAP	1991–96	1996	BPM5	Actual	G	B	G
Zambia	Zambian kwacha	Dec. 31	CY	1994	VAB	1990–92	1996	BPM5	Preliminary	G	B	G
Zimbabwe	Zimbabwe dollar	Jun. 30	CY	1990	VAB	1991, 1998	1996	BPM5	Preliminary	G	C	G

Note: For explanation of the abbreviations used in the table see the notes.

a. World Bank estimates including adjustments for fiscal year reporting. b. Country uses the 1993 System of National Accounts methodology. c. Original chained constant price data are rescaled. d. For Uttar Pradesh and Bihar.

	Latest population census (including registration-based censuses)	Latest demographic, education, or health household survey	Source of most recent income and expenditure data	Vital registration complete	Latest agricultural census	Latest industrial data	Latest trade data	Latest water withdrawal data
Romania	2002	CDC, 1999	LSMS, 2000	Yes		1993	1995	1994
Russian Federation	2002	LSMS, 1992	LMS, Round 9, 2000	Yes	1994–95	2000	2002	1994
Rwanda	2002	SPA, 2001	LSMS, 1998		1984	1986	2002	1993
Saudi Arabia	1992	Demographic, 1999			1983		2002	1992
Senegal	2002	DHS, 2004	ESASM, 1994		1960	1997	2002	1987
Serbia and Montenegro	2002	MICS, 2000		Yes				
Sierra Leone	1985	MICS, 2000	SHEHEA, 1989–90		1985	1993		1987
Singapore	2000	General household, 1995		Yes		2000	2002	1975
Slovak Republic	2001		Microcensus, 1996	Yes		1994	2002	1991
Slovenia	2002			Yes	1991	1998	2002	1996
Somalia	1987	MICS, 2000						1987
South Africa	2001	DHS, 1998	IES, 1994/95			2000	2002	1990
Spain	2001			Yes	1989	2000	2002	1997
Sri Lanka	2001	DHS, 1993	SES, 1995/96	Yes	1982	1999	2002	1990
Sudan	1993	MICS, 2000					2002	1995
Swaziland	1997	MICS, 2000	SHIES, 1994			1995	2002	..
Sweden	1990			Yes	1981	2000	2002	1991
Switzerland	2000			Yes	1990	1997	2002	1991
Syrian Arab Republic	1994	MICS, 2000			1981	1998	2002	1995
Tajikistan	2000	MICS, 2000	LSMS, 1999	Yes	1994		2000	1994
Tanzania	2002	AIS, 2003	LSMS, 1993		1995	1999	2001	1994
Thailand	2000	DHS, 1987	SES, 2002		1993	1994	2001	1990
Togo	1981	MICS, 2000			1996		2002	1987
Trinidad and Tobago	2000	MICS, 2000	LSMS, 1992	Yes	1982	1995	2002	1997
Tunisia	1994	MICS, 2000			1961	2000	2002	1996
Turkey	2000	DHS, 1998	LSMS, 2000		1991	2000	2002	1997
Turkmenistan	1995	DHS, 2000	LSMS, 1998	Yes			2000	1994
Uganda	2002	AIS, 2004	NIHS II, 1999		1991		2002	1970
Ukraine	2001	MICS, 2000	HIES, 1999	Yes			2002	1992
United Arab Emirates	1995				1998	1981	2001	1995
United Kingdom	2001			Yes	1993	1995	2002	1991
United States	2000	Current population, 1997		Yes	1997	1995	2002	1990
Uruguay	1996		ECH, 2000	Yes	1990	1997	2002	1965
Uzbekistan	1989	Special, 2002	FBS, 2000	Yes				1994
Venezuela, R.B.	2001	MICS, 2000	EHM, 2000	Yes	1997–98	1999	2002	1970
Vietnam	1999	MICS, 2000; DHS 2002	LSMS, 1997/98		1994			1990
West Bank and Gaza	1997	Demographic, 1995			1971			
Yemen, Rep.	1994	DHS, 1997	HBS, 1998		1982–85		1998	1990
Zambia	2000	EdData, 2002	LCMS II, 1998		1990	1994	2002	1994
Zimbabwe	2002	DHS, 1999	ICES, 1995		1960	1996	2002	1987

• **Fiscal year end** is the date of the end of the fiscal year for the central government. Fiscal years for other levels of government and the reporting years for statistical surveys may differ, but if a country is designated as a fiscal year reporter in the following column, the date shown is the end of its national accounts reporting period. • **Reporting period for national accounts and balance of payments data** is designated as either calendar year (CY) or fiscal year (FY). Most economies report their national accounts and balance of payments data using calendar years, but some use fiscal years, which straddle two calendar years. In *World Development Indicators* fiscal year data are assigned to the calendar year that contains the larger share of the fiscal year. If a country's fiscal year ends before June 30, the data are shown in the first year of the fiscal period; if the fiscal year ends on or after June 30, the data are shown in the second year of the period. Balance of payments data are shown by calendar year and so are not comparable to national accounts data for countries that report their national accounts on a fiscal year basis. • **Base year** is the year used as the base period for constant price calculations in the country's national accounts. Price indexes derived from national accounts aggregates, such as the GDP deflator, express the price level relative to prices in the base year. Constant price data reported in *World Development Indicators* are rescaled to a common 1995 reference year. See *About the data* for table 4.1 for further discussion. • **SNA price valuation** shows whether value added in the national accounts is reported at basic prices (VAB) or at producer prices (VAP). Producer prices include the value of taxes paid by producers and thus tend to overstate value added in production. See *About the data* for tables 4.1 and 4.2 for further discussion of national accounts valuation. • **Alternative conversion factor** identifies the countries and years for which a World Bank–estimated conversion factor has been used in place of the official exchange rate (line rf in the IMF's *International Financial Statistics*). Estimates also include adjustments to correspond to the fiscal years in which national accounts data have been reported. See *Statistical methods* for further discussion of the use of alternative conversion factors. • **PPP survey year** refers to the latest available survey year for the International Comparison Program's estimates of purchasing power parities (PPPs). • **Balance of Payments Manual in use** refers to the classification system used for compiling and reporting data on balance of payments items in table 4.15. BPM4 refers to the fourth edition of the International

Monetary Fund's (IMF) *Balance of Payments Manual* (1977), and BPM5 to the fifth edition (1993). Since 1995 the IMF has adjusted all balance of payments data to BPM5 conventions, but some countries continue to report using the older system. • **External debt** shows debt reporting status for 2000 data. *Actual* indicates that data are as reported, *preliminary* that data are preliminary and include an element of staff estimation, and *estimate* that data are staff estimates. • **System of trade** refers to the general trade system (G) or the special trade system (S). For imports under the general trade system both goods entering directly for domestic consumption and goods entered into customs storage are recorded as imports at the time of their first arrival; under the special trade system goods are recorded as imports when declared for domestic consumption whether at time of entry or on withdrawal from customs storage. Exports under the general system comprise outward-moving goods: (a) national goods wholly or partly produced in the country; (b) foreign goods, neither transformed nor declared for domestic consumption in the country, that move outward from customs storage; and (c) nationalized goods that have been declared from domestic consumption and move outward without having been transformed. Under the special system of trade, exports comprise categories (a) and (c). In some compilations categories (b) and (c) are classified as re-exports. Direct transit trade, consisting of goods entering or leaving for transport purposes only, is excluded from both import and export statistics. See *About the data* for tables 4.5 and 4.6 for further discussion. • **Government finance accounting concept** describes the accounting basis for reporting central government financial data. For most countries government finance data have been consolidated (C) into one set of accounts capturing all the central government's fiscal activities. Budgetary central government accounts (B) exclude central government units. See *About the data* for tables 4.11, 4.12, and 4.13 for further details. • **IMF data dissemination standard** shows the countries that subscribe to the IMF's Special Data Dissemination Standard (SDDS) or the General Data Dissemination System (GDDS). *S* refers to countries that subscribe to the SDDS; *S** indicates subscribers that have posted data on the Dissemination Standards Bulletin Board Web site [dsbb.imf.org]; while *G* refers to countries that subscribe to the GDDS. The SDDS was established by the IMF for member countries that have or that might seek access to international capital markets, to guide them in providing their economic and financial data to the public. The GDDS helps

guide member countries in disseminating comprehensive, timely, accessible, and reliable economic, financial, and socio-demographic statistics. IMF member countries voluntarily elect to participate in either the SDDS or the GDDS. Both the GDDS and the SDDS are expected to enhance the availability of timely and comprehensive data and therefore contribute to the pursuit of sound macroeconomic policies; the SDDS is also expected to improve the functioning of financial markets. • **Latest population census** shows the most recent year in which a census was conducted and for which at least preliminary results have been released. • **Latest demographic, education, or health household survey** gives information on the household surveys used in compiling demographic, education, and health data presented in section 2. CDC is Centers for Disease Control and Prevention, DHS is Demographic and Health Survey, FHS is Family Health Survey, LSMS is Living Standards Measurement Study, MICS is Multiple Indicator Cluster Survey, RHS is Reproductive Health Survey, and SPA is Service Provision Assessment. • **Source of most recent income and expenditure data** shows household surveys that collect income and expenditure data. HBS is Household Budget Survey; IECS is Income, Expenditure, and Consumption Survey; IES is Income and Expenditure Survey; LSMS is Living Standards Measurement Study; and SES is Socioeconomic Survey. • **Vital registration complete** identifies countries judged to have complete registries of vital (birth and death) statistics by the United Nations Department of Economic and Social Information and Policy Analysis, Statistical Division, and reported in *Population and Vital Statistics Reports*. Countries with complete vital statistics registries may have more accurate and more timely demographic indicators. • **Latest agricultural census** shows the most recent year in which an agricultural census was conducted and reported to the Food and Agriculture Organization. • **Latest industrial data** refer to the most recent year for which manufacturing value added data at the three-digit level of the International Standard Industrial Classification (revision 2 or revision 3) are available in the United Nations Industrial Development Organization database. • **Latest trade data** shows the most recent year for which structure of merchandise trade data are available in the United Nations Statistical Division's Commodity Trade (COMTRADE) database. • **Latest water withdrawal data** refer to the most recent year for which data have been compiled from a variety of sources. See *About the data* for table 3.5 for more information.

ACRONYMS AND ABBREVIATIONS

Technical terms

AIDS	acquired immunodeficiency syndrome
BOD	biochemical oxygen demand
CFC	chlorofluorocarbon
c.i.f.	cost, insurance, and freight
COMTRADE	United Nations Statistics Division's Commodity Trade database
CO$_2$	carbon dioxide
cu. m	cubic meter
DHS	Demographic and Health Survey
DMTU	dry metric ton unit
DOTS	directly observed treatment, short-course (strategy)
DPT	diphtheria, pertussis, and tetanus
DRS	World Bank's Debtor Reporting System
ESAF	Enhanced Structural Adjustment Facility
f.o.b.	free on board
GDP	gross domestic product
GEMS	Global Environment Monitoring System
GIS	geographic information system
GNI	gross national income (formerly referred to as gross national product)
ha	hectare
HIPC	heavily indebted poor country
HIV	human immunodeficiency virus
ICD	International Classification of Diseases
ICSE	International Classification of Status in Employment
ICT	information and communications technology
IP	Internet Protocol
ISCED	International Standard Classification of Education
ISIC	International Standard Industrial Classification
ISP	Internet service provider
kg	kilogram
km	kilometer
kwh	kilowatt-hour
LIBOR	London interbank offered rate
LSMS	Living Standards Measurement Study
M0	currency and coins (monetary base)
M1	narrow money (currency and demand deposits)
M2	money plus quasi money
M3	broad money or liquid liabilities
MICS	Multiple Indicator Cluster Survey
mmbtu	millions of British thermal units
mt	metric ton
MUV	manufactures unit value
NEAP	national environmental action plan
NGO	nongovernmental organization
NO$_2$	nitrogen dioxide
ODA	official development assistance
PC	personal computer
PM10	particulate matter smaller than 10 microns
PPI	private participation in infrastructure
PPP	purchasing power parity
PRGF	Poverty Reduction and Growth Facility
R&D	research and development
SDR	special drawing right
SITC	Standard International Trade Classification
SNA	System of National Accounts
SOPEMI	Continuous Reporting System on Migration
SO$_2$	sulfur dioxide
sq. km	square kilometer
STD	sexually transmitted disease
TB	tuberculosis
TEU	twenty-foot equivalent unit
TFP	total factor productivity
ton-km	metric ton-kilometer
TSP	total suspended particulates
TU	traffic unit

Organizations

ADB	Asian Development Bank
AfDB	African Development Bank
APEC	Asia Pacific Economic Cooperation
CDC	Centers for Disease Control and Prevention
CDIAC	Carbon Dioxide Information Analysis Center
CEC	Commission of the European Communities
DAC	Development Assistance Committee of the OECD
EBRD	European Bank for Reconstruction and Development
EDF	European Development Fund
EFTA	European Free Trade Area
EIB	European Investment Bank
EMU	European Monetary Union
EU	European Union
Eurostat	Statistical Office of the European Communities
FAO	Food and Agriculture Organization
G-5	France, Germany, Japan, United Kingdom, and United States
G-7	G-5 plus Canada and Italy
G-8	G-7 plus Russian Federation
GEF	Global Environment Facility
IBRD	International Bank for Reconstruction and Development
ICAO	International Civil Aviation Organization
ICP	International Comparison Programme
ICSID	International Centre for Settlement of Investment Disputes
IDA	International Development Association
IDB	Inter-American Development Bank
IDC	International Data Corporation
IEA	International Energy Agency
IFC	International Finance Corporation
ILO	International Labour Organization
IMF	International Monetary Fund
IRF	International Road Federation
ITU	International Telecommunication Union
IUCN	World Conservation Union
MIGA	Multilateral Investment Guarantee Agency
NAFTA	North American Free Trade Agreement
NATO	North Atlantic Treaty Organization
NSF	National Science Foundation
OECD	Organisation for Economic Co-operation and Development
PAHO	Pan American Health Organization
PARIS21	Partnership in Statistics for Development in the 21st Century
S&P	Standard & Poor's
UIP	Urban Indicators Programme
UIS	UNESCO Institute for Statistics
UN	United Nations
UNAIDS	Joint United Nations Programme on HIV/AIDS
UNCED	United Nations Conference on Environment and Development
UNCHS	United Nations Centre for Human Settlements (Habitat)
UNCTAD	United Nations Conference on Trade and Development
UNDP	United Nations Development Programme
UNECE	United Nations Economic Commission for Europe
UNEP	United Nations Environment Programme
UNESCO	United Nations Educational, Scientific, and Cultural Organization
UNFPA	United Nations Population Fund
UNHCR	United Nations High Commissioner for Refugees
UNICEF	United Nations Children's Fund
UNIDO	United Nations Industrial Development Organization
UNRISD	United Nations Research Institute for Social Development
UNSD	United Nations Statistics Division
USAID	U.S. Agency for International Development
WCMC	World Conservation Monitoring Centre
WFP	World Food Programme
WHO	World Health Organization
WIPO	World Intellectual Property Organization
WITSA	World Information Technology and Services Alliance
WTO	World Trade Organization
WWF	World Wildlife Fund

STATISTICAL METHODS

This section describes some of the statistical procedures used in preparing the *World Development Indicators*. It covers the methods employed for calculating regional and income group aggregates and for calculating growth rates, and it describes the World Bank's *Atlas* method for deriving the conversion factor used to estimate gross national income (GNI) and GNI per capita in U.S. dollars. Other statistical procedures and calculations are described in the *About the data* sections following each table.

Aggregation rules

Aggregates based on the World Bank's regional and income classifications of economies appear at the end of most tables. The countries included in these classifications are shown on the flaps on the front and back covers of the book. Most tables also include aggregates for the member countries of the European Monetary Union (EMU). Members of the EMU on 1 January 2004 were Austria, Belgium, Finland, France, Germany, Greece, Ireland, Italy, Luxembourg, the Netherlands, Portugal, and Spain. Other classifications, such as the European Union and regional trade blocs, are documented in *About the data* for the tables in which they appear.

Because of missing data, aggregates for groups of economies should be treated as approximations of unknown totals or average values. Regional and income group aggregates are based on the largest available set of data, including values for the 152 economies shown in the main tables, other economies shown in table 1.6, and Taiwan, China. The aggregation rules are intended to yield estimates for a consistent set of economies from one period to the next and for all indicators. Small differences between sums of subgroup aggregates and overall totals and averages may occur because of the approximations used. In addition, compilation errors and data reporting practices may cause discrepancies in theoretically identical aggregates such as world exports and world imports.

Five methods of aggregation are used in the *World Development Indicators*:

- For group and world totals denoted in the tables by a *t*, missing data are imputed based on the relationship of the sum of available data to the total in the year of the previous estimate. The imputation process works forward and backward from 1995. Missing values in 1995 are imputed using one of several proxy variables for which complete data are available in that year. The imputed value is calculated so that it (or its proxy) bears the same relationship to the total of available data. Imputed values are usually not calculated if missing data account for more than a third of the total in the benchmark year. The variables used as proxies are GNI in U.S. dollars, total population, exports and imports of goods and services in U.S. dollars, and value added in agriculture, industry, manufacturing, and services in U.S. dollars.

- Aggregates marked by an *s* are sums of available data. Missing values are not imputed. Sums are not computed if more than a third of the observations in the series or a proxy for the series are missing in a given year.

- Aggregates of ratios are denoted by a *w* when calculated as weighted averages of the ratios (using the value of the denominator or, in some cases, another indicator as a weight) and denoted by a *u* when calculated as unweighted averages. The aggregate ratios are based on available data, including data for economies not shown in the main tables. Missing values are assumed to have the same average value as the available data. No aggregate is calculated if missing data account for more than a third of the value of weights in the benchmark year. In a few cases the aggregate ratio may be computed as the ratio of group totals after imputing values for missing data according to the above rules for computing totals.

- Aggregate growth rates are denoted by a *w* when calculated as a weighted average of growth rates. In a few cases growth rates may be computed from time series of group totals. Growth rates are not calculated if more than half the observations in a period are missing. For further discussion of methods of computing growth rates see below.

- Aggregates denoted by an *m* are medians of the values shown in the table. No value is shown if more than half the observations for countries with a population of more than 1 million are missing.

Exceptions to the rules occur throughout the book. Depending on the judgment of World Bank analysts, the aggregates may be based on as little as 50 percent of the available data. In other cases, where missing or excluded values are judged to be small or irrelevant, aggregates are based only on the data shown in the tables.

Growth rates

Growth rates are calculated as annual averages and represented as percentages. Except where noted, growth rates of values are computed from constant price series. Three principal methods are used to calculate growth rates: least squares, exponential endpoint, and geometric endpoint. Rates of change from one period to the next are calculated as proportional changes from the earlier period.

Least-squares growth rate. Least-squares growth rates are used wherever there is a sufficiently long time series to permit a reliable calculation. No growth rate is calculated if more than half the observations in a period are missing. The least-squares growth rate, *r*, is estimated by fitting a linear regression trend line to the logarithmic annual values of the variable in the relevant period. The regression equation takes the form

$$\ln X_t = a + bt,$$

which is equivalent to the logarithmic transformation of the compound growth equation,

$$X_t = X_o (1 + r)^t.$$

In this equation X is the variable, t is time, and $a = \ln X_o$ and $b = \ln (1 + r)$ are parameters to be estimated. If b^* is the least-squares estimate of b, then the average annual growth rate, r, is obtained as $[\exp(b^*) - 1]$ and is multiplied by 100 for expression as a percentage. The calculated growth rate is an average rate that is representative of the available observations over the entire period. It does not necessarily match the actual growth rate between any two periods.

Exponential growth rate. The growth rate between two points in time for certain demographic indicators, notably labor force and population, is calculated from the equation

$$r = \ln(p_n/p_1)/n,$$

where p_n and p_1 are the last and first observations in the period, n is the number of years in the period, and ln is the natural logarithm operator. This growth rate is based on a model of continuous, exponential growth between two points in time. It does not take into account the intermediate values of the series. Nor does it correspond to the annual rate of change measured at a one-year interval, which is given by $(p_n - p_{n-1})/p_{n-1}$.

Geometric growth rate. The geometric growth rate is applicable to compound growth over discrete periods, such as the payment and reinvestment of interest or dividends. Although continuous growth, as modeled by the exponential growth rate, may be more realistic, most economic phenomena are measured only at intervals, in which case the compound growth model is appropriate. The average growth rate over n periods is calculated as

$$r = \exp[\ln(p_n/p_1)/n] - 1.$$

Like the exponential growth rate, it does not take into account intermediate values of the series.

World Bank *Atlas* method

In calculating GNI and GNI per capita in U.S. dollars for certain operational purposes, the World Bank uses the *Atlas* conversion factor. The purpose of the *Atlas* conversion factor is to reduce the impact of exchange rate fluctuations in the cross-country comparison of national incomes.

The *Atlas* conversion factor for any year is the average of a country's exchange rate (or alternative conversion factor) for that year and its exchange rates for the two preceding years, adjusted for the difference between the rate of inflation in the country and that in Japan, the United Kingdom, the United States, and the Euro Zone. A country's inflation rate is measured by the change in its GDP deflator.

The inflation rate for Japan, the United Kingdom, the United States, and the Euro Zone, representing international inflation, is measured by the change in the SDR deflator. (Special drawing rights, or SDRs, are the International Monetary Fund's unit of account.) The SDR deflator is calculated as a weighted average of these countries' GDP deflators in SDR terms, the weights being the amount of each country's currency in one SDR unit. Weights vary over time because both the composition of the SDR and the relative exchange rates for each currency change. The SDR deflator is calculated in SDR terms first and then converted to U.S. dollars using the SDR to dollar *Atlas* conversion factor. The *Atlas* conversion factor is then applied to a country's GNI. The resulting GNI in U.S. dollars is divided by the midyear population to derive GNI per capita.

When official exchange rates are deemed to be unreliable or unrepresentative of the effective exchange rate during a period, an alternative estimate of the exchange rate is used in the *Atlas* formula (see below).

The following formulas describe the calculation of the *Atlas* conversion factor for year t:

$$e_t^* = \frac{1}{3}\left[e_{t-2}\left(\frac{p_t}{p_{t-2}} \Big/ \frac{p_t^{S\$}}{p_{t-2}^{S\$}}\right) + e_{t-1}\left(\frac{p_t}{p_{t-1}} \Big/ \frac{p_t^{S\$}}{p_{t-1}^{S\$}}\right) + e_t\right]$$

and the calculation of GNI per capita in U.S. dollars for year t:

$$Y_t^\$ = (Y_t/N_t)/e_t^*,$$

where e_t^* is the *Atlas* conversion factor (national currency to the U.S. dollar) for year t, e_t is the average annual exchange rate (national currency to the U.S. dollar) for year t, p_t is the GDP deflator for year t, $p_t^{S\$}$ is the SDR deflator in U.S. dollar terms for year t, $Y_t^\$$ is the *Atlas* GNI per capita in U.S. dollars in year t, Y_t is current GNI (local currency) for year t, and N_t is the midyear population for year t.

Alternative conversion factors

The World Bank systematically assesses the appropriateness of official exchange rates as conversion factors. An alternative conversion factor is used when the official exchange rate is judged to diverge by an exceptionally large margin from the rate effectively applied to domestic transactions of foreign currencies and traded products. This applies to only a small number of countries, as shown in *Primary data documentation*. Alternative conversion factors are used in the *Atlas* methodology and elsewhere in the *World Development Indicators* as single-year conversion factors.

CREDITS

This book draws on a wide range of World Bank reports and numerous external sources, listed in the bibliography following this section. Many people inside and outside the World Bank helped in writing and producing *World Development Indicators*. The team would like to particularly acknowledge the help and encouragement of François Bourguignon, Senior Vice President and Chief Economist. The team is also grateful to those who provided valuable comments on the entire book. The poverty estimates were prepared by Shaohua Chen of the World Bank's Poverty Monitoring Group with help from Prem Sangraula and Johan Mistiaen. This note identifies those who made specific contributions. Numerous others, too many to acknowledge here, helped in many ways for which the team is extremely grateful.

1. World view

Section 1 was prepared by Eric Swanson and K. M. Vijayalakshmi. Eric Swanson wrote the introduction with input from Sulekha Patel and Saeed Ordoubadi. Amy Heyman, Masako Hiraga, and Vivienne Wang assisted in developing and preparing tables and figures. Valuable suggestions were received from members of the World Bank's Human Development Network. Yonas Biru and William Prince provided substantial assistance with the data, preparing the estimates of gross national income in purchasing power parity terms. The team is grateful to Guy Karsenty and Jurgen Richtering of the World Trade Organization for providing the market access indicators and to Wayne Mitchell of the IMF for providing the HIPC indicators in table 1.4. Vinoda Basnayake assisted in preparing the table.

2. People

Section 2 was prepared by Masako Hiraga in partnership with the World Bank's Human Development Network and the Development Research Group in the Development Economics Vice Presidency. Vivienne Wang provided invaluable assistance in data and table preparation. Sulekha Patel wrote the introduction, with input from Sarwar Lateef. Contributions to the section were provided by Eduard Bos and Emi Suzuki (demography, health, and nutrition); Shaohua Chen and Martin Ravallion (poverty and income distribution); Montserrat Pallares-Miralles (vulnerability and security); Barbara Bruns, Saida Mamodova, Raymond Muhula, and Lianqin Wang (education); Lucia Fort and Maria Estela Rivero-Fuentes (gender) and Eldaw Abdalla Suliman (social indicators of poverty). The team is also grateful to Rosario Garcia, Jens Johansen, and Olivier Labe at the UNESCO Institute for Statistics for their special effort to provide us with the education data. Comments and suggestions at various stages of production also came from Eric Swanson.

3. Environment

Section 3 was prepared by M. H. Saeed Ordoubadi and Mayhar Eshragh-Tabary in partnership with the World Bank's Environmentally and Socially Sustainable Development Network and in collaboration with the World Bank's Development Research Group and Transportation, Water, and Urban Development Department. Important contributions were made by Christian Layke, Daniel Prager, and Robin White of the World Resources Institute, Ricardo Quercioli of the International Energy Agency, Orio Tampieri of the Food and Agriculture Organization, Laura Battlebury of the World Conservation Monitoring Centre, Gerhard Metchies of GTZ, and Christine Auclair, Moses Ayiemba, Bildad Kagai, Guenter Karl, Pauline Maingi, and Markanley Rai of the Urban Indicators Programme, United Nations Centre for Human Settlements. Mehdi Akhlaghi managed the databases for this section, and Mayhar Eshragh-Tabary contributed with research and data analysis. The World Bank's Environment Department and Rural Development Department devoted substantial staff resources to the book, for which the team is very grateful. M. H. Saeed Ordoubadi wrote the introduction to the section with valuable comments from Sarwar Lateef, Eric Swanson, and Bruce Ross-Larson, who also edited the text. Other contributions were made by Susmita Dasgupta, Craig Meisner, Kiran Pandey, and David Wheeler (air and water pollution) and Giovanni Ruta and Kirk Hamilton (adjusted savings). Valuable comments were also provided by Azamat Abdymomunov, Julian Bandiaks, Zeljko Bogetic, Gohar Gyulumyan, Kirk Hamilton, Aurelien Kruse, Mark Lundell, Evgenij Najdov, Luc Razafimandimby, Giovanni Ruta, Marcin Sasin, Monica Singh, and Jean van Houtte.

4. Economy

Section 4 was prepared by K. M. Vijayalakshmi in close collaboration with the Macroeconomic Data Team of the World Bank's Development Data Group, led by Soong Sup Lee. Eric Swanson and K. M. Vijayalakshmi wrote the introduction with valuable suggestions from Sarwar Lateef. Contributions to the section were provided by Azita Amjadi (trade) and Ibrahim Levent (external debt). The national accounts data for low- and middle-income economies were gathered from the World Bank's regional staff through the annual Unified Survey. Maja Bresslauer, Kay Chung, Victor Gabor, and Soong Sup Lee worked on updating, estimating, and validating the databases for national accounts. The national accounts data for OECD countries were processed by Mehdi Akhlaghi. The team is grateful to Guy Karsenty and Andreas Maurer of the World Trade Organization and Sanja Blazevic, Arunas Butkevicius, and Aurelie von Wartensleben of the United Nations Conference on Trade and Development, for providing data on trade in goods; to Tetsuo Yamada for help in obtaining the United Nations Industrial Development Organization database; and to C. Patel for helpful comments.

5. States and markets

Section 5 was prepared by David Cieslikowski and Mahyar Eshragh-Tabary in partnership with the World Bank's Private Sector and Infrastructure Network, its Poverty Reduction and Economic Management Network, the World Bank Institute, the International Finance Corporation, and external partners. David Cieslikowski wrote the introduction to the section. Other contributors include Ada Karina Izaguirre and Kathy Khuu (privatization and infrastructure projects); Andrew Newby of Euromoney (credit ratings); Simeon Djankov and Caralee McLeish (business environment); Alka Banerjee and Isilay Cabuk (Standard & Poor's emerging stock market indexes);

Yonas Biru (purchasing power parity conversion factors); Esperanza Magpantay and Michael Minges of the International Telecommunication Union (communications and information); Peter Roberts (transport); Jane Degerlund of Containerisation International (ports); Maria Helena Capelli Miguel of the United Nations Educational, Scientific and Cultural Organization Institute for Statistics (culture, research and development, scientists and engineers); Anders Halvorsen of the World Information Technology and Services Alliance; Stephen Minton of International Data Corporation (information and communications technology); Dan Gallik of the U.S. Department of State (military personnel); Bjorn Hagelin and Petter Stålenheim of the Stockholm International Peace Research Institute (military expenditures and arms transfers); and Lise McLeod of the World Intellectual Property Organization (patents data).

6. Global links

Section 6 was prepared by Amy Heyman in collaboration with Eric Swanson and external partners. Substantial input came from Azita Amjadi, Jerzy Rozanski (tariffs), and Ibrahim Levent (financial data). Other contributors include Bernard Hoekman, Francis Ng, and Marcelo Olarreaga (trade); Betty Dow (commodity prices); Aki Kuwahara of the United Nations Conference on Trade and Development; Cecile Thoreau and Pauline Fron of the Organisation for Economic Co-operation and Development (OECD) (migration); Yasmin Ahmad, Brian Hammond, and Aimee Nichols of the OECD (aid flows); and Antonio Massieu and Azucena Pernia of the World Tourism Organization (tourism data). Mehdi Akhlaghi provided valuable technical assistance.

Other parts

Preparation of the maps on the inside covers was coordinated by Jeff Lecksell and Greg Prakas of the World Bank's Map Design Unit. The *Users guide* was prepared by David Cieslikowski. *Statistical methods* was written by Eric Swanson. *Primary data documentation* was coordinated by K. M. Vijayalakshmi, who served as database administrator. Gladys Gicker and Estela Zamora assisted in updating the *Primary data documentation* table. Mehdi Akhlaghi was responsible for database updates and aggregation. *Acronyms and abbreviations* was prepared by Amy Heyman. The index was collated by Richard Fix and Gonca Okur.

Database management

Database management was coordinated by Mehdi Akhlaghi with the cross-team participation of Development Data Group staff to create an integrated *World Development Indicators* database. This database was used to generate the tables for *World Development Indicators* and related products such as *WDI Online, The World Bank Atlas, The Little Data Book,* and the *World Development Indicators* CD-ROM.

Design, production, and editing

Richard Fix coordinated all stages of production with Communications Development Incorporated. Communications Development Incorporated provided overall design direction, editing, and layout, led by Meta de Coquereaumont and Bruce Ross-Larson. The editing and production team consisted of Joseph Costello, Elizabeth McCrocklin, Christopher Trott, and Elaine Wilson. Communications Development's London partner, Grundy & Northedge, provided art direction and design. Staff from External Affairs oversaw publication and dissemination of the book.

Client services

The Development Data Group's Client Services Team (Azita Amjadi, Richard Fix, Naomi Halewood, Gonca Okur, and William Prince) contributed to the design and planning of *World Development Indicators* and *The World Bank Atlas* and helped coordinate work with the Office of the Publisher.

Administrative assistance and office technology support

Estela Zamora provided administrative assistance and assisted in updating the databases. Jean-Pierre Djomalieu, Gytis Kanchas, Nacer Megherbi, and Shahin Outadi provided information technology support

Publishing and dissemination

The Office of the Publisher, under the direction of Dirk Koehler, provided valuable assistance throughout the production process. Randi Park coordinated printing and supervised marketing and distribution. Chris Neal of the Development Economics Vice President's office and Carl Hanlor of External Affairs managed the communications strategy, and the Regional Operations Group headed by Paul Mitchell helped coordinate the overseas release.

World Development Indicators CD-ROM

Programming and testing were carried out by Reza Farivari and his team: Azita Amjadi, Ying Chi, Ramgopal Erabelly, Nacer Megherbi, Shahin Outadi, and William Prince. Masako Hiraga produced the social indicators tables. William Prince coordinated user interface design and overall production and provided quality assurance.

WDI Online

Design, programming, and testing were carried out by Reza Farivari and his team: Mehdi Akhlagi, Azita Amjadi, Ying Chi, Shahin Outadi, and Nacer Megherbi. William Prince coordinated production and provided quality assurance. Cybèle Bourgougnon of the Office of the Publisher was responsible for implementation of *WDI Online* and management of the subscription service.

Client feedback

The team is grateful to the many people who have taken the time to provide comment on its publications. Their feedback and suggestions have helped improve this year's edition.

BIBLIOGRAPHY

AbouZahr, Carla. 2000. "Maternal Mortality." *OECD Observer* (223): 29–30.

AbouZahr, Carla, Tessa Wardlaw. 2003. "Maternal Mortality in 2000: Estimates developed by WHO, UNICEF, and UNFPA."

Ahmad, Sultan. 1992. "Regression Estimates of Per Capita GDP Based on Purchasing Power Parities." Policy Research Working Paper 956. World Bank, International Economics Department, Washington, D.C.

———. 1994. "Improving Inter-Spatial and Inter-Temporal Comparability of National Accounts." *Journal of Development Economics* 44: 53–75.

Allen, Richard, Salvatore Schiavo-Campo, and Thomas Columkill Garrity. 2004. *Assessing and Reforming Public Financial Management: A New Approach.* Washington, D.C.: World Bank.

Ball, Nicole. 1984. "Measuring Third World Security Expenditure: A Research Note." *World Development* 12(2): 157–64.

Barro, Robert J. 1991. "Economic Growth in a Cross-Section of Countries." *Quarterly Journal of Economics* 106(2): 407–44.

Beck, Thorsten, and Ross Levine. 2001. "Stock Markets, Banks, and Growth: Correlation or Causality?" Policy Research Working Paper 2670. World Bank, Development Research Group, Washington, D.C.

Behrman, Jere R., and Mark R. Rosenzweig. 1994. "Caveat Emptor: Cross-Country Data on Education and the Labor Force." *Journal of Development Economics* 44: 147–71.

Bhalla, Surjit. 2002. *Imagine There Is No Country: Poverty, Inequality, and Growth in the Era of Globalization.* Washington, D.C.: Institute for International Economics.

Bloom, David E., and Jeffrey G. Williamson. 1998. "Demographic Transitions and Economic Miracles in Emerging Asia." *World Bank Economic Review* 12(3): 419–55.

Brown, Lester R., and others. 1999. *Vital Signs 1999: The Environmental Trends That Are Shaping Our Future.* New York and London: W. W. Norton for Worldwatch Institute.

Brown, Lester R., Christopher Flavin, Hilary F. French, and others. 1998. *State of the World 1998.* Washington, D.C.: Worldwatch Institute.

Brown, Lester R., Michael Renner, Christopher Flavin, and others. 1998. *Vital Signs 1998.* Washington, D.C.: Worldwatch Institute.

Bruns, Barbara, Alain Mingat, and Ramahatra Rakotomalala. 2003. *A Chance for Every Child.* Washington, D.C.: World Bank.

Bulatao, Rodolfo. 1998. *The Value of Family Planning Programs in Developing Countries.* Santa Monica, Calif.: Rand.

Caiola, Marcello. 1995. *A Manual for Country Economists.* Training Series 1, vol. 1. Washington, D.C.: International Monetary Fund.

Chaudhury, Nazmul, Jeffrey S. Hammer, Michael Kremer, Karthik Muralidharan, and F. Halsey Rogers. 2004. "Teacher and Health Care Provider Absenteeism: A Multi-Country Study." World Bank, Washington, D.C.

Chen, Shaohua, and Martin Ravallion. 2000. "How Did the World's Poorest Fare in the 1990s?" Policy Research Working Paper 2409. World Bank, Development Research Group, Washington, D.C.

Collier, Paul, and David Dollar. 1999. "Aid Allocation and Poverty Reduction." Policy Research Working Paper 2041. World Bank, Development Research Group, Washington, D.C.

———. 2001. "Can the World Cut Poverty in Half? How Policy Reform and Effective Aid Can Meet the International Development Goals." Policy Research Working Paper 2403. World Bank, Development Research Group, Washington, D.C.

Collins, Wanda W., Emile A. Frison, and Suzanne L. Sharrock. 1997. "Global Programs: A New Vision in Agricultural Research." *Issues in Agriculture* (World Bank, Consultative Group on International Agricultural Research, Washington, D.C.) 12: 1–28.

Commission of the European Communities, International Monetary Fund, Organisation for Economic Co-operation and Development, United Nations, and World Bank. 2002. *System of Environmental and Economic Accounts: SEEA 2000.* New York.

Containerisation International. 2004. *Containerisation International Yearbook 2004.* London.

Corrao, Marlo Ann, G. Emmanuel Guindon, Namita Sharma, and Donna Fakhrabadi Shokoohi, eds. 2000. *Tobacco Control Country Profiles.* Atlanta: American Cancer Society.

Deaton, Angus. 2002. "Counting the World's Poor: Problems and Possible Solutions." *World Bank Research Observer* 16(2): 125–47.

Demirgüç-Kunt, Asli, and Enrica Detragiache. 1997. "The Determinants of Banking Crises: Evidence from Developed and Developing Countries." Working paper. World Bank and International Monetary Fund, Washington, D.C.

Demirgüç-Kunt, Asli, and Ross Levine. 1996a. "Stock Market Development and Financial Intermediaries: Stylized Facts." *World Bank Economic Review* 10(2): 291–321.

———. 1996b. "Stock Markets, Corporate Finance, and Economic Growth: An Overview." *World Bank Economic Review* 10(2): 223–39.

———. 1999. "Bank-Based and Market-Based Financial Systems: Cross-Country Comparisons." Policy Research Working Paper 2143. World Bank, Development Research Group, Washington, D.C.

de Onis, Mercedes, and Monika Blossner. 2000. "The WHO Global Database on Child Growth and Malnutrition: Methodology and Applications." *International Journal of Epidemiology* 32: 518–26.

Development Committee. September 22, 2003. SecM2003-0370: "Supporting Sound Policies with Adequate and Appropriate Financing: Implementing the Monterrey Consensus at the Country Level."

DKT International. 1998. *1997 Contraceptive Social Marketing Statistics.* Washington, D.C.

Doyle, John J., and Gabrielle J. Persley, eds. 1996. *Enabling the Safe Use of Biotechnology: Principles and Practice*. Environmentally Sustainable Development Studies and Monographs Series, no. 10. Washington, D.C.: World Bank.

Drucker, Peter F. 1994. "The Age of Social Transformation." *Atlantic Monthly* 274 (November).

Easterly, William. 2000. "Growth Implosions, Debt Explosions, and My Aunt Marilyn: Do Growth Slowdowns Cause Public Debt Crises?" Policy Research Working Paper 2531. World Bank, Development Research Group, Washington, D.C.

Euromoney. 2003. September. London.

Eurostat (Statistical Office of the European Communities). Various years. *Demographic Statistics*. Luxembourg.

———. Various years. *Statistical Yearbook*. Luxembourg.

Evenson, Robert E., and Carl E. Pray. 1994. "Measuring Food Production (with Reference to South Asia)." *Journal of Development Economics* 44: 173–97.

Faiz, Asif, Christopher S. Weaver, and Michael P. Walsh. 1996. *Air Pollution from Motor Vehicles: Standards and Technologies for Controlling Emissions*. Washington, D.C.: World Bank.

Fallon, Peter, and Zafiris Tzannatos. 1998. *Child Labor: Issues and Directions for the World Bank*. Washington, D.C.: World Bank.

Fankhauser, Samuel. 1995. *Valuing Climate Change: The Economics of the Greenhouse*. London: Earthscan.

FAO (Food and Agriculture Organization). 1986. "Inter-Country Comparisons of Agricultural Production Aggregates." Economic and Social Development Paper 61. Rome.

———. 1996. *Food Aid in Figures 1994*. Vol. 12. Rome.

———. 2003. *State of the World's Forests 2003*. Rome.

———. Various years. *Fertilizer Yearbook*. FAO Statistics Series. Rome.

———. Various years. *Production Yearbook*. FAO Statistics Series. Rome.

———. Various years. *The State of Food Insecurity in the World*. Rome.

———. Various years. *Trade Yearbook*. FAO Statistics Series. Rome.

Frankel, Jeffrey. 1993. "Quantifying International Capital Mobility in the 1990s." In Jeffrey Frankel, ed., *On Exchange Rates*. Cambridge, Mass.: MIT Press.

Frankhauser, Pierre. 1994. "Fractales, tissus urbains et reseaux de transport." *Revue d'economie politique* 104: 435–55.

Fredricksen, Birger. 1993. *Statistics of Education in Developing Countries: An Introduction to Their Collection and Analysis*. Paris: UNESCO.

Gallup, John L., and Jeffrey D. Sachs. 1998. "The Economic Burden of Malaria." Harvard Institute for International Development, Cambridge, Mass.

Gannon, Colin, and Zmarak Shalizi. 1995. "The Use of Sectoral and Project Performance Indicators in Bank-Financed Transport Operations." TWU Discussion Paper 21. World Bank, Transportation, Water, and Urban Development Department, Washington, D.C.

Gardner, Robert. 1998. "Education." Demographic and Health Surveys, Comparative Study 29. Macro International, Calverton, Md.

Gardner-Outlaw, Tom, and Robert Engelman. 1997. "Sustaining Water, Easing Scarcity: A Second Update." Population Action International, Washington, D.C.

Goldfinger, Charles. 1994. *L'utile et le futile: L'économie de l'immatériel*. Paris: Editions Odile Jacob.

GTZ (German Agency for Technical Cooperation). 2002. *Fuel Prices and Taxation*. Eschborn, Germany.

Gupta, Sanjeev, Hamid Davoodi, and Erwin Tiongson. 2000. "Corruption and the Provision of Health Care and Education Services." IMF Working Paper 00/116. International Monetary Fund, Washington, D.C.

Gupta, Sanjeev, Brian Hammond, and Eric Swanson. 2000. "Setting the Goals." *OECD Observer* (223): 15–17.

Habyarimana, James, Jishnu Das, Stefan Dercon, and Pramila Krishnan. 2003. "Sense and Absence: Absenteeism and Learning in Zambian Schools." World Bank, Washington, D.C.

Hamilton, Kirk, and Michael Clemens. 1999. "Genuine Savings Rates in Developing Countries." *World Bank Economic Review* 13(2): 333–56.

Happe, Nancy, and John Wakeman-Linn. 1994. "Military Expenditures and Arms Trade: Alternative Data Sources." IMF Working Paper 94/69. International Monetary Fund, Policy Development and Review Department, Washington, D.C.

Harrison, Ann. 1995. "Factor Markets and Trade Policy Reform." World Bank, Washington, D.C.

Hatzichronoglou, Thomas. 1997. "Revision of the High-Technology Sector and Product Classification." STI Working Paper 1997/2. OECD Directorate for Science, Technology, and Industry, Paris.

Heck, W. W. 1989. "Assessment of Crop Losses from Air Pollutants in the U.S." In J. J. McKenzie and M. T. El Ashry, eds., *Air Pollution's Toll on Forests and Crops*. New Haven, Conn.: Yale University Press.

Heggie, Ian G. 1995. *Management and Financing of Roads: An Agenda for Reform*. World Bank Technical Paper 275. Washington, D.C.

Heston, Alan. 1994. "A Brief Review of Some Problems in Using National Accounts Data in Level of Output Comparisons and Growth Studies." *Journal of Development Economics* 44: 29–52.

Hettige, Hemamala, Muthukumara Mani, and David Wheeler. 1998. "Industrial Pollution in Economic Development: Kuznets Revisited." Policy Research Working Paper 1876. World Bank, Development Research Group, Washington, D.C.

Hill, Kenneth, Carla AbouZahr, and Tessa Wardlaw. 2001. "Estimates of Maternal Mortality for 1995." *Bulletin of the World Health Organization* 79(3): 182–93.

Hill, Kenneth, Rohini Pande, Mary Mahe, and Gareth Jones. 1999. *Trends in Child Mortality in the Developing World: 1960 to 1996*. New York: UNICEF.

BIBLIOGRAPHY

IEA (International Energy Agency). 2002. *World Energy Outlook: Energy and Poverty.* Paris.

———. Various years. *Energy Balances of OECD Countries.* Paris.

———. Various years. *Energy Statistics and Balances of Non-OECD Countries.* Paris.

———. Various years. *Energy Statistics of OECD Countries.* Paris.

IFPRI (International Food Policy Research Institute). 1999. *Soil Degradation: A Threat to Developing-Country Food Security by 2020.* Washington, D.C.

ILO (International Labour Organization). 1990. *ILO Manual on Concepts and Methods.* Geneva: International Labour Office.

———. Various years. *Key Indicators of the Labour Market 2001–2002.* Geneva: International Labour Office.

———. Various years. *Sources and Methods: Labour Statistics* (formerly *Statistical Sources and Methods*). Geneva: International Labour Office.

———. Various years. *Yearbook of Labour Statistics.* Geneva: International Labour Office.

IMF (International Monetary Fund). 1977. *Balance of Payments Manual.* 4th ed. Washington, D.C.

———. 1993. *Balance of Payments Manual.* 5th ed. Washington, D.C.

———. 1995. *Balance of Payments Compilation Guide.* Washington, D.C.

———. 1996a. *Balance of Payments Textbook.* Washington, D.C.

———. 2000. *Monetary and Financial Statistics Manual.* Washington, D.C.

———. 2001. *A Manual on Government Finance Statistics.* Washington, D.C.

———. 2002. *Exchange Arrangements and Exchange Restrictions Annual Report, 2002.* Washington, D.C.

———. Various issues. *Direction of Trade Statistics.* Quarterly. Washington, D.C.

———. Various issues. *International Financial Statistics.* Monthly. Washington, D.C.

———. Various years. *Balance of Payments Statistics Yearbook.* Parts 1 and 2. Washington, D.C.

———. Various years. *Direction of Trade Statistics Yearbook.* Washington, D.C.

———. Various years. *Government Finance Statistics Yearbook.* Washington, D.C.

———. Various years. *International Financial Statistics Yearbook.* Washington, D.C.

IMF (International Monetary Fund), OECD (Organisation for Economic Co-operation and Development), United Nations, and World Bank. 2000. *A Better World for All: Progress towards the International Development Goals.* Washington, D.C.

Institutional Investor. 2003. September. New York.

International Civil Aviation Organization. 2002. *Civil Aviation Statistics of the World, 1999–2000.* Montreal.

International Road Federation. 2002. *World Road Statistics 2002.* Geneva.

International Working Group of External Debt Compilers (Bank for International Settlements, International Monetary Fund, Organisation for Economic Co-operation and Development, and World Bank). 1987. *External Debt Definitions.* Washington, D.C.

Inter-Secretariat Working Group on National Accounts (Commission of the European Communities, International Monetary Fund, Organisation for Economic Co-operation and Development, United Nations, and World Bank). 1993. *System of National Accounts.* Brussels, Luxembourg, New York, and Washington, D.C.

IPCC (Intergovernmental Panel on Climate Change). 2001. *Climate Change 2001.* Cambridge: Cambridge University Press.

ITU (International Telecommunication Union). 2003a. *World Telecommunication Development Report 2003.* Geneva.

———. 2003b. *World Telecommunications Indicators Database.* Geneva.

IUCN (World Conservation Union). 1998. *1997 IUCN Red List of Threatened Plants.* Gland, Switzerland.

———. 2000. *2000 IUCN Red List of Threatened Animals.* Gland, Switzerland.

Journal of Development Economics. 1994. Special issue on Database for Development Analysis. Edited by T. N. Srinivasan. Vol. 44, no. 1.

Kaminsky, Graciela L., Saul Lizondo, and Carmen M. Reinhart. 1997. "Leading Indicators of Currency Crises." Policy Research Working Paper 1852. World Bank, Latin America and the Caribbean Region, Office of the Chief Economist, Washington, D.C.

Kaufmann, Daniel, and Art Kraay. 2002. "Growth Without Governance." Policy Research Working Paper 2928. World Bank, Washington, D.C.

Kaufmann, Daniel, Art Kraay, and Massimo Mastruzzi. 2003. "Governance Matters III: Governance Indicators for 1996–2002." Policy Research Working Paper 3106. World Bank, Washington, D.C.

Klasen, Stephen. 1999. "Does Gender Inequality Reduce Growth and Development? Evidence from Cross-Country Regressions." World Bank, 2001, background paper for *Engendering Development—Through Gender Equality in Rights, Resources, and Voice.*

Knetter, Michael. 1994. *Why Are Retail Prices in Japan So High? Evidence from German Export Prices.* NBER Working Paper 4894. Cambridge, Mass.: National Bureau of Economic Research.

Kunte, Arundhati, Kirk Hamilton, John Dixon, and Michael Clemens. 1998. "Estimating National Wealth: Methodology and Results." Environmental Economics Series, no. 57. World Bank, Environment Department, Washington, D.C.

Lanjouw, Jean O., and Peter Lanjouw. 2001. "The Rural Non-Farm Sector: Issues and Evidence from Developing Countries." *Agricultural Economics* 26: 1–23.

Lanjouw, Peter, and Gershon Feder. 2001. *Rural Nonfarm Activities and Rural Development: From Experience toward Strategy.* Rural Strategy Discussion Paper 4. Washington, D.C.: World Bank.

Lewis, Karen K. 1995. "Puzzles in International Financial Markets." In Gene Grossman and Kenneth Rogoff, eds., *Handbook of International Economics.* Vol. 3. Amsterdam: North Holland.

Lewis, Stephen R., Jr. 1989. "Primary Exporting Countries." In Hollis Chenery and T. N. Srinivasan, eds., *Handbook of Development Economics*. Vol. 2. Amsterdam: North Holland.

Lovei, Magdolna. 1997. "Toward Effective Pollution Management." *Environment Matters* (fall): 52–53.

Lucas, R. E. 1988. "On the Mechanics of Economic Development." *Journal of Monetary Economics* 22: 3–22.

Mani, Muthukumara, and David Wheeler. 1997. "In Search of Pollution Havens? Dirty Industry in the World Economy, 1960–95." World Bank, Policy Research Department, Washington, D.C.

McCarthy, F. Desmond, and Holger Wolf. 2001. "Comparative Life Expectancy in Africa." Policy Research Working Paper 2668. World Bank, Development Research Group, Washington, D.C.

Midgley, Peter. 1994. *Urban Transport in Asia: An Operational Agenda for the 1990s*. World Bank Technical Paper 224. Washington, D.C.

Moody's Investors Service. 2003. *Sovereign, Sub-national and Sovereign-Guaranteed Issuers*. January. New York.

Morgenstern, Oskar. 1963. *On the Accuracy of Economic Observations*. Princeton, N.J.: Princeton University Press.

Morisset, Jacques. 2000. "Foreign Direct Investment in Africa: Policies Also Matter." Policy Research Working Paper 2481. World Bank, Washington, D.C.

Murray, Christopher J. L., and Alan D. Lopez. 1996. *The Global Burden of Disease*. Cambridge, Mass.: Harvard University Press.

National Science Foundation. 2003. *Science and Engineering Indicators 2003*. Arlington, Va.

Netcraft. 2003. *Netcraft Secure Server Survey*. [http://www.netcraft.com/].

NRI and World Bank. 2003. "Public Expenditure and Service Delivery in Papua New Guinea: Draft." World Bank: Washington, D.C.

Obstfeldt, Maurice. 1995. "International Capital Mobility in the 1990s." In P. B. Kenen, ed., *Understanding Interdependence: The Macroeconomics of the Open Economy*. Princeton, N.J.: Princeton University Press.

Obstfeldt, Maurice, and Kenneth Rogoff. 1996. *Foundations of International Macroeconomics*. Cambridge, Mass.: MIT Press.

OECD (Organisation for Economic Co-operation and Development). 1985. *Measuring Health Care 1960–1983: Expenditure, Costs, Performance*. Paris.

———. 1996. *Trade, Employment, and Labour Standards: A Study of Core Workers' Rights and International Trade*. Paris.

———. 1997. *Employment Outlook*. Paris.

———. 1999. *OECD Environmental Data: Compendium 1999*. Paris.

———. 2003. *Agricultural Policies in OECD Countries: Monitoring and Evaluation 2003*. Paris

———. Various issues. *Main Economic Indicators*. Monthly. Paris.

———. Various years. *International Development Statistics*. CD-ROM. Paris.

———. Various years. *National Accounts*. Vol. 1, *Main Aggregates*. Paris.

———. Various years. *National Accounts*. Vol. 2, *Detailed Tables*. Paris.

———. Various years. *Trends in International Migration: Continuous Reporting System on Migration*. Paris.

Organisation for Economic Co-operation and Development (OECD), Development Assistance Committee. Various years. *Development Cooperation*. Paris.

———. Various years. *Geographical Distribution of Financial Flows to Aid Recipients: Disbursements, Commitments, Country Indicators*. Paris.

O'Meara, Molly. 1999. "Reinventing Cities for People and the Planet." Worldwatch Paper 147. Worldwatch Institute, Washington, D.C.

Palacios, Robert, and Montserrat Pallares-Miralles. 2000. "International Patterns of Pension Provision." Social Protection Discussion Paper 0009. World Bank, Human Development Network, Washington, D.C.

Pandey, Kiran Dev, Katharine Bolt, Uwe Deichmann, Kirk Hamilton, Bart Ostro, and David Wheeler. 2003. "The Human Cost of Air Pollution: New Estimates for Developing Countries." World Bank, Development Research Group and Environment Department, Washington, D.C.

Pearce, David, and Giles Atkinson. 1993. "Capital Theory and the Measurement of Sustainable Development: An Indicator of Weak Sustainability." *Ecological Economics* 8: 103–08.

Pilling, David. 1999. "In Sickness and in Wealth." *Financial Times*, 22 October.

Plucknett, Donald L. 1991. "Saving Lives through Agricultural Research." *Issues in Agriculture* (World Bank, Consultative Group on International Agricultural Research, Washington, D.C.) 16.

Population Reference Bureau. 2002. *2002 Women of Our World*. Washington, D.C.

PricewaterhouseCoopers. 2003a. *Corporate Taxes 2003–2004: Worldwide Summaries*. New York.

———. 2003b. *Individual Taxes 2003–2004: Worldwide Summaries*. New York.

PRS Group, Inc. 2002. *International Country Risk Guide*. CD-ROM. December. East Syracuse, N.Y.

Rama, Martin, and Raquel Artecona. 2002. "A Database of Labor Market Indicators across Countries." World Bank, Development Research Group, Washington, D.C.

Ravallion, Martin. 1996. "Poverty and Growth: Lessons from 40 Years of Data on India's Poor." DECNote 20. World Bank, Development Economics Vice Presidency, Washington, D.C.

———. 2001. "Growth, Inequality and Poverty: Looking Beyond Averages." Policy Research Working Paper 2558. World Bank, Development Research Group, Washington, D.C.

———. 2002. "Counting the World's Poor: A Comment." *World Bank Research Observer* 16(2): 149–56.

Ravallion, Martin, and Shaohua Chen. 1996. "What Can New Survey Data Tell Us about the Recent Changes in Living Standards in Developing and

BIBLIOGRAPHY

Transitional Economies?" World Bank, Policy Research Department, Washington, D.C.

———. 1997. "Can High-Inequality Developing Countries Escape Absolute Poverty?" *Economic Letters* 56: 51–57.

Ravallion, Martin, Gaurav Datt, and Dominique van de Walle. 1991. "Quantifying Absolute Poverty in the Developing World." *Review of Income and Wealth* 37: 345–61.

Reddy, Sanjay, and Thomas Pogge. 2002. "How *Not* to Count The Poor." Working paper. Barnard College and Columbia University, New York.

Rodrik, Dani. 1996. "Labor Standards in International Trade: Do They Matter and What Do We Do About Them?" Overseas Development Council, Washington, D.C.

Romer, P. M. 1986. "Increasing Returns and Long-Run Growth." *Journal of Political Economy* 94: 1002–37.

Ruggles, Robert. 1994. "Issues Relating to the UN System of National Accounts and Developing Countries." *Journal of Development Economics* 44(1): 87–102.

Ryten, Jacob. 1998. "Fifty Years of ISIC: Historical Origins and Future Perspectives." ECA/STAT.AC. 63/22. United Nations Statistics Division, New York.

Sala-i-Martin, Xavier. 2002. *The Disturbing 'Rise' in Global Income Inequality.* NBER Working Paper 8904. Cambridge, Mass.: National Bureau of Economic Research.

Sen, Amartya. 1988. "The Concept of Development." In Hollis Chenery and T. N. Srinivasan, eds., *Handbook of Development Economics.* Vol. 1. Amsterdam: North Holland.

Shiklovanov, Igor. 1993. "World Fresh Water Resources." In Peter H. Gleick, ed., *Water in Crisis: A Guide to Fresh Water Resources.* New York: Oxford University Press.

SIPRI (Stockholm International Peace Research Institute). 2003. *SIPRI Yearbook 2003: Armaments, Disarmament, and International Security.* Oxford: Oxford University Press.

Srinivasan, T. N. 1994. "Database for Development Analysis: An Overview." *Journal of Development Economics* 44(1): 3–28.

Standard & Poor's. 2000. *The S&P Emerging Market Indices Methodology, Definitions, and Practices.* New York.

———. 2003. *Emerging Stock Markets Factbook 2003.* New York.

———. 2004. *Credit Week.* January. New York.

Taylor, Alan M. 1996a. *International Capital Mobility in History: Purchasing Power Parity in the Long Run.* NBER Working Paper 5742. Cambridge, Mass.: National Bureau of Economic Research.

———. 1996b. *International Capital Mobility in History: The Saving-Investment Relationship.* NBER Working Paper 5743. Cambridge, Mass.: National Bureau of Economic Research.

UNACC/SCN (United Nations Administrative Committee on Co-ordination, Subcommittee on Nutrition). Various years. *Update on the Nutrition Situation.* Geneva.

———. 2000. *Fourth Report on the World Nutrition Situation.* Geneva.

UNAIDS (Joint United Nations Programme on HIV/AIDS) and WHO (World Health Organization). 2002. *AIDS Epidemic Update.* December.

UNCTAD (United Nations Conference on Trade and Development). 2003. *The Least Developed Countries Report.* Geneva.

———. Various years. *Handbook of International Trade and Development Statistics.* Geneva.

UNEP (United Nations Environment Programme). 1991. *Urban Air Pollution.* Nairobi.

UNESCO (United Nations Educational, Scientific, and Cultural Organization) Institute for Statistics. 2003. *Global Education Digest 2003.* Paris.

UNESCO (United Nations Educational, Scientific, and Cultural Organization) and OECD (Organisation for Economic Co-operation and Development). 2003. *Financing Education: Investments and Returns—Analysis of the World Education Indicators.* 2002 ed. Paris.

UNICEF (United Nations Children's Fund). 2001. *Progress Since the World Summit for Children: A Statistical Review.* New York.

———. Various years. *The State of the World's Children.* New York: Oxford University Press.

UNIDO (United Nations Industrial Development Organization). Various years. *International Yearbook of Industrial Statistics.* Vienna.

United Nations. 1947. *Measurement of National Income and the Construction of Social Accounts.* New York.

———. 1968. *A System of National Accounts: Studies and Methods.* Series F, no. 2, rev. 3. New York.

———. 1990. *International Standard Industrial Classification of All Economic Activities, Third Revision.* Statistical Papers Series M, no. 4, rev. 3. New York.

———. 1992. *Handbook of the International Comparison Programme.* Studies in Methods Series F, no. 62. New York.

———. 1993. *SNA Handbook on Integrated Environmental and Economic Accounting.* Statistical Office of the United Nations. Series F, no. 61. New York.

———. 1999. *Integrated Environmental and Economic Accounting: An Operational Manual.* Studies in Methods Series F, no. 78. New York.

———. 2000a. *We the Peoples: The Role of the United Nations in the 21st Century.* New York.

———. 2000b. *The World's Women 2000: Trends and Statistics.* Department of Economic and Social Affairs. New York.

United Nations Economic and Social Commission for Western Asia. 1997. *Purchasing Power Parities: Volume and Price Level Comparisons for the Middle East, 1993.* E/ESCWA/STAT/1997/2. Amman.

United Nations Population Division. 2000. *World Population Prospects: The 2000 Revision.* New York.

———. 2002. *World Urbanization Prospects: The 2001 Revision.* New York.

———. 2002. *International Migration Report 2003*. New York.

———. Various years. *Levels and Trends of Contraceptive Use*. New York.

United Nations Statistics Division. 1985. *National Accounts Statistics: Compendium of Income Distribution Statistics*. New York.

———. Various issues. *Monthly Bulletin of Statistics*. New York.

———. Various years. *Energy Statistics Yearbook*. New York.

———. Various years. *International Trade Statistics Yearbook*. New York.

———. Various years. *National Accounts Statistics: Main Aggregates and Detailed Tables*. Parts 1 and 2. New York.

———. Various years. *National Income Accounts*. New York.

———. Various years. *Population and Vital Statistics Report*. New York.

———. Various years. *Statistical Yearbook*. New York.

U.S. Census Bureau. 1990. *1990 Census of Population Listing*. Washington, D.C.

———. 2000. *Current Population Report*. March. Washington, D.C.

U.S. Department of Health and Human Services. 1997. *Social Security Systems throughout the World*. Washington, D.C.

U.S. Department of State, Bureau of Verification and Compliance. 2002. *World Military Expenditures and Arms Transfers 2000*. Washington, D.C.

U.S. Environmental Protection Agency. 1995. *National Air Quality and Emissions Trends Report 1995*. Washington, D.C.

Wagstaff, Adam, and Harold Alderman. 2001. "Life and Death on a Dollar a Day: Does It Matter Where You Live?" World Bank, Washington, D.C.

Walsh, Michael P. 1994. "Motor Vehicle Pollution Control: An Increasingly Critical Issue for Developing Countries." World Bank, Washington, D.C.

Watson, Robert, John A. Dixon, Steven P. Hamburg, Anthony C. Janetos, and Richard H. Moss. 1998. *Protecting Our Planet, Securing Our Future: Linkages among Global Environmental Issues and Human Needs*. A joint publication of the United Nations Environment Programme, U.S. National Aeronautics and Space Administration, and World Bank, Nairobi and Washington, D.C.

WCMC (World Conservation Monitoring Centre). 1992. *Global Biodiversity: Status of the Earth's Living Resources*. London: Chapman and Hall.

———. 1994. *Biodiversity Data Sourcebook*. Cambridge: World Conservation Press.

WHO (World Health Organization). 1983. *International Classification of Diseases*. 10th rev. Geneva.

———. 1997. *Coverage of Maternity Care*. Geneva.

———. 2002b. *The Tobacco Atlas*. Geneva.

———. Various years. *Global Tuberculosis Control Report*. Geneva.

———. Various years. *World Health Report*. Geneva.

———. Various years. *World Health Statistics Annual*. Geneva.

WHO (World Health Organization) and UNICEF (United Nations Children's Fund). 2000. *Global Water Supply and Sanitation Assessment 2000 Report*. Geneva.

———. 2003. *The Africa Malaria Report 2003*. Geneva.

WITSA (World Information Technology and Services Alliance). 2002. *Digital Planet 2002: The Global Information Economy*. Based on research by International Data Corporation. Vienna, Va.

Wolf, Holger C. 1997. *Patterns of Intra- and Inter-State Trade*. NBER Working Paper 5939. Cambridge, Mass.: National Bureau of Economic Research.

World Bank. 1990. *World Development Report 1990: Poverty*. New York: Oxford University Press.

———. 1992. *World Development Report 1992: Development and the Environment*. New York: Oxford University Press.

———. 1995. "China's GDP in U.S. Dollars, Based on Purchasing Power Parity." Policy Research Working Paper 1415. Washington, D.C.

———. 1996a. *Environment Matters* (summer). Environment Department, Washington, D.C.

———. 1996b. *Livable Cities for the 21st Century*. A Directions in Development book. Washington, D.C.

———. 1996c. *National Environmental Strategies: Learning from Experience*. Environment Department, Washington, D.C.

———. 1997a. *Can the Environment Wait? Priorities for East Asia*. Washington, D.C.

———. 1997b. *Expanding the Measure of Wealth: Indicators of Environmentally Sustainable Development*. Environmentally Sustainable Development Studies and Monographs Series, no. 17. Washington, D.C.

———. 1997d. *Rural Development: From Vision to Action*. Environmentally Sustainable Development Studies and Monographs Series, no. 12. Washington, D.C.

———. 1997e. *Sector Strategy: Health, Nutrition, and Population*. Human Development Network, Washington, D.C.

———. 1999a. *Fuel for Thought: Environmental Strategy for the Energy Sector*. Environment Department, Energy, Mining, and Telecommunications Department, and International Finance Corporation, Washington, D.C.

———. 1999b. *Greening Industry: New Roles for Communities, Markets, and Governments*. A World Bank Policy Research Report. New York: Oxford University Press.

———. 1999c. *Health, Nutrition, and Population Indicators: A Statistical Handbook*. Human Development Network, Washington, D.C.

———. 1999d. *Toward a Virtuous Circle: A Nutrition Review of the Middle East and North Africa*. Middle East and North Africa Working Paper Series, no. 17. Washington, D.C.

———. 2000a. *Trade Blocs*. A World Bank Policy Research Report. New York: Oxford University Press.

———. 2000b. *World Development Report 2000/2001: Attacking Poverty*. New York: Oxford University Press.

BIBLIOGRAPHY

———. 2001. "Malaria at a Glance." Health, Nutrition, and Population Department, Washington, D.C. [www.worldbank.org/hnp/malaria].

———. 2002a. "Achieving Education for All by 2015: Simulation Results for 47 Low-Income Countries." Africa Region and Human Development Network, Education Department, Washington, D.C.

———. 2002b. *A Case for Aid: Building a Consensus for Development Assistance.* Washington, D.C.

———. 2002c. *Financial Impact of the HIPC Initiative: First 24 Country Cases.* [http://www.worldbank.org/hipc].

———. 2002e. *Globalization, Growth, and Poverty: Building an Inclusive World Economy.* A World Bank Policy Research Report. New York: Oxford University Press.

———. 2002f. *Private Sector Development Strategy: Directions for the World Bank Group.* Private Sector Development Network, Washington, D.C.

———. 2002g. *Social Protection in Latin America and the Caribbean.* Fact Sheet. Latin America and the Caribbean Region and Human Development Network, Washington, D.C.

———. 2002h. *World Development Report 2002: Building Institutions for Markets.* New York: Oxford University Press.

———. 2002i. *World Development Report 2003: Transforming Growth—Neighbor, Nature, Future.* Draft. Washington, D.C.

———. 2002j. *The Environment and the Millennium Development Goals.* Washington, D.C.

———. 2002k. *Poverty Reduction and the World Bank: Operationalizing World Development Report 2000/2001.* Washington, D.C.

———. 2003a. *World Bank Atlas.* Washington, D.C.

———. 2003b. "The Millennium Development Goals for Health: Rising to the Challenges." World Bank, Washington, D.C.

———. 2004. *Doing Business in 2004: Understanding Regulation.* Washington, D.C.: Copublication of the World Bank and Oxford University Press.

———. Various issues. *Global Commodity Markets.* Quarterly. Washington, D.C.

———. Various years. *Global Development Finance* (formerly *World Debt Tables*). Washington, D.C. (Also available on CD-ROM.)

———. Various years. *Global Economic Prospects and the Developing Countries.* Washington, D.C.

———. Various years. *World Development Indicators.* Washington, D.C.

World Energy Council. 1995. *Global Energy Perspectives to 2050 and Beyond.* London.

World Intellectual Property Organization. 2003. *Industrial Property Statistics.* Publication A. Geneva.

World Resources Institute, UNEP (United Nations Environment Programme), UNDP (United Nations Development Programme), and World Bank. Various years. *World Resources: A Guide to the Global Environment.* New York: Oxford University Press.

World Tourism Organization. 2002a. *Compendium of Tourism Statistics 2002.* Madrid.

———. 2002b. *Yearbook of Tourism Statistics.* Vols. 1 and 2. Madrid.

WTO (World Trade Organization). Various years. *Annual Report.* Geneva.

Zook, Matthew. 2000. "Internet Metrics: Using Host and Domain Counts to Map the Internet." *International Journal on Knowledge Infrastructure Development, Management and Regulation* (University of California at Berkeley) 24(6/7).

INDEX OF INDICATORS

References are to table numbers.

C

D

INDEX OF INDICATORS

INDEX OF INDICATORS

INDEX OF INDICATORS

N

O

P

INDEX OF INDICATORS

R

S

INDEX OF INDICATORS

INDEX OF INDICATORS